Cairo

EGYPT

Nile R.

R

A

ANGLO-
EGYPTIAN
SUDAN

Khartoum

White Nile

Ubangi R.

Congo R.

BELGIAN
CONGO

UGANDA

Lake Victoria

RUANDA-URUNDI
(Belgian Mandate)

Lake Tanganyika

TANGANYIKA
(Br. Mandate)

Red Sea

FR. SOMALILAND

BR.
SOMALILAND

Addis
Ababa

ITALIAN
EAST AFRICA

SOCOTRA
(Br.)

Mogadiscio

INDIAN OCEAN

KENYA

Nairobi

PEMBA
ZANZIBAR (Br.)
Dar es Salaam
MAFIA

SEYCHELLES

L. Nyasa

NYASALAND

NORTHERN RHODESIA

Zambezi R.

Lusaka

Salisbury

SOUTHERN
RHODESIA

MOÇAMBIQUE

COMORO IS.
(Fr.)

Mozambique Channel

MADAGASCAR

RÉUNION

MAURITIUS

BECHUANA-
LAND

Pretoria

SWAZILAND

Lourenço Marques

UNION OF

SOUTH

AFRICA

BASUTOLAND

TROPIC OF CAPRICORN

20

0

20

40

60

PROTEST AND POWER IN BLACK AFRICA

WRITTEN UNDER THE AUSPICES OF
THE CENTER FOR INTERNATIONAL AFFAIRS
HARVARD UNIVERSITY

PROTEST AND POWER
IN BLACK AFRICA

Edited by ROBERT I. ROTBERG and ALI A. MAZRUI

New York · OXFORD UNIVERSITY PRESS · 1970

In memoriam

Eduardo Chivambo Mondlane,
scholar and revolutionary
(1920-1969)

ACKNOWLEDGMENTS

Throughout the several years which elapsed between the conception of this volume and its completion, the editors—and their numerous collaborators—received devoted and efficient administrative, editorial, and secretarial assistance from Miss Stephanie D. Jones, Mrs. Jane F. Tatlock, and Mrs. Gwen McIntosh, for whose support no praise can be too lavish. We are also unstintingly grateful for the perceptive editorial guidance and criticism of Mrs. Shirley C. Quinn, Mrs. Marina Finkelstein, and Robert D. Erwin, who contributed to the ultimate preparation of the manuscript for publication. Miss Emily Barclay played a major role in the hectic final stages of this book's production, and the editors are particularly thankful for her mastery of the many tasks associated with the making of the index. The Harvard University Center for International Affairs, which at various times supported the research of the editors on nationalism, political development, and problems of ethnicity in Africa, has been a patient and generous sponsor of this volume. The editors also wish to acknowledge the bibliographical assistance of Miss Virginia Rowland. The particular debts of the individual authors are acknowledged, where appropriate, in the notes to each chapter.

R.I.R.
A.A.M.

Cambridge and Kampala
January 1970

CONTENTS

Bibliography

LIST OF MAPS

MAPS BY VAUGHN GRAY

NOTE ON ORTHOGRAPHY

In this volume proper names, foreign titles, acronyms, and Bantu usage conform to a pattern set—for the sake of consistency and intelligibility—by the editors, the publications staff of the Harvard Center for International Affairs, and the publishers. Pronominal concords are omitted from nonterritorial and nonlinguistic forms of Bantu nomenclature; genitival and adjectival agreement has been sought between nominals and their objects; and short titles rather than initials have been preferred for even the most well known African political parties in order to avoid readers' confusion. The imposed usage departs from the preferred style of some of the contributors but has the merits (and some of the defects) of simplicity and uniformity.

INTRODUCTION

The themes of this book are three: dissent, diversity, and reintegration. Throughout the modern history of black Africa, men alone and men in groups have refused to accept the ways in which their political, social, and economic parameters were defined by others. Like Americans, Asians, and Europeans, Africans devised or adapted a variety of mechanisms to cope with the strains of colonial and post-colonial conflict. In no instances were the modes of reaction unique to Africa in scope, intensity, or technique, but only in Africa was there such diversity, and were there so many examples of each of the many variations on the standard notions of protest. Africa has known episodes of resistance and rebellion which range along a continuum from the highly instrumentally revolutionary to the exceedingly expressive and particularistic. The fervor and ritual of religion and the secular reinforcement of class-based interests have often been used as matrices for political mobilization. Africans have also shown remarkable ingenuity in harnessing energies created by disparate and otherwise inchoate bodies of discontent to the distant and at first long deferred momentum of change. This book thus is an attempt, using the skill and knowledge of thirty-three African, European, and American authors, to describe and analyze the spectrum of African responses to perceived threats to their liberty and dignity as individuals and their self-government and self-expression as groups. Even in a book of some bulk, however, it has proved impossible to include examples of every form of dissent or, within the various categories, to provide exactly representative examples of each sub-type. Instead, in a search for generalizable observations about protest and the methods by which it may be articulated (and sublimated), this book offers close inspections of hitherto unexplored or obscure African manifestations of dissent, and re-evaluations of a number of their more widely known expressions.

There is no gainsaying that the introduction of Western norms and power, and accompanying controls and constraints, was everywhere in Africa questioned by the peoples affected. When the representatives of the nations of Europe demonstrated their desire to rule rather than merely to coexist commercially—an earlier pattern—Africans usually, but not invariably, managed to put up a show of resistance. This resistance was not, however, simply a primitive response to stimulus. It varied according to the nature of the alien thrust, the indigenous perception of the potency of that thrust, the structure of the society being defended, the political abilities of its leaders, and each side's differential access to modern instruments of combat. Although primarily thought of as martial, resistance was equally political, and in many areas a resistance of the mind rather than of the hands. Resistance, it should be said, is here defined as opposition to external hegemony and occupation prior to the time when an alien power has imposed upon a conquered territory a new administrative framework (whether or not fully effective) requiring obedience to alien values. Rebellion is the militant expression of discontent at this latter stage; we feel that the distinction which is often made between primary and secondary movements of resistance is seldom helpful.

Africans did not in every instance take up arms against the whites who during the nineteenth century began systematically to acquire territory. In many areas Africans were—understandably—naïve, and became aware of the nature of the European incursion only after it was too late to prevent the elaboration of an apparatus of administration. Elsewhere Africans perceived the situation correctly, but withdrew instead of attacking. Or, as a result of the defeats inflicted on African armies by Europeans, they negotiated in order to avoid further conflict. Then there were innumerable desultory clashes—whether in the upper Ivory Coast, the backwoods of Liberia or Sierra Leone, the Congo, or Somalia—of only parochial importance. Large-scale confrontations were statistically few, but each (like the resistance of the northern Nigerian emirates, the Tukolor of the Soudan, the peoples of western Angola, the slaving chiefs of Malawi, or the tribesmen of Eritrea and the Horn of Africa generally) had a significance which was at least regional.

Of the four examples of large-scale resistance included in this book, only one, the Abushiri movement discussed by Robert Jackson, was a reasonably unambiguous response to a European occupation. In this case the Germans, having made (questionable) treaties with African chiefs of the interior and forcibly compelled the Sultan of Zanzibar to accede to their demands, proceeded to garrison the coastal towns of Tanganyika. The peoples of the coast, led by prominent Arabs and assisted by tribesmen from the interior, responded by ousting the Germans. But, as Jackson shows, the resisters lacked unity of purpose, good leadership, widely acknowledged legitimacy, technological equality, and a positive ideological appeal to ethnically diverse groups which were fundamentally antagonistic. The ouster of the Germans was therefore but a temporary phenomenon, the combination of Arab and African soldiery being powerless to forestall the invaders permanently. In West Africa, however, Samori managed to preserve a wide measure of independence for more than a decade before finally succumbing to French rule. In staving off the French he and his numerous followers were more successful than any other indigenous state or group. As Yves Person shows, Samori imposed unity, maintained an ongoing organization well adapted to warfare against the French, gained a measure of technological parity, and understood—far more than Abushiri and others—the nature and requirements of modern resistance. Indeed, Samori tried to use political as well as martial tactics to oppose the French (and later the British and the Germans). Unlike Abushiri, and Minilik in Ethiopia, Samori knew better than to hope for ouster. He wanted to maintain the independence of the state in upper Guinée which he had established by conquest comparatively recently and had managed to extend despite French and British hostility. The legitimacy of the Samorian conflict, qua resistance, may therefore be questioned, but, by virtue of its timing, its conscious legitimization by modern West Africa, and its intrinsic interest as an example of Afro-European hostility, it deserves the kind of devoted analysis supplied by Person.

The legitimacy of Minilik's Ethiopian resistance to the Italian attempt to extend its conquest of Eritrea to include Ethiopia is hardly in question. Although Minilik's acceptance as king of kings and emperor of Ethiopia was not yet complete, he was the most powerful and the most widely acknowledged leader of a national determination to resist the massive and clearly perceived Italian aggression. Unlike confrontations elsewhere between whites and blacks, the conflict which reached its culmination at Adwa, in the highlands of Tigre, was between large, massed armies. Europe expected that such a battle would inevitably result in a salutary European victory. Sven Rubenson explains in some detail how the Ethiopians under Minilik managed, by the modernization of their state and skillful political manipulation, to transform Ethiopia and mount an electrifying campaign of resistance which dealt a defeat to Europe and Italy. Minilik staved off European domination until the subsequent rise of Fascism.

In Southern Africa, by comparison, the indigenous inhabitants were far less able to cope with the expansionist designs of the Anglo-Afrikaner attack. The Zulu blocked the British advance at Isandhlwana and the Sotho managed as a result of a number of campaigns to prolong an otherwise severely untenable position, but for the most part the design of African resistance lacked the technical and organizational attributes without which sustained opposition to foreign occupation was bound ultimately to prove difficult, if not impossible. As Anthony Atmore shows, Moorosi's defense of the Phuti realm was easily overwhelmed. No matter how desperate, his people could not alone even begin to regain their sovereignty. They could temporize, respond in a politically obstructive manner, and threaten to attack, but belated and uncoordinated assaults produced no more than pyrrhic victories and, ultimately, defeats. Atmore's essay also indicates how fine the distinctions are between resistance and rebellion. Although he follows the usual South African nomenclature and entitles Moorosi's militant dissent a rebellion, it is evident that the part of Lesotho under question had hardly been subjected to alien administration by 1879. In essence, Moorosi was attempting to prevent the articulation of an administrative structure, and, in the opinion of the editors, his movement may marginally be considered one of resistance.

Whereas resisters rejected what they anticipated, rebels, who had by definition experienced the constraints and exactions of the early phase of colonial rule, rejected what they knew. By rebelling they sought to reclaim their lost freedom, to oust the occupiers, to assert themselves, to reform the alien framework of their subordination, or, as in one case, to bare the extent of their despair. This is not to say that disillusionment was uncommon, but the energies that resulted therefrom were by and large channeled toward instrumental rather than expressive goals. The actual rebellions during the period of colonial rule in Africa were also few in number and scattered in incidence despite the complexity and authoritarian nature of the colonial regimen.

None of the rebellions succeeded permanently in reversing the fate of the indigenous peoples, but the Mahdiya ruled supreme in the Sudan for thirteen years, and recurrent episodes of Nyabingism between 1908 and 1928 testified to the refusal of the Kiga and Rwanda of British Uganda and German Ruanda to accept foreign domination without a struggle. Both of these movements, and Chilembwe's rebellion in Nyasaland, were organized by or around religious figures and were sustained by the mobilizing and sanctifying force of powerful religious observance; in general, however, their goals were secular, and the mechanisms of the rebellion rightly deserve to be discussed together with the Bai Bureh rising in Sierra Leone, the Zulu revolt in Natal, and rebellions like the Shona/Ndebele and Maji Maji which are so ably dissected elsewhere. All, except that led by Chilembwe, were mass movements, were demonstrations of agrarian economic disaffection (with merchant participation) tied to specific economic grievances, and achieved a measure of success before succumbing to European firepower. Leon Carl Brown explores the rise and success of the Mahdi and places his appeal and design squarely within the hallowed framework of revitalizing Sunni Islam. He does not deny the particularistic appeal of the Mahdi at a time of socio-economic tension, but he is equally persuaded that the transformational notion of Mahdism was especially congenial to the peoples of the Islamic fringe, whether in North or in sub-Saharan Africa.

Islam was an important element elsewhere in Africa, but, even where modern rebels may have been Muslims, Islam could not provide the organizing cement, especially in a context of antagonism like that generated toward the end of the nineteenth century in Sierra Leone. There, as LaRay Denzer and Michael Crowder inform us in the first detailed interpretation of the rebellion of 1898, Bai Bureh led Africans of the newly created Protectorate against Britons and their black allies from the long established Colony. They stress the complicated antecedents of Anglo-Temne/Lokko warfare and the involvement of Bai Bureh and other Africans of the Sierra Leone Protectorate in ongoing Anglo-French rivalry, and indicate the extent to which an individual British governor's determination forcibly to collect hut taxes precipitated the guerrilla movement led by Bai Bureh. Technically, it is true, Bai Bureh owed no allegiance to Queen Victoria and can therefore be considered a resistance leader; but most of Sierra Leone was subordinate to British administration. Without the decision to gather taxes, a martial reaction could probably have been avoided—hence the editors's decision to group the rising in Sierra Leone with the rebellions and not, as in the case of Lesotho, with the movements of resistance.

There is no such terminological difficulty with Shula Marks's analysis of the Zulu rebellion of 1906, when the collection of taxes also proved a precipitating factor. The Zulu had fought the British and the Afrikaners throughout the nineteenth century and had been defeated and subjugated. Zululand was annexed in 1897. But it was the decision to introduce a poll tax, and the unfeeling measures used to enforce its collection, which heightened the misery of a people who had recently experienced increasing impoverishment. This combination of circumstances, when added to a number of individual tribulations, proved conducive to small-scale rebellion—of a kind which was common to colonial Africa—and to the more disruptive insurgency led by Bambatha, a chief who, in the manner of Chilembwe, was resigned to revolt. The Nyabingi cult provided a different focus for rebellion. As Mrs. Hopkins explains, it was a spirit possession movement which by virtue of its ideological equation of supernatural power with material gain provided a ready vehicle for secular and, in this case, specifically anti-European activity. For nearly three decades the notion of Nyabingi incorporated the types of antagonisms which were endemic to a marginal border area whose populations were in the throes of externally induced social change. Problems concerning alien administration, taxes, and land rights exercised Africans, and the various Nyabingi and Nyabingoid leaders added a new para-religious dimension to the kinds of disparate protest which characterized the other movements of rebellion in Africa. The fifth essay provides a psychological context for Chilembwe's rebellion and argues that he rose in despair and with no real hope of secular accomplishment.

In most parts of Africa two axioms generally were well understood by the end of World War I: Rebellions were dysfunctional and doomed to failure for reasons discussed particularly by Mrs. Marks and Mrs. Hopkins; the white rulers were unlikely in the near future to board ships and return, as many had come, peacefully to their homes. A generation, or, in parts of West Africa, two or three, had grown up under European rule and had learned to adapt tolerably well to its constraints. Almost everywhere in tropical Africa the end of the war marked the beginning of a resigned acceptance by most of the inhabitants of their roles as colonial subjects—as inferiors who potentially could become equals. The new generation of Africans, and some of their elders, had come to understand the parameters of their foreign-dominated societal frameworks and were consciously attempting to make their destinies within them. Many adapted easily: the African in the administrative age learned the languages, customs, and organizational methods of his rulers. He studied in schools staffed by European secular and clerical teachers, worked for white district officers, road foremen, traders, and missionaries, and attended to the household needs of their families. All of these experiences naturally provided grist for mills of personal change. Africans, particularly those who chose to follow the paths of the West, relied upon the patronage of colonists to advance their own careers. Having become subjects, many chose at first to conform to what seemed to be the expectations of their rulers. Africans, at least those of the upwardly mobile or already upper classes, aspired to assimilation, and it was only when their assumptions about the nature of colonial rule proved false, and disappointment ripened into a new disillusionment, that the employment of multiple mechanisms of protest became common.

Africans, like most peoples, resented being subjugated. Then, once they were reconciled in a fatalistic way to the fact of their subjugation, they resented that reconciliation, the nature of the compromises that were daily made, and, perhaps most of all, the gross failures of colonialism to validate its own self-proclaimed moral justification for the assumption of hegemony. Africans resented being coerced, taxed without representation, and made subject to alien-imposed laws. They resented the denial of equality of opportunity in employment and education, the differential application of codes of justice, compulsory labor, corporal punishment, infringement of personal liberty (e.g., pass laws), and an entire battery of newly introduced measures of coercion and regimentation. Most widely, Africans resented being compelled to acknowledge their Western-ordained position of inferiority; discrimination and prejudice were bitter burdens to bear, no less so in regions where the absolute number of discriminatory acts was fewer than in those regions where settlers clustered. In sum, colonial rule introduced unwelcome changes of a kind that upset traditional social, economic, and political systems. And it was largely by way of expressing animosity toward these alterations—because the importance of traditional norms had been mocked or denied, or merely because the traditional order had been altered that Africans raised their voices and their fists in anger.

Most Africans are religious, and it is hardly surprising that indigenous dissatisfaction with colonial rule should have found a variety of religious contexts within which to elaborate and seek redress for generalized and quite specific sources of discontent. There were the pre-colonial cults, such as the Mumbo movement described by Audrey Wipper and the Nyabingi of Mrs. Hopkins, which were resurrected or redirected during colonial times as a functional source of security during periods of stress; they also played an important mobilizing role in a society anxious to cope with the persons and institutions which had made the old order crumble. However, even Mumbo, the most martially oriented of the sects discussed in Part Three of this book, was seeking indigenous reintegration as much as conflict with Europeans. It was not rebellious *per se*, although it did, on occasion, resort to force of arms. Utopian and eclectic, it represented an ingenious manner of adapting to, coping with, and protesting against new, complex, and intrusive strands of social change. There were a number of equally militant movements with which European administrations also clashed during the colonial era: the Kimbangu movement of the lower Congo, the Watchtower and Mwana Lesa disturbances of northeastern Zambia, the Prophet Harris movement in the Gold and Ivory Coasts, and numerous churches in South Africa come immediately to mind. But these groups, and the more than 2,000 independent churches which had been formed in black Africa before World War II, were for the most part subversive of colonial rule more because of their separate, disaffected witness than because of their violent intentions. Although many, it is true, refused on occasion to obey constituted white and black authorities (e.g., the Lumpa Church of Alice Lenshina), and there were clashes, most of these groups expressed protest primarily by the fact of their existence. But their importance to Africans was more because they were black-controlled during a period when whites dominated all spheres of activity—even (excepting the Islamic areas) the institutions of newly introduced religion. Andrew Roberts shows why and how the Lumpa church, which had aligned itself with black nationalists during the colonial period, nevertheless fought against a black government and was annihilated as an institution. From his analysis it becomes apparent that African independent churches were as much a response to a psychological awareness of inadequacy and impotence as to precisely delineated anti-colonial aspirations. Thus, the same factors which nourished separatism in Northern Rhodesia inspired Lenshina's followers during the period of that Protectorate's transformation into Zambia.

These are generally applicable conclusions which are supported by the remainder of the discussion of "The Religious Expression of Discontent." Two of the other chapters—Robert Mitchell on the Aladura Movement in Nigeria and Pierre Alexandre on Hamallism in Francophone West Africa—represent intermediate stages along a route leading to what James Fernandez has aptly called "The Affirmation of Things Past." Even if the particular religious movement was ostensibly anti-colonial, like Hamallism, or was the result of schisms from European-controlled churches, the message of Alar Ayong and Bwiti—two pre-colonial cults of Gabon—was that Africans must seek their salvation separately from whites, not that they must oppose white administrators or constituted governments martially. This was a putative sublimation, although in the cases of Alar Ayong and Bwiti more than Aladura and Hamallism—or a host of other African separatist churches—it was difficult to demonstrate the fullness of that revolutionary idiom.

During the years after World War I, when new churches were being formed in some profusion and traditional rituals were being invoked against the juggernaut of colonialism, Africans also began to adapt to their own uses the approved political techniques of their rulers. Using

the political concepts and languages of their respective rulers, they—
especially their educated elite—began to claim a democratic right to
participate in the governing process. At that stage they wanted to
achieve no more (but it troubled the colonial governments) than the
right to have their collective voice heard with respect to matters directly affecting the lives and actions of the indigenous population.
Thus the educated black lawyers, doctors, businessmen, clerks, evangelists, teachers, and journalists—the very men about whom Martin
Kilson writes in his essay on the National Congress of British West
Africa and the men to whom the ways of the whites had become familiar—established associations, congresses, and pressure groups in
order to seek the attainment of a variety of reforms. Even in the Portuguese and Belgian possessions, members of the emerging African
elite joined forces to express themselves throughout the period from
1920 to 1950. Their associations sought redress of grievances endured
by Africans; they petitioned and spoke up for representation; in the
settler-dominated regions they tried to counter every public move made
by organizations of whites to entrench their own privileges. They reacted against attempts to amalgamate or otherwise merge colonial
territories to the detriment of Africans. Naturally, too—as John Lonsdale's chapter on political associations in western Kenya makes perfectly evident—these associations also concerned themselves continually
with matters of immediate, even parochial, consequence to the African
elites and, often, to the masses.

These were gentle skirmishes with authority, like those in South
Africa, Northern Rhodesia, and Nyasaland, and this period of essential
constitutionalism has come to represent an intermediate phase in the
history of the rise of nationalism. It was the period when indigenous
leaders began to appreciate the essential futility of a strictly constitutional, *ad hoc*, and bascally elitist approach to the problems posed for
subject peoples by colonial rule. Nowhere in black Africa are the dilemmas of this period epitomized more dramatically than in the Lake
Province of Tanganyika. Andrew Maguire's contribution to this volume analyzes the search for new modes of opposition to British rule,
shows how the local leaders of what became the Tanganyika African
National Union moved faster than the embryonic national political organization, and provides clear evidence of the frustrations which led to
an escalating sense of urgency and militancy in that up-country, but
important, crucible of nationalism. Maguire takes us from the associa-
tional stage of conflict resolution to the birth of political parties, a
route traveled in many parts of Africa during the colonial era. In many
areas, too, political stratagems and the manipulation of a distant pub-

lic opinion were sufficient to ensure the triumph of indigenous quests for independence. Elsewhere, militancy shaded into violence. And nowhere more dramatically than in Cameroon did violence become a serious alternative. It is the struggle between the politics of violence and politics of peaceful persuasion at the end of the colonial epoch that is examined particularly with regard to its (ultimately beneficial) effects upon national integration in Willard Johnson's chapter on the *Union des Populations du Cameroun.*

In addition to adapting the general devices and mechanisms of interest aggregation to their own needs, Africans early discovered that Western notions of labor as a commodity could be used to express their own particularistic industrial as well as general economic and political grievances. By forming trade unions, withholding their labor, striking, etc., they could begin to influence the policies of white-dominated governments. As early as the 1890's African workers in Nigeria and the Gold Coast expressed their discontent militantly. During the 1930's, 1940's, and 1950's, there were industrio-political strikes on the Congo and Northern Rhodesian copperbelts, on the Kenyan waterfront, in the Sudan, and elsewhere. Only in South Africa, however, did a trade union movement develop a mass following and become a more than temporary focus for the articulation of African antagonism to the prevailing political and social system. Sheridan Johns analyzes the rise and fall of the Industrial and Commercial Workers' Union, a large national organization of black and coloured workers which from 1919 to 1927 seriously threatened to undermine white rule in South Africa. A failure of leadership and internal dissension, however, ended the effectiveness of the union, thereby muting the voice of African labor until the 1950's, when white and black South Africans used nonviolent tactics of mass mobilization, with but transient success, to bring pressure to bear on the *apartheid*-oriented government of their country. Leo Kuper's generally pessimistic chapter reassesses the possibilities of affecting the direction of South Africa's development by militant nonviolent means. Boycotts have been and can be employed as instruments of change in South Africa, but, as Dharam Ghai's account of the Bugandan trade boycott of 1959 makes evident, boycotts are blunt and imperfect weapons if the institutions and class of individuals being attacked are subject to constant redefinition and a certain ambiguity of instrumentality.

The energies of dissent can be focused more precisely when there is a strike for richer personal rewards which can be transformed into an assault upon the ways in which society distributes rewards in general. Robert Melson's account of the Nigerian general strike of 1964 clarifies these issues and provides a solid basis for an understanding of some of the class-based conflicts which eventually led to the Nigerian coups of 1966.

Even after the demise of colonialism, there were subsequent readjustments in the governmental alignments of tropical Africa which reflected the tensions of that era which had been left unresolved at, and in some cases were exacerbated by, the assumption of independence. The struggle for power, which in many instances has taken the form of ethnic and communal conflict (ideology has been important only for a few), has given recent African history a kaleidoscopic appearance. But most of the revolutions, rebellions, and coups discussed in Part Seven of the present book derived their posited legitimacy from the real or imagined grievances of the minorities or majorities disadvantaged as a result of the organizational modes of colonial rule or the scope and direction of the struggle for independence. René Lemarchand and Michael Lofchie examine the majoritarian—and bloody—upheavals in Rwanda and Zanzibar. In both cases, colonial-sanctioned social orders were reversed; in Rwanda, especially, a traditional caste system associated with an indigenous monarchy was exchanged, before actual independence and with the assistance of the European administering authority, for an indigenous republican government. Whereas the Rwandan transfer of power was sanctioned by processes of legitimacy as well as violence, when the dark-skinned Zanzibaris overthrew the elected Arab-dominated government of their independent island, force of arms was sufficient. Communal antagonisms had been exacerbated by the nature of the pre-independence electoral struggle and the short-sighted policies of the victorious Arabs. Status reversal was therefore abrupt, traumatic, and lasting—even after Zanzibar's merger with Tanganyika.

Crawford Young shows how the disorders and rebellions of the post-independence Congo emanated from the socially stressful situations in which Congolese of different categories found themselves. The Congo's insurrectionary potential grew as a result of a number of socio-economic and psychological crises; urbanization, unemployment, inflation, perceived iniquities in the distribution of power, and the inability of the new state to govern all played a part in stimulating the various outbreaks of the only lightly coordinated warfare that was the rebellion. His essay also reminds us of the continuity of change, particularly of the extent to which African methods of mobilization, and hence the rituals of rebellion, are similar across time and geographical space; the *simba* of the Congo, the Mau Mau of Kenya, the Maji Maji of Tanganyika, the Shona/Ndebele of Rhodesia, the Nyabingi, and even the

Zulu of Bambatha utilized forms and techniques which were strikingly similar and equally successful in the short term.

There have been coups and putsches of all kinds in Africa. In Nigeria, where the iniquities of misapplied federalism—essentially a British device which perpetuated the leverage enjoyed by the peoples of an educationally backward north in their dealings with advanced and aggressive southerners—poisoned the rational balancing arrangements in the wake of the general strike, census distortions, and a growing feeling of alienation among the urban masses and the professional classes, a coup was seen to be a democratic instrument capable of restoring power to its rightful holders. Both James O'Connell and Robert Melson (in his discussion of the 1964 strike) explain the complicated variables of the Nigerian equation; O'Connell charts the decay of constitutionalism which reinforced inherent factors of instability. Power, and the wealth that flowed from power, were maldistributed. Leaders lost legitimacy, that very quality without which no government, particularly a young one, can continue to govern without tyranny. O'Connell's analysis makes it possible to see how the first coup succeeded only in hastening the onset of national disequilibrium; a second coup flowed naturally from the consequences of the first, equally reflected pre- and post-colonial arrangements, and led almost inexorably to the secession of Biafra. Another instance of deprivation—Buganda within the new Uganda—became an example of privilege denied and potential secession aborted. A national solution—Ali A. Mazrui describes the process and its costs—was imposed upon a kingdom which during the colonial era had reigned preeminent among virtual equals and by its partially autonomous existence had contributed, contrary to most analyses, to national integration and political development. This was a denouement which the tiny Rwenzururu kingdom on the Ugandan slopes of Ruwenzori has managed to avoid since its successful secession in 1962. Martin R. Doornbos makes much of the crude ethnic conflict which gave rise to and sustains the breakaway state; he also offers explanations for its overwhelming appeal to the disadvantaged Konjo and Amba of the mountain. Beyond Ruwenzori, in Ankole in southern Uganda, similar ethnic disparities resulted not in a movement of secession but in successful conciliation and integration. Doornbos compares the differing social contexts of Ankole and Toro out of which the two movements (like those of the hill people of northeastern India) grew, and shows how local ethnicity can contribute to national unification.

Ethnicity, despite its widespread importance, explains few of the recent coups. Victor Le Vine compares the coups in three Francophone countries where exasperated and grasping soldiers took power after watching the politicians cope vainly, if at all, with the straitened economic and social circumstances inherited from the administrative age. His chapter provides a beginning for an understanding of that most common and Latin American of coups, the mere replacement of one elite by another. But, in the three Francophone states, the army also acted at the behest of other constituencies—even, to some degree, the masses—when the politicians had been seen to forfeit legitimacy, or to transgress the kinds of norms compatible with legitimacy. Politicians had condoned and participated in corruption, proved unable to remove the sources of persistent economic stress (and, especially in Dahomey, failed to placate the trade unions), mired their nations in constitutional instability, and seemed to prefer international attention to problem-solving at home.

Most coups, it is true, impinged only marginally upon the daily life of the ordinary man, in contrast to the very different situation in contemporary Tanzania. Ali A. Mazrui analyzes the international reasons for the promulgation of the Arusha Declaration and the articulation of socialism in one African country. In a closing essay, Yashpal Tandon describes the ways in which the Organization of African Unity has tried to handle interstate and interzonal conflict, and how, on two major and several minor occasions, it has proved incapable of offering the kind of mediating influence which is so acutely necessary if Africans are to maintain their integrity and developmental initiative during the remainder of the post-colonial period of national consolidation.

Part Six of the present book includes three essays: a discussion of the impact of a forthright anti-establishment journalist in colonial Angola, and two general descriptions of the literature of protest in Francophone and Anglophone Africa. The existing literature—the prose, poetry, and ephemeral tracts of artists and polemicists—represents only the initial outpourings of dissent. As both Gerald Moore and John Povey indicate, the end of colonialism hardly stemmed the flow of articulate criticism. With new sources of confidence, the writers of most of Africa continue outspokenly to examine the legitimacy of African goverments. For Africa has not seen the end of disenchantment, alienation, movements of protest, and controversy over the exercise and abuse of power. The discussions of readjustments which were prepared for this book are already analyses of past time. Some are implicitly predictive, and anticipate the kinds of instablities which may inhere in disestablished ex-colonies during a time of international stress. But if this book has demonstrated anything, it is the varied ways in which Africans have been and are capable of focusing and expressing their discontent, of finding violent as well as traditional modes of affirming their visions

of a meaningful past and a rewarding future. No all-embracing para-
digms can be constructed for protest and power in Africa; there we
find idiosyncrasy and universality, both of which can be described
and charted, and chronological continuity and contemporaneity. Let
the reader therefore consider this a sampler representative of Africa's
complex past and equally non-homogeneous future.

Robert I. Rotberg

PART ONE

RESISTANCE TO CONQUEST

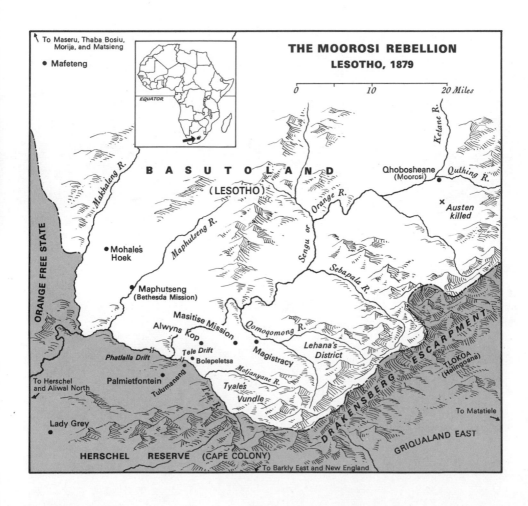

THE MOOROSI REBELLION
LESOTHO, 1879

0   10   20 Miles

To Maseru, Thaba Bosiu,
Morija, and Matsieng

● Mafeteng

EQUATOR

B A S U T O L A N D

(LESOTHO)

Qhobosheane
(Moorosi)

Quthing R.

Ketane R.

× Austen
killed

Orange R.

Sengu or

Mabhaleng R.

ORANGE FREE STATE

● Mohale's
Hoek

Maphutseng R.

Sebapala R.

● Maphutseng
(Bethesda Mission)

Masitise Mission

Alwyns Kop

Phatlalla Drift

Tele Drift

● Bolepeletsa

Magistracy

Qomoqomong R.

Lehana's
District

DRAKENSBERG ESCARPMENT

TLOKOA
(Helingoana)

Motjanyane R.

To Herschel
and Aliwal North

Palmietfontein

Tulumaneng

Tyales
Vundle

To Matatiele

Tele R.

● Lady Grey

HERSCHEL   RESERVE   (CAPE COLONY)

GRIQUALAND EAST

To Barkly East and New England

THE MOOROSI REBELLION:

LESOTHO, 1879

ANTHONY ATMORE

On the last day of 1878, the Phuthi chief Moorosi had his son Lehana rescued from the primitive lock-up at the magistracy in the Quthing district of British Basutoland. Lehana was to have been removed from Quthing by the Cape colonial government to serve a four-year sentence for horse-stealing by working on the construction of the breakwater at Cape Town. After his escape from jail he hid in the mountains, and his father disregarded the demands of the white authorities to surrender him to them.

By March 1879 the Phuthi were in what the Cape government called a state of rebellion. White troops, accompanied by African allies, moved against the recalcitrant chief. With less than three hundred men, Moorosi withstood a siege of eight months on his fortified mountain; he was shot dead in the final assault mounted by the colonial soldiers. Most of his kin and counsellors were killed. His people were largely removed from their country and sent to work on the colonists' farms in the Cape. Phuthiland was only saved from expropriation by the outbreak of a greater rebellion in Lesotho proper—the Gun War of 1880. Today there are remnants of the Phuthi group in Lesotho,[1] but there is no Phuthi chieftainship. As a separate tribal

A   Cape Blue Book in CO 51/207 in PRO
NA   Cape Town Archives Native Affairs Department Series

[1] For the period covered by this essay, I have used the toponym Lesotho in two senses: (a) for the country north of the Orange River, between the then uninhabited mountains (Maloti) and the Boer farms on the high veld, over which Moshweshwe ruled, and (b) in its present-day usage, for the whole of the country known until independence as Basutoland. I have kept this old European form in quotations, and in some instances in the text. Moorosi's country, Phuthiland (a term of my own devising) became known as Quthing (the name of a river) after it passed under British control. To conform with the usage in this volume, the prefixes of Bantu names have been dropped, and spellings brought up to date: thus Basuto becomes Sotho.

entity, the Phuthi were broken by the crushing of their rebellion of 1879.

This small yet dramatic conflict had its roots in long-standing troubled relations between tribesmen and colonists on this particular section of the turbulent frontier between black and white. Like all the racial wars in South Africa during the decade from the mid-1870's to the mid-1880's, the Moorosi affair only deteriorated into violence as the result of a final incident in a long chain of provocation from both sides. These wars between black men and white men in South Africa have about them an inevitability which was as apparent to discerning contemporary observers as it is to students today. As one moves from step to step, the outcome becomes both inescapable and predictable.[2]

The Phuthi were among the first Bantu inhabitants of Lesotho. They were, in origin, Nguni-speaking people from Natal who had trekked over the escarpment to the high veld, and then slowly moved south, toward the valley of the Orange.[3] Moorosi was born about 1795. During the *Difaqane* (times of trouble) he and his father played a role similar to, though less important than that of the Sotho great chief, Moshweshwe; they gathered scattered peoples under the protection of their overrule.[4] Moorosi was a short, alert man with fine features (perhaps denoting a part-Bushman ancestry) and a cunning, acquisitive, and highly temperamental nature. He entered into a close and generally subordinate relationship with Moshweshwe.

By the late 1840's the white colonists, followed, however reluctantly, by the Cape government, were encroaching upon Phuthi country. All that lay to the west of the Tele—the present southwestern boundary of Lesotho—became the native reserve later known as Herschel. During the Seqiti War, the last great Free State-Sotho conflict (which broke out in 1865), Phuthiland was invaded by a white commando force. Moorosi fled up the Orange Valley to the *qhobosheane* (mountain fortress), where he lived for the rest of his life.[5] After the

---

[2] In almost all cases the final result was defeat for the Africans. The significant exception was the Sotho, who emerged from the Gun War undefeated, albeit not victorious.

[3] See D. F. Ellenberger and J. C. Macgregor, *History of the Basuto: Ancient and Modern* (London, 1912), ch. 3; A. T. Bryant, *Olden Times in Zululand and Natal* (Cape Town, 1929/1965), ch. 37.

[4] See William F. Lye, "The Difaqane: The Mfecane in the Southern Sotho Area, 1822–1824," *The Journal of African History*, VII (1967), 107-31.

[5] G. M. Theal, *Basutoland Records*, II, 507, 526-27, 567: correspondence between Burnet and Wodehouse, Nov. and Dec. 1865. (*Basutoland Records,* henceforth BR, vols. I to III published Cape Town, 1883/1964, vols. IV to VI, unpublished manuscript in Cape Town archives; photostat copies in Maseru archives.)

Seqiti War, Lesotho was taken under British protection in 1868, and in 1871 was annexed by the Cape government; almost as an afterthought, Phuthiland was included in British Basutoland by Sir Edmond Wodehouse, the High Commissioner.[6]

The new administration for Phuthiland consisted of a Governor's Agent and three other magistrates, one of whom was stationed in the south of the territory, in Cornet Spruit district, which included Moorosi and his people. This magistrate, John Austen, was to become Moorosi's great adversary. Since 1853 Austen had been superintendent of the native reserve, in which capacity he had assumed chiefly prerogatives but with a pronounced bias in favor of the Boer farmers and the industrious Mfengu[7] and against the local Africans. There is little doubt that in the context of the politics of Lesotho and Phuthiland he was a formidable opponent. Nevertheless, the first few years of Moorosi's new position as a protected chief were relatively harmonious. Austen's residence in the town of Mohale's Hoek, north of the Orange, was farther from Moorosi's *qhobosheane* than when Austen was living in Herschel. So long as the Phuthi paid what the white authorities considered a reasonable amount of hut tax and refrained from stock thefts, Austen left Moorosi to his own devices.

This peaceful time, however, was short-lived. Though the Langalibalele rebellion of 1873 did not directly affect Moorosi, it ushered in a period of great disquiet among the whites in South Africa, who feared a general African uprising, and among the Africans, who feared that the whites were about to launch a final offensive against their independence.[8] As a result of the demand of the Kimberly diamond miners for African labor, which could only be obtained in exchange for firearms, by the mid-1870's most African groups were armed with guns.[9]

For details of Moorosi's fights with the Freestaters, and for his search for a defensible position, see Austen's report to Griffith, Quthing, 7 May 1879, printed in Cape A17, 1879 (henceforth A17/79) in CO 51/207 in PRO.

[6] For the Moorosi-Wodehouse meeting, see the evidence of Bowker and St. V. Cripps before the Select Committee on Basutoland Hostilities (henceforth BHC), A6/79. See also articles by D. F. Ellenberger in Sesotho, *Leselinyana* (*Little Light*), Dec. 1901 to Feb. 1902. Ellenberger founded Masitise mission in 1866. See Victor Ellenberger, *A Century of Mission Work in Basutoland, 1833–1933* (Morija, 1938), 142-44.

[7] Mfengu (Fingo) is a notoriously vague term. In this part of South Africa these people included Hlubi, Ngwane, and Tlokwa remnants.

[8] See, inter alia, British Parliamentary Papers, 1874, XLV, C.1025; 1875, LII, C.1342; Cape Town Archives series NA272, NA840; and CO3219.

[9] As an example, in the Cape Blue Book on Native Affairs, 1875, 7, Austen to Griffith, 21 Jan. 1875, Austen talks of "a sort of mania to be possessed of a gun and ammunition" among inhabitants of his district.

Another scare for black and white men alike ensued in 1876 when there was trouble in Griqualand East, the country south of the Drakensberg Range bordering Moorosi's territory, in which a brother of Letsie, the Sotho great chief, was involved.[10]

This trouble made clear the difficulty of administering Quthing from Mohale's Hoek, especially in times of crisis. Therefore, the Cape government agreed to the proposal of the Governor's Agent, Charles Griffith, for the creation of a new district comprising Moorosi's country, and to the appointment of Hamilton Hope as magistrate. Hope was a young man who had been clerk to the assistant magistrate at Mafeteng, in the large central Thaba Bosiu district.[11] Early in May 1877 Griffith and Austen visited Moorosi on his mountain to introduce the new magistrate to him and to his people. To the chief, this was indeed an unwelcome development. No longer would the Phuthi be able to go about their affairs in comparative isolation. Moorosi was fearful of this further extension of white power into his country. However, Griffith wore Moorosi down verbally and forced him to accept Hope and to acquiesce to the white men's choice of a site on which to build the magistracy. This submission earned an allowance of £50 a year from the white government, "in order to retain his influence on the side of the Government."

The issue that was to dominate Moorosi's political activities for the following two years had, however, been clearly raised; with the white men it was quite simply the issue of power and authority. In one small district, over one small group of people (about 5,000 all told), there could not be two sources of political power—two authorities to initiate changes—without constant friction and the eventual subjection of one by the other. In his dealings with whites, Moorosi showed less political acumen than most of the sons of Moshweshwe in Lesotho, who were prepared to hand over to the magistrates a large area of political shadow while keeping to themselves a vital core of political substance. Moorosi preferred direct action and was thus to precipitate a series of head-on collisions.

Hope opened a temporary office at an old store at Alwyns Kop, near the Tele River, but soon moved to the end of the wagon road, past

---

[10] For this (the Nehemiah) affair, see BHC appendices B and H. J. M. Orpen, an acknowledged authority on Sotho matters, wrote in appendix B, xxviii, " . . . there can be no doubt that the rankling sense of injustice, believed by the Basutos to have been done to Nehemiah *and all the other accused,* who had their property and *homes and fields* confiscated has had its serious influence on the state of feeling which has brought about the present rebellion" (i.e. Moorosi's).

[11] S9/1/3/3 Maseru archives (henceforth S9): Griffith to Hope, 28 Feb. 1877.

Masitise, at the point where the Qomoqomong River entered a deep gorge. This site was doubtless closer to Moorosi's mountain, but it was worthless as a defensive position. Hope had with him as clerk and interpreter Charles Maitin, the son of a pioneer French missionary, who had been born and bred in Lesotho (he later married a Mosotho), four constables to keep order around the court house, and nine policemen.[12]

Among Hope's first acts was to order one Raisa to appear before his court to answer charges of having destroyed a certain widow's cornfield. Raisa was an influential headman, one of Moorosi's war doctors and rainmakers, whose land was in the district of the chief's son, Lehana (known to the whites as Doda). Here Hope was treading on very dangerous ground. According to customary law, Raisa was exercising his rights over the woman's land, as she had refused to be *kenela*-ed (taken over by him) on the death of her husband—a close relative of Raisa.[13] It was a complicated matter which should have gone before Moorosi. Hope saw it as the kind of case in which European concepts of equity should override customary law. Raisa promptly refused to appear before the magistrate, who thereupon fined him for contempt of court. At this point Moorosi intervened.[14]

He and his sons, and a large following of armed men, gathered at the magistracy on June 22 and demanded a *pitso* (parley) with Hope. This took place the following day, but only after Hope had persuaded Moorosi to order his men to stack their guns and assegais. At Moorosi's request, Maitin read the official regulations in Sesotho. This procedure had become a formality at the annual Maseru *pitso*, and the mere reading did not imply consent.[15] Moorosi then raised the question of jurisdiction, in particular the case of Raisa. Turning to the *pitso*, he asked the people "do you obey me or this man?" They all cried out, "we obey Moorosi." At this mark of open disaffection the white men and their police withdrew into the magistracy, Moorosi's men regained their arms, and in the resulting excitement, with everyone shooting guns, one of the crowd was accidentally killed by a ramrod fired from a flint musket. Hope attempted to sort this matter out. The crowd dis-

[12] S9/1/3/3: Griffith to Hope, 11 June 1877.

[13] On this and other matters in the Moorosi story I am indebted to information supplied by Mosebi Damane in a series of conversations in London, Feb. 1965.

[14] This incident is described in detail in letters Hope to Griffith, 23, 25, and 26 June 1877, in Cape A49, 1879 (henceforth A49/79), 112-17.

[15] Cf. Charles Maitin's later comment on an annual *pitso*. "The net result of the meeting seems to have been an increased contempt for the Govt . . . the proceedings were opened by reading the laws and regulations, to which no one paid the slightest attention." Maitin's diary in possession of Chief Leshoboro Majara, 22 Sept. 1891.

persed, and Moorosi spent the following day, Sunday, thinking over his tactics.

He returned to see Hope on June 25. The argument between the two continued. Hope bluntly told the old chief that if he persisted in his attitude he was likely to be treated as a rebel. Moorosi maintained that he was supreme chief in Quthing and that the magistrate was his subordinate—a belief held by every Sotho chief, though seldom as explicitly stated. As Moorosi put it later, Hope "even said my conduct resembled that of Langalebalele [sic] and Moitheri.[16] I said, 'No chief, do not compare me to those who are dead.'" On the previous Saturday, when the man had been killed, Hope had turned on Moorosi with a similar fatal comparison. "Moorosi, supposing it had been either you or me who were dead, what would be said?," to which Moorosi replied, "The lips of you, chief, are fate-bearing, what you have said always comes to pass."[17]

Moorosi now brought up further complaints, all concerned with the exercise of authority: that dues payable on the allocation of land were no longer his prerogative; that Hope had kept him from exercising his jurisdiction over villagers who sold *joale* (beer)—that is, that he was rendered powerless to prevent the white man's money economy from trespassing upon one of the traditional bonds of hospitality, the giving of refreshment to travelers; that Hope had interfered with a case concerning one of his sons and a white trader over a stolen gun, which Moorosi had considered to be settled.

Hope told Moorosi that he, Moorosi, had no jurisdiction over such cases. The chief retorted that "he would never submit to this, he would preserve his independence and judicate in any case he chose." Hope reminded him that "it was too late to talk of his independence, he should have said this to Moshesh before Basutoland was given over to the Government," but Moorosi only replied that he had never given *his* country to the government.[18] When the magistrate warned him that his language was rebellious, Moorosi became very excited, told him that "you may kill me but I will not submit or resign any of my privileges," and left the magistracy in anger. Later the same day, however, Moorosi put out peace feelers; he had meant to intimidate Hope, but not to frighten him so much that he would panic and call in outside help. So he sent his confidential messenger, Mofetudi, to placate the magistrate. According to Mofetudi, the old chief should not have been

[16] Moitheri was implicated in the 1876 disturbances in Griqualand East. Both men had been *imprisoned,* not put to death. To Moorosi, imprisonment was a form of death. The same argument was used later when Lehana was put in jail.

[17] A49/79: Moorosi's statement, 16 July 1877, giving his version of the clash with Hope, 3-6.

[18] A49/79: Hope to Griffith, 25 June 1877, 114-16.

held responsible for his actions as he was under the evil influence of Mokojomela, his headstrong brother, and others.

It was a most diplomatic move at this stage of the row—Moorosi would have known that Hope had sent reports of the affair to the police camp at Palmietfontein, across the Tele in Herschel, and to Griffith in Maseru—to bring forward a scapegoat, and then to ask forgiveness on the plea that he had at last escaped from evil counsel. The submission came on the following afternoon, June 26. Hope made the occasion as formal as he could, standing, with Maitin, in the center of his little force of policemen. "[The magistrate] brought the matter to a crisis . . . would [Moorosi] submit to my authority or not . . . if he did, I would shake his hand as a faithful British subject, if not, he was a rebel, and I must treat him accordingly. At this, there was intense excitement as shown by the faces of the men . . . the chief made a most manly and complete apology, and promised never to oppose me again . . . we shook hands."[19] Moorosi claimed that he had given in "grudgingly . . . you have treated me unjustly in taking away from me that about which I had already given judgment. I can see that I am no longer anybody in this land . . . or anything to the people. Hope said I was; we shook hands, and cried 'Hurrah, God save the Queen.' "[20]

Thereafter, Moorosi and Lehana persuaded Raisa to submit to the authority of Hope's court. Perhaps they understood that any sentence would be nominal. Actually, however, Raisa was fined three sacks of kaffir corn (millet). Moorosi then ordered Raisa not to pay and, for the first time in his clashes with the white men, turned to Letsie for advice.[21] There is no direct evidence to illuminate the numerous meetings between the chiefs or their messengers. The few accounts in the official correspondence, based on informants' statements, are biased and unreliable. Judged by his public actions and pronouncements during this and the subsequent clashes between Moorosi and the white administration, Letsie behaved quite correctly toward the government, and always counseled Moorosi to be submissive.

Griffith meanwhile was admonishing Hope to act cautiously and with tact, to "substitute diplomacy and moral persuasion for physical force or high-handed proceedings," telling him that he was not in a position to promise any physical support "if Moorosi were forced into open resistance."[22] But Hope was anything but a tactful man. He had a reputation for being cruel and vindictive, even when compared with

[19] A49/79: Hope to Griffith, 26 June 1877, 117.

[20] Ibid.: Moorosi's statement, 16 July 1877.

[21] A49/79: Hope to Griffith, 5 July 1877, 119. Letsie, the great Sotho chief, was Moorosi's superior.

[22] S9/1/3/3: Griffith to Hope, 14 July 1877.

Austen; D. F. Ellenberger, who founded the Masitise Mission, wrote of him, many years later, that "he was harsh and impatient and the people feared him, more especially because he used to whip them unmercifully."[23] Meanwhile, Griffith also warned Letsie of the dire consequences if Moorosi continued his resistance to white rule. The great chief in turn sent his personal messengers to talk matters over with the old chief. There is no evidence of what was said and decided at this meeting, even whether Moorosi was given the burden of Griffith's message: "that whilst the Government has no intention of depriving him of his position as Chief it expects from him that he will place no obstacle in the way of his people availing themselves of their rights as British subjects to bring their complaints before the Magistrate."[24] The great chief's emissaries seem to have persuaded Moorosi to accept Hope's judgment and to order Raisa to pay the fine to the magistrate. At any rate, the messengers returned to Griffith with Moorosi's lengthy written statement (in Sesotho), giving his version of the clash between Hope and himself and "expressing his great regret that Mr. Hope should have misunderstood his sayings and doings, as he had not the remotest idea of insulting the Government or of behaving disrespectfully to the magistrate."[25]

Moorosi appeared to have made his peace with Hope, and all concerned breathed a sigh of relief. The government was prepared to "let bygones be bygones,"[26] and even Moorosi experienced the calm that follows a traumatic experience. His relations with Hope became "most satisfactory" and he was "most friendly" toward him.[27] The Raisa affair undoubtedly ended in victory for the white administration in Lesotho. Hope and Maitin had shown great fortitude in facing Moorosi and his armed men, and the old chief had given way to the arguments of the magistrate, Griffith, and Letsie. Nevertheless, Moorosi had proved that he could get away with a show of insubordination, backed by arms. To him, the important thing was not that he had lost a round, but that he had retired from the contest unscathed and was ready to fight another day.

In August 1877, war between the Xhosa groups (the Ngqika and Gcaleka) and the Cape colonists began. Griffith left Lesotho to take command of the colonial forces. His place as Governor's Agent was taken temporarily by Emile Rolland, who, like Maitin, was the son of

[23] Article in *Leselinyana*, June 1915.
[24] A49/79: Griffith to Sec. Nat. Aff. (SNA), 11 July 1877, 118; S9/1/2/1.
[25] A49/79: Griffith to SNA, 18 Aug. 1877, 2-3.
[26] A49/79: SNA to Griffith, 7 Sept. 1877, 6-7.
[27] A49/79: Private note Hope to Griffith, quoted in Griffith to SNA, 18 Aug. 1877, 2-3.

a French missionary; he had previously been assistant magistrate at Mafeteng and inspector of schools. The small detachment of white colonial soldiers left their camp at Palmietfontein, where they had been stationed since the early days of Cape rule over Lesotho, for the scene of the fighting. Both the war in the Cape and Griffith's removal caused much disquiet in Lesotho.[28]

Moorosi evidently decided that the unsettled state of affairs would provide a good opportunity for a further trial of strength with Hope. Thus, while Hope was absent from Quthing, attending the annual *pitso* at Maseru, Moorosi called upon his people, from the north as well as the Quthing bank of the Orange River, to attend his own *pitso* at the magistracy. Hope returned to find armed groups of men assembling at various villages, a spate of rumors about Moorosi's intentions, and a great deal of excitement.[29] According to Hope, it was rumored that Moorosi intended to force an acknowledgment from him that his own authority was superior to that of the magistrate, or to try to expel him from the district.

In a letter dated November 23, Hope agreed to talk to Moorosi and his people on December 3, on condition that they came unarmed. Moorosi replied in a Sesotho letter that he wanted to know from Hope about the proceedings at the Maseru *pitso*, and would come on the day that the magistrate had suggested, but "I will not leave my weapons at home when I go to a *pitso* to speak with a chief . . . ever since I was born it has been our custom. . . . A man does not leave his horns at home. . . . I used to go and visit even Moshesh with my weapons. . . . If the magistrate says I must leave my guns, then it is that he refuses to see me and we shall not meet. I do not want to walk stark naked. . . . I am coming to this *pitso* with a glad heart, as for arms, they are only the appendages of manhood."[30] This was direct and unambiguous, but the chief could not refrain from an enigmatic tailpiece: "Hope must not listen to what the lips say when he and I speak to each other, the great thing is the heart; the words of the mouth concern only the local question of our respective villages, they have no importance." Hope was forewarned that however seditious Moorosi's words might be, his heart was in the right place!

Hope admitted to Rolland that, in view of the unsettled state of the district, he had erred in fixing a date as close as December 3. He

---

[28] See petition of Letsie and others, enclosed in Rolland to SNA, 22 Sept. 1877, S9/1/2/1. "Letsie was so deeply affected [by the news of Griffith's departure] as to be immediately seized with violent pains and sickness and was seriously ill for some days."

[29] A49/79: Hope to Rolland, 24 Nov. 1877, 9–10.

[30] A49/79: Moorosi to Hope, Nov. 1877, 11. Trans. by Rolland.

therefore sent a telegram (by rider to Aliwal North) to that effect direct to the Secretary of Native Affairs at Kingwilliamstown.[31] Rolland then sent an admonishing letter to Moorosi, telling him he had no right to dictate to the government about the conducting of *pitsos,* and canceling the one fixed for December 3. To Hope he wrote that the situation in Quthing appeared most critical, that "everything is to be gained from delay . . . no advantage can possibly accrue from the *pitso,* which would give Moorosi an opportunity of being insolent, and of contrasting his large physical resources [armed men] with the [to African eyes] defenceless and weak position of the magistrate. He is trying to make use of these armed demonstrations in order to convince his people of his power and supremacy, being unaffected by the presence of the magistrate."[32]

The machinery for involving Letsie in Moorosi's affairs was also set in motion. But before Rolland's letters reached Quthing, Hope panicked; bands of armed men were roaming the district, excitement mounted. Hope took it upon himself to request the nearest colonial officer to send a detachment of soldiers to Palmietfontein, where he would meet them, and "have some of them there for a few days in order that Morosi [sic] . . . may be reminded by their presence in [the] neighbourhood that the Government has not lost sight of them." But he was still sensible enough not to ask for troops to cross the Tele and defend the magistracy; "if the men were marched into the district to meet Morosi's force, a collision would then inevitably take place."[33] (The Tele was a boundary line created by the white men for their own convenience, but it had been accepted as such by the Phuthi, and the crossing of it by white troops was in their eyes an act of war.)

Not all his colleagues realized this simple political truth as clearly as did Hope. As it was, the reappearance of the white soldiers at Palmietfontein caused something of a stir. Moorosi ordered his people who lived between the magistracy and the Tele not to come to the *pitso* (he had not yet received Rolland's letter canceling it), but to be on the alert with guns and horses ready to repel the soldiers if they should try to cross the river.[34]

As soon as he heard Hope's requests for the troop movements, Rolland countermanded them, perhaps out of pique that matters had been taken out of his hands:

---

[31] A49/79: Hope to Rolland, 24 Nov. 1877, 9-10, and Hope to SNA, 25 Nov. 1877.

[32] A49/79: Rolland to Moorosi, 12-13; Rolland to Hope, 28 Nov. 1877, 13-14.

[33] A49/79: Hope to SNA, 29 Nov. 1877, 8.

[34] A49/79: Rolland to SNA, 5 Dec. 1877, 8-9.

As a counter-demonstration to anything [Moorosi] may do, it is most in-adequate, and is only calculated to irritate and provoke the chief with-out overawing him. Moreover, the arrival of an armed force under such circumstances might produce a scene on both sides of the Telle, amongst a population so given to spreading false and exaggerated ru-mours. If [Moorosi] supposes that you have been instrumental in it, your moral influence with him will be greatly undermined.[35]

The composition of this moral influence which white magistrates were supposed to exert over their African subjects was never precisely de-fined; perhaps it was a matter of the heart about which Moorosi had earlier, oracularly, addressed himself to Hope.

Whether Rolland's assessment of the effect of Hope's actions was correct or not, by early December calm had returned to Quthing. Per-haps once again the diplomatic action taken by Letsie in sending Motlepu, his adviser on Phuthi affairs, to reason with Moorosi, had persuaded the old chief to rein in his warriors. The attitude of Letsie and the rest of the leaders of the Sotho *sechaba* (nation) counted for much in Moorosi's calculations; unless he felt that he had the support of his fellow chiefs, he was not prepared to risk a showdown.

Moorosi emerged from this incident with a reprimand from the Cape government; "he must not be led to believe that when he does wrong he has only to apologise to escape punishment . . . the next time [if any] he will be taught by other means than words, what his true position is."[36] Hope was able to report that, once again, Moorosi's attitude was conciliatory, the chief having sent to him for permission to hold a meeting on the *qhobosheane*, so that he could warn his people "to be careful to preserve order and quietness," although surely other matters would be discussed! Rolland considered this request "a very important concession on his part and a recognition of his position . . . I am fully satisfied that he will behave better in future."[37]

Yet by the end of January 1878 an even more serious clash was developing in Quthing. Hope had continued to press his magisterial powers to the utmost, in spite of Griffith's and Rolland's pleas for re-straint and caution. At the end of January he had given judgment against Maikela, a chief under Lehana (Doda), and four other men for hut tax payments due to be made by their widowed mothers, who had never previously done so. Maikela claimed that Austen had ex-empted them from paying, but had no written proof. Hope accordingly gave the men two weeks to go to Austen at Mohale's Hoek, and to get

[35] A49/79: Rolland to Hope, 30 Nov. 1877, 16-17.
[36] A49/79: SNA to Rolland, 9 Feb. 1878, 20.
[37] S9/1/2/1: Rolland to SNA, 25 Jan. 1878.

certificates of exemption from him; it is very likely that Austen would have given them as he was far less rigid in such matters than Hope. Certainly the whole notion of a woman's liability to pay the hut tax, which implied a right to land holding, was unacceptable to the Phuthi, who regarded women as legal minors without such rights.[38]

However, once convinced of his rectitude, Hope tore in where more experienced men might have feared to tread. Maikela and his companions did not go to Austen; perhaps they had misunderstood what Hope had told them—perhaps the Orange and other rivers were unfordable. Instead, Lehana assembled all his armed men in the Qomoqomong Valley, a few miles from the magistracy, ready to resist any move made by Hope either to arrest Maikela and the others or to lay hands on stock in lieu of a fine. Lehana had previously been to see Hope, who had tried to explain matters to him, emphasizing that the men had the right to appeal against his (Hope's) judgment to the Governor's Agent's court at Maseru.

But Lehana was in no mood to settle the matter peaceably. Hope reported that when Lehana went up to the *qhobosheane* to confer with his father, Moorosi admonished him for causing yet another crisis with the white man, and it is apparent that the Maikela affair was much more the business of Lehana than of his father.[39]

When, after the fourteen days had expired, Hope sent his policemen to serve a writ on Maikela, Lehana intervened and said that he would not allow any fine to be paid. The policemen asked him why the men had not appealed if they did not think the judgment just. Hope reported Lehana as saying: "I have nothing to do with *Makhoa* [white men], I only know Morosi." Having failed to serve the writ, the policemen then tried to drive off two head of cattle "believed to belong" to Maikela. By this time a large crowd had gathered, brandishing assegais, and the hills above the Qomoqomong were "swarming

[38] I am grateful for Mosebi Damane's opinion on this point.

[39] There are copious sources for the Maikela affair: the series of letters printed in A49/79, of which Hope to Rolland, 16 Feb. 1878, the source for much of this paragraph, is the first; Bowker's and Rolland's evidence before the Committee on Basutoland Hostilities, especially Rolland's reply to question 791; contemporary issues of *Leselinyana*; and D. F. Ellenberger's articles on Moorosi in 1915 issues of this newspaper. The role of Lehana in all the clashes between Moorosi and the white authorities is not easy to determine. Obviously he was a leading figure in most of them, but, when compared with other prominent Sotho at this time, there is little evidence about his character or motives, or even about his relationship with his father's more senior sons. The author has not, for example, been able to find any information about his mother. Perhaps he was, as the whites avowed, naturally "troublesome"; perhaps he was in the forefront of resistance just because of all Moorosi's major sons he lived closest to the magistracy.

with armed men." The policemen wisely abandoned their efforts to get hold of the cattle and withdrew to the magistracy, telling the crowd that they would be punished for their interference.[40]

Hope then issued a criminal summons against Lehana, Maikela, and others; sixteen men gave themselves up and were fined two head of cattle each, but Lehana, Maikela, and thirty-five of their followers fled with their stock into the mountains above the valley. The magistrate then sent a message up to Moorosi, demanding that the old chief arrest his son. Moorosi argued that he had no idea where Lehana was; Hope contended that he obviously did.[41] Rolland also wrote to Letsie, ordering *him* to arrest the offenders, and threatening that if he could not do so force would be used, however "terrible it would be that blood should be shed in the Lesotho."[42] It was made quite clear to Letsie that this force was to be largely provided by the Sotho themselves, as the Cape's white soldiers were still engaged in mopping-up operations on the eastern frontier. In other words, the *sechaba*'s loyalty to the white government was to be determined by Letsie's willingness to order his warriors to fight against their own kind.

Faced with the prospect of civil war, Letsie dispatched a high-powered mission, headed by his eldest son, Lerothodi, to Moorosi to tell him to advise Lehana to submit to Hope and accept his judgment; but the mission made little impression on the fears and suspicions of the old Phuthi chief.[40] Hope meanwhile turned to Ellenberger, who had returned to the mission station at Masitise after an absence of several years, for help in negotiating with Lehana. Ellenberger met Lehana in one of his fortified caves in the hills above Masitise, but could not persuade him to go to the magistracy. Lehana said he feared going to Hope, complaining that he would never listen to an African's side of the case: "When a man answers back the magistrate threatens him. It is better that Hope should kill me rather than I should be whipped like a dog."[44]

By this time Hope was in bad odor with all concerned—the Phuthi, the missionaries, and his government colleagues. Ellenberger years later wrote of Hope's "disgrace" at not being able to force his authority upon Lehana, and another missionary spoke of him as "un mauvais brouillon."[45] Also, at the beginning of the Maikela affair, Hope had

[40] A49/79: Hope to Rolland, 16 Feb. 1878.
[41] A49/79: Rolland to SNA, 6 Mar. 1878.
[42] S9/1/3/3: Rolland to Letsie, 6 Mar. 1878.
[43] *Leselinyana*, Apr. 1878.
[44] Ellenberger's article in *Leselinyana*, Dec. 1916.
[45] Paris Evangelical Missionary Society Archives, Paris (henceforth PEMS). Correspondence, 196, 1877–78: Germond to Casalis, 29 Mar. 1878.

sent Rolland two letters that Rolland had considered "unadvisedly written both with regard to direct expressions as well as to covert-implied [sic] sentiments."[46]

At this point James Henry Bowker, who had replaced Griffith as Governor's Agent, and who had held this post at the beginning of the white administration, arrived in Lesotho full of conciliation and good intentions, but determined to by-pass Hope in his dealings with Moorosi. He handled the situation with considerable adroitness, meeting his "old friend" Letsie at Morija on March 19 to discuss the righting of "old and crooked things."[47]

This coming of the white man to the great chief to discuss matters of state was more to the liking of the Sotho leaders than Hope's tactless actions. Letsie agreed to give strong support to Bowker to "put matters right for the Government."[48] Within a few days between six and seven hundred armed men had been assembled through his orders, and sent down to meet Bowker at Mohale's Hoek. At the Hoek, Bowker had hoped to hear of a successful end to the negotiations between Lerothodi and Moorosi from Austen; there was apparently no news which indicated that the negotiations had been successful, so he continued with Austen and the Sotho soldiers to the north bank of the Orange at Phatlalla Drift, where Lerothodi assumed command of the Sotho force, and where Hope joined the gathering.[49]

Bowker was wary of crossing the river into Quthing, which would have been seen by the Phuthi as an act of war. Although advised by his colleagues that "he could not pull through without fighting," Bowker was determined to avoid an open conflict if possible. As the head of the white administration in Lesotho, he had little money and fewer arms and ammunition. His sole force, Lerothodi's men, were wholly untried in action against their own kin. One missionary at least was doubtful whether they would fight Moorosi's men, "parceque le Gouvernement a en des torts évédents dans toute cette affaire."[50]

[46] S9/1/3/3: Rolland to Hope, 27 Feb. 1878. Hope's letters cannot be traced. They perhaps criticized Rolland for not allowing him to use force during the previous incident.

[47] S9/1/3/3: Bowker to Letsie, 14 Mar. 1878.

[48] *Leselinyana*, Apr. 1878. My informants, S. Pinda and M. Damane, are emphatic that Bowker, during this incident, and Griffith, when the Phuthi were in active rebellion, persuaded a reluctant Letsie to summon armed Sotho soldiers to fight for the white authorities only by warning him that if white troops from the Colony were involved, Phuthiland would be detached from Lesotho and settled by white farmers. In the event, this warning proved only too true.

[49] *Leselinyana*, Dec. 1915.

[50] PEMS Correspondence, 3, 1878–79: Dieterlen to Casalis, 2 Apr. 1878. For the Bowker quotation and much that follows, see evidence before BHC, especially answers 651 to 659. The kinship between Sotho and Phuthi was in some cases real, and in others was established by marriage bonds.

Bowker doubtless realized the measure of his men, and gave Moor-osi every chance to come to terms. But the old chief was afraid to meet Bowker at the head of such a large force and suspected treachery. He asked to be allowed to pay a fine, to which Bowker would agree only if Lehana brought the cattle in himself; Lehana and his father con-sidered this a trap.[51] Bowker sent Letsie's representatives up to the *qhobosheane*, keeping up a daily correspondence with them. After several days of uneventful parleying, Bowker told Lerothodi that "the things was [sic] played out," and that he must have a definite answer from Moorosi by the following Saturday when both Moorosi and Le-hana were to appear before him at Phatlalla.[52] Lerothodi, who had married one of Moorosi's daughters,[53] took this final demand to his father-in-law and returned, saying that the chief had agreed to come and talk, but that he was afraid "that he would be caught like Lan-galabelele" if he came unarmed.[54] However, unlike Hope in a similar situation, Bowker put no difficulties in the way of Moorosi's men being armed: "I was a soldier, and my people were armed, and I could see no reason why Morosi should not come armed." He had consulted Austen on this point. Lerothodi "was almost crying at the time for fear I would not agree; he said it was the only way of saving the country from a war. . . . I had never protested against armed meetings with native chiefs."[55] Moorosi therefore rode to Phatlalla with about seven hundred armed men, a force equal to Lerothodi's, and drew them up on the opposite bank of the Orange, where they stood "squarely behind Moorosi holding their arms to protect Doda."[56] On Lerothodi's and Austen's advice, Bowker called a *pitso* to settle the matter.

Moorosi had little to fear for his son's safety from such a formal, public assembly. It is not clear on what side of the river—in Lesotho or in Phuthiland—the *pitso* was held; the result of the proceedings, which accorded far more with Moorosi's sense of judicial process than the summary justice of the magistrate's courts, was that Lehana was fined twenty-four head of cattle,[57] Maikela ten, and the other men involved five or three head.[58] When compared with fines normally imposed by the magistrates' courts, these were not excessive; when

[51] *Leselinyana*, Apr. 1878.
[52] BHC, 658.
[53] Ibid., statement of S. Pinda, Mafeteng, 7 Oct. 1965.
[54] Ibid.
[55] Ibid., 659. The commissioners must have been somewhat alarmed by this statement, which was not strictly speaking correct: Bowker had on occasion criti-cized Griffith for holding such *pitsos*.
[56] *Leselinyana*, Dec. 1915. See also BHC, 791, Rolland's evidence.
[57] BHC, 567.
[58] *Leselinyana*, Dec. 1915. The official version was Doda, £100; Maikela, £25; S9/1/3/3: Rolland to Landdrost, Ladybrand, OFS, 11 Apr. 1878.

compared with the loot in cattle and other stock driven off by the government forces during the conflict of the following year they were innocuous. Yet Lehana had done no more than protect some of his men from what the Phuthi considered a miscarriage of justice.

The Maikela affair was the most dangerous to date of the various clashes between Moorosi and the white authorities: armed men had faced one another across the Orange. It had several important consequences. Because of the attitude of the Sotho "volunteers" toward the prospect of fighting their fellow Africans—an attitude doubtlessly emphasized by Lerothodi and Letsie's representatives in the course of their visits to Moorosi—the Phuthi had become convinced that no Sotho army would ever fight against them. The affair had also showed the solidarity of the Phuthi, their determination to support their chief, and Moorosi's determination to protect Lehana. However, the most dramatic consequence of the affair was the removal of Hope, a step agreed upon by Bowker and the Cape government.[59] Bowker considered that relations between Hope and Moorosi were anything but satisfactory and that Hope had acted "injudiciously." Rolland thought that Hope was "uncompromising."[60] The Phuthi must have looked upon the decision, coming a few weeks after the resolution of the last clash between the magistrate and their chief, as a considerable concession to Moorosi and a valuable point in his favor in the power game.[61] Nevertheless, Moorosi characteristically complained to Bowker about Hope's removal from Quthing, probably on the grounds that he had not been consulted. Moorosi believed that he was more than a match for Hope, who, though pig-headed, was a young man. Rolland later told the Basutoland Hostilities Committee that Moorosi thought that he could "manage" more easily with Hope, especially as his successor was to be Austen. Moorosi "knew Mr. Austen of old, and was afraid of him."[62]

By the spring of 1878 tensions had increased once again. For one thing, much of the Eastern Cape, Herschel, and Phuthiland was in the grip of a serious drought for the second season in succession, or perhaps longer. Even in Lesotho proper, which escaped the worst ravages, whites wondered whether the country would not be reduced to a desert like Karroo.[63] Moorosi's country was still suffering from the effects

[59] S9/1/2/1: Bowker to SNA, 25 Apr. 1878. See also BHC, 573.

[60] BHC, 572 and 795.

[61] Ibid., 795.

[62] Ibid., 796. Hope was transferred to Qumbu, one of the newly created Transkeian magistracies, in the Pondomisi chief Umhlonhlo's country. Umhlonhlo had Hope murdered in Oct. 1880.

[63] PEMS Correspondence, 1878–79, Ellenberger to his parents, 14 Oct. 1878, 118. At Shawbury, in the Eastern Cape, "the Natives say that never has such a drought been known . . . they attribute it to the country having recently been

of the drought at the end of the year, when Austen reported that very little grain had been reaped during the last three seasons, and that the people in Quthing had been saved from starvation by the purchase of grain in Griqualand East and "St John's Territory"—"the quantities that have been brought over the mountains on pack oxen and horses is almost incredible."[64] Good rains did not fall in Quthing until February 1879.[65] Drought does not lead people into rebellion, but it can be a contributing factor in the general atmosphere of discontent and in the despair that can force people to battle against overwhelming odds.

Against this background, Griffith returned to Lesotho as Governor's Agent in October 1878. On October 24 he announced to the annual *pitso* that the government would call upon the Sotho to give up their arms. He prefaced his remarks by a description of the Cape wars in which he had recently participated, stressing that the captured rebel chiefs had been sentenced to life imprisonment. He had been astonished to hear that Moorosi and the Phuthi had come to meet Bowker at Phatlalla armed with guns and assegais.[66] Griffith had been briefed by Sir John Gordon Sprigg, the Cape Prime Minister, on the policy he should adopt in carrying through disarmament in Lesotho. Sprigg expected difficulty from Moorosi, and promised to supply Griffith with a force to overawe him if necessary. Griffith replied that he had not the slightest doubt that Moorosi would refuse to give up his arms, and that he would resist any attempt to take them by force. He told Sprigg bluntly that at least two seven-pound mountain guns with ammunition and two "rocket-tubes" with rockets should be "collected quietly at Palmietfontein, and arrangements made for provisioning a sufficiently strong force at the same place when it becomes necessary to enforce the law."[67] But Sprigg neither sent the guns nor made any arrangements.

The Sotho who heard Griffith's announcement at the *pitso* were generally appalled; most of those who spoke at the meeting registered a shocked and uncomprehending protest, dismayed that Griffith should apparently compare them to the defeated Cape peoples. In their

---

taken over by the Colonial Government. Drought, they say, follows the white man wherever he goes." Wesleyan Missionary Society archives, London: Queenstown district 2823, W. S. Davies, 20 Nov. 1878. For a general commentary on the effects of severe drought, see C. W. de Kiewiet, *The Imperial Factor in South Africa* (London, 1937 and 1965), ch. VII, 151-52, 161-64.

[64] Cape Blue Book on Native Affairs, G33/79: Austen to Griffith, 30 Dec. 1878, 14.

[65] A49/79: Maitin to Griffith, 10 Feb. 1879, 20.

[66] A49/79: Report on Pitso, 29-30. Also in *Leselinyana,* Dec. 1878.

[67] Disarmament correspondence between Sprigg and Griffith, A30/82: Sprigg to Griffith, 5 Oct. 1878; Griffith to Sprigg, 16 Oct. 1878.

annual reports, written at the end of December, the white magistrates stated that they had received only a few reactions to the disarmament threat—the Sotho were considering the matter deeply and were seriously disturbed by it. No representatives of Moorosi were present at the *pitso,* but he and his people were fully informed by Austen of the intention to disarm them.[68]

As has already been pointed out, in November 1878 Austen arrested Lehana for stock theft, an act which became something of a *cause célèbre* in Sotho history. It has all the appearances of having been a trumped-up case. During the Maikela affair, while Lehana, Maikela, and their followers had been hiding from Hope and his policemen in caves in the mountains above Qomoqomong and Masitise in March and the early part of April, some of Lehana's men (from the caves) had raided white farms in New England, returning with a number of horses. Lehana was said to be "in command" of these men; one version of the story was that he had ordered them to steal from the white farmers.[69] The alleged theft had therefore taken place during the Griqualand East disturbances when the white forces and their African allies were, as usual, looting great quantities of stock. The theft might have been carried out in retaliation, or even in revenge for Hope's attempt to take cattle from Maikela's kraal when he refused to answer the charges against him. After Bowker's settlement with Moorosi, and Hope's removal, Lehana and Maikela once again went about their peaceful occupations in Qomoqomong.

Lehana's relations with Austen seemed to be cordial. It was known that the horses had been stolen, but the thieves could not be identified. Austen however kept on with his "secret service" investigations, working "quietly, sending his policemen there and here . . . without any noise."[70] Some stolen cattle (it is not clear if these were lifted in the same raid as the horses) were traced to some of Moorosi's "sons or grandsons," who were arrested by Austen. A mother of one of these cattle thieves complained to the magistrate that "she did not see why her son should suffer and Doda and the others escape."[71] On this woman's evidence, the theft of the horses was traced to Lehana's men.

Early in November 1878, nearly seven months after the alleged theft had taken place, Lehana and some of his men were arrested. Rolland later admitted to the members of the Committee on Basutoland Hostilities that this procedure, while "strictly legal" was a "harsh

[68] BHC, 823.

[69] For the events leading up to the arrest of Lehana see BHC, evidence of Rolland, 799-804.

[70] Ellenberger, article in *Leselinyana,* June 1915.

[71] BHC, 803.

measure" which did "occasion some feeling."[72] Lehana had not been caught red-handed, and had not been personally concerned in the stealing; he was an accomplice after the fact.

The trial was held on November 10. Austen's courtroom was filled to capacity. The prisoners denied the accusation, but Austen claimed that the evidence produced by his witnesses proved the charge against them. He sentenced Lehana to four years', and Nqatsha to two years' imprisonment.[73] Moorosi was present at the trial and left the court "grumbling and murmuring all sorts of abuse against Mr. Austen."[74]

Later, the members of the Committee expressed some surprise at the manner of the trial and the severity of the sentence passed upon Lehana. Rolland told Merriman, the chairman, that the magistrates in Basutoland had an unlimited power of sentencing, except that only a combined court could try cases punishable by death; there were no juries, prosecutors, or accessors. Each magistrate acted alone—"a man is sentenced to an extended term of imprisonment by the magistrate's own *ipse dixit*," except that the sentence was subject to review by the chief magistrate (the Governor's Agent), and there was a right of appeal to him but not to any higher colonial court. In reply, Merriman wondered whether it was satisfactory that this amount of power should be given to one man.[75] There is no doubt that Lehana's four years' imprisonment was an extremely severe sentence for a man who was merely "an accomplice after the fact," especially as the evidence was suspect, based more on hearsay than fact, and perhaps hastily gathered by Austen in an effort to incriminate Lehana and to eliminate him from the political scene. The Regulations for Courts of Law in Basutoland (Proclamation 41 of March 29, 1877) contained no stipulation concerning the accountability of chiefs for the actions of their followers, though such accountability could probably be inferred from Sotho law and custom. Austen, however, was not one to trouble himself with the niceties of law, be it English or Sotho. He wanted to revenge the "ignominious compromise" that he considered Bowker had been forced to make with Moorosi and Lehana over the Maikela affair earlier that year. With Lehana out of the way doing hard labor on the Cape Town breakwater, Moorosi might be induced to abdicate, and Phuthiland "reduced" to the submissive state of Austen's old district across the Tele.

Griffith gave his unqualified approval to Austen's decisions, and immediately wrote to the Cape government for authority to send the

[72] Ibid., 804.
[73] A49/79: Austen to Griffith, 20 and 23 Nov. 1878, 33-34.
[74] Ellenberger, *Leselinyana,* June 1915.
[75] BHC, 805-13.

prisoners to convict stations at East London or Cape Town.[76] Until arrangements for their "disposal" could be made, Lehana and his fellow prisoners were lodged in what Austen described as a "very insecure" lockup at Quthing magistracy. "It is a wonder," Austen wrote in his annual report for 1878, "that prisoners have not escaped through the [slender iron] roof continually."[77] In a prophetic comment he continued, "in the case of a disturbance the Magistrate would have to remove his family . . . and the result would be a general panic and stampede." Griffith repeated this prognostication in a letter to the Cape government written after Lehana's escape.[78]

Yet, in spite of the obvious risk, the prisoners remained in the little lockup for the rest of November and the whole of December. Only on December 23 did Griffith receive authorization to send Lehana to Aliwal North, en route to Cape Town, which authorization he relayed to Austen. If sent by special police delivery this letter should have reached Austen the following day; if by ordinary post, within a few days. (Members of the Committee on Basutoland Hostilities did wonder, in view of the seriousness of the case, why communications between Griffith and the Cape government had not been by telegram from Aliwal North to Cape Town and back.)[79] Austen, however, made no move. He may have been waiting for a detachment of white police from Palmietfontein to come to the magistracy to escort the prisoners to Aliwal North. From what he wrote in his annual report at the end of the year, Austen made no mention that a plot was afoot to rescue the prisoners:

> Since the trial and conviction of Doda . . . all commotion and excitement has subsided, and a general feeling of contentment seems to prevail. The chiefs appear to feel that their power is crumbling away. The wily old chief, Morosi [sic], seems to have cooled down entirely since the conviction of his sons. He came unarmed for the trial, nor was there a single assegai, or guns, seen amongst his followers (more than 100 men). He has sent several civil and very respectful messages to the Magistrate, and most of his principal sons appear anxious to co-operate with the Magistrate. The hut tax has been paid cheerfully notwithstanding the scarcity of food.[80]

The Phuthi must indeed have been remarkable people if the happy picture conjured up by Austen for the sake of his superiors and for

[76] A49/79: Griffith to SNA, 20 Nov. 1879, 33.
[77] Cape Blue Book on Native Affairs 1879, 16: Austen, 30 Dec. 1878, 14-16, in CO 51/205.
[78] S9/1/2/1: Griffith to SNA, 10 Feb. 1879.
[79] BHC, 819.
[80] Cape Blue Book: Austen, 30 Dec. 1878, 14-16.

those white colonists who troubled to read parliamentary papers had been literally true. No sooner, however, had he written his optimistic report than the tension which had been growing since Lehana's arrest dramatically broke into the open. It was widely believed in Quthing that on the first day of the new year white police from Palmietfontein would come to the magistracy to escort Lehana and the other prisoners to jail in the Cape.[81] If Moorosi had kept quiet until this time, it must have been because he had still hoped for a mitigation of his son's sentence as long as Lehana remained in Phuthiland. Conditions in and around the ramshackle lockup were not onerous, the prisoners were lightly guarded, and Lehana would have had ample opportunity to communicate with his friends and relations. But his removal to Cape Town was another matter—in the eyes of his fellow Phuthi it was a terrible fate reserved for rebels captured in battle. There seemed little possibility of Lehana ever returning alive.

Moorosi was under great psychological pressure to authorize the rescuing of the prisoners before it was too late. Lehana's mother is said to have upbraided him: "I don't produce children for the white man. You take this skirt and give me your trousers [a very short Basuto garment]."[82] An observation by a Methodist missionary in the Cape is illuminating in this context: ". . . the late rebellion in the Colony was fomented by women , , , they encouraged the men in every possible way and treated with scorn all the loyal natives, both male and female."[83]

On New Year's Eve Austen's Sotho police detachment watched over the prisoners while they were having their supper, then locked them in the jail and retired to their own quarters about sixty yards away. From there they could neither see nor hear what was going on at the lock-up.[84] They spent the rest of the evening making merry on Cape brandy (which was illegal in Lesotho), and "slept a peaceful sleep."[85] In the middle of the night Lehana and the five other prisoners were released from the lock-up by a well organized party of rescuers, who had crowbars to break the padlock on the jail door and spare horses on which the prisoners made a quick getaway.

Evidence later collected by Austen proved fairly conclusively that Moorosi had planned this rescue; one of the party is said to have

[81] Ellenberger, *Leselinyana*, June 1915.
[82] Statement of Likatana Sesoane, 21 Jan. 1966.
[83] Wesleyan Missionary Society archives, Queenstown district 2763, W. S. Davis, 15 Sept. 1878.
[84] S9/1/2/1: Griffith to SNA, 14 Jan. and 5 Feb. 1879.
[85] Ellenberger, *Leselinyana*, June 1915.

ridden the chief's favorite horse down to the magistracy.[86] It is remarkable that Austen could have been so deceived about the true state
of affairs in his district, and so negligent with the security of the
prisoners after he had just written about the deplorable condition of
the lock-up.[87] Griffith angrily demanded a full explanation,[88] and when
it arrived,[89] considered it unsatisfactory, and charged Austen and his
police sergeant with "great carelessness."[90] It is not impossible that
Austen had himself known what was afoot and had deliberately closed
his eyes to the rescue bid. This would not have been out of any
friendly feelings toward Lehana and Moorosi. On the contrary, he
would have realized that such a dramatic incident would lead to a
showdown with the old chief, resulting in his defeat and overthrow,
probably opening up Phuthiland to Mfengu and white settlement.

Lehana and his fellow fugitives took refuge in the mountains
around the upper Qomoqomong, in the caves which he and Maikela
had occupied during the troubles of the previous year. On the morning
after the rescue Austen sent to the chief, ordering him to assist in the
arrest of the prisoners and their rescuers. Moorosi retorted that he
could not possibly be held responsible for Lehana or know of his
whereabouts; as the prisoners had been in Austen's hands, "you should
know where they are. You can look for them."[91]

Austen then went ahead with his investigations to produce evidence which would break the old chief's power, offering a reward for
information leading to an arrest.[92] If Austen made life too difficult for
Lehana, Moorosi had plans to move his son further up the Orange, at
its junction with the Ketani, where another son, Masipudi, was living,[93] or to the comparative safety of independent Pondoland; messages were sent to this effect toward the end of January.[94] About the
same time Austen was able to report some success in the search for
the fugitives. The magistrate at Matatiele (Griqualand East) captured
one of Lehana's companions, Majerman (Majoematso?), and his evidence led Austen to arrest Mapara, one of the rescuers.[95]

By now Griffith was convinced of Moorosi's complicity in the

[86] Emma Ellenberger, Masitise, 17 Mar. 1879, printed in *Journal des Missions,*
translated by R. C. Germond in *Chronicles of Basutoland* (1967), 333.
[87] Cape Blue Book: Austen, 30 Dec. 1878, 14-16.
[88] S9/1/3/3: Griffith to Austen, 14 Jan. 1879.
[89] S9/1/3/3: Austen to Griffith, 21 Jan. 1879.
[90] S9/1/3/3: Griffith to Austen, 5 Feb. 1879.
[91] Ellenberger, *Leselinyana,* Aug. 1915.
[92] S9/1/3/3: Austen to Griffith, 11 Jan. 1879.
[93] NA276: Austen to Griffith, 25 Jan. 1879.
[94] S9/1/3/3: Austen to Griffith, 26 Jan. 1879.
[95] Ibid., 24 Jan. 1879.

affair.[96] He instructed Austen to continue to build up a case against the chief, but to do so quietly and tactfully. He was not to call for the assistance of the white troopers at Palmietfontein, except "as a very last resource . . . as I am afraid by you doing so it may precipitate matters."[97] But Griffith warned the Cape government that force might have to be used if Moorosi refused to answer the charges when these were brought against him. The March issue of *Leselinyana* (*Little Light*) reported that it was supposed that Moorosi wanted to fight— although he strongly denied this—and that his obdurate behavior was splitting his "nation" in two.

Up to the end of January 1879, however, all was peaceful in the country around the magistracy and the mission station. But the progress of the Zulu war was by this time casting its shadow upon affairs in Lesotho, and the news of the defeat of the British forces at Isandhlwana on January 22, with the heaviest casualties to white soldiers in any engagement so far fought in South Africa (some nine hundred white troops and five hundred of their African allies were killed), which reached Lesotho by telegram on January 27, hardened attitudes and reactions on both sides. Africans, who would have heard the news before its official arrival, were elated. Moorosi was doubtless encouraged to stand firm and defy Austen. Among the whites, "l'émoi, l'alarme, la consternation ont été grandes partout."[98] The Cape government determined on a show of white soldiers to overawe Moorosi, Griffith, quite independently, decided (like Bowker before him) to use the political authority and military forces of Letsie to bring Moorosi "to his senses." Early in February, on Sprigg's instructions, two troops of yeomanry militia were sent from Kingwilliamstown to reinforce the one troop of regular Cape Mounted Riflemen permanently stationed at Palmietfontein. Griffith first heard of this move, "fraught as it is either to give confidence to the Basutos or to frighten them into rebellion," from the Aliwal North newspaper (*Northern Post*), and complained bitterly to the government of being "kept in ignorance."[99]

As in the past, Letsie occupied a key position in the situation: Barkly, the magistrate at Mohale's Hoek, wrote that "the influence of Letsie is so great, that as long as [he] remains staunch in his loyalty, there is no fear of [the people] wavering in their allegiance."[100] In

[96] A49/79: Griffith to SNA, 28 Jan. 1879, 43-49.
[97] S9/1/3/3: Griffith to Austen, 26 Jan. 1879.
[98] PEMS Correspondence, 175: E. Ellenberger, Morija archives, 5 Feb. 1879.
[99] S9/1/2/1: Griffith to SNA, 5 Feb. 1879. See also "Life of General Sir E. Y. Brabant," typescript, Cape Town ACC 459, 73: The yeomanry were sent "to support the demand of the Government for Doda's surrender."
[100] NA 276, Barkly to Griffith, 15 Feb. 1879.

Quthing it was thought that unless Letsie took action against Moorosi, the sympathies of nearly all the people there would be on the old chief's side.[101] If Letsie were not put on the spot by the white authorities and involved on their side, then, it was thought, with the threat of disarmament and the news of Isandhlwana, he might join forces with Moorosi. Griffith visited Morija on February 6 and 7[102] and had long discussions with Letsie. He must have warned the great chief of the consequences of having to use white forces to pacify Quthing —the confiscation of land—and strongly urged him to use all his authority to induce Moorosi to surrender his son. As for Austen and other whites, they believed that there was collusion between Letsie and Moorosi, right up to the outbreak of fighting.[103] Austen wrote bitterly of "the farce played by Letsea's [sic] messengers to Morosi [sic], who saw the accused sitting on Morosi's mountain with guns and assagais [sic] in their hands, and defying the Magistrate and their paramount chief's orders." Rumors to this effect were rife. *Leselinyana* reported that such rumors were deliberately put out by Moorosi,[104] and Letsie thought fit to write to Austen to explain what his messengers had been up to—largely, it would seem, to escorting to Matsieng some of Moorosi's daughters to adorn Letsie's already large establishment of wives.[105] Even Rolland, a staunch supporter of the great chief's authority if not of his morals, admitted to the Committee on Basutoland Hostilities that Moorosi believed the Sotho would join him, because his messengers continually brought back reports of chiefs' grumbling about the threat of disarmament.[106] Austen and others argued that Moorosi would not have dared to take such an aggressive stance unless he were certain of Letsie's support. In the actual event, two thousand Sotho soldiers did take part in the fighting against Moorosi, although many of their leaders sympathized with him. After his death, even Austen was able to share this sympathy:

> The brave old Chief Morosi upon more than one occasion confessed that he had been victimised, but true to his obligations of loyalty to his supreme Chiefs [sic] would never mention names but allowed himself

[101] A49/79, Maitin to Griffith, 10 Feb. 1879.

[102] *Journal des Missions*, LIV (1879), 122; Edouard Casalis, Morija, 12 Feb. 1879. *Leselinyana*, Mar. 1879.

[103] See, for example, Austen's annual report for 1880, printed in Cape G20/81, 10-16; Henry Stevens, a resident of Herschel, reminiscences in possession of Rev. Paul Ellenberger, Masitise.

[104] *Leselinyana*, Apr. 1879.

[105] NA 276, Letsie to Austen, 9 Feb. 1879.

[106] BHC, 919-20.

to become the scape goat, and it has been roundly stated by Baputis, Basutos and Tambookies that what saved a large section of the Basutos from joining in the Morosi rebellion was their greed for loot.[107]

The Sotho later claimed that Griffith and Rolland had promised them that if they turned out with their guns against Moorosi, the threat of disarmament would be dropped. Thus, they were at one and the same time threatened and bribed by the whites to fight on their side.

As for Moorosi, the sending of the white reinforcements to Palmietfontein convinced him that his country was to be invaded;[108] that disarmament and even confiscation would be enforced as well as the surrender of Lehana; and that he himself would be tried and imprisoned. According to Ellenberger[109] the last straw for Moorosi was Austen's discovery that Ditlame, one of Lehana's half-brothers who had escaped with him, was in hiding in Phahameng. The magistrate and his police came to arrest him; Ditlame fled, and Austen fired on him. Moorosi then severed diplomatic relations with Austen, "since you have provoked us into war by shooting at my son. You want war and therefore we must fight." It is not clear when this incident took place. "From the day," wrote Ellenberger years later, "Ditlame was shot at by the magistrate, there was no other talk amongst the Baphuthi except war. Messengers were sent all over the country to tell the men to arm themselves in preparation for war."[110]

However, on Sunday, February 23, Ellenberger and a Swiss visitor rode past the magistracy on their way from Masitise to take the service at the chapel at Qomoqomong. They found Austen, Maitin, and the policemen hastily packing their belongings on horses and donkeys (it seemed that the white men's families had already been sent to Palmietfontein). Austen told them that they expected to be attacked at any moment, and as the magistracy was indefensible, they were abandoning it and taking refuge over the Tele.[111]

As Austen's party rode out of Quthing toward the Tele, it was watched by Phuthi scouts, who were seen "in all directions," and who were surely on the lookout for the anticipated attack from the white forces at Palmietfontein. "Had they been preparing for an attack upon Austen," wrote Griffith, "it would have been easy for them to have closed in upon him, and cut off his retreat altogether. In fact all the evidence . . . goes more to show that Morosi's people were

[107] G20/81, Austen's annual report.
[108] A49/79: Maitin, 10 Feb. 1879.
[109] Leselinyana, June 1915.
[110] Leselinyana, Aug. 1915.
[111] Ibid.

acting more on the defensive than the aggressive."[112] Rolland told the members of the Committee on Basutoland Hostilities that he thought that, had Austen remained at the magistracy, it would have had a "quieting effect," and that "nothing would have happened as long as Mr. Austen had remained."[113]

In the event, Austen's flight from the magistracy was a signal for a general uprising. Moorosi's men blocked the fords across the Orange and the Tele and watched the passes across the Drakensberg, capturing the great herds of cattle that many frightened people were driving into Herschel or Matatiele. On February 24, men under Moorosi's sons, Ratšuwanyane and Mqa, broke into the magistracy and Austen's house and plundered the contents; one trader's store was looted and the contents of another loaded on a wagon which was intercepted before it could reach the Tele.[114] Motsapi was in command of the border guard, and Ratšuwanyane established a camp near the mission station, trying to persuade the Christian Sotho who lived around it to join the rebellion; but the Christians generally listened to their missionary, who told them to remain faithful to the government which "Moshoeshoe had bequeathed them."[115] Lerothodi arrived at Masitise after an unavailing discussion with Moorosi on the mountain and stopped Ratšuwanyane's and Mqa's men from interfering with the Christians. Later Moorosi rode down, apologized to Ellenberger, and received a little homily on the evils of rebellion. The Phuthi retorted that the minister was right but they were forced by circumstances to fight."[116]

On February 27, Letsie was officially informed by Griffith that Moorosi "has thrown off the cloak under which he has been hiding for so long and has openly rebelled against the Government of the Queen."[117] He was "requested" to assemble his fighting men and send them down immediately to the Orange. Griffith made much of a supposed siege of the mission station and the need to relieve it. If there were any hesitations on the part of Letsie and his advisers to comply with Griffith's request—noncompliance would have been tantamount to supporting the rebellion—it was short-lived, and soldiers were

[112] S9/1/2/1, 5 Feb. 1879.
[113] BHC, 821-33.
[114] *Leselinyana,* Apr. 1879; Ellenberger, *Leselinyana,* Aug. 1915; S9/1/2/1, 26 Feb. 1879; Emma Ellenberger 17 Mar. 1879. D. F. Ellenberger stated that the actual men who looted the magistracy were "Ngunis" (i.e. Vundle) of Matushela. The son of Maitin, Cely Maitin, stated that Austen's house was plundered, but that his popular father's house, grain store, and horses were untouched: statement, 18 Nov. 1965.
[115] Emma Ellenberger, 17 Mar. 1879.
[116] Ellenberger, *Leselinyana,* Aug. 1915.
[117] S9/1/3/3: Griffith to Letsie, 27 Feb. 1879.

called out from all over the district of Thaba Bosiu. At the same time Molapo and Masopha sent contingents under their eldest sons, Jonathane and Lepoqo.

Griffith left Maseru on March 1 and joined the main body of Sotho soldiers on their way south. Appointed Commandant General of all the Cape forces, both white and African, that were gathering to attack the Phuthi, he was thinking in terms of a short campaign, one sharp blow to finish Moorosi. But he was still apprehensive over the loyalty of the Sotho; other whites shared this apprehension.[118] Ellenberger, writing later, suggests that Moorosi was in communication with Letsie's sons, the leaders of the Sotho forces—Lerothodi, Bereng, and Maama—and that he tried to persuade them to join him, and to prevent the white forces from crossing the Orange or the Tele. Griffith did not in fact invade Phuthiland until March 16. *Leselinyana* reported that the Orange was in flood, and that its waters delayed the Sotho soldiers who crossed it at the Phatlalla Drift. Further delay was caused by Lerothodi and Jonathane Molapo, who were at odds over their respective positions in the Sotho force.[119] Furthermore, the artillery which Griffith had long before asked the Cape government to have stationed at Palmietfontein had not yet arrived.[120]

While the opposing forces were waiting on the other sides of the Orange and the Tele, the Phuthi launched the first action of the war on March 5. Motsapi and other younger sons of Moorosi, who were guarding the river crossings, were impatient to attack in spite of the old chief's orders that the Phuthi were to remain on the defensive (he had learned his lesson fighting the Boers). They crossed the Tele and started to round up the white forces' cattle. There was a short skirmish with white soldiers, with a few casualties on both sides, and the Phuthi retired across the river to meet an angry Moorosi, who had come riding up from the camp near Masitise on being falsely told that the Cape forces had started the invasion: Ellenberger writes of him and his followers passing the mission in full battle array, chanting their war cries. This unsuccessful action seems to have persuaded Moorosi to give up his initial plan to try to prevent the enemy from crossing the rivers, and he, and most of the Phuthi forces, retreated up country to the *qhobosheane* and to various fortified caves.[121]

[118] Austen's various comments have already been noted. See also PEMS Correspondence, 190, 1878–79, Dieterlen, 3 Mar. 1879.

[119] G. Tylden, *The Rise of the Basuto* (Cape Town, 1950) 132, n. 24.

[120] Fanny Barkly, *Among Boers and Basutos* (London, n.d.), 73.

[121] *Leselinyana*, Apr. 1879; Ellenberger, *Leselinyana*, Aug. 1915. The Aborigines Protection Society's journal, *Aborigines' Friend*, June 1879, Casalis to Chesson, Paris, 31 Mar. 1879, 158; NA 276: Austen to Griffith, 26 Aug. 1879.

Moorosi then appealed to Lerothodi to intervene and to treat with Griffith on behalf of the Phuthi, but warned him that if the white troops entered his country he would fight to the death. On March 16 the Sotho contingent had been brought across the Orange, and were encamped two miles from the white camp at Palmietfontein—all except 700 soldiers who remained on the right bank of the river under Lerothodi to keep the rebels from crossing and to round up all the stock belonging to them on that side. The following day Griffith invaded Quthing, crossing the Tele with his entire force—400 white soldiers (100 regular Cape Mounted Riflemen and 300 yeomanry), 100 Herschel Mfengu, and about 1,200 Sotho.[122] Tylden states that Moorosi had about 1,500 men, "well armed and better shots than the rest of the Basuto [Sotho]," but probably this was an overestimate. He never had more than about 300 soldiers on the *qhobosheane* at any one time, but the Phuthi certainly showed themselves to be excellent sharpshooters.[123]

As they fell back on the *qhobosheane*, the Phuthi fought a series of sharp engagements with Griffith's advancing forces, in one of which a brother of Moshweshwe and several others of the Sotho contingent were killed.[124] By March 25 the Cape and Sotho forces (except those under Lerothodi, which remained on the opposite bank of the Orange) had reached the mountain and pitched camp at its foot. The flat-topped fortress, which is about one thousand feet above the waters of the Orange and Quthing at its base, has sheer rock faces on three sides. The fourth side falls in a series of ledges which were "strongly fortified by breast works built with large stones, and placed with great skill, so that the lower ones are commanded, and can in many cases be enfiladed by those above them; they are pierced with double rows of loop-holes and in most cases are situated on the verge of steep rocks, which render them almost inaccessible from below."

The mountain, wrote Maitin, "was crowded with stock of every description; there was a supply of water, though this was not plentiful, and stores of grain. Perhaps the most remarkable of Moorosi's arrangements was the large quantity of ammunition stored in caves and specially constructed magazines, which must have been diligently accumulated over the years."[125]

Griffith attempted to surround the mountain by positioning patrols

---

[122] A17/79: Maitin's diary, 10-11.

[123] Tylden, *Rise*, 131-32; A17/79: Maitin's Diary, 25 Mar. 1879, 12; ibid.: Griffith to Col. Sec., 24 Apr. 1879, 2; South Africa Correspondence, C2482, *Report on Capture of Morosi's Mountain*, 469, states that five hundred Phuthi had "threatened" Austen.

[124] A17/79: Maitin's diary, 22 Mar. 1879, 10-11.

[125] Ibid., 12.

around its perimeter, and by keeping up a desultory bombardment with his two little seven-pound guns, but, throughout the siege, the Phuthi were able to come and go from the mountain at night, taking up fresh supplies of grain and even animals. On the night of April 7 and into the next day Griffith launched a frontal attack, which was easily repulsed by the Phuthi, who inflicted losses on the Cape forces and their African allies.[126] He then handed over command to Colonel Brabant, who brought with him a more powerful field gun (a twelve-pounder) and reinforcements; for a time some six hundred white troops were in Phuthiland. The Phuthi constantly harassed their besiegers, on May 29 attacking the camp of a patrol and killing and wounding the soldiers as they slept in their tents.[127] On June 5, Brabant attacked the mountain again in force, but this failed as disastrously as the first assault.[128]

During the long winter, Moorosi made several attempts to come to terms with his adversary, venturing down the mountain with a white flag to the lowest line of defenses. The last of these parleys was with Prime Minister Sprigg in October. But the only terms offered were unconditional surrender, and Moorosi maintained that he preferred death to such a fate.[129] Brabant was replaced by a Colonel Bayly, the third change in Cape command, and on the night of November 19–20, the mountain was stormed by the Cape Mounted Riflemen, regular troops, who used ladders to scale one of the lightly defended rock faces.[130]

By then there were less than two hundred Phuthi soldiers left on the fortress. Twenty or more white troops were killed and fifty wounded during the eight months' siege. This was a high casualty rate in a "colonial" war. The Sotho and other "loyal" Africans suffered even heavier losses. It is impossible to determine the number of Phuthi casualties; it must have been several hundred killed, and many wounded. Austen counted thirty-eight bodies, including that of Moorosi, on the *qhobosheane* the morning after it was captured by the Cape forces.[131] Of the Phuthi leaders, Lehana alone escaped death or capture by fleeing up the Orange River Valley; much later he was pardoned, and he died in 1906.[132]

The gallant resistance of the Phuthi and their old chief earned the

[126] Ibid., Griffith to Colonial Secretary, 24 Apr. 1879, 2-6.

[127] Ibid., Court of Inquiry, 30 May 1879, 15-18.

[128] Ibid., Brabant to General, Colonial Forces, 7 June 1879, 21-31.

[129] PEMS Correspondence, 1879–80: D. F. Ellenberger to Director, 108; South Africa Correspondence, C2454: Sprigg to Frere, 24 Oct. 1879, 370.

[130] Ibid., 468-69.

[131] NA276: Austen to Griffith, 22 Nov. 1879.

[132] Information from M. Damane.

grudging admiration of many white men in South Africa, including the soldiers who fought against them. However, the length of the siege, continuing as it did through the bitter cold of the Phuthiland winter and into the spring, and the numbers of casualties they had suffered undermined both the morale and the discipline of the white soldiers. When Moorosi's body (shot through the neck) was brought down to the camp at the foot of the captured mountain, the army doctor had the head removed and sent down to Kingwilliamstown on its way to exhibition in a London hospital. This was not the only indignity suffered by the dead chief. The troopers got hold of the corpse and paraded it round the camp with a spear stuck up the rectum and then dismembered it, some of their African allies sharing in this last operation. The African soldiers no doubt valued parts of the body for their medicinal properties; the troopers had no such excuse. When news of the beheading reached Whitehall, hasty telegrams were dispatched to the Cape ordering the head to be returned and buried with the body. This instruction was presumably carried out, but no trace of the grave remains.[133]

At the end of the rebellion, Phuthiland was largely depopulated of men and beasts. Vast herds of cattle had been captured by and distributed among the white forces and their African allies. Known leaders of the rebellion who were captured were sentenced to terms of imprisonment; the ordinary men, women, and children were sent as laborers to white farms in the Cape. The only large groups remaining in Quthing were the Sotho Christians and Tyale's Vundle, who had just managed to escape being caught up in the rebellion. The Cape government determined to execute the usual punishment for rebellion and, despite the protests of Griffith, the missionaries, and the Sotho, began to confiscate much of the fertile land in Quthing. Austen served on the Land Commission which began to delimit the new white farms. Their occupation by colonists was prevented, however, by the outbreak of the Gun War in Lesotho in July 1880, and the successful Sotho resistance to the Cape's attempt to force them to disarm.

The Cape government learned nothing from its costly conflict with

---

[133] CO 48/493 Cape 1880: Frere to Sec. of State, 8 Jan. 1880, Sec. of State to Frere, 5 Feb. 1880; *Cape Argus,* 1 Jan. 1880; *Aborigines' Friend,* Apr. 1880, Rev. R. W. Barbour (Lovedale) to Fowler, 9 Feb. 1880, 221-22; Edwin W. Smith, *The Mabilles of Basutoland* (London, 1939), 245, quoting A. Mabille correspondence not accessible to the author of this present account; Tylden, *Rise,* 135 and n. 37; informants reluctantly confirm the story of the mutilation of Moorosi's corpse. Cely Maitin in his statement of 18 Nov. 1965, and S. Pinda (see n. 48 and n. 53) add that the Phuthi today believe that it was not actually the chief's body that suffered these indignities, but that another was substituted for it and that Moorosi was buried where he was killed, in a cave on his mountain.

Moorosi. Even before the chief had been defeated, it simultaneously demanded of the Sotho that they surrender their arms, double their hut tax payments, and consent to the confiscation of land which they had long considered to be part of Lesotho. Moorosi's rebellion had proved extremely difficult for the Cape forces to suppress; the wider Sotho resistance was to prove impossible. If Letsie had joined Moorosi in 1879, instead of grudgingly assenting to his people's resistance only in the middle of 1880, perhaps things would have gone differently for the old chief and his people; perhaps there would be a Phuthi chieftainship to this day.

The Moorosi rebellion was a comparatively minor episode in the great outburst of armed African protest against the relentless pressure of white rule in South Africa in the late 1870's. It shared with these conflicts a number of interrelated causes, one set of which were the psychological reactions of the two races to each other. The two sides were separated by a veil of misunderstanding. Whites and blacks had lived in close contact in Lesotho for many years, as they had in the Eastern Cape and Natal, and had learned by experience about the more superficial of each other's ways. Probably the Phuthi and their neighbors had made the greater effort to study their adversaries, and to accommodate themselves to their peculiarities; they tried to please. Some missionaries and a few administrators took a more than usual interest in the social and political environment of their charges and committed their findings to writing. But no one at this time, or for some time to come, studied the situation objectively with a view to formulating policies based upon substantial knowledge. Side by side with this lack of comprehension went fear: the whites feared what the Africans could do when they went on the "war path." The Africans had similar fears, sharpened by a religious terror that the white man could destroy a man's very spirit and that of his ancestors, and thereby disrupt the whole moral fabric of the tribe. (The mutilation of Moorosi's body must be seen against this background.)[134] Out of fear and incomprehension arose intolerance and its concomitant feeling of superiority; both these attitudes were felt and expressed in racial terms.

Such was the emotional background for racial war in nineteenth-century South Africa. There naturally were more specific causes for these outbreaks. As far as Moorosi was concerned, the two fundamental elements in the long conflict were loss of land and diminution of political authority. The Phuthi had lost land to the Cape authorities in the 1840's and 1850's and were threatened with further confisca-

[134] Cf. the illuminating remarks on "Cannibalism and Culture-Contact," in George Shepperson and Thomas Price, *Independent African* (Edinburgh, 1958), 9-11.

tions thereafter. The encroachment upon Moorosi's political power became particularly apparent after the appointment of the magistrate to the Quthing district. All of the crises which occurred at short intervals from 1877 to 1879 were about authority and who should exercise it in Phuthiland. Political authority in South Africa rested on the exercise of armed force and on the control of the available sources of economic wealth; that is, land, the products of the land, which throughout most of the nineteenth century meant cattle and other stock, and, to a lesser extent until the exploitation of mineral resources late in the century, labor. The white farmers and the African peasants and pastoralists wanted an exclusive use of the land and the use—if not the ownership—of the stock that grazed upon it. African chiefs and colonial farmers measured their prosperity in terms of area of land and head of cattle. The grounds for conflict were numberless. Disputes over land and stock were basic to nearly all of the racial wars until well into the second half of the nineteenth century.[135] This is especially true of the Sotho-Free State wars and the long series of "Kaffir" wars in the Cape.

Not merely did the magistrates and other government officials undermine the authority of a small chief like Moorosi within his own group, but they interfered with the relations between such a group and its neighbors. This divisive intervention in tribal affairs played a dominant part in the whole century of racial conflicts on the Cape eastern frontier from the 1770's to the 1870's. The whites attempted to play off one group of Xhosa against another; they settled "friendly" Africans on the lands of "recalcitrant" chiefs; they held certain chiefs responsible for the good order of a whole frontier region, when in fact their authority covered a more limited area. In Lesotho, the British annexation incorporated Moorosi in the *sechaba* of Moshweshwe and his successor to a far greater degree than ever before, with perhaps the exception of one period of his rule. The last-ditch stand of the Phuthi, when they "went it alone" in their desperate opposition to the white man's rule, was in defiance of the instructions of Letsie and was fought against Sotho as well as colonial soldiers. The people who ultimately benefited from the rebellion were the Sotho. After the Gun War, Quthing district was administered directly by Letsie, who sent one of his sons to be chief of the district.

The Phuthi reaction to the accumulation of white pressures was expressed in forthright and straightforward measures—a resistance

---

[135] At this time the colonial merchants, rather than the frontier farmers, were the chief protagonists of a policy of expansion. See Andrew Duminy, "The Role of Sir Andries Stockenström in Cape Politics (1848–1856)," *Archives Year Book for South African History, 1960,* II, 153-56.

which finally had recourse to arms. The Phuthi were an even less organized military people than the Sotho, though neither people had
anything like the complex system of age-group regiments developed
in Zululand. A chief and his immediate kin and trusted men simply
called out their able-bodied followers, in a kind of *levée en masse*, to
take up arms against the white foe and his allies. By the end of the
1870's these arms included a large proportion of rifles and other guns.
The warriors of Moorosi, as well as those of Lerothodi and the other
Sotho chiefs, were "doctored" to ensure victory for the *sechaba* and
individual invincibility. Compared with the Cape Africans, however,
prophets and prophetesses played only a minor part in Sotho (and
Phuthi) resistance.

In this respect, the courage and determination shown by the tiny
force of Phuthi warriors and their families in withstanding eight
months of siege are the more remarkable. They lacked the comforts
provided to men *in extremis* by the prophesies of a ministering priesthood. They had nothing but their loyalty to a much respected old
chief, and their obviously deep feeling for their homeland and their
people, to sustain them through the grim experience. There was never
really any prospect of the rebellion's succeeding, especially once the
siege was under way. If captured, Moorosi and the other Phuthi leaders would have been sentenced to life imprisonment. Rather than face
this fate or the humiliation of subservience to the white authorities,
Moorosi chose a course of action which could only have ended in
his death and the destruction of the Phuthi as a political entity. The
moving acceptance by Moorosi of this fate is a measure of the failure
of the peoples in this part of South Africa, black as well as white, to
come to a satisfactory political and social resolution of their conflicts
—or even to a reasonable *modus vivendi*.

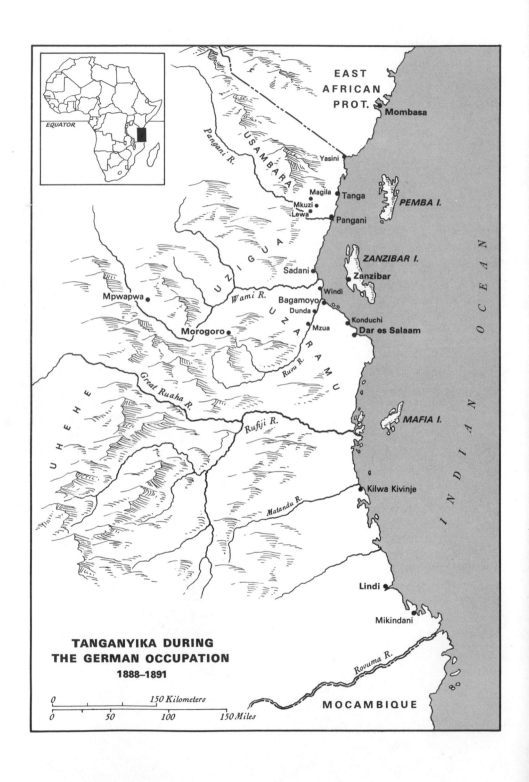

EAST
AFRICAN
PROT.

Mombasa

EQUATOR

Pangani R.

USAMBARA

Yasini

Magila • Tanga
Mkuzi •
Lewa •
Pangani

PEMBA I.

U Z I G U A

Sadani

ZANZIBAR I.

Zanzibar

Mpwapwa •

Wami R.

Windi

Bagamoyo
Dunda
Mzua

Konduchi

Dar es Salaam

Morogoro •

U Z A R A M U

Ruvu R.

Great Ruaha R.

U H E H E

Rufiji R.

MAFIA I.

I N D I A N   O C E A N

Matandu R.

Kilwa Kivinje

Lindi •

Mikindani

TANGANYIKA DURING
THE GERMAN OCCUPATION
1888–1891

Rovuma R.

MOCAMBIQUE

0   150 Kilometers
|___|___|___|___|___|
0   50   100   150 Miles

RESISTANCE TO THE GERMAN INVASION

OF THE TANGANYIKAN COAST, 1888-1891

ROBERT D. JACKSON

Between August 1888 and March 1891 the German Empire struggled to assert its rule over the coastal area of Tanganyika.[1] Although the Germans were ultimately successful, their task was far more difficult than anyone in Berlin could have anticipated. The initial thrust of their invasion was thrown back by hastily assembled African forces—probably more than 100,000—who remained in virtually complete control of the coast for over six months. These defenders were dislodged only by a reinforced German drive that required ten warships and thousands of Sudanese and Shangaan mercenaries. Even then, in spite of thousands of casualties and many defections in their own ranks, the African resistance forces were able to impede the invasion for nearly two more years.

How was such a massive resistance movement raised, and who were its most dedicated members? What motivated its leadership and adherents? Why were the coastal defenders finally unsuccessful in their bid to maintain their independence? In my opinion, the resistance was motivated by widespread disgust at German attitudes and policies, as well as a basic desire among most elements to retain the relaxed political and social arrangements that had existed under the Sultan of Zanzibar. Yet the cohesiveness and endurance of the movement were undermined by the question of long-term goals. Furthermore, for a variety of reasons, the coastal defenders failed to adopt the organiza-

[1] For the purposes of this article, the Tanganyikan coast includes the stretch of land between the town of Yasini and the Ruvuma River (the present limits of mainland Tanzania), and the hinterland to a distance of 150 miles. It was estimated in 1913 that the population of this area was 1,279,000. See Gerald F. Sayers (ed.), *The Handbook of Tanganyika* (London, 1930), 32.

tion and tactics necessary to counteract the superior firepower of the invading forces. Finally, the movement was weakened by the increasing efficiency of the German officials in dividing the African opposition through concessions and threats.

The viewpoint of the insurgents is best presented in a history written in Swahili by Hemedi bin Abdallah al-Buhriy, a participant in the early stages of the resistance.[2]

The Background of the Resistance

In order to understand the vehemence of the reaction to the German invasion, one must first examine the political, social, and economic character of the inhabitants of the Tanganyikan coast before the conflict. This examination will, of course, indicate what the Africans were defending, and it will also provide an insight into the inaccuracy of the German claims that the resistance they encountered was principally

---

[2] J. W. T. Allen (ed. and trans.), *Utenzi wa Vita vya Wadachi Kutamalaki Mrima, 1307 A.H.* (Dar es Salaam, 1960). Hemedi was a spiritual advisor to Abushiri, the chief resistance leader, and he provides us with a nearly precise chronology of events from June 1888 to July 1889, as well as a number of vivid descriptions of battles as seen through African eyes. His discussion of the motivation of the movement is somewhat less useful, however, for he writes from the viewpoint of a literate religious counselor and generally ignores the attitudes of the illiterate tribesmen who made up the vast majority of the resistance forces. Much can be added, however, by a careful reading of the available European sources. In this connection, it is impossible to overestimate the excellent work of Fritz F. Müller, stemming from his recent research in the previously unavailable documents in the Potsdam archives. *Deutschland-Zanzibar-Ostafrika: Geschichte einer deutschen Klonialeroberung, 1884–1890* (Berlin, 1959). Müller overlooks nothing in his exhaustive search for evidence of the African viewpoint, and I am greatly indebted to him for both facts and interpretation. A similar, though not so thoroughgoing, investigation of the available British documents in London by Norman Bennett has also been helpful. "The Arab Power of Tanganyika in the Nineteenth Century" (unpublished dissertation, Boston University, 1961). In addition to drawing together these key sources, I have added whatever useful evidence is in the officially published German Whitebooks and British Parliamentary Command Papers (*Weissbuch, vorgelegt dem Deutschen Reichstage*, Berlin, 1885–1902, 22 volumes; *Further Correspondence Respecting Germany and Zanzibar*, C. 5603 [1888], C. 5822 [1889]). There is also a wealth of detail to be found in the personal narratives of missionaries in East Africa at the time and in the memoirs of the officers of the German invasion force. I have preferred to use, where possible, British rather than German accounts, since the mutual antagonism between the two countries often led British commentators to reveal the distortions and omissions of the German writers. Whenever only German sources are available, I have tried to use them sparingly, and chiefly for matters of undisputed fact.

Arab slave traders reacting to an attack on their economic interests.[3] (The German Empire, of course, was an altruistic, "civilizing" force dedicated to the abolition of the East African slave trade.) The following survey will show, however, that slave trading was largely curtailed on the coast at that time, and that the few slave traders who remained played a very small part in the resistance. It should also show that the actual German motives were quite different from those announced to the world.

Socially and culturally, the coastal area was characterized by the dominance of Swahili, a term that referred not only to the language spoken by a large number of the people, but also to the complex and resilient amalgam that had developed from the constant intermingling of Arab cultural elements with those of the indigenous coastal peoples. There had been frequent migrations of Arabs to East Africa since well before the tenth century. These adventurers settled on the offshore islands and at favorable points along the coast, sometimes demonstrating their supremacy through bloody wars with the African population. The Arabs controlled the trade in ivory and the other products of the interior. They also established plantations worked by slaves whom they had captured or had purchased from the more powerful of the African chiefs.[4] Unlike the Europeans who eventually superseded them, however, these Arab immigrants had no aspirations to power or desire for land beyond what they themselves could utilize. They found that their ventures were most successful if they recognized and co-operated with the surrounding African rulers, and the Africans were in turn attracted by the religion and customs of the Arabs.

Over the course of centuries, the Arabs, who had no reservations about taking African wives and who were willing to associate with Africans on relatively equal terms, were gradually integrated into the coastal society. For this reason, a strong distinction between Arab and African did not develop on the coast. Although the more recently arrived Arabs could often be distinguished from the older inhabitants by their physical features, they too were quickly drawn into Swahili society, which by the end of the nineteenth century numbered nearly 200,000 individuals.[5] It is true that anyone of Arab ancestry continued to refer to himself proudly as an Arab and that most of the wealth

[3] This argument is presented, for example, by Georg Maercker, *Unsere Schutztruppe in Ostafrika* (Berlin [1893]), 7.

[4] On the early settlement of the Tanganyikan coast, see Gervase Mathew, "The East African Coast until the Coming of the Portuguese," in Roland Oliver and Gervase Mathew (eds.), *History of East Africa*, I (Oxford, 1963), 94-127.

[5] *Handbook of German East Africa* (n. p., 1916), 28-59. The same source estimates that in 1910 there were about 300,000 nominal adherents of Islam, found not only on the coast but in Usambara and Usagara as well.

was in the possession of such individuals, but the unifying factors of religion and custom far outweighed the divisive elements of heritage and disparity in wealth, especially since the wealthy of this society were not given to ostentation or haughtiness.

In fact, the social distinction that became most meaningful on the coast was not that between Arab and African, but rather between *Wamrima* ("people of the coast," whatever their origins) and *Washenzi* ("uncivilized people"—a pejorative term referring to the people of the hinterland who had not adopted the mixed Swahili culture). Even this distinction could not be rigidly applied, however, for the geographic division between the two cultural worlds was not sharp. Rather, as one progressed farther inland, the world of the *Wamrima* gradually faded and fewer and fewer Swahili characteristics were found. Yet even far into the interior there were occasional islands of coastal culture, especially along the caravan routes.

In the early nineteenth century there was a sudden increase of commercial interest in the interior of East Africa in response to the increased international demand for ivory and slaves. The first major penetration from the coast was made in the 1820's by coastal entrepreneurs along trails already traveled by such trading peoples as the Nyamwezi and Bisa. They took cloth and beads to trade for the great quantities of ivory and slaves that could be obtained in the area of Lake Tanganyika. Soon the word of the profits to be made spread to coastal Arabia, and a fresh influx of Arab traders, sponsored in part by Sultan Sayyid Said, began to follow the same trails inland. By the 1840's there was tension between the original coastal traders and the newer, purely Arab elements, and both were in conflict with the Nyamwezi, who sought to retain control of the trade in their homeland.[6]

By the 1860's, however, slave trading had nearly ceased in the Lake Tanganyika area, due largely to the exhaustion of ready sources and to the relatively greater ease with which slaves could be obtained to the south; henceforth most slave trading occurred in the Lake Nyasa area. Elsewhere increased emphasis was placed on alternate economic activities, especially the trade in ivory and the development of profitable plantations.[7] Soon, large numbers of Arab and Swahili traders were settling near the coastal towns to cultivate exportable crops, such as sugar, coconuts, and sesame, as well as rice and other staples. Eventually every coastal town, and particularly Bagamoyo and Pangani, was surrounded by plantations worked by thousands of slaves. By the

[6] For the history of this early commercial penetration from the coast, see Alison Smith, "The Southern Section of the Interior, 1840–84," in Oliver and Mathew (eds.), *History of East Africa*, I, 267-72.

[7] Bennett, "Arab Power," 8-9.

1870's whatever slave trading remained had been diverted to this purpose as a result of the decline of international demand and the prohibitions imposed by the treaty of 1873 between Britain and Zanzibar. Even Kilwa, which had once been the chief slave depot, by 1880 had found in rubber production a legitimate substitute for the slave trade. Within ten years rubber was the chief export of the entire coast, surpassing even ivory.[8]

It should be noted that the domestic use of slaves on the plantations was not only legal from the Arab viewpoint but was also sanctioned by tradition in the coastal economy. In comparison with the plantation slaves of the antebellum United States, those of East Africa played a considerably more legitimate and meaningful role in society. They possessed land of their own in the vicinity of their owner's plantation and were permitted to build and maintain individual dwellings for themselves and their families. Their obligations to their owners consisted of a month or two of work during the planting and harvesting seasons. Otherwise, they were at liberty to cultivate their own crops and to engage in any number of money-making activities. In time of conflict they were often called upon to serve as soldiers, and they could thus anticipate enriching themselves through plunder or even hope to win their freedom through noteworthy conduct.[9] None of the above is to imply that the life of a plantation slave was particularly pleasant; we can be sure that they all bore the scars, internal as well as external, dealt by the life of a human chattel. But it must be emphasized that by 1880 the trade in slaves had largely ended, and that German descriptions of the coast as a hotbed of Arab slave drivers and manacled Africans were flagrant distortions.

The most striking feature of the 1880's was the phenomenal growth of the towns of the coast in response to rapidly expanding legitimate trade. Accompanying this growth was a natural increase in the complexity of the coastal society as new trades and professions developed to meet purely urban needs. This period also saw the immigration of large numbers of Indians to the coastal towns to serve as the financiers and middlemen of the new commercial prosperity. The largest of the towns was Bagamoyo, with its permanent population exceeding twenty thousand constantly being augmented by thousands of transient caravan porters.[10] Pangani was next in prominence, having developed in

[8] J. M. Gray, "Zanzibar and the Coastal Belt, 1840–1884," in Oliver and Mathew (eds.), *History of East Africa*, I, 241.

[9] Wilhelm Wolfrum, *Briefe und Tagebuchblätter aus Ostafrika* (München, 1893), 82; Hugold von Behr, *Kriegsbilder aus dem Araberaufstand in Deutsch-Ostafrika* (Leipzig, 1891), 224-25.

[10] Rochus Schmidt, *Geschichte des Araberaufstandes in Ost-Afrika* (Frankfurt a. Oder, 1892), 185-86; *Deutsche Kolonialzeitung*, I (Aug. 25, 1888), 271-72.

ten years from "a large village of thatched huts and with little or no trade" into "an important commercial centre, of stone houses."[11] Kilwa, too, was growing, and large complexes existed at Tanga, Sadani, Lindi, and Mikindani. Interspersed between these coastal towns were numerous Swahili villages of fishermen, farmers, and petty traders, all of whom were gradually being drawn into the growing town economies.

Politically speaking, the population of the Tanganyikan coast was highly fragmented, a factor that was to weigh heavily in the failure of the resistance movement. Most of the towns, it is true, were relatively well organized in that they were ruled by councils of notables consisting of prominent Arab, Indian, and Swahili residents. The Arab and Indian notables customarily achieved this status through wealth, while the Swahili notables, called *jumbe,* were recognized for their authority as representatives of a particular quarter or segment of the population. Yet only a small minority of the coastal people lived in the large towns. Most continued to inhabit small, isolated villages that had only occasional communication with the coast or with one another. Each village was ruled by a Swahili chief (also called *jumbe*) who had risen to power in a variety of ways and who fiercely guarded his own domains against the inroads of surrounding *jumbe.* Occasionally a powerful chief would gather a few villages together and create a small kingdom (as in the case of Simboja of Usambara), but this was unusual.

It is evident that the main features of this political system remained unaffected by the strengthening of the Zanzibar sultanate under the Busaidi dynasty. This was so because the sultans had little desire to control the coast completely; it would have necessitated a far more complex administrative apparatus than they could have afforded. Their chief interest was in the profits to be gathered from East Africa, both through independent trading ventures and through the collection of customs duties in the ports. Although they nominated a *wali* (governor) in each of the large towns, this man was generally subordinate to the council of notables. As one *wali* explained to a German official, it was his practice "not to bother much about anything in the town, lest he upset the people."[12] It was far more important to the sultans that they gain recognition for the Indians to whom they had farmed out the task of collecting customs duties.

[11] J. P. Farler, "England and Germany in East Africa," *The Fortnightly Review,* LI (1889), 159. Farler had been Archdeacon of Usambara for the Universities' Mission to Central Africa since 1875 and had observed at firsthand the amazing growth that he described.

[12] Quoted in *Weissbuch,* IV, 13-14. See also Sir H. Bartle Frere, "Zanzibar: A Commercial Power," *Macmillan's Magazine,* XXXII (July, 1875), 279-80.

So long as the sultans restricted themselves to their interest in customs duties, the people of the coast were willing to recognize them and do them homage, for the sultanate was a symbol representing the loose legal and political structures that had preserved for each town and village its own autonomy and had permitted the commercial interests to carry on their trade with a minimum of interference. The sultans were also admired for their wealth and dignity and for the splendor of the occasions upon which they met with the coastal people and exchanged respects and gifts.[13] But there was not much regard for their power, for in fact they possessed little, as was demonstrated conclusively by Sultan Barghash's abortive attempts to increase his authority with British support in the 1880's. The coastal people acknowledged the sultan as their ruler, but only because he wisely limited himself to the policies that they themselves determined.

European contact with East Africa expanded greatly during the nineteenth century, spreading from commercial interests in Zanzibar to the establishment of missions and plantations on the coast and to the exploration of the interior. In particular, certain elements in Germany became interested in the colonial potential of the Tanganyikan coast and hinterland, and, in 1884 and 1885, representatives of the Society for German Colonization, led by Carl Peters, obtained the signatures of several of the lesser *jumbe* of Uzigua to treaties of dubious value. Upon presenting these to the Kaiser, the Society was rewarded with an Imperial Charter of Protection, which granted legitimacy to their endeavors despite the fact that the Sultan of Zanzibar had not been consulted. When the Sultan protested this infringement on his nominal control of the interior, he was quickly silenced by British verbal pressure and a display of German warships. In 1886 the European powers imposed a treaty upon him which limited his influence to the offshore islands and to a narrow band of coast, and which declared that the vast hinterland of this coastal strip was in the German sphere of interest. In the following two years, the agents of the German East Africa Company, which was an outgrowth of the Society for German Colonization, negotiated many more "protectorate" treaties with the peoples of the interior.[14]

It has often been asserted that the *jumbe* had little notion of the full implication of their signing these treaties, that they were befuddled with alcohol, and that, in any case, they were not the legal holders of

[13] It may be noted, for example, that Hemedi dwells very little on the power of Sultan Sayyid Khalifa in his formalized praise, but rather emphasizes his wealth, his wisdom, the beauty of his palace, etc. (Hemedi, *Utenzi*, 21-31.)

[14] See Müller, *Deutschland*, 220-86, for details of the expansion of German involvement in East Africa.

the land rights that they transferred to the German agents. There is, however, substantial evidence indicating that many of them had been warned far in advance of the German intentions, and that they understood most of the terms of the treaties.[15] From the outset, the Sultan had placed great difficulties in the way of the German treaty hunters, sending messengers ahead of them to warn the *jumbe* and interfering with their hiring of porters (at least one agent described with dismay his daily struggles to outrun the Sultan's adverse messages to the *jumbe*).[16] And those chiefs who did sign the treaties would probably have felt no qualms about repudiating them should the coastal people have placed pressure on them. But for the time being they were earning the gifts that the German agents brought and were paving the way for their own future security in the event that the Germans gained the upper hand in the struggle for control of the coast. It is also possible that some *jumbe* hoped to use the friendship of the Germans against neighboring enemies and, perhaps, even their help in re-establishing their *hongo* (local tolls on caravan traffic), which the coastal traders had denied them.

Whatever their original attitude toward the Germans, the peoples of the coast and interior were soon exposed to their bad behavior and ruthlessness. Word spread of their unpleasant conduct in Zanzibar, where, drunken and unruly, they continually expressed their ridicule for Islam. For example, a young Englishman in Zanzibar wrote to his parents in 1886 that, "This place is full of Germans. They walk the streets with the air of conquerors, taking any fruit &c that they want without paying for it and raping any women that they see—you can imagine the state the Arabs are in. . . . Two German sailors have already been stabbed."[17] And another observer described the following scene in Zanzibar:

> In March 1885 a large party of Germans were celebrating the Kaiser's birthday at a private house in Zanzibar when disturbances arose in the town and one of the party, who was drunk, went into the street and emptied his revolver into the crowd. The crowd closed in and seized him. General [Lloyd William] Mathews arriving found the German Consular judge himself drunk trying to rescue the German and assaulting the natives. . . . [The Germans also] publicly abused the Sultan and shocked the susceptibilities of the Mohammedans by their irreligion. "Why do you talk about your Allah?" said a German to a native; "That's your Allah," and he held out a rupee. Thus they came

[15] Ibid., 128, 528.
[16] Schmidt, *Geschichte*, 6-9.
[17] Quoted in Bennett, "Arab Power," 158.

to be known by the name of Adui Allah [Enemies of God], and were often so described in letters from the interior. They never sufficiently realized that the influence of the Sultanate on the mainland was to a great degree a religious influence.[18]

The story was also widely told of Rochus Schmidt, a German company agent who killed a man because he refused to carry his baggage and was, in turn, nearly killed by the *jumbe* of the man's village.[19]

But perhaps the most lasting impression was made by the conduct of the Germans who operated plantations, and particularly the tobacco plantation at Lewa, near Pangani, where three hundred contract laborers (that is, slaves) were treated so badly that the contracting Arabs began to complain of the workers' returning home exhausted and even crippled. The planters were then forced to obtain laborers through the neighboring *jumbe* in exchange for military assistance, but soon a strong faction of local chiefs warned them in forceful terms that any further expansion of their enterprise would be met by armed resistance. In March 1888 the head of the plantation wrote in desperation: "I am certain that there is a conspiracy to deprive me of all my laborers. The tale is told that we intend to drive away all the natives, to take away their land, and so forth."[20] And at the Company station at Dunda, near Bagamoyo, a delegation led by a local *jumbe* told the officer in charge, "You must leave here. We do not want any white men in this place. If you stay, soon many more will come and eventually white people will be the rulers of the land."[21] But the Germans managed to preserve their position at Dunda for a time by giving large gifts to another local *jumbe*. Finally, in April 1888, the *wali* of Bagamoyo ordered a notice to be published in all mosques that no one was to give assistance to the Dunda station, and the Germans were forced to curtail their operations there.[22]

The intentions of most of the German Company agents with regard to the coastal area were very clear. Far from wishing to set up peaceful trading colonies, they dreamed of establishing a great empire for Germany. They felt that their country was in desperate competition with Britain and France and were filled with the pride of national

[18] Robert N. Lyne, *An Apostle of Empire* (London, 1936), 96.

[19] The description of this occurrence in the British Foreign Office documents is quoted in Bennett, "Arab Power," 144. Schmidt gives his own version in his *Geschichte*, 10-13.

[20] *Deutsche Kolonialzeitung*, I (Mar. 31, 1888), 101. (All translations from the German are my own.) Concerning the Lewa plantation, see also Müller, *Deutschland*, 243-44.

[21] Eugen Krenzler, *Ein Jahr in Ostafrika* (Ulm, 1888), 89.

[22] Ibid., 91-100; Bennett, "Arab Power," 156-57.

power that was the legacy of Bismarck and the victory at Sedan.[23] But they feared that the German government was reluctant to seize the opportunity for empire; even the tactical espousal of humanitarian ideals failed to arouse the desired enthusiasm for colonies. The solution finally chosen was the negotiation of an agreement with the Sultan of Zanzibar, signed in April 1888, whereby the German East Africa Company would assume "the whole administration" of the Tanganyika coast on August 15, 1888 in exchange for a certain percentage of the customs duties collected in the future.[24] The terms of the agreement also made it clear, however, that this administration was "to be carried out in His Highness' [the Sultan's] name and under his flag and subject to His Highness' sovereign rights." From the Sultan's point of view, he was merely agreeing to farm out to the Germans the collection of export duties, as his predecessors had done to Indians for years. Although C. B. Euan-Smith, the British consul in Zanzibar, realized that the agreement promised substantially more, he felt that all would go well if the Germans handled themselves tactfully.[25] But the German agents had no intention of limiting themselves to the profits to be made from customs duties. They intended from the outset to challenge the sovereignty of the Sultan, and they intended to emerge victorious.[26]

Although the agreement was intended to affect the administration of the entire coast, no consultations were held with the coastal people, and the implications of the agreement were never made clear to them. In reality, the Germans intended to assume far more power than the Sultan himself ever had, and this the people were soon to find out. The Sultan slowly came to realize the full range of German intentions, but he was constrained by the British to co-operate with the Germans and to send the following letter to all his *wali:*

> I hereby order you to hand over to the German East Africa Company the house in which you now reside. Give them also your flag; they will unfurl it, as best suits them, together with their own flag, on the house which they will select. But both flags must fly side by side. Moreover, if you do not wish to be employed by the Company, return immediately to Zanzibar, and bring with you all the weapons and ammunition that belong to us.[27]

[23] For a few statements of the imperialistic motives of the German officials, see Schmidt, *Geschichte,* 1-2; Behr, *Kriegsbilder,* 1; G. Richelmann, *Meine Erlebnisse in der Wissmann-Truppe* (Magdeburg, 1892), vi; and an article by Carl Peters in the *Deutsche Kolonialzeitung,* I (June 23, 1888), 194.

[24] For the English text of the agreement, see *Further Correspondence,* C. 5603, 12-15.

[25] Ibid., 12.

[26] See, for example, Schmidt, *Geschichte,* 21-22.

[27] Quoted in Albert F. Calvert, *The German African Empire* (London, 1916), 111.

It is evident, however, that the Sultan also sent other letters, without the knowledge of the Europeans, asserting, "I have given him [the German] no more than control over the shipping. If he does anything else do not consent. If he wants land this is not in the agreement; kill them, let them not return. . . . Tell me not that you were frightened if they come and destroy you and make trouble."[28] These seemingly contradictory orders naturally put the coastal people on their guard and made them wonder if the Sultan was still in control of the changing situation in Zanzibar.

But whatever the reaction of the coastal people, the German agents were bent on conquest. They ridiculed the Sultan's weak authority and were determined to replace it with a strong, efficient administration. In their eyes, the coastal people were cowardly and worthless because they so willingly submitted to the rule of a Sultan who, after all, had no real power. It is perhaps characteristic of the imperial German mind that the agents assumed that their authority could simply replace that of the Sultan—that the populace was a passive mass properly resigned to some authority but having no voice in its form. In short, they totally misunderstood the system of mutual understanding and respect through which order was maintained on the coast.

The Growth of the Resistance

In August 1888, the German agents set out from Zanzibar to make preparations for the "transfer of power," as they put it, in the seven coastal towns of Tanga, Pangani, Bagamoyo, Dar es Salaam, Kilwa Kivinje, Lindi, and Mikindani. They were received calmly in most places, though they quickly antagonized their hosts by their impetuousness. In Pangani, for example, Wali Abd al-Gawy had the following encounter with Emil von Zelewski, described here by the Archdeacon of Usambara:

> [O]ne afternoon when taking his siesta in the Government House, a servant announced a young German [Zelewski] who had landed from a ship in the harbour. The Governor [wali] received him, and he at once proceeded to inform the Governor . . . that after the 16th of August the Germans would take over the administration of the country and the customs, but that they intended to employ him, only he would then cease to be in the service of the Sultan, and would receive his pay from the Germans. Also that he would be required to present himself four

[28] Hemedi, *Utenzi*, 35-37. One of the German agents confirmed that contradictory letters had been sent; see the *Deutsche Kolonialzeitung*, I (Oct. 30, 1888), 336.

times a day at the German office, to make his report and receive his instructions. The Arab restrained his indignation at such a gross insult, which he put down to the boorishness of the man, and merely replied that he had received no orders from his master the Sultan, and that he could not discuss the question. Of course the Governor told this story at his evening reception, with what effect upon the Arabs and British Indians present can well be imagined.[29]

In order to understand why this incident was so insulting to the *wali*, we must put ourselves in his position. He had never even met Zelewski, a man many years younger than he with nothing to recommend him but the fact that he was German, which was hardly a good recommendation in East Africa at that time. And yet Zelewski treated the *wali* as a minor bureaucrat, a mere hireling, and ordered him about. He was completely unaware that Abd al-Gawy was one of the most prominent men of the town, and was a "servant" of the sultanate only in the sense that he greatly respected the Sultan's splendor and wisdom. The *wali's* office was chiefly ceremonial, and only on rare occasions had he ever "made a report" to anyone. We can be sure that when Abd al-Gawy related this incident at his evening reception, his notable guests felt themselves to be equally insulted by Zelewski's attitude, foreseeing that the same arrogance would be displayed toward them.

The notables were further aggravated when the German agents announced that a ceremony to mark the change of power would be held in each of the seven towns on August 15. The key element of this ceremony was to be the removal of the Sultan's flag from the front of the *wali's* house and its placement, along with the German East Africa Company's flag, in front of the residence of the German agent. It was unwise, the Company felt, to leave the Sultan's flag in front of the *wali's* house and simply to raise another in front of their own building since "the presence of the red flag at two different points of the town would give occasion for misunderstanding among the populace."[30]

This plan naturally angered the notables. In the first place, the Germans seemed to be declaring again that the *wali* were mere civil servants whose allegiance could be changed without consulting them. Secondly, although the agents claimed to be representing only private interests and not the German Empire itself, the close resemblance of the Company flag to the imperial colors gave rise to the rumor that the coastal people were about to be made German subjects, an idea that

[29] Farler, "England and Germany," 346. From the German viewpoint, of course, Abd al-Gawy was "malevolent" and "slippery," and the proper cure for his disobedience was the application of more force (*Weissbuch*, IV, 8).

[30] Michahelles to Bismarck, Aug. 26, 1888, *Weissbuch*, IV, 11.

they found particularly distasteful.[31] Finally, the German houses, unlike the *wali's* residences, had been designed to look like fortresses, and the notables began to fear the loss of the influence that they had enjoyed through their easy access to the *wali*. Although it was chiefly the notables who were angered by the German flag-raising plans, the news soon spread to all levels of coastal society and was received with great dismay. For everyone on the coast, this was a desperate and confusing time. As Hemedi put it, "At Kilwa and Dar es Salaam there was a plague of Europeans. There was no free speech; they held the country. . . . In all the harbours wherever you looked you would see warships."[32] As the day for the raising of the Company flag approached, the *wali*, with the support of the townspeople, became increasingly intransigent. It was necessary everywhere to postpone the flag-raising until German warships could be made available for the protection of the agents.

In Pangani, for example, Zelewski called a meeting of the local notables on August 17 under the guns of the cruiser *Möwe* and presented to them a letter that he had specially obtained from the Sultan. It ordered the *wali* to acquiesce in the demands of the German company, including the transfer of the Sultan's flag. Abd al-Gawy, amazed at still another contradictory order from the Sultan, but wishing to avoid bloodshed, allowed the flag-raising to take place. As soon as the *Möwe* had sailed away, however, he declared his refusal to co-operate with Zelewski any longer, and it soon became clear that he had the full support of the notables of Pangani and the Sultan's soldiers. Zelewski immediately signaled to a nearby German warship, and a landing party of 110 men was sent ashore with orders to imprison the *wali* and the *akida* (the officer in charge of the Sultan's troops).

The German marines marched through the town to the mosque, where the people were celebrating the second day of 'Id al-Hajj, and caused such a disruption that the festal prayers could not be continued. From there they proceeded to the house of the *akida*, broke down the door, and seized him and his soldiers. Then they went to the *wali's* house, where they invaded the harem and caused great damage but could not find Abd al-Gawy, who had fled. Finally, they marched to the prison, tore down the doors, and released the convicts.[33] In the

[31] *Further Correspondence,* C. 5603, 68.

[32] Hemedi, *Utenzi,* 37.

[33] The foregoing narrative is taken from a list of grievances presented by the notables of Pangani in Zanzibar on Sept. 14, 1888. The most complete available copy of this document is the German translation in the Potsdam archives, reprinted in Müller, *Deutschland,* 544-46. It should be compared to the German version of the same events in *Weissbuch,* IV, 8-10, 16-20.

evening, Zelewski called   an assembly of the notables who had not
fled and announced: "We Germans shall take the place of [Sultan]
Sayyid Khalifa, and whatever happens in the future [in Pangani] shall
be regarded as the obstinacy of Sayyid Khalifa, for which we shall
send him to Germany in chains. And if you do not follow our orders,
we shall write to Zanzibar and send a ship with 800 men to destroy
Pangani and to seize you and send you to Germany."[34] The next day
the marines appeared at the *wali's* house, cut down the staff bearing
the Sultan's flag, and then embarked for Zanzibar, leaving behind a
small garrison under Zelewski.

Upset by the German actions, the notables left Pangani for their
nearby plantations and refused to comply with any of Zelewski's orders. Yet from the German viewpoint, a decisive victory had been
achieved, and the German reports described the ensuing period in
optimistic terms:

> In the first days after the landing many inhabitants had left the town,
> but the District Chief [Zelewski] let them know that they had nothing
> to fear and should return quietly. After a while they began to come
> back to their homes and to take up their customary occupations. The
> quick, confident intervention of the Imperial Marines seems to have
> made a lasting impression. . . . In the following days the contacts
> between [Zelewski] and the natives were good; legal hearings were
> held in consultation with prominent natives and tolls were levied with-
> out difficulty.[35]

But the same period was described quite differently by the people of
Pangani:

> [The Europeans] came to Pangani full of wrath; they fitted up the
> house and laid cannon. With the ship at Maziwe the whole town was
> humbled and the Europeans strode about the streets. The town was
> silent; no one spoke; not a free man said a word. The Europeans arose
> and charged the Moslems, demanding judgment against them. . . .
> Every morning he [Zelewski] and his twelve soldiers, Christians,
> walked about the town. If they saw any women, they seized them and
> did what they liked with them; when we asked them why they did
> this, they told us it was a German custom.[36]

A similar series of events occurred in the other coastal towns. The
flag-raisings were delayed everywhere because of the opposition of the
notables. In Bagamoyo, the German agents were able to remove the
Sultan's flag from the *wali's* house only by cutting down the flagpole,

---

[34] Quoted in Müller, *Deutschland,* 544.
[35] *Weissbuch,* IV, 10, 16.
[36] Hemedi, *Utenzi,* 41; Müller, *Deutschland,* 545.

an act greeted with understandable hostility by the people,[37] and in each town the Company was master of the situation only when a warship was in the harbor. At the southern ports of Kilwa, Lindi, and Mikindani, conflict was avoided because the *wali* quickly left for Zanzibar to present their complaints to the Sultan. Everywhere the people wished to follow the Sultan's leadership, for his wisdom was respected in such trying times; but there was confusion over the seemingly irrational directives which he had issued.

It was clear that the coastal towns were being ruined by the German actions. Economic activity was at a standstill, and the townspeople were virtually leaderless since most of the notables had fled to their plantations. The coast might have returned to normal if the Germans had been content with the power that they had already assumed. But they were not satisfied. They considered the Sultan's administrative apparatus to be hopelessly inefficient and felt that it had to be replaced by a "rational" governmental system. Above all, they intended to derive substantial profits from their labors. To this end, they instituted in each of the towns a number of regulations designed to increase their power and their income. They imposed a head tax, a burial tax, an inheritance tax, and road tolls; they required the town residents to register themselves at the Company station, prohibited the import of munitions, and declared the legal equality of the sexes.[38] Worst of all, they ordered all property owners to present themselves to the agents with proof of ownership of their land, or else have it confiscated. As the Germans undoubtedly knew, such proof of ownership seldom existed, since, in the Sultan's words, "Most of the land of our subjects is inherited property, and only a few of the land holders have written deeds."[39] The intentions of the Germans were made unmistakably clear by this last regulation; they wanted to take over the land—and thus the livelihood—of most of the coastal people.

It was the imposition of these regulations that began to unite the people of the coast in thoughts of resistance. Most people were already thoroughly disgusted with the Germans personally, and when the Company agents announced their intention to confiscate land and to charge unheard-of taxes, the people could bear no more. The residents of the towns gathered together, pooled their weapons, and sought the advice of the notables. Furthermore, many of the rural *jumbe*, who had never before paid much attention to the Sultan, now raised his flag as a symbol of resistance to German rule. These *jumbe*, foreseeing that the new fiscal regulations would eventually be applied to them, notified

[37] *Weissbuch*, IV, 11-13; *Further Correspondence*, C. 5603, 51-54.
[38] Müller, *Deutschland*, 362-65, 548, 550-51.
[39] Quoted ibid., 550-51.

the town notables that they were sending large groups of their best warriors to help defy the Germans. For example, a "powerful mountain chief" in Usambara immediately dispatched six thousand armed men to Pangani, declaring: "As for these Germans, we will never become their slaves, if we have to fight to the last man."[40] The notables, though not always happy to receive such large groups of untrained, poorly armed warriors, quartered them on the plantations and began the enormous task of organizing and provisioning them.

The first outbreak of armed hostilities against the Germans occurred in Pangani in September. For two weeks the people had endured the presumption of the agents, hoping for orders from the Sultan that might make their task clear. Meanwhile, Zelewski had aggravated the situation further by his inflexible application of the new regulations. Late in August he had sent notices to the land holders of Pangani, directing them to present to him proof of their ownership. When they failed to appear at the station, he had demanded that the Sultan send one hundred troops to force them to do so, a request that the Sultan complied with only at the insistence of the British and German consuls in Zanzibar.[41] These soldiers landed at Pangani on August 31 and were greeted joyously by the notables, who hoped that the Sultan had finally decided to take action against the Germans. To everyone's surprise, Zelewski ordered the troops to seize the notables. The soldiers, taking the initiative, refused, declaring: "We do not follow orders that are not lawful. The Sayyid sent us to determine who has opposed you in the administration of the tolls and to force them to desist. The Sayyid never ordered us to seize the notables and the inhabitants without cause."[42] Zelewski, furious at this "insubordination," ordered them to return to Zanzibar. Then he turned to the notables and told them: "These lands do not belong to the Sayyid, but to me. . . . Either you follow my orders or I shall send a letter to the German Consul to send a warship and soldiers to attack you."[43]

Despite Zelewski's threats, many of the notables continued to hesitate to take decisive action against the Germans until they had received specific orders from the Sultan. But before long, a radical faction

[40] Quoted in Farler, "England and Germany," 162. Further evidence of the widespread rural support for the resistance is provided by John Roscoe, who was a missionary in the interior in 1888; see his *Twenty-five Years in East Africa* (Cambridge, 1921), 36-38. It is entirely possible, of course, that some of the rural warriors came spontaneously and without any direction from their *jumbe*, who were, especially near the coast, sometimes too powerless to assemble a cohesive fighting force.

[41] *Further Correspondence*, C. 5603, 61-64; *Weissbuch*, IV, 16-20.

[42] Müller, *Deutschland*, 545.

[43] Ibid.

emerged under the leadership of a certain Abushiri, who succeeded in convincing the inhabitants of Pangani that at the very least coastal fortifications had to be built for protection against the threatened German naval attack.[44] The growing movement was then further radicalized by the arrival of large numbers of warriors sent by the rural *jumbe*. These men saw no need to spare Zelewski and his colleagues, and they joined with the militant wing of the Pangani notables in demanding their executions.[45] But on this issue, the moderate faction won out; pending orders from the Sultan, the Germans were locked in their house on September 4, and a guard was placed in front of it to protect them from the taunts of the rural warriors, who at least had the satisfaction of tearing down the Company's flag and ripping it to shreds.[46] For five days the Germans remained isolated, and attempts by German and British representatives to land and negotiate their release were turned back by gunfire from the new coastal fortifications.[47] The Pangani defenders remembered Zelewski's threat to summon a warship to bombard them, and they had no intention of allowing anyone but an official delegate of the Sultan to draw near the shore. Their determination was strengthened by the arrival of refugees from Tanga, where the first instance of indiscriminate German bombardment of a town had occurred on September 6.[48]

Back in Zanzibar, the German consul begged the Sultan to send his trusted general, Sir Lloyd Mathews, with a troop of soldiers to rescue the Company agents. The Sultan at first refused, declaring that, "The officials had driven the people into rebellion by their insults, and that he could not send his soldiers to fire upon the people."[49] But he finally gave way to the urgings of the British consul. Mathews arrived in Pangani on September 8, where he was greeted with joy by the notables, who had waited so long for decisive action from Zanzibar.

[44] Hemedi, *Utenzi*, 43-45.

[45] See ibid.; Müller, *Deutschland*, 545.

[46] See ibid.; *Weissbuch*, IV, 16-20. According to the German view presented in the latter source, this incident was interpreted as a hostile act by all the inhabitants of Pangani in retribution for the refusal of Zelewski to allow a dhow carrying a cargo of gunpowder to land at Pangani.

[47] *Weissbuch*, IV, 16-20; *Further Correspondence*, C. 5603, 64. The following description of the Pangani fortifications was given by the German officials: "In some places trenches have been dug, and several suitable houses have been fortified. In short, everything is prepared for battle. . . . At the small entrance to the harbor, entrenchments have been dug in such a way that the waterway can be raked with gunfire from three sides. These fortifications are filled with armed men day and night. (*Weissbuch*, IV, 18, 26.)

[48] Hemedi, *Utenzi*, 39; *Weissbuch*, IV, 20-22; *Deutsche Kolonialzeitung*, I (Oct. 20, 1888), 333-34, and I (Nov. 24, 1888), 379-80.

[49] Quoted in *Further Correspondence*, C. 5603, 61-64.

Confronted by "a regularly organized rebellion" of "8,000 men of all tribes under arms," Mathews calmed the situation by removing the German agents to his ship and agreeing to take five of the leading notables to Zanzibar to present their grievances to the Sultan and to the German and British consuls.[50] These grievances were presented on September 14, and although the German consul described the notables' assertions as "nonsensical," he agreed for the time being to restrict the German agents to the collection of customs duties "for four or six weeks" and to allow Mathews to mediate the differences.[51] Charged with this task, Mathews returned to Pangani on September 20, where he was again received warmly. But when it was learned that he intended to arrange for the eventual return of the Germans, the infuriated defenders—whose number had now grown to twenty thousand[52] —repudiated once and for all the moderate wing of the notables and gathered together at Abushiri's plantation to agree upon further action. The details of this assembly are not known, but its outcome was that on September 21 a delegation told Mathews that he must leave and declared that, "Their special object in expelling him was to prove to all other Europeans how determined they were never to admit them as their rulers."[53] At first Mathews hesitated, trusting to his soldiers, but when it became evident that even they would not protect him from the armed men who gathered around his house, he agreed to leave. Before embarking, he received a promise from the resistance leaders that they would protect the lives and property of the Indian inhabitants and heard the announcement of the new chief of the movement, Abushiri, that he intended "to raise all the other coast towns against the Germans."[54]

The people of the other towns needed little incitement, however. Events similar to those in Pangani had brought radical factions to the forefront, and the Germans had everywhere been driven out or isolated by the end of September. In Bagamoyo, where large groups of Swahili and Zaramu warriors had been gathering since the flag-raising in August, the Company agents were kept in a virtual state of siege until September 22, when a concerted attack was made on their house by eight thousand armed men under the leadership of a group of nineteen Swahili notables.[55] The Germans replied by landing a force of 260

[50] Ibid.

[51] *Weissbuch*, IV, 16-20.

[52] *Deutsche Kolonialzeitung*, I (Nov. 24, 1888), 379-80.

[53] *Further Correspondence*, C. 5603, 68.

[54] Ibid.; *Weissbuch*, IV, 25-26.

[55] For the events of September in Bagamoyo, see *Further Correspondence*, C. 5603, 69-73. These documents show that the circumstances of the attack were confused and that it may actually have been provoked by the German agents.

marines from the warship *Leipzig*, who stormed through the city "firing upon everyone who showed themselves," eventually killing over one hundred of the defenders. "The German attacking party escaped without any casualties, and . . . the rioters were killed when standing in groups on the beach under the heavy fire from the boats, most of them being only armed with spears and bows and arrows."[56] The defenders were forced to flee, and the Germans declared themselves masters of the utterly deserted town. A few days later, the German agent carried out a punitive raid on the surrounding villages, plundering and destroying them with his portable cannon and killing many of their inhabitants.[57] But these tactics of terror only increased the intransigence of the Bagamoyo *jumbe*, who rejected German demands that they return peacefully, saying that they had no desire to be German subjects. Even the Sultan, they declared, had treated them "as friends rather than as subjects."[58]

In Tanga, the German agents had been removed for their own safety in early September, and coastal fortifications were built by the townspeople to prevent their return. Dar es Salaam, which at this time was a relatively insignificant port with a population of less than one thousand, remained calm under the German cannon. This was because most of the land was already owned by the Sultan and there was no need for the Germans to initiate confiscation proceedings.[59] But toward the end of September there was considerable agitation caused by a mysterious "representative of the Sultan," who reproached the townspeople for their timidity.[60] Soon the Germans were masters of a deserted town as the Indian traders fled to Zanzibar and the Swahili residents gradually melted away. In Dar es Salaam as well as Bagamoyo, wrote the British consul, the Germans "are constantly threatened by attack, and should the men-of-war be withdrawn they would be at once attacked in force. There is absolutely no trade or movement at either place, in the neighbourhood of which there is great insecurity for life and property. . . . The Germans have on more than one occasion arrested and shot native tribesmen after subjecting them to a form of judicial inquiry."[61]

In the southern coastal towns there were no disorders until the German agents began to implement their new taxes and regulations, when the notables contacted the powerful *jumbe* of the surrounding

[56] Ibid., 71.
[57] Ibid., 76.
[58] Quoted in the *Deutsche Kolonialzeitung*, I (Dec. 8, 1888), 409.
[59] Müller, *Deutschland*, 390.
[60] Daniel von Cölln, *Bilder aus Ostafrika* (Berlin, 1891), 106.
[61] *Further Correspondence*, C. 5603, 95.

area, who agreed to join with them in driving out the German agents.[62] In Kilwa, a force of twenty thousand warriors assembled on September 21, and the Germans were given two days to leave.[63] When they refused, the notables assembled in the mosque and swore death to the Germans and then gathered their troops together for the final effort. For three days the two Company agents fired from their roof into the assembled crowd and managed to hold off several assaults. Finally one of them was killed by an Arab sharpshooter firing from a tree, and the other fled to his room and took his own life as the warriors of Kilwa streamed into the house. In Kilwa, as in most of the other towns, the notables declared that their only grievance was against the Germans, and that the British Indians were welcome to remain, since it was the notables' intention to carry on with customary commercial activities. In Lindi and Mikindani the Germans had the good sense to leave their stations when a similar ultimatum was presented to them. They escaped in a dhow, continually harassed by gunfire from the thousands of assembled warriors.[64] Finally, the people living around the Lewa plantation forced the German agents to flee and then systematically trampled their tobacco plants.[65]

The Resistance at Its Height

With most of the coast of Tanganyika under their control, the forces of the resistance had achieved their immediate goal. They had expelled the hated Germans and had assembled sufficient men, they thought, to prevent their return. But in the momentary respite that followed, the latent divisions within their ranks became apparent.

The original leaders of the resistance, and still one of its most important factions, were the town notables. From the beginning, they had urged the assembled warriors to be moderate, insisting that the advice of the Sultan be obtained before initiating any major action. They hoped for a swift and peaceful resolution to the conflict, since they feared that their wealth and power would be endangered by prolonged civil disorder. For this reason, they were prepared to contem-

---

[62] The main sources for the south coast at this time are *Weissbuch*, IV, 28-31; *Further Correspondence*, C. 5603, 70, 77-78, 87-89.

[63] This development was evidently quite sudden. One of the German agents, in a letter dated Sept. 18, reveals no anticipation whatever of the impending conflict. This letter was published in the *Deutsche Kolonialzeitung*, I (Nov. 3, 1888), 357.

[64] Ibid., I (Nov. 10, 1888), 359-60.

[65] Ibid., I (Dec. 1, 1888), 386.

plate a compromise with the German East Africa Company, perhaps allowing it to assume collection of the customs duties in the name of the Sultan.[66] Yet the majority of the resistance forces, against the advice of the notables, had rejected a similar compromise, offered by General Mathews in September 1888. As a result, the notables were increasingly unhappy with the radical tendencies of the movement and were beginning to speak against continued resistance.

But the most important faction, comprising the *jumbe* of the smaller towns, the common townspeople, and Swahili from the nearby villages, had no intention of surrendering in this moment of strength. They, too, continued to admire the Sultan and the orderly society he represented, but they no longer relied on him. They began to feel that they could take necessary action in his name, even if that action went against the directions given in his letters. This attitude was expressed by the people of Pangani to Bishop Smythies of the Universities' Mission when he visited there in November 1888:

> We are loyal to the Sultan of Zanzibar, but we know that he lives on an island and can easily be overawed by big ships and big guns; we cannot believe that it is his real wish that strangers should come into his dominions and cut down his flag or hoist another beside it; that they should beat his people, defile their places of worship, and insult their women.[67]

The less moderate of the townspeople went further and declared that their loyalty to the Sultan would end if he ever allowed the Germans to set foot on the coast again.[68] The chief motivation of this faction was their thorough hatred for the Germans, and it is doubtful whether many of its members had formulated detailed notions of what they thought the future political system of the coast should be. Rather, they probably hoped for the slow decline in influence of the prominent notables, for this could mean an eventual increase in their own freedom and prosperity.[69]

The largest faction, and the one most difficult to evaluate, consisted of the groups of warriors who had been sent to the coastal towns by the rural *jumbe*. Many of these men had undoubtedly joined the resistance primarily because their *jumbe* had ordered them to do so, but they probably also anticipated enriching themselves through plunder. Although some of them quickly adopted the anti-German sentiments of the townspeople, it is difficult to estimate how committed

[66] *Weissbuch*, IV, 76-78.
[67] *The Times*, Dec. 31, 1888, 8.
[68] *Further Correspondence*, C. 5603, 78, 89; *Weissbuch*, IV, 31.
[69] Müller, *Deutschland*, 368.

they were to a prolonged struggle. It is also questionable whether their *jumbe*, many of whom had stayed safely at home, were very deeply committed either. When the *jumbe* could see that the coastal people were in firm control of the situation, they offered help. This help might mean some practical experience at warfare for their young soldiers, and, in the event that the coastal defenders retained the upper hand, the *jumbe* could anticipate favors in the future from the resistance leaders, including the reinstatement of the local customs duties that had once been so profitable to them. But they undoubtedly continued to believe that, should the invader emerge victorious, they could simply retire to their villages and be left alone by the new German administration.

Finally there was the element of the resistance about which we know the most, the radical faction, consisting chiefly of aggressive leaders like Simboja of Usambara, Bwana Heri of Sadani, and Abushiri of Pangani. These men had developed an entirely new vision of the political future of the Tanganyikan coast and had rejected both the Germans and the Sultan. We shall dwell at some length on Abushiri, since we know a good deal about him and since he played a key role in the resistance.

Abushiri bin Salimu bin Abushiri al-Harthi was born in East Africa in about 1845, the son of an Arab father and an African (possibly Galla) mother.[70] His clan, the Harthi, of whose traditions he was undoubtedly aware, had been among the first Arab settlers in East Africa and had been the chief opponents to the growing power of the Busaidi dynasty in Zanzibar, choosing in many cases to move away from the coast rather than be forced to recognize the authority of the Sultan.[71] Abushiri grew up in the Swahili world of the coast, and throughout his life was more comfortable speaking Swahili than Arabic. As a young man, he had organized and led caravans to Lake Tanganyika, where he traded in ivory and probably also in slaves.

[70] The main sources for the background and personality of Abushiri are Hemedi, *Utenzi,* throughout; Oscar Baumann, *In Deutsch-Ostafrika während des Aufstandes* (Vienna and Olmütz, 1890), 135-46; and a quotation from Hermann von Wissmann's personal papers in Alexander Becker, *et al.*, *Hermann von Wissmann, Deutschlands grösster Afrikaner* (Berlin, 1914), 205-6. Abushiri's exact age is unknown; Euan-Smith estimated that he was 35 or 36 in 1889 (Bennett, "Arab Power," 199), while Behr thought he looked about 55 in the same year (Behr, *Kriegsbilder,* 334). The unlikely suggestion that Abushiri's mother was a Galla came from Wissmann, who interrogated him at length on these matters (Becker, *Hermann von Wissmann,* 205).

[71] Bennett, "Arab Power," 13. On the history of the Harthi clan, see Reginald Coupland, *East Africa and Its Invaders from the Earliest Times to the Death of Seyyid Said in 1856* (London, 1938), 22-23, 217, 296, 322, 455-56, 554.

With the profits from these ventures he purchased land for a sugar plantation not far from Pangani, where he began to play a role in the local politics. In the late 1870's he added greatly to his prestige by leading a contingent of the Sultan Barghash's troops in a successful campaign against the Nyamwezi chief, Mirambo, an achievement that he himself regarded as his greatest. But, back in Pangani, he was increasingly pressed by his Indian creditors. Action by the Sultan, in 1882, to force him to pay these debts, failed miserably, as Abushiri soundly defeated the Sultan's expeditionary force with an army made up of mercenaries and his own plantation slaves. It was this defeat, along with several others including one in the same year against the powerful Bwana Heri of Sadani, that convinced the Sultan to abandon his attempts to increase his power on the coast. Henceforth, Abushiri was an important man in Pangani, although he had to avoid Zanzibar where he would have faced severe punishment.

Despite being short and stout, Abushiri was, physically, an impressive individual. Hermann von Wissmann, who was later his arch-antagonist, wrote that he was clearly a man of extraordinary qualities, and compared the agility and speed that characterized his actions to those of a "springing panther."[72] Everyone who met him commented especially on his dark, intense eyes, which, in the words of the German explorer Oscar Baumann, "displayed something noble and reminded one of the peculiarly cold, almost cruel gaze of the Albanian mountain dweller."[73] He was an assertive, self confident man who declared without hesitation that he was one of the three most important men on the coast, the others being Tippu Tib and Mbarak al-Mazrui.[74] He was also a man of remarkable courage. On one occasion, for example, the Germans began a naval bombardment of Bagamoyo while he was engaged in a meeting at the French Holy Ghost Mission there. Although "shells from the German man-of-war were bursting around him, he entirely refused to listen to the prayers of his attendants to seek a place of safety until the negotiations were terminated."[75] Furthermore, Abushiri displayed unusual ingenuity. It was reliably reported that, lacking ammunition for a captured German cannon, he devised a

[72] Becker, *Hermann von Wissmann*, 205-6.

[73] Baumann, *In Deutsch-Ostafrika*, 137.

[74] Ibid., 138. On Tippu Tib, see Tippu Tib (trans. Wilfred H. Whiteley), *Maisha ya Hamed bin Muhammed el Murjebi yaani Tippu Tib* (Nairobi, 1958–59); Heinrich Brode (trans. H. Havelock), *Tippoo Tib: The Story of His Career in Central Africa* (London, 1907). On Mbarak, see Reginald Coupland, *The Exploitation of East Africa, 1856–1890* (London, 1939), 248-49, 253-55, 418, 457; Vincent Harlow and E. M. Chilver (eds.), *History of East Africa* (Oxford, 1965), II, 7-8, 136, 645.

[75] C. B. Euan-Smith, quoted in Bennett, "Arab Power," 199.

process for making his own shells, which were used with considerable effectiveness against German fortifications.[76]

While he was in Pangani, Abushiri exercised total control over the thousands of warriors assembled under his leadership. Baumann, who, in Abushiri's custody, arrived there with another explorer in October 1888, wrote:

> We landed and were immediately surrounded by people who greeted Abushiri respectfully, while they gazed at us with hostility. The city . . . was a scene of wild animated life. Everywhere could be seen fantastically dressed Arabs and Negroes, bristling with weapons; rifles and swords glistened in every shop; rebel bands surged through the narrow streets with loud war-songs and rifleshots. Many of the warriors let out cries of hatred and rage when they suddenly saw two Europeans, but all retreated timidly and respectfully before our escort, Abushiri, who passed through the excited crowds unruffled. The house of the German East Africa Company, which we passed by, stood plundered and empty; the toll station was half destroyed and a strong mast had been built for the Arab flag.[77]

Abushiri was firm in the assertion of his complete control, not hesitating to use a *kiboko* (hippopotamus-hide whip) on lazy or disobedient warriors.

Abushiri had developed very clear views on the nature of the resistance and its ultimate goals. He expressed these views in October to Baumann and his associate, Hans Meyer, whom he held captive for a brief time. Initially, he felt, the disturbances on the coast were to be blamed entirely on the German East Africa Company.

> If [he said] the Germans had come in friendliness, limited themselves to toll administration, and tried everything to win over the ruling class of Arabs, they would still be sitting peacefully today in the coastal towns. But these men . . . conducted themselves recklessly, tore down flags and raised others, gave us orders and regulations, and everywhere conducted themselves as though they were the lords of the land and we were their slaves. We observed these things for a while, and then we chased the whites away, as one chases away impetuous children.[78]

Abushiri also referred to the damage that had been done to legitimate trading interests on the coast: "The Indian financiers feared such precarious conditions and would not make any loans to us. But what

---

[76] J. Sturtz and J. Wangemann, *Land und Leute in Deutsch-Ost-Afrika* (Berlin, 1894), 44.

[77] Baumann, *In Deutsch-Ostafrika*, 142.

[78] Ibid., 138-39.

could we do without loans? How could we equip caravans without money? No one would help us, so we helped ourselves." Thus, the coastal people had united behind him, and he declared: "I will show the Europeans, just as I showed Mirambo, that I have an iron fist."[79]

Abushiri firmly rejected the leadership of the Sultan of Zanzibar. As he said to Baumann, "What do I care about the Sultan? I hate him and have not set foot inside Zanzibar for twenty years, since I would be immediately beheaded if I did. And now I respect him even less for disgracing himself by selling our land to foreigners."[80] Abushiri considered the coast an independent political entity. In his view, the first task was to prevent the Germans from establishing themselves in East Africa. After this was achieved, internal wars would be waged between the individual resistance leaders to determine the future of the new East African state.[81]

Yet even the dedication and charisma of Abushiri were hard pressed to hold the resistance together. The only sentiment shared by all the factions was a deep hatred for the invader. This feeling grew daily as the Germans employed a variety of terrorist tactics. For example, a *London Times* reporter wrote that, "Lately the German ships have been steaming two miles from the mainland coast at night and occasionally throwing shells promiscuously on to the land, with no idea of attacking an enemy, but simply to overawe the natives. . . . A day or two ago they killed four people sleeping in a hut near the shore. There is no pretense of shelling towns or attacking enemies."[82] But there were many other feelings that tended to divide the defenders and to undermine their will to continue the resistance. For instance, the notables were becoming increasingly uneasy about Abushiri's desire to renounce the Sultan and to become the ruler of the coast. They suspected that he would be just as tyrannical as the Germans were, and they dreaded the civil wars that would undoubtedly accompany the consolidation of his rule. Coastal business interests were also beginning to complain that the prolonged state of emergency was costing them profits, since the trading caravans were turning northward to Mombasa to avoid the war-torn towns.[83] And there was growing concern over the individuals who were using the disorder to further their own ends, especially debtors who had fled to Zanzibar to escape their obligations.[84]

[79] Hans Meyer, "Ueber meine letzte Expedition in Deutsche-Ostafrika," *Verhandlungen der Gesellschaft für Erdkunde zu Berlin*, XVI (1889), 89.

[80] Baumann, *In Deutsch-Ostafrika*, 138-39.

[81] Ibid., 139-40.

[82] *The Times*, Feb. 12, 1889, 11.

[83] *Weissbuch*, IV, 72.

[84] *Deutsche Kolonialzeitung*, I (Oct. 20, 1888), 334.

The continued presence of large numbers of rural warriors in the towns was also a cause for uneasiness. The notables suspected that these troops would indiscriminately plunder Arab and Indian business establishments if there were renewed hostilities, and it was doubted that they would be useful in the event of a concerted German attack, since they were so poorly armed and trained. Furthermore, although the notables (including the radical leadership) had sought to direct hostility against the Germans alone so as not to aggravate the British, the rural warriors consistently refused to recognize any distinctions among white men. They felt that all Europeans should be killed, or at least exchanged for a high ransom. These conflicting attitudes were revealed to Bishop Smythies during his visit to Pangani in November 1888 to insure the safety of the British missionaries at Magila. As he entered the town, he was greeted by Abushiri, who offered him full co-operation but warned him that the Swahili notables, "who have always been allowed a share in managing the affairs of Pangani, were not yet all agreed. It was also necessary to be very careful, because there were a great many natives from the interior in the town who would not distinguish between one European and another." Later, Smythies's house was surrounded "by an excited crowd, chiefly . . . of young men" who loudly expressed their desire to kill him. But Abushiri hurried to his assistance and "stood in the doorway downstairs and said that no one should enter unless they killed him first. He was able to keep the crowd back . . . until the other Arabs, with their soldiers, came up. He has said that his quarrel was with only those foreigners who had oppressed the people, that he had guaranteed the safety of the missionaries, and he would see me safe up to Magila, even if he had to fight his way up . . . It ended in three of the ringleaders being put in prison for a short time and all difficulties being composed."[85]

In addition to the growing factionalism, certain other weaknesses became apparent. First of all, the movement was poorly prepared for the impending German counterattack. Despite their obvious naval strength, everyone tended to underestimate the Germans and to consider them already defeated. Abushiri, for example, declared that the Company agents "came without weapons or soldiers, only with a letter from the Sultan, which meant nothing to us. . . . The English are surely wealthy and powerful, but the Germans seem to be very weak people (*wadogo dogo*)."[86] Related to this underestimation of German

[85] *The Times*, Dec. 31, 1888, 8. Euan-Smith wrote that similar restraints had to be applied to the rural warriors in Lindi by the town notables (*Further Correspondence*, C. 5603, 77).

[86] Baumann, *In Deutsch-Ostafrika*, 139.

strength was a failure to adopt the flexible organization and tactics of guerrilla warfare, which were indispensable in the face of the superior firepower of the invader. Instead, the townspeople built massive fortifications and prepared no secondary defenses whatsoever. This is partially attributable to the lack of experience of the resistance leaders in the subtleties of modern warfare and to the refusal of most of the warriors to submit to tedious drill and discipline. It should also be noted that the chief coastal advisor in tactical matters was Jahazi, a Comoroan who had served under the British in the Congo, where fixed fortifications and artillery barrages were the current mode. He had no experience with naval and marine strategies or with machine guns.

The movement was also weakened by the fact that no attempt was made to co-ordinate military operations in the coastal towns. It is evident that there was a certain amount of communication between them; for example, the attacks that had finally ousted the German agents in most places had occurred on September 21 or 22, indicating that each town was at least aware of the activities of the others. But there was no central planning or organized chain of command. This was so because of the mutual jealousies of the resistance leaders, and because different social elements dominated each of the towns. In Pangani, for instance, the leadership was firmly in the hands of Abushiri and his fellow notables, but in Bagamoyo the lesser Swahili *jumbe* had taken the lead. In the southern towns, the political power was held by the large bands of Yao tribesmen who made up the bulk of the resistance forces.

The first real test of the determination and cohesiveness of the movement occurred during November 1888 when supplies of food began to run out because of the enormous requirements of the masses of recently assembled troops. At first, the leaders visited nearby villages and requested contributions for the support of the warriors, but they found that the *jumbe* had only very small amounts of surplus food that they were willing to give. The *jumbe* observed that there had been no real fighting for over a month, and they refused to endanger the well-being of their villages for the sake of an army that no longer seemed to have any purpose. Many of the rural warriors returned home at this time, since they were rapidly becoming more of a burden than an asset. But the large groups of men who remained were growing desperate for food. Thus, with or without the consent of the leadership, bands of soldiers began to raid nearby villages and commandeer food supplies.[87] It might be argued that such tactics were necessary if the resistance was to be maintained, but they naturally

---

[87] *Weissbuch*, IV, 35; Müller, *Deutschland*, 434-35.

alienated large segments of the Swahili populace. These conditions were aggravated in December when the Germans clamped a blockade on the coast, ostensibly to stop the trade in slaves, but really to strangle the resistance by impeding the importation of weapons and provisions.

Abushiri, aware that decisive action was necessary to save the resistance from slowly crumbling, decided in late November to open a new front in Bagamoyo, where the Germans continued to occupy a single house. He had heard to his dismay that in that town "the people were considering yielding to the Germans" because of the growing famine and the intensive naval bombardment of the nearby villages.[88] In order to mold a more effective fighting force for this operation, he removed the remaining rural irregulars and replaced them with well-armed riflemen of Arab and Swahili extraction, whom he paid a wage only slightly less than that subsequently received by African soldiers in the service of the Germans.[89] With this new army, consisting of two thousand men and three cannon, he left Pangani on November 20.[90] A few days later Abushiri and his men made their first contact with the Germans when they opened fire on a warship passing near their camp in Windi. The ship replied with cannon fire and an assault party: "Cannon thundered like waves on a rock and houses were hit and fell down. There were many people on the reef opposing the entry of the Europeans into the town; but they came ashore with a crash of guns and many were struck and perished as they fell."[91]

Abushiri's troops retreated in face of this assault and proceeded south, finally arriving in the vicinity of Bagamoyo on December 4. For the next two days they repeatedly attacked the town, succeeding in mounting their cannon on a large stone house near the German building and, despite constant bombardment from a German warship in the harbor, in cutting off the agents from the sea with a line of trenches along the shore. But on December 7, Abushiri's men suddenly withdrew from their positions, evidently believing a rumor that the entire town had been undermined with German torpedoes. The official German reports of their evacuation state that they systematically burned and looted the town before leaving, but the Indian merchants who

---

[88] Hemedi, *Utenzi*, 49.

[89] Compare *The Times*, Jan. 17, 1889, 5; and Maercker, *Unsere Schutztruppe*, 48. Relatively large numbers of modern, breech-loading weapons were available on the coast, since they had been imported for some time by entrepreneurs in Zanzibar for use in the caravan trade.

[90] The sources for this and subsequent events in Bagamoyo are Hemedi, *Utenzi*, 49-51; *Weissbuch*, IV, 74-75, 85-86; *Further Correspondence*, C. 5822, 19-20.

[91] Hemedi, *Utenzi*, 49.

were present claimed that the destruction was actually done by German soldiers.[92]

Abushiri's men then built a large fort five miles south of Bagamoyo and from it continued to attempt to drive the Germans from the town. Their sorties were ineffective against the German cannon, however, and for the next month the major action was at Dar es Salaam where a force of over one thousand men had gathered under Sulaiman bin Sef, a notable of that town. It is difficult to determine the motives of the leaders of this group, but it has been suggested that they were infuriated that slaves taken from their plantations by the Germans were being used as laborers at the two German missions in the area.[93] On January 10 and 11, they made a concerted attack on the Company station and, although eventually forced to retreat, succeeded in destroying one of the mission stations. The other was attacked two days later, and three of the missionaries were killed and four taken prisoner. When Sulaiman bin Sef gave up his attempts to drive the Germans out of Dar es Salaam and divided his troops between Kilwa and Bagamoyo, these four were turned over to Abushiri.[94]

In the meantime, Abushiri had kept up daily attacks against the Company agents in Bagamoyo. During the night of March 3, 1889, he brought his cannon within range of the German station and, in the morning, initiated a major assault on the totally surprised enemy. The Germans quickly rallied, however, and Abushiri's men were forced to retreat, leaving their cannon behind. They returned from this battle, wrote Hemedi, "with heavy hearts and little desire for food for the sorrow that was upon them."[95] It was this defeat, along with Abushiri's increasing shortage of munitions and other supplies, that finally forced him to agree to a truce with the German admiral, Deinhard. Despite this truce, however, the Germans continued to raid the coastal towns, bombarding Sadani on March 23 and Konduchi on March 27. But little damage was done by these raids; at Sadani, for example, the entire population had left far in advance, removing the thatched roofs from their houses to prevent fire.[96]

April was a month of uneasy peace along the whole coast, with the northern towns maintaining their vigilance but with the southern

[92] *The Times*, Dec. 11, 1888, 5. Hemedi says, however, that Abushiri's men "prospered and took much booty." (Hemedi, *Utenzi*, 51.)

[93] *Further Correspondence*, C. 5822, 43-44; Müller, *Deutschland*, 436-37.

[94] A. Leue, *Dar-es-Salaam* (Berlin, 1903), 25-36; Cölln, *Bilder*, 107-120; Sturtz and Wangemann, *Land und Leute*, 57-61.

[95] Hemedi, *Utenzi*, 51. For a German account of this battle see Sturtz and Wangemann, *Land und Leute*, 43.

[96] *Further Correspondence*, C. 5822, 74-75.

leaders increasingly distracted by disagreements with their Yao allies and by the necessity of recapturing slaves who had run away during the battles against the Germans.[97] In Bagamoyo, Abushiri continued his drive to raise funds for the support of his army, depending chiefly upon the large ransoms paid to him for the release of the various missionaries whom he had imprisoned. But even this new money was not enough to support the kind of army he desired. At the end of April, when Hemedi came to him requesting forty experienced men for an attack on the German house, Abushiri was forced to admit that, "The men have not been raised. The war is breaking down; we must go and stir them up."[98] Increasingly desperate, Abushiri summoned his conjurers and asked them to forecast the outcome of his struggle with the Germans. He obviously expected a favorable answer, for he was infuriated when they warned him of impending disaster. He told them: "I do not believe it; the European will not come upon us; he cannot do so."[99] This was unwise, for the more superstitious of his followers, among them Hemedi, were deeply troubled by his seeming irreverence and feared that his words might be "an omen of disaster."

As the resistance movement slowly decayed from within, the Germans were preparing the assault that would finally crush it. In January 1889 the Reichstag had voted two million marks for the support of the Company in East Africa, and Wissmann had been appointed to recruit an army of Sudanese and Shangaan soldiers for an armed invasion of the coast. On April 28, 1889, the Company transferred its nominal administration to Wissmann, and in the next few days a total of seven hundred black recruits under German officers arrived in Bagamoyo, where they were drilled and issued weapons. In the meantime Wissmann contacted Abushiri and offered him ten thousand rupees to give up his resistance and leave the coast.[100] Abushiri was not so easily bought off, however. He informed Wissmann that he would agree to cease hostilities only if he were recognized as governor of the entire coast and if the Germans lifted the naval blockade and agreed to limit their activities to the collection of customs duties in the ports. He also demanded acceptance of a number of conditions, such as: "[The Germans] shall enter no private residences and shall have special respect for residences reserved for women. . . . Religion and everything that is connected with the religion of the land shall be respected. [The Germans] shall not enter mosques, and they shall not peer into them indiscreetly."[101] Wissmann, who considered these conditions "ridicu-

---

[97] *Central Africa*, VII (Apr. 1889), 60.
[98] Hemedi, *Utenzi*, 67.
[99] Ibid., 69.
[100] Bennett, "Arab Power," 212, 213.
[101] Becker, *Hermann von Wissmann*, 203-5.

lous," made the final preparations for the assault on Abushiri's fort, declaring that, "I expect more from a successful battle against him than from any easy peace."[102] As soon as the missionaries still remaining in Abushiri's custody had been ransomed, Wissmann was ready for the attack.

The Defeat of the Resistance

On the morning of May 8, 1889, a troop of one thousand men, consisting of three hundred Germans and the new black recruits, marched out of Bagamoyo toward Abushiri's fort. At the fort waited nearly an equal number of defenders, armed with modern rifles and several old muzzle-loading cannon. But Abushiri had made a fatal error: he had committed all his troops to the static defense of an armed fortress instead of adopting the flexible, harassing tactics necessary to overcome the superior firepower and organization of the invader. The Germans quickly blew holes in the wooden walls of the fort with their field guns, and the ensuing battle was a rout. The scene inside the stockade was chaotic:

> Wherever I put my hand [remembered Hemedi] there was a bullet.
> . . . The bullets went on coming with a monstrous whistling and all
> at once the Europeans flung themselves on the stockade. The place
> was full of Europeans and they watched all the paths; there was no
> way of escape and we wretches were in distress. Outside they sur-
> rounded us and their cartridges were ready for us. . . . When our
> leader [Abushiri] saw that we were defeated he was the first to flee.
> I was watching him there inside the stockade and I saw a good place
> to jump. . . . I commended myself to God and I bent down and ran.
> While we were showered with bullets men pursued us, opposing us like
> a storm. The cannon roared like thunder and we were hit as we fled.
> . . . We ran straight on, not turning at the sound of a rifle, and the
> bullets were like bees or drops of rain. . . . When we had gone some
> way we saw the stockade on fire; the Europeans were sacking it and
> doing as they wished. The whole stockade was on fire and they took
> the loot, and the corpses lay about unminded.[103]

The survivors, many of them wounded, reassembled a short distance away and took stock of their losses. A large number of the Arab

---

[102] *Weissbuch,* VI, 66-68.

[103] Hemedi, *Utenzi,* 69-71. For the European accounts, see *Weissbuch,* VI, 71-80; Behr, *Kriegsbilder,* 56-69; Johannes Hirschberg, *Ein deutscher Seeoffizier,* Part 3 (Wiesbaden, 1898), 83-100.

and Swahili soldiers considered themselves totally defeated and began to return to their homes or to Zanzibar. Hemedi, for example, bid farewell to Abushiri, saying, "Sir, I must take leave of you and go home; what has happened to us is the will of God. We must not oppose the Mighty's will."[104] Abushiri remained undaunted, however, and proceeded to visit the nearby villages to recruit new troops. But he found that the news of his crushing defeat at Bagamoyo, along with the continuing theft of food supplies by resistance members, had made the people hesitant to commit themselves.

Soon "peace parties" began to appear everywhere, consisting of plundered villagers, ruined businessmen, and disgruntled town notables. These groups contacted the invader and declared that they wished an end to hostilities, even if it meant than a German government would be imposed upon them. Nevertheless, the militant parties remained in power in the coastal towns, and preparations were made for the impending invasion. And yet the fatal mistake was made again of depending on fixed fortifications rather than mobile tactics. Within two months, the Germans, who had added machine guns to their arsenal, had won bloody victories at Sadani, Tanga, and Pangani, and declared themselves masters of these now utterly devastated towns.[105] In many cases, the exhausted people began to return to the towns after these battles to beg for peace, but substantial numbers, particularly around Bagamoyo, moved further inland and constructed forts from which to continue the resistance. In the meantime, the Germans devoted their energy to subduing the smaller villages in the vicinity of the towns. Usually they set out on small expeditions, looting, and burning every settlement that showed the least sign of opposition. Soon the news of these tactics spread to the remaining villages, and many *jumbe* made their way to the nearest German headquarters, signed a peace treaty, and received a German flag to fly over their houses.[106]

Because of these developments, it became increasingly difficult for the resistance leaders to stir up adequate support, and they began to resort to various ruses. This was the case with Upanga, a Pangani *jumbe* who attempted to recruit warriors among the Bondei people near Mkuzi. We know of his activities through H. W. Woodward, a British missionary at the Magila station. Woodward wrote the following report, the substance of which is probably accurate:

[104] Hemedi, *Utenzi*, 73. See also *Further Correspondence*, C. 5822, 96-97.

[105] Hemedi, *Utenzi*, 73-77; *Weissbuch*, VI, 80-89; Schmidt, *Geschichte*, 70-78; Hirschberg, *Seeoffizier*, Part 3, 106-20; Behr, *Kriegsbilder*, 151-66, 319-28; Richelmann, *Meine Erlebnisse*, 64-87.

[106] See, for example, Behr, *Kriegsbilder*, 116-17, 218-19; Richelmann, *Meine Erlebnisse*, 152-53; Schmidt, *Geschichte*, 68, 77.

[M]any people, foolishly listening to [Upanga] and his declarations of what should be when the coast men triumphed again, made a number rally round him. He had also plenty of money, it seems. He said the successful ones should be made chiefs, and take as many wives as they pleased when they returned, and so forth.

So, in spite of warnings, off they went to Mgambo, on the Pangani road, together with a number of Maholola. Before long, the Germans came out to attack them, and the coast leaders said to the Bondeis, "You stay in the village, and we will go out to fight."

They went out, but, instead of fighting, hid themselves in the woods, and left the Bondeis to their fate. The poor simple creatures thought they would be safe inside the stockade, and their astonishment was unbounded when they saw the German leader draw his men up outside the entrance, instead of keeping under cover as much as possible, according to the approved African fashion, and himself boldly *saw through* the supports of the door, and calmly walk in. They said their hearts failed them so, they could scarcely fire at all, for the white man was certainly a "Shetani [devil]," or a "Spirit," or "Jinni [water sprite]." They fled back to Mkuzi gunless and miserable, and the chief of Sega was left dead on the field.[107]

Such deceptive tactics naturally alienated whatever support the coastal leaders might still have had. One by one they yielded to the Germans or were hunted down and hanged.

Even Abushiri, failing to find adequate reinforcements in the coastal areas, was forced to seek new men and supplies far in the interior. At the end of June 1889 he attacked the German station at Mpwapwa, killing one of the agents and forcing the other to flee.[108] When word of this attack reached the coast, Wissmann decided to take a large expedition into the Mpwapwa area to reestablish German control.[109] This expedition was particularly important, for it was the first German contact with those major and minor *jumbe* of the interior who had previously given at least passive support to the resistance.

From the outset, Wissmann made it clear that he would tolerate no opposition, and he turned his cannon and soldiers on several villages to prove his determination. Within a few days the chiefs began to succumb to this pressure, as can be seen in the following description by a German officer who took part in the expedition:

Because most of the areas of the interior were taking part in the rebellion, more or less following momentary expediency, the Wissmann

107 H. W. Woodward, in *Central Africa*, VIII (Feb. 1890), 28-29.

108 Schmidt, *Geschichte*, 99-100.

109 The best descriptions of the Mpwapwa expedition are Wissmann's reports in *Weissbuch*, VI, 97-99, VII, 75-83. See also Schmidt, *Geschichte*, 101-35.

expedition was at first received with fear and mistrust. At Mzua, for example, the women and children fled and the men armed themselves and awaited us in the village. But they were made to understand that it was not the intention of the Imperial Commissioner [Wissmann] to take revenge on all those who could be accused of complicity in the rebellion. . . . As was later to become typical, Jumbe Simba of Mzua soon presented himself and his people, brought gifts, and asked for peace. . . . Every village asked for a Charter of Protection and a German flag, which, of course, they at first raised timidly, for they did not yet feel it wise to be considered complete friends of the Germans by the Arabs, Baluchi, and Wamrima who were still our enemies. It was still possible that the rebel party might once again gain the upper hand.[110]

On at least one occasion, the German expedition was received quite warmly by a major chief of the interior. Kingo of Morogoro, who had always been hostile to the coastal people because of their refusal to allow him to levy local customs duties, and who evidently also bore a personal grudge against Abushiri, welcomed Wissmann to his town and induced the surrounding chiefs to do the same. He also revealed the location of the stronghold of several of the fleeing Bagamoyo *jumbe* and led the Germans in an attack against it. As a reward he was given the two old cannon that had been taken from Abushiri's fort at Bagamoyo and was permitted to reinstitute his customs duties. Later he was also made a salaried official of the German government, a measure used frequently thereafter to ensure that the major chiefs of the interior would have a stake in the preservation of the new regime.

Wissmann arrived in Mpwapwa on October 12, 1889, where he began the construction of a large fort and received the peace delegations of the surrounding chiefs. In the meantime, however, Abushiri had been preparing another effort to expel the Germans. Finding it impossible to incite the people of the smaller villages, who had been intimidated by Wissmann, he turned to the southwest and established contact with the powerful leaders of the Hehe and other tribes, who agreed to give him contingents of warriors in exchange for whatever plunder they might take.[111] As Abushiri marched toward the coast with these eight thousand new troops, who were armed only with spears and shields, the remaining coastal leaders stirred up simultaneous ris-

[110] Schmidt, *Geschichte,* 107-8.

[111] It is not known whether Abushiri contacted the great chief Mkwawa to obtain his Hehe allies. There was a rumor on the coast that he had established "blood brotherhood" with a Hehe chief, but this chief was not identified by name. See *Weissbuch,* VI, 95-97.

ings in the area of Bagamoyo and Dar es Salaam.[112] The German garrisons, already understrength because of Wissmann's Mpwapwa expedition, were faced with a serious crisis and might well have been
overwhelmed had it not been for a fatal flaw in Abushiri's tactics. The
tribesmen who had joined him were not willing to wait until they
reached the coast to begin plundering, and Abushiri was unable to
prevent them from attacking the small Zaramu villages along their
route of march. Soon large numbers of refugees were pouring into
Bagamoyo with horrible tales of these attacks, which were naturally
blamed on Abushiri. The resistance movement was thus discredited,
and public opinion swung in favor of the Germans. Former allies of
Abushiri offered to be German spies, and many of the Zaramu refugees
volunteered to fight on the German side.

As Abushiri approached the coast, he divided his troops into several large sections, one of which encamped at Yombo, twenty miles
south of Bagamoyo. From here he sent letters to his allies, urging them
to join him in an assault on Bagamoyo and declaring that, "I have seen
my star. It has told me that I shall attack the Germans on October 20.
I shall attack all the stations on the night of the 20th. I shall conquer
the Germans, kill them."[113] Word of his plans reached the Germans
far in advance, however, and on October 19 they made a surprise attack on Abushiri's camp, killing over two hundred of his warriors during several hours of intense fighting. The Hehe, disillusioned by this
defeat, refused to help Abushiri any further and broke up into small
bands to return home, whereupon they were assaulted by the Zaramu,
who had been offered two rupees by the Germans for every warrior
whom they killed. Abushiri, increasingly plagued by elephantiasis, was
forced to flee northward, where he made a desperate attempt to ally
himself with the two remaining leaders of the resistance in the north,
Bwana Heri and Simboja. There is also evidence that he hoped to
reach Mombasa and to sail from there to Pemba, where he might once
again have raised an army.[114] But quick action by the Germans cut him
off from his potential allies, and he was forced to run from village to
village, constantly pursued by local chiefs who hoped to win the
10,000 rupee reward that had been offered for his capture. Finally one
of the chiefs, Magaya of Kwamkoro, lured Abushiri into his village
and had him seized and put in chains. Word was then sent to the
German headquarters in Pangani, and Abushiri was taken to the coast,

[112] See, for example, Leue, *Dar-es-Salaam*, 37-40; Hirschberg, *Seeoffizier*,
Part 3, 142-43. The major sources for the ensuing events are *Weissbuch*, VII, 78-
81; Behr, *Kriegsbilder*, 259-88; Richelmann, *Meine Erlebnisse*, 162-206.

[113] Hirschberg, *Seeoffizier*, Part 3, 149.

[114] *Weissbuch*, VIII, 11-12.

quickly tried, and hanged on December 15, 1889. It is significant that his last act was to deny that he had been personally responsible for the alliance with the Hehe warriors, which had brought so much destruction to the coast. His last words were: "I die a good Muslim!"[115]

With their chief antagonist eliminated, the Germans could devote themselves to the pacification of the rest of the coast and to the entrenchment of their administration. Simboja, the powerful chief of Usambara, had already capitulated because of Abushiri's defeat and because of his own failure to arouse the neighboring *jumbe,* Kimbanga and Kinyasi, to further resistance.[116] In February 1890 the Germans received his surrender, as well as a fine of ivory and gold for his previous co-operation with Abushiri, and appointed him Governor of Usambara at a salary of 100 rupees per month.[117]

But far more formidable was Bwana Heri, the Swahili "Sultan of Uzigua," who had defended for many years his one-man rule of Sadani and environs against the encroachments of the Sultans of Zanzibar.[118] He and his people had escaped the initial thrust of the German invasion because Sadani had not been one of the ports taken over by the German East Africa Company since it was not considered to be under the control of the Sultan. Nevertheless, when it became known that he too was opposed to the Germans, Sadani was bombarded and destroyed on June 6, 1889. Temporarily retreating from the coast, Bwana Heri soon returned to Sadani, and it was necessary for the Germans to stage a full-scale invasion to drive him out. In early November, Zelewski led a sweep of four hundred troops and six hundred Sukuma volunteers through Uzigua to Sadani, attacking any resisting villages. "Bwana Heri's opposition and his people's fanaticism forced us to use a harsh but necessary form of warfare: the destruction of crops and the burning of villages."[119] But Bwana Heri remained unshaken and moved his headquarters to Mlembule, about four miles inland from Sadani, where he won an impressive victory against a punitive expedition on December 27, inflicting eighteen casualties on the Shangaan troops of the Germans. Part of Bwana Heri's success can be attributed to his adoption of certain elements of guerrilla warfare, even though he continued to depend on strong stockades as the keystone of his defense. In the words of one German officer, "our efforts [to surprise Bwana Heri] were frustrated because his men had learned

[115] Schmidt, *Geschichte,* 162.

[116] H. W. Woodward in *Central Africa,* VII (Nov. 1889) 162-63.

[117] Schmidt, *Geschichte,* 175.

[118] Bennett, "Arab Power," 149-53. The best sources for the campaign against Bwana Heri are Schmidt, *Geschichte,* 152-56, 163-83; *Weissbuch,* VIII, 1-3, 16-17, 20-40.

[119] Schmidt, *Geschichte,* 155.

of our landing through spies and awaited us. They threw themselves against us in small bands and attacked our camps and resting places by day and by night. Although we always put them to flight, they gained in this way accurate knowledge of our movements."[120]

It was clear that such successful resistance could not be tolerated, and in early January 1890 Wissmann landed at Sadani with five hundred soldiers and five field guns and set out for Bwana Heri's fort at Mlembule. Here they were confronted by a stockade with "palisades four meters high" and "earthworks of a man's height" which successfully withstood the German cannon fire during the ensuing four-hour battle. From inside the fort came accurate and intense gunfire, punctuated by brief pauses during which the 1,500 defenders could be heard praying in unison. The Germans finally succeeded in storming the stronghold, with both sides sustaining heavy casualties. Bwana Heri, who had escaped with most of his men, fled further inland, but his resources were becoming exhausted. The scorched-earth tactics of the Germans had denied him necessary provisions, and he refused to raid small villages to replenish his food supply. After another serious defeat in March 1890, he agreed to accept the Germans as rulers of the coast and was in turn given a place in their administrative hierarchy.

With the northern coast fully pacified, the Germans could turn their attention to the southern towns.[121] Delegations from Lindi and Mikindani had already appeared in Dar es Salaam to express their desire for peace. But Wissmann felt that it was necessary to demonstrate his military might in these places, as well as in Kilwa, where seven thousand defenders remained intransigent. On May 1, 1890, a force of over seven hundred men with several field guns set out by ship for the southern coast, where they landed on May 3 and proceeded to march toward Kilwa. To their surprise, they were able to enter the town without firing a shot, because the three days of naval bombardment preceding their arrival had convinced the resistance leaders to give up the struggle. After this resounding victory, the remaining towns and villages quickly sent delegations to beg for peace.

Further inland, however, the Yao warriors who had made up the bulk of the forces in the southern towns returned to their villages and declared that they did not consider themselves defeated. Their most influential chief was Machemba, a man who had grown wealthy from the rubber trade. At first he had refused to support either the coastal resistance leaders or the Germans, but in the middle of 1889 he had

---

[120] Ibid., 163-64.

[121] For the accounts of this campaign, see *Weissbuch,* IX, 51-68; Hirschberg, *Seeoffizier,* Part 3, 204-29; Leue, *Dar-es-Salaam,* 68-82; Schmidt, *Geschichte,* 199-216; Becker, *Hermann von Wissmann,* 317-33.

decided that the invaders had to be repulsed.[122] Though the southern towns were eventually conquered, he resolved to continue the resistance further inland. Naturally, the Germans could not tolerate such independence, especially when Machemba attacked a German ally, Chikombo, a chief of the Makonde. But when the German district officer at Lindi wrote to Machemba, ordering him to present himself at the coast, he replied with a letter in Swahili which said:

> I have heard your words, but I do not see any reason why I should obey you. I should rather die. I have no relationship with you and I cannot recall that you have ever given me a pesa or a quarter-pesa or a needle or a thread. I search for a reason why I should obey you and I cannot find even the smallest. If it is a matter of friendship, I shall not refuse, today and always, but I shall not be your subject. . . . If you want to fight, I am prepared, but never shall I be your subject. . . . I shall not fall down at your feet, for you are a creature of God, and so am I. . . . I am Sultan of my people; you are Sultan of your people. Look here, I do not tell you that you must obey me. I know that you are a free man. Since I was born I have not set foot on the coast; shall I now go there because you call me? I shall not come. If you are strong enough, come and get me. I should rather lose your respect than surrender to you.[123]

Three German expeditions to punish Machemba for this impudence found it was impossible to make decisive contact with his warriors; they deserted every village as the Germans approached and constantly harassed the middle of their columns with surprise attacks.[124] But these expeditions caused great distress to Machemba's people by destroying their villages and crops, and he evidently decided that it was wiser to let the Germans have their way than to allow the destruction to continue. He presented himself at the Lindi station in March 1891 and signed an agreement that bound him to keep peace with his neighbors, to refrain from charging duties on caravan traffic, and to give up his modern weapons.[125]

The Germans could now consider themselves masters of the coast. But their control was based mainly on force; martial law was in effect everywhere. This meant that legal procedures were of the most rudimentary kind, employed more for their impact than for the achieve-

---

[122] Hugold von Behr, in *Mittheilungen aus den Deutschen Schutzgebieten,* VI (1893), 46; *Central Africa,* VII (Oct. 1889), 144-45.

[123] Quoted in Müller, *Deutschland,* 455-56.

[124] *Weissbuch,* IX, 89-97; Schmidt, *Geschichte,* 240-41; Tom von Prince, *Gegen Araber und Wahehe* (Berlin, 1914), 32-39.

[125] Schmidt, *Geschichte,* 241-43.

ment of justice. A striking example was one district officer's handling of
a particular case after the defeat of Abushiri at Yombo: "At this time
it was reported to me that one jumbe had captured the dreaded
Makanda, but that another jumbe had let him go. I gave the first
jumbe a reward and had the other one hanged, which made a good
impression on the people."[126] There was doubt in some minds, however, as to whether this was the proper "impression" to make; Michahelles, the German consul in Zanzibar, pointed out that, "Because of
the cursory hanging of Arabs, the coastal people have begun to consider all Arabs outlaws. One chief recently asked Wissmann whether
he should kill all Arabs without distinction."[127]

But such reservations did not move the young German officers,
for whom unrestrained force was the most effective mode of public
relations. Thus, hesitant or hostile Africans were threatened with a
drawn pistol, and soldiers were used to collect laborers to work on the
German fortifications.[128] When one officer found that the Gogo people
who lived near his station at Mpwapwa would not sell him cattle, he
placed barricades and armed guards around all the watering places,
giving the Gogo the choice of either relinquishing their cattle or watching them die of thirst.[129] Such methods of force were, of course, countered by violence, and on at least one occasion in the "pacified" towns
a German officer was shot dead by a hidden assailant.[130]

The German rule was also authoritarian. The young officers
thought of themselves as "small kings," and they frequently demonstrated this kingship by adopting the symbols and ceremonies prevalent in the region before the advent of the Germans.[131] Wissmann, for
example, gave the following description of his reception of a group of
five hundred surrendering Bagamoyo residents: "After an official act
of submission, in which, according to custom, the head and breast
[of the penitents] are covered with dust, I pardoned the people and
ordered rice and cattle to be distributed to them."[132] Even after such
initial gestures it was considered necessary to demand constant reaffirmation of the absolute authority of the German conquerors. In
Bagamoyo, the district officer decided that he had to prevent "a certain
passive resistance that could hinder the enforcement of necessary
regulations," so he ordered all Africans to greet any passing European

[126] *Weissbuch*, VII, 78-81.
[127] Quoted in Müller, *Deutschland*, 552.
[128] Behr, *Kriegsbilder*, 111, 238; Richelmann, *Meine Erlebnisse*, 194.
[129] *Weissbuch*, VIII, 12-15.
[130] Prince, *Gegen Araber*, 28.
[131] Wolfrum, *Briefe*, 90, 94.
[132] *Weissbuch*, VIII, 18-19.

so as to "demonstrate beyond question that we are the lords of the land."[133] The effect of this order was described by Baumann on a visit to Bagamoyo in 1890: "When a white man passes by, all coloreds, whether Arab, Indian, or Negro—even small children—stand up and salute militarily."[134] The exercise of such power naturally affected the German officers themselves; Michahelles complained that, "The martial law is ruining the young officers, for there is no legal limit set to their *bon plaisir*, and when their pasha-existence comes to an end, they will not be able to readjust to normal conditions."[135]

Eventually, of course, the Germans learned to employ certain positive measures to win African support. It has already been noted, for example, that many of the chiefs of the interior were allowed to re-establish their local customs duties and were made salaried officials of the German administration. These chiefs also received swords and other badges of office and proudly called themselves "men of the German Government."[136] One feature of the administration—the system of courts and judges that replaced the summary methods of martial law—seems to have been particularly effective in winning support. A British missionary in Usambara wrote in this regard that, "Many of [the chiefs of the interior] have debtors at the coast, or their children are unlawfully detained and made slaves by the coast men. Whenever the case is clear, they receive prompt and satisfactory assistance, and that at a minimum cost to themselves. So, although several villages have been burnt down, the whole country admits the justice of the act."[137]

After a while, the Swahili people began to make the best of the situation, bringing their crops to sell at high prices to passing German expeditions.[138] Some of the conquered towns even began to send detachments of men to fight on the German side in return for the right to plunder the resisting villages. The Germans also gained the cooperation of the Nyamwezi and Sukuma caravan porters, whose trade had flourished while the activities of the coastal entrepreneurs had been curtailed. And even the Arab plantation owners began to give their support when they saw that the German administration could be useful to them. They gladly accepted, for example, Wissmann's plan to establish a system of sesame oil mills that would depend upon their

---

[133] Richelmann, *Meine Erlebnisse*, 146-49.

[134] Quoted in Müller, *Deutschland*, 452.

[135] Ibid., 552.

[136] H. W. Woodward in *Central Africa*, VIII (Feb. 1890), 27; *Weissbuch*, VIII, 25.

[137] H. W. Woodward in *Central Africa*, VIII (Feb. 1890), 27.

[138] *Weissbuch*, VI, 101-4.

plantations for produce, even though the "negotiated" prices were sure to be low.[139] They were particularly happy to learn that the Germans had no objection to their continued use of slaves; in at least one town the district officer ordered that all runaway slaves be captured and returned to their plantations, explaining that, "Although this action seems to contradict our position on the question of slavery, it is necessary under present conditions. The caravan routes must be protected from the thievery of runaway slaves, and therefore I have chosen the lesser of two evils and shall return them to their owners."[140]

Thus, the ultimate defeat of the resistance was due not only to the superior military power of the Germans, but also to their increasing proficiency in the use of policies designed to win the support of the various factions of the movement. This would never have been possible, of course, had it not been for the nature of the coastal society, which was, in every sense of the word, pre-nationalistic. The chief allegiance of most of the people was to the family or, at most, the village, and in times of crisis it was to these units that they returned. The ruling elements of the society represented personal and local interests and generally saw their power solely as a means to wealth. The political arrangements of the coast, far from embodying either the will or the needs of the people, consisted of endless factionalism, family feuds, and conflict between the private armies of the notables. And the entire society was held together only by the tenuous compromise of many contradictory elements—commoners and notables, slaves and owners, coast and interior, and so forth.

This society had survived for so long before the coming of the Germans because it had never confronted an overwhelming external threat. There had been no reason to create central institutions, to establish an organized army (except for the Sultan's ineffectual police force), or to provide public services funded by regular sources of revenue. The sultanate, the one unifying element of the coast, was very weak and was, in fact, often merely the center of one more faction in the struggle for wealth and power on the coast. And yet it is important to note that the resistance movement initially united behind the Sultan's flag, if not behind the Sultan himself, for there was a natural inclination among the people to accentuate whatever elements would help them to unite against the invader. But the divisive characteristics of the coast were far stronger than this mere symbol. Even the widespread hatred of the Germans was unable to hold the movement together for more than a few months. The town notables began to fear that their

[139] Ibid., VIII, 23-25.
[140] Schmidt, *Geschichte*, 226.

wealth would be threatened by the rural armies, and their more aggressive colleagues, such as Abushiri, would demand too much power.
Most of the rural *jumbe* continued to believe that they could escape
the inconvenience of the new administration by retiring quietly to
their villages. And many of the Swahili townspeople were unwilling
to endure the hardships and expense of protracted warfare, especially
with the outcome so doubtful. All these elements learned to minimize
their feelings against the Germans when they contemplated the gradual destruction of the coast.

Could a stronger, more enduring resistance movement have been
created, given the nature of the pre-German coast? Perhaps so, if a
leader with greater than personal aspirations had arisen to unite the
people. Except for the Sultan, who had been rendered impotent, this
could probably only have been a religious leader at the head of an
Islamic revival (as in the Mahdist and Mullist movements to the
north), but one failed to materialize. Instead, religion became a curiously passive element in the struggle, for the people tended to attribute
their early defeats to the will of God and to resign themselves to German rule. Even if a leader had appeared, whether secular or religious,
he would have faced enormous difficulties, since it is clear that many
revolutionary social and economic measures would have had to have
been adopted if there were to be widespread popular support for a
long and arduous resistance. A positive program of change, comprehensive enough to serve as a unifying ideology, was needed to give
the general coastal populace a stake in the movement. For example, the
political base of the coast could have been expanded, the customs
duties from the ports could have been used for public works rather
than for splendid palaces, and the plantation slaves could have been
freed. And yet it is obvious that each of these measures would have
been explosive, since they attacked powerful vested interests. It is also
difficult to imagine that such a program would have been advocated at
this time, since it was usually the vested interests that led the resistance in each of the towns.

Abushiri, for example, failed to divest himself of his personal aspirations. He retained the character of a factional leader, especially in
announcing his intention to conquer the entire coast for himself after
expelling the Germans. He had the foresight to see that the coastal
society was too loosely organized to withstand the Germans, and this
is partially why he rejected the Sultan, who had proven to be ineffectual against the Europeans. Yet his own vision of a unified coast was
also imperfect. Although he began to use the terminology of the cohesive, defensible nation-state, he failed to advocate the revolutionary
changes in the coastal society that were essential for the creation of

such a state. Even though he displayed personal charisma, he did not have the status of a religious or traditional leader which would have enabled him to inspire something more profound than materialistic motives in his followers. It is evident that many other weaknesses also undermined his effectiveness as a leader. For instance, although he scoffed at religious zeal, he sought the advice of his holy men in a moment of crisis, and then compounded his inconsistency by rejecting their negative prophecy. He seems to have grown less courageous as well—he was the first to flee from the fort at Bagamoyo—and his health constantly deteriorated. Finally, he was unable to foresee that his alliance with the tribes of the interior would lead to widespread destruction on the coast and would cause him to lose whatever support he still possessed in the towns.

Despite these numerous weaknesses, the movement and its leaders endured for a remarkable length of time. Although no unifying ideology was developed to provide the basis for a long-range resistance, the widespread hatred of the Germans served as a strong motivation during the initial invasion. But the essential diversity of the coastal society soon made itself felt, and the factions that had always dominated coastal politics re-emerged and began to bargain with the invader. Farther inland, however, the Germans were to confront tribes that were far more cohesive than the coastal society. The Hehe, for example, who had already achieved unity and military proficiency in wars with the Ngoni, were able to resist large-scale German expeditions for years by the use of guerrilla tactics. It was this opposition, along with that of other tribes, that was greatly to inhibit the establishment of German rule in East Africa. As the Germans soon discovered, the resistance to their invasion of the Tanganyikan coast was only a prologue to many more lengthy and intense struggles in the interior.

SAMORI AND RESISTANCE

TO THE FRENCH

YVES PERSON

Without doubt, Samori Turé is one of the most impressive figures of pre-colonial Africa. He is one on whom the young nationalists of post-colonial Africa have placed great stress. To protect his great achievement—the African empire he had built up in the years from 1870 to 1887—Samori fought the French with skill and determination for fifteen years. However, the efforts Samori had to make in seeking to halt French military imperialism were so great that they led to the dissolution of his empire.

Samori's African Empire: The Dyula Revolution

Samori's achievement was the outcome of a social and political crisis which engulfed the peoples of the Guinea coast and the southern savannah in the nineteenth century and which was itself the outcome of a long period of disturbing change in the Western Sudan. To understand what happened and why, it is essential to review here a series of events which became known as the *dyula* revolution.

Malinké society, based in the West African forest from the Upper Niger to the Upper Sassandra rivers, had developed from a rewarding symbiotic relationship between the animistic masses, whose chiefs held military and political power, and the Muslim commercial minority,

ANS	Archives Nationales du Sénégal—Dakar
AOM	Section d'outre-mer des Archives Nationales—Paris
JORF	Journal Officiel de la République Française
NAS	National Archives of Senegal
PRO	Public Record Office—London

who assured the development and expansion of long-distance trade.[1] Political life was, in principle, the monopoly of the nobility, the descendants of the founding families. Sometimes a military regime gained control over a more or less extensive territory, but its hegemony was always short-lived. Malinké villages were grouped into *kafu* or *nyamaana* (small states) and ruled by chiefs. Malinké society included an ancient and very diversified working class that had been segregated into caste groups. Although the members of these castes were not necessarily scorned, they were always subjected to strict sexual segregation.

But there were also professional groups which did not belong to any castes, especially the Muslim tradesmen, the dyula. Religious tradition played an important role in the lives of the dyula, for without the influence of Islam these itinerant traders would have found neither lodging nor security during their long travels. The extreme individualism of the dyula, their competitive spirit, and their belief in material values was unusual for Africa. These qualities led them to play an important role during the colonial era. Yet the dyula were never a homogeneous group. They frequently established isolated trading centers among the Malinké and recruited neophytes from animistic ranks. Some were petty traders while others ran huge warehouses. These and the landlords were the "capitalists" of Malinké society.

Besides being involved in commerce in gold and in the import of products from the Maghreb and Europe, the dyula were specialists in the cattle, slave, and kola trades. The kola trade is particularly important because it was one of the moving forces in West African history. Kola is a product of the forest zone. There it is little appreciated, but this stimulant has, for centuries, been considered indispensable by the inhabitants of the Western Sudan. The kola trade routes, therefore, linked all the great centers of the Niger Valley with those of the forest. In this trade the dyula played a fundamental historic role because they were able to work out a harmonious equilibrium by abandoning all political functions to the animistic producers. This situation endured until the beginning of the nineteenth century. Why did this era of calm end suddenly in the second quarter of the century, and why did the Muslim traders attempt to impose their law by force?

The area between the Upper Niger and the Upper Sassandra rivers

[1] The history of the Futa-Dyalon and its repercussions on the Upper Niger and the Côte des Rivières has not yet adequately been studied. It is still necessary to look at Louis Tauxier, *Moeurs et histoire des Peuls* (Paris, 1936), bibliography; José Mendes Moreira, *Fulas da Gabu* (Bissau, 1948); and Jorge Veles Caroso, *Monjur-O Gabu e a sua historia* (Bissau, 1948). The best restatement is Jean Suret-Canale, "The Western Atlantic Coast (1600–1800)," in Michael Crowder and J. F. A. Ajayi (eds.), *A History of West Africa* (forthcoming).

was separated from the sea by an impenetrable forest and was comparatively isolated until the beginning of the eighteenth century. The northern trade routes of the Western Sudan provided its only exit to the outside world. To trade with Europe, large detours had to be made: to the east, through Kong, in order to reach the Gold Coast, and to the west, around what is now Futa Dyalon to reach the Gambia. Although there were direct routes to the coast through Sierra Leone and Liberia, these were rarely used.

This situation was dramatically altered after 1727 when the holy wars of the Fulani linked Futa Dyalon to the Western Sudan.[2] The dyula, as far as the Côte des Rivières (modern Guinée), were swallowed up by this movement. It was then that the village of Kankan, which stands at the crossroads of the major rivers, became a city and, in 1785, freed itself from the political domination of the animists of the Sankaran region. Kankan was soon recognized as the religious, intellectual, and commercial center for all the dyula groups from the Upper Niger to the edge of the forest. The Niger trade became more important in this region, and the political leaders, religious leaders, and wealthy traders all worked to expand European trade.

By the beginning of the nineteenth century the dyula trading centers had increased greatly in both size and number. The resulting growth in their wealth and cultural level, combined with revolutionary developments in the use of firearms, apparently caused the dyula to view the animists in a new light. Since virtually all the weapons passed through their hands, the dyula eventually thought of reverting to arms themselves in order to do away with the restraints of the animists and to impose their will on them. This movement became the dyula revolution and took the shape of holy wars.

Mori-Ulé Sisé, the initiator of the new *jihad* (holy war) movement received his early training in Futa Dyalon and was strongly influenced by its triumphant Muslim society. Although a native of Baté, the *kafu* of Kankan, he did not return to this area after leaving Futa Dyalon in 1825, but made his way to the deserted area of Toron (near Konyan on the edge of the forest), where he brought together a mass of adventurers, vagrants, and ruined dyula upon whom he imposed a strict religious discipline. It is from this new city, which he christened Medina, that he launched a holy war in 1835. In a short time, he crushed and forcefully converted to Islam his neighbors in Toron and Konyan. Mori-Ulé Sisé's conquests soon followed a meridian axis preparatory to taking control of a new kola trade route. To gain his objective he launched an attack against Sabadugu, on the Kankan road, but there

[2] On this question, see my forthcoming book, *Samori—Une révolution dyula.*

he met such strong resistance from the animists that he had to give up the project. He then turned his attention to the south, but the animists of Worodugu, with the help of Vakaba Turé, a dyula who had been trained by Mori-Ulé himself, turned him back. Mori-Ulé was killed in 1845 during the attack on Kurukoro.[3]

Mori-Ulé had tried to destroy the traditional animistic society by introducing foreign troops and by using superior military tactics. But the dyula of the region thought that they could improve their lot if, instead of fighting the animistic masses, they associated themselves more strongly with them. This is why Vakaba, having learned the methods of warfare from Mori-Ulé, came to the defense of the animists against his former teacher. Although he defeated Mori-Ulé, Vakaba spared the Sisé troops, with their help destroyed Nafana, and in 1846– 47 founded the strong Muslim state of Kabasarana, located near Odienné.[4] As conqueror, Vakaba demanded heavy tributes and the opening of trade routes, but not conversion to Islam. His kingdom soon extended for over two hundred kilometers along the axis of the kola trade route from Bamako to Mau (Touba), and, as it was supported by the indigenous population, it enjoyed a certain stability. This equilibrium was disturbed by the reigns of Vakaba's bellicose second son, Vamuktar, and of his brutal third son, Mangbe-Amadu, but the kingdom continued to exist.

While the Kabasarana kingdom was thus taking shape, the state of Sisé, Kabasarana's ally, revitalized itself under the leadership of Sérè-Burlay, Mori-Ulé's son, who reigned from approximately 1849 to 1858.

Taking advantage of internal wars, Sérè-Burlay succeeded in imposing his authority on the Bèrèté family—a dyula group firmly entrenched in the land west of the Dyon in the Konaté territory of Gundo (Upper Toron). Through the annexation of this country, he was able to intercept caravans on the well-traveled kola trade route from Kankan to Toma. But he soon had to put down a powerful revolt which was marked by the siege of Seydugu (c. 1851–53). In the midst of this battle Sérè-Burlay's troops captured the wife of a dyula aborigine named Laafiya Turé. Her son, the young Samori, joined the Sisé ranks in the hope of delivering his mother from captivity.

Between 1853 and 1855, Sérè-Burlay succeeded in holding off the Wasulunké of Dyèri Sidibé. This success convinced him that his power

---

[3] The history of the Sisé is reconstituted from oral traditions and can be followed in detail in the second part of *Samori*.

[4] Paul Marty's work on Kabasarana in *L'Islam en Côte d'Ivoire* (Paris, 1923) suffers from his use of administrative monographs and the fact that he did not work in the field.

was well consolidated and he made the same error as had his father before him: starting with a policy of moderation toward the original inhabitants, he reverted to a policy of forced conversion to Islam. This led, in 1859, to a massive revolt, during which he was killed.

The dyula, although in a minority, felt capable of imposing their own laws because of the development of new military tactics involving the systematic use of firearms and horses. The animistic society as a whole demonstrated a lack of political awareness which prevented them from recognizing the extent of their danger and mobilizing forces to meet the crisis. However, their reactions were enough to demonstrate to the dyula that they would not permit the erosion and destruction of their traditions and that the dyula could impose their will only insofar as they agreed to accept the main animistic traditions. Nevertheless the animistic masses still felt threatened and actively sought an innovative leader who both respected their freedom and understood the new political trends. The dyula of their region seemed to possess this quality—to combine a loyalty to their compatriots with a wider view of the world. This was particularly the case with Samori, which explains the magnitude of his triumph.

The Rise of Samori

Turé is one of the more important dyula clans of Sarakholé origin. From early times it was linked to commerce and to Islam. Samori's ancestors came from Sidikila, an ancient village near the goldfields of the Manding. By following the kola routes they had by the early eighteenth century established themselves in the lower Konyan region—especially in the village of Manyambaladugu. Intermarrying with the indigenous people, they eventually abandoned both commerce and Islam. This break was so complete that Laafiya, Samori's father, who was a farmer, an owner of cattle, and a pagan, retained almost nothing of the dyula tradition.

Samori, who was born about 1830, seemed to be destined for the life of a Konyanké animist. But his independent character led him to reject family restrictions to such an extent that he returned to the dyula way of life and, shortly before 1850, to Islam.

His life was strongly influenced by service in the Sisé army, which he had joined in 1853. He soon distinguished himself and acquired a flattering reputation as a fighter. But shortly before 1858, he broke with Medina and the Sisé because Sérè-Brèma, the new Sisé leader, hated him as much as Sérè-Burlay had esteemed him. Knowing that

he could not return to the life of a trader, Samori joined the Bèrèté of
Gundo in Konyan and assisted them in their campaigns in Konyan
and Kuranko. He finally broke with them but tried to establish himself
in the Upper Milo Valley in the name of the Bèrèté. When this tactic
failed in 1861, he went into hiding in the Simandugu mountains.

Samori's career might have ended here, but a revolt in Kuranko
and the aftermath of the Sisé wars so shook the hegemony of the
Bèrèté that he was able to restore himself to power. By the end of
1861 he led a small band whose duty it was to protect a mountain
village in Kamara country; he soon sought the assistance of his brothers, his childhood friends, and any adventurers who were free. It was
then that Samori began his remarkable maneuvering. He proclaimed
himself the defender of his animist Kamara "uncles" against Sisé imperialism, at the same time telling the Sisé that he was their ally
against the Bèrèté. Although the foundations of the state were based
on an alliance of the dyula and the animistic indigenes, his men indulged in such violence that some of the Kamara attempted to destroy
the new power. Samori put down this threat in 1862 and went on to
Sanankoro in the Milo plain, where his father had many relatives.

Sérè-Brèma, who had re-established the Sisé state, was attacking
the insurgents of the Upper Konyan who, in turn, were being helped
by the Kamara of Upper Dyon. Samori attacked these Kamara from
the rear and crushed them. He then called on the leader in Medina
to attack the Bèrèté from the north while he attacked from the south
in order to destroy their stronghold at Sirambadugu. During 1864–65,
this fortress resisted a strange coalition composed of the Sisé, the animists of Nantene-Famudu, chief of Sabadugu, and Samori's partisans.
Its fall marked the end of the Bèrèté's political power and consolidated
the authority of Medina in the Milo Valley.

Samori withdrew before the end of the "war" because he realized
that his newly formed army offended the Sisé and that he might become their next victim. In fact, Sérè-Brèma did attack him the following year, but Samori was wise enough not to engage in battle against
superior forces. Instead he sought refuge in the south, in the Toma
country (Tukoro). The Sisé were then, in 1866, the sole masters of
Konyan country; they advanced as far as Boola in the Guerzé (Kpelle)
country on the forest fringe without encountering any opposition.

Samori profited from this lull to extend his sphere of influence
toward the south. He reoccupied Sanankoro in 1867 when the Sisé
were fighting the Wasulu in the north. In the meantime the animist
Kamara had organized themselves in the Upper Konyan under the
direction of a very young king named Saghadyigi, who had taken
refuge on Gbankundo Mountain. From there Saghadyigi openly de-

fied the Sisé. According to Anderson it was because of the resulting
Musadugu War of 1868 that all this Muslim territory turned against
Sérè-Brèma, whose empire was then mutilated.[5] In a dozen years Saghadyigi was to build a strong animist state with frontiers extending
to the Guerzé forest and the Ivory Coast. Saghadyigi was thus offering
the Konyanké an alternative to Samori's rule, and we can be certain
that this did not please our hero. But, since his success depended on
the loyalty of the Kamara animists, Samori could not afford to engage
in a fratricidal war against Saghadyigi. Therefore, the new conqueror
turned away from the south, where he would have had to fight his
animist "uncles," and looked toward the north along the historic axis
of the kola trails.

From 1867 to 1870, Samori, the new *faama* (leader), took advantage of the existing peace to recruit massive groups of adventurers, to
arm and train them, and to organize them into *bolo* (troops of a hundred men). He also managed to inspire complete personal loyalty,
something which he never succeeded in doing among the inhabitants
of his native land.

Samori effected a reconciliation with the weakened Sisé and, in
1871, turned against Nantene-Famudu, who barred his path to Kankan.
During the ensuing three years of combat, his youthful army showed
its great strength by completely destroying the animist kingdom of
Toron. This gave Samori control over the Milo River Valley as far as
the Kankan frontier. In the distribution of the conquered lands, the
Sisé had to be content with the east bank of the Dyon; it was clear
that Samori had become the most powerful leader of the region.

As early as 1873 the new faama set up his residence at Bisandugu,
in newly conquered territory, to show that he was now working for
his own ends and no longer for his Kamara "uncles." As it was, he
did not hesitate to reverse his former policy and ally himself with the
Muslims, especially in the city of Kankan. This town had been assailed
by the Sankaran animists and its trade was now being ruined by their
blockade to such an extent that they sought help.

After the long siege of Kumban in 1875, Samori crushed the Sankaran. (He was shrewd enough ostensibly to dissociate himself from
the massacres which his allies perpetrated.) He then entered the Upper Niger Valley and subdued the area from Kouroussa to Siguiri,
during the period 1876 to 1878—the Burè district rallying to him and
bringing a substantial gold tribute. He then marched westward where
the Baléya and Ulada countries gave him access to the frontiers of

---

[5] Benjamin Anderson, former Secretary of State for the Treasury in Liberia,
gave the first testimony on the Konyan in his book *Narrative of a Journey to
Musardu* (New York, 1869).

Futa Dyalon and those of the Tukolor of Dinguiraye. Because the first assured him access to Sierra Leone, he concluded what proved to be a solid alliance with them. The Tukolor had just been placed under the supervision of Agibu, the brother of Shaykh Amadu.

During 1879 all of Samori's acquisitions were challenged. The nephews of Sérè-Brèma brought about a partial coup at Medina. They then demanded a renewal of hostilities, for they knew that otherwise Samori's hegemony could never be contested. Avoiding all direct provocation, but eliminating the Samorians of Sankaran, the Sisé army launched a powerful offensive toward the west which, in just a few months, brought them to the Upper Niger and then to Solimana on the road to Sierra Leone.

Samori tried as soon as he could to profit from the dispersion of his enemies and from the assistance which he received from some animists. By attacking the Sisé army from the rear, he defeated it almost without combat. He was then able to besiege Kankan (it had refused to help him). By the time the city fell in April 1881, Séré Brèma was also defeated and captured. While Medina was being destroyed and its population transferred to Bisandugu, Samori set up rainy season quarters at Gbelèba on the Kabasarana frontier. Here the unity of the new empire was sealed by matrimonial alliances with the Turé in Odienné, who submitted to the conqueror.

During these triumphal months, Samori had crossed a new threshold. All his adversaries had been eliminated, and he was the most powerful force on the Upper Niger. Although the animists of Saghadyigi still held the Upper Konyan and refused to ally themselves with him, they were reduced to a hopeless defensive. At this same time, the basic nature of the empire was undergoing tremendous changes because large Islamic centers had been integrated within it.

Samori was not one to let up after a number of successes. With his ranks swollen with soldiers from the vanquished armies, he marched at the end of 1881 against the people on the Fyé River who had helped Kankan and who now sheltered fugitives. He took Kényèra in February 1882 in spite of French intervention but at the cost of a trying siege. The French retreat enhanced Samori's prestige and allowed him to extend his authority to Kangaba and to a part of the Bambara country, between the Niger and the Bani rivers, which had seceded from the Tukolor. The Wasulu were easily subdued, and Samori left the care of the Niger to his brother Kémé-Brèma who was also preparing to occupy Bamako.

The conqueror then devoted all of 1883 to the elimination of Saghadyigi. The annexation of Saghadyigi's territory in Upper Konyan permitted Samori to use the edge of the great forest as his southern frontier from the Niger to Sassandra. The relative security of this boundary permitted him to free his forces for the task of expanding into the Western Sudan.

Since the French had closed off all expansion to the north, Samori changed the direction of his efforts in 1884 and deployed his troops to the east and to the west. This produced the most rapid conquest of his career. One of his commanders, after having crossed the Upper Niger, butchered the Hubbu revolutionaries on the Futa Dyalon frontier, and then destroyed Falaba, the capital of Solimana, before reaching the British outposts of Sierra Leone. Toward the east, another commander advanced as far as the Bagoé River where he came up against the advance guard of the strong Kénédugu kingdom of Sikasso. As will be seen, Samori's efforts to destroy Sikasso in 1888 began his downfall.

During Samori's rise to power, before the Sikasso crisis, his political ambitions were already limited by the European presence in Africa. Before discussing how this prevented the building of an empire on the foundation of the dyula revolution, we must describe the structure of the empire and define the society which was to be constructed.

The Construction of a State and the Failure of Islam

In the beginning the political problems which confronted Samori involved the construction of a centralized state in a land that for centuries had no stable organization, except that of the traditional *kafu*. Because of its remarkable permanence, this conservative organization was a powerful force. But a stable structure had to be established on a higher level. At first, Samori was content to perfect the methods adopted previously by the Sisé and Kabasarana: The army was quartered in the capital; in turn it was surrounded by a zone reserved for villages occupied by *sofa* (warriors) and agricultural captives. On the periphery, Samori's agents were installed in the principal centers and beyond were vassals who were forced to pay tribute and to join Samori's campaigning army.

This type of organization was practicable as long as the size of the state allowed for prompt intervention anywhere within its limits. After the conquest of Sankaran in 1875, however, the state became too large for this type of government and a new form, for which there was no precedent in the region, had to be found. Beginning in 1878, Samori organized the conquered territories of the north into military governments. The empire was thus divided into large regions which were occupied and governed by autonomous armies supported by tribute payments. There were never more than five of these autonomous territories and they were all located on the perimeter of the empire. The center of the empire and the forest border were governed directly by Samori and were policed by his large central army. In this section Samori developed a fairly elaborate administrative system which served as the model for each army chief who administered a regional government.

The entire empire rested on the shoulders of one man who had proved himself by his exceptional ability and who never ceased to reiterate that God had clearly designated him to secure order in the human world. Following the animistic tradition, Samori surrounded himself with a group of friends and relatives. This assembly finally became institutionalized as a council whose decisions Samori always seemed to accept even when he did not completely agree with them. What was remarkable and rather revolutionary was that the council members soon took on specialized tasks resembling ministerial functions—the secretariat, the treasury, justice, religion, and relations with the Europeans. The non-specialists acted as inspectors and oversaw the various regional governments.

The army was under the personal command of Samori. It influenced all aspects of society and was so important that it could not be subordinated to the bureaucratic apparatus. Since the empire was largely a product of conquest, it is no wonder that it was truly a military state and that the army received Samori's personal attention. He systematically organized the artisans of his domain, especially the blacksmiths, to serve the needs of his army, and he inaugurated long-distance trade, with the help of the wealthy businessmen, to insure the importation of horses and firearms for his army. The importation of almost six thousand repeating rifles replenished Samori's armaments, and soon his blacksmiths learned to make weapons of this model. This effort alone made it possible to modernize the army which, after 1888, adopted European techniques. All its main innovations took place between Samori's installation in Bisandugu during the year 1873 and the capture of Kankan eight years later; but they were still rough and needed to be refined as the state moved toward Islam.

Although Samori's return to the religion of his ancestors has never been questioned, it must be recalled that he started his career by defending his animist "uncles" against the Muslims. But beyond the territorial limits of this loyalty, Samori had fraternized with the Muslim inhabitants of the commercial centers. When he stated that "a woman alone should be able to travel as far as Kempu" (Freetown), he was indicating the kind of order that he intended to establish.[6] Finding this most attractive to their way of life, all the dyula from the traveling

[6] This statement is attributed to Samori by many independent oral traditions.

salesmen to the big merchants pledged him their loyalty and even served him as spies and propaganda agents.

The empire was thus dependent upon the massive loyalty of the traders to the imperial organization and upon a strong sense of personal loyalty to Samori which was inspired by his exceptional personality. Samori was very conscious of this fact, and it led him to worry about the perpetuation of his work. He recognized that the dyula, despite their present loyalty, would be unable to withstand the centrifugal tendencies of parochial animistic leadership. Fearing that the empire would crumble after his death, Samori sought a unifying force capable of cementing together the disparate elements he had assembled through military strength. It was only natural that he would turn toward Islam, because in it he saw the only available culture of any worth and the only available system of universal values. This former trader seems to have been most influenced both by his rivals, the Tukolor, and by his friends of Futa Dyalon, whose frontier he had reached in 1878. Although his egalitarian and individualistic efforts were in direct contrast to those of Futa Dyalon's strict Fulani aristocracy, the very existence of that triumphant Islamic state influenced Samori in much the same way that it had influenced Mori-Ulé at the beginning of the century.

Samori had received many Muslims into his ranks by 1881, when he annexed Kankan. In this same year he declared that conversion to Islam would be one of the conditions of the surrender of Saghadyigi. However, Samori did not insist upon this conversion until after the fall of this rival in 1883, when he became surer of his control.

At the beginning of 1884, while his troops were continuing an unprecedented war of expansion, Samori retired to Sanankoro to inaugurate reforms in his own territories. At the close of the month of Ramadan, he solemnly took the title of *Almami* (leader), which he borrowed from the Fulani of Timbo. He opened a network of Islamic schools in which he placed the sons of the more notable animists— whether or not their families consented.

After his treaty with France in 1886, Samori realized that he would have to quicken the pace of unification because of the threat of the colonial power to his empire.[7] In November, the Almami announced that all his subjects, including his family, had to convert to Islam.

Samori assumed that a triumph at Sikasso would quiet the malcontents in his kingdom and that he would finally be able to impose his own will. His defeat there in 1888, however, led many animists to stir up what came to be known as the "Great Revolt." It was during this

[7] See below, 99.

period that the Almami realized, with some surprise, that, despite his conversion to Islam, not all Muslims were faithful to him and that some animists—those who had been spared persecution—had remained completely loyal.

Samori seemed to ride out the crisis and learned a great lesson from it. From 1889 on, the ravaged empire was reconstructed on the basis of personal loyalty to Samori, and all efforts were united in the common cause of war against the French. The Almami and his entourage remained true to Islam, but they no longer sought to impose this religion upon the masses. As of 1893 in the east, the political and administrative structure of the new empire was simplified, and the army, although reduced in size, was perfected as a fighting force. Samori's effort to construct a new society, which was the point of the dyula revolution, was abandoned and with it the attempt to spread Islam. All his efforts and energies were devoted to meeting the French threat.

The French Menace and the Attempt at Alliance (1881–88)

Until 1881, during the time that his expansion to the north was advancing smoothly, Samori does not seem to have paid much attention to the European menace. He and the dyula tradesmen viewed the Europeans as a not very populous race of educated people who lived on small islands in the middle of the ocean and whose sole business was trade with the African coast. Similarly, the French in Senegal and the British in Sierra Leone, although they had heard vague reports about the conqueror, paid little attention to him.

In 1878 the French began consciously to occupy West Africa. It was their plan to advance from the upper Senegal River to Bamako on the Niger River. Thus they would pass through the Tukolor empire.[8] Samori, who lacked the prestige of al-hajj Omar, the former leader of the Tukolor, and who seemed to be active far to the south of their planned area of penetration, apparently did not worry the new conquerors.

[8] On the beginnings of French penetration to the Niger, the best study is the book of John Hargreaves, *Prelude to the Partition of West Africa* (London, 1964). See also John Hargreaves, "The Tokolor Empire of Segou and Its Relations with the French," in Jeffrey Butler (ed.), *Boston University Papers on Africa* (Boston, 1966), II, 123-46. A new interpretation can be found in J. I. Kanya-Forstner's "French Military Imperialism in the Sudan" (unpublished Ph.D. dissertation, Cambridge University, 1966). It is confirmed by Y. St. Martin's researches which are in progress in Dakar. The French never thought of an agreement with the Tukolor, only of provisional accommodations.

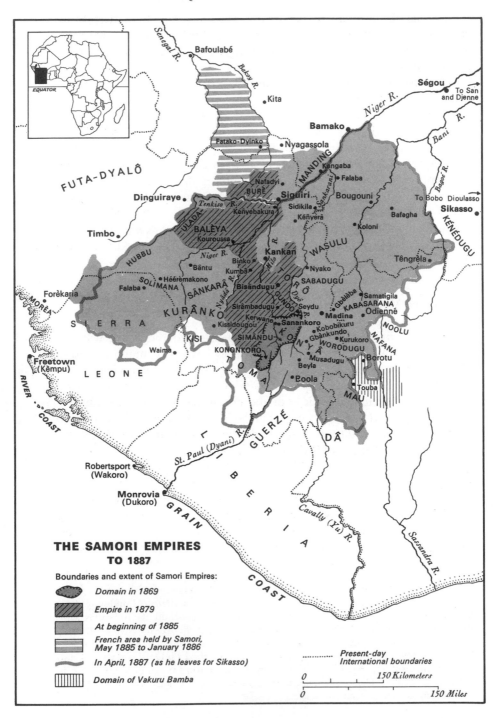

THE SAMORI EMPIRES
TO 1887

Boundaries and extent of Samori Empires:

- Domain in 1869
- Empire in 1879
- At beginning of 1885
- French area held by Samori, May 1885 to January 1886
- In April, 1887 (as he leaves for Sikasso)
- Domain of Vakuru Bamba

· · · · · · Present-day International boundaries

0   150 Kilometers

0   150 Miles

Thus, during the first stages of their advance, the French dealt only with the Tukolor. Bafoulabé was occupied in 1879, when Joseph Gallieni signed a treaty with Shaykh Amadu, at Nango. In 1881, a fort was erected in the old Malinké center of Kita. The command of the march on the Niger was given to Lieutenant Colonel Gustave Borgnis-Desbordes. With visions of grandeur, he was determined to be the man who would give the great river to France.

As early as 1881, Borgnis-Desbordes wanted to push his armies to Bamako but, because of an epidemic of yellow fever which swept through Senegal during the winter, he was ordered to limit his activity to reprovisioning Kita. Since he could not go up the Niger, he decided that any pretext would suffice for a battle. Upon his arrival at Kita, he learned that the commandant of the fort had sent a Senegalese lieutenant to Samori to prevent him from crushing the Kényèra rebellion. It was with great satisfaction that Borgnis-Desbordes discovered that the officer had been politely neglected by Samori. He thereupon decided that France had been insulted and, with a column of light artillery, crossed the Niger near Siguiri and surprised Samori's army at Kényèra on 26 January 1882. In spite of its superior armaments, the small French column, pressed on all sides, had to fall back in a less than glorious retreat. This victory greatly enhanced Samori's prestige. Thus Borgnis-Desbordes's ill-advised and abortive expedition served not only to consolidate Samori's position on the Niger but also to awaken the Africans to the danger of the French menace.

Unaware that it was the next French objective, Samori simultaneously planned to take the city of Bamako to gain access to the Sahel, where he hoped to find horses. Under the command of Samori's brother, Kémé-Brèma, the army was slow to attack, so slow in fact that it was caught unaware when Borgnis-Desbordes arrived on the bank of the river and occupied Bamako on 1 February 1883. The French column appeared so tired, sick, and short of rations that Kémé-Brèma thought that he could retake Bamako without telling Samori what had happened. But his army was dispersed and the establishment of French troops on the banks of the Niger could no longer be disputed. Samori strongly reproached his brother for having been so imprudent, but advised him to enter into friendly relations with the French. A type of *modus vivendi* was thus established on the Niger in 1884.[9] Borgnis-Desbordes now set his sights on the Tukolor capital of Ségu.

[9] This is evident from the comparison of oral traditions with the testimony of Gustave Borgnis-Desbordes (NAS, 3 B98 Dakar) and with that of Captain Pietri, *Les Français du Niger* (Paris, 1885). The best account, despite the bias of colonial historiography, is Jacques Méniaud, *Les pionniers du Soudan* (Paris, 1931), 2v.

The French had great difficulty in organizing an effective system of communications, and their conquest of the Western Sudan, on the pretext that it was necessary for building a railroad, was subject to violent criticism in the French National Assembly. The criticism was so great, in fact, that Borgnis-Desbordes was forced to call a halt to martial activity, despite his personal ambitions. He refused to return to the Sudan and had himself replaced by a modest interim commandant named Boilève. The new commandant began negotiations which could have led to a formal treaty with Samori, but he later broke off relations for fear of compromising French prestige. Boilève, in any case, had no thought of fighting. The calm that once more reigned along the Niger persuaded Samori that the French menace had abated. He therefore decided to concentrate his attention on fighting Tyèba. When the dry season began in 1884, a large part of his army was engaged in combat on the eastern front.

This action indicates that Samori underestimated the explosive force which was implicit in the existence nearby of a troop of virtually autonomous French colonial soldiers (*infanterie de marine, artillerie de marine*). The government of Jules Ferry, which was having its problems in Indochina and in Madagascar, wished to avoid unnecessary involvements in the Western Sudan where there were no obvious economic gains to be made. But the soldiers in Africa wanted to earn as much glory as possible, and they had no intention of following the orders sent from Paris.

Major Combes, an officer of lower rank who replaced Boilève, received no reinforcements, but the Burè country and its gold mines attracted him. He thought that Samori would be too preoccupied with Tyèba to interfere. In March, the major pushed the *sofa* behind the Niger and settled garrisons. At the end of May he left Bamako and proceeded toward Senegal. He was convinced that he would meet no opposition and scorned the alarmed reports of his subordinates. He was very surprised on June 6 when he learned that Samori had crossed the Niger at the head of a large army and was threatening to overwhelm the French garrison in Nafadyi (Séké). Although Combes had jeopardized everything by his rashness, fortune was on his side. After a quick march, he succeeded in freeing his men and bringing them back to Nyagasola in spite of Kémé-Brèma's army which had advanced behind him and barred the way to the Kokoro River.

Combes departed and left Lieutenant Étienne Péroz at Nyagasola —French prestige was then at its nadir. Because he had suffered great losses, the Almami decided not to make any frontal attacks against the French forts. But he exploited the situation and sent his forward column to within fifty kilometers of Bafoulabé. There was panic in Senegal, and an insurrection was feared. In Paris, the Tonkin debacle had forced Ferry out of office; attention was now turned to evacuating the Sudan.

But the French could not withdraw without first avenging the honor of the flag. Colonel Frey was ordered to seek out and chastise Samori. (This officer was an old-timer in Senegal and was against French expansion on the Niger.) Calm had returned during the rainy summer months, and the major part of Samori's army had returned to Sikasso to fight against Tyèba. In Nyagasola, Péroz, no longer besieged, had begun peace negotiations. Frey called a halt to these negotiations and, in an effort to destroy whatever enemy forces were in his reach, tried to surround Samori's army. This maneuver failed, in spite of the surprise attack at Fatako Dyinko on 19 January 1886, because their suppleness allowed them to escape. They retreated south of the junction of the Niger and Tenkiso rivers where Samori was waiting for them at Kényèba-Kura with a powerful army.

However, in his turn, the Almami realized (1) that he was caught in a pincers movement and (2) that he also would have to continue to fight Tyèba. This situation persuaded him to seek a treaty with the French. But Frey fully intended to pursue Samori past the river. This plan collapsed when Frey received news in January that the forts of Bakel and Kayes on the upper Senegal were endangered by Mamadu Lamin's insurrections. Because the French had to have peace on the Niger, they lost their desired initiative against Samori.

The final text of the resultant treaty, signed on 29 March 1886, was more concerned with peace and commerce than with the establishment of a French Protectorate. This pleased Samori, especially since he was then able to reopen trade in horses and firearms with the territory under French control. Although he had to forgo all rights to the lands north of the Niger and Tenkiso rivers, the Burè and the Manding in Kangaba were included on the condition that he would station no troops there. Samori showed his confidence in his new allies by entrusting to them his favorite son, Dyaulé-Karamogho.

There is no doubt that Samori acted in good faith toward the French because he needed peace in order to carry out his attack on Sikasso. He apparently gave extremely strict orders to his troops, most of whom guarded a very troubled and insecure frontier, for there were no incidents with the French that can be attributed to his men.

The treaty had raised a great cry in Paris against Frey, whose terms for peace were considered too lenient by the colonial party. The Ministry of Foreign Affairs demanded nothing less than a Protectorate which would both integrate Samori's lands into the French system and demonstrate to other nations the extent of France's hegemony in Africa.

Frey, who was unacceptable to the Sudanese faction organized by Gaston Brière de l'Isle and Borgnis-Desbordes at the Ministry of the Navy, was replaced by a young lieutenant colonel named Joseph Gallieni. Since Gallieni had to devote most of his time to the war in Senegal against Mamadu Lamin, Péroz, now a captain, was sent as the head of an autonomous mission whose objectives were to force Samori to abandon the special territorial clauses that were included in the treaty and to agree to a French Protectorate.[10]

Péroz stayed with Samori at Bisandugu from 14 February to 26 March 1887. The negotiations, contrary to Péroz's expectations, were extremely difficult. Samori was especially concerned about the new demands that his allies had made. He feared that if he let them take up quarters at Siguiri, they might menace his internal security, especially when he began his attack on Tyèba. Yet on 27 March he gave in to the French demands on the condition that they provisionally agreed not to occupy the disputed Siguiri territory. Péroz succeeded in all of the essentials, and Samori apparently did not realize that he had mortgaged his freedom. In addition, the delay in Samori's military timetable caused by these negotiations eventually proved disastrous to him.

The Sikasso Crisis and the Great Revolt (1887–90)

All the sacrifices that Samori had made could be justified only if the immediate freedom he gained could prevent his being surrounded as he was destroying Kénédugu. Samori did not expect any help from new allies, but he did expect the French to observe a benevolent neutrality.

His preparations had been finished for some time but the Bisandugu negotiations had made him lose three precious months of dry season weather. His army arrived at the fortress of Sikasso in the middle of May 1887. Samori found that Tyèba had made Sikasso much stronger than he anticipated; it was manned by an extremely aggressive enemy who lived off the surrounding land. His own provisions, on the other hand, were difficult to obtain. This situation was so hopeless that he was ready to lift his siege of Sikasso, but was saved from this embarrassing prospect by the arrival of his army of the west, which was armed with repeating rifles.

[10] The greatest part of Peroz's report was published by Joseph Gallieni, *Deux compagnes du Soudan français* (Paris, 1891), 223-94. The original seems to be lost. Cf. Étienne Péroz's reminiscences in *Au Soudan français* (Paris, 1889), which should be only provisionally accepted, with the Governor's in AOM, Senegal IV, 82.

The adversaries became immobilized in a war of attrition that lasted fifteen months. Contrary to previous tradition, the fighting did not stop during the rainy months even though Samori had drastically reduced his forces.[11] By making inhuman demands upon his porters, the Almami succeeded in the remarkable exploit of feeding, fairly regularly, ten thousand persons, half of whom were combatants—it is assumed that this number doubled during the dry season. His major assaults almost succeeded. His first was in January 1888. Then in June he ravaged all the exterior positions around Sikasso. He was, at this point, awaiting reinforcements from his vassals of Kabasarana. He finally had to lift the siege near the end of August 1888, more because of his position in general than because of his military position vis-à-vis the capital of Tyèba. He had lost many of his best men, including one son and his brothers Kémé-Brèma and Maninka Mori; his prestige was ruined; and his empire seemed to be falling apart. It is evident that Samori had not anticipated such an extended war, and the long-unsuccessful siege crystallized the discontent that had begun with the inauguration of his policy of Islamization. In addition, his subjects were filled with rage when they learned in 1888 that the next harvest would be requisitioned to satisfy the needs of the army.

This explosive situation was admirably exploited by the French. Gallieni had returned to the Western Sudan at the end of 1887, but the military situation had quieted down so much that he could devote his time to administrative and political concerns. Since he did not place any particular value on acts of military might as such, he wanted to turn the expansion of the Sudan away from the axis of the Niger to the rich lands of the Gulf of Guinea, and especially to the Futa Dyalon. Therefore, his principal obstacle was no longer the Tukolor empire but rather Samori's, which commanded the headwaters of the Niger. However, Gallieni could not immediately violate the treaty which had just been signed, and he wanted to avoid a military encounter. He hoped to achieve his ends by slyly working toward Samori's defeat at Sikasso.

Anticipating that such a defeat would bring about the immediate dissolution of the empire, Gallieni marched on Siguiri and began building a fort there in January 1888. (In the meantime Samori was thinking that the French would simply wait for the war to come to an end.) Gallieni had not been in Siguiri long before he created the suspicion

[11] These events have become known through oral tradition and the eyewitness reports of Louis G. Binger, *Du Niger au golfe de Guinée* (Paris, 1892). Also from correspondence relating to Major Festing, PRO, CO 806/308. One must be wary of the systematic ill will of Binger who went so far as to refute any possibility of success for Samori. (PRO, Confidential Print, Africa West, 34-40.)

that the Almami was responsible for an assassination attempt against Captain Louis Binger,[12] and his agents stirred up the Samori's subjects on the right bank of the river. On 23 May he ordered a column to advance toward Futa Dyalon. This column crossed the Samorian lands of the Upper Niger without warning and incited the populace to revolt. Finally on 18 June, before embarking for France, Gallieni signed a treaty of protection with Tyèba at Bamako despite the fact that this act could not be reconciled with the Treaty of Bisandugu.

This political action had remarkable results. The malcontents soon started uprisings on the periphery of Samori's empire, particularly on the frontier of Sierra Leone where some isolated Samorian garrisons were freed by the British in February 1888. This led to France's suddenly gaining control over all the Niger Valley. Then the Bambara, who had been sent to reinforce Samori's army of the west, mutinied. They were soon joined by the Sânkarâ and the Kuranko. All Samori's western empire was lost when the French Captain Roiffé, from the fort at Siguiri, succeeded in pushing the southern Wasulu into the insurrection. After all this, the rumor of Samori's death, which was spread in mid-July, shook the rest of the country and a good part of the Upper Konyan. By the end of August, Samori's army at Sikasso was cut off from the rest of the empire and one of his wives was turned over to the French. The empire was in ruins, Samori controlled only isolated sections—Kankan, the Milo Valley, Tukoro, Buguni, and Kabasarana. Only a long and complex struggle would have been able to revive the empire. Thus, the Almami returned from Sikasso in September 1888, restored his armies around Bougouni, and succeeded in crushing the Wasulu. He set up his headquarters at Nyako on the western frontier of Wasulu territory, and undertook systematically to rebuild his army. But another French action disturbed Samori's plans.

Gallieni, in effect, had turned over his command to Major Louis Archinard, an exceptionally ambitious officer and a disciple of Borgnis-Desbordes. Eager to gain personal glory Archinard attacked the Tukolor in Kundyan on 18 February 1889, thus violating their treaty with Gallieni. When Samori protested against frontier incidents, he was so sharply rebuffed that he believed he had no choice but to cede all the left bank of the Niger in order to gain time, not realizing that this would cut him off from Sierra Leone. Samori, therefore, signed the Treaty of Nyako on 21 February 1889, and Archinard made arrangements to meet him at Siguiri for formal ratification of the alliance.[13] Because of further incidents Samori did not go to Siguiri as he dis-

[12] Gallieni, *Soudan*, 553-69. Report and correspondence in ANS, 1 D90, Dakar.

[13] AOM, Senegal IV, 93, and V; ANS, 6 G203 and 208.

trusted the French and feared putting himself within reach of the insurgents who had taken refuge in the French zone. Furious, Archinard moved up the left bank of the Niger, occupied Kouroussa in April, and proceeded as far as the Ulada River on the Futa Dyalon frontier. During this march he sought to punish Samori's partisans in order to humiliate him publicly and gain his total submission. At the same time, as a slight gesture toward Samori, he had some of the most active insurgents executed.

Then, in May 1889, Samori denounced the treaty and sent it back to Siguiri. This reversal ruined Archinard's dream of hemming in Sierra Leone and expanding along the Niger. He returned to France in a rage but with the firm belief that he would sooner or later settle accounts with the man who had refused to be his pawn.

Samori had no desire to break with the French, but his faith in them had definitely been destroyed by Archinard's pride and Gallieni's intrigues. He finally saw that he must either submit totally—something unacceptable to the leader of the dyula revolution—or resign himself sooner or later to the possibility of a hopeless war. Samori prepared for the second alternative, but he needed time.

The "Great Revolt," triggered by the situation at Sikasso, also had to be put down as quickly as possible, and he turned his attention to it as soon as Archinard had returned to France. Dyaulé-Karamogho, Samori's son, who had visited France, attacked the Kuranko and broke their resistance in August. But other columns, which had attacked the Upper Konyan, were held in check. Samori marched to that area in person at the end of July. He took Musadugu and then the mountain fortress of Boronkènyi. He was at the Gbè by the end of November 1889, tracking down the last of the rebels, when the necessity of putting down a coup by his son Managbè-Mamadi forced him to return to the Milo. His generals then besieged the rebels at Borotu in the Sassandra basin. It was not until November 1890 that the last of the insurgents was captured, or expelled. Nevertheless, the "Great Revolt" was effectively crushed by the end of 1889.

The problem was now one of reconstruction. This was not an easy task because the reconquered empire did not resemble the pre-crisis state even though its territorial holdings remained essentially the same. The major part of Samori's domain was ruined and deserted because most of the insurgents had sought refuge either in the French sector, near the British colony, or in the remote districts of the great forest. Finally, the colonial menace, the only problem which had any importance for Samori, had become formidable. His dream of building a new society was shattered by the hard reality of colonialism. It was then that he decided to judge men and their actions solely in reference to their utility in the struggle against the French, not by their religion or ideology.

Since he had decided to abandon the Islamization of his people and to rebuild the empire on the basis of personal loyalty to himself, Samori proclaimed his young son, Sarankènyi-Mori, his heir. This was done on 27 August 1890 at Sanankoro in the midst of the cradle of the empire where animists and Muslims had gathered together to pledge their loyalty to Samori. From then on Samori prepared his men for the forthcoming struggle against the French. From 1890 the Almami proceeded to buy large quantities of modern arms, mostly from Freetown,[14] and his blacksmiths began to operate factories which could produce similar models. His own guard and a portion of the ever-growing army were regrouped in the European style and systematically trained by former African soldiers of the French and British forces. The empire was put on a war footing. Samori was certainly too aware of the enemy's power to hasten the confrontation which he judged to be inevitable. All the available evidence shows that he sought to gain time; but time ran out in 1891.

The Destruction of the Empire

Colonial historiography has helped to spread the legend that the rupture between Samori and the French began with the rejection of the Treaty of Nyako in 1889. This is not so. The Almami considered that his alliance with the French which dated from the Treaty of Kényèba-Kura in 1886 was still in effect, and a serious study of the events on the frontiers proves that civil, if not cordial, relations reigned until 1891 between the commanders of the French and Samorian forces.

Samori's destiny did not really depend upon a military balance on the frontier, but rather on the course of French politics. At the outset of the most active phase of the partition of Africa, known as the *course au clocher* (steeplechase), French strategy was centered on the line from Chad to Dahomey. The Western Sudan would, therefore, have been neglected except for the marine contingent which had made a fief of it and wanted to govern the territory in its own manner. In spite of certain hesitations, the Secretary of State for the Colonies, Eugène Étienne (the principal agent of French imperialism) gave Archinard a free hand. The fate of Samori was thus left to this activist.

By early 1891, Archinard had obtained his first goal, the defeat of

[14] AOM, Soudan VII, 1; PRO, CO 267/388; Sierra Leone National Archives (Freetown); Arabic letters book, 1891–93.

the Tukolor. Samori was his next objective. Since he believed that Samori was an unpopular tyrant and that his empire would fall apart at the first attack, Archinard decided to strike swiftly even though it was late in the season. Moving toward the Upper Niger region, Archinard's army occupied the city of Kankan on 7 April. Bisandugu was destroyed three days later.

Archinard then hastily retreated, leaving a garrison at Kankan. The fact that it was soon besieged was evidence that Samori's army had not fallen apart. On the contrary, Samori had reunited his followers at Misamaghana, prepared them for the supreme effort, and had accelerated his purchase of modern arms.[15] Archinard's attack had caught him off guard, but the rainy season would, he hoped, give him time to prepare for the counterattack.

Colonel Henri Humbert, Archinard's successor, had hoped to find glory in his African command but instead saw himself deprived of any freedom of action. Having received heavy reinforcements, he decided to put an end to the Almami with a frontal attack—striking in the Milo Valley at the heart of the empire. Samori apparently felt ready to take his chances with his modernized army and therefore resolved to bar the way to the French. Thus, all the conditions for a decisive battle were present by the end of 1891.

From the beginning Humbert had bad luck. The Western Sudan was infested with yellow fever, and his forces were not immune; and the greatest epizootic disease of the century also destroyed West African flocks, causing insurmountable provisioning problems. Nevertheless, the French arrived at Kankan on 6 January 1892 and, despite fierce resistance, finally occupied the ruins of Bisandugu on 13 January and the twin villages of Sanankoro and Kérwané on 26 January. Samori's arsenal on the cliffs of Tininkuru was attacked and overwhelmed on 14 February.

Humbert then discovered a very discouraging fact. The country that he was occupying was deserted and ravaged. Samori had ordered all dwellings burned and all inhabitants and food evacuated. Thus he inaugurated the terrible practice of burning the land, a practice that he continued for three years. This scorched earth policy was, in time, extended over large expanses of land and caused great harm to the people. It was, however, militarily effective. Humbert had to arrange a shuttle of convoys from Kankan to Bisandugu and Kérwané in order to provision his new forts. These convoys had to fight every foot of the way to and from their destinations. Weeks passed in this manner while Humbert was looking for a way out of this sterile and bloody land.

[15] PRO, CO 267/388.

Convinced that he had failed, Humbert returned to the coast on 9 April, leaving the garrison of Kérwané cut off from the outside world for almost seven months.

Humbert's sense of failure is easily explained by the fact that the most terrible battles ever fought in West Africa had given the French only two new forts, both of which were almost immediately isolated and besieged. In reality, however, it was Samori who had lost. He had succeeded in slowing down the advance of the French, but he had not paralyzed them, and the cost had been staggering. His troops had been decimated and he had lost many of his best leaders while the French had sustained only moderate losses.

The Almami did not have to wait for Humbert's departure to see that he was in no condition to dispute land titles with the French. He was aware of all the painful consequences of his position; the new forts were like cancers at the heart of the empire, and Samori understood that he could not defend his domain. To avoid capitulation, Samori had to find a remote region where he could hide and hold out in the hope that the storm would subside. Since he was nearly surrounded, he could look for shelter only on the southeastern frontier, in a region which later became the upper Ivory Coast. (He had prepared himself for flight during Humbert's approach by transferring his court to a provisional capital, Mahándugu, in the Kabasarana region.) On the extreme western frontier, Samori had to keep the road to Freetown open as long as possible in order to buy the maximum amount of modern arms from the British. In July 1892, as soon as possible, he left for the east.

It is quite obvious that the Almami had decided not to go through another bloody test of strength.[16] The scorched earth policy was reinstituted, and the zone of worthless land became even larger. The people were led, sometimes by force, to the eastern part of the empire, and Samori ordered his generals not to fight the French. His precious forces had to be kept for the conquest of new land instead of being wasted against a technically superior adversary.

It is in this context that we must place Combe's campaign, a campaign which colonial historiography had traditionally viewed as an extraordinary success.[17] Combes, who had fought against Samori and lost in 1885, wanted to trap his enemy and prevent him from hiding in

[16] This is completely confirmed by oral traditions as well as the logic of events. Unfortunately most colonial historiography has ignored the evidence.

[17] In fact this campaign was not well studied. A short extract of Combes's report was published in *Renseignements Coloniaux* which is the supplement to the *Bulletin du Comité de l'Afrique française*, V (Paris, 1896), 411-42. This source was used by all the following authors, especially Méniaud, *Pionniers*.

the east, so he organized a number of columns which barred movement along the Milo River and as far as the Toma forest. But Samori eluded pursuit, and Combes chose to risk an epic foray in the east. He was not able to engage the enemy in serious combat, however, until 10 April 1893, when a violent battle dispersed, but did not demolish, Samori's troops.

That Combes had failed to destroy the Samorians was evident, yet the colonial party in France succeeded in veiling this disagreeable truth by emphasizing the territorial gains which had been amassed. These gains were indeed spectacular since the Almami had offered no resistance. An enormous area, from the frontiers of Sierra Leone to the Dyon, including the forest fringes of Kisi and Toma, had fallen to the French. The road to Freetown, Samori's almost exclusive source of modern arms, was closed.[18] Two other Samorian armies, under Dyaulé-Karamogho, were still active in the Upper Konyan and eastern Toma regions on the road to Monrovia. But their position was precarious, and arms traffic was of little importance in that area.

At the beginning of 1894, Samori's authority went no farther west than Odienné and Tuba. This meant that he had completely lost his original territory, which had served as the matrix for the dyula revolution. Yet it was precisely at this time that the relentless pursuit by the French came to an end.

Théophile Delcassé, the new Secretary of State for the Colonies, was an imperialist who would not tolerate individual exploits which might hinder his overall plans. He wanted to concentrate all his available forces for a march first on Lake Chad from Dahomey and the Congo, and afterward to the Nile River. These plans excluded the conquest of the Western Sudan which, he believed, would benefit no one except the glory-seeking military. He, therefore, relieved the marines of their fief. In November 1893 he named the controversial Albert Grodet as the first civil governor of the Soudan.[19]

Grodet was sent to end the conquest. As early as January 1894, the Almami, recognizing the futility of his position, approached the

[18] One isolated Samorian column remained in the west on the outskirts of Sierra Leone. The chase after these "lost children" brought about the tragic Franco-British incident at Waima on 23 Dec. 1893. On this affair, see my papers, "L'aventure de Porèkèrè et le drame de Waima," and "Correspondances de la résidence du Kissi relatives à l'affaire de Waima," *Cahiers d'études africaines*, V (1965), 248-316; 472-89.

[19] The Grodet affair has never been objectively studied. The hostile version, in its most respectable form, can be found in the book of G. Bonnier, *L'occupation de Tombouctou* (Paris, 1926). For the Governor's career, see M. Blanchard, "Administrateurs d'Afrique Noire," *Revue d'Histoire des Colonies*, XL (1953), 411-20. This paper shows a strong hostile bias.

French through intermediaries. Talks at Bamako and Kayes lasted until July, when they were broken off by a threatened Samorian attack on Sikasso, the African ally of the French.

The Almami hoped to be quickly forgotten in the Western Sudan, and he left that region almost immediately. He had burned the bridges which tied him to his country and to his past, and with them he lost his *raison d'être*. However, he soon succeeded in acquiring new domains and was able to resist the French for several more years.

The Exodus and the New Empire (1892–96)

The conquest of the disunited lands of the east, where Samori decided to transfer his men and wealth at the beginning of 1892, proved difficult. And therefore, until 1894 Samori was engaged mainly in local warfare and was not in active combat against the colonial forces. In September 1892, he destroyed the chiefdom of Nafana and, in September 1893, that of Nkalakadugu, in Senufo country, because they were blocking the route to the east. Then, fearing that the arrival of the French in the Ivory Coast would cut him off from the hinterland, Samori undertook a feverish march to the east, where he came up against a new obstacle: the king of Sikasso, who held suzerainty over the Korhogo region, was trying to extend his sovereignty to the Senufo of the land along the lower Bandama River. After attacks and counterattacks Samori and Babèmba, the brother of Tyèba and the current leader of the Sikasso who was struggling against him, recognized that their duel was senseless in view of the rising tide of colonialism and, in October 1896, they signed a treaty of peace.

In January 1895 Samori returned to the east to help a troop of his followers who were attacked by a French column from the Ivory Coast. Although Louis Gustave Binger, the Governor, was concerned primarily with the economic development of this maritime zone, French imperial policy pressed for a liaison between the Ivory Coast and the Western Sudan. Thus there was consternation in Paris when it was revealed that Samori's troops had invaded and threatened to cut Bassam off from the Soudan, as well as the metropolis of Kong. While Binger was on leave in France during August 1894, he brusquely accepted the idea of military intervention in the Kong region, an idea that he had energetically fought before, and it was decided to reroute a column led by Lieutenant Colonel Parfait-Louis Monteil toward Bassam.

In March 1895, after many difficulties in the forest zone, Monteil's men attacked Samori's positions in the Dyimini. Although the Almami had had a long time to prepare himself, it was only because of his enormous numerical superiority that Samori was able to overcome the French. With a badly beaten and decimated troop Monteil, himself seriously wounded, returned to Satama (Dyammala) on 18 March. There he learned that Paris had disbanded his column and that he therefore had to abandon the Dyammala to the Samorians.

Many attempts to negotiate with Samori were thereafter begun on the Ivory Coast, but no one ever again considered using military action as a basis for negotiation. The defeat of Monteil had given Samori the security that he needed in the south. In September 1895 a cessation of all hostilities was advocated by Archinard for the immediate future. France's imperial strategy, strongly backed by this notorious imperialist, had many more urgent objectives.

Samori used this lull in hostilities to extend his new domain to the east. The Abron, who commanded the routes to Ashanti and the Gold Coast, had repulsed Samori's advances and had even taken the offensive. But the Samorians crushed the Abron forces during June 1895. All the savannah zone of the kingdom, as far as the Volta River, as well as the great city of Bondoukou and the route to Ashanti and the Gold Coast, thus fell into his hands. The Kulango kingdom of Buna paid tribute. In December 1895 Samori's army crossed the Black Volta River and easily subdued western Gonja as far as the White Volta. An alliance was also made with Wa, which helped to ward off the anarchic Dagari. Later the army interceded in the civil war being fought in Gurunsi by the Zerma conquerors. This action spread Samori's influence as far as the limits of the Mossi empire.

Samori did not go any farther east, and his new domain had reached its territorial limits by early 1896. In the west, the Mau (Tuba) had joined the French in December 1894, and Odienné followed in July 1895. The people of Noolu and Nafana were regaining their freedom at this time, and Samori's contact with the west was broken just as it had been along the whole frontier of the Western Sudan.

During 1896 Samori showed a strange lack of energy. It is evident that he was looking for a temporary solution and ways to prolong his respite and that he had given up the grand designs of the dyula revolution. This revolution was of no concern to the Senufo and other Voltaic people who now populated his new domains. Therefore, he was content to exact tribute to support his army. The army had been greatly reduced in size during the exodus, but it had retained its cache of modern arms and the number of soldiers who had been trained in the European style grew every day.

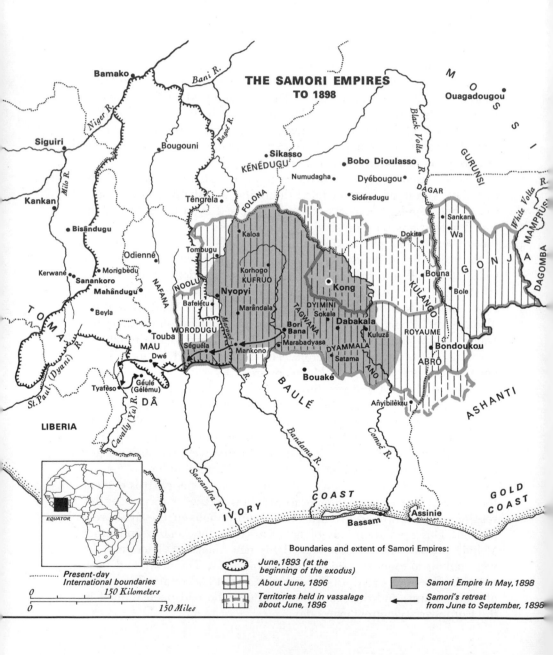

THE SAMORI EMPIRES
TO 1898

Boundaries and extent of Samori Empires:

June, 1893 (at the
beginning of the exodus)

About June, 1896

Territories held in vassalage
about June, 1896

Samori Empire in May, 1898

Samori's retreat
from June to September, 1898

.... Present-day
International boundaries

0   150 Kilometers

0   150 Miles

The End (1897–98)

Samori's isolation in the east could not have lasted forever. His fate depended ultimately on the race between the French and the British in West Africa.

The Almami seems to have joyfully welcomed the British entry into Kumasi in January 1896. The fall of the Ashanti brought his old partners—those who had earlier supplied him with arms from Sierra Leone—to his frontiers. Yet his joy was short-lived because the sale of arms had been prohibited and because the authorities of the Gold Coast had recourse to military measures which surprised him. He did not fear them as he feared the French, but he began to be suspicious of them.

Samori continued to put some distance between himself and the French. He succeeded in buying a few conventional rifles and some rapid-fire rifles from the Ivory Coast—much to the indignation of the military leaders in the Soudan. On the other hand, he tried to avoid any kind of provocation. That is why his army retreated toward the south as soon as the French had reached Gurunsi and recrossed the Black Volta. As his vassals in Buna hesitated in welcoming him, his son took the city by force in December 1896, effectively destroying the strength of the Kulango kingdom.

Samori's movement is easily explained by his desire to utilize the Franco-British conflict which was then entering a new phase. The authorities of the Gold Coast were disturbed over France's progress on the Niger, so they decided to spread out toward the north by going around the western end of the neutral zone. In December 1896, a number of British columns crossed western Gonja, which the Samorians evacuated at their approach, and headed toward Mamprussi and Wa. Captain Henderson, the leader of the western column, was under orders to arrive at Buna, one of the more disputed areas, at all costs before the French.

The warnings that the British sent to Samori's lieutenants were ignored because Buna was necessary to their strategy. The Samorians also held British power in low esteem, and the events of the period seemed to have proved them right. Henderson was foolish enough to cross the Volta; he was attacked by the *sofa* and forced to retreat to Wa, where he was besieged. He wanted to negotiate but instead was captured by Samori's son who took him triumphantly to Dabakala and presented him to Samori. But instead of joy, Samori received the prisoner with concern—he was not anxious to harm his relations with the British. The prisoner was freed on 4 May and sent back to Accra with letters filled with apologies. But the Almami kept the three field pieces taken at Wa. This was the first real artillery he had ever possessed.[20]

In the meantime Samori had to embark on a disciplinary campaign against Kong and Bobo which were in danger of erupting against him. He destroyed Kong on 18 May 1897, and his army continued on to Bobo. Samori succeeded in reestablishing his authority, but he was quite uneasy on arriving at Bobo when he learned that the French had built an outpost nearby at Dyébougou. He also feared an attack from the British in the south as a reprisal for the Wa incident. Samori again saw the possibility of being caught in a pincers movement. It was at this time that he attempted an admirable diplomatic maneuver.

Caudrelier, the French commander who had just organized the Niger-Volta region, had orders to arrive at Buna before the British. He had no orders to engage in combat with Samori, and the latter understood this situation very well. As early as July, Samori wrote to Caudrelier offering to give up Buna. It is evident that Samori wanted to assure himself of the goodwill of the French and at the same time wanted them to confront the British. He hoped that his opponents would be too worried about each other to care about him.

The Commander took him at his word and immediately ordered his deputy, Captain Braulot, to the Kulango capital, but the city closed its doors to him because Samori's son, who was supposed to be present at the transfer, had not yet arrived. The French and Samorians finally met on 18 and 20 August in sight of the city. Braulot, all his officers, and most of his men were massacred under very obscure circumstances. This event seems to have been perpetrated by the bellicose elements surrounding Samori's son who were aggravated by the presence of the French troops. The only certain fact was that Samori, whose plans were now shattered, was absolutely innocent.[21]

The Almami recognized that this act was unpardonable and feared that France would completely break off relations with him. He left Sidèradugu where he had been camped since July and hurriedly entered Dabakala, where a French mission, under the supervision of Nebout, had been waiting for him for two months. During the course of the interviews, which lasted from 5 to 23 October 1897, he tried to convince the French of his good faith, yet he obstinately refused

[20] For this question, see PRO, 69/278, confidential prints: WA: 516, 517 (Henderson's report: 21416).

[21] *Bulletin du Comité de l'Afrique française*, VII, especially Feb. and May 1898. AOM, Soudan IV, 6b, and Côte d'Ivoire IV, 1b. In *Samori*, I try to use oral traditions to throw light on the vexing question of the Buna affair.

to sign a treaty. He seems to have adopted an attitude of fatalism while trying to delay the inevitable.[22]

On 25 January 1898 Samori's men were attacked by the French column which occupied Kong. His men counterattacked and besieged the aggressor. This confrontation was inevitable because Samori could not allow his enemies to become entrenched near Dabakala unless he was resigned to capitulation. He knew that he was initiating the most dramatic moment of the whole adventure, but he was still deluding himself about his means of resistance. At the end of 1897, after the harvest, he had begun transferring his people to the Baulé frontier. Shortly after he lost Kong, Samori arrived in Bori-Bana and announced that he wanted it to be as strongly fortified as Sikasso had been. There he would wait for the French.

The events which followed proved the hopelessness of these projects. There were battles everywhere, and they always ended with the Samorians at a disadvantage. They had attacked the Tombugu fort in the west, and had been repulsed. The French outposts which were erected between Sassandra and Marawé threatened to cut off their last possible road of retreat.

The final decision of how to deal with Samori was left up to Colonel Audeoud, the commander of the French Soudan. Audeoud had to obey the order forbidding an attack on Samori but he thought that he might distinguish himself by receiving the unconditional surrender of Sikasso, then in the hands of Babèmba, Tyèba's brother, and which formed an annoying enclave in the middle of French territory. The young officer sent to accomplish this task was so seriously rebuffed that Paris decided to allow military action, and it was easy to spread this action into the territory held by Samori. After the massive mobilization of the whole Soudan and after a difficult siege, the French finally took Sikasso in a bloody assault on 1 May 1898.[23]

But Samori's actions were not dictated by Audeoud's plans. The fall of Sikasso had come as a terrible shock to the Almami; the taking of this supposedly impregnable city made him realize that on-the-spot resistance to the French would be suicidal. Since he had lost Kong and was not strong enough to retake it, and since the British forces had closed off any escape to the east, he decided to abandon the new empire. No sentimental link held him to the land, and he was confident that he could find a final asylum in the west, in Toma country, where some of his partisans still lived and where he would be close to his ancestral home in Konyan. To return to his native land, he had to pass

[22] AOM, Côte d'Ivoire IV, 1b (Nebout's report).

[23] See also an admirable work of colonially-biased historiography, Jacques Méniaud, *Sikasso* (Paris, 1935), and ANS, 1 D168.

across the edge of the great forest and skirt the French outposts at Touba. His first concern was to find asylum for the winter in a region where the next harvest could feed the great masses that had followed him.

Samori quickly headed west and on 18 June crossed the Sassandra River at Létu. He settled in the Dwé plain, which is the halfway point between Tuba and Man on the northern slope of the Dan range. With his complete army and about 100,000 followers, Samori found himself the master of only a small strip of land, but he had enough provisions to feed them all until the next harvest. This harvest would, he hoped, provide him with the necessary food for the march to the Toma country after the rains. Thus, within five weeks, Samori's empire had collapsed. The French reconnaissance troops saw nothing barring their way, so they marched as far as Baulé country, occupying Bouaké on 18 August 1898.

Another change in the French command brought this long drama to a quick end. Audeoud learned that General Edgar de Trentinian, who did not hide the fact that he wanted to put an end to the problem of Samori, would take over the command of the Soudan after the rains. Colonel Audeoud was enraged and decided to deprive his rival of the glory of suppressing Samori. Thus he ordered his men to track down the Almami by every means possible and without delay.

This decision pleased the field commander of the southern region, Lieutenant Colonel de Lartigue, who, without even assembling all his troops, attacked the mass of the Samorians at Dwé on 20 July. He was overwhelmingly defeated and chased to the gates of Touba.[24]

This imprudent act had some fortunate consequences for the French. Samori feared the nearness of his enemies, and this fear led to a senseless decision. He suddenly left his winter quarters and plunged into the forested area of the Dan mountains, where he was harassed by the local population. Within a few weeks he had lost all his food and his flocks. This led to a famine which killed the emigrants; his victorious army of 20 July disintegrated with amazing rapidity. His men dropped their weapons and deserted to the French. In this apocalyptic atmosphere, the survivors continued to push on toward the west. At the beginning of September, they attempted to cross the upper Cavally River at Tyafèso. They were surprised by French reinforcements which had come down from Beyla under Captain (later Governor) Henry Gaden. There, two-thirds of the remaining Samorians capitulated almost without a fight.

[24] The main source for the last campaign and Samori's capture is Lartigue's report published by the *Bulletin du Comité de l'Afrique française,* VII (Paris, 1898), 112-40. Cf. Henri Gouraud's memoirs, *Au Soudan* (Paris, 1939); correspondence in AOM, Côte d'Ivoire IV, 6b.

Having been driven back again into the thick forest of the Dan mountains, Samori was surprised, on 29 September at Géulé (Guelémou) by French reconnaissance troops. These troops had crossed the devastated zone in the west while the Almami had been waiting for an attack from Touba. Thus Samori finally fell into enemy hands. Realizing that his position was hopeless Samori had earlier offered to give himself up on condition that he could live at Sanankoro as a private person. But his actual capture made French concessions unnecessary.

Because he had been deprived of capturing Samori, Trentinian was very harsh toward him. He solemnly notified the Almami at Kayes on 22 December that he would be deported to Gabon. The old man, believing that his earlier negotiations were still valid, felt that he had been tricked and attempted to commit suicide before embarking from Saint-Louis. Samori died of bronchial pneumonia on 2 June 1900, on the small island of Ndjolé in the middle of the Ogooué River in Gabon.

The Importance of Samori

To his adversaries and the writers of colonial history, Samori was, despite his courage and loyalty, a slave merchant and a bloody tyrant —the very personification of evil. To young African leaders, he became one of the great heroes of the anticolonial struggle.

Neither of these two visions of the man is entirely accurate, but the second is closer to reality. Samori was essentially a man of battle and the builder of a state. His work answered the needs of a society in the midst of grave crisis. Events forced him to place himself in the path of the French colonizers. He then wasted most of his ability and strength in the continuous battle against them, even though that had not been his original purpose in assuming power. In fact, from the day on which his struggle against the French absorbed most of his time, the positive aspects of his work began to degenerate.

As a son of the Konyan, his first desire had been to save his own animistic society by regenerating it so that he could undertake the risks of the dyula revolution. But this was possible only through military means, and he soon began to make use of his tactical abilities and strategic genius, both of which were praised by the French. His superiority was manifested in 1885 in his struggle with Combes, and he was only deprived of the ultimate victory by the crushing technical superiority of his adversaries. The same tactical ability is seen in his politics. His policy was to accomplish his objectives through negotiation— not to use force unless all other means failed—but once compelled, he fought with the greatest obstinacy.

This able and energetic man was generally pragmatic. However, he sometimes became impassioned and then lost sight of reality. His most serious lack of judgment, as far as we can see, was the proclamation of a theocracy in 1886.

His personality was charismatic, and the loyalty and devotion that he inspired sometimes reached the height of fanaticism. Most of the charges of cruelty made against him do not seem to have any foundation, but we must admit that this hard realist used whatever means were at his disposal. When his life's work was in jeopardy, he would fall back on bloody terror as was evidenced by the treatment of the Wasulunké in 1888. Although it is true he resorted to slavery, he was by nature less cruel than were the Tukolor and the *faama* of Sikasso, the allies of the French.

What interests us most about his work is how a crisis can bring about the formation of a state through internal development and not through conquest. The dyula minority gained more than anyone else because the trade routes became safe and there were no longer any tolls to be paid. But the entire population profited from the end of domestic wars and the regularizing of trade over a large region.

Samori's actions and the admiration they inspired among his followers were in the best dyula tradition and encouraged the spread of Islam. The Islamization of the empire failed only when the dogmatic elements within Samori's court tried to impose Islam by force and thus shook the equilibrium of the Malinké world.

It is clear that the action of Samori, in spite of its revolutionary aspect, belonged to the traditions of his society. His conservatism, however, surprises us—for example, his scrupulous respect for the established local chiefs and other notables. It is, therefore, quite difficult to see him as the forerunner of modern nationalism. On the other hand, it is evident that his uprooting and moving of large populations might have been, without his realizing it, the prelude to the upheavals of the colonial era.

His work was condemned to failure because, in spite of all his energy and clairvoyance, he could not make up for his people's technical backwardness.

ADWA 1896:

THE RESOUNDING PROTEST

SVEN RUBENSON

Suspense

On Sunday, March 1, 1896, which according to the Ethiopian calendar
was Yekatit 23, 1888, and the day of Saint George, Ethiopians and
Italians met on the battlefield near Adwa to settle the question of
Ethiopia's survival as an independent state. Both sides knew that it was
at stake in the war, which had already lasted five months without major
encounters. How decisive "the day of Adwa" would be for the outcome of the war, how important a role it would come to play in the
history of both Ethiopia and Italy, was, on the other hand, impossible
for anyone to foresee. One of the many strange aspects of the Battle
of Adwa is, in fact, that the Italian commander in chief, General Oreste
Baratieri, who chose the date and place for the battle, neither wanted
it nor even expected it to take place.[1] Emperor Minilik and Empress
Taytu, on the other hand, greeted the news that the Italians were advancing with some surprise but also with deep satisfaction. For them
this was the god-given opportunity to bring the war to an end.[2]

[1] Roberto Battaglia, *La prima guerra d'Africa* (Torino, 1958), 736-37, 757.
This fascinating study is the latest comprehensive account and analysis of the battle
of Adwa by an Italian historian and will be referred to in this essay regarding
many points where I find no reason to take exception.

[2] Guèbrè Sellassié, *Chronique du règne de Ménélik II, roi des rois d'Ethiopie*,
II (Paris, 1932), 436-39; Bibliothèque Nationale, MS Collection Mondon-Vidailhet,
No. 82 (henceforth referred to as Mondon 82), Yosef to Mondon, 31 Mar. 1896,
31r.-40r. This collection of Amharic letters written by Minilik, his secretary Yosef
Niguse, and others to the Emperor's friend and contact man with other foreigners
in Addis Ababa is a most interesting source of information on the Ethiopian side
of the Adwa campaign. It has not to my knowledge been used before by any other
scholar.

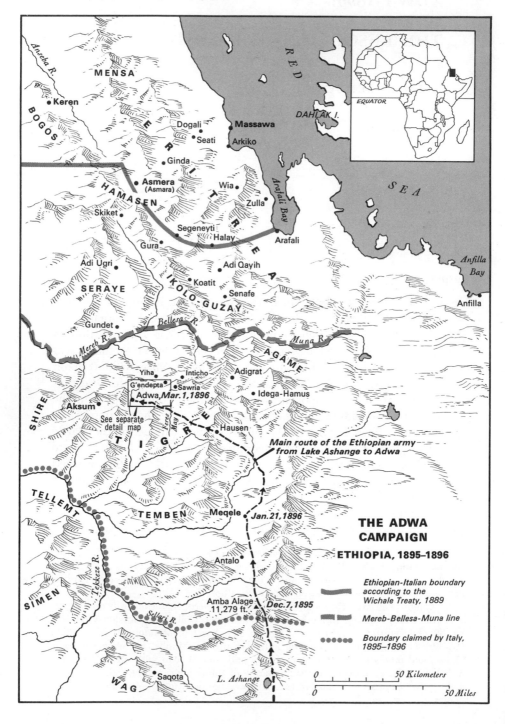

Aneeba R.

MENSA

• Keren

BOGOS

Dogali •   ● **Massawa**
      • Seati   Arkiko •

HAMASEN   • Ginda

Asmera   Wia •
(Asmara)   Zulla •
• Skiket

      Segeneyti •
Gura •   Halay •   • Arafali

Adi Ugri •   • Adi Qayih

SERAYE   • Koatit

IKOLO-GUZAY   • Senafe

Gundet •   *Bellesa R.*

      Mereb R.   *Muna R.*

      AGAME

SHIRE   Yiha •   Inticho •   • Adigrat

G'endepta □
• Sawria   • Idega-Hamus
Adwa, *Mar. 1, 1896*

• **Aksum**

See separate
detail map   Hausen •

T I G R E

*Main route of the Ethiopian army
from Lake Ashange to Adwa*

TELLEMT

TEMBEN   Meqele •   *Jan. 21, 1896*

Antalo •

SIMEN   *Tekkeze R.*

Amba Alage   *Dec. 7, 1895*
11,279 ft.
Selari R.

• Saqota   *L. Ashange*

WAG

RED   SEA

DAHLAK I.

Arafali Bay

*Anfilla
Bay*

Anfilla

EQUATOR

**THE ADWA
CAMPAIGN**

ETHIOPIA, 1895–1896

*Ethiopian-Italian boundary
according to the
Wichale Treaty, 1889*

Mereb-Bellesa-Muna line

*Boundary claimed by Italy,
1895–1896*

0   50 *Kilometers*

0   50 *Miles*

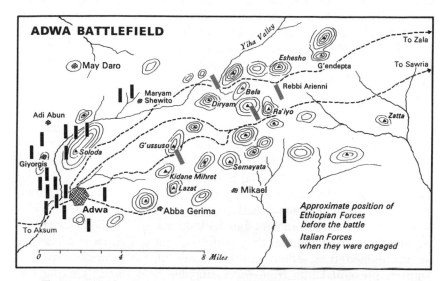

From several points of view the battle was long overdue. After the Italian surrender of Meqele fort on January 21, 1896, Minilik had marched his large army to new pastures east of Adwa: Feres May, Gendepta, and Yiha. Thereby he had avoided making a frontal attack on or laying siege to the fortified positions of the Italians at Idega-Hamus and Adigrat, and had placed himself in a favorable position to invade Eritrea. To be close enough to protect Eritrea in case of an invasion, Baratieri had countered by moving his army westward from Adigrat toward Adwa, selecting positions on a line of mountains west of Inticho. By February 13 this regrouping had been completed with the occupation and fortification of Sawria, about thirty kilometers east of Adwa and within sight of parts of the Ethiopian camp.[3]

During the weeks of these maneuvers there were no clashes between the two armies. This was in large part because negotiations for a peaceful solution of the conflict had been given a new chance by the circumstances of the surrender of Meqele. That the Italian garrison, entirely at the mercy of the Ethiopians, had been allowed to march out with its arms and return safely to its own side had created—and this was no doubt Minilik's intention—a favorable climate for negotiation.[4] As late as February 6, Minilik had offered to remain inactive at

[3] Guèbrè Sellassié, *Chronique*, II, 423-28; Oreste Baratieri, *Memorie d'Africa* (Torino, 1898), 301-16; Baratieri's dispatches and telegrams for this period are found in *Atti Parlamentari, 1895–96, Documenti Diplomatici, XXIII-bis, Avvenimenti d'Africa (Gennaio 1895–Marzo 1896)*, 213-49.

[4] *Doc. Dipl. XXIII-bis*, Baratieri to Mocenni, 26 Jan. 1896, 218; Baratieri to Blanc, 28 Jan. 1896, 222; cf. Mondon 82, Yosef to Mondon, 24 Jan. 1896, 11r.-18r.

Gendepta for six days to facilitate peace negotiations.[5] The terms for a future peace were specified once more by both sides. But the gap was too wide, and on February 12, exactly six days later, the negotiations broke down. Baratieri summed up the position: "The proposals which Your Majesty makes to our Government cannot be accepted, nor even discussed any longer. . . . Now it seems to me that the negotiations should be considered as closed and each of us is left free in his actions."[6]

There was now little reason to postpone action. Baratieri had increased his field army from 6,000 Italians and 10,300 locally recruited soldiers at Adigrat one month earlier to 535 officers, 10,620 Italian and 10,083 native soldiers at Sawria, and this in spite of the fact that he had been obliged to leave a strong garrison at Adigrat and to strengthen his extended line of communications.[7] He had been offered more reinforcements by his government but had shown great reluctance in accepting them. Agreeing that they might be sent to Eritrea as a reserve, he maintained that serious considerations of tactics and above all logistics prevented him from increasing his field force.[8] On the eve of the battle two weeks later, Baratieri's forces at Sawria had, in fact, decreased slightly: he had 20,170 men and 52 cannon.[9] Nevertheless Baratieri had no intention of taking the initiative. He had no other plan than to wait in the hope that Minilik would attack his fortified position.[10]

[5] *Doc. Dipl. XXIII-bis,* Baratieri to Mocenni, 7 Feb. 1896, 238-39. For the issues involved in the negotiations and the spirit in which they were undertaken, see below, 117.

[6] *Doc. Dipl. XXIII-bis,* Baratieri to Blanc, 13 Feb. 1896, 246-47. Cf. Mondon 82, Yosef [to Mondon], n.d., 25r.-26r., but most likely written either 21 Feb. or soon after this date. Yosef repeats almost literally, though in Amharic, the contents of the letter as reported by Baratieri, which proves that he was really in possession of the Emperor's correspondence at this time. (All translations of quotations from Italian, French, and Amharic sources used in this essay are by the author.)

[7] *Doc. Dipl. XIII-bis,* Baratieri to Mocenni, 14 Jan. 1896, 13 Feb. 1896, 190-91, 246.

[8] *Doc. Dipl. XXIII-bis,* Baratieri to Crispi, 15 Jan. 1896, 203; Mocenni to Baratieri, 3 Feb. 1896, 231-32; Lamberti to Mocenni, 6 Feb. 1896, 236-37. Cf. Baratieri, *Memorie,* 335: "A me, come è ovvio, non pareva vero di accettare."

[9] *Doc. Dipl. XXIII-bis,* Baratieri to Mocenni, 29 Feb. 1896, 283. Baratieri expected one more battery the very night before the battle; *Memorie,* 357. The strength of the Italian artillery is usually stated as fifty-six pieces. See Augustus B. Wylde, *Modern Abyssinia* (London, 1901), 198-99; G. F.-H. Berkeley, *The Campaign of Adowa and the Rise of Menelik* (Westminster, 1902), 267-69.

[10] Baratieri, *Memorie,* 341, "Quindi la prudenza elementare imponeva di aspettare sulla difensiva, finchè un attacco dei nemici contro noi in buona posizione. . . ." It is not within the scope of this essay to enter into the controversial issues of Baratieri's generalship in Africa or Prime Minister Francesco Crispi's lead-

Minilik also did not expect to strengthen his army. His call to arms had been obeyed throughout his realm. All of his great vassals, except those who had received security tasks elsewhere, had either preceded him or joined him in his march to the north.[11] At Meqele the reunion had taken place, and, thereafter, the Emperor had about 100,-000 men under his command, 70,000 to 80,000 with rifles, the remainder with swords, spears, and shields.[12] The artillery of the Ethiopian army was inferior to the Italian, at least in numbers, reportedly only forty-two pieces.[13] The very night after the peace negotiations had broken down, the two most important Tigrean allies of the Italians, Ras Sibhat and Dejazmach Hagos Teferi, defected with six hundred men and much valuable information about the position on the Italian side.[14]

The agitation caused by Sibhat's and Hagos's desertions to the Ethiopian side almost precipitated a battle on February 13.[15] Minilik was, however, as reluctant to attack the fortified Italian position as Baratieri was to offer battle in the field. The Emperor sent his new won allies to stir up the population of their districts and cut the Italian lines of communication.[16] This task they accomplished quite effectively, which led to some fighting behind the Italian lines.[17]

---

ership in Rome. The magnitude of Italy's defeat has made the question of whose fault it was the topic of many investigations and studies.

[11] Mondon 82, Yosef to Mondon, 1 Dec. 1895, 7r.-8r.; Guèbrè Sellassié, *Chronique*, II, 414, 416.

[12] Exact figures are not available, since the Ethiopians have traditionally been reluctant to count their troops. Estimates by Italians who visited the Ethiopian camp repeatedly vary from 62,000 to 90,000 rifles; *Doc. Dipl. XXIII-bis*, Baratieri to Mocenni, 19 Jan. 1896, 9 Feb. 1896, 13 Feb. 1896, 208-10, 242, 245. Wylde, *Abyssinia*, 199-200, mentions a maximum force of "at least 120,000 fighting men" and "at least 70,000 rifles on the field" the day of the battle. Whether this means that 50,000 men with rifles were absent when the battle started or that traditionally armed men were included in the first figure is not quite clear. On absence from the battlefield, see below, 121.

[13] Berkeley, *Adowa*, 268. Wylde, *Abyssinia*, 53, 204, maintains that the Ethiopian artillery was of superior quality to the Italian and served by well-trained people, but Battaglia, *Guerra*, 751, has come to the conclusion that it was inferior to its task and played little role at Adwa.

[14] *Doc. Dipl. XXIII-bis*, Baratieri to Mocenni, 13 Feb. 1896, 247; Guèbrè Sellassié, *Chronique*, II, 430-31.

[15] *Doc. Dipl. XXIII-bis*, Baratieri to Mocenni, 15 Feb. 1896, 251; Guèbrè Sellassié, *Chronique*, II, 431-32.

[16] Guèbrè Sellassié, *Chronique*, II, 432, states that this was decided on the advice of the Tigrean chiefs, but in Mondon 82, Yosef to Mondon, 21 Feb. 1896, 20r.-23v., it is reported simply as Minilik's instructions.

[17] *Doc. Dipl. XXIII-bis*, Baratieri to Mocenni, 16, 17, 18, 19, 20, 21, 23 Feb. 1896, 251-70; Mondon 82, Yosef to Mondon, 21 Feb. 1896, 20r.-23v.

In the main theater of war there was little activity. On February 20 a skirmish between outposts took place, and the following day Minilik awaited an attack in battle order all day long. On February 24 Baratieri made an "offensive demonstration" in the direction of Adwa, but stopped at a safe distance; on the next day Minilik marched out to find that the Italians had withdrawn again.[18]

But this situation could not continue indefinitely. On both sides supplies of food were giving out. The Italian army depended for provisions on a long line of communications, which was the Achilles' heel of its operations even before the local population started to attack it as a result of Sibhat's and Hagos's defection.[19] Toward the end of February the situation at Sawria was becoming desperate. Rations were cut to half and less at times; African troops received money but little or nothing could be bought from a hostile local population. "For our natives . . . hunger is no longer a threatening ghost but a daily reality."[20] On February 28 Baratieri informed his generals that the supplies would last until the second or possibly the third of March, and that there was little hope that they could be replenished.[21]

As for the Ethiopian side, both the supplies that had been laid in for this campaign and whatever personal provisions each soldier had brought along at the time of mobilization had been exhausted long ago, and the army was too large to live off the same district for any period of time.[22] The Italians reported a scarcity of food in the Ethiopian camp as early as December at Meqele,[23] but new supplies had become available as a result of the march to Adwa.[24] The Italian negotiator, Major Tommaso Salsa, returned to his own side on February 12 with the impression that the Ethiopian troops were provided for, although not abundantly.[25] As the days became weeks, the question of new supplies became, however, of overriding concern to Minilik. By the end of February he was sending detachments of his army as

[18] Doc. Dipl. XXIII-bis, Baratieri to Mocenni, 21 Feb. 1896, 26 Feb. 1896, 266, 274. Guèbrè Sellassié, Chronique, II, 433-36.

[19] Doc. Dipl. XXIII-bis, Baratieri to Mocenni, 28 Feb. 1896, 280.

[20] Battaglia, Guerra, 722; Berkeley, Adowa, 249-52. Both cite Italian sources other than the official dispatches. Even in his memoirs Baratieri speaks only of the future day when supplies would give out and makes light of the hardship endured, Memorie, 361-62.

[21] Baratieri, Memorie, 362, 469-70; cf. Battaglia, Guerra, 728.

[22] Guèbrè Sellassié, Chronique, II, 407.

[23] Doc Dipl. XXIII-bis, Baratieri to Mocenni, 20, 22, 24, 26 Dec. 1896, 69-78.

[24] See the interesting but probably exaggerated account of Balambaras Welde Amanuel's views in Berkeley, Adowa, 223-24.

[25] Doc. Dipl. XXIII-bis, Baratieri to Mocenni, 13 Feb. 1896, 245-46.

far as Shire, Tellemt, and Temben to collect provisions, and very considerable numbers were actually away for this purpose when the day of the battle finally dawned.[26] Though the situation was probably less desperate for the Ethiopians than for the Italians, because of the opportunity the former had to go in search of supplies, the scarcity of food is one of the main impressions which remains in the minds of the few survivors who are still alive. And when Minilik wrote of how he had resisted the temptations to attack the Italian position, he underlined his determination by admitting: "They [the Italians] had fortified themselves in an impossible place which was unsuitable for a battle. Though my army was starving, I remained encamped at Adwa. . . ."[27]

When Baratieri contemplated an alternative to "remaining," it was retreat. Three times in one week he reportedly gave orders for withdrawal, only to cancel them again in the hope that something better would turn up.[28] Minilik's alternative to "remaining" was a logical extension of the strategy adopted after the fall of Meqele. He had marched toward Adwa precisely to avoid a frontal attack on the fortified positions of the Italians at Adigrat. In spite of the difficulties and hazards involved, he preferred to continue the advance rather than attack the Sawria position. According to Minilik's secretary this decision was taken as early as February 21: "When His Majesty saw how difficult the position was, he said; 'I will not let my army be destroyed in vain. If I go to Asmara, will he [the enemy] not have to come out into the field?' So with the intention of marching to Asmara, he went down to Adwa, camped there, grouped the army, and started to arrange the supplies for transport."[29]

On February 23 Minilik sent some of his commanders, including Ras Mengesha Yohannis of Tigre and Ras Mekwennin Welde Mikael of Harer, to cross the Mereb Valley in advance with their troops. When they reported that there was no water in the river, they were recalled.[30] Since the valley could be crossed in two days, the lack of water was

[26] Guèbrè Sellassié, *Chronique*, II, 437-39. The chronicler has most certainly exaggerated when he wrote that two-thirds of the army were absent. Cf. Battaglia, *Guerra*, 723.

[27] Mondon 82, Minilik to Mondon, 11 Mar. 1896, 26r.-v.

[28] *Doc. Dipl. XXIII-bis*, Baratieri to Mocenni, 21 Feb. 1896, 267. For developments in this respect after 21 Feb., see Berkeley, *Adowa*, 255-58, and Battaglia, *Guerra*, 703-5.

[29] Mondon 82, Yoseph to Mondon, 31 Mar. 1896, 31r.-40r. The change of camp referred to must be the 21 Feb. withdrawal from Gendepta, where the camp was within sight of the Italian position, to Adwa itself, i.e., a few kilometers further west where the army would be right on the road from Temben and Shire to Asmara.

[30] Guèbrè Sellassié, *Chronique*, II, 435; cf. *Doc. Dipl. XXIII-bis*, Baratieri to Mocenni, 22 Feb. 1896, 459.

no insurmountable difficulty, but it was sufficient to make Minilik postpone the march.

Disappointment that Baratieri's "offensive demonstration" on the twenty-fourth had turned out to be precisely that heightened the suspense in the ranks of the Ethiopian army. Minilik is reported to have agreed to an attack on Sawria on February 26 but to have been dissuaded by Mengesha. Meetings of the generals in the Ethiopian camp on February 26 and 27 reaffirmed the decision to fight the Italians only if they left their position and to cross into Eritrea if they did not.[31] On Saturday evening—this was February 29, since it was a leap year —Minilik gave orders for the breaking of the camp on the following Monday, provided that the troops who were still dispersed to collect food supplies had returned by then.[32]

But on Saturday afternoon Baratieri had also made up his mind— to advance toward the Ethiopian lines. The evening before he had held a meeting with his four generals, explained the situation with regard to provisions, and suggested a retreat, possibly as far as Asmara. This was unanimously rejected by the generals, who all favored an attack. It was not a formal council of war; this was stressed by Baratieri himself at its opening.[33] Nevertheless the commander in chief, irresolute as he was, could not help but be influenced.[34] There was also the strong, though, according to Baratieri himself, not decisive, pressure for offensive action which emanated from Rome, including Prime Minister Crispi's notorious telegram of February 25: "This is a military phthisis, not a war: small skirmishes in which we always find ourselves facing the enemy with inferior numbers; a waste of heroism without success. . . . We are ready for any sacrifice to save the honour of the army and the prestige of the monarchy."[35]

Baratieri closed the meeting of February 28 with the words: "I

---

[31] Guèbrè Sellassié, *Chronique*, II, 436-37. Marcel de Coppet, the editor of the chronicle (437, n. 3), doubts that a firm decision in this direction was taken, but I can find no convincing reasons to disbelieve the chronicle. Cf. Battaglia, *Guerra*, 726, where the author accepts that Minilik intended to advance into Hamasen but only after having made a retreat across Tekeze (!) obviously to try to induce the Italians to follow in that direction.

[32] Guèbrè Sellassié, *Chronique*, II, 438. That they were expected to return that weekend was known to Baratieri, who began to report some arrivals on 28 Feb.; *Doc. Dipl. XXIII-bis*, 280-81.

[33] Baratieri, *Memorie*, 363-67, 469-71.

[34] *Atti Parlamentari, 1895-96, Documenti Diplomatici, XXIII-ter, Avvenimenti d'Africa (Marzo-Aprile 1896)*, Baldissera to Mocenni, 9 Mar. 1896, 13-14. This contains Baratieri's own list of reasons for ordering the attack.

[35] *Doc. Dipl. XXIII-bis*, 273. See Battaglia, *Guerra*, 716-21, for an analysis of the role played by Crispi as a prompter for more action.

am expecting further information from spies who should arrive from the camp of the enemy; when I have it I will take *a decision.*"[36] So he did, but the information which he cites as important in his memoirs can hardly have played a significant role. That some Ethiopian troops were absent raiding, that others were starving, sick, or even deserting the camp, that several of the Ethiopian chiefs would not fight for Minilik[37]—had not Baratieri been hearing and saying these same things for almost two months? If the last-minute information played any important role, it must have been rather more inviting. Did captured and released Italian spies or Ethiopian spies, ostensibly in Italian service but actually working for Minilik and his generals, really go and convince Baratieri that *the bulk of the Ethiopian army* had marched off to Aksum to celebrate the holiday, to collect food, or as the first stage of a retreat? There is much evidence to indicate that during the last weeks before the battle the Ethiopians were very actively disseminating information and rumors likely to induce the Italians to attack. The credit for having finally succeeded on the twenty-ninth is given by the Ethiopians, both by Minilik's secretary at the time and in local tradition today, to one individual, a poor man with a crippled hand who on his own initiative went to Baratieri and told him that: "All the army has gone to fetch grain; he is sitting there alone for you [to attack]; you have got him, today he will not escape, today is the day."[38] An Italian version of the information received runs: "The enemy has retreated to Aksum leaving a rear guard of 20-25,000 at Maryam Shewito; Ras Wele is dead, the King ill."[39]

Everything points to the conclusion that Baratieri, at least to some extent, had "allowed himself to be duped by the Shoan spies."[40] He decided to advance in the hope that there would be no battle or only a minor confrontation with 15,000 (note the further decrease) Ethiopians at Maryam Shewito.[41] What he wanted was not a battle but the opportunity for one more "offensive demonstration." It was the supposedly disintegrating, even absent, Ethiopian army that wanted the battle and could hardly believe the good news that their enemies were coming. Out of this absurd confusion came what Roberto Battaglia called "the most incredible and absurd battle that has ever taken place in modern history."[42]

[36] Baratieri, *Memorie,* 471.
[37] Ibid., 375-76.
[38] Mondon 82, Yosef to Mondon, 31 Mar. 1896, 31r.-40r.
[39] Battaglia, *Guerra,* 730.
[40] Berkeley, *Adowa,* 253.
[41] Baratieri, *Memorie,* 370-71, 405-6; cf. Battaglia, *Guerra,* 736-37, 757.
[42] Battaglia, *Guerra,* 731.

Battle

At 9 P.M. on February 29 three Italian brigades under Generals Matteo Albertone, Giuseppe Arimondi, and Vittorio Dabormida marched out of their positions, followed one and a half hours later by the reserve brigade under General Giuseppe Ellena.[43] Guided by the full moon they made their way toward the collection of rugged hills east of Adwa: Eshesho, Ra'iyo, Bela, Semayata, Abba Gerima, and many others. The landscape was fantastic; according to one observer, "like a stormy sea moved by the anger of God."[44]

The first objective was, before daybreak, to occupy a position on a group of hills between Mount Eshesho and Mount Semayata, about fifteen kilometers from Sawria and thus slightly more than halfway to Adwa. Baratieri had chosen the position for tactical reasons. With his superior artillery in position before the Ethiopians discovered what was going on, he might have hoped to battle successfully even against superior numbers, if challenged, and conveniently to slip away again the following night, if necessary. He probably hoped that the terrain would make it difficult for the Ethiopians to deploy their whole force, if by chance it was still at Adwa, while he would be able to keep the initiative and co-ordinate the action of his smaller army. In fact, the opposite occurred.

Already, during the night march, communications had broken down on the Italian side. Albertone's and Arimondi's brigades got mixed up so that the latter became seriously delayed. A faulty map, poor reconnaissance, vague and misunderstood orders left Baratieri with only half of his forces where he expected them to be. On the left flank Albertone advanced more than five kilometers beyond the position which he was supposed to occupy. This was erroneously called Kidane Mihret on his map, and, unable to find his bearings with certainty, he decided to push on to reach the real Kidane Mihret which his guides told him was much closer to Adwa. Crossing the ridge of hills where they were supposed to have stopped, both he and Dabormida on the right flank had seen not the plain of the map, but more

---

[43] Baratieri, *Memorie*, 376-82. For the following account of the battle I have used Battaglia, *Guerra*, 733-86; Berkeley, *Adowa*, 261-344; Wylde, *Abyssinia*, 196-225; Baratieri, *Memorie*, 370-457; Guèbrè Sellassié, *Chronique*, II, 438-48; Yosef's reports of 11 and 31 Mar. 1896, Mondon 82, 27r.-29r. and 31r.-40r. respectively (henceforth referred to as Yosef I and Yosef II with relevant passages referred to by specific folio numbers).

[44] Berkeley, *Adowa*, 270, quoting Lieutenant Melli.

hills and more mountains. Both pushed on, were lost among the hills, and were lost to each other and lost to the commander in chief.

The only action that Baratieri could possibly have taken to improve the position would have been to move Arimondi's brigade into the gap, but by the time he discovered what was happening, it was too late, and the Italian center remained grouped on and around Mount Ra'iyo.[45] Even if it were not immediately obvious to the Italian generals, the initiative had, in fact, passed from the Italian to the Ethiopian side as soon as the battle started.

Shooting began about five o'clock in the morning, when advance guards from Ras Mengesha's army encountered the approaching Italians, probably at Rebbi Arienni. The guards withdrew; both Dabormida at Rebbi Arienni and Albertone at Kidane Mihret could report that they had found these places unoccupied by the enemy, Albertone even stating that he had completed his occupation at six o'clock unbeknown to the enemy.[46] This was certainly incorrect. How early Minilik had received the first news about the approaching enemy is difficult to know, but by daybreak he had disposed his generals to meet the attack, and at six the battle began in earnest.

Ras Mikael of Wello, Ras Mengesha Yohannis, and Wagshum Gwangwil were ordered into action on the Ethiopian left wing in the direction of Maryam Shewitu. On the right wing Nigus Tekle Haymanot of Gojam was sent forward by way of Abba Gerima to attack Albertone on the flank. In the center Dejazmach Beshah Aboye was in position to meet Albertone's attack and return the heavy fire. Minilik must have seen that this part of the battlefield presented the first important challenge. He moved forward with overwhelming numbers: in the first line Fitawrari Gebeyehu—the regular commander of the Emperor's vanguard—Ras Mekwennin with his Harer troops and Fitawrari Tekle with troops from Wellega, followed by other units under the

[45] Wylde, *Abyssinia*, 206, 210-11, argues that Baratieri made a serious mistake in not advancing and closing the gap, thus strengthening the Italian position in the battlefield. The author, however, contradicts himself by stating that a successful operation of this kind would have led to still greater losses on both sides (pp. 218-19), which can only mean that the Italians would have been completely annihilated.

[46] Guèbrè Sellassié, *Chronique*, II, 438-39; Mondon 82, Yosef I, 27r., Yosef II, 33v. I see no reason not to accept the Ethiopian statements that shooting began at five, though the foreign sources report one hour later; see Battaglia, *Guerra*, 741, 744-50. The shooting was probably not reported to Baratieri because it was on a very small scale or even because the two advancing generals, who were in favor of a decisive action, did not want to risk an order to halt their troops. For the Ethiopians it was important to lure the Italians as far away as possible from their base at Sawria.

command of Ras Wele Bitul of Yeju, Ras Bitweded Mengesha Atkim, and others including Empress Taytu.[47] This disposition of the troops followed roughly the layout of the Ethiopian camp before the battle, and the necessary movements seem to have been completed without difficulty.[48]

At first Minilik led the battle from some point on Abba Gerima. From Mount Lazat, a lower hill in advance of this position, the Ethiopian artillery supported the advancing infantry. Between 8:00 and 9:00 A.M. the battle here reached its climax, and the first of Albertone's battalions began to retreat. Losses on both sides were high. It seems likely that several of the Ethiopian commanders who lost their lives in the battle, including Dejazmach Beshah and Fitawrari Gebeyehu, fell here, and that their demise led to some anxiety on the Ethiopian side. But fresh troops were thrown in; they pushed on, finally encircled what remained of the brigade, and rushed its artillery. Albertone was captured, and the Italian retreat developed into a rout.[49]

Little is known about what was happening on the Ethiopian left flank during these early morning hours. Yosef Niguse reports that the Italians were defeated "at once" on both flanks.[50] Whatever report of victory might have reached Minilik from the left could only have referred to Major Ludovico De Vito's battalion which had been sent by Dabormida to establish contact with Albertone's forces. This battalion moved over a ridge, clashed with Mengesha's and Mikael's forces, and was almost annihilated in less than half an hour. The remainder of Dabormida's brigade was, however, left intact. It remained strangely

[47] Mondon 82, Yosef I, 27v.-28r., Yosef II, 33v.-34r. Guèbrè Sellassié, though also present at Adwa, gives far less detail, only mentioning that Mengesha's guards were the first to be attacked and that Mikael's troops went into action at an early stage. Then he concentrates on the actions of Minilik and Taytu—whose active participation in the battle seems to have caused surprise and admiration, although it is not without precedent in Ethiopian history. The number of men involved can only be guessed at because of the troops away collecting provisions, but a low estimate would still reach 40,000-50,000, with at least two-thirds concentrated against Albertone's brigade.

[48] For the arrangement of Minilik's camp, see Wylde, Abyssinia, 201-2. The map in Battaglia, Guerra, opposite 790, is misleading with regard to the position of Mekwennin's and Mèngesha Atkim's forces which must have been much closer to Adwa.

[49] Battaglia, Guerra, 752-54; Berkeley, Adowa, 286-96. In spite of the serious Ethiopian losses, I find Major Giovanni Battista Gamerra's statements that "victory was shining on us" and that Minilik "gave order for a general retirement" (quoted from Berkeley) rather too sweeping. Gamerra reports the latter as a mere rumor. The statement by Guèbrè Sellassié, Chronique, II, 441, that some soldiers "began to hesitate" and were rallied by Empress Taytu cannot be used to support the idea that a general retreat was contemplated or ordered.

[50] Mondon 82, Yosef I, 28r.

inactive.[51] The attention of Mikael and Mengesha was called to the liquidation of Albertone's brigade, and they were then caught up in the advance against the main Italian position around Ra'iyo.[52]

The attack on this position followed immediately after the collapse of Albertone's resistance. Minilik crossed the Kidane Mihret area to the slopes of Semayata which brought Arimondi's and Ellena's position within view. It was, in Guèbrè Sellassié's words, "a new and still larger Italian army."[53] But it was a disorganized army, still less prepared for the onslaught than Albertone's brigade had been. The Ethiopian soldiers pushed on so fast that they arrived on the left of the Italian position together with the fleeing remains of Albertone's brigade. On their right the Italians expected no attack because they thought that Dabormida held the approaches in that direction. The Ethiopians rushed the position from all sides, using the difficult terrain to their best advantage. At noon Baratieri ordered a general retreat which gradually developed into a rout. Two attempts to organize cover for the retreat failed. The Ethiopians followed close on the heels of the withdrawing Italians through the Yiha valley. At about three in the afternoon Minilik could report back to the Empress that all was over in that section of the battlefield, but that he still heard firing on his left.[54]

In the valley of Maryam Shewito, mainly Tigrean forces had fought a holding battle against Dabormida's brigade while the Ethiopian attack on the center was carried out. When resistance broke down in the Italian center, additional Ethiopian troops were directed against Dabormida, who soon found himself encircled. Some very heavy fighting took place in this third section of the battlefield, mainly, it seems, between one and three in the afternoon. Then the retreat began here; but with the Ethiopians pressing on from all sides, there were few survivors from Dabormida's brigade. Sporadic shooting continued until after dark, and the pursuit of the fleeing was renewed on the following day.[55] The battle of Adwa was over.

The casualties were high on both sides. Italian estimates of their losses vary somewhat, mainly because of the uncertainty as to what

[51] Battaglia, Guerra, 767-68; Berkeley, Adowa, 284n, 320-24.

[52] In most Italian accounts the presence of Mikael's and, to a lesser degree, Mengesha's troops in the Ethiopian center has been noted.

[53] Guèbrè Sellassié, Chronique, II, 442.

[54] Battaglia, Guerra, 771-80; Berkeley, Adowa, 298-305; Guèbrè Sellassié, Chronique, II, 445.

[55] Battaglia, Guerra, 780-84; Berkeley, Adowa, 329-44. Guèbrè Sellassié, Chronique, II, 445, states that fighting continued until eleven in the night, but Yosef, Mondon 82, Yosef I, 27r., says that the cannon ceased at 5:00 and the rifles at 7:00 P.M.

happened to many missing soldiers from Eritrean units. Of their own people the Italians counted 289 officers and 4,600 soldiers dead, about 500 wounded, and 1,900 prisoners of war. Out of 10,600 Italians who entered the battle this means that no less than 70 per cent died or were injured. Their Eritreans fared somewhat better in the battle itself with roughly 2,000 dead, 1,000 wounded, and 1,000 prisoners of war, though the breakdown of these 4,000 is rather uncertain.[56] To some extent the lower losses of the Eritreans could have been the result of their greater ability to move fast in the terrain and to take care of themselves in the chaos of the defeat. But at least in the case of Major Giuseppe Galliano's battalion, treason on the battlefield was suspected.[57] It is understandable if Galliano's men were the least willing to fight. They were the ones who had received their lives and liberty from Minilik at Meqele. There were early rumors, vigorously denied, that Galliano as part of the surrender agreement had promised not to participate in the continuation of the war.[58] Yosef confirms that there was resistance in the Eritrean rank and file against entering the battle. The Italians are reported to have surrounded their "basha-buzuks" before the battle to prevent desertion, the latter saying: " . . . though we eat their money, we will not fight our country and our king."[59]

What the Ethiopian losses finally amounted to is also difficult to know. Yosef reports 3,886 dead on the battlefield,[60] which obviously represents the minimum figure. Wylde comes to "5,000–6,000 killed, and about 8,000 badly wounded, of whom perhaps a quarter died."[61] The losses of the Ethiopians may or may not have exceeded those of

[56] Battaglia, *Guerra*, 785, for the losses among Italians; cf. Berkeley, *Adowa*, 345-46, for various estimates including losses among the Eritreans. Yosef, Mondon 82, Yosef I, 28v., reports 1681 Italian prisoners of war, excluding Eritreans, in the first count but adds that there were also some more. Later, Yosef II, 38r., he reports the total Italian losses, dead and captured, at 10,785, which must include the 4,471 "basha-buzuks" also mentioned, though the text seems to indicate that these were in addition to the 10,785.

[57] Berkeley, *Adowa*, 301. See, however, the high praise given to De Vito's Eritrean battalion; ibid., 320-23.

[58] Berkeley, *Adowa*, 218-19; Wylde, *Abyssinia*, 52-53.

[59] Mondon 82, Yosef I, 28r., Yosef II, 36r.-36v. Yosef confirms that Minilik, in accordance with a proclamation made before the battle of Adwa, punished (mutilated) captured "basha-buzuks" who had been "pardoned" once, that is, after Amba Alage and Meqele.

[60] Mondon 82, Yosef II, 38r. Guèbrè Sellassié, *Chronique*, II, 447, offers a blank instead of figures.

[61] Wylde, *Abyssinia*, 212. Whether or not a number of fatally wounded have already been added to the number of dead here, it is obvious that the latter grew. Berkeley, *Adowa*, 346, reports 7,000 dead and 10,000 wounded without, however, indicating his source for this estimate, which is often repeated in Italian literature.

the Italians in absolute numbers; relatively speaking they were far less serious. Baratieri's army had been almost annihilated as a fighting force, Minilik's was intact. The Ethiopians had picked up thousands of rifles and captured all of their enemy's artillery.[62] There were no Ethiopian prisoners of war, and the battlefield remained Ethiopian. The victory was complete, the protest effective.

Shock and Relief

To the community of "civilized nations" the shock of Adwa was formidable. In Rome, Crispi's government collapsed in an uproar of abuse and outbreaks of violence. The Prime Minister and chief engineer of Italian colonial policy made no attempt even to defend his stewardship to his Parliament. The atmosphere in the Chamber was so tense that no one was allowed to speak at the reading of his formal resignation on March 5. In the streets and squares, shouts of "a basso Crispi," "via dall' Africa," and even "viva Minilik" were heard. Riots were reported at Milan, Turin, Pavia, and Naples. There were rumors that Crispi had been assassinated, fear that the monarchy might be overthrown. Baratieri was arrested and arraigned before a special court-martial.[63]

In London concern and doubt as to the accuracy of the reports were expressed in the newspapers: "'The latest accounts place the Italian loss in the battle of Adowa at a figure so high that we cannot but hope there is a serious mistake somewhere. . . .'" The figures "7,000 white and 2,000 native troops" are cited with the conclusion that ". . . the disaster has clearly been one of quite exceptional magnitude." Other things were unbelievable too; the way the attack was carried out "shows an almost incredible disregard of the rudimentary principles of military science. The motives which impelled General Baratieri . . . almost baffle conjecture."[64]

The predictable German reaction was that the British government should have come to the assistance of the Italians long ago,[65] which

[62] Wylde, *Abyssinia*, 212.

[63] See Battaglia, *Guerra*, 793-802, for some of the reactions in Italy. Note that he stresses the growing opposition to the war, the suspense and even the premonitions of disaster that gained momentum on 2 March before the news was made public.

[64] *The Times*, 9 Mar. 1896. For more information on this kind of reaction, see Richard Pankhurst, "How the News Was Received in England," *Ethiopia Observer*, I, 11 (1957), 357-63.

[65] See documents quoted in Ernest Work, *Ethiopia, a Pawn in European Diplomacy* (New York, 1936), 152-53.

Britain would most likely have found some way of doing, had it fore-seen the outcome. In France there were certainly those who before the battle had hoped for a minor setback for the Italians, but the feeling of European solidarity was also expressed: "No one here—I have not to take notice of this or that scatterbrained person, or a few habitually malevolent minds—wishes for the success of the Abyssinians at the price of the discomfiture of a civilized nation, from which it is possible to differ in aims and opinions without being supposed to cherish any ill will when that nation is face to face with a brave but barbarous foe."[66] The French government had avoided committing itself too deeply to Ethiopia's cause. No French (or Russian) officers partici-pated in the battle. Leonce Lagarde, the French Governor at Djibuti, seems to have given Minilik the impression that he did not believe in the possibility of a successful campaign.[67]

But the unexpectedness and the importance of the Ethiopian victory are best judged by the diplomatic and military activity that followed in its wake. As late as November 15, 1895, the British government had informed Lord Cromer in Cairo that it had decided to postpone the re-occupation of the Sudan indefinitely. On March 12, 1896, its instructions for the first step of the reconquest were issued. The sig-nificance of this was not lost on France. The Marchand expedition finally got under way. Lagarde was transferred to Addis Ababa and instructed to try to get Ethiopian forces under French officers moving toward the Upper Nile from the east. The stage was set for the "race" to Fashoda.[68]

For the Ethiopian nation the consequences of Adwa were in a cer-tain sense less obvious and less dramatic. The Italians immediately asked for peace negotiations.[69] Retaining prisoners of war as a guaran-tee that the Italians would this time be sincere, Minilik returned to Shewa (Shoa) with his army. The negotiations took time. The peace treaty was not signed until October 26, and even then the important and difficult issue of a permanent boundary was left open.[70] More grati-fying for Minilik was no doubt the eagerness with which British and French delegations arrived in his capital to compete for his friendship

[66] Pankhurst, "News," 357.

[67] Mondon 82, Minilik to Mondon, 1 Dec. 1895, 5v.-6v. The French had, of course, sold large amounts of arms and ammunition to Minilik, but so had the Italians themselves.

[68] Work, *Ethiopia*, 184-92, 247-51; cf. Ronald Robinson and John Gallagher, *Africa and the Victorians* (London, 1963), 345-54; G. N. Sanderson, *England, Europe and the Upper Nile* (Edinburgh, 1965), 242-49, 278-79.

[69] *Doc. Dipl. XXIII-ter*, Baldissera to Mocenni, 7 Mar. 1896, 10.

[70] Ministero degli Affari Esteri, *Trattati, Convenzioni, Accordi, Protocolli ed altri Documenti relativi all'Africa, 1825-1906* (Rome, 1906), 508-9.

and to negotiate boundaries for their possessions in the Horn of Africa.[71]

Minilik understood and appreciated the change of attitude of the European powers toward his country. Nevertheless, he would no doubt have smiled at the oft-repeated European definition of the significance of Adwa, namely, that it put Ethiopia on the map of the world. This was, of course, literally true with regard to the maps kept in the chancelleries of European capitals,[72] but Minilik and his subjects lived in another world with other realities. To most of them, the medieval map in *Mesihafe Aksum* with the Church of Saint Mary of Sion at the center was more relevant than Hertslet's *Map of Africa by Treaty*.

The Emperor spoke for his subjects as well as for himself in a circular letter to the European powers in 1891: "Ethiopia having existed for fourteen hundred years as a Christian island surrounded by a sea of pagans, I do not intend to listen quietly when governments from distant lands say that they will divide up Africa. I trust that God, who has protected Ethiopia until this day, will henceforth protect and increase her, and I have no fear that He will divide her and give her away to other nations."[73] For a nation with this attitude, the victory at Adwa cannot have come as a surprise. But it was certainly greeted with relief and gratitude, mingled with regret that it should have been so costly in human life.[74]

Protest Issues

The historical significance of Adwa is completely missed if it is viewed, as has so often been the case, as an eruption of "African savagery"—a sudden, inexplicable but successful rebellion by Italy's African vassal, Minilik. Regardless of its consequences, Adwa was no episode. It was the last dramatic act in a long play, the culmination of a struggle that had begun decades earlier. The Ethiopian protest was slow and patient, but unyielding.

[71] Work, *Ethiopia*, 249-60; Robinson and Gallagher, *Africa*, 359-66.

[72] The first and second editions of Edward Hertslet, *Map of Africa by Treaty* (London, 1894 and 1896, respectively), show Ethiopia as Italian, while the third edition (1909) has "put Ethiopia on the map." The French took exception to Hertslet's way of dividing Africa, but indicated a "French" Ethiopia instead, for instance, on *Carte générale des possessions françaises en Afrique, au premier janvier, 1895*, published by Augustin Challamel (Paris) for the French Chamber of Deputies.

[73] Foreign Office (hereafter referred to as FO): 1/32: Minilik to the "kings in Europe," 21 Apr. 1891, Public Record Office. (Translation from the Amharic original.)

[74] Guèbrè Sellassié, *Chronique*, II, 448. According to survivors whom I have interviewed, this reaction was not limited to Taytu and her circle.

Several elements in this protest are clearly discernible. It was a protest against direct military invasion and against Italy's self-assumed role as Ethiopia's "protector." On a deeper level it was a protest against the lack of sincerity so often and so clearly manifested by representatives of European powers and against the underestimation of, not to say contempt for, Ethiopia's political institutions and military potential.

The Italian invasion of 1895 had several forerunners. The story of encroachments on Ethiopian territory in the north could be said to have begun with the occupation, on behalf of Egypt, of the Keren area in central Eritrea by Werner Munzinger, the Swiss adventurer and former French and British consular representative, in July 1872. Emperor Yohannis, who had only recently been crowned after three years of civil war, protested to Cairo and several European capitals, requesting that the conflict be solved through arbitration. The response was half-hearted, and three years later Egyptian armies with Europeans and Americans as commanding or advisory officers invaded Ethiopia. This time Yohannis defeated the Egyptians decisively at Gundet and Gura. Nevertheless, the Egyptians kept some of the territory they had occupied, and a long period of uneasy truce and peace negotiations followed.[75]

Not until 1884, when the Egyptians had to evacuate their troops because of the Mahdist threat, was a peace treaty signed. This was for all practical purposes negotiated on behalf of the Egyptian government by British Rear Admiral Sir William Hewett. It was signed by Hewett for the British government and by an American governor of Massawa for the Egyptian government. The terms of the treaty included the restoration of the occupied areas and a formal guarantee that Ethiopian trade through Massawa, including the import of arms, would not be hindered or taxed. The port could not be ceded outright to Ethiopia because it was a Turkish possession.[76]

Before the end of the year, the British government had, however, agreed to let the Italians take Massawa, and, on February 5, 1885, the new masters arrived like a bolt from the blue. Yohannis's first reaction was that the British had somehow betrayed him. Perplexed by the suddenness of this new development on his doorstep and uncertain as to the extent of the betrayal, he again tried diplomacy first. He received the Italian emissaries, Vincenzo Ferrari and Cesare Nerazzini, who

[75] Sven Rubenson, "The Adwa Peace Treaty of 1884," *Proceedings of the Third International Conference of Ethiopian Studies* (Addis Ababa, 1969), I, 225-36.

[76] FO: 93/2/2; English text in Wylde, *Abyssinia*, Appendix II; Rubenson, "Adwa Treaty."

came to explain the new situation, in a sufficiently polite manner to make them think that they had allayed his fears.[77] But in a frank letter to Queen Victoria he expressed his disappointment and asked that the British government should explain its action.[78] He also turned to his vassal, King Minilik of Shewa, who for some years had been on friendly terms with the Italians and, pointing out the danger of the new development, urged a united stand to meet it. Minilik's response was positive inasmuch as he protested against the secrecy of the operation and the lie told to the population at Massawa, that is, that the Emperor had agreed to the occupation. He asked King Umberto to inform him personally about the whole truth and the reasons for the occupation.[79]

Of course, neither Yohannis nor Minilik expected that these protests would make any difference as far as the occupation of Massawa by a European power was concerned. Rather they were protests against the lack of sincerity shown by two supposedly friendly European governments.

The Italians, however, soon revealed that their aspirations went beyond administering the port. They began to fortify Massawa and to induce minor chiefs on the coast to ask for Italian "protection"; they occupied small harbors on the mainland such as Arkiko and Arafali and sent some irregulars thirty kilometers inland to Se'ati. Although these places had not yet been evacuated by the Egyptians, Yohannis and his governor of the northern borderlands, Ras Alula, regarded them—at least Se'ati—as Ethiopian territory by virtue of the Hewett treaty. Alula's protest could leave no one in doubt: " . . . the country belongs to the King. . . . Therefore clear out of Se'ati."[80]

Whether or not Se'ati, strictly speaking, belonged to Ethiopia is not the most important issue; it did not belong to Italy either. But it was to become the touchstone of the Italian-Ethiopian relationship. The Italian government was aware of its importance. In the instructions for the mission to be sent to Yohannis in January 1886, General Giorgio Pozzolini was informed that Hewett had promised Yohannis that the Egyptians would leave Se'ati and was instructed to weigh carefully the value of keeping it against the importance of calming the

[77] See Battaglia, *Guerra*, 163-68, 180-86, 215-28, for the developments of Ethio-Italian relations from 1885 to 1887.

[78] FO: 95/746: Yohannis to Victoria, 28 Aug. 1885.

[79] *Atti Parlamentari, 1889-90, Documenti Diplomatici*, XV, *Etiopia*, Antonelli to Mancini, 9 Apr. 1885, 191-92; Minilik to Umberto, 10 Apr. 1885, 194; cf. Battaglia, *Guerra*, 218; Work, *Ethiopia*, 62.

[80] Battaglia, *Guerra*, 220. See Rubenson, "Adwa Treaty," on possible interpretations of the Hewett Treaty.

Emperor's fear that it was being occupied as the gateway to the high-lands.[81]

Nevertheless, the conflict over Se'ati was allowed to lead to the so-called massacre at Dogali one year later. In September 1886 regular Italian troops were sent to fortify Se'ati. Alula's demand that they be withdrawn went unheeded. When reinforcements were sent, he attacked the small unit and cut it to pieces at Dogali on January 26, 1887.[82]

This was a stronger protest than the Italians and British had expected. The former wanted to march, if for no other reason to demonstrate their strength to "the barbarians."[83] The British government, prompted by a new letter from Yohannis to the Queen, offered to mediate. But when Yohannis was told to "apologize" for Alula's action, to renounce all rights to a strip of land along the whole coast, and to cede the Bogos province with Keren, his reply was a most emphatic "no." He expressed surprise that the British government could ask him to cede territory which had so recently been restored to him at their own instigation, and added:

> . . . when they [the Italians] wanted to begin the quarrel, they stopped the traders and came to the places in my country called Sehati and Wia and fortified them. . . . By making me appear to be the offender when I am not, are you not implying that I should give them the land which Jesus Christ gave to me? Reconciliation is possible when they are in their country and I in mine, but now, sleeping with our swords in hand and keeping our horses bridled, are we not with our armies as good as in combat already?[84]

The very harshness of this reply reveals that it was no longer a question simply of a protest against encroachment. It was an expression of bewilderment and anger because the British showed so little respect for signed agreements, so little gratitude for services rendered, and so little sense of fair play.

In the meantime Minilik had remained on fairly good terms with Italy's informal representative in Shewa, Count Pietro Antonelli. When war seemed inevitable because of the Dogali incident, he had offered to mediate and had even agreed to remain neutral if the Italians should decide to avenge their dead at Dogali. Yohannis accepted, but

---

[81] Archivio Storico dell'ex Ministero dell'Africa Italiana (hereinafter referred to as A.S. MAI): 36/3-31: Istruzioni per la missione d'Abissinia, 7 Jan. 1886.

[82] Battaglia, *Guerra*, 230-42.

[83] Ibid., 267-87.

[84] FO:/95/748: Yohannis to Victoria, 7 Dec. 1887 (translation from the Amharic original); Battaglia, *Guerra*, 287-94. See also David Mathew, *Ethiopia: The Study of a Polity* (London, 1947), 218-22.

the Italian government turned down Minilik's offer to act as a mediator. It is quite obvious that Minilik could not have succeeded and that he was, in fact, just as unwilling to let the Italians have their way as the Emperor himself. In the "convention of neutrality" signed by him and Antonelli in October 1887, Article 3 reads: "It shall be so that the Italian king shall not seize or touch a single place on Ethiopian soil."[85] Though Minilik would have preferred to stay out of an armed conflict, he was also concerned that no Ethiopian soil should be surrendered. In a more subtle way he had once more made his own protest. The "convention of neutrality" remained a dead letter.

Although both sides seemed prepared for a full-scale war in the first months of 1888, hostilities did not break out. Yohannis marched his army down to the now strongly fortified Italian positions at Se'ati. There he exchanged communications with General Di San Marzano on the causes of the conflict and the possibilities of reconciliation: "What would now make it possible for us to come to an agreement? Has not Christ distributed and made peace? Your country stretches from the sea to Rome, mine stretches from the sea to here, that is Ethiopia: there is no reason for us to quarrel."[86]

The principle that Europeans had no business in Africa as conquerors could hardly have been formulated more succinctly. Nevertheless the Ethiopian army withdrew without battle. News that King Tekle Haymanot of Gojam had been defeated and Gonder sacked by the Mahdists reached Yohannis, and he turned his attention to this conflict which, in terms of past Ethiopian history, was more fundamental and easier to understand.[87]

When Yohannis lost his life in the battle against the Mahdists at Metemma on March 9, 1889, Minilik inherited both conflicts and the problem of rebuilding Ethiopian unity under his own supremacy. Again the decision was made first to seek political rather than military solutions.

Antonelli was on hand with a treaty draft, and after some negotiating the Treaty of Wichale was signed on May 2, 1889.[88] By this

---

[85] A.S. MAI: 36/4-40 (translation from the Amharic original). See Sven Rubenson, "The Protectorate Paragraph of the Wichale Treaty," *Journal of African History*, V (1964), 243-83, where this "agreement" and the relations in general between Minilik and the Italians at this time are analyzed.

[86] Battaglia, *Guerra*, 313-21.

[87] For the role of the strained relations between Yohannis and his two most important vassals at this time, see Battaglia, *Guerra*, 347-49, 356; Rubenson, "Wichale Treaty," 272-78.

[88] Archivo Storico del Ministero degli Affari Esteri (A.S. MAE), Serie V, Trattati, Etiopia 3; Amharic and Italian texts in Sven Rubenson, *Wichale XVII: The Attempt to Establish a Protectorate over Ethiopia* (Addis Ababa, 1964), appendix.

time the Italians had gained a firm footing in the lowlands around Massawa. Minilik must have understood that nothing less than a major military campaign would suffice to dislodge them, and that this would be a risky undertaking as long as he had not consolidated his own position internally and come to terms with the Mahdists. Under the circumstances he was even prepared to give the Italians some more hinterland in exchange for peace and recognition. The important thing was now to draw the line and obtain the sanction of a solemn treaty for it. Italy's demands were rather excessive, and Minilik made two major adjustments. In principle the boundary should follow the edge of the plateau, but in the east it was to reach the coast at Arafali, thus leaving the coast to the east with the port of Anfilla in Ethiopian hands. Nevertheless the ceded territory included one major village on the plateau, namely Asmara, and most of the territories once occupied by the Egyptians in the west, including Keren. In area it amounted to more than one-third of what later became Eritrea, and, wrote Antonelli, "for the time being I believe that this must be sufficient for us."[89]

It was Minilik's mistake that he did not understand the transitionary character of this agreement, which included such phrases as "perpetual peace and constant friendship" (in the Amharic version "undiminishing love for evermore") and the stipulation that the agreed boundary could not be changed though the rest of the treaty could be modified after five years. While the Italians in the colony were still busy occupying their new territories, the government in Rome began to look for some way around the limitations to their expansion which had just been agreed upon.

A suitable opening was found in the stipulation that the boundary should be demarcated on the ground by delegates from both sides. While in Italy to receive the ratification of the treaty and negotiate a loan, Ras Mekwennin was asked to include in an additional convention a paragraph stating that the boundary should be demarcated on the basis of "actual possession." Great care was taken to avoid arousing Mekwennin's suspicion as to the real purpose of this new formula, and he could hardly have suspected that the intention was to tear up Article III of the Wichale Treaty and give Italy a legal right to still more Ethiopian territory. In the meantime General Antonio Baldissera was to advance beyond the line agreed upon with Minilik and to occupy as much territory as possible. This probably represents the highest level of duplicity reached by the Italians in their dealings with the Ethiopians: " . . . if ever an expression was used 'in bad faith,' if ever an imbroglio

[89] A.S. MAI: 36/6-53: Antonelli to Pisani, 14 May 1889. A.S. MAI, 36/5-48 contains the drafts of the treaty. For discussions about the boundary (Art. III), see Battaglia, *Guerra*, 375; Rubenson, "Wichale Treaty," 279.

or a trap was prepared by Europeans for Africans, it was without any doubt the 'additional clause' on 'actual possession.' "[90]

Presented with the additional convention and the actual occupation by Italian troops of all the territory as far as the rivers Mereb-Bellesa and Muna,[91] Minilik balked. He had sent his relative to Rome to bring back the ratified treaty as it stood, not to sign a new treaty. Nevertheless he would not disavow his representative; but "actual possession" would have to apply to the situation when the Wichale Treaty was ratified and the additional convention signed, that is, about October 1, 1889, not to the situation in February 1890 when Mekwennin and Antonelli reached Minilik's camp at Meqele. Minilik offered Antonelli some additional territory as far as Skiket, about twenty kilometers south of Asmara and thus only about one-fifth of the distance from there to the Mereb-Bellesa line, "in order to put an end to the bloodshed."

Antonelli accepted these provisions but the military in Eritrea and Crispi in Rome refused.[92] Negotiations broke down, the Italians remained at Mereb, and though Minilik turned south from the famine-struck Tigre, the relationship between the two countries must on the basis of the border issue be defined as a state of war. This lasted until 1896.

The issue that dominated Ethio-Italian relations between 1890 and 1896 was, however, not the boundary but the protectorate issue. In the original draft of the Wichale Treaty, Antonelli had included an article by which Minilik agreed to "avail himself of the government of His Majesty the King of Italy for all negotiations of affairs which he might have with other powers or governments." This was either not presented to Minilik in this form or rejected by him. In the Amharic text Article XVII contained no obligation for Minilik to conduct his foreign affairs through the Italian government, only an offer by the Italian government to assist Minilik with his communications with European governments. Though he must have been fully aware of the discrepancy and its significance, Antonelli did not change the Italian text accordingly.[93]

[90] Battaglia, *Guerra*, 379-83; for the quote from Battaglia, see 382.

[91] Ibid., 397-400, 403-7. An advance by General Baldassare Orero to Adwa in the end of January was regarded as too bold. His stay there lasted only a few days, but is significant as an indication of how far the new Governor of Eritrea was prepared to go.

[92] Ibid., 420-26. The Wichale Treaty was ratified 29 Sept., the additional convention was dated 1 Oct. but was re-worded once or twice soon after; ibid., 384.

[93] For this paragraph and the following on the protectorate issue, see Rubenson, "Wichale Treaty"; Carlo Giglio, "Article 17 of the Treaty of Uccialli," *Journal of African History*, VI (1965), 221-31; Rubenson, "Professor Giglio, Antonelli and Article XVII of the Treaty of Wichale," ibid., VII (1966), 445-57.

Article XIX stated that both texts, "agreeing perfectly with each other," were official and equally authoritative. This, of course, invalidated Article XVII in both its versions. Nevertheless Crispi used this article as the basis for declaring an Italian "protectorate" over Ethiopia in accordance with rules laid down in Article XXXIV of the Berlin Act and managed to get recognition of his protectorate from most of the signatory powers of this act. During the meetings in Tigre in the beginning of 1890, Antonelli managed somehow to cover up this matter. In July, however, the Emperor received letters from Queen Victoria and Kaiser Wilhelm in which he was told, plainly but politely, that he could henceforth, because of his treaty, approach the Italian government only.

It now became painfully clear to Minilik that Article XVII was nothing less than a threat to the independence and sovereignty of the Ethiopian nation. He began by protesting to King Umberto: " . . . I did not then [that is, when the treaty was signed] accept any mandatory engagement, and even today I am not the man to accept it, and you should not so much as ask me to do so. Now I hope that you will, for the sake of the honor of your friend kindly rectify the error committed in article 17, and make other friendly powers to whom you have communicated the article in question, aware of the error."[94]

When Minilik received no satisfactory reply, he proceeded himself to inform other European powers of the error. This caused the Italian government to send Antonelli once more to Minilik's court. He now had instructions to make concessions on the boundary issue if he could thereby induce Minilik to agree to some formula under which the "Protectorate" could be maintained. But Minilik would have none of it. Negotiations broke down in February 1891, and Minilik wrote to tell Umberto that he regarded Article XVII as annulled. Further negotiations and other envoys were equally unsuccessful. In February 1893 Minilik denounced the whole treaty, which would thus become void—as far as Minilik was concerned—at the end of the first five-year period.

With the letter to King Umberto in February 1891 and the circular letter to several of the European heads of state in April of the same year, the Ethiopian Emperor had made his position perfectly clear on both the protectorate and the boundary issues: He would not put up with any encroachments on his sovereignty or his territory. But he had taken no hasty steps and had been very careful to give no reasonable cause for complaint. In the unilateral definition of Ethiopia's boundaries he showed remarkable restraint on the northern frontier, allow-

[94] *Atti Parlamenti, 1890-91, Documenti Diplomatici, XVII, missione Antonelli in Etiopia,* Minilik to Umberto, 24 Aug. 1890, 10; Rubenson, "Wichale Treaty," 250.

ing the Italians not only the territory which he had ceded in the Wichale Treaty but also the additional territory which he had in vain offered in fulfillment of the "actual possession" clause in the hope of reaching a firm and lasting agreement.[95]

What remained to be done was to fight the idea of the "Protectorate" in every possible way. This Minilik did by keeping up correspondence with the powers that had only reluctantly or not at all recognized the Italian Protectorate, by receiving their envoys in Ethiopia, sending a mission of his own to Europe, applying for membership in the Universal Postal Union, and instituting a national Ethiopian currency. Secondly, it was necessary to prepare the country for a full-scale war with Italy by increasing the financial means of the state, enlarging the recruiting base for the army and above all arming it with modern rifles and artillery. This Minilik did by incorporating vast areas in the south and west into his empire, taxing these new provinces heavily in gold and ivory, and using the income largely for the purchase of arms. This does not mean that Minilik necessarily planned a campaign to retake the areas between the boundary he had agreed to and the Mareb-Bellesa-Muna line which had become the *de facto* border. There is at least no evidence of such plans before 1894. On the contrary Minilik seems to have been quite prepared to live with the *status quo*. He was well aware of the fate of other African rulers of the time and as eager as his predecessor not to give any grounds for the complaint that he was an aggressive neighbor.

The Di Rudini government, which succeeded Crispi's in the beginning of 1891, shared this attitude at least as far as the boundary question was concerned. It was more difficult for the Italian government to leave their "Protectorate" hanging in the air. Sooner or later Italy would have to establish it by force or give it up. But somehow or other no Italian government was prepared to draw this conclusion. Therefore Italian policy over the following years vacillated between attempts to patch up relations with Minilik and thereby save the "Protectorate," and attempts to win over his vassals and cause a civil war in Ethiopia. In December 1891 there was one early and greatly exaggerated success, the so-called Convention of Mereb. Ras Mengesha and a number of other Tigrean chiefs met with Nerazzini and the Italian governor of Eritrea at the Mereb River. Oaths and letters were exchanged to the effect that the two sides would from then on have common enemies and common friends. Ras Alula made no secret of his contempt for this kind of political activity at the solemn meeting itself.[96]

[95] See above, n. 73.
[96] Battaglia, *Guerra,* 506-17; Berkeley, *Adowa,* 36-37.

With Crispi back in government in December 1893, the pace accelerated. Colonel Federico Piano went to Addis Ababa as the last delegate of the self-styled protector, presented his credentials to the Emperor, and was, in effect, told that he might as well take the earliest possible opportunity to return to his own country.[97] Baratieri, who was now governor of Eritrea and who had always been against a *rapprochement* with Minilik[98] hardly needed Crispi's instructions: "Minilik's inexcusable behaviour compels [us] to prepare from now on a defense plan. As we did with Minilik against Yohannis, we should now encourage pretenders against Minilik. Mengesha in Tigre, Mekwennin in Harer, besides [being] ambitious persons, have serious reasons for hatred [and] revenge against the Emperor. If Minilik disappears, the empire could be divided into two kingdoms, one northern and one southern, under Italy's lofty protection, not to exclude other combinations which might be better for us."[99]

This was verily no new policy. It had been tried by Munzinger and the Khedive Ismail in the 1870's with Minilik. Unlike Crispi, Ismail had, moreover, been prepared to commit himself to *one* person and to do so some of the fighting himself. However, the policy had failed at a time when Yohannis and Minilik were actually rivals and both styled themselves King of Kings.[100] And if Crispi knew nothing about this, he might have recalled that all of Italy's efforts from 1885 to 1889 had not produced the desired result—an attack by Minilik on Yohannis.

Nevertheless, it was in the policy of sowing discord among the Ethiopians that Crispi and Baratieri placed their major hopes. Ras Mengesha of Tigre and Ras Mekwennin of Harer, the King of Gojam and the Sultan of Awsa, and many less important men were approached. And on all fronts success or imminent success was reported.[101] It did not seem to occur to Baratieri that Mengesha, who had become so disillusioned during his earlier short sojourn in the Italian camp that he had of his own free will submitted to Minilik and been reinstated as governor of Tigre, would hardly change sides again at the first hint. As for Mekwennin, he more than anyone else had had the opportunity of discovering the unscrupulous cheating of the Italians in connection with the Wichale Treaty and the additional con-

[97] Battaglia, *Guerra,* 572-73; Baratieri, *Memorie,* 43-45.
[98] Baratieri, *Memorie,* 48-49, 67.
[99] Battaglia, *Guerra,* 574.
[100] Sven Rubenson, "Some Aspects of the Survival of Ethiopian Independence in the Period of the Scramble for Africa," *University College Review* I, 1 (Addis Ababa, 1961), 8-24.
[101] Battaglia, *Guerra,* 575, 580-81; Berkeley, *Adowa,* 88-89.

vention. Nevertheless Nerazzini, who knew Ethiopia from the inside and had lived at Harer, proposed actively trying to bring Mekwennin into the Italian camp or, at least, to compromise him. For Baratieri the problem was already solved. He could, within a few days, report that Mekwennin had promised to revolt if Minilik began hostilities against Eritrea.[102]

The Italian government seems always to have believed the reports that were most favorable to its own cause. Minilik's "empire is, in appearance, a colossus, but in substance it has no base."[103] "A European conqueror . . . will have the whole country for himself and the way prepared. . . ."[104] Had not Colonel Piano, the highest ranking Italian officer ever to visit Minilik's camp or court, after his visit to Addis Ababa defined Ethiopia as "the colossus with feet of clay"?[105]

On December 14, 1894, a most unexpected revolt against Italian rule broke out in Eritrea. Bahta Hagos, governor of Ikolo Guzay, publicly proclaimed the liberation of his province from foreign rule. Three days later his irregulars were defeated, and he lost his life. Baratieri decided to make an additional demonstration of force and marched to Adwa, but found that he could not hold the place with available forces and withdrew. Mengesha followed into Eritrea, and an indecisive battle was fought at Koatit on January 12–14, after which Mengesha retired. Baratieri caught up with him at Senafe and shelled his camp, but the Ras managed to escape with his army to Tigre.[106]

This was the "small war," which might have remained an episode on the northern border but for two reasons. First, Mengesha had left behind in his abandoned camp at Senafe a number of documents which established beyond doubt that Bahta Hagos's action was part of a bigger plan by which Mengesha hoped to regain control of the lost provinces on the other side of the Mereb.[107] The plans must have had Minilik's blessing and had most likely been agreed upon in general terms during Mengesha's visit to Addis Ababa in June 1894. They showed that Minilik had begun to think of repaying the Italians in kind. Captured documents indicated, however, that Minilik had in September ordered Mengesha to restrain Bahta Hagos from action. Whether he later gave orders to act is uncertain.[108] It is also difficult

[102] Doc. Dipl. XXIII-bis, Nerazzini to Blanc, 26 Jan. 1895, 5-9; Baratieri to Blanc, 3 Feb. 1895, 21.

[103] Battaglia, Guerra, 570, quoting Traversi, Sept. 1893.

[104] Ibid., 580, quoting Capucci, Oct. 1894.

[105] Ibid., 622.

[106] Ibid., 594-606.

[107] Doc. Dipl. XXIII-bis, Baratieri to Blanc, 14 Feb. 1895, 23-26.

[108] Battaglia, Guerra, 597.

to know if the revolt was mainly the result of instigation or fundamentally a popular uprising against colonial policies, such as the expropriation of land for settlers.[109] Secondly, the easy and greatly exaggerated victories became an irresistible temptation for Baratieri to cross the Mereb-Bellesa-Muna line and annex the Adwa-Aksum area and Agame with Adigrat.[110]

The obvious lesson that Baratieri could have learned from the revolt—that his position was vulnerable at home and that he did not command the loyalty even of the chiefs in Eritrea—seems to have been entirely overlooked. Instead of consolidation, he chose expansion. Though he did ask for reinforcements from Italy for this purpose, he continued at the same time and increasingly to rely on Ethiopian disunity to avert the "big war" or win it for him.[111]

More than anything else it was this underestimation of both the Ethiopian polity and the individuals involved that caused the Italian defeat. Baratieri had been warned by Ras Sibhat and other Ethiopians,[112] and Nerazzini had at least in one of his memoranda told Crispi: "A national war against Ethiopia is a big war."[113] But somehow or other this had to be disbelieved and was disbelieved, for how could an African ruler, who had "rebelled against his superiors" in the last decade of the nineteenth century, possibly be strong—in European terms?

There is little purpose in speculating about the extent to which the Italians were deceived by wishful thinking or by deliberate deceit by some Ethiopian chiefs in the last stages of the conflict. There were Tigrean chiefs who fought for the Italians during part of the campaign, and there may well have been others who had at one point or another genuinely intended to side with the Italians or to remain neutral.[114] At the crucial moment, however, Minilik commanded the loy-

---

[109] Ibid., 582-93 makes a strong case for the second alternative and interprets the widespread Ethiopian proverb "From the bite of a black snake you may recover but not from that of a white snake" in terms of a choice between the Mahdists and the Europeans, in which the Ethiopian was bound to chose the former who only conquered and oppressed the individual while the white man destroyed everything, including the very structure of the society in which the black man lived.

[110] Ibid., 604-7; cf. Berkeley, Adowa, 73-79.

[111] Baratieri, Memorie, 161-68; Doc. Dipl. XXIII-bis, Baratieri to Blanc, 30 Sept., 4 Oct., 14 Oct., 25 Nov. 1895, 102-6, 131.

[112] Berkeley, Adowa, 119, 240.

[113] Doc. Dipl. XXIII-bis, Nerazzini to Blanc, 3 Feb. 1895, 19-21. But Nerazzini had only one week earlier spoken of Minilik's "disastrous policy of expansion" in the south and how it had weakened him; see above, n. 102.

[114] Baratieri, Memorie, 223, admits that he really did not know at all who would be with him, neutral, or against him.

alty of every important chief in the country, whether Amharan, Gallan, or Tigrean. Although there was plenty of internal strife and rivalry in the Ethiopian state at the time, there was, nevertheless, finally a unanimous protest against the unceasing interference of agents of foreign governments wanting to benefit from the lack of unity. At Adwa the Ethiopians told the Europeans that they preferred to carry on their quarrels themselves without interference.

Minilik must often have thought of Yohannis's advice and predictions ten years earlier:

> They [the Italians] are not a serious people; they are intriguers; and all this must be something which the English are doing to me. The Italians have not come to these parts because they lack pasture and abundance in their own country, but they come here because of ambition, in order to aggrandize themselves, because they are many and not rich. But with the help of God, they shall leave again humiliated and disappointed and with their honour lost before all the world. They are not a people who can frighten us; . . . If the two of us always remain united, we shall with the help of God overcome not only the weak Italians, but also the strong people of other nations. As Adam wanted to enjoy the forbidden fruit because of ambition to become greater than God, and instead found nothing but chastisement and dishonour, so it will happen to the Italians.[115]

Minilik had seen the dangers of disunity; he had experienced the falsehood of an Antonelli and a Crispi. As he marched toward Adwa something of Yohannis's defiance surged in the heart of the cautious politician:

> I find . . . that the Italians are impossible to deal with. Power is with God. But from now on no one will try to appease the Italians. I have endured all this until now so that the European powers would know how I have been attacked and not believe me to be the evildoer. This war does not worry me. The malevolent rumors disseminated [about the relations] between myself and Ras Mikael will not hurt us. As for them, the people of Europe who see their troubles will laugh at them.[116]

Nevertheless, Minilik kept the door open for negotiations, mainly through Mekwennin, all the way to Adwa. But in spite of the first serious defeat at Amba Alage and in spite of the fall of Meqele, the Italian position remained the same. All of the territory where the Italian flag

[115] *Doc. Dipl.* XV, Antonelli to Robilant, 26 Nov. 1885, 203-5.
[116] Mondon 82, Minilik to Mondon, 1 Dec. 1895, 5v.-6v.

had waved must be ceded and the yoke of the "Protectorate" accepted. Minilik asked for a radical modification of the Wichale Treaty and an Italian withdrawal to Mereb.[117]

The gap was too wide and the battle was fought. The ultimate protest, the willingness to risk and lose thousands of human lives, brought the desired outcome. Minilik, his generals, his soldiers, and his people secured the survival of the Ethiopian state and the right of its people to live their own lives.

"Africans have no fatherland."[118] To the propagators of colonialism, in Italy as elsewhere in Europe, this was once an article of faith. When Baratieri could not help discovering that something was moving in the Ethiopian society, he could find no better description for it than "a semblance of the idea of nationhood in the guise of hatred against the whites."[119] The language of Guèbrè Sellassié, the chronicler, may sound high-flown, but then he saw it from the African side: "On that day the master did not find his servant, the soldier did not find his officer; everyone marched straight forward to battle and towards the cannon as a monkey does who has seen a corn-sheaf. All the army was on fire with devotion for their country and the nation."[120]

In a certain sense the issue at Adwa was both the survival of an old nation and the creation of a new one. The importance of the battle as a decisive event in the history of Ethiopia can hardly be overestimated. The poems, the stories, the paintings—in almost every church —of the battle scene with Saint George fighting for the Ethiopians, and the fact that "Adwa Day" is the only national holiday not connected with the life and rule of the present Emperor, all testify to the place this victory over the Italian aggressors has in the hearts of the Ethiopians.

[117] See above, n. 6.
[118] Battaglia, *Guerra*, 313.
[119] Baratieri, *Memorie*, 48.
[120] Guèbrè Sellassié, *Chronique*, II, 440.

PART TWO

REBELLIONS AGAINST ALIEN RULE

THE SUDANESE MAHDIYA

L. CARL BROWN

Muhammad Ahmad, the Sudanese Mahdi, and the movement he created in the 1880's are well known in the Western world when compared with most major figures and events of African history. The period of the Mahdiya evokes memories of General Charles Gordon who died in January 1885 defending Khartoum against the Mahdists, of Kipling's fuzzy-wuzzies who "broke a British square," of Kitchener who won renown as commander in chief of the Anglo-Egyptian expedition which had successfully reoccupied the Sudan by 1898, and of an adventurous young man serving in the British army, Winston Churchill, whose *The River War* contains a thrilling account of the reoccupation campaign. The titles of books written by European contemporaries caught up in the Mahdist maelstrom—*Fire and Sword in the Sudan, Ten Years' Captivity in the Mahdi's Camp,* or *A Prisoner of the Khaleefa*—also suggest the romantic heroism and exoticism connected with the European image of the Mahdist movement. The inexplicable, wild Sudanese of the 1880's and 1890's were only dimly perceived as flesh-and-blood human beings wrestling in an intense and extraordinary fashion with recognizable problems of the kind likely to descend upon any society. Instead, these Sudanese assumed the impersonal role of Fate in a real-life drama wherein the manliness and religious convictions of a handful of Europeans were put to the test. To the extent that Europe was concerned with the other side, the Mahdi and his followers represented a doomed struggle of primitives against civilization, although their piety and amazing personal bravery were usually acknowledged. Only recently has sounder scholarship on the Sudan and

145

Islam—part of a generally more perceptive and sympathetic view of non-Western history—begun to modify the stereotype.[1]

In Sunni Islam the Mahdi (literally "the guided one") is the man whom God selects and guides in order to restore the faith at a time of cataclysmic trouble. The Mahdi, it is said, will "fill the earth with justice even as it has been filled with injustice."[2] It is true that in the orthodox doctrine of the theologians the role of the Mahdi is by no means clearly established. Even Sunni Muslim eschatology, which does provide for a final restorer of the faith before the end of time, does not clearly give this role to someone to be called the Mahdi. A more accepted Sunni Muslim version of the events preceding the Resurrection would have Jesus come to destroy al-Dajjal (the antichrist).[3] Theologians aside, however, the masses of Sunni Muslims have for centuries been strongly attached to a belief in a divinely appointed redeemer known as the Mahdi who would set matters right just when the forces of evil in this world appeared to be at their strongest.

To put it in a more general way, belief in a Mahdi can properly be classified as the specifically Sunni Muslim type of a general human

[1] The best example of both sounder scholarship and a more sympathetic view of the Mahdiya is the work of Peter M. Holt. See his *The Mahdist State in the Sudan 1881–1898* (Oxford, 1958). In addition, among his several articles on the Mahdiya which have appeared in various scholarly journals special attention should be called to "The Source-Materials of the Sudanese Mahdia," in *St. Antony's Papers: Middle Eastern Affairs* (London, 1958), 107-18. In this article Holt shows how certain of the more important contemporary Western accounts bore traces of "news-management" by Reginald Wingate, then director of Egyptian military intelligence. However, Wingate's "propaganda campaign" worked so well because it was attuned to the sentiments and prejudices of the day. The extent to which the Western outlook has changed in the direction of a greater willingness to accept the rest of the world can be seen by comparing the recent film *Khartoum* with *The Four Feathers* (based on the novel of that name written by A. E. W. Mason in 1902) which was produced in 1939. In the latter the "savage" Sudanese were simply part of the background. *Khartoum*, by contrast, came much closer to telling the story in terms of two strong-willed religious fanatics, the Mahdi and General Gordon. Nor should it be overlooked that an actor of the stature of Sir Laurence Olivier played the role of the Mahdi.

[2] No attempt is made in this chapter to cover the quite different Shi'i concept of the Mahdi, but it should be kept in mind that the historical development of the two is closely interrelated, just as the later reference to the Fatimids (see below, 162-63) suggests.

[3] See the articles "al-Mahdi," "al-Dadjdjal," and " 'Isa" in the *Shorter Encyclopaedia of Islam*. In the popular messianic beliefs of the Sudan the Mahdi was to appear before the second coming of Jesus. As a result, there were sporadic movements after the death of the Mahdi Muhammad Ahmad, instigated by persons claiming to be Jesus ('Isa). See Holt, *Mahdist State*, 22, 152; J. Spencer Trimingham, *Islam in the Sudan* (London, 1949), 158-59, and the additional references cited therein.

phenomenon—the messianic, millenarian expectation; a belief which should hardly be incomprehensible to anyone familiar with the Judaic or Christian tradition. The movement created by the Sudanese Mahdi, and other Mahdist movements in Islam, can usefully be compared with Christian and Jewish messianic cults of varying time and place such as the sixteenth-century millenarians anticipating the advent of Christ and the establishment of the true kingdom of saints, the Shakers, the American Millerites expecting the end of the world in 1848, and the Jewish messianic movement led by Sabetai Svei.[4]

A paradigm of messianic movements in the Semitic tradition (Judaic, Christian, and Muslim) would include the following characteristics:

1. Cataclysmic: The change which is believed to be imminent will be sudden, violent, and total.

2. Charismatic: The movement will be led by a divinely appointed individual with power and authority not to be explained or circumscribed by customary human patterns.

3. Sectarian: The individual adherent will be "called out." He must make his personal commitment to a new message, a commitment which is total and replaces previous obligations. Those not making such a personal commitment (even if they were co-religionists before the new message) are henceforth outside of the community, and in many cases to be fought as enemies.

4. Revivalist: There will be a return to the primitive simplicity of the "old time religion."

[4] There is a vast literature on messianic movements. Most of it is confined to a single religious culture, but there are several good studies comparing Christian and Jewish examples. Hardly any work exists on what can properly be called the Semitic (Judaic, Christian, and Muslim) tradition of messianic movements. Nor, except for a few tentative suggestions by pioneering sociologists, has much attention been given to the question of whether a decidedly different form and intensity in the messianic, millenarian, expectation is to be found in cultures based on the Semitic religious tradition as opposed to other cultures. Among books dealing with the general "messianic phenomenon" are: Norman Cohn, *The Pursuit of the Millennium* (London, 1957); Stephen Fuchs, *Rebellious Prophets: A Study of Messianic Movements in Indian Religions* (London, 1965); Sylvia L. Thrupp (ed.), *Millennial Dreams in Action* (The Hague, 1962); Ernst Troeltsch, *The Social Teaching of the Christian Churches* (New York, 1931); Joachim Wach, *Sociology of Religion* (Chicago, 1944); Max Weber (tr. Ephraim Fischoff), *The Sociology of Religion* (London, 1965).

5. Puritanical: All frivolity and self-indulgence will be forbidden (wine, tobacco, music, fine clothes, sexual libertinism) and an unremitting seriousness will be seen as the *summum bonum*. There are to be "no more cakes and ale."

6. Revelationist: A simplified scriptural doctrine will be accepted on faith. Previous theological formulations or attempts to create a new theology relying in large part on systematic reason are to be resisted.

The messianic, millenarian expectation is no rarity in human history, and it is especially marked in the Semitic religious tradition. The Sudanese Mahdiya is firmly within that tradition. The Western man who finds the Mahdi and his Sudanese followers odd betrays only an ignorance of his own cultural heritage. The common traits found in so many of mankind's millennial dreams deserve our attention if only to keep us from stumbling into egregious errors of interpretation. One is then less likely to assert glibly that this ethnic group, or that religion, or people at a certain level of economic development are especially prone to messianic movements.

On the other hand, the different patterns into which these movements fall according to the variables of time, circumstances, and cultural tradition are an essential next step in any serious analysis. The paradigm of messianic movements in the Semitic tradition, suggested above, applies perfectly to the Sudanese Mahdiya, and this, in itself, is important and useful to know. There remains the task of discovering what was specifically Sudanese, Islamic, and African about the Mahdiya. At the same time the problem of cause, or more precisely priority of causes, must be dealt with. Is the Mahdist impulse to be explained largely as a pattern of traditionally sanctioned responses to a body of "real" social, economic, and political problems? In that case, it might be argued, the historian would be advised to use the Mahdiya as a clear signal that important transitions and convulsions, yet to be determined, were taking place in Sudanese society. Or was the Mahdist impulse itself the major formative influence? Although obviously provoked and also shaped by the specific Sudanese environment, did the Sudanese Mahdiya by its own ideology and inner logic change Sudanese society?

It will be argued in this study that the Mahdiya can best be understood as another in a series of socio-religious movements on the Islamic fringe area of Africa,[5] that the Mahdiya conforms to a recog-

[5] A more precise definition of "Islamic fringe area" will be given below, 155-56, 160-61.

nizable historic type in Islamic Africa, arising in response to a distinctive set of social, political, and economic circumstances, and, finally, that the Mahdiya itself exerted a demonstrable influence on Sudanese society along predictable lines. Before illustrating these points it will be useful to present a brief sketch of Muhammad Ahmad, the Sudanese Mahdi, and of the messianic movement which he created.

Muhammad Ahmad was born in Dongola province in 1844, on a small island in the Nile River some five hundred miles downstream from Khartoum. His father and brothers were boat builders, but Muhammad Ahmad from an early age demonstrated an affinity for religious studies, a not inappropriate calling for one member of a family which claimed sharifian origins, that is, claimed to be descendants of the Prophet Muhammad. When Muhammad Ahmad was still a small child the family moved to a village located about twelve miles north of Khartoum. In terms of Sudanese history, these apparently mundane facts have considerable significance since within the Sudanese context itself there was a world of difference between the riverain peoples and the nomads to be found east and west of the Nile basin, not to mention the pagan tribes located in the Southern Sudan. To be from Dongola meant, therefore, that one's environment included sedentary agriculture, a limited degree of commerce and economic specialization, access to a modest urban culture, and a certain rudimentary educational system. Also, it was the riverain area which Egypt had been able to control and influence most effectively since Muhammad 'Ali had first turned his attention to conquering the Sudan in the 1820's. Beyond the accessible regions of the Nile basin, Egyptian control of the Sudan was slight and, in many cases, only established as late as the reign of Khedive Ismail (1863–79). It might be added that the "pagan" Southern Sudan was definitely not easily accessible even though the map shows the White Nile and its tributaries as intersecting the area. At about the ninth parallel the White Nile almost disintegrates into a great marshy swamp area without fixed watercourses.

As a child and young adolescent Muhammad Ahmad received the customary Sudanese education, which entailed memorizing the Qur'an and the simpler Islamic principles. This stultifying technique of rote learning at the feet of the village shaykh (religious teacher), who was himself the product of a hardly more formal education, was weak enough in such venerable centers of high Islamic culture as Egypt itself (where the traditional educational system was beginning to be attacked by Muslim reformers); one can imagine the intellectual level

of such education in an Islamic fringe area such as the Sudan.[6] Nevertheless, by the standards of the day Muhammad Ahmad would, like
so many other Sudanese during the years of Egyptian rule, have been
sufficiently prepared to attend the great mosque-university of al-Azhar
in Cairo as an increasing number of Sudanese had come to do.[7] It
seems quite plausible to speculate that had he attended al-Azhar, Muhammad Ahmad would never have declared himself to be the expected Mahdi and that his intense religious commitment would have
been expressed in other ways.[8] Instead, when he was seventeen years
old Muhammad Ahmad chose the more traditional Sudanese form of
religious training by becoming the disciple of one Muhammad Sharif,
a shaykh in the mystical Sammaniya religious brotherhood. After
seven years Muhammad Ahmad was permitted to become a religious
leader of the order in his own right, establishing his own residence
and in his turn teaching new disciples—while still, in accordance with
accepted Sufi practices, remaining subject to the overall discipline of
Muhammad Sharif.

A brief discussion of Sufism or Islamic mysticism and the great
Sufi *tariqa's* (religious brotherhoods) will clarify the later importance
of Muhammad Ahmad's Sufi training. In theological terms Sufism can
be seen as a reaction against the orthodox Sunni concept of a transcendent deity by Muslims seeking a more intensely personal relationship with an immanent God. The great Sufi brotherhoods which had
begun to appear in the twelfth century A.D. had institutionalized the
gnostic tendencies inherent in earlier Sufi mysticism through a hierarchy of shaykhs to whom blind obedience was due. This mass veneration of the Sufi shaykh—an aspect of saint worship in popular Islamic
beliefs, to use the terminology adopted by early European ethnographers—was diametrically opposed to a major tenet of Sunni ortho-

---

[6] Note, for example, the poignant story of Shaykh Muhammad al Khayr, an
early teacher of the Sudanese Mahdi. He was deemed so unlearned that finally one
of his students asked why they should presume to "seek knowledge" from him since
he knew even less than they. Shocked by this rebuff, Muhammad al Khayr went to
study for two years with Shaykh Husayn Zahra who had spent seven years at al-
Azhar. See Ibrahim Fawzi, *Kitab al-Sudan bayn yaday Ghurdun wa Kitshinir* [The
Sudan under Gordon and Kitchener] (Cairo, 1319/1901-2) 238-39, 314-15. This
story illustrates both the rudimentary, poorly institutionalized nature of education
in the Sudan and also the slow change being brought about during the period of
Egyptian rule, for Shaykh Husayn, as an alumnus of al-Azhar, symbolized new and
closer ties with Sunni orthodoxy.

[7] See Holt, *Mahdist State,* 37, and above footnote.

[8] This is not an implicit value judgment but an attempt to understand in secular terms the interaction of religious conviction and type of education. By comparison, in our own culture a graduate of Union Theological Seminary is unlikely to be
found conducting a revivalist tent meeting.

doxy as expressed by its most uncompromising theologians throughout the ages, such veneration of a mere mortal being considered by them a derogation from God's unity and transcendent authority. Indeed, it was to them the cardinal sin of *shirk* (association of anything with the Deity).

On the other hand, the Sufi idea of finding the way to God through an inspired mortal bore close comparison to the idea of a Mahdi. Sufi doctrine tended to be illuminist, seeking the real and true by other than rational means. In this way, too, it approached Mahdism, which relies on the nonrational authority of revelation as interpreted by a Mahdi to the exclusion of orthodox Muslim scholasticism. Although to a true Sufi, embracing the essential Sufi doctrine of *fana* (annihilation, that is, the state of losing one's imperfect individuality in the Divine Unity), the Mahdist concern with wordly revolution could only appear as a parody of true mystical religion, it can nevertheless be seen how Sufi training could predispose a religious activist toward Mahdism and how, at the same time, a general veneer of Sufi doctrine could predispose a Muslim population only lightly touched by the learned tradition into readily accepting a Mahdi. Thus, by his knowledge of the esoteric path to God and by his divinely inspired *baraka* (superhuman powers), the Sufi shaykh of a large brotherhood possessed an authority which, if he so chose, could easily be translated into political power.

To return to Muhammad Ahmad, in 1870 he moved to Aba Island in the White Nile south of Khartoum. Here, during the next few years, his fame as a pious mystic grew. He appeared to be well embarked upon a career destined to establish him as an important Sufi figure, at least within the confines of the Sudan. Instead, by 1881 Muhammad Ahmad had declared himself to be the expected Mahdi. What events can be adduced to explain or at least make somewhat more plausible this transition from Sufi leader to Mahdi? Some importance is usually attached to Muhammad Ahmad's break with his own shaykh, Muhammad Sharif, in about 1878. Among the varying accounts of the incident the most likely explanation would seem to be that in the best puritanical tradition, Muhammad Ahmad had protested against the luxurious festivities accompanying the circumcision of one of Muhammad Sharif's sons.[9] Whatever the exact cause of the dispute, it is clearly established that Muhammad Sharif banished Muhammad Ahmad, who was then accepted as disciple by a rival Sammaniya shaykh, al-Qurashi

[9] See Holt, *Mahdist State*, 38-40, for a treatment of the several possible causes of the dispute. R. A. Bermann, *The Mahdi of Allah* (London, 1931), 33-47, is an interesting and sympathetic attempt to recreate the atmosphere of the incident.

wad al-Zayn. When the latter—already elderly—died in 1880, Muhammad Ahmad emerged as his successor.

Undoubtedly this split with Muhammad Sharif must have had a great impact upon Muhammad Ahmad, because the presence of human failings in his master no doubt forced him to begin again his quest for religious purity and excellence. It seems reasonable to assume that had Muhammad Sharif been more ascetic and pious, Muhammad Ahmad would have satisfied his religious yearning by emulating his master within the existing Sufi tradition. On the other hand, disputes between master and disciple leading to new groupings of adherents around a rebel were hardly unusual among Sufi brotherhoods. There was nothing out of the ordinary about Muhammad Ahmad's being forced to leave his original master and join another, in a short time becoming a Sufi leader in his own right with a small devoted following.

Therefore, more than this dispute with his shaykh is needed to explain the ultimate step of announcing himself to be the expected Mahdi. (This can properly be separated from the question of why there was such an enthusiastic response to the Sudanese Mahdi, which can more adequately be explained in terms of the prevailing socioeconomic situation.) Obviously Muhammad Ahmad was a fervent, intense, totally committed religious figure. Given a different education, a happier experience with his first shaykh or a more halcyon Sudanese environment, he might well have acted out his religious commitment in personal asceticism and pietism. Quite a different set of experiences was, however, to mold his religious fervor in another fashion. Muhammad Ahmad came to feel that he had been called out to lead an errant, confused, and threatened people back to salvation. Thus, in March 1881 he confided to a few of his closest followers that he was the expected Mahdi, and three months later, in June 1881, he announced his mission openly, enjoining his followers to undertake the *hijra* (flight or emigration) to join the Mahdi.

This summons to the *hijra* marks the first step in what might best be called a reenactment of the Prophet Muhammad's role in the creation of the early Muslim community. Thus, the appeal suggested the famous *hijra* of Muhammad and his small body of followers, from an increasingly hostile Mecca to a new base of operations at Medina,[10] and the Mahdi interpreted his forced move from Aba Island to Jebel Qadir (to put some distance between himself and a central government which,

[10] The summons to the *hijra* as well as emphasis on *jihad* was equally important in the movement of 'Uthman dan Fodio and other West African Islamic reformers. See I. M. Lewis (ed.), *Islam in Tropical Africa* (London, 1966), 324-26, 412-13, 425-38.

having failed in its first attempt to arrest him, would, he presumed, surely move again) as a *hijra*.

The Sudanese Mahdi was to use other terminology borrowed from the golden age of Islam. The Prophet Muhammad had labeled those Meccans who had made the *hijra* to Medina *muhajirun* (emigrants). The Medinese followers of the Prophet were called *Ansar* (helpers). The Sudanese Mahdi used these terms as well—*muhajirun* being in this case those who had made the *hijra* with the Mahdi to Qadir as well as others such as the Baggara tribesmen who had emigrated to join him;[11] but the most common term (which has survived to this day) for describing the followers of the Mahdi was *Ansar*. Then, as events made offensive action possible, these moves were depicted as *jihad* (holy war). Muhammad Ahmad also evoked the lifetime of the Prophet and the period of the first four caliphs—the "rightly guided caliphs," a period which might aptly be called the Muslim patristic age—in asserting that he was by divine election the "successor of the Prophet of God"; his three principal subordinates were designated successors of Abu Bakr, 'Umar, and 'Ali. The fourth lieutenant in the Mahdist movement, who would have rounded out the historical parallel with the title "successor of 'Uthman," was to have been Muhammad al-Mahdi al-Sanusi, but the son of the founder of the Sanusi order rejected the invitation.

The Sudanese Mahdi also claimed to fulfill many of the signs associated with the coming of the Mahdi. He was of the family of the Prophet, his name was the same as that of the Prophet Muhammad, he possessed some of the expected physical signs such as a mole on his right cheek and the space between his two front teeth, and, when obliged to withdraw from Aba Island to Jebel Qadir, he renamed that mountain Masa in order to fulfill the prediction that the Mahdi would come from Jebel Masa. Furthermore, the Mahdist rising was co-ordinated with the beginning of the fourteenth Muslim century (1882), and it was a venerable Muslim tradition that the restorer of the faith would appear at the beginning of a new century.[12]

Muhammad Ahmad's efforts to establish a parallel between his movement and that of the golden age of early Islam, and his careful

[11] Holt, *Mahdist State*, 106.

[12] Peter M. Holt, in private correspondence with the author, has urged that not too much emphasis should be placed on Muhammad Ahmad's claims to fulfill the traditional signs. Muhammad Ahmad did evoke this argument in response to the *ulama* who used these criteria in an attempt to negate his claim. However, Holt continues, Muhammad Ahmad's major argument stressed his divine election communicated to him in colloquy with the Prophet plus the theological position that God was not constrained to follow rules laid down by men. The author would like to express his thanks to Dr. Holt for the above and the many other helpful comments he offered concerning the material in this chapter.

consideration of the traditional "signs" announcing the Mahdi's appearance serve to clarify several points about the movement. First, unlike several so-called nativistic movements studied by anthropologists, the Sudanese Mahdiya was a revolt within the framework of Islam, not a syncretistic movement which built on but nevertheless broke away from Islam. In addition, identification with primitive Islam also justified the tendency to deny most later theological tradition. When, for example, the Mahdi was asked which of the four schools of law accepted in Sunni Islam he wanted his adherents to follow, he replied that there was no longer any need for schools of law: "We have cast aside acting in accordance with schools of law and the opinion of learned men."[13] In fact, most of the learned heritage was viewed with suspicion as a defiled obstacle between the true believer and the pure religion as set out in the Qur'an and the *sunna* (tradition). Thus, it should be no surprise to learn that many standard books were repudiated and even burned in the period of the Mahdiya.

As in all such total religious challenges to the existing systems, the first mundane steps were of crucial importance. Had Muhammad Ahmad been successfully seized on Aba Island by the authorities he would have been dismissed as a harmless fanatic or even a madman. Muslim chronicles reveal a considerable number of these "false Mahdis" who, apprehended by the authorities almost as soon as they declare themselves, never again appear in the historical records.[14] A few

[13] Cited in Makki Shibayka, *Mukhtasar Tarikh al-Sudan al-Hadith* [A Short History of Islam] (Cairo, 1963), 74.

[14] For examples in the Sudan see H. A. MacMichael, *The Anglo-Egyptian Sudan* (London, 1934), 98-99, 176-79. For other parts of Islamic Africa see J. C. Froelich, *Les Musulmans d'Afrique Noire* (Paris, 1962), 200-210, Vincent Monteil, *L'Islam Noir* (Paris 1964), 294-97. As an example of how a traditional Muslim chronicler would handle the story of a "false Mahdi" let me cite a few lines from the Tunisian historian Ahmad ibn Abi Diyaf for the year 1860: "In those days there appeared in the Khumir mountains a man claiming to be from Baghdad named Muhammad ibn Abdullah, of sharifian descent. He was deluded into believing [literally: his tempter, i.e., Satan, told him] that he was the *iman*, the expected *mahdi*. Individuals from among the mountain goats [sic, i.e. those rough, hinterland folk] fell at his feet. It was like throwing straw on a lantern. It was said that he wanted to conduct Holy War in the Way of God [*al-jihad fi sabil Allah*], for a mad delusion suggested this to him." The French consul in Tunis wanted the man placed far away from the Algerian border, and—as it transpired—the Bey of Tunis wanted even more. A military expedition was immediately sent, and as the self-proclaimed Mahdi offered no resistance he was brought to Tunis and beheaded. See Ahmad ibn Abi Diyaf, *Ithaf Ahl al-Zaman bi Akhbar Muluk Tunis wa 'Ahd al-Aman* [A History of the Rulers of Tunisia, Their Contemporaries and the Fundamental Pact] (Tunis, 1964) V, 39.

Note the classic elements in this story: The man was named Muhammad ibn Abdullah (i.e. the same name as the Prophet), he was of sharifian origin, he was

early successes and a certain amount of time are needed to effect the
process in which thousands of potential adherents are swept through
the stages leading from doubt to detached interest to enthusiasm and
finally to unswerving dedication. The Sudanese Mahdi survived these
early challenges, and his first defeat—the abortive first siege of El
Obeid from September 1882 to January 1883—came late enough for an
already well established movement to absorb the blow to his power
and prestige without undue difficulty. Needless to say, when, in November 1883, the Mahdi's forces annihilated the Egyptian expeditionary army under its British commander Hicks Pasha, it became clear that
a strong, new political force had arisen in the Sudan. By this time both
the religious and worldly bases of the Mahdiya had been set. In order to
understand how and why such a movement could arise, and succeed,
there is therefore little need to trace the period from Gordon's return
to the Sudan in January 1884 until his death at the hands of the Mahdi's
forces on January 25, 1885. Nor is it necessary to deal with the early
death of the Mahdi in June 1885, his replacement by his principal
lieutenant Khalifa Abdullahi al Ta'ashi, and the relatively long period
of the Khalifa's reign until the Anglo-Egyptian reconquest of 1896–98.
Instead, having briefly sketched the rise of the Mahdiya as seen from
the career of its creator, Muhammad Ahmad al Mahdi, let us now re-
trace our steps, shifting emphasis to the Sudanese environment from
which the Mahdiya sprang.

A brief reference to early Islamic history is required properly to
distinguish the Sudan from the rest of the eastern Arab world.[15] The
Arab Muslim conquerors bursting out of the Arabian peninsula in the
seventh century managed within less than a decade to conquer all of
what now forms the Arabic-speaking world from Iraq to eastern Libya.
From that time, in spite of countless political vicissitudes, this large
region has served as the heartland of the Arabo-Islamic cultural world.
By contrast, the remainder of what is now the Arabic-speaking world
experienced a different development. The Maghrib—present-day Al-

---

calling for the *jihad*, and his would-be base of operations was a remote rural area
far away from the urban centers. Had this Tunisian "Mahdi" successfully resisted
the Bey's first military expedition a sizeable following would probably have quickly
coalesced around him; and, whatever his ultimate fate, his history would have
required more than a few lines in an Arabic chronicle.

[15] It should be pointed out that "the Sudan" is used in this chapter solely
to refer to the Eastern Sudan or roughly what is now the independent Republic
of Sudan, not to the classical "bilad-al-Sudan" of Muslim geographers—that broad
belt of Middle Africa between the Sahara and the tropical forests.

geria, Tunisia, Morocco, and Mauritania—was absorbed into the Arabo-Islamic world at a much slower pace. The process in the Sudan was slower still, being only gradually accomplished in the northern portions of the country by the steady infiltration of Arabic-speaking tribes. Effective Islamization had also been delayed; portions of the country had not begun to be absorbed into the Islamic world until the fourteenth century. Even to the present day most of the Southern Sudan lies beyond Arabism and Islam. Therefore, the Sudan of Muhammad Ahmad's time was an Islamic fringe area, just as much of the Maghrib had been a few centuries earlier and just as portions of Africa farther to the south are today. Nothing more clearly indicates the inchoate nature of Sudanese Islam at that period (and even later) than the indiscriminate manner in which the Sudanese Arabic term *faki* (corruption of the classical *faqih,* scholar or jurist) was used to label all categories of Muslim religious leaders and scholars, mystics, and saints, right down the social scale to "the ignorant hedge-priest and to the dubious dealer in charms and amulets."[16] Sudanese Islam still lacked an elaborate institutionalization and a long-standing, scholarly commitment to the Islamic learned tradition.

Nor was there a centralizing Arabic-speaking dynasty to accelerate the work of Arabization and social integration until the Egyptian conquest of the early nineteenth century.[17] But in the 1820's the Egyptian conquest of the Sudan delivered the *coup de grâce* to the important Muslim Funj dynasty. In one sense the Egyptian occupation was—to use the emotion-laden modern terminology—a form of imperialism. The conquest was brutal, its later administration was often harsh, and for most of the period its major aim was to use the Sudan in a fashion which would help the mother country, Egypt. Nevertheless, Egyptian rule also brought the Sudan within the context of a larger and more "advanced" Islamic world. The Sudan became part of a stronger, more institutionalized political unit—Egypt, itself still formally part of the Ottoman Empire. The Islamic cultural tradition—even if it had fallen upon hard days by comparison with its more illustrious past—became more readily available with the appearance of Sudanese religious judges, teachers, and administrators trained in

16 S. Hillelson, "Aspects of Muhammadanism in the Eastern Sudan," *Journal of the Royal Asiatic Society* (October 1937), 664.

17 This is not to deny that the Funj dynasty (mentioned below) did bring a certain amount of centralization. Also, although the Funj were not native Arab speakers, Arabic was the court language; and Arabization was undoubtedly facilitated during their long rule. However, the major distinction to be noted in this context is that the Sudan, alone among the countries which now form the Arab world, experienced no political absorption into a larger Arabo-Muslim unit until as late as the Egyptian occupation of the nineteenth century.

Egypt. Thereafter, a handful of Sudanese began to receive their higher education at al-Azhar in Cairo.[18] The Egyptian period also witnessed the creation of the new capital city of Khartoum at the junction of the Blue and White Niles, the inauguration of a steamer service, the introduction of the telegraph, and somewhat hesitant moves toward a more expansive trade policy. Although contemporary European observers were almost unanimously critical of Egyptian rule in the Sudan, it is nevertheless true that, seen in the broad sweep of Sudanese history, the Egyptian period brought the most effective "bureaucratic empire" the Sudan had known for centuries.

The revolutionary changes brought by Egyptian rule had an unequal impact on the several strata of Sudanese society. Many of the riverain tribes (including many people from Dongola, the Mahdi's home region) who had traditionally controlled commerce now found opportunities for expansion radically increased, and by the time of the Mahdiya a large number of these people were domiciled in the western Sudan (Kordofan and Darfur), with even more in the south. The latter were active in the slave trade, which was greatly extended by Egyptian penetration southward, and they felt economically threatened when attempts at suppression of the slave trade began in the 1860's. These riverain "frontiersmen" proved to be among the earliest and staunchest supporters of the Mahdi.

The new political and economic activities connected with Egyptian rule also produced an increased urbanism. In addition to Khartoum, there was the completely new town of Kassala, the provincial capital of al-Taka (now Kassala) province in the eastern Sudan. Other towns such as El Obeid, Suakin, Berber, and Dongola experienced appreciable increases in size and importance. On the other hand, as invariably happens in periods of radical change, certain towns increased at a slower pace or even declined. For example, Shendi on the main Nile north of Khartoum never recovered from the destruction caused by the Egyptians in 1822–23.

What was the population of these Sudanese towns during the Egyptian period? To the modern world they now appear to have been derisively small,[19] but the relative increase from what had existed be-

---

[18] These were not the first Sudanese students at al-Azhar. It had received a few Sudanese as early as the second half of the sixteenth century. See Peter M. Holt, "The Sons of Jabir and Their Kin," *Bulletin of the School of Oriental and African Studies,* XXX (1967), 150. More important than the slight increase in the number of Sudanese trained in al-Azhar following the Egyptian occupation was the capture of official religious posts by al-Azhar graduates, Egyptian and Sudanese, as a direct result of Egyptian rule (see below, 158).

[19] Contemporary estimates for the population of Khartoum at mid-century ranged from 14,000 to 52,000. In 1883 a careful observer (Colonel J. D. Stewart) estimated Khartoum's population at from 50,000 to 52,000. (Henry Russell, *The*

fore is impressive. Even if small, these towns now constituted a network of urban control over the much larger rural areas, both sedentary and nomadic—a control which readily made itself felt not only in administration and taxation, but also in commerce and education. A new class, largely foreign but with a sprinkling of Sudanese, was in charge.

The centralizing impulse of Egyptian rule also tended to distort the existing tribal and religious balances. For example, many of the Ja'aliyin, whose chief, Nimr, had assassinated Muhammad 'Ali's son, Ismail Pasha, in 1822, felt compelled to emigrate westward. Their riverain neighbors, the Shaiqiya, grew in political strength by serving as police and irregular soldiers for the Egyptian administration. The religious brotherhood of the Khatmiya under the Mirghani family cooperated with the Egyptians and achieved a marked growth in prestige and membership throughout the period. This rise in the fortunes of one brotherhood was not without its impact on others. The Majdhubiya, strong in the eastern Sudan, was among the brotherhoods most threatened by the rising fortunes of the Khatmiya. It is not surprising that its leader was soon found supporting the Mahdiya. Indeed, the greatest of the Mahdi's generals in the eastern Sudan, 'Uthman Diqna (Osman Digna), had been a member of the Majdhubiya order.

In addition to this inter-brotherhood rivalry which had been intensified by Egyptian rule, there was the incipient threat to the influence and position of all the brotherhoods with the arrival of al-Azhar-trained shaykhs to serve as judges, legal advisers, and teachers in the new administration. It has already been noted that from the advent of Egyptian rule small but increasing numbers of Sudanese began to find their way to al-Azhar for religious training. The slow intrusion of a more orthodox Islam based upon the learned tradition, as jealously guarded by the *ulama* (priestly) class, did not necessarily mean the end of Sufism and mass religious brotherhoods. There is no doubt that during this period most of the *ulama* in Egypt itself were members of religious brotherhoods. After all, the reformism of Shaykh Muhammad Abduh and the Salafiya movement with its harsh strictures against the brotherhoods was, itself, just beginning at the time of the Mahdiya. Even so, there can be little doubt that the imposition of an *ulama* class offered a clear threat to the social and political power then enjoyed by the leadership of the several brotherhoods in the Sudan.

A final point of considerable importance about the impact of Egyptian rule on the Sudan in its relationship to the rise of the Mah-

---

Ruin of the Soudan [London, 1892], 16.) Suakin, the major port on the Red Sea, had perhaps 8,000. Almost certainly, the few other important towns such as Shendi and El Obeid were even smaller.

diya is that in the ten to fifteen years before 1881 Egyptian power was declining. A brief reference to events in Egypt proper should make this clear. The advent of a dynamic but rash Westernizer, Ismail, marked an activist policy of economic buildup at home and attempts at expansion abroad (penetration into the Southern Sudan and the abortive campaign against Ethiopia), but this policy was financed by a vicious cycle of foreign loans with increasingly onerous terms. As a result Egypt was soon plunged into bankruptcy, European financial control (from 1876), and, finally, outright European control in the form of British occupation beginning in 1882. Ismail's laudable attempts to curb the slave trade had also induced him to appoint an increasing number of Europeans, and even a few Americans, as officials in the Sudan.[20]

The net result of all these policies for the Sudan was a growing imbalance between ambitious policies and the ability to perform. By 1882 the Egyptian hold over the country had been greatly weakened. Morale was undermined, pay often in arrears, efforts against the slave trade had been sufficient to disrupt and divert but not to destroy. In such a political climate the nomadic and semi-nomadic populations remotest from central control, and chafing under restraints imposed by Egyptian rule, began to sniff the telltale signs of *ma fish hukuma* (there is no government); the sedentary population began to wonder uneasily if the government would be able to mantain at least minimal public security—the implicit quid pro quo making even extortionate taxation bearable; certain groups began to hedge on their embarrassingly strong commitments to the regime; and other groups, bearing old grudges, waited for the time to strike.

The analysis above suggests that no monocausal theory will adequately reflect the complex totality out of which the Mahdiya arose. Embittered and resentful slave traders, tribal and brotherhood rivalries, a confused combination of new emerging classes and of old declining groups—all these played an important role in a movement which, itself, was strongly marked and shaped by the venerable Sunni Muslim tradition of Mahdism. No neat, simple theory will suffice, but on the other hand there are several historical patterns with which the Sudanese Mahdiya can claim affiliation. It is important to select the most satisfactory. This chapter began by placing the Mahdiya squarely within

[20] The European governors in the Sudan included Gordon, Governor of Equatoria Province and then Governor General of the Sudan during the years 1874–79, Romolo Gessi, Emin Pasha (Eduard Schnitzer), and Slatin Pasha, to name only the more illustrious.

the Semitic messianic tradition, but it was suggested that such a category was too broad to offer an adequate explanation. The Mahdiya might also be viewed as one of several traditionalist Islamic reactions to the impact of the Western world in modern times, for much that Egypt attempted to implement in the Sudan could be interpreted as surrogate Westernization. This view, quite useful up to a point, has certain disadvantages. It tends to exaggerate the importance of the Western impact as the dynamic factor and to discount the possibility of explaining the movement by reference to past Islamic history. A similar reservation should be entered regarding any attempt to depict the Mahdiya as an example of a traditional religious response by *any* premodern society (that is, characterized by near-subsistence economy, diffused political power, ascriptive social organization, and a single ethico-religious belief system—inflexible and theocentric—embracing all aspects of human behavior) to a body of challenges represented by the West. Such an approach would concentrate attention on its comparability with several other African movements being studied in this book, but, like the general Semitic messianic tradition, it is too broad a category. It would also squeeze out of proper perspective the extent to which Islam was an essential element in shaping the course of the Mahdiya.

What then of the possibility suggested in this chapter—the Sudanese Mahdiya as a socio-religious movement typical of the Islamic fringe areas in Africa? Such a theory could give the Islamic tradition its full importance. Further, by insisting on the importance of an historical *pattern* (which is to say, a variant on previous experience) there would be less chance of exaggerating the role of intrusive new factors. Without in any way overlooking new elements in the specific period of Sudanese history under consideration, one could avoid the anachronistic and illogical trap of pre-emptorily seeing the Mahdiya solely as another example of a general phenomenon, that is, the last-ditch fight of the pre-modern opposed to the modern world, or any similar moderno-centric fallacy.[21]

The historical pattern which perhaps best embraces and clarifies the Sudanese Mahdiya possesses the following major characteristics: It occurs on an Islamic fringe area which can be identified in two complementary senses. The Islamic fringe is, on the one hand, a phys-

---

[21] This unlovely neologism is intended to call attention to the following argument: Most present-day scholarship has overcome the unconscious implicit assumptions of ethno-centrism, but there is a danger now of exaggerating the similarity of men's problems and range of choices in the present age. People still are different, possessing differences which have been developed and are continually being modified according to the unique history of each society or culture.

ical border—the outer limits of *dar al Islam* beyond which lies the non-Muslim *dar al harb*. At the same time the fringe area is less fully integrated into the high Islamic tradition. The juxtaposition of Islamic and non-Islamic beliefs and values still prevails. The transitional nature of Islamization is usually to be explained by a variety of factors, including time (Islam introduced relatively recently into the area), intensity (the mode of introduction being often via a slow penetration of merchants and isolated groups or, at most, a military conquest leaving in its wake only a superficial political control system), and a low proportion of urban, or in some cases even of sedentary, population. This latter point calls attention to an important fact: Without a network of cities the fundamental educational and economic infrastructure creating and sustaining an *ulama* class is lacking. The Islamic fringe area is also, from the perspective of the urbanized Islamic high culture, an uncouth hinterland, a frontier.

The frontier motif suggests the next major characteristic of the Islamic fringe messianic movements: They usually partake of conflict, pitting the hinterland against the cosmopolitan centers. This is not to suggest a pattern of religiously led jacqueries. Nor would a Marxian framework positing non-urban groupings resisting more effective integration into larger economic units controlled from the cities offer an adequate description, although it would be quite useful up to a point. The underlying socio-economic tension in the Islamic fringe area is better depicted in political terms. These areas possess pockets of sedentaries, transhumants, nomads, and, often, mountaineers. Tribal organization is still intact. A considerable diffusion of political power is the norm, and at best the governments of the cites have made only tentative moves toward political centralization. In this situation of inchoate state structure and uncertain political stability the Marxian quest to isolate the progressive forces appears especially irrelevant. More important is the manner in which challenge to the existing power of the cities is mounted from the rude hinterland base. The townfolk and the sedentary agriculturalists closely tied to the towns, fearing anarchy most of all, adopt a wait-and-see policy. Then they come over en masse when the new challenger appears as the best candidate to restore order. Yet, the ultimate goal of the movement which appears to be directed against the towns, relying as it does upon forces of the hinterland seizing the opportunity to reassert their complete autonomy, is to create an even more effective centralization directed from the city. In all cases, the leaders of the movements are themselves products of the sedentary regions closest in touch with the Islamic high cultural tradition.

The historical pattern also reveals revolts conducted in the name of Islam. They may be heretical or schismatic, but these movements always ensure that the socio-political and ideological conflict be within an Islamic framework. As a result, the particularistic tendencies which are undoubtedly represented in these movements—indeed in pure material terms these tendencies dominate—are kept under control, and syncretist new religions do not result. Instead, the ultimate result is to facilitate the process of integration into Sunni Islam of the high cultural tradition, because the heretical or schismatic nature of these movements is evanescent and the Islamic context in which they are presented results in a net increase in Islamization.

The classic examples of messianic movements on the Islamic fringe of Africa are the rise of the Fatimids and the Almohades in North Africa. In general Islamic history the Fatimid dynasty is connected with Egypt, the founding of Cairo, and the great challenge which an aggressive Shi'ism posed for Sunni Islam. Quite a different picture emerges, however, when attention is directed to that area in North Africa where the Fatimids got their start as a political power, for the missionaries from the Middle East preaching the revolutionary Fatimid ideology (itself a product of the social and theological struggles growing out of the urban-based Islamic high culture) in North Africa did not gather converts in the cities or sedentary area of Ifriqiya (roughly modern Tunisia). Instead the Fatimid missionaries relied on the Kutama Berbers from the Lesser Kabylia, that rugged mountainous region lying within the triangle bounded by Djidjelli, Setif, and Constantine in Algeria. The Lesser Kabylia was only partially Islamized in the latter years of the ninth century when Abu Abdullah al Shi'i began his propaganda work there in the name of the Mahdi who was to come. Equally important, the Lesser Kabylia had never been brought under the political control of the city-based Muslim dynasties. The Aghlabids ruling from Kairouan had never attempted more than a policy of keeping this area under surveillance. In regional terms, the Fatimid revolt was a successful political challenge by the Islamic fringe area against the existing government of the cities. Yet the ideology for which they fought was universal and centralizing in its aims, and nothing was more normal than for the victorious Fatimids to move into the cities and work for a more effective political unification.

The Fatimids remained "Eastern" in leadership and outlook, and after a successful military campaign, the dynasty moved its political base to Egypt—establishing the new capital of Cairo in A.D. 969. Ifriqiya soon reverted to a staunch Sunni Islam and, in a sense, it might appear that the Fatimid period in North Africa left no lasting imprint. However, there can be little doubt that the imposing socio-political upheaval occasioned by the Fatimid period in North Africa had advanced the frontiers of effective Islamization. The Kutama and the other quondam supporters of the Fatimids did not remain Shi'i sectarians, but they did emerge from the experience more effectively integrated into Muslim culture.

The Fatimids had been a Mahdist movement. The first ruler, Ubaydallah, had assumed the title Mahdi and, as the name (from Fatima, the daughter of the Prophet) implies, the dynasty claimed descent from Muhammad. Emphasis was placed upon the Mahdi's possession of esoteric knowledge and power, and blind obedience was enjoined. In other respects, however, the Fatimid movement represents an intermediate stage between Mahdism as a political ideology and Mahdism as a puritanical, apocalyptical, and millenarian movement.[22] The full flowering of Mahdism as later seen in the Sudanese Mahdi is connected with the Almohades. Here again the historical pattern suggested above is clearly in evidence.

The man later to become the Mahdi of the Almohades, Ibn Tumart, was born some time between 1077 and 1087 in a small mountain town of the Anti-Atlas in southwestern Morocco. The many similarities between his life and activities and those of the Sudanese Mahdi a full eight centuries later are striking. Ibn Tumart was born into a family known for its piety. He himself was from an early age fully absorbed in religious studies. After a period of travels to further his religious education in Muslim Spain and the Middle East he returned to North Africa, and, as he made his way westward toward Morocco, he soon gained a reputation as a stern, censorious puritan. The Muslim chronicles are filled with references to his breaking musical instruments and wine jars and publicly rebuking highly placed officials for alleged religious laxity—often at the risk of his imprisonment or banishment. Near Bougie the famous meeting took place between Ibn Tumart and the man who was to become *caliph* (successor), Abd al-Mu'min. This famous warrior/administrator was to do for the Almohade movement what Abdullahi al Ta'aishi did for the Mahdiya. Abd al-Mu'min, at the time of his encounter with Ibn Tumart, was bound for the East seeking religious training; but when Ibn Tumart saw him he immediately recognized him as his chosen successor, and exclaimed, "The knowledge which you are seeking in the East is here. You have found it in the Maghrib."[23]

[22] See D. S. Margoliouth, "On Mahdis and Mahdism," *Proceedings of the British Academy* (1915–16), 213-33.

[23] Cited in E. Levi-Provençal, *Islam d'Occident; Études d'Histoire Médiévale* (Paris, 1948), 279. Abdullahi had also been a "seeker" before becoming converted to the message of the Sudanese Mahdi. In 1873 Abdullahi had written to Zubayr Pasha, "I saw in a dream that you are the Expected Mahdi and I am one of your followers; so tell me if you are the Mahdi of the Age, that I may follow you." Cited in Holt, *Mahdist State*, 44.

Later, still with only a handful of faithful disciples, Ibn Tumart arrived in Marrakech, the capital of the reigning Almoravid dynasty, where he sought to gain acceptance of his rigid puritanical ideas. Soon he realized that his stern preachings had placed him in some peril in Marrakech, and he retreated to his mountainous home in the Anti-Atlas. There the religious reformer took the ultimate step and declared himself to be the Mahdi. Again the pattern of conscious imitation of the Prophet's life is evident. His retreat into the mountains was deemed a *hijra* and those accompanying him were *muhajirun*. The term *Ansar* was also employed, and his later struggle to overthrow the Almoravid dynasty was depicted as a *jihad*.

At the same time it should be noted that the mundane base of the Almohades was tribal—the Masmuda Berbers, a hinterland mountain folk, were challenging the dynasty and the cities of the plains. Once victorious, however, these mountaineers moved to the cities and eventually established North Africa's most extensive empire.

Again, as with the Fatimids, superficial evidence might seem to suggest that nothing survived the Almohade experience. North Africa rejected the theological doctrines of Ibn Tumart, even in the mountain capital. "Ibn Tumart's grave still exists in Timmel, but his name and history is utterly forgotten."[24] In fact, the Almohade dynasty not only left behind a legacy of a political structure destined to survive in part until early modern times (and, it might be argued, even longer in Morocco proper), it also advanced the effective Islamization of North Africa's remotest regions.[25]

The Fatimids, the Almohades, and the Sudanese Mahdiya constitute the three major examples of a Mahdist movement in the suggested historical pattern. However, in socio-political terms the emergence of a self-declared Mahdi represents merely the ultimate step taken by certain puritanical protest movements. As Goldziher noted concerning Ibn Tumart, "the *mahdi* represents the summum of action to be taken to correct what is wrong in this world . . . It is the supreme application of the Muslim community's mission to 'command the good and prohibit the bad.' "[26]

A number of intense, puritanical Muslim reformers stopped short

[24] René Basset, "Ibn Tumart," *Encyclopedia of Islam*, II (London, 1927), 425-27.

[25] For example, it is related that Ibn Tumart taught his unlettered Berbers the *fatiha* (the prayer which constitutes the first chapter of the Qur'an) by giving each of them an Arabic name consisting of words from the *fatiha*. Then, by lining up in the proper order, the result of each giving his Arabic name would be a recitation of the entire Qur'anic chapter.

[26] I. Goldziher, *Le Livre de Mohammad ibn Tumart, Mahdi des Almohadès* (Algiers, 1903), 99.

of this ultimate step of declaring themselves to be the Mahdi, but in most other ways the movements that these reformers created also conformed to a historical pattern characteristic of the Islamic fringe area in Africa. In this sense attention should be called to the Kharijite activities in eighth-century North Africa, the nomadic-based Almoravid dynasty which sprang up in the eleventh century in the western Saharan region dividing North Africa from West Africa, the *chorfa* movements of sixteenth-century Morocco (properly *shurafa*—those claiming to be descendents of the Prophet Muhammad), and the reformist agitation of 'Uthman dan Fodio and later al hajj Umar in West Africa during the period extending from the late eighteenth century until the late nineteenth century. All of these, in spite of considerable differences in doctrine, are similar to each other and at the same time closely related to the three Mahdist movements cited. They were all rigidly puritanical, reformist movements relying on an essentially tribal base for major support and involving a challenge by the hinterland regions to the governments of the cities. All emphasized *jihad* even, in most cases, against nominal Muslims. Yet at the same time, in spite of the particularist nature of their mass support, all these movements extended acculturation into the high cultural tradition of Sunni Islam, just as in most cases they encouraged political centralization.[27]

These are the more important examples which could be cited to justify the idea that there is a historical pattern of puritanical Muslim protest on the Islamic fringe areas of Africa. From what has been said earlier it should already be clear how completely the Sudanese Mahdiya fits into such a pattern. First, there can be little doubt that the Sudan in the period of the Mahdiya fits the dual definition of an Islamic fringe area. By comparison with Egypt and the Middle Eastern heartland of Muslim culture, the Sudan was still very much in the process of being effectively integrated into the high cultural tradition. And there can be no doubt that the geographical border dividing Muslims from non-Muslims runs through the Sudan. The importance of the pastoral Baggara tribe as the military backbone of the Mahdist movement can hardly be overlooked, and there is considerable evidence that the Mahdiya was in many ways a revolt of the hinterland against the political control of the cities and their satellite, settled areas. For example, the first major defeat of the Mahdi's forces was

[27] This can only be a tentative list, subject to additions and corrections in view of the present rudimentary state of research for much of Islamic Africa. For example, can the movement sparked by al hajj Umar be deemed to involve in any significant degree action of the hinterland against the government of the cities? Perhaps not, but certainly he and his following conform to the pattern in other respects. Also, should the "Mad Mullah" of Somalia be included?

their failure to capture the fortified city of El Obeid. A contemporary European scholar summed up the Mahdi's military posture: "His strategy is elementary, but it is that which the country requires: no assaults on fortified towns, which are merely to be surrounded until famine opens their gates; no great battles, but a constant harassing of the enemy, surrounding him from a distance, then when he is exhausted, swooping down on him with all forces united to make an end of the affair."[28] The tribal and hinterland base of the Mahdi's support clarifies the tactics which led to the crushing defeat of Hicks Pasha and his army, the long siege of Khartoum, and the inability of 'Uthman Diqna, one of the Mahdiya's best generals, to capture Suakin on the Red Sea. A description of the siege of Khartoum, based on the account of four Christian prisoners of the Mahdi, appeared in the London *Standard* of March 4, 1885. The article contained the following revealing passage:

> The number of fighting men congregated before Khartoum seems to have been very fluctuating, sinking sometimes to seven or eight thousand, and again rising to forty and fifty thousand, according to the seasons and the requirements of agricultural pursuits, as no impediment was ever placed in the way of their going off, sometimes for weeks together—the fellaheen to look after their crops and harvests, the bedouins to graze their camels, and their flocks and herds. When in camp their time was wholly devoted to prayers, recitations from the Koran, and sham fights, often on a large scale. The actual number of properly drilled and disciplined troops, chiefly blacks from El-Obeid, was relatively small, nor did they seem to be implicitly trusted by the *Mahdi*. On the other hand, the enthusiasm of the Dervishes, as the *Mahdi's* true followers are styled, appeared to be wrought up to the highest pitch by the Prophet's fervent preachings, and to be in no way abated by the repeated checks they experienced before Omdurman.[29]

Yet, as the later history of the Khalifa's rule makes quite clear, the ultimate victors were not the forces of tribalism and particularism. The Mahdist state of Khalifa Abdullahi represented an effort at more effective centralization. Even in the time of the Mahdi himself, something approaching a regular army and bureaucracy began to emerge.[30]

[28] James Darmesteter, *The Mahdi Past and Present* (New York, 1885), 65-66. Darmesteter's book reveals occasional excellent insights, but the general tone is that of an arrogantly biased denigration of Islam and Muslim culture.

[29] Cited in Darmesteter, *The Mahdi*, 117.

[30] Holt has called the author's attention to a detailed study of the organization and practice of the Mahdist chancery by Abu-Selim (unpublished Ph.D. dissertation, "Majmū'at al-Nujūmī" [The Letter-book of al-Nujūmī], Khartoum, 1967). It is to be hoped that Dr. Abu-Selim's work on this important subject will become available in published form.

Evidence of the long-term more effective Islamization set in motion by the Sudanese Mahdiya is to be found today in the Sudan. Certainly, if the period of the Anglo-Egyptian Condominium involved in one sense a reaction against the Mahdiya, it was in no way a reaction against Islam. Instead, just as has been the case with modern Western colonialism in other Muslim countries, great strides were made in integrating the Sudan into the Sunni high cultural tradition. The forces of the Mahdiya also survived, and the posthumous son of Muhammad Ahmad al Mahdi, Sayyid Abd al Rahman, became the leader of a major nationalist grouping—the Umma party. In 1966–1967 a great-grandson of the Sudanese Mahdi was Prime Minister of the independent Sudan. There is little doubt that the political power of the Mahdi's descendants is based in large measure upon the continued veneration felt for this family by the descendants of the original *Ansar*. Yet, there already is considerable evidence to suggest that the religious followers of the Mahdi's descendants are merging imperceptibly into the greater Sunni community. Already, the *Ansar* are for all practical purposes equivalent to a religious brotherhood living in harmony with other brotherhoods, all within the framework of Sunni Islam. In the long run the *Ansar,* like the Khatmiya and other brotherhoods, may well fade away or split into other groupings, but it is already clear that one result of their appearance will be a more effective Islamization.

It has been suggested in this chapter that the Sudanese Mahdiya can best be understood by reference to the historical pattern of puritanical Muslim protest movements on the Islamic fringe areas of Africa. A few reasons why it is preferable to place the Sudanese Mahdiya in *this* historical pattern as opposed to others which might claim serious consideration have also been mentioned. However, it can properly be asked if the entire approach—that of seeking the most appropriate historical pattern—has any special value to recommend it over other possible methods of analysis and interpretation.

First, it must be admitted that a correct classification of phenomena into a historical pattern, in and of itself, merely offers somewhat greater order to a welter of data. The question remains whether the historical pattern can do more. Does it offer useful insights helping to explain some of the major problems facing historians of the Sudan as well as other parts of Africa? Quite possibly it does. For example, the historical pattern indicates that these protest movements, in spite of their particularist base, move along certain channels and provoke a body of reactions, all of which in the long run serve to advance Islamization in the area concerned. The same pattern does not seem to prevail with non-Islamic protest movements of a religious nature in Africa. A careful study of these movements can help to clarify the question of how Islam has spread—and is spreading—in Africa. Of course, one would want to push even farther in seeking the elusive "why." One would want to know why a certain pattern of social activities in an Islamic framework would have coalescent tendencies whereas approximately the same social activities in another cultural tradition might prove disruptive. There will be no easy answer to this question but it does at least underline the importance of Islam in African history.

According to the historical pattern a Mahdist movement (or a movement similar in every other way except that the leader stops short of declaring himself to be the Mahdi) occurs only given certain social situations. This would include a genuine difference in way of life between the hinterland and the urban areas, an incomplete political control over the entire country by the central government, a low level of economic integration, and several other factors usually associated with traditional or premodern societies. This suggests that the historical pattern of Mahdism as described in this chapter is to be found only in traditional or transitional Muslim societies in Africa. To the extent that Muslim societies in Africa achieve a certain level of political, social, and economic integration—that is, the process of "development" or "modernization"—movements such as the Sudanese Mahdiya will become increasingly unlikely.

More important for the future, however, it is clear that the Sudan —and other parts of Muslim Africa—will not move from one hermetically sealed epoch called "transitional" to another called "modern." Nor will these societies by becoming "modern" move into an earthly paradise where there is no need for patterns of social protest. Instead, new patterns of protest will evolve in response to new situations, and, if the work of previous historians and sociologists has any value, it can be predicted that there will be a certain lag between the changing situation and the institutionalized pattern of responses. The venerable historical pattern of puritanical Muslim protest movements on the Islamic fringe areas of Africa will still be an essential point of departure for the scholar attempting to assess the nature and direction of new traditions of protest in the several parts of Muslim Africa.

BAI BUREH AND THE SIERRA

LEONE HUT TAX WAR OF 1898

LA RAY DENZER AND MICHAEL CROWDER

In the early months of 1898 there was a general uprising against British rule in Sierra Leone. This was less than two years after the imposition of a British Protectorate over the hinterland of Freetown, the capital of the Sierra Leone colony. Sparked by the imposition of a hut tax in three of the five districts into which the Protectorate had been divided, the Hut Tax Wars, as they came to be known, were more than just a protest against a particularly obnoxious feature of colonial rule. They were rather a manifestation of African resentment against alien rule and of a "desire of independence," as Governor Frederick Cardew himself admitted to Joseph Chamberlain, Secretary of State

Research for this paper was carried out while Professor Crowder was Director of the Institute of African Studies, Fourah Bay College, University of Sierra Leone, and Miss Denzer was his Research Assistant. Research in the Sierra Leone Archives was conducted by Miss Denzer. Research in the Public Record Office, London, the National Archives of Senegal and the British Museum newspaper holdings at Colindale was conducted by Professor Crowder. The co-authors are grateful to the College and the Institute for the facilities which made research for this paper possible.

Archives sources:

ADCMP	Aborigines Department Confidential Minute Papers
ADLB	Aborigines Department Letter Book
ADMP	Aborigines Department Minute Papers
CO	Colonial Office
ECM	Executive Council Minutes
GCDSS	Governor's Confidential Despatches to the Secretary of State for the Colonies

for the Colonies, on 10 May 1898.[1] A few days earlier, Chamberlain had told the House of Commons that he no longer believed that the wars were due to the hut tax but that they were "a general rising against white rule."[2]

The wars themselves consisted of two separate but related risings: that of the Temne in the north, which broke out toward the end of February 1898; and that of the Mende and neighboring groups in the south, which broke out at the end of April. The Temne rising was under the leadership of an individual, Bai Bureh of Kasseh; that of the Mende was inspired and co-ordinated by a secret society, the Poro. Although the Temne restricted themselves to fighting the British forces and, with one notable exception, did not kill missionaries and traders, the Mende attacked every vestige of alien rule, murdering not only Europeans but also Africans dressed in European clothes. However, the underlying causes of the two risings were the same. And it seems fairly clear that Bai Bureh's highly successful stand against the British in the first two months of his war was an inspiration to the Mende.[3]

Bai Bureh's war against the British is the focus of this paper: why did he rise against them? Many of the reasons will apply equally to the Mende war. We shall then turn to Bai Bureh's career, starting with his early years as a war chief, when he acquired the military skills which he later used to such good effect against the British that it took them nearly ten months to defeat him. His career as chief of Kasseh follows: this brought him into direct involvement with the British administration of the Sierra Leone colony. Finally, we shall examine his war with the British, which, given the small size of his chiefdom and the limited forces at his disposal, was one of the most

GDSS	Governor's Despatches to the Secretary of State for the Colonies
GLLB	Governor's Local Letter Book
NACMP	Native Affairs Confidential Minute Papers
NALB	Native Affairs Letter Book
NAS	National Archives of Senegal
PRO	Public Record Office
SLA	Sierra Leone Archives

Journals:

| JAH | Journal of African History |
| SLS | Sierra Leone Studies |

[1] PRO, CO/267/438: Telegram of 10 May 1898, Governor to the Secretary of State.

[2] *Hansard,* 4th Series, LVII, 5 May 1898.

[3] Cardew made this point in various dispatches, both confidential and ordinary. Many of the witnesses whom Sir Donald Chalmers called before his Commission of Enquiry agreed.

brilliant campaigns conducted by an African leader against European forces.

The Building Up of Resentment

Britain had been established in Freetown since 1787. In 1895 it had concluded a treaty with France delimiting respective spheres of influence in the area. In 1896 Britain proclaimed a protectorate over the city's hinterland. Although the appointment of two traveling commissioners in 1890 had extended Freetown's influence over its hinterland considerably, in 1896 Britain exerted a strong, effective influence only upon chiefdoms near the colony, but very little on those distant from it.[4]

Authority over those chiefs who had entered into treaty relationship with the British was buttressed by the establishment of a paramilitary force known as the Frontier Police, stationed in various hinterland chiefdoms. The main functions of these police were to patrol the roads and to ensure free passage on them, to prevent traders from being molested, and, where possible, to avert the outbreak of war in those districts to which they were posted. But they were given no authority to interfere in the governments of the chiefs in whose areas they were stationed.

When the Protectorate was declared in October 1896, some chiefs had already made treaties of cession to the British Crown, some had agreed to British arbitration of their disputes with their neighbors. However, some chiefs who had made no treaties whatsoever with the British were also brought under British rule at this time. And those who had made treaties had certainly not envisaged the alienation of their sovereignty to a foreign power. They had agreed only to certain limitations on it.

Nevertheless, the declaration of the Protectorate unequivocally vested sovereignty in the British authorities in Freetown. The District Commissioners were given extensive judicial powers which seriously curtailed the judicial authority traditionally held by the chiefs.[5] They

---

[4] Parliamentary Papers 1899, LX, *Report . . . on . . . the Insurrection in the Sierra Leone Protectorate* (Chalmers Report), I, 11.

[5] The judicial powers delegated to the District Commissioners included: (1) trying all civil cases involving non-natives; (2) trying all land cases; (3) trying all criminal cases involving non-natives; (4) trying all cases of pretended witchcraft, faction or tribal fights, slave raiding or slave dealing; and (5) trying all cases of murder, rape, cannibalism, or offenses connected with Human Leopard or Alligator societies. For further explanation, see J. D. Hargreaves, "The Establishment of the Sierra Leone Protectorate and the Insurrection of 1898," *Cambridge Historical Journal*, XII (1956), 63-64.

could also direct arbitrary settlement of any question likely to cause a breach of the peace, even if it concerned local law and custom. The slave trade was abolished, and domestic slaves were free to leave their masters if they wished. For the chiefs, the Protectorate entailed not only the acceptance of the British District Commissioners, who were mainly young and inexperienced officers who interfered in every aspect of their administration, but it also contained provisions for the collection of taxes to support them, Governor Cardew having decided that the chiefs and people must help pay for their administration; this was done through a tax of 5/- a year for two-room houses and 10/- a year for larger houses. The tax became known as the "hut tax" since most of the houses in the Protectorate were huts. Collection was to begin on 1 January 1898 in the three districts of Ronietta, Bandajuma, and Karene (in which Kasseh lay).

In March 1897, Cardew wrote to the Secretary of State:

> The Protectorate Ordinance as far as I can ascertain is working smoothly and the authority and jurisdiction of the District Commissioner is being felt and accepted. I gather this from unofficial as well as official sources, but of course the crucial time will be when the house-tax is levied but with an adequate police-force and a sufficient complement of white officers I have no apprehensions as to the results.[6]

This optimistic assessment of the situation in the Protectorate was confounded less than a year later when the peoples of the Protectorate rose up in protest against the introduction of the hut tax in particular and the British administration in general.

At the beginning of hostilities, both the local administrators and the Colonial Office believed that the primary cause of the war was the imposition of the hut tax. Direct taxation by the colonial administration in any form had already proved itself very unpopular in Sierra Leone. In 1872, Governor John Pope Hennessey had made himself the best loved Governor in Sierra Leone's history by abolishing the house tax in the colony. "Today," he wrote to Sir Hercules Robinson of the Colonial Office, "I am the victim of popular ovations, bands, processions, religious services, public dinners and illuminations."[7] In the Gold Coast, direct taxation had led to riots. In neighboring Guinée, French attempts to collect tax in the Conakry region had met with resistance, which had only been overcome by "incarcerating the chiefs until their people had collected sufficient produce to meet half the

---

[6] SLA/GCDSS, 18/97: Governor to Secretary of State, 23 Mar. 1897.

[7] Cited in James Pope-Hennessey, *Verandah* (London, 1964), 143.

amount of the tax due."[8] To explain his ordinance and the tax, Cardew undertook three series of tours upcountry; these took place in 1894, 1895, and 1896. His tour in 1896 took him through the Karene district. At no meeting did the chiefs make any comment on the ordinance. To Cardew this meant acceptance, even if passive. However, Parkes, his shrewd Creole Secretary of Native Affairs, warned that from what he knew of the people, such passivity meant that "they would not consent."[9]

That Parkes was correct in his assessment became clear when, in mid-December 1896, a number of Temne chiefs including Bai Bureh, wrote to Captain Wilfred Stanley Sharpe, who had just assumed duties as District Commissioner for Karene. They complained generally about the new administration. Then, protesting their friendship for the Queen, they begged the District Commissioner "to tell the Governor that we are not able to observe the new laws and to pay house taxes."[10]

Later, in June 1897, while Cardew was on leave, a group of influential Temne chiefs who had been invited to Freetown for the Jubilee celebrations took this occasion to draw up a petition to the acting Governor. In it they expressed fears concerning their own status, judicial powers, and lands. They also asked for relief from the hut tax.[11] Neither this petition nor the earlier letter had much impact on the administration. Only Parkes, long associated with the chiefs, perceived that their grievances were such that "if it is decided to collect the hut tax during the coming dry season, considerable tact and patience will have to be exercised by the collectors in order not to alienate the loyalty and confidence of the natives concerned."[12]

However, Cardew did not relent in his intention to collect the tax,

[8] SLA/GCDSS, 10/98: Governor to the Secretary of State, 25 Feb. 1898. The French, however, were to contrast their collection of the hut tax favorably with that of the British. For instance, *Le Temps* of 13 May 1898, quoted in the *Daily Graphic* (London) of 14 May 1898, crowed: "We levy in French Guinea, as well as in our other West African colonies, a tax which has analogies with the English hut tax which has provoked the rising in the British possessions in Sierra Leone. But with us the tax is not oppressive, and its collection is made easier under such conditions that it has never excited discontent among the natives of our territories." (Translation in the *Daily Graphic*.)

[9] Evidence of J. C. E. Parkes, Chalmers Report, II, par. 850.

[10] Appendix XIV, Letter from Timini chiefs to Capt. Sharpe, 17 Dec. 1896, Chalmers Report, I: the signers of this letter were the following: Alikalie Morribah of Port Loko, Bai Foki of Mafokki, Bai Farima of Saffrako, Bai Kanarie of Tinkotupa, Bai Shakka of Dibia District, and Bai Bureh of Kasseh District.

[11] Hargreaves, "Establishment of Sierra Leone Protectorate," 66.

[12] SLA/NALB, 211/97: Parkes to Col. Sec., 14 Sept. 1897.

even though the Temne petitioners waited in Freetown for two months until his return in September so that they could present their grievances to him personally. He did concede that "it was desirable to grant considerable exemptions in view of the circumstances that next year would be the first year of its imposition, that natives were unaccustomed to be directly taxed by the government and that under the hope that their petitions against it might be entertained by [the Secretary of State] they had probably made no provision for its payment."[13] Therefore, the tax was made a uniform one of 5/- for all houses irrespective of size. The other grievances of the chiefs, except those concerning their authority in land disputes in their own territories, Cardew dismissed as unfounded and the result of gross misrepresentation as to the nature of the Protectorate Ordinance. He seems to have been blithely unaware of the seriousness of the situation created by his determination to collect the hut tax and his reluctance to change any part of the Protectorate Ordinance despite the numerous complaints presented to him about it. Joseph Chamberlain was to note a year later that "although I have supported Sir J. Cardew throughout I am a little afraid that he is inclined to be hard on the Natives and does not take sufficient pains to ascertain their views and to remove their suspicions."[14]

How gravely Cardew had misassessed the situation was brought out by his dispatch to Chamberlain of 8 October 1897:

> I do not apprehend that the chiefs will combine to forcibly resist the collection of the tax, for they lack cohesion and powers of organization, and there are too many jealousies between them for concerted action, but there may be isolated acts on the parts of some chiefs and their followers of forcible resistance to the tax which might spread to other tribes if not promptly suppressed by the Police. . . .[15]

Within six months a large part of the Protectorate had risen against the British.

As the war progressed, it became increasingly clear that the hut tax was only one of many causes of the rebellion, even though its collection had undoubtedly set it off. It is not even clear whether the tax as such involved real financial hardship for the people. The Temne chiefs in their petition had complained that prevailing prices for the produce of the Protectorate were exceptionally low, and Parkes him-

[13] SLA/GCDSS, 49/97: Gov. to Sec. of State, 8 Oct. 1897.

[14] PRO, CO/267/440: minute by Chamberlain of 9 Nov. 1898 on Sierra Leone Conf. Desp. 81, 13 Oct. 1898.

[15] SLA/GCDSS, 49/97: Gov. to Sec. of State, 8 Oct. 1897.

self confirmed this assertion.[16] They had also complained of the difficulty of obtaining labor for their farms; if they worked their domestic
slaves too hard, they could run away and obtain their freedom from
the British. The acting chief of Port Loko had protested to the District Commissioner at Karene that it would be hard to pay the tax:
"They were not allowed to buy and sell slaves as they did nine years
ago. There were no gold-mines, no quantity of palm-kernels or rice;
they could only just get their livelihood."[17] In the Colonial Office consideration was given to reducing the tax on the grounds that the people might be prepared to pay a lower one.[18]

Cardew, however, was able to marshal evidence from both official
and unofficial sources in support of his contention that the level of the
tax was not too high.[19] The Rev. J. A. L. Price, an American Negro
missionary who was the Secretary of the American Soudan Mission,
wrote Cardew that he did not think that the hut tax was "exorbitant
or oppressive."[20] Methods of collection rather than the tax itself were
put forward as the real cause of resentment. There were many allegations that brutality was generally used. The District Commissioner of
Karene dismissed such accusations preemptorily.[21] In fact officials had
received special instructions that nothing was to be done which might
irritate or hurt the people's feelings.[22] However, the Chalmers Commission of Enquiry which investigated the war proved that the arrogant behavior of the police and the misuse of their prerogatives had
long been a source of grievance to the people and chiefs of the Protectorate.[23]

It does not seem that direct taxation was repugnant to custom,
for chiefs throughout Sierra Leone were in the habit of imposing levies
on their people. However, the notion that people should pay a "rent"

[16] SLA/NALB, 211/97: Parkes to Col. Sec., 14 Sept. 1897.

[17] Evidence of Mala, the spokesman of the sons of the Port Loko chiefs who
were detained by the government in 1898, Chalmers Report, II, par. 1653.

[18] PRO, CO/267/437: minute of W. A. Mercer on Gov.'s telegram to the
Sec. of State, 5 Mar. 1898.

[19] The District Commissioner of Karene wrote him that it was certainly not
excessive: "A person only has to bring in a hamper of rice, half a dozen pineapples, yams, Kassada, firewood, etc., and a year's payment of tax is easily secured." SLA/CMP, 102-Enc./98, District Commissioner (Karene) to Col. Sec.,
10 Aug. 1898.

[20] PRO, CO/267/439: Conf. Desp. 59-Enc./98, Letter from Rev. J. A. L.
Price to Gov., 28 July 1898.

[21] SLA/CMP, 102-Enc./98: District Commissioner (Karene) to Col. Sec.,
10 Aug. 1898.

[22] SLA/CMP, 102-Enc./98: District Commissioner (Ronietta) to Col. Sec.,
4 Aug. 1898.

[23] Chalmers Report, I, 12-13.

to the government for houses which they owned seemed to them preposterous, and "an abnegation of their ownership rights in their own houses."[24]

There was considerable resentment also over the fact that the people of Rokamp, as Freetown was called in the Protectorate, were exempt from the tax. The District Commissioner of Karene insisted that everyone would continue to resent paying the tax as long as their compatriots in Freetown were exempt.[25] That the chiefs of the Protectorate were quite aware of this point comes out clearly in the Chalmers Report. For example, Creole traders in Port Loko told the local people that in Freetown no such tax was paid and they should not have to pay it either. They introduced the chiefs to lawyers in Freetown who could advise them about the tax. Indeed a British trader gave evidence to the Chalmers Commission that if the hut tax had been imposed on Freetown a year before its introduction into the Protectorate, there would have been no trouble.

Nor were the Creole traders the only outside interest group to oppose the tax. British traders in Sierra Leone were against it from the start, considering it detrimental to trade. They made their opposition clear to the Governor. The Manchester and Liverpool Chambers of Commerce, which represented most British traders in Sierra Leone, sent petitions to the Colonial Office asking for its repeal. Chamberlain even asked the Manchester Chamber of Commerce to suggest an alternative means of taxation.[26] Cardew, however, dismissed the opposition of merchants who "telegraph in the interest of trade"; he felt the administration of the colony was a matter of indifference to them as long as trade was good.[27] He even accused certain British traders of actively assisting the "insurgents" by selling gunpowder to them, naming in particular G. B. Ollivant's, the Sierra Leone Coaling Company, and Pickering and Berthoods. "The British Merchant out here has shown convincingly that he would not hesitate to sell arms and ammunition to the enemies of his country whenever he can get the chance. . . ."[28]

Chamberlain was so shocked by this news that he asked Cardew to find out whether there was sufficient proof of these allegations to

[24] Editorial entitled "The Madness of the Hut Tax," in *Daily Mail* (London), 6 May 1898.

[25] SLA/CMP, 102-Enc./98: District Commissioner (Karene) to Col. Sec., 10 Aug. 1898.

[26] Reuter's Liverpool representative in *Daily Graphic,* 13 May 1898.

[27] PRO, CO/267/438: Telegram, Gov. to Sec. of State, 9 May 1898.

[28] PRO, CO/267/438: Gov.'s Conf. Desp. of 28 May 1898, and Gov.'s Conf. Desp. 43, 31 May 1898.

prosecute the offenders for high treason.[29] Because of the difficulty of securing conviction, the disappearance of witnesses, and the fact that one of those to be tried had already been thanked by the Executive Council for his services to the government (lending carrier pigeons for use in the war), Chamberlain reluctantly agreed that there should be no prosecution.[30]

In Britain, traders pursued their opposition to the hut tax in the press, gaining a notable ally in the popular *Daily Mail* which "time and again . . . had called attention to the notorious hut tax."[31] Other newspapers, despite their preoccupation with the Spanish-American War, and, in Africa, with the Sudan and Anglo-French tension on the Niger, also found space to publish the merchants' views.[32] Mary Kingley, the celebrated traveler, came out in support of the merchants, describing the hut tax as "a piece of rotten, bad law from a philosophic as well as fiscal standpoint."[33] In the House of Commons, in May 1898, Davitt, the member for Mayo South, described the tax as a "blunder." And, while Chamberlain defended its imposition publicly, within the Colonial Office walls he had as early as April described it as a tax "which I strongly suspect ought never to have been imposed."[34]

Despite the general opposition to his tax, Cardew never—before, during, or after the war—countenanced its abolition. For him there was "a great principle involved in this struggle which is the right of the Government to compel the governed to contribute towards the support of the Government which ensures them the security of life and prosperity, just laws and all the other benefits of the most advanced civilisation."[35]

But as Cardew soon came to realize, the people did not want the so-called "benefits" of his government, and they were certainly not prepared to pay for what they did not want. They fought the government in order to regain their independence and be rid of what they considered an oppressive system of government. In a secret dispatch, Cardew himself attributed the war to "the desire for independence

[29] PRO, CO/267/438: Draft of reply dated 24 June 1898 to Gov.'s Conf. Desp. of 28 May 1898.

[30] PRO, CO/267/440: Gov.'s Conf. Desp. of 12 Oct. 1898 and Chamberlain's minute on it of 3 Dec. 1898.

[31] *Daily Mail* (London), 6 May 1898.

[32] For instance, see *Daily Telegraph* (London), 4 Apr. 1898; *Daily Graphic* (London), 6 May 1898; *Outlook* (London), 30 Apr. 1898.

[33] Letter to the editor in *Outlook* (London), 7 May 1898.

[34] PRO, CO/257/438: minute by Chamberlain on telegram from Gov., 21 Apr. 1898.

[35] PRO, CO/267/438: Gov.'s Conf. Desp. of 28 May 1898. Gov.'s secret despatch to the Sec. of State, 28 May 1898.

and for a reversion to the old order of things. . . . They are sick of the supremacy of the white man as asserted by the District Commissioners and Frontier Police."[36] T. Caldwell of the Church Missionary Society told Chalmers that he believed "that the country was ready for any excuse to throw off British rule, because they complained of having to clean roads, build barracks, and obey the Government in what they called their own country."[37] Rev. Price supported this view:

> The Temne people [the chiefs] do not want the English to rule in their country, or influence their customs in any way. . . . Their desire to throw off the English Power was not conceived last year nor the year before. They disdain the idea of being tributary. They want to dominate, hence the deep-rooted idea of slavery. For some years they have apparently been hesitating between two extremes, Rebellion or Submission, and the Hut Tax afforded them quite a pretext to decide one way. . . .[38]

If the hut tax was merely a pretext—a final straw—what were the underlying reasons the Temne, and later the Mende, decided on rebellion? In addition to the desire for independence, the complex of resentments falls under three main headings: (1) loss of authority and prestige by the chiefs, in particular their loss of judicial authority; (2) resentment at the abolition of the slave trade and the liberty offered to domestic slaves by the British; and (3) hatred of the Frontier Police. These grievances, given focus by the hut tax, were encouraged by the Freetown press and by Creoles living up-country.

The overriding grievance of the chiefs was their loss of authority under the new regime. They were now subjected to young District Commissioners who knew little of the areas which they were administering. In an interview with Lord Selborne, Parliamentary Secretary at the Colonial Office, Dr. Edward Blyden, the West Indian nationalist, said that "one main cause of the rebellion was the want of consideration shown by young District Commissioners in their dealings with the chiefs, many of them old men, who resented being dictated to by young men."[39] In particular, the chiefs resented their loss of ju-

---

[36] That the chiefs were anxious to regain their independence was confirmed by the District Commissioners of Karene and Ronietta in their reports to Cardew on the causes of the war. See their reports in SLA/CMP, 120-Enc./98, District Commissioner (Karene) to Col. Sec., 10 Aug. 1898; and District Commissioner (Ronietta) to Col. Sec., 4 Aug. 1898.

[37] Appendix E, Interview with Mr. T. Caldwell of the CMS Mission at Rogberi, 12 May 1898, Chalmers Report, I.

[38] PRO, CO/267/439: Gov.'s Conf. Desp. 59 of 28 July 1898; also its enc., letter from Rev. J. A. L. Price, 28 July 1898.

[39] PRO, CO/267/439: Gov.'s Conf. Desp. 57 of 2 July 1898, minute by Lord Selborne of 5 Aug. 1898.

dicial authority to the District Commissioners' courts. They were now deprived of that great proportion of their revenue which had hitherto been derived from fines imposed in the cases which they tried.[40] What legal authority was left to them was further reduced by the new sanctions on certain types of judicial procedure such as the "ordeal"—a form of physical torture used to determine guilt or innocence.

The chiefs also resented the tasks imposed upon them by the District Commissioners, such as building barracks for the Frontier Police, making roads, or collecting the hut tax. They were horrified by the provision in the Protectorate Ordinance that District Commissioners could punish them by flogging, a punishment which would disgrace them in front of their people. They felt that the Protectorate Ordinance had so reduced their authority in the eyes of their people that their wives, children, and domestic slaves would cease to obey them, and that they now lacked their former powers of punishment to enforce obedience.[41] Missionaries became the object of hatred in this connection. Not only did they expose "malpractices" to the British authorities, but in educating children, they taught them to despise their illiterate and "pagan" elders, thus arousing the jealousy of the uneducated.[42] (This grievance, however, was stronger in Mendeland where missionary efforts were concentrated, than in the Temne areas where Islam was making progress.)

Further, the prohibition on the internal slave trade deprived many chiefs of a major source of income from levying duties on slave caravans. This was particularly true in Kasseh, which lay astride the traditional trade route from Mendeland to Susuland. Although under the Protectorate Ordinance domestic slavery was not abolished as such, domestic slaves could obtain their freedom on application to the British authorities. This deprived chiefs and other owners of domestic slaves of an important source of labor and obviously weakened their control over their slaves.

Probably the most directly irritating aspect of colonial rule was, however, the behavior of the Frontier Police. Even before the imposition of the Protectorate they had far exceeded the powers delegated to them by either the colony's government or by the chiefs who had agreed to their being stationed in their chiefdoms. In spite of orders

[40] PRO, CO/267/438: telegram, Gov. to Sec. of State, 9 May 1898, minute by R. L. Antrobus referring to chief's memorials in Gov.'s Desp. 27603/97, 9 May 1898.

[41] Appendix J, letter from J. C. E. Parkes to Gov., 31 May 1898, Chalmers Report, I.

[42] SLA/CMP, 102-Enc./98; District Commissioner (Ronietta) to Col. Sec., 4 Aug. 1898.

from Freetown, far from just keeping the peace, they set themselves up as "little judges and governors";[43] they interfered in local disputes which were none of their business. Scattered over the hinterland, they were often unsupervised by senior officers who, when they made their tours of inspection, were inundated with complaints against these men. Parkes presented a volume of correspondence relating to complaints against the police to the Chalmers Commission.[44] One of the problems was that many of the Frontier Police were runaway slaves who had gained their freedom in Freetown, whence they were recruited. Chiefs thus resented the fact that they were open to arrest by men who had once been their slaves.[45] According to Parkes, the behavior of the police improved with the appointment of Cardew as Governor, although he told Chalmers that they were still not what they ought to be.[46] Regimental Sergeant Major George of the Frontier Police, however, defended the force against criticism, asserting that it was largely manufactured by Creole traders.[47]

The grievances against the police were exacerbated by the Sierra Leone press and the Creole traders in the Protectorate. The Freetown press had a surprisingly wide circulation in the interior; Creole traders subscribed regularly and conveyed the news to the largely illiterate chiefs. In this manner, British reverses became known to the African opposition during the wars.[48] Important chiefs, such as Bai Bureh, employed educated clerks, who translated the newspapers for them. When Almami Senna Bunde, one of the leaders of the revolt in the south, was captured in April 1898, some thirty copies of the *Sierra Leone Weekly News* were found in his house.[49] Taiama's Foray Vons was also well acquainted with Sir Samuel Lewis's attacks on the Protectorate Ordinance.[50] When a prisoner of Bai Bureh, W. M. Pittendrigh, the chairman of Freetown's Chamber of Commerce, recorded

---

[43] Chalmers Report, I, 13.

[44] Evidence of J. C. E. Parkes, Chalmers Report, II, par. 974.

[45] PRO, CO/267/438: telegram, Gov. to Sec. of State, 9 May 1898 with minute by R. L. Antrobus, 9 May 1898.

[46] Evidence of J. C. E. Parkes, Chalmers Report, II, par. 974.

[47] Appendix M, Letter from R. O. George, R. S. M. Frontier Police, to Adjutant, Frontier Police, n.d., Chalmers Report, I. These criticisms gained surprisingly wide currency before the publication of the Chalmers Report. In an editorial of the *Daily Graphic* (London) of 6 May 1898, the Frontier Police were criticized as the "worst of all rules, black rule backed by white authority, but without the efficient supervision of the whites."

[48] SLA/CMP, 102-Enc./98: District Commissioner (Karene) to Col. Sec., 10 Aug. 1898.

[49] PRO, CO/267/440: Gov.'s Conf. Desp. 68, 23 Aug. 1898.

[50] SLA/CMP, 102-Enc./98: District Commissioner (Ronietta) to Col. Sec., 4 Aug. 1898.

that the chief would look for articles on the Port Loko disturbances of February 1898, and that he put great faith in them.[51] There was even a limited circulation of English papers in the interior.[52] Cardew went so far as to request the restriction of the freedom of the press in the Colony because of the role he considered that it was playing in stimulating trouble in the Protectorate. With these constant communications between Freetown and the Protectorate, he asserted, "the disloyal sentiments contained in the Sierra Leone newspapers can be conveyed into and influence the minds of the natives."[53]

In much the same category as the Freetown press were the Creole traders of the Protectorate, whom Cardew accused of deliberately fomenting trouble. In this regard the district commissioners of Karene and Ronietta backed him.[54] So did the superintendent of the Soudan Mission, the Rev. E. Kingman, who wrote a letter to Cardew in which he laid great emphasis on the role of the Creole traders in inciting resistance.[55] Cardew, who greatly despised Creoles, insisted that the Creole traders not only incited rebellion but that they were also one of its causes by alienating the chiefs and people "with their loud and obtrusive ways, their contempt for the bushman and their property."[56]

That the causes of the war were as complex for Bai Bureh as indicated above is brought out in the text of the letter he signed, with other Temne chiefs, in December 1896. It is reproduced here as the prelude to our study of his role in the war:

> We received one letter here from Governor sent to tell us that the Queen now takes the whole of the Timini country. The palavers are all left now to Queen's part, so we read the letter and we know the law that he the Governor puts on us now, viz., not to *barter* any slaves again, nor to buy again, nor to put pledge again, so who ever do that if Government find you guilty of that with the slaves they will catch you and put you for seven years Gaol.
>
> So that again who get his own country and if the place is empty and there is no one to work, the Governor will take the place and give to another people to work farms there. This we come to you Captain, to beg the Governor, to make him don't do that to us. Because we did not make war in our country.

[51] Evidence of W. M. Pittendrigh, Chalmers Report, II, par. 436.
[52] Evidence of J. C. E. Parkes, Chalmers Report, II, par. 715.
[53] PRO, CO/267/440: Gov.'s Conf. Desp. 68, 23 Aug. 1898.
[54] SLA/CMP, 102-Enc./98: District Commissioner (Karene and Ronietta) to Col. Sec., 10 Aug. 1898 and 4 Aug. 1898, respectively.
[55] Appendix F, Letter from E. Kingman, Supt. of the Soudan Mission to Gov., 18 May 1898, Chalmers Report, I.
[56] PRO, CO/267/438: Gov.'s Conf. Desp., 28 May 1898.

Again to say we must pay for our houses, we are not able to pay for our own houses. Because we have no power and no strength to do so, so that please tell the Governor we beg him to be sorry for us, and to consider the old agreement he made with our fathers.

Suppose when your headman tells you to take up a heavy load, if you are not able to take it, you can only tell him by true words: "Master, I am not able to carry all this at once, I am too weak." Suppose you omit to tell him at the time itself that you are not able to carry the load, then when you tell him afterwards, he will ask you, "why did you not tell me at the same time that you are not able to do this?" This is why we tell you, Master, we are not able to pay for our house. Beg the Governor to leave us as we have been day before, because the law tells us that we must not take our load to go up country again, unless we pay duty.

Now the whole of the domestics we got before all stubborn and refuse to work for us. Now as we have no power to force them to work do, we beg you, Captain Sharpe, to tell Governor that we are not able to observe the new laws and to pay house taxes. Remember we all have been friends with the Queen for a long time. Also we beg the Governor must leave our woman palavers to ourselves because we are poor people, and because we do not get any power beyond our farm-work.

So, Captain, please beg the Governor to make him feel sorry for us, and beg him not to take any chief's waste land and give to any man or stranger. This we beg him, all this, we do not get slaves to work for us, and we cannot trade as the road is closed say if any body kill person or snake bites person and die, and all the witch palaver so the Chief must not talk palaver alone, except the Captain present, the Chief and the Captain talk the palaver—concerning all this we send to beg the Captain to tell the Governor not to pull the power to judge these matters out of our hands but to leave all these matters to ourselves both all the big palavers and all the small ones we beg may be left to ourselves, any matter are not able to settle them we will go take it to the Captain, Do, we all pray God by the Governor to allow this for us and not be so hard on us.[57]

The Early Years: Bai Bureh, the Warrior

Little is known of Bai Bureh's life.[58] He spent his childhood in the small town of Rogbolan in the chiefdom of Kasseh, which covers a

[57] Appendix XIV, Letter from Timini chiefs to Capt. Sharpe, 17 Dec. 1896, Chalmers Report, I.

[58] The main source for information on Bai Bureh's life is Elizabeth Hirst and Issa Kamara, *Benga* (London, 1958), which is based on oral tradition.

small area south of the junction formed by the Little Scarcies and Mabole rivers (see map). His father, a professional warrior, followed family tradition by sending his son to a well-known warrior training center at Pendembu Gwahun, founded by the great warrior Gbamelleh. So successful was Bai Bureh in his profession that his peers soon nicknamed him Kebalai, or "the man whose basket is never full," because of the number of men he killed in battle.[59] Since "Bai Bureh" is the title of office of the chief of Kasseh, not a personal or family name, he did not become known as such until he became chief in about May 1887,[60] by which time his fame as a war leader extended throughout much of modern Sierra Leone. It was this fame which led the elders of Kasseh to invite him to assume the post of chief. In the absence of a hereditary claimant, such a step was not against traditional custom.[61] However, the British with their theories of royal lineage and nobility, cast aspersions on Bai Bureh's right to rule because, to their way of thinking, he lacked the hereditary right.

Bai Bureh was a *kruba,* or war chief, whom other chiefs called upon to assist them in their wars. According to the traditional code regulating conduct in war, in return for his services he had certain rights of plunder. Among these was the right to enslave prisoners taken in battle—it is not certain whether he and his men had the right to all such prisoners or merely to a certain proportion. In English the name given to this transaction meant that one chief "bought war" from the other; Governor Cardew and his predecessors interpreted this literally, describing the system as one of acquiring "mercenaries."[62] Much more research into the nineteenth-century social and political structure of the Temne must be done before the term "mercenary," with all its derogatory implications, can be used with certainty to de-

[59] Ibid., 35.

[60] The date of Bai Bureh's assumption to office was previously fixed at about 1889 by Cardew in SLA/GDSS, 43/99: "Report on the Antecedents of Bai Bureh," 10 Feb. 1899. Christopher Fyfe, *History of Sierra Leone* (London, 1962), 501, accepts this date. However, the stipend records and letters of the Aborigines Department show that the office had been vacant since 1883, but that in May 1887, a messenger arrived in Freetown with Kasseh's treaty book in order to collect the stipend due for the intervening years on Bai Bureh's behalf. Also, by Aug. 1888, Bai Bureh was involved in a land dispute with Bai Inga. This was first mentioned in SLA/ADLB, 31/88: J. M. Baltby to Bai Bureh, 18 Aug. 1888.

[61] Hirst and Kamara, *Benga,* 42-45.

[62] SLA/GCDSS, 43/99: "Report on the Antecedents of Bai Bureh," Cardew to Sec. of State, 10 Feb. 1899. So too did the French. The Commandant de Cercle Mellacourie reported the difficulties experienced by his opponent Bokhari, for whom Bai Bureh fought, in recruiting soldiers "car le vieux dicton 'pas d'argent, pas de Suisses' s'applique dans toute la rigueur aux Tymenes." NAS/7G22/1/6: Commandant de Cercle Mellacourie to Lt. Gov. Senegal, 25 May 1883.

scribe Bai Bureh and other war leaders like him. The authors believe that it cannot be so applied because, for one thing, the position of war chiefs and warriors, as professional men, was clearly institutionalized. There were very few war chiefs, and only they possessed the right to request permission from other chiefs to travel through their chiefdoms to collect armed followers.[63] Furthermore, the occupation of warrior was specialized and boys were specifically trained for it in centers scattered throughout the chiefdoms.[64] Often boys were sent out of their own chiefdom to another for such training, thus acquiring "trans-chiefdom" loyalties. By the 1890's, political authority seems to have become concentrated in the hands of important military figures. Captain Sharpe, Karene's District Commissioner, observed that the war chiefs were the only ones who possessed any "real authority" and that one of them was worth fifty ordinary chiefs.[65] It would seem that the warrior system was a factor unifying the many Temne chieftains into a broad alliance for achieving politico-military ends, and that Bai Bureh's leadership of the Temne against the British was thus a result of his status within this military system rather than the result of his strictly political position as chief of tiny Kasseh.

Although Bai Bureh led the Temne against the British, it is not clear whether he was a Temne or a Lokko. He himself told Cardew that he was a Temne during an interview shortly before his deportation.[66] All administrative reports prior to 1899 also refer to him as a Temne.[67] Elizabeth Hirst and Issa Kamara, however, maintain that he was really a Lokko who intended to restore Lokko prestige in the Scarcies-Port Loko area.[68] Christopher Fyfe compromises by maintaining he was partly Lokko by descent.[69] Linguistic evidence tends to support those who claim Lokko descent, for it is maintained that Temne in the Scarcies-Port Loko area still sing war songs about Bai Bureh's exploits in untranslated Lokko.[70]

Bai Bureh was an adherent of traditional religion but he must also have been influenced strongly by Islam, for the Susu, Fula, and Mandingo, most of whom were Muslim, had migrated into the Scarcies

[63] Evidence of Capt. Sharpe, Chalmers Report, II, pars. 3349-50.

[64] Hirst and Kamara, *Benga*, 9-12.

[65] Evidence of Capt. Sharpe, Chalmers Report, II, pars. 3349-50.

[66] "Report on the Antecedents of Bai Bureh," SLA/GCDSS, 43/99: Cardew to Sec. of State, 10 Feb. 1899.

[67] E.g., SLA/ADMP, 110/82: T. Lawson to Gov., 16 Aug. 1882.

[68] Hirst and Kamara, *Benga*, 38-45.

[69] Fyfe, *History*, 432.

[70] We are indebted to A. K. Turay, a doctoral research student of the University of London presently engaged in field work on the Temne language, for this information.

and northern areas of Sierra Leone during the nineteenth century. Many Muslims from these groups had married Temne, Lokko, and Limba. Most important of all, as a war leader for the Muslim chief, Bokhari, in what Bokhari considered a *jihad* against Bokhari's own people, Bai Bureh must have been aware of Bokhari's desire to impose Islam on his followers. Nevertheless he seems not to have embraced the Islamic faith in terms implying anything other than the recognition of the abilities and influence of its adherents. Possibly he was a member of the *Kefa* or *Kefung* secret society, an elite group about which very little is known; membership supposedly endowed its members with abilities[71] which Bai Bureh possessed according to myth—such as his wondrous abilities to change into an animal in order to escape from his enemies and to live either underground or underwater for long periods of time.

Nevertheless, Islam affected his rule in a variety of ways, and he must have been profoundly affected by Islamic developments further to the north. Throughout his chieftaincy, he maintained an Arabic-writing clerk; the majority of his letters to the Aborigines Department (later known as the Native Affairs Department) were written in Arabic, as were the administration's replies. Hirst and Kamara suggest that there were close relations between Bai Bureh and a family of powerful Muslim traders who had immigrated into Temneland.[72] It was through influential Muslim leaders that he made various peace overtures to the British in 1898: once through the Alikali of Port Loko; at another time through the leader of the Muslims in Freetown.[73]

Before 1887, when he was installed as chief of Kasseh, Bai Bureh's contact with the British was indirect, always through the chiefs for whom he was fighting, and the result of his activities in "French-influenced" territory as war chief of the Temne forces in Bokhari's service. The areas which were involved in the struggle were the hinterlands of Forikaria and the coastal region stretching from Freetown to Conakry. The scene of constant, gradual change for centuries, this area was at the time undergoing three major internal developments: (1) the establishment of Islam as a major socio-politico-religious force; (2) the attraction of trade from the interior to the coast by means of the main river ports; and (3) the migration of Susu from the Forikaria and Mellakori riverain regions to the Scarcies and upper Limba countries, and their subsequent assimilation in the political

---

[71] Merran McCulloch, *Peoples of Sierra Leone* (London, 1950), 70.

[72] Hirst and Kamara, *Benga*, 13-18.

[73] SLA/NAMP, 154/98: Alfa Yanusa, Alikali of Port Loko, to Supt. of Native Affairs, 18 Apr. 1898; and SLA/GDSS, 219/98: Gov. to Sec. of State, 6 Oct. 1898.

systems within which they had settled. Conflict was a natural result
of such a situation. The evolution of events would probably have been
very much different had it not been for the external forces set in motion by the exigencies of European expansion and control.

Much of the conflict focused on trade relations. The Susu and
Temne, divided among themselves, were fighting to obtain footholds
on the rivers which commanded European trade. There was an attempt to divert the direction of the interior caravan trade from the
Mellakori River to the Scarcies rivers.[74] The internal slave trade was
still active and important, a major route running from Mendeland
along the road through Port Loko and thence to Mellakori.[75] Prisoners
of war were an important source of slaves; they could either be sold
or made a part of the domestic labor force. Either way they were a
great source of wealth to war chiefs such as Bai Bureh.

The disturbed state of the region's trade had an immediate impact
on the British and French, whose traders were active all along the
coast. Not unnaturally they made frequent demands on their governments for intervention. The French, furthermore, were anxious to establish their protection over at least the northern part of the area. In
Freetown, however, the British considered this area to be a part of the
natural hinterland of the colony, but the Colonial Office restrained its
administrators in Freetown from extending British responsibility there.

Kebalai first came to the attention of the British in Freetown in
1865 because of his role as Bokhari's war leader. Though Maligi Gbele
received support from the French in return for signing a treaty putting
his chiefdom under their protection, he was defeated and killed by
Bokhari's force, which was under Kebalai's command. As a result of his
success, Kebalai became Bokhari's principal war leader for many of
the campaigns which he launched during the next twenty years. Bokhari's victory over his French-supported rival suited British interests in
Freetown, for if they were unable to place Forikaria under their own
protection, they preferred that it should remain independent of another
power. Although the French made overtures to Bokhari, he did not co-
operate with them in the way they would have liked and remained
effectively independent until his subjects rebelled against him in 1876.

The cause of the rebellion was Bokhari's strict enforcement and
observance of the laws of the Qur'an.[76] The anti-Islamic reaction was
sufficiently violent that his people murdered his chief *imam,* and

[74] We are indebted to Allen Howard of the University of Wisconsin for this
information.

[75] PRO, CO/267/439: Gov.'s Conf. Desp. 59/98, 28 July 1898 with enc. letter
of Rev. J. A. L. Price; and "Report on the Antecedents of Bai Bureh. . . ." SLA/
GCDSS, 43/99: Cardew to Sec. of State, 10 Feb. 1899.

[76] SLA/ADMP, 64/83: T. Lawson to Col. Sec., 28 Sept. 1883.

eventually drove Bokhari himself out of his chiefdom.[77] He sought refuge in the British sphere of influence at Kambia, where Kebalai was then living. Bokhari sent for him and they made arrangements for Kebalai to go into the Scarcies interior and to Yonni country to recruit "warboys."[78] Kebalai gathered a large army of four thousand "warboys" and in January 1882, as has already been pointed out, led it in what from Bokhari's point of view was a *jihad* against his own subjects.[79]

In the meantime, Dowda, the Alikali of Forikaria, had usurped Bokhari's position as chief, and the French readily supported him. Although the early successes of Kebalai as Bokhari's commander suited British interests, they brought forth vehement protests from the French, who accused the British of actively assisting Bokhari. Mistakenly believing that Sattan Lahai and Bai Inga, the leaders of the Temne alliance supporting Bokhari, were under British protection, the French asked for their arrest as well as that of Kebalai, who had hitherto been a somewhat shadowy figure to them.[80] Governor Arthur Edward Havelock explained to the French that his treaties with the Scarcies chiefs merely specified terms of friendship but no formal protection; therefore he considered it completely beyond his political authority to arrest these persons.[81]

However, the geographical boundaries of the respective spheres of influence between the British and the French were becoming more strictly delimited, and international diplomatic lines were hardening. The British did not wish to provoke the French too much, and therefore the Governor warned the Scarcies chiefs to keep out of the war and to send Bokhari away from their country.[82] But at first the warnings had little effect. Sattan Lahai replied, explaining that he and his neighboring chiefs had been insulted by Dowda in 1876 when they tried to arrange peace negotiations between him and Bokhari at the latter's request.[83] The French were dissatisfied with such explanations

[77] NAS/7G/21/7/135: letter of Bokhari to Gov. Havelock which was forwarded to the French Consul in Freetown, 26 Jan. 1882.

[78] SLA/ADMP, 32/82: W. B. Harding to Gov. Havelock, 28 Jan. 1882; SLA/ADLB, 6/82: Gov. Havelock to Bai Inga, 24 Jan. 1882; SLA/ADLB, 7/82: Gov. Havelock to Alimami Colleh, 24 Jan. 1882; SLA/ADLB, 8/82: Gov. Havelock to Alimami Sattan Lahai, 24 Jan. 1882.

[79] See above, 185.

[80] SLA/GLLB, 81/82: Gov. Havelock to Bareste, 8 Mar. 1882; and NAS/7G/21/7.

[81] SLA/GLLB, 81/82: Gov. Havelock to Bareste, 8 Mar. 1882.

[82] SLA/ADLB, 6/82: Gov. Havelock to Bai Inga, 24 Jan. 1882; and 8/82: Gov. Havelock to Alimami Sattan Lahai, 24 Jan. 1882.

[83] SLA/ADMP, 26/82: with Encs. 3, 4, and 5, translations of letters from Alimami Colleh, Alimami Lunsenny, and Alimami Sattan Lahai, respectively, to Gov. Havelock, 2 Feb. 1882.

and indicated that if the British could not keep the chiefs in the area under control, the French would be forced to enter Kambia and arrest Bokhari themselves. Henceforth, British warnings took on sufficiently severe a tone to persuade Sattan Lahai and the chiefs of Kambia to expel Bokhari.[84]

Even after the departure of Bokhari from Kambia, the French (with some justification) continued to accuse the Scarcies chiefs of abetting Bokhari, especially as his war leader was still Kebalai.[85] This diplomatic wrangling between the French and the British was not brought to an end until mid-1885, when Bokhari was killed in battle, and Dowda became secure at last in his position as chief.

During the last three years in which Kebalai had led Bokhari's forces, his campaigns had been particularly bloody, especially by contrast with his restrained warfare against the British some fifteen years later. Pillaging and burning of villages was the order of the day. Adults taken prisoner were as often as not slaughtered. Toward the end of the war, in July 1885, there was an exceptionally violent campaign when Kebalai invaded the countries of Samo and Moria and took Gbarmooyah Island. His Susu opponents had hidden all their property and placed their wives and children on the island for safety. While Kebalai's warriors were on the island, the tide went down and it became impossible for them to cross by canoe until high tide. On the opposite bank, their opponents also waited for high tide to cross and defend their families and property. Before their eyes, the Temne killed everyone present on the island and burned all their property. When the tide finally came up, there was a violent battle in which the Temne were victorious. On their way back to their base, the Temne continued their destruction, burning every one of their opponents' towns in their path.[86]

In the course of the war, Kebalai had had his first contacts with Europeans. In 1882 he attacked Pharmoriah and captured a number of European traders whom Bokhari then held as hostages for three months in an attempt to secure French neutrality.[87] During his campaigns Kebalai had to contend with forces supplied with arms by the French; he clearly obtained his arms supplies through traders from Freetown and

[84] SLA/ADLB, 28/82: Circular from Gov. Havelock to the chiefs of the Great and Small Scarcies River Districts, 11 Apr. 1882; and SLA/ADMP, 29/82, with enc. 9, Memo from T. Lawson to Gov. Havelock, 13 Apr. 1882.

[85] SLA/GLLB, 267/82: Gov. Havelock to Bareste, 17 Aug. 1882.

[86] SLA/ADMP, 66/85: Memo from T. Lawson to Gov., 15 July 1885.

[87] SLA/GLLB, 267/82: Gov. Havelock to Bareste, 17 Aug. 1882. W. M. Pittendrigh, a trader, gave evidence to the Chalmers Commission that he had been held captive for three months by Kebalai. See Evidence of Pittendrigh, Chalmers Report, II, 428.

Port Loko. Above all, Bokhari's war gave Kebalai his best preparation for the brilliant campaigns which he was later to conduct against the British, and through his participation in it, he must have acquired from Bokhari some of the techniques of diplomacy necessary in dealing with Europeans. In 1887 he became chief of Kasseh, and although he was involved in wars over the next decade, none of them was on the same scale militarily as those he had fought for Bokhari.

Bai Bureh as Chief of Kasseh

When Kebalai was installed as chief of Kasseh in 1887, he assumed the name Bai Bureh and undertook the chiefdom's obligation of carrying out the terms of the 1871 treaty between Kasseh and the British. These included keeping the roads open to traders from the interior and the promise to refer any disputes with his fellow chiefs to the British Governor in Freetown. In return he received an annual stipend of £10 from the administration. Although on this occasion he did not question the terms of the treaty or the authority thus given to the British, as soon as the terms were invoked he showed how little they meant to him.

In the latter part of 1888, a land dispute broke out between Bai Bureh and his neighbor, Bai Inga. When it became apparent that war was about to break out, the acting administrator in Freetown reminded both chiefs of their treaty obligations to the British, and assured them that the newly appointed Governor, Sir James Shaw Hay, would settle the dispute on his arrival.[88] And soon after his arrival, Hay did summon the two chiefs to Freetown to discuss the dispute.[89] They agreed to submit the matter to three important Scarcies area chiefs for arbitration.[90] However, when Bai Bureh observed that the judgment of these chiefs was going against him, he made it clear that he would not accept their opinion. Deadlocked, they asked Hay to make the final decision, which he did, in favor of Bai Inga. So dissatisfied was Bai Bureh with the outcome that Hay had to warn him against preparing to fight with Bai Inga over the matter by sending a police officer to Bai Bureh with the message that whosoever broke the peace would be punished by the British authorities.[91] Bai Bureh finally yielded to this threat of British force.

Less than six months later, however, Bai Bureh came into more direct conflict with the British. Reports reached Freetown that he was organizing a strong war party to attack Moriah.[92] The Scarcies-Kambia

[88] SLA/ADLB, 38/88: Maltby to Bai Inga, 3 Oct. 1888.
[89] SLA/ADLB, 47/88: Gov. to Bai Bureh, 27 Oct. 1888.
[90] SLA/ADMP, 7/88: Memo from T. Lawson to Gov., 23 Nov. 1888.
[91] SLA/ADLB, 116/89: Gov. to Bai Bureh, 11 Mar. 1889.
[92] SLA/ADLB, 291/89: Parkes to H. C. Sawyer, 9 Aug. 1889.

area seemed to be in such a general state of confusion—with "warboys" patrolling the main roads leading from the interior to Kambia and Port Loko—that serious consideration was given by the British to the declaration of a protectorate over the area and the establishment of police posts at frequent intervals along the road.[93]

The situation deteriorated rapidly when a well-armed Susu war party led by Karimu, a Susu chief in upper Limba who was under treaty with the British, captured several towns in the country of the Limba.[94] The chiefs of upper Limba appealed to Bai Bureh to help them drive the invaders from their country. Bai Bureh assisted them, heading a coalition of Limba, Lokko, and Temne against the Susu. The Freetown administration was apprehensive lest the war extend into the French sphere and warned Bai Bureh against aggravating the extremely tense situation, reminding him that his chiefdom was in treaty relationship with the British. Their apprehension grew as Freetown came increasingly to suspect Karimu of collusion with the French.[95] Whatever the truth of this allegation, Karimu was able to retreat into the French sphere of influence with impunity and to receive support from Dowda of Forikaria.

Parkes feared that there would be a general uprising of Temne against Susu and tried to arrange peace talks. He summoned all the main chiefs in the area to the talks, but neither Bai Bureh nor Karimu came.[96] When the police constable arrived to summon him to the negotiations, Bai Bureh could not be found in this town. Parkes then told the chiefs who were friendly to Bai Bureh that if he did not return to his town in two days, he would be arrested.[97] Bai Bureh, however, remained out of reach of the short arm of Freetown. Parkes continued his attempts for negotiation even as he destroyed Karimu's stronghold at Kolunkureh, being "strongly of the opinion that an exhibition of force would be of incalculable benefit in increasing the prestige of the Government and maintaining peace for the future."[98] Finally, Parkes warned Bai Bureh that if he continued to make war he would suffer

---

[93] SLA/ADLI, 382/89: Parkes to Gov., 25 Sept. 1889. Parkes was instrumental in the foundation of the formal protectorate. For further information, see J. D. Hargreaves, "The Evolution of the Native Affairs Department," SLS 3 (1954), 168-84.

[94] SLA/ADLB, 397/89: Parkes to Alimami Bomboh Lahai, 14 Oct. 1889.

[95] SLA/ADCLB, 5/89: Parkes to Garrett, 30 Nov. 1889.

[96] SLA/ADLB, 432/89: Parkes to Garrett, 6 Nov. 1889; and SLA/ADLB, 446/89: Parkes to Sgt. Crowther, 16 Nov. 1889.

[97] SLA/ADLB, 446/89: Parkes to Sgt. Crowther, 16 Nov. 1889.

[98] SLA/ADLB, 450/89: Parkes to Garrett, 20 Nov. 1889; and SLA/ADCLB, 4/89: Parkes to Garrett, 24 Nov. 1889.

severe consequences.[99] Bai Bureh, however, continued to ignore the government's demands.

In mid-September 1889, after the police had reported that they had been unable to find Bai Bureh at Roballan, his chief town, Governor Hay sent another party to look elsewhere. The officer in charge was ordered to tell Bai Bureh that all the reports coming to the Governor were so unsatisfactory that as a treaty chief, Bai Bureh must "come to town without delay and explain otherwise [the Governor would] have to regard him as having broken his treaty."[100] He made it clear that every measure short of actual arrest was to be taken "to persuade" the chief to accompany the police to Freetown.[101] Although Parkes's letter, which the police were to deliver to Bai Bureh, acknowledged that Karimu had destroyed some of the towns of the Limba, Parkes also warned the chief that instead of accepting the Susu's invitation to make war, he should have advised them to consult with the government: "Take care Bey Boorey the Government have warned you once to be careful but it seems as if the time is fast coming when the things I told you would surely happen to you if you did not change will come to pass."[102] However, Bai Bureh was not found, and six months later the government had made no further progress in its attempts to bring about peace. Hay next instructed the police to arrest Bai Bureh if they could manage to do so without undue risk.[103]

For his part, aware of the dangers implicit in the government's letters to him and the escalation of activities in the interior, Bai Bureh sent Parkes a letter explaining his actions. The Governor replied that he found his answer unsatisfactory as it was not at all in accord with a recent report of his conduct[104] and ordered him to come to Freetown, or a place where a British authority was represented, to explain himself personally. If, however, Bai Bureh persisted in his activities, the Governor continued, the government would have no alternative to treating him as an enemy and would take every active measure against him.

Again government threats had very little effect. Two weeks later, there were reports that Bai Bureh was collecting "warboys" for an attack on Upper Sanda. By now the administration felt that even if Bai Bureh did come to them he would still continue his operations through

---

[99] SLA/ADLB, 450/89: 20 Nov. 1889.
[100] SLA/ADLB, 639/90: Gov. to Actg. Insp. Genl. of Police, 15 Sept. 1890.
[101] Ibid.
[102] SLA/ADLB, 640/90: Parkes to Bai Bureh, 15 Sept. 1890.
[103] SLA/ADLB, 182/91: Parkes to Insp. Genl. of Police, 8 Mar. 1891.
[104] SLA/ADLB, 223/91: Parkes to Bai Bureh, 2 Apr. 1891.

the agency of his lieutenants.[105] The Sanda patrol was instructed to assume the offensive only if absolutely necessary. If it met Bai Bureh's "warboys," it was to disperse them and call upon their leader to go to Freetown as directed.[106]

In May 1891 Hay brought the state of affairs in Sanda country before the colony's Executive Council. He explained that it was necessary to make a show of force in that area in order to disperse the "warboys," and that he had therefore instructed the police patrol to go to Sanda. The patrol had reached its destination early in May. At Tambi, a stockaded town within the British sphere of influence, it met opposition and was forced to retreat. It appears from the nature of the reports of this battle that although the "warboys" at Tambi were Karimu's, Bai Bureh's men also gave considerable trouble.[107] In any case, the unanimous opinion of the Executive Council was that Bai Bureh must not be allowed to defy the government with impunity and that force should be used to bring him to heel. Two days later the Council brought the matter up again, and considered the report of the Inspector General of Police, who maintained that the general war-like demonstration—the shouting, beating of drums, and war cries—obviously meant that the "warboys" intended to make war. The Council members concurred in the opinion that a defeat of the police might encourage the "warboys" to make more frequent raids, and they considered the possibility of stationing a strong police party in some adjacent town. It would remain there until "such time as active measures could be taken if it is not possible to send an armed force at this time of the year to disperse the band."[108] However, they had to postpone their demonstration of force because of the approaching rains.[109]

In the event, Bai Bureh continued his war operations in upper Sanda, and destroyed towns in Bai Inga's country. The Governor asked the Alikali of Port Loko to intercede with him, to urge him to stop the war, and to come to Freetown as he had promised to do.[110] Captain Edward Augustus Lendy, then the acting Superintendent of Native Affairs, warned Bai Bureh that if he did not come to Freetown, the government would in future treat him as an enemy.[111] The government was

[105] SLA/ADLB, 240/91: Parkes to Gov., 14 Apr. 1891.
[106] SLA/ADLB, 253/91: Gov. to Insp. Genl. of Police, 15 Apr. 1891.
[107] SLA/ECM, 14 May 1891.
[108] SLA/ECM, 16 May 1891.
[109] SLA/ECM, 23 June 1891.
[110] SLA/ADLB, 419/91: Actg. Supt. of Native Affairs to Alikali of Port Loko, 15 July 1891.
[111] SLA/ADLB, 450/91: Actg. Supt. of Native Affairs to Bai Bureh, 15 July 1891.

particularly anxious to restore peace in Bai Inga's area, as the war had blocked the Port Loko-Futa Jallon trade route.[112]

Meanwhile Bai Farima reported that Karimu's "warboys" had come as far as the outskirts of Kambia and were destroying various Limban towns nearby.[113] With the dry season, the situation deteriorated rapidly. Freetown therefore decided on a dramatic show of force to restore its authority in the area and recoup its prestige after the retreat from Tambi; the resultant expedition was primarily political in its objective. It was thought that Tambi had to be destroyed "no matter what the cost" because it had successfully resisted an attack by the police.[114] To ensure the success of the expedition, Freetown made what at first seems a remarkable decision: to use Bai Bureh's "warboys" as a "native levy." As Bai Bureh's objective was to defeat Karimu and drive him out of the country, in concert with the actions of the Limba-Lokko-Temne alliance, he agreed to collaborate with the British. The thought was that the British should ally themselves with peoples firmly based in the British sphere of influence, and against Karimu, who moved in and out of French territory. Captain Lendy, a European, was put in charge of Bai Bureh's "warboys" to ensure that action would be co-ordinated and that there should be no doubt in the eyes of the Africans that this was the Queen's war, not an African one.

At the last moment, London decided that the expedition should be conducted by the West India Regiment, commanded by Colonel Alfred Burden Ellis, instead of by the Frontier Police. At first, Ellis decided not to use Bai Bureh's "warboys." However, the administrator refused to dismiss them, fearing the political consequences of such a change.[115] In the actual expedition, Bai Bureh's "warboys," numbering some fifteen hundred, acquitted themselves well, although Captain Lendy and Bai Bureh had some initial difficulties in restraining them once Tambi was in sight. The attack, however, was disciplined, the "warboys" moving in concert with the police and regimental troops. They chased the Susu to the Scarcies rivers. Captain Lendy afterward praised Bai Bureh's command and the conduct of his "warboys," though his very laudatory account may have been partly designed to vindicate the original plan for a combined police and "warboy" operation against Tambi.[116] Peace

[112] SLA/ADLB, 454/91: Actg. Administrator to Alikali of Port Loko, 31 July 1891.

[113] SLA/EGDSS, enc. 3 to Desp. 414 (Dec. 19)91: Police Report from Kambia, 24 Nov. 1891.

[114] SLA/GLLB, 170/92: Administrator to Insp. Genl. of Police, 17 Mar. 1892.

[115] SLA/GLLB, 191/92: Administrator to Insp. Genl. of Police, 29 Mar. 1892; and SLA/GLLB, 194/92: Administrator to Col. A. B. Ellis, 31 Mar. 1892.

[116] SLA/EGDSS, enc. 2 to Desp. 169/92: Report of Capt. Lendy, 20 Apr. 1892.

was restored temporarily, and all the Scarcies chiefs, including Bai Bureh, agreed not to cross the Scarcies rivers again.[117]

The importance of the Tambi expedition to Bai Bureh was that it gave him and his "warboys" direct knowledge of the fighting techniques of both the Frontier Police and the West India Regiment, and not as opponents but as allies. He clearly did not consider that the experience placed him in the position of a permanent ally of the British nor as one who had recognized another's authority. Early in 1894, reports reached Freetown that Bai Bureh was about to attack Moriah, and the Governor, now Sir Frederick Cardew, had to issue a warning.[118] Although this attack never materialized, Temne "warboys" crossed the Scarcies into Benna on March 23. It later became clear that Bai Bureh had participated in this attack as the ally of Surakata, a Susu chief who had been at war with the French and had taken refuge in the British sphere. British authorities had allowed Surakata to stay in Kambia on his promise not to use the British sphere as a basis for incursions into French territory.[119] As a result of this raid on Benna, Surakata was expelled and Cardew ordered the arrest of Bai Bureh.

At this point, under Captains Sharpe and Alexander Tarbet, a party of fifty police was sent to detain Bai Bureh on charges of aiding Surakata. When they reached Roballan, they discovered that he had departed, leaving behind a number of "warboys" sufficiently large to resist the police force.[120] Not only did the "warboys" resist the police, they also humiliated them by jeering at them. Cardew feared that the result of this failure to arrest Bai Bureh "would have a bad effect in the Loko District and bring into contempt the authority of the Frontier Police."[121] He even proposed stationing a company of the West India Regiment in Port Loko to reinforce government authority, but Parkes reported from Port Loko that this step was not necessary, a view with which Cardew concurred after making a visit there himself early in June.[122]

After that Cardew wrote to Bai Bureh that he "could not overlook his offense in gathering his warboys together and resisting and insulting the police and that in consequence he must surrender himself unconditionally and that if he did not do so, [Cardew] would hold no further communication with him and when convenient effect his arrest."[123]

[117] SLA/ECM, 20 Apr. 1892.

[118] SLA/EGCDSS, enc. 1 to Conf. Desp. 37/94: Police report from Kambia, 24 Apr. 1894.

[119] SLA/ECM, 28 May 1894.

[120] SLA/GDSS, no number: Gov. to Sec. of State, 13 June 1894.

[121] Ibid.

[122] Ibid.

[123] SLA/GCDSS, no number: Gov. to Sec. of State, 13 June 1894.

From his place of refuge, Bai Bureh replied with an indignant letter in which he disclaimed any ill feeling against the British. He said that he had not refused to come to Port Loko, but that he feared to do so. He explained that when the police had come to his town, they had behaved in such a way that he feared what they might do to him. He claimed (in the language of his English-speaking clerk) that he did "not know what offence [he had] committed against the Government on account of which the policemen entered into [his] town and spoiled [his] goods and carried away a good number of [his] wives." He asked that Parkes and the Governor "do not refuse communication from me nor deny a hearing. You must not be vexed at me nor condemn me before you have heard from me. If you send me a letter of invitation to answer any charge I shall willingly go down; but for the present I am afraid as I very much suspect some evil."[124]

Subsequently, under a guarantee of safe conduct, a meeting was arranged at Port Loko between Bai Bureh and Cardew. There Cardew told Bai Bureh that he did not blame him for eluding arrest, for that was natural, but for gathering his "warboys" to resist the authority of the police and for having permitted them to menace and insult the latter.[125] Cardew ordered him to pay a fine of fifty guns within a month or be arrested and deprived of his chieftaincy "for a considerable period."[126] Cardew informed the Secretary of State that if Bai Bureh did not pay the fine, he proposed to deport him to Bathurst, Gambia, until the Anglo-French boundary question was settled and the rest was restored to law and order. Optimistically, he said that this would take no longer than a year.[127] Bai Bureh, however, paid the fine and thus escaped the planned punishment. Cardew asked the messengers bringing the fine "to exhort their chief to restrain in future his warboys from disturbing the peace of the country."[128]

From this time on, until the proclamation of the protectorate over the Sierra Leone hinterland in August 1896, Bai Bureh had very little to do with the British. He continued to draw his stipend,[129] and on one occasion wrote Parkes a letter assuring him and the Governor that he did not forget their warnings and was doing his best at Kasseh.[130] On

[124] SLA/NALB, 5 and enc./94: Bai Bureh to Parkes, 31 May 1894.
[125] SLA/GCDSS, no number/94: Gov. to Sec. of State, 13 June 1894.
[126] Ibid.
[127] SLA/GDSS, no number/94: Gov. to Sec. of State, 30 Aug. 1898.
[128] Ibid.
[129] SLA/NAMP, 26/94: Bai Bureh to Parkes, 9 Jan. 1894; SLA/NALB, 53/94: Parkes to Bai Bureh, 22 Jan. 1894; and SLA/AMP, 45/94: Administrative comments, 4 May 1894.
[130] SLA/NAMP, 362/94: Tr. of letter from Bai Bureh to Parkes, 12 Nov. 1894.

another occasion he requested financial assistance in order to repair roads and bridges in his area.[131] There were, however, indications that he was not content with British jurisdiction. Judging from the frequency of administrative reminders to him concerning his obligation to clear and repair the roads, it would seem that he was adopting the tactic of passive resistance as a means of showing his displeasure.[132] However, British influence continued to grow in Bai Bureh's area, and in two years' time he was to find the British uncomfortably close to him. In 1896, with the establishment of the five districts into which the country was divided, he was to discover that the headquarters of the district in which Kasseh was included was Karene on the north bank of the Mabole River in the chiefdom of Sanda, on the very borders of Kasseh.

Bai Bureh's War

Despite the obvious unpopularity of the hut tax, neither Cardew nor Captain Sharpe anticipated anything but a few isolated incidents of resistance to its collection. They certainly had no idea that, at least six months before its outbreak, the Temne chiefs of the Scarcies had already begun to plan their massive resistance.[133]

In late January 1898, shortly after he assumed office as District Commissioner, Captain Sharpe began collecting the tax at Karene. The first people asked to pay it were the Frontier Police. They protested on the grounds that they considered it unfair to have to pay taxes on houses they had been forced to rent as a result of the government's failure to provide them with barracks for their wives and children. But they gained no concession from Sharpe and had to pay, although with the greatest reluctance.[134] On the evening of the collection, rumors appeared that Bai Bureh was mustering his forces to oppose taxation and that he intended to attack the Karene garrison that same night. No attack materialized, but Sharpe's next preparations were made in an atmosphere of great uneasiness.

Sharpe then attempted to collect the tax in Port Loko, the largest

[131] SLA/NAMP, 354/95: Tr. of letter from Bai Bureh to Parkes, n.d., 1895.

[132] SLA/NALB, 579/94: Supt. of Nat. Affairs to Bai Bureh, 19 Dec. 1894; SLA/NALB, 65/95: Actg. Supt. of Nat. Affairs to Bai Bureh, 16 Feb. 1895; SLA/NALB, 218/95: Supt. of Nat. Affairs to Bai Bureh, 24 May 1895; SLA/NALB, 320/95: Supt. of Nat. Affairs to Bai Bureh, 22 July 1895; SLA/NALB, 448/95: Supt. of Nat. Affairs to Bai Bureh, 17 Sept. 1895; SLA/NALB, 524/96: Supt. of Nat. Affairs to Bai Bureh, 15 Sept. 1896.

[133] Evidence of Capt. Sharpe, Chalmers Report, II, pars. 3942-47.

[134] C. R. Morrison, "The Temnes and the Hut Tax War," *Sierra Leone Weekly News,* 13 Jan. 1934.

and wealthiest town in his district. Here traders refused to pay the tax for fear of reprisals against them by the local people, all of whom opposed the tax. After much palaver, Sharpe detained the leading chief of Port Loko, Bokari Bamp, and warned him that there would be serious consequences if his people molested the traders in any way. Later he released Bokari Bamp for a while on the chief's promise not to hinder the traders' payments even though he would not agree to vouch for his people's conduct. Some traders still refused to pay, and Sharpe detained them also. It was clear that the traders were still not entirely free agents because of the continued hostility and threats of the local people concerning what would happen if they did pay. Sharpe therefore summoned Bokari Bamp, who took a day to respond. When he did finally arrive at the District Commissioner's residence, he came with all his subchiefs and a thousand followers. Sharpe demanded an immediate reply to two questions: (1) Would he permit the traders to pay their taxes without fear of reprisals? and (2) Would he assist in the collection of taxes in Port Loko? "No," was the chief's categorical reply.

Almost immediately Sharpe had Bokari Bamp and four of his subchiefs arrested. He tried all of them summarily for inciting others to disobey, for refusing to collect the tax, and for attempting to overawe a public officer in the execution of his duty. Afraid of public response to their arrest, he sent them to Freetown as soon as opportunity arose, and then installed Sorie Bunki as chief in Bokari Bamp's stead.

All these events had taken place against a background of rumors that Bai Bureh was planning armed resistance. "Warboys" had kept Sharpe under surveillance from the bush along the way from Karene to Port Loko. On the night of his appointment, Sorie Bunki reported to Sharpe that messengers had brought news that Bai Bureh intended to attack Port Loko that night because of his co-operation with the government. The traders, advised of this attack by the subchiefs and themselves personally afraid of the consequences of an invasion by Bai Bureh, fled.[135] Most of the townspeople also fled. From the deserted town Sharpe wrote to the Governor that he could not return to Karene because of the danger of imminent attack by Bai Bureh. He also sent a messenger to the latter ordering him to collect his chiefdom's tax and have it ready when his party came to collect it.

Bai Bureh's "warboys" turned back the messenger, saying that if he wished to go to Karene the road was open, but if he wanted to go to their chief, there was no way.[136] Sharpe, convinced now that there

---

[135] Evidence of C. J. Warburton, Chalmers Report, II, par. 183-4.
[136] Evidence of Lance Cpl. Stephen Williams, Chalmers Report, II, pars. 7576-77.

could be no peace in his district unless Bai Bureh were removed from it, determined to arrest him. He requested an additional twenty veteran police from Freetown to assist in the arrest, because he felt that his own force was too raw and because only fifteen out of the force of sixty were presently available.[137]

Police reinforcements 'embarked on 16 February under the command of Major Tarbet, who in 1894 had already tried to arrest Bai Bureh. After great difficulty in obtaining a guide who would admit to knowledge of Kasseh, Tarbet set out with Sharpe and forty-six police. Their main problem was to discover Bai Bureh's location. What they did find was that the road to Karene was full of groups of armed men. To strengthen their force, they decided to ask the Frontier Officer at Karene to meet them at Kagbantama with as many men as he could spare. On their way, the officers tried to talk to some of the armed men they met on the road near Romeni. Only one would talk to the administrative party. While Sharpe was talking to this man, armed men began to surround him, and he decided he had better return to the column. He seized the man, thinking he could interrogate him later, but the "warboys" became so threatening that Sharpe finally released him.

As it went along, the "warboys" followed the column, jeering at it from all sides and throwing stones. The stoning became so intense that Tarbet ordered the police in the rear guard to open fire. Hearing these shots from the rear, soldiers at the head of the column rushed back to give assistance without orders to do so, leaving the carriers without any protection. The "warboys" then seized some of the latter, several of whom were later found to have been sold in French territory. The "warboys" themselves returned the fire, and only after several more volleys from the police did they retreat. This marked the opening exchange of Bai Bureh's war.[138]

At Kagbantama the force met the Karene party, whose officer reported that there were armed men all along the road to Karene. Tarbet therefore decided to proceed at once to Karene. While fording a river at Massoangball, the column was again attacked by Temne "warboys." Tarbet found Karene safe; however, this was of little comfort, since from Port Loko to Karene all the towns and all the villages except one were deserted. Everyone was in open revolt. The Karene-Port Loko road was now quite unsafe for messengers or small parties. The British had no indigenous allies: the people of Brima Sanda's chiefdom, which

[137] Letter from Capt. Sharpe to Col. Sec., 13 Feb. 1898, Chalmers Report, II, pars. 598-601.

[138] For full account of the day to day progress of the war, see LaRay Denzer, "A Diary of Bai Bureh's War," SLS, 23 (July 1968); 24 (Jan. 1969). Full details of archival sources for the account of the campaigns that follow are given there.

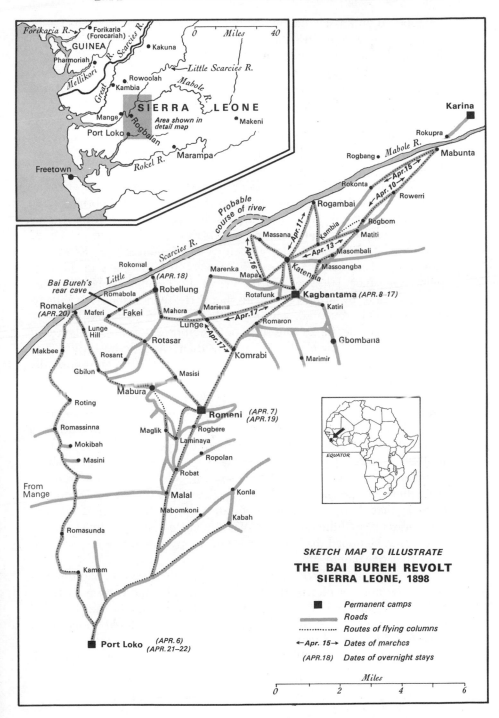

SKETCH MAP TO ILLUSTRATE

THE BAI BUREH REVOLT
SIERRA LEONE, 1898

■ Permanent camps
Roads
·············· Routes of flying columns
←Apr. 15→ Dates of marches
(APR.18) Dates of overnight stays

neighbored on Kasseh, had joined Bai Bureh, opposing their chief, who remained loyal to the British. It was clear to Sharpe and Tarbet that no British administration could function without the removal of Bai Bureh and a show of British force.

Meanwhile in Port Loko, rumors were circulating to the effect that Sharpe had been captured, taken to Bai Bureh, and killed. The threat of attack on the small garrison of police was ever present. In response they disarmed everybody in the town, not taking much trouble to distinguish between friendly and hostile Temne. There were one or two incidents.

All communication between Karene and Port Loko ended when the Temne captured most of the canoes at Rokupru on 19 February 1898 (see map). The only way to send messages to Freetown from Karene was by a circuitous route through Kambia or by carrier pigeon. On 22 February, Tarbet took a party of forty-eight police from Karene to Rokupru, where he had to cross his troops in four relays in the only remaining canoe. He staved off the fire of the Temne "warboys" on the opposite bank by firing rockets at them. He then rushed the village, but the Temne retreated, waiting until the police recrossed the river to fire on them again. During this confrontation it became evident that the Temne were much better armed than the administration had thought, being equipped with better guns than the Dane guns normally sold by the traders.

On his return to Karene, Tarbet requested reinforcements from Freetown. Cardew did not inform his Executive Council of the seriousness of the situation until this time, when he recommended that "a demonstration of force should be made to compel the natives to return to their allegiance."[139] The Executive Council finally agreed that a company of the West India Regiment should be sent to Karene to strengthen the police force there. Cardew then cabled the Secretary of State that there was armed resistance to the collection of the hut tax, and requested the use of the West India Regiment, adding optimistically that he hoped that the "service of troops will not be required for more than one month."[140]

Two days later Tarbet informed him that the situation had deteriorated. The number of armed warriors in the area had continued to increase and more and more villages on the Karene side of the river had come out in support of Bai Bureh. Meanwhile, Sorie Bunki appeared to have fled from Port Loko, although much later it was learned that he had been captured by supporters of the Temne warriors and murdered.

[139] SLA/ECM, 22 Feb. 1898.
[140] PRO, CO/267/437: tel. from Gov. to Sec. of State, 22 Feb. 1898.

Panic prevailed in the town and surrounding areas. Cardew ordered Sharpe to consult with the officer in command of the troops he was sending from Freetown to determine how many troops he would need to occupy the whole district. The country to the east of Kasseh feared attack from the Temne, but the country to the north supported them.

Major Richard Joseph Norris, the commander of the company of West India Regiment troops leaving Freetown, had instructions to remain at Karene "to support the Frontier Police who will thus be left free to operate in the Kassi District against the insurgents and to effect the arrest of Bai Bureh." If the police could not accomplish this mission, he was to give the District Commissioner what assistance he required and assume full control of operations. However, the District Commissioner was to retain his civil jurisdiction and to bring to trial any prisoners taken in battle. Cardew hoped that once the troops arrived, resistance to the administration's authority would collapse, and that the District Commissioner could then make an example of Bai Bureh, whom he described as a "great drunkard and a worthless character."[141]

The role the regimental troops were to play in the operations soon became an extremely controversial point in the tactics and strategy of the war. Cardew preferred the lightly equipped Frontier Police and was of the opinion that their numbers would be sufficient to bring Karene under control. According to him, the West India Regiment was only to garrison Karene and Port Loko in order to allow the police to concentrate on Bai Bureh's arrest, aiding them when they needed assistance. Because of their light field equipment, Cardew believed that the police could move more easily through the bush and that they would be an excellent match for the similarly unencumbered Temne. (For example, when Norris's company had left Freetown accompanied by 540 carriers and 912 loads, Cardew had felt compelled to complain to the officer in charge that such equipment was far in excess of what the expedition demanded.) However, when the troops arrived on the scene of field operations and saw how serious the actual situation was, their commander decided that lightly equipped police could not reestablish administrative control in the area, and that the government's only alternative was to use fully equipped troops in full force to impose its authority.

Norris disembarked with his troops at Robat on the Great Scarcies and marched to Karene without being attacked, although he was closely observed all the way. When he reached the Karene garrison, he found the men tense, fearful, hemmed in, and expecting attack at any moment. Food was in very short supply. Norris quickly concluded that the

141 SLA/GDSS, 10/98: Gov. to Sec. of State, 25 Feb. 1898.

country around the garrison was held by the Temne, and that the lack of food supplies would make it impossible for his company to stay more than three days in Karene. He suggested that Karene be evacuated since he felt that too much attention was being given to the question of maintaining communications with it. But Cardew objected violently that such an evacuation was politically impossible since it would "reveal great weakness and cause the rising to extend not only throughout the district of Karene but probably all over the Protectorate."[142] He was also very angry at Norris's decision to return to Port Loko, since his doing so prevented Tarbet and Norris from setting out on their planned expedition with the police.

In Karene, the situation became so serious that, on 2 March 1898, Sharpe asked Norris to declare martial law in his district and to assume full responsibility for Port Loko and Karene.[143] On the day following the declaration of martial law, Norris marched to Port Loko, twenty-five miles from Karene, in an attempt to restore communication between the two places. From hiding places in the bush along the road, Temne "warboys" constantly sniped at his column, every so often coming out in full attack. Only after intensive fighting did the troops drive them off. For ten consecutive hours, all the way to Port Loko, the company fought hard: they stormed and captured seven villages and three strongly fortified towns. Upon their arrival in Port Loko, Norris felt that matters were so grave he immediately requisitioned two additional companies from Freetown. He informed Cardew that he had decided to make Port Loko his headquarters and would wait there for further reinforcements before he determined his next moves.

As soon as Cardew received Norris's report, he conferred with Colonel Arthur Bosworth, the Commander of Troops in West Africa. They decided that only one company was needed as reinforcement. Cardew justified this decision on the grounds that he did not believe that Norris was as hard pressed as he made out, and that he could easily hold his own. Norris was furious at Cardew's intervention and his refusal to appreciate the seriousness of the situation in Karene.

The Temne attacked Port Loko three days after the declaration of martial law. Early that morning, the fire alarm sounded, and a house near the Church Missionary Society station was set on fire. This appeared to have been a signal for attack for, immediately afterward, "warboys" fired on the town from the direction of Old Port Loko. The tempo of their attack increased throughout the morning, and only after four and a half hours of steady battle did the regimental troops force

[142] SLA/GCDSS, enc. to 14/98: Gov. to Maj. Norris, 1 Mar. 1898.

[143] SLA/GCDSS, enc. 4 to 15/98: Report from Capt. Sharpe to Col. Sec., 2 Mar. 1898.

them to retreat. Once the attack subsided, the regiment set about enlarging and strengthening its position by clearing more of the surrounding bush and demolishing any huts within the area. Later that day, a company of reinforcements from Freetown arrived on the H.M.S. *Fox*. Norris took the opportunity to request assistance from the naval officer in charge for a combined attack on the Temne. Late in the afternoon all Temne "warboys" were driven out of Old Port Loko by shell fire from the *Fox*, supported by fire from the seven-pound gun manned by Norris's troops.

Norris straightaway requested another company and another seven pounder from Freetown, stressing that he could not return to Karene without more troops and more supplies. He proposed to distribute his troops in three directions: one company to garrison Port Loko; another to garrison Karene; and one to form a flying column under his command to patrol along the Port Loko-Karene road.

On the night of the sixth, Temne "warboys" attacked Karene itself, but the police drove them back. Captain Stansfield arrived in Port Loko bringing the new company of reinforcements which had disembarked at Robat. He reported that the Temne had attempted to burn his column by setting fire to the dry bush along the line of march, but that they had never actually attacked it. After receiving this report, Cardew ordered the Frontier Police to intensify their efforts to arrest Bai Bureh, and Sharpe to resume his political and administrative duties as soon as practicable.

Cardew was still optimistic that the situation was not nearly so serious as Norris and Sharpe maintained, gaining confidence from the fact that no reports had come in from Norris since the last reinforcements had arrived. He drafted an ambitious, but quite unrealistic plan for putting down the resistance and arresting its leaders. But before he could send his instructions, reports arrived from Norris, doubting whether he had sufficient troops to arrest Bai Bureh and requesting yet another company. Cardew, however, considered that Norris was exaggerating the seriousness of the situation and asked him to wait until he had seen how the operations of the two companies already under his command fared before requesting more. But Norris was soon asking for not one but two further companies because Sharpe, on his way to Port Loko with twenty police and twenty soldiers, had been seriously opposed at Malal by Temne "warboys" from newly constructed stockades. Sharpe now concurred with Norris that the police were "absolutely powerless" to quell the rising.[144] Cardew informed the Secretary

[144] SLA/GCDSS, enc. 2 to 17/98: Report from Maj. Norris to Gov., 9 Mar. 1898.

of State that he felt he could no longer shoulder the responsibility of withholding further reinforcements in the light of Norris's repeated requests even though he still contended that "the troops he had should have been sufficient to quell the disturbance had he made more use of them on the offensive."[145]

Actually, during the period from 23 February to 1 April, government forces had taken the offensive only once. Throughout this period it was Bai Bureh and his "warboys," estimated at three thousand, who held the initiative. Their tactics were simple but effective against the heavily encumbered troops of the West India Regiment whose officers knew little of the terrain over which they were fighting. They concentrated primarily on attacks on the columns, paying particular attention to eliminating the white officers. The insistence of Cardew that Karene be maintained as a garrison, and the consequent necessity of keeping the road open to it for supply and communication purposes, made the troops patrolling the road an easy target for ambush. Bai Bureh's strategy was primarily defensive and obstructive. His "warboys" avoided direct confrontation in battle; they preferred sudden raids, ambushes, and, in particular, attacks from behind stockades and war fences.

The stockades were built so that they supported each other and were generally positioned in places difficult to reach. They were never very large, usually from twelve to forty yards long, and were not visible from the opposite side of the road. Usually built out of blocks of trees, with a firing trench running the length of the stockade just inside the wall area, the stockades were placed on high ground so that the Temne were able to retreat swiftly down the slopes, if necessary. At times British troops were able to outflank the stockades, but because of the dense bush, this occurred only rarely.

The Temne maintained communication among themselves concerning the movement of the British troops by a network of spies and a system of signals: often three guns were heard by the troops whenever a column halted. By concentrating on ambush instead of open attacks, the Temne had the advantage since, except for the Kagbantama road, the entire countryside was dense bush. The roads were little more than bush paths. Generally speaking, the Temne used guerrilla hit-and-run tactics which were ideal for dealing with an extended column moving slowly along roads and paths it hardly knew.

Only once did the British go on the offensive before 1 April, and it was then that the Temne showed just how effective their tactics could be. A large British column consisting of 6 officers, 90 soldiers, and 640 carriers set out from Port Loko for Karene on 13 March. It had to oper-

---

[145] SLA/GCDSS, 17/98: Gov. to Sec. of State, 12 Mar. 1898.

ate in thickly wooded country interspersed with hills and intersected by rivers and swamps. On the first day's march, the column's commander, Major Buck, razed to the ground the villages and stockades of Ropolon-Rosannie, Robat, Malal, and Robant. He met with no opposition. He encamped at Mahera for the night and burned it to the ground as he left the next morning. On the second day, his column was greatly delayed going through the swamp, not reaching its destination of Butien until that afternoon, when it encountered heavy resistance. Temne, led personally by Bai Bureh (as it was later discovered) fired at them from stockades in the town as they approached. Only after long, intensive fighting did the troops succeed in taking the town. Later that evening, Temne again attacked the column and continued harassing it until dawn. As the column left Butien the next morning, it burned the village and proceeded unopposed to Kagbantama where it was ambushed. After a long battle, the soldiers dispersed the "warboys" and moved on toward Rotigon, where they were again attacked from five stockades which had been placed at intervals of fifteen yards on both sides of the road. The column was barely able to withstand this attack.

Consequently, when the "warboys" retreated the commander of the troops decided not to pursue them but instead followed paths through the bush on the windward side of the town. When the Temnes discovered that the troops were neither following them nor attacking the towns along the way, they suspected that they had inflicted severe damage. They set fire to the extremely dry grass and bush along the windward side of the road, and the country was in flames for a mile in every direction. To counter it, the troops were ordered to set fire to the bush on the leeward side of the path, which gave the company sufficient space to wait out the fire with little or no danger of attack. Nevertheless, the result was that it could not move until the next day.

Resuming the march at daybreak, the column encountered more intense resistance at the stockaded towns of Romaron and Katentia (one of Bai Bureh's strongest towns). Only after heavy firing with the "magazine" gun did the troops manage to disperse the "warboys." After this battle the column marched to Karene with no further resistance except for occasional Temne sniping. Although the column was able to destroy more stockades along the route, Bai Bureh's forces had by this time exacted a heavy toll.

Cardew was very alarmed by the systematic burning of villages and towns. If villages and towns were to be burned, he urged that they be carefully selected and limited to Bai Bureh's chief towns. Sharpe, however, supported Norris's decision and tactics, pointing out that before the column had started out Norris had advised the troop commander to use his discretion as to which towns to destroy. He assured

Cardew that only those towns which were fortified or offered resistance would be destroyed, and that all the officers concerned appreciated that this policy would be hard on the women and children. Nevertheless, "events necessitated the destruction of the principal towns of Bai Bureh's and of all villages where armed people met. The whole of his country had risen, and [Sharpe could] see no other way of punishing the offenders than by destroying their towns. . . ."[146] Criticizing the hut tax, a local correspondent of the *Daily Telegraph* noted sourly: "So far as we are informed, most of the huts on which he [the Governor] intends to collect the debts have been burnt down, if not by the people themselves, by the soldiers."[147]

On 17 March a company commanded by Major Stansfield, which had set out for Kambia from Karene, was driven back to Magbolonta, only six miles from Karene. This reverse was of such gravity that Cardew agreed that Colonel Bosworth himself should assume command in the field. Bosworth left on the evening of the nineteenth for Port Loko with a company consisting of 8 officers, 92 troops, 300 carriers, and a seven-pound gun. He decided that Port Loko was a more suitable base for his operations than Karene. Before determining what further operations would consist of, he asked Captain Carr Smith to report on his column's operations which had begun on 22 March. When Cardew received Bosworth's report, he concluded that the situation was so serious that he should go to Port Loko himself.

Meanwhile on 25 March, Carr Smith began his return to Port Loko, but the Temne opposed the troops so stubbornly outside of Matiti that they forced the column back to Karene. Carr Smith and one other officer were wounded, leaving the column under the command of its only other able-bodied officer. Receiving news of Carr Smith's retreat, Bosworth decided to march immediately for Karene in order to clear the road of opposition. He selected one hundred soldiers and four officers and took as little equipment as possible. He experienced strong opposition at Malal and Romeni but managed to push on to Kagbantama, where he met even greater opposition. By the time the troops had dispersed the "warboys," they were so exhausted that they were barely able to reach Karene. Bosworth himself collapsed and died from what was described as "heat apoplexy."[148]

The Temne tried to close the road again, entrenching themselves in stone stockades which were at least two feet thick; these had firing holes formed by inserting bamboo in them. They were almost bullet-

---

[146] SLA/CMP, 40/98: Sharpe to Col. Sec., 16 Mar. 1898.

[147] *Daily Telegraph* (London), 4 Apr. 1898.

[148] PRO, CO/267/437: Conf. Desp. 22, Gov. to Sec. of State, 31 Mar. 1898.

proof and the seven pounder had little effect on them. They were destroyed only after severe fighting and many British casualties.[149] It was obvious that continuous patrols would be needed in order to prevent the frequent reconstruction of the stockades.

Keeping the Karene-Port Loko road open had involved so many casualties and had so diverted the troops from their main aim of tracking down the leaders of the resistance that Major Burke, from the Port Loko garrison, once again urged the abandonment of Karene: "It will never be possible to take active measures against Bai Bureh with any chance of success as long as this station is occupied."[150] Despite Cardew's assurances that Burke was exaggerating the gravity of the situation, Bosworth's successor, Lieutenant Colonel John Willoughby Astell Marshall, found on his arrival at Port Loko that the troops were working under every possible disadvantage.[151] Political reasons, however, dictated that Karene should not be abandoned although the Colonial Office sympathized with the soldiers' point of view.[152] Chamberlain considered that "Sir J. Cardew is inclined to interfere too much in the details of the military action,"[153] and he later cabled Cardew not to interfere in the conduct of the operations.

Given the necessity of keeping the road to Karene open, Marshall decided to establish an auxiliary garrison at Romeni, as the best intermediate point between Karene and Port Loko. Once it had been established, he set out to implement a scorched earth policy in Kasseh country. From 1 to 10 April, he concentrated his attention on the road between Port Loko and Karene. Taking out a flying column each day, he razed every village which offered resistance to his advance. The Temne opposed him all the way, but by 10 April, he had gained complete control of the road. He left garrisons at Romeni and Karene which were to maintain the government's position and prevent further construction of stockades. He then extended his operations to the entire area, moving through the country systematically, destroying every village as he came upon it. Temne resistance was steady, increasing in strength after the fifteenth. Sometimes the column destroyed as many as twenty stockades a day, and fought three or four hard battles. The Temne offered par-

[149] Ibid.

[150] SLA/GCDSS, enc. 1 to 23/98: Report from Maj. Burke to Gov., 29 Mar. 1898.

[151] SLA/GCDSS, enc. 7 to 23/98: Report from Lt. Col. Marshall to Gov., 3 Apr. 1898.

[152] PRO, CO/267/437: minute by W. H. Mercer on Gov. to Sec. of State re Conf. Desp. 23, 2 Apr. 1898.

[153] PRO, CO/267/437: tel. from Gov. to Sec. of State, 4 Apr. 1898 with minute by Chamberlain, 4 Apr. 1898.

ticularly strong resistance at Katentia and Matiti on 11 April, at Kagbantama on 13 April, and at Mafouri on 25 April.

Once Marshall gained control of the country of Kasseh, he began operations in that of the Sanda. Wherever he was opposed, he destroyed the villages as he had done in Kasseh; where he was not, he assembled the villagers and explained to them what the troops were doing and that they would surely catch Bai Bureh soon. Toward the end of April, Marshall turned his attention to the countries of Bai Bureh's allies. By 13 May, he felt that the government had re-established control over the country. He sent letters to the chiefs warning them to desist from their hostile activities and to withdraw all their support from Bai Bureh.

By that time, of course, the war had spread to other parts of the Protectorate, and Cardew had requested a European battalion to deal with the situation in a telegram which had "a look of panic" about it.[154] By the end of May, however, Cardew was writing to the Secretary of State eulogizing Colonel Marshall's "energy, enterprise and endurance."[155] But Marshall's victory had been achieved only by using military methods that ruined much of Temne country and exhibited the civilization of the white man in its worst aspects. That Marshall had to resort to such methods is a tribute to the fighting skills of Bai Bureh who, as is appropriate for a guerrilla leader, remained a shadowy figure in the reports of the British campaigns. Nevertheless, it was clearly recognized that the length and stiffness of Temne resistance was due to him. While Cardew wrote optimistically that he hoped that "Bai Bureh's powers of resistance were completely broken," he acknowledged that "he will be a disturbing element till he is caught."[156] Still, the government could not contemplate the capture of Bai Bureh and other war leaders until after the rains, which in Sierra Leone fall with an intensity that made impossible British operations in Temne country. Thus there were only a few isolated incidents during the rains (May to October), the most serious of which was the attempt by a band of Temne "warboys" stationed at Robarrong to burn the Karene barracks.[157] This attack proved unsuccessful, and Cardew was not unduly worried, feeling confident that the situation was mostly under control in both the Mende and Temne areas. So sure was he that he made a provisional request for leave in October.[158]

Cardew rejected all attempts at mediation between Bai Bureh and

[154] PRO, CO/267/438: tel. from Gov. to Sec. of State, 5 May 1898 with minute by W. H. Mercer of 5 May 1898.
[155] PRO, CO/267/438: Conf. Desp. 39, Gov. to Sec. of State, 27 May 1898.
[156] Ibid.
[157] PRO, CO/267/440: Conf. Desp. 73, Gov. to Sec. of State, 17 Sept. 1898.
[158] PRO, CO/267/440: Desp. 174, Gov. to Sec. of State, 28 Aug. 1898.

the government, insisting that Bai Bureh's "submission must be precedent to any proclamation of a general amnesty,"[159] and offered a reward of £100 for information leading to his capture. However, he did inform the chief through intermediaries that his life would be spared if he surrendered.[160]

Although Cardew insisted on the surrender of Bai Bureh, he proposed to treat the people of the Karene district leniently. A general amnesty would be proclaimed in the district where "the insurgents have carried on their warfare on fairly humane principles. I do not say that they would have spared any of our troops had they fallen into their hands, but with the exception of the murder of the **Rev. W. J. Humphrey** [the Principal of Fourah Bay College], Chief **Suri Bonkeh** and a few other cases, they have refrained from killing non-combatants."[161] (Such leniency was not the case in the Mende areas where many European and Creole civilians had been murdered indiscriminately.)

Cardew continued to reject offers for mediation even though his optimistic assessment in June that there was "every hope that peace [would] soon be effected by the surrender of Bai Bureh"[162] had by early October proved unjustified. Freetown Muslims passed on letters from Bai Bureh, in which he expressed "every earnest desire for peace,"[163] to Sir Donald Chalmers, sole Commissioner conducting the enquiry into the causes of the Hut Tax War. Chalmers offered to mediate, much to the chagrin of Cardew who detested him and was sensitive to any action on Chalmers's part that might demean the gubernatorial authority. Meanwhile demonstrating his opposition to Cardew's uncompromising stand, Chalmers, as the Queen's Commissioner, wrote to Bai Bureh through the Secretary of Native Affairs and conveyed peaceful greetings to him: "He wishes peace for him and all this troubled country. He advises that for the good of all the people, Bai Bureh should listen with a good ear to the proposal which the Governor makes to him."[164] Mediation, however, proved impossible due to Cardew's insistence on unconditional surrender.

On 11 November Bai Bureh was finally tracked down in swampy, thickly vegetated country by a British patrol.[165] Under constant snip-

159 PRO, CO/267/439: no number, Gov. to Sec. of State, 28 July 1898.

160 PRO, CO/267/439: Conf. Desp. 45, Gov. to Sec. of State, 7 June 1898.

161 PRO, CO/267/439: no number, Gov. to Sec. of State, 9 June 1898.

162 SLA/GDSS, 110/98: Gov. to Sec. of State, 2 June 1898.

163 SLA/GDSS, 219/98: Gov. to Sec. of State, 6 Oct. 1898.

164 SLA/NALB, 447/98: M. G. Wingfield (Sec. to Chalmers) to Supt. of Nat. Affairs, 11 Oct. 1898.

165 SLA/GDSS: tel. from Gov. to Sec. of State, 12 Nov. 1898. Fyfe incorrectly gives the date as 16 Nov., see Fyfe, History, 590.

ing from Temne "warboys," Captain Goodwyn and forty troops caught up with him near Roballan. The Temne fired on the troops from a stockade. Two of the "warboys" rushed to the bush at the soldiers' return of fire, and the resulting drama ended the war: "Sergeant Thomas ran forward in pursuit of one who seemed to move rather slower than his companion. Getting close to him he shouted to him to stop or he would shoot, at the same time firing over his head. The man threw himself on the ground and was secured. He proved to be Bai Bureh."[166]   At 1:00 p.m. on 12 November, the elderly warrior, who had a striking face dominated by a very long aquiline nose and a remarkable protruding lower lip, was brought to Karene. He had lived in the bush for twenty-three weeks. Earlier in the month, Captain Goodwyn had destroyed his *fakai* (bush camp) and he had only narrowly escaped at that time.[167] In London, they were delighted: "The success will no doubt greatly simplify matters . . . it will no doubt much diminish any resistance by the natives all over the Protectorate," Mercer wrote to Antrobus on the fourteenth, "and the need either for a white battalion or for reinforcements from the Niger should be disposed of."[168]

It remained only to dispose of Bai Bureh. The government planned to bring him to trial in Karene since it felt that a trial in Freetown would cause too much popular excitement. Sharpe's original plan had been to try him for treason.[169] Cardew concurred and cabled the Secretary of State that he intended to try him for high treason or treasonable felony though he would not impose the death penalty.[170] The Colonial Office, however, doubted that Bai Bureh could be treated as a British subject, a necessary prerequisite for trying him for treason,[171] and instructed Cardew to delay proceedings. The local law officers opined that treason had not been committed by Bai Bureh since, in fact, he owed no allegiance to the Queen; therefore it was impossible to convict him of this charge. He was never brought to trial.[172]

Bai Bureh was detained while awaiting London's decision on Chalmers's recommendations. At first he was kept in Karene, but, after a Temne guard in the West African Regiment attempted to help him to

---

[166] PRO, CO/267: enc. to Conf. Desp. 273, Report of Capture of Bai Bureh from Lt. Col. Cunningham, Commanding Karene Dist. to Col. Woodgate, C. B., 23 Nov. 1898. Cf. the death of John Chilembwe, below, 342.

[167] Ibid.; also enc. report of Capt. Goodwyn.

[168] PRO, CO/267/441: tel. from Gov. to Sec. of State, 12 Nov. 1898 with minute of 14 Nov. 1898 by W. H. Mercer.

[169] SLA/CMP, 149/98: District Commissioner (Karene) to Col. Sec., 14 Nov. 1898.

[170] PRO, CO/267/441: tel. from Gov. to Sec. of State, 16 Nov. 1898.

[171] Ibid.; with minute by E. Wingfield of 16 Nov. 1898.

[172] Fyfe, *History*, 590.

escape, the District Commissioner decided to move him to the Freetown jail. There he received a special diet and was kept separate from the convicted prisoners. In April 1899, the administration removed him from the jail to a house on the outskirts of Freetown in Ascension Town, near the residence of the exiled Asantehene, Prempeh I, and kept him under guard. The Governor gave two reasons for his removal: first, there was a smallpox epidemic in the jail; and secondly, "the evil accommodation which that building affords at the best of times is an unnecessary addition to the punishment of political offenders of importance."[173]

Crowds flocked to the house hoping to catch a glimpse of this great opponent to British rule. Sir Matthew Nathan, the acting Governor, decided against allowing Bai Bureh to return to his own country, fearing that to do so might be regarded as weakness on the part of the government.[174] Instead he ordered him deported to the Gold Coast along with Bai Sherbro of Yonni and Chief Nyagua of Panguma. Neither of these two latter chiefs had taken part in the war, but the government greatly feared their influence. Both died in exile, but in 1905 Bai Bureh was allowed to return to Sierra Leone and resume his position. Then very old, he remained there without further incident until his death in 1908.

Conclusions

Like Samori in Guinée, Bai Bureh's sustained resistance to the British has made him a national hero of independent Sierra Leone.[175] In 1967, shortly after assuming power as Chairman of the National Reformation Council, Colonel Juxon Smith declared that his Council "had decided to work on the principles of three eminent Sierra Leone citizens—the late Prime Minister, Sir Milton Margai, the late Bai Bureh, and the late Mr. Isaac Theophilus Wallace-Johnson—that is, honesty, integrity and nationalism."[176]

Over the years, both before and after his capture, many myths have been woven about Bai Bureh. Many tales have been told of his magical powers, of his ability to disappear at will, or to live underwater. Cardew had reported that he was "regarded by the natives throughout the Protectorate, and I may add, by many in this Colony as a great Fetish man. For the stories current about him are that he had the power to

[173] SLA/GDSS, 135/99: Gov. to Sec. of State, 24 Apr. 1898.
[174] SLA/GDSS, enc. to Desp. no number/98: Gov. to Sec. of State, 10 Apr. 1898.
[175] See above, Yves Person, "Samori and Resistance to the French," 80-112.
[176] *Daily Mail* (Freetown), 1 Apr. 1967.

transform himself into animals and live under water. . . . "[177] However
fantastic the accounts that have grown up about him, most agree that
he was a superb soldier. Creoles spoke of him as the Big Black General.[178] Captain Braithwaite Wallis, Frontier Police officer, although
not in Karene district, wrote that Bai Bureh:

> besides being a man of acute intelligence, was a renowned and suc-
> cessful leader. . . . His name is now a household word for miles
> around, and in many villages mothers stilled their crying babies by
> whispering the name of their redoubtable Ethiopian into their infants'
> ears. This was the man who successfully defied the power of Great
> Britain for many months together, and thereby made for himself a
> name that will never die so long as the brave and misguided people
> whom he led remain a nation.[179]

However, one English writer, Elizabeth Hirst, has tried to show,
from oral tradition, that at heart Bai Bureh was a man of peace.[180] According to her and her co-author (and main informant), he had given
up fighting for a long time, taking a vow of peace which he broke
only when his sense of Lokko patriotism forced him into action when
Samori's *sofa* menaced the Lokko. While their thesis is apparently supported by some oral Lokko traditions, it conflicts with many Temne
traditions which emphasize Bai Bureh's essentially war-like character.
Moreover, the archival records reveal that he was almost continuously
engaged in war from 1865 until 1898. Indeed, many of the events recorded by Hirst and Kamara, none of which are dated, do not correspond with what the archives show clearly did happen. Since their
book is used in the schools, their portrait of Bai Bureh as a man of
peace and a model for Christian school children has gained wide currency in Sierra Leone.

It is essential, however, to contradict their thesis that Bai Bureh
gave up war for a long period of time both because it is not true, and
because it is clear that the major explanation for his success against the
British was his experience as a war leader—unparalleled in those parts
not only for its length but also for its continuity. Bai Bureh never suffered from that bane of generals—a long period of peace. The significance of his war with the British was that while many other Africans
had the will to resist European penetration, he was one of the few who
also had the skill.

[177] SLA/GCDSS, 277/98: Gov. to Sec. of State, 30 Nov. 1898.
[178] Appendix M, Letter from R. O. George, R. S. M. Frontier Police, to Adjutant, n.d., Chalmers Report II.
[179] C. Braithwaite Wallis, *The Advance of Our West African Empire* (London, 1903), 50-51.
[180] Hirst and Kamara, *Benga*.

THE ZULU[1] DISTURBANCES IN NATAL

SHULA MARKS

Introduction

On 8 February 1906 the Colonial Office in London received a startling telegram from the Governor of Natal, stating that two white police officers had been shot in an attempt to arrest a group of armed Africans at Trewirgie, a farm near the village of Byrnetown, to the south of Pietermaritzburg. The colonists of Natal were as dismayed, if rather less surprised. The imposition of a poll tax in September 1905 on all

This essay draws heavily on the author's Ph.D. thesis, "Black and White in Self-Governing Natal: An Assessment of the 1906-8 Disturbances" (University of London, 1967), of which it originally formed a part. The thesis has been published in revised form as *Reluctant Rebellion, An Assessment of the 1906-8 Disturbances in Natal* (Oxford, 1970).

ABM	American Board of Missions
AGO	Attorney General's Office, Natal
Col. Col.	Colenso Collection
MLA	Member of the Legislative Assembly
NLA	Natal Legislative Assembly
NNAC	Natal Native Affairs Commission
RCM	Richmond Court Martial
SNA	Secretary for Native Affairs
USNA	Undersecretary for Native Affairs, Natal
ZA	Zululand Archives
ZR	*A History of the Zulu Rebellion* (Stuart)

[1] The term "Zulu" today has a linguistic rather than a strictly ethnic connotation, though it is used in a loose sense to refer to all the chiefdoms and clans of Natal and Zululand. As a result of the conquest of Natal and Zululand by Shaka, the chief of the Zulu people at the beginning of the nineteenth century, the name became widely applied at least to those people actually incorporated into the Zulu kingdom. It fact the use of the term is fraught with difficulties. Many of the Africans

213

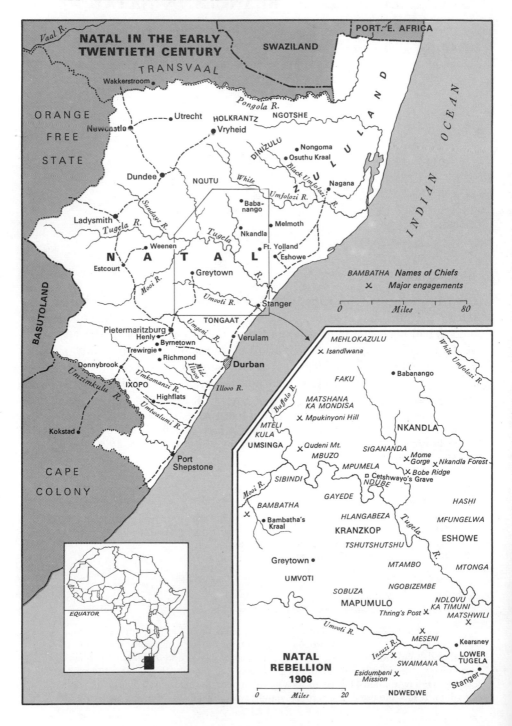

NATAL IN THE EARLY
TWENTIETH CENTURY

PORT. E. AFRICA

SWAZILAND

TRANSVAAL

Vaal R.

Wakkerstroom

ORANGE

FREE

STATE

Utrecht

HOLKRANTZ

NGOTSHE

Newcastle

Pongola R.

Vryheid

DINIZULU

Nongoma

Osuthu Kraal

Dundee

NQUTU

White

Nagana

Baba-
nango

Black Umfolozi R.

Umfolozi R.

INDIAN

OCEAN

ZULULAND

Ladysmith

Tugela R.

Sandaga R.

Tugela

Melmoth

Nkandla

Weenen

Ft. Yolland

Eshowe

N   A   T   A   L

Estcourt

Greytown

BASUTOLAND

Mooi R.

Umvoti R.

BAMBATHA   Names of Chiefs
    ✕   Major engagements

0   Miles   80

Pietermaritzburg

Henly

Trewirgie

Byrnetown

Richmond

Donnybrook

Umzimkulu R.

Umkomanzi R.

IXOPO

Highflats

Umtwalumi R.

Verulam

Durban

Illovo R.

Stanger

TONGAAT

Umgeni R.

Mid Illovo

Kokstad

CAPE

COLONY

Port
Shepstone

EQUATOR

MEHLOKAZULU

✕ Isandlwana

White Umfolozi R.

FAKU

Babanango

Buffalo R.

MATSHANA
KA MONDISA

✕ Mpukinyoni Hill

MTELI
KULA

UMSINGA

Qudeni Mt. ✕

MBUZO

NKANDLA

SIGANANDA

Mome
Gorge ✕

✕ Nkandla Forest

✕ Bobe Ridge

MPUMELA

□ Cetshwayo's Grave

NDUBE

Mooi R.

SIBINDI

GAYEDE

HASHI

BAMBATHA

✕

HLANGABEZA

Bambatha's
Kraal

KRANZKOP

TSHUTSHUTSHU

MFUNGELWA

ESHOWE

Tugela R.

Greytown ●

MTAMBO

MTONGA

UMVOTI

NGOBIZEMBE

SOBUZA

MAPUMULO

Thring's Post ✕

NDLOVU
KA TIMUNI

MATSHWILI
✕

✕
MESENI

Kearsney

Umvoti R.

Inzuzi R.

SWAIMANA

LOWER
TUGELA

Esidumbeni ✕
Mission

Stanger

NATAL
REBELLION
1906

0   Miles   20

NDWEDWE

adult males[2] in the multiracial colony was widely opposed by the African majority.[3] The long hot summer months of 1905-6[4] were full of disquieting rumors. Besides, the Africans had begun killing their white pigs, white goats, and white chickens, which many settlers feared to be a signal that white people would be next. Since the slaughter was said to result from an order by Dinuzulu, the son and heir of Cetshwayo, the last Zulu king, it appeared particularly sinister. Indeed, James Stuart, whose semi-official *History of the Zulu Rebellion* is still the essential starting point for any discussion of the disturbances, felt sure that the order had emanated from Dinuzulu and that "its underlying intention . . . was that the natives of Natal and Zululand should rise against the white man. Its purpose was to warn as well as to unite by use of a threat."[5]

---

of Natal were refugees from the Zulu kings and for most of the nineteenth century would almost certainly have denied the appellation "Zulu." As late as the first decade of this century, the true "Zulu" contemptuously called the Africans of Natal "Amakafula" (Kaffirs) and still call them "Amalala" (apparently the name of one of the streams of migration into Natal). By the beginning of this century, however, it is clear that certain non-Zulu groups even in Natal were beginning to class themselves as "Zulu"—perhaps partly in response to a European tendency to classify them in this way. For some it was a more self-conscious assertion of nationalism, an attempt to overcome the tribal divisions which beset African society in Natal. Under pressure from the white settlers and their government, even Africans in Natal looked back to the days of Shaka with nostalgia. Both traditionalist and Christian Africans in Natal were turning to the representative of the Zulu royal house, Dinuzulu, to save them from white rule, as witness the many stories associated with his name casting him in a messianic role. As we shall see, during the disturbances the rebels made wide use of his name, war badge, and war cry, in an attempt to create a more unified opposition to the government which could transcend the "tribal" disunities in the colony.

The alternative term to Zulu—Nguni, or Natal Nguni—would be somewhat pedantic in the context of the 1906 disturbances and perhaps create as many problems as it solves. For a discussion of some of the terminological problems involved see Marks, "Natal, the Nguni and Their Historians," *Journal of African History,* VIII (1967), 529-40.

[2] Except those Africans who were liable for the hut tax and indentured Indian laborers.

[3] The population of Natal in 1904 was: Whites—97,109; Africans—904,041; Coloureds (people of mixed European and African descent as well as a number of Mauritian immigrants) and Asians—108,604.

[4] The Natal summer runs from October to March and is both hot and humid. For the Africans the last few months of the year are frequently a lean period before the new season's crops are ripe. The 1905-6 summer appears to have been particularly hot and oppressive.

[5] James Stuart, *A History of the Zulu Rebellion, 1906, and of Dinuzulu's Arrest, Trial and Expatriation* (London, 1913), 105. (Henceforth cited as ZR.) Stuart, a magistrate, was a captain in the Natal Field Artillery, and acted as in-

The course of the "Zulu disturbances" in Natal may be divided into three stages, which will be briefly summarized here as an introduction to their more detailed description and analysis below. The first phase began when magistrates trying to collect the poll tax at the beginning of 1906 were met by angry Africans waving sticks and shouting war-cries.[6] The killing of the two white policemen seemed the signal for widespread revolt against white rule. The atmosphere was further inflamed when it was learned that the armed men were members of an independent African sect,[7] it being generally believed that the African separatist churches had as their goal the white man's overthrow not only in the church but in the state as well. Therefore, on 9 February martial law was declared throughout Natal and the military alerted.[8]

For almost two months after this initial episode, armed forces under the command of Colonel Duncan McKenzie in the south and Colonel George Leuchars in the north marched through African locations,[9] burning crops and kraals and confiscating cattle. As the result of sum-

---

telligence agent with McKenzie's column both in 1906 and 1907. An able Zulu linguist, he was appointed Secretary to the Natal Native Affairs Commission in 1906-7, and Assistant Undersecretary for Native Affairs in 1909. He was personally responsible for collecting much of the evidence against Dinuzulu even before his arrest and clearly believed in Dinuzulu's guilt.

[6] In 1906 Natal and Zululand were divided into forty-one districts each under the jurisdiction of a magistrate. Though the functions of the magistrates were mainly judicial and they were appointed by the Department of Justice, many of them had no legal training. They were responsible also for collecting taxes and announcing new laws. Their activities with regard to the African population were directed by the Department for Native Affairs. In many respects their position was analogous to that of a district officer in other African colonies, with the crucial difference that they were chosen from the settler community and a major part of their time was occupied in dealing with the white section of their magistracy. Most magistrates were unable or unwilling to maintain an unbiased attitude in dealing with the conflicting claims of black and white; those who did try to be impartial were generally branded as "negrophiles" by the whites in their district who were politically powerful enough to secure their removal.

[7] The African Presbyterian church was founded by P. J. Mzimba, who broke away from the Free Church of Scotland Mission at Lovedale in the Eastern Cape, in 1896. It was spread in Natal by John Sibiya, who had also broken away from the Church of Scotland. It is not clear how much—if any—jurisdiction or control either Mzimba or Sibiya had over the men at Trewirgie. For further details see Marks, "Christian African Participation in the 1906 Zulu Rebellion," *Bulletin of the Society for African Church History*, II (1965), 55-72.

[8] References for this general account will be found in the more detailed analysis below. It is based very largely on Stuart, *ZR*, and Marks, "Black and White in Self-Governing Natal."

[9] In Natal, as in the rest of South Africa, the term "location" referred to land reserved for the exclusive use of Africans. In Natal, the locations or reserves amounted to just under 2.25 million acres (of a total of 12.5 million acres) vested in a specially established trust.

mary trials, chiefs were fined and, in some cases, deposed and removed from their tribes[10] for alleged "seditious intentions," for allowing their people to possess assegais, or for failing to hand over persons branded as rebels by spies. On 15 February two of the participants in the shooting of the policemen were themselves summarily shot; on 2 April after trial by court-martial at Richmond, twelve more men were shot for the same offense. At the end of March the Governor informed the Colonial Office that the rebellion was at an end and that the field forces were about to be demobilized.

The first signs of overt African resistance came on 3 April, when Bambatha, a minor chief who had been deposed by the government, captured the regent who had been appointed by the government in his stead. On the following day, Bambatha fired on the magistrate who had been sent to investigate the situation and on 5 April he engaged in a skirmish with a police rescue force, killing three of its members. Then, accompanied by a section of his Zondi people, as well as by one Cakijana who was widely believed to be an emissary from Dinuzulu, he made his way into the fortress-like Nkandla mountains, where he set about raising an army.

Troops under the general command of Colonel McKenzie were immediately dispatched to the Nkandla area to ferret out the rebels. Through a series of converging movements on the rebel hideouts, McKenzie brought this second phase of the disturbances to an end on 10 June with the Battle of Mome Gorge. Bambatha and most of the important African leaders were killed, and a large number of the rank and file were also killed or captured. Once again the Governor believed that the disturbances were at an end.

Within a few days, however, reports were received that Africans in the Lower Tugela and Mapumulo divisions were disaffected, and troops were dispatched to that area. After several skirmishes and what were somewhat ambiguously termed "sweeping movements," this phase of the disturbances was also brought to an end. The long process of rounding up the rebels and trying them by courts-martial began. Martial law came to an end on 17 September 1906, well over a month after the last armed encounters. In all, more than three thousand Africans had lost their lives in these uprisings and some thirty whites were killed. Not a single white woman or child was harmed.[11]

[10] In Natal "tribes" were primarily administrative units ruled over by chiefs, some of whom were hereditary and others of whom were appointed by the government. In general the nucleus of the "tribe" consisted of kinsmen tracing their descent from a common ancestor, but it also contained many non-kinsmen. The term "chiefdom" is probably more appropriate.

[11] Stuart, ZR, 540-52, for the white casualties; the number of African dead is not known exactly, but between three and four thousand was the official figure.

Despite the end of martial law and the appointment in 1906 of the Natal Native Affairs Commission to inquire into African grievances, the government continued to track down participants in the disturbances. Many had fled to Zululand; some found refuge at Dinuzulu's headquarters. The denial of a general amnesty contributed to the bitterness and poverty caused by the upheaval of 1906. In 1907 two chiefs who had fought on the government side were assassinated and other "loyalists" feared for their lives. Most whites, especially those with vested interests in Zululand—which had only just been opened up to white settlement—joined the "loyal" Africans in believing that Dinuzulu was behind the continued unrest in Zululand proper and that he was planning further rebellion. Finally, at the beginning of December 1907, martial law was again declared and Dinuzulu was arrested.

In November 1908, after a long, drawn-out preliminary examination, Dinuzulu was brought to trial before a specially constituted court, on twenty-three separate charges of high treason. The government of Natal went to great lengths to prove that he had been the chief instigator of the disturbances of 1906, largely on the basis of evidence gathered while martial law had been in force in Zululand. It had been prolonged specifically for this purpose. He was found guilty on two and one half counts: hiding Bambatha's family during the rebellion, sheltering rebels during and after the disturbances, and possessing unregistered firearms. He was sentenced to a fine and four years' imprisonment. However, one of the first acts of the Union government in 1910 was to release him, at which time he was permanently exiled from Natal-Zululand.

The Poll Tax as a Cause of Rebellion

This then, in barest outline, was the Natal rebellion of 1906, "the last tribal revolt on South African soil"[12] and the most severe crisis faced by self-governing Natal during its short history. Not surprisingly, these events were variously interpreted by contemporaries. The Governor of Natal, for example, had little doubt that the Christian Africans had been responsible, and that the rebellion had had as its mainspring the cry, "Africa for the Africans."[13] This view was shared by John Buchan, who, some four years later, based his novel *Prester John* on the Natal disturbances, though curiously enough his tale bears a closer resemblance to the later Chilembwe uprising in Nyasaland.[14] Stuart agreed that the part

[12] W. K. Hancock, *Smuts I. The Sanguine Years 1870-1919* (Cambridge, 1962), 224.

[13] Government House Records, Natal Archives, Pietermaritzburg GH 579: Sir Henry McCallum to Lord Selborne, British High Commissioner in South Africa, 27 Aug. 1906.

[14] See below, Robert I. Rotberg, "Psychological Stress and the Question of Identity: Chilembwe's Revolt Reconsidered," 337-73.

played by Christian Africans had been prominent,[15] but felt that the outbreak was rather more the "inevitable" result of the "attempt made to impose the European character and civilisation on the native races"[16] —a view well in accord with the social Darwinism of his day.

As for the military men in Natal, they had long prophesied a Zulu uprising. They saw the disturbances as "a golden opportunity" to inflict the most severe punishment on Africans who, they felt, had been "insolent" and "out of hand" since the end of the South African War (1899 to 1902).[17] The Natal government and army were both convinced that the first outbreak of violence had to be dealt with as swiftly as possible, and that they were saving the whole of South Africa from "the nameless barbarities which the savage mind alone can conceive."[18]

Other observers were less sure. From the Orange Free State, ex-President Martinus Theunis Steyn talked of Natal's "hysterical" handling of events,[19] while other South African statesmen, none of whom could be accused of being overly sympathetic to the black man, all expressed concern lest the methods used by Natal to suppress the rebellion would only spur it on.[20] Harriette Colenso, daughter of the famous Bishop John William Colenso of Natal, and an ardent protagonist of the Zulu people, went even further in suggesting that the Africans had been virtually goaded into revolt.[21] A more moderate view point was expressed by Archdeacon Charles Johnson, an Anglican

[15] Stuart, ZR, 420.

[16] Stuart, ZR, 513.

[17] Stuart Papers (Killie Campbell Library, University of Natal, Durban), Col. H. T. Bru-de-Wold to J. Stuart, 22 Jan. 1913; Cd. 3027: Further Correspondence Relating to Native Disturbances in Natal (1906); Encl. 4 in desp. 97: Col. Duncan McKenzie to Department of Militia, 15 June 1906.

[18] Col. Duncan McKenzie in his introduction to Walter Bosman, The Natal Rebellion of 1906 (London, 1907), v.

[19] Merriman Papers (South African Public Library, Cape Town), No. 160: M. T. Steyn to J. X. Merriman.

[20] See, for example, Merriman Papers, Nos. 93, 123, and 147, and W. K. Hancock and Jean van der Poel (eds.), Selections from the Smuts Papers (Cambridge, 1966) XI, nos. 289, 293-96, 303, 305-6.

[21] For Harriette Colenso, see S. Marks, "Harriette Colenso and the Zulus, 1874-1913," Journal of African History, III (1963), 403-11. A missionary, Harriette spent most of her long life fighting for the two causes dearest to her father's heart: the break-away Colensite Church of England in Natal and the defense of the Zulu people and especially the Zulu royal family. Through her brother, Francis E. Colenso, who lived in London, she was able to bring her views to the attention of radical-humanitarian pressure groups in Britain, notably Liberal and Labour backbenchers and the Aborigines Protection Society. Her numerous pamphlets from the late 1880's onward shed interesting light on Zulu politics in the late nineteenth and early twentieth centuries. In 1888-89 and again in 1906-8 she spent much of her time and formidable energy, as well as most of her private income, in defending Dinuzulu against the government's charges of high treason.

missionary in Zululand, who declared that while the rebellion was the result of

> a combination of causes, among which were the attitude of the white man towards the black and the gradually growing antipathy of the black man towards the white . . . he thought that the last straw was the way in which the Government commenced to deal with the first indications of disaffection. He considered that the measures which were adopted were nothing more than an invitation to people who were irritated to go on to worse.[22]

The African case was put rather more simply, albeit dramatically, by one Dhlozi, who was not himself a rebel, when he stated to the Natal Native Affairs Commission that

> The reason for the rebellion was that the Natives felt themselves over-burdened and considered that they might as well fight and be killed straight away. . . . If any nation as strong as the British should appear, the natives would fly to it owing to the heavy troubles that afflict them.[23]

A compatriot, Socwetshata, added: "Happy are those who fought and are dead."[24] No greater protest could be made.

The very diversity of interpretation suggests some of the many strands involved in the disturbances. Each view finds some echo in the events of 1906. With the passage of time, however, these views must be put into perspective: New questions are being asked about colonial rebellions. If the older interpretation of rebellions as the "inevitable" result of the contact between primitive peoples and civilization was an oversimplification and distortion, so probably was the over-ready inclination of the radical-humanitarians to see only the provocative actions of the army without considering the varied reactions of the Africans themselves to the military presence. Nevertheless a detailed examination of the actual course of the disturbances does support the view that in many cases the Government of Natal's handling of an already explosive situation did precipitate revolt.

[22] Natal Native Affairs Commission (henceforth NNAC), 1906-7: Evidence, 91. The evidence and report of the NNAC of 1906-7 is an invaluable source on the social and economic as well as the political condition of Africans at the turn of the century. The Report of the Commission was published as a British Command Paper (Cd 3889) but the evidence was apparently published solely for official use; only a few copies are available.

[23] NNAC: Evidence, 709.

[24] Ibid.

It is also essential to point out that, even before the appearance of the field forces, there had been a deep undercurrent of hostility between black and white. In large measure this feeling is to be traced to the land and labor policies adopted by successive Natal governments and to the increasingly rigid and autocratic approach of the administration to the African population. Also, the rapid expansion of Natal's white population in the last decade of the nineteenth century and Natal's annexation of Zululand in 1897 had made the white man's presence far more obvious and far more onerous than it had been in the early days of the colony. At the same time the economic expansion of South Africa as the result of the mineral discoveries on the Rand had greatly increased the demands for labor of industrialists, farmers, and the government. While, however, settler and governmental pressures can be seen as the underlying and precipitating causes of African dissatisfaction prior to 1906, the imposition of the poll tax at the end of 1905 can be considered as an underlying, predisposing, and precipitating cause. In its relationship to the entire structure of land and labor policies it formed part of the underlying causation; in imposing a new and heavy burden of taxation on the shoulders of an indigent population (not all of whom rebelled against it), it was certainly a predisposing factor; finally, by providing the occasion for the defiance of governmental authority by certain groups and for the declaration of martial law, the poll tax was undoubtedly the precipitating cause of the 1906 disturbances. Despite Stuart's dismissal of the poll tax as "merely a contributory cause and not the most important of those that have been cited,"[25] most Africans at the time attributed the disturbances to the imposition of the tax. It was from that moment that "things began to go wrong."[26]

Indeed, so close was the link between reaction to the tax and the 1906 disturbances, they have frequently been called the "Poll Tax Rebellion." Although the disturbances arose out of a number of complex causes which varied from tribe to tribe, and indeed from group to group within the African population, it was the poll tax which had set off the batch of nervous rumors about an impending uprising at the end of 1905 and which had led to the spate of white animal killing in the most densely populated rural districts of the colony—a reaction very similar to the cattle killing among the Xhosa in the Eastern Cape in 1856.[27] To

[25] Stuart, ZR, 520.

[26] NNAC: Evidence of Nkantolo, 711.

[27] In 1856, following the prophecy of a young Xhosa maiden, Nonqause, thousands of Xhosa tribesmen slaughtered their cattle and destroyed their corn in the hope that this would miraculously cause the whites to be driven into the sea. Though the aim of the movement was clearly extremely hostile to the white man, the cattle killing was not accompanied by any physical violence to whites.

take this up in greater detail, many Africans linked the tax with the un-popular 1904 census, which magistrates had promised would have no sinister repercussions: the poll tax was thus regarded as a distinct breach of faith on the part of the government.[28] The translation of poll tax into Zulu as a "head tax" was also rather unfortunate and led to wry remarks among Africans that a leg and arm tax would follow. However, in introducing the poll tax bill in the Natal Legislative Assembly in 1905, the Minister of Native Affairs had asserted that ". . . the natives of this Colony will hail the present Bill, if it is made law, with pleasure. . . . I can assure [members] . . . that if this bill is made law there will be no difficulties as far as the natives are concerned."[29] Magistrates in many parts of the colony were also initially sanguine as to the ease with which the tax would be collected.[30] Nevertheless, when, at the end of January and February 1906, they actually attempted to collect the tax, they were generally met with passive resistance and even, on occasion, as has already been touched on, by open defiance. Thus, on 22 January, the acting magistrate of Mapumulo was met by angry gesticulating men of Ngobizembe's tribe, many of them armed with sticks; in the same district the followers of Swaimana and Meseni also refused to pay the tax. Furthermore, though in September 1905 the magistrate of Nkandla had stated that the reports of the forthcoming tax had not roused "the slightest sign of disloyalty" in any of the chiefs or headmen to whom it had been announced,[31] in January 1906, Sigananda's people in that division maintained that they could not afford to pay the tax, apparently shouted their war cry, and did a war dance in front of the magistrate.

It is difficult to know how to interpret this early passive resistance to the tax, or indeed even the more violent expressions of hostility. Some of the protesting chiefs and their people were later involved in the disturbances and did fight against the white forces. But several others who also protested against the tax and at first refused to pay it later remained neutral, and some, like Sibindi and his followers, even remained conspicuously loyal to the government and provided men to fight on its side.[32] Moreover, at the same time that the Africans were voicing their protests against the tax, its white opponents were holding several very

[28] NNAC: Report, 34.

[29] Natal Legislative Assembly (henceforth NLA), *Debates*, XXXIX, 27 July 1905, 704-5.

[30] Secretary for Native Affairs (henceforth SNA) (files in the Natal Archives, Pietermaritzburg), SNA 1/1/325 2302/05: Summary of magistrates' reports, n.d. (*c*. 11 Sept. 1905).

[31] Ibid.

[32] SNA 1/1/367 1116/07: Report of Magistrate of Krantzkop. See also B. Colenbrander, "The Bambata Rebellion," unpublished manuscript (Killie Campbell Library, Durban).

noisy meetings in Pietermaritzburg and Durban.[33] For Africans, however, there were few ways of expressing opposition other than by passive resistance. Whether Africans were allowed to express their views or not depended to a large extent on individual magistrates—as did the adequacy of the information they received as to when and by whom the tax had to be paid.[34]

Partly as a result of the failure of the government to listen to their complaints, several chiefs in 1906 sent messages to Dinuzulu to find out what he was going to do about the tax. Nor were these chiefs only from Zululand; messengers came from prominent chiefs as far south as Tilonko[35] and Sikukuku in the Ixopo division of Natal. Dinuzulu's replies to these messages would appear invariably to have been proper: He pointed out that his people had been the first to pay the tax, and completely denied the rumor, which was supposed to have emanated from him, that all white animals were to be killed. More than one witness at Dinuzulu's subsequent trial on charges of high treason affirmed that "If Dinuzulu had refused to pay the Poll Tax we would have fought and died" and that "Dinuzulu was the Peacemaker between us and the Government. He stopped what might have taken place. . . ."[36] Indeed, Sir Charles Saunders, Commissioner for Native Affairs in Zululand, maintained throughout the disturbances that Dinuzulu's example in paying the tax had prevented the disturbances from spreading through Zulu-

[33] See NNAC: Evidence, *passim.*, for example, H. Bazeley, 462, and H. A. Smith, 506.

[34] SNA 1/1/333 54/06: Circular, 22 Dec. 1905. In Zululand, where the Commissioner for Native Affairs, Sir Charles Saunders, was a capable and not unsympathetic paternalist, the following circular was issued to magistrates in December 1905.

> Chiefs are now distinctly warned that no excuse will be accepted and any opposition to the Tax will be most severely dealt with; that the chiefs themselves as the government's representatives amongst their people will be held personally responsible that the tax is promptly paid on the dates fixed . . . that any neglect in this respect will be regarded as an indication that they are not fitted for their positions and responsibilities as chiefs and render it incumbent upon the government to seriously consider whether they should not be deprived of their positions and the status attached thereto.
>
> No discussion in connection with the matter should be entered into, the chiefs merely being informed that the foregoing are the Government's final words of warning and the sooner any people liable for the tax prepare to meet it, the better it will be for all concerned.

[35] Also spelled Tilonkwe and Tilongo.

[36] Colenso Collection (henceforth Col. Col.), 98 (Natal Archives, Pietermaritzburg). Records of Dinuzulu's Defence Precognitions, C. Renaud: Sibhamu ka Mboro of Chief Matuta (Babanango Division), Ndabankulu ka Lukwazi of Chief Lubudhlungu, Madikane ka Mfingeli of Chief Mnyombe, and Mjinji ka Kutshwayo of Chief Sigananda (Nkandla Division).

land,[37] but his view as to Dinuzulu's participation became less favorable later.[38]

Even overt signs of defiance were not taken equally seriously by all the magistrates. As will be seen later, some, if anything, overreacted; others took an opposite path. Chief Ngokwana's tribe, for example, was initially reported disrespectful and insolent; two weeks later it was apparently "paying well," after a simple reprimand by the Commissioner for Native Affairs.[39] A. J. S. Maritz, the magistrate of Entonjaneni, who tried Sigananda's men for breach of the peace, thought so little of that episode that he dismissed the men with a caution.[40] The conflict in magisterial views as to what constituted "rebelliousness" was to persist throughout the disturbances and to become even more marked once the troops were in the field.

The government was clearly in a difficult position over the collection of the tax, having imposed it with little consultation, even with those magistrates who were closest to African public opinion, and despite the advice of others who had pointed out that it would probably aggravate African poverty and undermine family life. It now found itself faced with widespread opposition. Apart from military preparations —and even in this respect at the beginning of 1906 the active militia had been reduced and the militia reserves were still disorganized—there is little indication that the government had considered what it would do if its authority were challenged over the collection of the tax. James Stuart, at that time First Criminal Magistrate in Durban and responsible for convening meetings of African urban workers to announce the tax, was one of the few to face the issue squarely. After a couple of turbulent meetings at which Africans had vigorously voiced their opposition to the tax, he wrote to the Minister for Native Affairs:

> On getting refusal, compulsion in some form or other may have to be resorted to, but is it desirable to resort to force when, as I think, the whole people are not only opposed to the tax, but regard it as oppressive and as calculated to disturb their social system. . . . I as one whose duties bring him into close contact with the natives venture to think that the passing of this act brings the Colony . . . face to face with a grave risk which cannot be too well considered beforehand.[41]

[37] Natal Native Affairs Department, *Annual Report,* 1906, 14.

[38] By August 1907, if not earlier, Sir Charles Saunders had become convinced that Dinuzulu was responsible for the continued unrest in Zululand and would have to be removed.

[39] Zululand Archives (henceforth ZA), 34. (Pietermaritzburg): Reports, Magistrate, Umlalazi Division, 24 Jan. 1906, and 5 Feb. 1906.

[40] ZA 34: Confidential Report 16/06, 7 Apr. 1906.

[41] SNA 1/4/14/, C 43/05, 8 Nov. 1905. For the Government of Natal's justification for the poll tax see Marks, *Reluctant Rebellion,* ch. 5.

Far from considering the risk, however, the sole response of the Minister was to reprimand Stuart for holding meetings of Africans and allowing them to get out of hand: his not proceeding through the traditional chieftainly authority (non-existent in the urban centers) was regarded as a far greater threat to the security of the colony than a possible explosion over the tax.[42]

The Incident at Trewirgie: February 1906

One of the most important instances of early defiance over the collection of the poll tax occurred on 7 February 1906, when Chief Mveli of the Funzi tribe brought his people to Henly to pay their tax to the magistrate of the Umgeni division, T. R. Bennet. On hearing from the chief that some twenty-seven armed members of his tribe had taken up a position almost two miles away, the magistrate sent a European trooper, who spoke no Zulu, and two African messengers to discover the reason for their behavior. Both the African messengers were relatives of the chief; one of them, Jobe, was his brother.

On arrival, the emissaries addressed themselves to the leaders of the group, Makanda and Mjongo, and asked what was going on. According to Jobe, their reply was: "We have como to the Chief or magistrate who is collecting the money. We shall refuse our money for the Poll Tax." They were then asked why they were carrying assegais, and answered: "These assegais, it is our day today. There will be blood today." At this point the rest of the men moved forward suddenly—whether to hear what was being said or for some less innocent purpose is not clear—and the messengers fled.[43]

Mjongo and his men then went back to their homes on Henry Hosking's farm, Trewirgie, near Byrnetown. The following day, 8 February, a detachment of fifteen policemen, including two Africans, was sent to arrest the twenty-seven men accused of being in unlawful possession of arms. Under Subinspector S. K. Hunt, the police arrived at dusk, having lost their way earlier in the day, and, despite Hosking's advice, decided to proceed with the arrests. At the huts, about a mile away from the farmhouse, they asked for the wanted men; Mjongo and two others were found immediately and handcuffed. The police then began their search for the others, who were some distance away from the kraals.[44] According to the court-martial evidence of Mbadi, one of the accused,

[42] Ibid. Minute by H. D. Winter.

[43] The evidence and judgment in the Richmond court-martial (henceforth RCM) is enclosed in despatch [confidential] CO 179/234/19935: Governor (Natal) to Secretary of State, 11 May 1906.

[44] Ibid.

After Mjongo had gone we decided to follow him. Then one police trooper saw us and turning round called the others. The police came and . . . said "Go home, go home."

We noticed that they had drawn their revolvers; they were in front of us, so we drew back to the rocks, saying that we had done no harm in the location. They said: "You have been carrying assegais." We said: "There is no harm in that. Mveli sent us back." We said, "Let Mveli come here, we will talk to him. It is no good your coming here armed." . . . They told us to lay down our assegais and we said, "How can we do so when you have drawn your firearms. . . ." The others then shouted, "You have come for our money; you can shoot us. We won't pay," and "We would rather die than pay."[45]

When Mjongo was released by the police to try to quiet the men who were flourishing small shields and assegais, he was pulled down among them. The police then apparently rode their horses into the group, who believed that they were trying to trample them down; this did nothing to improve the temper of the Africans.[46] Eventually the police returned to the huts, followed by the men, some of whom, according to their evidence, had agreed to discuss matters there or at Hosking's farm, while others wished either to join or to rescue the two men already arrested.[47]

However, they trooped down after the police in twos and threes, according to Stuart "jeering and taunting . . . [them] in the most insolent manner," and, according to some African witnesses, singing and praying as they had done outside Henly.[48] Suddenly one of the Africans grabbed hold of the bridle of the policeman in charge of prisoner Ngcubu. Subinspector Hunt immediately fired his rifle, and the other police followed suit. In the ensuing scuffle, four Africans were wounded and two of the police, Subinspector Hunt and Trooper Armstrong, stabbed to death. The following day, 9 February, martial law was declared throughout the colony.

In what followed, the declaration of martial law played an important role, for in a sense martial law is the abrogation of law. Under it, any acts carried out "in good faith" by the Governor, the commandant of the militia, or their subordinates, in an attempt to put down the disturbances, would be indemnified later by an Act of Parliament. Once there was "no law" in Natal, the normal restraints of society could be loosened. The element of force took on a new significance. As well as

[45] RCM: Similar evidence was given by other accused, 17 Mar. 1906.

[46] RCM: Evidence of Mambuka and Ubuwini, 17 Mar. 1906.

[47] RCM: Evidence of Mbadi and Mjaja, 17 Mar. 1906.

[48] Stuart, *ZR*, 122-6, gives an account of the affray. RCM: Evidence *passim*, 15 and 17 Mar. 1906.

being a response to aggression, whether overt or covert, it could in turn become its cause, although not, of course, its only cause. Reactions were varied. Thus, many tribes who witnessed troops marching through their locations took the government's advice and remained quiet—or even responded to appeals for aid from the whites. And the same was true of those tribes who found themselves attacked by the "rebel forces" in the second phase of the disturbances, when the rebels under Bambatha attempted to force other peoples to join them; some responded positively, others fled to the nearest magistracy or to the bush. Nevertheless, where there was a background of tension and conflict with white authority, administration, police, or settlers, fears were aroused simply by the appearance of white troops on the scene: Africans would arm and doctor themselves for war, sometimes, it would appear, purely in self-defense; such steps in turn aroused fresh apprehensions on the other side, and forces would be sent to deal with a new outbreak of "rebellion." In much of what follows there is something in the nature of a self-fulfilling prophecy: fearing, perhaps half wanting, rebellion, the colonists and their leaders by their actions gave substance to their fears. For, although the picture concerning the events on Hosking's property which emerges from the court-martial evidence is not absolutely clear and there are obviously great difficulties in interpreting the evidence of the accused, it would appear from this incident that the murder of the magistrate or the police officers had not been premeditated, nor was there any intention to massacre whites. Even if one follows the official account of what occurred, or Stuart's rendition, the Africans did not, despite their jeers and gesturing, strike first. The first shot had been fired by Hunt at a handcuffed prisoner.[49] On 7 February, the three messengers from the magistrate to the armed men had escaped unscathed; nor is it clear why, if, as was alleged, the group had intended murdering the magistrate, it should have taken up a position two miles away from the magistracy. Indeed, some of the group maintained that they had been ordered to stop there by Mveli himself—presumably because they were carrying assegais, although this was not illegal, and because he wished to stop them from voicing their opposition to the poll tax before the magistrate. According to both Nomkuba, the sister of Makanda, and Mantayi ka Mjongo,[50] himself one of the accused, they were on their way to pay their taxes when they were ordered to stop. Had they gone on to the magistracy, it is conceivable that an incident no more serious

[49] Cf. SNA 1/6/28 4356/06: Petition of Ngcuba sentenced to twenty years' imprisonment and thirty lashes. Minute by the Assistant Commissioner of Police to SNA: "Trooper van Aardt informs me that he believes that the prisoner was shot by Subinspector Hunt. *This would be the first shot fired.*" (My italics.)

[50] RCM: Evidence, 15 Mar. 1906.

than those already described as having taken place in Mapumulo and Nkandla might have occurred. Once it was reported, however, the magistrate could not ignore the fact that these men were armed, but his sending relatives of the chief as the only Zulu-speaking messengers was perhaps unfortunate, as they were likely to share the chief's views on the dissident minority in their midst.

The crucial mistake would appear to have been the sending of so small a detachment of police to arrest Makanda, Mjongo, and their supporters the following day. Furthermore, Subinspector Hunt was not well suited to his task. Knowing no Zulu, and apparently convinced beforehand that this was going to be the start of a widespread uprising, he felt that he had been selected as "bait" by the government.[51] His own somewhat extreme views on the "native problem" may have influenced his behavior. Thus, in a letter to his family shortly after his arrival in Natal in the early 1890's, he had written of "licking the niggers into shape" and "knocking hell out of them."[52] It is possible that ten years in Natal had mellowed Subinspector Hunt's approach to Africans. The tradition, however, that lives on of him as an autocratic, overbearing man seems to have been borne out by the African evidence at the court-martial.

Yet whatever the truth about the police handling of the matter, it can also be argued that after all twenty-seven armed men had appeared in defiance of the poll tax, and that such an act was in itself sufficient indication of hostility to the government.

Again, the picture is more complicated. While it would appear that the immediate reason for the group's defiance was their chief's order to join other members of the tribe in paying the tax, the fact that they were, as has already been mentioned, all members of an independent church, was significant. Although it did not mean that they were necessarily anti-white, it did mean that they were estranged from their chief and his other followers who were pagans.[53]

Actually, there had been a fairly long history of antagonism between Christian converts and pagans in the Funzi tribe. Thus in 1896 a case had been taken from the Native High Court[54] to the Supreme Court, in which tribesmen who were orthodox members of the Euro-

---

[51] Personal communication from K. Hunt, grandson of Subinspector Hunt, drawing on entries in his unpublished diary which I have not been able to see.

[52] Letter from S. Hunt to his parents in Dorset, 15 Feb. 1896, kindly shown me by K. Hunt (Rhodes University).

[53] See Marks, "Christian African Participation," 55-72.

[54] In Natal and Zululand there was a separate court system for Africans who were governed according to customary law. Purely African cases were first heard in chiefs' courts, from which there was an appeal to magistrates' courts and then to the Native High Court. In 1898 cases could be taken from there to the Supreme Court of Natal, which dealt with all final appeals in Natal.

pean controlled Wesleyan Methodist church had alleged that they had been victimized by their chief, at that time Hemuhemu, Mveli's father. Apparently as a result of the complaints of some of the older members of his tribe that their wives and daughters "stayed out late" when they attended services, Hemuhemu had forbidden public services and private prayers. The penalty for infringing this command had been set at a £2 fine or a beast, and, when a local missionary came to hold services in the location, the chief had actually sent his private policeman to note the names of those who attended. While Chief Justice Sir Walter Wragg of the Supreme Court had found in favor of the Christians in this instance,[55] the complaint of the chief that they were disrespectful of his authority is a familiar historical theme. That the conflict did not die down in 1896 was borne out by a letter written by Joseph Baynes, a member of the Legislative Assembly, to the magistrate of Richmond in the middle of 1904 in which he transmitted the complaints of "respectable kraalheads" in the area about the disruptive effects, especially on the women, of a Christian sect operating from Trewirgie under Mjongo, at that period a sawyer with Makanda in the Enon forests.[56] By this time, however, the Christians complained of what appear to have become members of the independent African Presbyterian church.

In some ways, the 1906 episode also suggested a continuance of this aspect of the conflict. It is difficult to say how much antagonism was directed against the chief as the representative of the government, and how much as the representative of rejected tribal tradition. Mbadi's statement—"Let Mveli come here, we will talk with him"—suggests that the defiance was primarily directed against the chief and not the government. Mveli's own prompt reporting of the incident to the magistrate—unlike Bambatha's subsequent behavior—and his alacrity and zeal in hunting out the rebels, as well as his expressed wish to remove their women and children,[57] may well have represented an attempt on his part to consolidate his hold over the tribe and to rid himself of an unruly and undermining element in its midst.

Whatever the complexities of the incident, the fact that it involved members of a separatist sect and that two police officers had been killed undoubtedly increased white fears and made the incident appear particularly ominous. Taken against the background of rumors and isolated incidents of resistance to the poll tax, this was the last straw. It led to the swift declaration of martial law over the entire colony within hours

[55] Reported in the Proceedings of the Natal Missionary Conference, July 1896.
[56] It formed part of the evidence in the Richmond court-martial; see G. D. Alexander, Nel's Rust, to Magistrate, Richmond, 15 July 1904.
[57] Prime Minister [Confidential] (Natal Archives) (henceforth PM) PMC 101/88: McKenzie to Prime Minister, 15 Feb. 1906.

after an event which in normal circumstances would hardly have warranted more than the reinforcement of the local police force.

The participants in the killing of Hunt and Armstrong were soon to suffer dearly for their actions. On the day that martial law was declared, troops were mobilized and a column under McKenzie was dispatched to Thornville Junction, Richmond, and Elandskop. Together with Mveli and five hundred of his men, they searched the Byrnetown area and the Enon forest. On 15 February, just a week after the initial incident, two of Mjongo's men were captured and, after trial by drumhead court-martial, shot in the presence of Mveli and his men.[58] The remaining participants were rounded up in the weeks that followed and tried by a court-martial which sat from 12 to 17 March. Another twelve were sentenced to death and, after some delay as a result of protests from the Colonial Office, were shot before assembled tribesmen and chiefs from the Midlands and Southern districts of the colony on 2 April. Several others were sentenced to twenty years' imprisonment at hard labor, confiscation of property, and lashes.[59] Finally, three remaining participants, who had been too badly wounded after a brush with the troops hunting them out in February to be shot by order of the Richmond court-martial like the others, were put to death after a trial by the Natal Supreme Court in September 1906. Mjongo was hanged on this occasion.[60]

These events undoubtedly had a profound effect on the people in the surrounding areas. According to Stuart, news of the drumhead court-martial on 15 February "which was regarded as just and proper by every loyal Native" spread at once far and wide.[61] Having dealt with these rebels, McKenzie then found it necessary to turn his attention to other chiefs and tribes in the district concerning whom "there had been many adverse reports." Interviews were held with chiefs regarded as defiant in some way, who were reported to have been reluctant to pay the poll tax, or who were said to have had their tribes "doctored" for war. From the evidence that he had received from settlers and military spies, McKenzie was convinced that his action had "nipped in the bud" a widespread conspiracy of the black man to rise against the white.[62] Ultimatums were delivered to various chiefs to hand over their "rebellious" subjects and to search their tribes for assegais. Failure to comply meant the confiscation of cattle and, not infrequently, the burning of

[58] Stuart, ZR, 138.

[59] RCM: Sentence, 19 Mar. 1906.

[60] Cd. 3247, *Further Correspondence Relating to Native Disturbances in Natal* (1906), No. 46: Governor to Secretary of State, no. 2, 7 Sept. 1906.

[61] Stuart, ZR, 138.

[62] CO 179/233/12460, encl. 2 in desp. 41: Col. McKenzie to Col. Bru-de-Wold, 11 Mar. 1906.

crops and kraals. "Rebels" were tried before specially constituted courts set up by McKenzie, and sentences of death, twenty-five years' imprisonment, and fifty lashes were not uncommon, although they were generally modified by the Governor in Council.[63]

While some of the magistrates appear to have considered these proceedings essential to combat the growing restlessness of the tribes in their district, others were less sure. Thus, in a private letter to the Undersecretary for Native Affairs, J. Y. Gibson, the magistrate of Richmond, who was soon forced to resign from this position for being too sympathetically inclined toward Africans in general and for opposition to the Richmond court-martial in particular, wrote:

> Men are still being continually arrested under Martial Law, but I have no idea what the charges are against them. I have discovered the spirit of Titus Oates prevailing to a certain extent and it is not possible at present to determine the extent. . . . A large number of men were taken away from my division, I hear, and tried at Ixopo. I have not been informed who they were or what they had done. Only occasional information reached this office in regard to some individual said to have been seen with one or more assegais. . . . There is a general belief . . . too that it is intended to send the force to deal with Tilonko, In the meantime, complete peace appears to reign, the people being all most amenable and anxious to do right. . . . They are all poor people in this division and heavy fines and exactions are ruining them completely. . . . [64]

As the troop movements were extended throughout the Midlands and the Southern districts of the colony, many chiefs and tribes began to feel apprehensive. These fears were perhaps most marked among members of Tilonko's and Msikofeli's[65] tribes in the Ixopo and Richmond divisions. Both chiefs headed large and important peoples, and both were extremely unpopular with their white neighbors, who probably resented their independent attitude and coveted their land. Thus, from the outset of his career as head of the Kuze tribe in 1897, Msikofeli had been faced with the opposition of the magistrate and local settlers who for some years had been agitating for the breakup of his chiefdom.[66] In the Richmond area, suggestions for deposing Tilonko because of his alleged reluctance to pay the poll tax came from white residents even

[63] See, for example, Report in *Natal Witness*, 17 Mar. 1906, and CO 179/234/16020, encl. in desp. 60, 11 Apr. 1906: Sentences of Umtwalumi court martial and Governor's modifications.

[64] SNA 1/1/338 940/06, 24 Mar. 1906.

[65] Also spelled Msikofeni. Miskofeli is almost certainly incorrect.

[66] See, for example, SNA 1/1/302 1810/03: Minute by Magistrate F. E. Foxon.

before the declaration of martial law and before there was any evidence
of his, or his tribe's, overt hostility to whites.[67] On 12 February there
were reports that members of Msikofeli's and Tilonko's tribes had taken
up arms—according to Stuart, and even McKenzie—because they feared
the arrest of their chiefs.[68] The moving of all of the Europeans in the
area into a laager further increased their apprehensions: according to
tho one local resident who did not join the flight from the farms, the
African population now "seemed to have one idea and that was the
troops were coming to kill them all."[69] Now that the whites had moved
out, Chief Msikofeli openly expressed the fear that the troops had
come to wipe out him and his people.

Despite the reports that the two tribes had armed themselves, on
the following day the Minister and the Undersecretary for Native Affairs risked meeting these chiefs to reprimand them for their unruly
conduct before the magistrate collecting the poll tax.[70] The meeting
passed without incident, and both the tribes began to pay the tax without further ado. By early April the Embo people, including Tilonko's,
had paid nearly all their taxes.[71] Yet, though Tilonko and Msikofeli
played no further part in the disturbances, whites continued to agitate
for the break-up of their tribes. Five months later, when virtually all the
troops had been demobilized and the disturbances were at an end,
Tilonko was summoned before the Minister of Native Affairs. He went
voluntarily to Pietermaritzburg, where he was tried by court-martial
behind closed doors for sedition and public violence.[72] He was found
guilty, fined five hundred head of cattle (later reduced to two hundred
and fifty by the Governor, who thought that the original sentence would
inflict the punishment on his tribe), deposed from his position, and deported with the ringleaders of the disturbances to St. Helena.[73] Msikofeli, who had handed over all the men wanted by the military in the
early days of the disturbances, was not dealt with as harshly, merely

[67] Defence Department 51, correspondence HJ 1288/06 V 2815/06: Mr.
Power Mid-Illovo to Minister for Native Affairs (henceforth MNA), 23 Mar. 1906;
SNA 1/1/335 365/06: H. Nicolson, Richmond, to MNA, 31 Jan. 1906. See also
petitions from white residents in SNA 1/1/341 1489/06, 1/1/339 1180/06, and
PM 61 888/06.

[68] Stuart, ZR, 139, Cd. 2905, *Correspondence Relating to Native Disturbances
in Natal (1906)*, encl. 1 in no. 31: McKenzie to Bru-de-Wold, 25 Feb. 1906.

[69] SNA 1/4/16 C 106/06: E. A. Garland to F. E. Foxon (Magistrate, Ixopo),
18 Feb. 1906.

[70] Cd. 2905, 14, no. 25: Governor to Secretary of State, 16 Feb. 1906.

[71] SNA 1/1/367 1116/07: Report of Magistrate H. C. Colenbrander.

[72] CO 179/236/31497: Governor to Secretary of State, 4 Aug. 1906. Cd. 3247,
nos. 9, 18, 21, 25, and 39 (July-Aug. 1906).

[73] CO 179/236/28634: Governor to Secretary of State, Cd. 3247, no. 42, desp.
193, 11 Aug. 1906.

being fined in cattle and having his chiefdom divided into three. Yet much of Natal's argument for a dangerous conspiracy—which could only be dealt with by martial law and military action—rested on the cases of Tilonko and Msikofeli. It is an interesting footnote to Tilonko's "rebellious and dangerous" character that, on the day following the arming of his men and their assembling at his kraal, he sent an apology to the neighboring white farmer lest his tribesmen had inadvertently trampled his tobacco during the night's activities.[74]

Bambatha's Rebellion

During the first phase of the disturbances, when there was no overt resistance to the white forces, fear of punishment may well have cowed would-be rebels. It has been stated as a psychological "law" that, with "the strength of frustration held constant, the greater the anticipation of punishment for a given act the less apt that act is to occur."[75] And certainly this dictum would appear to have been borne out in the early weeks of the "rebellion," when for nearly two months white forces were able with impunity to march through locations, fine and depose chiefs without trial, confiscate large numbers of sheep and cattle, burn crops and kraals, and flog all Africans whom the military men considered "insolent." Trials were held under martial law for offenses as vague as those of "insubordination or contempt or defiance of public authorities, or menaces or seditious language or acts inciting to insurrection."[76] All this time the ordinary courts of the colony were functioning normally. By the end of March, McKenzie considered that he had sufficiently "impressed" the Africans in the Midlands and South Coast to be able to demobilize his forces.

In terms of the subsequent history of the disturbances, however, McKenzie's operations, and those of the troops under Colonel George Leuchars who were operating in the Mapumulo area principally against Chief Ngobizembe and his tribe, may well have been converting latent hostility into open aggression. There appears to be a point at which punishment intended to deter aggressive action can actually become its cause, where the punishment for minor offenses is so disproportionate that people feel they may as well commit major ones. Moreover, for punishment to act as a deterrent, people must feel they have something

[74] CO 179/237/44376: Evidence in court-martial of Tilonko, 20 July 1906. G. Pople (Resident Overseer, tobacco farm), 37.

[75] J. Dollard. L. W. Doob, N. E. Millar, O. H. Mowrer, and R. R. Sears, *Frustration and Aggression* (New Haven, 1961), 38.

[76] Cd. 2905, *Correspondence Relating to Native Disturbances in Natal (1906 24*, encl. 2 in no. 30: Bru-de-Wold to Leuchars, 23 Feb. 1906.

to lose—whether it be property, status, or family comfort and happiness. In the next phase of the disturbances, which saw the first open defiance of the government, there appears an element of despair and desperation, so well expressed before the Natal Native Affairs Commission by one Mvinjwa—not himself a rebel—when he talked of Bambatha, the chief of the Zondi people and the leader of the rebellion:

> They were like Bambata. He went to extremes simply because he was tied hand and foot by the network of troubles in which he found himself. He then strayed off in revolt. He was very much like a beast which on being stabbed rushes about in despair, charges backwards and forwards and, it may be, kills someone that happens to be in his path.[77]

To modern African nationalists Bambatha has become a great national hero, and, of course, in the simple sense that he resisted oppressive European rule and attempted to unite behind him the chiefs and people of many tribes, he is rightly so regarded. Unfortunately, however, Bambatha himself left no record of what he was trying to do and therefore—in analyzing his motives and aims—we are dependent on the very imperfect assessments of administrative officials and the less imperfect but still inadequate views of his *induna* (headmen) and followers. From these records one does not get a picture of a man with a clear plan of action. Despite his frequent use of Dinuzulu's name, war cry, and war badge, and his attempt to bring the ex-king of the Zulu into the rebellion, one's predominant impression is that of a man goaded beyond endurance who was using the king's name as a centralizing device and making an appeal to Zulu national feeling, but who was prepared to die fighting—probably in the knowledge that his chances of success were slender in the extreme.[78]

Already very unpopular with his white neighbors, who called him "Bellicose Bambata the Chief of Misrule,"[79] Bambatha was in the course of 1905 involved in two faction fights and, on being brought before the Undersecretary for Native Affairs at the end of the year, was warned that any future misbehavior would probably lead to his deposition.[80] Bambatha's suspicions of white intentions had been revealed in 1904 when he had questioned the motives for having the census. At the time of the promulgation of the poll tax, however, he made no open complaint to the magistrate of the division; but considerable discontent

[77] NNAC: Evidence, 713.
[78] For Bambatha's early life, see Stuart, *ZR*, 157-60. Stuart and most older authorities spell the name "Bambata." Where possible I have followed the most recent orthography here and elsewhere.
[79] *Greytown Gazette*, 27 Jan. 1906. See also issue of 10 Feb. 1906.
[80] SNA 1/1/324 1912/05: Memorandum USNA, 3 Nov. 1905.

was expressed by the Zondi tribesmen, led by one of their *induna,*
Nhlonhlo.[81] The protests of people living on private lands and, like
Bambatha himself, heavily in debt were, not surprisingly, the loudest.
As a result of this opposition, Bambatha's people were the last to be
called upon to pay the tax in the Umvoti division, and the magistrate,
J. W. Cross, decided to make the magistracy itself, Greytown, the center
of collection.

On 22 February, the day appointed for the collection of the tax,
Bambatha, as was customary among many tribes, arranged to meet his
men outside Greytown, but found at the rendezvous that some of the
younger men, suspicious of the change of venue, had arrived armed
with assegais and shields. Still others had failed to bring the money, or
were likely to contravene borough regulations which prescribed that
Africans wear European-type clothing within the municipal area.[82] Apparently swayed by the fears of those who thought that if he went to
Greytown he would be arrested,[83] and perhaps by the thought that he
could better control the wilder elements in the tribe if he remained with
them, Bambatha sent on those members of the tribe who were prepared
to pay the tax; about ninety-seven paid, and fifty-three were exempted
on this occasion.[84] He himself remained about two miles from Greytown
with those men who had refused to lay down their arms and sent an
apology of ill health to the magistrate.

According to Stuart,[85] Bambatha's mistake at this point was in not
reporting what had occurred to the magistrate, as Mveli had done under similar circumstances. From this time he became more and more
closely associated with the armed section of his tribe, and it became
more and more difficult for him to respond to messages from the white
authorities instructing him to report to the magistrate. That Bambatha
failed to have much confidence in the assurances of his local magistrate
may, in part, have been related to the personality of Cross. Although
Cross had been in the colony some forty years, and had by 1906 been
in government employ for over thirty, he was something of an alarmist
and tended to believe exaggerated stories of African unrest. It was apparently for this reason that he had been temporarily removed from a
magistracy near the Pondoland border in 1897.[86] Despite the fact that

[81] Stuart, *ZR,* 160.

[82] Ibid., 161.

[83] CO 179/241/33767, encl. 1 in Report No. 2: Evidence of Folekile (Bambatha's daughter) before J. Stuart, 18 July 1907.

[84] *Greytown Gazette,* 3 Mar. 1906.

[85] Stuart, *ZR,* 164.

[86] CO 179/200/23628, desp. [confidential]: Governor to Secretary of State,
9 Oct. 1897, and CO 179/200/24495, desp. [confidential] 2: Governor to Secretary
of State, 23 Oct. 1897.

he spoke Zulu fluently, his tactless remarks to the Africans assembled to welcome him to his new post at Greytown in 1904 (he had informed them that the land was the white man's and not theirs) had even led to a private reprimand from the Natal cabinet.[87] In the same year the Governor had expressed doubts as to the wisdom of his deposing Acting Chief Njengabantu.[88] Like so many magistrates of his generation, Cross believed that a freer use of the lash for the punishment of infringements of beer-drinking regulations and the Masters and Servants Acts, and as a means of preventing faction fighting, would vastly improve "native" behavior in Natal.[89] He was unlikely to have viewed with sympathy Bambatha's troubles with his people or his own past history of unruliness, whatever their economic causes.

The chief's troubles were increased by the fact that on the night of the tax collection a false rumor had spread that his tribe had surrounded Greytown and intended to attack it.[90] All the whites spent the night in laager, and extra police were sent to the area to deal with the "emergency." At the same time the Umvoti militia were called out. Members of Bambatha's tribe now became even more determined to prevent their chief giving himself up to white authorities. The feelings of the Zondi were expressed by one of Bambatha's followers before the Greytown court-martial:

> The white people should they want the Chief must take him from our hands . . . our wish is that the Chief should not be shot as a buck [nor] as a beast or an ox driven to the slaughter house.[91]

Bambatha's position became more difficult not only because of his own action, or inaction, and because his previous friction with the authorities had made him fear punishment, but also because, as the days passed, the nature of "punitive action" in different parts of the colony became clearer. His original reluctance to report the presence of armed men in his tribe had occurred only a week after two of Mjongo's followers had been shot for their part in the Trewirgie affray; troops were still in the Ixopo and Mid-Illovo districts hunting out the rest of that armed

[87] CO 179/229/19920, desp. [confidential] 2: Governor to Secretary of State, 2 May 1904.

[88] SNA 1/1/314 2193/04: Minute of Governor to Sir Henry McCallum, 28 Oct. 1904.

[89] SNA 1/1/367: Reports of Magistrates, 11 Jan. 1907; SNA 1/1/344 2386/06: Minute by J. W. Cross, 27 Aug. 1906; and NNAC: Evidence of J. W. Cross, 627 ff.

[90] Stuart, ZR, 162.

[91] SNA 1/6/28: Greytown court-martial, evidence of Gadupi, 4 July 1906, 21. Similar evidence was given by Nhlonhlo, Saka, and Hanise.

band and burning their crops and kraals. While Mveli had reported the defiance of this group in his tribe and had later apparently welcomed the opportunity of ridding himself of dissident elements in his location, this solution may well have appeared increasingly impossible to Bambatha as the troop movements continued and came closer to Greytown.[92] The proceedings against Ngobizembe in neighboring Mapumulo on 5 March may also have increased Bambatha's determination to evade the clutches of the police and armed forces sent to arrest him on 9 March. Two days later he made his way into Zululand and, ultimately, to Dinuzulu's headquarters at Nongoma.[93]

Much was made of this last fact by the government of Natal in 1907–8, when it was discovered that Bambatha had left his wife and children at Dinuzulu's headquarters for safekeeping. It was widely belived at the time of the disturbances and afterward that he had been given arms and ammunition by Dinuzulu and had been actively encouraged by him to start a rebellion in Natal, being assured of Dinuzulu's future active support. The evidence for and against such a view —which was rejected by the majority of members of the special court which tried Dinuzulu—cannot be considered here. Whatever happened at Nongoma, however, at the end of March Bambatha returned to Natal accompanied by Ngqengqengqe, one of Dinuzulu's messengers, and by Cakijana ka Gezindaka, who was believed to be one of his *induna*. Cakijana was soon to become a key figure in the rebellion as Bambatha's "right hand man."

It is difficult to know at exactly what point Bambatha made his momentous decision to oppose the white man with force.[94] The evidence of both Ngqengqengqe and Cakijana seems to suggest that the decisive moment came when he returned to his tribe and discovered that Magwababa, his uncle, had been appointed regent in his place. At this point Ngqengqengqe, who had ostensibly been sent by Dinuzulu to find a doctor for him in the Greytown district, returned to Zululand—without the doctor—as he feared trouble. On this, his evidence is consistent and straightforward.[95] There are, however, many variants of Cakijana's evidence. In his first deposition, before members of Dinuzulu's defense counsel, which he subsequently repudiated, he stated that on the fourth day after he had accompanied Bambatha from his father's home—also to

[92] Stuart, *ZR*, 164, suggests the comparison.

[93] Ibid., 166.

[94] Stuart suggests that this happened when Bambatha was at Nongoma. He accepts the evidence—rejected by the Special Court—of Bambatha's wife and children that Dinuzulu openly instigated Bambatha to rebellion.

[95] CO 179/244/3062, Confidential A in desp. [secret], 5 Jan. 1908, contains Ngqengqengqe's evidence at Dinuzulu's preliminary examination.

look for Dinuzulu's doctor—he came upon Bambatha talking to some members of his tribe. At this point he was told: "Go back, we are still talking. I have found that the white people have placed some other person in my place." Only after this conversation did Bambatha appear with guns.[96] This would suggest that it was only after he had heard of Magwababa's appointment that he decided to take up arms—although Cakijana's later evidence, given both while he was detained at Nkandla jail after his arrest and at his own and Dinuzulu's trial, stated that he had been instructed by Dinuzulu to join Bambatha in order to start a rebellion. The difficulties of interpretation are considerable since, in both instances, Cakijana, an extraordinarily shrewd character, was giving the evidence he expected his audience to want—in the first instance he was talking to Dinuzulu's defendants, in the second to his prosecutors. (It is interesting that Cakijana's father reported to Dinuzulu's defense team that Cakijana said he had joined Bambatha when the latter was surrounded by white troops after he had attacked Magwababa and that as a result he, Cakijana, "could not escape"; this was also Cakijana's first version of his evidence.)[97] It is clear however that Bambatha's first openly hostile move was on the evening of 2 April, when he captured Magwababa, whose life was saved only by Cakijana's intervention.[98]

There had long been a rift between that section of the tribe which now supported Magwababa as regent and the younger followers of Bambatha, a rift which had in fact been revealed at the time of the poll tax collection when Bambatha had identified himself with the more turbulent members of his tribe and was described by one of his followers:

> We dogs of Bambata had no quarrel with the government. Bambata's quarrel was with his father Magwababa because Bambata alleged that Magwababa was the means of getting him deposed.[99]

Once Bambatha attacked Magwababa, a government appointee, it was inevitable that his quarrel would be with the government, a fact of which he must have been aware. His final decision to oppose the white man with force by attacking the magistrate and the police sent out to arrest him on 4 April may have been prompted further by a feeling that he might as well be hanged for a wolf as a lamb and die fighting. He followed up the capture of the regent by looting a hotel and the house

---

[96] Col. Col. 98: Statements to Samuelson.

[97] Col. Col. 98: Mankulumana and Mgaqo prosecutions, 38. Evidence of Gezindaka ka Nomaqonqota.

[98] CO 179/234/11743: Governor to Secretary of State, no. 49, 3 Apr. 1906.

[99] SNA 1/6/27, Greytown court-martial: Evidence of Gwazi Zulu, 3 Aug. 1906, 138.

of a white man in a search for arms. Two days earlier, the shooting before the assembled Africans of Richmond of twelve of Mjongo's men was an awful example of the white man's punishment, an example which would have acted as a spur to a man who felt by this time that he had nothing to lose. By 3 April Bambatha may have considered that he had no alternative to armed rebellion. The government of Natal, however, denied that there was any connection between Bambatha's taking up arms and the Richmond court-martial, maintaining that the time difference between the two events was too small. This contention fails to recognize the fact that the sentences had been announced several days earlier and had received widespread publicity as a result of the Natal cabinet's resignation when the British Secretary of State for Colonial Affairs requested further information about the Richmond executions.[100]

At any rate, on 5 April Bambatha fled to the dense Nkandla forests on the borders of Natal and Zululand, an area which had more than once served as a royal sanctuary. From the tactical point of view, this area could hardly have been improved on for defensive warfare. After a few days in hiding Bambatha began to build up a rebel army. Here, apparently, his plan was to keep to the forest, sending messengers to chiefs to join him, and using Dinuzulu's name as his authority and maintaining that he possessed his support.[101]

Bambatha seems to have had little intention of attacking the Europeans in the open; it was simply a matter of waiting for them to come into the bush and then taking them unawares.[102] Despite an attempt by Bambatha to force the Africans in the area to join him, however, he met with little success until Sigananda and his Cube tribe, one of the largest in the Nkandla district and the guardians of the royal grave of Cetshwayo, decided to throw in their lot with the Zondi. At first accompanied by only his own Zondi followers—they were reported to be about two to three hundred strong—Bambatha now quickly began to attract in-

---

[100] When the imperial government heard of the Richmond court-martial sentences, it asked that the shooting be delayed pending the receipt of further information in Whitehall. Natal, which was a self-governing colony, greatly resented this "interference" in their handling of the disturbances, and the cabinet handed in its resignation to the Governor. Protest meetings were held all over Natal and messages of sympathy poured in to the government of Natal from all over South Africa. White equanimity was restored when Lord Elgin, the Secretary of State for the Colonies, approved the sentences, ostensibly satisfied by the further information that he had received from the Governor, and the cabinet withdrew their resignations. See Marks, *Reluctant Rebellion*, ch. 7.

[101] CO 179/234/16019, encl. in desp. 60, 11 Apr. 1906: Statements of Vava and Hlangabesa, Bambatha's messengers.

[102] Stuart Papers (Killie Campbell Library): "Native Habits and Customs in Time of War." Evidence of Nzuze ka Mfela futi (ex-Chief Sigananda).

dividuals from the Nkandla chiefdoms. For the first time since the declaration of martial law on 8 February, a resistance movement was being built up. For this reason, the disturbances as a whole are frequently referred to as the "Bambatha Rebellion."

Sigananda's tribe had already signified their opposition to the poll tax. Shortly thereafter Sigananda's heir, who was in effective control of the chiefdom, was fined for failing to provide eight men for compulsory labor for the Department of Public Works.[103] When Bambatha fled to this area, Sigananda, together with the other chiefs in the neighborhood, was ordered by the Commissioner of Native Affairs to arm his men and hunt out the rebels, and on 8 April Sigananda's messenger reported to the magistrate that Bambatha had entered his ward.[104] However, after an apparently halfhearted and brief attempt to find Bambatha, the attitude of the Cube changed. One of Sigananda's sons, who had given the information to the government that Bambatha had been seen, was victimized by the Cube people, and on 13 April Saunders began to suspect that Sigananda had joined the rebels. By 16 April Bambatha was apparently moving about freely among the Cube, who had all been "doctored" for war by Bambatha's Sotho war doctor, the whole force then consisting of twelve to fourteen companies, according to one estimate—or about 700 to 1,000 men. Sigananda sent messages to the warriors of the surrounding chiefs—Ndube, Mpumela, Makubalo, and others—and, while the chiefs did not join, members of their chiefdoms began to filter toward the rebel army.

Despite statements to the contrary, poverty appears to have been among the root causes of Cube discontent.[105] Sir Charles Saunders, who discounted the rumors that it was Dinuzulu's messages which had led Sigananda's people to rebel, also pointed out that Sigananda and his chief son and heir, Nkabaningi, were "paupers."[106] As in the case of Bambatha, exceptional poverty was one of the clues to the above average frustration felt by the Cube people and their leaders, and therefore to their low threshold of resistance in the face of an appeal to take up arms. The high correlation between low economic status and criminality, both because of the higher level of frustration and because of the lesser "inhibiting influence of anticipated punishment," has frequently been noted. At the same time, people who have been ground down by poverty for generations do not usually rebel against their lot. It is the recently poor and the recently conquered who are most prone to "do something about it." It should be remembered that the Nkandla-Nqutu

103 CO 179/234/18854, encl. 9 in desp. 79: CNA to PM, 28 Apr. 1906.
104 Ibid.
105 Stuart, ZR, 202; Bosman, The Natal Rebellion, 48.
106 CO 179/234/18854, encl. 9 in desp. 79: CNA to PM, 28 Apr. 1906.

area of Southern Zululand had only relatively recently come under colonial rule. Unlike the Africans of Natal, the Zululanders had more recent memories of a "glorious past." That they should in so many cases have responded to Bambatha's call is hardly surprising. In the case of Sigananda, especially, these memories must have proved a potent spur to action.

Sigananda, a venerable old man, reputed to have been about ninety-seven years old, had been an *udibi* or mat-carrier during the last campaigns of Shaka's army.[107] He was also said to have witnessed the killing of Retief at Dingane's kraal. Be that as it may, he had had a more recent history of loyalty to the Zulu royal family, having been closely involved in the troubles of the 1880's. It was he who had granted Cetshwayo sanctuary in his flight from his enemies in 1883. In the 1888 disturbances he had been held in Eshowe jail on a charge of treason.[108] In a sense he was among the oldest living representatives of Zulu military pride and tradition. For such a man, it must indeed have been difficult to become reconciled to European rule. Certainly a message he is reported to have sent to Dinuzulu in reply to his instruction that he should pay the poll tax fits in with this interpretation. He is reported to have accused Dinuzulu of cowardice in not openly fighting against the white man—a message which Dinuzulu, a younger but perhaps wiser man, rejected with the words· "He is bodaring [talking nonsense] when he says I am afraid. Who can fight the white man? I have been sent over the seas by 'them'. I do not want my children to suffer."[109]

On the other hand, the Natal government maintained that secret messages from Dinuzulu to Sigananda, instructing him to look out for Bambatha, led to his change in attitude.[110] While, in fact, Dinuzulu admitted to having sent such a message, he maintained that it was sent before the outbreak of violence—before he knew that Bambatha intended starting a rebellion—and when he thought that Bambatha was simply looking for land on which to settle. At the court-martial of Sigananda and his sons, evidence was given which suggested that Cakijana's claims that he had been sent by Dinuzulu had made considerable

[107] Bosman, *The Natal Rebellion*, 109.

[108] CO 879/30/370, encl. 1 in no. 50, p. 86: Return of untried prisoners, 3 Sept. 1888 (African Confidential Prints).

[109] *Natal Mercury*, 2 June 1908. Evidence of Maliba Sijulana (Chief Lubudlungu) at Dinuzulu's preliminary examination. In 1888-89 Dinuzulu was charged with treason against the newly established British regime. Though he denied the charge, and the issues were in fact extremely complex, he was found guilty and exiled, with two of his uncles, to St. Helena. He returned to Zululand in Jan. 1898, but no longer as Zulu king.

[110] Stuart, *ZR*, 202.

impact on the Cube.[111] How important this factor was in the light of the visit of Dinuzulu's chief adviser, Mankulumana, to the Cube, in an attempt to disillusion them, is difficult to gauge. On 23 April Mankulumana arrived at the Nkandla stronghold and, according to his version of what happened, was given a very hostile reception by the Cube, who refused to let him see Sigananda.[112] Although some considered this visit simply a part of Dinuzulu's double-dealing and thought that he had probably sent other more sinister messengers simultaneously,[113] the Commissioner for Native Affairs was sure at the time that Mankulumana's visit, while not affecting the Cube decision to rebel, materially affected the decision of other tribes in the division and that "rebels from other tribes appear to be melting away."[114]

Another interpretation was given to the actions of the Cube tribe by some of its members. Thus Polomba, the *induna* of the tribe, stated at the time of his court-martial that the tribe was only recognized to be in open rebellion after the arrival of the troops, and that when they did not report Bambatha's trail (which Sigananda maintained had become imperceptible) they were treated forthwith as rebels.[115] Cakijana, a highly unreliable witness but one who in every other way tended to implicate Dinuzulu in the disturbances, maintained in May 1908 that when Mankulumana addressed Sigananda's tribe they replied:

> We have no answer for you only that we have been armed by Matshiqela [Saunders] and we are now armed for good and intend fighting for he fired on us while we were still looking for Bambata.[116]

Several other defense witnesses in the Dinuzulu trial gave similar evidence,[117] and at the court-martial of Sigananda and his sons even the counsel for the prosecution maintained that their fault lay in attempting to remain neutral (instead of actively assisting the European

111 SNA 1/6/26, Nkandla court-martial: Evidence of Polomba, 29 June 1906, 11-12.

112 CO 179/234/18854, encl. 9 in desp. 79: CNA to PM, 28 Apr. 1906.

113 See, for example, *Address of the Attorney General, The Trial of Dinuzulu on Charges of Sedition and Treason . . . held at Greytown, 1908-1909* (Pietermaritzburg, 1910), 19-20. CO 179/233/22649, Annex A in desp. 106: R. H. Addison (magistrate) to CNA, 20 May 1906. Stuart, *ZR*, 203.

114 CO 179/234/18854: Enc. CNA to PM, 28 May 1906.

115 SNA 1/6/26 MSS: Evidence of the Nkandla court-martial, 29 June 1906, 9.

116 AGO 1/7/68 (Attorney General's Office, Natal Archives): Statement Cakijana, Krantzkop, 20 May 1908.

117 For example, Col. Col., 98: Precognitions of R. C. Samuelson. Evidence of Ndabambi ka Lumungu and Nkamanga ka Tshibu-tshibu.

forces), for "of course [in war] there is no such thing as neutrality."[118] Although Stuart denies that the Cube were first fired upon by the white forces, it does appear as if it were simply assumed that they were in rebellion once they failed to hand Bambatha over, and the evidence of some of the tribesmen that they were fired upon by the troops when they were still looking for the rebels does have to be taken into consideration. To expect a man with Sigananda's background to relish handing Bambatha over to the white forces was probably expecting too much—or too little—especially when one considers that in the days of Mpande Sigananda had fled to Natal for fear of his life and had been succored by Jangeni, Bambatha's grandfather.[119]

It would thus appear that at first Sigananda had tried to remain neutral; but his poverty, the tribe's opposition to the poll tax, and his own memories of past glory and the laws of hospitality, had made him reluctant to pursue Bambatha in any very enthusiastic fashion. When he and his people realized that if they did not hand Bambatha over they would be regarded as rebels, and were perhaps so regarded already, they decided to throw in their lot with the rebels, although admittedly some of the outlying sections of the tribe might not have been fully aware of the decision.

After Sigananda, the most influential chief to join Bambatha was Mehlokazulu of the Qungebe people, another man with roots deep in the Zulu past. In many ways the motives which induced him to throw in his lot with the rebels in the Nkandla forests appear to have been similar to those which had initially spurred Bambatha into action. Once again, Mehlokazulu had a long history of past conflict with the authorities, both British and colonial. He had first gained notoriety at the time of the Zulu War of 1879, when he crossed the border of Natal in order to kidnap two of the adulterous wives of Sirayo, his father, who had fled to the colony. This incident had provided Sir Bartle Frere with one of his pretexts for war against Cetshwayo in 1879. Prominent in the Zulu War and in the tussles between the Zulu royal family, both against the British and against Zibhebhu, Dinuzulu's arch-rival, Mehlokazulu's existence during the 1880's and early 1890's was turbulent and harried. He was driven from district to district as now one loyal chief, now another, accused him of offenses, such as cattle stealing, against their white neighbors. He settled for some time in the New Republic, in Faku's location, but ran into trouble there when a Boer farmer accused him of insulting his wife: He was imprisoned at Vryheid for the of-

118 SNA 1/6/26, 59: Prosecutor Major W. A. van der Plank's address to the court, July 1906.

119 Bosman, *The Natal Rebellion*, 108. Mpande was Dinuzulu's grandfather. He ruled from 1840 to 1873.

fense.[120] Finally, he returned to the Nqutu district where his father's people lived, and, in 1893 when Sir Marshal Clarke became Resident Commissioner in Zululand and British attitudes toward the Zulu royal family and their adherents became less uncompromising, he was appointed as the chief of his father's tribe. It was felt that restoring him to a position of responsibility might ensure his loyalty.[121]

From that time Mehlokazulu does indeed appear to have led a peaceful, law-abiding life—until the time came to pay the poll tax at the beginning of 1906. On the day appointed to pay the tax, he failed to appear before the magistrate with his men, and the magistrate was disposed to take a serious view of the matter.[122] Nevertheless, for the first three months after the proclamation of martial law, Mehlokazulu made no openly hostile move, despite many rumors that he was planning to do so. As the armed forces drew nearer to his district, however, Mehlokazulu apparently became apprehensive about white intentions toward him. These apprehensions increased as rumors spread among the whites that he had been sending messages to Chief Kula in Umsinga division and that they were planning a joint action against the whites.[123] There were close ties of kinship and friendship between these two chiefs, and it is true that Mehlokazulu had sent messages both to Kula and to Dinuzulu about the poll tax.[124] It is not unlikely that these communications were attempts to ascertain whether joint opposition to the tax was possible. It must, therefore, have been with considerable fear and trembling that Mehlokazulu saw the arrest of his friend and neighbor by the white forces on 8 May.

Kula, one of the most important of the government-appointed chiefs in Natal, headed an amalgam of tribal fragments formed into a "new tribe" by the British administrator, Sir Theophilus Shepstone, in 1869.[125] Conspicuous in their loyalty to the government both in 1879 and during the Anglo-Boer War, his people had always considered themselves the "government's tribe"—a fact which tended to draw on it the enmity of its neighbors, both African and Boer. At the end of 1905 and the beginning of 1906, there were several reports by spies of pending faction fights among the many tribes of the very densely populated

[120] Zululand Archives, 22 R 618/1891: Information from Majolo ka Sirayo (according to magistrate taking down the information, "a very hostile witness" to Mehlokazulu). He was Mehlokazulu's brother.

[121] ZA 22 R 2472/93.

[122] SNA 1/4/15 C 59/06: Magistrate to USNA, 25 Jan. 1906.

[123] CO 179/235/20725: Governor to Secretary of State, desp. 95, 18 May 1906.

[124] *Times of Natal.* Evidence of Magadisa, 29 Feb. 1908 (report of Dinuzulu's preliminary examination).

[125] SNA 1/4/12 96/03: Memorandum USNA to Commandant of Militia 1903.

Umsinga district, where Kula's was by far the largest. Perhaps as a result of the arming of young men for these fights, and also because this was an area where Africans had been killing white animals from October 1905, white farmers in the area, predominantly those of German and Dutch descent, began to express their fears of being "wiped out."[126] At the beginning of March there was a "panic" among the white settlers in Kula's division over "nothing definite," which was followed in turn by the arming of one of the sections of Kula's tribe under the *induna*, Mabulawa, "who feared arrest."[127] At the same time, the magistrate of Umsinga division, with whom Kula's relationship was of the worst, sent frequent complaints about the chief's behavior to the Minister for Native Affairs, although "he furnished no specific charges." In part, the magistrate's suspicions may have been roused by his chief informant, who was a man from Sibindi's tribe, a tribe which had been involved in many boundary disputes with Kula's people.[128] Finally, Kula was summoned before the Minister for Native Affairs at the end of March and was warned that if he did not mend his ways his fate would be similar to that of the chiefs the government had already dealt with.[129]

Apparently awed by this warning, Kula returned to his people and handed over Mabulawa, despite the obvious dissatisfaction of the rest of the tribe at this action. In fact at this point his uncle, Mtele, led the dissidents into open rebellion, being joined by another small tribe in the division. Though with some reluctance, Kula, however, continued to do his duty as a government servant, and on 4 May reported Mtele's rebellion. A few days later, when the local magistracy had been reinforced with militia reserves from Helpmekaar and by the Natal Mounted Rifles, Kula, with several of his leading men, once more made his way to the magistracy to tell of further developments in his tribe. On the advice of the magistrate, the officers decided to transfer him to the officer commanding the troops at Helpmekaar, where, after being questioned, Kula was detained in custody. Despite orders from the head of the defense headquarters in Pietermaritzburg to the chief leader of the reserves in Helpmekaar that Kula should be released immediately, as he had been arrested while visiting a magistrate and should have been regarded as holding a safe conduct,[130] the leaders of the reserves at Helpmekaar telegraphed to headquarters that the release of the chief

---

[126] SNA 1/4/14 C 45/05: Magistrate, Umsinga (A. E. Harrington) to USNA, 22 Oct. 1905.
[127] SNA 1/1/337 726/06: Lt. Sgt. C. J. W. Stringer, Natal Police, to Subinspector Maxwell, Dundee, 8 Mar. 1906.
[128] SNA 1/1/338 886/06: Interview of Kula with MNA, 26 Mar. 1906.
[129] Ibid.
[130] SNA 1/1/341 1493/06, 9 Mar. 1906.

would spread the rebellion among adjoining tribes and would "cause grave condition amongst our men which we will not hold ourselves responsible for."[131] According to the resident magistrate and neighboring magistrates, the Boers (and the surnames of the leaders of the reserves at Helpmekaar bear out his interpretation) were seeking to avenge themselves on Kula for his services to the British during the Anglo-Boer War.[132]

In the face of this threat of mutiny from the reserves, Kula was removed to Pietermaritzburg, where he was held for the duration of the disturbances.[133] A few days later another portion of his tribe, under his brother Manuka, joined Mtele in open rebellion.[134] This may have been the result of resentment at the government action in removing their chief, or lack of adequate control once Kula had been detained; to the local settlers it was evidence that Kula himself had been fomenting rebellion all along. However, the government considered that there was insufficient evidence to prove this, for, although Kula was deposed and removed from his tribe at the end of the disturbances, he was not brought before either a civil or military tribunal.[135]

Other chiefs, and Mehlokazulu in particular, were left, however, to draw their own conclusions from Kula's visit to the magistrate and his consequent arrest. Mehlokazulu's followers feared that his would be a like fate. Almost immediately after Kula's arrest, when the column of Lt. Col. D. W. Mackay (the officer in charge of the troops in the district) marched through the Nqutu district, they urged him to hide in the forests to save his life and cattle. When he was instructed by the officer commanding to provide men to fight that portion of Kula's tribe which had rebelled and crossed the Buffalo River, he refused and fled with his wives, cattle, and a few followers to the bush.[136] The majority of his tribe apparently took no further action on either side. The magistrate of Nqutu tried his best to keep up negotiations with Mehlokazulu and to persuade him to return to his tribe, but, according to one witness, Mehlokazulu's reply was: "I can't go back now. I have been surrounded by troops. I do not know what harm I have done."[137]

[131] *Times of Natal*, 12 Sept. 1906.

[132] SNA 1/1/343 1627/03: Private letter to MNA, 29 May 1906.

[133] Stuart, *ZR*, 320-24.

[134] Ibid., 324

[135] Cd. 3247, *Further Correspondence Relating to Native Disturbances in Natal (1906)*, Governor to Secretary of State, no. 60. 28 Sept. 1906.

[136] CO 179/251/10868: C. de B. Persse to Secretary of State, 27 Mar. 1908.

[137] CO 179/235/20725: desp. 95, Governor to Secretary of State, 18 May 1906; Col. Col. 98. Mankulumana and Mgwaqo Prosecutions, 83 ff.; Evidence of Magadisa. See also *Times of Natal*, 29 Feb. 1908 and CO 179/235/22649, encl. in desp. 106: CNA to PM, 26 May 1906.

It was at this time that the government found it necessary to instruct the magistrates of Dundee, Ladysmith, Estcourt, Greytown, and Krantzkop[138] to assure chiefs in their divisions that they need not worry about being interfered with; in Nqutu division, however, where the magistrate asked permission of the government to hold a meeting to allay the fears of the chiefs, Mackay instructed the Commissioner for Native Affairs to "discontinue any further diplomatic negotiations" with Mehlokazulu. The conference of chiefs was apparently not held either.[139] Finally, after a few days in the bush, Mehlokazulu decided on 18 May to throw in his lot with Bambatha and made his way to the Nkandla stronghold. (It is possible that his action was partly influenced by the burning of Cetshwayo's grave by white troops on the previous day.) He was joined by members of Faku's tribe under Lubudlungu, who had been armed in accordance with the instructions of the magistrates to guard the fords when Mtele and others had crossed into Zululand. The story of the tribesmen was that after Mehlokazulu's flight they had seen their kraals burning and, thinking that this was rebel action, had gone to see what was happening, but were fired on by the white troops. They therefore "ran away and . . . joined Mehlokazulu and went to Nkandla with him, without Faku's orders."[140] This may, of course, have been a convenient excuse on the part of men who had already decided to rebel against the government; that most of the Africans of Zululand were reluctant to fight against their fellows in Natal, despite previous tribal enmities, was an undoubted fact. Whether this in itself constituted rebellion depends on one's point of view. Their situation is reminiscent of that of the Boers in the Cape at the beginning of the South African War in 1899.

The plaint of Faku's men, however, that they were fired on by the white troops when they were in fact assisting them is to some extent supported by a very interesting correspondence between the Commissioner for Native Affairs in Nkandla and the magistrate of Nqutu, C. F. Hignett, in which reference is made to the white troops "trying to goad the whole population" into rebellion and to the difficulties the magistrates had in protecting "people who one knew perfectly well were faithful to us."[141] Hignett's words are strikingly supported by a long,

[138] PMC 102/231, 16 May 1906.

[139] PMC 102/228: no. 143, CNA to PM, 25 May 1906.

[140] Col. Col. 98. Precognitions of R. C. Samuelson: Nduma ka Ziningo (brother of Faku); and Col. Col. 98, Mankulumana and Mgwaqo Prosecutions, 83 ff.; Evidence of Magadisa. See also CO 179/235/20725: Governor to Secretary of State, desp. 95, 18 May 1906.

[141] ZA 28. Papers Relating to the Zulu Rebellion. CNA to C. Hignett, 14 June 1906, agreeing with the sentiments originally expressed by Hignett. I have not found Hignett's original letter.

and, for him, unusual letter sent by Archdeacon Johnson, the Anglican missionary at St. Augustine's in the Nqutu district, to the secretary of that organization in London. He wrote:

> Many thinking people have been asking themselves "What are we going to do with this teeming native population?" Some stronghanded men have thought that the time was ripe for the solving of the great question. They knew that there was a general widespread spirit of dissatisfaction amongst the natives of Natal, Freestate and Transvaal, but especially in Natal, and they commenced the suppression of the rebellion in the fierce hope that the spirit of the rebellion might so spread throughout the land and engender a war of practical extermination. I fully believe that they were imbued with the conviction that this was the only safe way of dealing with the native question, and they are greatly disappointed that the spirit of rebelling was not strong enough to bring more than a moiety of the native peoples under the influence of the rifle. Over and over again it was said, "they are only sitting on the fence, it shall be our endeavour to push them over"; and again speaking of the big chiefs, "We must endeavour to bring him in if possible." Yes, they have been honest and outspoken enough—the wish being father to the thought, they prophesied the rebellion would spread throughout South Africa; had they been true prophets, no doubt the necessity of solving the native question would have been solved for this generation at least.[142]

Archdeacon Johnson was a highly respected member of the Natal community. He was one of the four non-official members of the Native Affairs Council set up by the government of Natal after the disturbances. He was no wide-eyed novice or fiery philanthropist. Johnson had been in Natal since the age of seven, and justly described himself as "no negrophilist in its narrow rabid sense . . . [but] a colonist and proud of that position."[143]

It could also be argued, however, that it was only the already disaffected and the guilty who would allow themselves to be provoked into aggressive action by the troops. The case of Chief Matshana ka Mondisa would appear to illustrate both the degree of military provocation and this latter point. Although the majority of his tribe assisted the government forces at Nkandla and the chief himself remained in touch with the authorities ever since Bambatha had fled to the district, some members of the tribe broke away under five of his sons, with whom Matshana had been having considerable difficulty for

[142] Letters 1906, no. 71, 24 July 1906. Society for the Propagation of the Gospel Archives (London).
[143] Ibid.

several years.[144] During the third week in June the tribe was fined five head of cattle per rebel. This fine was promptly paid by Matshana to Mackay, and he was given a "complete discharge." But a week later, a further column under Lt. Colonel J. R. Royston swept through Matshana's ward, gathering up "almost every beast it could find." According to the Commissioner for Native Affairs in Zululand, Royston's "handling of the matter in view of what had already happened under Mackay and Colonel George Leuchars (to whom Matshana had rendered every assistance) was, to say the least, extraordinary." The civil authorities immediately reassured Matshana and his people that their cattle would be restored to them. Although this had not been done by December 1906, no further members of the tribe joined the rebels.[145]

In the midst of offensive operations it must have been very difficult, in any case, for the troops to distinguish between black friend and black foe, even had they been willing to make the effort. With many of the contingents, especially those of volunteers from outside the colony, there was often only one European who spoke or understood the Zulu language.[146]

For them, it must frequently have seemed impossible to draw the distinction between "goading into rebellion" and "taking the necessary precautions." In the Nkandla-Nqutu area, where there undoubtedly was open rebellion—whatever the initial reasons for its outbreak—from the European point of view, that rebellion had to be stamped out as swiftly as possible. The terrain was extremely difficult to operate in, the Mome forests and the Nwandla mountains constituting a natural stronghold, with steep cliffs, deep gorges, and dense bush. If, in the course of the converging movements considered necessary for surrounding the rebels and hunting them out, other, more or less innocent, chiefs and tribes were dragged into the hostilities, it could be held that this was an unfortunate but unavoidable concomitant of warfare.

The Third Stage: Rebellion in the Mapumulo Division

It is, however, more difficult to accept these arguments in the case of the third stage of the disturbances—the outbreak of "rebellion" in the

[144] SNA 1/1/323 1741/05: Interview between magistrate and members of Matshana's people.

[145] SNA 1/1/360 4208/06, 8 Jan. 1907. Cf. Stuart, ZR, 397, where he calls the episode "a mistake."

[146] See, for example, ZA 34, CR 34/06: R. H. Addison to PM, 28 June 1906.

Mapumulo division. On 10 June McKenzie inflicted a crushing and decisive defeat on Bambatha and his followers at the battle of Mome Gorge. Most of the leaders of this phase of the disturbances, including Bambatha himself—whose head was cut off for purposes of "identification"—and Mehlokazulu, were killed. The Governor believed that this blow had brought the rebellion in Zululand to an end, and that there was "no chance whatever of the rebellion spreading into Natal."[147] But on 18 June Africans of Mapumulo attacked Thring's Store, killing a trooper as well as destroying some wagons at Otimati River; it was reported that hundreds of tribesmen had taken up arms.

The timing of this action was the more surprising as Mapumulo, a very densely populated, almost entirely African, area, had been among the first of the districts reported to be disturbed by the poll tax. After the initial refusal on the part of the followers of Ngobizembe, Swaimana, and Meseni to pay the tax, and a subsequent meeting of the Minister for Native Affairs with chiefs in the area, a strong body of police had been sent there at the beginning of February. Following further adverse reports from the division, where tribes had had themselves "doctored" for war, a second column of the field forces had been mobilized under Leuchars especially to deal with them. At the end of February Leuchars delivered an ultimatum to Ngobizembe to hand over within six days three hundred men who had shouted war cries, danced, and brandished sticks in front of the magistrate in January.[148] Ngobizembe protested that, after the lapse of nearly six weeks, it would be impossible to find all the offenders in the allotted time. He handed over only twenty of the culprits, and, as a result, on 5 March Leuchars bombarded Ngobizembe's kraal with artillery fire from a distance of two hundred yards.[149] This was reported to have had a "splendid effect." Leuchars, who had been Secretary for Native Affairs, was congratulated by the Governor of white Natalians on his superb understanding of the "native mind," and all over Natal the Africans were reported to have "changed their attitude of studied insolence to one of thorough submission."[150] Ngobizembe immediately surrendered with a large portion of his tribe, and plans were made to send him to northern Zululand. Half his lands were confiscated and the people thereon placed under adjacent chiefs. He was further fined 1,200 head of cattle and 3,500 sheep and goats. Mounted troops "drove" the country for further "rebels" and cattle. No opposition was shown to these

[147] CO 179/235/24596; Governor to Secretary of State, 16 June 1906.
[148] Cd. 2905, *Correspondence Relating to Native Disturbances in Natal (1906)*, Governor to Secretary of State, desp. 30, 2 Mar. 1906.
[149] Cd. 2905, Governor to Secretary of State, desp. 37, 9 Mar. 1907.
[150] Ibid.

disciplinary actions, although Bambatha, at this time deposed from his chieftainship, was in the neighboring Umvoti bush, watching no doubt with some interest.

While Ngobizembe's was the most drastic fate in Mapumulo at this time, Leuchars also demanded that the "rebels" from Meseni's and Swaimana's chiefdoms be given up. Meseni himself had not actually been present at the time of the alleged defiance of his people over the poll tax. (He had been attending a trial at the Stranger magistracy.) Nevertheless, for not handing over more than fifty-five of the hundred men demanded by Leuchars for trial by court-martial for their participation in the defiance of the Mapumulo magistrate, he was imprisoned without trial for six weeks.[151] The opportunity was also taken to limit his jurisdiction to those of his people in the Mapumulo-Ndedwe divisions, ostensibly as punishment for his part in a 1905 faction fight.

In March, Ndlovu ka Timuni, another chief in the Mapumulo division, was summoned to Stranger for having failed to appear before the magistrate on two previous occasions and was, "owing to a mistake," detained for more than a month before he too was released without trial.[152] The arbitrary nature of these proceedings was further illustrated by the case of acting Chief Geveza of the Cele people. Arrested for failing to obey a command to report to Leuchars, who apparently wanted him to be present when Ngobizembe's deposition was read out, he was sentenced under martial law to three months' imprisonment. Geveza's tribe was, in fact, divided between the Krantzkop and Mapumulo divisions, and it would appear that the original summons to hear the deposition had gone to the *induna* of the Mapumulo section of the Cele, Geveza himself residing at Krantzkop. The Krantzkop magistrate himself thought that this was the most likely explanation for Geveza's behavior.

Although the bulk of Leuchar's column, which had been operating in the Mapumulo-Lower Tugela River area, was demobilized in the middle of March, small numbers of troops, especially the Umvoti Mounted Rifles, were retained there. These were later supplemented by a garrison of the Natal Mounted Rifles and the Durban Light Infantry, who were sent there because of the rumors of rebelliousness among the tribesmen, although nothing of a definite nature was proven at this stage. At the end of April some of Ngobizembe's men joined Bambatha in the Nkandla forests.[153]

By the middle of April there were indications that the presence

[151] Stuart, ZR, 344-46.
[152] SNA 1/4/16 C 125/06: Col. Leuchars to Commandant of Militia, 20 Mar. 1906, and Memorandum of Magistrate T. Maxwell, Mapumulo, 2 Apr. 1906.
[153] Stuart, ZR, 318, 344.

of the troops in the Mapumulo and Lower Tugela divisions was not entirely beneficial. The magistrate of the neighboring Krantzkop division wrote to the Undersecretary for Native Affairs that Chief Tshutshutshu, who had men in both divisions like Geveza, had complained that several members of his tribe had been unjustly flogged by the troops at Mapumulo and that he (the magistrate) had heard several other complaints of a similar nature.[154] The young men of Tshutshutshu's tribe were later described as having been "insolent and insubordinate" during the initial poll tax collection, but during the actual outbreak of violence in the division to have been "loyal and zealous" in hunting out rebels.[155]

On being asked for an explanation of these allegations of unjust floggings, the head of the Umvoti Mounted Rifles replied to the commandant of the militia that:

> The natives in question were punished for insolent behaviour and for not showing the required respect for the King's uniform. Strong measures had to be resorted to to teach the natives who had utterly got out of hand . . . to pay their respects to the white man.[156]

This action was fully approved by the commandant of the militia[157] and apparently roused no further comment at the time. Yet a few weeks later Sir James Liege Hulett, a man who had held various responsible positions in the colony—having been a member of the Natal Parliament since responsible government and Secretary for Native Affairs in 1899, as well as being one of the largest sugar farmers in the colony with considerable interests in Zululand—was to write earnestly and urgently from his sugar estates in the neighborhood of Mapumulo to the Prime Minister of the serious state of affairs there. Once again, these words cannot be dismissed as those of an attention-seeking negrophile and have to be quoted at some length:

> The native population is absolutely docile and quiet throughout the district, [though] how long they will remain so depends upon the government; if they are to be harried by irresponsible men who act as demi-Gods and who, armed with a kind of self-imposed authority, think it the correct thing to flog unoffending people . . . then the area will be drawn into the area of disaffected with the result that the [European] people [here] . . . will have to leave their homes, wives and

154 SNA 1/1/340 1224/06: Magistrate A. W. Leslie to USNA, 19 Apr. 1906.
155 SNA 1/1/314 3263/08: Report of Magistrate, Krantzkop, 27 Aug. 1906.
156 SNA 1/1/340 1224/06: Minute, Captain Moe to Commandant of Militia, 30 Apr. 1906.
157 Ibid. Commandant of Militia to Minister of Justice, 1 Aug. 1906.

plantations to the mercy of an outraged foe. . . . Pray let us have a level-headed man at the head of affairs at Mapumulo and put a stop to this nonsense of having every man in uniform requiring every native to conform to his idea of what salutation consists of. This [illegible] people is being driven into rebellion and it speaks volumes for [their] good sense . . . that they have not risen.[158]

A few days later ministers heard from another source that the troops were using their leather stirrups to impress upon the natives "due respect" and to obtain information, and gave as their unanimous opinion that this "should immediately be put to a stop."[159]

Even in peacetime, the extent to which Natal magistrates resorted to the lash was greater than in any of the other South African colonies at this time. As de Kiewiet has remarked, the temptation for a small, insecure white population to resort to rule by terror was immense.[160] In the absence of consent, the Africans of Natal were governed by a thinly veiled use of force, even in peacetime.[161]

In all the South African colonies except Natal, sentences involving flogging had to be reviewed by a judge of the supreme court. In 1907 in Natal, where there was no such check, one in every four hundred of the total male population was flogged, exclusive of young boys sentenced to birching;[162] during the disturbances, according to the *Times of Natal*,[163] seven hundred Africans had their backs lashed to ribbons and four thousand seven hundred sentences, including lashes, were carried out before the government itself put an end to this "judicial violence."[164] The paper continued: "We wonder if any official record exists of the number flogged, so to say on sight, during the . . . expedition . . . in that year."

In Natal there was little of the lynching and public violence which has characterized race relations in the southern states of the United States; nevertheless, this form of legalized brutality appears to have constituted an adequate substitute and was, in many ways, probably

[158] PM 60 575/06, 20 May 1906.

[159] CO 179/235/22649, Governor to Secretary of State, 1 June 1906. Publ. Cd. 3027, desp. 54.

[160] Cornelius W. de Kiewiet, *The Imperial Factor in South Africa* (2nd ed.; London, 1965), 36.

[161] See, for example, Supplement to the Natal government *Gazette*, 5 June 1905, Report of the Prison Reform Commission, 317, which talks of the "cult of the lash."

[162] Nathan Papers, MSS 401, (Rhodes House). Copy, Minutes of Nathan to SNA, 25 Oct. 1907, 247; to PM, 6 Jan. 1908 and 28 Jan. 1908, 255; to Attorney General, 31 Dec. 1908, 258; and Nathan Papers 368 to Selborne, 11 Dec. 1908.

[163] *Times of Natal*, 28 Jan. 1908.

[164] Stuart, *ZR*, 404.

the outcome of the same psychological factors. It is beyond the scope of this essay to explore this aspect of settler mentality; nevertheless, in finally prompting into action those Africans who had already watched their cattle confiscated and their kraals destroyed, it cannot be ignored. It would also go a long way toward explaining the "puzzling" feature[165] of this last phase of the disturbances—why it was that after the rebellion was so clearly a hopeless and dying cause the chiefs in the Mapumulo-Lower Tugela area should suddenly have taken up arms, especially after many of them had already paid their poll taxes and had suffered for their previous recalcitrance. If the "doctoring" of tribes in January and February, regarded by Stuart as revealing the most hostile intentions to the white man, was intended as a preliminary to war,[166] it is difficult to explain why more of the Mapumulo men did not either join the Nkandla army or rise at the same time when the bulk of the forces was engaged there.

Stuart's explanation of this very odd course of action is that messengers were sent from Dinuzulu's uncle, Siteku, to Meseni, Matshwili, and Nklovu ka Timuni, inciting them to rise only after the Battle of Mome Gorge.[167] Yet this hardly seems a sufficient reason for their curious action, especially as the Commissioner for Native Affairs himself found these allegations "most unsatisfactory"; he had had a long interview with Meseni and Ndlovu ka Timuni when they surrendered and, despite the most careful examination on the question of whether they had been encouraged from Zululand, "they gave not the slightest hint that that was so."[168] Many may have been induced to take up arms by the rumor that the Africans had been successful at Mome Gorge and that all the white soldiers had been killed which was apparently circulated in the Mapumulo area by survivors of Mome Gorge.

That this rumor could long have lasted in face of the overwhelming disaster inflicted on 10 June, however, seems most unlikely. A member of Chief Ngobizembe's people in this division appeared to be giving the general African view when he told the Natal Native Affairs Commission that:

Before they had an opportunity of making any reply and stating that they thought the taxes already existing were heavy enough, they were threatened with being shot. They thereupon paid, but while they were

[165] Papers of American Board of Missions in Natal (American Zulu Mission) in Natal Archives: ABM 111/1/3, 348 ff.: J. D. Taylor to Rev. D. W. Drew, ed., *The Friend* (Bloemfontein), 30 June 1906.

[166] Stuart, *ZR*, 347.

[167] Ibid., 347-48.

[168] AGO 1/7/52: Minute by CNA on statements made by Ndlovu and Meseni before J. Stuart, 20 and 21 July 1906.

still paying hostilities broke out. It was a matter of curiosity on their side as to whether the government really wanted this tax or whether they wanted their lives.[169]

The Mapumulo rebels were to pay dearly for their uprising: about 1,500 Africans were killed, 1,300 prisoners taken, and thousands of people rendered homeless and starving by the burning of their crops and kraals in the division.[170] Even after the surrender of the chief leaders of the rebellion there, and long after the government considered such action to be necessary, these "punitive measures" continued.[171] The Governor referred to the "sweeping actions" and "mopping up operations" in this division and neighboring Lower Tugela as "continued slaughter," and Frederick Graham, at the Colonial Office, a man not given to hyperbole, called it a "massacre."[172] While many atrocities had been ascribed to the troops in other areas, it could be argued that these were generally in the heat of battle. In this area, the atrocities continued long after the heat of battle had burnt out. They were eventually stopped only as a result of action by the government.[173]

Conclusions

There were those, even in 1906, who saw the entire rebellion as deliberately contrived by the government, the white settlers, or, indeed, by that bogey of left-wing thought in the early twentieth century, the Transvaal mine owners, for the purpose of grabbing the Africans' land and forcing them to work in the goldfields. There is little evidence to support such views. Both the government and the settlers feared rebellion as much as they were determined to stamp it out completely once it occurred. Their blundering, misunderstanding, and insensitivity must, however, be counted among the factors which led to the flare-up of violence in 1906. There is more evidence, but even this perhaps in the very nature of things is not absolute, that once the military men

[169] NNAC: Evidence of Mavandhla, 698.

[170] SNA 1/1/371 1862/07: Report Magistrate Farrer, Mapumulo, to MNA, 28 June 1907.

[171] PM 61 829/06: G. Armstrong, MLA, and M. S. Evans, MLA, to PM, 13 July 1906.

[172] PM 61 815/06: Governor to PM, 10 July 1906; and CO 179/236/24787: Minute 10 July 1906 on tel., Governor to Secretary of State, 9 July 1906, no. 1.

[173] PM 61 829/06, 815/06 as above. Proclamation in Government *Gazette*, no. 3552, 12 July 1906. ABM 111/1/3 Letterbook: J. D. Taylor to MNA, 9 Sept. 1906; to Judson Smith 13 July 1906 (Boston Sec. ABM); to F. F. Churchill (MLA), 13 July 1906; to Marshall Campbell, 21 July 1906.

were in the field they exacerbated the situation considerably. Although it is true that in the long run the mine owners profited from the 1906 disturbances, as the number of Africans forced onto the labor market of the mines grew from 17,900 in 1906 to 34,200 in 1910,[174] it was certainly not only the rebellion which caused this. Nor, of course, can one argue from this that the mine owners were in any way directly or indirectly responsible for this result, however much they had wanted to increase their labor supply. Among neither blacks nor whites is there much evidence of a conspiracy, although much of "cross purposes rampant on a sea of rumor."

Nevertheless, the official view in Natal that the campaigns were conducted with the utmost humanity and the contention that only swift action saved thousands of white women and children from being murdered by black hordes also does not bear much scrutiny. Of both extreme views it can be said "not proven." The words of the veteran Cape politician, John X. Merriman, summed up the feeling of the more liberal element in South Africa, when he wrote to Goldwin Smith in September 1906:

> We have had a horrible business in Natal with the natives. I suppose the whole truth will never be known, but enough comes out to make us see how thin the crust is that keeps our Christian civilization from the old-fashioned savagery—machine guns and modern rifles against knob-sticks and assegais are heavy odds and do not add much to the glory of the superior races.[175]

If the rebellion had not added "much to the glory of the superior races," it had inflicted a shattering blow on the African population of Natal and Zululand. From the military point of view, the army had indeed "solved" the "native question" for their generation. Although there was some change of heart among a handful of white Natalians on the subject of their treatment of the African population, and an attempt was made to "reform" the "native policy," there was little change in the poverty-stricken and depressed conditions of African life. Among whites outside Natal the disturbances illuminated the dangers of allowing a small white community to handle a question so vital to the rest of southern Africa. The growing movement toward a unification of South Africa in order to ensure the dominance of the white man was given a considerable spur forward. But on the positive side, Africans too were increasingly realizing the need for political unity. While all over south-

---

[174] C. E. Axelson, "The History of Taxation in Natal prior to Union" (unpublished thesis for M. Commerce, Natal University College, 1938), 160.

[175] Merriman Papers (Cape Town Public Library), no. 202, 16 Sept. 1906.

ern Africa the futility of opposing the white man by force of arms was realized once and for all, the need for education, for new political organizations, and modern political weapons was appreciated more widely than ever before. In the formation of the South African Native National Congress in 1912 (later to be renamed the African National Congress) the lessons of 1906 were writ large.[176]

[176] In deference to Natal's recent experiences, John Dube of Natal was elected first president of the Congress, and Dinuzulu was made an honorary vice-president. Cf. also the remark of a Christian African at a meeting held in Zululand to explain the new Congress: "I thank Bambata. I thank Bambata very much. Would this spirit might continue. I do not mean Bambata of the bush who perished at Nkandhla but I mean this new spirit which we have just heard explained." From Marshall Campbell Papers (Killie Campbell Library), Bantu Section, Letter from District Commissioner, Zululand, n.d., R 156/1912/32.

THE NYABINGI CULT OF

SOUTHWESTERN UGANDA

ELIZABETH HOPKINS

The coalescence of traditionally diverse populations in opposition to European rule has been a recurrent feature of the colonial process. In the Mfumbiro region between Lake Kivu and Lake Edward there was, however, an unusual, if not unique variant, for the polarization of anti-European sentiment into active and co-ordinated resistance occurred before the local implementation of administrative control. The immediacy of the response, the degree of regional and tribal coordination and, above all, the effectiveness and duration of resistance, distinguish the Nyabingi cult from similar movements of protest.

The matrix for protest was familiar: an initial claim to superior supernatural powers, later used to validate claims to a monopoly of secular control. The idiom for political opposition—an indigenous possession cult—is again not without historical parallel in Africa. What is striking is that, despite a strong parochialism of method and purpose, the Nyabingi cult succeeded in immobilizing the administrative efforts of three colonial powers for nearly two decades, until its final suppression in 1928. That a traditional possession cult, without significant ideological modification, could remain such a tenacious and effective vehicle for opposition to alien rule ensures the Nyabingi cult a distinctive position in the history of colonial Africa.

The Cult of Nyabingi

The cult of Nyabingi was one of a number of possession cults found throughout the western interlacustrine area which celebrated leg-

I acknowledge with gratitude the support of The Social Science Research Council during my two periods of field work in Uganda.

endary heroes called *emandwa*. While in a number of cults the *em-andwa* could be summoned by any initiated member, in the Nyabingi cult access to the spirit was limited to the *bagirwa*, or specialists, each of whom claimed to have been selected by Nyabingi as her medium and therefore to have the exclusive power to invoke her presence and to interpret her will. In consequence, there were no initiation rites or communal rituals to provide a more egalitarian focus for cult activity.

As in other *emandwa* cults, the presence of the spirit was marked by possession, but the diagnostic behavior, to confirm the claim of privileged access to the spirit, was more elaborate and demanded greater skill. Among the techniques associated with possession by Nyabingi were the assumption of a stylized trembling movement, ventriloquism, and the ability to hold a "dialogue" with the spirit in an esoteric language and in falsetto.[1] Other eccentricities of behavior reinforced these attributes of possession. Emin Pasha, describing similar specialists in the court of Bunyoro, observed that they were "most striking figures" who "vie with one another in eccentricities." One "grunted every minute," another "spoke in the highest falsetto," while a third "sat down beside one of [Emin's] company, and wanted her shoulders rubbed and her head bent."[2] This erratic behavior, intensified by its supernatural associations, could easily be parlayed by a skilled practitioner into more pervasive claims of influence. Muhumusa, one of the more forceful and feared of the Nyabingi leaders, was acknowledged by colonial officers to be "an extraordinary character":

> By dint of years of training, she has acquired a high falsetto voice and professes inability to walk normally, her method of position being on tip-toe in a crouching position with the aid of two sticks. . . . The chiefs with scarcely an exception trembled whenever her look was directed toward them. She also made most noticeable efforts to exercise some form of hypnotism over me.[3]

Basic to the demonstration and revalidation of the claimed power of the *bagirwa* was the ability to evoke supernatural forces to punish those who angered or ignored the spirit or who failed to accede to Nyabingi's demands for offerings. Once their power to curse had been demonstrated by a few strategic acts of misfortune, the mere threat

[1] For a more detailed description of the cult ritual consult Marcel Pauwels, "Le culte de Nyabingi (Ruanda)," *Anthropos*, XXXXVI (1951), 337-57.

[2] Georg Schweinfurth, F. Ratzel, Robert W. Felkin, and G. Hartlaub (eds.), *Emin Pasha in Central Africa* (London, 1888), 285.

[3] NAF Seditious Movements: District Commissioner Kigezi to District Commissioner Bukoba, 9 Jan. 1937, Kigezi District.

of such action was sufficient to ensure that further demands for grain, livestock, or beer would be met. So strong was local belief in the ability of an offended *mugirwa* (specialist) to inflict violent physical illness that any sudden acute pain was called *nabingi amuunbe* or "Nyabingi has cursed me."[4] Evidence given during the trial of a cult leader in 1938 confirms the critical role of the curse in establishing the reputation of a *mugirwa*:

> The Acc. used to ask people forcibly to offer to him cows in the way of frightening them. There was also a Munyarwanda man called Kabundami who refused to give the Acc. a cow but afterwards this man was killed by a lion because the Acc. used to say that as the man had refused to offer him a cow he would not live long. Therefore this was a surprise to other people and immediately they began to fear Acc. very much.[5]

While the threat of acute illness served as the major technique for intimidation, an aura of supernatural power was also cultivated to reinforce the claims of the *bagirwa* to curative and malevolent powers. As J. E. T. Philipps reported, "Every attempt is made to surround the simplest action with supernatural significance."[6] The studied eccentricities of behavior also provided a major psychological barrier between the *bagirwa* and ordinary Africans.

The influence of the *bagirwa* was further strengthened by secular conventions which marked their social distance as important political leaders. All relied on restricting the access of outsiders to specific cult channels by remaining in seclusion in their encampment and by receiving suppliants within the sacred hut. Some were never seen by their adherents, while others only appeared publicly on litters—a prerogative of royalty in the interlacustrine area—shrouded in bark cloth or with their faces veiled. This public posture unquestionably created social distance by manipulating the traditional symbols of royalty. It also reinforced the claims of the *bagirwa* to unique supernatural powers through depersonalization and, for the male cult leader, through the affectation of a female pattern of dress.

Finally, physical violence or the threat of physical violence was also used to consolidate the authority of the *bagirwa* both within the cult and among non-adherents. Philipps states that force was "fre-

---

[4] Captain J. E. T. Philipps, "The Nabingi: An Anti-European Secret Society in Africa in British Ruanda, Ndorwa and the Congo (Kivu)," *Congo*, IX (1928), 316.

[5] Eishengyero Court 60/39, Ankole District, Statement of Second Witness; Statement of Fourth Witness.

[6] Philipps, "Nabingi," 317.

quently" used against those who showed evidence of disloyalty.[7] Non-adherents who resisted the movement and its demands for allegiance and gifts were also subject to punitive raids in which their property was destroyed or confiscated. While the claims of a *mugirwa* to supernatural power were in themselves a major incentive for compliance, they were unquestionably reinforced by the presence of a sizable armed following in his personal entourage. Testimony elicited during the trial of Ndungutsi in 1938 indicated that he was accompanied by some sixty men who conspicuously displayed the traditional weapons —the bow and arrow and shield—long after they had been eliminated by political conditions and by the administrative pressures of *pax Brittanica*.[8]

As the reputation of a *mugirwa* increased, his ability to exact offerings from the local population also grew. This in turn meant an enlargement of his personal entourage, for the tribute permitted the elaboration of a redistributive network based on personal patronage. The allocation of cattle, in particular, provided an effective way of attracting supporters. One witness stated:

> I know that my cattle died of 1936 rinderpest and when I was in sorrows then there came to me a munyarwanda man and told me that I should not cry because of my cattle died as there was a new king at a village called Kibeho . that he is saving people by giving them cattle as presents. On receiving this information I went and joined Acc. . . . where he gave me a heifer Kahogo as present, which was offered to him by one called Mazosio.[9]

Thus the entry of a *mugirwa* into a new territory was marked not merely by his acquisition of goods but by the promise of the distribution of beer and cattle. As in the secular system of authority, economic action was used to support political claims.

The ascendancy of Nyabingi over other *emandwa* cults in the Mfumbiro area was based in large part on the distinctive hierarchical pattern of the cult structure. By restricting access to the spirit to the *bagirwa*, the cult provided considerable leverage for the economic, political, and psychological manipulation of followers and for the extension of control over those who did not voluntarily seek the protection of Nyabingi. The continuity of the movement was further facilitated by the belief that were a leader killed or removed from an area, the spirit of Nyabingi would select another host. Thus the death or dis-

---

[7] Ibid.
[8] Eishengyero Court 60/39, Ankole District, Statement of Third Witness.
[9] Eishengyero Court 60/39, Statement of Second Witness.

appearance of any given leader did not threaten the cult itself. This ideology of a shifting locus of supernatural power was unquestionably central to the rapid acceptance of the Nyabingi in areas which had successfully resisted secular control by adjacent kingdoms.

Origins of the Cult

The origins of the Nyabingi cult are obscure but two persisting traditions serve to illuminate the character of the cult during the colonial period. In one version, the cult was introduced into Rwanda during the last half of the nineteenth century by two Rwanda cattle traders returning from Uzinza, a kingdom to the southeast. When misfortune befell those refusing to acknowledge Nyabingi, the reputation of the cult and the recruitment of adherents rapidly accelerated. The response eventually became so widespread that the "enormous flow" of gifts and fees seriously disrupted not only the traditional Rwanda cults but the collection of royal tribute as well.[10]

The movement entered a more activist phase when local cult leaders, protesting the defection of so many of their adherents, appealed to the Rwanda chiefs for support. The *bagirwa* countered by urging the Hutu of the area to rebel against the privileged position of the Tutsi. As the cult continued to grow and to encourage such openly seditious sentiments, it became of direct concern to the *mwami*, the ruler of Rwanda. In response to appeals of the local chiefs, he sent an expedition against the Nyabingi. Although the cult leader and many of his entourage were killed and their livestock confiscated, unrest continued for the spirit of Nyabingi was reported to have "moved on." Soon a *mugirwa* claiming the powers of Nyabingi and effecting dramatic cures appeared in another area. Again, as the cult gained members, it became more explicitly political in character, stressing its protective role toward the Hutu and the iniquities of the Tutsi superstructure. As before, local chiefs soon complained to the *mwami* of their weakening authority but it was only when labor and tribute were no longer given in the dissident area that the *mwami* again marched against the cult. The leader and his adherents were killed and the countryside in the rebellious area destroyed, but once again a girl from the subjugated area was rumored to have received the spirit of Nyabingi and the influence of the cult moved northward. This pattern of extortion, disruption of existing channels of labor and tribute, and subversion against the Tutsi, followed by retaliatory expeditions and the execution of the cult leaders, continued as a cyclical

[10] Philipps, "Nabingi," 313 ff.

phenomenon in northern Rwanda throughout the final years of the precolonial period.

The second tradition of origin places the focus for cult development and activity north of Rwanda in Mpororo. In this version, Nyabingi was a historical figure who ruled Ndorwa-Kajara before the formation of Mpororo. In the dynastic accounts of the Hororo, Kamurari, the founder of Mpororo, found the region ruled by an "Amazon Queen," Kitami. By procuring the royal drum from Kitami, Kamurari obtained control over the heartland of Mpororo.[11] According to this version, Kitami was only later apotheosized as the spirit Nyabingi. J. M. Gray, in contrast, feels that the name Nyabingi, "she who possesses many things," was an alternative title to Kitami.[12] He also suggests that the usurpation of her authority by the invading Hororo provided the key to the recurrently seditious character of the Nyabingi cult:

> After her death she became immortal and continued to issue her decrees through the mouths of her Bagirwa (lit. "those who initiate"), who were almost invariably women. The doctrines preached by these Bagirwa were those of the old regime. It is therefore not surprising to find that the latter-day rulers of the land regarded them as enemies and made war upon them. It is also not surprising to learn that upon occasion devotees of the cult rose in rebellion and killed leaders of the invading races.[13]

Rwanda sources, in contrast, assert that Nyabingi was either a royal princess of Ndorwa or—perhaps a later ideological expediency—a Hutu attached as a servant to the Ndorwa court.[14] In either event, as in the Abashambo legends, she never married and, under varying circumstances, met a sudden and violent death. Marcel Pauwels, who provides certain linguistic evidence in support of the northern origin of the cult, asserts that before 1865 and the accession of Rwabugiri as *mwami* in Rwanda, the Nyabingi rarely carried their activities south into Rwanda.[15]

In the origins as perceived in this version, we also find a key to the politically volatile role which the cult played in Rwanda during the latter half of the nineteenth century: "Il est également à noter que les Batutsi du Ruanda ne montrent aucun enthousiasme pour ce

[11] H. F. Morris, *A History of Ankole* (Kampala, 1962), 17.

[12] Sir John Milner Gray, "A History of Ibanda, Saza of Mitoma, Ankole," *Uganda Journal*, XXIV (1960), 176.

[13] Ibid., 177.

[14] Pauwels, "Culte," 337.

[15] "*Bingi* est de Gihororo (Ruhima); en Kinyaruanda on dirait *Byinshi*," ibid., 337, 341-42.

culte de Nyabingi; mais cela n'est pas étonnant puis qu'il est censé honorer une princesse étrangère dont la famille fut fréquemment en guerre avec les rois du Ruanda."[16] Although it is not clear under what circumstances Philipps acquired his version of the Nyabingi legend, the corroborative evidence of the presence of the cult in Mpororo would seem to point to a northern rather than southern origin. Here the only puzzling discrepancy is May M. Edel's statement that the movement reached the Kiga, who are territorially contiguous to Mpororo and in an area designated today as Ndorwa, from Rwanda. Her informants in 1933 seemed in accord that the movement had been recently introduced into their area by Rwanda moving in from the south.[17] Yet the claims of the bagirwa to the Ndorwa tradition could only encourage Kiga identification with the cult. The royal idiom of the Ndorwa tradition also provided a more effective validation of both the political pretensions and the patterns of centralization which the cult imposed without hesitation in the more acephalous areas.

Early Political Techniques of the Nyabingi Cult

The earliest European reference to Nyabingi confirms the presence of the cult in Mpororo during the final years of the nineteenth century. Although Stanley had alluded to reports in Karagwe of an "Empress of Ruanda," it was only during his expedition of 1889 that reports were first heard of the "Wanyanvingi."[18] It is apparent that during his second expedition Stanley retained the impression that Rwanda was "Unyavingi." To judge from his location of the territory, however, he was actually describing Mpororo: "a large, compact country, lying between the Alexandra Nile [the Kagera River] and the Congo watershed to the west, and reaching to within one day's long march to the Albert Edward."[19] The confusion is compounded by his observation that "the late Queen has been succeeded by her son, Kigeri," for at no time was the Rwanda throne under the control of a woman.[20]

The final journey of Emin Pasha north in 1891 provided important information on the position of the cult in Mpororo:

> The Queen of Mpororo . . . said to be a woman named Njavingi
> . . . has never been seen by anyone, not even her own subjects. All

16 Ibid., 342.

17 May Mandelbaum Edel, The Chiga of Western Uganda (New York, 1957), 154-55.

18 Henry M. Stanley, Through the Dark Continent (New York, 1878), 454.

19 J. Scott Keltie, The Story of Emin's Rescue as Told in Stanley's Letters (New York, 1890), 140-41.

20 Julian Gorju, Entre le Victoria l'Albert et l'Edouard (Rennes, 1920), 145-55.

that they ever get to know of her is a voice heard behind a curtain of bark cloth. Such theatrical practices have gained for her, throughout Karagwe, Nkole etc., the reputation of a great sorceress, capable of bewitching people and also of benefiting them.[21]

Her authority over the chieftaincies of Mpororo was, however, far from monolithic. Emin Pasha observed, "[she] appears to be acknowledged by part of her subjects only." As for her ability effectively to control those areas of Mpororo which she claimed, Emin noted:

> The whole of Mpororo has fallen into a complete state of lawlessness, owing to the circumstances that the Queen has no authority whatever, and there is no protection whatever for the subjects.[22]

Yet his diaries indicate that those chiefs who did acknowledge her suzerainty were fearful and anxious to avoid her anger.

A partial explanation for these discontinuities in control lies in the political state of Mpororo at that period and in the *modus operandi* used by the *bagirwa* to gain the obedience of the existing Mpororo chieftaincies. In consequence of raiding from the adjacent and more centralized kingdoms of Rwanda, Nkore, and Buganda, Mpororo had become depopulated, a "no man's land." The ascendancy of the Nyabingi cult in this area appears to have been in large part a response to the severe dislocations caused by these external political pressures. Exploiting the existing instability, the leaders of the cult were able to assert an uncontested if nominal claim to sovereignty over Mpororo, though their actual control over the Hororo chieftaincies was at best erratic. This failure of the cult to provide a viable focus for political unification despite the external stimulus for consolidation is of particular interest, given the later role of the cult in the more acephalous areas of Kigezi to the west.

It is also apparent from Emin's account that the incumbent Nyabingi was well aware of the tenuous character of her claim to power. Nevertheless, she was clearly determined to impose control over the entire Mpororo area. In fact, she hoped to manipulate Emin to this end. Exploiting the vulnerability of Emin's caravan and its need for guides, porters, and fresh supplies, she urged Emin to remain in Mpororo "to set the country in order, so that Njavingi might rule again." As an inducement for such services, Emin was told to "pillage wherever I liked, seize people and confiscate cattle."[23]

[21] Georg Schwitzer, *Emin Pasha, His Life and Work* (Westminster, 1898), II, 173, 177.

[22] Ibid., 182.

[23] Ibid., 177.

If Emin's information is correct, control over the fragmented chieftaincies of Mpororo required secular techniques which he himself had observed:

> Queen Njavingi has repeatedly called in the aid of her more powerful neighbour, King Ntali of Nkole, to punish her rebellious chiefs, and on such occasions he pillages their respective districts. Something of the kind happened here three months ago, the northern part of Makovoli's district being laid waste; he therefore hastens now to make his peace, quite neglecting us in his anxiety.[24]

Thus it is clear that the effective domination of the Hororo demanded not merely the familiar cult techniques of secular intimidation or threatened supernatural vengeance but the manipulation of a larger intertribal context. By exploiting the raiding patterns of adjacent, more powerful kingdoms, the *bagirwa* acquired a far more efficient executive machinery than could have been generated internally, given the competing claims of an hereditary chiefly structure. The basis for cult power thus rested both on the threat of supernatural retaliation and on the enlistment of a more powerful polity (in this case, Nkore) as an ally in the exploitation of this unstable and vulnerable area.

The pattern of cult expansion into Mpororo reflects the structural limitations of such a movement. Unable to compete for control of the core areas of Rwanda or Nkore, and presumably unmotivated to exploit the acephalous, predominantly agricultural Kiga, the cult was restricted in the precontact period to marginal but centralized areas on the periphery of the larger pastoral states. As such, the motives for intimidation were there, as well as the mechanisms for the accumulation of goods through existing redistributive networks. To utilize these networks, however, it was essential either to displace the Hororo chiefs or to obtain their tacit co-operation. Whereas to the south, in Rwanda, the cult stood in active opposition to the existing chiefly structure, in the Mpororo area the strategy for control emphasized the incorporation of the indigenous chiefs into the larger cult structure as local representatives of Nyabingi.

Despite continuing intertribal unrest and the expansion of European colonial activity, Mpororo remained under the nominal control of the Nyabingi cult throughout the final decades of the nineteenth century.[25] The earliest colonial references to the cult come from the adjacent territory of Ankole, which was established as an administrative district at the end of 1898. In the political reports for 1901, refer-

[24] Ibid.

[25] Ewart S. Grogan and Arthur H. Sharp, *From Cape to Cairo* (London, 1900), 168 ff.

ence is made to the "disturbed state of a place east of Buchika under a chief named Muhumuzi."[26] Perhaps even more illuminating is a report that cattle captured by German patrols after a punitive expedition against a local chief "are now with Navingi, chieftainess of Omupundi."[27]

Thus, by 1901, the cult had moved within the orbit of the German administration and appeared to be manipulating the Germans to consolidate its position against the secular chiefly structure. Two years later the Germans were openly drawn into the political network of the cult when two *bagirwa* near the border sought the support of Lieutenant Weiss of the Anglo-Belgian Boundary Commission. One, on the German side, was concerned with suppressing local dissidence; the other, in British territory, saw the presence of the Boundary Commission as an opportunity to overthrow her weaker rival to the south. Weiss refused to help either one and urged the latter to return to her own country.[28] Also south of the border at that time was the *mugirwa,* Muhumusa, who within a few years would achieve notoriety in both British and German territories. In 1903, however, she was fully cooperative with the survey party. From Weiss's account it is clear that even at that time she exercised considerable authority over her followers.

The open co-operation of the cult leaders with these alien intruders reflects the political focus of the cult at the time of contact. Whether intent upon consolidating the small, weak chieftaincies of the Mpororo area or upon subverting the central authorities of the larger kingdom of Rwanda to the south, the cult represented throughout the region the major vehicle for opposition to the established authority structure of each tribe. The initial response of the *bagirwa* to the European betrayed no re-alignment of cult interests which would place the cult in opposition to colonial rule. Their action reflects, on the contrary, a consolidation of existing political contests to accommodate this new political perimeter. Cult intent was, however, to be rapidly redefined during the initial years of colonial overrule. With this realignment, the parochial concerns of the indigenous period were cast aside to permit a co-ordinated intertribal action which openly and simultaneously challenged the suzerain claims of three colonial powers. Yet it is in the traditional expectations of the cult leaders and in the tactical and ideological resilience of its indigenous history that we must seek an explanation for the character of cult activity during the colonial period.

[26] Letter C/28, Racey to Johnston, 2 Mar. 1901, Ankole District.
[27] Ibid.
[28] Gray, "History," 178.

Muhumusa

At the beginning of the twentieth century, northern Rwanda was controlled by a series of refractory chiefs who refused to acknowledge the suzerain claims of the incumbent *mwami*, Musinga. Foremost among them was the *mugirwa*, Muhumusa, whose position in the traditional Rwanda structure had unquestionably facilitated her rapid ascension to unchallenged regional prominence among the *bagirwa* of the Nyabingi cult. A widow of the late *mwami*, Rwabugiri, Muhumusa was, according to M. J. Bessell, also the mother of the designated heir, Bulegeya, who had been an infant at the time of Rwabugiri's death in 1894.[29] Bulegeya's selection was, however, successfully challenged by Musinga, and Muhumusa was forced to flee northward, at last finding a safe refuge in Ndorwa, the mountainous area of southeastern Kigezi. There, by the borders of Ruanda, she was removed from any further harassment by the new *mwami*.

Undeterred by her defeat, Muhumusa decided to use Ndorwa as a base of operations from which to reassert a claim to the throne. To secure her position there, as an intruder, it was necessary to acquire local political influence, for the Kiga were fragmented into isolated, hostile hamlets by internecine feuds. Unless her reputation could transcend the xenophobic predispositions of the Kiga, it would have been impossible for Muhumusa to maintain her organizational network or to contact her supporters in Rwanda.

It was in order to achieve such authority that Muhumusa turned somewhat ironically to a cult which had proven in Rwanda an effective vehicle against her late husband and against the Tutsi chiefly structure. In the Ndorwa area, on the periphery of Mpororo, however, the cult represented a viable agency for unification, not sedition.

Although Muhumusa's activities were not initially anti-European, her considerable influence with local chiefs in German Ruanda marked her as a potential political threat to the newly imposed colonial administration. Moreover, increasing German control in Ruanda and German recognition of the legitimacy of Musinga made the movement by implication hostile to German authority as an extension of the existing chiefly structure.

In 1907 the German Resident capitulated to Musinga's demand that Muhumusa be driven from northern Ruanda, for he recognized the importance of consolidating the authority of the Rwanda throne.[30]

---

[29] M. J. Bessell, "Nyabingi," *Uganda Journal*, VI (1938), 73-86.
[30] William Roger Louis, *Ruanda-Urundi, 1884-1919* (Oxford, 1963), 146.

It was not until the following year, however, that Muhumusa, while in German Mpororo, was arrested by the Germans and detained in Bukoba for two years. Although the official charge was that she had conspired against Kisiribombo, the chief in whose territory she was apprehended, Bessell refers to Kisiribombo as an "influential adherent" and ascribes her visit to German Mpororo as an effort to enlist military support for her claim to the Rwanda throne.[31]

Upon her release in 1910, Muhumusa returned to British Ndorwa where she strengthened her forces by recruiting two notorious Rwanda outlaws. Although they were attracted to her services by motives of personal gain, not political commitment, her choice revealed considerable tactical acumen, for one was a Hutu and the other a Twa. By selecting as her lieutenants men who represented non-Tutsi strata of Rwanda society, she maximized allegiance within her following and muted the issue of royal factional interests in favor of a more generalized image of liberation. It was at this time also that Muhumusa again proclaimed her son Bulegeya to be the rightful *mwami* and, with considerable popular support, began a peaceful advance on the capital. The Germans, by now quite sensitive to her political potential and presumably concerned by her rapid resumption of cult activity, quickly intercepted her and forced her final retreat to Ndorwa.[32]

The Occupation of Kigezi

During the three years of quasi-civilian British occupation which preceded the appointment of a District Commissioner in 1913, the administration of Kigezi was assumed by a Special Mission under the charge of a single European officer. Handicapped both by his small military force and by the tenuous international status of the mission, the Political Officer was assigned to Kigezi primarily to validate the British claim to effective occupation of the area, not to supervise the population or to impose any fiscal or administrative requirements. However, his relationship to the local population, his response to openly defiant acts, and the decision, perhaps inevitable, to employ Ganda as government agents, were all critical in defining the character of subsequent civilian administrative patterns in Kigezi.

The problem of effective administration was further exacerbated by the geopolitical character of the district. At the time when the British assumed control of Kigezi, northern Ruanda and the adjacent

---

[31] Bessell, "Nyabingi," 78.
[32] Ibid., 80.

British areas of Bufumbiro and Rukiga were areas of political marginality, territorial and ethnic ambiguity, and physical inaccessibility. They had, in consequence, become a refuge for fugitives from both British and German authorities and from the pressures of the indigenous political system.

Efforts at control were further complicated by the arbitrary character of the international boundaries which defined both the southern and western margins of Kigezi district. Although the international boundary to the east was later revised to conform to the natural and indigenously recognized barrier of the Kagera River, Kigezi's borders remained subject to the original international agreement, which had placed political concessions and compromise above the ethnic or political realities of the region. In consequence, the international boundaries arbitrarily transected two of the three major tribes of the district, the Kiga and Rwanda, creating an artificial political barrier in the existing networks of communication within ethnically homogeneous areas. Only the Hororo, who occupied northeastern Kigezi, retained their traditional political integrity during the colonial period.

The ethnic heterogeneity of the district further exacerbated the task of early administrative control. While two of the three tribes spoke mutually intelligible languages, all were culturally and politically distinct: the Hororo of Ruzumbura formed the westernmost extension of Mpororo, an ethnically homogeneous region of small autonomous chieftaincies; the Kiga represented a mountain enclave of acephalous peoples within the interlacustrine area; and the Rwanda, the northernmost extension of the kingdom of Rwanda, whose capital now lay well to the south, in German territory. Moreover, all three tribes brought with them the legacy of Rwanda's efforts to expand northward into areas occupied by the Kiga and the Hororo. Although these invasions had been successfully resisted, they had created the conditions for mutual distrust during the colonial period and for the priority of tribal identification to district affiliation.

The lag in time between the final clarification in Europe of the international boundaries of the Mfumbiro area and their actual demarcation in East Africa also led to local political tensions. During the years in which the boundaries were surveyed and marked, the disputed territory along the Congo and Ruanda borders was avoided by each colonial power. With the delineation of these borders, previously undisturbed patterns of raiding were suddenly recast as acts of international hostility, to be avenged by the aggrieved colonial power in order to validate its claim to effective authority. Intervention during this period was, however, arbitrary, occurring only in response to protests initiated by local administrators. Such protests, in turn, were only elicited by the more spectacular acts of indigenous aggression, such as raids which involved not merely the confiscation of cattle but the murder or abduction of women.[33]

While such sporadic regulative action might have had some effect, for the most part the traditional political networks continued to operate without interruption, both because of the limited visibility of events from the British post at Kumba and because control of these networks was not at the time considered a responsibility of British claims to suzerainty. In August of 1911, however, a series of events occurred which could not discreetly be circumvented by the officer at Kumba, for they represented a direct challenge to his authority.

Muhumusa 1911

In retreating to Ndorwa after her unsuccessful march upon the Rwanda capital, Muhumusa had been forced to redefine both her political goals and her strategy. The alignment of German forces in support of Musinga had signaled the futility of any further action with regard to the Rwanda throne. Furthermore, this shifting balance of power in German Ruanda had been complemented by the British occupation of Kigezi during the years of Muhumusa's detention in Bukoba. Returning to Ndorwa after an absence of two years, Muhumusa was confronted both by a loss of influence among the Kiga and by the British political post at Kumba. In addition, although earlier military routes had avoided Ndorwa, the Anglo-German Boundary Commission in 1911 crossed the center of her putative territory, erecting boundary pillars.

The conjunction of the failure of the Rwanda offensive, Muhumusa's deteriorating position among the Kiga, and the threatened encroachment of the British into Ndorwa transformed the Nyabingi cult under Muhumusa into a militant and explicitly anti-European movement. Proclaiming herself Queen of Ndorwa, liberator from European domination, Muhumusa, in August and September of 1911, began a series of raids against the Kiga who refused to give her cattle or resisted her claims to authority. Although ostensibly her intention was to drive all Europeans from the area, her efforts during this initial campaign were directed only against the Kiga. The testimony of one Ganda chief does suggest, however, that the ideological focus for punitive action was the degree of local co-operation with the British:

[33] E.1981: Annual Report of the Provincial Commissioner, Western Province, 1911, Entebbe Archives.

> When she came in August . . . she had many Ruanda people with
> her and also Ruhiga people. She gave out that she had much power
> and that if anyone would follow her, she would drive out the Euro-
> peans. . . . She did no harm to those people over there until she
> reached the country of those who were willing to be under the Euro-
> peans.[34]

Directly confronting this conflicting claim to sovereignty, Muhumusa
demanded cattle from local loyalist chiefs as a symbol of their renunciation of British affiliation. Any ambivalence about continuing contact
with European agents was met with a series of ruthless and punitive
raids in which villages were burned and pillaged. All those who resisted
were killed or driven to seek refuge elsewhere.

Her *modus operandi*, and the pattern of her advance into central
Kigezi from the Ndorwa area, are most effectively revealed in the following affidavit by the Agent:

> I first heard of her in last August of this year. In that month a Chief
> . . . came and told me that Muhumusa was stopping him from coming
> to me; that she, Muhumusa, said that he and other Chiefs belonged
> to her and not to me. I sent for Ruagalla, the big Chief to confirm
> this, which he did.
> . . . When Ruagalla came to me he complained to me that Muhumusa
> had sent word to him and others to take cattle to her. Ruagalla asked
> me, as they were hitherto under British Protection, whether this was
> right.[35]

When Ruagalla and other chiefs refused to change their allegiances,
Muhumusa began a series of attacks which laid waste to the district
and forced their displacement northward to areas adjacent to the
British post at Kumba.

Her success in intimidating the Kiga soon led Muhumusa to be
more audacious and less oblique in her efforts to eliminate the British
threat to her suzerain claim. The bitterness generated by the failure
of the British post to take action, despite local appeals for protection,
unquestionably accelerated support for the movement. The Political
Officer was handicapped, however, not merely by the size of his forces
and his isolation but by the indeterminate status of the area occupied
by Muhumusa—then designated "Eastern Rukiga"—and by the international range of her operations.[36]

---

[34] E.2196: Affidavit of Y. Basajabalaba, Government Agent, 6 Dec. 1911,
Entebbe.
[35] Ibid.
[36] E.2196: Affidavit of E. H. Reid, 10 Dec. 1911, Entebbe.

By the end of September, however, Muhumusa had attained a position of "complete ascendancy" over the Kiga. As a mark of her confidence, she moved her fortified headquarters well within British territory. Her encampment now represented a direct challenge to colonial control for it was located within a few miles of the Kumba post. From there, Muhumusa openly confronted the British by threatening to burn down the post which had, by that time, become swollen with refugees and their livestock.

Faced with such an unambiguous act of insolence, E. H. Reid, the Political Officer, found it necessary "in the interests of British Prestige" to take military action against her. On 28 September, a combined force of the King's African Rifles, the Uganda police, and local loyalist levies quietly encircled her encampment and attacked without warning. The confrontation was both brief and successful. The decisive factor appears, however, to have been the expectations and morale of Nyabingi's adherents, not the efficiency of the British forces.

Critical to the rapid routing of the encampment was "the particular legend which obtained the greatest credence among the local Bakiga . . . that the bullets of the Wazungu [Europeans] would turn to water against her."[37] When the ammunition of the British forces proved clearly superior to Muhumusa's claims of immunity, resistance broke and her followers fled. Muhumusa herself was wounded in the foot and captured.[38]

The arrest of Muhumusa created further political complications, for the area in which she was captured—although internationally recognized as British territory—had not yet been officially incorporated into the Uganda Protectorate. In consequence, the Principal Judge in Entebbe ruled that the Political Officer had no jurisdiction to prosecute Muhumusa through the courts of the Protectorate.[39]

After the arrest of Muhumusa, nominal peace returned to the district and chiefs previously ambivalent or aligned with Muhumusa once again came to the British post to acknowledge their subordinate position within the British superstructure. The detention of Muhumusa in the Kigezi area continued, however, to generate unrest. Kikeri, a Tutsi chief, refused to submit to British authority, protesting "his deity says he will die if he should go into Kumba to see the White Man."[40] More indirectly, rumors reached the British officer that Kikeri was organizing a plot to rescue Muhumusa which involved the importation of "numbers of Ba-ruanda" and the "murder of loyalist chiefs." Again,

[37] E.2196: Reid to Chief Secretary, 30 Nov. 1911, Entebbe.
[38] Bessell, "Nyabingi," 80-81.
[39] E.2196: Reid to Chief Secretary, 13 Oct. 1911, Entebbe.
[40] E.2196: Affidavit of Y. Basajabalaba, 6 Dec. 1911, Entebbe.

however, the Political Officer was handicapped by the jurisdictional limitations to his authority:

> As Kikeri is at present in territory still nominally German I am disposed to leave him for the present in the hopes that either [his followers will] disperse quietly, or, should he raid the local natives, that they may settle him by themselves.[41]

Responding to a warning from the Resident of Ruanda, Reid did prepare for a possible invasion by strengthening the installations at Kumba and by deploying patrols of Ganda agents and "local natives" along the road to German Ruanda. These patrols, it was felt, would ensure "ample warning of any attempt at rescue en route." Once Kikeri had advanced into British territory, Reid would then seek his arrest. Beyond this, Reid could do little but affirm that should Kikeri continue to maintain his "uncompromising attitude," punitive action would be initiated once the new frontier had been established and the ceded territory formally transferred to Great Britain.

To remove the most immediate catalyst for continuing political unrest, the Chief Secretary suggested that executive action be taken against Muhumusa to permit her transfer to Mbarara, in the adjacent district of Ankole, where she would be confined "until the District Commissioner is sure of her reformation."[42] The Governor concurred, but ordered rather that she be transferred to Kampala, for Mbarara "is too near her own country." The Political Officer, observing that Muhumusa, "having been always served by a number of attendants, is quite incapable of doing anything for herself and cannot, in fact, walk more than a few hundred yards," sent with her a small retinue of four personal servants and "a few head of cattle." Upon her departure, Reid observed to the Chief Secretary that it was "most undesirable in the interests of future peace that she should ever be permitted to return to the country where her influence [had] caused such loss of life and destruction."[43] Muhumusa remained near the court of the Kabaka of Buganda until her death in 1945.

The advisability of permitting Muhumusa to return to Kigezi was periodically reviewed by the central administration. Each time, however, the action was rejected by both the local chiefs and British officials for it was feared that her continuing reputation could easily polarize further political unrest. In reviewing the tenacity of her repu-

---

[41] E.2196: Reid to Chief Secretary, 13 Oct. 1911, Entebbe.

[42] E.2196: Chief Secretary to Governor, 18 Oct. 1911, Entebbe.

[43] E.2196: Governor to Chief Secretary, 19 Oct. 1911. Political Officer to Chief Secretary, 13 Oct. 1911, Entebbe.

tation nine years after her removal from Kigezi, the Provincial Commissioner observed:

> So far as I know, no limit has been fixed to the detention of Muhumusa. It would, in my opinion, be a grave mistake to allow her ever to return to Kigezi for I am confident she would, in a very short time, be the cause of serious trouble. The cost of building another hut for her [in Kampala] would be trifling . . . the cost of suppressing a native outbreak in Rukiga, which Muhumusa would be quite capable of causing about the middle of the next beer drinking season might be very considerable, not only in money but in lives.[44]

German Ruanda

While the Nyabingi movement in Kigezi presented a unitary threat to British control, the German Residency in Ruanda faced a series of open rebellions by dissident Hutu and Twa in the more independent northern areas of their territory. The successful rout of Muhumusa in 1910 was only the first of a number of such encounters. It was followed in 1912 by renewed opposition to the Rwanda chiefly structure led by fugitive cult leaders who, after the arrest and deportation of Muhumusa, fled south to resurrect and manipulate earlier anti-Musinga sentiment among the northern Hutu.[45]

The role of Ndungutsi, while pivotal, is somewhat ambiguous. Ugandan sources regard him to be no more than an influential lieutenant of Muhumusa. Rwanda sources, however, view him as one of Muhumusa's sons, by Mibambwe IV, Rwabugiri's successor, who had been killed within a year of his succession. In supporting Muhumusa's claim to the throne for her son, Bulegeya, mentioned earlier, Ndungutsi had thus been reinforcing the political aspirations of his mother and half-brother. It is suggested that upon his retreat to Ruanda his commitment to the interests of his half-brother became increasingly attenuated as he vacillated between claiming the title for Bulegeya and for himself.

By manipulating Tutsi clans on the succession issue and by promising to emancipate the Hutu from their position as servants to the Tutsi, Ndungutsi soon acquired popular support throughout German Ruanda, the "open or passive support of many important chiefs," and "enormous popularity" among the Hutu of northern Ruanda.[46] As

[44] E.2196: Provincial Commissioner, Western Province to Provincial Commissioner Buganda, 15 Jan. 1920, Entebbe.

[45] Louis, *Ruanda-Urundi*, 154.

[46] Ibid.

his influence increased, he gained sufficient strength to initiate the characteristic raiding pattern of the *bagirwa* of the Nyabingi cult. Now, however, the axis of expansion was reversed and raiders moved south from Rukiga.

Although the increasing influence of Ndungutsi was the source of considerable anxiety for Musinga, it did not actively engage the German authorities until rumors reached Gudovius, the German Resident, that Ndungutsi claimed that the Germans "were harmless" and that under his protection only water would come from their guns.[47] The similarity of this claim to those of the Maji Maji rebellion of 1905 could only impress upon the Germans the need for prompt repressive action. Therefore, on 5 February 1912 a German police officer and fifteen troops were sent to form "emergency posts" in the area immediately south of the "troubled region." In this manner Gudovius hoped both to discourage further expansion of the raiders to the south and to create an intelligence network in the threatened area. Northern Ruanda remained, however, under the control of the cult.

On 8 April, guided by two Tutsi "spies," Gudovius moved a detachment of thirty men into the rebel area. In order to surprise Ndungutsi and to prevent his retreat into British territory, they moved by secret forced night march from Kigali. The body of the force encircled the encampment while Gudovius, with a small escort, attacked directly. Most of the persons within the encampment, including, it was reported, Ndungutsi, were slaughtered. At the same time, forces which had been left to the south under the command of a German officer began to move through the rebellious area, destroying villages and killing those who resisted.

The stated intent of the expedition had been the "punishment" of the insubordinate populations by imposing "the greatest possible damage until complete submission."[48] Once subdued, the region was to be placed under the administration of loyalist chiefs from central Ruanda. The attack on Ndungutsi and against the dissident areas to the south was so ferocious, however, that organized resistance rapidly collapsed. As a punitive rather than political measure, the Germans continued to lay waste to the area although Gudovius later reported that "less violence" was required because the population was, by then, "thoroughly intimidated and 'obedient'."[49] By 20 May martial law was lifted. Sporadic acts of violence continued against patrols and caravans but they were isolated occurrences and betrayed no organized or ideologically incited resistance to German rule. Control of northern Ruanda

47 Ibid., 155.
48 Ibid., 156.
49 Ibid., 157.

remained tenuous, however, for the limited German staff could only govern through Musinga's representative, and his influence in these outlying areas traditionally had little reality beyond the annual tribute acknowledging his suzerainty.

Ndungutsi

During the period between the arrest of Muhumusa in 1911 and the outbreak of World War I, sporadic resistance to European rule continued in the Kigezi area. The major impetus for unrest was the continuing presence of an individual claiming to be Ndungutsi. Whether he was in fact Ndungutsi is uncertain as the Germans claimed he had been killed in the action of 1912. What is significant is that a Tutsi identified as Ndungutsi, the son of Muhumusa and the rightful heir to the Rwanda throne, re-entered Kigezi from the south, proclaimed himself "King of Rukiga," and was apparently accepted as such by at least "several minor chiefs."[50]

Hostility toward European overrule initially was expressed by the refusal of cult-influenced chiefs to carry out governmental orders and by a general recalcitrance toward agents and loyalist chiefs. By December, however, protest had become both more organized and more overtly anti-European: after threatening to burn Kabale, two chiefs began a series of open attacks upon loyalist chiefs. Acting on the appeal of one of the chiefs so harassed, the District Commissioner was drawn once again into direct confrontation with the forces of Nyabingi. His efforts to send an expedition against Bukola, an ally of Ndungutsi, were defeated by the tactical retreat of the dissident chief. Upon his return to Kabale station, the district officer made an effort to appease Bukola by sending him a message affirming his desire for peace and stating that "he should come and meet me and tell me his grievances." Bukola replied that "he did not want any dealing with the English, that he was Ndungutsi's man." His subsequent attack on "friendly natives" engaged in road construction convinced the district officer of the need for more forceful measures.[51]

The actual confrontation was far from decisive, however, for the rebel chiefs, having by now reached a more realistic measure of the power of Nyabingi, retreated at the approach of British troops. As the district officer's military force was small, he contented himself with firing the abandoned kraals and confiscating thirty-one head of cattle.

[50] H. R. Wallis, *The Handbook of Uganda* (London, 1920), 94.
[51] E.2471: District Commissioner to Provincial Commissioner, 10 Mar. 1913, Entebbe.

Before leaving, he reassured the fugitive chief that "if he would come in I would forgive him and return his stock." This limited and seemingly ineffectual action was later to have considerable effect, however, for the rebel chiefs subsequently submitted to British authority in Kabale. Fully as relevant in breaking the force of the resistance was the arrest in January 1913 of "Ndungutsi" in the adjacent district of Ankole. In response to local administrative pressure, Ndungutsi was promptly removed from Mbarara to Busoga, in eastern Uganda.[52] With Ndungutsi in detention, the residual power derived from Muhumusa was effectively extinguished. The open confrontation of the District Commissioner with Ndungutsi's leading chiefs, compounded by the arrest and removal of Ndungutsi himself, suggested to other less powerful chiefs the expediency of "offering their submission" to this new and superior power.

Protectorate Reforms

At the end of 1912 Kigezi was formally incorporated into the Uganda Protectorate and political responsibility for the area transferred from the temporary supervision of the Special Mission to a more formal district administrative structure. At this time, as well, a number of innovations were introduced in order to standardize the local administrative operation and to bring it into greater conformity with other areas of Uganda. Foremost among these was the appointment of six chiefs "selected by the natives themselves" to serve as governmental representatives in the acephalous areas.[53] "Native Agents" from Buganda were then assigned to reside nearby and instruct them in their duties. In contrast, in the centralized areas of Bufumbiro and Ruzumbura, the authority of the traditional chiefs was recognized in the expectation that their hierarchies could be readily absorbed into the larger district structure. In these areas as well, however, agents from Buganda were placed in supervisory positions.

Although the fiscal and political demands of the British in Kigezi were initially minimal, the response of the population to the extension of the administrative network was unpredictable and often quite volatile. This was perhaps inevitable, for the decision to assume control of the region had been unilateral, the expectations of the inhabitants were thought irrelevant, and the burden of effecting the incorporation was left largely to individuals whose interests were firmly aligned with their European masters.

[52] E.3173: "Report on Ndungutzi," 25 Apr. 1913, Entebbe.
[53] E.3314: Annual Report of the Provincial Commissioner, Western Province, 1912-13, Entebbe.

As intruders, the Ganda agents derived their legitimacy solely from the colonial superstructure. As F. G. Burke noted in another context, "his powers in fact were limited only by his accountability to the District Commissioner."[54] In this unnatural skewing of channels of responsibility and validation lay the primary dangers of the Agent system. By presenting an alien and often extortionate barrier between the European staff and the indigenous population, the agents exacerbated local mistrust of British motives.

These dangers seem to have been well understood by the British. Thus the Governor in 1910 urged that very great care be taken to select "suitable and reliable" men as agents; other administrators warned of the need to regulate the size and character of the personal entourage permitted the Agent, for "cases of extortion and petty annoyance to natives are in most cases traced to the Buganda followers of those Agents."[55] Despite local resistance the Ganda had, by the end of 1913, imposed an effective system of private extortion.

In response, the powers of the agents were "defined and restricted."[56] The actual reforms adopted reflected both a concern with extortion and political intimidation and with the dangers of alienation and resentment inherent in the institution of the Agent itself. The District Commissioner urged 1) the reduction of personal retainers (apart from officially assigned armed followers) to three, and 2) the introduction of judicial responsibilities into the local councils. By expanding the local chiefly functions to include the official adjudication of minor criminal offenses, it was felt that the newly imposed system of political centralization could be more effectively validated. The Agent system itself was not questioned, however, by the British for they felt that the Kiga would not be able to govern themselves "for many years" and that the removal of the Ganda would only lead to political chaos.[57]

The increasing regularization of relations between the British authorities and the indigenous chiefs was reflected in the growing confidence of the British. The successful action against Ndungutsi at the end of 1912, and the voluntary capitulation of his local representatives in Kigezi after his arrest unquestionably encouraged the British to use similar techniques to extinguish further acts of political unrest. The

[54] Fred G. Burke, *Local Government and Politics in Uganda* (Syracuse, 1964), 35.

[55] E.1047: Governor to Chief Secretary, 5 Sept. 1910; District Commissioner, Ankole to Chief Secretary, 25 Aug. 1910, Entebbe.

[56] E.3314A: Annual Report of the Provincial Commissioner, Western Province, 1913-14, Entebbe.

[57] E.3851: "Scheme for the Organisation of Rukiga, 1914," Entebbe.

deployment of military expeditions into recalcitrant areas and the con-fiscation of abandoned livestock led to the submission of other unruly chiefs. The firm disciplinary action taken against Nyindo, a major Tutsi chief, for his role in the abduction and revenge murder of a Tutsi from German Ruanda, was also strategic in reaffirming the dominant political position of the British in Kigezi. It was assumed by the British that the severity of their action would suggest to local populations the wisdom of modifying traditional patterns of raiding and retaliation and of seeking recourse to the court system of the Protectorate. In reality, however, it led merely to the development of displaced pat-terns of aggression and to techniques for evading British detection of continuing acts of personal vengeance.

In 1913 the first major effort was also made to extend disciplinary practices to the acephalous populations of Rukiga. However, their resistance to any formal judicial inquiry into their notorious predisposi-tion to homicide, and their unerring retreat into swamps or across the border into German East Africa upon the appearance of any British patrol, led to the application of the Collective Punishment Ordinance of 1909 to justify the seizure of any livestock left behind in their sud-den flight. The imposition of collective fines of this character when communities proved un-co-operative in the location and indictment of criminals became so common a practice that a separate ordinance, the Kigezi Prevention of Crime Ordinance, was promulgated in 1914.

The War and Anti-European Activity

For the British officer in Kigezi, 1914 was a year of crisis and ultimate desperation, for, with the inclusion of Kigezi in the East African theater of operations, the gradually emerging district structure was abruptly dislocated, then abandoned. The first months of 1914 had been charac-terized by an absence of political unrest and increasing support for the British judicial structure. By mid-year the district officer was encour-aged to introduce a more odious aspect of colonial administration: the collection of taxes. At the end of 1914, 10,000 taxpayers had been en-rolled, the majority of whom were Kiga.[58] As no pressure was applied in outlying areas, it was only the Kiga, by virtue of their geographic centrality, who were vulnerable to such unwanted administrative reforms.

In July of 1914, the Tutsi chiefs of southern Kigezi once again began to defy British authority. During that month, an Agent was attacked "near the German border" and one of his followers killed. In addition, Nyindo, the leading Tutsi chief, had refused to come to

[58] Annual Report, Kigezi District, 1914-15, Kigezi Archives.

Kabale where several cases had been lodged against him. The final provocation, however, was an unambiguous affront to British authority: the release "by armed force" by several southern chiefs of a prisoner being sent to Kabale. These "fits of foolishness," each perhaps a minor irritant in itself, marked the onset of wide-scale unrest which was to prove totally disruptive to civilian administration in Kigezi.[59]

The outbreak of World War I on 1 August 1914 marked a second resurgence of anti-European activity, for the political discontent which had characterized the initial years of British rule was exacerbated by the position of Kigezi within the East African theater of operations. Local military action in this area was probably unavoidable, for controversy over the region north of Lake Kivu had resulted in a comparatively heavy concentration of Belgian and German military forces which were still intact at the outbreak of the war. The immediate consequence of the war was the rapid polarization of local British and Belgian personnel against the German officers in Ruanda. This in itself did much to aggravate local unrest for the European no longer presented a monolithic image of suzerain power or of common political purpose.

The perceptions of the European in Kigezi, a border area, had never been confined to the administration which claimed direct jurisdiction but encompassed as well the politics and actions of colonial personnel in adjacent territories. This international orientation, characteristic perhaps of any border area, was further encouraged by the long-standing controversy over the demarcation of both the Congo and German borders and by the ethnically arbitrary character of the boundaries once established. Continuing ties of tribal identification and of marriage, kinship, and friendship eroded the reality of these political distinctions.

The additional dislocations of World War I, particularly the offensive movement of German troops against installations in Kigezi and the Belgian military occupation of the district in 1915, gave the tribes in this area a unique opportunity to observe the concurrent operation of three colonial powers in the area. Rather than illuminating the relative strength of any given power, the fluctuation in personnel served mainly to weaken the legitimacy of all foreign claims to territorial control. In this respect Kigezi was particularly vulnerable for Belgian forces had been granted immunity from British supervision. As the District Commissioner noted at the end of 1915:

> The district is still under military control, and up to a recent date has been entirely occupied by the Belgians, which has at times been a

[59] P.11: Monthly Report of the District Commissioner, Kigezi, May 1914, Fort Portal; July 1914, Fort Portal.

source of considerable embarrassment to the local Administrator. Offenses committed by Belgian troops against British natives are not punishable by British Courts. . . . It is not surprising that the natives have begun to wonder to whom the country now belongs.[60]

The conjunction of these conflicting images of colonial power did much, once again, to generate an increasing sense of the vulnerability of the British position, and with it the belief that liberation from British overrule could successfully be effected.

The immediacy of the East African campaign was particularly serious in Kigezi for, at the onset of the war, the district had only been subject to civilian administration for two years. Rather than consolidating the district against a common external threat, as in Ankole, the threat of open conflict brought these initial exploratory efforts at civilian control to a "standstill."[61] Far more serious than the threat of outside attack were the internal disruptions which both led to and were made possible by the deterioration of the civilian structure. Politically, the most serious consequence of the war was the alignment of the Tutsi chiefs in the southern sector of Kigezi with Musinga of Ruanda, and, by extension, with the German authorities. This shift in allegiance led to a resurgence of anti-European, and, more specifically, of anti-British sentiment throughout the southern and central portions of the district, culminating in a series of attacks on local patrols, Ganda agents, and even, in one dramatic instance, on the Anglo-Belgian installation at Chahifi. Nyabingi again provided the idiom for protest.

While the seemingly random incidents of July 1914 could be dismissed as eccentricities of Tutsi temperament, the events of August left little ambiguity as to the underlying pattern of dissent. Foremost as an index of growing disaffection was the exodus of numbers of Tutsi from southern Kigezi. While some migrated to Belgian territory, the majority crossed into German East Africa to reaffirm their allegiance to Musinga. Most significantly, Nyindo, the Tutsi chief, was among the defectors. While the Provincial Commissioner professed no alarm or surprise at the loss of this ranking British chief, the action could only have further eroded the slipping prestige of the British in southern Kigezi. The events of August betrayed an increasing arrogance toward the British. As was the case in July, a prisoner being sent to Kabale under escort was released "by armed force" by one of the Tutsi chiefs. Similarly, efforts on the part of the District Commissioner to apprehend fugitive criminals in the southern sector of the district were met with open and irreverent evasion. In one instance, a night march of

[60] Annual Report, Kigezi District, 1915-16, Kigezi.
[61] Louis, *Ruanda-Urundi*, 198.

ten hours was made to ensure a surprise arrest, but the chief "and all his people and cattle had already fled into Belgian territory."[62] The increasing recalcitrance of both the Kiga and Rwanda in border areas, provoked initially by the thrust for more effective fiscal and political supervision during the prewar months of 1914, was sharply exacerbated by the political dislocations of World War I.

Resistance, evolving spontaneously as a response to the instability of the period, initially employed the major indigenous technique for political defiance in both the centralized and non-centralized areas: physical evasion. The pattern of retreat and concealment had unquestionably proved an effective tactic for the Kiga in dealing with Rwanda's political expansion. Similarly, the characteristic interlacustrine idiom for political insubordination was essentially passive: to remove oneself, one's followers, and one's cattle from the offending patron or chief. In using the international boundary as a means of political evasion, the border populations were merely absorbing into their traditional repertory a new but highly effective constraint on the movements of a suzerain power. The political dynamics behind the fastidiousness of the colonial powers were probably not understood, for intertribal relations were traditionally predicated on the assumption of political expansion and the constant flux of borders. What was appreciated, however, was the predictability of such fastidiousness.

The political uncertainties and increasing local unrest occasioned by the onset of the war were to have an additional ramification: the reappearance of the Nyabingi cult, dormant since the arrest of Ndungutsi in January of 1913. The resurgence of cult activity in central Kigezi appears to have received its initial impetus from Ruanda, most probably from dissident Tutsi who, in addition to actively participating in German military raids into British territory, continued to urge the Hutu in southern Kigezi to rebel against British authority.[63] In choosing the idiom of Nyabingi to generate dissent among the local Hutu, the cult leaders were, of course, exploiting a political technique which had proved highly successful in the pre-colonial period. The weakness of British control was reflected in the rapidity with which the possibility of liberation from British overrule was accepted, not merely by border Hutu, but by the Kiga of central Kigezi.

Thus, in August 1914, rumors originating in German Ruanda reached Kabale that Muhumusa had escaped from Kampala and that she and the Germans would soon appear to drive out the British. The imminence of her arrival seemed confirmed by the appearance of

[62] P.11: Monthly Report of the District Commissioner, Kigezi, Aug. 1914, Fort Portal.

[63] Annual Report, Kigezi District, 1914-15, Kigezi.

several "female 'witches' of the Mamusa type" who claimed that their powers were superior to those of the British. With these developments, the District Officer at last acknowledged the necessity for action and resolved to repress the movement before it could further "inflame the natives with anti-European ideas."[64]

The arrest of Changandusi, a prominent *mugirwa*, near Kabale at the end of August and the failure of either Muhumusa or the Germans to appear broke the force of the resurgent movement in central Kigezi and did much to discourage correlative but independently organized acts of civil disobedience against the British. The position of Changandusi within both the traditional and modern colonial structure revealed, however, both the vulnerability of British authority and their defective access to popular sentiment, for she was the mother of Katuleggi, a Tutsi chief near Kabale.

With the arrest of Changandusi and the deterioration of cult influence in central Rukiga, the focus of unrest shifted once again southward to the Ruandan border. Although the idiom of protest remained secular in this region, anti-British activity was now undertaken not by local residents but by raiding parties of Tutsi based in German East Africa and organized under German direction. At the beginning of October, the District Officer was attacked by "three hundred Batusi"; then on the following day, a "raiding party of some 1500" destroyed several villages before being driven once again into German territory.[65] At the center of this paramilitary activity was Nyindo. Although their military sophistication was limited, the threats of these raiders kept the people of southern Kigezi in a state of anxiety and terror.

The final months of 1914 witnessed the deterioration of any pretence at administrative control in the Kigezi district. Nevertheless, the region north of the border area remained relatively quiet throughout the critical years of World War I. Pressures from disaffected Tutsi chiefs in German East Africa did, however, continue to threaten the political stability of the entire district, not merely that of the border populations.

Other difficulties also arose from the needs of the war. Although normal judicial and fiscal expectations had long since been abandoned, the war did bring comparable demands on local resources: food for troops stationed in the area and labor, particularly as porterage. In much of the region the response to British military requirements was apathy or evasion. In the border areas, however, which had remained under the influence of fugitive Tutsi chiefs, virulent anti-British sentiment soon manifested itself in open resistance. The persistent refusal

[64] Ibid.

[65] E.3314B: Annual Report of the Provincial Commissioner, Western Province, 1914-15, Entebbe.

of these populations to work or to bring in food was supplanted in December of 1914 by open rebellion in the Kyoga Valley. Marked initially by the murder of a chief sent to claim a quota of porters, subsequent messengers sent by the District Officer to investigate the murder were "driven back and had arrows fired on them." Not content with a defensive strategy, men from Kyoga Valley also made two attacks "in large numbers" on the headquarters of the local Agent.[66] Although the District Commissioner conceded that passive hostility might be "somewhat overlooked," such open contempt for British authority required punitive action. The arrival of British troops led to a massive and rapid depopulation of the valley toward the frontier. "Between 400 and 500 armed Bahororo" remained behind to harass the patrol. In the confrontation which followed, 38 Hororo were killed.[67] The livestock captured were later converted retroactively into a political fine.

The violence at Kyoga and the regular implementation of a system of collective fines against recalcitrant communities led to a prompt decrease in overt demonstrations of hostility to British rule. While the threat of British action unquestionably served to deter any further obstruction of British authority, the hostility remained. When it again erupted, the degree of co-ordination and local support accorded the rebels throughout Kigezi attested to the intensity and pervasiveness of anti-colonial sentiment.

In the early months of 1915 considerable political instability was generated in the interior of Kigezi by Katuleggi, the son of Changandusi, who had followed Nyindo into Ruanda after the arrest of his mother. From German territory he organized a series of raids which thrust deep into Rukiga. Although there is no evidence of his continuing alliance with the cult, his anti-British sentiments were openly expressed in the harassment of official runners and messengers.[68]

The British response to Katuleggi reflected a new and more realistic measure of their political handicap under such marginal adminstrative conditions. Rather than insist that he be apprehended and brought to trial, it was now felt that he had been "dealt with" when he had been driven back into German Ruanda. The elimination of political agitators by forcing them across international boundaries became increasingly favored as a technique for political action.

In July of 1915 central Kigezi was again subject to the influence of

[66] E.4526: District Commissioner to Provincial Commissioner, 11 Apr. 1915, Entebbe.

[67] E.4526: Acting Superintendent of Police to District Commissioner, 28 March 1915, Entebbe.

[68] E.3314B: Annual Report of Provincial Commissioner, Western Province, 1914-15; 1915-16.

Nyabingi with the appearance of a female *mugirwa* who proclaimed that she had "driven out the English." Anticipating that her presence would "doubtless produce the customary foolishness amongst the savages," the British resolved to deal with her "as soon as her whereabouts are definitely known."[69] There is no record of her apprehension; however, reference is made in the annual provincial report to the "prompt and firm" suppression of several *bagirwa* by military action. Philipps implied in 1919, however, that the presence of the cult in Kigezi had been uninterrupted since the arrest of Muhumusa in 1911, for "on the death or deportation of each apostle or local personification, another representation is possessed by the spirit."[70] By July 1916, although the activities of the Tutsi chiefs, Katuleggi and Nyindo, had been contained, new opposition to British control arose in the Congo to the west of the Kigezi district. With this shift in the locus of resistance from Ruanda to the acephalous areas of the eastern Congo, the Nyabingi cult once again assumed ascendancy.

Resurgence of the Cult in 1916-17

The resurgence of the cult as the dominant idiom for political protest represented a major ideological shift in anti-colonial activity. Earlier resistance had come primarily from disaffected Tutsi chiefs who, under pressure from Musinga, saw in the divisive international oppositions of the war an opportunity to shift the regional balance of power and, in so doing, both to reaffirm their identification with central Rwanda and to exploit the greater degree of autonomy from colonial supervision permitted under German rule. Although these Tutsi had manipulated the colonial context for their personal ends, they did not challenge the validity of colonial control itself. In addition, their claim to authority rested firmly within the matrix of both the indigenous and colonial political structures. They were not intruders or rebels, intent upon seizing power where no legitimate claim lay. Finally, their actions against the British and their appeals to their followers were totally secular in character. In contrast, the authority of the leaders of the Nyabingi cult was predicated on supernatural power and lacked support from the indigenous power base. Having no legitimacy within the traditional secular hierarchy and therefore no claim to possible recognition within the colonial system, the cult could emerge in full opposition to colonial rule.

[69] P.145: Monthly Report of the District Commissioner, Kigezi, July 1915, Fort Portal.

[70] E.3314C: Annual Report of the Provincial Commissioner, Western Province, 1915-16, Entebbe; NAF B: "Report on Nabingi," 31 July 1919, Kigezi.

The recrudescence of the Nyabingi movement as a serious threat to the political stability of Kigezi occurred early in 1916, with the appearance of Ndochibiri on the southern borders of the district. Unlike the earlier leaders who had entered Kigezi from the south as Tutsi aristocrats, Ndochibiri [lit. "two fingers"] was Congolese in origin, of the Hunde tribe, and reputedly an epileptic. His activity as a *mugirwa* had begun after the onset of World War I and the deterioration of the Belgian administration in the eastern Congo. There, in the name of Nyabingi, he had attacked both the local Belgian installations and the German posts in adjacent Ruanda.[71]

In January 1916 Ndochibiri began his operations in British territory with a strategic attack on the Anglo-Belgian installation at Chahifi;[72] this was the fort which had provoked the sole German offensive action in the western theater a year before. Presumably, if Chahifi could be taken, Ndochibiri's superiority to both the German and the Anglo-Belgian forces would be simultaneously demonstrated. Supported by "over two thousand fanatics" and the sacred emblem of the cult, a white sheep,[73] Ndochibiri and his followers besieged the fortification for five hours under heavy machine gun fire, retreating only after capturing three rifles and some ammunition. Certainly the most auspicious aspect of the attack was the remarked ability of the sacred white sheep "to defeat all attempts at marksmanship at comparatively close quarters." In describing the assault on Chahifi, the Provincial Commissioner reported the "prophet" as "severely wounded," adding that "one may hope [this] will keep him quiet for a time."[74]

Although no mention is made of further harassments by Ndochibiri, his continuing presence in British territory was defined as provocative by the British government. In February an unsuccessful punitive expedition was organized to effect his capture.[75] In addition, to enhance the colonial image, all those who had been forced to contribute cattle to the cult, presumably under pressure of supernatural punishment or physical coercion, were compensated. Through this measure, an effort was made both to gain the goodwill and gratitude of the loyalists and to encourage others to oppose Ndochibiri. The

[71] Bessell, "Nyabingi," 82; NAF B: "Report on Nabingi," 31 July 1919, Kigezi.

[72] Although Philipps, "Nabingi," places the date of this initial raid in January 1915, the local political memoranda and monthly Provincial Reports to Entebbe indicate that his movement into British territory did not occur until January 1916.

[73] In the *emandwa* cults of Rwanda a sacred white sheep guards the upper slopes of Mount Muhavura where the spirits of faithful initiates are believed to be taken after death. (Philipps, "Nabingi," 313.)

[74] Ibid., 318; E.2471D: Monthly Report of the Provincial Commissioner, Western Province, Jan. 1916, Entebbe.

[75] Annual Report, Kigezi District, 1916-17, Kigezi.

seizure of livestock, in itself a well understood sanction within the traditional systems of the pastoral interlacustrine area, was thus manipulated to secure political allegiance to the colonial superstructure. To this end, the image of the extortionate cult leader, ruthless, self-serving, punitive, was balanced against that of the intrusive yet benevolent, concerned administration. Both represented unwanted encroachments into economic autonomy; but the British at least carried the promise of political protection and of liability should that protection fail.

Ndochibiri's sphere of operations was centered on the southwestern borders of Kigezi. In January 1916, however, evidence of the existence of the Nyabingi cult was discovered considerably to the north of the area of Ndochibiri's activities, in areas which had been virtually abandoned by the British since the outbreak of the war. The base of operations for this second *mugirwa*, an unidentified female, was also the Congo. Her intent, however, was not to challenge British authority but, by evading British detection, to pass through the tenuously administered areas of northern Kigezi to Ruzumbura. Ruzumbura, openly neglected by British authorities, offered a perfect locale for cult activity unmolested by colonial intervention. There is no reason, therefore, to attribute to this *mugirwa* any conspicuous anti-British motive. Rather, she appears to have been manipulating the cult for personal aggrandizement. Regrettably for this particular entrepreneur, she and her "large following" chose to traverse Kigezi near the Kumba post. She was discovered and detained and her following was forced back into the Congo. To discourage further local interest in the cult and to compensate those who had been victims of extortion several "temples" were burnt and "a large number of cattle that were recently stolen [were] recovered and returned to their owners."[76]

In April, raiding again erupted in southern Kigezi with renewed incursions by rebel Tutsi chiefs and with the resumption of "looting" under Ndochibiri's leadership. Both received "military attention," but in both instances the raiders evaded the British patrols.[77] The operational pattern of Ndochibiri had changed significantly in the months following his initial assault on Chahifi, for his activities were no longer directed at British installations themselves but rather at Kiga who resisted the material demands of the cult. To what degree anti-European sentiment determined his raiding pattern is not clear. His most serious attack, in April, in which he "ravaged the country" within a few miles of a border post, suggests that his aggression was directed against

[76] Kigezi Correspondence, District Commissioner to Provincial Commissioner, 7 Feb. 1916, Kigezi.

[77] E.2471D: Monthly Report of Provincial Commissioner, Apr. 1916.

loyalist Kiga and that it was an oblique but unambiguous challenge to British authority.[78]

After Ndochibiri's raid, an effort was made to counter his increasing influence and to deter his return to Kigezi. While British forces had failed to capture Ndochibiri, it was at least hoped that a border post would "force him to confine his attentions to the Congo."[79] Although discovered and driven briefly back across the Congo border in July and October of 1916, Ndochibiri had gained sufficient support to move freely through Kigezi.

In November, efforts to apprehend Ndochibiri became more concerted and for the first time involved a co-ordinated strategy on the part of British and Belgian authorities. The maneuver failed, however, for Ndochibiri was by then sensitive to the limitations of the European forces and skilled in anticipating their action against him. It was this tactical acumen which enabled him to evade, for over four years, the intensive efforts of the British and Belgians to capture him.

At the end of 1916 Ndochibiri remained at large, a continuing threat to the political stability of the district. The year had seen, however, the effective removal of most of the dissident Tutsi chiefs who had returned to British territory with the advance of Belgian forces into German East Africa. In May of 1916 Nyindo surrendered and was removed to Mharara and then to northern Uganda. With his capitulation, other dissident Tutsi chiefs also placed themselves under British jurisdiction.[80] With the exception of Ndochibiri, other *bagirwa* were similarly contained by being driven back into their forest refuges or into the Congo.

The Nyakishenyi Rebellion, 1917

With the displacement of the rebel Tutsi chiefs from southern Kigezi, the cult of Nyabingi became the dominant modality for protest against British rule. This shift in personnel and motive also heralded a major shift in sphere of operations. Whereas the earlier impetus for protest had come from Rwanda to the south, the Congolese origins of the new *bagirwa* and their reliance upon the Kayonza forest as a refuge from both British and Belgian patrols increased the political prominence of the areas to the north of Kabale, particularly that of Kinkizi to the northwest. By February 1917 political activity had been virtually eliminated south of Kabale. Only one rebel chief, Buego, remained

[78] Annual Report, Kigezi District, 1916-17, Kigezi.
[79] Ibid.
[80] Annual Report, Kigezi District, 1916-17, Kigezi; E.2471D: Monthly Report of Provincial Commissioner, Western Province, Dec. 1916, Entebbe.

uncaptured but his arrest was regarded as "only a matter of time."

British efforts to alienate the people of Kigezi from the movement failed, however, as did efforts to arrest Ndochibiri. His success in resisting capture was based both on his tactical skill in avoiding British patrols and on the tacit co-operation of the Kiga. Their sympathy permitted him to assume control of an elaborate communications network which, despite the acephalous and even xenophobic character of the area, had existed in the pre-colonial period. Thus, each move of the British and Belgian patrols was reported to him, enabling him when pressed to retreat with his entourage into the mountainous rain forest which defined the Congo-Uganda border. As Philipps observed:

> The difficulties are such as to almost negative any military proposition. A vicious circle of spies surrounds the slightest movement of any military force. The element of fanaticism in Nyabingi adherents and terrorism of those who are not, renders every local native at least unreliable and provides a refuge for members of the cult.[81]

The effectiveness of the network also inhibited the flow of information to the British. Ganda agents were "grossly" and, Philipps implies, deliberately misinformed, while local Kiga could not be coerced into revealing the movements of Ndochibiri. Only through "endless tact and secrecy" was Philipps able to obtain any reliable information concerning Ndochibiri.

No activity directly ascribed to Ndochibiri was reported in 1917, but events revealed not merely the degree of general disaffection which the cult had generated in northeastern Rukiga, but an organizational skill which betrayed the presence of this leading *mugirwa*. Sporadic and small-scale raiding, initiated at the border, erupted periodically throughout 1917. In April, a Kiga chief from the border areas attacked a village in central Rukiga, surrendered to the Agent, then escaped. The arrest of other raiders in July pointed more directly to a Congolese origin for this activity.[82]

These raids, however, did little to prepare the British officer or his agents for what was to be the most serious and concerted operation of the cult during the colonial period. On Sunday, 12 August 1917 at 6:30 A.M., the headquarters of Agent Abdulla at Nyakishenyi was attacked by what was initially identified as "a horde of Bakiga and Bahororo from the adjacent country."[83] The force, estimated at 1400 men,

[81] NAF B: "Report on Nabingi," 31 July 1919, Kigezi.

[82] E.4526: District Commissioner to Provincial Commissioner, 22 Apr. 1917, Entebbe; P.253, Monthly Report of the District Commissioner, Kigezi, July 1917, Fort Portal.

[83] E.4526: District Commissioner to Provincial Commissioner, 31 Aug. 1917.

represented the followers of seventeen Kiga and Hororo chiefs. Not since Ndochibiri's initial attack on Chahifi in 1916 had indigenous anti-European sentiment been able to generate a co-ordinated force of that magnitude.

The attack, although employing traditional techniques for dealing with local recalcitrants, was unprecedented in its savagery; in addition to looting and burning the residences of the inhabitants, the raiders murdered and mutilated sixty-three members of the community while only fifteen were injured.[84] The ferocity of this action, which involved the indiscriminate slaughter of unarmed men, women, and children, may have in part represented an extension of the raiding patterns of the western Congolese tribes. Also relevant, however, given the local recruitment of the raiders, was the tribal identity of the victims. Although some of those massacred were Kiga, the majority were Ganda and Nkore: direct appendages of the alien and much resented Agent system. The explicitly anti-European character of the attack was reflected in the symbolic destruction of the courthouse, the Anglican church, and the mosque. In addition, five poll tax registers, the case books of the native court, and five books of poll tax tickets were destroyed. Also the day chosen for the attack, Sunday, was probably not fortuitous. Curiously, the European rest house, although situated near other buildings which were razed, remained untouched.[85]

Initially the District Commissioner claimed that "the cause of the massacre is obscure [although] there is every reason to believe that the affair was engineered by a 'Nabingi' or witch doctor named Kaigirwa,"[86] who was reputed to be the "sister" of Ndochibiri. The incontestable solidarity of local participation could thus be rationalized in the following manner:

> As might be expected among unsophisticated savages the powers of superstition are enormous. This explains the influence of the local witchdoctors, who suitably combine their claims to supernatural powers with promises of liberation of the natives from European rule and restoration to their former condition of a) absence of obligations and b) freedom to plunder and loot their neighbours, a pastime much favoured by sections of the Bakiga.[87]

Although no evidence of Ndochibiri's direct participation in the raid was contained in the political reports of 1917, the *modus operandi*

[84] Annual Report, Kigezi District, 1917-18; E.4526: District Commissioner to Chief Justice, 8 Sept. 1917.

[85] E.3814: District Commissioner to Provincial Commissioner, 14 Sept. 1917, Entebbe.

[86] Ibid., 31 Sept. 1917.

[87] Ibid.

and size of the attack suggested his organizational skills. In 1919 Philipps did obtain information which confirmed Ndochibiri's role in the massacre. According to these sources, after his rout from Kigezi in 1916, Ndochibiri had retreated to Kisali on the Congo frontier. There, to secure his position locally, he had contracted an alliance with the frontier chief. From this base, with the aid of the "chief's daughter," Kaigirwa, and her Kiga husband, Luhemba, he organized the attack on Nyakishenyi.[88] Although the initial impetus for the massacre may be attributed to these *bagirwa*, the size and intertribal composition of the attacking force clearly betrayed the extent of local support which the cult commanded. Certainly one of the most striking features of the raid was the secrecy which shrouded its organization, particularly when the scale of the operation is considered. As Philipps noted, "Not a suspicion of the plot leaked out beforehand despite the fact that the British native political Agent and his [Ganda] followers had Bakiga wives and boys."[89]

Of the hundreds participating in the raid, only twenty-two were arrested. Rebel casualties were estimated at about one hundred, but attempts to apprehend other participants met with little success.[90] British action with regard to the leaders was, however, somewhat more efficient. Of the seventeen local chiefs who had led the attack, three were killed and seven arrested, with only seven remaining "at large." The other fifteen chiefs who were apprehended only confirmed the degree of local solidarity both in the attack and in resisting subsequent action by the British. Three were women "believed to have aided and abetted a witch doctor in engineering the rebellion"; as members of the *mugirwa's* personal entourage they were more obvious during the attack and, presumably, more defiant in its aftermath. The remaining twelve chiefs were rather lamely rounded up after "stolen property" was found in their houses.[91]

In the weeks following the attack, additional information on the raid was obtained from raiders who were "becoming tired of hiding in the swamps . . . and are not adverse to giving other people away." Yet by the end of August only three hundred of the local rebels had returned to their villages. The others, the District Commissioner assumed, had "betaken themselves to other parts where they doubtless hope to escape arrest for complicity in the rebellion, and to avoid taking their share in the rebuilding of dwelling houses, etc. destroyed

[88] Philipps, "Nabingi," 95.

[89] Ibid.

[90] E.4526: District Commissioner to Chief Justice, 8 Sept. 1917; District Commissioner to Provincial Commissioner, 31 Aug. 1917, Entebbe.

[91] E.4526: District Commissioner to Chief Justice, 8 Sept. 1917, Entebbe.

by them."[92] From those who did surrender, however, the popular motives for the massacre emerged:

> The rebellion was an attempt by a section of the residents of Naki-shenyi to free themselves from European rule, and to restore former conditions of independence; and absence of obligations in the shape of Poll Tax and Labour.[93]

Nor was the choice of Agent Abdulla a matter of pure chance. Agent Abdulla was the most active of the Ganda in the suppression of local unrest and in the pursuit of the intrusive *bagirwa* and Tutsi rebels. Short of an attack on the British posts themselves, his destruction would most effectively have symbolized the ascendancy of the cult over the intrusive colonial structure. Although his elimination had a decided tactical advantage for the *bagirwa*, Abdulla's zealousness in dealing with political irregularities must also have been displayed by his local administration. The population under his jurisdiction would thus have been subject to inordinate administrative demands. Efficiency in such political contexts breeds vulnerability: communities initially compliant were being increasingly exploited by a staff reluctant to test its strength in more recalcitrant or distant areas. The exploitation of the Nyakishenyi area by Abdulla made the population particularly responsive to promises of emancipation by the Congolese *bagirwa*.

To judge from the political reports, support for the cult was initially elicited from the lowest echelon of chiefs. These men, selected by the British, were by virtue of their local origins and position in the colonial hierarchy both more closely identified with the people of the area and more vulnerable to the hostility evoked by British demands for food and labor. The strength of the Nyakishenyi revolt lay with these men. Once they had pledged support to the *bagirwa*, their organizational framework, although the creation of the British, provided the necessary matrix for effective protest.

To convince the general population of the merits of driving the Europeans from the area required little effort. The following affidavit, submitted to the District Commissioner, was regarded by him to be "typical of many":

> Our chiefs told us "we see you are tired of work, we have made a plan to kill the Baganda and the Europeans, so that they may leave the country and we shall be independent as we were before. You will pay

[92] Ibid.; P.254: Monthly Report of the District Commissioner, Kigezi, Sept. 1917, Fort Portal.

[93] E.4526: District Commissioner to Provincial Commissioner, 21 Sept. 1917, Entebbe.

no more tax and we will serve Nabingi who used to rule over us
before." When we heard what the chiefs said, we agreed, as we did
not want to do any work.[94]

The appeal of this ideology of protest is striking, for it was based on a
series of premises whose distortions and inaccuracies must have been
evident to those whose support was being sought. The Nyakishenyi
area had not fallen within the indigenous thrust of the cult in Mpororo
to the east nor would it have been subject to the later advance of Muhumusa into Ndorwa from the south. The Kiga of this area therefore
had no model for the operation of the cult and, in addition, no reason
to appreciate the merits of supplanting one centralized system of tribute with another. We must assume, therefore, that they in turn regarded the cult instrumentally, as a mechanism for ridding the area of
the hated and burdensome colonial structure. To drive out the British
was not to achieve independence, but rather to face another series of
tributary demands from the *bagirwa*. The dubious merits of such a
shift in masters must have been balanced by the belief that the requirements under Nyabingi would be either lighter, more palatable, or more
easily evaded.

Receptivity to the cult, it is true, was enhanced by the familiarity
of its reputation in the central areas of Rwanda and Mpororo. Moreover, the *emandwa* cult was within the tradition of the Kiga, although
the autochthonous *emandwa,* as might be expected in an acephalous
society, had failed to transmute their religious influence into claims of
political ascendancy. The political focus of the Nyabingi cult, derived
from the model of the interlacustrine chieftaincies, was thus foreign to
the Kiga. The cult also represented for the Kiga an intrusion of personnel; their xenophobic predisposition, in itself, would militate against
their acceptance of Congolese *bagirwa* as their masters.

What then was the perceived advantage of the cult over British
rule? Here the British records are of little value for it was in their political interest to project as unfavorable and unsympathetic a view of the
movement as possible.

There is *no* evidence in the political reports of *any* cult activity in
the Nyakishenyi area before the attack on 12 August. From this conspicuous silence one can assume that the characteristic earlier Nyabingi pattern of harassment and intimidation or of punitive raids had
not been applied in this area. To the contrary, Ndochibiri appears to
have used northern Rukiga as a tactical extension of his forest base.
The co-operation of the population in this region, both in communicating the presence of patrols and in protecting his movements, was
more important to him than their potential material wealth. Ironically,

[94] Ibid.

in accelerating their attempts to apprehend him, the British had un-questionably reinforced this redefinition of the *mugirwa's* relationship to his adherents. Far from being an intrusive religious figure claiming political domination over the existing structure, and prepared to en-force his claims with threats of supernatural and physical punishment, the *mugirwa* needed the support of the local population to evade yet another series of political pressures. In order to achieve their goals, *bagirwa* now turned to the political channels erected by the British themselves, and sought the aid of local, British-appointed chiefs. The structure created by the British system was thus used to unite the Kiga against British rule.

The motives of the Congolese *bagirwa* need little amplification. What is curious is the degree of solidarity exhibited by the local Kiga and Hororo populations, not merely during the raid but in the period of preparation and the subsequent period of investigation. Tradition-ally, in both Mpororo and southern Kigezi the people had feared the extortionate and punitive tactics of the Nyabingi. With the tactical shift of Ndochibiri, the *bagirwa* emerged in contrast as sympathetic leaders. By confining their activity to a direct confrontation of British rule rather than turning against dissident or uncooperative Africans, as did Muhumusa, the local population became, in effect, spectators to an open contest between the British and the cult leaders.

As Ndochibiri proved himself capable of evading even the most concerted efforts of the British and Belgian forces, his popular appeal could only increase. Moreover, he became a vicarious symbol of defi-ance for the docile yet politically restless Kiga who chafed under the requirements of British administration. Thus, when the call came to co-operate with Ndochibiri in a raid upon the most efficient and therefore most threatening of the Ganda agents, it was reinforced by his repu-tation and by his proven skill in avoiding apprehension for a year and a half. Under such circumstances, even the direct subordinates of Ab-dulla were induced to join him.

The solidarity exhibited during the period of secret preparation, involving as it did the forces of seventeen local chiefs and the com-plicity of the Kiga in Abdulla's entourage, is a striking testimony to the degree to which the raid had engaged the imagination of the entire population of the area. Such unanimity of support could never have been borne, as the British implied, of intimidation.

After the devastating loss of prestige suffered at Nyakishenyi, the British attempted to salvage their reputation and to re-enlist the sup-port of the local Kiga by awarding compensation for lost livestock, by rebuilding damaged property, and by taking punitive action against those who had participated in the revolt. Also, in October, five Kiga chiefs were tried during a special session of the High Court at Kabale on the technical charge of "unlawful assembly." Four of the accused were sentenced to ten years rigorous imprisonment and the fifth to five years.[95] Additional efforts were made to apprehend two elusive Kiga chiefs who continued to harass the Ganda in Nyakishenyi. To provide an additional incentive for information leading to their arrest, a reward of ten head of cattle was offered. "Run to earth" in Ruzumbura in November 1917 on the basis of information furnished by "a native of Nakishenyi," they were publicly executed in Kabale in February 1918. In addition, an effort was made to penalize "the peasantry" who had participated in the raid by assigning additional disciplinary duties, preferably in "rebuilding the habitations they destroyed."[96]

Compensatory and punitive tactics failed, however, to gain public support for the suppression of the movement. Intelligence reports from the Belgian post at Rutshuru indicated that Kaigirwa had in November moved from her Congo base into Kigezi. A reward of twenty head of cattle was offered for information leading to her arrest, yet no reports were forthcoming. The refusal of the Kiga to be tempted by such a reward lay as much in their active sympathy as in any fear of retaliation. Given prevailing support for the movement and the solidarity of anti-European sentiment, the notoriety and wealth of the reward would bring little pleasure, considerable danger, and certain disgrace.

The revolt at Nyakishenyi had repercussions considerably beyond northern Rukiga. The southern and southeastern sections of Kigezi, quiescent since the arrest of the leading Tutsi chiefs, now began to show "signs of active sympathy" with the rebels against the British. Within a few days, while on tour the Agent at Butale was challenged by a border village which refused to let him pass. Although this was interpreted as "merely an isolated expression of ill will by the inhabitants of a small village," the District Commissioner proceeded promptly to Butale with twenty police. The inhabitants of the village fled into the swamps "at the first signs of our approach" but sixty goats and three head of cattle were captured. The action of the village was initially perceived to be idiosyncratic and without political provocation for "tax is not being in any way pressed in these parts, and the calls for labour [are] few." By the end of the year, however, it was apparent that Nyabingi was providing an increasing focus for resistance.[97]

[95] E.2471E: Monthly Report of the Provincial Commissioner, Western Province, Nov. 1917, Entebbe.

[96] P.38: District Commissioner to Provincial Commissioner, 29 Sept. 1917, Fort Portal.

[97] Philipps, "Nabingi," 319; P.253: Monthly Report of the District Commissioner, Kigezi, Aug. 1917, Fort Portal; E.4526: District Commissioner to Provincial Commissioner, 31 Aug. 1917, Entebbe; Annual Report, Kigezi District, 1917-18, Kigezi.

The Reassertion of British Control

The ferocity of the Nyabingi resurgence in 1917 and its organizational elaboration provoked a number of administrative adjustments designed both to contain the cult's influence and to discourage any further overt expression of anti-European hostility. Primary among these was the application of the 1912 Witchcraft Ordinance to cult practitioners. Whereas previous *bagirwa* had been dealt with extrajudicially as political prisoners, in 1917 those that were apprehended were charged with the exercise of witchcraft.

By avoiding any attempt to designate a specific series of actions as witchcraft, the ordinance provided a flexibility of interpretation which could include a wide variety of actions as potentially indictable. In addition, by defining the charge in terms of "professing," "pretends to be," or "holds himself to be," the ordinance circumvented any need to consider either the phenomenological reality of witchcraft or the causality of the actions in which the accused engaged in an attempt to control supernatural forces. Such phrasing eliminated any need to document the consequences of the actions of the accused. The *intent* of the accused, whether elicited verbally or inferred from behavior or from the objects which the defendant was alleged to have manipulated, became the basis for conviction. Given the supernatural matrix of the Nyabingi cult, both as the idiom for leadership and in the patterns of intimidation used to secure adherents, the movement, while secular in intent, could be readily proved to manipulate "supernatural powers" and so to be subject to prosecution under the Witchcraft Ordinance.

The degree to which the administration consciously planned to influence local sentiment by defining cult activity as an act of witchcraft is not clear. Given their simple rubrics in dealing with traditional supernatural categories, the British officials may well have failed to appreciate the cult's position within the indigenous religious structure. The *bagirwa* were preeminently curers, powerful if specialized mediaries, but not, in any technical sense, witches. The conditions for their anger or pleasure were well understood and openly declared, their role being confined to the satisfaction of cult interests. Theirs was not a general skill to be applied, for a fee, to the personal grievances of any applicant. Until revised in 1957, the ordinance failed to distinguish between black and white magic and designated all attempts to manipulate supernatural power as potentially indictable. By avoiding any statutory designation of the attributes which were to characterize an act of witchcraft or enchantment, the ordinance retained a flexibility of interpretation which enhanced its value as an administrative tactic.

The British use of "witchcraft" as an instrument for more effective political control in Kigezi would seem to have been directly correlated with a growing administrative awareness that cult support had not been extorted under threats of punishment or death but that it represented a general and quite voluntary response to perceived political grievances. As suppressive political measures had proved ineffective, the redefinition of cult protest as an act of witchcraft provided new leverage for British authorities in dealing with political resistance in Kigezi. Well aware of the futility of applying political or military measures to problems of civil disobedience and alarmed by the increasing alienation which such measures provoked, the British chose to transmute a political contest into a juridical frame of reference.

The application of the Witchcraft Ordinance to the Nyabingi cult, although patently a political decision, provided a jural idiom which minimized British intervention and opposition to local leadership and local political values. Psychologically it was far preferable to the alternate charge of "unlawful assembly" which emphasized the polarity of local and British interest and did little to foster a climate of local cooperation. By moving from a political action to a jural act reasserting public order, a homogeneity of value and purpose could be claimed which could subsequently be invoked to alienate the population from further acts of political rebellion. Moreover, the association of the cult with witchcraft—a traditional crime of high emotional valence—once accepted, would secure a common identification with the maintenance of the public order and with further British action against cult activity.

At issue, really, was the relative strength of local identification with the definition of the cult as a criminal or anti-social activity or, conversely, with the legitimacy of the claim of the cult leaders. Prosecution under the Witchcraft Ordinance was thus a conscious tactic—a tactic as much of indoctrination as of political control. However, in 1917 its effectiveness remained to be established.

During that year three men and three women were convicted under the Witchcraft Ordinance. The application of the ordinance immediately led to certain penal complications for it became necessary to construct additional accommodations for female prisoners. An additional problem, intrinsic to the ordinance itself, was the difficulty of obtaining adequate evidence for conviction. Liability, inasmuch as it required evidence of intent not of action, rested exclusively on the testimony of witnesses. Yet belief in the power of the practitioners and fear of reprisal were such that few were willing to testify. Prosecution under the Witchcraft Ordinance thus often served only to aggravate the political situation for, when released on grounds of insufficient evidence, the *mugirwa* could return in triumph, proclaiming the superiority of the forces of Nyabingi over those of the Europeans.

The restricted powers to sentence under the Witchcraft Ordinance also created serious political problems, for the *bagirwa*, even if convicted, could not be detained for more than a year. By 1918 the implications of this restriction were well appreciated for certain *bagirwa* convicted in 1917 were due to be released. Recognizing that "these fanatical women are a curse to the country" and that the movement could only be controlled by their removal, the British developed the convention of extending the period of detention extrajudicially by requesting deportation at the expiration of sentence.[98]

For similar reasons, the repatriation of the *bagirwa* deported earlier as political prisoners to other areas of Uganda was strongly resisted by local British administrators. For example, in 1917 the Governor urged the return of Ndungutsi as a clement act. In informing the District Commissioner of this request, the Provincial Commissioner revealed both his concern with the tenacity of cult influence and his continuing fear of the volatile nature of Kigezi district:

> Unless you can assure me that you consider Ndungutzi's former power has gone and that he will be without influence on his return and that there will be no risk of his causing trouble again, I can not take the responsibility of recommending his return. These fanatical witch doctors, with their sacred sheep, are a menace not to be despised and even an upstart like Ndochibiri whose influence compared with Muhumusa and her offspring was trifling, caused very serious trouble for a lengthy period. Please give the question your very careful consideration with due regard to the safety and welfare of the natives of the district under your administration.[99]

Similarly, the District Commissioner, on sentencing a *mugirwa* for witchcraft, stressed that it was "essential for the peace and good order" that she be detained 250 miles from the district for "at least" three years "to prevent her from exercising her evil influence on the said District."[100]

By the end of 1917 the political viability of the Nyabingi cult was conceded to be an issue of public sentiment. In contrast to the initial encroachment of Muhumusa into a fearful and reluctant Rukiga, the cult was now openly embraced as an alternative to British occupation.

[98] NAF B: Provincial Commissioner to Chief Secretary, 22 July 1918, Kigezi.

[99] P.233: Provincial Commissioner to District Commissioner, 3 Sept. 1917, Fort Portal.

[100] Kigezi 13/16, Affidavit by Additional District Magistrate, 9 Sept. 1918, Kigezi.

The increasing absorption of the cult into the local political matrix required as well the revision of British strategy. Whereas the earlier phase of the movement was contained by direct military assaults on cult leaders, control now required the conversion of the population at large. It was for this reason, above all, that the District Commissioner emphasized the expansion of formal educational facilities to combat "the influence of witchdoctors." Although such efforts to undermine indigenous religious practices seem strikingly displaced given the virulence of the movement at the time, it was recognized that only by prolonged, systematic, and early indoctrination could the sentiments supporting resistance by the cult be changed. Only when they had been effectively undermined would the *emandwa* cults cease to be a potential political danger.

The 1919 Rebellion

The political memoranda of 1918 little suggest the character of the events to come. Only one incident offered even oblique evidence that the passivity which had followed the Nyakishenyi rebellion might be a superficial and temporary adaptation. This occurred when the efforts of the District Commissioner to introduce a formal educational system into southern Kigezi were countered by the Tutsi chiefs who, in a formal resolution, stated that although they "realized the value of their children being literate [they] were opposed to obtaining the advantage at the price of Christianity."[101] The political importance of this conservatism as an index both of increasing resistance to further assimilation and of the continuing strength of traditional religious practices seems to have been unappreciated by the District Commissioner. Nor was the gradual deterioration of relations between the colonial government and the people of Kigezi perceived by the local administration, which proceeded to consolidate the reforms instituted after the war with little understanding of the tensions they might create. It was these tensions and the insensitivity of the European officers to the increasing abuses perpetrated by the Ganda agents which underlay the resurgence of cult activity in 1919.

No overt activity occurred against the British until April 1919, yet, in the preceding months, several signs of growing alienation betrayed an increasing antipathy toward European rule and the possibility of violence. By early 1919, the station at Kabale "was avoided by Bakiga wherever possible" while court activity also sharply declined during

[101] Annual Report, Kigezi District, 1918-19.

this period. One major source of rising anti-European sentiment was natural, not political: the sudden concurrence of severe epidemics of influenza and cerebrospinal meningitis, a conjunction of events which readily received a magico-political interpretation. "The extreme suddenness of death [in both instances] led numbers to attribute the scourges to alien influence."[102]

Far more critical, however, in explaining the increasing antipathy toward European rule was the introduction of several administrative innovations which severely dislocated the already strained relationship between the indigenous population and the Ganda agents. Foremost among these was the introduction of Luganda as the official language of Kigezi, presumably in the interests of administrative efficiency. In retrospect the innovation was recognized by the District Commissioner to be "a distinct political error": "The local population has been submerged, incoherent and voiceless. Their attitudes, needs and aspirations have only reached the Government indirectly coloured by Baganda intermediaries [who constitute a] small but noisy oligarchy."[103]

In addition to the control exercised by the Ganda as interpreters, the activities of the Agent and his petty chiefs were becoming increasingly corrupt and overbearing as their power grew. At the end of 1918 a number of changes were made in the gombolola (subcounty) system which further increased the power of the Ganda in administrative positions. These were implemented by the incumbent district officer without the approval of the Provincial Commissioner, who had strongly opposed early efforts to "Buganda-ise" the district.[104]

The resentment of the local population over the introduction of these alien practices was inevitable for they brought with them "innumerable cases of abuse and oppression."[105] In addition to extortions of tribute and labor claimed as a prerogative of office and the establishment of elaborate nepotic networks, the Ganda also manipulated their judicial powers in an arbitrary and abusive manner. That the local populace was less than docile in the face of such abuses is suggested by the District Commissioner's observation: "The Mwalimu bears nineteen spear wounds since August 1919, but appears not to have learnt wisdom therefrom."[106] It was these abuses, both judicial and administrative, which formed the political context for the events of 1919.

[102] Annual Report, Kigezi District, 1919-20; E.3314G: Annual Report of the Provincial Commissioner, Western Province, 1919-20, Entebbe.

[103] Annual Report, Kigezi District, 1919-20, Kigezi.

[104] P.309: Provincial Commissioner to Treasurer, 20 Oct. 1919, Fort Portal.

[105] Annual Report, Kigezi District, 1919-20.

[106] Monthly Report of the District Commissioner, December 1919, 302.

The first evidence of the recrudescence of cult activity, dormant since 1917, occurred on 10 April 1919 when an unidentified "Ruanda Nabingi" established himself on the northern slope of Muhavura mountain. From this base he organized three hundred followers in an attack on government-employed road laborers near Chahifi, the scene of the initial assault by Ndochibiri at the beginning of 1916. The attack proved unsuccessful, and the government forces, now alerted to the rebel's presence, captured him three days later. He was promptly convicted under the Witchcraft Ordinance and sentenced to the maximum punishment of one year.[107]

However, by early June reports reached Kabale that Ndochibiri had been joined at Buitwa, his Congo refuge, by four other *bagirwa*, including Luhemba and Kaigirwa. The conjunction of so many leaders and the report that twenty-five rifles had been seen at that time convinced the District Commissioner of the seriousness of this latest cult activity. Similarly ominous was the sudden deterioration of British intelligence contacts; after the meeting in Buitwa further information about the *bagirwa*'s movements suddenly became most "difficult to obtain." Alerting the Belgian Resident at Kivu to the immediate danger of some action by the *bagirwa*, the District Commissioner urged that "even should no disturbances occur, these rebels should be hunted mercilessly in our respective districts [for] their death or capture will alone ensure peace."[108]

In contrast to the earlier apathy exhibited by the Belgian administrators, the Ruzizi-Kivu officer now promptly agreed to co-operate. The logistics of locating and apprehending Ndochibiri were fully appreciated by the Belgians for they had also, "on many occasions," made unsuccessful efforts to capture him. In Belgian territory, as in British, his tactical skill depended both on the effectiveness of his communications' network and upon the measures which he took to evade detection. There, as in Uganda, it would appear that he was "always informed of our slightest movements." Again, as in Uganda, the implicit solidarity of local support was not acknowledged by the authorities. Rather, the failure of information to reach Belgian officials was attributed to Ndochibiri's malevolent reputation: "He is held in terror by the native population . . . and no one dares to denounce his gathering from the additional fear of reprisals."[109]

To overcome both the efficiency of Ndochibiri's network and the inability of patrols and loyalist chiefs to determine his movements, the

[107] Ibid., Apr. 1919.
[108] E.4526: District Commissioner to M. le Commissaire de District, Ruzizi-Kivu, 7 June 1919, Entebbe.
[109] Ibid., M. le Commissaire to District Commissioner, 18 June 1919.

District Commissioner in June resorted to rather extraordinary political measures: the deployment of local Africans "in plain clothes" to obtain information leading to Ndochibiri's arrest. To increase their incentive for efficiency, a "large reward in cash or stock" was offered. Such inducements proved perhaps sufficiently tempting for, with the murder of one intelligence agent who had been keeping them under observation "not wisely but too well," Ndochibiri and his followers retreated once again into the refuge of the Kayonza forest.[110]

Convinced that the reputation of both colonial administrations and the stability of the area depended upon the prompt arrest of Ndochibiri, the District Commissioner "after a careful study of the methods of the rebel . . . throughout his murderous career" devised an elaborate strategy which anticipated the major features of Ndochibiri's *modus operandi*. To achieve this, the British and Belgians organized a joint operation which would entice him from his forest base and effectively manipulate his intelligence network for their own purposes.

> The measures adopted were to surround the forest with patrols leaving one attractive bait which might give an opportunity of engaging his force in the open and cutting off his retreat. . . . It appeared probable from his past tactics that his opening raid would have an objective in which success would be both certain and easy, to instill confidence into his followers for future operations. It was . . . unlikely that he would at first risk collision with any armed force.[111]

On the night of 19 June 1919, a British intelligence agent reported that a Nyabingi "priestess," presumably Kaigirwa, had crossed into British territory with a force of six hundred recruited from "border nationalities." Ndochibiri had by that time secretly entered the Kigezi area and was at Ruagara Hill opposite the Kabale station, where, with Luhemba, the husband of Kaigirwa, he was engaged in consolidating his support for a large-scale attack against the British through ceremonies of blood brotherhood with "leading Bakiga."[112]

As in the earlier Nyakishenyi rebellion, the co-ordination of the Kiga in the Kabale area was essential to the *bagirwa*'s plan of attack, for the first and most strategic phase of the operation required the seizure of the district station at Kabale. This was then to be the signal for "a general rising all over the District."[113] The preparatory tactics of Ndochibiri—his undetected entry into the station area and his consoli-

---

[110] Ibid.; P.302: Monthly Report of the District Commissioner, June 1919, Fort Portal.

[111] E.4526: District Commissioner to Provincial Commissioner, 25 June 1919, Entebbe.

[112] Philipps, "Nabingi," 320.

[113] Bessell, "Nyabingi," 83.

dation of control through blood brotherhood with influential Kiga—
suggest the mechanisms and scale of organization which underlay the
earlier massacre at Nyakishenyi.

The British, however, now more alert to the possibility of an impending attack than in 1917, succeeded in intercepting a messenger returning to Kayonza forest. From the information obtained from this
hostage and by noting fires in the uninhabited forests near Kumba, the
British were able to locate the encampment of Ndochibiri on 23 June.
Attacking without warning, British troops surprised and killed both
Ndochibiri and Luhemba. Philipps reports that before the *bagirwa* died,
they deliberately broke their rifles, crying "we will not look upon a
white man, he shall not have our [iron] but a curse."[114]

The decision of the British to publicize their success by the display
of both bodies for one day at Kabale station[115] was an index of their
prolonged frustration and their fear at renewed unrest following the
death of these leaders. Their concern was well placed for Kaigirwa with
the major body of followers, by dispersing and moving only at night,
successfully evaded both the British troops and a detachment of Belgian
police which was sent to the border to cut off their retreat. Although the
District Commissioner attributed his failure to elicit local co-operation
once again to "terrorism," the ability of such a large group to infiltrate
a heavily patrolled area without detection by loyalist chiefs or military
patrols would rather suggest a high degree of local support and sympathy.

To further impress upon the Kiga populations the supremacy of
their power, the British captured the sacred white sheep and transported it alive to Kabale where it was publicly burnt on 2 July as a
"precautionary measure." To witness the event, the Provincial Commissioner convened a *baraza* of "leading chiefs"; before disposing of
the sheep he "gave [the chiefs] a lengthy anti-Nyabingi lecture . . .
and begged them not to listen to Kaigirwa who will only lead them to
trouble." Considerable care was taken that all the skin, flesh, and bone
of the animal be consumed by the fire to ensure that its potency had
been fully neutralized.[116]

Somewhat ominously, the property of the District Commissioner

[114] Philipps, "Nabingi," 320.

[115] E.4526: District Commissioner to Provincial Commissioner, 25 June 1919,
Entebbe. Bessell reports that the notorious two-fingered hand of Ndochibiri was cut
off and exposed publicly at Kabale "for a time . . . to show all and sundry that
the famous fighting leader was well and truly dead." ("Nyabingi," 83.) In addition, his head was later sent to England where "it may now be seen at the British
Museum." (Ibid., 84.)

[116] E.4526: Monthly Report of the Provincial Commissioner, July 1919; Philipps, "Nabingi," 321.

was subsequently subject to a series of mysterious accidents: On the night of 12 July a portion of his house fell in, between 15 July and 20 July his small flock of sheep sickened and died although other sheep in the area were not affected, and on 29 July a smoldering ridge pole was discovered in his house at dawn. Philipps does not reveal, however, what effect these incidents had on the morale of either the Kiga or the District Commissioner who was, it should be remembered, the sole European officer in Kigezi.

Sensitive to the continuing anger of Kaigirwa, whose hatred of Europeans was now compounded by her personal loss and by the need to validate her new ascendancy to the position of "leading Nyabingi,"[117] the British officers attempted to undermine the appeal of her anticipated return by rewarding those who had actively participated in the apprehension of Ndochibiri.

On 8 July, Kaigirwa made one final attempt to mobilize the population of Kigezi against the Europeans. Her commitment to the success of the operation must have been high for her own reputation as a *mugirwa* was at stake and the prestige of the cult itself was threatened. In addition, of course, her own motives for revenge would on this occasion have been particularly intense. Despite these pressures, the retaliation of Kaigirwa was brief and abortive. A chance encounter with an isolated police patrol proved a sufficient deterrent: Kaigirwa and her party hastily retreated, announcing as they departed that they "would wait for vengeance until the government relaxed their precautions and forgot their presence."[118] No further reference to Kaigirwa occurs in the political memoranda, although Bessell reports that she was "eventually rounded up during the same year and . . . killed resisting capture."[119] Sporadic unrest by raiders from the Congo continued throughout July. On 23 July, seven Hunde appeared on the southeastern edge of the Kayonza forest where they "tried to make trouble with the local Wanya-ruanda." They were "suitably dealt with at once." The scale of the organization is evinced by the simultaneous appearance on that day at Itenbero of "Nabingi malcontents with twenty-eight rifles."[120]

The response of the colonial administration to this continuing unrest in western Kigezi was to arrange a joint withdrawal from the international border.

[117] E.4526: Provincial Commissioner to Chief Secretary, 5 July 1919.

[118] E.4526: Monthly Report of the Provincial Commissioner, Western Province, July 1919, Entebbe.

[119] Bessell, "Nyabingi," 83.

[120] E.4526: Monthly Report of the Provincial Commissioner, Western Province, July 1919, Entebbe.

On communicating with the Commissaire de District Kivu-Ruzizi he caused Kisalu to be burnt out and the inhabitants removed further from our frontier. Following this arrangement our natives in Kinkizi-Kayonza have been simultaneously moved back from this storm center. While one cannot hope for any permanent result from this action, it has nevertheless had a salutary effect.[121]

Further unrest was anticipated with the receipt of a dispatch from Mulera in Ruanda reporting that a successor to Ndochibiri had been "ordained" at Kiante. In an effort to rally the cult adherents after the death of Ndochibiri, this *mugirwa* now claimed to be able to protect his followers against bullets by merely holding out his hand.[122] He did not, however, appear in British territory.

Although the focus for cult activity in 1919 was the southwestern sector of Kigezi, in July a "priestess" did penetrate as far as northeastern Ruzumbura. This was the first time a *mugirwa* was observed in Ruzumbura, and government action was swift: "She has been at once apprehended and imprisoned, and will be deported."[123] On the night of 31 July a Tutsi chief who had been a valuable source of information for the British was murdered by two of his servants who, after burning the house over his body, fled into the Congo. The action was "announced" by the cult as "one of vengeance on an 'informer.' "[124] No further evidence of cult activity was reported until 9 September when a *mugirwa* was said to be "five hours south of Lake Bunyonyi with a large following of malcontents." To discourage any action in Kigezi, the District Commissioner wired requesting twenty police from Mbarara "at once."[125]

Despite these instances of continuing cult action, with the death of Ndochibiri and the rout of Kaigirwa, the major organizational focus of the movement had been broken. Whether in response to the increasingly prompt action of colonial authorities or as a result of the absence of the charismatic leadership and tactical skill of Ndochibiri, the attacks of the *bagirwa*, although widely distributed, grew increasingly desultory and uncoordinated. In contrast to the dramatic and district-wide confrontations planned by Ndochibiri, the *modus operandi* of the surviving cult leaders deteriorated into a series of short forays from foreign bases. In addition to reflecting the absence of the organizational talents of Ndochibiri, this new pattern of raiding in-

[121] Ibid.
[122] Ibid.
[123] Ibid.
[124] Ibid.
[125] Ibid.: Telegram from Provincial Commissioner, 2 Sept. 1919, Entebbe.

creasingly betrayed motives of personal gain. Rather than providing a framework for the expression of local opposition to British rule, the *bagirwa* now reverted to a pattern of extortion and intimidation. This tactical shift unquestionably exacerbated the growing disenchantment of the Kigezi populations with the movement. At the same time, the disillusionment itself probably set the conditions for the resumption of these exploitative techniques.

Neither the District nor Provincial Commissioners harbored any illusions as to the strength of Ndochibiri's support or of the imminence, at the time of his death, of an organized and district-wide rebellion. The District Commissioner observed: "I am of the honest conviction that a very serious general rising . . . had been most narrowly averted," and the Provincial Commissioner stressed: "I realize that, at Entebbe, it is not possible for you to form any idea of the very serious nature of this Nabingi propaganda nor of the narrow escape we have had from a serious native outbreak. . . . I am deeply grateful the worse did not befall us."[126] One European officer and a police establishment of thirty-five men, both realized, could offer little resistance to any widespread rebellion.

Recognizing that the focus for most of the local anti-British sentiment was not the demands of the British government itself but against the agents and that real grievances did exist with regard to the exploitation of their prerogatives of office, the British in 1919 undertook a serious reform of the Agent system. Prominent among these reforms were the immediate withdrawal of the prerogative of labor tribute and the dismissal of agents implicated in serious abuses.[127] By the end of the year the District Commissioner had effectively disassociated himself from any responsibility for having created conditions for revolt: "Their [the agents'] overbearing and domineering attitude to the local populations had without doubt been the direct cause of more than 90 per cent of the so-called local 'rebellions' in a country where [the] European Government has never been personally unpopular."[128]

Years of Accommodation and Alienation: 1920-27

Despite the measures taken in 1919 to stabilize administration along the borders and to control the abuses of the agents, in September 1920

[126] E.4526: District Commissioner to Provincial Commissioner, 25 June 1919, Entebbe; ibid.: Provincial Commissioner to Chief Secretary, 5 July 1919, Fort Portal.

[127] P.309: Provincial Commissioner to Treasurer, 20 Oct. 1919, Fort Portal.

[128] Annual Report, Kigezi District, 1919-20, Kigezi.

political unrest erupted once again in southwestern Kigezi. Again, the impetus for revolt was the Nyabingi cult with its base of organization in Belgian territory. The locus of the movement had once again shifted, however, for whereas Ndochibiri had moved from the Congo into the heart of central Rukiga, the new cult activity emanated from Ruanda, southwest of Lake Bunyonyi. The analogous character of the terrain was readily appreciated by both the cultists and their British adversaries: "These are wild mountain frontier areas which are practically unadministerable. Neither the Germans, the Belgians nor ourselves have ever succeeded in obtaining tax or labour from these people owing to the nature of the country."[129]

Although no leader emerged during this period of instability to challenge the skill or reputation of the Congolese *bagirwa*, the climate of opinion was such that even the most trivial incident could "trigger" the highly volatile and embittered population. The mere rumor of the impending arrival of a "Nabingi emissary" was, for example, sufficient in many areas to precipitate open resistance, and any efforts by the district administrator to enforce intrusive regulations only widened the chasm between local interests and colonial intent.

When in October disturbances once again began to assume "alarming proportions," the District Commissioner, recognizing the general alienation which such unrest betrayed, chose to focus on relieving the underlying conditions which had generated such widespread discontent. Whereas 1919 had been spent in "breaking rebellious organizations," now rehabilitation, not further military action, was emphasized. It was even suggested by Philipps that the effect of Nyabingi might be neutralized by the encouragement of other, "more innocuous" cults within the traditional magico-religious system: "Since purely military measures have proved useless against the Nabingi it would appear that a considerable influence might be enlisted for European administrations by more sympathetic handling of the conservative Rwanda *kubandwa* cult and the powerful but innocuous local fortune telling, rainmaking institutions which enter so deeply into the life of these people. So might Greek meet Greek and the Devil take the hindmost."[130]

While the basic premise for cult unrest remained that of "all native politics," that is, that the "alien Government is only temporary," a number of more specific grievances and issues were also exploited by the new Nyabingi leaders: the enforcement of township regulations, the capture of fugitive criminals, and the continuing anxiety over labor and taxes. A recurrence of an epidemic of cerebrospinal meningitis was

[129] E.4526: District Commissioner to Provincial Commissioner, 17 Sept. 1920, Entebbe.

[130] Annual Report, Kigezi District, 1919-20, Kigezi; Philipps, "Nabingi," 321.

again readily manipulated by the Nyabingi so as to increase local alienation from British rule: "There is a belief current among the native population that the germs of this disease are buried in the ground by European and alien agents as a punishment."[131] Under such politically volatile circumstances, the District Commissioner conceded that "a certain amount of political uneasiness" had to be anticipated. In the absence of any overt aggression against either the British or their representatives, however, no offensive action to suppress the cult was taken in 1920.

Although both the provincial and local officers now displayed considerable sensitivity to the signs of continuing alienation, difference of opinion among the British officials continued, both as to the nature of the unrest and the most effective ways of neutralizing it. The Provincial Commissioner affirmed the need for "drastic measures" in the event of any resurgence of overt hostility. To avert any local participation in activities planned by *bagirwa* in Ruanda, he therefore convened the "leading people" of Bufumbiro and Rukiga while on tour in Kigezi:

> In full Baraza today I . . . spoke to them on the matter and warned them that this was the second year in succession that trouble and unrest had arisen in the country from the "Nabingi" movement and that if they again participated in the movement or did not take steps to prevent dangerous people from crossing the border and stirring up trouble here, the Government would next time take severe punitive measures in the confiscation of stock and imprisonment of offenders. I pointed out to them that this annual unrest and trouble would not be tolerated and that gave them a clear warning on this matter.[132]

Given the pervasiveness of unrest and a population said to be in "an electric and inflammable state of mind," such an ultimatum required a considerable degree of bravado. However conscientious or disciplined the military or police forces might be, they were ultimately defenseless against a population of several hundred thousand distributed over several thousand square miles.

In contrast, the District Commissioner argued that "the best remedies and safeguards against future trouble" would be to combine more regular systemic changes with a continuing tolerance for local unrest and an acknowledged capitulation to certain long-standing grievances. He advocated five measures:

[131] E.4526: District Commissioner to Provincial Commissioner, 17 Sept. 1920; Kigezi Correspondence: District Commissioner to Provincial Commissioner, 1 Nov. 1920, Kigezi.

[132] Ibid.: Provincial Commissioner to Chief Secretary, 13 Nov. 1920, Kigezi.

1) The gradual civilization of the district;
2) The levelling up of administrations on both sides of the two international frontiers;
3) Abstention from the pressure of tax or labour in frontier areas;
4) Increasing toleration of the Rwanda *imandwa* [an anti-Nyabingi
   institution];
5) Employment of Tutsi, the hereditary rulers, whenever possible.[133]

Clearly, the suggested deferment of fundamental administrative
requirements and the wide-scale social reforms implicit in this list
represented a major departure from earlier administrative policy.
Token deference was made to the external impetus for political unrest;
but his conditions suggested that the District Commissioner was fully
aware that such resistance was neither superficial nor intrusive and
that it in fact represented a pervasive antagonism which could only
be weakened by a gradual attitudinal reform. This in turn would require certain prompt concessions in the most volatile areas, considerable tact and patience where resistance was met, and a gradual stand-
ardization of administrative practices, particularly in the immediate
border areas.

The five major points of reform were rather perfunctorily conceded
by the Provincial Commissioner. Immediate efforts were made to substitute "where possible indigenes for aliens in the control of local affairs." The replacement of the Agent in Bufumbiro was recognized to
be both a political imperative and most feasible for this area which, in
spite of a history of political turbulence, was regarded in 1920 as "by
far the most progressive County in Kigezi."[134] Only two qualifications
were now regarded as essential for the office of Agent: that the candidate be a Tutsi, that is, "anti-Nyabingi," and that he be of the royal
family. As a final stipulation, it was also suggested that "if possible,
he be acquainted with Ugandan fiscal and judicial methods and have
a knowledge of Kiswahili."[135]

Tutsi affiliation was specified in an attempt to gain the support of
that segment of the Rwanda population which had little enthusiasm
for the Nyabingi movement. By appointing a member of the royal clan,
traditional lines of political identification would be reinforced, not disrupted, and existing Tutsi sentiments toward the cult, already congruent with British interests, could be manipulated in the event of further
cult activity. However, the appointment of a Tutsi as chief, although

---

[133] E.4526: Provincial Commissioner to Chief Secretary, 13 Nov. 1920.
[134] Annual Report, Kigezi District, 1919-20; Kigezi Correspondence: Provincial Commissioner to District Commissioner, 24 May 1920, Kigezi.
[135] Ibid.: District Commissioner to Provincial Commissioner, 15 Nov. 1920,
Kigezi.

politically strategic in one respect, represented considerable political risk for, by reinforcing the traditional lines of privilege within the Rwanda hierarchy, the British rendered themselves vulnerable to identification with the hated aristocracy and to further alienation on the part of the Hutu majority.

During 1921, no political disturbances occurred in Kigezi. Although it is not clear whether the period of quiet reflected concerted British efforts to introduce a number of preventive and deterrent measures or, alternately, an internal shift in the dynamics of local political relations, the activities of the *bagirwa,* when they did occur, were strikingly apolitical in nature. It is possible that the reinforcement of the district police establishment with twenty men from Ankole and the co-ordinated patrol of the southwestern frontier by British and Belgian detachments provided a sufficient display of force to deter any open cult activity.

A major reform of the 1912 Witchcraft Ordinance also occurred in 1921 which facilitated its application in Kigezi. Although prosecution under the Witchcraft Ordinance had proved the most effective political instrument for inhibiting the activities of the cult leaders, the British conceded in this year that the penalty provided in the Witchcraft Ordinance was "no longer adequate as a deterrent."[136] The maximum sentence was increased from one to five years, thus empowering the courts to remove any potentially disruptive leader for long enough to undermine both his authority over his adherents and the residual structure of cult organization. In addition, although the ordinance carefully avoided classifying witchcraft as either a felony or a misdemeanor—it is referred to only as an "offense"—the severity of the increased sentence brought the application of the ordinance well within the range of felony. The enhanced sentence further provided a technical basis for claiming exclusive jurisdiction over all witchcraft cases, for the maximum sentence in itself would warrant the removal of such cases from the local African courts.

The 1921 amendment further secured the probability of conviction by making "possession of witchcraft articles" a punishable offense. Absent in the principal ordinance, the addition of this clause unquestionably increased the efficiency of prosecution for, provided such tangible evidence could be recovered, the onus of proof of innocence was now on the defendant. Moreover, the admission of such evidence eliminated the need to rely upon reluctant or intimidated witnesses. The revision provided, however, for a maximum penalty of only six months. This, as one Provincial Commissioner noted in the 1950's, "renders it virtu-

[136] E.2156: Governor to Secretary of State, 23 Apr. 1921, Entebbe.

ally useless as a protection to the community in which the pretended witch is living."[137]

As 1922 remained a year of political tranquility, the few practitioners of Nyabingi apprehended were dismissed as "of the witchcraft variety and without any political significance."[138] In evaluating the continuing quiescence of the movement, the District Officer stressed the relevance of the gradual incorporation of the area into a larger attitudinal framework, and urged an even lighter sentence for those convicted under the Witchcraft Ordinance. This laxity of the British in the prosecution of the less dangerous *bagirwa* had, however, repercussions, for it was rapidly exploited by the cult leaders. Ever concerned with the size of their following, the *bagirwa* claimed that the relaxation of British control represented a capitulation to their superior power. In particular, when they did not receive maximum sentences, the *bagirwa* used their early release to enhance their reputations and to demonstrate the potency of Nyabingi over the Europeans.[139]

Although no political activism was reported in the political memoranda of 1922, a *mugirwa* moved into the Kigezi area from Ruanda at the end of the year urging others "to go out and kill the white man and drive him from the country."[140] With her arrival, the first syncretistic elements appeared in the ideology of the movement, for she commanded "on threat of immediate death" that the "old Nyabingi custom" of no cultivation or cooking on Monday be restored. Her influence was such that over a year later the District Commissioner observed: "The fear of the power of the 'Nabingi' is so great that with very few exceptions the people keep strictly to this command." Many attempts were made to apprehend this *mugirwa* once her anti-European focus and power became apparent, but by the time systematic action was taken against her "the sect [was] too well guarded to allow of it."[141]

In 1923, Kigezi district remained politically quiet. The few arrests made were of a "non-political" nature, leading the District Commissioner to interpret the absence of the more virulent forms of cultism as "encouraging proof of the advancement of the District."[142] His confidence, however, was premature. During a tour of Bufumbiro at the end of December 1923, the local strength of the movement at last reached

---

[137] District Court 22/21, Ankole District; Attorney General 789: Provincial Commissioner, Northern Province to Secretary for African Affairs, 14 June 1955, Entebbe.

[138] Annual Report, Kigezi District, 1922.

[139] District Court, 7/24, Kigezi District.

[140] District Court, 32/34, Kigezi District.

[141] District Court, 7/24, Kigezi District.

[142] Annual Report, Kigezi District, 1923.

the attention of the British authorities. In response, the District Commissioner warned both the chiefs and the populace against participation in the movement, emphasizing that any further activity would be met with prompt repressive measures and heavy punishments for those implicated. Despite British precautions, even the chiefs were found to be involved. No measures were taken against them, but they were warned that "in future" any evidence of association with the movement would result in their dismissal.[143]

The year 1924 witnessed a subtle but significant deterioration in the local administration of Kigezi, as a consequence of both the growing disaffection of incumbent chiefs and the increasing encroachments of the larger protectorate network. Disaffection was marked among the parish chiefs by a growing alienation from the *saza* (county) and *gombolola* chiefs themselves as well as from the British superstructure. The District Commissioner noted: "in each Saza I visited there were numerous complaints by the Chiefs about their Bkungu, these cases were tried by me and in almost every case were proved and exemplary punishments meted out 'on the spot.' "[144]

The discipline and education of chiefs remained a continuing concern for the British administration. Even more serious, however, was the evidence of increasing unrest on the part of the population at large. One significant index of this growing alienation was renewed difficulty in the collection of the poll tax; in Bufumbiro, for example, the people of one area proved so recalcitrant that an *askari* (soldier) was stationed there "to help matters." In Ruzumbura, to the north, the District Commissioner reported in October "approximately 3,330" tax defaulters of whom "over 2,000" had gone to Buganda.[145]

Within this socio-political context, the cult of Nyabingi quietly but discernibly began to regain its strength in 1924. In April 1924 the District Commissioner observed that "minor," i.e., non-political, cases of Nyabingi were becoming increasingly common. Attributing the increase in cult activity "to the fact that too lenient sentences have been inflicted in the past," the British tried to suppress the movement by exemplary sentences in the "several serious" cases that were brought to their attention.[146] In addition, by defining cult activity as "an evil practice," government propaganda attempted to appeal to the incipient Christianity of the district. Both directly and indirectly efforts were

[143] MIN 89/26, Tour Bufumbiro, Dec. 1923, Kigezi.
[144] Kigezi Correspondence, District Commissioner to Provincial Commissioner, 7 Apr. 1924.
[145] Kigezi Correspondence, District Commissioner to Provincial Commissioner, 5 July 1924 and 7 Oct. 1924, Kigezi.
[146] Ibid., 7 Apr. 1924.

made to establish a climate of opinion which, it was hoped, would alienate the "agriculturists" from the movement.

Although by 1925 cult activity was regarded as politically inconsequential, it remained a continuing problem in Kigezi. It was assumed, however, that cult support would "doubtless disappear with the spread of education." The District Commissioner acknowledged the "large amount of witchcraft being practiced" but affirmed that a new and intensive campaign against practitioners and the increasing prosecution of those found in possession of ritual articles had had "good results" leading to a "noticeable diminution of this danger."[147]

However, in 1927, eighteen cases charging possession of witchcraft articles were tried in the District Court. The tribal distribution of the defendants revealed that "Ruzumbura country is probably the worst in this respect followed closely by Bufumbiro, the Bahororo and Banyaruanda being the two tribes most versed in their practice."[148] Although administrative hostility to local magico-religious practices was presumably stimulated by the recognition of the potentially volatile role of such specialists, no mention was made in the reports of 1927 of the political genesis of such activity, or more specifically, of the continuing strength of the Nyabingi cult. From their indifference, one can only assume that the British staff was totally unprepared for the events of 1928.

The 1928 Rebellion

While cult activity had remained a peripheral administrative consideration during the decade following the death of Ndochibiri in 1919, suddenly, in 1928, the cult of Nyabingi erupted once again as the organizational focus for open and widespread anti-European resistance. The extent of its appeal, the suddenness of its recrudescence, and the degree of organization which it manifested must be viewed both as responses to then current administrative practices and as consequences of the growing alienation of local chiefs from the district administrative structure.

The earliest evidence of renewed cult activity was reported from Kinkizi county in northwestern Kigezi, where the Ganda Agent had been rebuked in the preceding year for losing control of his district. The extent to which this had in fact occurred is evidenced in the arrogant centrality of the cult operation. As with Chandugusi, the leading

---

[147] E.3314P: Annual Report of Provincial Commissioner, 1927, Entebbe; Annual Report, 1927, Kigezi.

[148] Kigezi Correspondence, District Commissioner to Provincial Commissioner, 1 July 1922, Kigezi.

mugirwa was revealed to be the mother of the *gombolola* chief at Ka-
yonsa. The District Commissioner, upon learning that the cult had been
operating "right under the nose of Agent Sulimani," moved quickly to
apprehend the *mugirwa*. "Unfortunately, as so very frequently happens,
suspicion had been aroused of the intention of my search with the result that a particular chair used in these seances, a drum, and a special
iron wand were made away with before they could be seized with the
remaining things."[149] Despite the absence of these key ritual objects,
the woman was arrested and convicted after being charged with the
possession of witchcraft articles. The *gombolola* chief himself, it was
tersely noted, "has been recommended for dismissal."

At the same time, the District Commissioner reported "an insid-
ious recrudescence" of the cult to the south in Rukiga. Although initially the district officer was unable to obtain sufficient information
from the Kiga to locate or arrest this southern *mugirwa*, he was aware
of the virulence and potential danger of this new leader who openly
proclaimed the superior power of Nyabingi and his intention to drive
Europeans from the land. Pressing both the symbolic claims of the
1922–23 resistance and a more secular exhortation to resist British demands for tax and labor, the *mugirwa* called for immediate action
against British rule. "One of the curious decrees is that no work (i.e.,
in shambas [gardens]) may be done on a Monday or Tuesday—these
two days being set apart for 'Nyabingi' of course—and it is amazing
how very generally this is observed by the Rukiga natives."[150] The
prominence of this proscription in the ideology of protest was attributed by the Provincial Commissioner to "the action in the past of certain C.M.S. evangelists who some years ago tried to prohibit the pagan
Bakiga from working in their gardens 'on the Lord's Day' and is in the
nature of a reprisal."[151]

In addition, a curious and presumably intrusive motif found in
other African rebellions, notably in the Maji Maji of Tanganyika and
the Allah-water of the Dinka of the Sudan, was incorporated into the
ideology of this new *mugirwa*, for he claimed that the bullets of the
Europeans, when confronted with the powers of Nyabingi, would be
"rendered harmless."[152] The degree of influence which he exercised
over the local population was reflected in the inability of the British to
elicit any information as to his location from even the more loyalist or
assimilated Kiga.

[149] Ibid., District Commissioner to Provincial Commissioner, 1 Feb. 1928.
[150] Ibid.
[151] E.3173: Provincial Commissioner to Chief Secretary, 29 Apr. 1928, Entebbe.
[152] Ibid.

Despite an auspicious beginning, the 1928 movement was destined to be brief for, although a co-ordinated action against the British was planned by the *bagirwa*, they exhibited little of the tactical sophistication of their predecessors. Nevertheless, their initial advance into the Kabale area was ingenious. Bessell reports that "for some days beforehand the Nyabingi war-anthem, 'the Queen has come to her country' was continually sung by a man from the top of the hill facing the station."[153] This, it may be imagined, served not merely to encourage the Kiga of the area but to erode the morale of the sole European officer.

The injudicious decision of the *bagirwa* in February to convene three hundred followers for an "armed witchcraft dance"[154] in the hills a few miles from Kabale led to a prompt and ill-fated confrontation with the forces of the District Commissioner. Although Bitura, the most influential of the leaders, escaped and fled south into Ruanda, his two sons were arrested and sentenced to the maximum punishment of five years. One of the most striking indices of the extent of the influence of these *bagirwa* was a large water pot confiscated at the time of their arrest. Used as an urn for votive offerings, it contained 305 shillings, almost entirely in cents. The degree of their power was also evidenced during the trial of Kamunda: "In order to get [the witnesses] to speak it was found necessary to place the accused in such a position that the witness would neither be facing him or could see him."[155] His position as a "great" *mugirwa* was also established during the trial, for those present at his unsuccessful flight from British authorities testified that he had been carried by "large numbers" of his followers. This, the assessors noted, "would not be done if he were a witchdoctor of minor importance."

Later intelligence reports confirmed that the intent of the cult leaders in moving into the Kabale area had been to co-ordinate a direct attack on the British station and mission headquarters at Kabale. Their planning had in fact gone so far as to allocate, on paper, the houses and contents of both the station and mission to various favored members of the immediate entourage.[156] We are dealing then, in this final phase of the movement, with men who had clearly spent sufficient time in the colonial educational system to acquire the skill of literacy and the mannerisms of European bureaucracy.

The confiscated plans also revealed that the local *gombolola* was

[153] NAF Seditious, "Nyabingi" (n.d.), Kigezi.

[154] E.3173: Provincial Commissioner to Chief Secretary, 29 Apr. 1928, Entebbe.

[155] Kigezi Correspondence, District Commissioner to Provincial Commissioner, 8 Feb. 1928, Kigezi; District Court 9/28, Kigezi. The East African shilling contains one hundred cents.

[156] Annual Report, Kigezi District, 1928.

to be the initial focus for attack, to be followed by the capture of the mission headquarters, then the district station. Presumably this order of advance was selected with a concern for the relative vulnerability of each installation and a concomitant likelihood of success. It did, however, reveal a curious myopia as to the presumed response of the district officer when alerted to the presence of "large excited and armed gatherings" in the adjacent hills. In confirmation of this priority, Bessell reports that the cultists, before their dispersal, succeeded in killing three minor loyalist chiefs.[157]

With the arrest or escape of the Kigezi *bagirwa,* the seat of the Nyabingi movement shifted into Ruanda. There, in March of 1929, a series of attacks were made upon Belgian chiefs in border areas only fifteen miles from Kabale. During this action, which was regarded by the District Commissioner as "undoubtedly coordinated" with the abortive rising in Kigezi, six Belgian chiefs were murdered and the region along the frontier burned and looted. The leader directing these operations was reported to be Ndungutsi. However, as he was "carried from place to place with his face veiled," the District Commissioner conceded that "proof of identity may be difficult."[158]

Although the activities of the cult in northern Ruanda remained a potential political threat to the Kigezi administration, the district was quiet after the initial arrest of the leaders in February 1928. However, British officers continued to co-operate in the location of cult leaders who remained at large.

It was further recognized that active measures would have to be taken to impress upon the population that the administration "will not tolerate these Nyabingi outbursts." The Provincial Commissioner therefore suggested in April that a collective fine of seventy-five head of cattle be levied against those resident in the area where the "secret dances" had been held. There is no indication, however, that this punishment was implemented. However, despite British efforts, the cult continued to receive the tacit support of both local populations and chiefs. When two "priestesses" entered Kigezi in August, for example, their presence was not reported by the local chiefs.[159]

By now sensitive to the futility of any precipitous or categorical handling of popular sentiment, the British consoled themselves with an

[157] Kigezi Correspondence, Provincial Commissioner to Chief Secretary, 29 Apr. 1928, Kigezi; Annual Report, Kigezi District, 1928, Kigezi; Bessell, "Nyabingi," 84.

[158] Kigezi Correspondence, District Commissioner to Provincial Commissioner, 30 Nov. 1928, Kigezi.

[159] E.3173: Provincial Commissioner to Chief Secretary, 29 Apr. 1928; Kigezi Correspondence, District Commissioner to Provincial Commissioner, 3 Oct. 1928.

interpretation of the cult which both justified their ineffectiveness and offered a promise of its eventual dissipation:

> The leaders are fanatics aided by elementary, but locally terrifying, stock in trade developed from the natural phenomena of hypnotism, ventriloquism and mental suggestion. The followers are principally the terrorised, also the aggrieved. It must be emphasized that every local grievance, whether real or imaginary, and every misapprehension, is greedily exploited, hence the need of going slow, of constant personal contact, with the peasantry, and seeing under the surface in Kigezi.[160]

Even so, the District Commissioner could not foresee the final suppression of cult influence as long as the "present generation" of cult adherents survived.

The inability of the Belgians to control cult activity in northern Ruanda presented a continuing political threat to Kigezi. In anticipation of further unrest a police superintendent was transferred to Kabale to provide a second European officer. The police establishment remained, however, far below the figure regarded as adequate during the earlier periods of resistance. Further political instability was created by fugitives driven north by the raiders in Ruanda, who continued to seek refuge in Kigezi. The disturbances themselves, however, did not at any point break across the frontiers into British territory, presumably because of local disaffection with the cult rather than any fastidiousness on the part of the Rwanda *bagirwa* themselves. Although the British attributed this welcome immunity to their increasing accommodation to local grievances, of far greater relevance was the persisting inability of the *bagirwa* to effect their claims to superior power. Their failure, in 1928, to attack Kabale, compounded by their subsequent arrest by or flight from the British, unquestionably did much to undermine the force of the movement, however congruent with existing local sentiment.

One index of this growing disillusionment with cult efforts to challenge British authority was the dramatic increase in the number of converts to Christianity in the months following the suppression of the Nyabingi movement. As was later disclosed, this new enthusiasm for Christianity was motivated far more by political expediency than by the demonstrable merits of Christianity:

> A recent roundup of those terrorized into tribute to Nyabingi "priests" is alleged to have caused a mass-production of Christians. It was due principally to action indiscriminately taken against both credulous pagans [as well as] avaricious malcontents [and] the real organizers

160 Annual Report, Kigezi District, 1928, Kigezi.

of the Society. . . . The pagan therefore feels the need of some
protection. Baptism and a Hebrew name seem to him to offer a kind
of alibi.[161]

A further impetus for conversion appears to have come from the
"boys in charge of Protestant bush churches, ambitious to gain merit
with their employers by a fat convert-roll," who readily recognized the
exploitative potentialities of pagan anxiety. To impress upon the un-
initiated the advantages of Christianity, they circulated rumors that the
government had warned that "those who did not become Christians
[within six months] would be considered as sympathisers with the
Nyabingi and thrown into prison."[162] Lest the pagans in confusion stray
into Catholicism, the rumors further stipulated that such protection lay
in seeking "the Government religion," i.e., Protestantism.

Although no further political unrest occurred in Kigezi after the
initial eruption in February, investigations revealed the scale of the
planned revolt, its anticipated co-ordination with other regions and the
degree of popular sympathy which it had elicited in each area.

> The movement [was] not only both synchronized and widespread, but
> also [showed] signs of a quite cunning, if elementary organization.
> Manifestations of differing importance, but [using] the same tactics,
> varied only to take advantage of local weaknesses, occurred in the
> same period in Uganda, Belgian East Africa and even in Tanganyika
> Territory.[163]

The seriousness and scale of this latest manifestation of cult activity
prompted the British abruptly to institute a number of major administrative reforms in an effort to eliminate certain long-standing local
grievances. By such action, it was felt, the impetus for further rebellion
would be effectively undermined, for the key to cult popularity was believed to lie in the articulation and manipulation of these grievances.

Of foremost importance was the removal of the Ganda agents
who were reluctantly recognized to be "chauvinists to a man," indifferent to local expectations and local customs and intent upon "Ganda-
ising" the district rather than developing it within a more familiar and
sympathetic frame of reference.[164] Acknowledging the tensions which

[161] Kigezi Correspondence, District Commissioner to Provincial Commissioner,
3 Oct. 1928, Kigezi.

[162] Philipps, "Confidential Note" (n.d.), Kigezi; Annual Report, Kigezi District, 1928, Kigezi.

[163] Annual Report, Kigezi District, 1928, Kigezi.

[164] Kigezi Correspondence, District Commissioner to Provincial Commissioner,
3 Oct. 1928.

their arrogance and abuses had engendered, the Provincial Commissioner resolved to replace them in Rukiga and Ruzumbura by the end of 1929.

In a second major thrust to correct local political tensions, Swahili was once again instituted as the official language of the district. Local resentment toward the earlier adoption of Luganda, both as a symbol of alien domination and as a barrier to communication between the local population and the District Commissioner, was, of course, intimately drawn into the constellation of hostilities associated with the agents themselves. Facilities for instruction in Swahili were "somewhat vaguely if not reluctantly" provided by the missions in August.[165]

Meanwhile, the dislocations caused by the continuing unrest in Belgian Ruanda were exacerbated by conditions of famine in Belgian territory and by the completion of the Kabale-Rutshuru road into the Congo. By October the southwestern portion of the district was subject to a heavy influx of immigrants from both Ruanda and the Congo. With their arrival, the political stability of the area deteriorated, and this led to an increase in the incidence of frontier raids for women and food as well as cattle. An effort to control the situation was undertaken in October with the prohibition of any further settlement in the frontier areas. By forcing immigrants to move farther into the district, the impetus for local raiding and counter-raiding was, it was felt, "considerably reduced."[166]

The Redefinition of Cult Intent

With the containment of the *bagirwa* raiders beyond the southern borders of Kigezi, the threat of the Nyabingi movement as a locus for organized opposition to British dominance was permanently eliminated. Whether in consequence of the failure of a new leader of sufficient stature to emerge; as a direct response to the increasing accessiblity of colonial political and religious values; or, as claimed by the British, because of "the removal of a number of grievances, petty enough to the European [but] actual and infuriating to the African, and easily exploitable by the Nya-bingi,"[167] the cult lost its political dimension after 1928.

This shift in focus was evident as early as June 1929 when two of the more prominent participants in the 1928 rebellion escaped from

[165] Annual Report, Kigezi District, 1928.

[166] P.510/3: Monthly Report of the District Commissioner, Kigezi, Oct. 1928, Fort Portal.

[167] Annual Report, Kigezi District, 1928, Kigezi.

the Belgian prison at Kigali. Previously detained without trial for a year at Mbarara, they were reported upon their escape to have moved northward into the mountainous border country, swearing to "do their worst to make things unpleasant" for the British. The populations of the border area were, at that time, particularly vulnerable to such agitation for "owing to drought, [they had] neither contentment arising from a full stomach, nor [were they] actively engaged in agricultural pursuits which, in most parts of Africa are shown to be one of the simplest and most effective antidotes against privy conspiracy and rebellion."[168] Yet despite the appeals of the escaped leaders for vengeance, no overt opposition to the British ensued.

With the loss of its traditional role as a vehicle for political protest against the established authority structure, Nyabingi assumed new importance as a curative cult. As such it retained a position of prominence among the *emandwa*. By virtue of this adjustment the cult remained, at least for the ruthless and avaricious, an effective vehicle for personal intimidation and extortion.

> That it has considerable influence is apparent from the large number of alleged "witchcraft" cases submitted by Native Courts. On inquiry, it is generally found that they are not genuine cases of witchcraft, but mere charlatanism on the part of imposters who are well aware of the fear inspired in the credulous, and who play upon their fears for their own personal gain.[169]

Traditional cult sanctions were now parlayed into a more naked appeal for personal power. That the threat of the wrath of Nyabingi continued to inspire such fear is in itself significant, for the appeal of the cult in the 1930's must be measured against the promptness of government action in the detection and prosecution of *bagirwa*, the extension of missionary influence, and the direct appeal of various British administrative reforms. The persistence of the powers of the cult is reflected, as in so many other instances of witchcraft, both in the reticence of those so exploited to report the oppressive activities of the *bagirwa* and in their reluctance to testify as witnesses for fear of punitive action either to themselves or to their families or property. As the police noted, "Only when demands of witchdoctors become so exhorbitant that [it is] utterly impossible to appease them are reports of malpractices made."[170] The number of cases prosecuted thus provides little insight into the scale of cult activity.

[168] Minute 79/29: District Commissioner to Provincial Commissioner, 29 July 1929, Kigezi.

[169] Annual Report, Kigezi District, 1930, Kigezi.

[170] Annual Report of the Uganda Police, 1932, Entebbe.

In an attempt to eradicate the cult itself, efforts were made to suppress local support through a policy of "ridicule, stripes and small sympathy with the duped."[171] The effectiveness of this new tactic was reflected in the "considerable" reduction of cases of extortion by practitioners of Nyabingi. Where arrests were made, they seemed to involve those practitioners whose avariciousness had led them to accumulate either a conspicuous flock of sheep or a notoriously large sum of money, both pursuits which would eventually attract the attention of the local chiefs. To these *bagirwa* "scorn and imprisonment [were] meted out, in the hope that they would take themselves less seriously on release."[172]

By 1934 the movement had, at least by all overt indices, been effectively suppressed. The decreasing incidence of Nyabingi cases from 1930 to 1933 and their total elimination by 1934 did not reflect a decline in cult activity, however, but rather an increasing sensitivity on the part of the practitioners to the tactical importance of evasion. By becoming both more circumspect in their operation and increasingly apolitical in focus, the *bagirwa* discouraged detection or intervention by local chiefs. These major shifts in operational tactics may therefore represent no more than an accommodation to increasing bureaucratic control on the district level.

Early in 1935 rumors originating in the Rukiga and Ndorwa *sazas* revealed that Ndungutsi was once again active along the eastern borders of the district. It was the opinion of the District Commissioner, however, that Ndungutsi was "at present merely a name": "I have been told by middle aged chiefs that they have heard of Ndungutsi all their lives and that if he still exists he must be a very old man."[173] Although both the district officer and the Provincial Commissioner stressed the diminished influence of the movement in consequence of "the spread of education and the realization of European power,"[174] Ndungutsi remained at large throughout the year. To do so, the tacit support of the local populations was essential.

By virtue of his reputation and the co-operation which it encouraged, Ndungutsi successfully evaded the British authorities until the end of 1938. The District Commissioner of Ankole, by then fully sensitive to the uncertainties of prosecution under the Witchcraft Ordinance, ingeniously arranged his detention, by force of arms, on an irrefutable and easily substantiated charge: failure to pay poll tax.[175]

171 Annual Report, Kigezi District, 1933, Kigezi.

172 Ibid.

173 NAF, Quarterly Report of the Assistant District Officer, 30 Sep. 1935, Kigezi.

174 Annual Report, Western Province, 1935.

175 Annual Report, Ankole District, 1938.

Thus, despite British claims to increased administrative efficiency and to the ameliorative effects of Christianity and education, the detection of such cult leaders during the mid-1930's remained contingent upon the alignment of local sentiment. Where the *mugirwa* succeeded in demonstrating the efficacy of his power, the fear of his wrath far outweighed the discomforts of his extortionate demands. The official position, emphasizing as it did the "progress of Christianity and education" and the political implications of an increasingly efficient communications system, placed a premature confidence in the ability of the local chiefs to apprehend *bagirwa* "before their influence [became] great enough to cause serious trouble." Although local authorities stressed the inevitability of cult decline with "the advance of civilization," the central police more realistically assessed such assertions as little more than an acknowledgment by the civilian officials of their basic helplessness in instituting any controls which would seriously influence local attitudes toward "the problem."[176]

Although the activity of the Nyabingi leaders remained confined to instances of personal extortion after 1928, their influence in Kigezi remained viable into the early 1950's despite decades of prompt, punitive action, a campaign of public ridicule, and a series of administrative and judicial restrictions designed both to deter the practitioners themselves and those who might seek their power. The tenacity of the cult, especially in the 1930's, impressed upon the authorities both the irrelevance of repressive methods and the critical roles of education and, by implication, of shifting values in the ultimate erosion of such beliefs. It was the missions, ironically, which were to provide the subsequent matrix for political unrest with the emergence of a virulent, evangelical sect of the Anglican church, the *balokole* or "Twice Born." This sect, which encouraged both a defiance of local administrative directives and an open confrontation with local chiefs, was designated "subversive" and made subject to prosecution in the district courts. Although under close surveillance after 1939, the leading adherents succeeded in provoking open disturbances in 1942 and 1946.

Conclusion

The transformation of the Nyabingi cult into a vehicle for colonial opposition may be viewed as a response to a series of shifting political contexts: 1) its initial position in the indigenous political network of the Mfumbiro region, 2) the conditions which defined both the impetus

[176] NAF, Bessell, "Nyabingi" (n.d.), Kigezi; Annual Report, Kigezi District, 1935; Annual Report of the Uganda Police, 1935, Entebbe.

for and the nature of its expansion into the acephalous areas of Kigezi, 3) the degree and nature of support encountered in this region, and 4) the factors underlying its decline and redefinition as a curative cult manipulated primarily for personal, not political, gain.

Although similar to other possession cults throughout the inter-lacustrine area, the cult of Nyabingi had by virtue of its ideological equation of supernatural power with material gain always contained the seed of secular disruption. In Rwanda this was manifested by direct competition with the chiefly structure for the existing tributary chan-nels; in Mpororo, by an attempt to incorporate the established chief-taincies and their networks of labor and tribute into a larger suzerain relationship. In both areas the secular dimension of cult activity was thus already well established in the precolonial period.

While the initial activity of the *bagirwa* in Rwanda was directed toward establishing personal influence through the flow of gifts, once this intrusion was challenged by the *mwami* and his local representa-tives, the cult became an explicit instrument for regional resistance, cleverly manipulating the existing antagonisms of the Hutu to consoli-date local support against the secular chiefly structure.

In Mpororo, in contrast, instead of dividing or disrupting the ex-isting political system, the cult sought control by establishing a higher level of political organization—one which would co-ordinate the frag-mented and politically autonomous chieftaincies of the area. Here cult ascendancy was envisioned as an act of political centralization, that is, the absorption of these independent chieftaincies into a political unit coterminous with their existing ethnic identification as Hororo.

As the accounts of Emin Pasha indicate, this effort proved unsuc-cessful for the cult leaders who, despite their considerable influence, failed to realize more than nominal control over the Mpororo area. Al-though unable to override the existing political loyalties of the Hororo, the cult did provide a precedent for unification during the pre-colonial period.

The failure of the *bagirwa* to consolidate the Mpororo area was in large part due to the absence of any polarity of political identification beyond these local hereditary chieftaincies. Nyabingi itself provided the only model for unification but, as such, lacked the opposition of interests which had proven such an effective part of cult support in Rwanda. The rapidity with which the cult was later embraced by the acephalous Kiga in turn rested on the introduction of the colonial frame of reference. A condition for the political viability of the cult would thus seem to be an opposition to a larger, competing set of political demands.

Although the colonial context introduced an opponent of unprece-dented scale and technological superiority, the modality for resistance was derived from cult activity during the precontact period, for it reflected both the legacy of subversion in Rwanda and the manipulation of larger political networks in Mpororo. In addition, the Mpororo pattern of incorporating the raiders of Nkore as an executive organ of the cult provided both the vocabulary and the precedent for further efforts to breach traditional ethno-political alignments in the name of Nyabingi.

The distribution of the cult in the precontact period was conspicuously restricted, due both to the systemic limitations of the cult operation and the material interests of the *bagirwa*. Until the colonial period, no effort was made to penetrate the mountainous, acephalous areas of Kigezi or to challenge directly the core areas of the larger kingdoms. Rather, cult activity ranged through areas politically peripheral and territorially marginal to these kingdoms: in the northern and loosely administered provinces of Rwanda and in Mpororo, a buffer zone between the kingdoms of Nkore and Karagwe. Both regions were, however, centralized. Both were joined as well to these more powerful kingdoms in an attenuated tributary or garrison relationship. It may in fact be argued that the political discontent and anxiety of these areas, their fear of greater incorporation, and their resentment of their position of marginal exploitation made them particularly vulnerable to the attentions of the *bagirwa*. In addition, of course, their centralized networks for the collection of tax and labor and their predominantly pastoral focus provided strong economic incentives for cult activity in these areas. The acephalous and agricultural Kiga, in contrast, afforded little economic interest or organizational potential for the traditional *bagirwa*. Only with the political pressures of the expanding colonial frontier and with the introduction of patterns of centralization by the colonial power could the cult turn with success to this previously inhospitable area.

The extension of the Nyabingi cult into Kigezi under Muhumusa was primarily a defensive action, first against the forces of Musinga, then against the actions of the German officials. Whereas the expansion of the cult in earlier contexts had been motivated by a desire to enlarge the tributary structure which the *bagirwa* commanded, the concern of Muhumusa was not with the richness or vulnerability of the area but rather with seeking refuge from further political harassment. In her retreat northward she was forced into a region which not only lacked the exploitative potential of Rwanda and Mpororo, but also had no tradition of political subordination under either secular or supernatural leadership.

The absence of a model for political centralization, although it inhibited the rapid absorption of the Ndorwa area into the cult orbit, did prove structurally advantageous in one respect, for it eliminated the need to contest an existing political base whose leaders would view the activities of the *bagirwa* as a direct threat to their control of privileged interests. The virulence of the cult in Rwanda and Mpororo thus had no analogue in the Kiga area where conflicting allegiances to indigenous political institutions were absent. In Rukiga, rather, the issue was autonomy, the maintenance of local enclaves of agnatic kinsmen against the incursions of other Kiga, or the encroaching boundaries of Rwanda. One would assume in such a situation that any effort to superimpose a centralized structure would be resisted, let alone the predations of a fugitive and politically disabled cult leader from Rwanda.

In assessing the response of the Kiga to Muhumusa, the role of the cult in northern Rwanda would appear critical. The commitment of the Hutu to the cult as a mechanism for liberation from Tutsi domination, inasmuch as it created a barrier to Rwanda expansion, may have provided a major impetus for the passive acceptance of Muhumusa in Kiga areas.

Although there is sufficient evidence of the intimidatory tactics of Muhumusa and of her ruthlessness toward non-adherents, she clearly was able rapidly to absorb southeastern Kigezi into her tributary network. Whether this should be viewed as open and voluntary support is, however, another matter. More likely, the motive for nominal adherence was fear of her reputed supernatural or secular powers. Equally compelling were the activities of her entourage. Presumably also the rewards of cult allegiance—absorption into the patronage system—tempered the resentment of many Kiga toward her tributary demands.

The acceptance of the Nyabingi cult by the Kiga was also encouraged by certain structural and contextual factors. Foremost among these was the existence of similar *emandwa* cults within the magico-religious system of the Kiga. The cult, although intrusive, could thus be easily incorporated into an existing system. The political dimension of cult activity, although without parallel among the Kiga *emandwa*, was also implicit in the incipient ranking by reputation and territorial range which characterized the *emandwa* systems of the region. This existing hierarchy, though relevant only to reputation, again prepared the Kiga to accept the claims of Muhumusa to political ascendancy.

Additional leverage for pressing political claims came from the very nature of cult power. Secular attempts to incorporate the Kiga had met with fierce resistance, but, as religious specialists, the *bagirwa* could activate the one role which in the egalitarian Kiga society had the greatest potential for prestige and influence. Moreover, the existing reputation of the cult and its known importance in the adjacent areas of Mpororo and northern Rwanda must also have disposed the Kiga to accept the claims of Muhumusa.

The internal structure of the cult in itself provided an important model for political centralization. With access to Nyabingi confined to the individual claiming to be the personification of the spirit, cult participation was in itself hierarchical, for all others were dependent on the *bagirwa* to intercede in contacting the spirit. This systemic advantage was unquestionably compounded by the personal attributes of the early *bagirwa* who were not only supernaturally powerful but royal Tutsi. As such they entered Kigezi with a domestic entourage and life style commensurate with their secular origins. These accoutrements of royal status could not fail to impress the simple Kiga and to reinforce the validity of the *bagirwa's* political claims or the privileged inaccessibility of such power. In addition, the Mpororo legend which placed the origin of the cult in the royal court of Ndorwa unquestionably strengthened both this parameter of cult power and the legitimacy of Muhumusa's claim to southern Kigezi.

Other factors, by virtue of their discontinuity from traditional political expectations or existing social alignments, decreased the perceived dislocations of existing institutions by the cult, and, by implication, the resistance of the Kiga to its advance.

The general eccentricities of behavior displayed by the *bagirwa,* which served to validate the exclusivity of their claims, unquestionably provided a psychological obstacle of considerable proportions, for they were without precedent in the traditional political or religious roles of the Kiga. The tenacity of Muhumusa's reputation for over three decades after her arrest reveals the full impact of these mannerisms on the Kiga.

Additional mechanisms for displacement, highly effective although inadvertent, were 1) the high proportion of female *bagirwa*, a factor which directly undercut the traditional patrilineal authority structure of the Kiga, and 2) the external origins of the major cult leaders. As Rwanda or Congolese they avoided any factional indentification with either local territorial segments or local clans, affiliations which could readily have undermined their claims to universal allegiance.

The rapid transformation of the Nyabingi cult in Kigezi into a vehicle for anti-European protest occurred largely in response to the motives of the leading *mugirwa*, Muhumusa. Embittered by her treatment by the Germans in northern Ruanda and threatened by British encroachment into Ndorwa, she set aside the earlier issue of the Rwanda throne to marshal her energies against these new intruders. The anti-European focus of the movement, so striking in its rapid growth, was thus no more than a deflection of the existing political dynamics of the region. The comparability of grievances and aims and the success of traditional operational tactics in dealing with both the local Kiga and with the British may in part explain the conservative character of the cult after contact and the delay in the intrusion of syncretistic elements until the second decade of resistance. Certainly the ideology of protest which supported cult activity in Rwanda could be applied to the colonial situation virtually without modification.

The personal hostility of Muhumusa to Europeans does not, however, provide an adequate basis for co-ordinated regional protest. The increasing degree of popular support for the movement, beyond the personal entourage of the *bagirwa*, attests to an increasing degree of general resentment at the presence of the British.

Because of the attenuated character of initial colonial occupation, sensitivity to Europeans and discontent with their demands were generated by a limited series of incidents and issues. Spared any intrusion of mining or settler populations, the economic issue was not land, but rather the early attempts of the British to obtain taxes and labor from the people of the district. Although efforts to collect taxes or recruit labor were unsystematic and irregular, particularly during the war years, the tendency of the administration to counter early recalcitrance with "rigorous police operations" created a degree of hostility which bore little relation to the amounts actually collected. By 1917 the administrative structure in central Kigezi had stabilized sufficiently to permit a more effective and regular exploitation of the adjacent populations. The degree of resentment which these demands elicited is amply verified by the scale and unanimity of the Nyakishenyi rebellion.

The second major source of political tension was the presence of the Ganda agents. The tendency of these men to maximize their personal gain through bribery, administrative abuses, and extortion; their lack of identification as aliens with Kiga interests; and their manipulation of their intercalary position between the British and the Kiga generated an atmosphere of frustration, anger, and fear on the part of the Kiga. This in turn increased their vulnerability to the counterclaims of the *bagirwa*, who promised to drive not merely the inaccessible British from the area, but also their hated representatives. Given the hostility of the Kiga toward these alien chiefs and the tangibility of their grievances, it is not surprising that the major focus for acts of organized violence was the Agent, not the European administrator. Their role in providing the major impetus for open resistance is further confirmed by the geographical distribution of cult-incited violence; it was concentrated in central and northern Rukiga, areas which lacked a traditional chiefly structure which could provide either a buffer between the Agent and the people or a direct channel of access to the British officer. Here the presence of the Agent under such circumstances was oppressive and vulnerable to abuse.

If the activity of the early *bagirwa* was motivated more by personal aggrandizement than by ideology, the response of the Kiga was also instrumental. Although aware that the demands of cult allegiance represented in one respect yet another erosion of their traditional autonomy, the Kiga clearly assumed that in aligning themselves with the *bagirwa* conditions under the suzerainty of the cult would be improved: either less oppressive, less threatening to their life style, or, alternately, more easily evaded. Support of the cult thus became a conscious strategy by which the Kiga sought to reinstate at least a measure of their independence.

The modality of local resistance throughout most of the period of cult activism confirms this interpretation for, with the exception of the isolated, large-scale operations of 1916, 1919, and 1928, open harassment of loyalist chiefs, agents, or British personnel was undertaken only by the immediate entourage of the *bagirwa* and then most frequently in brief forays from bases in other territories. The role of the population at large, although clearly sympathetic to the cult, was passive, devoted either to providing the essential intelligence network to protect cult movements or to evading by non-compliance or physical withdrawal the demands of the British superstructure and its local representatives. On those occasions where activism occurred, it was either a regional attempt to co-ordinate local anti-British sentiment or independently expressed as isolated and spontaneous acts of resistance to demands for tax or labor. Similarly, cult allegiance was manifested by local chiefs for the most part in inefficiency, evasion, and failure to perform orders, not in an open challenge of British authority or overt noncompliance.

However instrumental the motives for local support of the Nyabingi cult, the sympathy and co-operation which the cult elicited were crucial to its success: to its effectiveness in confronting any given British tactic, to its evasion of detection, and to its tenacity over time. Not only did this network of co-operation ensure that information about European movements and plans would be conveyed to the *bagirwa,* but it constricted and distorted the flow of information to the British. The scale of support also proved a major constraint on anyone who might oppose the *bagirwa* or serve as an informant, for opposition to the cult brought the threat of disgrace and even death.

The solidarity of support evidenced in this communications' network was not, however, a simple response to the political expediencies of the Kiga. The tenacity of the movement, despite periodic defeats of often devastating proportions, attests to the resilience of the cult itself. In addition to an internally generated predisposition on the part of the Kiga to align themselves with cult interests, there were a number of systemic and situational factors which also contributed to the enduring reputation of the cult.

Although the cult was graced with an ideological resiliency in the potency of the spirit after the death, defeat, or flight of any given *mugirwa*, the success of the major *bagirwa* and their sustained skill in evading British capture unquestionably generated considerable enthusiasm and support for the cult and a high degree of vicarious identification with the *mugirwa* in question, who became, for the more passive, a symbol of defiance to colonial rule.

The actions of Ndochibiri, who clearly attained the status of a folk hero before his capture and death in 1919, played a major role in the tenacity of cult influence during the colonial period for they confirmed the legendary power of the Nyabingi. Moreover, his abandonment of the exploitative tactics of the early *bagirwa* marked a major shift in the focus of cult activity since his concern was not with consolidating tributary networks, but rather with enlisting local support in opposition to colonial rule. The economic motives of the earlier *bagirwa* were supplanted by an ideology of political emancipation. Ndochibiri's shift from an emphasis on submission to one of local co-operation, symbolized by his egalitarian consolidation of support through blood brotherhood with local chiefs, may have been a response to the absence of an indigenous model for centralization in Rukiga. Such considerations had not deterred the more imperious Muhumusa, however, who had subdued the southern Kiga before the introduction of the British superstructure which Ndochibiri so cleverly manipulated. Far more relevant in defining Ndochibiri's egalitarian approach were his acephalous Congolese origins, the new conditions for opposition created by the tightening of British control, and their more systematic harassment of the *bagirwa*. Unlike Muhumusa, who could move freely on the periphery of British influence, Ndochibiri faced a co-ordinated interterritorial political network which imposed artificial restrictions on his movements. The intimidation and fear upon which the earlier *bagirwa* had based their influence had little place in such a world. Success could no longer be defined in terms of a reluctant capitulation to tributary demands; it required a real measure of support, an active and voluntary co-operation with the cult organization, and a willingness to protect the more activist members from British detection. As a measure of cult identification was unquestionably higher and less intimidatory under Ndochibiri, the tenacity of Muhumusa's reputation and the selection of Ndungutsi, not Ndochibiri, as the symbol of cult immortality, appear even more curious. One can only assume that the activities and the origins of these *bagirwa*, although less palatable, provided a higher degree of congruence with the traditional cult image.

Although the actions and expectations of the *bagirwa* and the displacement of cult power from any specific carrier, both intrinsic cult features, unquestionably contributed to the tenacity of the cult in the colonial period, other more fortuitous factors also proved critical to the enduring strength and periodic resurgence of the Nyabingi cult.

The character of colonial administration in the area also, if inadvertently, facilitated the success of the movement. Most critically, the European image was not monolithic. As the Mfumbiro area fell under the jurisdiction of three colonial powers with different languages, different administrative policies, and different images of their role in this area, the implicit political heterogeneity of the situation was invested with administrative reality. Moreover, the administration of each territory was not a self-contained operation. Each political power openly competed for the region as an extension of its existing colonial interests. The factionalism which this competition generated, and its eruption into open conflict during the early boundary disputes and World War I, could only erode the impression of inevitability and immutability which attends unchallenged colonial expansion.

The political position of the Mfumbiro region also proved a fortuitous, yet significant, feature of cult tenacity. For each colonial power, the Mfumbiro region represented an economic and political hinterland. This marginality to both the interests of the colonial powers and to the capital of each territory resulted in an attenuated pattern of administrative supervision within which intervention in local affairs was sporadic and often arbitrary, creating not merely an acknowledged situation of weakness, but limited access to popular sentiment or discontent.

The geographical delineation of southwestern Uganda to accommodate British claims south of the first degree parallel resulted in an administratively vulnerable definition of Kigezi district. In addition to isolating the district from other administrative centers within the protectorate, it increased its exposure to three other territories. Thus the geographic position of Kigezi, combined with the defective supervision which characterized the entire region, lent itself readily to the manipulation of international boundaries as vehicles of evasion. Given the weak administrative structure, the defective channels of communication, and the administrative encumbrances of "international" appeals for co-operation, the borders themselves provided an effective constraint on colonial action against the movement. The region itself, an area of rugged volcanic mountains, impenetrable forests, and lava caves also provided a natural refuge for the cult and a formidable barrier against effective colonial supervision. These natural advantages, again fortuitous, played a critical role in the protracted evasion of the British officials.

Although all these factors serve to clarify the tenacity of the cult in Kigezi, the degree of regional co-ordination exhibited during certain phases of the movement requires further amplification. To accept the cult as the most promising vehicle for local protest is one thing. To submerge traditional or intertribal suspicion and hostility in a common effort to eliminate Europeans is another. This new level of political identification—one which aligned the indigenous population in common opposition to the colonial intruders and which overrode traditional barriers of language and tribe—was, in a very real sense, a creation of the colonial powers themselves.

The intrusion of a colonial power, disruptive under any circumstances, was exacerbated in this instance by the assignment of homogenous populations to three separate administrative systems: Uganda, German East Africa, and the Belgian Congo. This fragmentation of traditionally autonomous groupings, in addition to creating centrifugal pressures to reaffirm the traditional unit at the expense of the international boundaries, succeeded in severely dislocating the existing political networks and the traditional dynamics of intertribal opposition. In such circumstances, it is not surprising that traditional hostilities or even predispositions to intertribal xenophobia were submerged to create a new level of political identification.

Given this pressure for more inclusive identification, the Nyabingi cult provided several organizational advantages: 1) the leader was not of the local tribe, thereby avoiding the dangers of factional identification with any local territorial segment or kin group, 2) the leaders were often women, undercutting the patrilineal authority structure which characterized the region, and 3) the cult, by projecting the source of power onto a supernatural level, both manipulated the existing pan-tribal institution of the *emandwa* cult as a framework for unification and removed cult allegiance from competition with existing secular political affiliations.

Although intertribal co-ordination of the movement was essential to its sustained opposition to three colonial powers, the irregular distribution of the cult suggests that the local political context was as critical in defining its more virulent manifestations as any inherent feature in the cult itself. The appearance of the cult as a vehicle for anti-European resistance was confined to the egalitarian populations of central and northern Kigezi and to the Hutu-dominated areas of northern Ruanda and southern Kigezi. The ethnic alignments of both these populations support the position of analysts who feel that an acephalous tribe under the pressure of colonial rule is particularly susceptible to such movements.

Perhaps fully as critical, however, was the degree of local identification with the lower level of the colonial administrative hierarchy. In the acephalous areas of Kigezi the British relied on the introduction of men from another tribe. Therefore, no intertribal political tensions between local chiefs and rebel leaders were created. The opposition of indigenous to colonial interests was in consequence much more salient.

These dynamics of opposition would, in turn, explain the immunity of the Hororo and the Tutsi to cult allegiance. Ruzumbura, in spite of the high degree of cult activity at the end of the nineteenth century, remained indifferent to colonial opposition and to the activities of the *bagirwa* in adjacent areas. Here, however, the chiefly structure was not merely recruited locally but had, from the earliest period, managed to maintain a considerable degree of autonomy. With the virtual abandonment of British supervision during the war, the Hororo had little occasion to protest either the presence of the British or the character of local control.

Similarly the Tutsi, long the object of cult activity in Rwanda, had little incentive for identifying with Nyabingi regardless of their resentment of the European. Sustained resistance, as we have noted, did occur among the Tutsi in British areas, but it was secular in nature and primarily an affirmation of their identification with Musinga in German East Africa. In defying the international boundaries which had severed the kingdom of Rwanda, the hostility of the Tutsi to the colonial political situation was explicitly anti-British with pro-German sentiment serving as a vehicle for reasserting their ethnic identity with core Rwanda. Also inhibiting cult activity in Tutsi areas was the character of the local chiefly structure. As in Ruzumbura, southern Kigezi had maintained both a greater degree of autonomy from British supervision than central Kigezi and a basic continuity between indigenous and colonial chieftaincies. The cult therefore remained, as traditionally defined, a vehicle for protest against the chiefly system. The major factor behind differential response to the cult therefore appears to be more immediately a consequence of the continuity and degree of representativeness of local chiefly personnel, not the degree of centralization. By implication, however, one would expect a higher degree of congruence between these variables in centralized areas.

The force of the Nyabingi cult may be put in one final perspective by examining the factors contributing to its sudden displacement in 1928 as a vehicle for anti-European sentiment. Although the redefinition of the cult at that time was rapid and final, its loss of political focus was a response to a complex series of pressures, some of which had been initiated a full decade before.

With the death of Ndochibiri, British policy toward the cult underwent a striking tactical change. Suppressive military measures, which had only aggravated the polarity of colonial and local interests, were replaced in 1919 by a strategy of positive indoctrination designed to undermine the reputation of the cult and to correct the conditions which had generated political unrest. In addition to a greater accommodation with regard to tax and labor demands, the local administrative structure was itself subject to major reforms: Agents who were known to have abused their positions were immediately removed, and additional measures were taken in preparation for the eventual replacement of the entire Agent system by locally recruited chiefs.

These positive reforms represented one aspect of British action against the cult; efforts were also made at this time directly to challenge cult activity and the existing reputation of the cult leaders. Although popular sentiment continued to identify with the *bagirwa* throughout the 1920's, the increasing efficiency of the district administration, greater efforts at interdistrict and international co-ordination, and the tightening of the communications' network within the district created more effective conditions for the detection and capture of cult practitioners. In addition, with a more systematic application of the Witchcraft Ordinance and the deportation of the more important *bagirwa,* a jural context was established which directly and forcefully challenged the claims of the cult leaders to greater power. Finally efforts were made to engage local support through the return of extorted cattle, the depreciation of cult powers, the confiscation of cult objects, and public exhortations to renounce cult affiliation. Although in isolation such propaganda would have been without value, the increasing control demonstrated by other political and judicial measures and the evidence of benign intent implicit in the various administrative reforms all served to undermine the reputation of the *bagirwa* and to support British claims to political ascendancy. Moreover, the affirmation of British strength through administrative reforms offered a positive alternative to cult affiliation. Identification with the encroaching world of the Europeans became a matter of political expediency if not of conviction.

The failure of cult leaders to command a position of political prominence after the 1928 rebellion was not only a consequence of British action per se but also reflected the increasing disillusionment of the Kigezi populations with the disparities between the claimed goals and actual achievements of the cult in resisting the encroaching colonial powers. The inability of later *bagirwa* to generate anti-British sentiment in Kigezi reflects the degree to which this apathy was already entrenched among the acephalous populations. Although the intensification of repressive colonial measures after the death of Ndochibiri had in large part set the conditions for an eventual rejection of the movement, their efficacy required the alienation of local populations from the movement itself. The swift and decisive action of the British in suppressing the 1928 rebellion provided the critical catalyst for accelerating this growing disaffection. The dispatch with which they routed such a highly organized operation dramatically confirmed for the Kiga the futility of further resistance. It was this disillusionment alone which contained the continuing activism of *bagirwa* beyond the borders of Kigezi.

The reputation of the Nyabingi cult was unquestionably compromised by the repeated failure of the *bagirwa* effectively to challenge the British occupation, but other factors also contributed to the decline of the cult in the late 1920's. Foremost among these was the increasing incorporation of local Africans into the colonial administrative structure and into the local mission hierarchies. Through recruitment into these organizations, Africans were also absorbed into the underlying incentive system of the colonial power. This process was of particular significance in the acephalous areas where the movement of local Africans into the higher levels of the chiefly structure for the first time created a vested local interest in the colonial bureaucracy and an effective channel for the direct expression of local discontent. This new participation in the formal political network seriously undermined the vicarious displacement of political sentiment previously provided by cult participation. Nyabingi offered no promise of a return to traditional autonomy for the local Kiga but rather an alternate pattern for centralization—one in which the monopoly of power remained in the hands of the alien *bagirwa*. The British, in contrast, had created new channels for status and mobility and given the promise of local self-administration. While the Kiga could not, in any event, hope to regain their traditional autonomy, the British at least offered a more viable channel for political expression.

This attitudinal shift, so critical for the dissolution of the movement, was further reinforced by the emergence of a local African elite. The substitution of new criteria for prestige and power, inevitable with the acquisition of positions of local prominence, directly undermined the indigenous traditions of privilege which had validated the claims of the *bagirwa* to political ascendancy. The colonial superstructure itself became the major vehicle for political participation. With this increasing identification with the colonial power, the prospect of cult dominance and the promise of a new order of political unity within an alien traditional idiom could offer little ideological competition to the perceived rewards of mobility and local recognition of the existing British system.

An additional weakness of the Nyabingi cult was inherent in its ideology: despite its magico-religious matrix, the cult remained secular in intent. Offering no passive or vicarious alternative to open resistance, its repeated failure to rout local British officials could only confirm the futility of open opposition and the irreversibility of the colonial process. Resistance to European occupation, where it occurred, reverted to the traditional acephalous idiom: to tactics of evasion or to independent acts of covert aggression. Although no efforts at open rebellion were organized after 1928, by the mid-1930's arson, an offense which lent itself admirably to the evasion of detection or prosecution, was being systematically employed against local authorities in Kigezi. Arson had been traditionally employed as an integral feature of the raiding complex, but this earlier context offered no precedent for its emergence as a major modality for political discontent. Its transformation suggests, however, the relevance of the strengthening colonial context and a need for increasing circumspection in defying British rule.

The sudden dislocation of the cult from its enduring role as a vehicle for political protest marked the end of co-ordinated opposition to British rule in Kigezi. No further effort was made to challenge the presence of Europeans; rather, local political energies, confirming the premise of European occupation, were channeled into a manipulation of and movement within the system itself. This stability and increasing efficiency of the district administrative structure as it moved into the 1930's, the increasing local tolerance of the many inconveniences and restrictions which its continuing presence implied, and the expansion of options for direct participation eroded both the original stimulus and conditions for local resistance.

With this attenuation of local resentment there was no longer a felt need for either an open or a vicarious rejection of the colonial superstructure. The polarity of focus, so critical to the endurance of the cult in both the precontact and early colonial periods, was lost in the growing congruence of colonial aims and African needs. Within this changing context the cult of Nyabingi could offer no viable alternative, either structurally or ideologically, to the process of colonial expansion. The abandonment of the cult was thus in a very real sense inevitable, for its relative weakness had been repeatedly demonstrated and the world which it promised was no longer real or desired.

PSYCHOLOGICAL STRESS AND

THE QUESTION OF IDENTITY:

CHILEMBWE'S REVOLT RECONSIDERED

ROBERT I. ROTBERG

In early 1915 a number of Africans led by John Chilembwe rose against the established order of the Protectorate of Nyasaland, killed three whites, wounded two others, and, for at least a brief time, threatened radically to stem the growth of settler power. The course of the rising and the social, economic, and political circumstances which preceded it and made it possible are by now well known and are summarized below. But the critical questions—precisely why its American educated leader, hitherto a respected member of the community, fomented revolt, and what he and his followers intended by so doing—continue to perplex students of this rising, of protest movements in Africa, and of revolution everywhere.

Did Chilembwe seek to make himself king of Nyasaland in the manner of Christophe of Haiti, Prester John (of the book by John Buchan), or the hero of George Heaton-Nicholls's *Bayete!*?[1] If victorious, what then? Or did he anticipate defeat and plan with that

[1] Buchan's *Prester John* was first published in London in 1910. Heaton-Nicholls's work, which was written with apparent prescience in 1913, was not published until 1923, in London. It describes the rise and triumph of Nelson Balumbata, a chief's son who attends a Negro seminary in Virginia, returns to South Africa, and soon obtains a widespread religious following among Africans. He understands that organization is strength in the South African context, and under his direction Africans withdraw all of their labor from white employment, thus forcing the ruling whites to agree to grant full adult suffrage to Africans. Balumbata enters Parliament with his African supporters, becomes the power behind the white-led cabinet, and subsequently, after much intrigue, leads a successful military revolution with Arab and American assistance. An earlier version of this paper was enriched by the comments and suggestions of John Demos, Hans Hofmann, Bruce Mazlish, Joseph S. Nye, William Griffith, Stanley M. Elkins, George Shepperson, and my fellow members of the Boston Group for Applied Psychoanalysis.

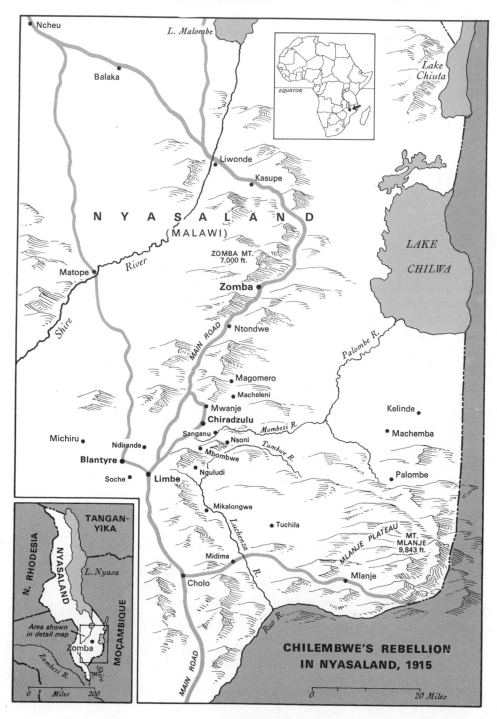

CHILEMBWE'S REBELLION
IN NYASALAND, 1915

contingency in mind? Did Chilembwe seek martyrdom and merely intend his rebellion as a flamboyant gesture of protest? What did he want? And why did he care? Were there psychological factors which presupposed revolt? What, in sum, gave a sense of purpose to the rising and sustained Chilembwe throughout the period of its gestation and emergence?

These questions can probably never be answered indisputably. Rebels sometimes make demands of authority in writing, justify their actions in printed or diary form, or are called upon to explain their deeds to a tribunal or a commission of inquiry. But for the Nyasa rising of 1915 there now exist no explanations or tracts by Chilembwe, nor is there reliable testimony by those of his followers who were later summarily tried for participating in the conspiracy. Similarly, there exist no first-hand accounts by persons who could claim an intimate acquaintance with Chilembwe or a real appreciation of his motives. On the other hand, there is no dearth of contemporary assertion and contemporary or nearly contemporary speculation. There are reminiscences by whites and at least two lengthy African views of the rising which, from internal and external evidence, hardly seem capable of having been manufactured. The reminiscences and one African account, that by Andrew G. Mkulichi, a rebel, were used by George S, Mwase in a book which has recently been published. Its detailed reconstruction of the events of 1915 depends in turn upon the testimony of Wallace Kampingo, another of the rebels.[2] A reconsideration of Chilembwe's motives is also assisted by newly discovered contemporary data—primarily the papers of a mysterious African shopkeeper named Haya Edward Peters. Future advances in our understanding of the Chilembwe phenomenon will obviously depend almost exclusively on the finding of contemporary materials, if any, which are today unknown.

The main events of the rising are not in dispute. On the night of 23 January 1915, after a period of preparation that lasted no more than two months, the "battalions" of Chilembwe's small army of conspirators issued forth from the small church at Mbombwe, the headquarters of his Providence Industrial Mission. Some battalions went south to Blantyre and Limbe, the white-dominated commercial centers of the Protectorate. Another headed toward the estates of Nsoni and Midima. Two other patrols or platoons, for the term battalion grossly overestimates their size, effectiveness, and purpose, followed the twisting

[2] George Shepperson and Thomas Price, *Independent African, John Chilembwe and the Origins, Setting and Significance of the Nyasaland Native Rising of 1915* (Edinburgh, 1958); George S. Mwase, *Strike a Blow and Die. A Narrative of Race Relations in Colonial Africa*, ed. Robert I. Rotberg (Cambridge, 1967).

paths northward to the nearby vast estates of Alexander Livingstone Bruce.[3] A message was also dispatched to Ncheu, 110 miles northwest of Mbombwe, where Filipo Chinyama had promised to foment a complementary revolt. Finally, Chilembwe sent a courier to German-ruled East Africa with a communication about the rising.

The rebels first drew blood at Magomero, the headquarters of the Bruce estate. There William Jervis Livingstone, the manager of the estate, and his wife were entertaining Mrs. Ranald MacDonald, the wife of a customs official. In a nearby house occupied by the custodian of the local rifle club's ammunition supply, were Mrs. Emily Stanton and Mrs. Alyce Roach. The four women were accompanied by five children. Duncan MacCormick, an estate employee, was alone in a third house. None had any forewarning of the attack, although their servants, at least some of whom later demonstrated their loyalty to the women and children involved, certainly knew for what purposes the battalion had come.

The rebels wanted Livingstone's head, and, after a slight skirmish, during which Livingstone was wounded, one of the attackers forced his way into a bedroom where Mrs. Livingstone was vainly attempting to revive her husband, and—she later recalled—"with an axe proceeded to cut off my husband's head."[4] By this time MacCormick, alerted by his servants, had come to the assistance of the Livingstones. But the rebels met his advance with spears, and he died beside William Livingstone. Throughout the attack, however, none of the women and children at Magomero was in any way harmed or molested, and Mrs. MacDonald's attempt forcibly to halt the rebels' attack was ignored. In addition, aside from the arsenal, the existence of which had helped to prompt the attack, the rebels looted no property and returned to Mbombwe with only a few rifles, some ammunition, and Livingstone's head. It was placed atop a pole in the Mbombwe church.

While the attack at Magomero was taking place, the second battalion shed blood at Mwanje, another section of the Bruce estate. These members of the battalion speared Robert Ferguson, the stock manager, on his bed, but he managed to stagger a few yards to the house of the section manager. There John and Charlotte Robertson's preparations for bed were interrupted, and a running gun battle ensued until the

[3] The exact size of Chilembwe's army is unknown. Modern estimates range from two hundred to nine hundred men; contemporaries judged his cadre to number several thousand, but they may have blurred the distinction between followers or supporters and men under arms.

[4] GOA 2/4/14: Statement of Katherine Livingstone, 2 Feb. 1915, Zomba archives. A lengthier account of these and the following events will be found in Robert I. Rotberg, *The Rise of Nationalism in Central Africa* (Cambridge, 1965), 87-90.

Robertsons escaped into a cotton field. The Robertsons could never explain why they should have been attacked and Ferguson killed. The battalion may have hoped to find a cache of arms or may have intended simply to safeguard the line of retreat from Magomero. In any event it returned empty-handed to Mbombwe.

The raid on the isolated planters at Nsoni and Midima never took place, but telephone lines between Zomba and Tete and Blantyre and Mikalongwe were severed. The battalions which were primed to attack the *boma* in Blantyre and commercial establishments in nearby Limbe failed to act. Similarly, after vainly waiting for the Nsoni/Midima battalion to join them, the seventy rebels who had been instructed to break into the arms warehouse in neighboring Mandala were able to complete their mission with only partial success (seizing a few rifles and seven hundred rounds of ammunition) because supposedly loyal African watchmen and soldiers turned against them. The untended *boma* at Chiradzulu, a mere five miles from Mbombwe, was never threatened;[5] the rebels likewise refrained from attacking the numerous whites who lived without protection on prosperous estates within a twenty mile radius of Mbombwe and Magomero; and the men of Mbombwe resorted to arms again only on 26 January when they severely wounded Father Swelsen, a Roman Catholic priest, and set his Nguludi mission on fire. It is impossible to guess whether the rebels under Filipo Chinyama really intended—as Mwase reports[6]—to make their way southward to join Chilembwe; before they could even attack the Ncheu *boma* an alert administrator learned of their intentions from several loyalist chiefs and arrested Chinyama and company without a struggle. Nor is it possible to say whether or not Chilembwe and Chinyama expected their initiative to stimulate a mass uprising among the peoples of southern Nyasaland. Only thus could the rebellion have succeeded, but Chilembwe spent the days of the revolution meditating atop a hill near Mbombwe. He seems, furthermore, to have prepared no line of defense and to have failed to fortify his mission station. More surprisingly, although the possibility of failure was discussed, no systematic retreat was planned or put into effect.

The uprising was short-lived. By 26 January hastily raised white volunteers had pressed an attack on Mbombwe, where they were resisted only for a day. Many of the rebels fled, or attempted with little success to mingle with noncombatant villagers; Chilembwe himself was finally persuaded to leave his hill and seek refuge in neighboring Moçambique; and, after the expenditure of much dynamite, whites

[5] An allusion by Mwase indicates that an attack on Chiradzulu conceivably may have been intended. Mwase, *Strike a Blow*, 37, 43.

[6] Ibid.

managed to destroy the thick-walled church at Mbombwe. On 3 February Chilembwe was killed by a small patrol north of Mlanje, and, by the end of March, forty rebels had lost their lives on the scaffold or before firing squads and about three hundred had been imprisoned.[7]

The ease with which the rising was suppressed immediately encouraged confident drawing of conclusions about its origins: Why, observers and antagonists asked themselves, had Africans risen so unexpectedly? What moved the rising's presumably fanatical leader, of whom few had hitherto heard? And what had he and the rebels expected to achieve?

General answers to the first question proved easiest to supply. The attack on Magomero obviously implied hostility toward Livingstone and the Bruce estates. It was accepted in settler and official circles that Africans who had worked for the estate or lived within its three hundred square miles might justifiably have complained about the way in which they had been treated. Livingstone's rule had been especially iniquitous and objectionable, and he had in a wanton manner destroyed prayer houses of the Providence Industrial Mission. Even the official commission of inquiry, whose report could hardly have been expected to be critical of settlers, felt compelled to say that "Livingstone's treatment of natives was often unduly harsh and apart from this the general system of estate management was not satisfactory."[8] The members of the commission and their contemporaries were also forced to acknowledge that whether on or off the lands owned by Bruce, Africans felt systematically discriminated against, were subjected to severe curtailments of their personal liberty, and almost always were treated by whites with disrespect. Subsequent investigations have substantiated these accusations and emphasized the extent to which Africans resented their cruel rejection by the official society of white-ruled Nyasaland. Their social and psychological grievances were real and keenly felt, and are not to be underestimated.

But the existence of social and psychological grievances is insufficient to explain with what intent Chilembwe transformed a widespread and rather discontinuous energy of disaffection into the actuality of revolution. The then Governor of Nyasaland was naturally the first person (of whom we have any record) to commit his conclusions to writing. On the day of Chilembwe's death he reported to the Colonial

[7] S 1/946/19: Statement of Sir George Smith.

[8] *Report of the Commission Appointed by His Excellency the Governor to Inquire into Various Matters and Questions concerned with the Native Rising within the Nyasaland Protectorate*, 6819 (1916). For a further discussion of social grievances, see Shepperson and Price, *Independent African*, 225-30, 384; Rotberg, *Rise*, 27-36, 39-45, 53-54, 78-80; Mwase, *Strike a Blow*, 29-33.

Office that the various papers and books which had been seized in Chilembwe's house "prove and disclose a wide and well-organized movement to attack and massacre the whites."[9] A few weeks later the official responsible for the administration of the Blantyre district probably spoke for many of his colleagues when he opined that "John Chilembwe wanted to become King of Nyasaland." (The Yao chief, Malemia, believed that Chilembwe wanted to be "the Governor.")[10] Unlike some observers, however, this administrator advanced the paradoxical but perceptive explanation that Chilembwe "and his educated accomplices must have persuaded themselves that there existed a general disaffection towards Europeans which would result in a widespread rising following immediately on his first attack on the white men . . . [but] with the exception of the attack on Magomero there can never have been a more irresolute and half-hearted rising. It seems clear to me that there existed no real desire to kill Europeans among the bulk of John Chilembwe's followers. . . . My own belief is that, with the exception of the ringleaders, no one knew what Chilembwe contemplated, and the bulk of his followers did not know for what they were called out. That they were animated by no common grievance against the Government or Europeans as a whole I feel sure."[11]

The commission of inquiry, whose members were all local men naturally sympathetic to their peers, finally presented its official report early in 1916.[12] The commission decided that "The objects of the rising were the extermination or expulsion of the European population, and the setting up of a native state or theocracy of which John Chilembwe was to be the head." But it failed to define any of these terms or to demonstrate the nature of the information which indicated such un-

[9] CO 525/61: George Smith to the Colonial Office, 3 Feb. 1915. PRO. Much, if not all, of the correspondence and books referred to by the Governor failed to survive a fire in Nyasaland's Secretariat in 1919. For a further repetition of the Governor's reaction, see Reginald Charles Fulke Maugham, *Nyasaland in the Nineties and Other Recollections* (London, 1935), 55-56, and, on the derivative nature of Maugham's evidence, Shepperson and Price, *Independent African*, 467, n. 74. But Shepperson and Price may unintentionally have been misled into thinking that the Governor's published statement (ibid., 219-20) was written in 1915 rather than 1919. See below, n. 13.

[10] Quoted in Shepperson and Price, *Independent African*, 251.

[11] L. T. Moggridge, Annual District Report, 31 Mar. 1915, Zomba archives.

[12] The chairman of the commission was Judge Robert William Lyall Grant, the leading jurist in the Protectorate. He was joined by Aubrey Marriott Dalway Turnbull, the Assistant Chief Secretary of the Protectorate; Joseph Charles Casson, Superintendent of Native Affairs; the Hon. Arthur George Bernard Glossop, Anglican Archdeacon of Likoma; and Claude Metcalfe, the General Manager of the British Central Africa Company, which owned numerous large estates in the Shire Highlands.

equivocal conclusions. Indeed, presumably because such a conclusion was in no way controversial, the commissioners saw no need either to supplement or modify their bald statement. If today it begs innumerable questions, the chief of which must be to reconcile Chilembwe's methods and the scale of his operations with his possible goals, then it reflected the locally acceptable stereotype and, in ruling circles at least, was never openly challenged. Nyasaland, moreover, was embroiled in war against the Germans, and most whites were readily prepared to accept the commission's findings as definitive. Sir George Smith, who was still the Governor of Nyasaland in 1919, saw no reason to modify his original views, or to take issue with the commission, when he submitted a chapter on his country to Sir Charles P. Lucas's *The Empire at War*, a five volume compilation of essays from the far-flung colonies of the Crown. "The movement," Smith wrote of Chilembwe's rising, "was designed [unquestionably] for the massacre of whites in the Shire Highlands . . . and for the suppression of white rule." Smith also believed that "however ill conceived . . . the rising was full of potentiality."[13]

During the two decades between World Wars I and II, Chilembwe's rising retained some local notoriety. Certainly the administration was alert for any recrudescence of similar activity, and the Criminal Investigation Division of the protectorate's police force maintained a steady surveillance of those of Chilembwe's followers who had been released from prison. They also scrutinized the activities of African churchmen, particularly those of separatist persuasion, and watched all other educated Africans as a matter of routine. But no whites questioned the orthodox interpretation of the rising—indeed, there was no compelling reason why any should have—and beyond Nyasaland's borders even the historical fact of the uprising was little known.

However, a medical officer in Kenya, Norman Leys, had served in Nyasaland and was concerned to explain the nature of African grievances in the former colony, as well as to set the Nairobi riots of 1921 in a fuller context. He understood the problems and aspirations of Africans far better than many of his white contemporaries and appreciated the many factors that drove Africans to rebel (and yet ap-

---

[13] George Smith, "Nyasaland and General Northey's Campaign," in Charles Prestwood Lucas (ed.), *The Empire at War* (Oxford, 1925), IV, 259; S 1/946/19: "Governor Smith's contribution to Charles Lucas's history of the war," Zomba archives—which seems to be a copy of the original draft. The bracketed word in the text was contained in the draft but not in the published version. The file in which the draft is found was opened in 1919: there is no reason why Governor Smith should have written about the war in 1915 when it still raged on the borders of his Protectorate. See n. 9 above.

proved of the brutal suppression of all revolts). The short chapter on Chilembwe's rising in his *Kenya* was thus written with a modicum of compassion and the advantage of a degree of hindsight. Leys derived his summary—for it is no more than that—from the report of the official commission and conversations with the Rev. Mr. Robert Hellier Napier of the Blantyre Mission and "many of the survivors of the rising" who were in prison in Zomba. According to Leys, Chilembwe's inspiration came from the Old Testament; every week he preached sermons "in which the example of the Jews in their national struggle with Egyptians, Philistines and others was held up for their admiration and imitation." Chilembwe's plan "was to get the people on the estate to murder their masters, and then to bring about a general rebellion. He had a list of all the Europeans [then 821] in the country, of whom some were to be killed out of hand; others, including the women and children, were to be expelled from the country; while a few, men and women, were to be allowed to remain as teachers, but without political authority." The great majority of the rebels, Leys believed, were "serfs surrounded by people living rent-free." Although Chilembwe, he wrote, "no doubt dreamed of an Africa for Africans . . . the bait he tempted his followers with was land of their own, and release from the necessity of work without wages in order to pay rent and taxes."[14] Like his predecessors, Leys essentially agreed that Chilembwe had sought to destroy white rule and become king of Nyasaland. And this was the view that by and large prevailed until 1958.[15]

[14] Norman Leys, *Kenya* (London, 1924), 328-30.

[15] The intervening literature is, in any event, sparse. The Rev. Dr. Alexander Hetherwick of the Blantyre Mission in Alexander Hetherwick (ed.), *Robert Hellier Napier in Nyasaland: Being His Letters to His Home Circle* (Edinburgh, 1925), 91, blamed the rising on "private grievances" (although Napier joined the Mikalongwe Volunteers in their suppression of the rebellion, Hetherwick includes only an uninformative snippet from Napier's correspondence of this period) and ascribed it to the members of a "Native American Baptist Mission." In his own memoirs, Hetherwick repeated his conclusion that the rising was the result of some "private grudge." *Romance of Blantyre* (London, 1931), 213. The Rev. Dr. Donald Fraser in *The Future of Africa* (London, 1927), 89, merely mentioned the incident in passing. In his memoirs, Sir Hector Duff, a sometimes Chief Secretary and acting Governor in Nyasaland, stated that "Chilembwe had no personal cause of grievance either against the Nyasaland government or against Europeans as a race, to whom, indeed, he was indebted for everything that raised him above the level of his fellows. . . . I don't believe the man was a natural villain. . . . [He simply] persuaded himself that Heaven had commissioned him to deliver Nyasaland from the foreign yoke." *African Small Chop* (London, 1932), 49-50. Daniel Thwaite, *The Seething African Pot: A Study of Black Nationalism, 1882-1935* (London, 1936), 63-65, drew on Leys, added nothing new, and included a number of erroneous details, some of which were repeated in Cyril L. R. James, *A History of Negro Revolt* (London, 1938), 48. L. S. Norman, a planter who oversaw an estate in the Shire

African testimony and writings have been more equivocal than those of whites. Their conclusions give pause to those who would readily accept a simple, direct explanation of Chilembwe's behavior. The first public intimation of Chilembwe's attitude toward whites and the efficacy of rebellion came in August 1914 when a frightened man approached Philip Mitchell, then a raw recruit to the Colonial Service who was temporarily in charge of the Chiradzulu *boma*, with a confusing story about the intentions of John Chilembwe. By the time that Mitchell had become Sir Philip and had governed Uganda and Kenya, he could remember little about this obscure incident on the eve of World War I. It seems, however, that the man must have been one Eugenio of Matuta village, an African teacher in the employ of the Roman Catholic Montfort Marist Fathers Mission at Nguludi. A later recollection of Eugenio's testimony by Bishop Auneau of the Mission —that Chilembwe "intended to kill all the Europeans of the country, as well as those Africans who would not join him, and then make himself spiritual and temporal head of Nyasaland"—seems repetitive of the stereotype and less acceptable than Mitchell's immediate report to L. T. Moggridge, his superior in Blantyre: "A boy from the Nguludi Mission has made a long rambling statement, the gist of which is that the Azungu [whites] are said by John Chilembwe to be going to attack the natives in November and that before they get a chance the natives must attack the Azungu. They are to go to Zomba and make the Boma bugles blow the alarm in the middle of the night, while John Chilembwe's people squat outside the doors of the European houses and kill the owners as they come out on hearing the bugle."[16] Neither Mitchell himself nor his successor, although they cross-examined Africans assiduously, censored Chilembwe's correspondence, and kept their ears to the ground, managed to confirm Eugenio's story or to learn anything more about the supposed conspiracy. Milthorp, Mitchell's replacement, merely gathered that Chilembwe was telling Africans not to work for whites, but in Milthorp's view rebellion was not being contemplated. Indeed, on several occasions Milthorp and Moggridge, the Blantyre Resident, assured the Governor, who for his part was prepared to deport Chilembwe on the slimmest evidence of suspicion,

---

Highlands, provided very interesting details about white reactions to the rising and accepted as fact that a massacre had been planned in "Rebellion," *Blackwood's Magazine,* CCXX (1931), 862-73. Norman reiterates these conclusions in his *Nyasaland Without Prejudice: A Balanced, Critical Review of the Country and Its Peoples* (London, 1935), 37-38.

[16] GOA 2/4/14: Mitchell to Moggridge, 18 Aug. 1914; Auneau to George Smith, 3 Feb. 1915, Zomba archives. Bishop Auneau's account is quoted in Shepperson and Price, *Independent African,* 248-49.

that there was "little to be feared from this man." Furthermore, Moggridge, blinded by common prejudice, was confident that "Our native is a very poor hand at conspiracy and concealment; if there are more than two or three in the business it will certainly be given away. . . ."[17]

After the rising, statements were collected—it is not known in what form, under what circumstances, or by whom—from a number of African participants and the white survivors. Lupiya Zalela (alias Kettleo) reported that "They . . . agreed to bring the war on Saturday and kill all the Europeans first, so they went to Magomero to kill the Europeans. Mr. Livingstone was killed because he did not pay us well for our work. . . . Chilembwe sent messengers to various churches saying 'The Europeans are to kill the natives on Monday, 25 January; What shall we do? Tis good that we begin the war and kill the Europeans before they begin.' The people agreed." The testimony of Duncan Njilima, who was immediately afterward executed for high treason and for being an accessory before the fact, agrees substantially: "I went to John Chilembwe . . . and he said 'The Europeans want to seize and kill all natives this year. I want all natives, before the Europeans come, to attack and kill them.' I refused and said . . . 'what will you take with you to fight?' John Chilembwe said that there were boxes of ammunition at Magomero. 'Many people will go to Magomero to take the rifles and ammunition' . . . 'We will take sticks.'" Abraham Chimbia recalled that Chilembwe had said that "the Europeans were making slaves of us and getting us killed in war." Mrs. Alyce Roach said that she had been given a note (the author is unspecified) to take to the Chiradzulu boma. It said: "tell all white men that the chiefs of all tribes have agreed to kill them because they have so cruelly robbed us of our Mother land."[18] These are, in sum, statements of a defensive as well as an offensive character and say nothing directly about Chilembwe's ultimate aims. But then, too, their contents are in essence based on hearsay of a very incomplete kind.

Two personal statements by contemporaries of Chilembwe are of great importance despite the fact that they were made from memory many years after the event. Kalindi Morrison Malinki worked with both Joseph Booth, Chilembwe's first mentor, and Chilembwe himself. He subsequently became Nyasaland's first African Seventh-day Adventist pastor. Sometime during the early 1950's he recalled that "Things went

[17] GOA 2/4/14: Milthorp to Moggridge, 29 Aug. 1914; Smith, minute of 21 Oct. 1914; Moggridge to Milthorp, 24 Oct. 1914; Moggridge to the Chief Secretary, 11 Dec. 1914; Zomba archives.

[18] S 10/1/2: statements of Lupiya Zalela, 26 Jan. 1915; Abraham Chimbia, 24 Feb. 1915; Alyce Roach, 30 Jan. 1915. See also Mrs. Livingstone's statement in Shepperson and Price, Independent African, 296. S 2/18/22: statement of Duncan Njilima, 17 Feb. 1915, Zomba archives.

well for a few years when, later, Chilembwe hated the European. His
hatred grew more bitter that he definitely made up his mind to destroy
all the Europeans in Nyasaland. But, as he could not do all this by
himself, he at once got busy interesting all his believers and his friends
to join him in his plan. 'The European is here to make you his slave
for ever, let us get rid of him,' he told them. One day John Chilembwe
came to my house. 'Why do Europeans trouble us?' he asked. 'Let us
plan to kill them all!' "[19]

The second statement is of an entirely different character. Entitled "Maziko a Prov. Ind. Mission. Chiradzulo. Nyasaland. 1900.
A.D.," it was compiled from memory in 1951 by Andrew G. Mkulichi,
one of Chilembwe's followers, and contains a fairly full account of
Chilembwe's life and influence. According to this source, after Chilembwe's famous letter of November 1914[20] had failed to elicit any stir
of recognition of African grievances on the part of the government,
Chilembwe feared that he would soon be arrested and killed. "He
then began strong teaching" counseling revolt, and read out, among
other portions of the New Testament, Acts 20:32: "And now brethren,
I commend you to God, and to the word of his grace, which is able
to build you up, and to give you an inheritance among all them which
are sanctified," and finally strengthened his followers with the words:
"We ought to suffer persecution. . . ." Mkulichi also reported that
Chilembwe frequently reiterated three points: "I hear the crying of my
Africans. My people are destroyed through lack of knowledge. It is
better for me to die than to live."[21] If the gist of this account—not all
of which has been quoted—is credible, Chilembwe courted martyrdom,
not a kingdom, and only acted out of despair, not avarice. Mkulichi's
account narrows Chilembwe's fear of being killed by whites to a specific point in time, thus moderating the otherwise paranoid dimension
circumstantially attributed to his behavior by the few Africans who
made statements immediately after the rising.

Both of these statements were among the many elicited especially
for the pioneering study of Chilembwe by Shepperson and Price. In
the course of their very thorough survey of the rich and disparate
evidence, they advanced a number of hypotheses to explain Chilembwe's behavior. First, to them it was a harmful simplification to
specify the aims of the rising as no more than anti-European and pro-

[19] Quoted in Shepperson and Price, *Independent African,* 468, n. 84. The
statement was collected for the authors by Pastor S. G. Maxwell.

[20] The letter demanded that the administration of the Protectorate should heed
African grievances before it was too late. For the letter see ibid., 234-35; Rotberg,
Rise, 82-83; Mwase, *Strike a Blow,* 33-34.

[21] Quoted in Shepperson and Price, *Independent African,* 239, 285, 472, n. 136.

independent-African government. "No doubt these were the objects which Chilembwe and his lieutenants, as well as the majority of his convinced following, set themselves, if the Rising should prove successful. Yet it is by no means clear that Chilembwe believed it would be successful, and one aspect of the Rising, as a symbolical gesture to show that Africans in the Protectorate would not always accept passively the spate of changes and discriminations which the rush of European rule was heaping on them, [was] . . . suggested. It was one way—perhaps the only way—of forcing upon the government and settlers of the Protectorate an independent African point of view. Thus the aims of the Rising appear to have been twofold: first, if successful, the creation of an African state in Nyasaland, with strongly theocratic elements and selected European guidance; second, if unsuccessful, a gesture of protest . . . against what were conceived as the intolerable aspects of European rule." On the point of "selected European guidance" the authors subsequently reiterate—on the basis of what evidence is uncertain—that Chilembwe's concept of the future Nyasaland was not multiracial, although "he apparently considered that that state which would emerge from a successful rising would accommodate some Europeans as mentors and specialists." In their concluding chapter Shepperson and Price go on to say that Chilembwe and his followers were "confused in their aims: they wanted both to destroy and to preserve; to stage both a demonstration and a revolution; to assert a traditional dignity by martyrdom, and by the same activity to mould a new community." They make the important distinction that the prospect for which Chilembwe began to fight was "one of founding a nation rather than of restoring the fortunes of the tribes." At another point in their analysis the authors emphasize the equally critical conclusion (also obvious, but often overlooked) that Chilembwe "wanted to break the European monopoly of the power, wealth, and dignity which their culture conferred, not to reject that way of life."[22] Unlike their white predecessors, Shepperson and Price refused to accept a simple reading of Chilembwe's character. They examined it with a full awareness of and deference to its complexity, and, from a number of different angles, saw how Chilembwe might well have wanted to make a gesture as well as to oust his rulers. Their variety of rich sources led in no conclusive direction, however, and they were thus forced to accept the validity of both main postulates while indicating a slight preference for the possibility that Chilembwe consciously played the precarious role of martyr.

Fortunately a reconsideration of Chilembwe's aspirations need not rest with Shepperson and Price's admirable, if wisely ambivalent, con-

[22] Ibid., 254-55, 400, 415, 409, 429.

clusions. The full text of George Simeon Mwase's "A Dialogue of Ny-asaland, Record of Past Events, Environments and the Present Outlook within the Protectorate" which was originally written in 1931–32, has now been published. Based upon the evidence of a leading participant in the rising, it contains a graphic account of the events leading up to the rising, and the rising itself, that can hardly have been invented.[23] Without question it provides the fullest African explanation of Chilembwe's motives and aims. Mwase, for example, flatly says that "John had no intention of rebelling against the Government itself. . . . His personal aim was to fight white Planters, Traders, and other white settlers within the country." He grieved for his country and his fellow Africans, but determined to act only after his famous letter to the *Nyasaland Times* failed to bring promises of amelioration. The conspirators, Mwase wrote, "all came to the conclusion, that by not answering us on our request, means death on us." They all said, Mwase reported, that "it was better for all of us to die, than to live and see all these troubles"—the last two words possibly referring to World War I. In early January (Mwase supplied a precise date) the conspirators held a decisive meeting. There they decided "'to strike a blow,' or else . . . to be buried alive alternately." And it was on this occasion that Chilembwe specifically referred to the example of the abolitionist John Brown, "who after losing his hope, in succeeding the request in writing . . . he determinate to strike a blow and lose his own life, than, as he said, [it] was too good for him and was ['] out of sight and reach.'" Mwase then recorded: "John said, this case stands the same as that of a Mr. John Brown. . . . 'Let us then strike a blow and die,' for our blood will surely mean something at last." (Somewhat later in his narrative, Mwase specifically says that Chilembwe is the Mr. John Brown of Africa, and also compares him favorably with William Prynne, the Puritan pamphleteer, and Sir Roger Casement, the Irish patriot.) Subsequently Mwase quotes Chilembwe as saying "I did not mean you to succeed and defeat whitemen, no, not at all, that is not my idea even when I am standing here now. This [action] is only a hint to the whitemen, that the way they treat our country men and women is to grieve the whole country, and on behalf of all our country people, we choose to die for them."[24]

Chilembwe's "instructions to his army," as given by Mwase, strengthen the above suggestions about the intentions of the leader, intensify the impact of Mkulichi's much briefer account, and reinforce the suspicions put forward by Shepperson and Price.

---

[23] For the provenance and assessment of the document, see the editor's introduction in Mwase, *Strike a Blow*, xxxiii-xxxiv, xxxix-xl.

[24] Ibid., 29, 35, 36, 43, 79-80.

You are all patriots as you sit. Patriots mean[s] to die for Amor Patria. This very night you are to go and strike the blow and then die. I do not say that you are going to win the war at all. You have no weapons [guns?] with you and you are not at all trained military men even. One great thing you must remember is that Omnia Vincit Amor so for love [of] your own country and country men, I now encourage you to go and strike a blow bravely and die.

This is only way to show the whitemen, that the treatment they are treating our men and women was most bad and we have determined to strike a first and a last blow, and then all die by the heavy storm of the whiteman's army. The whitemen will then think, after we are dead, that the treatment they are treating our people is almost [most] bad, and they might change to the better for our people. After we are dead and buried. This blows means "non sibi sed patria."[25]

According to Mwase, Chilembwe willingly sought martyrdom. "He knew at the beginning that his idea of striking a blow on a whiteman meant his death." Chilembwe had no weapons; whites had many. His army was small and untrained. Mwase compared his action to that of a person, armed only with a maize stalk, who intrepidly and absurdly attacks a lion at his prey. He wanted glory, says Mwase—"He wanted to win heroic, and nothing else." Furthermore, he specifically wanted to draw attention to the grievances of his people by protesting, and, after failing to do so by his letter, the only way in which he could draw attention to his protest was by attacking the government with a "maize stalk." "He did," Mwase began a long parable of explanation,

as the old story say, that in a place, somewhere in the North, a lot of monkeys found plenty of fruits food and they were enjoying and living upon that food. One day a huge elephant came over to that forest, where, after entering into the fruit forest, instead of eating the fruits with monkeys, the elephant began to knock and cut down the fruit trees and chewed even the roots of the trees. This kind of action, the elephant repeated often times. The trees were finishing falling. One day the elephant was again doing the same thing. One of the monkeys approached the elephant personally, and ask him to stop felling down the fruit trees, as they, the monkeys, had no other food to live upon— and told the elephant the better way was for him to eat the fruit of the trees in the same way they were eating, by plucking off the fruits only, and have the trees to yield more fruits for next year, and so forth. The elephant paid not a slightest attention to that, now he made a worse of felling the trees he was doing. Monkeys being a small kind of animals, never went on with the matter, although the matter was a grave one, but through fear, he went away.

[25] "Not for oneself but one's country." Mwase, *Strike a Blow*, 48-49.

Next day the monkey came again and sat on one of the fruit trees in the forest, just by the side of the elephant road. The elephant again came passing the same road, a poor monkey then gave a deadly slap on the elephant tail, that slap made the elephant look behind and saw that the slap had been inflicted on his tail by a tiny monkey. He caught him, and asked him, what he meant by it. Monkey replied, I did not mean anything Sir. [The elephant asked:] Why and what made you to slap me? I am too tiny and weak, [the monkey said,] to go on discussing with you and I thought it the best, to give you a signal of my poor slap, that you may understand that the action of felling fruit trees do us a great harm; and I choose to die by being tramped by you, than to die with hunger. The elephant said, you are a fool, poor little monkey, you knew you have no strength to fight me, so as you have made up a fool of yourself, by touching me with you tiny hand. I will now crush you into powder. The monkey was then crushed and finished.

Next day the elephant passed that road again, and when he arrived near that tree, where that monkey was, remembered that slap which he received from a tiny monkey, and for what the tiny animal bravely slapped him, and when he saw the rest of monkeys about eating the fruits from the trees, he thought, if I will fell more fruit trees, surely, these tiny monkeys will look at me as a bad man, though they have no words to speak or power to fight with me. So the elephant at last became [took] pity on the little animals and never fell more fruit trees, but he kept eating in the way the small animals were eating. At the end, the elephant became a big friend and a protector of the small animals."[26]

Mwase's account lends color and circumstantial evidence to the case for a gesture rather than a bid for power. But it can be argued that Mwase, who wrote in 1931–32, may well have wanted to put a more acceptable gloss on Chilembwe's motives for patriotic reasons. Mwase had already engaged in the desultory politics of self-assertion, and he may have felt that the advancement of educated Nyasas had been inhibited by the government's opinion of Chilembwe as a crass, self-serving opportunist. Mwase never once considers whether Chilembwe accepted the inevitability of failure. But this may simply be ex post facto reasoning, and, even if Mwase did not see the inherent contradiction, he was clearly troubled by Chilembwe's willingness to invite assistance from the Germans. Mwase does not attempt to explain why Chilembwe, if he wanted merely to make a gesture, bothered to co-ordinate his plans with Chinyama, and why Chinyama (according to Mwase) was expected to march south from Ncheu to the Blantyre district, attacking planters in the Zomba district en route. Additionally,

[26] Ibid., 73-76.

the reader is devoid of means to discover on what grounds Mwase asserted his belief in Chilembwe's search for martyrdom. The instructions and statements which he quoted, however, contain too many plausible components to have been concocted wholesale. It has been shown that the rebel Wallace Kampingo was Mwase's primary informant,[27] and it is an allowable assumption that Mwase renders Kampingo's memory (however accurate or inaccurate it may have been) with a high degree of faithfulness. Certainly few Africans of (in the Western sense) limited educational attainments and experience—for Mwase was no more advanced than many of his contemporaries—would, despite the marching song, have known enough about John Brown to forge a new myth with such seeming verisimilitude.

Before deciding the extent to which Mwase's attractive and romantic hypothesis should become the orthodox interpretation, it is essential to scrutinize the whole body of evidence as well as the conclusions of the record. Moreover, it is especially important that whichever explanation of the intentions of Chilembwe wins favor accords well with what we know of the latter's personal history and his psychological makeup. Unfortunately, of Chilembwe's formative years we can learn very little. He was born in "the time of Livingstone"—during the 1860's or early 1870's—to a Yao father and a Cowa (or possibly a Mang'anja) mother. Chilembwe later, as a student in America, said that his father was a "king," but this was the fanciful talk so beloved of an expatriate. His mother, however, had previously been married to a Yao with some chiefly connections, and she herself bore a name with historically regal overtones. She may conceivably have set Chilembwe on the road to prominence by precept, or by reminding him of a real or presumed heritage. Indeed, according to Mkulichi's account, Chilembwe's prenatal behavior foretold greatness. Chilembwe had twisted and turned in the womb to an unusual degree and was thus, in his mother's view, intended to "turn" future events. In this connection there is some scientific evidence that maternal emotional stress increases fetal activity and leads to reduced birth weight and irritable, hyperactive infants. Furthermore, infants reported by their mothers to be very active as fetuses were somewhat more advanced on motor test items than those reported to be less active in the fetal stage.[28] Or, more probably, does this reported recollection of Chilembwe's mother merely signify a later attempt by biblically

[27] Ibid., xxix.

[28] T. W. Richards and H. Newberry, "Studies in Fetal Behavior III," *Child Development*, IX (1938), 79-86; Lester W. Sontag, "Effect of Fetal Activity on the Nutritional State of the Infant at Birth," *American Journal of Obstetrics and Gynecology*, XLVIII (1944), 208-14.

knowledgeable Africans to equate Chilembwe with John the Baptist, his putative namesake? Passages from Luke, particularly 1:41 ("And it came to pass, that, when Elisabeth heard the salutation of Mary, the babe leaped in her womb; and Elisabeth was filled with the Holy Ghost.") are analogous, and Mkulichi, or even Chilembwe himself, may have wanted to suggest links between the two Johns. Chilembwe would often have pondered the relevant remainder of Luke, particularly 1:48-53 and 76-80, and could himself have used this supposed affinity with the first John to win waverers to his side in 1915. Had his mother not said that he had emerged into the world feet first—an unnatural and precocious sign?[29]

A few years after his birth, Chilembwe and his family moved from Sanganu, in the Chiradzulu district, to what became Blantyre. By the accident of this residence Chilembwe—conceivably thrust forward by an ambitious mother—became a student and catechumen of the Blantyre Mission of the Church of Scotland. This event took place about 1890, or a few years before, and may have implied a conscious desire by Chilembwe or his parents to learn more about the ways of the whites who had so recently (missionaries arrived in 1876, planters followed, and the Shire Highlands became a British Protectorate in 1889) settled in their midst. As his biographers aptly described the milieu, "Chilembwe spent his early years in an atmosphere of great insecurity and change. It was an atmosphere full of the keenness of the contrasts between the new gospel of peace and brotherhood which the missions were preaching and the evident injustices and disturbances of both European and African society at a time of rapid social change. The new education which the missions had brought with them provided much of the stimulus and the means for observant Africans like Chilembwe to apprehend these contrasts."[30]

In 1892, in the midst of this ferment, a missionary of unorthodox persuasion arrived on the scene to challenge the Blantyre church. He was Joseph Booth, a British fundamentalist of apocalyptical religious vision. After a commercial and agricultural career in England and the Antipodes, he had heeded the evangelical call and, soon thereafter, entered Nyasaland with a determination to establish a self-supporting Baptist church on lines pioneered by William Carey in India. From his Zambezi Industrial Mission on the outskirts of Blantyre, Booth attempted to spread the egalitarian ideas that immediately made him anathema to the established Scottish missionaries and to the colonial

---

[29] Mkulichi MS., cited in Shepperson and Price, *Independent African*, 45.

[30] Ibid., 41-42. The discussion of Chilembwe's early years is based on both ibid., 41-46, 442-44 and Mwase, *Strike a Blow*, 12-24. They are not in complete agreement about details, but the general outline is clear.

administration.[31] He criticized the comfortable life led by European missionaries in the midst of African poverty, paid Africans somewhat higher wages than did the mission or the government, and soon attracted a small but devoted following. In this group, which included several potential Scottish converts, was John Chilembwe. Whether Booth's personality, wages, or message, or some dissatisfaction with the Scots, wooed Chilembwe is not known. Booth's daughter recalled that he "had heard of Father as being a kind, white man." He came with a note which read: "You please carry me for God. I like to be your cook-boy."[32]

It is clear that Chilembwe and Booth were soon *en rapport*. He became Booth's faithful house servant (Booth had recently become a widower), and in that capacity also cared for Emily and John Edward, the evangelist's young children. As his knowledge of spoken and written English improved, he interpreted for Booth, was baptized, and later taught in schools of the Zambezi Industrial Mission. He became the mainstay of the new church as he was the linchpin of Booth's household. Emily remembered Chilembwe's qualities: "Without his faithfulness and dependability I doubt very much if I could have survived, or if Father could have completed . . . the buying of land for a mission station. . . . Father was able to leave me in his care. He was kind and infinitely patient."[33] Sometime after Chilembwe's death, Booth wrote of their first days together: "The writer doubts if any human being he has known has had a greater influence on himself than this same Native Youth. His many touching acts of kindness and thoughtfulness during the first 18 months of the writer's residence in Nyassaland, before any other White Comrade assisted. . . . Certainly the writer and his little daughter being alone would have died but for Chilembwe's never wearying tender help. . . . He joined me in a time of Distress and Sickness . . . [and] soon won my heart more than I could have believed possible."[34]

There is no doubt that Chilembwe was influenced beyond measure by what was, for the time and place, a most unusual contact with a white household, and through it, with a corner of the West. Guided by Booth, Chilembwe could not help but appreciate that the typical British approach to colonial problems was not invariable. Booth was among the earliest whites to enunciate a clearcut doctrine of "Africa

[31] For details, see Rotberg, *Rise*, 61, 64-66.

[32] Emily Booth Langworthy, *This Africa Was Mine* (Stirling, 1952), 40.

[33] Ibid., 40-41.

[34] Joseph Booth, "re John Chilembwe the Yao Native Messenger to the Negroes of the U S A," unpub. holograph seen in photostatic form through the courtesy of Harry W. Langworthy.

for the African"; indeed Chilembwe joined him in 1897 in proposing an African Christian Union of Nyasaland, the objects of which were to be "equal rights, political, social, and economic, for Africans as well as Europeans; the development of African education along the technical lines of the European world; independent African activity in all economic fields; a just land settlement; the encouragement of a pro-African press and literature; and the growth of independent African Christianity."[35] By this time Chilembwe had, if the term is not too loaded, become an *évolué* with perhaps some appreciation of the precariousness of his position between traditional and white society. Already the few whites who looked upon Nyasaland as their home resented and feared the emergence of Western-educated Africans. A color bar was in the process of erection. Indeed, even if Chilembwe had not gone to the United States, his association with Booth and the isolation that often oppresses the marginal men in any society might themselves have provided the necessary inspiration for the makings of a revolutionary.

A profile of the American experience, to the extent that we can recapture it, is essential for an understanding of the possible motives of 1915. Booth asserts that Chilembwe "volunteered" to go with him to the United States in order to disprove Arab-disseminated rumors (then circulating among the Yao) about the fate of the African slaves who had been transported to the United States. Many Yao apparently believed that "for hundreds of years Whites had taken shiploads of slaves to U S A & other places & eaten them there, for they never came back."[36] But even if this widespread attitude of doubt provided the main motivation for Chilembwe's voyage abroad, it is also evident that Booth (who presumably paid for most of Chilembwe's passage) wanted very much to exhibit Chilembwe before the committees and church groups to which he expected to appeal for funds. And either Chilembwe alone, or both jointly, may have decided that Chilembwe's stature and potential for good would be enhanced by further study in an American institution of higher learning. In any event, they traveled together in 1897 via London and Liverpool to New York, Richmond, and Baltimore, later visited Washington, Brooklyn, and Philadelphia, and by early 1898 Chilembwe, supported by New York Negro Baptists, had been enrolled as a student in the Virginia Theological College and Seminary in Lynchburg, Virginia.

His experiences in western Virginia, and wherever he traveled

---

[35] Quoted in Shepperson and Price, *Independent African,* 79. Booth's book, *Africa for the African,* was published in Baltimore in 1897.

[36] Booth, "re Chilembwe."

along the eastern seaboard, could hardly have lessened whatever antipathy he may already have harbored toward whites. In Richmond, mobs of young white men followed and frequently stoned Booth and Chilembwe for walking together, sitting together on the same public park benches, and living in the same Negro household.[37] In Virginia, as elsewhere in the South, Negro voters were systematically being deprived of their suffrage by the poll tax, literacy requirements open to interpretation, and other recently introduced legislation. Segregation, sometimes accompanied by violence, was then being extended into new areas of routine and endeavor. And lynching was a common occurrence. Although little direct evidence survives, Chilembwe could hardly have escaped some confrontation with these harsh facts of Negro existence. In the same way, he could not have avoided becoming acquainted with the different methods utilized by Negroes to respond to the prevalence of white power. He probably heard or read of the slave rebellions. He conversed with a number of the leaders of the independent Negro churches, may have been influenced by his discussions with John L. Dube, the experienced and later militant proto-nationalist, religious separatist, educator, and publisher from Natal, and was probably conversant with the radical ideas of some of the men who subsequently founded the National Association for the Advancement of Colored People.

It is unclear, however, what Chilembwe studied, or whether he followed any set course during his two years in the Lynchburg college. The nature of his reading is unknown, although his biographers reasonably suppose that it may have included the well-known autobiography of Frederick Douglass. It is, in fact, sensible to argue that the image that recurs in Mwase's account—that Chilembwe urged his followers to "strike a blow and die"—derives from Douglass. In 1892 Douglass had published a final, completely revised version of his popular autobiography. An analysis of John Brown, a central figure in the author's life, occupies sizable portions of the second part of the book. Douglass dissects Brown's character, motives, and strategy in a way that may well have appealed to Chilembwe. He also refers specifically to a conversation he had had with Brown before the raid on Harpers Ferry and, in so doing, he uses the very form of words that—if Mwase is to be believed—became the *leitmotiv* of the rebellion: "Our talk was long and earnest; we spent the most of a Saturday and a part of Sunday in this debate—Brown for Harpers Ferry and I against it—he for striking a blow which should instantly rouse the country, and I for the policy of gradually and unaccountably drawing off the slaves

[37] Ibid.

to the mountains, as first suggested and proposed by him."[38] Chilembwe may somehow also have known of Brown's conversation with
Mrs. Mary Stearns in Boston: "Oh," he said, "if I could have the money
that is smoked away during a single day in Boston, I could strike a
blow that would make slavery totter from its foundations."[39] But whatever the source of inspiration for the particular and admittedly obvious
image, Chilembwe could only with difficulty have avoided learning
of Old Brown's raid on Harpers Ferry. It is not very far from Lynchburg, and the raid, celebrated as it was in song and poetry, was widely
if erroneously credited with having precipitated the Civil War, the
emancipation of the slaves, and the welcome years of reconstruction.
Louisa May Alcott had christened Brown "St John the Just"; for Ralph
Waldo Emerson, Brown had made the "gallows glorious like the cross,"
and Henry David Thoreau described Brown as "an angel of light."
At the time of his deed, Julia Ward Howe had told her sister that "The
attempt, I must judge insane, but the spirit *heroic*. I should be glad
to be as sure of Heaven as that old man may be, following right in the
footsteps of the martyrs, girding on his sword for the weak and the
oppressed. His death will be holy and glorious—the gallows cannot dis-
honor him—he will hallow it."[40]

Negroes of Chilembwe's acquaintance may conceivably have
viewed the deed with a greater sense of proportion, but Chilembwe
may still—as Mwase asserts—have incorporated the folk myth into his
own psyche. Certainly John Brown was a folk hero in late nineteenth-
century America; that he had struck a great and heroic blow for freedom and liberty, and that martyrdom was a just reward, were widespread sentiments. As late as 1931 Mwase—if his own understanding
of Brown's actions was in any way compatible with that of Chilembwe—
believed that by being against slavery and fighting his own government, Brown's name "won a great fame. Up to this time all the military
troops march on with a song of Mr. John Brown actions and deeds, although his actions and deeds were seen as criminal offences. Many
years after, wise people examined them, and found that they were
worth while. So they published them out, and made it known to
everyone, and after all they formed a song out of his actions and
deeds. The song is still living now. . . ."[41]

Although he was awarded the degrees of A.B. and B.D. *in absentia*
in 1901, Chilembwe returned to Nyasaland in 1900 (the date is in

[38] *Life and Times of Frederick Douglass: His Early Life as a Slave, His Escape from Bondage, and His Complete History* (New York, 1962 ed.), 319-20. See
also Shepperson and Price, *Independent African*, 450, n. 53.

[39] Quoted in J. C. Furnas, *The Road to Harpers Ferry* (New York, 1959), 366.

[40] Quoted ibid., 343, 381.

[41] Mwase, *Strike a Blow*, 79.

dispute, and his own deposition gives "Feb. 1900" as the date of the opening of the Providence Industrial Mission)[42] as an ordained representative of the National Baptist Convention. The events of the subsequent fourteen years would provide grist for a number of analytical mills but, as with so many facets of Chilembwe's career, the existing evidence is more tantalizing than conclusive. For the first few years, assisted by American Negroes from the National Convention, he certainly concentrated on the difficult problems of establishing his unique mission. Gradually he transformed a collection of mud huts into a proper station, opened a chain of out-schools (he reported seven in 1914),[43] constructed the solid station church, planted crops, and gained adherents throughout the Shire Highlands and Moçambique, where he occasionally preached. Chilembwe also seems to have turned his station into an outwardly Western community; he insisted upon European affectations and the wearing of clean, neat Edwardian attire. Chilembwe's African biographer commented favorably upon his sobriety and his habits of industriousness. "He liked to see his country men work hard and prosper in their undertakings, also to see them smart, such as Negro fellows he had seen in America."[44] Outwardly, at least, Chilembwe accepted the techniques of advancement so favored by the black bourgeoisie, preached no disturbing millennial doctrine, and, when whites put their impressions on paper—which was rarely—the Chilembwe of this period was viewed in a respectable light.

It is arguable that Chilembwe initially believed that the attainment of African power and of enhanced social and political opportunity depended upon the ability of Nyasas to demonstrate commercial ability and responsibility. It was with such ends in mind that he helped in 1909 to establish the Natives' Industrial Union.[45] Its objects were said to be "the promotion and protection of Negroes Christian

[42] S 2/22/34: Chilembwe to Resident, Chiradzulu, 12 Jan. 1914. Mwase (*Strike a Blow*, 23) says that Chilembwe reached Blantyre in July 1899, which might accord with a February 1900 date for the opening of the mission, but it would conflict with Booth's assertion ("re Chilembwe") that his protégé spent two years at the Virginia Seminary and with the fact that a letter contributed by Chilembwe was featured in a late 1900 issue of the *Central African Times*, a newspaper published in Blantyre. An unpublished thesis cited in Shepperson and Price, *Independent African*, 454, n. 1 gives the date of Chilembwe's departure from the United States as 23 Jan. 1901. This date accords well with the recollection of Lewis Garnett Jordan, *Sabbath Recorder* (6 Feb. 1911), 171, cited ibid., and might conceivably be acceptable if Chilembwe meant to write 1901 instead of 1900 in his admittedly noncontemporary deposition.

[43] S 2/22/34: Chilembwe to Resident, 12 Jan. 1914.

[44] Mwase, *Strike a Blow*, 27.

[45] This date is clear from evidence in the Peters Papers (originals in the Malawi archives), among which is the "Rough Rules and Regulations etc. etc." of the Union, which is dated 14 Aug. 1909.

work in the Country, the collecting and recording of commercial information and . . . the establishment of a Court of Arbitration. Communication with the public Authorities on subjects affecting the Commercial and Planting Community, or such other things as occasion may require." A kind of co-operative was envisaged, a five per cent dividend ("or thereabout") being half-promised. Whether the Union ever functioned as a co-operative, however, is not ascertainable. We have records in English of meetings throughout 1909, but no account of the business of or discussions at these meetings. It is also assumed that the Union continued to exist through at least 1911, when its name became the African Industrial Society; its purposes seem to have been as nebulous as those of the Union. But again no positive evidence is available. Was it a "talk shop" in the manner of the later welfare associations? Or was it a façade for a conspiracy of some kind? All we know is that Chilembwe participated in some of the meetings during 1909 and may have been instrumental in organizing the Union (along lines sketched by Booth years before). In a letter to the mysterious Haya Edward Peters which could just barely refer to conspiracy as well as to the Union, Chilembwe said: "I want to remind you, that you must stand as a man, and be not discouraged or be coward enough, but stand in God's His own will. Please don't you be tired to preach the gospel of Native, Industrial, Union to every Christian man and to every Christian women. You can reach them by writing to them, and telling necessity of being a member, of the said Union. I think the future of the Christians is very largely depends on true understanding that when Christian join with Christian, and are blought [sic] in continous contact with men of intellectual and spiritual strength; it will benefite both part. Should also enterpert the meaning of the greate intercessory prayer, in the same literal way. that they all may be one, that the world may believe."[46]

Chilembwe's name was not, perhaps for good reason, on the list affixed to the earliest invitation (of 9 April 1909) to Africans to join the Union. Peters seems originally to have had the idea of a Union, and he was joined by Joseph Bismark, an African businessman, A. M. Chisusi, an African photographer, James G. Kuuji Mlanga, and Justin K. Somanje, whose name was later deleted. Two weeks later, at the first meeting of the Union, Bismark took the chair, and among the new members present were Cedric Massangano, headmaster of the Blantyre Mission; Thomas M. Massea; Harry K. Mate[i]cheta, who was later ordained by the Blantyre Mission; Asher M. Matipwile, possibly a relation of the Yao chief, Moses Matache; and Nelson Kabweza. At

---

[46] Peters Papers: Chilembwe to Peters, holograph, 5 July 1909. All of Chilembwe's letters to Peters were taken by hand by Chilembwe's nephew, Morris.

the second meeting on 15 May, Chilembwe, who became chairman, and John Gray Kufa Mpantha joined the others and several new recruits. The yearly dues were set at 12/- (which was later to become £5), Bismark was appointed treasurer, and an argument ensued, interestingly enough, about photographing the members. Chisusi wanted to practice his profession, but the members "strongly pointed out that photos should not be taken." But by the end of June, Morris Chilembwe; John Wesley Mlanga; Ardwell Mlenga; Ruben N. Funsani; "David Livingstone," a sometime colleague of Chilembwe during their days with Booth; Kalindi Morrison Malinki, the Seventh-day Adventist; D. B. O. (a relation of Filipo?) Chinyama; Charles Scott Kwikanda; and Stephen Nsomo had also joined. It is true that many of these men were involved in the uprising of 1915, and the most prominent among them formed the innermost circle of the cabal. Nevertheless, there is no reason to assume that these men were scheming, or that they were doing any more than muttering criticisms of the established regime. Chilembwe did tell Peters that "everything is hard on us," and then went on: "Please don't you think that it requires [sic] to have more than hundred members of the said union meetings. How many have we now let me know all particles?"[47] But the intent of his message may be more innocent than its mystery would suggest.

The key to an understanding of Chilembwe's actions and thoughts during the six or seven years before the uprising probably lies with a solution to the conundrum of Haya Edward Peters. Very little was known about Peters until 1968, when Bridger Pachai discovered that the real name was Peter Mlelemba.[48] He was born in the Blantyre area in about 1875, thus making him a contemporary of Chilembwe, and attended the Blantyre Mission School, perhaps with Chilembwe. He completed his studies, however, at the Zambezi Industrial Mission at Mitsidi. Later, during 1905–6, he was employed by the British Central Africa Company (Kabula Stores) and is subsequently reported to have mined mica in the Kirk Range of central Malawi with a white businessman. When this venture failed, Peters (properly Mlelemba) purchased (it is not known how he obtained further capital) the Nangafuwe Estate near Ndirande on the outskirts of Blantyre. He sold

[47] Peters Papers: Chilembwe to Peters, 7 May 1909. Statements in a number of other letters from Chilembwe could imply a conspiracy but none do so specifically.

[48] I am greatly indebted to Professor Pachai of the University of Malawi for making his findings known to me at some length and for corresponding on these and other matters relevant to this essay. Pachai's information was largely derived from inquiries in Magomero, Kaduya (near Mlanje, and the Blantyre area, and several oral responses, among which were those of Willie Gray Kufa Mantha, the son of one of the men executed in 1915).

timber, grew chillies and tobacco, and ran a small store. He was among the two or three leading indigenous businessmen in the Blantyre area. By 1914 he also had a little school for fifty boys and girls, but lacked training in the Scriptures. He claimed to be studying by correspondence with a firm in London "in order to help my brethren."[49] His father died in 1910 at Nangafuwe, and there is correspondence about family and business matters between Haya Peters and a brother named J. B. Warren Peters.

The use of a European-sounding name was not uncommon among the educated class of Nyasas; Bismark, Gray, Isa Macdonald Lawrence, Charles Domingo, and several other *évolués* were all known by their non-African names. Furthermore Mlelemba seems to have had a light complexion. He wanted to be recognized as an *assimilado,* and positively refused to be known by his African name. Hence the adoption, not only as a *nom de plume,* of the name Peters. But traces of all of these other men appear in missionary records, contemporary correspondence, and the surviving official records. Only the Peters clan escaped notice and even avoided being implicated in the uprising, largely, it seems, because Haya Peters himself was then on an elephant hunting expedition along Malawi's northeastern border with Moçambique. When Peters learned of the uprising (it is still not known whether he anticipated a rising, but Pachai cogently believes that he did not), he fled through Moçambique to German East Africa where he was eventually captured by the British command. Later he was allowed to proceed to South Africa.[50] Some years later Peters returned to Nyasaland and was employed as a clerk in the Blantyre *boma.* He was murdered in 1940 near Blantyre because of some domestic quarrel.

If we cannot as yet precisely delineate the extent to which Peters participated in the planning of the rebellion, we can at least seek to estimate the extent of Peters's influence upon Chilembwe's ideological development. From a reading of their correspondence it appears that Peters was the more forceful and the stronger of the two—he clearly dominated Chilembwe—but this appearance could be explained by the peculiar nature of their financial relationship (for which, see below, 366), and/or by the fortuitous circumstance that our image of Peters is derived almost entirely from the construction and tone of

[49] He enclosed two photographs with his letter "to proved that I am a colored man." Peters Papers: Peters to Messrs. Watch Tower Bible & Tract Society, Allegheny, Pa., 7 July 1914. He had read the latter's *Plan of the Ages,* a tract.

[50] Malawians apparently believe that Peters influenced the work of Clements Kadalie (see below, Sheridan W. Johns, III, "Trade Union, Political Pressure Group, or Mass Movement: The Industrial and Commercial Workers' Union of Africa," 695-754.) but no positive evidence at present connects him with the Industrial and Commercial Workers' Union.

Chilembwe's outgoing letters. No letters survive from Peters to Chilembwe. Nevertheless, the sense of their relationship seems evident, and Chilembwe certainly treated Peters's ideas with profound respect. The earliest extant letter from Chilembwe to Peters concludes: "I had not thought, that here in Africa can be found few heads so wise as you & [Domingo]. Certainly your Schemes are the source of spiriturs Illumination in this dark country and your words not with . . . standing are wonderfull preservation of this benighted people. I may die tomorrow but the trueth remaineth that you shall be counted one of the Africa sages. Believe me God is able."[51]

This letter may contain, as do later ones, a hint of conspiracy, but if so the rising was a far more calculated and premeditated exercise than has generally been accepted.[52] Moreover, the only extensive expression of Peters's views indicates that he was a man of forward, emancipatory, but hardly revolutionary, views. The "Rough Rules" is in Peters's hand, not Chilembwe's (although the ideas could have been those of either, or even of Joseph Booth), and attached thereto is an explanation of the importance of the Union which seems to have been the text of a sophisticated speech delivered by Peters at an early meeting of the members of the Union. It is again in his unmistakable hand (although his style had somewhat altered by 1914) and is of uncommon interest:

> If a black man becomes a lawyer a Doctor a minister or an ordinary teacher, his professional duties would not ordinary bring him in a touch with the portion of the community, but rather confine him to his own role. Industrial education, however, would soon recommend itself to the white Nyasaland. This distorts my real meaning. All such training has its place and value in the development of a race. Mere training of the hand without mental and moral education would mean little for its welfare of any race, all are vital factors in the harmonious plan, but; while I do not propose that every individual should have hand training, I do say, that in all my contact with men, I have never met one who had learned a trade in youth and regretted it in manhood, nor have I ever seen a father or another who was sorry that his children has been taught trade. There is still doubt in many quarters as to the ability of the negro, unguided, [and] unsupported, to hew [out] his own path and put into visible, tangible, indisputable forms the products and signs of civilisation. This doubt cannot be extinguished by mere abstract argument, no matter how ingeniously and convincingly advanced. Quietly, Patiently, doggedly, through summer and winter sunshine and shadow, by self sacrifice, by foresight, by

---

[51] Peters Papers: Chilembwe to Peters, 20 Oct. 1908.
[52] See Rotberg, *Rise*, 80.

honesty and industry, we must reinforce arguments with results. One farm bought, one house built, one home nicely kept; one man the largest taxpayer and depositor in the local Bank, one school or church maintained, one factory running successfully, one truck garden profitably cultivated, one patient cured by a negro Doctor, one sermon well presented, one office well filled one life cleverly lived—these will tell [more] in our favour than all the abstract eloquence that can be summoned to [plead] our cause. Our pathway must be up through the soil, up through swamps, up through forests up through the streams and rocks; up through commerce, education and religion! In my opinion we cannot begin at the top to build a race any more than we can begin at the top to build a House. If we try to do this, we shall reap in the end the fruits of our folly.

Did Chilembwe share this belief in the efficacy of a gradualist approach? Did he thus accept inwardly as he espoused outwardly that notion of change which would least disturb whites and the ideology of colonial rule? Did he thus identify with his oppressor? Or did Peters and Chilembwe, from whom Peters may conceivably have obtained the ideas and very words for his speech, simply adopt as their rationale the appealing and stirring (but in no sense radical) views of America's leading and most celebrated Negro? There can be no doubt that Booker T. Washington inspired Peters's speech to the members of the Union. The message and the very construction are unmistakably stamped with the imprint of Washington's lush oratory. Indeed, a careful comparison of the above text and Washington's speeches and writings reveals what Peters may not have told his colleagues—that nearly every word had first been uttered by Washington.[53] If Chilem-

[53] The speech by Peters is especially derivative of Washington's oft-stated views on the importance of industrial education. In particular, see Booker T. Washington, *The Future of the American Negro* (Boston, 1899), 61-81, 123, 200-244, which Chilembwe might have read and/or purchased in America and transported to Nyasaland. Booker T. Washington's "Industrial Education for the Negro," in *The Negro Problem* (New York, 1903), is a more succinct and dramatic statement of the same views, and pp. 16-17 contain the germ of the first six sentences of Peters's text.. More directly, pp. 28-29 of the same essay spell out this doctrine of "deeds not words" in phrasing identical with nearly all of the remainder of Peters's text. "There is still doubt," both began, and they conclude "up through commerce, education and religion!" Indeed, the exclamation point and all but a few of the intervening words are identical. Washington, of course, was not adverse to repeating his most well-rounded and memorable constructions. The above words were originally voiced by Washington in Brooklyn, in a speech on "The Educational and Industrial Emancipation of the Negro," delivered on 22 February 1903 before the Brooklyn Institute of Arts and Science. It appears in E. Davidson Washington (ed.), *Selected Speeches of Booker T. Washington* (Garden City, 1932), 111-12.

Washington's speeches were often published in pamphlet form and distributed widely. Either Chilembwe or Peters could have obtained copies from the National

bwe were influenced by Peters, it is evident that these thoughts of Washington influenced his outward conformity far more than the shape of his inner conflict and the subsequent urge to rebel. On the evidence of 1915, Nat Turner and William E. Burghardt Du Bois were far more Chilembwe's men than was Washington.

It is easier to demonstrate the effect upon Chilembwe of other aspects of his dealings with Peters, particularly the psychological stresses that are revealed by their correspondence. Sometime in 1908, when Chilembwe was (according to his own statement) "pennyless," he decided to open a little store. From Peters he borrowed £50, and apparently also promised to pay interest on the unpaid balance of the loan, a sum which amounted to 1/- per pound per month. But £50 proved insufficient to build and stock a store, and Chilembwe went bankrupt. Only then did he begin to appreciate the leech-like quality of his creditor. Tenaciously Peters clung to the scrap of paper which Chilembwe had signed; monthly he dunned Chilembwe, eventually, over about six years, extracting not only the principal, but a grand total of £42 interest—much of it in turn begged from the National Convention and other American friends. There is no doubt that Chilembwe was harried mercilessly by Peters, with whom he nonetheless remained friendly: for example, from 1909 Chilembwe began pleading for time and some sympathy. "If you really wish to help your poor people, Let us limit this you shall not lose every penny." "Brother, trust in God, and also in me. . . . Please have faith on me." Again "I hope you will not forget to remember that when a man havn't got money he cannot create money." "I know next December was our agreement and it will not go beyond that, but the time of your grace is needed you had been so good in the beginning toward this first African Church, and I hope you will be the same to the end. You understand me that it is motto in my heart to live honestly before God and my fellow countrymen." In 1912 when £23 was still outstanding and Chilembwe was forced again to seek help in the United States, he wrote with an even heavier heart than before: "The remainder I am searching and I shall pay you only give me time. My word I value and if you not value yours I am not responsible. . . . Pray for me that I may not fail, for the money in my heart I value nothing. For I

Baptist Convention (before whom Washington often spoke) or from the Negro missionaries who labored alongside Chilembwe. Or even from Booth. Indeed, it is known that Washington and Booth corresponded in 1902 and 1903 about a scheme to colonize American Negroes in East Africa. Moreover, Washington's most prominent African disciple was John Dube, whom Chilembwe had known in the United States. For further details, see Louis R. Harlan, "Booker T. Washington and the White Man's Burden," *The American Historical Review*, LXXI (1966), 459-63.

have weighed the world and its riches and find nothing. Comparing the love I got for my people and our God. And as for you my dear friend I owed a great thanks I shall never forgot the kindness you showed me in this world and in the world yet to come. . . . I remain in prayer that God may raise some friends to loose me the chain prepared for my neck. God bless you."[54]

Of what oppression were the links in this chain forged? Chilembwe was never freed from his worries about money, the correspondence continuing in a similar vein through March 1914, and in 1913 Peters threatened to take his debtor to court. "To go to the law with me My dear Bro. Peters," Chilembwe advised, "we will gain nothing it will be simply to mock ourselves."[55] But money was only the most obvious of Chilembwe's many anxieties. The chest complications which had hastened his departure from the United States, and which had troubled him since, grew particularly severe after about 1909. His sight also began to fail. Continuously he complained of feeling unwell. In 1911 he wrote plaintively to Peters: "My Dear Brother as usual I am suffering with the Asthma and being on heaviest weather and atmosphere being so high has coursed a dreadful pain in my system so that I had been trying the medicine from both white [and] black Doctors. But proved resultless till I give up for using the medicine for fear it will poison me. . . . I am almost too weak but in the spirit there is a hope of long living."[56] At his death he was emaciated and cut a very poor figure.

It would not be amiss at this point in our discussion to consider the possible psychoanalytic interpretation of Chilembwe's problems. Despite the paucity of hard data, the insights of psychoanalysis may at least be suggestive. Certainly if we are to make the fullest possible use of the available evidence, it is necessary in this case to attempt to go beyond the inherent limitations of a strictly documentary approach.

It has long been accepted that in many patients asthma, which was first described in clinical detail in the seventeenth century, can be a severe psychosomatic disorder. Immunologic sensitization is suspected of invoking an initial attack of bronchial asthma, but the exposure of sensitized persons to sensitizing allergens does not always produce an attack, and individuals often exhibit asthmatic symptoms when they are not exposed to the allergens. Emotional stress often

[54] Peters Papers: Chilembwe to Peters, 15 Sept. 1909, 21 Oct. 1909, 12 Mar 1910, 13 Nov. 1910, 24 Apr. 1912.

[55] Ibid., 9 Mar. 1914. Blackmail cannot absolutely be ruled out, but the nature of the debt is spelled out at such length, and referred to so frequently, as to discredit such an otherwise attractive hypothesis.

[56] Ibid., 9 Feb. 1911.

stimulates an attack, and the frequency and severity of asthmatic attacks is clearly related to the state of the patient's emotions. Furthermore, chronic emotional disturbance can prolong the symptomatology despite the best medical care. All we know, albeit at secondhand, of Chilembwe's childhood is that he may have been unusually close to his mother, conceivably even overdependent. (We have no information about his father, his father's role, or his father's presence or absence in the childhood home. It is unlikely, however, that Chilembwe would have seen much of his father during the years of his youth; his mother's society stressed matrilineality and emphasized no decisive role for fathers.) If this is so, it conforms to our knowledge of the non-physiological dimension of asthma. Franz Alexander, whose findings are widely accepted, says that the nuclear psychodynamic factor "is a conflict centering in an excessive unresolved dependence upon the mother."[57] As a defense against such an infantile fixation, a variety of personality traits—aggression, ambition, hypersensitivity, and so forth—may develop. Asthmatics have been described as anxious and insecure, and a classic report indicated that bronchial asthma occurred when the patient's security was threatened or when there was a temptation to act in a way which would cause the mother's love to be withheld.[58] Unfortunately, we know too little about Chilembwe's formative years and the nature and timing of his first attacks to decide whether the above clinical findings apply directly to his case, or even whether reference can be made to Western findings when a retrospective analysis of African psychopathology is being attempted. It is nevertheless very tempting to accept the relevance of further research, the conclusions of which do not depend on a purely psychoanalytic interpretation of the presumed childhood relations of Chilembwe and his mother: it has been shown that the repression of aggressive feelings and the internalization of hostility is often associated with a high incidence of asthma, and that severity and frequency of attack are linked

[57] Franz Alexander, *Psychosomatic Medicine: Its Principles and Applications* (New York, 1950), 133.

[58] See Thomas M. French, Franz Alexander, *et al.*, "Psychogenic Factors in Bronchial Asthma," *Psychosomatic Medicine Monographs* I (Washington, 1941), 1-92; C. H. Rogerson, D. H. Hardcastle, and K. Duguid, "A Psychological Approach to the Problem of Asthma and Asthma-Eczema-Prurigo Syndrome," *Guy's Hospital Reports,* LXXXV (1935), 289-308; E. B. Strauss, ibid., 309-16; Margaret W. Gerard, "Bronchial Asthma in Children," in Franz Alexander and Thomas Morton French (eds.), *Studies in Psychosomatic Medicine: An Approach to the Cause and Treatment of Vegative Disturbances* (New York, 1948), 243-48; Thomas French and Adelaide Johnson, "Psychotherapy in Bronchial Asthma," ibid., 249-58. See also Edith H. Freeman, Ben F. Feingold, Kurt Schlesinger, and Frank J. Gorman, "Psychological Variables in Allergic Disorders: A Review," *Psychosomatic Medicine,* XXVI (1964), 543-75.

in a crude but positive way with the magnitude of the hostility repressed.[59]

Even if it is premature to suppose that the incidence of asthma by itself led to rebellion, it is not unwarranted to suppose that a host of personal afflictions, each by itself inconclusive, tugged fitfully at the sinews of Chilembwe's spirit during the fateful few years before the uprising. Collectively they would have oppressed a troubled mind and encouraged a dramatic, all-redeeming response to affliction—especially when the doleful social conditions prevalent in the Highlands and the real troubles of his parishioners would only have magnified the impact of the afflictions and increased the stresses to which Chilembwe was subject. It is also worth wondering whether the rebellion occurred when Chilembwe was in the throes of what Erik Erikson, in analyzing the psychological gestalt of Martin Luther, has called a "crisis of generativity." It occurs "when a man looks at what he has generated, or helped to generate, and finds it good or wanting, when his life work as part of the productivity of his time gives him some sense of being on the side of a few angels or makes him feel stagnant."[60] Luther suffered physically, or psychosomatically, during this stage, as did Chilembwe, but it may be even more important that Chilembwe believed that his own end was near. The act of rebellion, then, may in Chilembwe's eyes have been invested with the attractive glitter of redemption. For him—at a time of psychological crisis—it may have been seen as an obvious, even the only, alternative. After all, his preachings and his written protestations had produced no amelioration of white attitudes, on the northern front Africans daily lost their lives, and action was the only clear alternative to stagnation. In a more generalized way, if Chilembwe were indeed succumbing in 1914 to the stress of his mental and physical circumstances, then the act of rebellion contained within it the seed of psychic liberation. He had withheld his feelings for some time, at least in terms of the dominant white society, and rebellion provided an outlet—a "safety valve"—as well as a means of expressing hostilities. By the end of 1914, tensions had clearly accumulated to a dangerous level.

[59] Mildred Creak and Joyce M. Stephen, "The Psychological Aspects of Asthma in Children," *Pediatric Clinician of North America* (Aug. 1958), 731-34; Hyman Miller and Dorothy W. Baruch "A Study of Hostility in Allergic Children," *American Journal of Orthopsychiatry*, XX (1950), 506-19. See also Sidney S. Kripke, "Psychologic Aspects of Bronchial Asthma," *American Journal of Diseases of Children*, C (1960), 935-41.

[60] Erik H. Erikson, *Young Man Luther: A Study in Psychoanalysis and History* (New York, 1958), 243. Cf. Erik H. Erikson, *Identity and the Life Cycle* (New York, 1959), 97, 156-58. I am conscious that my interpretation of Erikson's "crisis of generativity" may not precisely agree with his own.

It is also relevant to inquire whether Chilembwe, in the clinical sense, may have identified with his aggressor. He had unquestionably adopted white values and standards, as Mwase makes clear. Chilembwe tried to dress well and to adhere to Western conventions of behavior. He strove for a respectability which—within his own milieu at least—he seems to have achieved. He married a woman who, according to several accounts, was of mixed parentage—a half-caste. And there is a somewhat prurient letter to Peters that indicates Chilembwe's interest in other girls of mixed blood: "Now concerning the half-cast [sic] girl mentioned in your letter I regret Sir, to say Walker has arrived yesterday with a tedious report that girl is used by a whiteman . . . and that the girl has already conceived. And it leaves me in hope that you will try another chance."[61] Nevertheless, there is no evidence to show that Chilembwe's identification was pathological. He does not seem to have been truly submissive in the "Sambo" sense, nor can his identification be equated with the transference analyzed in the classic studies of concentration camp experiences—except in the sense that resignation exemplified by a willingness to be killed, "to strike a blow and then die," is submissive.[62] But it is at least suggestive that identification with the aggressor has been defined as representing, on the one hand, a preliminary phase of superego development (which Elie Cohen and others have shown can be altered and/or resumed under extreme conditions later in life)[63] and, on the other, an intermediate stage in the development of paranoia. A person "introjects some characteristic of an anxiety object and so assimilates an anxiety experience which he has just undergone. Here, the mechanism of identification or introjection is combined with a second important mechanism. By impersonating the aggressor, assuming his attributes or imitating his aggression, the child transforms himself from the person threatened into the person who makes the threat." Furthermore, "reversal"—the transformation of acceptance into aggression—is said to complete "what introjection and projection have begun, and the result is the development of paranoid delusions," which would help to explain African testimony about Chilembwe's state of mind on the eve of the rebel-

[61] Walker was probably the name of an African messenger. Peters Papers: Chilembwe to Peters, 22 Feb. 1911.

[62] For "Sambo," see Stanley M. Elkins, *Slavery: A Problem in American Institutional Life* (Chicago, 1959), 81-89, 130-33. For concentration camps, see Bruno Bettelheim, *The Informed Heart: Autonomy in a Mass Age* (Glencoe, 1960), 177-235, which draws on his own and the experience of others.

[63] Elie A. Cohen (trans. M. H. Braaksma), *Human Behavior in the Concentration Camp* (New York, 1953), 136. For further references, see Elkins, *Slavery,* 113-18.

lion.[64] Did Chilembwe, having identified, project the hostility which he himself suffered back upon the obvious aggressor?

If psychological factors contributed to the decision to rebel, then it is arguable that the very act of rebellion was more important to Chilembwe than the immediate consequences of that act. Chilembwe's state was such that he could easily have persuaded himself—especially after the outbreak of World War I and the refusal of the government to heed his protest—that oppression of Africans and the spirit was imminent, that his own life had in any event reached a point of no return, and that by sacrificing his own life in a good cause he could achieve something at last. Whether or not Chilembwe's spirit had plumbed the depths of despair, the example of John Brown—especially as seen through the popularly distorted prism—would probably have seemed worthy of emulation. Mwase's account, the recollections of Mkulichi, the fact that Chilembwe meditated atop Chilimangwanje hill throughout the critical days and nights of the rebellion, the symbolic taking of Livingstone's head (the precise reason for doing so is uncertain), the failure to attack other isolated planters, the way in which the white women and children were well treated and used as messengers, and the fact that the rebellion was so half-heartedly organized and involved so few Africans—and presupposed no widespread tribal revolt—all tend to substantiate the hypothesis that the rising of 1915 was intended as a gesture, as the "only way to show the whitemen," in words Mwase attributed to Chilembwe, "that the treatment they are treating our men and women was most bad." Recall too, that Chilembwe was credited with saying: "They whitemen will then think, after we are dead, that the treatment they are treating our people is [most] bad, and they might change to the better for our people [a]fter we are dead and buried."[65]

But is it legitimate to dismiss the conclusions of the commissioners of inquiry, and other contemporary or nearly contemporary white verdicts so cavalierly? Does not some of the African testimony collected after the rebellion discredit Mwase's reconstruction? And how are we to reconcile the planned attacks on Blantyre, Limbe, and so forth, and the second front that was supposed to be opened up by Chinyama, with a putative gesture? Moreover, a "much thumbed" military manual —the nature of which is, however, unspecified—was found in the

---

[64] Anna Freud (trans. Cecil M. Baines), *The Ego and the Mechanisms of Defense* (New York, 1966), 113, 120-21. See also: Guy E. Swanson, "Determinants of the Individual's Defenses Against Inner Conflict: Review and Reformulation," in John C. Glidewell (ed.), *Parental Attitudes and Child Behavior* (Springfield, Ill., 1961), 5-42.

[65] See above, 351.

Mbombwe church after the uprising, and there is evidence that Chilembwe trained stretcher bearers and planned the storage of guns.[66] If the gesture were meant to fail, would Chilembwe have even bothered to raid the arsenal in Blantyre or to sever telephone lines? Then, too, there is the letter to the Germans: A few days before his followers rose, Chilembwe sent Yotam S. Bango, a courier, through Moçambique with a letter—no copies of which have ever been found—which the Nyasan authorities assumed had been intended to solicit the assistance of the German regime in the struggle against the British government. Whether by design or not, Bango delivered the message to the Bezirksamtmann of Tunduru who, in turn, according to an ambiguous letter from him in Swahili that Bango conveyed back to Nyasaland, claimed that he had transmitted Chilembwe's message to the Provincial Commissioner in Lindi (who seems to have received it) and the Governor in Dar es Salaam.[67]

There are only three ways of reconciling the divergent strands of evidence. Either Chilembwe wanted to overthrow white rule but was realistically prepared to have his actions interpreted merely as a gesture of protest; was determined to protest in such a way that the whites would take notice but also hoped that he might, God willing, by some fluke succeed and become king of Nyasaland; or, eschewing any ambition to erect a theocracy on the ruins of British Nyasaland, simply wanted to maximize (or be seen by his followers as trying to maximize) the effectiveness of his protest. Mwase's evidence accords best with the last proposition and least well with the first unless we are prepared to assume that Chilembwe deliberately misled his followers or that Chilembwe wanted one thing and his disciples another. The psychological evidence strongly supports the third proposition. And since nothing emerged at Bango's trial, or in the Nyasaland records, which hints at a conspiracy, Chilembwe may merely have written of his plans in order to gain German acquiescence if the rising happened to succeed.[68] He may not have asked for guns or ammunition. The existence of a military manual and the cutting of telephone wires need not imply anything other than a desire to enhance the possible effectiveness of a

[66] Shepperson and Price, *Independent African*, 261, call it a military manual, citing the diary for 1915 of The African Lakes Co. But Norman, "Rebellion," 867, refers only to "books bearing on the subject of military operations" having been studied.

[67] The discussion of this episode follows that in Robert I. Rotberg, "Resistance and Rebellion in British Nyasaland and German East Africa," in Prosser Gifford and William Roger Louis (eds.), *Britain and Germany in Africa* (New Haven, 1967), 688. It was said that the incriminating reply had been found "on a path," where Bango had presumably discarded it.

[68] S 2/8/19: trial of Yotam Bango, Zomba archives.

protest. Nor does a second front necessarily imply an aggrandizing rather than a reforming zeal. Indeed, Chinyama himself may have been operating independently, that is, he may have rebelled for reasons quite distinct from those of Chilembwe and simply co-ordinated the two movements in order to enhance their overall impact.

The socio-economic conditions then prevailing in the Shire Highlands obviously would have given the suggestion of rebellion an immediate appeal to upwardly mobile Africans of the emergent middle class, landless immigrants from Moçambique, and employees of white landowners. But rebellion as an instrument of protest could not have appeared to these different groups as either the only or the most promising of solutions to their collective dilemma. In order to foment revolt, a charismatic figure was necessary who could persuade disparate groups of possible followers that rebellion would provide the only sensible way of alleviating their self-perceived discontent. It is likely that Chilembwe, who radiated (newly discovered?) sources of incandescent illumination, reminded his possible recruits of the overweening nature of white oppression and of the conceivably dismal future that awaited Africans under continued colonial rule. Such arguments could have been powerful, yet it still seems probable that only the conjunction of two factors gave them an overwhelming appeal. The outbreak of World War I and the refusal of the authorities to heed Chilembwe's written protest were in themselves ominous acts; they tolled the bells of doom for Africans, or at least would have been perceived in that manner by persons already disturbed by their fate. It is also worth suggesting that decisions based on such collective perceptions could only have been precipitated by the declarations of a charismatic leader whose own perception of reality had become unavoidably distorted and/or heightened. The rebellion, as has been argued elsewhere,[69] would probably not have occurred when and as it did had the world war not broken out, but equally—as the discussion of Chilembwe's psychology has implied—only the state of Chilembwe's mind and spirit, with its possible manifestation of the syndrome of reversal (given the descriptions of his paranoia), encouraged him to equate the outbreak of war with the imminence of existential doom and thus to provoke a call to arms.

Finally, can we ever know precisely what Chilembwe intended to achieve by his call to arms? If, lacking an unambiguous testament, we cannot, it seems evident that Mwase's words must carry great weight. From a psychological point of view his description alone speaks to Chilembwe's condition better than any case which one could construct for an intended theocracy. From what we know of the character and

[69] See Rotberg, *Rise*, 80-81; Shepperson and Price, *Independent African*, 238.

course of the uprising itself, it seems inconceivable that Chilembwe could have expected that he would succeed in overthrowing the established order. Certainly with the bulk of the Protectorate's army away on the northern front, that he and his followers could have done much more than they did is obvious. They could easily have massacred whites in some number in their isolated farm houses and, by enlisting the support of the servants in Blantyre, in the houses in town. They could easily have held the white women and children hostage, but they refrained from so doing. If rural Africans had truly risen (the masses failed to participate in any way and it is wrong to argue that Chilembwe acted on behalf of, or was in the vanguard of an aroused peasantry[70]), the Protectorate would have been indefensible until loyal troops could have been released from the war. But nothing was done along these lines, nor, if we except the rather garbled testimony of Norman, even planned.[71] His followers need not have themselves wanted martyrdom (in the eyes of John Gray Kufa the prospect would not have seemed very inviting), and, in the final analysis, this duality of intention could well have overshadowed and confused Chilembwe's personal quest for martyrdom and psychological redemption. He did, however, want to become the Mr. John Brown of Africa, and thus struck a resolute, if very premature, blow for freedom in colonial Africa.

[70] The leaders were not peasants nor, in the usual sense of the term were their followers. See also Rotberg, "Resistance and Rebellion," 689-90.

[71] Norman, "Rebellion," 869-70.

PART THREE

THE RELIGIOUS EXPRESSION

OF DISCONTENT

THE GUSII REBELS

AUDREY WIPPER

Resistance to alien control in southwestern Kenya was first demonstrated in 1905 and 1908 when the dominant Gusii[1] staged two revolts. Only after disastrous confrontations with modern weaponry did the indigenous people change to more passive forms of resistance. Prominent among these were millennial cults.

Of special significance was the earliest sect in the area, the cult of Mumbo, which had its beginnings during the first decade of British

This analysis is limited to material gathered mainly from administrative records. I visited Kisii in June 1966 and spoke wth several ex-chiefs who had been in charge of the district when Mumboism was at its height. I also spoke with the local authorities and some of the inhabitants. In this way I was able to check certain information and acquire more.

The original draft of this paper was presented at a Conference of the East African Institute of Social Research, Makerere University, Kampala, Uganda, in January 1966. Considerable revisions have been made, and data collected through interviews added.

Research for this paper was conducted during 1964–66 with the support of a Canada Council pre-doctoral fellowship. I am indebted to John Kesby, Robert A. LeVine, John Lonsdale, Anthony Oberschall, and Edmund Vaz for helpful criticism.

All provincial and districts reports can be found in the Kenya National Archives.

[1] The Gusii, a pastoral-agricultural people now numbering more than 500,000, belong to the Bantu-speaking language group. Composed of seven autonomous tribes that recognize Mogusii as their ancestor, they formerly banded together to wage war on the Kipsigis. Otherwise, each tribe went its own way and fought over cattle, women, and territory. In addition to the common ancestor shared by all Gusii, each tribe recognizes its own founder.

377

occupation.[2] A pan-tribal pagan sect, Mumboism prophesied the early departure of the Europeans and the coming of a golden age during which the elect would be blessed with abundance and the wicked overthrown. In its symbolism, Mumboism was nativistic, as it rejected European customs and advocated a return to the old prophets and the old ways. Its message stressed the lost glory and dignity of the tribe that were to be re-established in the millennium. From another and more revealing perspective Mumboism was both revolutionary and utopian, rejecting the colonial regime, tribal authority, and traditional mores, and introducing new norms and leadership roles. Although it engaged in sporadic collective protest, the cult was concerned mainly with prophecies, dreams, ritual, and ecstatic behavior.

Mumboism has often been presented in a stereotyped way that obscured much of its basic content. The colonial administrators and the missionaries saw it simply as an atavistic, irrational, vicious movement, grounded in perversions and superstitions. Albeit in a more restrained manner, this negative view has been carried over to the academic world. Thus, B. A. Ogot overlooks any aspects of the cult that do not fit his description of it as "fanatical and non-programmatic . . . [a cult whose] leaders preached complete rejection of everything European and a return to the African way of life."[3] John Lonsdale, another historian, writes of the cult's "reactionary appeal . . . the rebellion had to be backward-looking, rejecting all things European. . . . Mumbo was a political aberration. A return to the Old Africa was not yet the key to the future."[4] Little evidence was, however, presented for these allegations, and no serious study of the cult was undertaken.

Therefore, in an attempt to understand the nature of Mumboism, this essay will explore its message and activities, the basis of its support, and the way in which the agents of social control reacted toward it. Two propositions are basic to my argument. They are presented as assumptions from which some of the more particular statements follow: (1) Discontent and protest are manifested in many forms and when one fails another will, other conditions being equal, be tried; (2) For discontent to result in protest, general grievances need to be sparked by particular grievances.

[2] The simple spelling for tribal words is used. Instead of adding different prefixes to distinguish different forms such as "Nyamumboites" or "Omamumbo," the word "Mumbo" is used throughout the paper.

[3] B. A. Ogot, "British Administration in the Central Nyanza District, 1900-1960," *Journal of African History*, IV (1963), 249-73.

[4] John Lonsdale, "A Political History of Nyanza 1883-1945" (unpublished Ph.D. thesis, University of Cambridge, 1964), 190, 363.

Let us turn now to the immediate background. We are concerned here with development in a relatively remote area of Kenya, South Nyanza, formerly called South Kavirondo. Separated from the main arteries of communication and cut off from contact with the West by lack of European settlement, it was an area whose inhabitants continued in their traditional ways of life for a longer time than tribes in more settled regions. By 1938, for example, there were still no political associations in the area and the tribes had little contact with other tribes. They were therefore slower than either the Luo in Central Nyanza or the Kikuyu in Central Province in articulating political opinion.[5] Even in 1949, Philip Mayer noted that "outside the immediate neighbourhood of the township and of the two main mission stations, Christians are few and literacy is rare among adults."[6]

It was into this isolated area that, in the early 1900's, the British attempted to extend their control. The reaction was a protest which found its center in the Kisii Highlands, also known as Gusiiland. Located some fifty miles south of the equator and some thirty miles inland from Lake Victoria, the Highlands were bordered on the south by Tanzania; on the east by the District of Kericho, the tea-growing country of the Kipsigis tribe; on the southeast by the vast plain of the nomadic cattle people, the Masai; and on the west and north by the Nilotic Luo. Softly rolling hills, a pleasantly cool climate, and fertile, rain-drenched valleys make the Highlands a delightful green oasis amid the semi-arid lowlands of the west and the hot savannahs of the east.

A Gradual Awareness

Three factors in particular contributed to the region's gradual awareness of an outside world, undermined the basis of traditional life, and set the stage for the development of millennial movements: (1) British penetration and political reorganization; (2) the missions; and (3) the Carrier Corps and forced labor.

1. British Penetration and Political Reorganization

British administration was not established in South Nyanza until 1908. Their first efforts sparked local rebellions, which led to two punitive

---

[5] *South Kavirondo Annual Report 1938.*
[6] Philip Mayer, *The Lineage Principle in Gusii Society* (London, 1949), 4.

expeditions, in 1905 and 1908.[7] These dealt harshly and effectively with the rebels, the 1905 affray being described as "not so much a battle as a massacre." Both confrontations ended in the Gusii's total defeat.

When a message arrived in 1905 of a Kisii revolt (Europeans at that time referred to the Gusii as "Kisii"), a detachment of one hundred African police under W. Robert Foran and a company of the Third King's African Rifles under Captain Jenkins were immediately dispatched to quell the rebellion. Foran vividly described the encounter:

> Then came word that the Kisii were in open revolt. Almost immediately a small punitive force was sanctioned, though reluctantly by Sir Charles Eliot [the Commissioner of Kenya from 1901 to 1904]. . . .
>
> The tribesmen did not understand the power of modern weapons and had yet to encounter the white man in combat. They boldly attacked the small force of 200 askaris with masses of spearsmen. Captain Jenkins formed [a] square and gave battle. He let the attack have a good dose of lead, but this did not halt their more determined advance. They ran straight up to the rigid wall of fixed bayonets. Their losses were great. The machine gun was kept in action so long during this sharp engagement that it became almost red-hot to the touch. Before the Kisii warriors were repulsed, they left several hundred dead and wounded spearsmen heaped up outside the square of bayonets. This

[7] W. Robert Foran, *A Cuckoo in Kenya* (London, 1936); F. H. Goldsmith, *John Ainsworth, Pioneer Kenya Administrator 1864-1946,* ed. J. M. Silvester (London, 1959); G. H. Mungeam, *British Rule in Kenya 1895-1912* (Oxford, 1966); W. Lloyd-Jones, *K.A.R.—Being an Unofficial Account of the Origins and Activities of the King's African Rifles* (London, 1926). Both Robert A. and Barbara B. Le-Vine and Philip Mayer refer to a 1907 punitive expedition. (See LeVine, "Nyansongo: A Gusii Community in Kenya," in Beatrice B. Whiting [ed.], *Six Cultures* [New York, 1963], 89, and Mayer, *Gusii Bridewealth, Law and Custom* [London, 1950], 2). However, Ainsworth, Foran, Lloyd-Jones and the carefully documented study of Mungeam, together with *The Times Index,* confirm beyond doubt that the date of the revolt was 1908.

There is also some confusion about a third revolt. I have found no actual description of the revolt. Mayer refers to a 1916 expedition: "Two punitive expeditions (1907 and 1916) served to break resistance, and administration since then has gone on smoothly enough with a notable expansion of services since the beginning of the 1930's." LeVine, on the other hand, speaks of a 1914 expedition ("An Attempt to Change the Gusii Initiation Cycle," *Man,* 179 [1959], 120). Neither LeVine nor Mayer documents his sources. The district records of South Kavirondo and the district and provincial annual reports for that period do not mention a punitive expedition. I also checked *The Times Index* and found no reference to either a 1914 or 1916 expedition. The LeVines's reference may pertain to the time the Mumboites mistook the British evacuation of Kisii in the face of German advance for the millennium, whereupon they ransacked the government offices and missions.

was not so much a battle as a massacre, but wholly unavoidable under the circumstances. It was an urgent case of decimating that determined attack or else being completely wiped out by the Kisii warriors.

The lesson was effective. The Kisii withdrew into the hills, while we buried their dead and succoured the wounded. Our casualties were negligible, only a few askaris being slightly wounded by spears or arrows. We camped in a commanding site near the scene of the fight, and confidently awaited the outcome of events. Early next day the leading chiefs came in and surrendered unconditionally, the tribe being sentenced to pay a heavy fine in cattle and sheep for their past misdeeds.

Foran goes on to describe the 1908 revolt.

On the march between Karungu to Kisii I observed that the latter tribe, the Gusii, were displaying obvious signs of unrest. [It had been decided to move the district administrative center from Karungu on Lake Victoria to Kisii, a distance of about fifty miles inland as the crow flies.] They deserted their villages and crowded the hill-tops at our approach; while all the warriors were fully armed. Straws on the wind, but showing which way it blew! Trouble was definitely brewing. I reported what had been seen to Northcote, the acting district commissioner at Kisii Boma [Swahili for a compound, in this case referring to the administrative headquarters] and he promised to go out next day to investigate what was troubling the tribe. . . . [An interlude of one or two days passes.] I was in pyjamas so put on a dressing-gown and went across to his bungalow. Ainsworth [the Provincial Commissioner] was very agitated. He told me a runner had come through from the Kisii Boma that afternoon, reporting the Kisii were in open rebellion, killing Indian and Somali traders and that Northcote had been speared dangerously in the back while out in the district investigating the state of affairs about which my letter warned him. Immediately he received my note, Northcote mounted his mule, collected half a dozen askaris, and set forth to probe the cause of the unrest among the tribesmen. The Kisii, seeing how small was his escort, suddenly attacked. A spear thrown by one of the warriors struck the district commissioner in the back, severely wounding him and only just missing the spine. His men opened fire, drove off the Kisii, and then carried Northcote back to the Boma. . . .

Ainsworth ordered me to collect all available police, stores and ammunition for a month, also the necessary porters. I was to march at dawn, or earlier if possible, to the relief of Kisii Boma, which was reported to be surrounded and being attacked by the warriors of the tribe. . . .

[In Kisiiland] every village was deserted and the warriors massed on the hill-tops; but they made no attempt to interfere with our advance. They had not forgotten their experience when attacking the 1904 [correctly 1905] column under Captain Jenkins. The closer we got to the Boma the denser became the masses of Kisii spearmen; yet they still hesitated to dispute our progress. . . .

[Later, after the Gusii had asked to surrender] we were astonished to see heavy clouds of smoke arising from the neighbourhood of the road to Kendu, followed by the sputtering of machine-guns and rifle-fire. . . . [Foran had sent a message to the commander of the Kisii Expeditionary Force en route to Kisii informing him of the tribe's willingness to surrender and that they were now peacefully returning with their livestock to their villages. To his amazement this information was ignored. "Another medal cheaply won," remarked a British officer on learning that the Expeditionary Force was going to fight anyway.] We made our way towards the headquarters of the Kisii Expeditionary Force to report ourselves and receive instructions. The [Kings] Africa[n] Rifles were putting in some strenuous work—burning villages, devastating standing crops, capturing livestock and hunting down the bolting warriors. It was tough luck on the latter, for I have no doubt they were under the impression that the tribal surrender had been accepted and no war would take place. . . .

While waiting for a chance to report ourselves we heard that the main column had already burned a great many Kisii villages, as well as capturing over 4,000 cattle on their march from Kendu [Kendu Bay on Lake Victoria] into the country of the tribe. . . . Meanwhile the main column pursued the Kisii about the country, burning villages, destroying crops and capturing both prisoners and livestock. . . .

On the way back to the Boma a large body of Kisii warriors again boldly attacked, forcing us to open fire upon them with rifles and macine guns. We heard afterwards that twenty-five men were killed in that short, sharp engagement. They followed us almost up to the outposts around the Boma, only withdrawing when we fired three volleys over their heads.[8]

A series of telegrams conveyed the results of the expedition to the Colonial Office in London where, for some time, there had been concern over the handling of punitive expeditions which, in the absence of official policy, had been left pretty much to the man on the spot.[9] On February 1, 1908, a telegram received by the Colonial Office read: "Result of operations in Kisii to 28 January cattle captured 5,636 sheep and goats 3,281. 100 Kisii killed. No further casualties on our side. Operations suspended as several clans wish for peace. Kisii reported

[8] Foran, Cuckoo, 177-78. Foran also describes the 1908 revolt in The Kenya Police 1887-1960 (London, 1962), 27-29. Lonsdale, "Political History," 176, suggests that this expedition was undertaken on behalf of the neighboring Luo whose cattle were stolen by Gusii living in the hills.

[9] The following account of the Colonial Office's reaction has been taken from Mungeam, British Rule, 171-80. For the individual documentary references, see Mungeam. Thanks is due John Lonsdale for bringing this account to my attention.

generally demoralised." Two days later a telegram reported the number of dead Kisii had increased to 160 and that the commanding officer hoped soon to meet the main body of Kisii. At that point Winston Churchill, the Colonial Undersecretary, intervened:

> I do not like the tone of these reports. No doubt the clans should be punished; but 160 have now been killed outright—without any further casualties, and the main body has not yet been encountered. . . . It looks like butchery, and if the H. of C. gets hold of it, all our plans in E.A.P. will be under a cloud. Surely it cannot be necessary to go on killing these defenceless people on such an enormous scale.

Churchill then sent a telegram to Sir Donald Sadler, the Governor of Kenya.

> Much regret to observe large numbers of Kisii killed in recent operations. Rely upon you to confine bloodshed within narrowest limits consistent with safety of force and restoration of order. Impress immediately upon O. C. that every effort should be made to induce the enemy to submit peacefully after the most severe lesson they have received and mercy should be extended to all not personally concerned in original outbreak. I shall expect a full report upon any causes of discontent which may have provoked rising

Churchill's suspicions turned out to be correct. A letter from Northcote to his father two days after his attack stated that the incident had been exaggerated—it was only the Kitutu who had attacked—and that far too severe repressive measures had been used. Lieutenant Colonel Mackay, the commanding officer, later sent in a report that confirmed what the previous telegrams had indicated:

> From the date I commenced active operations to the end of the expedition on 6 February 1908, the enemy suffered heavily. They lost over 7000 cattle captured and 5000 sheep and goats were taken, many living and cattle Bomas were burnt while over 200 casualties were inflicted on the enemy, who were completely demoralised fleeing with their families into the Kavirondo country for personal safety.

This controversial episode was not allowed to drop with Churchill's admonitions, but was carried on by R. Popham-Lobb, another British official, who had for some time been incensed over the tactics employed by punitive expeditions. Popham-Lobb calculated the losses suffered in six operations in Kenya during a five-year period (1902–6) to be 2,426 Africans killed as against the administration's loss of 179 killed and wounded. He estimated that since the number killed and wounded was probably three times the number killed, the "enemy" had suffered casualties forty times as great as had the administration.

Popham-Lobb dispatched a long report to the Colonial Office a year after the event, in which he urged close scrutiny and supervision of military operations. He attacked the colonial administration and used the 1908 expeditions as a prime example of needless slaughter:

> The whole episode betrays a degree of administrative ineptitude and a vicious misuse of force on the part of the Administration which deserves the gravest censure, and a Governor so lacking in a sense of his responsibilities with regard to native races under his care that he is able to see in the result of such methods only a "complete success" . . . .

Despite Popham-Lobb's attack, no investigation was undertaken and no punishments were meted out. This was due in part to the lateness of Popham-Lobb's report, for it was considered unwise after a year to reopen the whole question. Instead, a set of Lugard's "Instructions for the Control of Expeditions" was sent to the East African authorities for their consideration.

From the above documents, the following conclusions can be drawn:

1. Spears and shields were no match for machine guns, bayonets, and rifles. When their villages were burned to the ground, their crops demolished, their livestock captured, their warriors killed, and their prophets shown to be impotent in the face of a much superior force, the Gusii suffered the humiliation and demoralization of complete defeat. Pacification showed the futility of armed resistance and closed off the possibilities of revolt and direct challenges to the colonial power.

2. Neither the 1905 nor the 1908 revolt was a haphazard skirmish that happened to occur when a spear slipped or a gun went off. Both were premeditated and planned, determined, and persistent on the part of the Gusii.

3. These military expeditions must have proved a shattering experience for this hitherto unmolested tribe; they furnished a rude awakening to the realities of foreign conquest. Not only did they lay the basis for British rule in South Nyanza, but they gave Africans a first contact with Europeans which must have made the Europeans appear to be objects both of fear and hatred. Is it any wonder that with such a violent beginning, British rule should, in turn, have been violently attacked some fifty years later?

4. Since the Gusii had indicated a desire to surrender, the very need for the 1908 expeditionary attack can be seriously questioned. The commanding officer probably found, after his troops had marched miles across difficult country, that he had a company of trigger-happy soldiers itching for some action. The attack suggests that considerable truth lay in Sir Charles Eliot's contention that punitive expeditions were often needlessly waged by British officers who were hungry for medals.

Evidence suggests that the military seized upon a minor incident to show the Africans brutally who was master. Northcote's spearing appears to have been used as an excuse to perpetuate widespread destruction against a whole community regardless of its participation in the disturbance. Out of all proportion to the danger involved, the military decided on the systematic employment of violence to establish beyond doubt the insurgents' utter powerlessness. Nor was this an isolated incident. Popham-Lobb, Churchill, and other officials knew only too well that these tactics were being used consistently in the colonies.

5. The geographical location of the revolts almost assured the involvement of the Bogonko clan. Kisii (the administrative center) was situated in the middle of Kitutu Location, an area occupied by the Kitutu tribe. Ainsworth's reports clearly singled out the Kitutu tribe as the protagonists. He stated as a matter of fact that the trouble was confined to the Kitutu: "In a few words, it is evident that the Kitutu did not want a station near them. They resented the white man intruding amongst them. They were extremely ignorant and isolated, and the witch's medicine showed it was bad for them if the European remained, and that it was good for the Kisii that he should die."[10] In the Kitutu tribe the Bogonko was the largest clan, comprising more than half of the location's population.[11] Since it was also the most powerful clan, its warriors probably led the attack. Subsequently this area was to become the center of Mumbo activity. (The various links between protest by revolt and the reasons for Bogonko support of Mumboism will be traced in a later section.)

With the advent of the British, Gusii society was politically reorganized: the villages where the young warriors had lived while making forays upon a neighboring tribe's cattle were abolished; allegiance to clan and tribe no longer entailed military duties; territory was divided on the basis of tribal units with the result that the seven Gusii tribes were allocated to seven subunits known as locations, an

[10] Mungeam, *British Rule*, 175.
[11] See below, 410.

administrative unit like a county, and central authorities were introduced into a traditionally chiefless society. In making these changes,
the British used the indigenous structure, placing chiefs and headmen
responsible to them in charge of areas roughly coinciding with tribal
units. Usually the chiefs were chosen from traditionally powerful clans
whose right to rule was accepted by the people; sometimes, however,
out of ignorance, the British would appoint an individual who had secured their favor but whose credentials marked him as insignificant in
the eyes of his fellow Africans. Other times, rival contenders from
within the same clan or between two powerful clans contested the
chieftainship. "Government backing [and threats of dismissal] replaced the consensus of the elders as the sanction for chiefly action,
the scope of such action being immeasurably widened by Government's requirements."[12] Thus a basis for inter- and intraclan rivalry
was engendered.[13]

Under the new system, the chiefs had wide powers—some traditional, some new—and considerable autonomy in the management of
the locations. Each reported directly to the District Officer and District Commissioner. During Mumboism's most active period, the chiefs
also held judicial powers (until the African Tribunal Courts were established in the 1930's, and even after that informally they exercised
wide judicial powers). They provided not only advice and warnings
but meted out punishment. Commenting on the scope of chiefly
power, R. A. LeVine wrote:

> Location chiefs, who act as constables and informal courts of first in-
> stances, go far beyond their formal powers, incarcerating young men
> for insolence to their fathers, threatening legal sanctions against hus-
> bands who neglect their wives, punishing their personal enemies with
> legal means at their disposal. Gusii judicial leaders do not fear the ad-
> verse opinions of their fellowmen because they know that their judicial
> authority is respected and even feared by the entire group. Chiefs and
> Tribunal Court presidents are the most powerful individuals in Gusii-
> land; immoderate criticism of them to their faces is considered impolite
> as well as simply unwise.[14]

This concentration of power meant that the chiefs could act auto-
cratically and few would dare to challenge their action.

[12] Lonsdale, "Political History," 27.

[13] See Carl G. Rosberg, Jr. and John Nottingham, *The Myth of Mau Mau*
(New York, 1966), 80-84, for a similar explanation. The role of chief in Kisii dis-
trict is examined by LeVine, "Nyansongo," 89-94. This discussion is based on
LeVine's analysis.

[14] Robert A. LeVine, "The Internationalization of Political Values in Stateless
Societies," *Human Organization,* XIX (1960), 52.

Much prestige also came to be attached to being in a chief's employment. His retinue included a host of assistants: clerks, elders of the tribunal court, tribal police, headmen, personal bodyguards, and, as befitted an important person, any number of household retainers. Assistants often took advantage of their position and ordered people about on matters having nothing to do with the government of the location.

Most chiefs were wealthy before taking office, but if they were not they soon rectified this condition. While a chief did not have the actual right to appoint personnel, he was in a key position to influence choices. Nor did chiefs fail to exercise this influence, as can be seen by the many officials who were their kinsmen. Obviously, a chieftainship was viewed as a political plum, a position that could be used to enhance an individual's as well as a clan's power, prestige, and wealth. Thus the office of chief was much sought after, and its loss could well foster envy and bitterness on the part of the unsuccessful.

Militating against any direct challenge to the chief and governmental officials was the authoritarian structure of Gusii society.[15] Command relationships were a part of everyday life, a person of higher rank being entitled to order a lower-ranking person to do his bidding in any sphere. Thus, wealth, prestige, and political position traditionally endowed their possessor with broad powers of command. As LeVine put it, deferential behavior on the part of lower status persons was pronounced and had been that way in the past as well: "A soft voice and downward glance constitute traditionally proper demeanor for someone talking to an elder, chief, or other figure of importance."[16]

2. Impact of the Missions

As the power and authority of the administrative center was extended to the hinterland, missionaries followed. In reaction, a number of semi-religious, semi-political sects developed in Gusiiland. They formed a loose network of small, locally organized groups with little or no co-ordination except for shared anti-European sentiments and a belief in a millennium when their prophets would return and banish the foreigners forever. In a very general way, these sects resembled each other in their organization as well as in their belief in the god Mumbo and various indigenous prophets.

The first missionaries to arrive, the Seventh-day Adventists (the Adventists), landed at Kendu Bay and opened a mission station nearby at Genia in 1907. The second group, the Mill Hill Fathers (the Fa-

15 Ibid., 53.
16 Ibid.

thers), founded a mission at Nyaribari near Kisii in 1911. Besides introducing Christian teachings which challenged the basis of traditional thought, the missionaries also opened schools and hospitals. As elsewhere, their educational efforts produced a group of young men who became increasingly divorced from indigenous social control. Year after year, the annual reports noted the growing rift between the students and tribal authority. The 1921 Report, for example, stated: "The mission boys appeared inclined to impose on newcomers in an endeavour to get support for an attitude of independence from tribal authority . . . any attempt [must be prevented] on the part of the mission boys to regard themselves as a separate community." The 1924 Report complained that the mission adherents "are too much inclined to consider themselves as a class apart and consequently entitled to different treatment from other natives and to a certain extent to be outside the authority of ordinary native law and custom." In 1926, S. O. V. Hodge, the acting District Commissioner, wrote that the elders "complain of the lack of respect shown by mission boys to their elders and betters. This is repudiated by the boys themselves who in their turn complain of the drunkenness, laziness, and unprogressiveness of the older generation." Thus the cohesion of tribal society was weakened since many of the new Christians believed that in shaking off old communal obligations they had rid themselves of tribal control. Not only did they refuse to make tax and bride-wealth payments, but they scorned the authority of chiefs, elders, and headmen.

No doubt the rivalry between the Adventists and the Fathers was still another factor that disturbed Africans since their differences were more obvious than their common ground of Christianity, and, although open disagreement among the missionaries themselves rarely came to the fore, disagreement among their converts was often violent.[17]

3. The Carrier Corps and Forced Labor

The third factor of change was the recruitment of men for the Carrier Corps. This aroused the inhabitants of Nyanza to the events occurring around them and gave thousands of men new experiences and ideas. What happened was that, with the progress of World War I, it had become necessary to recruit porters to transport equipment for the German East Africa campaign. A large portion of the responsibility fell upon Nyanza. The task of acquiring porters for the Corps, referred to as "a suicidal system of supply," was with great reluctance undertaken by John Ainsworth and, according to Lord Cranworth, it

[17] *South Kavirondo District Annual Reports, 1913, 1921, 1922, 1924, 1926, and 1928.*

"nearly broke his heart" for "he was not unaware of the privations and casualties which must inevitably be suffered by those he loved. . . ."[18] Carrying heavy loads through tsetse- and mosquito-ridden swamps and over sun-baked savannah in humid tropical weather was one of the toughest, most grueling assignments of the war. Ainsworth estimated that of the 162,000 Africans recruited for military labor, 24,000 died—although other estimates of the number dead were much higher and the government's conservative figure was strongly criticized.[19]

Nyanzan porters served with distinction and their effort was singled out as one of the factors that helped to win the war. They were affectionately eulogized in the following paraphrase of Kipling's "Gunga Din."

> Oh, the Lindi road was dusty
> And the Lindi road was long
> But the chap w'at did the hardest graft,
> And the chap w'at did most wrong,
> Was the Kavirondo porter with his Kavirondo song
> It was "Porter njo hapa!" [Porter, come here!]
> It was "Omera, hya! Git!" [Omera, come on!]
> And Omera didn't grumble,
> He simply did his bit.[20]

The experience of the Carrier Corps—which was not forgotten—had a profound effect upon the Africans' attitudes toward employment. A district annual report states, for example, that in 1914 many young men had been tricked into coming to the district station to "cut grass," whereupon they had been seized and sent off to the Corps.[21] When rumors spread in 1938 of an impending second world war, the Gusii displayed anxiety and hardly anyone turned up for the annual administration-sponsored sports meet. Even after a lapse of twenty-four years no Gusii intended to be so deceived again!

It was also no secret that the administration forced young men to leave the district and seek work in other areas. Although leading colo-

[18] Lord Bertram Francis Cranworth, *Kenya Chronicles* (London, 1939), 73-74.

[19] Goldsmith (*Ainsworth, Pioneer*, 100) simply mentions that other figures are higher but he does not provide them. Norman Leys, a medical officer in Kenya, wrote in 1924 that the British recruited 350,000 porters in all for the German East Africa campaign, of whom 150,000 were recruited from Kenya. The officially recorded deaths totaled 46,618; 1,743 killed and 44,875 dead of disease. The relatives of 40,645 dead men were untraced, Norman Leys, *Kenya* (London, 1924), 287. See also Rosberg and Nottingham, *Mau Mau*, 30-31.

[20] Goldsmith, *Ainsworth, Pioneer*, 95-96.

[21] *South Kavirondo District Annual Report 1938.*

nial officials attempted to stop this practice, individual District Commissioners appeared to have had considerable leeway in the administering of their areas.[22] Thus, the District Commissioners of South Nyanza in 1915 and 1920, respectively, wrote: "Lately in order to fulfill Labour requisitions, force has had to be applied i.e. the young men have been rounded up during the night"; and "There is no use in blinding the fact that the majority of this labour [5,000 men] was not voluntary—it was ordered out by Chiefs and Elders, under instructions from me, in the hope that once the young men have taken the plunge, and find that they do not die in masses, and are not starved and ill-treated, there will be a more or less steady flow of voluntary labour in the future.[23]

Origins and Development of the Cult of Mumbo

The exact date of Mumbo's origins is hard to pinpoint. There is a legend that Onyango Dunde, a Luo of Alego Location (which lies on the eastern shore of Lake Victoria), was given the message in 1913. One evening when sitting in his hut, Onyango was accosted by a gigantic snake so big that when it stood on its end in the lake, its head reached into the clouds. (One version has the snake coming from the clouds.) The snake swallowed Onyango and then regurgitated him, unhurt but shaken. This appeared to have been the snake's way of obtaining Onyango's attention because it immediately began to speak:

> I am the God Mumbo whose two homes are in the Sun and the Lake. I have chosen you to be my mouthpiece. Go out and tell all Africans— and more especially the people of Alego—that from henceforth I am their God. Those whom I choose personally, and also those who acknowledge me, will live forever in plenty. Their crops will grow of themselves and there will be no more need to work. I will cause cattle, sheep, and goats to come up out of the lake in great numbers to those who believe in me, but all unbelievers and their families and their cattle will die out. The Christian religion is rotten [mbovu] and so is its practice of making its believers wear clothes. My followers must let their hair grow—never cutting it. Their clothes shall be the skins of goats and cattle and they must never wash. All Europeans are your enemies, but the time is shortly coming when they will all disappear from our country.
>
> Daily sacrifice—preferably the males—of cattle, sheep, goats, and

[22] For an example of intervention by higher officialdom, see below, 416.
[23] South Kavirondo District Annual Reports 1915, 1920. See also Seaton, Lion, 194.

fowls shall be made to me. More especially do I prefer black bulls. Have no fear of sacrificing these as I will cause unlimited black cattle to come to you from the Lango, Masai, Nandi and Kipsigis. Lastly my followers must immediately slaughter all their cattle, sheep and goats. When this is done, I will provide them with as many more as they want from the lake.

Having spoken thus, the snake disappeared into the lake, and Onyango set out to spread Mumbo's words. He soon gathered a fairly large following.[24]

From Alego Location in Central Nyanza, Mumboism spread quickly to neighboring locations and thence to South Nyanza, carried by some mission-trained men in the absence of the Adventist missionaries. (The Adventist mission, though staffed mainly by Canadians, had its headquarters in Hamburg, Germany. During World War I, the missionaries were all interned.) Mumboism's millennial message fitted in well with Adventist teachings such as "Watch and pray, for the end of the world is at hand." The District Commissioner of Kisii spoke of a new religion, "Mumbo," making its appearance in his district in 1914–15.[25]

The sect's existence became patently evident on September 19, 1914, when the Germans invaded Kisii from what was then German East Africa and the British vacated the town in order to mobilize resistance and return. Believing Mumbo's prophecy that the British would soon depart, the local inhabitants mistook their temporary exodus for the millennium and looted the town and the neighboring missions. They ransacked all the government buildings and houses, the missions of Nyaribari, Nyanchwa, and Asumbi, and the trading centers of Riana and Rangwe. District Officer P. M. Gordon recorded the event:

Thus it was that the Africans who gathered on the surrounding hills to watch the battle of Kisii, and as evening fell, saw the rival forces draw off to the north and south, felt assured that the prophecy was fulfilled. The Europeans had gone forever! . . . Their works, their offices, and Missions must be cast out. In this spirit of frenzy the empty Missions and trading centres, and offices were plundered, sacked and

[24] "The Cult of Mumbo in Central and South Kavirondo," by "Nyangweso" in *The Journal of the East Africa and Uganda Natural History Society*, 38, 39 (May, Aug. 1930), 13-14. "Nyangweso" must have been a British administrator since he had access to administrative files. He might have been District Commissioner S. O. V. Hodge, who was the District Commissioner of South Nyanza at that time.

[25] KSI/27: District of South Kavirondo Administrative Records, Kenya National Archives.

burned. The sight of the [King's] Africa[n] Rifles marching back in good order the following morning must have been a severe shock.[26]

Even the heavy fine of three thousand head of cattle levied by the administration and the dispatch of many Kisii to work outside the location did not kill the movement. The following year, the chiefs reported an increasing number of adherents. Again many were sent out of the district to work.

In the years from 1915 to 1920, the cult spread rapidly, causing the British anxiety. As the District Commissioner put it in a letter, if the sect were left unattended "in an affair of this sort incalculable harm may be done and the position in time become so bad that the whole district be utterly inflamed and disorganized."[27] Not knowing with what it was dealing, the administration questioned the chiefs and missionaries and sent informers into the sect's schools.

In 1920 another group, closely resembling Mumbo, was reported. It had been started by an old woman, Bonairiri of Kitutu Location, and it believed in the return of the prophet Zakawa. Zakawa was a great Kisii medicine man and prophet who, when the Uganda Railway was begun, had collected the Kisii, gone to the site of the present district headquarters, and prophesied where the police lines, the hospital, the office, and the District Commissioner's house would be built. He had also prophesied that over the course of years the young men would be disarmed and prove a greater source of revenue to their parents than the girls (who brought a bride-price), because they would receive wages for their work. He had also predicted the departure of the Europeans. When most of his prophecies came true, Zakawa's reputation as a seer was established. Whether he had actually uttered these prophecies is immaterial, since everyone believed that he had.[28] Later his influence was enhanced by a belief that he was still alive: apparently he had died during a great beer-drink around 1902 but because he had not had a regular funeral, it was thought that he had not truly died and would return.

At the outset, Bonairiri sought permission from the chief to start a school where she could instruct her followers. The chief took her to the District Commissioner who refused her request. In mid-October,

[26] "An Outline of the History of the District of South Kavirondo—Kenya Colony 1870-1946," in *South Kavirondo District Annual Report 1946.*

[27] KSI/27: Letter, 21 July 1915. District of South Kavirondo Administrative Records, Kenya National Archives.

[28] Zakawa's repute has grown with the attainment of independence, for time has confirmed his prophecies about the white man's departure. I talked with two ex-chiefs and they spoke admiringly of how Zakawa had been proved correct.

1920, the chief reported that Bonairiri had collected a small group to whom she was preaching Mumboism. The administration dispersed her school. In November, it appeared that she had been joined by exponents of Zakawaism.

With the addition of Zakawaism, the movement was strengthened. In December 1920 District Commissioner H. E. Welby reported that all the people of Kitutu location were attending Bonairiri's school and that most, especially the old men, believed in Zakawa's return.[29] Two days before the predicted reappearance of Zakawa and the departure of the white man, the District Commissioner, worried about Mumboism's rapid growth and the restlessness that it was causing, disbanded Bonairiri's school and rounded up the ringleaders. Consequently, Bonairiri was found insane and confined to a mental institution; her husband, Owura, whom Welby described as "chiefly responsible for the ready adoption of the dangerous part of the teaching"; her son, Marita, said to be "the most active agent in spreading the dangerous part of his mother's and father's teachings"; and Ongeri, the son of Maraa, the witch doctor responsible for the spearing of District Commissioner Northcote during the 1908 rebellion, together with another woman, were in 1921 all deported to Lamu, an isolated Arab town about eight hundred miles away on the coast of Kenya.[30]

Repression, however, did not mean the end of the movement. During the 1920's there were outbreaks of Mumboism in Karochuonyi, Kasipul, and Kochia locations of South Nyanza. In 1927, the District Commissioner of Kisii wrote that the natives of Majoge Location were resurrecting Mumboism and that it was spreading rapidly to Bassi, Nyaribari, and Kitutu locations. (These locations form the northeastern section of South Nyanza and border one another.) The administration made the ringleaders move their huts into Kisii village where they could be watched. In 1931, the Local Native Council passed a resolution forbidding the practice of Mumboism.

However, the District Commissioner expressed the fear that should there be a serious famine or some other calamity the cult would recruit many followers and trouble would ensue. And as predicted, it was in the early 1930's, during a serious economic depression brought on by drought, famine, and an invasion of locusts, that the last widespread resurgence occurred. Thus, in 1933, the chiefs and members of the Local Native Council reported an alarming spread of the cult into all areas of South Nyanza. The climax was reached in November

[29] CN/43: Letter, 5 Dec. 1920. Central Kavirondo Political Records, Kenya National Archives.
[30] *South Kavirondo District Annual Report 1921.*

at the District Sports Meet when twenty armed young Mumboites defied the order of the senior Kisii chief to disperse. The nine ringleaders were promptly arrested and, after a judicial inquiry, deported to Kipani (another isolated settlement on the Kenyan coast). Within a few months, little was heard of Mumboism.

The movement did not die out completely, however. There was evidence of its activity in 1938 and 1947. Finally, in 1954 during the Mau Mau emergency, it was proscribed.[31] But in 1963 Ogot estimated that there were still about five hundred practicing Mumboites:[32] my own investigations in June 1966 revealed that the cult was extinct. Local people could recall its existence but none knew of any recent activities. When asked whether any members were still alive, several mentioned Marita, Bonairiri's son, but no other name was given.[33] Ex-Chief Musa Nyandusi wrote in January 1967, "Marita Ogwora is the only survivor who is alive, others were old and died. Since they were arrested by the British Government, they never practised their cult."[34]

During its time, Mumboism had its geographic center in the district of Kisii in the locations of Kitutu, North Mugirango, Nyaribari, Bassi, Majoge, and Wanjare; it had also spilled over into the neighboring locations of Gem, Kasipul, Karochuonyo, Kochia, and Kaniamwa. It had even recruited members as far away as the Luo location of Gwassi, on the shores of Lake Victoria.

Two general observations can be made about Mumboism's pattern of development. First, its growth coincided with years of agricultural depression. Its greatest activity occurred immediately after

[31] *East African Standard,* September 17, 1954.

[32] Ogot, "British Administration," 249-74.

[33] I located Marita with some difficulty, having to drive over miles of narrow, hilly, dirt roads muddied from the "long rains" and so eroded that the car often straddled a deep gully. Eventually what were called "roads" petered out to trails, and finally driving had to be abandoned. After a hike across country, I found Marita's home. Marita was absent and a boy was sent to find him. Marita returned but refused to talk to me, feigning tiredness, although it was early afternoon. Despite my pleas that we could have a "restful talk," he insisted: "I'm very tired, I must have my rest." Aside to his companions he said: "What's a European doing here? We're going to die." My guide, a young welfare worker, was amused at the old man's fears. He explained: "They're afraid. They've never seen a European come to this primitive place." This statement was surprising since Marita lived only fifteen miles from Kisii. It served, however, to underline the remoteness of the Highlands.

Although Marita's refusal was exasperating, it was understandable. His contact with whites had been limited to the British who had deported and imprisoned him and his parents. Even though Kenya had achieved independence, he still feared and distrusted white people.

[34] Personal letter to the author from ex-Chief Musa Nyandusi, Jan. 23, 1967.

World War I and in the early 1930's, both periods of serious hardship when people pressed by drought and famine sought supernatural help in controlling the elements. Of these periods, Lonsdale wrote:

> Traders took advantage of concerted tax-drives to lower the prices offered for African cattle, huts were occasionally burned to encourage payment, and widows, unlike those in Tanganyika, had to pay the full rate of tax on their huts. Inefficient tax-registers and collection in both the reserves and settled areas not infrequently led to double-payment of the taxes of migrant workers.[35]

Second, the movement developed erratically. There were sudden flareups when membership expanded greatly—churches were built, schools opened, and feasts held. These florescences sparked government concern, and it would respond with repression, causing the sect to lie dormant for some time only to blossom forth in a nearby area with another leader.

Little is known about the actual organization of local groups. Sometimes the Mumboites built their meeting places on hilltops, at other times they met in their home compounds in a hut set aside for this purpose. The following describes such a meeting place:

> . . . The meeting place of the cult consisted of a beautifully swept enclosure adjoining the High Priest's Boma and capable of seating some two hundred people. From the next boma to that of the High Priest ran a made path, four feet wide and trenched at the sides. . . . The enclosure was surrounded by a well-built dry stone wall. In the centre was a little semi-open hut about six feet in diameter, finished with white mud. . . . There was no door, it appeared symmetrical all round. . . . In the centre of the hut was a phallic altar-post, bearing traces of blood-stains. . . . The High Priest's daughter produced some unpleasant animal relics from a hole in the wall in the enclosure. In the Western corner a bush plant (Nyaluthkoth) had been planted. . . . In the Eastern corner was a small length of inner wall covered with dry grass, from which a shrub was growing so as to leave a covered but hollow space between the walls.[36]

The members were divided into two orders. The first order, the priests, were older, established men, usually the head of a *boma*, who were "called"—by being possessed—in a way similar to Onyano, the founder. It was believed that the spirit of Mumbo wandered the land

---

[35] Lonsdale, "Political History," 14; *South Kavirondo District Annual Reports 1921, 1933.*

[36] "Nyangweso," "Cult of Mumbo," 15-16.

until it found a suitable person to enter. Supposedly invested with supernatural powers that enabled them to cure all kinds of illnesses and even resurrect the dead, such people were in great demand. The second order consisted of the priests' dependents and any others who wished to join.[37] Members were also distinguished on the basis of their tasks, be it sect leader, evangelist, food provider, teacher, prophet, or any of a variety of ritual specialists.[38]

Message and Activities of the Cult

In order to try to explain the sect's tenacity despite administrative repression, let us look at its message and basis of support.

First of all, its message. Mumboism articulated an aggressive stand against foreign domination: "The Christian religion is rotten; all Europeans are your enemies." The movement proclaimed a set of values to which all "true Africans" should adhere, and it attacked the administrators as bearers of false values. The British were charged with being alien intruders and corrupters of the traditional way of life, and the chiefs with being agents of the intruders and traitors to that way of life.

The chiefs were treated with particular contempt. For example, at the District Sports Meet after twenty Mumboites in warriors' garb openly defied both the senior Kisii chief and an important Luo chief sent by the District Commissioner to stop their dancing, District Commissioner E. R. S. Davies reported:

> . . . I believe that they have all intrigued against the authority of the chiefs and headmen and deliberately hindered them in carrying out their duties by insults and threats, and claiming greater powers . . . When I arrested Muchirongo the day after the meeting of Mumboites at Kisii, I heard him abusing the chiefs, some of them individually by name and all of them collectively in a way that showed me that such teaching was dangerous to peace and good order, and inciting enmity between his followers and government. He and those who thought like him were without doubt intriguing against constituted power and authority . . . Moreover the chiefs are evidently afraid of it and realize that they are the special objects of hatred and scorn.[39]

[37] Ibid.

[38] PC/NZA 4/5/7: Based on a letter, 8 Dec. 1933, Intelligence Reports, South Kavirondo District, Kenya National Archives.

[39] PC/NZA 4/5/7, Intelligence Reports of the Provincial Commissioner, Nyanza, Kenya National Archives.

Given the powerful position of the chiefs, the authoritarian structure of Gusii society, and the fact that the order had come directly from the District Commissioner, this defiance was particularly bold and disrespectful.[40] Also, its conspicuous style—the men being decked out in fighting attire (perhaps symbolizing the former revolts) and participating in traditional dances (perhaps denoting loyalty to traditional values)—suggests premeditated action designed to antagonize as well as to convey a message.

The millennial dream was the movement's chief tenet; with minor variations, it was held in common by the different local groups,[41] and appeared in the prophecies, visions, and dreams of cult heroes, both living and dead. It promised the destruction of the colonial order: the present world was soon to undergo a great cataclysm at which time a terrible vengeance would befall the enemies of the Mumboites, all of whom—the administrators, missionaries, and chiefs—would be overthrown and a kingdom of the Mumboites established.

Several versions recounted how this transformation was to proceed. In one, all water would be turned into blood and only Mumbo's followers would have drinking water, provided by him. All white people would disappear, leaving the Africans as sole survivors. In another, the founder was to be snatched up into heaven by fire, from whence he would dispense food to his followers. A third story recited how a certain Abachi tribe (an unknown tribal name) would descend from the north and exterminate the white man with sharp knives. Even the exact number each Abachi would kill (twenty white men apiece) was specified. Another story that circulated during World War I and had some basis in fact predicted that the Germans were soon to invade and cut off the arms of men in clothes, presumably Europeans and Westernized Africans, and particularly chiefs and mission converts. The Mumboites would escape unscathed because they were the Germans' friends. Still another story recounted that Zakawa's return was to be followed by days of darkness and a plague of locusts, after which the white man would be no more, and Zakawa, together with a sect priestess, would occupy the district headquarters. Given the frustrated ambitions of the Bogonko clan it is not surprising that the apocalypse they envisioned was both catastrophic and violent.[42]

What was the Mumboite utopia to be like? As with the Marxian utopia only the barest outlines were specified, but in contrast to that utopia, work was not given a prominent place. It was, in short, to be a life with an abundance of material goods, a relaxed happy life free

[40] See above, 386.
[41] For one version of the origins' legend, see above, 390.
[42] See below, 410-11.

from worry in which the Mumboites could smoke *bhang* (Indian hemp) as much as they wanted. They would be blessed with an unfailing supply of sheep, cattle, and goats and their unattended crops would grow plentifully. Food would be showered upon them from heaven or arise of its own accord from Lake Victoria. They would be reunited with their dead, especially their great warriors and prophets and their god Mumbo.[43] The crippled would be cured.

When was this paradise to be reached? Although the date was not usually specified, it was believed to be near at hand. There were reports that the Mumboites were buying lamps, in preparation for the end of the world when all would be dark. Some faithful followers, believing Mumbo's promise of food in the millennium, stopped cultivating their gardens, a few killed all of their livestock as he had ordered, and others refused to comply with the government demand for road construction, saying that since the Europeans were soon to leave, roads would no longer be needed.[44]

One of the most revealing aspects of this dream was its reversal theme. In the promised land the superior-inferior positions of the Europeans and the Africans were to be reversed; the poor were to become rich and the weak strong. The politically dominant would suffer terrible punishments: They would die, be damned, be turned into monkeys, have their arms cut off, or be eaten by the great snake Mumbo. This theme appeared in a number of stories. For instance, part of the myth stated that actually the black man had been created first and white man second but that Zakawa and Mumbo had purposely put the white man over the black. Zakawa's sorceries were also credited with originally bringing the white man to Africa. This situation was soon to be righted with the return of Zakawa and other prophets, who would banish the white man forever. No information is available as to why this topsy-turvy state of affairs had originated, but in similar sects it came about, so the explanation goes, to test the black man by trials and tribulations—a purification through suffering. Only those who had truly followed Mumbo's edict—"Go tell all Africans . . . that henceforth I am their God"—would be saved.

It was not only within the cult that this theme predominated.

[43] This vision of the wealth-to-come is not surprising since among the Gusii a man's social status and hence his influence in community affairs largely depended upon his wealth. An *omanda* (rich man) was respected and listened to, but an *omoraka* (poor man) was despised and ignored. Robert LeVine, "Wealth and Power in Gusiiland," in *Markets in Africa*, ed. P. J. Bohannan and George Dalton (Evanston, 1962), 523.

[44] KSI/27: the District Commissioner of South Nyanza to the Provincial Commissioner, letter, 2 Dec. 1927, South Kavirondo Political Records, Kenya National Archives.

Similar stories circulated elsewhere in South Nyanza. For example, a rumor that gained some currency among the Gusii and Kipsigis during World War II was that of the "Queen's dream." The Queen of England was said to be really a prophetess who dreamt that a black baby with wings would be born. The social order would then be reversed and the black races would take command. In an effort to prevent the baby from being born, the government was supposed to be trying to make the Africans sterile by distributing European blankets and tea, which were believed to possess magical properties that could bring impotence.[45] What the cult did was to take such rumors and stories and give them form and coherence by linking them to a set of related ideas.

Whatever else they did, these stories certainly portrayed the blacks' dislike of the whites, and they transferred the power to determine men's destinies to the black man. Since he will occupy his rightful position, he will control instead of being controlled. The reversal theme can be viewed as an effort to come to terms with the fact that the white man possessed superior ability to cope with the physical environment and had far greater material wealth than the African. This myth transformed the humiliating aspects of defeat into virtues, for Mumboism credited its own prophets with having put the African into a subordinate position. The colonial era, soon to be terminated, was to be considered merely an interlude in the chain of events leading to the assumption by the Mumboites of their predestined superior position.

In spite of Mumboism's blatant rejection of Christianity and white men, Christian influence is, however, evident in its teachings. Bonairiri preached that woman came from the rib of man. The millennial concept appears to be derived from Christian eschatology since there is no mention in either traditional Gusii or Luo religion of a Day of Judgment, there being rather the traditional principle of retribution whereby evildoers were punished here and now. The belief that the Mumboites would be provided with food by their god at the millennium is reminiscent of the Lord supplying manna to the Children of Israel during their progress through the wilderness to the promised land. Though a traditional custom, the sacrifice of animals may well have been reinforced by the Old Testament practice. A number of precepts such as one will go to heaven by praying to Mumbo, one should not steal, one should not insult people, one should honor the aged, and one should not go about naked, have a Christian flavor about them. Al-

[45] PC/NZA 4/5/2: Intelligence Reports of the Provincial Commissioner, Nyanza, Kenya National Archives.

though some of these practices were part of traditional life, the very fact that they were singled out as explicit rules suggests Christian contact.

The "origins" story (Mumbo the sea serpent swallows Onyango Dunde) also sounds as if it came straight from the Old Testament account of Jonah and the whale. A Luo tale, however, also tells of an important elder being swallowed by a sea serpent.[46] Mumbo's legend may be based either on Luo or Biblical cosmology, or it may have originated independently. Probably, however, since there were parallels between the Christian and traditional myths, these parallels became the basis for a new one.

The strongest Christian influence is, however, in the concept of Mumbo. Did the Gusii, the main supporters of Mumboism, have any similar ideas? Or even more relevant, did the tribe in which the myth originated, the Luo, have such an idea in their traditional beliefs? The Gusii are said to have had a snake god called Kiboyi.[47] According to LeVine the word *Nyasaye*, which is equivalent to our concept of "luck" or "fortune," is often heard among the Gusii, who believe that it is a Luo word diffused via the missionaries. Events over which an individ-

---

[46] John Ainsworth, one-time Provincial Commissioner of Nyanza Province and later Chief Commissioner, speaks of the origins of the sea serpent myth and, though there is no mention of Mumbo, the similarities between his account and the above story leave no doubt but that they are related. "The people of the Kisumu district have a superstition that a big serpent lives in the lake. In the far distant past one of their most important elders was out in a canoe when it sank and the occupants were lost. Sometime afterwards the elder returned to his people and said that when the canoe was upset he was swallowed and subsequently thrown upon an island. He afterwards asked the serpent to take him to his people and the snake agreed. He was again swallowed and later ejected upon the shore of the mainland. The serpent is said to visit a piece of woodland near Yala River. It can be heard on certain nights passing over the land to the woodland where the people place offerings of fowls and eggs. It is unlucky for anyone to see the reptile which is held sacred."

Ainsworth gives his interpretation of what is said to be Mumbo rearing its body from the lake: "At times clouds of midges (winged ants) known as 'lake flies' emerge from the Lake. They look, from a distance, like water spouts." From Goldsmith, *Ainsworth, Pioneer*, 74.

A water snake also appeared in the mythology of the Maji-Maji Rebellion of 1905–6 in what was formerly German East Africa. The battle cry *maji maji* (the Swahili word for water) was said to have reminded the insurgents that they were serving a pagan water-snake spirit whose prophets had incited the first acts of defiance and who provided protection by a magical medicine that turned bullets into water. From George Shepperson and Thomas Price, *Independent African* (Edinburgh, 1958), 420.

[47] P. M. Gordon, "An Outline of the History of the District of South Kavirondo."

ual has no control are attributed to *Nyasaye*. However, absent from Gusii thought is any notion of a creator-spirit.[48]

Whisson maintains that the concept of a creator-spirit was present in Luo cosmology before the Christian idea of a creator was introduced. *Nyasaye*, however, is a Bantu rather than a Nilotic term, and the Luo, like the Alur (another Nilotic tribe), appear not to have had a clear idea of a personal god until they came into contact with the Bantu. To some extent *Nyasaye* was equated in Luo thought with the sun. It was considered a good thing for all people to be out of bed by dawn, when simple supplicatory prayers were offered to the rising sun. An old man might say "Rise well for me that I may be at peace." Younger people might ask that a good prospective mate be brought to their notice during the day. Similarly, prayers were offered at night as the sun set. *Nyasaye* was seen not only in the sun but in other large and extraordinary phenomena—in the moon, in large rocks, in big snakes, in elephants, and in awe-inspiring objects of nature. The creator-force was not personalized in any way. It belonged to the cosmology of a nomadic people to be worshipped wherever men were, not only in a temple or in a sacred grove.[49]

[48] LeVine states that traditional Gusii religion consists of an ancestor cult which co-exists with beliefs in a witchcraft-sorcery complex. The Gusii do not have an organized cosmology in the sense of a comprehensive set of conceptions of the universe and the beings and forces in it. The spirits of the ancestors are the major supernatural beings recognized by the Gusii. LeVine, "Nyansongo: A Gusii Community in Kenya," 73-78.

Ex-Chief Ooga, who was a chief during the period of active Mumboism, maintained that the Gusii were sun worshippers. He said that they looked at *Engora* (the sun) and asked *Engora* to help them. To my question whether all the Gusii worship the sun or only the Mumboites, he replied, "all people of Gusii." "The word 'Mumbo' of 'Nyamumbo' means God," he said. "When the missionaries came they translated the word God into the Swahili 'Ombamumbo', or the abbreviated form 'Mumbo'." From an interview with ex-Chief Ooga, June 28, 1966.

[49] Whisson maintains that the attributes of *Nyasaye* were those of a moral god. "He brought health and wealth to those who live according to the customs of the tribe. . . . He would help the diviners in their good works but not in their evil works, and was the final power that directed the universe, an idea that cannot be easily aligned to the presence of evil in the world, nor to the idea that some have expressed that a thief, before setting out on a raid, would request the protection of God. The *ajugoa* [diviner] would, through his divinations with cowries and other small objects, possibly suggest that the wrath of *Nyasaye* was responsible for some misfortune, but this would be unlikely, other more easily approached forces being more commonly divined. The rainmakers appear to have the power to coerce *Nyasaye* in their particular function which is hard to separate from pure magic. . . .

His function therefore in the field of social control was one of directing men to follow in the ways of the tribe, for he would visit with disease those who sinned against the customs of the tribe, and those who so fell might expect his judgment.

Mumboism seems to have taken from the indigenous religion the idea that the creator-spirit dwells in Mumbo. However, in Mumboism the traditional view of a vague life-force that fills wondrous objects is gone; in its place is the omnipotent Christian figure who clearly promises eternal life to his followers and damnation to unbelievers. Here the Luo creator-spirit has changed from a depersonalized force into a personal god with the attributes of the God of the Old Testament. He is a commanding and demanding patriarch who requires exclusive worship from his children and lays down rules that must be followed: "I am the God Mumbo . . . go and tell all Africans . . . that henceforth I am their God. Those whom I choose personally, and also those who acknowledge me, will live forever in plenty . . . but all unbelievers and their families and their cattle will die out . . ."[50] Hence, a new culture form emerged from combining indigenous and Western ideas.

Mumboism often also turned to the past for inspiration: fresh meaning was imbued into tribal ways; old dreams were animated with a new vitality. Since Mumbo had ordered a return to the old ways, the converts were directed to reject the new religion of Christianity, to sacrifice daily, let their hair grow long, wear clothes of skins, and never to wash. Old tribal dances were revived. The most venerated Gusii warriors and their most militant anti-British leaders were claimed by the movement. Zakawa the great prophet, Bogonko the mighty chief, and Maraa the instigator of the 1908 rebellion became its symbols, infusing the living with the courage and the strength of past heroes.

Furthermore, leaders bolstered their own legitimacy by claiming to be the mouthpieces of the deceased prophets, an effort in which their descendants were especially successful. Nyamachara and Uriogi, the sons of Zakawa, for example, revived a belief in their father's re-

---

The power that ruled the universe was not beyond visiting the individual man to bless or punish." Michael Whisson, "The Will of God and the Wiles of Men," in *Proceedings of the Conference of the East African Institute of Social Research* (Jan. 1962), 3.

The concept of Mumbo could, in part, be derived from the traditional view of God. However, the very wording of his commands bears such a strong resemblance to the Old Testament patriarch that it suggests that the Old Testament was the main influence. Besides, Whisson's statement about rainmakers having power to coerce *Nyasaye* makes him appear not quite omnipotent. On the other hand, as John Lonsdale pointed out in conversation—the article on Mumbo (from which this quotation was taken) was written by "Nyangweso," who was obviously a British administrator, and he may well have translated Mumbo's edicts into the Christian idiom.

[50] "Nyangweso," "Cult of Mumbo," 13-17.

turn, as a result of which, pilgrims came to their village bearing gifts of livestock, and some even reported that they had seen Zakawa. In a similar vein Ongeri, the son of Maraa, spread his mother's teachings, and Nyakundi, the son of Bogonko, established himself as the medium of communication with both his father and Zakawa. Thus, with the progeny of Gusii heroes supporting the movement, blood ties as well as symbolic links with the past were established. Here was an especially powerful group whose prestige and authority could well be used to arouse, strengthen, and weld the various disunited cults into solid anti-British opposition.[51] The legitimacy conferred by the ancestors—especially the Gusii heroes—was of particular significance because among the Gusii ancestor spirits are the major supernatural beings.[52]

However, the cult's advocacy of a return to the old ways can be given different interpretations. Identification with indigenous values obviously meant the rejection of Europeans, especially of the missionaries who insisted upon the wearing of clothes and on cleanliness. But the rejection of European clothes was probably also connected with the chiefs' practice of employing as assistants youths who dressed in European or Swahili apparel, "the donning of which is popularly supposed to increase their cerebral powers."[53] Usually these boys had obtained an elementary education, a knowledge of Swahili, and were converts to Christianity. They were useful to the chiefs on two counts: first, they could translate from the vernacular into Swahili (many chiefs could not); second, they had become acquainted with Europeans, and chiefs in working with the British preferred assistants who had some knowledge of the white man's ways. Consequently, the youths held a position of status as associates of chiefs, missionaries, and administrators. Thus, if the chiefs were viewed by the Mumboites as European lackeys, doubtless the mission converts were viewed as equally contemptible. In addition, the youths' behavior was not likely to endear them to their tribesmen. With their knowledge of the outside world they could qualify as sophisticates among their illiterate countrymen. There were countless complaints about their "swelled heads" and one can imagine how obnoxious some were in lording it over their fellows. Therefore, the cult's rejection of European clothing may also have been tied up with its refusal to recognize these youths' claims to superiority.

To sum up, Mumboism's stories, myths, and prophecies repre-

[51] CN/43: Letter, 5 Dec. 1920. Central Kavirondo Political Records, Kenya National Archives.

[52] See above, n. 48.

[53] *South Nyanza Annual Report, 1910-1911.*

sented the wishes and dreams of peasants for wealth, happiness, freedom, and the punishment of their enemies. Here was a way of coping with a world in which they lived but which they did not understand. Having in some ways been catapulted into the twentieth century, for which their traditional beliefs had not prepared them, they were at pains to explain it. Beginnings of doubts about the efficacy and veracity of their indigenous beliefs were met by the cult's provision of answers to the pervasive questions of the times. The answers, concocted of traditional and Christian teachings, claimed legitimacy by rejecting Christianity and resurrecting the old prophets while, at the same time, utilizing certain attractive features from what was viewed as the West's powerful religion. The message of Mumboism was a skillful attempt to reconstruct a disintegrating world by combining traditional and Western ideas and thereby obtaining the best of two worlds.

The cult's ideology also attempted to restore pride in traditional ways and promised a new self-respect based, in part, upon downgrading Europeans and upgrading Africans. It provided an explanation and a ray of hope in a promise of a better tomorrow. In the words of one District Commissioner: "The melancholy fact remains to be stated, that a large number of men and women in this district do find, at any rate, spiritual and physical satisfaction in these base fraudulent practices."[54] Hence, the ideology represented first and foremost a way of righting the colonial system with all of its inequalities and injustices, and thus provided the means to adapt to a rapidly changing social order.

Given these beliefs, what were the means which the Mumboites employed to bring their millennial dreams to fruition? They appeared to rely heavily upon magic and ritual to solve their problems: if the proper rite were performed Mumbo would bless them. Priests sacrificed to Mumbo to ensure protection against drought and invasions of locusts. The usual practice was to present a priest with a sheep or goat which he sacrificed to Mumbo with the prescribed oblations. Sometimes it was specified that such offerings should be black, at other times white. Feasts were held periodically. Together with their integrative function, they may have symbolized the disappearance of economic privation during the millennium. The priests also performed ceremonies to appease the spirits, control the elements, cure sickness, and restore life.

This concern with magic was rooted in traditional beliefs. Illness, death, and various kinds of disaster were dealt with by sacrifices and oblations which were carried out by a host of supernatural specialists:

[54] PC/NZA 4/5/7: Intelligence Reports, South Kavirondo District, 8 Dec. 1933, Kenya National Archives.

professional sorcerers and witch-smellers in the area of medicine, rain-makers and hail-stoppers for weather protection, magical detectors for theft control, and other part-time experts who executed rituals for removing different kinds of curses and providing protection against specific misfortunes.[55]

Resistance to the British appeared to be largely symbolic, as in the refusal to wear European clothes or to eat European food. It was believed that no harm could come to anyone protected by a Mumbo cloak and cap of skins. District Commissioner Campbell obviously understood the significance of Mumbo garb when he wrote:

> As regards the men . . . I personally interviewed them all and they pro-fessed Mumboism. Each was wearing a "mumbo" cloak of goat skins sewn together also a hat of skins. . . . I am glad to say that for the time being my action has squashed the movement as those who fool-ishly paid cattle etc. to the teachers now see those men in prison await-ing trial and in consequence of my having burnt their cloaks and hats before their eyes I do not anticipate any immediate recrudescence among the Kisii.[56]

With the government's efforts to repress the sect, resort was had to less obvious signs of membership. One chief, for example, who would not be able to admit membership and keep his job, wore a badge of goatskin under his ordinary clothes. This was a most ap-propriate symbol since the British had let it be known they did not favor the wearing of skins.[57] These tactics had probably been abetted by Maraa's counsel. According to ex-Chief Ooga, however, Maraa after the revolt of 1908 changed her tack, exhorting her people not to fight the Europeans by force because God had told her during the night that the Europeans would go. God himself was going to fight them and the people should trust in Him. They should also try new ways—of talking and cleverness—to rid themselves of the foreigners.[58]

Ecstatic behavior—"being possessed"—which was manifested by trembling, uttering a stream of unintelligible words, and falling down, was also much in evidence. Assistant District Commissioner S. H.

[55] LeVine, "Nyansongo: A Gusii Community in Kenya," 77.

[56] KSI/27: Letter, 26 Nov. 1918. District of South Kavirondo Political Rec-ords, Kenya National Archives.

[57] Ex-Chief Ooga explained it this way: "At that time most of the people wore skins. When I went to the DC's I wore a blanket but when I was at home I wore skins. The DC said 'When you come to my office you are to wear a blanket. If you want, you can wear skins at home.' Few people wore blankets at that time, 1914. People started to wear blankets after the war. Men came back with cloth." Interview, 28 June 1966.

[58] See above, 380-83.

Fazan reported that an informant had described possession as follows: "Mumbo comes when dark clouds are in the West. He possesses people and makes them tremble. Sometimes he comes at night when a man is asleep. Signs of possession are trembling and speaking unintelligible words."[59] Possession is still practiced among the Gusii, sometimes being linked to sun worship as well.[60] *Abarogi* (diviners) become possessed when they shake gourd rattles during the initiation of a new diviner.[61]

Possession among the Mumboites could also have been influenced by its Luo membership. According to Luo beliefs, spirits live in people most of the time and, when not possessing someone, return to their several homes, in the sun, in trees, rivers, or in the mythical water snake, Mumbo, whose home was Lake Victoria. These spirits, *juogi*, were believed to give the person possessed the power to prophesy and, after suitable experience, the power to cure people possessed by the same kind of spirits. In all likelihood, possession, whether it was purely Gusii in origin or Luo-influenced, was reinforced by the Christian practice of "receiving the spirit," and the traditional powers given the possessed were extended to include the miraculous powers of Jesus Christ. Although I have no direct evidence of this connection, such is the case in a present-day sect—Legio Maria—which originated in a nearby area.

The Mumboites were great smokers of *bhang* and consequently were harassed by law enforcement officers. An informer reported that they smoked secretly during specific hours set aside each day (4 and 5 A.M. and 7 and 9 P.M.), probably with a guard posted, and hid their pipes on the mountain during the day.[62]

It is interesting to note that the cult also made several attempts to abolish both female and male circumcision,[63] in 1920 ordering that it be suspended for nine years. Apparently the order was carried out, at least in Kitutu and North Mugirango locations, for the year 1921. But dissatisfaction with this arrangement led to its resumption the fol-

[59] KSI/27: His informant is anonymous. "Report of Investigation Made Concerning the Worship of Mumbo," 31 July 1915. District of South Kavirondo Political Records, Kenya National Archives.

[60] "Nyangweso," "Cult of Mumbo"; Henry A. Owuor, "Spirit Possession Among the Luo of Central Nyanza, Kenya" (typescript copy). East African Institute of Social Research Library.

[61] A personal letter from LeVine, 14 Aug. 1967.

[62] CN/43: Ochio, an informer, reported this to District Commissioner Storrs Fox on 23 Aug. 1921. Central Kavirondo Political Records, Kenya National Archives.

[63] The material used here on the attempt to abolish circumcision is taken from LeVine's "Initiation Cycle," 117-20. I have drawn extensively from his article both here and later in the paper.

lowing year. When, in 1922, many children died during the period of seclusion, their deaths were attributed to the violation of custom in 1921.

This was an attempt at a radical innovation, especially when it was tried as far back as 1920. Writing about the Gusii in 1959, LeVine stated:

> Although fairly progressive agriculturalists, they are behind other Kenya Bantu tribes in westernization, owing partly to isolation and partly to cultural conservatism. One of the major foci of this conservatism is the initiation cycle, involving genital operations for boys and girls. . . . Although missionary activity and the use of European clothing have altered the ritual content of the initiation to some extent, and school attendance limits its duration for some boys, there has been no general trend against initiation in Gusiiland, no long-term indication that its universality and cultural significance have been impaired.[64]

And that was written nearly forty years after this initial attempt!

Circumcision is among the most important events in the life of the Kisii. The ceremony marks the assumption of an adult role with its rights, duties, and higher status. It is an integral part of the whole fabric of mores, customs, and practices that order traditional society Philip Mayer, in a detailed study of the initiation rites, describes the community's involvement:

> . . . the initiation cycle is woven into the life of the neighbourhood in such a way that nobody remains altogether unconcerned. Children too young to be initiated themselves are occupied in carrying food or running errands; . . . The older boys and girls, who have already been initiated but are not yet married, play a very important part, indeed, apart from the actual operation and the adults' beer parties, they organize and carry out most of the rites and celebrations themselves. . . . The young married people are less closely involved, but maturity brings the right to be entertained at the beer-drinks with which all parents celebrate their respective children's entry into and emergence from seclusion. Among the old people, some will be needed to take part in the ritual, for instance, in blessing the novices at the end of seclusion and burning the bedding.[65]

Had this order been followed important changes in Gusii culture and social relations would have ensued. Boys and girls well below the usual age might have been circumcised, and if they had failed to fulfill kinship and other obligations of adult status the meanings of initiation for the child and his family could have been substantially

[64] Ibid., 117.

[65] Philip Mayer, "Gusii Initiation Ceremonies," *Journal of the Royal Anthropological Institute*, LXXXIII (1953), 9-10.

altered. The age-grading of children would also have been disturbed and, if a considerable number of prepubertal boys and girls had waited the nine years to be circumcised, some would have indulged in sexual relations and offspring would have resulted, thereby violating the mores that initiation must precede sexual activity. Besides, Gusii distinctiveness is maintained by their language and culture rather than administrative autonomy. Circumcision is one of the most important customs integrating all Gusii and setting them off from the surrounding Luo. The order to abolish circumcision, therefore, was *strongly anti-traditional.*

It is also possible that incest and the "communal enjoyment of women" may have been practiced, as these activities are mentioned in five separate accounts.[66] The most reliable data came from an old man convicted of incest with his daughter in 1938 and sentenced to two years' imprisonment with hard labor. He gave as his reason his membership in the cult.[67]

A strong argument can be made for dismissing such allegations. First, there is a paucity of evidence. Second, the Gusii lived in a generally hostile and suspicious environment where malicious gossip was rife.[68] And third, given this milieu, together with the administration's

[66] At first, I was inclined to view these allegations as name-calling. There were, however, five separate accounts that reported the same practices. Granted, hearsay forms the bulk of the evidence but then it would almost have to, given this kind of activity.

The evidence all comes from government documents. District Commissioner Kenyon-Slarey in a letter dated 16 Apr. 1920, wrote: "It is said that they enjoy all women in common and regard incest as natural."

Assistant District Commissioner Bond wrote 6 July 1930 (CN/43: Central Kavirondo District Political Records) that he had rounded up a number of "incorrigible Mumboites." He listed their names and then in discussing the different people mentioned that: "A dangerous character at large is Ochoondo, daughter of Obeto with whom he is believed to have incestuous relations. [Obeto was the leader of the cult.] She is believed to be a future priestess and from her behaviour in handling some of the objects would appear an initiate now. I did not arrest her as I had no place for her in camp and she can always be got hold of."

District Officer Gordon wrote: "Bhang was an invariable practice of Mumboism; incest was often so." *South Kavirondo District Annual Report 1946.*

The article by "Nyangweso" also mentions the practices of incest and the communal enjoyment of women. "According to the elders this is the old religion (if any) of the Luo but there were in their day no such rites as incest or what appeals to them most, the feeding of crocodiles with good meat."

I realize that once such accusations are made, other people may take the same view without any fresh evidence.

[67] *South Kavirondo Annual Report 1938.* This evidence is strong because it came directly from a member and was not merely someone's opinion.

[68] Robert A. LeVine, "Socialization, Social Structure and Intersocial Images," in Herbert Klein (ed.), *International Behavior: A Social Psychological Analysis* (New York, 1965), 64.

need to justify its repression of the sect, it would not be surprising if many accusations were exaggerated. On the other hand, to dismiss the accusations prima facie might lead to overlooking a significant dimension in the development of protest. What is needed is to look beneath the rhetoric to investigate each accusation for whatever truth there may be in it. In reference to sexual practices the questions to be answered are: (1) did the population, in general, regard them as deviant and (2) did the Mumboites engage in them to a greater extent than non-members?

The answer to the first question can be stated quite simply: for the Gusii, marriage provided, and still does, the only acceptable sexual outlet. All other relationships were regarded as deviant, although viewed with varying degrees of disapproval.[69] Feelings of sexual avoidance and embarrassment between persons of adjacent generations were at the core of Gusii morality. They were strongest between father and daughter or daughter-in-law, next strongest between father and son, less between mother and son, and weakest between mother and daughter or daughter-in-law. LeVine does not spell out the taboos governing the father-daughter relationship, but, having elaborated the father-son relationship, he states that the former is even stricter. Hence, father-daughter incest would be abhorrent to the Gusii. It was viewed as an affliction caused by ancestor spirits which must be propitiated by sacrificing an expensive animal like a sheep or a goat.[70]

No information is available on what the ambiguous phrase the "communal enjoyment of women" entailed. However, according to tradition, sexual relations were surrounded by norms of privacy. Adultery, especially on the part of the wife, was believed to bring severe supernatural sanctions, and premarital sex, though engaged in, was not approved by the older people. Girls had misgivings and feared gaining the reputation of a "slut" and young men did not consider it proper to fornicate with girls whom they intended to marry. Thus both incest and "communal enjoyment" were regarded as deviant by the Gusii.

As for the second question, evidence suggests that at least some Mumboites indulged in these practices. Scholars have written about sex as an area of particular tension for the Gusii. LeVine and Mayer

---

[69] I use LeVine's description of sex in Nyansongo ("Nyansongo," 50-52, 58-72) as typical of Gusii. Granted that it is a study of only a single community, but unless special factors exist that would make it non-representative, there is no reason why it should not provide a satisfactory guide for distinguishing deviant from non-deviant practices.

[70] Ibid., 57.

have noted the aggressive sexual behavior of both men and women.[71]

Obviously not all Gusii were satisfied with the established norms, least of all youths whose sex life was stringently curtailed and whose sources of adventure and status had been cut off. Since young people were prominent in the cult, it is reasonable to expect that they would push for new arrangements. Therefore, given a culture area with less than satisfactory norms which impinge, in particular, upon an age group prone to experimentation, it would not have been surprising if deviant practices had developed.

No data are available on how widespread these practices were, whether they were carried out as part of the ritual, and if so, what were the accompanying beliefs. Since the movement was composed of small, autonomous groups, it provided ample scope for each to go its own way. The possible significance of this behavior will be discussed later.

Basis of Support

Tribal support for Mumboism came mainly from the Gusii and a few Luo and Kuria.[72] Aside from tribal affiliation, were there any special categories or strata of people for whom the movement had special appeal?

The core of support for Mumboism appears to have come from the Bogonko clan, the largest and wealthiest clan of the Kitutu tribe. This tribe consisted of seven alien clans linked to the dominant Bogonko lineage, whose allegiance had been bought by providing them with cattle for bridewealth. The political structure of the Kitutu developed from mutually benefiting patron-client relationships founded on the warrior tradition. In the era immediately prior to the British occupation, the Bogonko clan was at the peak of its prestige, having subordinated the seven alien clans to itself and having formed the beginnings of a "state" system with a hereditary chieftainship. This was the most advanced system of political authority, in the sense of a centralized, hierarchical structure clearly demarcating the political from other spheres, to be found among the seven Gusii tribes. Some of its elders were even recognized as authorities not only within the clan itself but throughout the whole tribe.[73]

[71] LeVine, "Gusii Sex Offenses: a Study in Social Control," *American Anthropologist*, LXI (1959), 965-90; Philip Mayer, "Privileged Obstruction of Marriage Rites Among the Gusii," *Africa*, XX (1950), 113-25.

[72] PC/NZA 4/5/7: South Kavirondo Intelligence Reports 1930–36, Kenya National Archives.

[73] Even today this clan is quite exceptional. Its size is enormous: eighteen subclans (none of the other clans have more than four) and more than 30,000 people. Mayer, *The Lineage Principle*, 11-15, 28-31.

When the British came, the position and influence of the Bogonko clan suffered. It is submitted that they became the leaders of protest against the colonial regime, as the center of Mumbo activity was in Kitutu Location where, as previously stated, more than half of the population belonged to the Bogonko clan. Furthermore, the clan was well represented in the Mumbo sect, Bogonko being a cult symbol and his son, Nyakundi, having been imprisoned for Mumbo activities. It is also submitted that the resentment of the Bogonko clan was primarily *political*, arising from their resentment over the administration's by-passing of their chief (possibly because of the clan's support of the revolts). This has been noted by LeVine.[74] Indeed, the Bogonko's lack of general grievances has been pointed out in numerous sources. In contrast to the Kikuyu situation, for example, there was an acute land shortage among the Gusii and the Luo of South Nyanza.[75] Nor did economic grievances seem to have been root causes. And general anti-British sentiments cannot serve as sufficient explanation because all Kenyan Africans experienced the same system of colonial rule, and some protested and others did not.

But it can be argued that alien rule impinged on some to a greater extent than on others; and that those who felt its burdensome aspects more were consequently more highly motivated to protest and, if need be, to suffer the consequences of their militancy. In the case of the Bogonko clan, the members appear to have used general anti-British sentiments to further their own political purposes.

Numerous data support this hypothesis—that the grievances were mainly political and clan-based. Thus, the choice of symbols—Bogonko, the clan's great warrior, and Maraa, the *laibon* (ritual leader) who ordered the spearing of the District Commissioner which led to the 1908 revolt—emphasizes political protest. In addition, one may note that support for Mumboism also came from people who had something to lose under the British system, for example the tribal ritual specialists for whom there was no room in the mission churches. Thus, though the mission churches could provide a place for the priest-like head with a set of customary duties, they excluded the charismatic prophet who sought to cure psychological and physical disorders.[76] In Mumboism, where there was an emphasis on communicating with the supernatural, possession, and the curing of illnesses, there was room for this type of leader.

There were also those who aspired to a new role in a changing society. Thus, a surprisingly large number of leaders were women:

[74] LeVine, "Initiation Cycle," 24.
[75] Cmd. 4556: *Report of the Kenya Land Commission* (1934), 292, 297.
[76] Lonsdale, "Political History," 354.

Bonairiri, the chief exponent of Zakawism; Kibiburi, considered a dangerous agent by the administration and deported to Lamu; Obondo, mentioned in administrative correspondence as a future priestess; and Okenyuri, the wife of a cult leader described as "the most attractive agent who works the mystical and oracular interviews with Mumbo," and Maraa. Traditional society has many middle-aged or elderly female diviners. This is the most important role a woman can occupy outside the family and, although a respected position, it does not endow her with extraordinary powers or prestige.[77] The cult may have adapted this role to that of priestess.

Young men were especially prominent in the cult. Chief Orinda, in charge of a location where the cult was strong, said: "The sect consists only of young men. There are no old men in the sect or practically none." Unmarried girls joined the sect. Chief Mahangain reported that the elders were refusing to attend *barazas* (public meetings) and "that the young men are preaching to the effect that it will only be a short time before white men go, that they will have a free fight, and it will be a case of the survival of the fittest.[78] This sounds as if the young were openly challenging the elders' authority.

There is an apparent inconsistency here. Earlier, we noted that the District Commissioner had stated in 1921 that Zakawaism was especially attractive to the old men and that almost all in Kitutu Location had joined. Here (in 1919), we note that chiefs say that only young men join and hardly any older people. How is this discrepancy to be explained? It could be that the composition of the membership varied by area or by time, or that Zakawaism had a particular appeal for older people, because of its links with the great Gusii prophet, that Mumboism, in general, did not have. Lacking evidence, we can only conjecture.

Why did women and youths support the cult? What was there in it for them? At the heart of the traditional authority system were the ancestors and the elders. In death as well as in life the ancestors were regarded as being intimately bound up with the welfare of the clan. Only the elders, because of their close lineage relationship to the ancestors, were able to ascertain the ancestors' will and, when necessary, make the required propitiations.[79] This gave them much power and permitted them to exercise strong social sanctions. One of the functions of ancestor worship was to keep respect and power in the hands of the elders who, because of their wisdom, were believed to possess the necessary attritubes of authority.

But the cult established other criteria for leadership. In keeping

[77] LeVine, "Nyansongo," 76.

[78] KSI/27: Letter by District Commissioner Campbell, 6 Feb. 1919, District of South Kavirondo Political Records, Kenya National Archives.

[79] LeVine, "Nyansongo," 75-77, 92-94.

with its reversal theme, youths and women, both occupying low status in the traditional authority structure, figured prominently as leaders. They claimed greater powers than the elders. They communicated with the ancestors, interceded on behalf of the members with other supernatural agencies, and made many of the decisions that in traditional society belonged to the elders. Thus, in rejecting age and sex, two major attributes of traditional leadership, and in introducing new norms and leadership roles, the cult in essence rejected tribal authority.

Both mission and Mumbo youth were rebelling against tribal authority, and some of the latter were engaging in activities highly disapproved of by the older generation. Joining either the movement or the mission provided new activities, and both supported, even if unintentionally, rebellion against tribal authority. Both groups attracted young people and, although the Mumboites clearly disliked the educated mission students, the cult recruited many of them. Two choices were presented to young people: (1) to join the cult which was to take an aggressive stand against the foreigners and to defy the chiefs and elders; or (2) to join a mission where one could become literate and perhaps acquire a job with the administration. Joining a mission had the added advantage that one was not forced to leave the district to go to work.[80] One group of young people chose to accommodate to the colonial system while the other chose to reject it. Although any number and combination of factors could have accounted for the difference in choice, it is possible that geographical proximity was the crucial factor. Did it simply depend on whether the mission or the cult was closer to the individual's home? As evidence is lacking, we can only speculate.

The cult therefore recruited a clan with political grievances; people whose traditional positions were threatened by the incipient order; and those who, like women and youth, were laying claims to new roles. No doubt as in any amorphous, heterogeneous movement, the psychologically unstable, the shiftless, and the malcontents joined, but they do not appear to have formed its mainstay.

Attitudes of Agents of Social Control Toward Mumboism

In examining the nature of the sect and its development, a crucial dimension is the way in which the agents of social control—British administrators, chiefs, headmen, tribal police, and missionaries—saw it and dealt with it. Once the sect had established itself as anti-British, the administration used a number of repressive tactics to eradicate it.

---

[80] *The South Kavirondo District Annual Report 1915* notes that "it is often the case that a lad describes himself as a 'mission' boy merely that he may escape being sent out to work."

Deportations, imprisonments, fines, forced labor, and a variety of harassments were employed whenever the sect appeared to be gaining members.[81]

By and large, the administration viewed the cult leaders as exploiters of credulous peasants—as persons who manipulated an environment of superstition and fear for their own ends. District Commissioner Hodge said:

> Apparently the reason for the cult springing up again was that Onkenyuri and Omwega had most of their cattle confiscated after the previous Mumbo trouble and thought that now was a suitable opportunity of restarting the cult and thereby again amassing stock. The fee for becoming a Mumboite is a goat—a higher grade in it requires a cow.[82]

And, in 1934, the District Commissioner of South Nyanza, E. R. S. Davies, stated:

> The general opinion which I form on the present evidence is that the promoters of the movement and their devotees are parasites addicted to *bhang* smoking who want to obtain food for nothing and have used unscrupulously certain prophecies of the past and a fear of locusts, over which they are believed to have power. They on the other hand claim to be teachers of a true religion persecuted by the chiefs who attribute evil and sedition to them.[83]

Some administrators even feared that the Mumboites would cause another uprising. District Commissioner Campbell wrote: "I think that there is little doubt that most have been preaching sedition, though it may be difficult to get evidence." Later in the same letter he reported that Chief Nsungu had said: "It is exactly this sort of thing that might lead to the murder of an officer and another Kitutu War" [an obvious reference to one of the Kisii revolts].[84] In the previous year the District Commissioner had written: "There is no question but that Mumboism may become an extremely dangerous political force. . . . If such warnings are totally neglected there is a possibility of the events which occurred at Blantyre being repeated in this Protectorate."[85] (In 1915, Africans led by John Chilembwe had revolted near Blantyre, formerly Nyasaland, now Malawi. The revolt had lasted less than two

[81] See CN/43: Letter, 6 July 1930. Central Kavirondo District Political Records, Kenya National Archives.

[82] PCN ZA4/5/7: 8 Dec. 1933. Intelligence Reports, South Kavirondo District, Kenya National Archives.

[83] Ibid., 8 Jan. 1934.

[84] KSI/27: Letter by District Commissioner Campbell, 6 Feb. 1919. District of South Kavirondo Political Records Kenya National Archives.

[85] Ibid., Letter 26 Nov. 1918.

weeks and been completely crushed, yet it was a portent for other colonial administrations.)[86]

The hostile reaction on the part of the administration naturally hardened the sect's view toward it. Men were often arrested, detained, and deported on mere suspicion and on charges that would not have been upheld under normal conditions in British and American courts of law. For instance, a District Commissioner in a letter to his Provincial Commissioner admitted that he had insufficient evidence to have four people deported. He wrote " . . . it is difficult to get any weight of evidence against individuals of actual sedition."[87] Nevertheless, they were deported.

In spite of its repressive tactics, the administration did not present a monolithic front in its handling of the cult. It stressed a pragmatic approach and attempted to abide by the rule of law, even though often disregarding civil liberties. An interesting case occurred in 1918 when District Commissioner Campbell sent some Mumboites out of the district on a project using compulsory labor. The Provincial Commissioner wrote:

> The Assistant District Commissioner here reports that you have sent in a batch of 28 men under escort for work at Magadi. As you are aware labour is not to be forced even for Government purposes without the sanction of His Excellency. Neither Chiefs nor District Commissioners can deport men from their Districts except they are being transferred from one jail to another under warrant. In the circumstances, I am ordering the return of the men and shall be glad of an explanation.

In defending his action, District Commissioner Campbell wrote:

> In this matter I feel bound to say that I consider the headman acted with extraordinary loyalty and energy. It requires some pluck on the part of a chief to boldly tackle a wholesale and vicious movement such as this, surrounded by superstition, illwill and mysterious "dawa" [magic]. In acceding to their suggestion to send the riff-raff out to work and try the teachers it seemed to me and still does that in the interest of Government, the step taken was a wise one and that under the Native Authority Ordinance Section 5 (1) and (2), 6 (1) a legal one. I cannot agree that sending men such as these to Magadi for six months work for good wages can be described as "deportation" and when natives in a reserve are misbehaving themselves I do not understand how the operation of sending them out for a few months work

---

[86] For an analysis of Chilembwe, see above, Robert I. Rotberg, "Psychological Stress and the Question of Identity: Chilembwe's Revolt Reconsidered," 337-74.

[87] CN/43: District Commissioner H. E. Welby on 5 Dec. 1920. Central Kavirondo District Political Records, 1920.

can be placed on the same footing with "forcing labour" when all and sundry have to be called upon. . . .

The Provincial Commissioner then wrote both John Ainsworth, the Chief Native Commissioner (the highest official in charge of native affairs) and the acting Chief Secretary to report the District Commissioner's action. The Chief Native Commissioner wrote the acting Chief Secretary supporting the Provincial Commissioner's reprimand; he too viewed the District Commissioner's action as *ultra vires*. In his letter, the chief Native Commissioner displayed considerable knowledge of Mumboism and, since he felt that it was neither a political nor a subversive cult, he suggested ridicule instead of repression.

> Personally I failed to detect in it any disloyal or harmful tendency and formed the opinion that to take official notice of the matter was likely to do more harm than good. Sometime ago, I saw some of the so-called teachers and followers when I came to the conclusion that the best way to deal with the subject was to ridicule rather than take serious notice of it. . . . Personally I deprecate any repressive action by the Government until and unless we are satisfied that the cult has become such as to lead to disloyalty or that it is dangerous to peace and order in the districts concerned.
>
> Any hasty or ill-considered action in a matter of this description is likely to create an impression in the native mind that the Government fears the teaching when it becomes imbued with exaggerated importance and may on that account alone become highly desirable.
>
> I believe that the best policy is to keep in touch with any such movement as this and allow it to have full scope until we are satisfied that it is necessary to take steps to deal with it. . . . [88]

For their part, acting as agents of the administration responsible for law and order, the chiefs and headmen viewed the sect with hostility. If it disrupted the community, they were required to deal with it, and it was they who were blamed for not forewarning the District Commissioner. Administrative records report: "All the Kisii chiefs and many of the Luo chiefs . . . were unanimous in advising the suppression of the cult" and "The trial [of Mumboites] was well attended by the general public. About 150 assessors (chiefs and tribal elders) recommended the deportation of the eight accused and the imprisonment for six months of another."[89] Even if they had sympathized with the cult, the chiefs as civil servants could not afford to let the administration know it. The evidence confirms, however, that they were anti-

[88] This correspondence can be found in KSI/27: District of South Kavirondo Political Records, Kenya National Archives.

[89] The above excerpts were from PC/NZA 4/5/1: Intelligence Reports, 8 Dec. 1933 and 8 Jan. 1934, respectively. Intelligence Reports, South Kavirondo District, Kenya National Archives.

cult. They had much to lose if its goals were achieved; the cult's elect and not the administration's appointees were to be the potentates in the new order. Thus, having accommodated themselves to British rule and standing at the top of the native authority structure, they were certainly going to look askance at any group that advocated a change.

Not unexpectedly the missionaries were also against the cult. Father Scheffer of the Asumbi Catholic Mission wrote the District Commissioner fully supporting his action in sending the Mumboites out of the district on work projects. His view was consistent with the missionary perspective.

> I have heard reports to the effect that Mumbo people, taken by you, have been sent back from Kisumu. What a pity! Mumbo people were responsible for all the looting in September 1914.[90] They were responsible for a good amount of trouble to their respective chiefs at the time the latter were recruiting government labour.
>
> At the present they still are opposed to the progress of civilization and from information received they are an immoral and drunken lot.
>
> One of their many prophecies was that in 1914 when the crops would be in the *wasungu* [white man] would leave the district. This very phophecy made some people think that Mumboism was of German origin and if I had anything to say in the matter, I would stamp out anything of that kind, and the manner I would try to stamp it would be to make them see something of the world. It would convince them that the *wasungu* had come to stay and they would have to submit to the higher authority.[91]

It is not surprising that the missionaries were against Mumboism since the missions probably lost many members to the sect. Although there is no information available on how many of the members of Mumbo had formerly belonged to a mission, other independent sects in Kenya have posed serious threats to missions.

By and large, then, the agents of social control viewed the cult negatively. They wanted peace and stability, whereas Mumboism continually provoked unrest and· lawlessness. The sect upset established ways: youth challenged chiefs and elders, women challenged men, and the sect challenged foreign domination and traditional life. It is difficult to say whether the repressive tactics of the colonial power actually brought an end to the cult or whether it died out because of, among other things, the failure of its millennial prophecies.

Our image of the early phase of the colonial era has been formed by the writings of European administrators and missionaries, since it was their views and evaluations of tribal life that have been dissemi-

[90] See above, 371-72.

[91] KSI/27: Letter, 1 Dec. 1918, District of South Kavirondo Political Records, Kenya National Archives.

nated. They defined the cults as consisting of "deluded," "hysterical" people under the sway of a leader whose "diseased brain" was centered on self aggrandizement. Action was thought to be motivated by "the black and blood-stained forces of sorcery and magic stirring the vicious hearts of wicked men."[92]

Whether or not any of these accusations is true, it should be noted that the history of sects and other nonconforming groups shows that new and different groups whose ways and motives are unknown tend to be regarded by the established order with suspicion and, at times, outright hostility. That such suspicion was largely inappropriate in the instance being studied here is clear for the following reasons:

1. Doubts about the veracity of many accusations were voiced from the lowest to the highest administrative levels. Chief Orinda stated frankly that he did not like the people of Mumbo but continued:

> On the other hand much that has been said against them is not true. They cultivate like other people and they do not kill stock, and they give no trouble at all when they are wanted for work. They come to work at once. Their teaching is good. They teach men not to steal, or use insulting language, or to laugh at old men, or to walk about naked.[93]

An informant, sent to one of the sect's schools, reported:

> I don't know that they do any harm except to say that the *wasungus* will soon return to their own country. They do not kill all their cattle in preparation for the millennium. They have little feasts at their bomas from 10 days to monthly intervals and occasional big ones for which they foregather at Betis' boma. [They had been accused of killing all their cattle in preparation for the millennium. Probably some of the more fervent believers did, but the more prudent did not.][94]

While most administrators viewed the sect as dangerous, retrogressive, and a menace to law and order as well as to morals, a few refused to characterize it as all bad. Assistant District Commissioner Fazan, after investigating the sect, wrote:

> . . . most of them have stock, and they cultivate shambas. They all either wear clothes, or more than one goat skin, so that they live up to the precept not to go naked. A man called Wadi, who is the chief of

[92] For an example of this kind of writing see Philip Mitchell, *African Afterthoughts* (London, 1954), 242-48, 254-55, 260-68. The words in quotation marks were all used in Sir Philip's account of African cults. Sir Philip was the Governor of Kenya from 1944 to 1952. He came to Kenya after thirty years of Colonial Service, mostly in East and Central Africa, where he gained repute as a liberal administrator.

[93] KSI/27: Statement, 19 July 1915, District of South Kavirondo Political Records, Kenya National Archives.

[94] Ibid., Statement, 23 Aug. 1921 by Ambrose Ajuang.

Chief Orinda's retainers and has most of the actual work of collecting porters to do [for the Carrier Corps], states that the Mumbo people give no trouble whatever, and that their readiness to turn out for government labour is conspicuous. For my part I can add the testimony that I have more than 40 of them confined in my camp at the present moment. None of them are reported to have resisted the summons to appear, and nobody has made any attempt to escape. Therefore they do not seem to me to be intractable.

I investigated a charge of assault (or grievous hurt) against them and found that the persons who brought the charge were more culpable than the persons charged. The persons who brought the charge were mission boys.

By the foregoing remarks I do not mean to vindicate Mumboism. I am aware that a large amount of damage has probably been caused by it. But it is possible that the attitude of the persons concerned may be loyal in one place and disloyal in another.

I should not even like to say they are not disloyal here, but I have found no evidence of it.[95]

2. The administration's accusation that the Mumboite rituals exploited credulous Gusii does not stand up to examination. A comparison of their fees with those charged by the *omari* (witch-smellers, the traditional practitioners), shows that the Mumboites charged the usual fee, a cow (worth about $42) or a goat or goat meat ($5)[96] On the other hand, the issue of who was a true or false prophet, a true or false witch doctor, is complex and beyond the scope of this paper.

3. While it is true that the Mumboites smoked *bhang*, so did many others in Nyanza. John Ainsworth, Provincial Commissioner of Nyanza in 1908, commented on this practice:

All the Kavirondo, particularly the Luo are great smokers of tobacco which is grown in this country. . . . It is also a custom amongst the men at times to smoke *bhang* obtained from a species of Indian hemp which is cultivated in the country for this purpose. *Bhang* smoking produces a state of semi-madness or intoxication. . . . Some few months ago I instructed all DC's to call in all chiefs and inform them of the dangers of *bhang* smoking and point out to them that a great deal of crime in the country was due to its use.[97]

In 1921 Senior Commissioner H. R. Tate wrote: "*Bhang* smoking and witch-craft are prevalent all over the District and are difficult to stop."[98] Anyway, the administration's belief that *bhang* encouraged the

[95] KSI/27: 21 July 1915. District of South Kavirondo Political Records, Kenya National Archives.

[96] Robert LeVine, "Omoriori: Smeller of Witches," *Natural History*, LXVII (1958), 142-47.

[97] *Nyanza Province Annual Report, 1907-1908.*

[98] *Nyanza Province Annual Report, 1920-1921.*

outbreak of hostilities because of its aggression-arousing tendencies is debatable.[99] *Bhang* may release aggressive tendencies or it may produce a state of euphoria.

4. It is true that the cult looked to the past by calling upon its heroes for support and inspiration, so in a symbolic sense it can be called "retrogressive." There is no evidence, however, that incest and the communal enjoyment of women were ever part of the approved traditional life. The smoking of *bhang* was indulged in by other Gusii. Unless "retrogressive" is used in some absolute moral sense, it appears to have little meaning here. Rejection, rather than regression, is a more suitable designation. The cult could not banish Europeans but it could symbolically reject them—particularly the mission converts. Instead of "regressing" to the old ways, the movement rejected or attempted to reject several important tribal mores: circumcision and the authority of the elders.

With these labels the colonial administrators and missionaries made the Mumboites appear basically different from the majority of Africans. They considered their protest childlike and primitive—irrational behavior aroused by the prophecies and incantations of witch doctors. These explanations detracted from the dignity and rationality of the African and served to exonerate the administration while by-passing the important question of whether, in fact, genuine grievances existed.

Failure to consider the time perspective in interpreting actions can sometimes lead to error. The Gusii were defeated in battle. For them to persist with this tactic would have been futile. Obviously an alternative to the spear had to be found. Groping for ways to cope with the formidable intruders, they turned to a belief in the millennium which had been promised by the powerful white man's religion. Under the circumstances this can hardly be construed as irrational conduct.

A Later Phase of the Movement

During the 1950's groups similar to Mumbo appeared sporadically. But none had any lasting impact. In 1952, a millenarian movement inspired by the Adventists emerged in various parts of the Highlands.[100] When Mumboism was proscribed in 1954 another cult in the same area,

---

[99] CN/43: District Commissioner H. W. Welby, writing to the Provincial Commissioner, 5 Dec. 1920 expresses this fear. Central Kavirondo Political Records 1920, Kenya National Archives.

[100] Robert A. LeVine, "Witchcraft and Sorcery in a Gusii Community," in *Witchcraft and Sorcery in East Africa*, ed. John Middleton and E. H. Winter (London, 1963), 230.

known as *Dini ya Mariam,* was also proscribed. (*Dini* is the local word for sect and the literal translation was the Sect of Mariam.) Mariam Rogot of Kabondo Location was its chief protagonist. Accompanied by her husband, Paul Adika, she had wandered the countryside preaching her own brand of evangelism. She spoke of the imminent end of the world, carried out baptisms, and incited ecstatic behavior among her followers. *The South Nyanza Annual Report, 1954* described the group as follows:

> Led by a half crazy woman named Mariam Rogot, this sect which originates from a small group of renegades from the Roman Catholic missions, displays a marked similarity to the Mumbo religion which had with difficulty been stamped out many years before. In June Mariam Rogot, her husband and one other were removed from the District on Detention orders, and this prompt action had the required effect so that by the time the sect was formally proscribed in September the movement had almost died out and gave no trouble during the remainder of the year.

In 1958 Mariam and her husband were sentenced to a month's imprisonment for holding illegal meetings. On release they recommenced their preachings, whereupon they were restricted to Nyamira substation in the Kisii Highlands. Despite the optimistic note in the 1954 report of the cult's imminent demise, the 1959 report concluded with: "There is no doubt that Mariam still has disturbance potential particularly among the very emotional and less stable bodies of fanatical religious thought." And in 1960 it was reported that Mariam and Paul had been de-restricted early in the year and had remained relatively quiet. Their activities included preaching on a number of occasions and attempting to amalgamate three other sects.[101]

Of a different order were the later visionary experiences and efforts to abolish circumcision originated by the Bogonko clan in and before 1957.[102] LeVine discusses the short-lived 1957 attempt and states that it was only the most recent example. Information is not available on earlier ventures.

The 1956 initiation ceremonies began as usual in October but instead of stopping as was customary in December, they continued on into January. The Gusii explained this strange occurrence by telling how a youth from the Bogonko lineage saw three old men with long hair, sitting in the middle of the Echarachani River drinking beer. They ordered him to return with his father and when he did, the old men said:

[101] *South Nyanza District Annual Report, 1960.*
[102] See n. 63.

We are tired of living in the water. You tell the people of Bogonko and Kitutu to resume circumcision of their children and continue until seeding time [April-June] then stop. This is to give us, the people of the water, a chance to circumcise our own children. Go tell all people in Gusiiland to obey that rule.

The old men disappeared and the father and son spread the story in Kitutu. This order was plausible because it came from a source that commanded respect: the old men appeared to be a composite of ancestor spirits and living lineage elders which would make them particularly powerful wielders of supernatural sanctions.

The following evidence links this episode to Mumboism and to the Bogonko clan:

1. The order was reported by a Bogonko youth and directed to the Bogonko clan.

2. This attempt to change the initiation cycle was opposed by the chiefs because of its association with Mumboism. When the chief of Kitutu Location heard of the vision, he immediately said it was an attempt by the Bogonko people to resuscitate Mumboism, and the elders took the same view. Since this occurred during the "emergency," when "Mau Mau" posed a severe threat both to the British and to the chiefs as civil servants, it is understandable that the chiefs should frown upon any renewal of a movement that had overtones of militant Mumboism. Furthermore, it is likely that the chiefs saw the instructions to abandon circumcision as a threat to the established order.

3. This event was not unique and did bear a striking resemblance to earlier Mumboism.

   (a) The order to suspend circumcision was the same as that ordered by the Mumboites in 1920; even the same period of time, nine years, was designated. Thus in 1957, in spite of previous disastrous consequences, the suspension of initiation was patterned on an earlier effort.

   (b) The 1957 attempt was carried out in a manner reminiscent of the origins' myth. In both cases, spirits making their home in the water issued instructions that if followed would have introduced a radical change in tribal ways. Besides, the instructions were issued through a medium. This pattern of oracular presentation was deeply rooted in tribal ways.

   (c) Geographically, both places where the events occurred were historically significant. Kitutu is a traditional source of cultural innovation. The Echarachani River flows through an area where the heroes of Kitutu are celebrated in myth and song, and it is the region where Gusii military success and civil leadership reached their greatest heights in pre-British days. Furthermore, visions had been experienced at that particular river before. And Lake Victoria, the site of the previous revelation, has a prominent place in African folklore.

(d) The mouthpiece of the ancestors was a youth, and youths were important in the sect.

Interpretation and Conclusions

Let me present a possible interpretation of the evolution of Mumboism. As I have indicated, the evidence is patchy and insufficient; therefore, the explanation is speculative.

When the Gusii saw that there was no way to fight the administration militarily, the thoughts and hopes of some turned to the "other world" of which the missionaries had talked: If only they worshiped the true god and followed the proper rituals, their problems would be solved. Hence, their political protest took the form of a new subculture with an ideology that advocated a withdrawal from the world of action. Thus the turning inward to fantasy and to the world of the senses.

As for specific action directed toward ousting the British or acquiring an education or engaging in any concrete projects that would provide the means for the desired material goals, there was little. Some evidence suggests passive resistance. There were complaints that the Mumboites refused to comply with compulsory labor and to pay their taxes. But, by and large, anti-British activity was limited to sporadic collective protest, like the looting of Kisii in 1914, agitation, and the symbolic rejection of the foreigners.

Mumboism presents a curious paradox: on the one hand, it glorified the tribe, while on the other, it attempted to abolish important tribal mores. How is this contradiction explained? Why did its members engage in behavior that ran counter to the moral sentiments of those around them? Why did they pursue conduct that marked them off as "bad Gusii"?

Although military defeat was humiliating for all Gusii, it was even more so for the Bogonko clan, which, as has already been pointed out, probably suffered the brunt of the destruction. To add insult to injury, this proud and formerly dominant clan had to suffer the appointment of a chief from a subordinate clan. At the same time its members were in a highly structured colonial situation that provided few legitimate channels for the expression of grievances. So unlike the other Gusii the Bogonko's feelings of hostility-aggression gave rise to their continual protest in one form or another; first in Mumboism and, when its millennial hopes failed to materialize, in attempts to abolish circumcision and other tribal mores. The effort to abolish circumcision, closely linked as it was to tribal identity, was particularly aggressive, attention-gaining, and extreme, and perhaps mirrored the desperation of a clan long bedeviled by feelings of bitterness and long prevented from asserting itself. At first, its aggression was directed toward the foreign rulers, but later it acquired a negativistic strain lashing out at the tribal system itself and was marked by a shift from collective goals to more individualistic, hedonic values.

This negativism may have been abetted by the growing land pressures that had begun to be felt by the 1950's. *The Kenya Population Census, 1962* showed that the districts of Kisii, Kisumu, Nairobi, and Fort Hall were the country's most densely populated areas. Hence, the tensions that gave rise to the earlier protest were exacerbated by economic pressures, well known to be particularly potent fomenters of unrest.

The general patterning of activities supports this interpretation. Narcotics, ecstasy, visions, and passivity fit together and reinforce each other. Escapism and passivity were encouraged by the smoking of *bhang* which, in turn, abetted visionary states. Religious ecstasy or possession was seen, in part, as communicating with ancestral spirits.

What was the nature of Mumbo? My understanding of the cult suggests that although many of the elements attributed to it were undoubtedly present, its major dimensions were different from those generally posited. I would argue that:

1. Its goals were utopian and revolutionary rather than traditional and regressive;

2. Its message combined and modified, in an eclectic fashion, strands from different belief systems. Given the peasants' view and understanding of the world, Mumboism represented an ingenious way of adapting to, and coping with, a new, complex, and confusing situation rather than a curious mixture of irrational ideas or a retreat into past beliefs;

3. Its members exhibited deep admiration of, and desire for, European material goods rather than a rejection of all things European;

4. Its activity gave evidence of deeply rooted patterns of behavior motivated by strong desires rather than meaningless, ephemeral, spur-of-the-moment action;

5. Its main support came from people with social and political grievances rather than from a motley collection of "riff-raff," "parasites," "drunks," "sodomites," and the insane and hysterical.

The movement held aloft a vision of a future life in which the oppressed would be elevated and the oppressors put down. It advocated radical change: hence it was, in important aspects, anti-traditional. It would reverse the power structure, abolish circumcision, and broaden clan and tribal allegiance to encompass pan-tribalism. This ideology did not aim to change the present order but to abolish it and usher in a new social order.

The Mumboites held highly ambivalent feelings toward Europeans which can probably best be epitomized as a love-hate relationship. Coupled with a deep admiration for Western man's technology and material goods was a deep hostility, for his very superiority had caused the devaluation of the tribal way of life. The underlying theme in visions, stories, and utterances was the longing of Mumboites for "all those wonderful things" which Europeans possessed. What the members really wanted was not a return to the old way of life but the life of the European, at least as far as material goods were concerned. In his vision of heaven, the priest, Mosi, found his entry announced by an explosion of light after which he approached God on a motorbike accompanied by five Europeans.[103] Advocating in a few specific and highly symbolic ways a return to the past, the cult nevertheless represented a drastic break with the past. It looked to the past for inspiration, but to the future for a pattern of life. When the new order arrived, Muchirongo, Bonairiri, and Zakawa were not going to live in their mud and wattle huts; they were going to collect the tax, occupy the district headquarters, and, no doubt, drive the District Commissioner's Land Rover.

The leaders articulated deeply held sentiments common to the masses of peasants. Their hopes, wants, fears, and resentments were unchangeable factors; they persisted despite the appearance and disappearance of leaders. These sentiments usually remained dormant until a spokesman brought them to the fore by giving them some form and substance, even if a loose one, and, to our minds at least, one full of contradictions. In large part this explains Mumboism's tenacity and the administration's difficulty in stamping it out for, whenever the administration tried to chop off its head, it found itself battling a hydra. Groups sprang up here and there wherever a local prophet appeared. When one set of leaders was deported, others came to the fore. There was little organization which the administration could seize, the movement being what is sociologically called "expressive." People were bound together by an amorphous structure of shared sentiments and beliefs with little formal organization or program.

[103] PC/NZA 4/5/2: Intelligence Reports of Provincial Commissioner, Nyanza, Kenya National Archives.

Mumboism was yet another attempt on the part of the Gusii to rid themselves of the foreigners. More specifically, it was an attempt on the part of a dissatisfied, ambitious clan to assert itself and to retrieve its former dominant status. The argument that support for the movement came from those with strong anti-British feelings needs to be qualified. It is a facile generalization that obscures both the complexity of the colonial relationship and the *quid pro quo* realities of the day-to-day struggle for power and dominance. It presents a one-sided view of the African-British relationship which vastly underplays the Africans' dexterity in handling the British. It is perhaps too obvious to point out that Africans, like people everywhere, are interested in power, wealth, and prestige. It should be borne in mind that British administrators were few in number and that they had to rely upon support from the indigenous leaders. From the first days of the British occupation alliances were made between the British and the African chiefs, who often helped the British to bring areas under their control while enhancing their own position by the subjugation of their traditional enemies with the help of the British.

In South Nyanza, it was not just a case of the British using Africans but of particular African rivals for chieftainships securing their positions by acquiring British backing. The British provided a new structure of power and prescribed rules within which the age-old power struggle continued. Those chiefs who learned early how to handle the British in order to achieve their own ends came out on top. Tribal and clan rivalry continued as it had for centuries, only now another, foreign, dimension had to be taken into account. Consequently, those clans and subclans whose positions were enhanced and whose claims were supported by the administration tended to be pro-British. One can hypothesize that had the British supported the Bogonko clan's claims to chieftainship, the Bogonko would have worked with the administration and, being dominant, would not have protested.

The first challenge to European authority in South Nyanza came from Mumboism. Its undisputed stance against alien rule indicated an uncompromising position. Its attempts to find new ways to cope with the foreign invaders were fumbling, experimental, and ineffectual. Compared with the Kikuyu and Luo who, by the 1920's and 1930's, were pressuring and petitioning the colonial administration and the British government to redress their grievances, the Gusii were politically unsophisticated. And, although Mumboism's protest eventually fizzled out because of severe repression and the dissipation of its energies upon individualistic, hedonistic goals, it still represents the beginnings of African political protest in Gusiiland, the articulation of grievances, and the building of embryonic trans-tribal allegiances.

THE AFFIRMATION OF THINGS PAST:

ALAR AYONG AND BWITI AS

MOVEMENTS OF PROTEST

IN CENTRAL AND NORTHERN GABON

JAMES W. FERNANDEZ

The malaise that gives rise to protest movements is composed of various feelings of disparity; often the greatest disparity is that felt between "the past" and "the present." The times are out of joint, and protest movements arise to set them right. But the ways in which they do so are not always as exclamatory as the conventional meaning of the term "protest"—a gesture of extreme disapproval of existing conditions —might lead us to believe. Consider, for example, a rather bizarre feature of the two Gabonese movements discussed below: their compulsiveness about the timing of ceremonial events. Highly industrialized peoples living under the rhythmic compulsions characteristic of their milieu have frequently commented on the more casual or nonexistent sense of time among peoples in traditional societies. And in the colonial situation, as everyone knows, jokes of various degrees of disparagement were frequently made about the indigenous sense of time, while more sober administrators, charged with efficient conduct of office, wrote seriously about the matter.[1] However, in the *esulan* (meetings) of the Alar Ayong movement which I attended between 1958 and 1960, there was always an elaborate insistence on an exact timetable: throughout the day each meeting was assigned its appropriate time. This is also true of Bwiti, the religious movement in which every chapel contains an old alarm clock that dictates when the rituals must proceed. I have known leaders of Bwiti to carry an alarm clock about with them wherever they go, their rationale being that all events

Research in northern and central Gabon was undertaken from July of 1958 to July of 1960. It was supported by a Foreign Area Training Fellowship of the Ford Foundation.

[1] R. P. Briault "La Notion du Temps Chez les Noirs," *Dans la Forêt du Gabon* (Paris, 1936), 114-28.

in heaven are exactly timed and that their own prayers and rituals must therefore follow suit. Or friendly discussions on the trail or in the village will suddenly be cut off by the clatter of a bell more usually associated with a sleepy dawn than with diurnal devotions.

What are we to understand by such practices? They clearly indicate a response to European values and an attempt to obtain by imitation the temporal aspect of European organizational efficiency. As it is carried out the imitation seems inconsequential—a ritual form with negligible content. But the crassly imitative features of these two movements (and the matter of timing is just one example) are part of a much larger attempt to reorder the universe—an attempt to build a cultural framework within which the membership can contentedly live. The totality of these rituals creates a substantial sense of reality for the cult membership vis-à-vis the outside world to which it is reacting. As a contribution to a fuller understanding of the phenomenon of protest and in an attempt to suggest its more positive aspects we will examine certain features of cultural re-organization found in these two movements. We may call the process microcosmogony.

Alar Ayong: The Regrouping of the Clans

The Alar Ayong movement (*alar*: to unite; *ayong*: clan) had its origins in the Cameroun in the middle and late 1930's and its greatest influence among the Fang of the northern Woleu-Ntem, Gabon, in the later 1940's and early 1950's. The Bwiti movement—which is an adaptation of the traditional ancestral cult of the southern Gabonese people, notably the Mitsogo of the Ngounie—dates on the other hand from the turn of the century. It has been most significant among the Fang of the southern Woleu-Ntem, the Gabon estuary, and Lambarene. Both movements, then, arose outside Fang territory.

We shall not dwell on this fact except to note that, in attempting to revitalize themselves,[2] societies in a state of malaise are frequently open to "extra-processual" influences. Whatever the origins of the movements, however, in the 1940's and 1950's Alar Ayong was the revitalization movement among the Fang of northern Gabon, while Bwiti played this role for an even longer time among the Fang of central Gabon (see map).

As can be seen from this map, the distribution of the two movements in Gabon has been complementary. This fact has been related to the relative progressiveness of the northern Fang resulting from

[2] P. J. Bohannan has discussed this phenomenon in "Extra-Processual Events in Tiv Political Institutions," *American Anthropologist*, LX (1958), 1-12.

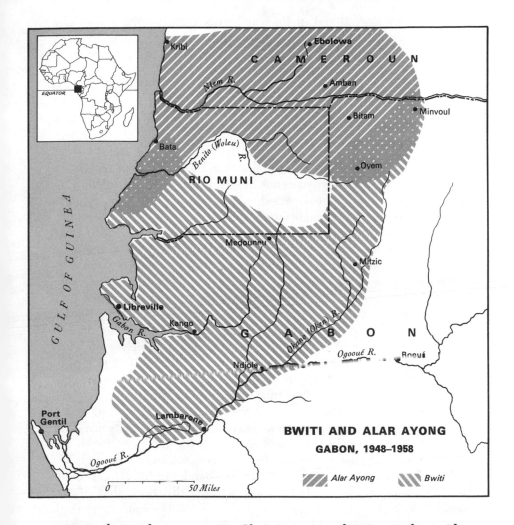

EQUATOR

Kribi

CAMEROUN

Ebolowa

Ntem R.

Amban

Bitam

Minvoul

Bata

Benito (Woleu) R.

RIO MUNI

Oyem

Medouneu

Mitzic

Libreville

Gabon R.

Kango

GABON

Okano (Oken) R.

Ndiole

Ogooué R.

Booué

Port Gentil

Lambarene

Ogooué R.

BWITI AND ALAR AYONG

GABON, 1948–1958

GULF OF GUINEA

Alar Ayong

Bwiti

0   50 Miles

a more thorough exposure to Christian evangelization and a wider participation in such economic activities as cash-cropping.[3] The assumption is that Alar Ayong appealed to a more developed population than did Bwiti, a cult whose traditionalism and employment of the arcane had less appeal in the more modernized districts. This is true enough but, at the same time and without denying important differences between these two movements, we would emphasize that, as they both developed among the Fang, they were revitalistic affirmations of Fang culture and shared the same overall intention. In the en-

[3] Georges Balandier, *Sociologie Actuelle de l'Afrique Noire, Dynamique des changements sociaux en Afrique centrale* (Paris 1963), 241.

thusiasm they engendered, there was hardly room for more than one of these movements in the same area. But it should also be pointed out that probably no more than twenty per cent of the population in either area participated in these movements.

The Alar Ayong movement rested on an ideological reexamination of the Pahouin past insofar as that past was contained in genealogical histories, legends, and myths. Originally this re-examination took place among the Ntumu and Bulu dialect groups in the Southern Cameroun; it was these groups which had received the most intense American and German Protestant education.[4] The efforts of the native ideologues revealed an unexpected degree of organization in the clan relationships of the colonial period, which had hitherto been thought of as extremely scattered and disorganized.

Some time during World War II, this conscious attempt to mine the folklore of the Fang past resulted in a desire both to disseminate the "facts" of that past and also to accomplish the clan reunion suggested by these facts. In this desire, the indigenous groups were helped by the American Presbyterian Mission Press, which printed accounts of the meetings—*esulan*—of clan regroupment in *Mefŏe*, its vernacular press. The press also printed and circulated *Dulu Bon be Afri Kara* ("The Journey of the Children of Afri Kara"), which is the most literate summary in the vernacular of research into the Pahouin past. Like the Alar Ayong movement itself, this account rests on genealogical history, legend, and myth—both traditional and revised.

The Fang, more than most African peoples, preserve long patrilineal genealogies averaging ten "names," and in some instances reaching twenty "names," or generations. Usually the genealogies begin with the informant himself and proceed backward through his father, his father's father, and so on, to the founder of his clan. Though the first name in the genealogy has traditionally been that of the founder, in recent decades genealogies have reached into mythology and the clans have established their divinity by citing the efficient god, Zame ye Mebege, as the final name and hence the founder. Thus for the clan Bukwé in northern Gabon, genealogies now generally tail off in the following fashion: Nguema Bukwé, Bukwé Ndong, Ndong Zame, Zame ye Mebege. In recent years these genealogies have been losing

---

[4] The Americans, particularly through the lexicographical work of A. I. Goode and others, encouraged in the Bulu an interest in their past. They also encouraged and published historical accounts in the vernacular, such as *Nnanga Kon* (Ebolowa, 1948). Since the Cameroon Bulu Mission was established after the Americans had been expelled from Gabon by the French in the late 1880's, there has always been mistrust between the American missionaries and the French authorities.

importance, but they had a crucial function in the pre-contact era, and were highly stressed in the education of the young.

This was so because the classic Fang social organization consisted of dispersed clans—patrilineally related, exogamous social units of common ancestry—which were, probably because of the dispersal processes of rapid migration, scattered about in small villages and not all represented in an integral area of clan lands. Feuds, disputes over marriage payments, rapine and small-scale attacks between villages of different (and sometimes the same) clans were characteristics of Fang equatorial life. The internecine strife that prevailed and the dispersal of social organization meant that there was uncertainty about one's allies and relatives. What certainty there was existed in the genealogies, for it was only through them that proof of common clan membership and degree and depth of relationship could be established. Knowledge of the genealogy was therefore more than the crucial source of one's identity: It had survival value.

Associated with the genealogies were myths, legends, and historical testimony concerning the origins of the Pahouin; the origins and dispersal of the various dialect groups, the Bulu, Ntumu, Ewondo, Okak, Fang, Meke, Mven, and others; and historical evidence as to the activities, places of residence, and migrations of the principal names found in the genealogy. The intellectual founders of Alar Ayong, the *lettrés* among the Ntumu and the Bulu (often pastors or catechists), studied all these materials to arrive at a revised and integrated version of the Pahouin past. The present took on a new shape when these intellectuals discovered a historical basis for the regrouping of the dispersed and greatly disorganized clans.

The basis for reorganization was found in the fact that some genealogies showed the fission of clans; hence, matrix and derivative clans could be distinguished.[5] On this basis clans could be reunited and the chaotic dispersal of recent times rectified. There is little evidence among the Fang of Gabon of any aboriginal ceremony or ritual which had grouped together all the lineages of any clan. Yet conditions were such that, when representatives of Alar Ayong made their way through the forests in the late 1940's, most villages readily acceded to clan reunions. In the particular Alar Ayong ceremony to be described below the great clan Essalan (Cameroun), also called Maban, is shown

[5] Discussion of the general problem of segmentation in the Fang patrilineages can be found in Balandier, *Sociologie*, 102-42; for a discussion of the problem of fission into new clans and the problem of matrix clans, see J. W. Fernandez, "Redistributive Acculturation and Ritual Reintegration in Fang Culture" (unpublished Ph. D. dissertation, Northwestern University, 1962).

reuniting its Gabon derivative clans—Odjip (Oyem district), Essan (Minvoul district), and Esseyan (Libreville district).

The genealogies out of which this reconstitution of the present by affirmation of the past took place seem to have been employed with skill and veracity. But it is also clear that the traditional genealogies offered sufficient gaps and vagaries to allow for the interpolation of much newly created material. Thus, the printed version of the Alar Ayong legend found in *Dulu Bon be Afri Kara*, although resting on real genealogical materials, added a great deal to the Fang past.[6] We can, however, identify a common plot symbolizing the origin and migration of the Fang ancestors from the northeast through a treeless savannah, where there was little water, no wild game, and a constant shortage of food, to arrive at length at an *adzap* tree which blocked their further passage. They were forced to chop a hole in the tree through which they then passed, one by one, to find themselves in a dense equatorial forest which was too much for their technology. However, they soon fell in with the autochthonous Bukwé (pygmy peoples) who instructed them in the ways of the forest. Finally they built their own village. But family quarrels, which the various legends usually detail at length, began and *ndebots* (minimal segments) broke away from each other, moving off to found what were to become the various dialect groups of the present Pahouin.

Various interpretations have been given to this legend. Some scholars find evidence of Egyptian origins.[7] And, though they speak a neo-Bantu language, it is true that the Fang are originally a Sudanic people of savannah origin. But it is the penetration of the equatorial rain forest, which is represented in the legend both symbolically and directly, that most interests the Fang themselves. Genealogical research anywhere in Fang territory soon discloses that every one of the more than one hundred fifty clans traces its origin to *adzap mboga* (the pierced tree) where, in general, the first ancestor in the genealogical line is supposed to have lived. The legendary account of ancestral difficulties in adapting to the rain forest is heartily appreciated, for the Fang still do not feel fully at home in the forest and not only marvel at the pygmies in this respect but regard them as an important source of forest magic and medicine. The reference in the traditional legends to family conflict evokes a satisfying explanation for fractionalism and dispersion. It also provides the basis and rationale for regroupment.

---

[6] As recounted in J. W. Fernandez, "Folklore as an Agent of Nationalism," *Bulletin of the African Studies Association*, 2 (1962), 3-8.

[7] Anta Diop, *Nations nègres et Culture* (Paris 1948), *passim*.

The Alar Ayong elaboration of this legend which is printed in *Dulu Bon* traces the African back to the flood, and accounts for such customs as circumcision, polygyny, and relationships to women. But in particular it discusses the vicissitudes and strife which led to the splitting away of the six sons of Afri Kara, Fan Afri, Oka'ga Afri, Mevu m'Afri, Nden Afri, Bulu Afri, and Ntumu Afri, who are the founders of the various dialect groups of the Pahouin. The passage through the *adzap* is recounted as well as the first encounter with life in the equatorial forest. The coming of the Germans and their replacement by the French is also discussed to bring the legend up to date.

Thus, in the Alar Ayong version, the genealogical legends are founded on biblical events which establish the Fang origin as coeval with that of other biblically based civilizations.[8] They conclude with modern historic facts which give the whole account a convincing ring. Furthermore, although it recounts the quarrels which resulted in the dispersion of the clans, the published legend offers a continuity to the Pahouin past which must have been a source of confidence and identity to those repeating it. Thus this version of the legend has a more positive emphasis than did the earlier legends of malediction and frustration which were the first response to colonial domination. There is a certain nobility in the struggles recounted in *Dulu Bon*—the account has the air of a wonder book of old romance. In addition, by reporting the internecine strife of Europeans and the repeated battles of the Germans and the French, the new legend implicitly compares them with the strife of Africans, thus making it difficult for Europeans to assume any superiority, or the Africans any inferiority, in the matter of social cohesiveness.

This reworking of the Fang ancestral legends represents, then, a basic kind of protest. In response to times out of joint, it knits together past and present. It affirms the present relevance of the past, and of its characteristic social organization as a way of equipping the Fang for the challenges of the present. As a specific illustration of how this was done, let us turn to a description of an *esulan ayong* (a clan meeting), held in August 1958.

This particular meeting—which the author attended—took place almost a decade after the height of the movement and well after most of the political ambitions tied to it had passed into abeyance or been satisfied by other means. One week before the three-day meeting, the following notice, in French, was posted in Endama village, district of Oyem:

[8] Georges Balandier in his account of his years in Africa, *Afrique Ambiguë* (Paris 1957), 179, has discussed the psychological function of the Christianization of Fang legends.

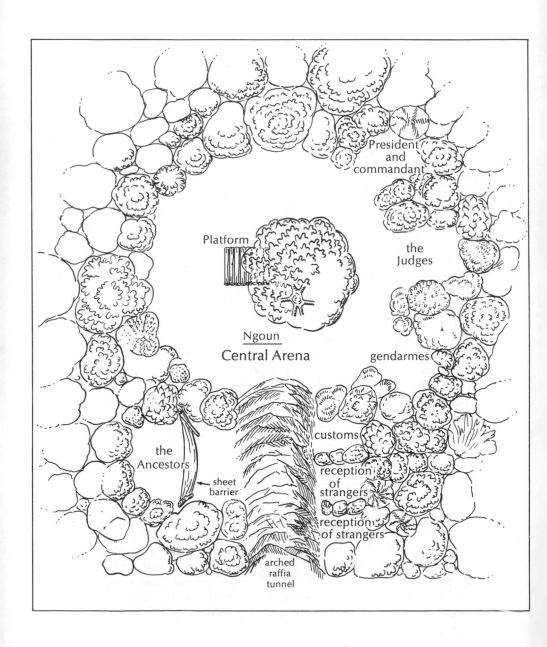

President
and
commandant

Platform

the
Judges

Ngoun
Central Arena

gendarmes

the
Ancestors

customs

reception
of
strangers

reception
of strangers

→ sheet
barrier

arched
raffia
tunnel

Wednesday 6/8/1958 The reunion begins at 9 in the morning—optional attendance. Attendance on this day is prohibited to women who will be occupied in bringing foodstuffs in from the plantations for strangers. The day will be devoted to preparation of the meeting grounds and of the emplacement of administrative echelons.

Thursday 7/8/1958 Gathering at 8 in the morning sharp. The various ranks in the hierarchy will enter their respective emplacements accompanied by their secretaries.

Friday 8/8/1958 The women may this day enter the meeting ground where they will hear all that is said. This day will be designated Day of the Clan Genealogy—*Jour d'Endan Ayong.*

The first day, at which I was not present, was spent in clearing out the reunion site in the deep brush back of the village (see diagram). Late that afternoon there was an *enyengé* (a dance of welcome to the participants).[9] It was also announced that the particular forest containing the reunion site was sacred to the ancestors. Hence no weapons of any kind, and no spitting, sneezing, or coughing could be allowed. In the middle of the *ngoun,* or central arena, was a small speaker's platform. Woven palm fronds arched over this platform, as well as over the separate galleries and over the entrance to the reunion ground itself. Since these fronds are also employed in traditional religious ceremonies, particularly in the ancestral and anti-witchcraft cult, the atmosphere was evocative of traditional practices and attitudes toward the supernatural. Compared to the brightness of the village clearing, the meeting grounds seemed a dark chamber in the forest until the eye adjusted to the obscurity.

The first two galleries near the entrance were reserved for women and for strangers whose credentials were being examined. The third was the station of the gendarmes. To the left as one entered was a long gallery reserved for the ancestors. Halfway down its length there was a white cloth hanging, behind which only the leaders of the reunion were allowed to penetrate. It was said by a member of a clan not involved in the ceremonies that the skulls of clan ancestors were displayed behind this cloth, as was usual in the periodic forest rituals of the Fang ancestral cult.[10] This was denied later by Ayong informants who cited the Roman Catholic and Protestant prayers and hymns sung during the meetings as evidence of a modern Christian orienta-

[9] The dance of *enyengé* has provoked great interest on the part of observers who have gone to some length to account for its connection with Alar Ayong. Was it invented for this movement and does it have a special, recondite significance? My own data indicate no special status for *enyengé* among the many dances which the Fang invent, adopt, and circulate annually.

[10] As detailed in Gunter Tessmann, *Die Pangwe* (Leipzig, 1913), II, 115-25.

tion. The other galleries were reserved for the various dignitaries and functionaries of the Ayong—the presidents and the commandants with their secretaries and "adjoints," the judges, the customs men, and the gendarmes.

Thursday was spent in selecting the membership of these various groups from the approximately sixty men in attendance. Only the commandant who had called the *esulan* and the president who had been held over from a former meeting and who was to be replaced, had already been selected. For most of the participants this was the first *esulan* they had attended since the height of the movement in the late 1940's and early 1950's.

On Friday morning, I was ushered in before the ceremonies began. Flowers hung on all the arches and in the trees, and the site had a festive air. I was searched by a gendarme for weapons and admonished not to cough, sneeze, or spit. I was then escorted to the gallery of the presidency and presented to the notables of the clan. All the officers and bureaucratic officials then gathered in the center to sing, first a Catholic hymn, then a Protestant hymn, followed by a prayer from each of the two persuasions. This was concluded by the "Reunion Song" in Fang.

> Brothers O Brothers we have come together for a reuniting of hearts.
> We have left behind our villages and our houses
> We have left behind our women
> We have come to have a reuniting of hearts.[11]

This brief chant accompanied by soft clapping was followed by a word of admonition from the oldest man of the three host villages who urged the assembly to face each other with open hearts since they were all of the same clan in the presence of their common ancestors. Then the men dispersed to their appointed places. The six oldest men entered the gallery of the ancestors along with a man whose face was painted white, the color of the shades themselves. The presidency was occupied by the four presidents who were in charge of the reunion; they were accompanied by their secretaries. The judges, the customs officers, and the gendarmes also went to their appropriate places. Four local pastors who were in attendance took their places in one of the guest galleries.

The first order of business was the matter of my presence, which was considered by frequent exchanges of notes written and delivered

[11] The Bulu-ized Fang version is the following: "Bobezang, Bobezang bia ti zu efulan minlem, bia mania lik menda mangan, bia mania lik bininga bangan, bia ti zu efulan minlem."

by schoolboy secretaries to the non-literate dignitaries and passed from one leafy gallery to another in what seemed to me a factitious flurry of tropical bureaucracy. Toward the end of the negotiations and communications, the president came forward, mounted the platform, and explained in a loud voice the purpose of my visit and my identity. I was then permitted to photograph each echelon of the organization in turn. This was followed by more passing of notes dealing with judgments taken the day before on clan disputes—judgments which were to be communicated to the chief of the district. Very soon, however, the oldest man came forward and announced from the platform that everything said and done from then on would be in the presence of the ancestors, for the genealogy was to be recited and the ancestors would each be called by name. This recital of ancestors common to the various derivative clans took some fifteen minutes; this was followed by a lecture on the origins of the various derivative clans and their common bond in the great clan Maban-Essalan. The lecture was based on materials learned from the Camerounian intellectuals.

The women were then ushered in. After they had been settled, the president of the Ayong and three of the chiefs of village mounted the platform to speak to the women about the brideprice.[12] The president said in effect: "Our fathers paid 300 francs for a woman and ten to twelve children resulted from that marriage. Now we must pay sixty to eighty thousand francs and these women give our clan few or no children. The clan asks that you women should stop running about and stay in your villages. You have a woman's representative in our Ayong. You should decide to get together and send her to the Commandant in Oyem and promise him that hence forward you will limit the brideprice to 10,000 francs." Each of the men who addressed the women became very heated in admonishing them, all in a similar vein. It then being well past noon the morning session of the *esulan* was adjourned. The afternoon and final session turned again to the selection of officers.

How are we to interpret the significance of such meetings and of the Alar Ayong movement in general? In the late 1940's when the movement was at its peak and when representatives were coming

[12] It might well be argued from the frequency of complaints on this issue that their relationship with their intransigent women has been the greatest preoccupation of the Fang men, far surpassing any other political and economic issue. The emotional nature of the admonishment to the women in the *esulan* surely bears this out. For economic reasons—the amount of potential savings and investment capital tied up in the brideprice—both colonial and newly independent governments have tried to limit the marriage payment, without notable success. Its attempts to reduce the brideprice is evidence of one aspect of the modern outlook of Alar Ayong.

down into Gabon and Spanish Guinea and holding frequent reunions, the colonial authorities tended to take an alarmist view of such proceedings and to regard Alar Ayong as an attempt to replace colonial organization with an adapted indigenous organization: In seeking to elect its own officers, Alar Ayong seemed to be trying to replace the officially appointed and approved chiefs.[13] Was Alar Ayong another manifestation of premature attempts by the Camerounians to obtain independence while under trusteeship? The presence of *lettrés* in the organizing circles convinced some administrators that Alar Ayong was much more than a spontaneous revitalization developed by thoughtful members of Ntumu-Bulu society. More devious elements must, they thought, lie behind it. The *côté secret* was frequently referred to, the presence of *nègres de Paris* was decried, and a probable understanding between Alar Ayong, and the *Union des Populations Camerounaises Rassemblement Démocratique Africaine,* and the communists, with whom the *Rassemblement* was then collaborating, was suggested.[14]

There can be no doubt that Alar Ayong did have political implications and that Camerounian politicians did seek to push it in a more politically instrumental direction. The creation in 1948 in Ebolowa, the Cameroun, of the *Union Tribale Ntem-Kribi* to bring together all the Alar Ayong movements was undoubtedly primarily a political effort. This superior body which represented a joining of clan committees and councils was never, however, recognized by the administration; nor did it achieve the reality or the vitality possessed by the Alar Ayong on the clan level. There was also the suggestion of a relationship between the Alar Ayong movement and the *Congrès Pahouin* (see below, 453-54) but this was never proved. Be that as it may, a decade later, at the time of the meeting described above, it was apparent that the authorities of Gabon and Spanish Guinea (Rio Muni) had overemphasized the menace. Alar Ayong was virtually defunct. In a report written in the late 1940's, a French administrator with long experience in Gabon, Edouard Trezenam, had seriously questioned the tendency of Camerounian administrators to see the movement as

---

[13] Some of the administrative archives dealing with Alar Ayong are available. Brian Weinstein has acquired Edouard Trezenam's reports from Libreville on Alar Ayong. These include a letter from the Governor of Gabon to local administrators advising them to support with all their authority the customary chiefs, regularly nominated, against attempts by Alar Ayong to advance new authorities. "Affaires Politiques et Sociales Libreville," 30 Dec. 1948.

[14] In Trezenam's report (above) this *côté secret* is mentioned with some fascination. "Rapport à M. le Gouveneur, Chef du Territoire du Gabon sur le Regroupement des Fangs," 30 Mar. 1948, Boué.

primarily a kind of *festivité*—a diversion.[15] But in the end this is what it had become—at least in the main.

Since most of the data on the Alar Ayong movement comes from colonial administrators, the tendency has been to emphasize its instrumental nature in the strictly political sense.[16] My research into Alar Ayong and my presence at a reunion leads me, however, to emphasize its expressive quality—a release of enthusiasm about the past and about the present achieved by genealogical myth-making and by creating in the forest precincts of the *esulan* a microcosm in which all is perfectly organized, with the Fang themselves occupying all the important posts. In this microcosm the women, whose "liberation" in the colonial period had created such a problem in African life, are once more in their place, listening submissively as the men lay down the law. In this microcosm the ancestors, who have been neglected by the evangelical process, are once again present and, moreover, alerted to their responsibilities by the meaningful intonation of the genealogy, which is *la pièce maitresse* of the entire movement. The fact that the reunion grounds themselves have a remarkable similarity to the *elik Bieri* (forest enclosures) employed in the ancestor cult cannot be ignored. The Alar Ayong was indeed a *festivité* in the sense that it sought suspension of disbelief; it created a microcosm in which the Fang could dwell if only briefly and obtain gratifying diversion; and it sought solemnly to affirm a reality more than it attempted to change existing conditions.

But this affirmation was not simply a return to the past, to old organizations and to old religious beliefs. The ancestor cult and the ancestors themselves were included to a degree hitherto unknown. The syncretisms with the colonial world, the emphasis on a timetable for example, is also obvious in this account. Georges Balandier has argued that new forms of solidarity based on hierarchy have tended to replace the older, egalitarian reciprocities in the clan movement.[17] Though, in fact, observation of the exchange of messages in the reunion showed that exchanges between bureaucratic groups in their various galleries still depended more on reciprocal and symmetrical

[15] This discussion appears in the second report by Trezenam, 25 Sep. 1948, Boué, 31.

[16] On balance the most comprehensive previous account, that of Georges Balandier, takes the instrumental, power-oriented, view of these movements. But it would be unfair to him and unfair to his commitment to "wholistic" sociology, not to point up his frequent mention of the ambiguities involved and the satisfactions of religious expression and revelation bound up in these movements. He also recognizes how basic to them is their search for autonomy. "Le Sens des Changements Socio-Culturels en Pays Fang," *Sociologie Actuelle,* 255-83.

[17] Ibid., 245.

relationships than upon hierarchical and asymmetrical ones, the syncretisms taking place were moving in the hierarchical direction. Nevertheless, beneath all this, Alar Ayong affirmed the relevance of the ancestors and the relevance of the clan, together with the genealogies and the organization of social life that they encouraged.

Bwiti: A New Search for an Old Salvation

The elaboration of a microcosm in which to dwell, which we saw in the Alar Ayong reunion in the forest galleries, is even clearer in Bwiti. There are other similarities between these two movements—a fact which accounts for their complementary distribution: a preoccupation with ensuring the presence of the ancestors, a concern for the fertility of their women, and an interest in genealogy and genealogical events. But, generally, these similarities in form are given different emphases and different functions by the two movements. Bwiti is a confessed religious movement, engaging a much greater portion of the participants' time than Alar Ayong and determined that cult membership be the primary commitment. Symbolism and ritual are more richly elaborated in Bwiti than in Alar Ayong although, as we have shown, the Alar Ayong movement was the result of a high degree of creative intelligence applied to the Fang past.[18] We might distinguish these movements by saying that in the one we see an affirmation of organization and in the other, Bwiti, the affirmation of spiritual communality. This generalization, despite its aptness, should not be taken so literally as not to admit an overlap. It is a question of emphasis in the total configuration of the two movements.

For example, we have seen the way Alar Ayong emphasizes genealogy. We also find extensive use made of genealogy in Bwiti. The individual member recites his genealogy in his personal prayers, offered outside the chapel before the full ritual begins in the early evening. Since within the chapel itself only prayers for the entire membership can be made and the membership is drawn from many clans indiscriminately, and since genealogy is the chief symbol of clan membership, its use within the chapel would not be appropriate.[19] The

---

[18] The variations in creative intelligence applied in the ritual organization of Bwiti are found in J. W. Fernandez, "Symbolic Consensus in a Fang Reformative Cult," *American Anthropologist*, LXVII (1965), 902-27. The point to be made is that although these movements have been constructed by only a very few individuals, appreciation for what has been elaborated is widespread among participants.

[19] Balandier, *Sociologie Actuelle* talks about generalization of ancestry, that is, the extra-genealogical search for ancestry, within Bwiti. The Bwitists, in pro-

belief is that as each ancestor is cited, he is alerted to the needs of his descendant. Since the Bwitists invariably conclude the genealogy with the name of God, the father of the clan founder, the attachment of the Bwitist to deity is affirmed. The genealogy in Bwiti, therefore, serves to affirm the ties of the worshipper to his ancestors and to God, two relationships brought into doubt in the colonial situation, mainly by evangelization. But no attempt is made, as in Alar Ayong, to reconstruct a former social organization through the genealogy. In the use made of the genealogy itself, we see the distinction between an affirmation of a communal spirituality and an affirmation of organization.

Among the Fang, Bwiti is considered a reinterpretation of the ancestor cult found among the Mitsogo and Massango peoples of the Ngoumé region in southern Gabon. The origins of Bwiti are, however, more difficult to establish than those of Alar Ayong. It appears to have made its first appearance among the Meké-Fang of the Ogooué around the turn of the century, but it received its real impetus around Libreville and along the estuary at the time of World War I.[20] The Okoumé lumber camps, which had appeared in great numbers in the estuary region at the turn of the century, had brought together men from a number of tribes and provided ideal conditions for the diffusion of the cult. Like Alar Ayong, Bwiti was regarded with suspicion by the administration as a manifestation of autonomy with positive political designs.[21] And in certain of their branches, the Bwitists did participate in politics; they may actually in the 1940's have provided "cells" for the organization of the party of Léon Mba, the first president of Gabon—the *Comité Mixte Gabonaise* (later the *Bloc Démocratique Gabonaise*).

We are concerned here, however, with the affirmations being made in the spheres of myth and ritual—the essential aspects of Bwiti.

---

hibiting the use of genealogy within the chapel, are also reacting to the individualization of the ancestral cult by which, because of the missionary onslaught, the apparatus and powers of the cult have fallen into individual hands for selfish use (222-30).

[20] Traditional Bwiti (MBuiti) is mentioned by Paul du Chaillu in the 1860's among the Massango-Mitsogo. *The Country of the Dwarfs* (New York, 1872), 238-45. French missionaries reported Bwiti among the peoples of the Lambaréné region at the turn of the century in the *Journal des Missions Evangéliques de Paris*, XXIX (1904), 435. This would include the Fang and is probably the earliest date that it appeared among them.

[21] A special, privately circulated report on the Pahouin, emphasizing Bwiti, was put out about 1930 by the Governor of Gabon, Vuillaume. In this report the Bwiti custom of taking *eboka* and the putative need for child sacrifice are given emphasis beyond any political implications of the cult. Vuillaume saw Bwiti as rapidly brutalizing the Fang race.

To capture these we need to return to the early colonial period and to recollect the attitudes toward the Fang then current. In that period lies the source of what has been called the Fang "quest for salvation," a quest arising out of their sense of dissatisfaction with the distribution of life's goods and out of their attitude toward immorality. Their affirmation of a communal spirituality should be understood in this context.

In the nineteenth century the Fang were engaged in a slow conquest of western Equatorial Africa. They were therefore particularly susceptible to cultural shock as the Europeans, by conquest, first pacified them and then imposed a culture on them which was, in material possessions, vastly richer than their own. The state of malaise—the sense of deprivation and impotence—that this engendered in the Fang has led Balandier to call them "conquerants en disponibilité,"[22] a people with a sense of a past but with a depressing sense of the future.

One of the first tasks a conquered people undertakes as a consequence of the culture shock of finding themselves in a colonial situation is to reexamine and rephrase the past in an attempt to explain how they "got there." Hence from almost the earliest period of contact, Fang folklore gives plentiful evidence in stories and legends of the manifest technical superiority of the white man. These *Ntangan ye Nsutmot* (Whiteman-Blackman) stories have many variants.[23] A very common one, told by old men in the districts of Oyem and Mitzik in the late 1950's, explains that after the efficient God, Zame ye Mebege, son of the primordial and final God, Mebege, created the world and

[22] This is a phrase frequently employed by Balandier in his *Sociologie Actuelle*. Since the Fang "conquest" of Gabon was accomplished piecemeal, not by tribal-wide, highly organized, military expeditions like the Zulu under Shaka, it is unlikely that the Fang were stirred, like the Zulu, with memories of a glorious military past. Discussions with Fang indicate that they remember more vividly the internecine strife and bloody feuds of intervillage life in the nineteenth century. On the other hand, the Fang have always had a strong sense of superiority over the other Gabonese tribes, the *bilobolobo* as they call them—the speakers of gibberish. The other Gabonese tribes reciprocate with a strong dislike which has replaced the earlier fear of a Fang onslaught.

[23] These attempts to elaborate new myths and legends by which the ascendancy of the European is explained are mentioned widely in the early literature and are recorded in Henri Trilles, "Proverbes, Légendes et Contes Fang," *Bulletin de la Société Neuchatel de Géographie*, XVI (1905), 93-104. The advantages enjoyed by the Europeans were either traced directly to the oversight of God and an unlucky happenstance, which comes to the same thing, or to some failing or frivolity of the African which lost him his patrimony. We discuss below the degree to which part of the Fang response to the imposition of European control was a search for moral failings in themselves. The biblical story of Ham's failure to cover the nakedness of Noah, his father, Genesis 9:22-25—for which he was cursed—was repeated to me orally in Africanized form.

man, he left them to their own devices. Soon he noticed that there was considerable turmoil and that his two human creatures needed further instruction. He called them together and decided first to talk to Whiteman. Whiteman listened patiently. Then God turned to Blackman who was squabbling with his brothers, and was inattentive and impatient. Shortly before God could finish all that he had to say, He was called away to heaven, never again to reappear directly in the affairs of man. Thus Blackman was left without vital information that Zame had intended to give him. He was left, as the storytellers usually conclude, unable to discover anything and unable to complete anything because he lacked the necessary "words of God." Whiteman profited enormously, as is evident, from all that he had learned. One does not have to point out the congruence of this tale with the missionaries' efforts to spread the "bonnes nouvelles."

The point is that tales of this kind testify to a very early sense of deprivation and impotence among the Fang vis-à-vis Europeans. What Whiteman gained in his extended and attentive interview with God were the powers of organization and the means by which to escape the savage state. Blackman continued to labor under an earlier and inadequate patrimony. These tales and other more direct orally derived data from the early contact period give evidence that the Fang were painfully conscious of how their disorganization and savagery appeared to Europeans. The Alar Ayong and Bwiti movements were efforts to find some sort of affirmation in the midst of such malaise through organizational capacity and communality of spirit.

But we must be careful how we interpret this myth-making of the early colonial period. Many of the myths seem to focus on material superiority, which has caused some students of the Fang to interpret their activity as being devoted entirely to a search for material well-being. Though there is plenty of evidence for this, it is not the only animus which inspired the Fang, and it is not at all a satisfactory motive for understanding Bwiti notions of salvation.

Since the Fang were at one time a migrating people, one can gain insight into this world view by inquiring as to how they conceived of their migration—which moved to the southwest, toward the ocean. Henri Trilles, who was among the earliest to gather the folklore of the Fang, speaks of a widespread myth in which they envision themselves and, more particularly, their legendary ancestors, the heroes of the Mvett cycle of legends, as being pursued by a monster crocodile.[24]

[24] Henri Trilles, *Totemism Chez les Fang* (Munster, 1912). I was never able to elicit this myth from my informants. The Mvett troubadour legends of the famous epigonae, the clan of Egong, are reported at length by Ndong Philippe in *Réalités Gabonaises*, 1-6 (1960-1966).

Family quarrels again and again provide this crocodile with the opportunity to decimate the Fang population. Trilles and others have interpreted the crocodile as symbolic of the Sudanic peoples, probably the Fulani, whose expansion drove the Fang out of their original savannah home. In this legend we see the Fang thinking of themselves not simply as conquerants but primarily as a displaced population fleeing from their original homeland. But of greater interest is the way in which their own quarrels debilitate the Fang and open them to the ravages of inimical forces. This notion is congruent with Fang ideas of the operation of malevolent supernatural forces. When men are overwhelmed by evil, it is to a large extent their own fault—because they have weakened themselves.

These concepts give us a better grasp of the moral discomfort experienced by the Fang in contemplating their social disorganization in a situation of colonial subordination. "Contemplation" is here used advisedly. We have seen this discomfort as a motive behind Alar Ayong. Much earlier, at the time of the origin of Bwiti, V. Largeau had also referred to the sense of inadequacy felt by the Fang because of their scattered condition and their frequently expressed need to reunite and interpenetrate.[25] Because of their moral sensitivity on this issue, which was coupled with a remarkable interest in abstract thought, Largeau was inspired—in contrast with other African cultures—to call the Fang outlook a philosophic culture.[26] In the same period the missionaries were noting this reflective quality among the Fang of the estuary. The missionaries saw the Fang sense of moral imperfection expressing itself in respect to their relation to the deity whom they recognized as having abandoned them because of their imperfections. The Fang saw their new and correct relationship with the deity as an extreme desire for salvation.[27]

It is not surprising that the myth-making designed to account for European superiority should have been energized by feelings among the Fang of moral inadequacy and a search for salvation. Frequently their response to the missionaries' evangelical efforts was that the very migration of the Fang to the sea had been a search for salvation from the god who dwelled there and who, although in the traditional view otiose and entirely careless of mankind, was now considered to have a new-found relevance. This spiritual, rather than economic, rationale for the migration toward the sea comes up, it is true, in the context of missionary endeavor and, it may be argued, has little rele-

[25] V. Largeau, *Encylopédie Pahouin* (Paris 1904), 4.
[26] Ibid., 16.
[27] The *Journal des Missions Evangéliques* (see n. 20 above) yields extensive testimony from missionaries about this desire, particularly the reports of the *tournées* (1895-1905).

vance except in that context. On the other hand, for the Fang this was an influential context within the colonial situation. The missionaries had more intensive contact with Africans than any other European group and were therefore highly influential in the formation of the African self-image. It is not surprising, therefore, to find that this rationale of the migration had considerable importance in Bwiti and was even reflected in the layout of the Bwiti chapel (see below, 449).

Mythologically, it would seem, the migration of the Fang has a transitional character. If we read the mythological materials right, they were in flux between the savannah country of contentment on the other side of *adzap mboga,* where brothers lived peacefully before the eviction and pursuit by the monster crocodile, and the sea which was to offer a new salvation. At the sea brotherly harmony would again prevail, and there, influenced by the "bonnes nouvelles" of the missionary, they could come to know God and resolve the great question of death.[28] Clearly Bwiti was an institution which responded to this search for a new salvation in the midst of a compound malaise. At the same time, it affirmed an old salvation, a noble spirituality which could be found in the past as well as achieved again in the future. In a sense it suppressed the transitional situation and tied together the past and the future. That this affirmation could take place at all is partly due to the decline of European moral authority and hence to a decline of moral pressure upon the Fang. Albert Schweitzer has, for example, written at length about the decline of European moral authority as a consequence of the dissolute behavior of segments of the colonial population and of the internecine strife which the African observed in World War I.[29] The affirmations of Bwiti, then, were not only more easily accepted but could even be considered to counter a manifest European immorality.[30]

---

[28] H. M. Bôt ba Njock has written in this connection, "Les Fang, visiblement chassés de ce pays d'adoration d'après la tradition avaient eu la promesse de retrouver la sécurité, la paix dans un autre pays situé vers l'ouest," in "Prééminences Sociales et Système Politico-Religieux dans la Société Traditionnelle Bulu et Fang," *Journal de la Société des Africanistes,* XXX (1960), 161-62.

[29] Albert Schweitzer, *On the Edge of the Primeval Forest* (London, 1955), 97. I have discussed this same decline in "The Sound of Bells in a Christian Country; The Quest for the Historical Schweitzer," *Massachusetts Review,* V (Spring, 1964), 537-62.

[30] As we see later on, the Bwitist occasionally implicates the fallen character of the European. Dorothea Lehmann, writing about Alice Lenshina's Lumpa cult in Zambia, talks about a Biblical puritanism in her belief that sets a rigid standard for her own followers while it implicitly criticizes the whites on the basis of theirs. John V. Taylor and D. Lehmann, "Alice Lenshina Mulenga and the Lumpa Church," in *Christians of the Copperbelt* (London 1961), 248-68. See also below, Andrew Roberts, "The Lumpa Church of Alice Lenshina," 513-68.

But if such changes in European moral authority made the affirmations of Bwiti easier to accept, they did not ease the feelings of Bwitist and Fang generally that life, if not themselves, had been invested with a surfeit of evil. The consequences of that evil, the disease, poverty, and general deprivation in which the African lived, were before their eyes daily. Among the Fang, as elsewhere in Africa, their relative deprivation in the colonial situation, coupled with the destruction of the old anti-witchcraft agencies, caused a demonstrable increase in witchcraft activity.[31] In some chapters of Bwiti and among some cult leaders we find the elaboration of a grandiose mythology of evil in which the old Fang beliefs in witchcraft and the witchspirit, Evus, are syncretized with biblical history to produce an account (in which the devil as Evus plays the major role) of why the world and particularly the African is in such dire straits. P. Bekale has recently given us such an account.[32] One wonders, upon reading it, whether in the Manichaean drama that he presents the principle of evil and the power of darkness are not a great deal more real and ever present than the power of good and light.

In any case, evil is omnipresent and, in the midnight *évangiles* (sermons) which are characteristic of Bwiti ritual, the membership is frequently lectured on the circumambience of evil (as if the many precautions taken during the ritual itself did not keep this in mind): They are reminded that it is the rivalry and covetousness among brothers, the adultery, the laziness, the gambling, the drinking, and the other immoralities that have weakened the Fang and enabled evil, the Evus, to assert himself. At the same time, it is made clear that Bwiti protects its membership against the surfeit of evil in the world not only by ritual devices but also through its social requirements. It prevents immorality from making inroads on the strength of the membership.[33] Moreover, it is frequently reiterated that the Fang once lived in a moral state with their brothers, in fertile connubiality with their wives, and in devoted worship of their ancestors. All this Bwiti attempts to recapture, and the individual member is constantly urged to a more perfect membership by being presented with affirmations of the past morality of his antecedents.

[31] The increase in witchcraft accusations and sensed witchcraft activity has been widely remarked in the anthropological literature. I have discussed this increase among the Fang in the introduction to the Bwiti manuscript of P. Bekale. J. W. Fernandez and P. Bekale "Christian Acculturation and Fang Witchcraft," *Cahiers d'Etudes Africaines*, VI (1961), 244-70.

[32] Ibid.

[33] The distinction is made between two classic forms of evil among the Fang: *nsem* (ritual sin) and *ebiran* (social sin, aggressiveness and egoism). Cf., ibid., 260.

It must also be mentioned that the *évangiles* which carry the burden of the above message also frequently comment on the European way of life which constitutes such an attraction to the African. The leaders of the cult frequently repeat that Bwiti is a forest religion, that it employs in its rituals items taken out of the forest, and that, therefore, it is the natural religion of the Fang, who are a forest people. In this respect Bwiti is contrasted with the European religions which use alien ritual elements such as bread, wine, and candles. This contra-acculturative point is frequently extended to a critique of all the material aspects of European life which, it is argued, constitute a threat to the morality and dignity of the Fang way of life.[34]

In contrast to the mythology of the Alar Ayong movement, which was elaborated intellectually and was to a large degree independent of any ritual characteristics, in Bwiti mythology and ritual are closely intertwined, reflecting and reinforcing each other. This is so much the case that informants called upon to recite the mythology will frequently intersperse their recital with songs and dances taken out of the ritual. Thus, while one is hearing of the origin of the world as the sky spider, Dibodia, drops his egg upon the great primordial ocean, or of Evus, the principle of evil, tricking Eve into eating the apple and then having intercourse with her, the informant will intersperse this account with the songs or dances appropriate to the portions of the ritual in which these events are being celebrated.

In fact, the entire sequence of the all-night rituals, usually held weekly on Saturday nights from six in the evening to six in the morning, is a two-phased recreation of mythical reality. Thus, until midnight the members dance creation and birth—the creation of the world and the creation of man as well as the birth of Adam and the birth of Christ.[35] These events are variously developed in song and dance; the system is not highly stereotyped. That is, these themes are as often presented simultaneously as serially and on succeeding evenings the order and the themes may be changed. After midnight the dancing represents death and destruction: the destruction of men's hopes in a benign world, the expulsion from paradise, the flight from the savannah into the rain forest, and the death of Christ. It is also after mid-

[34] J. W. Fernandez, "Unbelievably Subtle Words: Representation and Integration in the Sermons of an African Reformative Cult," *Journal of the History of Religions*, VI (Aug. 1966), 43-69.

[35] Something of the Christianized aspect of the myth and ritual can be found in J. W. Fernandez, "The Idea and Symbol of the Savior in a Gabon Syncretist Cult," *The International Review of Missions*, LIII (1964), 281-89. There is a high degree of creativity in Bwiti. Balandier interviewed a cult leader excited by a recent trip to Libreville where he had learned new versions of the basic mythology as well as new ritual. *Afrique Ambigué*, 242.

night, and after the *évangile*, that the membership established *esamba* (reunion) with the ancestor spirits which have been attracted into the cult house from the deep forest. It is in this reunion that the distinction between individual, living cult members is obliterated. All became *nlem mvore*, one heart.[36] The significance of this achievement (there is a reference to a union of hearts in the theme song of Alar Ayong) will be realized when placed in the context of the increasing mistrust and suspicion between brothers brought about by the disintegration of the extended family in contemporary society. Its significance will also be realized when seen in relation to the guilt felt in the abandonment of the ancestors as a consequence of Christian evangelization. Bwitists affirm that "one-heartedness" among living Fang and between living Fang and their dead ancestors was once the condition of Fang life and that it is recaptured in Bwiti. In the morning hours after the conclusion of the rituals of 6 A.M., the feeling of *nlem mvore* is particularly strong.

The affirmation of that spirituality among the members of Bwiti is first and foremost the reaffirmation of bonds of one-heartedness among the living and between them and the dead. It is achieved by emphasis on ritual creativity and by down-grading the appetite for material well-being, which the Bwitists believe is such a curse in contemporary Africa and which leads to such profound feelings of inferiority. The ritual and songs are themselves syncretic elaborations of a mythology reconciled with Christianity.

Most of this ritual creation is too elaborate to be discussed here; there are, for example, over one hundred and fifty songs in the major branches of the cult and more than a dozen basic dances. However, in the context of the discussion of the microcosmogony of Alar Ayong, reference should be made to the spatial organization of Bwiti worship. One key to the understanding of that organization is to note the place and role of women within it. A diagram helps us appreciate the intricate organization of the chapel as a microcosm. We note first that the chapel has a male and female side and that each of these sides is further associated with other elements so that we get a binary set of opposed qualities in the chapel:[37]

male	female
death	birth
sun	moon
white	red

[36] Reference to the ritual manner of achieving one-heartedness is made in Fernandez, "Symbolic Consensus," 905.

[37] This dual organization of values is discussed in Fernandez, "Redistributive Acculturation."

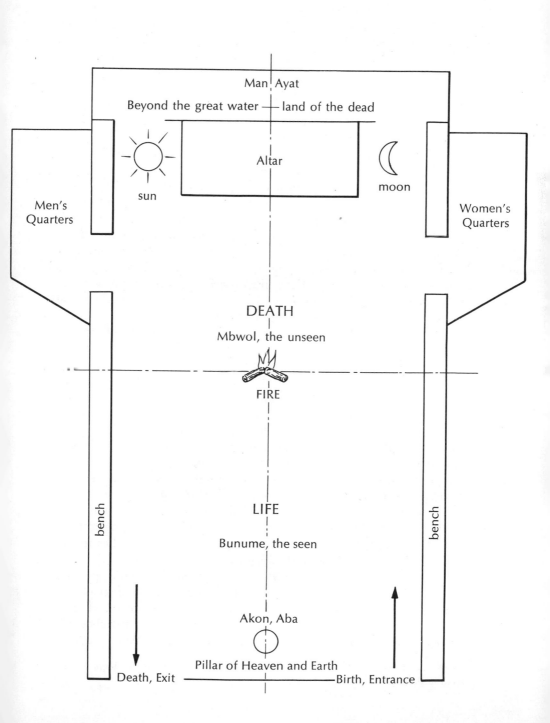

The chapel is also bisected in the opposite dimension so that we have a life and a death portion, or a "this world" and "other world" division, as it is sometimes called. Behind the altar is a very sacred area called the *mang* (sea). This is the abode of the great gods in keeping with the Fang myth which speaks of the Fang migration toward the ocean as a search for God. The progress of ritual moves from the *akon aba* or *adzap mboga,* which stands at the entrance of the chapel, to the *mang.* It is here that the sacred music is played which represents the voices of the deities, principally the female deity, Nyingwan Mebege. On either side of the chapel and opening into it are the two dressing chambers where male and female members robe and where they perform the particular rituals by which they create or prepare the cult, *akomnge engosi.* The point is often made that it is impossible to dance Bwiti in just one or another side of the chapel. For Bwiti is something created by both sexes. Thus women, in contrast to the situation in Alar Ayong, have a complementary and highly functional role in the Bwiti cult. Cult leaders affirm the great part Fang women have played in the past as complements to Fang men. The contrast is frequently drawn between this former state and the suspicion, frustration, adultery, and venereal disease that are part of contemporary Fang life.

The Bwiti cult has as one of its objects the restoration of fertility and the birth of children, an objective arising from the declining birthrate of the Fang.[38] It is accomplished by a ritual which is symbolic of sexual activity, although no direct physical contact between the sexes is allowed to take place for such would be a clear defilement of worship. In this symbolic production and celebration of creativity, the women play an important role. They perform such rituals as introducing the female principle of creation by bringing in the substance of the female deity of the universe, Nyingwan Mebege, from a sacred pool in the deep forest. Men and women together ritually create a universe, a microcosm as it were, in which they can dwell with dignity, with a sense of moral adequacy, and in one-heartedness. They may hope that the ritual will produce well-being, harmony, fertility, and good fortune in the everyday world. But the most powerful affirmation lies in the ritual reproduction of these spiritual realms.

In this account of Bwiti the degree to which an ecstatic spiritual state is sought by means of dance and through consumption of the alkaloid *eboga* (*Tabernenthes eboka*) has not been emphasized. The Bwitists pride themselves on the reality of the religious experience obtained by their methods, with the boost of this drug. They contrast

---

[38] The demographic census and declining birthrate among the Fang is discussed in Balandier, *Sociologie Actuelle,* 92-102.

the power of their religion to obtain religious transport with the meager powers of missionary Christianity. "Can Christianity bring the visions or the mingling with the dead that is characteristic of Bwiti?" they ask. Bwitists go on to boast that Bwiti offers its membership a knowledge superior to that available elsewhere in the underdeveloped world. It is called by them a "science" of the ancestors and of things beyond death. This boast implies that Bwiti is a spiritual answer to the material inferiority imposed by the European. It is an answer that is, in some sense, morally superior. An anecdote would serve our understanding here. On several occasions Bwitists have explained my white skin to me in the following way:

> Human beings normally have black skin. Black is the color of sin and all human beings live in sin. Now, Whiteman has a white skin because he has died once and paid in dying the penalty for his sins.[39] He has also gained thereby much of the knowledge that God holds beyond death. But Whiteman tends to forget that advantage. You see the blemishes, the moles, the freckles that cover his skin. These are sins creeping back on him. We Bwitists die [obtain ecstatic release] in our cult. We go beyond death. We show this in painting our faces and arms white with kaolin [as in the actual practice]. This shows how we go beyond death to the science of the other world. Whereas Whiteman has forgotten the source of his knowledge, we have not.

This version of the affirmation of a noble spirituality, which embodies both admiration and depreciation of the white man by reference to spiritual realms and spiritual values. It indicates the complexity of the attitudes involved in Bwiti, both against and for the colonial situation, both against and for the past condition of the Fang. This complexity, which may appear dissonant in discussion, is easily incorporated into the intricacies of the myth and rituals by which the new moral universe of Bwiti is created.

Analysis: Microcosmogony and Modernization

Protest is commonly understood in the negative and, depending upon one's commitment to the social order, usually in the pejorative sense, as involving gestures of extreme disapproval of existing conditions. In

---

[39] There is some material on the European being taken as a *revenant* (ghost) of the dead. Among the Fang the European at first was, according to the folklore, said to be some kind of fish because he came from the ocean and smelled peculiarly. Because of his odor and appearance it was also said that he was a corpse recently risen from the grave.

an effort to gain a fuller understanding of the phenomena of protest, we have introduced materials from two movements in Equatorial Africa. In particular, as Webster permits us to do, we have placed emphasis upon protest as "an affirmative statement or solemn declaration of adherence." In this case the adherence and the affirmation are for things past. Colonial domination meant many things to the Fang and gave rise to many reactions. Among other things it means a deprecation of the Fang past and a denial of their place in the present. In this situation, as clearly seen in these two cults, protest consisted of an affirmation of things past and the creation by microcosmogony of a small world of cult activity in which the membership could dwell sealed off from the frustrations of the present. Both movements created microcosms, literally carved them out of the forest, in which the membership could dwell ritefully in festivity. But the affirmations made in the two cults differ: Alar Ayong affirms a past organization; Bwiti a past moral spirituality. By diagram and discussion, I have endeavored to make clear how, at least momentarily, self-sufficient universes were created which totally preoccupied the membership.

When such facts are advanced, it is usually argued that they are epiphenomenal. The flights and fancies of the imagination as it builds symbolic universes out of frustrations are interesting but represent a "displaced ingenuity."[40] Much more relevant are the "structural factors"; those economic and political events involved in the search for wealth and power. It would be foolish to deny the importance of such structural explanations. But on the other hand analysis from this point of view can itself bias understanding. Political and economic motives can be exaggerated, and affirmative, creative, and expressive satisfactions bound up in protest movements can be overlooked. At the time that I studied Alar Ayong and Bwiti, I estimated that these latter satisfactions were of dominant interest to the members. It was the microcosmogonic aspects of the cults which attracted them.

In the case of the Fang, the view has frequently been put forward that in the colonial period the Fang were driven by a desire for European goods and a desire for increments in power. Hence their major calculations immediately before and during the colonial period were made on the basis of commercial and political advantage. I do not

[40] E. J. Hobsbawm, *Primitive Rebels* (New York, 1965), 163. Hobsbawm's perceptive account of nineteenth- and twentieth-century social movements in Europe suffers from his failure to understand how the religious features of these movements, to which he makes plentiful reference, provided a reality of their own. He resists seeing, in other words, how forms acted upon provide content. For Hobsbawm, content is only present where there is a manifest and instrumental social and political program.

want to deny the energizing animus of acquisitiveness, whether for goods or power, either in the case of the Fang or in the human equation generally. There is ample evidence of the Fang's envious eye for European material goods. Certainly much of the early colonial history, as in the uprising of Emana Tole, the Ogowe partisan who attempted by reuniting the clans to reassert the Fang position as middlemen in the rubber trade, shows us that this acquisitive motive was, indeed, powerful. But the stimulus for the two protest movements is not compelling cupidity—certainly they do not resemble anything like a cargo cult or an underground revolutionary movement based on desire for material advantage. I believe them to be more satisfactorily understood by reference to the two affirmations which have here been distinguished.

Outside these cults, of course, the idiom of Fang reaction to the European could be very much economic and political. Attempts, and in the early days armed attempts, to organize in the face of colonial domination were frequent, though usually of minor significance. The French administrators were ever ready to detect the appearance of organizations inimical to their interest—the archives yield much data on administrative sensitivity and precautions. Of course, the administration had its own notions as to what would constitute a more efficient organization of the Fang. In 1947 the Governor of Gabon called a Congrés Pahouin at Mitzik.[41] This was held to assist in administration-oriented reorganization—village regroupment and more efficient transmission of administrative directives to the villages. But the Fang's own sense of organization did not conform to that of the administration and the Congrés escaped administrative control. In the subsequent decade Fang politicians came to agree with the administration that the regroupment of the small and scattered Fang villages was called for and actively pressed for that result.[42] Like the various mutual aid societies and associations that appeared among the Fang under the évolués, these attempts at organization are, to be sure, all manifestly political or economic. But they do not have the deeper qualities of affirmation characteristic of the two movements we have discussed. This analysis would be inadequate if we tried to understand the one group of movements by the other and if we did not carefully distinguish their different emphases.

It may be useful in an analysis of these different emphases to have

[41] Balandier discusses the Congrés in Sociologie Actuelle, 198-203.

[42] J. H. Aubame, the leader of the opposition party in Gabon before independence, the Union Démocratique et Sociale Gabonaise, wrote a pamphlet on this matter in 1947. Renaissances Gabonaises (Brazzaville, 1947). He and his party strongly supported regroupment during the 1950's.

in mind a bipolar continuum in which the two poles are an instrumental emphasis on the one hand and an expressive emphasis on the other. (The same approach can be seen in the literature which talks about the search for instrumental or consummatory satisfactions).[43] Instrumental emphasis means that the movement has a realistic awareness of the political, social, and economic forces external to itself and is attempting to advance its interests and increase its share of economic and political power, and that it is ready to curtail immediate satisfactions for future benefits to its interest. A movement of expressive or consummatory emphasis, on the other hand, is preoccupied with present satisfactions—with having its needs currently satisfied, most often in symbolic ways. It tends to be self-isolating and self-indulgent in the sense that it tends to ignore external realities. It is ontogenetic in the sense that through its often ritualistic activities it creates a world in which the membership can dwell, in which they can adjust to their difficulties, if only for the time being. There are surely many difficulties in such a simple scheme, but it does alert us to a basic problem of analysis.

In point of fact no movement is ever entirely instrumental or expressive. That is implied in speaking of emphases. The problem of analysis is to indicate emphasis, but it must avoid reductionism in interpretation. For example, Carl Rosberg and John Nottingham have recently published a salutary study of Mau Mau in which they attempt to counteract the popular delectation with the barbarous and atavistic aspects of that polymorphous movement by placing it in the long term context of Kikuyu and Kenyan nationalism.[44] But they themselves risk a new myth by concentrating on an instrumental interpretation of events. They either ignore or give short shrift to expressive or consummatory aspects of the phenomena—the symbolic issues, for example, bound up in such matters as circumcision and oathing. Their interpretation may be a natural consequence of the dialectic they are engaged in with previous atavistic interpretations and of the discussions they held with a coterie of politically sophisticated informants. At the same time one feels that the analysis would be more adequate and run less risk of stereotypes if it would confront the question of instrumental-expressive emphasis.

It must be admitted that an instrumental bias runs through Western analysis of protest movements. It may be, simply, that we are always more interested in politics than we are in religion. It surely is

[43] See especially David Apter, *The Political Kingdom in Uganda* (Princeton, 1961), 85-91.
[44] Carl Rosberg and John Nottingham, *The Myth of Mau Mau* (New York, 1966).

because we are more interested in meaningful change in the objective world of resource and power distribution than in largely subjective changes of state. Our own structural perspective in the analysis of facts may make all social scientists "political" scientists. In any case, this bias is certainly present in the published materials previously available on the two sects discussed here. Most of these earlier materials are administrative in origin or written under adminstrative auspices, and it is quite understandable that it is the political implications of these movements which should have been carefully sifted. But the sifting was often too careful, as in the reports of Trezenam; what he saw as a high degree of political intent turned out, as some of his earlier interlocutors had suggested, to be a form of *festivité*.

At the time in which I studied these movements in Gabon, the expressive or consummatory emphases were very clear. The materials I gathered, some of which I have presented, confirm this emphasis. But to avoid those pitfalls in analysis which I have suggested I must indicate something of their instrumental concerns, subordinate though they may be. In the first place, both Bwiti and Alar Ayong as I knew them were in a stage of post-florescence, the latter much more so than the former. Alar Ayong in the late 1940's and early 1950's was actively used by Camerounian and Fang nationalists in an effort to mobilize sentiments for independence across frontiers. I say "used" because Alar Ayong in origin and in procedure had another more expressive *raison d'être* which persisted long after the nationalists had discovered it. As an instrument for the mobilization of nationalist sentiment and for the organization of the independence movement, it proved, in the long run, too inert and too self-indulgent. The instrumentalism present in Alar Ayong in the late 1950's was limited to attempts to discuss and report opinion on minor problems posed by the district administration. For the most part, the participants in Alar Ayong were living in their own microcosm. Important events in the growing nationalist drive were taking place elsewhere.

As for Bwiti, though it ante-dated the nationalist drive in Gabon and appeared for quite other reasons of cultural conservatism among the *déracinés* in the coastal towns and lumber camps, it too was used in the late 1930's and 1940's as a convenient structure for early political mobilization.

Once again the term "used" is appropriate, for the culture of this movement was deeper and richer and more preoccupying than can be explained simply by regarding it as an instrument of political mobilization. By the 1950's the political parties in Gabon had sufficient freedom of public movement and sufficient momentum no longer to need this religious movement as a cover. A high degree of party loyalty to the *Bloc Démocratique Gabonaise* was, however, preserved in Bwiti, and party organizers at voting times were careful to visit chapels of cult leaders and to mobilize their votes. In return the *Bloc Démocratique Gabonaise*, which in the late 1950's became the governing party in Gabon, extended protection to Bwiti, which was then under attack by missionaries and certain *évolués* as an unacceptable form of cultural atavism. Once again it was considered self-indulgent by many of the young elite who objected to all-night dancing and other ritual "foolishness" when the energy of every citizen was needed in the building of the modern Gabon.

Within the microcosm they had constructed, however, the members of Bwiti were finding, and have continued to find, plentiful satisfaction. Its basis was a simple solidarity. In both Alar Ayong and Bwiti we find an emphasis upon and a ritual achievement of the "reunion of hearts"—one-heartedness among all participants. One might say that these movements were protesting against conditions in the late colonial period which led to suspicion and anxiety in the relationship of one Fang to another and in the relation of all living Fang to their dead ancestors. One may interpret the microcosmogony which resulted as a protest against the mistrustful and dispiriting conditions of the colonial world. The small worlds being created were to a considerable degree a symbolic reconstruction of the world which it is supposed the Fang lived in before the European imposed his foreign dilemmas. For these reasons we have talked about these movements as affirmations of things past. It is this conscious affirmation bound up in ritual satisfactions that provided most of the appeal which they possessed for their membership.

One may talk at length about the affirmations made by a subordinate society to console itself for its condition, but the prevailing question in the mid-twentieth century is: What is the contribution made by these movements to modernization? By modernization is usually meant Westernization in a nationalistic context. This means, in turn, the learning of values and skills characteristic of the members of Western European nations, though the broader definition would be any modification of traditional behavior which would be adaptive to and permit full engagement in the modern world. The microcosmogony we have observed in these two cults would seem to be, frankly, so self-preoccupied and self-indulgent as to be incompatible with modernization and the materialism it implies. In its intellectual, religio-aesthetic creativity it has offered a compensatory participation which may well act to divert the participant from the pressures of modern life. But if the microcosmogony has released participants from the pressures of the modern world, it has also given them some chance to make adjustments to their plight. For neither of these movements has engaged the participants fully nor is it entirely self-isolating except for a few adepts. Practically all members have had to return from the microcosm to engagement in the modernizing African scene for the larger portion of their lives.

The question is whether their participation in these microcosms has better enabled them to participate in the modern world. Are these movements recreative in that sense? There are as yet no easy answers nor convincing measures. Alar Ayong has passed, but it would seem to have been the more modernizing movement. The criticism that is frequently directed against Bwiti by the new ruling elites—that its waste of energies in all-night dancing is a great drag on nation-building—is telling. Yet there is sufficient evidence of effective instrumental political action in the history of Bwiti to confuse our judgment. Or suppose we take the attitude toward women of the two movements. In Bwiti, women are offered an equal and functional place in the proceedings and no attempt is made to re-institute, as in Alar Ayong, old forms of domination and subordination. Here the Bwiti attitude would seem to be the more modern one. We are only suggesting a whole range of new problems for analysis. In this essay evidence has been offered of affirmation through microcosmogony in two movements of protest in central and northern Gabon. Students of modernization with their commitment to a macrocosmic order should not forget the possibility and the viability of such microcosmic affirmations.

RELIGIOUS PROTEST AND SOCIAL CHANGE:

THE ORIGINS OF THE ALADURA

MOVEMENT IN WESTERN NIGERIA

ROBERT CAMERON MITCHELL

African religious movements[1] have long been recognized as potential vehicles for social protest in the colonial situation.[2] Despite an occasional attempt to categorize all such movements as "religions of the

[1] This is a general term used to refer both to instances of religious collective behavior and to the rise of African independent churches. Although there have been Islamic movements, this study is limited to those of Christian origin, which comprise the vast majority of such movements. The field work on which this chapter is based was undertaken in Western Nigeria in 1960–62 and 1965–66. The author gratefully acknowledges support or assistance from the following sources: The Foreign Area Fellowship Program; The Council for Intersocietal Studies, Northwestern University; The Nigerian Institute of Social and Economic Research, Ibadan; and Vanderbilt University.

[2] Among those studies which emphasize the role of social protest in the rise of religious movements are the following: Georges Balandier, "Contribution à une Sociologie de Dépendance," *Cahiers Internationaux de Sociologie,* XII (1952), 47-69, and many subsequent publications of Balandier including *Sociologie Actuelle de l'Afrique Noire* (Paris, 1963); Paul Bohannan, *Africa and Africans* (New York, 1964), 25-30; James S. Coleman, "Nationalism in Tropical Africa," *The American Political Science Review,* XLIV (1954), 404-26; Père Dufonteny, "Les Sorciers comme Chefs du Rébellion," Semaine de Missiologies, *La Sorcellerie dans les pays de Mission* (Brussels, 1937), 700-788; Thomas Hodgkin, *Nationalism and Colonial Africa* (London, 1956), 94; André Retif, "Pullulement des Églises Nègres," *Études* (Paris), CCCII (Sept. 1959), 186-95; Robert I. Rotberg, "The Rise of African Nationalism: The Case of East and Central Africa," *World Politics,* XV (1962), 75-90; B. I. Sharevskaya, *Religionznaya politika Angliyskogo Imperializma v Angliyshikh Koloniyakh Afriki* (The Religious Policy of British Imperialism in British Possessions in Africa) (Moscow, 1950); George Shepperson, "Ethiopianism and African Nationalism," *Phylon,* XIV (March 1953), 9-19, and "The Politics of African Church Separatist Movements in British Central Africa, 1892-1916," *Africa,* XXIV (July 1954), 233-47; Endre Sik, *Histoire de l'Afrique Noire* (Budapest, 1964), II, 52, 59, 71, 78, 130-31, 292-93. Most of the examples cited by these sources are from parts of Africa other than West Africa.

oppressed,"[3] this potential was by no means universally realized. As Michael Banton has written:

> The extent to which any religious movement expresses protests varies from time to time and one cannot easily be compared with another. . . . At times it is impossible to demonstrate that the element of protest is of any significance at all.[4]

In this paper I shall use the term "social protest" to refer to criticism, opposition, or hostility toward whites in general or the colonial regime in particular, expressed either manifestly or covertly, and I shall differentiate it from religious protest, which limits its criticism to the spiritual sphere. It is recognized, of course, that social systems are interrelated and that it is impossible to treat religious systems as self-countained entities. Nevertheless, I hope to demonstrate that a distinction between social protest and religious protest is valid. It is my contention that religious protest is universal to African religious movements and that only under certain conditions of general societal strain—when alternate avenues of protest are unavailable—does religious protest become social protest.

Sometimes, as in the case of the Ethiopian type of independent church described first by Bengt Sundkler in connection with the Zulu of South Africa,[5] the independent churches start as a result of specific criticism of the mission churches. Since the Ethiopian churches characteristically developed by schism from an already existing church, the grievances against missionary domination were clearly articulated and an air of protest maintained.

The other major type of independent church in Africa, which Sundkler calls the "Zionist" type,[6] is quite different. The Zionist or prayer-healing churches developed around particular prophets, stressed emotion and spontaneity in their rituals, were loosely organized, and emphasized healing and God's help for the believer in this life. Even in South Africa, the Zionist churches did not start as manifest protests against white domination in mission churches, although the theology of the messianic movements with their Black Christ certainly embodied the black-white tensions in the society. The Zionist appeal in South Africa, as it has been elsewhere in Africa, was generally in the

---

[3] Vittorio Lanternari, *Religions of the Oppressed: A Study of Modern Messianic Cults* (New York, 1963).

[4] Michael Banton, "African Prophets," *Race*, V (1963), 50. Much of the essay by Banton concerns itself with matters of social protest, however.

[5] Bengt Sundkler, *Bantu Prophets in South Africa* (2nd ed.; London, 1961), 55.

[6] Ibid.

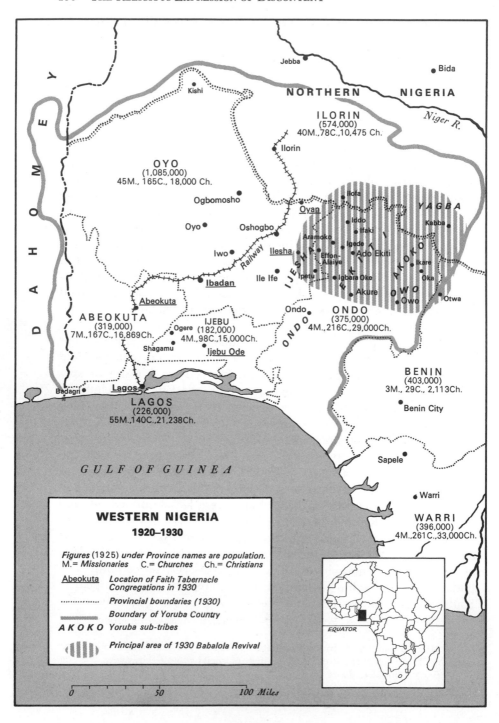

Jebba

• Bida

Kishi

NORTHERN   NIGERIA

Niger R.

ILORIN
(574,000)
40M.,78C.,10,475 Ch.

• Ilorin

OYO
(1,085,000)
45M., 165C., 18,000 Ch.

Ogbomosho

Ilofa

Oyan

YAGBA

Iddo

Kabba

Oyo •

Oshogbo

Aramoko

Iffaki

Igede

IJESHA

Ado Ekiti

AKOKO

Iwo •

Ilesha

Effon-
Alaiye

Ikare

Ibadan

Ile Ife

Ipetu

Igbara Oke

EKITI

Oka

OWO

Abeokuta

Akure

Owo

Otwa

ABEOKUTA
(319,000)
7M.,167C.,16,869Ch.

Ogere •

IJEBU
(182,000)
4M.,98C.,15,000Ch.

Ondo •

ONDO

ONDO
(375,000)
4M.,216C.,29,000Ch.

Shagamu

Ijebu Ode

Badagri •

Lagos •

LAGOS
(226,000)
55M.,140C.,21,238Ch.

BENIN
(403,000)
3M., 29C., 2,113Ch.

• Benin City

GULF OF GUINEA

Sapele •

• Warri

WARRI
(396,000)
4M.,261C.,33,000Ch.

WESTERN NIGERIA
1920–1930

Figures (1925) under Province names are population.
M.= *Missionaries*   C.= *Churches*   Ch.= *Christians*

Abeokuta   *Location of Faith Tabernacle*
           Congregations in 1930

·············   *Provincial boundaries (1930)*

           Boundary of Yoruba Country

AKOKO   *Yoruba sub-tribes*

           Principal area of 1930 Babalola Revival

EQUATOR

0   50   100 *Miles*

positive attractions the new Zionist churches offered—specifically, healing ånd protection from witchcraft.

This essay contains a case study of some independent churches of the prayer-healing or Zionist type in Western Nigeria, a country whose colonial experience was relatively untraumatic. Through an examination of the origins and early development of these churches an attempt is made to specify the nature of the religious stresses and strains within Nigerian Protestantism, the general social conditions that led to the development of these churches, and the extent to which they can be identified with social protest. My conclusion is that these churches essentially represent a protest that remained within the religious sphere. Their followers rejected neither Europeans nor the colonial regime as such. Basically they wanted a religion which satisfied their daily needs better.

The Aladura Movement

The subject of this case study then is not a specific African independent church, but a set of churches of a common type but of differing origins which arose among the Yoruba in Western Nigeria, beginning in 1918. These churches, which comprise three main subtypes and many splinter groups, have enough similarity in their origins, beliefs, leadership, and rituals to be known locally by the same term; the Yoruba word *aladura*. Aladura means "one who prays" and is the Nigerian equivalent of South African "Zionism." The aladura churches have in common their initial emergence as prayer groups in mission churches; their emphasis upon the power of God to protect, heal, and help the believer in this life; the designation of their leaders as prophets; their practice of possession in the form of speaking in tongues; and their emphasis upon visions as a means of revelation and on personal holiness as the distinctive Christian style of life. I shall use the phrase the "aladura movement," to refer to the development and growth of these various aladura churches.[7]

Before delving into the complexities of the origins and doctrines of the individual variants of the aladura movement, something of an

[7] Literature on the aladura in general includes Geoffrey Parrinder, *Religion in an African City* (London, 1953), John B. Grimley and Gordon E. Robinson, *Church Growth in Central and Southern Nigeria* (Grand Rapids, 1966), 299-317, and J. D. Y. Peel, "A Sociological Study of Two Independent Churches among the Yoruba of Nigeria" (unpublished Ph.D. dissertation, University of London, 1966). More specialized works will be footnoted as they are referred to. Peel has since published *Aladura: A Religious Movement Among the Yoruba* (London, 1968).

overview is necessary. Between 1918 and 1930 three separate aladura churches were formed by former members of the existing mission churches in Western Nigeria. The first aladura church, called originally Faith Tabernacle but later known as the Christ Apostolic church, began in 1918 and separated from the Anglican church in 1922. The second, the Cherubim and Seraphim Society, became a separate church about 1927, and the third, the Church of the Lord (Aladura), finally became an independent church in 1930, although its founder lost his position in the Anglican church in 1926. By 1930 these groups could boast small congregations in the capital city of Lagos and the major interior towns, especially Ijebu-Ode, Abeokuta, and Ibadan. Their members were relatively few, although their activities, particularly the open-air meetings of the Cherubim and Seraphim in Lagos and nearby cities, had attracted the attention of the public. In 1930 the Faith Tabernacle variant received a considerable impetus from a mass healing movement led by Prophet Joseph Babalola, hereafter referred to as the Babalola Revival.

The Origins of the Faith Tabernacle (Christ Apostolic Church)

In an attempt to understand the dynamics behind the emergence of the aladura movement in the 1920's and the kind of protest that it manifested, a description of the origins of the Christ Apostolic Church in the Faith Tabernacle is given here in some detail. It is a complex story, involving a number of characters rather than a single charismatic leader. Its pattern will be compared with the origins of the Cherubim and Seraphim and the variants of the Church of the Lord.

The Faith Tabernacle may be said to have had its beginnings in St. Saviour's Anglican Church, Ijebu-Ode, during the worldwide 1918 influenza epidemic.[8] Some time before the epidemic, in response to a vision received by "Daddy" Ali, the church's sexton, a special prayer group had been founded in the church by some of its leading members, and with the support of its pastor, the Rev. S. J. Gansallo, an African. At first the group met after the Sunday service, but later, in response to requests from the congregation, also met on Monday evenings. The leader of the prayer band was J. B. Eshinshinade,[9] a

---

[8] J. A. Ademakinwa, *Iwe Itan Ijo Wa Lati Eqbe Okuta-Iyebiye Ijo Faith Tabernacle, Apostolic Church de Christ Apostolic Church* (History of Our Church from Diamond Society, Faith Tabernacle, Apostolic Church to Christ Apostolic Church) (Lagos, 1945) is a major source for the early history of Faith Tabernacle. It is supplemented by interviews with many of the participants. References to this work will be to its short chapters and not to pages.

[9] Eshinshinade's name was originally Shadare. He changed his name during the 1920's and his later name is used exclusively here.

goldsmith, whose piety was held in high respect in the church, where he was an officer, and in the community.

When the influenza epidemic struck Ijebu-Ode, Sophia Odunlami, an educated girl of nineteen who resided in a village four miles from town, fell ill. After five days she had certain supernatural experiences, which included hearing a voice which proclaimed: "I shall send peace on this house and to the whole world. The World War is ended. . . ."[10] Another message apparently instructed her to tell all those who believed in God that if they washed in a coming rainfall they would be healed. Sophia was an Anglican and she told her message to her local pastor, the Rev. I. B. Ogunmefun. Word of her revelation subsequently traveled to the prayer band in Ijebu-Ode, which sent for her. Addressing the whole congregation after an evening service, she told them that a rain would soon fall and that it should be used with faith for healing. Her message made a profound impression upon the anxious assemblage. Many used the subsequent rainwater and praised its effectiveness. No one was more impressed than the prayer band members who regarded her vision as a confirmation of the earlier vision of "Daddy" Ali. She was invited to join the group.

At about the same time, a government order closed all public buildings, including churches, for the duration of the epidemic in order to prevent its spread. The Rev. Mr. Gansallo obeyed this order and went to his village, an act which many of his Church members regarded as desertion. In contrast, the Rev. S. A. Phillips, an African and the school headmaster, led a procession of Church members about the town praying for deliverance from the epidemic. The prayer group, following Phillips's rather than Gansallo's example, intensified their efforts during the epidemic.

This experience of divine help in time of need through a revelation by a layman, coupled with the failure of their pastor in the time of crisis, led the prayer group directly to question aspects of the Anglican faith they had formerly taken for granted. The idea that God could provide for His faithful in their life on earth, especially during time of danger, sickness, or adversity, and prevent attacks of witches had lain behind the original formation of the prayer group. They knew that many otherwise staunch members of mission churches resorted to traditional diviner-healers when faced with difficult situations for which the mission churches offered no immediate solution, not even a hospital. Now they had dramatic confirmation that the acts of healing and promises of help against the "evil one" contained in the New Testament had contemporary meaning. In 1919 their ecclesiastical dis-

[10] Interview with Mrs. Sophia Odunlami Ajayi, May 1962.

quiet and theological discoveries were given form and a new source of legitimation through a young man, David Odubanjo, who then joined the prayer group.

Odubanjo was a fellow townsman, well educated and ambitious, who had been away in Warri in government employment.[11] In 1917 he had been given a copy of a periodical published by a small American faith-healing group called Faith Tabernacle. Reading this paper, *Sword of the Spirit,* Odubanjo was greatly impressed by the personal experiences printed in it. They testified to the power of prayer alone to heal and to provide for worldly needs, and condemned the use of any medicine whatsoever. Odubanjo began to correspond regularly with Pastor J. Clark, the American leader of Faith Tabernacle. Latent ministerial ambitions were apparently raised in him, for as one aladura historian wrote: He "began to dream that he was preaching and baptizing people."[12]

Odubanjo then put his faith to a rather unique test. With a practicality characteristic of him, he decided that if he could increase a government war bonus of £25 which he had just received to £50 he would resign his government work in order to preach his new belief. Owing to the outbreak of a local conflict, the Adubi War in Abeokuta, he was twice able to sell barrels of gunpowder which he had bought for £30 in Warri for £60 in Ijebu. The test proving successful, he returned to Ijebu-Ode. There he came into contact with the prayer band. Invited to a meeting, he preached the Faith Tabernacle doctrine of healing without medical aid. The group was so impressed that they accepted him as leader.[13] In 1921 Odubanjo moved to Lagos where he formed a second branch of the prayer group, leaving Eshinshinade as the leader in Ijebu-Ode.

At the time of Odubanjo's arrival in their midst the prayer group numbered only nineteen members. They chose a name, the Diamond (*Okuto Igbaiye*) Society, on the basis of a revelation received by Eshinshinade, and on July 5, 1920 commenced regular meetings.[14]

[11] A brief biography of Odubanjo has been written in Yoruba by A. M. Onoshinwo, *Itan Kukuru Nipa Igbesi Aiye Eni Iwo David Ogunleye Odubanjo* (The Short Life History of the Rev. David Ogunleye Odubanjo) (Odogbolu, *c.* 1959). The account which follows is based primarily upon Ademakinwa, *History,* 1-3.

[12] Ademakinwa, *History,* 3.

[13] Ibid., 13. Ademakinwa states that "They all resolved that Odubanjo be accepted as the leader of the band. Pastor Eshinshinade willingly stepped down for Odubanjo." It is likely that this is an oversimplification of what actually happened.

[14] *The Diamond Society Minute Book,* No. 1, July 5, 1920–May 1921 (Shadare Papers, Ijebu-Ode). I am grateful to T. Shadare, the son of the

The minute book they kept provides access to their activities and discussions during the first two years of their existence. During this time they assimilated the Faith Tabernacle teachings, were ejected from the Anglican church, and established several branches in other cities, most particularly in Lagos.

The main concerns of the society as reflected in the minute book were the doctrine of healing without medicine and their relationship to non-Christians. Their sources of authority were the doctrines of Faith Tabernacle as given in *Sword of the Spirit*, correspondence with Pastor Clark, and personal visions, particularly those received by Eshinshinade and Miss Odunlami.

At one point soon after the Society's foundation the two sources of authority apparently came into conflict. An entry which stated that "we could use any medicine (*ogun*) that is revealed to be applied to any sick person" was crossed out and in the margin was written "we mustn't use any type of medicine."[15] On the whole the Faith Tabernacle doctrine triumphed; the exception was the use of blessed water, which the leaders sometimes encouraged the sick to drink. Each meeting featured testimonies, sometimes from the newspaper *Sword of the Spirit*, most often from their own members, of victories won through faith—jobs received, sicknesses healed, and personal problems solved.

After a time of debate and prayer, the Society adopted a policy of separation from non-Christians. Odubanjo articulated this policy in his sermon of November 2, 1920: "As Christians we should not mix with pagans, but try to see how we can influence them with our ways."[16] This meant that they forbade their members to attend ceremonies, such as those for the dead, which are important communal and familial expressions of solidarity in Yoruba culture.

Since the Society required its new members to abstain from the use of both traditional and modern medicine, it differentiated itself

---

late J. B. Eshinshinade (Shadare) for permission to use this source. Shadare listed sixteen of the original male members for me and gave their occupations. The breakdown is as follows: five traders (three "educated" including Odubanjo), two goldsmiths, two craftsmen, one farmer, one teacher, and five schoolboys (mostly sons of members).

[15] *Minute Book*, No. 1, Sept. 7, 1920. The passage that was crossed out read: "We could use any medicine (*ogun*) that is revealed to be applied to any sick person—when one person was sick it was revealed to one man what medicine to use and the person was healed. When another was sick the same medicine was used and didn't work."

[16] Ibid., Nov. 2, 1920. Among the issues they discussed in their meetings during this time was whether they should go to *Ita-oku*, festive ceremonies celebrating various anniversaries of the death of relatives, or eat *Ileya* meat, meat consecrated and eaten as part of a Muslim festival.

from the Anglican congregation of which it was still a part. There was no conscious antagonism toward fellow Christians or the pastor, but as they immersed themselves more and more deeply in their type of Christianity, they developed a form that was more rigid and demanding than the Anglican persuasion and which eventually led to a clash with the Church authorities.

About half their rules covered behavior and attitudes which would be considered as prohibited for Christians in any part of the world: adultery, envy, polygyny, bribery, hatred, and so forth. Eight more involved traditional practices, some of which were already proscribed by the mission churches—such as sacrifices and going to *babalawos*[17] for divination. Others involved prohibitions peculiar to the Diamond Society, such as the rule against participating in so-called "contributions societies." Twelve of the rules were puritanical, defining as immoral dancing and drumming, debt, drinking, cigarettes, cards, gambling, "interest in money," not keeping the Sabbath, "too much ornament," and chewing kola nuts. Finally, there were rules against the use of medicine and "getting into company with non-Christians."

The American Faith Tabernacle group did not practice infant baptism which was the customary form of baptism for the Anglican church. Ademakinwa, the aladura historian, states that this influenced the society to search the Bible to see if infant baptism was correct and it was concluded that it was not.[18] The Ijebu-Ode Society then noticed that a number of the infants baptized in the Anglican congregation died soon after. This not uncommon event in African society was interpreted as evidence of God's displeasure at the following of an unbiblical practice and led to a boycott of infant baptism.

Tension had been developing between the members of the society and Gansallo, their well educated, somewhat worldly pastor. He was unsympathetic to their form of radical Christianity, particularly the prohibition against the use of all medicines. The issue of infant baptism brought these disagreements into the open.

The Rt. Rev. Melville Jones, the Anglican missionary Bishop, had been sympathetic to the Society's endeavors, as he knew and respected Eshinshinade, a member of the Anglican Synod. Jones visited the society to try to settle the differences between them and Gansallo. Both their minute book and the Bishop's later recollections agree that healing without medicine and infant baptism were the issues that were

[17] The *babalawo* (Yoruba, "father of secrets") is a central figure in Yoruba religion. A priest of the Ifa cult, the *babalawo* is a diviner-healer most frequently consulted at times of sickness or uncertainty.

[18] Ademakinwa, *History,* 17.

amicably discussed, although the Bishop added that he cautioned them on the use of visions for revelation.[19] A later visit to the group by Isaac Oluwole, the Assistant Anglican Bishop, who was in direct charge of the Ijebu area, proved more stormy.[20]

The Society's response to both visits was to remain steadfast in its beliefs and practices. The Bishop then asked Eshinshinade to resign his seat as a member of the Synod. Oluwole further required that members of the Society who were teaching school resign their jobs and children of members of the Tabernacle leave the Anglican school.

The Diamond Society of Faith Tabernacle, as the Ijebu group was called, held its first meeting as a separate Church on January 22, 1922. The minute book explained the event as follows:

It is a day noted for the separation of the Diamond Society from the C.M.S. Church brought about by the persecution from the said C.M.S. members, St. Saviour's Church, Ijebu-Ode.[21]

They also established a school for their children.

At the time of the break, Odubanjo's Faith Tabernacle group in Lagos (the name Diamond Society was used only in Ijebu-Ode) and the small group in the inland Yoruba city of Ilesha also separated from the Anglican church. Odubanjo's organizational skills soon manifested themselves in his recruitment of members for the Lagos branch, his maintenance of constant contact with Pastor Clark as well as with leaders of other sects in Western countries, and his co-ordination of the increasing number of small Faith Tabernacle congregations in major Nigerian cities.

The growth of the Faith Tabernacle in the 1920's came about al-

[19] The Diamond Society recorded the Bishop's remarks: "The Bishop said it was not a sin to use a medicine. . . . It [infant baptism] could in fact not be found in the Bible, nevertheless, but we could find out whether it is right or not. But now that circumcision has been replaced by Baptism it is fit that children should participate in it." *Minute Book*, No. 2, Sept. 13, 1921. Bishop Jones concluded his address to the Anglican Synod about the Faith Tabernacle as follows: ". . . It appears that the name of the society and a considerable part of the movement are founded on dreams and visions. It is not surprising that if they are unwilling to take the Work of God as the final Court of Appeal, they should go seriously astray. In any case, our Church, which teaches and believes in Infant Baptism, cannot come into line with such a Society." *Minutes of Proceedings of the Third Session of the First Synod of the Diocese of Lagos, May, 1922* (Lagos, 1922), 13.

[20] Jones, ibid., claimed Oluwole was anxious to keep the group in the Church. A. M. Onashinwo, interview, May 1962, remembers Oluwole declaring: "No! I won't allow Ijebu to spoil anything. I am in charge of Ijebu." It is clear that Oluwole was much less conciliatory than Jones.

[21] *Minute Book*, No. 2, Jan. 22, 1922.

most entirely because government clerks and private traders, who had become Faith Tabernacle adherents, recruited friends and relatives in the cities to which they were transferred by their employers. By 1930, after nearly a decade of separate existence, the Faith Tabernacle consisted of about seventeen branches located in administrative centers all over Nigeria. It had perhaps as many as eight hundred members. Several of these branches were formed by Yoruba immigrants to northern cities such as Jos, Zaria, and Kaduna. The branches established in Yorubaland numbered only six: Ijebu-Ode (1920), Lagos (1921, two branches), Oyan (c. 1924), Ibadan (1925), and Abeokuta (1928).[22] These newer branches contained the majority of the members.

The new converts were typically young men and their families who were residing as "strangers" in places away from their hometowns. They were for the time quite well educated, and their positions, though junior because of their age, were relatively rewarding. They were in a position to harbor ambitions, and their residency away from their homes brought about a marginality as "strangers" which made it easier for them to question the mission Christian faith that they had been raised in and at the same time made them more vulnerable to misfortune and anxiety.

In considering what form of protest was embodied in the rise of the Faith Tabernacle churches of the aladura movement, it must be noted that, if anything, they expressed less political protest than was exhibited by some members of mission churches. Nowhere did their doctrines touch on colonialism. In the 1920's and 1930's their leaders co-operated with the colonial authorities except on the occasion of compulsory vaccination campaigns, when the newspapers would occasionally report the forcible vaccination of some of their adherents. Many of their members, including Odubanjo, were in government employ and they were well thought of by their employers.

Nor was the Faith Tabernacle a movement of protest against European culture in general. When its children were ejected from the mission schools in Ijebu-Ode it established its own school on the pattern of and for the same purpose as the mission schools. It should be noted that at this time Eshinshinade evinced some misgivings about

[22] The map shows the towns in Yorubaland that had Faith Tabernacle congregations in 1929–30, before the revival. Several commercial or governmental centers in other parts of Nigeria where there were small colonies of Yoruba were also reported to have small branches of Faith Tabernacle at this time, including Minna, Zaria, Onitsha, Benin, Jos, Kano, Kaduna, Port Harcourt, Makurdi and Enugu. Ademakinwa, *History*, 19-26, describes the expansion of the church. J. Ade Aina, *Odun Medogbon Ijo Aladura Ni Ilu Ibadan* (The Silver Jubilee of the Establishment of the Aladura Church in Ibadan) (Ibadan, 1949) describes the history of Faith Tabernacle in that city in detail.

education, but it is significant that he was overruled.[23] Other schools were started in Lagos and Ibadan during the early period.

Finally, the Faith Tabernacle was not a protest against European religion as such. Its relationship with the American Faith Tabernacle and Pastor Clark and with other similar foreign religious bodies is indicative. Its members objected only to a particular manifestation of Christianity. An examination of their relationship with Clark will offer a chance to describe more exactly the critique of Christianity as practiced by the missions which was embodied in the Faith Tabernacle churches.[24]

Why was Clark's religion so attractive to the Nigerians? From 1919 to 1925 the Nigerian Faith Tabernacle groups voluntarily submitted themselves to the guidance of the American Pastor Clark in all matters of importance. They urged him to send a missionary, a request which was beyond the resources of the tiny Philadelphia sect. Even after Clark's church had divided over his alleged adultery and the Nigerians had declared their independence from the competing American factions, they retained a love for Clark, who had taught them God's way, and urged the American elders to give him a chance to repent.

At first glance Clark's religion might appear rather repugnant to prospective African adherents. It was partly cast in the sectarian mode by its insistence on total commitment, its strong belief that it alone possessed scriptural authority, and its puritanical rules concerning personal conduct, none of which naturally demonstrated much sympathy for important African customs like polygyny. Although most African independent churches of the Zionist type have taboos, these usually involve personal sex morality or dietary restrictions and are often *pro forma*. Far from forbidding dancing, they typically encourage it.

Secondly, Clark's religion lacked elements which have characterized other types of independent religious groups in Africa. It did

---

[23] One early Faith Tabernacle member said that "At the beginning Faith Tabernacle said the Lord doesn't write. We thought a man who bought a newspaper was a heathen." Interview with Rev. Ibidapo, Mar. 1962. This was a short-lived and not very general prejudice. Several of the Faith Tabernacle members were pupil teachers, and a school was quickly founded in Lagos. Ademakinwa, *History*, 21-22. A school was held in Akinkeni village outside Ibadan by the Faith Tabernacle just two years after the first Ibadan group was founded in 1925. Aina, *Silver Jubilee*, 11. These ventures did not last long, owing to financial difficulties, but they were the progenitors of the very large school system of the Christ Apostolic church.

[24] The sources for the Faith Tabernacle relationship are personal interviews and the correspondence between Odubanjo and Clark contained in the Odubanjo Papers, Christ Apostolic church, Lagos.

not offer compensation for earthly suffering by possession (it vigorously opposed speaking in "tongues");[25] by office holding (its simple polity involved a leader and elders); by a messianic figure (Clark claimed no divine powers for himself); nor in apocalyptic promises (when the members of the Lagos branch migrated in 1922 to Ebute Metta following a prophecy by "Jesus of Agege" that Lagos would fall into the sea the next year, Clark ordered them to return to Lagos).

Furthermore, the American Faith Tabernacle did not consider visions as a source of divine knowledge. Prior to Odubanjo's arrival the prayer band had been steadily receiving and following such revelations, but it appears that they neglected visions following their contact with Clark. Not until 1928, after they had separated from Clark and had had correspondence with another overseas sect, did they regret their earlier lack of visions. They then attributed their slow growth to this prohibition.[26]

What then was the attraction of the American Faith Tabernacle group to the Nigerian aladura? It lay in the American group's doctrine of God's power to help and heal, which answered a crucial religious question for the Africans, a question which the mission churches failed to answer satisfactorily. This question was: How can God help me to attain my life's destiny in this world?[27] Traditional Yoruba religion provided a wide range of religious practitioners, chief of whom were the babalawos, or diviner-priests of Ifa, who were available for consultation in times of sickness and distress. Through divination they would locate the causes of the problem—perhaps the evil machinations of a witch or an unwitting slight by the sufferer of a deity or

[25] H. W. Turner is incorrect when he attributes a Pentecostal belief in the "second baptism of the Spirit" to the American Faith Tabernacle. H. W. Turner, African Independent Church (Oxford, 1967), I, 10; II, 3. It was against Pentecostalism and had a pamphlet denouncing the practice. Interview with T. Shadare, May, 1962.

[26] In their letter to Eshinshinade, Odubanjo and Mensah, another leader in Lagos, described their dissatisfaction with their previous policy and the effect it had on the Nigerian Faith Tabernacle: "We believe that if our people in Philadelphia have [sic] been practicing this gift, the sudden downfall of Pastor Clark [he was accused of adultery and the American church split] would have been revealed to them. . . . People are running after the Society of Seraphim [the Cherubim and Seraphim] simply because the leaders there use [sic] to prophecy through visions and dreams. . . . But if we elect to have all these gifts in the church today there would be no room for the hundreds of people that follow the Seraphic society. . . ." Mensah and Odubanjo to Eshinshinade, Aug. 13, 1928, Odubanjo Papers.

[27] For a cogent presentation of how Yoruba traditional religion poses and answers this question see E. B. Bolaji Idowu, Olodumare: God in Yoruba Belief (London, 1962), 169-201.

ancestor. They would then prescribe appropriate sacrifices and medicines to relieve the situation.

Islamic clerics performed these same functions using Islamic formulas, but the mission Christian priests lacked an equivalent set of procedures. They emphasized instead the prospect of life after death or recommended hospital care, which was then largely unavailable.[28] As a consequence, many of their members and adherents sought out the services of traditional practitioners when faced with a medical need. This resort to traditional religion was seen as apostasy by the members of the Faith Tabernacle. What excited them about Clark's teaching was its offer of divine help in this world, an offer which provided a functional alternative for the activities of the traditional diviner-priests. Considering the relative unavailability of Western medicine, that Clark's teaching required abstention from both Western medicine and traditional medicine was of little consequence. It met their crucial religious need in Christian terms.

The doctrine was especially appealing because it was legitimated by "European" authority. The search for overseas sponsorship is a characteristic of the Zionist type of independent church.[29] It is quite

[28] An illuminating insight into the missionary message of the early period is contained in the following quote from a report by a Church Missionary Society (Anglican) missionary in Abeokuta to the Society's London headquarters in 1851: "I had a very pleasing conversation with four elderly men. . . . The topic of my discourse with them has been the exposition of their folly for spending their money for making sacrifices that they may neither sick nor die. . . . Thus I told them sickness and death came into the world . . . and shall or will be in the world until the end of time . . . there is nothing to be done to drive sickness and death from this world. . . ." (A2/0.49 (b) C. M. S. Archives, London; attributed to the Rev. David Hinderer but not in his handwriting.) A book for missionaries which emphasized that "some knowledge of the African mentality is . . . necessary . . ." contained a sermon outline on healing which differentiated between real illness (go to a doctor) and the sickness of heart that Jesus healed (repent and have faith). A. L. Kitching, *The Presentation of the Gospel to the African* (London, c. 1900), 12. In Yorubaland the Anglican church had no hospital and the Methodists, Southern Baptists, and Roman Catholics only had one hospital each by 1930.

[29] Sundkler, *Bantu Prophets*, 48, 55. See also the description of conquered peoples taking the conqueror's deities for their own in Melville Herskovits, *The Human Factor in Changing Africa* (New York, 1962), 419. The search for spiritual power in Africa by Africans subjected to contact with the West has tended to direct itself toward the West in various ways. The first white man to enter Ibadan (in 1851), a C. M. S. missionary named David Hinderer, noted with disgust how every scrap of paper he discarded was seized and used to make charms. The so-called *Sixth and Seventh Books of Moses* has had a ready sale in Nigeria for forty years or more. H. L. Ward-Price, *Dark Subjects* (London, 1939), 200. H. W. Turner, "Searching and Syncretism: A West African Documentation," *International Review of Missions*, XLIX (1960), 189-94.

clear that the aladura, unlike the earlier Nigerian "African" churches, were not merely rebelling against European leadership as such. They were seeking spiritual power and did not hesitate to look upon the West as the obvious source of such power.

European legitimation was not without its drawbacks, however, and not all of the Nigerian aladura leaders shared Odubanjo's predilection for European contacts. These negative feelings were brought out when, after their break with Clark, they actually entertained an American missionary of another Church. This man, Pastor C. R. Myers, was sent by the Faith and Truth Temple of Toronto, Canada, to establish a mission in Upper Volta. This group's principal distinction was a taboo against eating pork. He visited Nigeria on Odubanjo's invitation, arriving sometime in 1928 with his wife, a daughter, and several other young missionaries.[30] Myers was impressed with the Faith Tabernacle church and visited many of its branches. His home Church was annoyed at his delay, however, and cut off his funds. Then his fellow missionaries died. But he had impressed the Lagos Faith Tabernacle. Its members held a meeting in March 1929 to decide whether Odubanjo should resign and be replaced by Myers,[31] but apparently they decided that Myers should merely work in their midst. Myers then got the Nigerian church to support him and to send two of its members with him to Upper Volta. This trip was a disaster, and Myers and the Nigerians returned on November 22. During the journey Myers's wife had died in childbirth in a hospital. Besides this evidence of a lack of faith in God's healing power, the Nigerian companions reported that he had "treated them badly." The Faith Tabernacle church separated from him, but he pathetically continued to try to found a Church in Nigeria.[32]

Despite their disappointment over Clark and his adultery and their bad experience with Myers, Odubanjo continued to address inquiries to a number of European and American sects. This was to have important consequences for the revival of 1930–32 when one of these sects, the Apostolic church, answered Odubanjo's call for help. A growth toward spiritual independence on the part of other leaders, however, may be seen in the pre-revival reply of I. B. Akinyele, the

---

[30] Ademakinwa, *History*, 68-72.

[31] D. O. Odubanjo, *Diary 1929*, entry for Mar. 8, 11, 1929, Odubanjo Papers.

[32] In 1931 he turned up as the American vice-consul in Lagos and acted as a guarantor for the Apostolic church delegation. In 1934 it was noted that he had left a wife and child unsupported in Oshogbo and had traveled to Akure to try to found a church. Resident, Ondo to Commissioner of Police, Ibadan, June 5, 1934 (Oyo Prof 3/357, National Archives, Ibadan). All archival references will refer to the Nigerian National Archives, Ibadan, unless otherwise noted.

Ibadan leader,[33] to a letter from Odubanjo which enclosed literature from yet another overseas group:

> I received the cards and pamphlets with thanks. . . . I cannot yet form any opinion but my advice is that we should be slow indeed to adopt any foreign method, there are hundreds of them. We are just coming into contact with them . . . we should be careful of *imitation*, we should strive to be *original* ourselves.[34]

The very large religious revival led by the young prophet, Joseph Babalola, which swept northeastern Yorubaland from 1930 to 1932, succeeded in making the Faith Tabernacle indigenous. Ironically, the success of this revival finally aroused the opposition of the colonial authorities and culminated in the arrest of Babalola, making necessary an invitation to "yet another" overseas Church to assist the Faith Tabernacle leaders in creating a Church out of what had suddenly become a mass movement.

Babalola was an Ekiti Yoruba who in 1928 had received a call from God to preach. At the time, he had been a roadroller-driver employed by the government. The month before his call he had spent a sleepless week:

> I did not fell sleeping [sic] for a complete week both day and night and I was happy, I was reading books from evening to day break and where I was reading in the Bible was the book of Psalms from chapters one to 150 every-day. I did not feel sickly and I saw nothing.[35]

After the call, which he tried to resist, he went about preaching in northeastern Yorubaland. In 1929 he made contact with the Faith Tabernacle leaders in Ibadan.[36] They sent him to Lagos, where he greatly impressed Odubanjo and Eshinshinade.[37] Eshinshinade bap-

[33] Akinyele, a member of the early educated Ibadan elite, later rose to become the Olubadan (King) of Ibadan and his brother became the Anglican bishop of Ibadan. He was one of the founding members of the Faith Tabernacle in Ibadan and was later the president of the Christ Apostolic church for many years until his death in 1964. See J. A. Ayorinde, M.B.E., "Oba Sir Isaac Babalola Akinyele I.T.," *Odu* I, 2 (Jan. 1965), 78-82.

[34] Akinyele to Odubanjo Jan. 27, 1930, Odubanjo Papers; italics in the original.

[35] J. A. Medaiyeshe, *Biography of the Late Great Apostle and Prophet Joseph Ayo Babalola* (Okene, c. 1960), 2.

[36] The available evidence strongly suggests that he did not first go to Ilesha as H. W. Turner has written. Turner, *African Independent Church*, I, 17.

[37] Odubanjo wrote in his diary at the time: "Since the days of the Apostle, I have not met with any man of his type who has direct dealings and intercourse with the Holy Spirit . . ." Odubanjo, Diary 1929, Dec. 20, 1929, Odubanjo Papers.

tized him, and he thus became associated with the Faith Tabernacle.

The revival began at a Faith Tabernacle leaders' meeting in Ilesha in July 1930 when a routine healing suddenly mushroomed into a widespread revival with thousands of people pouring into Ilesha with receptacles to hold the water blessed by Babalola, which was believed to have great curative powers. In August 1930 mention of the revival appeared in the *Nigerian Daily Times*:

> A "Prophet" is said to have put up an appearance at Ilesha, whose power of healing by prayer has been testified by many who have been healed. Two well-known figures in Ibadan who have nearly lost their sights have completely recovered; pilgrims mostly consisting of lames, blinds, deafs and all kinds of invalid [sic] are crossing Ilesha everyday by motors to receive this wonderful healing.[38]

He left Ilesha in September and for the next eighteen months he traveled throughout northeastern Yorubaland and the revival continued unabated. The Yoruba subgroups of the Ekiti and Akoko were particularly responsive to Babalola. His avowed intent at first was to call people to a "deeper spiritual life," as a British missionary observer termed it, and not to the Faith Tabernacle as such; hence the appellation "revival" which I have applied to his movement.[39]

The general theme of his utterances involved the following elements: (1) The Christian God has power to heal and protect; (2) idols and charms no longer have power; (3) God hates bad things such as adultery and witchcraft; (4) unless people repent something bad will happen; and (5) people should confess their sins, give up their idols and charms, and drink water that has been blessed so as to receive healing and protection. The "something bad" that would happen without repentance apparently involved apocalyptic occurrences which would strike towns. An African Anglican critic of the revival, the Rev. T. A. J. Ogunbiyi,[40] who visited the town of Effon Alaiye, where Babalola had had a great success, claimed that this prophecy was instrumental:

[38] *Nigerian Daily Times*, Aug. 28, 1930, 4.

[39] Nomenclature presents difficulties here as "prophet movement" and "witch-finding movement" are used in the literature to refer to movements somewhat similar to Babalola's. "Revival" is also the term used by the aladura historians such as Ademakinwa.

[40] Ogunbiyi will also appear below in connection with the origin of the Cherubim and Seraphim Society. He was one of the founders of the Christianized Reformed Ogboni Association. E. A. Ayandele, *The Missionary Impact on Modern Nigeria* (London, 1966), 260-78.

At Efon . . . he [Babalola] started to tell them of God's wrath coming on the people in the world and that the hills surrounding the town would melt and be destroyed. His excellency [the Alaiye or King of Efon] informed me that the warning terrified him so much that he joined them [Faith Tabernacle] so that evil might not befall his town.[41]

I have described the religious and social factors behind the Babalola revival in some detail elsewhere[42] and will here only summarize the conclusions of that study as they relate to the type of protest involved in such a widespread popular movement, which culminated in the arrest and imprisonment of the prophet.

The basic dynamic behind the revival was religious. This was recognized by both European missionary and government observers, who were impressed with Babalola's sincerity and, in the revival's early months, saw nothing in his work that threatened the existing order. To the crowds that pressed to hear him, Babalola offered deliverance from sickness and the powers of evil—defined as evil spirits and witchcraft. Of course the depression, the recent imposition of income taxes, and general social change in northeastern Yorubaland contributed to the feeling of uncertainty which generated the tremendous response to Babalola's message, but both Babalola's message and the elicited response were defined in religious terms.

It has been observed that religious mass movements frequently change character as they develop[43] and the Babalola revival was no exception. Owing to the lack of repression by the authorities and the internal religious discipline supplied by the leaders of the Faith Tabernacle, the revival did not move in the direction of a manifest social protest, as have other African movements. In its case the change was from a non-denominational emphasis on religious renewal toward the deliberate establishment of a separate Church. This organizational aspect was a threat to the mission churches, of course, and the missionaries subsequently became critics of the revival.

It was the revival's sheer persistence after more than a year and the rise of a few secondary prophets (not connected with Babalola) who criticized taxation that finally led British administrators to try Babalola. He was sentenced to prison for six months on a charge of witch accusation. The important point is that he was jailed only be-

[41] T. A. J. Ogunbiyi, *Asiri Joseph Babalola Aladura ni Efon Alaye ni Ile Ekiti* (The Secret of Joseph Babalola in Efon Alaye in Ekitiland) (Ibadan, *c.* 1932), 3-4.

[42] Robert Cameron Mitchell, "The Babalola Revival: A Non-Arrested Prophet Movement," forthcoming.

[43] See Sylvia L. Thrupp (ed.), *Millennial Dreams in Action: Essays in Comparative Study* (The Hague, 1962), 23.

cause of the possibility that the revival might lead to social protest, not because it had actually done so. The secondary prophets were marginal and easily controlled, and even the act of repression against Babalola failed to encourage the other aladura churches to criticize Europeans and the colonial system. Thus, despite provocations such as Oshitelu's apocalyptic visions, which will be discussed below, the preachings against taxation, of a very few secondary prophets, and the mobilization of a large segment of the population in a time of economic uncertainty, social protest failed to materialize. The Babalola revival was essentially a mass continuation of the aladura religious search for a more satisfying form of Christian expression.

The fact that the Apostolic church, a British Pentecostal church, was invited to come to Nigeria by the beleaguered Faith Tabernacle further establishes its lack of anti-white feelings. It should be noted that the agreement on whether to receive the Apostolic church and, further, to change the Faith Tabernacle's name to the Apostolic church, was not made without considerable discussion and some apprehension. The first Apostolic missionaries arrived in 1932 and were very successful in helping the Nigerian church to obtain land, build schools, train its leaders, and receive the Pentecostal baptism of the Holy Spirit. Nevertheless, tension arose within the Nigerian church when the missionaries began to achieve control. The split which occurred about 1939 was defined on religious grounds—that by using malarial prophylactics the Apostolic missionaries were showing a lack of faith in God's power to protect them from illness. The old Faith Tabernacle anti-medicine doctrine, which is still held strongly by the resulting Christ Apostolic church, was the defining point for the church's further quest for religious independence.

The Origins of the Cherubim and Seraphim Society

A similar concern for a religion that offered assistance to the believer in this world was manifested by the remaining two aladura variants which emerged in the 1920's: the Cherubim and Seraphim Society and the Church of the Lord (Aladura). These groups lacked involvement with an overseas group, however, and in their beliefs and practices they developed an even more indigenous expression of Christianity. They utilized a wide range of symbolism in their services; their members wore distinctive white gowns; visions and special revelations were given particular emphasis; polygyny was permitted, and although resort to traditional medicine was prohibited, Western medicine was generally allowed in conjunction with prayers and holy water.[44]

The Cherubim and Seraphim Society was founded in Lagos in 1925 by an itinerant religious figure, Moses Orimolade Tunolashe, and a young woman, Christiana Abiodun Akinsowon (later Mrs. C. A. Emanuel). Tunolashe was a native of Ikare, a small town in northeastern Yorubaland. Born about 1885 of pagan parents, he had been regarded from birth as spiritually precocious or unusual.[45] According to his sister's account, he was baptized into the Anglican church, and despite never learning how to read, he had somehow memorized vast portions of the Bible. In his early years he seems to have suffered from a physical ailment which made it difficult for him to walk and, for a period of years around 1910, he sat "in one place" sometimes not talking to anyone for weeks, at other times talking and telling people that he would one day be famous. About 1915 he began to preach against "idol worship" and prayed for people who brought their ailments and problems to him. In the process he "cured" himself of his own physical ailment. In the early 1920's he arrived in Lagos, where he appears to have found lodging in various mission compounds. Living from hand to mouth, he preached and received alms.[46] By 1925, however, he had apparently built up something of a local reputation so that when Miss Akinsowon went into a trance he was called to come to her assistance.

Miss Akinsowon was born in Porto Novo, Dahomey, in 1907. Her mother was "half Yoruba and half Dahomey"; her father, an employee of a European trading firm, was a Yoruba.[47] She was brought up in the Methodist church in Dahomey, where her father was a lay preacher and the secretary of the local congregation. When she was about twelve she went to live with her aunt and uncle, Mr. and Mrs. Moiett, in Lagos, where she attended school and joined their Church, the Anglican church. She was confirmed about 1923.

Before describing the actual founding of the Cherubim and Seraphim Society it is necessary to say something about the religious and social situation in Lagos in 1925. The Faith Tabernacle, as we know, already had a branch in the city. Like the mission church congrega-

---

[44] General discussions of the Cherubim and Seraphim may be found in Parrinder, *Religion in an African City;* Peel, "Sociological Study"; and in a popular, inaccurate, account: Anonymous, "Cherubim and Seraphim," *Nigeria Magazine* (Lagos), 53 (1957), 119-34.

[45] Interview with Tunolashe's eldest sister, Idanaringiya, Apr. 1962.

[46] Interview with the Rev. Canon M. Fawehinmi, Feb. 1962. James Bertin Webster says that Tunolashe stayed with J. K. Coker at Balogun Square in 1921.

[47] Interview with Christiana Abiodun Akinsowon (now Mrs. Emanuel), Jan. 1962. For a discussion of Yoruba ethnicity in Porto Novo see Godfrey Parrinder, "Some Western Yoruba Towns," *Odu,* 2 (c. 1956), 29-34.

tions—Roman Catholic, Anglican, Methodist, and Baptist—the African churches were especially strong in the city. These were independent churches of Sundkler's Ethiopian type that had separated from the mission denominations as early as 1888.[48]

The newspapers for the year tell of still further religious influences: "Our religious activity is a mere farce and our domestic life is even worse in most cases. . . . The Apostles of Russellism [Jehovah's Witnesses] declared that the world will come to an end this year. . . ."[49] An advertisement for the *Sixth and Seventh Books of Moses* and other occult literature appeared regularly. In April one Dr. Ishola was reported to have begun a new religion, Isholaism, "A brand of unitarianism."[50] Also in April came a report from Abeokuta about a certain religionist in "distinctive dress" who practiced an "increasingly notorious form of swindling" by going to the market place where "he always has revelation to make . . . [and] a few minutes' harangue which he calls a Sermon."[51] There were independent, aladura-type prophets.

As for the social situation, the years 1924 to 1926 were a time when Lagos suffered heavily from the bubonic plague and other epidemic diseases. The visit of the Prince of Wales to Lagos in April 1925 had to be postponed because of the plague, and a month later the British Governor's "at home" had to be canceled because of yellow fever.[52] The plague affected the hinterland as well. A report from Ogere, the home village of the founder of the Church of the Lord, depicted the aftermath of the plague there in November 1925:

> I am stricken with awe when I was walking through the narrow streets of Ogere for there are no voices in many parts to be heard save the deep groanings of the bereaved.[53]

According to her later testimony, for two weeks before June 18, 1925, Miss Akinsowon had been visited in visions by a mighty angel who took her on heavenly journeys. She lost her appetite but kept these experiences secret. On June 18, with some companions, she fol-

[48] See James Bertin Webster, *The African Churches Among the Yoruba 1888-1922* (Oxford, 1964).

[49] Editorial, *The Nigerian Spectator,* Jan. 10, 1925.

[50] Ibid., Apr. 4, 1925. The *Sixth and Seventh Books of Moses* is an occult work, commonly used in West Africa, which originally appeared in medieval times. It is published in various editions, the most common being that of Delaurence of Chicago.

[51] "Abeokuta Column," *The Nigerian Spectator,* Apr. 11, 1925.

[52] Ibid., Apr. 18, May 16, 1925.

[53] Ibid., Nov. 14, 1925.

lowed the colorful Roman Catholic Corpus Christi procession through the streets of Lagos and into the cathedral. Just as the Bishop lifted the chalice in the Mass she saw her angel again. Stricken with fear she implored her companions to leave the service and go home with her. She described what followed during an interview in 1962:

> I felt cold and headache. I was nervous. When I got home I began to work, but I was always looking over my shoulder like this. (RCM: You were really afraid?) Yes, too much, I can't eat, can't say anything to anybody, can't tell anyone. The same night he [her angel] came and took me to heaven [in dream]. After that on Thursday I went into the trance entirely [that is, went to heaven entirely].[54]

The angels appear to have had the intent of taking her away with them permanently. This would suggest that the experience should be seen in light of the Yoruba cultural definition of *emere*. *Emere* are people who are believed to consort with "spirit fellows" in heaven. These heavenly fellows eventually call the spirits away from the earthly bodies and the people die prematurely. In her experience the "spirit fellows" become "angels."[55]

Her aunt and uncle sent for the Rev. Mr. Ogunbiyi, who was their Anglican pastor. He failed to come, so they turned in desperation to Tunolashe. He came and prayed. After prayer Miss Akinsowon supposedly recovered enough to open the Bible for him to read and interpret. The two chapters she chose were Hebrews 3 and 11. The angels then left her and the "old man" said "Salvation enter your house. Get

[54] Interview with Christiana Abiodun Akinsowon (1962). See also C. Abiodun Akinsowon, *Iwe Iran tabi Isipaya Orun Ti Olorun fi han Nipashe eyi ti a da Egbe Mimo Kerubu ati Sera fi Sile* (The Book of Heavenly Vision Revealed by God by which We Found Out the Cherubim and Seraphim Society) (Lagos, 1960).

[55] I regret that I did not see the parallel between her experience and that of the *emere* type early enough to have questioned her about it. The parallel is quite clear in this description of the *emere* belief in Idowu's book on Yoruba religion: "The Yoruba believe that there are companies of *Elere* or *Emere* (also called *elegbe*)—'Wandering spirits of children given to the prank of entering into pregnant women and being born only to die for the sheer relish of the mischief.' Anyone of them who is being sent on this errand of mischief must covenant with his 'companions' that on a named date he would 'return to his normal life'; that is, he must die from this world." Parents try to prevent this by consulting the oracle who prescribes a sacrifice. "This sacrifice is found necessary when the person is very ill and is in danger of dying . . . [it alters] the agreement made between the person and his 'companions.'" Idowu, *Olodumare,* 123. Informants told me that *emere* are usually women and that their contracted date of return is often just before marriage. Miss Akinsowon was precisely at this age when stricken.

instruments to sing. You should not make curse in the compound again. (It is a holy place.)" He had, then, persuaded the angels to release her.

This resolution of Miss Akinsowon's condition caused a stir and people began to come to them, both for prayer and visions. Mrs. Emanuel later wrote that while she was in the trance the angels had shown her various mysteries and taught her many prayers and how "water [could] be sanctified for various diseases." By September, three months after her trance, a society was formed by the two visionaries. It was, however, definitely not at this time regarded as a separate Church. Daily the society worshiped morning and evening (and all night on Saturday) with the exception of Sunday morning, which was reserved for the members' attendance at their regular churches.

The two leaders seem to have complemented each other during this time, although Tunolashe appears to have gained the wider reputation. An Anglican clergyman who knew him during his earlier days of penury in Lagos recalled how surprised he had been upon a visit to the city in 1925 when he was told that a person now had to have an appointment to see the "wondrous prophet."[56] A contemporary account described Tunolashe's activity as seen by a number of the educated class:

> Another Prophet "Moses" by name was busy during the week holding open air revival services. He professes to have been translated to the worlds above where he saw a vision and was taught to read though he attended no school. He advances ability to invoke angels and prescribes prayers of his own creation to meet all conditions and desires. . . . Many throng around him; some of whom we regard as intelligent and sensible people. . . . He has found a disciple in an ordained minister of a particular denomination who heads the procession of religious fanatics to be seen holding meetings at Cemetery Street on Thursday evenings.[57]

There were several distinctive characteristics of the early Cherubim and Seraphim Society, the full name given to the society by revelation in March 1926. Its members adopted distinctive white gowns, employed drums and dancing in their worship, prayed spontaneously, and sought guidance through visions. According to informants the major attraction of the society was its open denunciation of witchcraft and its offer of protection from witches through prayer and holy water.

> He dispelled from our minds the fear of witchcraft. By prayer. He said that they [witches] were powerful, but God's power was greater. This

56 Fawehinmi, interview.
57 Ebute Metta Column, *The Nigerian Spectator*, Sept. 1, 1925.

was a real attraction! In the Church [Anglican] no one said that in the open. (RCM: Did the Cherubim and Seraphim preach against Europeans?) They did not preach against them—rather they said that the Europeans had love for Africans, but Africans themselves have no love for one another [meaning that they practice witchcraft against each other].[58]

He challenged witches openly. In previous years we were very afraid of them. There were thousands in Lagos.[59]

There also was some emphasis on ideas of an eschatological nature,[60] although it is difficult to know how important these ideas were to the preaching of Tunolashe or Akinsowon. Akinsowon's original experience contained nothing of this kind. An informant reported Tunolashe as referring to the second coming in these terms: "Whoever is unholy let him continue, but I am coming with my reward to give to every man according to his deeds." Shodeinde, one of the early leaders, referred to the present as the "time for the sealing and the ingathering of the chosen few" in a letter to a Lagos newspaper in October 1925.[61]

With time, the mission churches became increasingly critical of what they termed the spiritual excesses of the movement. These included the late night meetings, the fervor of the worship services, "indiscriminate" visions, "frauds," and alleged immorality among the members. In February 1928 a letter was sent to all Methodist churches by the chairman of the district declaring the movement to be "hostile to the spread of Scriptural Holiness." At the Anglican Synod of that year, Bishop Jones accused the movement of meeting "superstition with superstition."[62] Miss Akinsowon stopped attending St. Paul's Church in 1928; that year may be considered the date of the Cherubim and Seraphim's emergence as an independent church.

In the same year, the two founders separated through a "misunderstanding." By 1930 three separate branches were registered with the government. The movement continued to spread to several of the Yoruba cities in Western Nigeria and to villages in the vicinity of Lagos. Tunolashe died in 1933, and the leadership of his section passed to another man who was accorded the title *Baba Aladura* (Father of Prayer).

[58] Interview with Hector E. Ladejo, May 1962.
[59] Interview with A. Adefowoju, May 1962.
[60] I use this term in the sense of doctrines relating to the end of the world. For a helpful discussion of the terms eschatology, chiliastic, and millennial, see Norman Cohn, *The Pursuit of the Millennium* (London, 1957), xiii.
[61] *The Nigerian Spectator,* Oct. 3, 1925.
[62] Ibid., June 25, 1928.

Very occasionally Cherubim and Seraphim followers would come to the government's attention when, in bursts of fanaticism, they would destroy traditional shrines without the "owner's" permission or a prophet would claim to identify specific people as witches. Striking the traditional shrines could be interpreted in the interior areas, as it was in Ondo in 1927, as an attack on native law. This sort of reaction was not restricted to the aladura, however, and in these same areas mission Christians provoked far more court cases by destroying shrines or disobeying traditional customs. Witch-finding did not characterize mission Christianity, of course, and there was a specific ordinance against this practice under which Babalola was convicted in 1932.

The most serious case of witch-finding by a Cherubim and Seraphim prophet occurred in 1931. An official file was then opened which offers a glimpse of the government's interpretation of the Cherubim and Seraphim at the time when the Babalola revival was beginning to cause them some concern. The case involved a prophet whose accusation of three people led to the death of one of them. The prophet was a member of Tunolashe's section of the movement. The police reported that: "The society is a purely religious body of fanatical type. . . . They concern themselves in no way with political affairs. . . . It is their opposition to paganism which causes trouble."[63] It further stated that with the exception of Tunolashe's followers the society did not support extreme fanaticism. The only action taken against Tunolashe was to warn him against condoning accusations of witchcraft.

The Oshitelu Movement

The third of the three original aladura variants is the Church of the Lord (Aladura). Its founder, Josiah Olunlowo Oshitelu, was a first-generation Christian from Ogere, an Ijebu town some twenty-three miles west of Ijebu-Ode. He had become a catechist-teacher in the Anglican church and seemed destined to be ordained into the priesthood when his career was interrupted by supernatural visitations in the form of visions and voices.

Oshitelu had been born after his parents had lost a number of children in infancy. Turner's description of his parents' reluctance to discipline him[64] because of certain prophecies by the traditional diviner who had been consulted at his birth, suggests that he may have been defined by his parents as an *abiku* child, a cultural definition re-

[63] CSO 27103 S/5. See also the *Nigerian Daily Telegraph,* May 22, 1931.
[64] Turner, *African Independent Church,* I, 35. This recent comprehensive work is on the Church of the Lord (Aladura).

lated to the *emere* condition suggested for Miss Akinsowon. These children were believed by the Yoruba to be animated by a malicious spirit that repeatedly allowed itself to be born to the same woman only to die after a short time.[65]

The future Primate of the Church of the Lord (Aladura) received his first vision on May 17, 1925 (just a month before Miss Akinsowon fell into her trance in Lagos). At the time, he was working in the village of Erukute as a teacher-catechist. The vision revealed to him a large eye "reflecting as a great orbit of the sun."[66] This experience unsettled him as he believed it was caused by evil powers. He took a leave from church work and finally consulted one "elder," Samuel Shomoye, a local aladura-like figure who interpreted the experience as a "call to service" by God. After reading psalms and, much prayer and fasting, Oshitelu's visions and voices became systemized as God's revelation to him personally. On August 18, 1925, God told him: "I will anoint you as my prophet, even as Elijah anointed Elisha with oil in the olden days, so it shall be unto you."[67] These and similar messages prompted him to develop his own spiritual exercises which his Anglican supervisor defined as "erroneous," and, on April 19, 1926, he was dismissed as a teacher-catechist.

The next three years were spent developing his powers and studying under Shomoye, who was establishing an aladura church of his own on a local scale. Although there was no contact with an overseas group such as the Faith Tabernacle, Oshitelu seems to have had a certain familiarity with Masonic symbolism and especially with the *Sixth and Seventh Books of Moses*.[68]

After a time Oshitelu's revelations began to include references to a church which he would found and to an apocalyptic occurrence

[65] The *abiku* phenomenon is attributed to both male and female children. *Emere* are believed to be the cause of the *abiku* phenomenon according to Idowu. *Olodumare*, 196. In suggesting the connection between these metempsychological concepts and the founders of the Cherubim and Seraphim and the Church of the Lord the inference is that, if these concepts are in fact involved, they may have influenced adults' definition of the individuals and thus the individuals' definition of themselves.

[66] M. Sam Wobo, *A Brief Résumé of the Lifecourse of Dr. J. O. Oshitelu, Psy. D.* (Shagamu, Nigeria, 1955).

[67] Ibid.

[68] Oshitelu's early experiments with "secret writing" and "seal words" suggest that the *Sixth and Seventh Books of Moses* had a direct influence on him during the period 1925–30. See also Turner, *African Independent Church*, I, 44; II, 73-76. The defensiveness of Oshitelu's foreword to his *The Book of Prayer with Uses and Powers of Psalms and Precious Treasures Hidden Therein* (Ogere, Nigeria, 1960) is striking in its virtual admission that he is duplicating Western occult literature.

which would overwhelm those who failed to repent and join the righteous. On June 3, 1929, he recorded the following revelation:

> The day of destruction has come . . . tell the people of Judah your God has come. . . . He has been waiting long for the power of God, he's been searching for knowledge of the Almighty. . . . The righteous Elijah hath come. . . . I was put on a high mountain and given authority to own from Ogere to Ijebu-Ode to Ikorody [sic] to Abebkuta to Ibadan to Owode [Yoruba towns and cities]. . . . Ogere is the appointed place. . . . We shall build a house of God in Judah and make every part of it a happy place, to make known the glory of god.[69]

On June 9 he began holding open air services in Ogere, his home village. Among the points he made were the following:

> Hear the Gospel of Joy! ye Christians. You have strayed away and you have not obeyed my commandments. You have profaned my name, and disregarded my power. . . . The world is old and broken and would be changed immediately. . . . He who abhors divine healing will not be saved. Believe in God, and put not your trust in native Doctors. . . . Come, come remedies for your Sundry ailments are procured for you.[70]

Harold Turner has summed up Oshitelu's original message as "an offer of blessings in all one's troubles through faith in God alone, with judgment for those who fail to respond," and points out its resemblance to the teachings of the other aladura.[71]

Oshitelu officially inaugurated his Church in Ogere on July 27, 1930, with ten members. July 1930 was, of course, the time when the Babalola revival began in Ilesha, some miles to the north of Ogere. During the height of the revival Oshitelu became associated with the Faith Tabernacle for six months and helped to bring the revival south to Ibadan and Abeokuta.

Oshitelu's reputation seems to have spread first to the Faith Tabernacle group in Ijebu-Ode, and visits were exchanged in the summer of 1930. During his visit to Ijebu-Ode in August 1930, Oshitelu claimed that God had revealed to him that there were eighteen witches and one wizard among the members of the Faith Tabernacle church there.[72] A revelation of this sort did not endear him to the stern Eshinshinade, but Oshitelu's great capacity for visions impressed others in the Faith Tabernacle circle and he was invited subsequently

---

[69] Turner, *African Independent Church,* I, 45.

[70] Wobo, *Brief Résumé.*

[71] Turner, *African Independent Church,* I, 46.

[72] Josiah Olunowo Oshitelu, *Private Journal,* Oshitelu Papers, 135. I am grateful to H. W. Turner for typescripts of these and other Church of the Lord documents.

to Ibadan to join in the revival already begun by the prophet Daniel Orekoya.

In Ibadan, Oshitelu was acclaimed for his visions and, by his account, recognized as the spiritual superior of the other revivalists. In fact, Orekoya was the principal revivalist and healer.[73] Oshitelu led the way to the large city of Abeokuta, however, where a revival began, but Orekoya became the leading revivalist and continued the work after Oshitelu returned to Ogere in November.

The collaboration between Oshitelu and the Faith Tabernacle leaders came to a dramatic conclusion during a meeting called to air the differences between the two parties. The minutes of this meeting, held on January 23, 1931, contain a series of charges against Oshitelu, condemning as unscriptural his visions, his witch-finding, his acceptance of polygyny, and especially his use of "Holy Names." The Faith Tabernacle emphasis upon biblical authority was incongruent with the personal authority Oshitelu felt God had granted him. The two sides separated, with two of the lesser Faith Tabernacle leaders choosing to join Oshitelu.

As the Babalola revival swept forward in Ekiti-Akoko and governmental and mission authorities grew increasingly concerned with its possible threat to law and order, Oshitelu, too, came under government scrutiny. In August 1931 a prophetess unconnected with Babalola had preached against taxes in Akure, occasioning a small riot. She was incarcerated and, when the incident was investigated, Babalola was exonerated. But it was alleged that one of the influences promoting such a challenge to the colonial authority was *Awon Asotele*, a printed set of the prophecies of Oshitelu.[74]

This booklet was but one of three extraordinary booklets of proph-

---

[73] Oshitelu suffered from a pronounced tendency toward self-aggrandizement which in this case led him to exaggerate his actual role.

[74] A high government official described the situation as one in which Babalola, "who takes no part in any form of political agitation," afforded an opportunity to a number of "unprincipled persons, mainly young men, for carrying on agitation against Government, Native Authorities and the missions under the guise of religious teaching. . . . They . . . give utterance to so-called prophecies which are, for the most part, culled from a pamphlet by Woli [prophet] J. O. Oshitelu of Ijebu Remo entitled *Awon Asotele*. . . . A translation of some passages is attached. A favorite subject of such preachers is tax, and they have generally urged the people not to pay more than 3/— while one of them fixed the amount at 1/—. . . . Babalola blames the pamphlet for much of the agitation. He says it has been in circulation for some eight months in large numbers and is sold by persons representing the printer. It has nothing to do with him and he condemns its contents as bad." Secretary, Southern Provinces, Enugu, to the Resident, Oyo, Aug. 31, 1931 (Oyo Prof. 3/357). It is interesting to note that this protest was not against taxes as such, but against the level of the rate which was felt to be high during a time of depression.

ecies written in Yoruba and published by Oshitelu in 1930–31. The apocalyptic character and poetic urgency of these works may be seen in the opening paragraph of one of them:

> The world perishes! The world perishes! Heaven is Spoiled; the sons of men are corrupt to the uttermost; the day has got to its middle; The world has got to its middle; the sun has got to the center in the sky; the end has come to all people. How difficult will the end be?[75]

Well might the government be concerned with such utterances, especially if they were in fact linked with the tax disturbances. Since these prophecies comprise the sole evidence of overt anti-government sentiment on the part of the aladura, apart from the activities of the occasional secondary prophets mentioned earlier, they demand a close examination.

The following are the most specifically anti-government of the 13 verses which the police selected from the total of 159 in the *Awon Asotele*:

51 Shagamu, Iperu and Ode: (Kaajaa) these towns will be destroyed utterly and those whose minds are not right with God will be destroyed.

139 The day is coming when the Government will be demanding taxes on goats and sheep every year. As a result of this, domestic animals will be at liberty to feed in the open places without anybody to claim their ownership.

141 The Europeans are coming for secular studies and knowledge of God in Africa.

149 Epidemic of smallpox is coming to the land of Africa. So much that all the Europeans in the continent will die of it.

150 Those who collect taxes and money on land, and on other things, [sic], the judgement of God is awaiting them.[76]

As Turner has pointed out, the other two pamphlets contain "possibly more inflammatory sections" proclaiming various other events connected with the coming end:[77]

> Lagos, a worldly town . . . a side of it shall sink. The white man takes another's property by force; the time is coming when epidemic of

[75] J. O. Oshitelu, *Ifihan ati Asotele Nipa Ohun ti o Nbowa si Aiye* (Disclosure and Prophecy About the Things Coming to the World) (Ogere, Nigeria, c. 1930), 1.

[76] J. O. Oshitelu, *Awon Asotele Ohun ti yio Bere si Sele lati Inu Odun 1931 lo eti Ki Odun Mefa* (Prophecies About Things to Happen in the Year 1931, and Six Years After) (Ogere, Nigeria, c. 1930).

[77] Turner, *African Independent Church*, I, 28-29.

smallpox shall be let loose on the Africans and the white people among them shall perish.

All these churches [mission churches] shall be destroyed . . . because they know not any other thing but money. . . .

Islam shall be destroyed. . . . [78]

A section entitled "Prophecy about Foreign Countries" contains an interesting distinction between the Europeans who are to die (by smallpox) and the Americans:

1. The Americans are coming for my great glory. Ye Africans are their mothers; people of brown complexion shall be their fathers in this region. That is the reason why people of black and brown complexions are to be in their land.

4. The Americans shall come and the Indians shall be destroyed; there shall be no more Europe and European nation.[79]

The question arises: do not these prophecies indicate a manifest criticism of Europeans and colonial rule? The answer is "yes" and "no." "Yes" in the sense that overtly Europeans and tax collections are called under God's judgment. "No" in the sense that these verses formed only a tiny fraction of Oshitelu's prophetic output and must be seen in the context of his message of judgment for *all* unrepentant segments of society.

The origin of these ideas bears examination. Turner ascribes Oshitelu's apocalyptic preaching and the millennial aspect of his self-interpretation as the "forerunner of the Lord," to the American Faith Tabernacle church's belief in the millennium. This is doubtful, as this was one of the least emphasized of the American tenets and one which its Nigerian followers largely ignored. As was mentioned earlier, when it was declared in Lagos in 1922 that Lagos would fall into the sea, Clark had told the Nigerians to disregard this prophecy. The end was not immediately imminent according to Clark. The idea of apocalyptic events most probably represents the influence of the Jehovah's Witnesses who were at this time active in Nigeria.[80] The allusions to the

[78] Oshitelu, *Disclosure and Prophecy;* J. O. Oshitelu, *Isipaya tabi Ifihan Awon Ohun ti Mbowa She* (Revelation or Disclosure About the End of Time) (Ogere, Nigeria, *c.* 1930). The second work is a second part of the first pamphlet, although it has a different title.

[79] Oshitelu, *Disclosure.*

[80] The presence of the Jehovah's Witnesses or Russellites in Nigeria at this time has been mentioned above. An indication of their approach is given in the following quote from H. L. Ward-Price, a very knowledgeable and sympathetic colonial officer who knew Yoruba: "I have heard Jehovah's Witnesses deliver, by

coming of the "Americans" in Oshitelu's prophecies would seem to reflect the impact of the Garvey movement on West Africa, an impact that has also been noted in Congo religious movements of this time.[81] Ultimately, of course, these ideas are biblical in origin, and Oshitelu's prophecies have strong biblical overtones.

What is most significant here is that the presence of apocalyptic ideas to a greater or lesser degree in the aladura preaching did not occasion social protest. These ideas *are* potentially explosive in their ability to legitimate radical questioning of existing social arrangements. Nevertheless, such questioning did not ensue in the mainstream of the aladura movement. The major prophets—Tunolashe, Akinsowon, Babalola, and Oshitelu—failed to develop ideas in this direction.

As a result of the allegations regarding the influence of his prophecies, Oshitelu was questioned closely by the local British officials in Sabongidda-Ora, a non-Yoruba town in Mid-Western Nigeria where he was conducting a revival, and his house in Ogere was searched in his absence. In the end, on advice of Crown Counsel, no proceedings were instigated against him owing to the evident similarities between his prophecies and those of certain Old Testament figures.[82] His subsequent published prophecies contained no further references to taxes or Europeans, and all the contemporary witnesses agree that he was always apolitical in his preaching and work.

Expansion of the Church of the Lord proceeded very slowly during the 1930's and 1940's and somewhat faster in the 1950's and 1960's, especially in the Ijebu and Lagos areas. A total of about seventy-two branches with 10,000 members was counted in Nigeria by 1962,[83] plus

---

means of loudspeakers in the market places, terrible prophecies of the impending fall of the white man's Government in a Universal War, and the destruction of all kings, both black and white, and ministers of religion. . . . [Government left them alone] But though revolutionary ideas of this kind in Nigeria may appear to go to ground and die, yet there is a chance that the seeds so planted may crop up years later as troublesome weeds in the Colony's political and religious harvest-fields." *Dark Subjects*, 240.

[81] Efraim Andersson, *Messianic Popular Movements in the Lower Congo* (Uppsala, 1958), 229. The possible influence of Garvey's movement on Oshitelu's thought is a matter of conjecture which bears further investigation. A Lagos branch of the Garvey movement was organized in the fall of 1920 with much of its top leadership coming from the African type of independent churches. James Coleman wrote that, although the organization soon became moribund "the ideas propagated by Garvey had made a deep impression on some Nigerians who would not embrace the movement openly." James S. Coleman, *Nigeria: Background to Nationalism* (Berkeley, 1958), 191.

[82] Resident, Oyo, to Secretary, Southern Provinces, Enugu, Sept. 23, 1931 (Oyo Prof 3/357).

[83] Turner, *African Independent Church*, II, 14.

branches in other countries mentioned earlier. Turner has detailed eighteen direct secessions from the Church during this period, not including some secondary secessions and semi-independent congregations.[84]

Conclusions

In the introduction to this essay it was asserted that it is possible to distinguish religious protest from social protest and that while the aladura movement in its three variants involved religious protest, it did not express social protest to any significant degree. Protest as such was said to refer to manifest or latent criticism, opposition, or hostility toward some situation. Religious protest was differentiated from social protest in terms of the relative bounds of focus. Social protest involved criticism, opposition, or hostility directed toward an array of institutions other than the religious—in colonial territories, most especially, political institutions. The historical data presented on the origins of the aladura movement examined the self-definitions and actions of the aladura leaders and, to a lesser extent, the self-definitions and actions of their followers, with particular reference to such mani festations as might be identified with the exhibition of social protest.

All the leaders defined themselves as exclusively religious, and the Faith Tabernacle and Cherubim and Seraphim leaders had the non-political nature of their missions confirmed by confidential governmental reports. Babalola was finally jailed after two years of revivalism only because of British fears of what might happen if this movement continued to "unsettle" people, not because of any existing social protest. Oshitelu, of course, was regarded as potentially inflammatory by the government, but he disavowed any political intent and, as no further action was taken against him, it must be assumed that the government felt that he posed no further threat. None of the leaders, again with the exception of Oshitelu, criticized the colonial regime, its policies, or white people in general. Indeed, the Faith Tabernacle had a long involvement with white religious groups. Oshitelu's statements were made in the context of a pre-existing rhetoric (of the Bible and the Jehovah's Witnesses) and of his message of universal destruction. None of the leaders attacked traditional authorities as such, although their campaign against traditional religion touched upon an aspect of traditional life which supported the traditional political system.

[84] Ibid., 104-7.

There were, admittedly, secondary aladura or lesser prophets, particularly in Ekiti during the Babalola revival. As we have seen, a few of the latter went beyond the religious message of repentance and the cleansing of witchcraft to advocate the reduction of taxes. This showed the potentially inflammatory nature of the aladura message, but only a very few secondary aladura engaged in social protest of this kind. Despite the severe effects of the depression, they did not gain any following, and they were universally repudiated.

What about the followers of aladura? Did they perceive the aladura leaders as critics of the existing social or political order and respond to them on that basis regardless of how religious the leaders themselves saw their mission? In answering this question I shall distinguish people who were merely adherents—temporary followers attracted especially by the mass movements of the revival—from members—people who consciously left their former religions and joined the aladura churches. The *adherents* saw Tunolashe, Akinsowon, Babalola, and Oshitelu, and their lieutenants as wonder-workers—healers and diviners who could help those who needed help to attain their life's desires. Sometimes these people brought specific illnesses or problems to the meetings; at other times their needs were more diffuse, and they wanted reassurance in the face of an unsettling personal situation. At times, a whole community was motivated to go and drink Babalola's holy water in order to cleanse itself of tensions regarding witchcraft. But the people's need, and the remedy which they saw offered, was defined within the framework of supernatural powers. It was not generalized to the social or political order in any significant way.

The *members* of the aladura churches similarly defined their situations in religious terms, although those who joined came mostly from the existing mission churches and their responses carried with them an element of protest against their former churches. The mission churches were condemned as harboring witches, as fostering hypocritical recourses to traditional practitioners by their lack of spiritual power to overcome evil, and as charging money for God's free gifts. But there is no evidence that the recruitment of these members involved any protest against the social or political order, or that their protest against mission churches generalized a protest against all European institutions.

It might be argued that although the aladura movement implied no manifest social protest, it did represent a latent negative response to the imposition of colonial rule—that in protesting against the white man's religion, a vote was implicitly recorded against his political dominance. It is difficult to disprove such a contention, involving as it does assumptions about deep-seated, unarticulated dispositions. All that can be said is that the emotional tenor of the churches does not seem to suggest such a conclusion, that the members of these churches and their leaders participated in Nigerian society at all levels without difficulty, and that at the time when the aladura movement began there were alternate means available to record such protest in a more direct fashion. Religion was by no means the only mechanism available for self-expression in the Nigeria of the 1920's.

What motivated the aladura leaders and their early followers, therefore, was a desire to reform existing mission Protestant Christianity[85] to make it more relevant to the needs of daily African life. Each of the three variants tried to stay within the bounds of mission Christianity at first but was ousted by the mission churches. Once separate, the aladura variants each maintained Christian identification and looked to the Bible and to Christian tradition for the legitimation of its practices. What was it in Protestant Christianity that led to the aladura movement?

The answer to this question may be put into the framework of a strain analysis[86] which seeks to identify points of incompatibility within Protestantism, as a cultural and social system, which are directly related to the form and content of the resulting aladura movement. Although the incompatibilities which will be cited are "conflicting principles always present" in almost every religious system, it is argued that they were especially salient and conflictful in the situation under review because one side of each dilemma was a part of the traditional Yoruba world view unrecognized by the mission churches.[87]

[85] The Roman Catholic church was rather small in Western Nigeria and little is known of the effect of the aladura movement upon it. As far as is known most of the aladura leaders and members in the early period were former members of Protestant mission churches, particularly the Anglican church, which was by far the largest of these churches.

[86] The intent of this brief exposition is to identify points where members of Protestant mission churches have conflicting sets of expectations. For a discussion of this approach to the study of change see Wilbert E. Moore, *Social Change* (Englewood Cliffs, N. J., 1963), and Neil J. Smelser, *Theory of Collective Behavior* (New York, 1963), 47-66. Clifford Geertz uses this approach in contrasting the *moderen* interpretation of Javanese Islam with the *Kilot* interpretation. *The Religion of Java* (New York, 1960), 148-61.

[87] Histories of mission Christianity have hitherto paid slight attention to missionary theology and its relation to African traditional religion. C. P. Groves discusses this problem only at the conclusion of his monumental work, *The Planting of Christianity in Africa* (London, 1958), IV, 348-52. For the situation of the mission churches in Nigeria the following touch on this topic: J. F. A. Ajayi, *Christian Missions in Nigeria, 1841-1891: The Making of a New Elite* (London, 1965), 8, 14-18, 264; Grimley and Robinson, *Church Growth*, 280-81; and Parrinder, *Religion in an African City*. See also Idowu, *Olodumare*, 209-13; S. S. Farrow, *Faith, Fancies and Fetich* (London, 1926); J. Olumide Lucas, *The Religion of the Yorubas* (Lagos, 1948); James Johnson, *Yoruba Heathenism*

In the cultural dimension there were three important and related incompatibilities of world view. In answer to the question, how can God help me in the difficulties of this life—sickness, joblessness, sterility—mission Christianity emphasized life after death but traditional religion offered supernatural help in this life through diviner-healers. In answer to the question, what is the nature of evil, the missionaries saw evil as an abstract principle with special reference to morality, but traditional religion posited real powers, such as witches, that were at work spoiling men's destinies. Finally, in answer to the question, how does one approach God, the missionaries emphasized subjection to God's inscrutable will, but traditional religion, despite its fatalistic tendencies, promoted supplication for help from ancestors or divinities. The American Faith Tabernacle belief appealed to its Nigerian followers because it emphasized God's help in this life; it saw evil as personified power, and it offered an approach to God which involved active supplication for God's help.

In the social dimension two important incompatibilities may be described. They are not obvious from the historical data presented earlier. First, mission churches were preclusive in their membership requirements. Full communicant membership involved various requirements including, for men, a monogamous marriage and, for all, a measure of literacy. Church membership in one denomination was regarded as incompatible with membership in a second denomination.[88] Traditional religion, on the other hand, was inclusive; cult membership involved few prerequisites, and multiple cult membership was common. People faced with particular difficulties might even be advised by a diviner to change cults.[89] The aladura variants in their

---

(London, 1899); William Bascom, "African Culture and the Missionary," *Civilisations*, III (1953), 491-504; and William B. Schwab, "The Growth and Conflicts of Religion in a Modern Yoruba Community," *Zaire*, VI (1952), 829-35. The indigenization of Christianity was often a topic at the early Anglican Synods and the claim was sometimes made that that church was actively involved in relating Christianity to local customs. An editorial in the Anglican layman's magazine, *In Leisure Hours*, in 1926 made such a claim with reference to the use of African music, African dress by members of the Synod, and motions made at the last Synod calling for study of traditional customs and for "serious effort to discourage usage of charms and juju and kindling in their place a true trust in God and in the power of prayer." The reality of the situation was perhaps better expressed in the syllabi for the first and second class catechist exams, published in the preceding issue of *In Leisure Hours*, which included no reference to traditional religion or customs at all. XVII, 194 (June 1926), 1.

[88] Grimley and Robinson, *Church Growth*, 296, 337-38, Webster, *African Churches*, 46-47.

[89] William Bascom, "The Sociological Role of the Yoruba Cult Group," *American Anthropological Association*, Memoir 63 (1944), 42-45.

attempt to stay within the mission churches were following a variation of the traditional principle of multiplicity. Of course, the Faith Tabernacle was even more preclusive than the mission churches in its membership requirements, but the other two aladura variants were far more flexible in this regard, as was the Babalola revival before its institutionalization in 1932.

Second, scope was not provided for female leadership in the mission churches, but traditional religion offered certain leadership roles to women. The Anglican church at this time gave women no seats in the Synod, none in the district councils, and none in parochial committees. Nor were they even given the franchise.[90] Although, as in traditional religion, men were still dominant on most levels, the aladura churches offered far more scope to women, as the presence of Miss Akinsowon and Miss Odunlami among their founders suggests.

An examination of Islam's position among the Yoruba at this time suggests that cultural factors were more important in the aladura movement than were social factors. Islam was fast making converts in Yorubaland, but it did not spawn a parallel movement toward indigenization;[91] it did not give much scope to women; nor did it look with favor upon multiple religious allegiance. Islam required less of a sharp break with traditional social patterns, such as polygyny, than did mission Christianity, of course, but it was incompatible with the practice of traditional magic and religion.

The reason why there was no movement within Islam parallel to the aladura movement and why very few Muslims joined aladura churches seems to lie in the provision within the Islamic framework of a functional alternative to the cultural emphases of traditional Yoruba religion. The *alfa* (Muslim priest) offers divination and healing services similar to those of the *babalawo,* but of an Islamic character. Muslim theology provides for the personification of evil spirits and the acceptance of the reality of witchcraft, and although orthodox Islam is more systematically fatalistic than traditional religion, the Yoruba variety of Islam allowed full play to the worshippers' supplicatory needs.[92]

[90] Bishop Isaac Oluwole, "Address to Diocesan Synod, Lagos, May 1921," *Western Equatorial Africa Diocesan Magazine,* XXVI (Aug. 1921), 212-15.

[91] Humphrey J. Fisher, "Muslim and Christian Separatism in Africa," in "Religion in Africa" (Edinburgh, 1964), mimeo., 9-23.

[92] J. Spencer Trimingham, *Islam in West Africa* (Oxford, 1959), 24, 36-7, 221-22; J. Spencer Trimingham, *A History of Islam in West Africa* (London, 1962), 230-31. Trimingham in another publication notes that in the Akoko area of northeastern Yorubaland, an area strongly affected by the Babalola revival, the number of Muslims was diminishing with marginal Muslims becoming Christian. These people were turning, not to the Anglican church but to the aladura churches. A missionary wrote to him: "The Aladuras seem to have captured the

These incompatibilities within Protestant Christianity would not lead to strain if the new Christians were fully socialized into the mission definitions, or if they were at least offered compensation such as access to mission hospitals, education, or a separate Christian community apart from the tensions of traditional life. From early in the twentieth century, however, the Yoruba began turning to Christianity and Islam in such large numbers (their traditional religions gave way before the attractions of these "civilized" religions) that adequate socialization was impossible.[93] An enormous burden was placed on the very limited missionary resources, and the output of well-trained African leaders was small. Furthermore, the Anglican church was continually decrying its low spiritual state and its need for spiritual revival.[94] Under such circumstances the incompatibilities within Christianity became genuine points of strain.

Thus far, it is only the strains within the Protestant religious system that have been discussed. Attention must now be directed to the strains in the social, economic, and political realms. The influenza epidemic and the depression of 1930, previously mentioned, were im-

---

soul of Western Nigeria in a way we have not. While much of their practice and belief is unhealthy, we might be able to learn much from them, particularly from their beliefs in healing, from their use of native music and dancing, and from their practical belief in prayer." This is a support for my argument that the aladura and Yoruba Islam may be seen as functional alternatives to each other and to the traditional *babalawo*. J. Spencer Trimingham, *The Christian Church and Islam in West Africa* (London, 1955), 50-51.

[93] A perusal of the Anglican Synod reports for the years 1905–30 will yield numerous recognitions of this problem by that church over this period of time. Perhaps the clearest statement on the subject in this period was made in 1921 in an article "Needs of the Yoruba Mission." Statistics were presented for 1895 and 1920, showing an enormous growth of baptized Christians from 7,500 to 60,000 and inquirers under instruction from 1,200 to 17,000. The number of European male missionaries engaged in evangelistic work remained about the same from 1895 to 1920, about ten. The number of African clergy and teachers increased from 115 to 649 over this period. The number of members and catechumens per African churchworker (including both clergy and teachers) increased from 76.3 in 1895 to 118.6 in 1920. The article implies that the quality of African churchworkers was lower in 1920 and pleads for a larger missionary staff. *Western Equatorial Africa Diocesan Magazine* XXVI, 196 (April 1921), 84. Data for the Methodists are not available to me at this time, but Grimley and Robinson present data for 1914 and 1934 which show an increase in the African churchworker (ordained and unordained pastors) -member (presumably only those baptized) ratio from 36.7 to 160.2. Grimley and Robinson, *Church Growth*, 327.

[94] For representative statements regarding the Anglican church: R. Kidd, "After Twenty Years," *Western Equatorial Africa Diocesan Magaine*, XXI, 137 (May 1916), 157; C. W. Howells to Canon Wakeman, July 25, 1925, CMS (Y) 2/5, 40. For the Methodist church: Oliver J. Griffen to Headquarters, London, July 28, 1925, WMMS 1/4/10.

portant influences in the rise of the original Faith Tabernacle group and the Babalola revival. Other plagues and a depression occurred during the 1920's, which had no direct effect on the development of the aladura churches but may have contributed indirectly.

Politically, it was a time of ferment in Lagos with Nigerian participation in the developing National Congress of British West Africa, the controversy over the government's treatment of the *Eleko* (King) of Lagos, the elections to the new Legislative Council and to the open seats of the Lagos Town Council, and the activity of Herbert Macaulay's Nigerian National Democratic party, Nigeria's first thorough-going political entity.[95] This rise of political consciousness was in a context of greater freedoms of the press, assembly, speech, and movement than in most of the rest of Africa.[96] Thus, the situation was relatively unrepressive and was characterized by various means of political expression. Those whose religious beliefs were touched by nationalism had recourse to the already existing "African" type of independent churches.[97]

In conclusion, therefore, we can point to a number of factors in the society as a whole and in the Protestant religious systems in particular which led to the emergence of the small aladura groups in the 1920's and to the Babalola revival in 1930. Chief among these was the ideological schism between Protestantism and traditional religion and the inability of the Protestant system to relate its beliefs and practices to the people's concern for worldly spiritual help. As the size of the churches increased and the people became more accustomed to the Western factor in their culture, the latent functions of Protestantism had less attraction and the manifest differences became more burdensome. The failure of Western culture to provide alternate means of controlling sickness and an economic depression which caused considerable relative deprivation, for example, in those areas like Ilesha where cocoa had been more recently introduced, were powerful external factors which reached their height in 1930 and, in conjunction with both types of internal strains, touched off the 1930 mass movement.

[95] Coleman, *Nigeria*, 169-229.

[96] Ibid., 113.

[97] Webster, *African Churches*; Coleman, *Nigeria*, 91-112. E. A. Ayandele (*The Missionary Impact*, 176-77) offers a convincing critique of Coleman's conclusion that there were no "causal relationships . . . between Christian missionary activity and the rise of nationalism." Ayandele discusses Ethiopianism as a Christian expression of African nationalism characterizing both the mission and the African type of independent church. His conclusion that West African Ethiopianism "never became anti-government, and although it was anti-white it was not on the same scale as in Central and South Africa" parallels the conclusion for the aladura of this study.

The aladura movement as a whole was not a revitalization movement in the sense of a conscious attempt to reconstruct a new culture—it was a Christian indigenization movement. Nor did it take the more radical religious forms of millenarianism, nativism, or messianism. With a few minor exceptions it accepted Christianity, Western civilization, and British rule. It would seem that the external sources of strain were not severe enough to transform religious protest into social protest.[98] Religious strain, as such, is a basic stimulus for the formation of African independent churches, though not the only stimulus, and bears more thorough analysis than it has heretofore received.

[98] This argument can be cast in the framework of Smelser's typology of collective behavior. Smelser says: "For any given empirical case of strain, the exact level of generality which must be reconstituted to overcome the strain depends on two things: a) the seriousness of the initial conditions of strain, and b) the adequacy of the facilities at each level to meet the conditions of strain," *Collective Behavior*, 69. I am suggesting that the strain in the religious system did not coalesce with strains at other points in the social system. Because of this the protest did not generalize to include other groups nor was it directed at the values of the legitimacy of opposing groups. Smelser tends to put all religious movements in colonial areas into his value-oriented movement category which, of course, is incorrect for the aladura.

A WEST AFRICAN ISLAMIC MOVEMENT:

HAMALLISM IN FRENCH WEST AFRICA

PIERRE ALEXANDRE

In 1951 or 1952 one of my Togolese friends remarked that the Tijani order, of which he was a devout member, had been born at about the same time as the French Revolution. This was intended as a political comment, a hint that the order was democratic and progressive and not, in contrast to the prevalent official contention, reactionary, conservative, or anarchistic. Actually, the French colonial administration—whose representative I happened to be—was at the time still nervously trying to sort out the "good" Tijanis from the "bad" and had just begun to wonder whether the "bad" ones of yesterday—the Hamallists or Hamawis—were not showing signs of becoming the "good" ones of the future. (This, after all, had happened before with the Omari branch of the order, as thoroughly "good" in 1914 as it had been "bad" fifty years earlier.) But, in fact, the colonial redemption of the Hamalliyya was to lose its point very quickly, with the unexpectedly swift collapse of the colonial regime itself. Hamallism had certainly contributed to this collapse, even though its contribution was not in itself decisive.

Regular Tijanism, under al-hajj Omar Tall's leadership, had for a generation been the most effective force opposing the rise of the French colonial domination in West Africa. It had, in fact, been the only large-scale, organized, hierarchical organization at a supratribal level. Then, because even after military defeat Tijanism retained its members and organization, the French colonial administration came to a more or less explicit agreement with it and in 1914 turned the Omari Tijaniyya into a kind of established church with a quasi-official status. "Reformed" Tijanism—the Hamalliyya—was at first preeminently a religious, nonconformist, dissident movement. But insofar as it was directed against an officially recognized, semi-officially supported "church," it was bound, willingly or not, to assume a political significance. If regular Tijanism in the late colonial period was, so to speak, rather "High Church," Hamallism could be considered "chapel." The very looseness of its organization made it relatively immune to legal repression, especially as long as it phrased a deep-seated reaction to political and social frustrations in outwardly religious terms.

After the 1946 reforms had opened modern, legitimate channels of political expression, the Hamalliyya gradually merged into the opposition party, *Rassemblement Démocratique Africain*, which took over its political role for a thirteen-year period (1945–58).

The Tijani Order: Historical Background

The Tijani order spread south of the Sahara during the lifetime of its founder, Si Ahmad al-Tijani. A Moor from Trarza, Muhammad al-Hafiz b. Mokhtar, took the *wird* at the Fez *zawiya* about 1789, returned home, and converted his tribe, the Idaw 'Ali,[1] before the turn of the century. He met with strong opposition from the Fadeli and Bekka'i branches of the Qadiriyya, so that the Tijaniyya remained practically confined to the white nomadic tribes of the desert[2] and *sahil* (arid) zones and did not encroach upon the Sudan proper for more than a generation. Introducing the Negro peoples of the savannah, and the upper reaches of the Senegal and Niger rivers to Tijanism was to be the life work of a Fulani from Fouta Toro, al-hajj Omar Tall.[3] Toward the middle of the eighteenth century Fouta Toro had become a Muslim kingdom under Fulani rulers belonging to the Qadiriyya. A member of a scholarly family of the ruling caste,[4] Omar was born in 1794. He received a good education and traveled widely around West Africa to attend the lessons of various scholars. He was probably initiated into the Tijaniyya before his pilgrimage to Mecca (1828–33). Coming back from Arabia he stayed some time in Sokoto and married the daughter of the ruler, Muhammadu Bello.[5] In 1840 he settled down at Dinguiraye

---

[1] Alternative spellings in other French sources: Ida Ou Ali, Ida Ouali. The *wird* is to be initiated; a *zawiya* is a seat of a Sufi order.

[2] The so-called "Moors" (Maures) or Ba'idan "white" (French sources: Bidanes).

[3] Al hajj 'Umar b. Sa'id al-Futi; French sources: El Hadj or Hajj Omar. For facility of reference all names of places and persons will be given in the usual spelling of the French sources.

[4] Most French sources present him as a "Toucouleur" or "Toucoulor." This is a French mispronunciation of a Wolof mispronunciation of the toponym "Tekrur." The so-called "Toucouleurs" or "Tukolor" are a branch of the Fulani—or "Peuls," or, more properly, Fulbe.

[5] He is said to have conferred the Tijani *wird* on Muhammadu Bello, a fact which has been denied by the Nigerian Qadiris.

(Guinée) and opened a *zawiya*, around which he began to build up his military and political power, launching raids upon the neighboring Qadiri states and cities as well as against the pagan tribes. In 1851 he proclaimed a *jihad* and conquered the Bambara state of Kaarta, establishing his capital at Nioro.

Just at the same time, however, the French, under General Léon C. C. Faidherbe, were working their way up the Senegal Valley from Saint-Louis in an effort to open up and protect the commercial routes to the interior. After several indecisive skirmishes and abortive attempts to parley (Faidherbe was trying to avoid an open conflict), Omar besieged the French outstation of Médine so successfully that it was down to its last rounds of ammunition when relieved in 1856. There followed three years of hard fighting between the French and the Tijani army. Beaten at Guémou in 1859, Omar refused to accept a treaty. He stopped his attacks on lower Senegal and turned instead against the Muslim (Qadiri) kingdom of Maçina on the Upper Niger. The invasion was successful, but, after his defeat by the French, Omar had lost prestige and in 1863 he had to face a joint revolt of the pagan Bambara of Kaarta and the Fulani of Maçina, stimulated by the Qadiri shaykh, Ahmad al-Kunti. In somewhat mysterious circumstances,[6] Omar was defeated and killed in 1864.

After his death the empire he had built was divided among his three sons, and unsettled conditions prevailed for a generation in the Western Sudan. French colonial penetration, halted after the Franco-Prussian War, was not resumed until the 1880's, at which time the French had Omar's successors as their main opponents. However, they were able to make good use of both the rivalries within the Tall family and the hostile memories still alive from the days of Tijani expansion. Thus, in 1890, influencing Aguibou Tall against his cousin Ahmadou, they achieved the conquest of the former Tijani empire by occupying Maçina.

Paradoxically, the French victory was actually to facilitate Tijani expansion in West Africa. France's principal opponent in the 1890's was a Qadiri, the Malinke Samori Turé.[7] But the Algerian branch of the Tijaniyya, which for several decades had been supporting the French in North Africa, sent emissaries to preach similar co-operation in West Africa. So the French colonial administration was able to win the support of the Omarian Tijanis and to support them in its turn. Tijanian dignitaries, such as al-hajj Seydou Nourou Tall and al-hajj

---

[6] At the beginning of the twentieth century there were still some people who refused to admit that he was dead and professed to believe that he was alive and hiding in Syria or Arabia, waiting to return to West Africa as a Mahdi.

[7] See above, Yves Person, "Samori and Resistance to the French," 80-112.

Malik Sy, were given quasi-official positions as recognized leaders and representatives of the West African Muslims. Minor *moqqadmin* (*marabouts officiels*) were given similar positions at provincial and divisional levels, sitting on native courts, *conseils de notables,* and so forth, or being appointed village headmen, *chefs de canton* or even *chefs supérieurs.* The Tijaniyya thus came to be considered as reliable and loyalist in contrast to the Qadiriyya, which had come under official suspicion after the rise of its Muridist splinter branch in Senegal.[8] Hamallism was to develop in direct opposition to this idyll.

Development of Hamallism

In 1900 a sharif from Touat, Si Muhammad uld Ahmad uld Abdallah al-Akhdar, had come to live in Niorodu-Sahil. He criticized both the Idaw 'Ali and the Omarian branches of the West African Tijaniyya for reciting the *Jawharat al-Kamal* prayer of the *wazifa* (special rosary) twelve times instead of eleven, as had originally been prescribed by Si Ahmad al-Tijani. He therefore used a rosary with the beads grouped 11-19-20-20-19-11 instead of 12-18-20-20-18-12. He was ostracized by the regular Tijanis who accused him of being under the influence of the Moroccan *zawiya,* which was considered anti-French. The administration of French West Africa watched him closely but could find no motive to intervene, inasmuch as, despite his great learning, he had little success with the local Muslims and was supported mainly by a small group of Wolof from Senegal living in Nioro as traders.

On his death in 1909 al-Akhdar was replaced by his favorite disciple, Hamahu'llah b. Sharif Muhammad b. Sidna Omar, who was to become famous as the shaykh of *"tidjanisme différencié"* or *"tidjanisme réformé,"* later called *"tidjanisme-onze-grains"* or, more plainly and strikingly, "Hamallism."[9] Hamallah had been born in 1883 or 1884,

[8] The Muridists were a splinter group of the Qadiriyya founded at Diourbel (Senegal) in 1886 by Shaykh Amadou Bamba Mbacki (d. 1927). Amadou Bamba opposed the economic and political privileges of the *citoyens des quatre communes,* especially the Saint-Louis creoles. He built up a kind of theocratic agrarian communism on the basic creed "work is prayer." Today's 400,000 Muridists control about 40 per cent of the groundnut production in Senegal and wield an important political influence. They are said to support Dr. Mamadou Dia against President Senghor.

[9] The terms Hamalliyya, Hamawiyya are seldom found in French sources. In the vernaculars (Fulani, Soninka, Mandinka, More, etc.) the order seems to have been usually called "Hamallah's way." "Hamallah" is a kind of compromise between a regular transliteration (hence the [h]) and the most common African pronunciations such as 'amala, 'amalaw, amalu. "Hamallah" is the usual French and ajami spelling of the name of the man who in the Arabic transliteration was born "Hamahu'llah b. Sharif Muhammad b. Sidna Omar."

the son of a Moorish trader from Tichitt and a Fulani woman of servile condition. He had a prepossessing figure, and was dark-skinned and handsome. He received a fairly good Qur'anic education in Nioro but never became an outstanding scholar: the level of *'ilm* (Islamic cultural) teaching had dropped sharply after the French conquest, with many learned teachers fleeing to Morocco. One of the first to join al-Akhdar's small group, he soon showed signs of a deep mysticism which probably earned him more prestige among the *hasanyeh* (warrior) and *zanaga* (pastoralist) Moors than would have scholarship. Born locally and with an African mother,[10] he was in a better position than his master to influence the Africans.

The differences between Hamallah's teaching and regular, non-reformed Tijanism do not seem very clear, even to such experts as Captain Paul Marty.[11] There was of course the obvious difference in the use of the eleven-bead rosary, but the shaykh claimed on apparently solid ground that this was a return to Tijani orthodoxy. He certainly put more stress on faith and mystique than on learning, an approach which suited both his own personality and the milieu and time in which he lived. In fact, little is known about the actual content of his teaching. When the colonial authorities came up against him they were unable to build a case: reports from spies only mentioned rather abstruse theological dissertations interspersed with ecstatic episodes during which the shaykh claimed to meet 'Ali, the Founder, or even the Prophet himself. Despite the fact that Hamallah had fallen under official suspicion as early as 1912, Marty's report of 1916 was definitely in his favor and exonerated him from any charge of political agitation.

This mystery, which certainly helped to arouse administrative suspicion, is understandable if one looks at the shaykh's methods. He lived a secluded life, never preaching in public, and, in later years, led prayers only in his own mosque. He never went on *ziara* (gift collecting) tours, nor did he solicit gifts from people who came to visit him. What gifts they brought were immediately distributed among the poor, Hamallah himself, as a report had it, always taking care to remain "ostentatiously modest and ascetic." Although he made himself readily available to pious visitors, he taught only a select few who were then sent away to teach others in a similar way. His teaching was there-

10 Later in his career he claimed descent from the Prophet through 'Ali. Genealogies of this type are quite common in West African Islam, even among pure-blooded Africans.

11 Of the *Affaires Militaires Musulmanes* (AMM). The AMM corps, disbanded after 1962, was a crack intelligence unit whose officers received a very high degree of scholarly training in languages and Islamology.

fore of a markedly esoteric nature, in keeping with the original intents of Si Ahmad al-Tijani, but in contrast to the usual methods of the Omari branch. Hamallah also used to send written messages—not through the government mails—to minor Tijani marabouts, explaining how the West African Tijaniyya had gone wrong and offering to bring them back to the unadulterated Way.

Hamallah's methods proved efficient. More and more village marabouts began using the eleven-bead rosary; more and more refused to accept the Omari shaykh's authority. Many traveled to Nioro, often without an official permit,[12] to attend Hamallah's *zawiya*. A number of the poorer people began to refuse to pay the *zakkat* (tithe) or to render the traditional *prestations* (a French administrative euphemism for illegal taxation in kind and labor) to the men they began to call the "French" or *nasara* ("white man," or "Christian") marabouts. Poems vaunted Hamallah's humility and gentleness of heart in contradistinction to the harshness, pride, and cupidity of the regular Tijani and Qadiri marabouts.

These events brought against him the joint hostility of the "regular" Tijanis, who had the ear of French officialdom, and of the local faction of the Qadiriyya, represented by the *maraboutique* (or Zawiya tribe) called Tenwajib.[13] Thanks to the *pax Gallica,* this tribe had built up a kind of religious monopoly among the local Moors, from which it derived considerable material benefits. The Omari Tijanis had more influence among the half-emancipated, sedentary *haratin* (serfs) and the Fulani, and they too found their economic interests and political influence threatened by Hamallah's unworldly behavior. Increasingly the Tenwajib began to initiate provocations and even bodily attacks against Hamallah's followers, and, in 1912, the "regular" Tijanis used their connections with the Governor General's office in Dakar to trump up a charge against Hamallah of hostility to the French and of maliciously endangering public order.

Official inquiries did not substantiate this accusation, Marty's 1916 report even claiming that the shaykh's followers were rather more reliable, from the French point of view, than the other Moors. In 1917, however, a fight between "regular" and "reformed" Tijanis broke out in Bamako, and the administration was dismayed to find that Hamallah's influence had spread so far into the savannah. Dakar issued a standing order to all administrators to keep a close watch on Hamallists.

---

[12] The *laissez-passer,* compulsory up to 1946 for people who wanted to travel outside their home district.

[13] "Tenouadjib," "Tinouaziou" in some French sources.

Hamallah and the French Administration

After 1918, because of the situation in Morocco and in Syria, the French became even more cautious. In 1922, al-hajj Malik Sy, the highly respected head of the West African Tijaniyya, died: he had not belonged to the Tall clan[14] and had acted as a kind of moderator in the quarrel. His death was followed by a new schism of the order in Senegal and a renewal of incidents in the *sahil*: Nioro, 1923, Kiffa, 1924. New inquiries were made about Hamallah's attitude vis-à-vis the French. No overt act of hostility could be ascribed to him, but the reports[15] all insisted on his aloofness: he never visited the district office except when summoned, never attended *Quatorze Juillet* festivities, and refused to send his sons to the French school. The Monié report (1924) quoted a number of anti-French poems in Arabic or Fulani, composed by his followers. In 1925, the Rif War generated a kind of John Buchan complex in French officialdom: administrative reports teemed with hints of a worldwide Muslim uprising supported by the Bolsheviks and/or the British Intelligence Service. Since new official inquiries failed to uncover enough evidence to bring Hamallah before a court, Governor Terrasson de Fougères signed an executive order, under the *indigénat* code, deporting him for ten years.

Thus, in 1925, Hamallah was sent to Mederdra in southern Mauritania, which was near the famous *zawiya* of the Ahil Shaykh Sidya. Perhaps there was an expectation that the famous scholars at the *zawiya* would have a good influence upon him. In fact it was the other way round: he remained uninterested in scholarly pursuits while his reputation for piety brought him new local disciples. Meanwhile his followers in the Soudan Français, no longer subject to his direct authority, became more violent, if not anarchistic. New incidents occurred, culminating in the Kaédi riots of 1930, where about thirty persons were killed during an assault on the district office. Although the leader, one Yakouba Sylla (of whom more later) was disavowed by the shaykh, the Governor General ordered that Hamallah be sent to the lower Ivory Coast for the rest of his sentence.

Hamallah's reaction was to start using the two-*rek'a* (genuflection) abbreviated prayer, lawful only in case of war, constraint, or urgent ne-

[14] Malik Sy was a Wolof.

[15] André, 1923 (CHEAM), quoting Lieutenant Seydou Jerma-Koy, later paramount chief of the Jerma; Marty, 1923 (CHEAM), files of *Le Centre de Haute Études Administratives sur l'Afrique et l'Asie Modernes*, University of Paris.

cessity.[16] Then his followers in Soudan changed both the *qibla* (direction), praying with their faces to the west (whence he was expected to return), and the *shahada* (prayer) saying " . . . and Hamallah is our shaykh" instead of " . . . Muhammad racul Allah." The openly Spartakist trend started by Yakouba Sylla spread eastward and incidents with the Tenwajib multiplied. What dismayed the administration even more was to discover that Hamallism was no longer "une mystique des illettrés." Supported by the two leading Senegalese politicians, Galandou Diouf and Lamine Guèye,[17] members of the *évolué* group—teachers, clerks, medical assistants—began to intervene in his favor. The Governor General considered a pardon and sent Chief Administrator Beyries to visit Hamallah and ask him to promise to conform if he were allowed to come back to Nioro. The shaykh refused to compromise on what he declared to be a matter of faith. Even when he finally came home, in 1935, he continued praying with only two *rek'a*.

In 1936 the *Front Populaire* government in Paris brought a change of policy to the French colonies. By this time the district officers had realized some of the social roots of Hamallah's success and explained them in many reports: "an attempt towards social liberation . . . expresses the confused and still insecure aspirations of lower class and poorer condition people";[18] "reaction of an unhappy and hopeless mass";[19] or, from a usually hostile source, "overwhelming desire to free themselves from [the] material and moral servitude that both native society and colonization, the latter with its materialistic machinery and large-scale economy, bring to bear upon them . . . Hence [this] affirmation of nonconformism enabling [the adepts] to achieve [the] deep hidden wishes of an anxious multitude."[20]

In 1937, Governor General Marcel de Coppet issued a secret instruction to the effect that district officers should "advise the keepers of tradition to show more tolerance, more understanding of the moral and material needs of the native masses [who are] all too often destitute and discouraged." In keeping with the instruction, he dispatched the head of the Omari branch, al-hajj Seydou Nourou Tall, on a peace mission to Nioro. An uneasy truce within the tijaniyya ensued, with Hamallah resuming the normal, five-*rek'a* prayer.

But the situation remained tense. That year for the first time, a European, the geologist Jacquet, was killed in the desert. His murderers were said to belong to the Hamawiyya. The Tenwajib—who were

16 Qur'an, IV: 102.
17 Lamine Guèye was usually supported by the Qadiris, Diouf by the Tijanis.
18 Captain d'Arbaumont, 1937 (CHEAM).
19 Rougier, 1937 (CHEAM).
20 Nicolas, 1943 (CHEAM).

no party to the truce negotiated by al-hajj Seydou Tall–became more offensive than ever, repeatedly raiding the Hamallist villages and camps,[21] beating men, stealing cattle and camels, and abducting women and children. As for the agreement within the estranged branches of the Tijaniyya, its fragility was demonstrated when the highly respected *tierno* ("learned man" in Fulani) Bokar Salif Tall went to visit Hamallah and publicly accepted his *wird*. He was repudiated by his clan, denounced as hostile to the administration, and the *évolués* among his disciples were disciplined by transfer or demotion in the civil service.

Then came the war and with it a tightening of administrative control. The colonial authorities were probably more sensitive than the Africans to the German propaganda in Arabic whose mainly antisemitic themes were, on the whole, irrelevant in the West African context. Some of it nevertheless did have some influence, especially in the *sahil* region where people speak Arabic and have many contacts with Morocco and Algeria. The French capitulation, in June 1940, came not only as a surprise but also as a very direct and personal blow since thousands of West African *tirailleurs* had been taken prisoner. The Europeans and *évolués* were furthermore divided by the conflict between Gaullists and Vichyites.[22] Wild rumors circulated and a panicky atmosphere prevailed all over French West Africa.

In this overtense psychological context the Assaba incident was interpreted as the beginning of a general uprising. On August 25, 1940, the Commandant of Nioro heard that a Hamallist band, led by three of the shaykh's sons, had attacked the main Tenwajib encampment, butchering more than four hundred people, mainly women and children as many of the men were absent at that time of year. Captain Joseph Rocaboy, specially charged with the inquest, found evidence of an incredibly savage slaughter: Qur'ans and other religious books had been torn to shreds or defiled with human blood, the corpses had been dismembered and beheaded. Rocaboy's *goumiers*[23] rounded up

[21] According to some of my African informants, the Camel Corps officers (*méharistes*), in charge of the nomadic populations, condoned those raids and refused to prosecute because they disapproved of the *Front Populaire* policy and opposed de Coppet's plan of putting the nomadic districts (*subdivisions nomades*) under civilian control.

[22] The *évolué* group was quite conscious of the meaning of Hitler's racialism and supported de Gaulle, but many Europeans were against him, in many cases for precisely the same reasons. After the failure of *Opération Menace* (September 1940) the Vichyite administration relied heavily on African chiefs and kept a suspicious watch on *évolué* officials who were deprived of most of the privileges they had been granted under the regime of the Third Republic.

[23] *Goumiers:* semi-irregular levies, used as a military police in nomadic districts.

the murderers without encountering any serious resistance. It seems that, after years of more or less unrequited Tenwajib provocations, the attack had been triggered by a rumor that the Germans were landing in Dakar to oust the French.[24]

The repression was severe: thirty-three leaders (including Hamallah's sons) were shot and six hundred rank and file were imprisoned throughout French West Africa.[25] Yet once again it was impossible to unearth any direct evidence against the shaykh himself. In fact, he publicly disavowed and condemned the massacre as contrary to the spirit of his teaching. Nevertheless Governor General Boisson sentenced him to deportation for ten years and, spirited onto a plane, Hamallah was flown to Chassaigne, south of Oran, Algeria. In 1942 the Algerian administration complained that, "despite the darkness of his skin," he had a bad influence upon the local Muslims,[26] and he was sent to a small, dreary spa, Vals-les-Bains, in the Cévennes. There he started on a campaign of protest fasts which eventually resulted in his death, at Montluçon (Allier) hospital, on January 16, 1943.

The French repression did not solve the Hamalli problem. On the contrary the deportation of the shaykh's followers helped to disseminate Hamallism at a time when economic and political conditions made the population especially receptive. The executions and Hamallah's deportation had been carried out with the utmost discretion: the families refused to mourn the dead and instead spread the rumor that they had fled to Syria or Mecca and would eventually come back with the shaykh as a Mahdi. In August 1941 a Hamallist band stormed a café in Bobo Dioulasso—then in the upper Ivory Coast—killing six Europeans. In the *sahil* the Hamallists were adopting queer and spectacularly unorthodox practices: shouting prayers instead of chanting them, tattooing their cheeks with the shaykh's cattle-marks, later on organizing orgiastic sessions with group fornication and sodomy.

In 1943, after the Gaullist takeover, the Governor General of West Africa ordered the commandants to pursue a policy of appeasement. This proved nearly impossible: there was no central restraining authority left, and the local, un-co-ordinated factions were in many cases on the verge of open rebellion. Moreover an undermanned administra-

[24] De Gaulle's abortive attempt to invade Senegal took place on Sept. 23. "Yet it had been planned in July and decided on August 3" (W. S. Churchill, *Mémoires sur la deuxième guerre mondiale,* [Paris, 1949] II, 168-69), and both Berlin and Vichy were aware of it: this might be the origin of the rumor.

[25] Another consequence was a decree detaching the Hodh region from the Soudan colony and incorporating it with Mauritania. This was to become a source of friction between Mauritania and Mali after independence.

[26] Chassaigne is in the sphere of influence of the Tlemcen *zawiya* of the Tijaniyya.

tion, with a war on its hands and *la Métropole* occupied, could not afford to be either patient or liberal. Public order *was* in danger, so the repression went on, and resentment piled up.

Postwar Hamallism

After 1946 a new situation obtained: the new constitution provided modern channels for political expression and lessened the former omnipotence of the colonial administration. Up to 1951 there were still violent incidents in the Soudan, Upper Volta, Ivory Coast, and Niger, but Hamallism, on the whole, dispensed with the anarchistic character it had acquired after Hamallah's deportation. To a very large extent it became integrated with the *Rassemblement Démocratique Africain,* the biggest and most efficient opposition party in French West Africa. The fight against colonial authority went on but it was henceforth an organized fight—and a far more equal one.

Two trends must be distinguished at this point, both of which played a constructive part in *Rassemblement Démocratique Africain* politics up to independence.

The first was the popular Spartakist trend, as exemplified by Yabouka Sylla's splinter group, mentioned earlier. Yakouba Sylla was a Soninke disciple of Hamallah's, who, after a mystic vision of the Prophet's daughter, Fatima, started a puritanistic, egalitarian movement in Kaédi district. This movement rejected the authority of chiefs and traditional marabouts, and refused to observe the existing social distinctions between tribes and social groups. To gain admission his followers had to make a full public confession of their sins, renounce all finery and fancy clothing, and give all their jewels to the community. They built separate villages where everybody worked in common, the earnings being handed over to the local head of the sect. (This primitive socialism was strikingly reminiscent of the Murid sect, founded in Senegal at the turn of the century by the Qadiri *seriny,*[27] or learned man, Ahmadou Bamba.)[28]

The Yakubist villages consisted chiefly of people who had previously lived in a dependent position: slaves fleeing from their patrons, wives or concubines fleeing from their husbands, youth fleeing from their parents. They appropriated land, waterholes, and cattle, refusing any attempt to have such matters—or indeed any matter—brought to court, on the grounds that even Qur'anic courts were controlled by the Unfaithful. They went farther and rejected even the *sharia,* claiming that learning perverted the purity of the Faith. The rejection

[27] French sources: *serigne.*
[28] In fact Muridism may well have been the inspiring source of Yakubism.

of all recognized authority led in due time to a conflict with the colonial administration, and, after the Kaédi riots of 1930, Yakouba Sylla, who had been disavowed by Hamallah, was deported to the Ivory Coast, where he eventually became an economic power to be reckoned with (just like Ahmadou Bamba in Senegal). Yet his influence endured in the northern savannah zone and spread eastward to reach the Niger colony in the late 1930's. After 1946, the *Rassemblement Démocratique Africain* used this influence both to isolate the chiefs who supported— and were supported by—the administration and to further its own brand of African Socialism.

The second trend was the intellectual one, exemplified by the late convert, Tierno Bokar Salif Tall, who died in 1940, and his *évolué* disciples, who include such famous people as Presidents Modibo M. Keita and Diori Hamani, al-hajj Ahmadou Hampate Ba, member of the UNESCO executive council, Boubou Hama, Minister of Education of the Niger Republic, and many others. A learned man like Bokar Tall was certainly closer to Hamallah than Yakouba Sylla or the would-be Songhai Mahdi, Moussa Aminou (killed in a riot near Gao in 1949). He derived from the intellectual and mystical content of Hamallah's teaching the notion that Islam—or, perhaps more precisely, reformed Tijanism—was a religion that an African could be proud of *qua* African. This was elaborated on by less mystical and certainly more practical men who came to see in "differentiated Tijanism" a kind of national religion, an Africanized Islam. The test case occurred in the late 1940's when graduates from al-Azhar tried to propagate reformist doctrines and to set up a purely Arabic school system: they were considered un-African, and Hamallist intellectuals such as Ahmadou Hampate Ba countered their action with a deliberate attempt to Africanize Qur'anic teaching, using the vernaculars in Qur'anic schools and translating parts of the Qur'an into Fulani and Bambara. The politicians stressed the egalitarian character of Hamallism, its rejection of foreign authority, and its failure to insist upon strict orthodoxy. Many of these politicians, if not most of them, had only a French education and were quite unable to appreciate the fine points of Tijani doctrine. The important thing for them was that Hamallah rejected the colonial establishment while the Omari Tijanis accepted it, indeed were part of it.

Hamallism ceased to be a problem for the French when the political pressure went down following the 1946 reforms and when the *Rassemblement Démocratique Africain* split from the French Communist party in 1951. In fact, in the years just preceding independence it came to be considered a barrier against Arabic influence and was valued accordingly. Little is known of its evolution after independence. On the whole it seems to have lost most of its significance and to have been integrated with the other varieties of West African Islam. I have, however, heard of isolated instances—in Mali, Upper Volta and Niger—where small Hamallist groups have resumed an attitude of opposition to the new establishment similar to that which they had vis-à-vis the French administration before independence. This is a trait shared with some of the Bantu protest movements: in Congo (Brazzaville), for instance, the Matswanists have fallen foul first of the French administration, then of Foulbert Youlou's government, and now of "scientific socialism." The big difference in the cast of Hamallism is that, from the doctrinal angle, it was seldom fundamentally different from the prevalent (and rather vague) Muslim orthodoxy, a fact which ought to have facilitated its demobilization after independence.

Evaluation of Hamallism

One striking fact about Hamallism is that Hamallah himself would probably have denied that there was such a thing. He was primarily if not exclusively a religious leader. He never seemed to have directly meddled with politics. As mentioned above, the French colonial authorities were unable to provide any reliable evidence of open hostility on his part. He did not attack them: he just deliberately ignored them, and some official reports show traces of an almost comical exasperation at his attitude, taxing him with hypocrisy and damning him for not damning France. He certainly disliked the French but he probably disliked even more those Muslims who co-operated amicably with them. Those he considered traitors, and they, in their turn, used their influence with the French against him, also calling him a traitor—to another system.

Another interesting point is that his influence spread so far away from the *sahil* and its nomadic society, to agriculturalist Negroes whose islamic orthodoxy was most questionable and who were not likely to understand much of his attempts at theological reform. In some cases their ancestors two or three generations before had violently and often heroically opposed the forcible imposition of Tijanism or even of Islam:[29] it came as a surprise to see them adhere to an ostensibly ultra-Islamic movement.

The new factor was, of course, the colonial situation itself; and this was at least implicit in the official reports which, from 1930 on,

[29] There was a school of opinion among French administrators which opposed the practice of selecting the chiefs of pagan populations from among the Muslim tribes. This school expounded the theory that French colonization was, or should have been, a liberation of the pagan peoples from Muslim tyranny. See J. Brevié, *Islamisme contre naturisme au Soudan Français* (Paris, 1923), and Robert Delavignette, *Les paysans noirs* (Paris, 1931).

insisted upon the emancipatory aspects of hamallism. The French methods of *administration directe*—or direct rule—were so erosive that they rapidly became self-destructive. Some administrators, army officers chiefly, therefore advocated a policy of indirect rule and preservation of the traditional structures; the more liberal civilian administrators, however, sought to destroy the same structures because they judged them oppressive. The actual policy vacillated between those extreme views and continued to aggravate the fundamental ambiguity of the situation, especially in the *sahil* and in the most strongly hierarchical societies of the savannah. Thus the official emancipation of the *haratin* did not give them any means of livelihood, since their masters kept their herds even without any labor to tend them. The *pax Gallica* put the *hassanyeh* out of a trade, destroying the former balance between them and the marabout tribes. The latter, although struck deep by the slaves' emancipation, came off rather better: while their influence was considered potentially dangerous, their religious pursuits were held to be relatively innocuous and were encouraged, or, at least, not interfered with. The religious field thus became a rather privileged one, as far as freedom of expression (strictly repressed in political and economic matters) was concerned. This is, of course, reminiscent of the position of Christian missions in other parts of Africa, where religion was also the least obstructed channel of expression. In many cases, in fact, they acted as a kind of mitigating power between their African converts and the colonial administration, but they reacted strongly—sometimes even calling in the secular arm of colonial law—if and when some of their flock left them to build up schismatic churches, even if the schism was not compounded with heresy.

In Hamallah's case the missions' place was taken by the *marabouts officiels* of the Omari Tijaniyya. They probably resented al-Akhdar as a foreign competitor, so to speak. As for his Wolof supporters in Nioro, they may well have been motivated in part by tribal hostility toward the Tukolor and local Moors. Hamallah's position was different as he was local-born and half Fulani. Yet his movement was certainly not an Africanist one at first. That it became one was not the shaykh's doing: the first symptoms appeared hundreds of miles away from his *zawiya* and grew most spectacularly after he had been deported. His order nevertheless did possess from the start some very convenient factors:

—It was both open and exclusive: open, since any Muslim could adhere without distinction of tribe or social standing, exclusive, since joint membership in another order was prohibited.

—As a new institution in the making it was still supple, not sclerotic, as was the regular Tijaniyya: here was a chance of social mobility for its members, all the more so since the shaykh did not put the same weight on scholarly education as did the establishment, both Islamic and colonial.

—While it largely ignored everything French (colonial), it did condemn and reject in very fierce terms those Muslims who had accepted the colonial order.

Here we meet with another ambiguity: although colonial authorities considered him a revolutionary, Hamallah was in most respects a reactionary since his avowed aim was a return to the purity of olden times. However, his influence was objectively subversive, even if it failed to appear so to saintly, peaceful, tolerant Tierno Bokar Salif Tall.

One of the most specific administrative accusations against Hamallah was that he did not approve of the chiefs appointed by the colonial government. It was not until very late (in fact I could find no instances before World War II) that there were Hamallist candidates for official chieftainships. While the shaykh was alive, his followers merely "withdrew": in this sense they could very well be called *khareji* (withdrawn). They did not collide with the administration until they started to set up their own parallel and separate systems. Up to that moment harassed administrators could but report generalized negative attitudes—sons refusing to obey their fathers, youths their elders, wives their husbands—against which even the *Code des Sanctions Administratives* (*indigénat*) was not a very efficient weapon. The first serious incidents were not directed against European commandants or even against their native policemen and messengers, but rather against other Muslims, then against African chiefs who, in the French system as elsewhere, occupied a very uncomfortable position (with many compensations, it must be added). Yet the colonial administration was bound to intervene long before that point since *l'ordre public colonial*, as it was aptly termed, was undoubtedly troubled when litigants refused to attend native courts, or when young men refused to pay bride-wealth, or girls to marry according to their father's choice. All this is familiar enough: President Jomo Kenyatta and André Matchoua (or Matswa) were once as warmly commended in missionary or official reports as Hamallah had been by Captain Marty in 1916.

Hamallah's case differs from that of the leaders of Christian or syncretic schismatic movements such as Kitawala, Kimbangism, or Matswanism, insofar as, in the political and social field, he was less a leader than a kind of catalyst. Simon Kimbangu and André Matswa directly and publicly addressed the masses, while Hamallah never taught more than smallish groups in the seclusion of his *zawiya*. As far as can be ascertained this teaching was political only by implication, which seems to have also been the case with Kimbangu. John

Chilembwe seems to have mixed politics and religion to a far larger and more evident extent,[30] and Matswa was, at first, openly and consciously political. Kimbangu split away from a fundamentalist mission; Matswa had first been trained by the Roman Catholic church, then had traveled to Europe—Chilembwe had gone to the United States—and was influenced by the League of Human Rights, a French left-wing, politico-philosophical group. Hamallah came from a religious body which could be considered fully Africanized; many of his followers, however, especially among the Yakubist faction, were first-generation Muslims and comparable in this respect to the recent Christian converts who made up the bulk of the following of Chilembwe, Kimbangu, and Matswa. Chilembwe was killed leading an open rebellion; Hamallah, Matswa, and Kimbangu never personally engaged in physical violence, and there is no proof that Hamallah and Kimbangu actually condoned its use by their disciples. All three were removed by the colonial authorities, and in each case this removal seems to have enhanced the charismatic and supernatural character of their authority and prestige. At the beginning of his career Matswa was an exponent of orthodox French political radicalism just as Hamallah originally espoused orthodox Tijanism. Hamallah's heterodoxy was in fact a theological moot point which could be appreciated only by learned Muslim scholars and was of no interest for most of his rank-and-file followers. It can be argued that this was also the case with Matswa's political ideas when he came back to French Equatorial Africa after a long stay in France: the local French were almost the only people who could have understood and discussed them (did, in fact, try to discuss them for a time). This probably explains why Matswa fell back to a religious wording of his protest and eventually assumed a prophetic posture. His initial modernity was anachronistic in the Congo of the late 1930's (it would have been up to date in Senegal).

The most important of the traits which set Hamallah apart from other contemporary leaders of messianistic-prophetic protest movements is the fact that he did not borrow anything from European sources—from colonial and missionary innovations. His interpretation of Tijanism was in no way syncretistic. It did not significantly differ in form or content from the teaching of previous Muslim reformers in West Africa. Yet it triggered a popular reaction which conformed in its overall structure and history with the pattern of most Afro-Christian protest movements. The common factor would seem to have been the colonial situation itself.

[30] See above, Robert I. Rotberg, "Psychological Stress and the Question of Identity: Chilembwe's Revolt Reconsidered," 337-74.

THE LUMPA CHURCH

OF ALICE LENSHINA

ANDREW D. ROBERTS

Between July and October 1964, shortly before Northern Rhodesia obtained independence as Zambia, over seven hundred people were killed in fighting between members of the Lumpa church, founded by Alice Lenshina in 1955, and the recently elected government of Northern Rhodesia, dominated by the United National Independence party. The Church has since been banned, and Lenshina herself is still restricted. This conflict raised important questions about the relationship between separatist churches and political nationalism in Africa and thus about the whole character and role of such churches. To some extent, the conflict was itself a painful illumination of this problem; on the other hand, it has made it very difficult, at least for the time being, to pursue inquiries. For the most part, the present study is not based on direct observation. It was undertaken after I had returned from doing other research in the Northern Province of Zambia;[1] this had been the scene of the heaviest fighting, and for this very reason any systematic research on the Lumpa church was out of the question, even had I intended it. Thus I have had to rely mainly on the limited written sources, and in particular on the accounts of the Church published by Dorothea Lehmann and Robert Rotberg in 1961.[2] But in

---

[1] Between Mar. 1964 and July 1965 I conducted research in Zambia on the precolonial political history of the Bemba, with the support of a Carnegie Fellowship from the University of Wisconsin and as an affiliate of the then Rhodes-Livingstone Institute, Lusaka. This essay was written in 1966 and does not take account of later developments.

[2] Robert I. Rotberg, "The Lenshina Movement of Northern Rhodesia," *Rhodes-Livingstone Journal*, XXIX (1961), 63-78; Dorothea Lehmann, "Alice Lenshina Mulenga and the Lumpa Church," in John V. Taylor and Dorothea Lehmann, *Christians of the Copperbelt* (London, 1961), 248-68. (All of Part IV

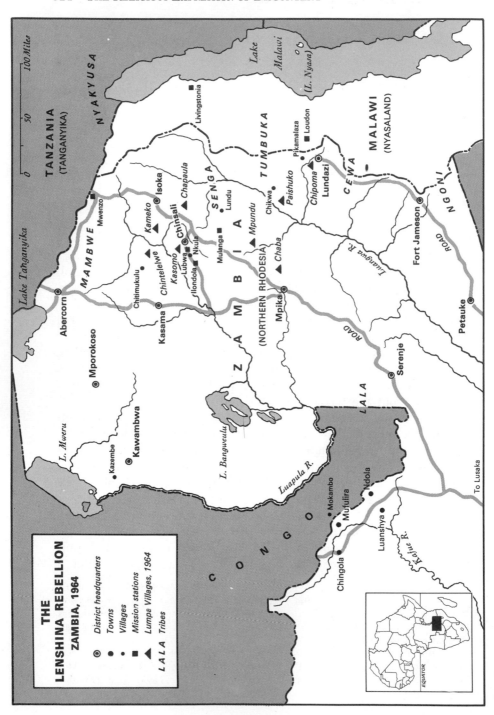

THE
LENSHINA REBELLION
ZAMBIA, 1964

◎ District headquarters
• Towns
• Villages
■ Mission stations
▲ Lumpa Villages, 1964
L A L A Tribes

order to place such descriptions in the perspective of the final catastrophe I have sought to outline the local social and religious context; to note the affinities of the Lumpa church with certain earlier popular movements in the area; and to sketch its history against the background of Zambia's advance to political independence. Such a survey will, it is true, make it all too clear how little is yet known in any detail of the religious and social basis of Lumpa belief and worship. In particular, there is very little information of any kind on the internal organization of the Lumpa church—a most important subject which perhaps will never properly be elucidated. And on many points there is disagreement or doubt among the sources, based as they are, for the most part, on hearsay evidence. Nonetheless, even the present restricted analysis may serve to guide further speculation and research on the history and sociology of this and comparable movements.

The Background

The Lumpa church was syncretic, mingling elements of belief and practice which were European and African in origin. It was a sect, in-

---

of *Christians of the Copperbelt*, "Some Independent Churches," in which this account appears, is by Dr. Lehmann; my references to this part are given simply as "Lehmann" while I refer to the parts by Taylor as "Taylor.")

I have also drawn on two accounts which are not generally available: Rev. L. Oger, W. F., "Lumpa Church: a Study of the Lenshina Movement, 1955-1960" (mimeograph, Serenje, 1960); and Christine M. Woods, "Alice Lenshina Mulenga: a Bemba Cult Leader" (unpublished M.A. thesis, University of Edinburgh, 1961). Fr. Oger's study is largely based on information he obtained when stationed at Ilondola, near Lenshina's headquarters; he reproduces some documents of the Lumpa church, including several hymns. (A summary of this study has been published: L. Oger, "Le Mouvement Lenshina en Rhodésie du Nord," *Eglise Vivante*, XIV [1962], 128-38; and "Lumpa-Church," *Notes [et] Documents* [1961], 401-10). The thesis by Miss Woods (now Mrs. Heward) is based primarily on contemporary press reports and interviews with three missionaries of the Church of Scotland who met Lenshina or her followers: Rev. F. Macpherson, Rev. K. Mackenzie, Rev. J. G. Fraser. Mrs. Heward summarized her thesis in "The Rise of Alice Lenshina," *New Society*, IV (13 Aug. 1964), 6-8.

There is one primary source, cited by Lehmann, 268, which I have not seen: this is a manuscript, "What I think about Lenshina," by Sandy Rain. I have not seen H. Charles Chéry, "Les sectes en Rhodésie du Nord," *Parole et Mission*, VII (1959), 578-94; nor have I been able to refer to all the relevant press reports.

I am very grateful to Fr. Oger and Mrs. Heward for kindly enabling me to consult their full-length studies. I am also indebted for information and advice to the Rev. Kenneth Mackenzie; Dr. Dorothea Lehmann, Dr. Audrey I. Richards, Mr. P. Harries-Jones, Mr. H. W. Langworthy, Rev. Fergus Macpherson, Prof. T. O. Ranger, Prof. R. I. Rotberg, and Dr. D. L. Wilson.

asmuch as it seceded from a parent Christian church (the United Church of Central Africa), but it was not, however, a mere replica, under African leadership, of the parent church: it drew its inspiration both from European Christianity and from important features of African social and religious experience. The Lumpa church was heir to two traditions in the modern history of Zambia: movements toward African Christian independence, and movements toward the eradication of witchcraft and sorcery; in both of these traditions, as in the Lumpa church, prophecy has on occasion played a crucial part. The interplay of these traditions to a large extent constitutes the history of the Lumpa church. I shall therefore briefly mention some manifestations of these traditions after summarizing the relevant social and religious background.

The Lumpa church was founded among the Bemba inhabitants of the Chinsali district in northeastern Zambia. The Bemba belong to the belt of matrilineal peoples which reaches across Central Africa from Kasai, in the Congo, to the Indian Ocean.[3] They number about 150,-000 and practice a form of slash-and-burn cultivation in the woodland which covers the well-watered but infertile plateau between the Luangwa Valley in the east, and the Luapula Valley (part of the Zambia-Congo border) in the west. This is still the only important means of subsistence in Bembaland; there is no cash crop.

The religious beliefs of the Bemba were, and to some extent still are, centered on the traditional political system.[4] They live in villages of a hundred or more people under the immediate authority of a chief or hereditary headman. Above the village level, the Bemba are governed by a network of territorial chiefs, under a single paramount chief, Chitimukulu. This paramount chief, and to a lesser extent the other senior chiefs, may be called "divine kings" inasmuch as their ritual purity and physical health are thought to affect the fertility of land, livestock, and people. Moreover, they alone, with some aid from their councillors, can obtain the blessings of their ancestors, the great chiefs of the past, upon their land and people. A creator god, Lesa, is recognized, but he is virtually a *deus otiosus* and has no special cult. There are, however, other tutelary spirits in addition to those of the dead chiefs—the *ngulu,* chthonic deities who are worshiped at water-

---

[3] The economic, social, and political institutions of the Bemba have been intensively studied by A. I. Richards: see especially her *Land, Labour and Diet in Northern Rhodesia* (2nd ed.; London, 1961).

[4] For Bemba religious beliefs see Richards, *Land, Labour and Diet,* 351-80; see also A. I. Richards, *Chisungu: a Girls' Initiation Ceremony among the Bemba of Northern Rhodesia* (London, 1956); J. H. West Sheane, "Some Aspects of the Awemba Religion and Superstitious Observances," *Journal of the Royal Anthropological Institute,* XXXVI (1906), 150-58; Ian G. Cunnison, *The Luapula Peoples of Northern Rhodesia* (Manchester, 1959), 222-25.

falls, rocks, and caves. Sacrifices can be arranged only by the local chief, but *ngulu* reveal themselves to anyone in dreams or through spirit possession. They foretell disasters, give advice on hunting, or simply remind people to worship them.

These two kinds of spirits, those of the chiefs' ancestors and the *ngulu*, are thought to look after the communal welfare of the Bemba. The fortunes of individuals have, however, been subject to two other kinds of mystical power: the approval or anger of personal ancestors and the operation of magic.[5] Major personal misfortunes, such as deaths in the family, were often attributed to the anger of ancestors provoked by disrespectful or other wrong behavior toward those in authority. Other misfortunes might be attributed to sorcery. Charms have been widely used, for example to keep granaries full or to ensure success in hunting and fishing. But if someone were too successful, or stood too much upon his "rights," he was thought to be using black magic—to be a sorcerer. Diviners, or perhaps a person possessed by a *ngulu*, would identify the suspect, and the charge would be confirmed or denied by a poison ordeal administered only by a chief. This ordeal was indeed a reflection of the extensive mystical power exerted by Bemba chiefs, not only in the "public" sphere of communal ritual but also in the "private" sphere of magic and sorcery. As a result, sorcery probably did not have for the Bemba the pervasive power with which it is credited in other Central African matrilineal societies, such as the Cewa or the Lele, where chiefs are either relatively weak or non-existent.[6] In the hierarchical society of the Bemba, social order was primarily secured not through processes of accusation, ordeal, and punishment, but through conformity to their ideal values of *umucinshi* (respect, deference) and *umano* (social sense), and through the observances due to the tutelary spirits.

[5] See A. I. Richards, "A Modern Movement of Witch-Finders," *Africa,* VIII (1935), 448-61. There are also two accounts by White Fathers of Bemba sorcery and divination: Rev. L. Molinier, "Croyances superstitieuses chez les Babemba," *Journal of the African Society,* III (1903), 74-82; and Rev. E. Labrecque, "La sorcellerie chez les Babemba," *Anthropos,* XXXIII (1938), 260-65.

The Bemba word for both witchcraft and sorcery, as commonly distinguished, is *ubuloshi;* in fact, witchcraft seems much less important to the Bemba than sorcery, the deliberate use of magic for antisocial ends. The distinction between witchcraft and sorcery is not so much a social reality as an analytic convenience: its limitations are noted in a discussion of some recent studies: V. W. Turner, "Witchcraft and Sorcery: Taxonomy versus Dynamics," *Africa,* XXXIV (1964), 314-24.

[6] Cf. M. G. Marwick, *Sorcery in its Social Setting* (Manchester, 1965); Mary Douglas, *The Lele of the Kasai* (London, 1963). Among the Cewa, in contrast to the Bemba, the ordeal was administered "at the behest of chiefs and village headmen . . . to whole village populations at a time . . . as a routine measure of social hygiene." (Marwick, *Sorcery,* 87). But see Mary Douglas, "Witch Beliefs in Central Africa," *Africa,* XXXVII (1967), 72-80, esp. 79-80.

Under colonial rule, however, it is likely that beliefs in the power of magic tended to gain ground among the Bemba, as perhaps among some other African peoples, while beliefs in the efficacy of the chiefs and their ancestors diminished.[7] Large-scale labor migration to the Copperbelt aggravated tensions inherent in the structure of Bemba villages and undermined the always precarious rural economy; and life in the towns, where the Bemba became involved in a worldwide economy, brought new and mysterious hazards while also bringing opportunities for personal gain and feelings of jealousy. Thus the people increasingly found themselves in situations of insecurity for which sorcery was the conventional explanation. With wages, charms could be bought, but as Audrey Richards observes, "Wherever protective magic is freely bought and sold there is an atmosphere of mutual suspicion between individuals. Protective magic, like protective armaments, increases the sense of insecurity it was bought to end."[8] At the same time, the old checks on sorcery had been removed: it was illegal to make charges of sorcery, and chiefs could not administer the poison ordeal. And though the traditional system of chiefs was used by the government in its rural administration, their political and religious authority was severely curbed. The old communal rituals were held less and less frequently, and, as perspectives extended beyond Bembaland, it was harder to believe that Bemba spirits were accountable for the changes and chances of life. It is not at all clear that accusations of sorcery among the Bemba increased as a result of modern social change,[9] but it does seem that for them at least there was good reason to believe that sorcery was a more potent social evil than in the past.

---

[7] This paragraph is based on A. I. Richards, *Bemba Marriage and Present Economic Conditions* (Livingstone, 1940), especially 28-40; A. I. Richards, "Tribal Government in Transition," *Journal of the African Society*, XXXIV (Oct. 1935), supplement; Richards, "Witch-Finders," 448-61; and Taylor, 67-77.

[8] Richards, "Witch-Finders," 457, 459.

[9] Writing of the Ashanti, Goody has pointed out the difficulty of demonstrating either an increase in witchcraft accusations or an increase in insecurity and anomie, even if a connection is presumed between the two: Jack Goody, "Anomie in Ashanti?," *Africa*, XXVII (1957), 356-62. Turner has stressed that since not only social but also physical disease prompts witchcraft accusations, "waves" of such accusations may often call for explanation in medical rather than sociological terms: "Witchcraft and Sorcery," 315-16. Mitchell has noted in Salisbury, Southern Rhodesia, that personal misfortune tends to be attributed to the displeasure of ancestral spirits rather than to sorcerers or witches for the very practical reason that nothing legally can be done about the latter, whereas it may well be possible to appease the dead through acts of atonement or compensation: J. Clyde Mitchell, "The Meaning in Misfortune for Urban Africans," in M. Fortes and G. Dieterlen (eds.), *African Systems of Thought* (London, 1965), 192-202.

It was this background of religious and magical belief which for many years conditioned popular reactions to colonial rule in northeastern Zambia. Christianity and modern secular education alike were slow to develop in this remote and sparsely populated region. Social services were in any case grossly neglected by the Northern Rhodesian government, and in Bemba country there were no government schools or hospitals before the 1950's—such facilities were provided instead by missions. Since 1899 the Roman Catholic White Fathers had extended a network of mission stations throughout Bemba country. The only Protestant missions were those of the London Missionary Society, near Mporokoso in the far northwest, and the Lubwa Mission, near Chinsali, founded in 1905 by David Kaunda from the Free Church of Scotland Mission at Livingstonia in Nyasaland.[10] But the impact of missions on the Bemba, whether in terms of conversion or of secular education, has been rather limited. Some acquaintance with elements of Christian belief is fairly widespread, and numerous Bemba have been baptized; relatively few, however, are regular churchgoers. Few Bemba chiefs have become Christians, and these are not the most senior. Roman Catholicism is the predominant form of Christianity in Bembaland, but it is in no sense an "established" church. As for secular education, by 1952 there were only two or three hundred Bemba children in the seventh year of primary school, and until 1954 there was only one (junior) secondary school, run by a Catholic order, in all of Bemba country.[11]

It is thus not surprising that modern, secular political associations did not develop in Bemba country until the late 1940's, with resistance to plans for federating the Central African territories; and that such associations did not acquire a popular character until the 1950's.[12] Instead, the Northern Province witnessed a number of movements which sought answers to modern problems in the realm of the supernatural. Some proclaimed an African derivative of European and Christian teaching; some professed to eradicate witchcraft and sorcery; some

[10] For some aspects of the early history of missions in Northern Rhodesia see Robert I. Rotberg, *Christian Missionaries and the Creation of Northern Rhodesia, 1880-1924* (Princeton, 1965).

[11] As late as 1953 for the territory as a whole, children in the fifth year of primary school numbered only 17 per cent of those in the first year, and those in the seventh year numbered 4 per cent of those in the first year. Northern Rhodesia Government, *Report on African Education, 1952* (Lusaka, 1953), 47. For the history of secondary education in Zambia, see Trevor Coombe, "The Origins of Secondary Education in Zambia," *African Social Research,* 3 (1967), 173-205; 4 (1967), 283-315; 5 (1968), 365-405.

[12] For early political associations in Zambia, see Robert I. Rotberg, *The Rise of Nationalism in Central Africa* (Cambridge, Mass., 1965), 124-34; and Richard Hall, *Zambia* (London, 1965), 118-21.

combined both of these appeals. All may be seen as attempting, however naïvely, to develop new forms of authority and social cohesion in the face of often complex and bewildering social change. Such movements offered relief and hope in just those areas of experience where the strains of modern life were most acutely felt. Baptism assuaged the guilt and fear caused by neglect of the spirits; puritanical moral codes made good the damage done to older customs; doctrines of salvation promised dramatic reversals of European and African fortunes; and by attacking sorcery such movements attacked the very evil against which there had seemed least defense.

In 1919 there was a short-lived but dramatic response in the Northern Province to an African "Watchtower" movement—an indirect derivative of the American-based Watchtower Bible and Tract Society, otherwise known as Jehovah's Witnesses.[13] "Watchtower" preachers urged their fellow Africans to seek salvation through baptism and foretold imminent perdition for Europeans. Among the Mambwe, to the north of the Bemba, there flourished from 1917 to 1939 an independent church that was indirectly inspired by the Watchtower Society. Under its leader, Anok Simpungwe, the Church set itself apart from other Mambwe by the highly abstemious conduct of its members. Eventually they rejected all earthly authority, and the head village was burned down on government orders.[14] In 1925 among the Lala in the Central Province, the "Watchtower" message inspired the Mwana Lesa movement. This movement ended abruptly when an ordeal by water was used to detect sorcerers and many suspects were drowned.[15]

The Bemba, it seems, were hardly affected by these movements, but in 1934 they responded eagerly to the *mucapi* anti-sorcery cult introduced from Nyasaland.[16] The cult leaders, the *bamucapi*, effected mass purifications village by village, using a mirror to detect sorcerers and inducing people to give up all their charms, whether malevolent

[13] Rotberg, *Rise*, 66-68, 136, 139-40; J. R. Hooker, "Witnesses and Watchtower in the Rhodesias and Nyasaland," *Journal of African History*, VI (1965), 99.

[14] William Watson, *Tribal Cohesion in a Money Economy* (Manchester, 1958), 198-203.

[15] Rotberg, *Rise*, 142-46; L. H. Gann, *A History of Northern Rhodesia* (London, 1964), 232-34; Taylor, 26-27. It might be said that baptism, by total immersion, had become an anti-sorcery technique.

[16] Richards, "Witch-Finders," describes the *bamucapi* as observed by her and Bronislaw Malinowski in a village in Chitimukulu's area, near Kasama. I know of no evidence of pre-colonial witch-finding movements among the Bemba. No doubt there have always been among the Bemba, as even now, individual diviners of sorcery who, like the *bamucapi*, kept on the move to escape the resentment or disappointment they left behind them.

or not. The sorcerers were made to take the *mucapi,* a soapy solution of redwood powder which was said to react fatally on those who took it and then relapsed into evil ways; many people took it simply to clear themselves of the possibility of being accused of sorcery. The *bamucapi* made a real advance on the Bemba forms of sorcery control: not only did they promise to eradicate sorcery once and for all, but instead of killing sorcerers, they enabled them through purification to rejoin society and once again become trusted members of their communities. And the new procedure had overtly European-derived features—the *bamucapi* and their assistants went about their business in the brisk manner of clerks and hospital dispensers, and they preached sermons which spoke of the washing of sins and the second coming of their Founder. The support obtained by the *bamucapi* represented no mere retreat into a "tribal" past but a real desire to relate modern innovations to Bemba experience in a meaningful way. The *bamucapi* appeared, however briefly, to offer a means of obtaining a more effective communal well-being than did the attenuated forms of politico-religious rituals. The *bamucapi* themselves may have been more interested in making money, for they also sold new protective charms, yet they seem for a time to have generated a feeling of integration into a new and synthetic spiritual order which was more satisfying, in colonial conditions, than the precolonial beliefs alone could ever be. George Shepperson, remarking on the Christian elements in the *mucapi* cult, has suggested an affinity between such cults and contemporary independent African churches.[17] But, as B. G. M. Sundkler had already observed in South Africa, such churches are often themselves deeply involved in the struggle against sorcery.[18] In both senses, the *bamucapi* may be seen as forerunners of the Lumpa church.

The *bamucapi* did not stay to reap the fruits of popular disillusion; by the end of 1934 they had moved north into southern Tanganyika. For several years afterward there seem to have been no new religious or quasi-religious movements in the area. In 1935, the Watchtower Bible and Tract Society was finally allowed to send a European representative to Northern Rhodesia, and over the next two decades the Society gained followings in several communities, including the Mambwe, which had earlier adopted African versions of "Watchtower" teachings. The Society forbade involvement in politics, but was at pains to disavow civil disobedience. It eschewed the fierce millennial preaching of prophets such as Mwana Lesa, but it enjoyed massive

[17] George Shepperson and Thomas Price, *Independent African* (Edinburgh, 1958), 413.

[18] B. G. M. Sundkler, *Bantu Prophets in South Africa* (2nd ed., London, 1961), 255, 261, 264, 350-53.

support as a religious organization which, in sharp contrast to the mission churches, was to all intents and purposes in African hands. Again unlike the missionaries, the Society's preachers appeared to accept the efficacy of witchcraft and magic. In 1951, Ian Cunnison suggested that the Society's success in Northern Rhodesia accounted for the virtual absence of separatist churches there.[19] However, an independent "Watchtower" movement, the *bamulonda* (Watchmen), emerged in the Luapula Valley in about 1947; like Simpungwe's church among the Mambwe, this was distinguished by a strict moral code.[20] In 1950, the Mwakalenga church, apparently an offshoot of the separatist African National church in Nyasaland, developed near the Tanganyikan border.[21] And in 1951, in Bemba country, there was a breakaway from the Roman Catholic church—the *bana bamutima* or Children of the Sacred Heart. This movement, led by Emilio Mulolani, sought to create a fellowship akin to that of the early Church. It was much occupied with giving to the poor, and it endeavored, at a time of uncertainty and strain in family life, to strengthen the nuclear family by encouraging closer association between husbands and wives. This was an attempt, also made by the Jehovah's Witnesses, to achieve a new and essentially modern equality between men and women. Such a trend was obviously liable to misinterpretation and misrepresentation: rumors of outrageous promiscuity led the government in 1961 to cancel the registration of *bamutima* branches in the Kasama and Mporokoso districts.[22]

The Origin and Growth of the Lumpa Church

On September 18, 1953, at Lubwa Mission near Chinsali, the Rev. Fergus Macpherson of the Church of Scotland was visited by a woman who claimed to have risen from the dead.[23] Macpherson heard of her

[19] Ian G. Cunnison, "A Watchtower Assembly in Central Africa," *International Review of Missions*, XL (1951), 456-69 and *Luapula Peoples*, 205-7; Lehmann, 230, 236-37.

[20] Lehmann, 167, 238-47.

[21] [White Fathers], *Notes [et] Documents* (1963), 385-86.

[22] Kasama District Notebook, 280, National Archives of Zambia; Lehmann, 106-8, 113, 167, 191, 286. There is also a short account by Rev. L. Oger, W. F., "Mutima Church of Emilio Mulolani, 1955-1962" mimeograph, n.d.; Fr. Oger kindly allowed me to make a copy.

[23] The following four paragraphs are based on Fergus Macpherson's own account, "Notes on the Beginning of the Movement," in "The Alice Movement in Northern Rhodesia," confidential occasional paper of the International Missionary Council Department of Missionary Studies (August 1958), 2-5. As Rotberg notes

arrival shortly before the beginning of the midweek service and asked her to wait to see him afterward. When the service began, Macpherson found that the church was unusually full, and he noticed a woman "sitting against the wall, on one of the pews, looking very ill and weak." This was Alice Lenshina Mulenga, a woman of about thirty-three,[24] who lived with her husband and children in Kasomo village, a few miles from Lubwa. Lenshina herself was illiterate,[25] but she had once been a catechumen at the mission, and her husband, Petros Chintankwa Mulenga, had once been employed there as a carpenter.[26] After the service was over, Lenshina told Macpherson that she had been very ill; she had died not once but four times—the last time only two days before. Each time she had revived after mourning for her had begun. She had been called by Jesus to a river, where he told his people, "Send her back. Her time has not yet come." Jesus then told her to visit the white people,[27] who would have a message for her. The interview between Lenshina and Macpherson was watched from outside the church by some of the people who had come with Lenshina from Kasomo, so Macpherson asked her to come back the following Sunday and discuss her story with him in private. She duly returned and recounted her experience, adding that Jesus had taught her some new songs, one of which ran, "We will not cross the river until our hearts be washed." He had also shown her the "Book of Life": he had laid it on her head-cloth, and Lenshina showed Macpherson the yellow mark of its moisture. Macpherson now told Lenshina that he could not pass judgment on her story, but that she should give thanks to God

---

("Lenshina," 66), there are conflicting accounts of Lenshina's visionary experience. The various versions are compared in H.-J. Greschat, "Legend? Fraud? Reality? Alice Lenshina's Prophetic Experience," *Africana Marburgensia*, I (1968), 8-13.

[24] Rotberg, who interviewed Lenshina in 1959, deduced that she was born in 1919 or 1920 ("Lenshina," 68). Lenshina's age in 1953 is given as 29 by the *Report of the Commission of Enquiry into the Former Lumpa Church* (Lusaka, 1965) (hereafter cited as *Report*), 3. The same source gives Lenshina's full name as Alice Lenshina Mulenga Lubusha—Lubusha was the name of her father, the paternal grandson of a Chitimukulu (Peter Harries-Jones with Jacques Chiwale, "Kasaka: a Case Study in Succession and Dynamics of a Bemba Village," *Rhodes-Livingstone Journal*, 33 [1963], 64). Lenshina may be a Bemba version of *regina* (queen), but I do not know whether Lenshina took this name before she acquired any eminence. Cf. Macpherson, "Notes," 2; Lehmann, 265.

[25] *Report*, 3.

[26] Northern Rhodesia Government, "Background to the Lenshina Disturbances" (mimeo., Lusaka, 1964) (hereafter cited as "Background"), 1. This handout was printed in *Kwacha* (the fortnightly paper of the Information Department), 19 Aug. 1964 and 2 Sept. 1964.

[27] It is worth noting that Lenshina spoke not of *basungu* (the ordinary word for Europeans) but of *bena kubuta* (literally, "people of whiteness") which is not a term for Europeans at all—*buta* connotes goodness as well as literal whiteness.

for her recovery and serve Him from now on. She agreed to resume instruction for baptism, to attend church regularly for worship, and to gather people for prayer in her village.

In November 1953 Lenshina was duly baptized, with the name Alice, by the Rev. Paul Mushindo, the African minister at Lubwa. Throughout the following year, she remained in close touch with the Church leaders at Lubwa. Some of them, including Macpherson, visited Kasomo, where large congregations gathered from the neighborhood to hear Lenshina teach the gospel. Many came with her to the church at Lubwa, and several leading Christians there shared Macpherson's wish to give scope to Lenshina's apparent spiritual gifts, thereby keeping the "movement" within the Church. The mission lorry took Lenshina's choir to the nearby court of the senior Bemba chief, Nkula, and they seem to have sung there the songs which Lenshina said had been taught to her by Jesus at the river.

In November 1954 Macpherson went on leave. He then began to receive reports from Lubwa which indicated that Lenshina was straying far from the mission fold. Not only was she now calling on sorcerers to give up their evil charms; she was herself baptizing people and had attracted several who had been suspended from membership in the United Church of Central Africa, the Church to which the mission at Lubwa belonged.[28] It has been alleged that Lenshina, through holding services at Kasomo, had collected large sums in Church offerings and was unwilling to hand them over to the Lubwa Mission.[29] At all events, it seems that by 1955 there was little or no contact between Lenshina's following and the mission. Some time in that year Alice Lenshina and Petros Mulenga were suspended from Church membership, and the mission at Lubwa joined the White Fathers at the nearby mission of Ilondola in declaring Lenshina a heretic.[30] The final break came with an evangelical campaign in September and October 1955, during which African evangelists from Lubwa tried to reclaim Lenshina's followers. By that time Lenshina had her own ministers, who told their people to have nothing to do with the evangelists. The mission also took the unusual step of calling on members of the Church

[28] Macpherson, "Notes," 3. It is widely accepted that Lenshina claimed that God had specifically charged her with the eradication of witches and sorcerers, but, as Mrs. Heward notes, it is not clear when she began to make this claim, although the Rev. Kenneth Mackenzie saw a pile of anti-witchcraft charms at Kasomo late in 1954 (Woods, "Cults," 23).

[29] Report, 4.

[30] Rotberg, "Lenshina," 72, n. 2; Heward, "Rise," 6. The White Fathers declared Lenshina's followers to be apostate in November 1955: Oger, "Lumpa Church," 21. It seems that for both missions the heresy consisted in teaching that there are separate ways to salvation for Africans and Europeans.

at Lubwa to renew their vows: only four hundred did so out of about three thousand.[31] Many Lenshina followers were consequently suspended from the sacrament of Holy Communion, and Lenshina rightly regarded this as tantamount to excommunication.[32]

Macpherson had been much impressed by Lenshina. He was convinced that she sincerely believed that she had risen from the dead and desired to give thanks to God for this deliverance.[33] He was sure that Lenshina had not started as a heretic or schismatic, and he believed that "In the relatively dormant condition of the Church in Chinsali district, Lenshina's 'ministry' might have been an instrument of refreshment because in the beginning she seemed anxious to utter a call to renewal of life and confession of sin." However, the enthusiasm she evoked "called for more pastoral activity than was available. . . . The growth of heresy in the 'movement' and its break with the Church, I believe, resulted not only from the appearance of malcontents who took over the movement for their own ends, but also from the unhappy fact that what might have been a revival movement found the Church so tied to its set practice and so wanting in zeal and vision that it had not the strength of will to enable it to contain 'Alice'."[34]

Early in 1955, Macpherson returned to Northern Rhodesia, this time to work at Mwenzo Mission near the Tanganyikan border. In the course of a tour in the Isoka district, he encountered, not far from Chinsali, a village of Lenshina's followers. As night fell, they began to sing hymns—not the rigid tunes and stilted Bemba of the Lubwa hymnal, but hymns which drew freely on the expressive resources of real Bemba and on the striking musical art of traditional Bemba singing. "This was indigenous praise, simple, evangelical, and not in any sense heretical in its message. The Lenshina movement seemed to me to underline solemnly the need to give full place, in the life of the Church, to indigenous praise and expressions of worship. Lubwa had tended, perhaps unconsciously, to reproduce the formal solemnity of Church life in Scotland in the earlier part of this century."[35] These re-

[31] *Report of the Foreign Missions Committee to the General Assembly of the Church of Scotland, 1955*, cited by Rotberg, "Lenshina," 65, n. 1.

[32] *Report*, 4.

[33] It is worth noting that the Bemba word for "to die," *ukufwa*, is commonly used as hyperbole for "to faint." There is no good evidence that Lenshina is or was an epileptic. Rotberg mentions a story that she had fallen ill after eating poisonous mushrooms but is himself skeptical of it ("Lenshina," 68 and n. 1).

[34] Macpherson, "Notes," 4.

[35] Ibid. I heard a very similar account of the singing of Lenshina followers from a White Father, Rev. Lavertu, at Mulanga Mission, Chinsali district; see also *Notes [et] Documents* (1961), 403. The White Fathers' reflections on the lessons

flections were supported by W. Vernon Stone, who joined the Lubwa Mission staff in 1956. Stone acknowledged that Lubwa had failed to appear as other than an "outside-run, outside-financed organisation." He stressed that the "Alice movement" had become very far from orthodox, but he also emphasized that it satisfied a genuine desire for African participation in the life of the Church—a desire which could only be met through African leadership.[36]

The stages by which Lenshina and the Lubwa mission drifted apart are not very clear, and it is hard to say what opportunities there might have been to keep her in the United church. It was ironical that the mission should have faced its first crisis of sectarianism at just the period when a long established tradition of severe paternalism was yielding to the influence of a younger generation of missionaries. But it may not be unfair to suggest that it was perhaps easier for the one or two European missionaries resident there to take a broad-minded attitude than for the African catechists whose commitment to Christianity, to which they owed their social position, had been made through its manifestation in the particular environment of Lubwa. Such men, however dedicated, can have had only a very limited idea of the history of Christianity and the diversity of Christian experience. But whatever the reasons for the breakdown in communication, by 1956 Lenshina's following had become a Church of its own which could scarcely be accommodated within the United Church of Central Africa.

Lenshina's church derived its authority, not from the United church, but from Lenshina's own charisma. Its gospel was derived as much from Lenshina's visionary experience as from study of the Bible. It may also be that God was believed to speak to her even after her original visions. According to reports received by Stone and the White Fathers, those who wished to join her church were assembled under the tree where she had "died" in September 1953. They were made to turn their backs to her while she played on a reed pipe; its "unearthly sounds" were then interpreted by her.[37] Such reports are not well au-

---

to be learned from Lenshina were very similar to those of the Lubwa missionaries: cf. Oger, "Lumpa Church," 22-25. There is an interesting account by a White Father with Bemba experience of the use of genuinely African hymns; he suggests that dancing might also be introduced into worship, Rev. C. van Rijthoven, "African Culture at the Service of Religion," *African Ecclesiastical Review*, IV (1962), 320-26. Taylor also notes the importance of dancing for Africans as a form of religious expression, Taylor, 291.

[36] W. Vernon Stone, "The 'Alice Movement' in 1958," in "The Alice Movement in Northern Rhodesia," 5-10.

[37] Oger, "Lumpa Church," 3-4; Stone, "Alice," 5-6.

thenticated, but it is clear enough that Lenshina was believed to be divinely inspired.

Lenshina's actual manner and appearance were by no means sibylline. To Europeans who met her while she was at the height of her power and reputation, she seemed a quiet, motherly woman, usually to be seen with a baby in her arms. Lehmann called her "a healthy, rather plump and happily relaxed village matron."[38] Yet to her fellow Bemba there was nothing astonishing about the manner of Lenshina's leadership. It was, to be sure, a new form of leadership as befitted times of change, but it had roots in Bemba tradition. As a woman in authority, she was no stranger. In this matrilineal society the social role of women had always been considerable—a key part in the structure of Bemba ritual was played by the *banacimbusa*, women (often of royal descent) who supervised the girls' puberty rites. There were also the *bamukabenye*, "wives of the relics," who looked after the royal relic houses; and certain *banamfumu*, mothers of chiefs, held small chieftainships of their own and were accorded much of the deference and ceremony due to male chiefs. And as a host to spiritual visitations, in the recent past if not also in the present, Lenshina had her analogues among those to whom the spirits revealed themselves through dreams or possession. Moreover, it was, as we have seen, characteristic of people so possessed that they should expose sorcerers.[39]

From the early stages of her mission, Lenshina gave members of her following authority to preach. In the early years at least, such *badikoni* ("deacons") sought to give the impression while preaching that they too were divinely inspired; they preferred to consult the Bible in the privacy of their own homes.[40] It was apparently easy to obtain Lenshina's permission to preach, and this may well have helped to attract into the church a number of doubtful characters as well as political nationalists in search of a platform. But it was surely also true that, like any independent African church leader, Lenshina attracted people who felt excluded from full participation in the life of mission churches. (As early as 1932, Merle Davis had noted that the experience of the Copperbelt whetted the ambitions of African church officials for a greater share in shaping mission policy.)[41] In any case,

[38] Lehmann, 254. A British journalist who visited Kasomo in 1955 or 1956 gave a vivid description of "Lenshina and Child, within the foundations of her Church, surrounded by her black and ragged adherents," Cyril Dunn, *Central African Witness* (London, 1959), 36.

[39] Oger reports that Lenshina was indeed thought to be possessed by a *ngulu* but he gives no name to it: "Lumpa Church," 1.

[40] Stone, "Alice," 9.

[41] J. Merle Davis (ed.), *Modern Industry and the African* (London, 1933), 370.

there were in Lenshina's church several former mission evangelists and catechists, who had been discharged at a time of financial difficulty, and Stone considered these to be "a steadying influence on the movement."[42] The influence of such men, as well as of Lenshina herself, may be detected in the fact that the Church continued to draw heavily on the tradition of liturgy and religious vocabulary of the Scottish mission, even after it came to include a large number of former adherents of Roman Catholic missions.[43] By 1959, the organization had improved: there was a "carefully regulated hierarchy," and applicants were examined by Petros Mulenga (who does not seem to have preached himself but acted as the Church treasurer). But the preachers do not seem to have been expected to understand Scripture; some acquaintance with Lenshina's doctrines as expressed in her hymns appears to have sufficed.[44] Indeed, local choirmasters were key, if subordinate, members of Lenshina's organization. As Lehmann observed, "The most important medium in the Lumpa congregations is not the spoken but the sung word."[45]

The message of Lenshina was typical of Christian revivalism the world over, with one significant addition—the injunction against sorcery and witchcraft. Her hymns called sinners to repentance:

> Shout to the desert, shout:
> Leave beer and witchcraft.

She preached a puritanical moral code. Her followers were to forswear polygamy, tobacco, beer, and "all primitive dances," and they were not to engage in sorcery or divination. The rules of her Church, which were codified in 1957, listed these prohibitions along with others taken from the Decalogue; they also included exhortations to prayer and to quiet and unselfish living.[46] How far this morality was actually enforced is uncertain. The strictures against drink, at least, had a limited effect, but in 1956 the District Commissioner at Chinsali commented

[42] Stone, 8.

[43] Lehmann, 261.

[44] Rotberg, "Lenshina," 74.

[45] Lehmann, 255; and 256-59 for the texts of some hymns. The rules for Lenshina's choirs are given in the *Report* as Appendix C. Oger, presumably referring to the earliest days, says that deacons had to go to Kasomo each month to learn new hymns. He also says that there were "senior deacons" in charge of a number of churches: "Lumpa Church," 16.

[46] Lehmann, 253, gives an English text which appears to be an original. A similar version, which is clearly a translation, is given in the *Report*, 17. Another translation, obviously from the same Bemba original, is given by Oger together with the Bemba text, which is dated Kasomo, 13 Dec. 1957, "Lumpa Church," 26-27. A rather different list was sent to the Governor, Rotberg, "Lenshina," 71.

(on what evidence I do not know) on "the new high sex morality" under Lenshina's influence.[47] Lehmann noted the importance of this moral discipline on the Copperbelt as "a strong unifying force among people of such varying spiritual backgrounds."[48] And she also stresses that the moral impact of Lenshina went deeper than the externals of behavior. The hymns, several of which are highly poetic, seem to echo a mystical experience. They warn of the fires of hell which await the evildoer, but they also dwell on the sorrow of being estranged from God and describe the joy of those who are made clean and are united with their Savior in the "new Zion."

> You who love the land of darkness,
> let us break through, be saved.
> He will help us in everything,
> he will take us out of evil,
> when, when?
>
> Come all near,
> it is my Father,
> he calls us.
> Stand all in a line!
> Those who stay behind should look at us, the brothers.
> Our Father stretched his arm out
> You are blessed, you who have been given.
> Now shout with joy, you blessed ones.
>
> Gather all together for the Lord.
> We shall be spread out far and wide in the beautiful country;
> We shall always roll in the dust, [the greeting for a chief]
> hallelujah, always.
>
> You, the mountain of refuge which stands in this world,
> you, the highest mountain.
> Those who fail to climb this mountain,
> they shall be cut to pieces.
> But you who have climbed the mountain
> rejoice, sing.
> You are fortunate, you have found the refuge.[49]

This doctrine of regeneration was central to the belief and practice of Lenshina's church, and it claimed that she herself could effect such regeneration. The theology, while recognizably Christian in out-

[47] Rotberg, "Lenshina," 71; Lehmann, 266, 274.
[48] Lehmann, 266-67.
[49] Ibid., 257-58.

line, remained ill-defined. The hymns speak frequently of Jesus as a Savior, and they occasionally refer to the Crucifixion and Second Coming. But some hymns represent Lenshina herself as the Savior, sent by God as a result of the failure of other churches to achieve His purposes.[50] The Crucifixion does not seem to be invested with the redemptive power which orthodoxy ascribes to it, and this is borne out by the absence of any form of Communion in Lenshina's church.[51] The principal sacrament administered by Lenshina was baptism. This was performed, in the name of the Father, Son, and Holy Ghost, by sprinkling water from a supply which was said to have been "given" to Lenshina and supposedly never diminished.[52] Moreover, it seems that only Lenshina herself could baptize.[53]

Through baptism, sinners were purified of their past delinquencies and gained assurance of salvation. And of such repentance and hope for redemption there was persuasive and visible proof. Immediately before baptism, each adherent had to confess to any previous use of magic, black or white, and hand over such charms as he or she possessed. Piles of these charms accumulated in a hut near Lenshina's house at Kasomo, testifying both to her success in extracting them and to her immunity from any malevolence which they might have contained.[54] But the important point is that, like the *bamucapi* and some African "Watchtower" preachers,[55] Lenshina addressed herself with equal zeal to ridding people of both malevolent and protective charms. From the point of view of society as a whole rather than of any one individual, all magic is fraught with danger inasmuch as it may be suspected of favoring one man at another's expense. Thus, to gain complete immunity, all must be surrendered. More than many revivalists, Lenshina preached a *social* gospel. She attacked the use of magic as she attacked beer-drinking or polygamy, because it gave rise

[50] Oger, "Lumpa Church," 6-7.

[51] Rotberg, "Lenshina," 72. In fact, Lenshina forbade her followers to partake of Communion on pain of death, Stone, "Alice," 7.

[52] Lehmann, 264. Oger reports another, and not specifically Christian, formula. He says that rainwater was used; "Lumpa Church," 4.

[53] Lenshina told Lehmann that only she could baptize (Lehmann, 261), but Rotberg says that one of his informants was baptized "by one of Lenshina's priests" ("Lenshina," 74). The *Report*, 4, says that baptism was performed by Lenshina or Petros; the government handout quotes "an authority on comparative religions" [sic] as saying that the baptizers were usually Petros and "capitao Matamanga" ("Background," 2).

[54] Rotberg, "Lenshina," 70; Oger, "Lumpa Church," 3-4; Lehmann, 253, 261, 266; Dunn, *Central African Witness*, 36.

[55] Gann, *History of Northern Rhodesia*, 235; no details of time or place are given. In the early 1930's there were recurrent "Watchtower" campaigns against sorcery in the Mumbwa district, west of Lusaka.

to quarreling and ill-feeling; and on this score it seems that Kasomo village had possessed a bad reputation. Apparently Lenshina was not above issuing her own protective charms,[56] but, as with the *bamu-capi*, these were no more than supplementary to the main process of purification. She certainly had little need to use such methods, at least in the first few years, because her very presence could be felt as a force for goodness and peace, especially among the diseased who might well think themselves victims of witchcraft. Lehmann noted in a Copperbelt town in 1958 that people suffering from sickness or injury, or from personal anxieties, came to seek out Lenshina. She did not make any promises or gestures of healing, nor did she issue detailed advice, "but one could clearly see the relief which the people felt when telling her about their troubles, and their gladness to be admitted to her presence."[57]

It was, of course, in her attitude to protective magic that Lenshina differed most sharply from the missionaries. To them, it was harmless superstition; to her, as to anyone with a belief in the power of magic, it was (unless issued by her) as socially disruptive in its way as sorcery. It was her peculiar strength that she acknowledged the power of magic: instead of ignoring it, she claimed to conquer it. It is true that in 1919 Donald Fraser, a Scottish missionary in Nyasaland, had called on the people of Loudon district to deposit their "instruments of witch-craft" in Loudon church and he met with a great response.[58] But this initiative was not repeated,[59] and, in any case, no missionary could admit the effectiveness of sorcery even were he to admit the existence of sorcerers. A missionary required not only a surrender of implements but a surrender of beliefs. Lenshina, on the other hand, actually fortified such beliefs by the dramatic way in which by her ceremony of baptism she associated a person's sinful past with the practice of sorcery.

[56] Heward, "Rise," 6 (and Woods, "Cult," 21), based on information from the Rev. J. G. Fraser.

[57] Lehmann, 263.

[58] Stone, "Alice," 6; Agnes R. Fraser, *Donald Fraser of Livingstonia* (London, 1934), 193-95. I owe this reference to Dr. K. J. McCracken. Fraser himself thought he was leading a campaign against "witch-doctors," but 152 people gave up their implements, and most of these were probably not diviners at all but ordinary people seeking escape from the burden of diviners as well as sorcerers. They clearly regarded Fraser as a powerful new protector and took it for granted that his aid was to be obtained in exchange for giving up the old forms of protection. Fraser can thus be seen as the unwitting leader of a proto-*mucapi* cult.

[59] In eastern Tanganyika, however, the Church Missionary Society at one time encouraged "witchcraft confessions," T. O. Beidelman, "Witchcraft in Ukaguru," in J. Middleton and E. H. Winter (eds.), *Witchcraft and Sorcery in East Africa* (London, 1963), 95.

Yet, it would be misleading to argue that people joined Lenshina's church simply because she offered superior protection against sorcery, and that the Christian sentiments of the hymns were only a veneer. Many earnest Christians were troubled by fears of sorcery,[60] and Lenshina must have eased their burden while meeting their real need for a Church. And to a large extent their feelings could be shared by those who had not been Christians. As in the *mucapi* cult, the release from the power of sorcery was felt by all as a moral deliverance from a realm of evil. Evil was not thought of as original sin—a concept alien to Bantu beliefs—but as a malign mystical power capable of possessing people and of being manipulated by them. Not only individual moral or physical weakness, but a far more generalized sense of individual weakness in the face of hostile circumstance was likely to be blamed on such malignancy, especially, as we have seen, when traditional forms of social control were gravely weakened. And in associating their own and others' wrongdoing with the action of sorcerers, Lenshina's followers were not so far removed from those who, whether in the first century or the sixteenth, engaged in a battle with Satan. One might indeed say that Lenshina exchanged the heritage of Calvin for that of Martin Luther—especially since the feeling of benediction and deliverance from the trammels of sin inspired, as with Luther, a new and ardent hymnody in which all could share.

As an anti-sorcery cult, Lenshina's church was certainly more firmly based than the *mucapi* cult twenty years earlier. But the *bamucapi* had introduced two important innovations to Bemba techniques of sorcery control. They sought not simply to control it but to eradicate it by the taking of *mucapi*. They did not inflict penalties on those whom they exposed as sorcerers—though they were ready enough with dire threats for backsliders. Lenshina also sought to eradicate sorcery, and being baptized by her, like taking the *mucapi*, was also said to mean instant death to any who reverted to sorcery.[61] But Lenshina went beyond the *bamucapi* in dispensing altogether with accusations of sorcery as a part of the purifying process. She thus kept much more clearly within the law than did the *bamucapi*. Indeed, in this respect, Lenshina had been preceded by the Bwanali-Mpulumutsi cult which flourished in southeastern Northern Rhodesia and southern Nyasaland in 1947, an area where the *bamucapi* were also remembered. In this cult, as in Lenshina's, confession replaced accusation. After confession, a medicine was administered which, like the *mucapi* solution, reacted on backsliders, but the medicine also provided immunity to the truly

---

[60] Cf. Lehmann, 98-103.

[61] Oger, "Lumpa Church," 13. This threat is presumably to be linked with the warning against Communion, see n. 51 above.

penitent. Indeed, the cult went beyond Lenshina's in that no other charms were issued.[62] It may be that Lenshina knew of this cult, but it would not be surprising that two fairly distant areas with similar experiences of anti-sorcery activity should independently have made similar advances in technique.[63] It is also significant that in the Bwanali-Mpulumutsi cult, though to a lesser extent than with Lenshina, the more refined technique was evidently associated with a fuller and more explicit appeal to Christianity than had been made by the *bamucapi*.[64] Popular beliefs had been exposed, however partially, to another twenty years of mission influence and were that much more responsive to a Christian type of doctrine and the Christian technique of salvation.

By 1956 it seems that most people in Chinsali district belonged to Lenshina's church.[65] We have already seen that in 1955 the congregation of Lubwa fell from three thousand to four hundred. But Lenshina's influence was also considerable among the numerous Roman Catholics in the area. The White Fathers' mission at Ilondola, seventeen miles from Lubwa, had not been founded until 1934, but it had several missionaries in the field, a large school program, and had built up a much larger following of baptized members and catechumens than had Lubwa. In 1953 these numbered 5,915 and 1,694 respectively; in 1958, 1,300 of the former were counted as apostates to Lenshina, and in 1960 only 918 catechumens remained. There were similar defections from the neighboring White Fathers' missions at Mulanga and Mulilansolo, and in 1955–56 the Abercorn Diocese, which included these missions, lost 3,400 baptised members and 2,000 catechumens. (These losses were, however, partly offset by the recruitment of new catechumens, and by 1960 Ilondola had 6,391 baptized members.)[66]

[62] M. G. Marwick, "Another Modern Anti-Witchcraft Movement in East Central Africa," *Africa*, XX (1950), 100-112, especially 108, 111-12 .

[63] It is more likely that Lenshina made contact, in 1953 or 1954, in Ufipa (southwestern Tanganyika) with a witch-finding group called "Wachauta." They were apparently of Bemba origin, but their technique had little in common with Lenshina's—their medicine made those who took it have fits. (Information from A. E. M. Shorter, W. F.; see R. G. Willis, "Kamcapi: An Anti-Sorcery Movement in South-West Tanzania," *Africa*, XXXVIII [1968], 1-15.) All the same, it may well be that such contact is what gave rise to the story reported by the White Fathers that Petros gained inspiration from a visit to southern Tanganyika. As Rotberg notes, there is no evidence to support the suggestion that Petros learned from a Nyakyusa cult, Rotberg, "Lenshina," 68.

[64] Marwick, "Another Movement," 112.

[65] Macpherson, as quoted in Lehmann, 252.

[66] These figures are taken from the White Fathers' annual statistics, kindly supplied to me by Fr. Oger. See also *Notes [et] Documents*, 19 (1961), 404, 410. The figures I give do not correspond to those given by Rotberg, "Lenshina," 64-65.

The speed with which Lenshina's church grew suggests that she was remarkably successful in cleansing her home area of sorcery. But it is inherent in anti-sorcery movements that their work is never done; inasmuch as the results of their work fall short of their claims and the sorcery-free millennium fails to arrive, so the need for a bogey persists. Besides, although Lenshina's followers might themselves be immune from sorcery, Lenshina had a mandate to redeem the world as she knew it, and those few—missionaries and their adherents—who had failed to come forward to be purified by her were naturally suspected of sorcery.[67] Thus accusations were made against outsiders, even if such accusations formed no part of the cleansing process. In the course of 1956, Kasomo was visited from time to time by the Rev. Pascale Kakokota, an African priest at Ilondola, in attempts to recall former Roman Catholics to the mission church. In September, a Lenshina follower called Joseph Mumba accused Fr. Pascale of being a "wizard."[68] Fr. Pascale informed the magistrate at Chinsali, and the accuser was duly sentenced to a month's imprisonment. This provoked Lenshina's first brush with civil authority. She and her husband, Petros, went to Chinsali with several hundred followers and demanded that the prisoner be released, or else simply fined. The crowd dispersed after six people had been arrested, but some days later many Lenshina followers gathered to demand the release of all prisoners.[69] Lenshina herself told the people to go home, but encouraged by Petros they stayed, and he, with sixty-four others, was arrested. He was sentenced to two years' imprisonment with hard labor and received a further six months from the Native Authority Court of the Bemba paramount chief, Chitimukulu, which also imposed short sentences and fines on several others. Thereafter, the demonstrations ceased.[70]

This incident threw some interesting light on the evolution of Lenshina's church. It testified to the confident self-assertion of her followers. It also indicated that her authority might on occasion be less effective than that of her husband. The movement's rapid growth had provoked a spirit of communal strength and called for leadership gifts other than those which had distinguished Lenshina. Yet although the

[67] Oger notes that missionaries were the "enemy" to whom Lenshina's hymns so often refer; "Lumpa Church," 7-8.

[68] This is the word used by Rotberg, "Lenshina," 76, and the *Report*, 7. Presumably the word used by Mumba was *muloshi*, a witch or sorcerer.

[69] Rotberg, "Lenshina," 76.

[70] Heward, "Rise," 7, based on *Central African Post*, 24 Sept. 1956, and a broadcast by the Chief Information Officer as reprinted in the *African Eagle*, 16 Oct. 1956. Rotberg, "Lenshina," 76, says Chitimukulu imposed the two-year sentence, but this was beyond his powers. Lehmann, 252, says Petros was sentenced to three years' imprisonment.

mass action showed that Lenshina's church was a force to be reckoned with, the accusation which led to it may perhaps be seen as reflecting the basic weakness of any movement which claims to reform the whole human condition—it cannot admit its own (inevitable) shortcomings but must project them on the outside world. Inasmuch as it was an anti-sorcery cult, Lenshina's church was perhaps especially prone to this weakness. And, in course of time, scapegoats were no longer enough; doubts grew within the movement as to its own efficacy. The subsequent history of Lenshina's church bears out this generalization.

By the end of 1955, Kasomo had been visited by something like sixty thousand pilgrims.[71] In the last few months of 1956 up to a thousand pilgrims came to Kasomo each week.[72] These pilgrims carried Lenshina's gospel home with them, and congregations of Lenshina's followers began to spring up in villages all over northeastern Zambia and among migrants in the towns of the Copperbelt and others further south. During 1955 the Lenshina movement gained a considerable following not only among other Bemba and Bisa in the Chinsali, Kasama, and Mpika districts but among other tribes in the Isoka and Lundazi districts. In August and September 1956, twelve men in long white robes, calling themselves the twelve disciples of Lenshina, toured the Copperbelt making converts to the movement.[73] In 1958 the Registrar of Societies knew of 60 Lenshina churches in the Chinsali district, 20 in Kasama, 20 in Mpika, 23 in Lundazi, 6 in Isoka, and 3 in the Kawambwa district (toward the Luapula Valley). There were 9 on the Copperbelt, 4 in Lusaka, and 3 in Broken Hill.[74] By 1956 Lenshina's church had become known as the "Lumpa" church, from a Bemba verb stem meaning both "excel" and "go far."[75]

From the statistics on the location of its congregations, it is possible to draw some very general inferences about the forces favoring or inhibiting the expansion of Lenshina's Lumpa church. There are two salient characteristics about the rural areas in which it seems to have spread. First, they are all areas within which the Bemba language is generally understood. Thus, in the east, the Church found a following among the Senga and other Tumbuka-speaking groups, but these peoples tend to speak Bemba on the Copperbelt and have in

[71] Lehmann, 266, quoting a district officer's report of 1955.

[72] Ibid., 250. There was even a group of Cokwe whose rural home is on the Angolan border, a thousand miles from Bemba country.

[73] Report, 4; Manchester Guardian, 10 Sept. 1956.

[74] Rotberg, "Lenshina," 75, n. 2, lists the numbers by district and gives "Kasomo" 20. This is presumably a misprint for Kasama.

[75] Cf. White Fathers' Bemba-English Dictionary (London, 1954), s.v. -lumpa; also Lehmann, 252-53, where various meanings are given.

any case been for some time in contact with the Bemba and other peoples of the plateau. The Lumpa church does not seem to have made an overwhelming impression south of the Lundazi district, which is roughly the northern limit of the Nyanja-speaking Cewa. (It may also be that the recent experience in Cewa country of Bwanali and Mpulumutsi tended to cool enthusiasm for a cult that so much resembled theirs.) The second notable feature of the area of Lumpa expansion is that the Church had not proved attractive to Jehovah's Witnesses. Where the Witnesses were relatively numerous, as in the lower Luapula Valley to the west, in the Abercorn district to the north, or in the Serenje district to the south, the Lumpa church made little impact. It has been asserted that no Witnesses went over to the Lumpa church,[76] and this conclusion seems very probable since they already enjoyed one of the main advantages which Lumpa had to offer—membership in a community independent of white control. It is probable, then, that language and local religious history largely determined the general areas of Lumpa predominance. Nonetheless, the reasons for the success or failure of the Lumpa church in any particular area would only emerge from a study of local politics and sociology.

The expansion of the Lumpa church attested to its strength as a Christian church as well as an anti-sorcery cult. It seems that Lenshina alone (and possibly her husband and one or two others) had the power to absolve people from the power of sorcery through baptism, and she began to tour the country for this purpose. With money collected from the faithful, Petros bought two five-ton trucks,[77] and in 1956 Lenshina made the first of her visits to the Copperbelt[78]—she made later visits in 1958 and 1961–62. She also seems to have made annual visits to the Lundazi district.[79] But the devotion of her following did not depend solely on such visits. They built pole-and-mud churches and gathered for frequent services, sometimes two or three times a week, singing Lenshina's chants and hymns and listening to their black-gowned deacons preaching stories and messages derived from Scripture.[80] Marriages were performed by the deacons,[81] and people desiring baptism were given instruction.[82] Funds were raised by

[76] Report, 9.
[77] Heward, "Rise," 7.
[78] Report, 5.
[79] Paul Clairmonte, "Lumpa Church Based on Fear," The Times, 6 Aug. 1964. Clairmonte was an administrative officer in the Lundazi district during the late 1950's.
[80] Lehmann, 250, describing a service at Nchanga mine; Rotberg, "Lenshina," 74.
[81] The Lumpa marriage rules are given in the Report as Appendix A.
[82] Lehmann, 261.

charging a penny for baptism[83] and by taking collections, but officials were paid no fixed salary.[84] The choirs, under their choirmasters, met regularly for practice and formed an inner core of devotees who maintained contact between congregations by traveling and correspondence.[85] The devotional atmosphere created at a Lumpa service by alternating edifying discourse and harangue, with solo, choral and congregational singing, could clearly be intense. Even Lenshina herself might be interrupted in the middle of a sermon by someone starting up a hymn.[86] There does not seem to have been any ecstatic behavior or symptoms of spirit possession. But some converts to the Church said that they had been prompted to visit Lenshina by dreams,[87] and it is likely that many of her followers thought they had had similar experiences.

Lenshina's gospel doubtless had more appeal for the illiterate villagers and migrant laborers and their families than for the small minority of Africans in Northern Rhodesia with modern skills and some literary education. The rule that widows were free to remarry whom they chose, or not to remarry at all, may have made the Church especially attractive to women. Yet her followers included clerks, mechanics, and builders, as well as ex-catechists. And in certain respects her Church was clearly a force for "modernization." This followed from its Christian character. Churches were built, newsletters were circulated, subscriptions and church dues collected. All of this activity, reaching from the far northeast to the towns of the Copperbelt and beyond, took place on an essentially non-tribal basis. An administrative official in Lundazi observed that the Lumpa church was the first modern influence to stimulate any general activity in the Luangwa Valley, where missions and schools had met with little or no response. "One noticed the long, strongly built pole-and-mud churches, which sprang up

[83] Oger, "Lumpa Church," 13; Richard Chellah (an administrative assistant at Chinsali) as reported in the *Central African Post*, 12 Sept. 1956. He adds that special blessings and cures were also sold, at 2/— for adults and 6d. for children (Woods, "Cult," 24).

[84] Lehmann, 262; cf. Rotberg, "Lenshina," 70. Oger says that deacons were paid £9 a month: "Lumpa Church," 16.

[85] Cf. the choir rules in the *Report*, Appendix C. In December 1964 I found in the remains of Lenshina's house at Kasomo a list of the choir members there, in which each member's Christian (or European) name was followed by a clan name. This is noteworthy, since Bemba clans are unimportant as corporate groups and clan names are not used as personal names, but I do not know what importance the Lumpa church attached to them.

[86] Lehmann, 260. Lehmann, 255-61, gives the fullest account of Lumpa worship, but see also Rotberg, "Lenshina," 74.

[87] Rotberg, "Lenshina," 73-74. Taylor, 279-87, notes the importance of dreams in the spiritual histories of individual Africans.

everywhere, and yet efforts to persuade the villagers to build themselves new huts, or grain bins, often proved abortive, and always long drawn out." There was also a great increase in divorce cases, due to Lenshina's prohibition of polygamy.[88]

Much the most impressive physical testimony to the Lumpa church was (and indeed still is) the monumental church at Kasomo. This was begun in 1956 and completed in 1958. (Lehmann noted that labor for it was organized in the same way as tribute labor for a chief: whole villages came in, with supplies of food, for days at a time.)[89] The church was built in yellowish burnt brick, on lines similar to, but slightly larger than, the procathedral at Ilondola (which itself was much larger than the Lubwa church). The cement floor measures 169′ 8″ x 39′. Pillars line the long nave; at the east end is a raised platform and a preaching stand. (Men and women sat on opposite sides of this stand, as in mission churches.) The walls and clerestory were decorated with paint, and small windows were glazed and painted yellow.[90] An inscription on the foundation stone tells of Lenshina's rise from the dead and her divine mission. Above the massive west door the words are carved, in Bemba, "Come unto me all ye that labor and are heavy laden, and I will give you rest." For several years this appeal dominated the surrounding low bush, and the building itself still does so today.

The Lumpa Church and the Rise of Nationalism

The rise of the Lumpa church coincided with the growth of African nationalist politics in Northern Rhodesia. The main stimulus to modern political organization in that part of Africa had been the preparations for federation between the two Rhodesias and Nyasaland; this was achieved in 1953. In the same year Lenshina had her first visions.

In view of the supposedly political role of separatist churches elsewhere in Africa, it is important to inquire how far the Lumpa church encouraged or drew strength from African political protest. This is not an easy matter to determine. It is, however, clear that the local environment was exceptionally "politicized." For several years, the Chinsali district has had a reputation for political volatility. This can be attributed largely to the relatively high educational level of the district, and also, perhaps, to its extreme backwardness in other respects. In these respects, Chinsali resembles other celebrated areas of political

[88] Clairmonte, *The Times*, 6 Aug. 1964.
[89] Lehmann, 265.
[90] Ibid., 264-65; Rotberg, "Lenshina," 75.

activity such as the Nkhata Bay district in Nyasaland, or Kerala in South India. In 1953 Chinsali was the only district in the Northern Province where school children numbered over 70 per cent of those of school age, and the school at Lubwa had been the first in the Northern Province to hold the Standard VI examination for entry to secondary schools.[91] Lubwa itself was the center of political discussion in the Northern Province. Since the 1940's there had been a Chinsali African Welfare Association. In 1950, a member, the Rev. Paul Mushindo of Lubwa, speaking on behalf of the Welfare Association, expressed a hope for eventual African government. (Subsequent members were Kenneth Kaunda and Simon Kapwepwe, both former pupils at Lubwa who had returned to teach there.) Early in 1952, the Association "rejected federation outright since no-one knew what 'partnership' would mean in practice."[92] And in 1950 Kaunda had formed a branch in Chinsali of the Northern Rhodesia African Congress, founded in 1948.[93] In the months before federation was inaugurated in 1953, there was a campaign by the Congress to mobilize rural opinion against it, and Chief Nkula from near Chinsali, like the other two most senior Bemba chiefs, Chitimukulu and Mwamba, was very sympathetic.

It may well be, as Macpherson suggests, that, from the first, Lenshina gained support from the politically ambitious. One of her earliest followers was Kaunda's brother Robert, also a member of the Chinsali Welfare Association.[94] It is also probable that Lenshina attracted many people who felt that the churches had not done enough to resist the federation.[95] Moreover, many people may well have been disillusioned with the African National Congress because its tactics had proved unequal to preventing the imposition of the federation. Once the federation was established, the Congress was somewhat at a loss, and it took time for new strategies and objectives to emerge.[96] For many people, the Lumpa church undoubtedly fulfilled a continuing need for an organization in which they could feel free of European domination. And, as Macpherson observes, Lenshina's status was enhanced when the

[91] Northern Rhodesia Government, *Report on African Education, 1952* (Lusaka, 1953); Hall, *Zambia,* 136.

[92] Rotberg, *Rise,* 230, 239.

[93] Kenneth Kaunda, *Zambia Shall Be Free* (London, 1962), 40.

[94] Rotberg, *Rise,* 239; Heward, "Rise," 6. Robert Kaunda seems to have remained a member of the Church until at least the middle of 1963. Soon afterward, he settled at Livingstonia; it is not clear whether he remained in touch with the Lumpa church in Chinsali (*Parade* [Salisbury], Sept. 1964).

[95] Rev. Colin Morris, as reported in the *Northern News* [Ndola], 2 Oct. 1964.

[96] A. L. Epstein, *Politics in an Urban African Community* (Manchester, 1958), 161, 190, n. 1; Hall, *Zambia,* 158-59, 173. Kenneth Kaunda had left Chinsali for Lusaka in August 1953. Kaunda, *Zambia Shall Be Free,* 55, 60.

District Commissioner at Chinsali called her in after hearing of her visions and told her to "watch her step."[97]

There is, however, no clear evidence that Lenshina herself had any special, political views beyond a generalized resentment of European domination and the conviction that, through her, Africans could work out their own salvation. A great many stories and rumors about her visions and teachings gained currency, and it is hard to say which accurately reflect her own beliefs. Rule II of the Lumpa church forbids racial discrimination, and at an interview with the press in Lusaka in June, 1956, she declared that "white and black should love one another."[98] But it is also true that at Chitimukulu's village in 1957 Lenshina said in a sermon that it was the Europeans who crucified Christ.[99] And it was said by her followers that the Lord had given Lenshina a book specially for Africans, since the Europeans had hidden the book that the Africans should have seen.[100] One Lumpa leader told Lehmann that "one day soon Mama Lenshina will give us our own Bible."[101] Such beliefs fostered the interest of Congress members in the Church, and during these early years, Lenshina does not seem to have objected to her followers belonging to Congress, although she did not approve of them holding office.[102] In the late 1950's the Lumpa church seems to have supported a protest campaign mounted by the Congress in the Chinsali district,[103] but, as one chief explained, "teachers and educated people join the Lumpa church for nationalist reasons, but though they are politically minded Lenshina herself does not want politics."[104] Lehmann stresses that "the essential emphasis of Lenshina's hymns and sermons is strongly pietistic and other-worldly . . . the most frequently repeated phrase is unequivocal: 'Do not look for the things of this world.' "[105] This theme was to become crucial in the relations between the politicians and the Lumpa church.

[97] Macpherson, "Notes," 3-4.

[98] Oger, "Lumpa Church," 10; Woods, "Cult," 39. Sir Stewart Gore-Browne, who had lived for over thirty years on a large estate at Shiwa Ngandu, fifty miles south of Chinsali, was invited by Lenshina to attend the opening of her church at Sioni on 30 November 1958. (Letter from Alice Lenshina to Sir Stewart Gore-Browne, in the Gore-Browne papers. I owe this reference to Robert I. Rotberg.)

[99] I owe this information to Dr. Audrey Richards who heard the sermon; she was misreported by Lehmann, 165. Lehmann adds that Lenshina's followers were asked to pray for Europeans since they had committed this terrible sin.

[100] Rotberg, "Lenshina," 67; Stone, "Alice," 9.

[101] Lehmann, 261; cf. 226.

[102] Report, 6.

[103] Rotberg, Rise, 273.

[104] Lehmann, 165. This seems to have been the Bemba chief, Chikwanda, from near Mpika; cf. ibid., vii. Oger makes the same point: "Lumpa Church," 11.

[105] Lehmann, 165-66.

The Lumpa church, then, was not, except accidentally, an organ of political protest. And when trouble did break out in 1959 it was perhaps due as much to the internal as to the external politics of the Church. To be sure, Lenshina's submission to the government would seem to have been qualified at the best of times and inspired more by pragmatism than principle. The incidents at Chinsali in 1956, which resulted in the imprisonment of her husband, certainly increased Lenshina's suspicion of the government. In 1957, presumably in an attempt to secure governmental approval of the Lumpa church, she sent a list of its rules to the Governor; in another such list, submitted to the District Commissioner at Chinsali, Rule I reads: "Lumpa Church is a church in which to worship God and his son Jesus Christ. It is not an organisation to make unruly behaviour with the laws of the country."[106] But this very insistence suggests that the point was not always appreciated by Lumpa members. During a state of emergency late in 1956 which followed strikes and disturbances on the Copperbelt, the Lumpa church there was regarded by many whites as the Congress party at prayer.[107] Lenshina herself and her followers (whether Congress members or not) had good reason to suspect government motives, if only because they were aware that the Church—rightly or wrongly—was seen as a challenge to white domination. (It was hardly surprising that in 1958 and 1959 Lenshina declined to register the Church under the Registration of Societies Ordinance.)[108] However, such mistrust is rather different from open defiance, or the deliberate espousal of political goals. And it was essentially this chronic defensiveness—amounting to a persecution mania—which determined the Church's relations with the government in 1959, and, indeed, subsequently. It was aggravated both by the growth of tensions within the Church and by a marked change in the position of the Lumpa church within the community.

The Lumpa church seems to have achieved its greatest influence by 1959, when its membership was probably between 50,000 and 100,-000.[109] It may be doubted, though, whether its organization was adequate to control and co-ordinate so large and extensive a movement.[110] And by 1959 the Church seems to have been faced with the problem not so much of accommodating the influx of new adherents as of rallying the faithful and stemming a growing disillusion. No doubt, like

[106] Rotberg, "Lenshina," 71; Lehmann, 253.

[107] Lehmann, 254. Lehmann gives the date as 1957, but this is a mistake. Cf. Hall, *Zambia*, 177-78.

[108] "Background," 5. But Oger, writing in 1960, says that the Church was registered by the government: "Lumpa Church," 4.

[109] Cf. Rotberg, "Lenshina," 63, n. 1; Oger, "Lumpa Church," 4.

[110] This was the view of the Commission of Enquiry in 1965, *Report*, 5.

any anti-sorcery cult, the Lumpa church ran into the problems posed by the apparent persistence of sorcery.[111] Its techniques might be more sophisticated and encourage a more genuine sense of spiritual security than the nostrums of the *bamucapi* or the atrocities of Mwana Lesa but, insofar as Lumpa followers continued in fact to be troubled by the ills that had previously beset them, there would be a tendency to suspect that Lenshina's techniques of individual and social regeneration were not quite all they were made out to be. The rumors of the forthcoming "black" Bible or of the second coming of Christ on a black cloud[112] were symptomatic of a millenarian expectancy which was clearly beyond Lenshina's ability to satisfy. From December 1954, Lenshina had issued seeds at sowing time and blessed them and had also issued charms to guarantee full granaries;[113] it seems that by 1956 some people were blaming her for crop failures or even the normal annual food shortages.[114] There may also have been some dissatisfaction with other leaders. (It is doubtful whether—as several Europeans believed—Petros actually masterminded Lenshina's church as a carefully planned hoax, but he had made questionable use of church funds.)[115]

In 1958 there was a specific disappointment. In the course of that year, the great church at Kasomo was completed, and after several postponements it was finally opened with great ceremony in November.[116] Lenshina may have promised that when the church was finished Christ would come. At all events, this belief was held by several people, and a special pillar was built on which He could alight. Thousands of Lenshina's followers gathered at Kasomo, some coming from the Congo and Southern Rhodesia. No proper arrangements had been made for their food and shelter. The rains broke and the crowd which filled the church for the ceremony and the expected revelation was wet, tired, and querulous. Christ did not appear, and one suspects that

111 This weakness in anti-sorcery cults has been stressed by Mary Douglas, "Techniques of Sorcery Control in Central Africa," in Middleton and Winter (eds.), *Witchcraft and Sorcery in East Africa,* 123-41. See also Douglas's note on Lenshina, "Against Witchcraft," *New Society,* 13 Aug. 64.

112 These beliefs were current by 1956: Oger, "Lumpa Church," 2, 6; Peter Fraenkel, *Wayaleshi* (London, 1959), 69.

113 Report of the Rev. P. B. Mushindo, as quoted in Lehmann, 250; Oger, "Lumpa Church," 14.

114 Heward, "Rise," 8, and Woods, "Cult," 21, 31, based on information from the Rev. J. G. Fraser who was at Lubwa from 1956 to 1958.

115 Rotberg, "Lenshina," 68; Stone, "Alice," 7-8; Oger, "Lumpa Church," 1; "Background," 5.

116 Heward, "Rise," 7, is evidently mistaken in giving the date as 1959. The date on the church is 1958, and it was in regular use when Rotberg visited it in mid-1959; Rotberg says it was "built" by Nov. 1958.

many may have gone home with their faith in Lenshina considerably shaken.[117]

A falling-off in spontaneous devotion may in part account for an increasing use of compulsion on the part of Lumpa leaders toward their congregations and toward nonmembers. In 1959 Lenshina visited the Lundazi district. According to Clairmonte, who was then a district officer there, "an old man was ordered to bring her tribute. He failed to do so, and Lenshina so far usurped the chief's authority as to give the man a 'case' seated in state in one of her churches. He was dragged there quite illegally by two *simapepas* [i.e. *bashimapepo,* a local term for Lenshina's priests], censured as though he had committed a crime, and then beaten up by them. The chief and his court officials witnessed this and yet took no action." This was apparently only one of several similar cases.[118] The Lumpa church, having gained great power, was loath to see it questioned or slighted.

There was, though, a more fundamental reason why the Lumpa church should have come to arrogate governmental functions and disregard the authority of chiefs. Lenshina claimed to provide an answer to the troubles, not just of individuals, but of society at large. Her concern with sorcery as well as with the more obvious manifestations of human sinfulness plainly showed this. The Lumpa church had its own means to personal salvation and communal harmony. Implicitly at least, these rendered superfluous all other techniques of social control. Insofar as it was millenarian, the gospel of the Lumpa church was inherently anarchic—like that of the Anabaptists, or like Marxist prophecy. No other authority, whether derived from ancestral spirits or Acts of Parliament, was truly valid, but instead it was positively dangerous, inasmuch as it represented a refusal to join with the Lumpa church in being absolved of sorcery. Hence the trouble in Chinsali in 1956; hence also the situation in Lundazi. As Clairmonte remarks, "There was no standing aside, in the villages there could be no secrecy. The villager either belonged to the Lumpa Church or he did not."[119] And in practice—again like many another analogous movement—the Lumpa church was theocratic because it recognized no source of authority other than its own. It may be that this theocratic tendency was nourished by the very tradition of chieftainship with which Lenshina competed. Her Bemba followers had been brought up in an environment where great political and religious authority had been vested in

[117] Stone, "Alice," 6; Rev. Levesque, W. F., Mulanga mission, 28 Apr. 1965; Heward, "Rise," 8, and Woods, "Cult," 42, based on information from the Rev. J. G. Fraser.

[118] Clairmonte, *The Times,* 6 Aug. 1964.

[119] Ibid.

chiefs, and, even though this authority was no longer fully exercised, it may still be said to have been very much a social ideal.

Lenshina might disclaim any wish to "make unruly behaviour" but, like the Jehovah's Witnesses and many other independent churches such as that of Anok Simpungwe, the Lumpa church engaged in politics by the very act of eschewing participation in the larger political structure.[120] As early as 1956 Lenshina's followers were said to believe that "Lenshina will rule over all the chiefs," that she alone would hear cases.[121] And by 1959 the Lumpa church had seriously undermined the Native Authorities. In Chinsali as well as in the Lundazi district, chiefs were virtually powerless to enforce the law among members of the Church. Whole villages had gone over to Lenshina, and new ones were formed without seeking the local chief's permission, as traditional law had always required. In particular, Kasomo (now known to Lumpa members as "Sioni") was a law unto itself. I do not know what became of the hereditary headman there, but he was clearly of small account beside Lenshina, whose substantial house, surrounded by a stockade, like that of a Bemba chief, faced down the long avenue leading to the church. Yet Lenshina herself, in matters concerning the external relations of the Lumpa church, was probably of less account than her husband Petros. He was released from jail early in 1959, and he seems to have become a prime mover of resistance to governmental interference.

The population of Kasomo had grown to include many people from other districts who had settled there without obtaining the necessary permission of their own chiefs.[122] This breach of the law provoked Chief Nkula and the administration to take action against Kasomo in May 1959. Nkula sent his *kapasus* (constables) to evict the illegal residents. Both the *kapasus* and the District Commissioner's messengers were rebuffed with threats of violence, and eventually the District Commissioner told Lenshina herself to remove the immigrants, otherwise he would use force. This warning had no effect; a unit of mobile police was sent to the village, and it was attacked by a crowd hurling spears and stones. A number of arrests were made, and the offending villagers were removed.[123] No one was killed, but Lenshina herself fled in the direction of the Lundazi district, and her deacons advised her followers to carry arms in self-defense. One of her elders wrote a letter to the government about this time which eloquently expresses the Church's growing fatalism:

120 Cf. Cunnison, *Luapula Peoples*, 206; Watson, *Tribal Cohesion*, 201.
121 The Bemba chief, Makasa, received this report on 21 July 1956 from an old catechist: Oger, "Lumpa Church," 50.
122 Rotberg, "Lenshina," 77.
123 Ibid.

Therefore if it be God's wish or that he means us to suffer under the hardness of your hearts and by the power of your kingdom, we cannot stop you.

Our blessings may come from above by your temptations. What we know is to do the will of God who sent Lenshina back to us since we are led and guided by Him through the Lord Jesus Christ whom he sent to suffer under the hand of the Jews and who led Moses to suffer under the hand of Pharo. And if it is meant that we are led by Lenshina we shall suffer under the hand of Queen Elizabeth II who is in power now.

Let it be as the Father wills to do upon his people, whether we like it or not.[124]

Thus by the end of 1959 the Lumpa church was confirmed in its hostility to the government, at least in the Chinsali and Lundazi districts, the main rural areas of its influence. (The reaction of Lumpa churches on the Copperbelt to these developments is not clear.) During the next three years, however, there do not seem to have been any further clashes with the government. This was perhaps mainly because by this time nationalist politics confronted the government with a far graver challenge; one administrator later admitted that in the face of this challenge the activities of Lenshina's followers were "largely ignored."[125]

The nationalist cause in Northern Rhodesia gained new strength following the political crisis in Central Africa in 1959. Kaunda's Zambia African National Congress (which had broken away from the African National Congress in October 1958) was banned and Kaunda himself jailed. But further secession from the African National Congress formed the basis of the new United National Independence party, founded toward the end of 1959. When Kaunda emerged from prison early in 1960, his prestige greatly enhanced, he took over the leadership of the Independence party. The Independence party inherited and extended the support which the Congress had originally attracted in the Northern Province; the Bemba in particular had stood fast behind Kaunda, Kapwepwe, and other leaders who had refused to follow the path of compromise taken by the African National Congress. Thus the administration was challenged most severely just where the Lumpa problem was most acute, and it is likely that some

---

[124] "Background," 6. This source says that Nkula had visited Lenshina with the District Commissioner and that Lenshina herself called on the "foreign" villagers to register their move but was ignored. The *Report*, 8, says the trouble arose over the registration of Kasomo itself; as on some other historical points, this source confuses as much as it clarifies.

[125] Clairmonte, *The Times*, 6 Aug. 1964.

officials were all too ready to turn a blind eye to Lumpa illegalities. It did not help matters that the turnover of officials, which was high enough elsewhere in the country, was especially rapid in the Chinsali district.[126] Probably none of the administrators there in the later 1950's and early 1960's had any familiarity with the district, its people, and its problems. Chinsali was a "trouble spot" which officials were only too glad to leave.

In 1960 and 1961 the Independence party was busy establishing branches all over Northern Rhodesia. In 1961, following concessions made by the British government to the federal government concerning a new constitution for Northern Rhodesia, the Independence party launched a massive campaign of civil disobedience in the Northern and Luapula Provinces. During August and September, roads were blocked and schools (often the only familiar signs of government) were burned.[127] The struggle now was no longer against the federation as such; it aimed at the early creation of an independent African government. The impact of this struggle on the Lumpa church was profound. While the political campaign was at its height, Lenshina herself was absent from the Chinsali district. Early in 1961 she left for an extended tour of the Copperbelt and other towns in the south, and she did not return to Kasomo until May 1962. On her return, the District Commissioner, Chinsali, noted that she had lost much support during her absence. Later, a government account estimated that her following in the Chinsali district fell during her absence from 70 per cent to 10 per cent of the population; it also reported that most of these dissidents joined the Independence party and the United Church of Central Africa.[128]

This period was thus of critical importance in the history of the Lumpa church. Further research in Zambia is plainly needed if we are to understand the apparent large-scale shift of allegiance away from Lenshina and toward the institutions of the larger society— whether the Independence party or the missions. But it is clear enough that Lenshina's prolonged absence from Chinsali was a major error

[126] Between 1950 and 1963 fourteen different officials served in turn as District Commissioner at Chinsali: Chinsali District Notebook, II, 30 (National Archives of Zambia, Lusaka, KTQ 2/1); cf. Kaunda, *Zambia Shall Be Free*, 59.

[127] Rotberg, *Rise*, 312; Hall, *Zambia*, 201-9.

[128] "Background," 7. I do not have any United National Independence party statistics to check this statement, but I gather that there was no large or sudden return to either the Lubwa or the Roman Catholic missions. By this time, the Lubwa primary schools were under governmental management, so that it was possible for former Lumpa mission members to send their children to them without necessarily returning themselves to the mission fold. For the losing of support, see Chinsali District Notebook, II, 208 (National Archives of Zambia, KTQ 2/1).

of judgment. From 1958 at least, it seems that the Church had been losing support due to a growing disillusionment with Lenshina. And during just this period new life was injected into nationalist politics. We have already seen that although Lenshina's aims were not at all "political" in a nationalist sense, many Lumpa members had strong nationalist sympathies. Membership had been one way of asserting independence of European domination, and in the early years it was by no means irreconcilable with membership in the Congress. But such members may well have been dismayed by Lenshina's continuing, and perhaps increasing, dependence on beliefs in magic and in miracles. And by 1962 it was evident that political action would have the most influence; the wind of change was blowing in Whitehall and Lusaka as well as in Chinsali. Early that year there was convincing proof of the Independence party's strength when as a direct result of its violent action in 1961, the British government revised its constitutional plans once again: this time, the Independence party was able to agree to participate in a general election to be held in October 1962. From April to June, the Independence party agents were hard at work registering voters,[129] and they evidently gained the kind of mass support which Lenshina had attracted in 1956 and 1957. It is true, as Kaunda later admitted, that some of his agents used strong-arm methods,[130] but this policy received no support from the leaders, least of all from Kaunda himself, and it is therefore doubtful whether the agents would have been so assertive if they had not had a large measure of public support. The Independence party indeed achieved a cultural revival among the Bemba similar to that of Lenshina seven years before. Singing, for example, played an important part in the Independence party as well as in Lumpa activities: local Independence party agents and followers set Bemba and mission or "Watchtower" tunes to words that were racy, poetic, or eulogistic.[131]

Lenshina's reaction to this development was to hold a rally at Kasomo on her return in May 1962, at which she told a thousand of her followers to take no part in politics.[132] There were rumors that Lenshina had made some sort of alliance with the white settler United Federal

[129] David C. Mulford, *The Northern Rhodesia General Election, 1962* (Nairobi, 1964), 40-43, 52.

[130] *Northern News*, 6 Aug. 1964; Clyde Sanger in *The Guardian*, 7 Aug. 1964.

[131] There is room for a study of the role of music in African independent churches and African political movements. This aspect of protest is of course familiar from the American context. Sally Belfrage, in *Freedom Summer* (New York, 1965), has some perceptive observations on the importance of group singing for civil rights workers in Mississippi in 1964.

[132] Chinsali District Notebook, II, 208.

party, or had told her people to support the African National Congress.[133] Such rumors were unfounded, but they were naturally encouraged by Lenshina's long absence in the towns. The local administration was certainly widely assumed to be in league with the United Federal party; furthermore, it had failed to show itself as unequivocally hostile to Lumpa-initiated acts of violence as to those of the Independence party. It was thus not surprising that some victims of Lumpa violence despaired of redress through official channels and decided instead to take the law into their own hands. Passions rose high, and in July 1962 five small Lumpa churches in the Chinsali district were burned down.[134]

The 1962 election gave Northern Rhodesia its first African government, a coalition between the Independence party and the National Congress. The colonial administration became the servant of African politicians, and there was no longer cause for a major conflict between them. And, in the Northern Province at least, there was considerable rapport between the Independence party and the chiefs. The basis for such agreement had long been there, inasmuch as many chiefs had openly opposed plans for amalgamation and federation.[135] The chiefs' role as agents, through the Native Authority system, of the colonial government had compromised their role as spokesmen for popular fears of land alienation, and they were naturally resentful when Congress, and later the Independence party, threatened to subvert all civil authority.[136] But after the Independence party's accession to power such tensions naturally abated, and chiefly authority became more, rather than less, secure than before.

However, these major political changes simply aggravated existing tensions in the Lumpa church, especially in the rural areas. Government by the United National Independence party was doubly abhorrent: it aroused the hostility with which the Church by now regarded all civil authority, and it was feared as a rival in the struggle for the people's undivided loyalties. The colonial government, of course, had

---

[133] Report, 6-7.

[134] Chinsali District Notebook, II, 208.

[135] In 1953, the Mambwe paramount chief was deposed, and leading chiefs of the Ushi and Bisa suspended, for organizing resistance to the government; in the same year, Chitimukulu, the Bemba paramount chief, flew to London with other chiefs from Northern Rhodesia and Nyasaland in a last-minute attempt to stave off federation. Mwamba, the second most senior Bemba chief, had raised his voice against amalgamation in 1944 (when he held the Nkolemfumu title) and against federation in 1950. Cf. Watson, Tribal Cohesion, 219 and n. 1; Rotberg, Rise, 202, 230.

[136] In 1958, Chitimukulu banned the Congress from his area and was rewarded by the Governor with a chiming clock: Hall, Zambia, 174.

never aspired to being a popular government; it derived its legitimacy from Westminster, and its local support, inasmuch as it had any, from among the European minority. The United National Independence party, however, like many other African political parties, hoped to embody a truly national will. It was not content to represent sectional interests, even if these constituted a parliamentary majority, but sought to establish a new conception of political legitimacy and to mobilize the whole population in the task of creating a nation where none had existed. In a profound sense, the United National Independence party saw itself as Zambia—the name to be given to an independent Northern Rhodesia—and those who withheld support from the United National Independence party were implicitly regarded not just as political opponents but as enemies of the nation. This belief was earnestly held by many United National Independence party officials. Members of the new government and the more senior and responsible party workers recognized that this belief could not justify a disregard of the country's established laws and liberties. But such distinctions and limitations were less easily appreciated by the many zealous party workers in the constituencies. And once African self-government had been achieved, it seemed to many that the United National Independence party was entitled to enforce its claims to nation-wide support.

This "total" commitment to the cause of the United National Independence party found a ready, if perhaps temporary, response among the peoples of the Northern Province. Indeed, the pressures making for the "one-party state" can come from below as well as from above. Just as the traditional character of Bemba chieftainship, uniting political and religious authority in a hierarchy headed by a "divine king," may have served as a model for the Lumpa church, so too it may have predisposed the Bemba to accept a new political authority which in an important sense had claims to spiritual as well as physical power. (The actual erosion of the authority of Bemba chiefs under colonial rule need not be thought to invalidate this argument, for popular conceptions of authority commonly survive the decline or even removal of the regime which originally reflected them.) Besides, the societies of the Northern Province, like many others in Africa, were relatively undifferentiated. In precolonial days there had been, at least on the plateau, little economic specialization, nor were there many groups with particular local, ethnic, or cultural ties.[137] And Bemba so-

[137] The secret *butwa* society flourished in Northeastern Rhodesia in precolonial days, but according to Campbell, whose accounts are the main source of information on *butwa*, it did not operate in Bembaland: Dugald Campbell, *In the Heart of Bantuland* (London, 1922), 99-100. Cunnison gathered that in the Luapula region *butwa* denied external authority over its own organization. He was struck by the parallels with the Jehovah's Witnesses. *Luapula Peoples,* 207.

ciety in particular was spatially very mobile, with frequent movement between villages over considerable distances, and groups from tribes conquered in the last century were easily and rapidly assimilated into this homogeneous society.[138] Nor had sixty years of colonial rule done much to change this picture. Education and economic development had made little general impact, and the main change, labor migration, had hardly begun to alter the social structure despite its effect on the way in which it worked. There was thus little predisposition to see politics as a matter of competition and conciliation between different kinds of enduring interests. To be sure, pre-colonial Bemba politics were highly competitive, but they were essentially palace politics, based on personal rivalries within the royal clan, whose members were transferred from one chiefdom to another, rather than on structured competition between different areas.[139] There was, then, little encouragement to take a pluralistic view of politics, and the tribe continued to be a most important focus for political sentiments. Since the United National Independence party was far and away the most powerful party in the north, since several of its national leaders were Bemba, and since it had the blessing of the tribal authorities, to be for the United National Independence party was to show oneself a good Bemba, with the corollary that to oppose the United National Independence party was to declare oneself a foreigner, observing alien customs.

In such an atmosphere, it was inevitable that the quarrel of the Lumpa church with the government, with party officials, and with local chiefs should become even more bitter. At one time the Church had enjoyed mass support of the kind which the United National Independence party now commanded; now it increasingly felt itself to be a persecuted minority. No longer could it presume upon the relative indifference of an administration distracted by "agitators" or upon the impotence of chiefs in face of its own claims to secular authority. Instead, it found its autonomy progressively curbed and undermined. And the effect of such opposition was to strengthen the determination of the Church to retain, and indeed increase, its control over the earthly as well as the spiritual destinies of its members.

This problem had also come to involve a matter more fundamental than voter registration or party membership. Like many other Afri-

---

[138] Cf. Richards, *Land, Labour and Diet*, 119, 156; and A. D. Roberts, "A Political History of the Bemba to 1900" (unpublished Ph.D. dissertation, University of Wisconsin, 1966), 31-32.

[139] Cf. Roberts, ibid., *passim;* Richard P. Werbner, "Federal Administration, Rank, and Civil Strife among Bemba Royals and Nobles," *Africa,* XXXVII (1967), 22-49.

can independent churches, the Lumpa church faced a crisis over land. The Church's stronghold around Kasomo constituted a community more or less separate from the society around it. Similar communities had developed as Lumpa followers, in defiance of Bemba custom and Native Authority orders, left their own villages to form new ones which were exclusively Lumpa. These new communities needed land of their own in order to provide themselves with the means of subsistence.[140] Moreover, the shifting cultivation of the Bemba obliges them to occupy new land from time to time, as cultivation sites are gradually exhausted. Thus Kasomo and other villages needed to expand into areas hitherto unoccupied by them, and perhaps partly occupied by non-Lumpa villagers. And friction between shifting cultivators, which is generally uncommon in the sparsely populated Bemba woodland, was most likely to erupt in an area, such as that around Kasomo, where a mission and a district headquarters, with schools, shops and roads, tended to attract a cluster of villages. In this part of Africa, control over the use of land has traditionally been the prerogative of chiefs, and colonial rule had confirmed chiefs in the exercise of this prerogative. It would seem that for a time Lumpa followers were able to disregard such claims, but by 1963 chiefs were in a much better position to enforce them. Lenshina herself had apparently tried to lease a plot of land (where and from whom is not clear), but this was taken as proof that she wished to set up a kingdom of her own.[141] Whatever the political implications of her request, there can be little doubt that its rejection had important economic implications: her followers now felt that their livelihood as well as their religious and political autonomy was threatened.

Nonetheless, it was the political issues which remained the immediate cause of friction. Throughout 1963 there were several violent incidents in the northeast, especially in the Chinsali district, between supporters of the Independence party and supporters of Lenshina. These incidents culminated in large-scale fighting which bordered on civil war during the last two weeks of December.[142] In April and May 1963, Lumpa churches were burned in both the Chinsali and Lundazi districts. Local Independence party officials sought to compel people to join the party, demanding the production of party cards as a test of loyalty to the new order. Such illegal action provoked reprisals by Lumpa members, and destructive raids by one village on another became fre-

[140] Cf. Watson, *Tribal Cohesion*, 203; also Sundkler, *Bantu Prophets*, 69, 91-92, 104, 130.

[141] *Report*, 9. The date of this request is not given. The context merely indicates that it was made some time between 1959 and 1964.

[142] The next two paragraphs are mainly based on the *Report*, 11-12.

quent. The preservation of law and order was threatened, and if the Lumpa church felt itself beleaguered, the authority of the Independence party to participate in government was called into question if its leaders could not control their wilder subordinates. Kaunda, now Minister of Local Government, was approached by both Independence party officials and Lumpa leaders in an attempt to reach some agreement. In June 1963 Kapwepwe, then Minister of Agriculture, conferred with local leaders from both camps and their respective grievances were aired. Lumpa leaders complained that Independence Party Youth Brigade members banned their churches, that Independence party officials compelled Lumpa members to attend political meetings instead of going to church on Sundays, and that they demanded to see party cards and threatened those without them. Independence party leaders, for their part, claimed that Lumpa leaders organized the burning of party cards, that the Lumpa church expelled any members who had party cards, that Lenshina had declared that no Christian could belong to the Independence party, that Lumpa members said that Independence party members who had been killed during the resistance campaign of 1961 would not go to heaven, and that Lumpa members attacked Independence party members. Kapwepwe rebuked both sides, and for a few weeks calm prevailed. But in August there was more violence; in the Kasama district, two Lumpa churches were burned on the orders of an official in Chitimukulu's Native Authority (he was later imprisoned). Another meeting of leaders took place and they agreed on certain measures to prevent further trouble. This agreement was approved by Kaunda, when he himself came to visit Chinsali.

However sincere this accord may have been, neither side seems to have had much power to enforce it. Many local people, and not only Independence party members, believed that there was a conspiracy among the Independence party's enemies (the National Congress leader, Harry Nkumbula; Sir Roy Welensky of the Federal party; and Moise Tshombe of Katanga) to support Lenshina in setting up a "state within a state" which would effectively discredit the Independence party. Lumpa leaders, for their part, were convinced that the Independence party intended to crush their church once and for all. In early October 1963 six people were killed and thirty-two wounded in a fight in the Luangwa Valley. In the last two weeks of December there was bitter raiding and fighting in the Chinsali district, in the course of which nine people died. Two were followers of Lenshina killed in an attack by Independence party supporters on a Lumpa prayer meeting at Chibonga village on 22 December. Kaunda returned to Chinsali and engaged in long discussions with Lenshina (with whom he had once been at school). One of the main points at issue was the recent rapid spread of illegally-formed Lumpa villages, mainly in the Chinsali and Lundazi districts, but also in Isoka, Kasama, and Mpika.[143] Eventually Lenshina agreed to tell her followers to return to their original villages by 18 January 1964. "At Dr. Kaunda's instigation, eleven teams of representatives of both sides toured the entire district of Chinsali to inform the people of this decision."[144]

The Final Conflict

During the first six months of 1964 there was an uneasy truce. The federation was dissolved at the end of 1963, and in January 1964 a second general election was held in Northern Rhodesia, on a broadened franchise. The Independence party won a handsome majority and formed an all-Independence party government under Kaunda as Prime Minister. Nothing now stood in the way of achieving political independence, and in May Britain agreed that 24 October 1964 should be the date for the transfer of authority. The tensions and bitterness which had characterized the whole period of federation, and especially the last few years, now subsided. In the rural areas at least, the political atmosphere was at once more relaxed and more purposeful than it had ever been before. For the Lumpa church, however, the advent of independence was an ominous prospect after all the irresponsible threats made by local United National Independence party followers. People in the Church believed that a life-and-death struggle was at hand, and they began to make due preparations. New, all-Lumpa villages continued to be formed and some surrounded themselves with stockades,[145] evoking the days (still vividly remembered by a few old men) when warriors and slave-raiders roamed the plateau.

This period of consolidation and fortification against the outside world was clearly crucial to the subsequent conflict. As yet, however, very little is known about it. It seems highly probable that by this time there was an acute crisis of leadership in the Lumpa church. Signs of strain had been showing since 1956; they recurred in 1959; and the collisions between the Lumpa church and the United National Independence party throughout 1963 must have severely aggravated them. Meetings with government ministers placed Lenshina

[143] *Northern News*, 24, 27, 29, and 31 December 1963, dates this from Oct. 1963; "Background," 8, to November; the latter source gives figures of villages by districts: Chinsali, 22 (5,500 adults); Kasama, 6 (1,200 adults); Lundazi, 6 (1,100 adults); Isoka, 3 (450 adults).

[144] *Report*, 12; cf. *Northern News*, 31 Dec. 1963.

[145] Ibid. I am not sure when the first Lumpa stockades were erected; it does, however, appear that the government did not attempt to inspect them until fighting broke out in mid-1964.

and other leaders in the position of at least appearing to make concessions. These must have provoked heated debate among both the leaders and the rank and file. It is certainly clear that Lenshina was unable to persuade her people to return to authorized villages. It is doubtful whether she made any attempt to do so, because she would thereby have visibly diminished her authority (it is not necessary to suppose that her non-co-operation simply reflects the ascendancy of Petros). It is very likely also that internal difficulties were a factor making for still greater hostility to government. Such "displaced aggression" was noted by Sundkler as characteristic of South African independent churches.[146] Certainly the Church officials at Sioni and elsewhere in the Chinsali and Lundazi districts were determined to resist any further attempts by the government to assert its authority over the followers of the Lumpa creed.

As the sense of persecution deepened, so too did the belief of the members of the Lumpa church in their own invincible purity as an elect destined for salvation. The leaders of the Church, including Lenshina, raised the morale of their congregations by painting glowing pictures of Heaven, and by issuing chits which others described as "passports to heaven."[147] They spoke in terms of leading a holy war against the forces of darkness. The voice of Winston Churchill, rallying Britain against Hitler, croaked scratchily from old phonographs.[148] Cries of "Jericho!" resounded from pulpits and anthills, and it may even have been believed by some that by crying "Jericho!" in face of attack a Lumpa member could turn bullets into water.[149] There were also reports that Lumpa members sought immunity from bullets by smearing themselves with urine, or by eating excrement.[150] Certainly, they were exhorted to look forward eagerly to death, as a gateway to eternal joys, and two men are said to have attempted suicide as a result.[151] There may also have been a degeneration in Lumpa ritual. Tales of barbaric practices in Lumpa villages began to circulate, and

[146] Sundkler, *Bantu Prophets*, 173.

[147] *Northern News*, 4 Aug. 1964; Musosa Kasembe, "How the Lenshina Surrendered," *Drum* (Central African edition), Oct. 1964. A photograph printed in *Drum* shows a typed "passport" which seems to be dated as early as 30 Sept. 1960. The text is partly indecipherable: what there is would be appropriate enough for a religious identity card that could be shown to fellow Lumpa members, in imitation, perhaps, of political party cards.

[148] Kasembe, *Drum*, Oct. 1964.

[149] *New York Herald Tribune*, 6 Aug. 1964; *Time*, 7 Aug. 1964.

[150] *Northern News*, 4 Aug. 1964; Kasembe, *Drum*, Oct. 1964. Bryan Wilson noted that pollution with excrement was a protective device in the Munkukusa anti-witchcraft movement in the Congo in the 1950's, "Peril in Martyrdom," *Observer*, 16 Aug. 1964.

[151] Kasembe, *Drum*, Oct. 1964.

the Rev. Colin Morris, chairman of the United Church of Central Africa, later said "There is abundant evidence in Lumpa villages that revolting witchcraft rites were being practised."[152] It may be that the anti-sorcery element in Lumpa belief was re-emphasized at this time in new forms of exorcism. And in view of the history of certain other politico-religious movements, such as Mau Mau, it would not be wholly surprising if, under extreme stress, there were deliberate efforts to strengthen internal ties and sever those with nonmembers, especially relatives, by enforcing acts which, through the very disgust they aroused, reinforced the members' awareness of belonging to a group wholly cut off from the rest of society with its traditional taboos and restraints.

It is important to point out, however, that it was the core area of Lumpa support, in the eastern part of the Chinsali district and the western part of the Lundazi district, which was the scene of whatever increase in irrational behavior can be discerned. There is no indication that Lumpa congregations on the Copperbelt shared in this rising hysteria. They consisted not of villages practicing subsistence agriculture, but of people engaged, for the most part, in wage labor in towns or on the mines. Life in the municipal locations and mine compounds precluded the evolution of Lumpa congregations into residential groups. A few Lumpa churches may have existed in squatting communities outside the locations, but such hand-to-mouth existence would hardly have been consonant with the ordered and seemly life demanded of Lumpa members. Further research is needed on these urban Lumpa congregations; in particular, it is not at all clear how far they conflicted with the United National Independence party. But it seems that they continued to display very much the same sober yet fervent character which so impressed Lehmann at Chingola in 1958, and they made no violent attempt to resist involvement in the processes of government and politics.[153]

Despite the proliferation and reinforcement of unauthorized Lumpa villages throughout the first part of 1964, the government did not seek to enforce the agreement reached in January for the dispersal of these villages. There were Native Authority orders for the control of village formation, but their legality was in doubt. The Chinsali

[152] As quoted in the Northern News, 2 Oct. 1964. Morris visited Lumpa villages in the course of the fighting in Aug. 1964 and returned to the Chinsali district later in the year.

[153] Cf. Lehmann, 254-64. My own impressions of the Lumpa church in the towns are derived from letters to Lenshina from deacons and members in Mufulira, Ndola, and Lusaka in 1963 and 1964, which I retrieved from the remains of Lenshina's house at Kasomo in Dec. 1964.

Rural District Council, which replaced the local Native Authority at the end of 1963, ordered the destruction of unauthorized villages, but this order was not officially approved.[154] When fighting next broke out, it was prompted by another issue—school attendance.

Some time in the first part of 1964, Lenshina forbade her followers to send their children to school. It has been said that this decision was taken after Lenshina (who was illiterate) and her deacons had disagreed with some of her more educated followers over the interpretation of the Bible.[155] This seems very plausible. The role of the Bible in the Lumpa church had always been rather equivocal. It was probably seen by some as a challenge to Lenshina's own, more direct revelation, and those who hoped for a "black" Bible can hardly have put much faith in the "white" one. The Bible was usually invoked by way of greeting ("Yours in the Bible") in letters to Lenshina from urban followers,[156] but it is not at all clear how much it was actually used, let alone how it was interpreted. It is at least apparent that not all Lumpa followers were so ignorant as to be taken in by the increasingly wilder promises made by their leaders, and some, at least in the rural areas, may well have been alarmed at the bellicose atmosphere of siege fostered by the leaders. But in any case, in their progressive withdrawal from the outside world, Lumpa communities wanted eventually to assert control over the minds of their youngest members. True to a theocratic logic, Lenshina spoke of children being "educated by God."[157] And this ambition, more perhaps than any other, alienated non-members of the Church. Not only was education, as the path to worldly success, as highly valued here as elsewhere in Africa, it was at this time very much a political issue. United National Independence party branches were busy rebuilding schools which had been destroyed in 1961, and this work was considered a declaration of faith in the new Zambia. Furthermore, education was, as elsewhere, very much a family matter. The formation of Lumpa communities had already begun to divide families against themselves, but separate education proved the breaking point. "When the children were stopped from going to school, relatives hid in the bush and assulted the youngsters or tried to drag them back to school, or back to their original villages."[158]

[154] Report, 12.

[155] Kasembe, Drum, Oct. 1964.

[156] Such a greeting occurs in seven of the eleven letters to Lenshina collected at Kasomo in 1964.

[157] Kasembe, Drum, Oct. 1964. Years before, in 1956, it was reported that Lenshina's people said "We want a Lenshina school not a European one": letter of catechist to Chief Makasa, 21 July 1956, quoted by Oger, "Lumpa Church," 50.

[158] Kasembe, Drum, Oct. 1964.

The trivial incident which sparked off the catastrophic debacle in July and August 1964 reflected very clearly one aspect of the predicament of the Lumpa church. On 25 June 1964, a boy from a Lumpa village, Kameko in the northern part of the Chinsali district, was walking through a non-Lumpa village, Kasanta, when he was struck by his uncle, a United National Independence party member who was angry at seeing his nephew absent from school. The boy went home and reported his uncle's assault to the people of Kameko, whereupon fifteen young men from Kameko ransacked Kasanta village.[159] That the boy was chastised by his uncle illuminates the extent to which the Lumpa church was setting itself outside society. The uncle was presumably the boy's mother's brother—the Bemba call a father's brothers "fathers."[160] Among the Bemba, a man has rights of guardianship over his sister's sons, and these rights were particularly invoked when it came to sending children to school and supporting them there. Thus a fundamental principle of Bemba family organization came into conflict with a nascent principle of Lumpa organization—obedience to Lumpa authority regardless of other political or social ties. It would be rash to infer a great deal from a single incident, and in general the intensity of local feeling against the Lumpa church must have varied according to the relationships (in terms of kinship and other bases of association) between local United National Independence party agents, village headmen, and Lumpa villagers. Nonetheless, the point illustrated by the Kameko incident may well be crucial to an understanding of the depths of fear and hatred which were revealed by the events of the next few weeks. No longer was it, if indeed it ever had been, simply a United National Independence party-Lumpa quarrel; it was becoming a quarrel between the Lumpa church and the whole society from which it arose.

The attack by Kameko village on Kasanta brought in the police, who made several arrests on 26 June.[161] A patrol visited Kameko; it was attacked by spearmen and had to withdraw. During the next two weeks, the police managed to contact Lumpa deacons, and a few Lumpa members were prevailed upon to surrender their weapons. Meanwhile, the incident had persuaded the government that Lumpa

[159] *Report,* 12, 20.

[160] A mother's brother is *nalume;* a father's brother is *wishi,* the word for father. Conversely, there is no special word for a mother's sister—she too is *nyina;* but a father's sister is *nyina senge.*

[161] The ensuing narrative is based on the *Report,* 20-35, and also on information obtained from eyewitnesses by Robert I. Rotberg. For some contemporary reflections on the Lumpa fighting and its causes, see Andrew Roberts, "The Lumpa Tragedy," *Peace News,* 4 Sept. 1964.

villages could no longer be tolerated. On 9 July it resolved to enforce their dispersal if necessary. Kaunda visited Chinsali on 13 July in yet another attempt to achieve this object by persuasion, but the suspicions of the Lumpa leaders were now too deeply entrenched to allow any response. Lenshina herself sought to avoid meeting Kaunda by feigning illness, but eventually she did meet him at the district offices but made no compromises. Kaunda then ordered the administration to tour Lumpa villages, giving the inhabitants a seven-day deadline for returning to their old villages. And soon afterward the District Commissioner at Chinsali gathered together representatives of the Roman Catholic church, the United church, Jehovah's Witnesses, and the Lumpa church. Africans from the first three groups urged Lenshina to obey the government. But Lumpa unwillingness to cooperate resulted in police patrols being sent out to demonstrate the government's firm intention to break up the villages by one means or another. These patrols naturally stiffened yet further the Lumpa spirit of resistance.

In retrospect, it is clear that by this time the battle lines had been drawn. The government had finally resolved to break up the Lumpa villages, but within their stockades Lenshina's followers were prepared to meet force with force. The ultimate test of the government's determination came on 24 July, when a European police inspector and an African constable were killed at Chapaula, a Lumpa village near Chinsali (but in the Lundazi district) which had earlier chased away two district messengers. The District Commissioner, Chinsali, tried in vain to retrieve the inspector's body, and on the following day he returned to Chapaula with three platoons of mobile police, including European officers, and requested the villagers to lay down their arms. Instead, the police met a hail of spears, arrows, and bullets from muzzle-loaders. They retaliated, and after an hour and a half took the village, having killed twenty-seven and wounded fifteen; a few of the casualties were women. Meanwhile, the government decided to reinforce the police in Chinsali district with two battalions of the Northern Rhodesia Regiment. They arrived on 29 July, and the following day the first battalion occupied Sioni (Kasomo), after a fierce battle in which spears, arrows, and guns were thrown and fired with reckless bravado against automatic riflefire and tear gas—eighty-five people were killed. Lenshina herself was nowhere to be seen.

There is not space here to recount in detail the course of this conflict, nor indeed would such an account advance the present attempt to analyze the character and development of the Lumpa church. It will be enough to note a few salient points. On 29 July, it was reported that Lumpa members in Lundazi district were ready to resist the government, and early on 3 August a Lumpa party from Chipoma, a nearby Lumpa settlement, overran the Lundazi police station and did much damage to the township before retiring.[162] On the following day, the army took Chipoma, and the figures of the Lumpa losses indicate the suicidal recklessness with which so many Lumpa villagers faced modern weapons: 81 were killed, and 43 wounded, and only 11 prisoners were taken. As the army and the police gained control around Chinsali and Lundazi, and along the main roads, Lumpa members regrouped in the Luangwa Valley and on the Muchinga escarpment to the west. Also on 3 August, some of the many Lumpa members in the Senga chief Chikwa's village, northwest of Lundazi, killed the chief; on the same day a Lumpa party killed 17 and captured 50 people at Pikamalaza, near Chipoma. These attacks were soon bloodily avenged. On 7 August, Senga villagers killed 40 people at Paishuko—the target of a government operation which had been planned for the sixth but had then been postponed.[163]

There were no incidents in the Kasama district, and Lumpa churches on the Copperbelt seem to have offered no provocation. But news of fighting in the north understandably inflamed anti-Lumpa feeling in the towns, and on 2 August Lumpa churches were attacked in Ndola and at the Roan Antelope mine, near Luanshya. Some prominent Lumpa members were said to have left the Church, and one Lumpa deacon in Chifubu township, Ndola, was reported as saying:

We have been trying to avoid discussing this situation. It is regrettable that followers of our Church have been involved in unfortunate acts of violence in the Northern Province. The best thing now is for our members to cooperate with Government forces in ending the troubles.[164]

Elsewhere, however, the government could not hope for such co-operation, and the Lumpa church was banned on 3 August.[165]

On 11 August, Lenshina, who had eluded the army and police for two weeks, gave herself up to a European civil servant from Lusaka at Chintelelwe, a Lumpa village in the Kasama district which was not stockaded and had not been involved in the fighting.[166] She was flown

[162] Thus the *Report*, but according to an informant of Rotberg's the attack came from Chapaula, far to the north, which had been attacked by government forces ten days before.

[163] The army attack was apparently postponed "as investigations were in train with the object of devising some alternative method of conducting this type of operation in such a manner that the number of casualties could be reduced": *Report*, 27.

[164] *Northern News*, 3 Aug. 1964. The 500-strong Lumpa congregation at Mufulira sent Lenshina a letter deploring the violence at Chinsali (ibid., 30 July 1964).

[165] Ibid., 4 Aug. 1964.

[166] *Times*, 14 Aug. 1964; Kasembe, *Drum*, Oct. 1964. *Cintelelwe* means "shade," so the name may be an allusion to the Lumpa hymn "Great tree, a shade to make us all happy," cited by Lehmann, 260.

to Ndola and on 12 August was placed in custody, with her husband Petros (who seems to have been captured at the same time) and their children, at Mumbwa, west of Lusaka. Meanwhile a group of clergymen led by Colin Morris flew up from the Copperbelt and moved around the Chinsali district unarmed in an effort to induce Lumpa members to disarm.[167] On 13 August, leaflets bearing a message from Lenshina urging her supporters to surrender were widely distributed. Reactions to such overtures were mixed, but over the next two weeks several Lumpa members gave themselves up. The pressure to do so was now very great. On the twenty-first, the government was authorized to destroy Lumpa villages—stockades, houses, and granaries. This prevented Lumpa groups from re-occupying their villages, as they had begun to do, and compelled them to take to the bush where they lived on roots and berries, supplemented by game and occasional raids on villages. A month or more of this precarious existence began to wear down their resistance. Between 21 and 25 September, 560 Lumpa followers surrendered in the Chinsali district; most had belonged to a large group based near the border between the Chinsali and Lundazi districts, in the area of the Senga chief Lundu.[168] But a prolonged attempt to track down a similar group further down the valley, west of Chikwa's, was only ended when, on 10 October, a large Lumpa group resisted a platoon of police and in the ensuing fight lost 60 dead and 28 wounded; 95 were captured.

This engagement, which took place only two weeks before independence, was the last of the "Lumpa War." There remained the massive task of "rehabilitating" the captives. Their first and most urgent need was physical recovery. Many had been reduced to walking skeletons, and several months later many survivors were still not fit to leave the rehabilitation centers at Katito, near Abercorn, and Makali, north of Petauke in the Eastern Province. But far more difficult was the problem of resettling the former Lumpa followers within the communities they had rejected. Understandably, these villages were little inclined to accommodate people whom they had come to fear as beasts or devils in human shape; similarly, many of Lenshina's followers preferred the security of Katito and Makali to the hazards of making a new life among former enemies. The Lumpa villages in the Kasama district were quietly dispersed in September 1964.[169] But in March 1965 there were almost four thousand people at Katito, and in September there were still thirty-two hundred, though there was

---

[167] Clyde Sanger, *Guardian*, 7 Aug. 1964; *Times*, 11 Aug. 1964.
[168] *Report*, 32, 34.
[169] Ibid., 34.

no compulsion to stay.[170] By October, those at Makali were successfully resettled, but many remained at Katito.[171]

In addition to this large community of Lenshina followers under government care and supervision there was another over which the Zambian government had no control. Many Lenshina followers, instead of surrendering to the government, had made their way into Katanga, settling at Mokambo, just across the border from Mufulira. By September 1965 there were about two thousand there,[172] many making baskets and growing vegetables for sale in Mufulira.[173] The Congolese authorities seem to have made no objections, though they obstructed a journalist who tried to visit the settlement in July 1966.[174] Several members of this Lumpa colony wished to return to Zambia but were dissatisfied with the slow progress of resettlement schemes. In October they threatened to march on Mufulira, and there were further reports of restlessness in December. In July 1966 the government intercepted letters from some Mokambo exiles urging friends and relatives to join them but by October several had left Katanga and gone back to their home districts. In March 1967 it was reported that Lenshina followers in Mufulira were crossing over to pray with their fellows in Mokambo and to take them food. Some Mokambo exiles were still afraid of reprisals if they returned to their home areas (one of these was a woman who had left her husband and children behind in the Chinsali district and would not return despite their entreaties).[175]

The problem of reintegrating former Lumpa members into the community at large was, of course, closely connected with the problem of what to do with Lenshina herself, and whether the ban on her church might eventually be lifted. Lenshina, with her husband and seven other leaders of the Church, had been detained in Mumbwa under emergency regulations. In March 1965 the Attorney General stressed that the Lumpa faith was still strong in the rehabilitation centers, and that Lenshina could not yet be safely released. Lenshina herself appeared to agree with this. Meanwhile, a Commission of Enquiry was appointed to investigate the history of the Lumpa church and to make recommendations as to the future of its former members "with a view to the preservation of public security."[176] The four members of the Commission included, astonishingly, the Rev. Pascale Ka-

---

[170] Northern News, 26 Mar. 1965; Report, 15. An account of Katito appeared in The Times, 13 Apr. 1965.

[171] Times of Zambia (successor to the Northern News), 9 Nov. 1966.

[172] Africa Digest, Dec. 1965.

[173] Times of Zambia, 13 Oct. 1966.

[174] Ibid., 16 July 1966.

[175] Ibid., 6 July 1966, 13 Oct. 1966, 23 Mar. 1967.

[176] Northern News, 23 Mar. 1965, 24 Mar. 1965; Report, 1.

kokota, who had been accused of sorcery by a Lumpa member in 1956.[177] In September 1965[178] the Commission published its report. This threw very little new light on the nature or history of the Lumpa church; it did not even refer to the various works already published on the subject. It recommended that the ban on the Church, and the detention of Lenshina and other leaders, should continue until all former Lumpa members had been reintegrated into society. The Commission suggested that the rehabilitation centers should be regrouped into smaller "interim settlement areas," but was otherwise disappointingly vague.[179] By the end of 1966 the ban had been lifted on Lumpa meetings in rural areas, but they were still proscribed on the Copperbelt. Lenshina was still in detention, and a lasting solution still seemed distant.

Conclusions

As an example of religious protest in modern Africa, the Lumpa church is of special interest in that its growth coincided with the development of a successful national movement for political independence. At one time, there was a tendency to regard independent churches in Africa as safety valves for frustrated sentiments of anticolonialism. However, since independent churches have outlasted colonial rule, more interest has been taken in their essentially religious character.[180] James Fernandez has recently argued that the rise of nationalist parties and the advent of political independence have relieved independent churches of a political burden—instead of having to provide a focus for generalized feelings of frustration, they have become more specifically religious and limited in their aims. He thus discerns a trend away from "expressive" and toward "instrumental" behavior.[181]

[177] The other members of the Commission were Mr. Justice Whelan, Mr. Henry Makulu (chairman of the Public Service Commission) and Canon Mulenga of the Universities' Mission to Central Africa. None is named in the *Report*.

[178] *Zambia Mail* (Lusaka), 24 Sept. 1965. The *Report* itself is not dated (apart from giving the year of publication).

[179] *Report*, 16.

[180] E.g., Michael Banton, "African Prophets," *Race*, V (1963), 42-55. In a recent study of two independent churches in western Kenya, it is noted that one of these (the Church of Christ in Africa) declined to be "used" by nationalist politicians: F. B. Welbourn and B. A. Ogot, *A Place to Feel at Home* (London, 1966), 20.

[181] James W. Fernandez, "African Religious Movements—Types and Dynamics," *Journal of Modern African Studies*, II (1964), 531-49. His argument leans rather too heavily on Paul Raymaeker's "L'Eglise de Jésus-Christ sur la terre par le prophète Simon Kimbangu," *Zaire*, XIII (1959), 675-756. Kimbangu's church was the "nonpolitical" survivor of Kimbanguism.

But this line of argument also has obvious limitations. First of all, it tends to perpetuate the older theory inasmuch as it implies that "politics" is simply a matter of being hostile to Europeans and getting rid of them. It may well be that the "political" feelings of impotence or oppression which nourished religious movements in colonial days will be just as strongly felt under an independent government.[182] Second, the very distinction between religion and politics, though to some extent inevitable, masks the important fact that religion can be political in character and vice versa. Not only may a church encourage or thrive on sentiments of political protest, it may also, depending on its social basis, organization, and aspirations, be a body of political significance. And just as churches may retain their political character in the postcolonial era, so too governments and political parties may retain a quasi-religious character as forces for "total mobilization." Indeed, if nationalist movements are to survive and complete the work of nation-building, they cannot simply play Martha to the churches' Mary. As T. O. Ranger has pointed out, the task of new African governments "is to maintain mass enthusiasm and to demonstrate that they can institutionalize and make permanent their answers to the problem of how to increase effective scale without destroying African communalist values more successfully than the primary resistance leaders or the millenarian cults "[183]

These reflections indicate two ways in which religion and politics may react on each other in independent Africa. First, the more or less inevitable disappointments of independence may encourage participation in supernatural rather than political procedures for changing the world. This may be especially likely when an African government is in fact relatively unconcerned with maintaining "mass enthusiasm"; when politics, one might say, is insufficiently "religious." The Kwilu rebellion in the Congo seems to illustrate this possibility (I develop this point below). Second, a political movement which is highly charged with nationalist enthusiasm is most apt to compete and perhaps conflict with popular religious movements. Such a political movement may attract much support that might otherwise go to religious movements, but it is simultaneously and inevitably drawn into rivalry with existing religious movements which have acquired political signifi-

---

[182] Welbourn and Ogot observe that independent churches may protest against nationalist as well as colonial governments. Welbourn argues that the need for locally-based institutions in which to feel "at home in the impersonal wilderness of a mass society" is likely to increase under African governments: *A Place to Feel at Home*, 8, 144-45.

[183] T. O. Ranger, "Connexions between 'Primary Resistance' Movements and Modern Mass Nationalism in East and Central Africa: II," *Journal of African History*, IX (1968), 641.

cance, whether they articulate specific political protest or simply claim extensive, if not exclusive, authority over their members. This second possibility is plainly illustrated by the history of the Lumpa church.[184] Ironically, indeed, the crisis of the Lumpa church arose largely because it had originally articulated "political," nationalist protest but then ceased to do so. Far from resulting in an inoffensive quietism, this estranged the Church from the larger society and thus made it more of a political problem than ever before.

It may be convenient to recapitulate briefly the main points in this analysis of the history of the Lumpa church. Like many other separatist churches in Africa, it began as a movement combining a revival of African leadership and local African culture with an all-out attack on sorcery. What was unusual was that it arose at a time and place in which modern political sentiment and organization were also beginning to develop. This conjunction was poignantly demonstrated in the meeting between Alice Lenshina and Kenneth Kaunda in Chinsali at the end of 1963. The strange counterpoint of their very different careers illustrates the diverse ways in which Lubwa Mission helped to shape African responses to colonial rule. The mission had been founded by Kaunda's father, and the Kaunda home there was called Galilee.[185] Kaunda and Lenshina had for a time been together in the school at Lubwa. Later, between 1948 and 1953, Kaunda established a rural beachhead of Zambian nationalism in the Chinsali district; he then moved to Lusaka to direct the movement's growth at the national level. Meanwhile, Lenshina had her visions. As a result she also was baptized in the Lubwa church but then broke away to establish a spiritual rival to Lubwa—Sioni. Eventually, this also became an overt political challenge paralleling Kaunda's national leadership.

This conjunction, in place as well as time, of political and religious responses to colonial rule was perhaps the main reason for both the rise and fall of the Lumpa church. Throughout its history the Church was clearly sustained in part by a genuine religious fervor which, though often narrow and ignorant, was as recognizably Christian as some older manifestations of the faith. This religious commitment was perhaps never very widely shared, but it was the Church's most enduring form of support and provided the rationale for its transformation into a theocracy. For the first few years, the Church also enjoyed mass support, both as an anti-sorcery cult and as an all-African, "anti-

---

[184] In an article on the Lumpa church, Fernandez does in fact give greater weight than in "African Religious Movements" to the possibility of tension between nationalist governments and religious movements, James W. Fernandez, "The Lumpa Uprising: Why?" *Africa Report*, IX (1964), 30-32.

[185] Kaunda, *Zambia Shall Be Free*, 8.

white" organization, at a time when African political resistance was still ineffective. But the appeal to the fear of sorcery brought in the diminishing returns inherent in the nature of sorcery beliefs, and the political appeal of the Church declined as mass nationalism grew as an effective force for political change and a vehicle of cultural revival. But this did not mean that the Church simply relapsed into decent obscurity as a minor Christian sect. The fact that it had gained and lost mass support as a movement against sorcery and against European domination had a profound effect on its character as a Church.

The struggle against sorcery involved Lenshina in an increasing dependence on magical techniques, since only good magic (whether antelope horns, baptismal water, or human urine) is acceptable to the believer in bad magic, and belief in any form is likely to last only a short time. Had the movement been merely an anti-sorcery cult, it would doubtless have faded away like others before it. Being more than this, it survived. But as a Christian sect, the Church's capacity for teaching and ritual was very weak,[186] and it continued, in the face of adversity, to require nourishment from beliefs in magic. Lenshina was thus caught up in a vicious circle in which she was obliged to promise, and was expected to supply, ever more extravagant marvels: an end to sorcery, a "black" Bible, the Second Coming, immunity to bullets. And inasmuch as the Church was a consciously African organization, enjoying politically motivated support at a time of rising resistance to colonial rule, both the Church and the government were bound to regard each other with suspicion, if not hostility. Thus, from at least the time of its first clash with the government in 1956, the Lumpa church felt obliged to protect itself by developing those theocratic tendencies which are latent in any prophetic and millennial movement.

This trend to autonomy was further stimulated by the decline in mass support following popular disenchantment and disillusion with the Church as a means to a future free from sorcery and European interference. In an increasingly unfavorable, indeed hostile, environment, the Church had to find a new basis for survival. One aspect of it was the proliferation of new magical beliefs; another was the progressive withdrawal from the world at large into an increasingly self-sufficient and disciplined community. The phases of this withdrawal, following the original religious secession, were, successively, political (culminating in the break with the United National Independence party in 1962), economic (the demand for land), and social (the clash over schools and family responsibilities in 1964). But this total with-

[186] In this respect, there is a striking contrast between the Lumpa church and, for example, the two Kenyan churches described by Welbourn and Ogot in *A Place to Feel at Home*.

drawal from Zambian society by the Lumpa church encountered an ideal of total commitment to that society by the Independence party, and it was this head-on collision which provoked the bloodshed of 1964.

This tragedy—and for a disaster so entirely human in its causes this word is peculiarly apt—seems to have no close parallel.[187] There is a startling early similarity, even in point of time, between the Lumpa church and an independent church in Southern Rhodesia, the Guta ra Jehovah.[188] Its founder was a woman, Mai Chaza, who had a vision in 1952—a year before Lenshina's. In 1954 she made her followers abandon all magical charms; in 1956 there was a mass confession of witches; and in 1958 she obtained healing water from "Zion," after which her village, like Lenshina's, was named. Mai Chaza died in 1961, but she is said to have left a new Bible. It would, of course, be most interesting to know if there was any contact between the Guta ra Jehovah and the Lumpa church. This is quite possible since Lenshina had several followers in Southern Rhodesia which she visited. But the more important point is perhaps the difference between the historical and political situations north and south of the Zambezi River. In Rhodesia there is a mythos of tribal resistance without parallel in Zambia, and the Guta ra Jehovah specifically invoked Shona history and religion in a way that the Lumpa church never did for the Bemba. And though the relations of the Guta ra Jehovah with African political parties have not always been cordial, it has clearly not faced anything like the challenge with which a triumphant United National Independence party confronted the Lumpa church.

The Lumpa church also contrasts interestingly with the history of popular movements in Kwilu, Lower Congo. Here, between 1930 and 1956, there had been a succession of more or less millennial and anti-sorcery cults. In 1959 the *Parti Solidaire Africain,* ostensibly a modern and "instrumental" political organization, seemed, paradoxically, to continue this tradition for it gained votes by promising that "independence would be an era of leisure, plenty and happiness." Disillusion came swiftly and harshly, and the people turned to Pierre Mulele, who, like most African messiahs, began to create the good society at the

---

[187] Fernandez in "Lumpa Uprising" gives the Chilembwe rising and "Mau Mau" as examples of movements which have turned violent under extreme pressure. Perhaps more relevant to the Lumpa church is the example of the Ras Tafari movement in Jamaica, which fell foul of the police and by 1958 was dominated by "the cult of criminality and violence," M. G. Smith, Rex Nettlefold, and Roy Augier, *The Ras Tafari Movement* (Kingston, 1960), 19. (This thoughtful account could profitably have been studied by the authors of the *Report* on the Lumpa church.)

[188] I owe my information on the Guta ra Jehovah to Professor T. O. Ranger.

grass roots, enforcing a strict puritanical code as well as instilling new magical beliefs.[189] In Kwilu, then, as in Chinsali, a political party gathered mass support which had earlier gone to religious movements. But unlike the Independence party, the *Parti Solidaire Africain* did not have to contend with an existing movement (the latest had been suppressed in 1956). Furthermore, Kwilu, like the Congo in general, was politically inexperienced when compared with Northern Rhodesia and the Chinsali district in particular. The *Parti Solidaire Africain* operated as the improvised tool of an elite rather than as a genuine mass party. It would have been more successful had it been less hardheadedly "political" and attempted instead to meet the popular needs for a new world view and a new style of life. The situation in Chinsali was exactly the reverse: the United National Independence party was led by fully engaged politicians in close touch with the grass roots, and it had the popular flavor so lacking in the *Parti Solidaire Africain*—in a sense, the United National Independence party was for a time a new form of folk culture. But far from having the field to itself, the United National Independence party confronted a religious movement which was very much alive and was itself making political claims. Both Church and Party were competing for total allegiance. As I have argued, it was their similarities as much as their differences which brought them into conflict.

We may conclude that although to date there have been few if any parallels with the Lumpa conflict, it has considerable significance for the future. Wherever governments or dominant parties are actively concerned with fostering the sentiment of nationalism, there is bound to be some tension between these governments and the leading religious organizations, whether or not these are primarily "expressive" in orientation. (The Anglican church, not a notably expressive institution, has had its troubles in Africa.) As Fernandez notes, expressive movements are inherently ill-fitted to adapt to the "larger situation,"[190] but the important point is surely the extent to which a religious movement has established itself as a powerful and diffused social force, acting in several spheres of life so that there is an association between religious beliefs, residence, economic behavior, education, and so forth. The Lumpa church, in the rural areas at least, had obviously gone far along this road, and we see that other groups in Zambia are traveling in the same direction. Most important are the Jehovah's Witnesses, who, in central Zambia at least, are particularly to be found among

[189] Renée Fox, W. de Craemer, and J. M. Ribeaucourt, "The Second Independence: A Case Study of the Kwilu Rebellion in the Congo," *Comparative Studies in Society and History*, VIII (1965), 78-109.
[190] Fernandez, "African Religious Movements," 548.

the "progressive" farmers and craftsmen, and who form something of an economic as well as social group. Like the Lumpa church, the Witnesses abjure party politics, but they pay their taxes. Yet if their religion is hardly syncretic or expressive in the sense in which the Lumpa faith was, the Jehovah's Witnesses are recognized as a powerful force which could give the Zambian government a very difficult time. In the course of 1966 there were various minor clashes between Witnesses and the government, mainly due to the refusal of Witnesses to let their children salute the national flag at school or sing the national anthem. There has been a good deal of fiery talk, and there seem to be people on both sides who would welcome a showdown.[191] The situation in Zambia is not, of course, wholly typical. More than many African countries, it is torn by racial, economic, and ethnic divisions, and its sense of nationhood is too newly, and tentatively, won for apparent defiance to be regarded with equanimity. But it is likely that wherever the regimes of new nations seriously seek to retain a popular character they will conflict to some extent, sooner or later, with religious movements which have, for whatever historical reasons, taken firm root in African soil.

[191] See the *Times of Zambia* for June, July, and Oct. 1966. For the witnesses, see Norman Long, *Social Change and the Individual* (Manchester, 1968), esp. 200-236.

PART FOUR

THE EMERGENCE OF PRESSURE GROUPS AND POLITICAL PARTIES

THE NATIONAL CONGRESS OF

BRITISH WEST AFRICA, 1918–1935

MARTIN KILSON

The Formative Years, 1918–21

The idea for the National Congress of British West Africa is generally said to have originated in discussions in 1914 between Joseph Ephraim Casely Hayford, a Ghanaian lawyer and the first vice-president of the Congress, and Dr. R. A. Savage, a Nigerian medical doctor, who was practicing in Ghana and also editing the influential newspaper, *Gold Coast Leader*. A few Sierra Leoneans also participated in the initial discussions on an organization of black African elites, especially Mr. (later Sir) L. E. V. M'Carthy, a lawyer. But nothing material resulted from these discussions, presumably because of the onset of World War I.[1]

In 1918 the initiative for what was then called both the "congress movement" and the "conference movement" was resumed. This occurred in Ghana when the *Gold Coast Leader* issued a call for a conference to consider, among other things, means for achieving greater African participation in colonial government.[2] This newspaper gave the particulars of how, when, and under what leadership a conference of emergent black West African elites should be held. Similar discus-

I am indebted to the Ford Foundation Foreign Area Training Fellowship Program, to Professor Robert Bowie and the Harvard University Center for International Affairs, and to Thomas Hodgkin and the Institute of African Studies at the University of Ghana, for funds which enabled me to do research in Sierra Leone (1959–60) and Ghana (academic year 1964–65) on the history of the Congress. I am also indebted to Professor J. H. Nketia and Richard Greenfield, Director and Senior Research Fellow, respectively, of the Institute of African Studies at the University of Ghana, for research facilities which enabled me to complete this paper during the summer of 1968.

[1] David Kimble, *A Political History of Ghana* (Oxford, 1963), 375.
[2] *Gold Coast Leader*, Feb. 2, 1918.

sion of the machinery of such a conference took place in the Sierra Leone press, especially in the *Sierra Leone Weekly News*, whose editor, Cornelius May, permitted the newspaper to be used virtually as the organ of the incipient "conference movement." The Nigerian press was also involved in these discussions, particularly the *Lagos Weekly Record*, whose editor, Thomas H. Jackson, became the secretary of the Lagos group concerned with furthering the "conference movement."

Inasmuch as the idea of the Congress was Ghanaian in inspiration, the elites in Sierra Leone and Nigeria left the work of launching the organization to Ghanaians. It was not, however, an easy matter for the Ghanaian initiators of the "conference movement" to get the idea off the ground. A local organization, the Aborigines' Rights Protection Society, already existed. It had since 1898 been the spokesman for a coalition of educated Ghanaians and politically assertive chiefs.[3] Though the Society was not exactly opposed to the "conference movement," it hesitated at the prospect that its position as quasi-official representative of articulate African interests might be superseded by a new organization. Consequently, a rather bitter hassle ensued between those educated Ghanaians backing the "conference movement" and those behind the Society. This resulted in delaying the formal organization of the Congress until 1920.[4]

The groundwork for the initial meeting of the Congress was laid by stages. In Ghana in mid-1918 a network of local committees, based on the administrative provinces in the southern part of the country, was formed. The Western Province Committee, headquartered at Sekondi, was led by J. E. Casely Hayford, the lawyer involved in the original discussions of 1914; the Central Province Committee, based at Cape Coast, was led by H. Van Hein, a wealthy merchant; and the Eastern Province Committee, based at Accra, was directed by Thomas Hutton-Mills, a lawyer. These committees were supported in their preparatory work by voluntary associations like churches, social clubs, and professional groups.

The same process was followed in Sierra Leone, and with striking success. From its inception in May 1918, the Sierra Leone Committee of the British West African Conference enjoyed the support of professional associations like the Sierra Leone Bar Association, there being in fact a close overlap in the leadership and membership of the Committee and the Bar Association. A. S. Hebron, president of the Bar Association, was a member of the Committee; M'Carthy, a joint sec-

---

[3] Cd. 6278: H. C. Belfield, *Report on the Legislation Governing the Alienation of Native Lands in the Gold Coast Colony and Ashanti*, 1912.

[4] See Kimble, *A Political History of Ghana*, 376-80.

retary of the Bar Association, was secretary of the Committee and its main organizing officer.[5]

Other voluntary associations such as the Anti-Slavery and Aborigines Protection Society, in which church leaders were prominent, the African Progress Union (Sierra Leone branch), the Ladies' Pastoral Aid Association, the ratepayers' associations, and the Universal Negro Improvement Association (Sierra Leone branch) all participated in the work of the Committee.[6] Again, there was often overlap in membership or leadership between these voluntary bodies and the Committee. Cornelius May, treasurer of the Anti-Slavery and Aborigines Protection Society, was a prominent member of the Committee; the Rev. J. B. Nichol and the Rev. R. R. Reffell, vice-presidents of the Anti-Slavery and Aborigines Protection Society, were members of the Committee; and E. S. Beoku-Betts, a prominent member of the Bar Association and secretary of the Anti-Slavery and Aborigines Protection Society, was a leading figure in the Committee.[7] The Muslim community in Freetown, the capital city, was also represented in the Committee through one of its modernized leaders, Almamy Jambarnya. The African mayor of the Freetown City Council, S. J. S. Barlatt— a lawyer—most of the African councillors, and one African-nominated member of the Legislative Council, J. H. Thomas, were also associated with the Committee.

The Mayor's decision to join the Committee elicited the following reaction from the editor of the *Sierra Leone Weekly News*: "Apart from the increase in prestige that his high position will bring to it, the Committee is likely to find Mr. Barlatt's conspicuous ability a valuable asset in the important work in which it is engaged."[8] The Committee further benefited from the fact that several of the associations that supported it were themselves pursuing goals quite like its own. Thus the aims of the Universal Negro Improvement Association (often known as the Garvey movement) included the following:

1. That the principle of self-determination be applied to Africa and all European controlled colonies in which people of African descent predominate.

2. That all economic barriers which hamper the industrial development of Africa be removed.

3. That Negroes enjoy the right to travel and reside in any part of the world, even as Europeans now enjoy that right.[9]

[5] *Sierra Leone Weekly News*, Feb. 8 and 15, 1919.
[6] See, e.g., *Sierra Leone Weekly News*, Mar. 1, 1919.
[7] *Sierra Leone Weekly News*, Mar. 15, 1918.
[8] *Sierra Leone Weekly News*, Dec. 14, 1918.
[9] *Sierra Leone Weekly News*, Jan. 25, 1919.

The Sierra Leone Committee's broad ties with voluntary bodies in the modern sector of colonial society attracted rather envious attention from the preparatory committees in the other British West African colonies. This was noted with some pride in an article in the *Sierra Leone Weekly News*, which remarked that the Committee "was being extolled in the Gold Coast and Nigerian press for having taken the lead in the movement, and being held up to the good example of the other British West African Colonies."[10]

Yet the initiative for founding the Congress was recognized by all concerned as belonging to the Ghanaians, and it remained their task to consolidate arrangements for the inaugural conference. These arrangements were finally made by early 1920; all delegates were requested to convene in Accra in early March, 1920. Sierra Leone was represented at the conference by M'Carthy, Dr. H. C. Bankole-Bright, the youngest member of the Sierra Leone Committee, and F. W. Dove, a lawyer and businessman. There were six representatives from Nigeria, including E. G. Shyngle, a lawyer, and the Rev. J. G. Campbell; only one delegate came from Gambia, E. F. Small, a businessman. Ghana had the largest delegation, some forty, which was led by Hutton-Mills and Casely Hayford, both of whom were nominated members of the Legislative Council.

Analytical data on the occupational background of 35 members of the Ghanaian delegation show that 15 were lawyers (43 per cent), 2 doctors (6 per cent), 2 educators (5 per cent), 2 journalists (6 per cent), 3 clergymen (8 per cent), 8 merchants (23 per cent), and 3 chiefs (8 per cent).[11] Lawyers and merchants clearly predominated in the Ghanaian delegation—as they did in the other delegations—constituting 66 per cent of this group. Thus the inaugural conference of the Congress was very much an affair of the emergent bourgeoisie, and this influence was to pervade both the proceedings of the conference and the subsequent evolution of the Congress.

J. E. Casely Hayford, who was elected vice-president of the Congress in 1920, articulated the emergent bourgeois nature of the Congress in his supporting remarks to the inaugural address by Hutton-Mills, president of the Congress. He insisted on the right of the rising elites—the "educated Africans" or "intelligentsia" as he called

---

[10] *Sierra Leone Weekly News*, Feb. 15, 1919.

[11] LaRay E. Denzer, "The National Congress of British West Africa: Gold Coast Section" (unpublished M.A. thesis, University of Ghana, 1965), 89-90. Miss Denzer's data also show close kinship ties to high-ranking traditional families and chiefs for some 40 per cent of the 35 members of the Ghanaian delegation she studied. These data go far to explain the perpetual ambivalence displayed by the Ghanaian emergent elites towards chiefs, supporting them and coalescing with them in some circumstances and opposing them in others. Cf. Kimble, *A Political History of Ghana, passim.*

them—to lead African peoples in modern development, and he rejected those who "supposed that the educated African is a kind of impediment in the way of successful administration . . . and would like to see direct dealing with the untutored native, without the medium of his educated brother." Indeed, Casely Hayford considered that as "the African advances in education and intelligence, naturally the higher grade of educated African becomes the leader of his people . . . The time will never be when it will be possible to dissociate the educated African from his uneducated brother."[12]

Apart from the natural right of the rising bourgeoisie to lead the movement for modernity in Africa, Casely Hayford saw this movement as legitimate only to the extent that it was reasoned, peaceful, and constitutional. "In all that we do," he remarked, "and in all that we say, we must for ever remember those words 'Be Constitutional' . . . In the name of Heaven, let us be constitutional." But in return for this adherence to the pattern and principles of government associated with British society, the rising elites requested concessions from the colonial government. According to Casely Hayford, the primary concessions desired were greater African representation in the legislative and executive branches of government, wider African participation in commerce and industry, and a larger African presence in the administration of the colonies, including especially an end to the "anomaly that a black man—however well educated and whatever his merits—is relegated in rank, salary, and emoluments, to an inferior position to that of the European."[13]

During the two weeks of the conference's proceedings (March 15-28) the issues emphasized in Casely Hayford's address—all of special concern to the rising elites—dominated the attention of the delegates. This may be seen from the official program of the conference:

 1.   Legislative (including Municipal) reforms and the Granting of the Franchise, and Administrative Reforms with particular reference to Equal Rights and Opportunities, by the Hon. J. E. Casely Hayford, M.B.E., Barrister-at-Law (Gold Coast).

 2.   Alien Problems—By F. W. Dove, Esq. (Sierra Leone).

[12] J. E. Casely Hayford's address, along with other documents, can be found in *Report of the Proceedings of a Meeting Held in London Between the League of Nations Union and the Delegates of the National Congress of British West Africa* (London, 1920). See also Magnus J. Sampson, *West African Leadership* (London, *c.* 1950), 57-91. Data on the Nigerian branch are lacking. For the Gambia, see J. Ayodele Langley, "The Gambia Section of the National Congress of British West Africa," *Africa*, XXXIX (1969), 382-92, which was published after the present article had reached the proof stage.

[13] For comparative data on salaries of African and European civil servants, see John Maxwell, *The Gold Coast Handbook 1928* (London, n.d.), 485-86.

3.   Commercial Enterprise with particular reference to (1) The Scheme of the Empire Resources Development Committee, (2) Banking, (3) Shipping—by Leslie M'Carthy, B.A., Barrister-at-Law (Sierra Leone).

4.   Judicial Reforms with particular reference to an Appellate Court—by Akilagpa Sawyerr, B.A., Barrister-at-Law (Gold Coast).

5.   West African Press Union—by Dr. F. V. Nanka-Bruce, M.B. (Gold Coast).

6.   Sanitary and Medical Reforms with special reference to Segregation System and the Position of the African Medical Practitioner in the Government Service—by Dr. H. C. Bankole-Bright (Sierra Leone).

7.   The Policy of Government in relation to the Land Question— by the Very Rev. Patriarch J. G. Campbell (Nigeria).

8.   The Right of the People to Self-Determination—by E. F. Small, Esq. (Gambia).

9.   Representation of West African Views in London—by Prince Tata-Amonu, Barrister-at-Law (Gold Coast).[14]

Political Methods of the Congress

Insofar as the leadership of the Congress committed the organization to a reasoned and constitutional approach to politics, the Congress remained rather limited in the kinds of political methods it might employ. This in turn restricted the issues it might embrace, for issues conducive to non-constitutional actions were *ipso facto* beyond the pale of legitimate consideration. This was, in a crucial sense, unfortunate, because if the Congress were ever to expand beyond its strictly bourgeois basis to include popular forces like wage laborers, cash-crop farmers, subsistence peasants, artisans, clerks, and the ubiquitous petty traders, it would have to assume the risk of acting non-constitutionally in certain situations. Moreover, such situations, created by popular forces, were well nigh everywhere during the formative years of the Congress, assuming the form of workers' strikes, anti-Lebanese riots, anti-chief riots, cocoa "hold-ups" or boycotts, and anti-tax riots.

In a situation of modern colonial transformation where a rural populace must increasingly respond to market forces rather than to customary obligations, the marked proclivity of traditional rulers to translate customary claims into modern benefits (for example, cash, concrete houses, marketable crops, automobiles,) provoked popular insurgence of one form or another. For example, in the Benin Province

14 *Sierra Leone Weekly News,* Mar. 27, 1920.

of Nigeria in 1918, peasants were "stirred up . . . by [a district chief's] malpractices to resist his authority . . . On this . . . occasion it was a mighty explosion which required an escort of soldiers for him." Typically, the malpractices and abuses by the chief concerned included "diverting carriers to his farm for personal services to him . . . compelling the villagers to hunt for him without payment, forcing the people to contribute large amounts of food as presents, imposing arbitrary fines on the people and exacting forced labor for the construction of personal houses for himself and his relations."[15]

Similar peasant outbursts against the abuse by chiefs of the modern authority which they derived from colonial rule started in the early 1920's in Sierra Leone and Ghana.[16] In Ghana, where popular complaints centered on (1) personal use by chiefs of modern resources which were obtained through the colonial administration and (2) distortion of the chiefs' traditional relationships and role by the colonial administration, the outbursts were intensely violent and resulted in bodily harm to the chiefs and the burning of their property. A report on Ashanti for 1920 noted that "this was the case at Offinsu and Kumawa, where the Head Chiefs were severely mauled, and had to spend a month in hospital for treatment of their injuries . . . At Bekwai the Head Chief succeeded in making good his escape, and at Denjiasi the timely appearance of the Provincial Commissioner prevented any serious outrage. At Agogo and Aguna, violence was threatened at one time, but wiser counsels prevailed and the case was brought to the government. The Head Chiefs of these various Divisions were declared destooled, and at the same time heavy punishment was inflicted on those guilty of riot, and in the case of Offinsu, of arson, and of grievous bodily harm on the person of the Head Chiefs. One common feature in these destoolments is the charge of maladministration of Stool [Native Authority] revenues."[17]

[15] Philip A. Igbafe, "The District Head System in Benin 1914-1935," *Odu*, III, 2 (Jan. 1967), 12, 16.

[16] For the Sierra Leone situation, see Martin Kilson, *Political Change in a West African State* (Cambridge, Mass., 1966), *passim*.

[17] Colonial Office, *Report for Ashanti 1920* (London, 1922), 21-22, 24. Commenting on the underlying causes of peasant outbursts, the report observed that "generally, Native Affairs in Ashanti have reached a stage of transition. A new generation which has grown up under the British Administration of Ashanti is coming to the fore. *Prima facie* also native institutions which suited the environment of the old order are hardly likely to be adapted as they stand to the radically changed and changing conditions of the present . . . Communications also break down the isolation [and] extend the horizon beyond the village or the tribe. The great factors of modern progress—Trade, Education, and Christianity— all tend to enhance the importance of the individual, and thus inculcate a sense of the equity of personal reward, of private property, and of the right of bequest."

More articulate elements among the lower orders of colonial society were also insurgent in expressing their particular needs and grievances. In 1927–29 in the Owerri, Calabar, and Warri provinces of Southern Nigeria, traders rioted against local taxes which they considered unfair.[18] In the Gold Coast, cocoa farmers launched boycotts of European cocoa-buying firms because of low purchasing prices. The boycotts occurred first in 1914 (the year the Congress was conceived) when some farmers in the central province refused to market cocoa at prevailing prices;[19] again in 1918 (the year the preparatory committees for the founding of the Congress were formed) when hardly half of the cocoa crop was marketed;[20] in 1921 (the year after the Congress's inauguration) when Akwapim farmers in the eastern province of the Gold Coast organized a widespread boycott of the cocoa-buying firms;[21] and in 1930–31 (the period of the Congress's decline) when farmers in the southern province organized a widespread "hold-up" of cocoa through the Gold Coast and Ashanti Cacao Federation. In Ashanti the "hold-up" was effective in Bekwai and Bompata in the eastern province of Ashanti, and in Sunyani in the western province of Ashanti.[22] Finally, in Sierra Leone in 1919 a rather spontaneous coalition of wage laborers, petty traders, and artisans staged, in the wake of a railway workers' strike, a destructive riot against Lebanese merchants in Freetown, causing some £250,000 property damage.[23] As one observer recorded the events: "The community of Freetown woke this morning and found the City all in confusion and wild consternation. Organized bands of ruffians and irresponsible men were reported to have concentrated at different centres

[18] Igbafe, "The District Head System in Benin 1914–1935," 19; Margery Perham, *Native Administration in Nigeria* (London, 1937), *passim*.

[19] *Report on the Central Province for the Year 1914* (Accra, 1915), 3.

[20] *Report on the Agricultural Department for the Year 1918* (Accra, 1919), 11.

[21] *Report on the Eastern Province for the Year 1921* (Accra, 1922), 5. It is noteworthy that the element of political awareness in the cocoa "hold-up" was quite explicit. For example, in 1921 the Akwapim farmers "started an Association amongst themselves early in December forbidding any persons selling cocoa until such a time as the price rose to 15s. a load . . . [and] with very few exceptions, it was impossible to purchase cocoa in any Akwapim village. It is needless to say that the general impression amongst the farmers was that the local 'hold-up' was responsible for influencing the European market thereby also influencing the local market. . . ."

[22] *Reports on the Eastern and Western Provinces of Ashanti for the Year 1930–31* (Accra, 1931), 1, 20. *Report on the Eastern Province for the Year 1930–31* (Accra, 1931), 15.

[23] Kilson, *Political Change in a West African State*, 106-8. R. Bayley Winder, "The Lebanese in West Africa," *Comparative Studies in Society and History*, IV (1962), 300.

where they made forcible entry into several premises occupied by Syrians, broke open their stores and took away whatever they could lay hands on. A large quantity of cotton goods, rice, palm oil and cash were looted."[24]

As already intimated, the Congress was incapable of seizing the political opportunities provided by the many acts of popular insurgence undertaken at that time. The myopic political consciousness at the bottom of this failure was amply illustrated by the proceedings of the inaugural conference; the various speakers were oblivious of the widespread popular stirrings in colonial West Africa. The conference related to the colonial problem strictly in class terms—as a problem of the emergent black bourgeoisie.[25] One qualification to this conclusion might be the tendency of the Congress's leadership to accept some chiefs as part of the emergent elites; and to the extent that some chiefs were responsive to popular forces in colonial society—which was seldom—it might be argued that the Congress was at least imperfectly aware of these forces. Yet one must look hard to find in the many resolutions of the 1920 conference evidence of this awareness; only three categories of the conference's resolutions even touched on matters of popular concern: the resolutions concerned with (1) the land question, (2) administrative reform, and (3) the so-called Syrian question.[26]

Concern with the land question was directed mainly toward strengthening the position of chiefs vis-à-vis government in matters of the grant or lease of mining, timber, and other commercial lands to European firms—and the peasantry might be said to benefit only indirectly from any reinforcement of African capacity to stave off outright colonial alienation of valuable land. In regard to administrative reforms, the conference was concerned mainly with reducing arbitrariness on the part of European field administrators in their relations with chiefs and educated Africans. Here, too, it might be claimed that any reduction in the arbitrary nature of colonial rule contains at least some indirect gain for the African population in general. In regard to the Syrian question, the Congress had the interests of the emergent new elites exclusively in mind, for African merchants and entrepre-

---

[24] *Sierra Leone Weekly News*, July 19, 1919.

[25] For a viewpoint that fights shy of a class analysis of emergent social and political power in modern African societies, preferring instead an ambiguous and analytically amorphous notion of status, see Kimble, *A Political History of Ghana*, 136-37.

[26] Resolutions of the inaugural conference of the Congress are found in *Report of the Proceedings of a Meeting Held in London Between the League of Nations Union and the Delegates of the National Congress of British West Africa* (London, 1920).

neurs had long resented the keen competition of Syrian and Lebanese businessmen. On this issue, the leaders of the Congress, not unlike other emergent bourgeoisie elsewhere in the modern world, struck out viciously against a politically weak, foreign, commercial group—portraying the Lebanese as "undesirables and a menace to the good Government of the land"—and requested the colonial authorities to consider whether they "should be repatriated from the West African colonies."[27]

The outlook and status of the Congress's leadership closely shaped its political action. This action has been characterized as that "of an intermittent pressure group rather than a political organization."[28] Thus, the Congress relied on techniques like memorials and deputations to the colonial and metropolitan governments. Within six months of the termination of the inaugural conference, the Congress mustered £10,000 to dispatch a delegation to London to confer with the British government on matters contained in the conference's resolutions. Much enterprise went into their endeavor, including a conference with the British League of Nations Union, in order to arouse support for the Congress from liberal Britons. Furthermore, two extensive petitions were submitted to the British Crown and the Colonial Office which reiterated the resolutions of the inaugural conference.[29] But all this was not enough to force a favorable response from the British government, and the Congress's deputation returned to Africa with nothing to show for its effort.

The Territorialization of the Congress

The immediate cause of the failure of the Congress's deputation to London was the unwillingness of the British government and the several colonial governments to treat the Congress in pan-territorial terms. This response was largely justified, insofar as the Congress's general demand "firstly to effect a Union between the four colonies" was illusory.[30] Such illusion stemmed directly from the emergent bourgeoisie's exalted sense of its calling—its natural right to lead the

[27] Ibid.

[28] Kimble, A Political History of Ghana, 399.

[29] See Memorandum of the Case of the National Congress of British West Africa (London, 1920). See also The Humble Petition of the National Congress of British West Africa by Its Delegates Now in London (London, 1920).

[30] F. W. Dove's supporting address to the inaugural conference of the Congress, in Report of the Proceedings of a Meeting Held in London Between the League of Nations Union and the Delegates of the National Congress of British West Africa.

masses into modernity—as well as of the real potential of its own modern attributes. More particularly, the rising elites were victims of a false consciousness in regard to the political capacity of their class. Like many rising classes, they assumed that the process of self-discovery as a class generated enough momentum to realize both the aspirations and the objective needs of the class. But, alas, the political context within which the rising elites were shaping their world outlook did not allow their false consciousness to fulfill itself. The colonial governments throughout British West Africa, possessing the power to shape the limits of political change, made it clear to the leaders of the Congress that whatever advances were to be made toward greater African participation in government would be made only within each individual colonial territory.[31]

Accordingly, in 1922, 1924, and 1925 the colonial governments in Nigeria, Sierra Leone, and Ghana, respectively, promulgated new constitutions providing for increased African representation in the legislatures and a limited franchise. For the Congress, the major organization of the rising black elites, these constitutional changes were a mixed blessing. In Ghana, for example, the grant of elected representation was counter-weighted by a provision which brought three chiefs into the legislature: they were to be elected by newly established Provincial Councils of Chiefs acting as electoral colleges. Moreover, the Provincial Councils were granted quasi-legislative functions, especially the right to enact bylaws for Native Authorities and the right to advise on certain legislation before the Legislative Council. Thus, these changes helped to accentuate the differences already existing between the articulate, more forceful chiefs and the leaders of the Congress.[32]

Another mixed gain for the Ghanaian section of the Congress, stemming from the 1924 Constitution, concerned the franchise. The new franchise enabled some three thousand persons to qualify as voters, which meant that for the first time a class of Africans other than lawyers, merchants, clergymen, and well trained educators had formal or institutionalized access to colonial government. The new voters included clerks, primary school teachers, some artisans, cocoa brokers, and a few other quasi-elite elements. Thus the Congress was afforded the first constitutional occasion to extend its activity beyond the confines of the bourgeoisie proper. In doing so, however, the Congress actually intensified the gap between itself and the lower orders of society, such as peasants, wage laborers, petty traders, and cash-

[31] See *Correspondence Relating to the National Congress of British West Africa*, Sessional Paper No. X of 1920–21 (Accra, 1922).

[32] See Kimble, *A Political History of Ghana*, 491-97, *passim*.

crop farmers, none of whom were covered by the new franchise. In order to contest elections in the Legislative Council, the leaders of the Congress had to fashion makeshift political parties like the Mambii party, which supported the candidacy of a Congress leader in Accra, and to ally with voluntary associations that comprised some of the newly enfranchised elements (for example, the Accra Ratepayers' Association and the Cape Coast Ratepayers' Association.)[33] In short, although this new political activity around the 1925 franchise spurred the Congress to reach out beyond its usual clientele, at the same time it did not appreciably lessen the gap between the new elites and the popular forces in the lower classes. This situation was to persist to the end of World War II, at which time a new kind of educated African was to alter the political map of modern Ghana.[34]

In Sierra Leone, the endeavor of the local leaders of the Congress to work within the rules of the game as set by colonial authority was rather more creative than in Ghana. This was due in part to the more compact nature of the new elites in Sierra Leone as well as to the greater variety of modern voluntary associations available to it. Soon after the return of the Sierra Leone delegation to the British government in October 1920, the local section of the Congress began to broaden its contacts with the new elites. Members of this stratum who hitherto had displayed little or no interest in the Congress were now brought within its fold. Like the initial organization of the Sierra Leone section of the Congress, this was achieved partly by taking advantage of overlapping ties among leaders of the new elite type of voluntary organizations. For example, Dove, a leading figure in the Congress, exploited his ties with the Old Boys' Association of the Wesleyan Boys High School, of which he was a former president. In February 1921, he put these ties to test: "At the request of Principal Roberts, Mr. F. W. Dove . . . visited his alma mater on Thursday . . . 3rd February. Mr. Dove saw the classes at work and afterwards addressed the whole school at the Assembly Hall. His reference to the work of the delegates to England was gratifying . . . In the afternoon of the next day the Old Boys' Association gave a public welcome to Mr. Dove . . . Several old boys attended. Mr. C. D. Hotobah During, President [and prominent lawyer] addressed the gathering and gave a warm welcome to Mr. Dove on behalf of the Association. Mr. Dove spoke lengthily on the work of the delegates to England . . . He urged that the fund of the Congress should be well supported by everyone in the gathering."[35]

[33] Ibid., 451-55.
[34] See David Apter, *The Gold Coast in Transition* (Princton, 1955), 165-68.
[35] *Sierra Leone Weekly News*, Feb. 12, 1921.

Other associations of this type were also brought within the range of the Congress's concerns. Where overlapping membership links did not exist to facilitate this co-operation, the Congress made use of the so-called "mass meeting," usually called "public meeting" in the contemporary press. These meetings attracted many influential persons who might otherwise not have found a direct contact with the Congress. As one account of a "public meeting" held by the Congress reported: "A largely attended gathering crowded the Wilberforce Memorial Hall [Freetown] at a Public Meeting on Monday afternoon [April 4] convened to receive the Report of the Delegate to England, Dr. H. Bankole-Bright. There was no standing room in the hall. On the platform were the Chairman, the Hon. J. H. Thomas [nominated member of the Legislative Council who hitherto had been associated with the Congress], E. S. Beoku-Betts, Professor O. Faduma [a teacher at Fourah Bay College, Freetown, who was associated with the preparatory committee several years earlier], Messrs. A. Tuboku-Metzger [a lawyer hitherto not associated with the Congress] and Songo-Davies [a retired senior civil servant hitherto not associated with the Congress], besides the Tribal Chiefs. Dr. Bright occupied about two hours presenting his Report, which was received with cheers."[36]

The Sierra Leone section of the Congress also received a spur to greater political activity from the provisions of the 1924 Constitution.[37] The new constitution provided for three elected African members of the Legislative Council—the number of eligible voters was about 1,350. The first election campaign in September–November 1924 afforded the Congress an opportunity to reach beyond the established new elites to the lower middle classes—to clerks, small shopkeepers, school teachers, artisans, and so forth. In the rural settlements just outside Freetown, such elements formed organizations, like the Kissi Committee of Young Men, in order to support Congress candidates.[38] In Freetown these same groups, sometimes in coalition with the established new elites, organized or rather reactivated ratepayers' associations as a means of mustering support for the Congress's candidates. One of these associations, the West Ward Ratepayers' Association, backed the candidacy of E. S. Beoku-Betts, secretary of the Sierra Leone section of the Congress.[39] The political interest generated by this electoral activity was both solid and genuine; in the 1924 election some 89 per cent of the registered voters cast their votes. Some-

36 Sierra Leone Weekly News, Apr. 9, 1921.
37 Order in Council, Jan. 16, 1924, Laws of Sierra Leone.
38 Sierra Leone Weekly News, Sept. 27, 1924.
39 Sierra Leone Weekly News, Sept. 27, 1924.

what surprised by this outcome, the Governor, Sir Alexander R. Slater, remarked that the voting figures "are striking and encouraging facts, testifying to the fact that the franchise is highly prized, and that the class of persons placed on the register appreciated the system of secret ballot, and were fully competent to use it."[40] All of the Congress's candidates were successful in the 1924 election and repeated this success in the three subsequent elections before World War II.[41]

Apart from the success of the Sierra Leone section of the Congress in broadening its influence and organization among the new elites—both upper-level and lower-level—it was no more succesful at penetrating the lower orders of colonial society than its counterparts in Ghana and Nigeria.[42] By the 1920's the urban area of Freetown contained a reasonably well developed network of voluntary associations organized by the lower orders of society. For example, by 1925 some 13,415 persons belonged to voluntary associations like the Mixed Kru Tribal Association (founded in 1900, with 75 members in 1925), the Kru Tribe Seamen's Union Friendly Society (founded in 1916, with 650 members in 1925), the Ekewam Keyarati Mandingo Muslim Society (founded in 1918, with 97 members in 1925), the Seamen's Defensive Union Friendly Society (founded in 1916, with 76 members in 1925), the Martha Davies Confidential Benevolent Association (founded in 1910), and the John Bull Line Co. Society (founded in 1915, with 72 members in 1925).[43] Thus, had the emergent bourgeoisie in the Congress properly understood the political requirements of a nationalist penetration of West African societies in the period between the two World Wars, they would have found a ready-made network of lower-class voluntary associations through which to effect such penetration. The available records indicate that there was only one occasion when the Sierra Leone section of the Congress even managed to approximate such a penetration of the wider society. This occurred in January and February 1926 during a rather violent strike by the

[40] *Sierra Leone Weekly News,* Dec. 13, 1924.

[41] See *Sierra Leone Weekly News,* Nov. 1, 1924; Nov. 9, 1929; and Aug. 18 and Nov. 10, 1934.

[42] The success of the Sierra Leone section of the Congress at embracing the upper-level and lower-level new elites was quite striking. For example, in the 1934 election of African members of the Legislative Council, all Congress candidates, some 3,263 persons, were influenced to register in the Urban District and 1,312 in the Rural District. *Sierra Leone Weekly News,* Nov. 10, 1934.

[43] *Sierra Leone Blue Book 1926* (Freetown, 1927), 270b-70c. I. M. Ndanema, "The Martha Davies Confidential Benevolent Association," *Sierra Leone Bulletin of Religion* (Dec. 1961). For the special political dynamics of lower class voluntary associations, see Kilson, *Political Change in a West African State,* 108-23, *passim.*

Railway Workers' Union. Several leaders of the Congress—presumably the more radical in nationalist orientation—sought to mobilize a favorable public opinion behind the strike among the new elites and also to collect a benefit fund for the strikers which they succeeded in doing in the amount of £ 1,000.[44]

Not surprisingly, the colonial government was deeply perturbed by this effort of a segment of the Congress to join forces politically with the lower classes. Concerned with what the Governor described as the "serious character of the strike in that it revealed a widespread defiance of discipline and revolt against [colonial] authority," the government publicly reprimanded the Congress's leaders and decided that no additional constitutional concessions for the new elites would be forthcoming beyond those granted in the 1924 Constitution.[45] It was even contemplated that the advances under the 1924 Constitution should be reversed, but the Governor, quite sensitive to the potential dynamics of emergent nationalist politics in the interwar years, rejected this proposal. Governor Slater's defense of his position is worth quoting:

> In my opinion the harm that demagogues of the type of Dr. Bankole-Bright and Mr. Beoku-Betts can, and undoubtedly do, cause is to some extent mitigated rather than accentuated, by the fact of their membership of the Council. Their sense of responsibility as legislators is, it is true, painfully low but it is occasionally discernible . . . In my judgment, to oust from the Legislative Council the members who were chosen of the people less than two years ago would, by making martyrs of them, increase their power for harm far more than continued tolerance of their presence can do . . . It would . . . in all probability antagonize the moderate section on whose tacit, if timid, support we can now depend . . . *It would tend to drive underground the disorderly and undisciplined elements always unhappily present in the Colony of Sierra Leone and thereby gravely enhance the danger arising from such elements* . . . I consider that the more dignified course for the Government to adopt is . . . to refuse to let that deplorable exhibition of political perversity deflect us . . . from our course of seeking patiently to educate public opinion by the means deliberately adopted in 1922.[46]

In the end, the colonial authorities' policy of, as it were, constitutionally overwhelming the emergent elites of the Congress with their

[44] *Sierra Leone Weekly News*, Feb. 13, 1926.
[45] Dispatch of Sir A. Ransford Slater to the Rt. Hon. L. S. Amery, Apr. 20, 1926 (in Sierra Leone Archives).
[46] Ibid. (Italic added.)

status and role in the Legislative Council succeeded rather well in both Sierra Leone and Ghana as well as in Nigeria. In Sierra Leone, this policy had a rather peculiar effect on the Congress's ability to embrace an incipient group of new elites from the Sierra Leone hinterland, which was administered as a protectorate. The majority of the new Sierra Leonean elites who controlled the Congress were descendants of liberated slaves who called themselves "Creoles." They had always jealously guarded their special status in colonial society—a status which had been created by early contact with and the unflinching support of Christian missionaries, reinforced by a grudging measure of special treatment from the colonial government since the early nineteenth century.[47] Though the 1924 constitution offered the Creole elites a major political concession through the franchise, it also offered concessions to the incipient new elites, or rather their chief spokesmen, in the protectorate. The Creole elites never quite accepted the latter concessions (especially the representation of Protectorate chiefs in the Legislative Council) as legitimate, claiming, among other things, that British protected persons were ineligible as members of a Legislative Council founded originally for British subjects. Even those Creole leaders of the Congress whom the Colonial government considered radical were opposed to Protectorate representation in the legislature. For example, E. S. Beoku-Betts, who was associated with Dr. Bankole-Bright in favoring the railway workers' strike in 1926, argued that "from a constitutional point of view an anomaly has been created, for so long as the Protectorate remains such, the Paramount Chiefs are aliens and not British subjects—and it is contrary to the fundamental principle of the British Constitution for aliens to legislate for British subjects: they owe no allegiance to the King and it is a moot point whether they can properly take the oath of allegiance. . . ."[48]

This sort of legal hairsplitting typified the political response of the leaders of the Sierra Leone section of the Congress, all Creoles, to the issue of the administrative and political absorption of the Protectorate, despite the overwhelming legal precedent in favor of such absorption.[49] Moreover, the leadership of the Congress confronted a veritable impasse insofar as the colonial government was determined to pursue the closer integration of the Protectorate with the central government. As a result, the Congress was unable to spread its influence and structure to the incipient new elites, including educated chiefs, in the Protectorate. The Congress was blindly hostile to the first

[47] See Christopher Fyfe, A History of Sierra Leone (London, 1962).

[48] E. S. Beoku-Betts, "The New Legislative Council from a Constitutional Standpoint," Sierra Leone Weekly News, Aug. 23, 1924.

[49] Cf. Order in Council, Mar. 7, 1913, Laws of Sierra Leone.

modern political organization to emerge in the Protectorate—the Committee of Educated Aborigines. The Congress charged the leaders of the Committee of Educated Aborigines with attempting to "impeach the broadmindedness and integrity of the Congress,"[50] when they proposed that the government give greater attention to modern development in the Protectorate relative to the Colony. When in 1925 another group of educated Sierra Leoneans in the Protectorate formed the Sierra Leone Aborigines' Society, which was basically more conciliatory toward the Congress than the earlier organization, the leaders of the Congress again stood firm on their attitudes about Creole supremacy.[51] In this way, then, the Congress deprived itself of a major opportunity to embrace a valuable addition to the political capability of the Sierra Leonean new elites. In the end, the leaders of the Sierra Leone section of the Congress became as smug and shortsighted about their new status in the colonial legislature and administration as did their Ghanaian counterparts. The frosting of elected representation was taken as the cake of political power. Illusion thus became reality, as it often does when emergent elites fail critically to confront their own false consciousness.

Conclusion. A Theory of Emergent African Nationalism

By "emergent African nationalism" I mean, of course, the nationalist politics associated with the Congress between the two World Wars. During this era nationalist politics labored under two prominent limitations, neither of which the rising bourgeoisie who dominated the politics of this period could surmount.

One limitation was the hesitation of the colonial government to admit fundamental change in the structure and behavior of colonial political systems. This hesitation was less a function of ideology—though it was partly this—than a reflection of simple empirical fact: colonial government was still powerful enough to have its way in matters of political change, and like most ruling groups the colonial oligarchy of administrators, technicians, and expatriate firms preferred to have their way as long as circumstances permitted. Thus, whatever constitutional change took place was limited by the colonial oligarchy's decision to hang on to power. This was precisely the situation regarding the constitutional changes granted to Nigeria, Sierra Leone, and Ghana in 1922, 1924, and 1925 respectively. Interestingly enough, although the rising nationalist elites were ostensibly unhappy with this

[50] *Sierra Leone Weekly News*, Sept. 16, 1922.
[51] *Sierra Leone Weekly News*, Mar. 14, 1925.

limited form of constitutional advance, they rather soon adjusted to it and integrated at that level of national politics where they were capable of participating.

The second and more crucial limitation in the interwar years concerned the nature of the rising elites which fashioned emergent nationalist politics. These elites were created rather explicitly in the image of their maker—the colonial oligarchy, including the Christian missions. Naturally flattered, if not obsessed, with the special status they had vis-à-vis the black masses of peasants, workers, and petty traders, the emergent elites became victims of what may, in Marxist terms, be called a false consciousness. They extrapolated from the facts of their special attributes or status a political approach which their objective power (socio-economic and political) could not in fact realize. This was evident in the very idea of the Congress as a vanguard body for the creation of pan-territorial or pan-African politics and administration in a colonial setting.

But the political expressions of false consciousness are not to be taken at face value; they were merely excuses for not taking decisions that the group or class concerned was ideologically incapable of taking. Thus the Congress offered the emergent black bourgeoisie a convenient, albeit unconscious, excuse for not seizing the more truly radical or revolutionary political possibilities available to it. These opportunities were, after all, virtually legion in the 1920's and 1930's—workers' strikes, peasant outbursts against chiefs in colonial administration, anti-tax riots by petty traders, anti-Lebanese riots by coalitions of workers, traders, and fledgling artisans, and so on. Moreover, insofar as the lower-class elements in colonial society in the interwar period possessed a modern-type infrastructure of organizations all their own, the rising elites could derive a real political advantage by embracing these popular forces.

Nowhere in West Africa did the emergent elites in the interwar years reach out politically to embrace the insurgent popular forces. Yet the emergent elites in the Congress, as well as in other organizations in this period, persisted in considering their nationalist politics as the most progressive mode of politics available. In reality, however, the politics of emergent African nationalism was a politics of compromise and accommodation, and, though the elites concerned might project this politics in terms suggestive of something more radical (like the pan-territorial politics of the Congress), they ultimately and rather quickly retreated from such fancy and returned to first principles, namely, political survival.

POLITICAL ASSOCIATIONS

IN WESTERN KENYA

J. M. LONSDALE

Among the Luo and the Luyia people of the old Nyanza Province, western Kenya, memories of African resistance to the imposition of colonial rule have been the property not of the political associations but of the popular religious cults and independent churches. In preserving these legends the independent churches buttressed their prophetic and radical role by emphasizing the identity of the ordinary illiterate men and women of the countryside who had gained least from the colonial situation.

The leaders of the early political associations, on the other hand, sought personal acceptance and recognition from the rulers of a colonial society from which they had gained much. The early politicians' indignation was fired not by corporate memories of resistance but by the frustration of their individual great expectations. Here two occupational groups were prominent: official chiefs and mission school teachers.

But a word of caution is in order. Despite the distinction that has been drawn between the independent churches and the political associations, it would be unjust and misleading to describe the political groups as made up of collaborators. In western Kenya it is more useful to see both those who resisted colonial rule and those who exploited it as two groups of innovating leaders.

Under the British, the position of the early Luo and Luyia chiefs was full of potential difficulty. At the same time it contained an equal potential for self-advancement. In the past, except in the Luyia Wanga tribe, to be a chief was generally a personal attribute, though it tended

589

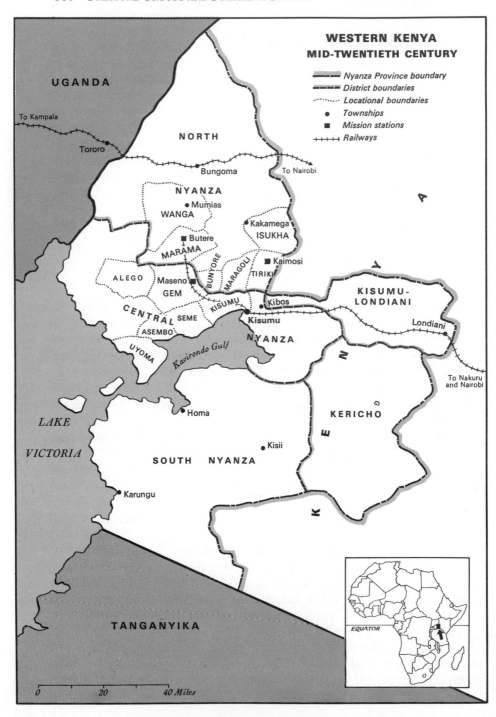

WESTERN KENYA
MID-TWENTIETH CENTURY

Nyanza Province boundary
District boundaries
Locational boundaries
• Townships
■ Mission stations
+++++ Railways

to remain within the senior or largest clan in each settlement.[1] The British, however, wanted a more predictable system and as few regular authorities as possible. They therefore looked on the territorial settlements of both the Luyia and Luo peoples as tribal units and set over each an official chief—often the settlement's previous leader. As a result, the chief's position became much more secure as it depended upon government approval rather than popular consensus. Furthermore, with the growth of the cash economy and opportunities for education, new opportunities developed for the long-term consolidation of the chief's family's position. There is no doubt that many chiefs became petty despots.[2]

However, in the early years the path to local dictatorship was not sure nor was the exercise of such power necessarily long-lived. Thus, before the Native Authority system was finally elaborated about 1910, the administration of western Kenya was plagued by a myriad of clan elders, all clamoring for official recognition and direct access to the District Commissioner. If anything, this competition for office grew more violent as official chiefs were confirmed and their opportunities were increased. Though the clans were now denied their traditional weapon of secession from the territory of an overweening chief, non-co-operation and litigation remained effective techniques to turn against a chief whom the British expected to preside over a quiet and orderly "location." In turn, the chief's traditional counter-measures of hospitality and arbitration became harder to employ, as the British came to consider them bribery and corruption respectively. In sum, an official chief was playing for far higher stakes than before; he had new means to ensure that authority remained in his lineage. But these very advantages meant that the chief's office was probably the focus of fiercer intrigue and jealousy than before.

In the first years of British rule it seems likely that the chiefs' opportunities outweighed their duties, among which the collection of the hut tax was prominent. However, with poor communications and little motor transport, it was some time before this tax was fully assessed. There also was little competition from rival educated groups, for what little education existed was available more readily to the chiefs' own clans than for others. In addition, the labor which the chiefs called out was initially used to obvious local benefit.

By the outbreak of World War I, however, many of these favor-

[1] The best discussion of Luo chieftainship is to be found in B. A. Ogot, *A History of the Luo People,* I (Nairobi, 1967). There is nothing comparable for the Luyia.

[2] B. A. Ogot, "British Administration in the Central Nyanza District of Kenya, 1900–60," *The Journal of African History,* IV (1963), 253, 255.

able conditions no longer obtained, and the demands of the war itself put the chiefs under increasing pressure, both from the administration and their own people.[3] During the five war years, when the total population of Nyanza Province was slightly over one million,[4] nearly 200,-000 adult males were recruited for military or civil employment, and by 1918 the province had provided over 50,000 head of cattle for feeding the forces. Most of the burden had fallen on the Luo and Luyia peoples.[5] In 1918, one official noted that demobilized military Carrier Corps personnel (porters) were responsible for "anti-chief feeling" and that "they had lost their trust in the European."[6]

At that time, most of the local opposition was of a rather negative character. In North Nyanza, men fled either westward across the Ugandan border or on to the European farms to the east in order to avoid compulsory recruitment and tax increases; in South Nyanza many attempted to seek refuge at mission stations.[7] To the chiefs such flights must have seemed alarmingly like the secessions through which pre-colonial leaders had most frequently lost power.

Nor did peace bring any relief. By 1920 taxation had been raised and the tax registers were much more accurate. The white administrative staff had been greatly increased, and the motorcycle was as much in use as the foot safari. Both mission and village schools had undergone tremendous expansion, but the chiefs' patronage opportunities for their literate products remained confined to one or two clerical positions in each "location." Above all, the chiefs were under increasing pressure to recruit labor for use outside African areas. In marked contrast to the pre-war period, when Nyanza Province had earned most of its revenue from domestic agriculture, the government in the post-war period committed itself to the concept of "labor supplying districts," in which the Luo and Luyia districts were certainly included. Colonial officials were instructed to keep lists of chiefs who were "helpful" in this respect.[8]

For those chiefs who were sensitive to the feelings of their people

[3] KNA, PC/NZA.3/66/1: John Ainsworth (Provincial Commissioner, Nyanza) to Chief Secretary, 30 Mar. 1914.

[4] Hugh Fearn, An African Economy (London, 1961), 43, suggests a figure of about 1.25 million for the 1930's.

[5] Nyanza Province Annual Reports, 1915–16, 1918–19.

[6] KNA, DC/NN.3/2: District Commissioner, Central Nyanza, cited in C. M. Dobbs, "History of Wanga Domination in Marama."

[7] Nyanza Provincial and District Reports; Dr. Clive Irvine, interview with the author in Nairobi, Aug. 1966. KNA, DC/KSI.3/2: notes by Rev. Father Scheffer in South Nyanza Political Records.

[8] Despatch to the Governor of the E.A.P. relating to Native Labour and Papers connected therewith, Cmd. 873 (1920).

—and they were probably in the majority—the position became increasingly intolerable. In the years before the war, many of them had been genuine leaders. Now they were only too obviously agents of the government, their major task being to ensure a steady supply of labor to European-owned farms. Therefore, soon after the war, some chiefs began to consider how they might restore their former freedom of action and at the same time ensure that the forces of progress were no longer harnessed exclusively to the advantage of the immigrant communities.

If after World War I the chiefs were seeking to recover their earlier powers—not in the name of reaction but of increased progress— their educated allies in the mission organizations were trying to transfer the relative freedom they knew in their churches to more secular fields: All the leaders of western Kenya's first political association were adherents of the British-based Church Missionary Society[9] which had successfully extended its activities from Uganda to Nyanza in 1906. In addition there was a galaxy of other missions of various persuasions, the largest being the Roman Catholic Mill Hill Mission, locally based like the Church Missionary Society in Uganda. But even by 1920 their adherents represented only a tiny minority of the population.

Considerable division marked the Christian communities. Division by mission denomination often coincided with kinship groupings, a segmentation which was part of traditional Nyanzan politics. But there was another division, very much more fluid and difficult to define. Broadly speaking, there was on the one hand a small Christian "establishment," and on the other a larger number of Christians who found that their literate status did not confer corresponding political or economic advantage in a society in which lineage seniority long remained the primary avenue to political success. In some areas there was a pronounced church-and-chief alliance, with the local church elders and teachers being drawn in the main from the same lineage as the chief, with some of the younger chiefs sitting on pastorate councils. There were also Christians who taught at the central mission schools, and who seem to have been satisfied with the status of a post consciously distant from more traditional concerns in society that involved very close relations with the white man's world.[10] Their interests were

[9] For early Church Missionary Society policies in Nyanza, see F. B. Welbourn and B. A. Ogot, *A Place to Feel at Home, a Study of Two Independent Churches in Western Kenya* (London, 1966), 21-28; J. M. Lonsdale, "A Political History of Nyanza 1883–1945" (unpublished Ph.D. dissertation, University of Cambridge, 1964).

[10] Oginga Odinga, *Not Yet Uhuru* (London, 1967) is in its early chapters the story of the author's rebellion against the attitudes of such men.

at one with the chiefs. There were also many literate persons in minor clerical and supervisory posts, content with the existing pattern of social rewards, who felt that protest was best expressed in demands for higher status for incumbent local African officials. In short, the Christian establishment is here defined as enjoying a comfortable and congenial relationship with the secular African elite, whether defined in traditional or in new official terms.

However, there were many Christians who were by no means "establishment men." Many were humble members of society with no political role and no political interest, but some were men of spirit and enterprise who chafed at white missionary control or at the prevailing distribution of privilege in African society, or at both. Some tried to use their position in the church as a means of exercising territorial, secular authority over small Christian communities in defiance of the local chief.[11] Others acted as the political champions of their clans in land disputes, or tried to use the ecclesiastical discipline of church councils against Christian chiefs. If these rebels succeeded in their aims,[12] they were usually happy enough to join the ranks of the establishment and become respectable.

One must therefore be careful before generalizing about a Christian—that is, educated—interest or party. As in political conflicts everywhere, common fronts could be maintained for a limited time to achieve a limited purpose. In this the Christians of Nyanza—the Anglican adherents of the Church Missionary Society in particular— were helped by a common heritage which fostered individual initiative and corporate self-confidence. Church Missionary Society work in Nyanza had been started in 1906 by one remarkable man, John Jamieson Willis, later Bishop of Uganda, and carried on by another, Archdeacon Walter Edwin Owen. From the start, Willis had applied the then liberal policies of the Uganda church, of which Nyanza was an Archdeaconry.[13] Therefore, in contrast to Church Missionary Society work elsewhere in Kenya, where its growth was inhibited by the "settler" environment, Nyanza Anglicans were early given considerable local responsibility, Willis having formed a church council while all the council members were still schoolboys. His first converts had been encouraged to preach in their home areas and in the labor lines

[11] Correspondence in KNA (Kenya National Archives) file PC/NZA.3/30/2; Michael Whisson, "The School in Present Day Luo Society" (unpublished Ph.D. dissertation, University of Cambridge, 1963).

[12] As in the case of Luyia opposition to the Wanga hegemony discussed below, 619.

[13] For full discussion of the Uganda context, see John V. Taylor, *The Growth of the Church in Buganda* (London, 1958).

at Kisumu almost immediately after baptism. Financial self-support on the part of each congregation was a continuing principle.

In the early years these local responsibilities had also been complemented by links with the diocesan headquarters at Kampala, Uganda, surely at that time the most exciting place in East Africa for any politically sensitive African. Thus, African delegates to the annual synod in Kampala met with their fellows in dignified surroundings in which Africans far outnumbered Europeans, close to the decorous life of the Kabaka's court and Bugandan Lukiiko or Parliament. The Luo and Luyia delegates to these synods—Nyanza remained part of the Uganda diocese until 1921—were deeply impressed with the relative political independence enjoyed by the Ganda as compared with the situation in Kenya.[14]

These Nyanza Christians had two points of reference by which to judge their position. By comparison with their secular chiefs they had tremendous freedom of action. The missionaries openly and indeed proudly admitted that much of the church organization, extension, and discipline was the unaided work of their young Luo and Luyia adherents.[15] Many new converts learned the rudiments of their faith, and the technical skills of reading and writing that went with it, without even seeing a missionary.[16] For many, the somewhat incongruous title of Native Anglican church which was given to the organization of pastoral affairs really meant something. They were not noticeably under the direction of an alien missionary society.

Politically, however, as the years went by, the chiefs came under increasingly obtrusive European supervision, as the policies which they had to carry out became harsher. Some Christians reacted by obstructing older chiefs in their duties and by well-founded complaints against their arbitrary powers.[17] Others, in co-operation with younger, educated chiefs, sought the more far-reaching solution of gaining for their chiefs the independence enjoyed in their own sphere by village catechists and teachers. The model they chose for this independence was taken from their other point of reference: Buganda. This kingdom had all the advantages which their own political authorities lacked. Up to World War I the Christian and political elites of colonial Nyanza had gained much; their expectations were rising. But for the chiefs these expectations had been dashed by the war and the in-

[14] Ex-Senior Chief Jonathan Okwiri, interview with the author in Uyoma, Central Nyanza, Apr. 1963.

[15] For instance, John Jamieson Willis, "Kavirondo 1916," *Uganda Notes,* 18 (1916), 20-23, quoted in Welbourn and Ogot, *A Place to Feel at Home,* 24-25.

[16] A. M. Elverson, *A Cast-Away in Kavirondo* (London, 1920).

[17] *Nyanza Province Annual Report,* 1922–23.

creasing allocation of public resources—African labor chief among them—to the development of the settler economy. Even the African church leaders felt a sense of relative deprivation when they looked to Buganda, the historical origin of their new community.

Genesis of Political Protest in Western Kenya

By 1920, the mood of many ordinary Luo, Luyia, and Kikuyu was ugly. These were the people most exposed to the rigors of the colonial situation in Kenya. They had given of their best in men and substance during the recent war. They were being dragooned onto European farms, which were at the same time encroaching on more African land. Taxes were being raised. A Registration Ordinance was introduced, and Africans had to carry the hated *kipande*, or pass. After a brief post-war boom, the local economy slumped. Not only was African produce hit, but struggling European farmers attempted a one-third cut in the wages paid to their African laborers. In addition, inflation followed on a horribly mismanaged conversion from the Indian rupee to a sterling-based local currency. The East African Protectorate became Kenya Colony and, at a stroke, all African land rights appeared to be extinguished.[18]

The personal advantages of chiefs and literates were overwhelmed by this catalog of disasters. Education, adherence to the rulers' systems of belief, chiefs' representations at periodic meetings with the District Commissioner, enthusiastic encouragement of cash crops—all these manifestations of initiative, all these promises of status—achieved nothing but an intensification of the European presence. It was a classical revolutionary situation, with one major difference. Revolutions are commonly directed to taking over the political center of a community in order to achieve social and economic ends. In Kenya the political power was then based in the European rather than African community: an African political community did not yet exist.

In any colonial protest movement it is difficult to disentangle the specifically anti-colonial elements from the stimuli provided by more purely social concerns. For example, if an association under educated leadership insists on its right of access to the administration on the grounds that official chiefs are not fully representative, is it in fact implying that the chiefs are ineffective mouthpieces of *protest*, or that older and often ill-educated chiefs are no longer representative of local *society?* In most cases, no doubt, these implications are inseparable

[18] Carl G. Rosberg, Jr. and John Nottingham, *The Myth of "Mau Mau"* (New York, 1967), 62.

and amount to the same thing, but the distinction is worth bearing in mind. In western Kenya it seems that the associations were at times more preoccupied with political protest, at others, with the question of social change. When colonial pressures receded, social conflicts would come into the open, reflecting the tensions of social change rather than of the colonial situation. When political protest was next required, its leaders tended to be among the newer groups which had emerged in the intervening period of social debate.

In a very real sense, the story of the Luo and Luyia political associations between the wars is the story of a hesitant and contradictory shift in the goal of political protest from something like secession to-ward—but not to—revolution. Within the limits of this trend, the atmosphere and aims of political protest and the experiences of the Luo and Luyia differed greatly in the period from 1920 to the early 1930's. The variations were almost entirely due to the fact that, at the outset of modern political activity in the 1920's, most of the Luyia tribes were directly under Mumia, the Wanga chief who was their paramount chief, but the Luo chiefs all had independent access to the district administration. The existing system of Native Authority had been proved to be inadequate. In advocating changes, the Luo sought to implement the Luyia arrangement, while the Luyia tried to break out from the bonds of the Wanga hegemony.

For both Luo and Luyia, the first frenetic burst of modern protest occurred in late 1921 and early 1922, coinciding with similar activity in Nairobi and Kikuyu.[19] However, for a few months prior to the outbreak, the chiefs and the Christian establishment had been engaged in fairly explicit skirmishing for the honor of sole popular leadership. In 1920, Luyia chiefs, at a regular meeting with their District Commissioner, had argued that emigration from the African areas for work on European farms would prompt further white demands for African land since the settlers would say that the African areas were being under-utilized.[20] In this, they were articulating a popular fear. At about the same time, Luo chiefs in Central Nyanza succeeded in persuading the administration to alter the boundary between North and Central Nyanza so that all of the Luo were in two districts, Central and South Nyanza, whereas, previously, some had been in North Nyanza and therefore under the domination of Mumia and his Bantu subordinates. In further response to Luo requests, the government instituted a chiefs' quarterly council under the chairmanship of the District Commissioner. During the same period, the Luo chiefs also made an important concession to traditional sentiment. For one of the first

[19] Ibid., 35-55.
[20] *Nyanza Province Annual Report, 1920–21.*

acts of the new council was the formal recognition of village headmen, thus conceding the justice of a demand that had been current since the establishment of official chiefs.[21] Early in 1921, the Central Nyanzan chiefs seem to have decided that the constitutional forum of the council was not enough: Chief Daniel Odindo of Asembo, another early product of mission education, at that time summoned a secret meeting of his colleagues, with the apparent intention of pressing for a council under African chairmanship.[22]

Meanwhile, the Christian establishment had also been active, the Church Missionary Society school at Maseno being both the local focus of activity and the main channel of communication with African sentiment elsewhere. The loss of Protectorate status in 1920 caused a strong reaction within this establishment—a desire, in defiance of the traditional lack of Luo unity, for a paramount chief. At this stage popular thinking on the functions of a paramount chief were not particularly clear, but two points were certain: as far as the Christians were concerned, by virtue of treaty relations with government he would be able to protect African land from further alienation,[23] and he would be "the nominee of the Maseno Mission natives and under his wing mission natives will have a secular prestige and authority which they have not got under the present regime." Interestingly enough, the originators of this campaign were Ezekiel Apindi and Jacob Ochola, both of whom had represented the Luo at the Uganda diocesan synod. And behind them was Mathayo Onduso, the recently dismissed chief of Gem Location and son of Odera Ulalo who had twenty years earlier been *de facto* paramount chief over most of Central Nyanza.[24] It is possible that the Luo Christians had been emboldened to entertain this ambition by the Provincial Commissioner's approval of Archdeacon Owen's suggestion that his church councils be allowed to discuss political matters. "As a means of expressing semi-educated native opinion," the Commissioner thought that this would be "eminently preferable to the alternative of the young Kavirondo forming a political asssociation of their own which would be subject to no moderating influence."[25]

[21] *Central Nyanza Annual Report,* 1920–21.

[22] *Central Nyanza Nine-Month Report,* 1921; information from ex-Senior Chief Jonathan Okwiri.

[23] S. H. La Fontaine, District Commissioner, Central Nyanza, to the Provincial Commissioner, Nov. 1920, cited in KNA.PC/NZA.3/31/1/2: C. M. Dobbs, Provincial Commissioner, Nyanza, to Colonial Secretary, 6 July 1930. La Fontaine wrongly discounted this preoccupation with land rights in his report.

[24] Ibid.; and information from ex-Senior Chief Jonathan Okwiri.

[25] Owen Papers: N. A. Kenyon-Slaney to Owen, 23 Nov. 1920. Kavirondo was the name which was then applied indiscriminately to both Luo and Luyia.

It seems justifiable to conclude from this account that the Christians were consciously competing with their chiefs for political leadership. It would seem no less likely that one of the chiefs' motives in trying to develop their own quarterly council was a desire to head off this challenge. But the fact that both Chief Daniel Odindo and ex-Chief Mathayo Onduso had been schoolmates of the militants among the schoolteachers and catechists and were now members of the same congregations, meant that an alliance would not be difficult. Indeed the successful demand for a paramount chief would fulfill the ambitions of both parties in providing an educated and much more independent local authority. But for the time being, it might be politic for the chiefs to remain in the background.

The Young Kavirondo Association, 1921–23

After some months of preparation, during which their organizers toured by bicycle around the mission centers, the Luo decided to come into the open on 23 December 1921, with a mass meeting held under the auspices of the Young Kavirondo Association near the village of Lundha, North Gem. The leaders of the Young Kavirondo Association were closely associated with the Church Missionary Society center at Maseno. The president was Jonathan Okwiri, from Uyoma, who had been a headman in the military Carrier Corps during World War I and was now on the staff of Maseno School. Benjamin Owuor, of Seme location, dresser at the mission hospital, was the Association's secretary. Simeon Nyende, treasurer, was an evangelist in his home location of Gem. Joel Omino, cousin of the Anglican chief, Yona Orao, of western Kisumu, was the Association's typist and clerk to the headmaster of Maseno School.[26] Only one chief was present, but incognito. Some Kikuyu observers and some Luyia were also there. It was an impressive gathering of several thousand, both Christian and non-Christian. Worried government officials called up a police detachment but they were courteously but firmly[27] told by the Luo leaders that no official demands could be formulated under such pressure. The officials were

[26] For Okwiri's account of the origins of the Young Kavirondo Association, see Odinga, *Not Yet Uhuru*, 25-28. This corresponds in all essentials with his information given to the author in Apr. 1963. Beauttah's account is given in Rosberg and Nottingham, *Myth*, 59-60, 63-64. The analysis in my "Archdeacon Owen and the Kavirondo Taxpayers' Welfare Association," East African Institute of Social Research conference paper (1963), was derived entirely from official and missionary documents.

[27] Officials who subsequently served in Nyanza regarded Okwiri as a "real gentleman."

forced to withdraw, and the Young Kavirondo Association drew up a ten-point memorandum for submission to the government. The first point contained the demand for a paramount chief: "We want to have an organization, and a President in our country."[28]

Harry Tate, the Provincial Commissioner, decided to get to the bottom of the trouble and summoned an official *baraza* (assembly) at the Kisumu locational center of Nyahera, on 7 February 1922, a little over a month after the mass meeting at Lundha (and a month or so before the arrest of Harry Thuku and the subsequent riot in Nairobi).[29] Because of the official nature of this meeting, the Luo chiefs appeared at last in their true colors. Of the fourteen main speakers at Nyahera, seven were chiefs and four others held, or had held, officially recognized positions as headmen or tribal elders. As an indication of the flexibility of Luo tactics and the closeness of the partnership between chiefs and leading Christians, no Young Kavirondo Association office-holders appear to have spoken: evidently they trusted the chiefs to state their case forcibly enough.[30]

Judged by the number of times they were reiterated, the main grievances in order of importance were: the chiefs' lack of power generally; a hatred not only of higher taxes but of the hut tax as well, the latter being regarded as a tax on women; the obligation to perform unpaid local labor and the imposition of the Registration Ordinance; fears for the security of land, with the change of status to that of a colony being seen as a renewed threat; and the poor standard of education offered by missions which were not sufficiently under African control. The demands made at Nyahera remained the basis of Luo protest for the next twenty years and were voiced by chiefs and schoolteachers alike.

Chief Daniel Odindo opened the meeting with the demand that in future the District Commissioner should come to chiefs' meetings only when invited; this, he argued, had been the practice some twenty years earlier, soon after the establishment of the administration. After other speakers had made the same demand and—perhaps—confidence was increasing, an ex-headman named Okingo came to the point: "We Joluo want our own baraza alone. When Government has given us this privilege we shall choose our Chief to be over us all. We want a ba-

[28] Odinga, *Not Yet Uhuru*, 27. The original document does not appear to have survived.

[29] For the importance of Harry Thuku see Rosberg and Nottingham, *Myth*, 37-65.

[30] These conclusions are drawn from Owen Papers: Tate, circular letter to officials and missionaries, 8 Feb. 1922. This letter appears to be a verbatim account of the *baraza* proceedings. Subsequent quotations of points made at the meeting are taken from this letter.

raza like the big Nairobi Council of Europeans."[31] Only such an independent body of chiefs would be strong enough to present their people's case. One chief, Ndeda of South Gem, made it quite clear that the mass meeting at Lundha had not been the work of the minority of educated people alone: "It was a meeting of the people," he said. At present, the chiefs were too much creatures of government to be able to speak for their people. As Chief Ogada of North Gem pointed out, "the Government calls us Chiefs when we are only Headmen and treated as such. Chiefs are independent persons and Headmen are under the District Commissioner."

Chiefs were not alone in protesting that their position was a fraud. Daniel Olilo, who was then a minor clerk, joined with the chiefs by asking why officials established permanent camps in the rural areas. At Nyahera, which was one such camp, he said they had "a District Commissioner and a Chief in one location. Which is the bigger man?" he asked, "District Commissioner or Chief? . . . . when the District Commissioner is here the Chief does not exist."

In addition to their desire for higher status, the chiefs were also anxious to have their load of unpopular duties lightened. Several objected that they had seen nothing of the reward they had been promised for their wholehearted co-operation in the war effort. Two speakers maintained that it should be no business of the chiefs to turn out labor; others demanded that when labor was forced to work on local roads it should at least be paid. The implication behind several of the statements was that there would be less unpaid labor, fewer demands for thatching grass for government camps, and certainly less provision of free food for officials on tour, if the chiefs could have their own council free from interference from the District Commissioner.

Ten of the fourteen speakers made specific reference to the high incidence of taxation. A point that rankled was that, in contrast to the practice of John Ainsworth, the Provincial Commissioner before the war, there had been no consultation before the recent increase. All were indignant that the hut tax was virtually a tax on women; they felt that a poll tax on all adult males would be much fairer.[32] Similarly, the Registration Ordinance and the *kipande* had been introduced without prior notice. Okingo, one of the *kipande*'s critics, revealed an interesting distrust of Nairobi, as the symbol of central government. He seemed to think that the local officials would not have

[31] Okingo was presumably referring to the Colony's Legislative Council; but he might have been referring to the Convention of Associations, dubbed "the settlers' parliament."

[32] This continued to be a grievance until the government finally replaced the hut and poll tax with a universal poll tax during the course of World War II.

thought of such a dreadful system and was rather surprised that they had allowed Nairobi to do such a thing. (In later years this sort of naïveté about the mechanics of the administration was to disappear, and government had to wage a continuous battle to prevent appeals by the associations directly to the Governor or even to the Secretary of State in London.[33]

But for the time being, the sense of the meeting was that the local administration could be more easily controlled than the central government. The mechanism of control had both negative and positive features. First, fewer powers must be given to white officials. As Chief Odindo explained when demanding a chiefs' council under African chairmanship, "When we desire to discuss the affairs of our various locations we do not want the District Commissioner to be present, and only want him to come in when we invite him." Also on the negative side, the chiefs wanted greater security for their land. Government assurances were not enough for, as Chief Okelo complained, "the Europeans in charge of our country are changed time and again." Title deeds for the tribal land, vested in local representatives, would give the necessary security. In any case, as Chief Ogada put it, "The Government has begun to eat our country." It is doubtful whether the Luo representatives were asking for individual title deeds; it is more likely that, taking their precedent from Buganda, they knew that hitherto any legal security for African land had been contingent on the signing of a solemn agreement between the colonial authority and an African ruler. Unfortunately, the demand for title deeds was not elaborated—the suggestion here is that it was in some way connected with the desire for a paramount chief.

But defensive arrangements were not enough. If the administration were to be challenged effectively, it had to be challenged on its own ground. Better education was essential if Africans were to speak with confidence; in this conviction both the older generation of non-Christians and the younger men were united. Ex-Headman Okingo wanted to see much more African control over the sort of education provided: "The Government has let the Missions come and teach us. We want to teach ourselves. We don't need to be taught by the Missions alone; we want our own schools. The Missions don't teach us safi [pure] teaching. We want our own schools. Our own teachers are able to manage them." Okingo was evidently perturbed by the fact that, in conformity with governmental thinking at the time, most missions laid as much stress on vocational training as on literacy. "Pure"—literary—education was what counted. He may also (the tone of his

---

[33] For the comparable "battle of the petitions" in Nyasaland, see Jaap van Velsen, "Some Early Pressure Groups in Malawi," in Eric Stokes and Richard Brown (eds.), *The Zambesian Past* (Manchester, 1966), 404-7.

voice cannot be recaptured in the report) have implied objection to the religious content of mission education, for a later speaker, John Omolo, who was in charge of a Church Missionary Society school, took him up: "Okingo said that we don't want Mission Schools. I say that we want both Mission and Government Schools. If we are only Mission boys the Government may think that the Missionaries prompt us when we put forward representations. The Government should build us a Native Finishing-off school—a College. I get small pay from the Mission. The Government would pay me much better." Omolo was pressing for the recognition of an authentically African voice in the same strain as the chiefs were demanding their own council. Again, there is disappointingly little elaboration of the speakers' arguments, but there is later evidence to suggest that Okingo, in asking for "our own schools" and Omolo, in wanting governmental schools, may have been asking for similar institutions.

Eight years later, when a Government African School was under discussion for North Nyanza, a member of the Local Native Council urged that it be financed from Local Native Council funds alone: if the central government helped out, European children might be educated there.[34] Discussing a similar project in 1934, the South Nyanza Local Native Council was unanimous in demanding that the word "Government" be deleted from the name of the Government African School proposed for their district.[35]

If Luo demands were at this stage not particularly well formulated, they had nevertheless stimulated an effective organization of associated interests and aimed at a logical political solution to the overbearing demands of the central government by the institution of a paramount chief and an independent council. By contrast, the Luyia, apart from the negligible number who had joined the Young Kavirondo Association, contented themselves with expressing dissent without creating an institution for the continued exertion of pressure. A week before attending the Nyahera baraza to hear the Luo grievances, Harry Tate, the Nyanza Provincial Commissioner, had met Luyia representatives at Mumia's baraza. From his record of the meeting,[36] it seems fairly clear that the Luyia chiefs felt that they already had a representative mechanism in the Wanga paramountcy under Mumia: thirteen chiefs were present; only one spoke—Mulama, half-brother of Mumia. Of the remaining five speakers, only one held an

[34] Cited in Nyanza Province Annual Report, 1930.
[35] KNA, PC/NZA.4/5/7: South Nyanza Monthly Intelligence Report, Dec. 1934.
[36] Owen Papers: Tate, circular letter to officials and missionaries, 8 Feb. 1922. There were two letters on the same date, one describing the Nyahera meeting, the other the one at Mumia's baraza.

official position as headman. The rest were schoolteachers. There was only one grievance: the high rate of taxation. This suggests that the Wanga paramountcy really did act as an effective buffer between the demands of the government and the expectations of the people, and that the Luyia chiefs did not feel their position of popular leadership to be so gravely threatened as did their Luo colleagues. When a teacher remonstrated against a possible rise in poll tax to offset the abolition of hut tax, Chief Mulama felt obliged to intervene by suggesting, "Divide the rich and the poor into two divisions, one paying a high and one paying a low tax."[37] After further discussion, the idea of a graduated poll tax was abandoned, but Mulama did enter a powerful plea on behalf of the poorer, indeed voiceless, sections of his people. He urged that "the halt, blind and maimed people" should not be entered on the tax register. If a complete register was administratively expedient, then "old and decrepit people were not to be worried for their tax" and, in any case, "the people should not have the tax increased on them again without due notice."

This first foray—the *baraza* at Nyahera—by the people of western Kenya into modern politics was notably successful. In the following months high government officials, including the Governor (who arrived *without* a police escort),[38] announced a number of important concessions at further mass meetings. Thus Governor Sir Edward Northey announced the abandonment of the policy of building permanent camps for the use of officials on tour; he went some way toward meeting the Luo demand for a paramount chief by agreeing to a joint annual council of Luo chiefs from Central and South Nyanza districts; he lowered the hut and poll tax from 16 to 12 shillings. Tate, and other officials, had apparently urged that some reduction should have been made as soon as the economic situation deteriorated. "Instead, the reduction was wrung from Government after violent native agitation had manifested itself. The natives not unnaturally drew their own conclusions."[39] A further concession was embodied in Secretary of State Winston Churchill's dispatch of September 1921, which forbade any direct administrative action in recruiting African labor for private employment, and placed certain restrictions on the use of compulsory labor for public purposes.[40] After some delay, the necessary policy

[37] This was perhaps only a minor concession, as it could be argued that the wealthier members of the community found the hut tax a heavier burden than poorer men who would have fewer wives and dependents.

[38] The Luo felt this to be in conscious contrast to the police intimidation at the Lundha mass meeting of 23 Dec. 1921; information from ex-Senior Chief Okwiri, 6 Apr. 1963.

[39] *Nyanza Province Annual Report*, 1922–23.

[40] Cmd. 1509 (1921): *Despatch to the Officer Administering the Government of Kenya Colony and Protectorate relating to Native Labour*, 5 Sept. 1921.

changes were effected. It was soon clear to settlers that the chiefs in Nyanza fully appreciated the purpose of this concession as they gave only the minimum of assistance to European labor recruiters.[41] No doubt the government was reacting to stronger pressures than those exerted by the people of western Kenya, that is, to the African political disturbances in Kikuyu and Nairobi and the lobbying by missionary and parliamentary groups in England,[42] but the Luo and Luyia must have felt that their protests had been of some avail. Protest had been effective. What was needed now was both a continuing, recognized channel for expressing African views in official quarters and greater local participation in the practical affairs of administration and development.

The government, too, appreciated this need. But it was not at all clear as to how it could best be satisfied. Early in 1922, the Chief Native Commissioner remarked that the tendency to hold mass meetings which made recommendations directly to the government seemed to "show the rapid growth in the Reserves of a feeling that the Kiamas [councils] and Chiefs as at present constituted do not represent the feelings and opinions of a considerable mass of the Natives.'" The answer seemed to be the provision of "some body in which the young educated Natives could feel that their views would adequately be considered."[43] His alarmingly liberal, and thus temporary, predecessor, O. F. Watkins, had suggested that the mere representation of opinion would not be enough. He had proposed a system of African District Councils, capped by a General Council for the Colony as a whole, with the object of attracting "the younger and more vigorous brains among the natives and lead them to take an active part in their own administration, and thus to ensure that they are for the Government and not against it."[44]

The government's dilemma was very real. "Native agitation," it had to be admitted in private, was rather alarming. Clearly it was pref-

---

[41] Correspondence in KNA, PC/NZA.3/20/4/3: "An Inquiry into the Alleged Discouragement of the Free Flow of Labour from Nyanza, 1925."

[42] For the latter, see Roland Oliver, The Missionary Factor in East Africa (London, 1952), 248-57; Marjorie Ruth Dilley, British Policy in Kenya Colony (New York, 1937), 227-32.

[43] KNA, DC/KAJ.9/1/1/1: G. V. Maxwell, Circular No. 3, 9 Jan. 1922.

[44] Owen Papers: O. F. Watkins (acting Chief Native Commissioner) to Owen, 7 Feb. 1921. In a proposal amazingly liberal for this period, Watkins saw his proposed District Councils as a training ground for future African participation in the Legislative Council. He reminded his officials that if the current Indian demands for a common roll were successful, some Africans would be enfranchised. It was therefore "imperative that they should be trained to take an intelligent interest in the politics of the Colony." See his circular No. 44 of 27 June 1921: Copy in KNA, Coast Province file 54/1447. It is not surprising that he did not retain his post for long.

erable that the younger spirits should express their views in public, with officials present, rather than incite each other to wilder thoughts in secret meetings.[45] But it was difficult to see how these young men could be given any power. Would not the official chiefs have justified cause for resentment if their powers were usurped in any way, and were not these same chiefs the foundation of all good government? In any case, judging by their criticisms of current government, these young men might well urge policy changes that could not be agreed to by Nairobi. There would then be an embarrassing clash between the central government and the proposed District Councils, and the government's position would be worse than ever. For if the young men became disillusioned with their local administrative powers, they would surely turn their attention more exclusively to the question of African representation at the real center of power in Nairobi. (It was not until 1925 that Local Native Councils, first mooted in 1921, were instituted.)

Be that as it may, the government's first official reaction was to ban the Young Kavirondo Association. It could tolerate the expression of grievance through the recognized chiefs, but the calling of meetings, sometimes in secret, and obstruction of the administration could not be countenanced. However, the Provincial Commissioner shrank from the formal and provocative act of a legal order against the Association; instead he tried to get the missionary societies to do the work for him. Until the government decided what its response to the Young Kavirondo Association's expressed grievances was to be, missionaries were asked "to instruct their pupils and adherents to abstain from all participation" in the Young Kavirondo Association.[46] The Provincial Commissioner followed up this request by asking missionaries to warn their adherents, "either directly or indirectly," that they might be liable to deportation.[47] The Roman Catholic Mill Hill Fathers, the Friends' Mission, and other, smaller American missions fell in with the

[45] See the remarks by F. Longland (Provincial Commissioner of Tanganyika's Eastern Province) to Governor Sir Mark Young, 25 Apr. 1939, referring to the Tanganyika African Association: "It is difficult to know the ambitions of the Association, which appear to be vague or nebulous. Of one thing the Association seems to be sure: that an official letter complete with reference no. . . . is the passport to all things. In short, African clerks who have become more or less familiar with official ways and official jargon seek to use these things for some purpose which is not quite clear to themselves. They seem to be groping for they know not what. In a confused way they seem to reason that they have the tools (official letters and officialdom generally) and they will make something. They do not plan the something and find the tools to make it." Minute on a Secretariat Minute Paper 21728, Tanzania National Archives.

[46] Owen Papers: Tate, circular to missionaries, 8 Feb. 1922.

[47] Owen Papers: Tate, circular to missionaries, 19 Feb. 1922.

Commissioner's suggestion. The Roman Catholics "actually decided to bar from their direct assistance and influence any adherents of their faith, connected with the body [Young Kavirondo Association]."[48] The Friends' Mission feared "the spirit of unrest" and tried "to induce quietness and steadiness" amongst its members.[49] The small American Nilotic Independent Mission near Kisumu warned its adherents not to associate with the Young Kavirondo Association.[50] None of these missions had as yet fostered a lively indigenous church, but they cannot have looked with favor on an association whose leaders were all members of a rival denomination.

The Church Missionary Society was in a quite different position, since the association's leadership was almost identical with the leadership of the Native Anglican church. Any collaboration with the government in suppressing the Young Kavirondo Association would have "risked losing the friendly understanding with the Natives upon which the success of our [Church Missionary Society] work depends."[51] In any case, the Church Missionary Society was facing its own crisis of confidence—its adherents were protesting the transfer of the mission's farm to a commercial company.[52] In this delicate situation, Owen suggested to the Provincial Commissioner that "ways and means of advising and controlling the Association" would be preferable to banning it. He thought that the encouragement of African initiative, which was the basis of the Native Anglican church, might have equally beneficial results in the political sphere. His mission's policies allowed the development of a constructive African leadership; surely the government would welcome co-operation from such enlightened men.[53]

Luo Organizations: The Kavirondo Taxpayers' Welfare Association and the Local Native Councils, 1923–33

After some hesitation, the administration decided to let Owen go ahead and, early in 1923, the Young Kavirondo Association was remodeled as the Kavirondo Taxpayers' Welfare Association, with Owen as president. In African eyes, the Kavirondo Taxpayers' Welfare Association was the same organization as the Young Kavirondo Association;

[48] *East African Standard*, 24 Nov. 1923: Special Report, "Native Organizations."

[49] Kaimosi Mission Papers: Emory Rees to Secretary, American Friends' Board of Foreign Missions, 5 Oct. 1923.

[50] Daniel Olilo, interview with the author at Nyahera, 14 Apr. 1963.

[51] Owen Papers: Owen to Tate, 23 Nov. 1922.

[52] Correspondence in Maseno Diocesan papers (Kisumu), file "Maseno Ltd."

[53] Owen Papers: Owen to Tate, 23 Nov. 1922.

Owen had merely joined them.[54] The Young Kavirondo Association's officials retained their posts in the new association with Jonathan Okwiri becoming chairman. Owen remained the effective head of the Kavirondo Taxpayers' Welfare Association until the mid-1930's. This fact alone casts more light on the nature of early Luo protest than any amount of analysis of their grievances. Owen's character was, admittedly, unique. At that time, he was one of the very few missionaries who was willing to carry the logic of his religious teaching into the political sphere. He delighted in controversy with both Europeans and Africans, urging on both a social conscience. Many European settlers referred to him as the Archdemon of Kavirondo.[55] He referred to himself as "a blister, a local irritant that stimulates, that brings inflaming matter to a head, and discharges it, and heals."[56] For all that, he was still a European and one who had worked closely with the settlers' Convention of Associations for a short period in the early 1920's. One is tempted to suggest that Owen's relations with the Kavirondo Taxpayers' Welfare Association represented for the Luo the sort of position they had envisaged for their administrative officers in their demands for their own council at the Nyahera *baraza*. He was a colleague in development—political, social, and economic; he was not a ruler. Through association with Owen, Luo chiefs and the Christian establishment were achieving, or appeared to be achieving, that responsible incorporation into their own government which they so much desired.

The response was remarkable. By the end of 1923, its first year, the Kavirondo Taxpayers' Welfare Association had mustered five hundred full members—paying a three shilling entrance fee and a two shilling annual subscription, and being "of good report among their co-religionists"—and about five thousand associate members—paying 2/- to enter and 1/- annually, "without distinction of creed or tribal origin." Despite the continuing depression in European and African farming, the Association banked £175. There were seventy branches throughout the three Nyanza districts.[57] Members and associates had to promise to undertake such sanitary measures as digging earth latrines, killing rats, keeping wells clean, and not adulterating milk with cows' urine. In addition, they undertook to plant trees, to provide them-

[54] Okwiri, Olilo, and John-Paul Olola, in several interviews with the author, 3 Apr. and 6 May 1963, 27 Apr. 1965.

[55] C. G. Richards, *Archdeacon Owen of Kavirondo* (Nairobi, 1947), 27.

[56] As remembered by L. B. Greaves, "Missions and Colonial Administration," *Corona*, III (Jan. 1951), 15. I owe this reference to Ben Kipkorir.

[57] *Nyanza Province Annual Report*, 1923; *East African Standard*, 23 Nov. 1923; T. J. Jones, *Education in East Africa, A Study . . . under the Auspices of the Phelps-Stokes Fund* (New York, 1925), 123-25.

selves with beds, and not to marry girls under sixteen. Full members had to do rather more, for they also had to furnish their families with bed-clothes, they had to wear clothes themselves, and keep themselves from drunkenness. The program bears the marks of Owen's deep respect for Booker T. Washington and the early enthusiasm of the Luo is eloquent witness to the Association's faithful reflection of the aspirations of humble men. But the Kavirondo Taxpayers' Welfare Association looked beyond sanitary welfare. The insertion of the word "Taxpayers" in its title was no accident. Good government was also its concern, and at the time this meant the search for closer co-operation between the people and the administration. All official chiefs became vice-presidents of the Association for life. White officials were accorded the same title, attending meetings by invitation. This practice soon lapsed, but the Kavirondo Taxpayers' Welfare Association continued to send to district headquarters notice of its agenda and minutes of its meetings until its virtual demise during World War II. The Governor himself was asked to act as its patron, but declined.

To the Association, good government was synonymous with development—development in the interests of the African community rather than for the Colony as a whole, for even after the government's adoption of the so-called dual policy, settler interests were only too often equated with the Colony's well-being. So the Kavirondo Taxpayers' Welfare Association began to act as a counterweight to the government's preoccupation with the provision of services for the white community. It organized plowing matches; it drummed up support for Nyanza's first agricultural show; members formed syndicates to establish water-powered maize mills on the rivers, and the sale of hand-operated mills rose markedly. Members were noted for their keenness in setting themselves up in trade, and the Association appointed Shadrach Osewe, an Anglican evangelist, as an itinerant development officer—he was paid £5 per month to supervise tree planting, rat killing, and so on. By 1935 the Association had accumulated £500 to provide sixteen scholarships annually for needy pupils at Maseno school.[58]

Owen had sold his idea of remodeling the Young Kavirondo Association to the administration with the argument that concentration

---

[58] Details of the KTWA's activities may be found in: *Nyanza Province Annual Reports*, 1923, 1924; KNA, PC/NZA.3/30/1: Owen to Registrar-General, 13 May 1926; Correspondence in KNA, PC/NZA.3/23/10, "Native Mill-Sites in Native Reserve"; Owen Papers: Owen to editor, *East African Standard*, 10 Mar. 1928, and Owen to the Assistant Secretary of the International Missionary Council, 29 Apr. 1935. It is interesting to note that the young Oginga Odinga used to accompany Shadrach Osewe on his evangelistic tours: Odinga, *Not Yet Uhuru*, 41.

on welfare activities would relegate politics "to their proper place."[59] For a couple of years his argument seemed to have been justified. The Provincial Commissioner acknowledged that Owen, through the Kavirondo Taxpayers' Welfare Association, had "done much to restrain political agitation, and the Administration owes him a debt of gratitude."[60] However, this view seems to have stemmed from a fundamental misunderstanding of welfare activity. Welfare, self-help and self-improvement, agricultural and commercial development schemes, all these are the proper concern of a modern government. The Kenya administration of the day was devoting little effort in these directions. The Kavirondo Taxpayers' Welfare Association was filling the gap. It was performing governmental functions and was doing so in co-operation with official agencies. It was a time of hope. The government had made its concessions to African political demands; the political atmosphere was now relatively friendly, at least in Nyanza; the Kavirondo Taxpayers' Welfare Association was, in a sense, urging the administration to live up to "all that was best in British government."[61] In short, welfare activity was deeply political activity.

Initially, the chiefs and the Christian establishment seem to have worked together within the Kavirondo Taxpayers' Welfare Association. Chief Ogada of Gem, who had been one of the Young Kavirondo Association's possible candidates for the paramount chieftainship, was used as a sort of proto-paramount chief. He was Owen's legate to Paul Mboya's South Nyanza branch of the Kavirondo Taxpayers' Welfare Association;[62] he maintained links with Association members in Nairobi, causing some police alarm in the process;[63] and he was the Association's spokesman before the East African Parliamentary Commission in 1924.[64] But this cordial relationship did not last long. Its continuance was dependent, in part, upon recent memories of combined protest in the tense and exciting days of the Young Kaivrondo Association; in part, upon the government's withdrawal of pressure on the chiefs to perform unpopular administrative duties; but most of all, perhaps, upon the lack of any alternative focus of political activity. But memories faded. In 1924 with the implementation of the dual pol-

[59] Owen Papers: Owen to editor, *East African Standard*, 25 July 1923.

[60] *Nyanza Province Annual Report*, 1924.

[61] Welbourn and Ogot, *A Place to Feel at Home*, 19. I am suggesting a parallel between the aims of the Kavirondo Taxpayers' Welfare Association and the Welbourn and Ogot analysis of the aims of religious revival in East Africa.

[62] Ex-Senior Chief Paul Mboya, MBE, interview with author at Homa Bay, 1 May 1963.

[63] KNA, PC/NZA.3/31/2: Criminal Investigation Department to Commissioner of Police, 30 Sep. 1925.

[64] Owen Papers: Owen to Governor Sir Edward Grigg, 25 Apr. 1927.

icy of development in both the European and African areas, chiefs were instructed to press cotton cultivation on their people. Cotton gave little financial return for the very hard work involved, and the chiefs' methods were often harsh. Kavirondo Taxpayers' Welfare Association members protested. Owen, realizing that such an issue would split his membership, urged the Provincial Commissioner to conduct investigations before the association was forced to make its own.[65]

At last, in 1925 the government introduced its Local Native Councils. Each locational chief was a member ex officio; in addition each location had one or two unofficial members, nominated by the government after a rudimentary form of election. In Central Nyanza, Kavirondo Taxpayers' Welfare Association members were in a majority on the Local Native Council.[66] Both Africans and white officials had great hopes for the Local Native Councils. Officials anticipated that the ground would be cut from under the political associations.[67] African enthusiasm can best be measured in terms of hard cash: by 1929 the Local Native Councils of North and Central Nyanza had each voted about £ 10,000 for the establishment of government schools in their district, the money to be raised from a voluntary assessment in addition to the normal rates.[68] Recurrent expenditure was mainly for grants to mission schools, the payment of scholarships, and a host of improvements—local roads, medical dispensaries, tree nurseries, agricultural services, and so on.

Local Native Councils thus demonstrated local enthusiasm for development, carrying on the tradition of the Kavirondo Taxpayers' Welfare Association, but they had little power. Their deliberations were presided over by the District Commissioner. They could pass bylaws, but they could not influence general legislation. Local taxes could make up some of the deficiencies in government services, but councillors' representations could scarcely influence the government to

[65] Owen Papers: Owen to Provincial Commissioner, 2 Aug. 1924.
[66] *Central Nyanza Annual Report*, 1924.
[67] *Nyanza Province Annual Report*, 1925.
[68] Ibid., 1929. The assumption that such schools would be under Local Native Council control has already been mentioned in the discussion of the Nyahera *baraza* of Feb. 1922. By 1942 the Central Nyanza Local Native Council had been persuaded that its education fund should be used for building day primary schools rather than a boarding school; by this time it was clear that Government African Schools, taking boarders, were not under Local Native Council control. The Local Native Council said that the change "appealed to all because the schools would be cheap, convenient, *African-controlled* and more in number, and yet have the ability to give equal and the same education as is obtainable in the expensive Mission or Government boarding schools." From KNA, Secretariat File ADM.4/1/3: Central Nyanza Local Native Council Memorandum to Governor Sir Henry Moore, 13 Feb. 1942. (Italics mine).

provide more. Officials often had to remind councillors that they were subordinate to the Colony's legislature and the administration reserved the right to withhold approval of any Local Native Council resolution. There were compensations, however. Local Native Councils could, with governmental approval, turn down private Europeans' applications for land in African areas.[69] They could also employ Europeans to perform such tasks as the supervision of a scheme to clear tsetse-infested bush.[70] With increasing confidence over the years, they could also upbraid a European departmental officer for sloppy accounting.[71] If Local Native Council minutes often betrayed frustration over the narrow limits of Local Native Council competence, there was still occasional justification for the hope that, with patience, such competence might be extended. And debates on the annual budget estimates became increasingly lively and well-informed. Thus, even if within narrow, constricting limits, councillors were taking an active share in the development of their own areas. The noisiness and enthusiasm of Local Native Council elections attested to the importance of sharing in these local satisfactions. The leaders of the Young Kavirondo Association and Kavirondo Taxpayers' Welfare Association, both Luo and Luyia, have maintained that their early political agitation was responsible for the institution of Local Native Councils;[72] and in many respects these local government bodies did fulfill the aspirations of the first politicians, especially of those who were either official chiefs or Christians whose lineage position enabled them to win in local elections.

The Kavirondo Taxpayers' Welfare Association forum continued to provide an opportunity for African discussion of wider issues of government policy. But after 1925 the Association no longer represented a common front. The alliance between Christian leaders and official chiefs remained effective on general issues, but in the day-to-day activities of the association there was growing acrimony and tension. There were two main reasons for this development, one endemic in the fragmented nature of Nyanzan society, and the other resulting from governmental pressure upon its official chiefs. First, the often rough-and-ready methods employed by the chiefs in collecting taxes and in performing their other administrative duties gave ample oppor-

[69] Dobbs, memorandum dated 29 Oct. 1926, in Provincial Commissioner's file 40/9, "Mill Hill Mission," Nyanza provincial offices, Kisumu.

[70] *Native Affairs Department Annual Report* (1932), 41.

[71] *Nyanza Province Annual Report,* 1941.

[72] KNA, Secretariat File ADM.4/1/3: Kavirondo Taxpayers' Welfare Association Memorandum to Governor Sir Henry Moore, 13 Feb. 1942; information from interviews with ex-Senior Chief Jonathan Okwiri at Uyoma, Apr. 1963; John-Paul Olola at Kibos, May 1963; Pascal Nabwana, OBE (ex-chairman, Elgon Nyanza African District Council) at Kimilili, 10 Apr. 1965.

tunity for complaints and dramatic exposures of the abuse of authority. Intrigue was possible for anybody whose sense of justice was sharpened by the social antagonisms of kinship rivalry. And for Kavirondo Tax- payers' Welfare Association members, their civic sensibilities trained in the debates of church and Association meetings, Archdeacon Owen was always at hand as a willing, indeed impetuous, advocate of the common man against the hand of authority.

During the late 1920's, in his dual position of churchman and president of an African political association, Owen took up numerous complaints of wrongful tax collection or misuse of compulsory labor by the chiefs.[73] Officials were exasperated. After an investigation by Owen into an allegation that a Luyia chief was using compulsory la- bor for his private benefit, the District Commissioner warned that "a tendency is growing up among the natives of Bunyore [a Luyia loca- tion] to look upon Archdeacon Owen as the executive authority. If this state of affairs goes on we shall have a decidedly bolshevik ele- ment in the District, who will endeavour to be a law unto them- selves."[74] Personal feelings were naturally ruffled, as the Provincial Commissioner pointed out: "He [Owen] contends that there is nothing personal in his attacks, that they are only directed against the sys- tem, but the individuals he pillories find it very difficult to regard it in the same light."[75] The malefactors in Owen's pillory were the official chiefs, Chief Ogada among them, who were also vice-presidents of the Kavirondo Taxpayers' Welfare Association. The Provincial Commis- sioner might take some pleasure in drawing attention to the "curi- ous, not to say humorous situation of the President of the Kavirondo Taxpayers' Welfare Association, an Association described by the Presi- dent as a 'forum for airing complaints,' invoking the aid of the Ad- ministration to take action in regard to the alleged illegal acts of the two Vice-Presidents of the same Association and calling public atten- tion to the circumstances in the press . . . [produced] a Gilbertian state of affairs."[76] But for the continued vitality of the Kavirondo Tax- payers' Welfare Association the implications were serious indeed.

[73] The Provincial Commissioner had at least two files devoted exclusively to Owen's "inquisitions" on these topics: 42/1, "Compulsory Labour under the Native Authority Ordinance, 1927–28," and 62/3, "Tax-Collection-General, 1925– 27." Both these remain in the Kisumu provincial offices, not having been trans- ferred to the KNA.

[74] Provincial Commissioner's file 42/1: F. G. Jennings (acting District Com- missioner, North Nyanza) to Dobbs, 19 Nov. 1927.

[75] Provincial Commissioner's file 62/3: Dobbs to Chief Native Commissioner, 12 July 1927.

[76] KNA, PC/NZA.3/30/1: Dobbs to Chief Native Commissioner, 22 Mar. 1928, commenting on Owen's letter to editor, *East African Standard*, 6 Mar. 1928.

The second threat to the Kavirondo Taxpayers' Welfare Association came from the government's pressure on the chiefs. Administrative officers were justifiably dismayed at the thought of chiefs, in their capacity as members of the association, taking part in investigations designed to show up administrative irregularities. The climax came with the publication in the local press in December 1927 of the Association's memorandum to the Hilton Young Commission on Closer Union in East Africa.[77]

Among other things, the association called for "a new spirit" to animate administrative officers. Such a statement violated all civil service norms in that junior officials—the chiefs—were publicly criticizing their superiors. The subcommittee responsible for drafting the memorandum had included, besides Owen and other Church Missionary Society missionaries, the Luo chief, Ogada, the Luyia brothers of Mumia, Chief Mulama and Chief Murunga, two members of the Maseno staff— Ezekiel Apindi and Benjamin Owuor—and Joel Omino, clerk to the Central Nyanza Local Native Council. All were either in full governmental employ, or attached to a mission which received generous government grants. The situation was intolerable. The Provincial Commissioner sent for the three chiefs; they denied any responsibility for the more outspoken passages of the memorandum.[78] Owen's close friend, Dr. Norman Leys, maintained that the chiefs had been "browbeaten. . . . When protest involves personal ruin, whether protesters are white or black, protesters are few."[79] Leys's point was well made, for the Chief Native Commissioner summoned the senior Church Missionary Society officials in Nairobi and gave the impression that the mission's grants were endangered by Owen's activities. Accordingly, the Church Missionary Society warned Owen against any further fireworks.[80]

This episode highlighted the fact that there were two modes of protest open to Africans, the choice between them depending upon the protesters' relationships with the colonial authorities. Chiefs, for all their subordinate position, had direct access to the white officials. The nuances of their working relationships are difficult to resurrect, but the administrators' daily decisions were always influenced to some degree by their knowledge of the workings of "the native mind," gleaned from contact with chiefs and interpreters. They could well judge the

[77] *East African Standard,* 31 Dec. 1927.

[78] KNA, PC/NZA.3/1/9: Dobbs, notes of interviews, 9 Jan. 1928.

[79] Sidney Webb Papers, held at The London School of Economics: Dr. Norman Leys, Memorandum for Labour Party Advisory Committee on Imperial Questions, Nov. 1930.

[80] Owen Papers: Rev. Harry Leakey to Owen, 31 Jan. 1928.

extent of the diplomacy needed before a policy could be implemented and often urged a judicial caution on any matter affecting social sensibilities.[81] It is difficult to judge the extent to which chiefs knew how much influence they exerted on colonial policy-making—even if at a lowly level. But their continual demands for more consultation, and their harking back to such consultation in their complaints at Nyahera, suggests that they were well aware of the possibility. This form of protest was undramatic but, for this very reason, likely to be effective in a situation in which the government's overriding concern was to maintain the appearance of unchallenged control.[82] Established administrative channels were proof against publicity. In addition to the backroom satisfactions of the civil servant, chiefs still had the traditional satisfactions of local leadership, to which the continuing scramble for office and pleas by subordinate clans for separate administrative locations, each with its own chief, bore witness.

The Local Native Council was an adequate forum for those who felt themselves to have the status necessary to effect change by protest from within, especially if council meetings were not the only occasions in the year when they could gain the ear of the authorities. Chiefs and the Christian establishment could still co-operate on the broad issues of African political concern.[83] They could agree on such specific issues as the need for some mechanism to safeguard their land from alienation, more government attention to African agriculture, a more liberal system of tax exemption for the needy and widows, and for more consultation of African opinion before enacting legislation, both through a strengthening of the system of Local Native Councils and through direct African representation on the Legislative Council.

[81] As for instance, the government's dismay at provocative missionary tactics over the female circumcision issue in Kikuyu. For a sensitive study of the restraints in a local administrator's position, see T. H. R. Cashmore, "Studies in District Administration in the East African Protectorate, 1895–1918" (unpublished Ph.D. dissertation, University of Cambridge, 1965).

[82] This sentiment animated Provincial Commissioner Tate's protest cited on 604 above. In such a situation a chief might well reason with the Egg of Head:

> In speaking out one loses influence.
> The chance for change by pleas and prayers is gone.
> The chance to modify the devil's deeds
> As critic from within is still my hope.

Barbara Garson, *MacBird!* (Harmondsworth, 1967), 35.

[83] Besides the frequent minutes of meetings and memoranda to be found in KNA, PC/NZA.2/554, PC/NZA.2/565, and DC/CN.8/2, the Kavirondo Taxpayers' Welfare Association's main policy statements from 1923 to 1931 were its memorandum to the East African (Ormsby-Gore) Commission, 1924, in the Owen Papers; the memorandum to the Hilton Young Commission, cited above; and Ezekiel Apindi's evidence before the 1931 Parliamentary Joint Select Committee on Closer Union in East Africa.

Equally, the younger educated chiefs, at least, could acquiesce in demands that the government institute specific training schemes for chiefs, and that it publish all relevant ordinances and regulations in Swahili so that Africans would have a much better knowledge of their rights, obligations, and "civil liberties." Such measures would raise the status of the chiefs as local spokesmen, give them an increased standing in the civil service hierarchy, and make them better qualified for the higher salaries and pensions that they were also demanding. Equally, an appointment as chief would become more acceptable to those members of the Christian establishment who had already experienced the missions' teacher training courses and the exposition of the printed word in classroom and church. Above all, chiefs and teachers in the Kavirondo Taxpayers' Welfare Association could agree, from their positions within or without the local administrative hierarchy, that as organs of local government the Local Native Councils needed more power.

This demand was most clearly expressed by Ezekiel Apindi in 1931 when giving evidence before the Committee on Closer Union in London,[84] and on his return when he explained that evidence before the Central Nyanza Local Native Council. Apindi's evidence, together with that of the two other official African representatives from Kenya, Chief Koinange of the Kikuyu and James Mutua of the Kamba, revealed a good deal of uncertainty as to how Africans could best exercise a larger voice in the government. He argued that the leaders of the Young Kavirondo Association had aimed "not to separate from the Government, but to help themselves under the Government" and, in accord with this aim, Apindi now asked that, in time, Africans should have the same number of seats as Europeans on the Legislative Council in recognition of their numerical strength in the country. But Apindi does not seem to have imagined that the African representatives would be able to exercise any decisive influence over this center of power. Rather, he agreed with Chief Koinange[85] that Africans would maintain a watching brief in the Legislative Council to see that there was a fair distribution of services between the racial communities. In Apindi's view, separate fiscal arrangements would be still more desirable:

> We would like a native budget in our country, and not the National Budget. We want a native budget, separate and distinct from the National Budget. We would like to know how it is worked. Also we would

[84] *Joint Select Committee on Closer Union in East Africa, Vol. II, Minutes of Evidence,* Commons 156 (1931), Questions 4063, 4068–4077, 4084–4085, 4088–4094, 4110–4118, 4135–4138, 4140–4143.

[85] See Chief Koinange's evidence. Ibid., Question 4060.

like our matters to be settled separately from the Legislative Council. On my side I may say this, that if you had one who would stand on the native side as adviser to look after native affairs, and all matters must be under him, and the natives must settle their matters separately from what is happening now in our country, that is what we would desire, because all our matters are now settled in the Legislative Council without our being consulted at all.[86]

With this aim presumably in mind, he went on to ask for a tiered system of Native Councils "which would lead up to the controlling government of the country" and suggested that Provincial Native Councils be instituted as a start. His wish for closer bonds between Provincial Commissioners and the Governor[87] might be taken as another way of by-passing the settler-dominated Legislative Council. In all this, Apindi seems to have been the faithful representative of articulate Nyanza opinion.

In July 1933 the Nyanza administration did hold an informal provincial native council composed of delegates from four Local Native Councils. Major Clarence Buxton, District Commissioner of South Nyanza, observed that the council's discussion on some points "indicated that natives were not satisfied that under the unitary system [of government] they received adequate return for their taxation or attention to their problems." The Provincial Council, Buxton thought, was "an institution which in effect treats interests on the separatist basis," and that Africans were probably right in thinking that its resolutions would carry more weight than those passed by a Local Native Council. But the paradox was that a form of separatism was the means to closer incorporation in the government: "there are many natives sufficiently awake to appreciate the importance of getting the closer attention of Government to their needs, by closer access to the Central Authorities."[88] The paradox owed its existence almost exclusively to the fact that it was then inconceivable—both to Africans and others—to imagine a Legislative Council not dominated by white settlers.[89] As Apindi explained to his Local Native Council on his return from London, "if Council ask for something, the District Commissioner can tell them that Legislative Council, which is composed of settlers and others who wish to take the country, does not agree." He thought the Local Na-

[86] Ibid., Question 4068.
[87] Ibid., Question 4110.
[88] KNA, PC/NZA.4/5/7: *South Nyanza Monthly Intelligence Report,* July 1933.
[89] KNA, PC/CP.8/5/3: The Kikuyu Central Association was alone in envisaging a future in which there would be an African majority in the legislature. KCA to Sir Samuel Wilson, 30 May 1929.

tive Council should have absolute discretion, with the District Commissioner acting in an advisory capacity only. The councils were "powerless so long as they were not allowed to elect a paramount chief."[90]

Luyia Organizations: The North Kavirondo Taxpayers' Welfare Association, 1924–35

Whether chiefs or teachers, Luo politicians had been seeking a wider unity for their people and a spokesman of greater weight within the government than their locational chiefs. Political realities were a cruel reflection of the difficulty of realizing these aspirations. Not only were there growing strains within the alliance between chiefs and the mission element, there were denominational splits too. Originally Kavirondo Taxpayers' Welfare Association membership had been open to all, irrespective of creed; but it was clearly under Anglican guidance. About a year after its formation, the Catholic Mill Hill Fathers started a Native Catholic Union for their adherents. The Native Catholic Union had broadly the same welfare objectives as the Kavirondo Taxpayers' Welfare Association but was rarely involved in politics.[91] The Kavirondo Taxpayers' Welfare Association had also intended to include both Luo and Luyia, but in 1924 Owen was forced by the pressures of tribal opinion to form a North Kavirondo Taxpayers' Welfare Association for the Luyia. The North Kavirondo Taxpayers' Welfare Association's main strength was in the area of Anglican influence, western North Nyanza, centered on the Church Missionary Society station at Butere in Marama Location. The locational chief, Mulama, brother of the paramount chief, Mumia, was the Association's vice-president, but the North Kavirondo Taxpayers' Welfare Association soon ran into an explicit and angry clash with the Luyia chiefs.

As already indicated, the Native Authority system imposed upon the Luyia was very different from that of the Luo. Mumia, chief of the Wanga tribe, was officially paramount over all the North Nyanza district. Until the establishment of a district appeal court in the 1930's, he

[90] KNA, PC/NZA.4/1/1/1: Minutes of Central Nyanza Local Native Council, 19 Aug. 1931.

[91] The Native Catholic Union differed from the Kavirondo Taxpayers' Welfare Association in advocating the continuation of the hut and poll tax in preference to a universal poll tax. Officials thought that Native Catholic Union opposition to the poll tax was in deference to missionary wishes; KNA, PC/NZA.3/48/6: H. R. Montgomery to Provincial Commissioner, 26 June 1925. The missionary director of the Native Catholic Union supported the hut tax as both a crude form of graduated income tax and an economic disincentive to polygamy; Rev. H. G. Farmer to editor, *East African Standard*, 4 Aug. 1928.

had performed this judicial function, but otherwise had exercised little real authority after the transfer in 1920 of the district headquarters from Mumia's village to Kakamega, twenty miles away. Nevertheless, Mumia himself retained a revered position in the affections of most Luyia people. In 1931 Ezekiel Apindi was instructed by the North Nyanza Local Native Council to ask for Mumia's appointment as "guardian of the soil" against settler encroachment.[92] But this affection did not include his brothers and other relatives who had in 1909 been "temporarily" imposed as agents of the government over many Luyia locations, mainly in the north, west, and southwest of North Nyanza.[93] In 1909 North Nyanza had been a turbulent district and it was thought that only the Wanga had sufficient appreciation of the administration's requirements to maintain order. But in the 1920's the Wanga agents were still in office. This was not for any lack of local Luyia opposition. From the first there had been incidents of non-co-operation and affrays, often instigated by families that had exercised power or influence in the localities before the establishment of the Wanga hegemony. At first the government was disinclined to tolerate what it termed this "self-determination" movement—since its Wanga agents were "undoubtedly intelligent, capable and progressive."[94] But as popular revulsion grew more extreme, officials had to admit that they could not but sympathize with the movement "which seems a perfectly natural one and inevitable, and the only thing [that they could do was] to control it and guide it with as little friction as possible."[95] Also, by the 1920's, many representatives of locally influential families had been educated, and the Local Native Council provided a forum in which their newly articulated demands could be heard on a basis of equality with the Wanga members of council. By the early 1930's, the government had come round to the view that "the astuteness of Mumia, allying himself with the newcomers, in the early days of the European occupation of Kavirondo, must have given him an overwhelming advantage" in presenting Wanga territorial claims. Other tribes, by contrast, had been "too shy to send representatives to early district commissioners.[96] In 1928 Mu-

---

[92] KNA, DC/NN.3/2: North Nyanza Local Native Council abstracts, 24 Mar. 1931.

[93] The main source of information about the establishment of the Wanga hegemony and subsequent Luyia opposition to it is a series of memoranda by C. M. Dobbs, Provincial Commissioner of Nyanza, 1930, based on old political records. Ibid. There is a brief account in John Middleton, "Kenya; Administration and Changes in African Life, 1912–45," in Vincent Harlow and E. M. Chilver (eds.), *History of East Africa*, II (London, 1965) 373-77.

[94] *Nyanza Province Annual Report,* 1923.

[95] Ibid., 1929.

[96] Ibid., 1932.

lama was excommunicated for polygamy[97] and by 1935, all the Wanga agents had been replaced by locally born chiefs. In most cases, popular feeling had been led by the mission elements, and all of these had some connection with the North Kavirondo Taxpayers' Welfare Association.

Luyia Organizations: The North Kavirondo Central Association, 1932–35

In 1931 gold had been discovered in the densely populated southeastern corner of North Nyanza, leading to an influx of European farmers turned prospectors.[98] The Kenyan government was now faced with an extraordinarily embarrassing situation. It was unthinkable—in European circles in Kenya at any rate—that prospecting and digging should be prohibited. Yet only a few months earlier, in 1930, the Native Lands Trust Ordinance had ostensibly set aside reserves "for the use and benefit of the native tribes of the Colony for ever." Under pressure from the Labour government in London the administration of Kenya had been forced to incorporate in the Ordinance the provision that for any land excluded from the reserve for any public purpose other than communications, an area equal in extent and, if possible, in value should be added. Another important clause stipulated that no lease could be granted nor exclusion made before the Central Land Board had obtained the views of the Local Native Council and Local Land Board (which had African representation) in the area concerned. Any objection on their part was to be referred to the Secretary of State in London. In any case, no lease could be granted in any area under beneficial occupation.

The area of the goldfields was clearly "under beneficial occupation"; it was thickly populated and closely cultivated. However, the government argued[99] that mining operations might be short-lived, and that permanent exclusion of land from the reserve, entailing the addition of equal areas of land in exchange, would be unnecessarily cumber-

[97] Mulama, a Christian, was on the local Anglican church council. One of his Luo accusers was so heated that, when presenting charges to Owen, "it was only by the grace of God that [Owen] was prevented from punching him." Owen to District Commissioner, North Nyanza, early 1921. Cited in KNA, DC/NN.3/2: Dobbs, "History of Wanga Domination in Marama." KNA, DC/NN.10/1/3: C. B. Thompson (District Commissioner, North Nyanza) to Lloyd Feild-Jones (Provincial Commissioner), 1 May 1929.

[98] For the economic history of the gold mining, see Fearn, *An African Economy*, 123-50; Dilley, *British Policy*, 264-74, discusses the episode as a matter for imperial concern.

[99] Legislative Council *Debates*, 20 Dec. 1932, 510.

some. Instead, the affected areas might be temporarily excluded, with compensation to those evicted being paid in cash rather than in other land. The government argued, further, that it would be "merely a farce" to consult the North Nyanza Local Native Council on these changes: "It would simply add to their aggravation to consult them because, on every single occasion, if we went to the natives concerned or the Local Native Council, they would say 'We do not want to do it'; and we should then have to say: 'It doesn't matter whether you want to do it or not; it has got to be done.' "[100] With scarcely a dissenting voice, the Native Lands Trust (Amendment) Ordinance, incorporating these major changes to the principal Ordinance (itself enacted such a short time before), was rushed through the Legislative Council in December 1932, just before the Christmas parliamentary recess.

There was a first-class row in the English press and parliament over the betrayal of the imperial pledges to consult African landholders and to add land to reserves. The Africans of western Kenya were no less concerned and scarcely less articulate. Not only were Europeans claiming their land and sometimes destroying their crops and huts in the search for gold, but their representatives in the Local Native Council were powerless to stop this influx; indeed, they had not even been consulted. A more strident political voice was obviously needed, and it appeared in the form of the North Kavirondo Central Association. It was led, in the main, by schoolteachers who allied not with individual chiefs but with one chiefly family only, the Wanga; it relied on petitions to the Secretary of State and co-operation with the Kikuyu rather than a privileged association with the missionary and administrative authorities; and it aimed at the reform of the Local Native Council's composition, not merely an enhancement of its powers. These new political perspectives were not prompted solely by the unprecedented crisis of the gold rush.

In addition, the North Kavirondo Central Association had to move into new paths because the approach used by the Kavirondo Taxpayers' Welfare Association was not open to it. First of all, the North Kavirondo Central Association received no European advice; second, the Luyia official chiefs, conscious of the fact that their local positions had only recently been confirmed as against the Wanga agents, were suspicious of any fresh moves to promote Luyia unity. This negative attitude meant that the North Kavirondo Central Association could not engage in large-scale welfare projects. In any case, such schemes were increasingly the responsibility of the Local Native Council, being financed out of local rates. As a consequence, the administration pro-

[100] Chief Native Commissioner, Armigel de V. Wade, ibid., 512.

hibited the collection of fees by the new Association, arguing that the submission of petitions involved little expense;[101] this prohibition no doubt acted as a further deterrent to any chief contemplating support for the Association. The end result was that, in contrast to the Kavirondo Taxpayers' Welfare Association which had, with official African support, achieved its successes within the local arenas of district and provincial administration, the North Kavirondo Central Association had to turn elsewhere for allies.[102]

These observations need some amplification, for they are important. The personal and missionary factor must be considered. During 1932 and 1933, when mining activity was confined to prospecting and alluvial operations, local African opinion was hurt and enraged by the encroachments, but it was also rather bewildered. But Archdeacon Owen, who over the years of controversy had refined his means of contact with the English press and parliament, was able to swing into immediate action, mainly through his dispatches to London "direct from the front line."[103] He was also able to provide both the Luo and Luyia branches of the Kavirondo Taxpayers' Welfare Association with the formal rules for presenting a petition to Parliament. The resultant petition protested against the terms of the Native Lands Trust (Amendment) Ordinance and expressed its "appalling surprise that His Majesty's Government should go back on its word given to the natives of Kenya in which our only hope lies."[104] If the gold had to be mined, then the petitioners asked that operations be conducted by the state or a public utility company,[105] with a percentage of royalties being paid into Local Native Council funds. The Native Anglican church councils also cabled word of their distress to the Archbishop of Canterbury.[106] But the gold rush continued unabated. Having at least one European on their side must have given the members of the Kavirondo Taxpayers' Welfare Association some comfort;[107] and Owen's knowledge of the constitutional channels of protest enabled the Kavirondo Taxpayers'

[101] KNA, PC/NZA.4/5/5: *North Nyanza Monthly Intelligence Report,* Aug. 1934.

[102] There is a summary of North Kavirondo Central Association activities in Rosberg and Nottingham, *Myth,* 161-63, 177-78, 186, 218.

[103] Owen Papers: Rev. Handley Hooper (CMS Africa Secretary) to Owen, 6 June 1933.

[104] Printed in full in *Kenya Land Commission Evidence,* III (Nairobi, 1934), 2137-2139.

[105] This suggestion seems to have been first made in a letter from W. McGregor Ross to Owen, 10 Jan. 1933, Owen Papers.

[106] Ibid.: Owen to Hooper, 10 Feb. 1933.

[107] Their dismay when Owen refused to help in the drafting of the parliamentary petition is discussed below.

Welfare Association to avoid methods which would have invited official repression.

The North Kavirondo Central Association had no such help. The core of the goldfields, in the eastern locations of North Nyanza, was in the Friends' African Mission sphere of influence. All the early North Kavirondo Central Association leaders were Friends' African Mission adherents. The Friends' African Mission, recruited from America's Middle West, had an apolitical tradition. It was at this time gravely understaffed; it was also rent by theological dissension between its older "Fundamentalist" and its younger "Modernist" missionaries.[108] The expatriate members could not discuss these questions among themselves, let alone take their African adherents into their full confidence. There were external difficulties too. The area, for long the special preserve of the Friends' African Mission, was being invaded by Catholic influence and by the Salvation Army. Many of the Friends' brightest pupils defected to the Church Missionary Society school at Maseno, which then enjoyed an unchallenged academic reputation in Nyanza. To crown it all, the Friends' African Mission was also facing the new problem of separatism among its followers. It was clearly in no position to take constructive action. It did not even take the relatively simple step of keeping American and English Quakers informed of local developments in the gold mining crisis.[109] It is not surprising then that the mission never adopted a collective attitude, one way or the other, on the problems of the North Kavirondo Central Association.[110]

In addition, it seems that members of the North Kavirondo Central Association thought that the threat to their land was so serious that no European could be trusted to present a strong enough case.[111] It is possible that this natural feeling was reinforced by the way in which Owen, on advice from London, had refused to help in the drafting of the Kavirondo Taxpayers' Welfare Association parliamentary petition on the grounds that a less grammatical African production would carry more weight.[112] However, a more fundamental reason for the lack of European help for the North Kavirondo Central Association lay in

[108] John A. Rowe, "Kaimosi: An Essay in Missionary History" (unpublished M.A. thesis, University of Wisconsin, 1958).

[109] Kaimosi Mission Papers: American Friends' Board of Foreign Missions to Friends' African Mission, 6 Mar. 1933; Owen Papers: Ross to Owen, 18 Jan. 1933.

[110] KNA, Secretariat file ADM.35/2/2/1: *Nyanza Province Monthly Intelligence Reports*, May, June, 1939.

[111] Pascal Nabwana, OBE, ex-Senior Chief Jeremiah Segero, and Moses Muhanga (onetime secretary of NKCA), interview with the author at Kimilili and Kakamega, 20 Apr. 1965.

[112] Owen Papers: Owen to Hooper, 10 Feb. 1933.

its aproach to the problem of attracting support. The Association had started in a small way in 1932, and through 1933 and 1934 it was still struggling for popular recognition against a background of administrative opposition.[113] Several of its leaders were fined and imprisoned for obstructing miners and uprooting their stakes to claims. Being unable to attract mass support, the Association then turned to the ruling dynasty of the Wanga tribe, so recently stripped of its former glories. Though Mumia was now paramount chief in name only and both bitter and in despair at his loss of power and the invasion of European prospectors,[114] his brothers were more resourceful. Early in 1935 Murunga addressed a mass meeting of the North Kavirondo Central Association urging Luyia unity;[115] in June of the same year, Mulama accepted the title of paramount chief from the Association. The administration dismissed him from the chieftainship of Marama, replacing him with a local man, a member of the North Kavirondo Taxpayers' Welfare Association who had been prominent in earlier campaigns against Mulama.[116] This episode typified the difference between the two associations. The North Kavirondo Taxpayers' Welfare Association, an alliance between locally influential families and the Christian establishment, was delighted at the removal of the last representative of the Wanga hegemony. The North Kavirondo Central Association, while holding no brief for direct Wanga rule over non-Wanga locations,[117] sought to capitalize on the only possible focus for Luyia unity and, by selecting the extremely able Mulama, to ensure that the post of paramount chief would really mean something in administrative terms after the death of Mumia.

There was, thus, powerful local opposition to the North Kavirondo Central Association.[118] Furthermore, apart from Mulama, its activists

[113] North Kavirondo Central Association pamphlet *Avaluhya—"Kinship,"* translated by the Friends' African Mission at Kaimosi: copy in KNA, DC/NN. 10/1/2. The pamphlet starts with an historical introduction followed by copies of petitions to the Secretary of State.

[114] KNA, PC/NZA.3/31/1/2: Dobbs to Colonial Secretary, 23 July 1930; Owen Papers: Owen to Hooper, 24 Jan. 1933.

[115] North Kavirondo Central Association, *Avaluhya*.

[116] KNA, PC/NZA.4/5/5: *North Nyanza Monthly Intelligence Reports*, June, July, 1935.

[117] Exemplified by its appointment of a non-Wanga, Chief Sore of Isukha, as assistant paramount chief.

[118] The North Kavirondo Central Association's difficulties may be illustrated by reactions to its choice of Baluyia as the name for the peoples previously known as the Bantu Kavirondo. This was derived from *oluyia*, the fireplace where clan elders congregated, and therefore rejected by chiefs as "an assertive appellation which a number of young men had given to themselves." KNA, Secretariat file ADM.4/1.III: Provincial Commissioner to Chief secretary, 5 Sept. 1940.

were not men of major standing and its base in the eastern locations of North Nyanza was more than usually rent by lineage and denominational factionalism. The Association's president, Andrea Jumba, was a Friends' African Mission schoolteacher in Tiriki, but support from local Friends' African Mission adherents was difficult to mobilize, for many of the mission's teachers, like Jumba, originated from the neighboring location of Maragoli, and this the Tiriki resented.[119] Erasto Ligalaba, the North Kavirondo Central Association's first secretary and probably its moving spirit, was employed in Nairobi as a compositor on the government Swahili newspaper, *Habari*. As such, he was a new phenomenon in Nyanzan politics: hitherto all political leaders had been locally employed, and it is perhaps significant that Ligalaba's activity in Maragoli, his home, did not last more than a few months. There was as yet no close contact between rural and urban politics in western Kenya of the kind then developing among the Kikuyu. On the other hand, Ligalaba's successor as secretary, John Adala, came both from a small mission, the Church of God, and a small location, Bunyore, though his post as teacher in the district's Government African School did give him wider contacts.[120] Of the Association's members, only John Adala and two others were members of the North Nyanza Local Native Council.[121]

This last point is vital. The Luo Kavirondo Taxpayers' Welfare Association was able to campaign for increased Local Native Council powers because it was well represented on that body. If the North Kavirondo Central Association was to achieve any power it had to work for more radical reforms. This it did on two fronts, internal and external. Internally, it engaged in some minor welfare schemes as a demonstration of what a paramount chief would consider his governmental duties.[122] But it carried the implications of its demand for a paramount chief much further. Not content with echoing Apindi's complaint that the Local Native Councils did not have enough say in the expenditure of local rates, the Association demanded that these be administered jointly by the North Kavirondo Central Association and Local Native

[119] Andrea Jumba, interview with the author in Tiriki, 13 Apr. 1965.

[120] John Adala, interview with the author in Nairobi, 27 Apr. 1965.

[121] KNA, PC/NZA.4/5/6: Notes of meeting between District Commissioner and North Kavirondo Central Association Committee, 18 May 1938, in *North Nyanza Monthly Intelligence Report*, May 1938.

[122] For example, by building improved watering facilities in competition with the Colony's Health department; as reported in KNA, Secretariat file ADM. 35/2/2/1: *Nyanza Province Monthly Intelligence Report*, Jan. 1940. The North Kavirondo Central Association had been allowed to collect funds to build a meeting hall. Another source of finance was the (African) North Kavirondo Chamber of Commerce, which was associated with the North Kavirondo Central Association.

Council.[123] For, again in direct contrast with the early Kavirondo Tax-payers' Welfare Association, the North Kavirondo Central Association argued that the Local Native Council was unrepresentative, being packed with chiefs and their nominees.[124]

After 1936, when it became apparent that the goldfields were very small, the North Kavirondo Central Association found it still more difficult to arouse local support—until threats to African land were renewed just before World War II. Therefore, it turned to outside help. In contrast to the early Kavirondo Taxpayers' Welfare Association, the North Kavirondo Central Association was remarkable for the number of petitions sent directly to the Secretary of State in London in contra-vention of the regulation that all representations should be forwarded through the district administration.[125] The local impasse could also be circumvented by other means, especially contact with the Kikuyu and Luo. The North Kavirondo Central Association's links with the Kikuyu dated from the start of the Association. Many miners brought with them Kikuyu employees, some of them members of the Kikuyu Central Association. By mid-1933, some Luyia were paying subscriptions of two shillings to these Kikuyu Central Association members, to get a "docu-ment from King George." Ligalaba, the North Kavirondo Central Asso-ciation's first secretary, was acquainted with Kikuyu leaders in Nairobi, and by June 1934 he, Andrea Jumba, and other members of the Asso-ciation were in direct contact with the Kikuyu Central Association's headquarters in Nairobi.[126] The Kikuyu politicians had of course long experience of protest over land alienation; the North Kavirondo Cen-tral Association leaders were conscious of this and felt that they and the Kikuyu were now fighting "the same battle."[127]

But, after the initial flurry of activity, the North Kavirondo Central Association's continuing external contacts seem to have stemmed more

[123] KNA, DC/NN.10/1/2: North Kavirondo Central Association to Secre-tary of State, 24 July 1936.

[124] Legislative Council Debates, 9 Mar. 1937, cols. 195-96.

[125] Assistant Chief Luka Lumadede Kisala (onetime vice-president, North Kavirondo Central Association) in interview in Maragoli, 12 Apr. 1965, told me that the North Kavirondo Central Association ensured that the District Commis-sioner's copy was always posted well after the one addressed to London.

[126] KNA, PC/NZA.4/5/5: North Nyanza Monthly Intelligence Report, June 1933; Kaimosi Mission papers: Friends' African Mission Secretary to missions in Kikuyuland, 27 May 1933; Christian Council of Kenya Papers: Fred Hoyt to Kenya Missionary Council Race Relations Committee, 2 Mar. 1934; KNA, DC/NN.10/1/2: Goldfields Police to Criminal Investigation Department, 20 June 1934; and information from the several North Kavirondo Central Association leaders interviewed in Apr. 1965.

[127] Ex-Senior Chief Jeremiah Segero and Moses Muhanga, interview with author at Kakamega, Apr. 1965.

from the ambitions of ex-Chief Mulama than concern over gold mining. The government had made it clear that it would not appoint a paramount chief to succeed Mumia, arguing that the development of the Local Native Councils had made such an appointment redundant.[128] Mulama therefore needed different legal and social precedents for his case. Accordingly, only three months after his dismissal from the chieftainship, he sought advice from the Kabaka of Buganda. He considered visiting England to present his case; failing satisfaction there, it was rumored that he would have favored secession to Ethiopia.[129] The North Kavirondo Central Association was forbidden to collect funds for Mulama's passage to England, so he turned to the next best forum, the Colony's Legislative Council. He enlisted the aid of the Indian member, Shamsud Din, who, in the debate on the Native Authority bill, argued that the Imperial British East Africa Company's treaty of 1889 with Mumia justified the resurrection of an effective Wanga paramountcy in North Nyanza.[130]

Nairobi was at last becoming a focus of political attention. The North Kavirondo Central Association's acute land grievances, Mulama's ambitions, and the obstruction of such local channels of communication as the missions, chiefs, and the Local Native Council had forced the Association to look beyond the locality. There was another factor in the situation: the influx of Europeans had created a local market for African produce. African producers and small traders combined in the North Kavirondo Chamber of Commerce to exploit this opportunity, in rivalry with established Indian shopkeepers. In this commercial enterprise the Luyia discovered a new community of interest with the Luo Kavirondo Taxpayers' Welfare Association such as had not existed since the stirring days of the early 1920's.

The New Kavirondo Taxpayers' Welfare Association and the Kisumu Native Chamber of Commerce

But it was a very different Kavirondo Taxpayers' Welfare Association. By the early 1930's, the chiefs and the Christian establishment were no longer on cordial terms with one another. And during the decade many of the Kavirondo Taxpayers' Welfare Association's educated leaders had achieved their goal of responsible incorporation in the colonial

[128] KNA, DC/NN.3/2: Speech by acting Governor Armigel Wade, 15 July 1935, at Kakamega.

[129] KNA, DC/NN.10/1/2: Memorandum, "Present Activities of the NKCA," 9 Oct. 1935.

[130] Legislative Council *Debates*, 9 Mar. 1937, cols. 179-82.

system and its ancillaries. Some, including Jonathan Okwiri, Paul Mboya of the South Nyanza branch, and Paul Agoi of the North Kavirondo Taxpayers' Welfare Association, had become locational chiefs. Their ability and commitment to progress commended them to both the administration and the people. Others, such as Simeon Nyende and Ezekiel Apindi of the Kavirondo Taxpayers' Welfare Association and Jeremiah Awori[131] had become ordained Anglican priests, exercising full pastoral responsibility at least until 1945, when the death of Archdeacon Owen seemed to rob the Church Missionary Society of some of its liberal momentum.[132] Still others found opportunities in the steadily increasing number of posts available in governmental agencies—in the veterinary, agricultural, medical, postal, and railway services, and in government schools. Such positions carried little weight in local politics; they were not daily concerned with the life and land of the villages. And with the progressive raising of educational standards, many younger men must have found local political horizons somewhat constricting, even if they were not yet thinking in national terms. Finally, partly in accord with his general desire to encourage African initiative and partly because of ill health, Owen withdrew from active politics in 1936.

But there was a growing body of men, enterprising and relatively well educated, who instead of increasing satisfaction experienced growing frustration. These were the African small traders. With them, one can begin to talk of a section of African society with economic interests which were both readily definable and in conflict with the interests of many of the chiefs and other establishment figures who had figured so largely in the early leadership of the Kavirondo Taxpayers' Welfare Association. Thanks to the withdrawal of the chiefs and the Christian establishment, after about 1935 the Luo traders and their organization, the Kisumu Native Chamber of Commerce, virtually took over the Kavirondo Taxpayers' Welfare Association. By World War II the Kavirondo Taxpayers' Welfare Association and Kisumu Native Chamber of Commerce were indistinguishable, with the same secretary and an overlapping membership.

As with the North Kavirondo Central Association, local conflicts had wider implications. Resentment of the chiefs' economic advantages provoked African thinking on the real meaning of Britain's declared policy of trusteeship. Traders who were members of insignificant lineage groups sought to eradicate kinship as the basic constituency of the Local Native Council elections. They also sought support from Kikuyu

131 Father of W. W. W. Awori, prominent in the Kenya African Union after World War II.

132 Welbourn and Ogot, *A Place to Feel at Home*, 27.

Central Association leaders who were mobilizing their Kikuyu clans in defense of their land. The traders' general failure to achieve economic progress prompted close consideration of the central government's agricultural and marketing policies. As in the months before the emergence of the Young Kavirondo Association in 1921, as in the early Kavirondo Taxpayers' Welfare Association's protests against the abuse of chiefly authority, and as in the North Kavirondo Taxpayers' Welfare Association members' campaign against the Wanga hegemony, there had been disputes on internal social matters between the Christian establishment and the chiefs, so now the political associations of western Kenya questioned the bases of local society. But in the late 1930's these questions were of a much more radical character, because they identified the pillars of local society with the props of colonial rule.

The Kisumu Native Chamber of Commerce had been founded in 1927 by John-Paul Olola, whose home location was Alego in Central Nyanza, but whose government service as an agricultural instructor had brought him possession of a freehold farm near Kisumu, on the site of an old government farm at Kibos. He was a remarkable man, passionately interested in climatic and soil conditions, rainfall, and the progress of his exotic crops, such as oranges and pineapples.[133] He had a wide range of contacts throughout the province, dating from his days as an inspector, and possessed considerable organizational ability, and, rare in African traders of those days, competence in bookkeeping. His first venture was a dairy co-operative, but he soon branched out into other activities such as milling maize and making ghee.

Retail trading and produce marketing was then almost entirely in the hands of Indians who had the advantage of long experience and well-established credit facilities. The chiefs were the African middlemen: they retained some of their traditional control over local markets; they capitalized on the desire of the Indian traders for influential contacts in the rural areas; because of close contact with the administration, they tended to put larger acreages than most under cash crops, cultivating them with departmental advice.

The men who joined Olola's Kisumu Native Chamber of Commerce had no such advantages. At an early Kisumu Native Chamber of Commerce meeting in 1931, a member declared that "there was rigid misunderstanding between the Native Chiefs and the Native Traders . . . because the Native Elders who have power and authority to [ad]minister the reserves were very badly misled by the Chiefs who are in the habit of telling them before attending the Local Native Council's meeting and in every occasion that they should not attempt

[133] Olola's diaries record such details over a number of years. I am indebted to him for allowing me access to his private papers.

to say anything against the Indians who are trading in the reserves, because the Indians have induced them with bribes, but the poor Native traders mean to develop their country, which the majority of the Chiefs have not yet realised."[134]

This protest clearly raised issues of local government, which will be considered later. But the marketing nexus between the chiefs and the immigrant entrepreneurs raised a wider issue, that of trusteeship, which had in 1930 been reiterated as the cornerstone of British East African policy.[135] In 1932 Olola had opened a branch of the Kisumu Native Chamber of Commerce in South Nyanza. According to the District Commissioner, Olola posed "as champion of native rights as expressed in the Memorandum on Native Policy. He gets resolutions passed by his Chamber of Commerce urging Government to deport the Indians and to punish Chiefs who accept bribes from them and allow the erection of [ghee] separators."[136] The Kisumu Native Chamber of Commerce went on to suggest that the encouragement of African trade should be just as much a function of government as the promotion of African agriculture,[137] and that the practice of granting produce-buying licenses to Indians was "not the procedure of lifting up the natives at all."[138] African traders should instead enjoy positive discrimination in their favor; they should be "considered as learner traders," paying smaller licenses than immigrants.[139]

Local disabilities raised wide questions. They also prompted wider contacts. Olola's main associate in the Kisumu Native Chamber of Commerce was Zablon Aduwo Nyandoje, who had been a clerk in the office of the District Commissioner in Kisumu, and then in a firm of Indian lawyers. His clan, the Kanyakwar, had originally lived somewhere near Kisumu but had been displaced at the turn of the century by disease, war, and the establishment of the administrative station. Galvanized into action by the arrival of the Kenya Land Commission in 1932, the clan had presented its claims for land, including part of Kisumu township, and for their own official chief. Zablon Aduwo was one of the few literate members of the clan. John Daniel Odele was another. Odele had been down to Nairobi to present the clan's claims

---

134 John L. Riddoch papers, privately held: T. G. Nyaoro, in minutes of Kisumu Native Chamber of Commerce meeting, 19 Apr. 1931.

135 Cmd.3573 (1930), *Memorandum on Native Policy in East Africa.*

136 *South Nyanza Annual Report,* 1932.

137 Zablon Aduwo Nyandoje (secretary, Kisumu Native Chamber of Commerce) to editor, *East African Standard,* 27 Jan. 1934.

138 KNA, PC/NZA.4/1/2/1: Kisumu Native Chamber of Commerce to Governor Sir Henry Moore, 18 Sept. 1940.

139 KNA, PC/NZA.2/565: Kisumu Native Chamber of Commerce to Provincial Commissioner, 26 Apr. 1938.

to the chief Native Commissioner. His fare had been paid by the Kikuyu Central Association and he had discussed his people's predicament with the Kikuyu.[140] At this time the Kikuyu Central Association, through its associate, the Kikuyu Land Board Association, was mobilizing Kikuyu clans to present evidence to the Land Commission.[141] One can only speculate as to whether the Kikuyu Central Association would have helped Odele and his clan had there not been this fortuitous coincidence of interests. Certainly the Kanyakwar's claim was not a big issue of policy. But the coincidence did open a new channel of communication between Nyanza and the Kikuyu.

The social origins of Aduwo, a member of an oppressed clan, and Olola, with his farm some fifty miles away from his home location, were probably not typical of the Kisumu Native Chamber of Commerce's membership as a whole. But they did dramatize the small trader's concerns, especially the need to circumvent the privileged economic connections of lineage dominance and administrative office. The Kisumu Native Chamber of Commerce adopted two tactics, the one social, the other political. Its first explicit clash with the old Kavirondo Taxpayers' Welfare Association leadership had occurred in 1931, when Ezekiel Apindi was selected by the administration to represent Nyanza before the Closer Union investigation in London. The Kisumu Native Chamber of Commerce had then protested that Apindi was not sufficiently outspoken, that Africans had not been consulted on the choice, and, above all, that he was too closely involved in the mission hierarchy.[142] The distrust of the European nomination of African representatives was a political suspicion,[143] but Apindi's social standing as a member of the Christian establishment added to the Kisumu Native Chamber of Commerce's objections.

There is little doubt that some Christian leaders exploited their privileged position within the educational system to secure a disproportionate share of the limited school opportunities for their kinsmen and clients—Archdeacon Owen was increasingly worried by this development.[144] Also, together with the official chiefs, they took the lead

[140] Kenya Land Commission Evidence, III, 2148-59.

[141] Rosberg and Nottingham, Myth, 145. ·

[142] KNA, PC/NZA.4/1/1/1: Minutes, Central Nyanza Local Native Council, 1 Apr. 1931; Riddoch Papers: Minutes, Kisumu Native Chamber of Commerce, 19 Apr. 1931; and information from ex-Senior Chief Jonathan Okwiri and Olola.

[143] For Kikuyu distrust of Chief Koinange, on similar grounds, see Parmenas Githendu, "The Story of Parmenas Mockerie of the Kikuyu Tribe, Kenya," in Margery Perham (ed.), Ten Africans (London, 1963), 166.

[144] Terence Ranger, "African Attempts to Control Education in East and Central Africa, 1900-1939," Past and Present, XXXII (1965), 84.

in commercializing their land, in erecting Western style houses, and in enclosing fields on which they employed laborers.[145] In so doing, they affronted traditional attitudes to communal land ownership; their neat hedges made many of their kinsmen fear that they were becoming "black settlers."[146] The arrival of the Kenya Land Commission in 1932 brought into the open the hopes of those who were politically and socially privileged, and the fears of those who were not. The Kavirondo Taxpayers' Welfare Association called for a land register, "protected by an Order-in-Council of His Majesty, King George," which would record the territory of each clan.[147] This was opposed by nearly every speaker at a public meeting with the Commission.[148] The Kisumu Native Chamber of Commerce also submitted a memorandum attacking the idea.[149] The Kavirondo Taxpayers' Welfare Association had made no mention of individual title deeds—Owen himself, whom the Kisumu Native Chamber of Commerce accused of influencing the Kavirondo Taxpayers' Welfare Association in this respect,[150] regarded such deeds as premature[151]—but the Association's critics evidently feared that individual freehold would be the outcome of any land registration.

Representatives of both the dominant clans which held the original rights to their land, and of those clans which held land as tenants and clients, opposed any form of registration. The former feared that their clients would too easily win the unchallengeable rights to land that were customarily acquired only over several generations of good behavior; tenants on the other hand feared that their subordinate status would be unalterable once recorded on an official form. The Kisumu Native Chamber of Commerce's opposition to registration stemmed from the viewpoint of the underprivileged: "without a proper safeguard the wealthier tribes may subsequently legally dispossess poorer tribes and sub-tribes and individuals." Land tenaciously preserved by clan elders "would gradually be slipping from our hands by sale to richer tribes and individuals or by costly procedures on each transfer or initial costs." With individual titles, "the natives would cease to think of the tribe as a whole and . . . selfishness would be developed in the native's character."

145 Owen Papers: Owen to secretary, International Missionary Council, 29 Apr. 1935. This is also the impression gained by the author while visiting elderly church and political leaders at their homes in 1963 and 1965.

146 Ex-Senior Chief Jonathan Okwiri, interview with the author in Uyoma, Apr. 1963.

147 *Kenya Land Commission Evidence*, III, 2139.

148 Ibid., 2166-2172.

149 Ibid., 2144-2147. The quotations below are from the memorandum.

150 Ibid., oral evidence of Zablon Aduwo, 2169.

151 Ibid., Owen's oral and written evidence, 2190-2197 and 2198-2204 respectively.

But the Kisumu Native Chamber of Commerce's apparent championship of minor lineages was in this respect at odds with its members' interests as traders. Both Luo and Luyia Chambers of Commerce were untiring in their demands that traders be allowed loans from Local Native Council funds or commercial banks,[152] being as often reminded by the administration that customary conditions of land tenure could offer no form of security in return. A few years later the traders seem to have admitted the force of this argument, and the Kavirondo Taxpayers' Welfare Association—now dominated by Olola and Aduwo —accepted the Land Commission's recommendation that land registration be introduced progressively through clan and family toward individual tenure.[153] Nevertheless, these new men were determined that this concession should not play into the hands of the official chiefs and dominant clans. In late 1936, with Olola in the chair and Aduwo as secretary, a Kavirondo Taxpayers' Welfare Association meeting appeared, innocently enough, to carry on its former leadership tradition in suggesting that the security of a land register would not be complete until it was vested in a paramount chief.

When all holders of rights in land had been registered the meeting "asked that a suitable African be engaged as a HEAD, to hold responsibility for these duties, and that the power of the right holders be pro tected by ORDER IN COUNCIL." Echoing Ezekiel Apindi's sentiments of five years previously, the meeting urged that no European should have any power of management over African land, "because the District Commissioners, besides their own decisions, have so many advisers from the different parts of the communities, whose intentions are to deprive natives of their lands." What was wanted was "A NATIVE HEAD CHIEF whose duties will be to deal with the Lands matters etc."[154] But in the 1920's a Luo paramount chief would have been chosen by the Christian establishment in concert with the incumbent chiefs. These men were no longer active members of the Kavirondo Taxpayers' Welfare Association. The Kavirondo Taxpayers' Welfare Association-Kisumu Native Chamber of Commerce might want a paramount chief to perform the same defensive political functions, but they certainly did not see him as an establishment figure—the establishment had proved itself incapable of promoting the interests of anyone out-

[152] Riddoch Papers: Minutes, Kisumu Native Chamber of Commerce, 19 Apr. 1931; *Central Nyanza Monthly Intelligence Report*, Oct. 1931: Provincial Commissioner's file ADM.12/2/4, Kisumu; KNA, PC/NZA.4/5/5: *North Nyanza Monthly Intelligence Report*, May 1936; KNA, PC/NZA.4/1/2/1: Kisumu Native Chamber of Commerce to Governor Sir Henry Moore, 18 Sep. 1940.

[153] KNA, DC/CN.8/2: Minutes, Kavirondo Taxpayers' Welfare Association, 25 Oct. 1936; ibid.: Notes of Kavirondo Taxpayers' Welfare Association interview with Provincial Commissioner, 14 Nov. 1938.

[154] Ibid.: Minutes, Kavirondo Taxpayers' Welfare Association, 25 Oct. 1936.

side its circle. The Kavirondo Taxpayers' Welfare Association-Kisumu Native Chamber of Commerce continued to discuss the appointment and by 1939 they had concluded that only candidates sponsored by the Association should stand for election for the posts of paramount chief and president of the Local Native Council.[155] In their last recorded debate on the subject, the Kavirondo Taxpayers' Welfare Association-Kisumu Native Chamber of Commerce proposed that the Rev. Simeon Nyende—then carrying on a bitter land dispute with the dominant lineage of Gem Location—should be the Luo paramount chief, with Olola as president of the Local Native Council. The Provincial Commissioner, noting that the Luo backed the North Kavirondo Central Association's choice of ex-Chief Mulama as the Luyia paramount chief, rightly concluded that such proposals would mean "the overthrow of all the existing native authorities."[156]

The Kavirondo Taxpayers' Welfare Association-Kisumu Native Chamber of Commerce and the North Kavirondo Central Association occupied very similar positions in their neighboring societies. The North Kavirondo Central Association had claimed that the Luyia Local Native Council was unrepresentative. The Kavirondo Taxpayers' Welfare Association-Kisumu Native Chamber of Commerce did too. Their argument here was of a piece with their initial rejection of a land register. Local government representation was biased in favor of the larger clans, they felt, and took insufficient account of those enterprising individuals who might make their living outside their natural lineage constituency. As John-Paul Olola put it at a meeting in March 1937,

> the elections to Local Native Council's made in reserves, is the one [way] of defiling Africans and decrease of the Africans' progress. The reason is that a best man who owns good knowledge and well understanding, cannot win a majority in any vote in the reserves, as most of these best people live outside the reserves, and for that, whenever they appear at home, the elders seem to be ignorant of their abilities, otherwise they report them unnecessarily to the Administrative Officers on creating disturbances in the reserves. Actually speaking these are the types of people that can carry out the Government orders among the natives and can try to avoid the abuses arising in the part of justice etc.[157]

Earlier, the Kavirondo Taxpayers' Welfare Association-Kisumu Native Chamber of Commerce, with John Adala of the North Kavirondo Central Association present, had discussed radical electoral reforms

---

[155] Ibid.: Minutes, Kavirondo Taxpayer's Welfare Association, 16 Dec. 1939.

[156] Copy in KNA, DC/NN.10/1/2: Provincial Commissioner to District Commissioner Central Nyanza, 10 June 1940.

[157] KNA, PC/NZA.2/565: Minutes, Kavirondo Taxpayers' Welfare Association, 25 Mar. 1937.

to meet this kind of objection. They considered that the current system of electing councilors to represent "family and group" interests produced too many representatives who were qualified to do little more than claim their travel allowances; instead there should be something approaching a communal roll which would secure the representation of other interest groups in addition to the lineages. The Association proposed that one third of the Local Native Council membership should be "selected by the mutual consent of Government"; a further third to be "elected by the majorities of the African pagans"; and a final third to be "selected by the Africans of the best advanced, that is to say Native Agricultural, clerks, masons, etc."[158] The demand was repeated a year later,[159] and again refused. Not only would the paramount chief be a challenge to the local establishment; he would be responsible to a council which would reflect other than purely tribal interests.

Co-operation Among Political Organizations, 1936–40

For all their radical social views, the administration was probably correct in describing the associations as representing only minorities in these years. Economic change had not shaken fundamental loyalties to the lineage as the primary social unit, and townsmen had as yet made little impact on Nyanza sentiment. Nevertheless, by the late 1930's Luo and Luyia political associations had shaken off their earlier establishment features; they were free to mount an unequivocal attack on govmental policies should it be necessary. It has already been suggested that their local difficulties opened the eyes of both the North Kavirondo Central Association and Kavirondo Taxpayers' Welfare Association-Kisumu Native Chamber of Commerce to wider possibilities. In the last three years before World War II direct governmental action greatly accelerated this process, and at the same time ensured that the associations' protests would voice mass opinion locally. For the policies of the government suddenly seemed to pose a new threat to all that the ordinary African held most dear—his land, his crops, and his cattle.

As traders, the leaders of the Kisumu Native Chamber of Commerce had shown a developing racial consciousness in their resentment of the Indian stranglehold on produce marketing. By the same token, they were alert to governmental restrictions on crop production itself. Protesting against restrictions on African coffee growing, the Kisumu Native Chamber of Commerce urged that Africans were "only black with our skins but not our crops as well."[160] So, when the government,

[158] KNA, DC/CN.8/2: minutes, Kavirondo Taxpayers' Welfare Association, 14 Sep. 1935.

[159] Ibid.: Minutes, Kavirondo Taxpayers' Welfare Association, 25 Oct. 1936.

[160] Riddoch Papers: Joel Omino, in minutes of Kisumu Native Chamber of Commerce meeting, 19 Apr. 1931.

alarmed at the rate of soil erosion in the increasingly overcrowded African reserves, implemented measures of soil conservation and cattle culling in 1938 and 1939, it was moving into a very sensitive area. African opposition was most dramatic elsewhere in Kenya, especially among the Kamba and Taita peoples, with the Kikuyu Central Association playing a crucial co-ordinating role.[161] Nyanzan politicians already had links with the Kikuyu Central Association, forged from local discontents. These were now strengthened, and in a much wider cause.

The initiative seems to have come from the Kikuyu. In September 1938, Jesse Kariuki, the vice-president of the Kikuyu Central Association, visited ex-Chief Mulama in company with the most outspoken Indian member of the Legislative Council, Isher Dass. It was rumored that Mulama paid £12 into Kikuyu Central Association funds.[162] The emissaries warned against the forthcoming Highlands Order-in-Council. A few months later, the visit bore fruit in a joint Kavirondo Taxpayers' Welfare Association-Kikuyu Central Association memorandum to the Secretary of State, protesting that the Order closed all possibility of African expansion outside the reserves.[163] The government's soil conservation and cattle culling measures were indeed designed to contain the growing African population within the reserves. To Africans, it seemed rather that the policy would mean that their work "for Lands, Education and Agriculture would be put back further than ever"; none of these could go forward "without cattle, goats and sheep." These remarks were made in March 1940, at a meeting in Nairobi between representatives of the Kikuyu Central Association, North Kavirondo Central Association, and Kavirondo Taxpayers' Welfare Association which marked the climax of the growing co-operation between Nyanza and Nairobi.[164] During the course of this activity, the Kavirondo Taxpayers' Welfare Association had published a joint statement with the Kikuyu Central Association newspaper, *Muigwithania*. Zablon Aduwo described this as having been drafted in conjunction with the "Kenya African Intertribal Association."[165] There seems to be no other evidence that this association in fact existed. But its formation would have been

---

[161] For discussion of government's land usage measures and the whole range of African opposition, see Rosberg and Nottingham, *Myth*, 163-78.

[162] KNA, PC/NZA.4/5/6: *North Nyanza Monthly Intelligence Report*, Sept. 1938.

[163] Isher Dass read part of the memorandum into Legislative Council *Debates*, 21 Apr. 1939, cols. 286-88.

[164] KNA: DC/NN.10/1/2: "The Conversations of the KCA, KTWA and A(baluyia) NKCA," 4 Mar. 1940; present were Jesse Kariuki, Joseph Kang'ethe, and George Ndegwa of the Kikuyu Central Association; ex-Chief Mulama and Moses Muhanga of the North Kavirondo Central Association; and Zablon Aduwo.

[165] KNA, DC/CN.8/2: Zablon Aduwo Nyandoje to Provincial Commissioner, 2 Dec. 1939.

the logical outcome of the African reaction to governmental policies that were unprecedented in the extent of their interference with the daily life of the mass of rural Africans.

While the Nyanzan associations were groping toward a common African front for the whole Colony, they were also finding that the new governmental measures were generating a popular outcry that had not been heard since 1922. North Kavirondo Central Association support seems to have expanded rapidly in the hitherto quiescent northern locations of North Nyanza, following on the fencing off of a pilot soil conservation scheme. This and other measures were represented as but the prelude to alienation of the land to Europeans. And, ominously enough for the government, some official chiefs appeared to think that the depth of popular dismay was sufficient to warrant their tacit collaboration with the North Kavirondo Central Association.[166] The Kavirondo Taxpayers' Welfare Association-Kisumu Native Chamber of Commerce found similar issues to exploit in Central Nyanza. The administrative authorities began to chafe at the growing popular obstruction of their policies. Then the war came. The Provincial Commissioner warned that opposition could no longer be tolerated. The North Kavirondo Central Association announced its voluntary liquidation less than a month after the proscription of the Kikuyu Central Association.[167] Only after the District Commissioner warned against the dangers of political activity going underground did the Provincial Commissioner spare the Kavirondo Taxpayers' Welfare Association-Kisumu Native Chamber of Commerce.[168] Neither Luo nor Luyia politicians were particularly vocal during the war years, and at its end a younger and better educated generation took the lead in nationalist organization. But when the nationalists sought local mass support it was to the issues of soil conservation and land consolidation that they turned, and it was the leaders of the North Kavirondo Central Association and Kavirondo Taxpayers' Welfare Association-Kisumu Native Chamber of Commerce on whom they depended for local insights and whose increasingly radical language they used.

Conclusion

In conclusion, we may return to the beginning of this essay. There a contrast was drawn between the independent churches and the political associations of the inter-war years. The former enlisted the enthusi-

[166] KNA Secretariat file ADM. 35/2/2/1: *Nyanza Monthly Intelligence Reports,* July 1939, Feb., Apr. and Mar. 1940.

[167] KNA, DC/NN.10/1/2: District Commissioner, North Nyanza, to Provincial Commissioner, 17 June 1940.

[168] KNA, DC/CN.8/2: Kenneth Hunter to Sidney Fazan, 13 June 1940.

asms of ordinary folk while the latter mobilized their leaders. The churches were confused in their attitudes to modernity and unwilling to work within a political system which they scarcely understood. The early politicians on the other hand were eager for progress and hoped to manipulate a political system in which they already enjoyed a recognized status. And, as we have just seen, even their more radical successors, the traders, initially saw the key to political power in reshaping the political system, in securing election by "the Africans of the best advanced." They did not consider the alternative—the mobilization of popular pressures from "the majorities of the African pagans."

If the churches voiced the cries of a confused society, the politicians' confusion did not arise until much later with their realization that their modern aims, which had been sought by closer acceptance within the colonial system, could be completely gained only by sweeping that system away. On the local level this realization was in direct response to the government's programs for agrarian change. Hitherto the government had allowed the local African authorities a certain amount of initiative. But soil erosion was too alarming a problem to allow of African solutions. And improved husbandry was so technical an issue that it was assumed that it could only be controlled by the European officers of the central government. Progress, it was argued, could come only if the reins of colonial authority were tightened.

The colonial system might have been reformed by decorous debate. It could be swept away only by popular pressure. The tribesmen of western Kenya had opposed the imposition of colonial rule as warriors; they now opposed the government's agrarian dictates as peasants. Here was the mass support which the politicians needed. And in eliciting the popular symbols for their revolutionary new tactic of doing away with colonial rule altogether, some among them turned to the memories of armed resistance and the inspired groping of the independent churches as the keys to the mass African self-confidence that was now required.[169]

[169] For the importance of the African memories of resistance in later politics, see Terence Ranger, *Revolt in Southern Rhodesia, 1896-7: A Study in African Resistance* (London, 1967), 345-86. For connections between western Kenya politicians and the churches in the 1950's, see Odinga, *Not Yet Uhuru,* 133; Welbourn and Ogot, *A Place to Feel at Home,* 20, 59-61, 68; KNA, DC/NN.11/1: G. H. Webb, "Report on the Mumias Division of North Nyanza" (1957).

THE EMERGENCE OF THE TANGANYIKA
AFRICAN NATIONAL UNION
IN THE LAKE PROVINCE

ANDREW MAGUIRE

The Tanganyika African National Union actually began in the Lake Province of Tanganyika years before its official founders proclaimed its birth in Dar es Salaam in 1954. Before the name of Julius Nyerere was known in Mwanza, Shinyanga, Bukoba, or even in Musoma a few miles from his own home—not to mention in the rest of Tanganyika—the leaders of the Lake Province branch of the Tanganyika African Association had articulated the ideological principles and perfected the organizational techniques on which the Tanganyika African National Union later built its power throughout the territory. The leaders of the Association in the Lake Province—the most prominent of whom were Paul Bomani, Isaac Bhoke Munanka, and Saadani Abdu Kandoro—were Tanganyika's first full-time political organizers: they were the first to move from words of petition to direct action; they were the first to organize on an inter-tribal basis; they were the first to forge the essential political link between town and countryside; they were the first, in short, to transform a tradition of diffused and sporadic protest into the dynamism of modern African nationalist politics.

This is not to suggest that the impulse toward a full-fledged nationalist type of political action was not felt elsewhere in Tanganyika before 1954. It was. But outside the Lake Province this impulse suffered from one or both of two inadequacies. Either it failed to move beyond the discussion of principles and drafting of memoranda by an elite few to the organization of a truly indigenous political movement; or, where organization of a political base was successfully effected and action taken, the political impulse failed to transcend the parochial issues and the tribal identification which had prompted its initial local success.

639

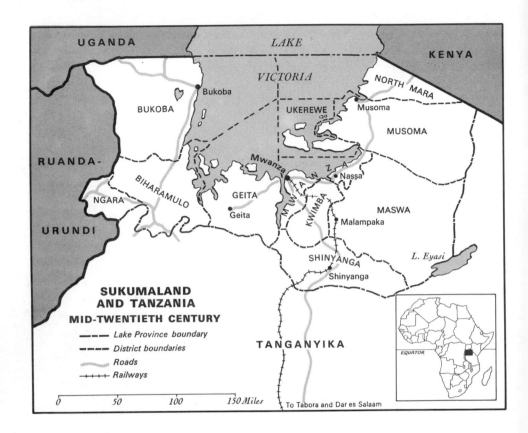

The Tanganyika African Association, which was founded with the help of British civil servants in Dar es Salaam in the late 1920's, generally suffered the shortcomings of an "elitist" organization. Its members were mainly government servants, commercial clerks, teachers, and traders. Despite some "modest forays" into politics in the 1930's, the Association "remained for long little more than a mutual benefit society, a social organization catering for urban Africans."[1] Political activity took the form of articulating African opinion on those occasions when a special governmental commission or United Nations mission specifically called for an expression of views. Members of the Association gave evidence in 1933 to a special commission established by the British Parliament to report on the administration of justice in Tanganyika; in 1947 they protested proposals for the formation of an East

[1] This was the assessment of the then Governor, Sir Donald Cameron. Quoted in Ralph A. Austen, "Notes on the Pre-History of TANU," *Makerere Journal*, IX (1964), 2.

African High Commission which incorporated revisions regarded as favorable to white settlers in Kenya and prejudicial to Tanganyikan interests; they wrote petitions to the United Nations Visiting Missions to Tanganyika of 1948 and 1951; they produced memoranda in 1950 for Governor Twining's Committee on Constitutional Development and for a visiting Minister of State for Colonial Affairs.[2]

But, despite a collaboration between graduates of Makerere College and ex-servicemen which revitalized the leadership of the Association in postwar Dar es Salaam and directed the attention of the organization to more frankly political concerns, the Association's activities —except in the Lake Province—remained largely insulated from the countryside. Though it claimed thirty-nine branches in 1948 and five thousand members in 1951, and though the United Nations Visiting Mission of 1951 found branches of the Association in "practically every town of importance" that it visited,[3] these up-country outposts often contained little more than a handful of civil servants who, when transferred from Dar es Salaam or some other major center where they had been nominal members of the Association, established a "branch" by virtue of their presence in the new location. Except in the Lake Province, branches of the Association neither influenced nor were influenced by rural Africans.

Equally prejudicial to the development of a full-fledged nationalism was the fact that tribal associations, which developed strength in some areas in the inter-war and post-war periods, suffered a "parochial" limitation. Like the Association, tribal unions catered first to town dwellers—in this instance to those who wished to preserve their identity and to participate in some scheme of mutual benefit after a disrupting move from the security of rural life into an unknown urban environment. Unlike the Tanganyika African Association outside the Lake Province, these associations occasionally did organize town-rural coalitions productive of effective political action, but they were of local interest.

Thus, in 1951 in Kondoa, the leaders of the Warangi Union combined agitation for the removal of a chief with resistance to the government's soil conservation measures. In 1951–52 the Kilimanjaro Chagga Citizens' Union demanded and received, then successfully contested, the election of a paramount chief. In the same years, Kirilo Japhet galvanized thousands of Meru tribesmen into a citizens' union to protest the eviction of African families from land alienated by the government

[2] George Bennett, "An Outline History of TANU," *Makerere Journal,* VII (1963), 1-2; Judith Listowel, *The Making of Tanganyika* (New York, 1965), 186-94.

[3] Bennett, "Outline History of TANU," 2.

to a European concern—a case which Japhet took directly to the United Nations in 1952. However, even in such rare instances of direct political action by a tribal union, the particular cause, and the tribal character of the resulting political effort, forestalled the translation of locally inspired action into organized intertribal nationalist activity. Although the Meru land case, which became a "byword among politically conscious Africans . . . widely known and talked about . . . from one end of the Territory to the other,"[4] unquestionably became one of the more powerful symbols of incipient Tanganyikan nationalism, it remained for the precocious political organizers of the Lake Province to number it among those local issues with territory-wide implications which could be exploited for purposes of pan-tribal political mobilization.

Why should the Lake Province have served as a cradle of Tanganyikan nationalism in the years before 1954? Why should this up-country region, more than seven hundred miles from Dar es Salaam and one of the last inland areas of East Africa to be "opened up" by explorers, traders, and administrators, have provided the principal testing ground for nationalist-oriented political organization in advance of the formation of the Tanganyika African National Union?

Size and wealth provided an initial reason. Provincial Commissioners of the Lake Province often pointed with pride to the fact that the territory which they administered equaled Nyasaland in size. Further, its relatively heavy population, about two million, and its natural wealth made it accountable for well over half of Tanganyika's total agricultural and mineral production. The Lake Province had cattle and smaller stock animals; it produced coffee, cotton, and a host of lesser crops; it mined diamonds and gold; there was a small but growing fishing industry; commercial and service occupations proliferated where towns sprang up at the interconnections of roads and railroad, railroad and lake steamer. It has been as true in East Africa as elsewhere that where economic stakes are high and where a significant portion of the population is involved in economic life, politics is an ever-present possibility.

A second factor, closely related to the first, was that an unusually overbearing administration—even by the relatively rigorous standards of British colonialism in Africa—produced an early political counterreaction in the Lake Province. While the economic promise of the province was unquestionably considerable, British agricultural experts forecast desiccation of the land if existing cultivation methods were not radically altered to conform with "rational" principles of land utiliza-

4 United Nations, Trusteeship Council, Official Records (Supplements), *Visiting Mission to Trust Territories in East Africa: Report on Tanganyika*, 1954 (T/1169), 88, 54-55.

tion. This prompted the administration during the post-war years to undertake in the Lake Province—especially in Sukumaland—one of Britain's major efforts at colonial economic development. At the same time, the administration concentrated on the introduction of English-style local governmental institutions—an effort which, unhappily, made it easier to impose unwelcome agricultural policies from above than for the participation in democratic institutions from below.[5]

Third, and this factor is again dependent on the first two, the Lake Province had political "entrepreneurs" with nationalist inclinations who were willing by nature, and able in the circumstances, to organize associations committed to effective political action. Mwanza in particular —which, though small, was one of Tanganyika's major urban centers— attracted younger, educated members of Tanganyika's emerging, nontraditional elite. As elsewhere in Tanganyika, these potential leaders might have remained isolated from the people of the countryside. But in the Lake Province the negative reaction produced among the people by the administration's development policies gave those from the town who had a political bent an entrée into the surrounding rural areas. Given this entrée, the forging of an initial political link between town and countryside was further facilitated by the fact that the relatively modest educational and occupational attainments of those who comprised the elite of Mwanza and other Lake Province towns, as distinct from major centers like Dar es Salaam, did not divorce potential leaders from close personal and economic ties with rural people. At the same time, among the rural people of the relatively developed Lake Province, there was a considerable number with enough economic and political sophistication to permit them to move easily into contact with town life and town-based leadership.

Once the political leaders had forged links between town and countryside, they found themselves able both to exploit for nationalist purposes the possibilities for mass support inherent in the larger tribal

[5] For details on the administration's post-war programs for economic and political development see the author's *Towards Uhuru in Tanzania: The Politics of Participation* (Cambridge, 1969), 17-42; Hans Cory, *The Indigenous Political System of the Sukuma and Proposals for Political Reform* (Kampala, Uganda, 1954); B. J. Dudbridge and J. E. S. Griffiths, "The Development of Local Government in Sukumaland," *Journal of African Administration,* III (July 1951), 141-46; Elspeth Huxley, *Sorcerer's Apprentice* (London, 1948), 176-81; J. Gus Liebenow, "Responses to Planned Political Change in a Tanganyika Tribal Group," *American Political Science Review,* L (June 1956), 442-61; D. W. Malcolm, *Sukumaland: An African People and Their Country* (London, 1953); N. V. Rounce, *The Agriculture of the Cultivation Steppe* (Cape Town, 1949); J. V. Shaw, "The Development of African Local Government in Sukumaland," *Journal of African Administration,* VI (Oct. 1954), 171-78. The body of this essay is based in part on material presented at greater length in the author's *Toward 'Uhuru,'* especially chs. 3, 5, and 6.

units within the province, *and* to transcend tribal identifications by establishing an intertribal organization throughout the province based on a central principle of protest which rejected the very existence of the colonial regime itself. In other words, given the presence in the province of not one but two large and dominant tribal units (the Sukuma and the Haya) plus a host of smaller tribes, these leaders combined the extensive support and emotional élan occasionally engendered by a politically active but parochial tribal association with the inter-tribal membership and nationalistic ideological impulse previously characteristic only of elitist groups. It was the genius of Lake Province politics, and its contribution to Tanganyikan political history, that this achievement came in the two years before the formation of the Tanganyika African National Union and that it predated by three to four years the Tanganyika African National Union's own consolidation of a mass basis of support in geographically diverse rural areas.

Beginnings

As elsewhere in Tanganyika, the proto-nationalist politics of the voluntary associations emerged first in the towns. It was in the towns of the Lake Province—Mwanza and Shinyanga in Sukumaland, Bukoba and Musoma—where traders, artisans, clerks, salaried domestic and industrial employees, and civil servants lived and worked. It was in the towns that they gathered together to discuss common ideas and mutual grievances and, eventually, to organize in furtherance of their own interests. The towns were populated by Africans of a multiplicity of tribes; the membership and leadership of the associations reflected this diversity. There were civil servants originally from Northern Rhodesia, Nyasaland, the Congo, or some other part of Tanganyika where mission education had made an early start. There were Muslim "Swahili" traders in the townships who had, or whose fathers had, traveled the trade routes from Zanzibar and the coast to Tabora, Lake Tanganyika, and Lake Victoria. There were representatives of local tribal groups who, by dint of chiefly relationship or proximity to a mission school, had received some education or who, formally uneducated, had themselves become Swahili-speaking traders.

Politically, the Tanganyika African Association was the most important of numerous African-led associations, unions, and welfare groups operating in Mwanza during the late 1940's. Frequently dismissed at the national level by Tanganyikans and European observers as the Tanganyika African National Union's mild predecessor, the Association in Mwanza was never reducible to civil servants giving tea parties. Unhampered by tribal, religious, or occupational prerequisites of membership, the Association bridged a diversity of parochial interests. From its formation in February 1945 the Mwanza branch concerned itself with the rights, welfare, and advancement of urban and, subsequently, of rural Africans. The opening of the Association office in Mwanza—which was soon to become the provincial headquarters of the organization—marked the beginning of the first phase of post-war African nationalist politics in the Lake Province.

For the first years, the Association's branch in Mwanza differed little from branches of the Association elsewhere. It catered to an urban elite, and concerned itself mostly with African interests in the town: social questions, mutual benefit activities, night school classes, township rules and regulations, municipal facilities, labor problems, and town government. The Association lacked a permanent office and had no full-time staff, but meetings were convened more or less regularly (once a month in a member's house) and were moderately well attended (about thirty persons per meeting). Membership may have reached one hundred by 1946; it continued to expand gradually into the early 1950's when, under fresh impetus, it began to climb more quickly.

By 1947, in addition to Mwanza, eight other at least nominal outposts of the Association existed in the Lake Province. Because of its size and central location, the prior existence of the government's provincial offices, and the presence of a functioning branch of the Association, Mwanza seemed the natural site for a provincial Tanganyika African Association headquarters. In April 1947, Joseph Chombo, a medical officer who was the enterprising secretary of the Association of Mwanza, called for a provincial conference to be held in Mwanza the following month. Despite an emphasis on education and economic advancement, Chombo's letter of invitation to the Association's leaders throughout the province had the character of a political manifesto with its contention that Africans must "unite and push forward," that "no one else will liberate us . . . other than we ourselves." Lamenting that members had not often enough in the past gathered to discuss and act in unity through the Tanganyika African Association, "the great voice of all we Africans," Chombo noted that the Association was weak also because it lacked paid officers and a permanent headquarters. Though the Association had the largest membership of any organization in the area, Chombo emphasized that its importance was not yet recognized and respected by many Africans—a situation which he urged be rectified for the benefit of both urban and rural Africans.[6]

---

[6] Chombo to "Honorary Secretaries" of the Tanganyika African Association in Biharamulo, Bukoba, Missungwi (in Mwanza district), Musoma, Ngara, and Ngudu (in Kwimba district), Apr. 25, 1947, files of the Lake Province adminis-

Representatives from eight of the Association's branches from Bukoba to North Mara attended the two-day conference. A wide variety of items were vigorously debated in striking anticipation of issues which were to become prominent in the politics of the later 1950's. Participants expressed suspicion and resentment of non-Africans who monopolized trade and took African land; opposition to specific tax levies combined with dissatisfaction and misunderstanding regarding the use of Native Authority revenues; opposition to specific natural resources measures combined with a growing distrust of the administration's intentions concerning African well-being and advancement; and dismay at the increasing identification of Native Authorities with the administration.[7] The demand for self-government was not yet explicit and the Association still hoped to enlist the support of Native Authorities in the rural areas. Still very much a compilation of grievances, the minutes of the conference were presented to the Provincial Commissioner by African leaders who were more suppliants than revolutionaries. As yet the pressure of undesired governmental programs was not sufficiently great, nor African sentiment in rural areas sufficiently aroused, to galvanize a miscellany of complaints into focused opposition to the colonial system itself.[8]

Though exhilarated by the provincial conference, the Association's grander plans for a permanent headquarters, full-time staff, and recruitment of rural Africans appear to have slipped quickly into the background, because of the stubborn practical difficulties involved. Tanganyika was not yet at that stage when full-time politics would be either a profitable political or a sound financial undertaking. Therefore, the leaders of the Association found themselves returning to the more pedestrian role of raising an occasional objection, periodically forwarding a complaint, or consulting at the invitation of the administration regarding African appointments to the Township Authority.

Another milestone in the development of the Association in the Lake Province was passed in 1948 with a petition by members of the Shinyanga branch to the first United Nations Visiting Mission to Tanganyika. The petition pleaded eloquently for more educational oppor-

---

tration of the Government of Tanganyika (transferred from Mwanza to the National Archives, Dar es Salaam, in 1965). (Original in Swahili.) I would like to express my gratitude to the Government of the United Republic of Tanzania for permission to conduct the research upon which this essay is based and, in particular, for permitting me to consult government documents relevant to the period under study.

[7] The term "Native Authority" refers to the Chief, or the Chief in Council—the statutory authority of local government under British Colonial Administration.

[8] Minutes of a Provincial Conference of the Tanganyika African Association held in Mwanza, May 17–18, 1947, Lake Province files. (Original in Swahili.)

tunities, greater participation of Africans in administration and government, a higher standard of living, provision for African competition with Asian traders in the towns, full African control of trade in rural areas, higher wages for mine workers, and a greater share of the revenues earned from Tanganyika's mineral wealth. The petitioners asked for "full freedom in speech . . . in publications of all sorts and in public life" and they pleaded for an end to the "heart-breaking . . . color bar . . . if good social relation and mutual agreement between the different Nationalities [in the territory] . . . are to be put into practice."

The Shinyanga document set forth keenly and clearly that to accomplish any African advancement fundamental changes in the relations between rulers and ruled were required. The petitioners understood that the alleviation of specific grievances would not be sufficient, that an equality in rights, opportunities, and status *generally* would be required. Nor did the Shinyanga document avoid the crux of the matter —the exercise of political power. While expressing "heartfelt thanks" for "all the British people have so far done," and while acknowledging that changes would take place "in accordance with the supervision of the British Government," the petitioners expressed "thanks and gratitude to the United Nations *for securing us freedom.*" Though they did not state explicitly the goal of independence, the petitioners pointed unmistakably toward self-government:

> We wish, even at present, that the Native Authority be given more power to run its own affairs. . . . We are of the opinion that once we are given a chance surely we can prove our ability and nobody will regret it. . . . We wish the whole African public and not the few as at present, to be allowed a fair part in the administration of their country—in other words, Africans should be consulted in all forms of bills and proposals and their choice should seriously be considered; by that way we trust the democracy as embodied in the United Nations Charter and the Trusteeship Rules would be readily complied with.

Not yet aware that "democracy" would require nothing less than the departure of the colonial rulers, nor that Africans themselves might disagree over the means and structures of enhanced African participation, the Shinyanga group nevertheless posed the fundamental political questions of power, authority, and consent which were to underlie the specific controversies and dominate the political struggles of the 1950's. The Shinyanga petition was a most unusual document in the Tanganyika of 1948. It clearly stated the essential issues between mature colonialism and aggressive nationalism years before nationalism itself had come of age.[9]

Three years later, in a petition to the 1951 United Nations Visiting Mission, the Association's provincial headquarters in Mwanza defined the political goal of Tanganyikan Africans as complete independence—the first time in Tanganyikan history that this goal was so clearly specified. Asking the mission to consider the views of Africans as well as of the administration, the Association stated:

> The Africans must now have a big say over the rule and public funds of the Territory in order to enable them to acquire independence in the near future. In fact it is high time that Africans should be given an opportunity to start shouldering the rule of the country.

Specifically, the Association requested increased African representation in the Legislative Council; immediate introduction of the elective principle for all public bodies (for example, Provincial Councils, the Land Utilization Board, the Cotton Board); responsible posts for Africans in administrative and technical cadres; abolition of ninety-nine year leases of Crown Lands to non-Africans and the restriction of European settlement; a single educational system with Swahili rather than English the medium of instruction; better education for Tanganyikans including overseas training in countries other than England for lawyers, engineers, doctors, and teachers (perhaps with direct financial assistance from the Trusteeship Council of the United Nations); and finally, in the economic sphere, encouragement of African co-operatives, loan banks for Africans, a percentage of mining and estate revenues to be directed to local Native Treasuries, and free trade with the rest of the world to make imported goods less expensive and reduce the cost of living.[10]

The Mwanza petition was even more strongly worded than the petition from the Association's headquarters in Dar es Salaam. Though the Dar es Salaam petition made some similar and some additional points, there was no language comparable to Mwanza's explicit: "to acquire independence in the near future." Yet, however eloquent, language can never be the whole of politics. The truly decisive political development was to come a year later with the advent of full-time political organizers—men who differed from their predecessors not as much in background as in their singular vocational commitment to politics as a way of life.

[9] The petition, dated Aug. 20, 1948, was reproduced in full in United Nations, Trusteeship Council, Official Records (Supplements), *Visiting Mission to Trust Territories in East Africa: Report on Tanganyika*, 1948 (T/218). (Italics mine.)

[10] United Nations, Trusteeship Council, Official Records, "Petitions from Tanganyika," T/Pet. 2/103, Oct. 1951. (Mimeographed.)

The New Politics

In the early 1950's, the Association in the Lake Province transformed itself under new leadership into a thoroughly activist, even militant, organization. In rural areas specific grievances relating to Asian and Arab domination of the economy and a general dissatisfaction with Native Authorities and the European administration permitted, indeed prompted, political activation of the people of the countryside. Bent on translating a variety of existing discontents into a potent political force, the Association broadened its base of support and intensified its effort to articulate the political views of Africans to higher authority.

The new brand of politics angered the administration, which continued to be preoccupied with its own strenuous efforts to inject principles of English local government into the Native Authority system and to transform the economy. The interests of the administration and of African politicians then polarized. Misunderstandings compounded a widening gap in loyalties and outlook. Denied the political leverage that it sought by administrators who turned a deaf ear to the complaints of political leaders and rejected their appeals for a role in local government, the Association in the Lake Province turned to attack the colonial regime itself. Amidst the maze of rules and orders then obtaining in the Lake Province, it was not a difficult task to link the aspirations for freedom from colonial rule of the more sophisticated elite with the desires of the ordinary rural farmer for freedom from rules which prevented him from cultivating his land as he saw fit.

Thus it was that intense and highly organized political activity (of the sort usually associated with the later phases of the Tanganyika African National Union's development) flourished in the Lake Province for at least two years before the Tanganyika African National Union was formed. The subsequent appearance of the Union in mid-1954 required little more than a change of letterhead. The Tanganyika African National Union in the Lake Province was basically the Tanganyika African Association under a new name; for the Association had already achieved—in leadership, membership, organization, style, and ideology —the status of a full-scale political movement.[11]

[11] In the early 1950's two other associations—the Lake Province Growers' Association of cotton co-operatives and the politically oriented Sukuma Union— also played important roles in the rural areas in transforming latent discontent into organized political action. For a detailed account of the growth and activities of these two organizations see the author's *Toward 'Uhuru,'* 75-113, 122-31, 143-49. For an even fuller treatment of the Sukuma Union, see the author's "Toward 'Uhuru' in Sukumaland: A Study of Micropolitics in Tanzania, 1945-1959" (unpublished Ph.D. dissertation, Harvard University, 1966), 103-61; 211-49.

The architects of the invigorated Lake Province Association of the early 1950's were Paul Bomani, Bhoke Munanka, and S. A. Kandoro. In 1967 these men were, respectively, Minister of Commerce and Co-operatives, Minister of State (President's Office), and Area Commissioner (Bagamoyo) in the government of the United Republic of Tanzania. Because of the importance of their political roles, a description of their personal backgrounds is relevant.

Bomani, the son of a Sukuma Seventh-day Adventist teacher and preacher, was born and educated at a mission in Musoma district. In 1944, after nine years of school, including a teacher training course, he was expected by the Adventists to follow in his father's footsteps. Though he wanted to continue his education at Tabora, Tanganyika's finest secondary school, at Makerere College in Uganda, and possibly at a foreign university, his way was apparently blocked by the disappointed Adventists. The older Bomani then took a job at the Mwadui diamond mine in Shinyanga, and Paul became a clerk at the company store. In 1947 Paul became treasurer-accountant of the African Traders Co-operative Society in Mwanza; and in 1949, managing secretary. In the early 1950's he founded the cotton co-operative movement and organized the Lake Province Growers' Association—later to become the giant Victoria Federation of Co-operative Unions. A member also of the Tanganyika African Association and of the Sukuma Union, Bomani became president of the latter in 1951 and of the Association in 1952. One of Mwanza's outstanding figures, he also served in those years on the Township Authority and the Lake Province Council.

Munanka, a Kuria from North Mara district to the east of Lake Victoria, completed Standard X and a two-year clerical course at the Tabora School. Posted to Mwanza as a government clerk in 1948, he became a member of the Tanganyika African Association but did not become prominent until after his resignation from government service in January 1952. Never happy as a civil servant, Munanka found his forte in active politics. He was elected vice-president of the Association in January 1952 and president after Bomani went to study in the United Kingdom in October 1953.

Kandoro, the son of a Manyema trader-farmer and a native of Ujiji (a town on the Tanganyikan side of Lake Tanganyika), completed a teacher-training course at a school near Mwanza in 1944 before taking up a post in the Native Treasury in Tabora. He resigned his government post in 1946 to become a trader. The initiator of various associations of a semi-political or political nature in the Ujiji-Tabora area (including a branch of the Tanganyika African Association in 1944), he took his political predilections with him on trading trips, traveling sometimes as far as Mwanza, Musoma, and even Nairobi. He sold chairs, oil, and utensils at the town markets where he traveled, but he also talked politics, and in Mwanza he met Bomani and Munanka. He recalls addressing a large meeting in the Mwanza community center where people were "surprised to see a man who sold chairs at the market wanting to govern."[12] He claims to have questioned the validity of alien rule as early as 1947 and to have pushed for the reorganization and rechristening of the Tanganyika African Association in early 1952. In that year Bomani and Munanka asked him to become secretary of the Association in the Lake Province. In 1953 he moved his home from Ujiji to Mwanza, the better to devote his efforts to his new post.

With Kandoro's election as provincial secretary in mid-1952, the top leadership of the Association moved for the first time into the hands of men who were not, or who were not still, civil servants. No longer was the Association to be the avocational interest of men whose major energies were absorbed elsewhere; the Association would be the work of men who served as full-time political organizers, who dedicated the major portion of their energies to the fostering of African enterprises and associations with an economic or political cutting edge. No longer would the Association simply register grievances or present petitions or organize in ad hoc response to a particular need in a particular locality; the Association would become a full-scale political movement led by men motivated by a singular passion for the most fundamental political change of all—self government. From the time of their first all-night political discussions in Mwanza in 1951–52, Bomani, Munanka, and Kandoro defined their goal explicitly, simply, and powerfully: "to search for ways to release the country from enslavement . . . to work for an end to alien rule."[13]

In January 1952, Kandoro and Munanka wrote to the headquarters of the Tanganyika African Association in Dar es Salaam proposing that the Association's name be changed to dramatize the Association's transformation into a more strident political organization. In February, Bomani, Munanka, and Kandoro met with representatives of the Association's branches in Shinyanga and Bukoba to decide on bylaws for the Lake Province organization which would serve temporarily until bylaws could be established for Tanganyika as a whole.

Aside from the rather pedestrian outline of the organizational structure and of the duties of officeholders, the bylaws specified that provincial meetings be held four times yearly, that officers be elected annually, and that entrance fees and annual subscriptions be 6d. and

---

[12] S. A. Kandoro, interview, Nov. 21, 1964.

[13] S. A. Kandoro, *Mwito wa Uhuru* (The Call of Freedom) (Dar es Salaam, 1961), 19. (All quoted material from Kandoro has been translated by the author from the original Swahili unless otherwise noted.)

4d. respectively. A permanent provincial office in Mwanza would be staffed by a full-time salaried secretary who could not accept part-time employment elsewhere. The drafters explicitly laid down that no provincial officers could be government servants or work for European or Asian concerns—a ruling dictated certainly by the need that they felt to make politics itself a full-time occupation, but also, perhaps, by a desire to avoid untoward influence or pressure from employers who might not be entirely sympathetic to the activities of the Association. The drafters of the bylaws delineated no political aims of the Association as such, but they did state specifically that "the Provincial Branch has the right to appeal to the United Nations if the Colonial Office or the Dar es Salaam [Tanganyika Government] Secretariat are unwilling to listen, to give assistance, or to forward representations to higher authority."[14]

Throughout 1952 resentment against the administration mounted, most notably on issues posed by compulsory destocking, taxes on cattle and cotton production, and agricultural regulations. Responsibility for the enforcement of the myriad regulations and for the prosecution of transgressors rested in the first instance with chiefs and headmen, and popular dissatisfaction with Native Authorities grew apace. In January 1953 Munanka and a delegation of the Association's representatives met with the Provincial Commissioner to urge that destocking and livestock taxation be abolished and that the people themselves—rather than Native Authorities alone—be more thoroughly consulted on legislative questions. The outcome of the meeting was unsatisfactory from the Association's point of view: aside from reiterating the necessity for the legislation in question, the Provincial Commissioner maintained that the people were properly consulted through public meetings held by Native Authorities and increasingly through new local councils. These were the established channels through which the Association should register its views.[15]

While the Association stepped up its activities at the provincial headquarters in Mwanza, the branches in Shinyanga, Geita, Nassa, Bukoba, Ukerewe, and Musoma became increasingly active. There were minor outposts in smaller centers as well. While each branch concerned itself with the issues common to all parts of the Lake Province—princi-

---

[14] Minutes of a meeting to draft bylaws for the Tanganyika African Association, Lake Province, Feb. 1952, Sukuma Union files, privately held, Mwanza, Tanzania. I am indebted to former officers of the Sukuma Union for permission to consult papers relating to the history of the organization.

[15] "Notes on Meeting Between the Provincial Commissioner, Mwanza, the Deputy Provincial Commissioner, Malya, and the African Association on Friday, 13th February, 1953," Lake Province files.

pally natural resources legislation and growing disenchantment with Native Authorities and the colonial administration—each involved itself in problems particular to its own locality: cattle trading in Shinyanga, boat service and access to grazing reserves in Geita, arbitrary prosecution procedures and restrictions on African trade in Nassa, and rules pertaining to coffee cultivation and food crops in Bukoba. On the other hand, branches sometimes transcended the local environment to make suggestions of a territorial nature, as when the Shinyanga branch proposed the use of Swahili in the Legislative Council and greater African representation in all governmental bodies.

While the Association in the Lake Province assumed the posture of a forceful political organization with full-time leadership, regular meetings, and extensive membership, the territorial headquarters of the Association in Dar es Salaam "was without a president, and no meetings were held during the second part of [1952]."[16] In view of the fact that the Association in Dar es Salaam had become "dormant," the leaders in the Lake Province district discussed the possibility of asking that the territorial headquarters of the Association be transferred to Mwanza.[17] Julius Nyerere took over the presidency of the Tanganyika African Association in 1953 and the headquarters remained in Dar es Salaam, but "the next year was spent in drawing up a new constitution and in seeking the support of the tribal authorities for the new organization,"[18] Meanwhile, without help from Dar es Salaam, the Association in the Lake Province rapidly became the single most powerful, anti-colonial political force in Tanganyika.

In August 1953, however, the administration made its first overt move against the development of African political activity. Governor Twining ordered "that in future members of the senior and junior services . . . might not be members of political associations."[19] Though the ruling applied to all races, there can be no doubt that it was directed primarily at the members of the Tanganyika African Association. Based, of course, on the British principle of an impartial civil service, the ruling, nevertheless, made no sense in Tanganyika in 1953 unless it was designed to cripple what the government regarded as a developing "opposition" movement. Ironically, the leadership of the Association in the Lake Province—by far the strongest branch of the Associa-

---

[16] Quoted from J. Clagett Taylor, *The Political Development of Tanganyika* (Stanford, 1963), 95, and based on Colonial Office, *Report on the Administration of the Tanganyika Territory for 1952,* 39.

[17] Joseph K. Petro, "Political History of TAA Shinyanga," a paper prepared for Kivukoni College, Dar es Salaam, 1964; and Petro, interview, Nov. 1964.

[18] Taylor, *Political Development of Tanganyika,* 95.

[19] United Nations Visiting Mission, 1954, 75.

tion in the territory—was not at all affected by the new ruling. Although some branches, such as Shinyanga, lost leaders who were also civil servants, the provincial leaders, in conformity with the bylaws framed in 1952, were full-time employees of the Association.

In fact, the Lake Province branch of the Association accelerated its activities soon after the new regulations came into force. In September Kandoro joined Kirilo Japhet, the Meru spokesman at the United Nations the previous year, and Abbas Sykes, the territorial secretary of the Tanganyika African Association, in a political tour of the Lake Province. For almost a month they traveled from Bukoba to Musoma publicizing the specifics of the Meru land case and seeking support for the Association. A turning point for the Association, this was the first time in Tanganyikan history that top political leaders systematically barnstormed town and countryside alike over an extensive geographical area. Japhet had organized the Meru, and the Sukuma Union had launched some political touring earlier in the year; but the Association now started to break the ground for a national movement which would seek to unite tribe with tribe, and to integrate town and countryside in the name of freedom from colonial control for all Tanganyikan Africans. Membership in the Association was open to every African as it had always been, but the style of recruitment was new. Full-time politicians now went out to obtain members. They embarked on political tours intended to recruit mass support. They sought to establish a hierarchy of provincial, district, branch and sub-branch organizations. Concerned as always with specific complaints and grievances, the ideology of the new politics offered something more: the crux was the unifying, simplifying, overwhelming desire for an end to alien rule.

In the final months of 1953, while Nyerere and other leaders in Dar es Salaam discussed the need to replace the Association with a truly political organization, Munanka and Kandoro pushed the Lake Province organization vigorously forward. Representatives from throughout the province attended provincial meetings in Mwanza in October and again in November. Munanka and the secretary of the Association's branch in Bukoba, Sylvester Herman, argued the Association's case against alienation of land to non-Europeans, destocking, livestock taxation, and outmoded Native Authority structures before the Royal Commission on Land[20] during hearings in Mwanza. New branches of the Association sprang into activity outside the major towns once the seri-

[20] The Commission—more properly entitled the East African Royal Commission—held hearings on land and population problems throughout Tanganyika, Kenya, and Uganda during 1953–55. (A Sukuma chief, David Kidaha Makwaia, was one of the eight Commissioners.) The Commission's report (Cmd 9475) was presented to Parliament by the Secretary of State for the Colonies in June 1955.

ousness and extent of the Association's political efforts became more widely known.

In December 1953, antagonism became evident in Bukoba. As in Sukumaland, opposition to compulsory regulations with regard to soil conservation and the minimum cultivation of food crops had grown. In Bukoba there were particular complaints against banana weevil and coffee mulching rules and, during 1953, "political agitators . . . had much success in propaganda." Native Authorities were also under criticism in Bukoba, and the government felt that politicians were stirring up trouble between the aristocratic Hinda and commoner Hangoma populations. By December matters were critical enough in the government's view to justify a ban on public meetings "in the interests of law and order."[21]

Nevertheless, Ali Migeyo, the Association's president in Bukoba, held a large public meeting that month which police disbanded with tear gas. The Bukoba branch of the Association telegraphed the Lake Province headquarters that tear gas had been used to disperse a meeting of the Association, and Kandoro called an emergency session in Mwanza to discuss the matter. The meeting, which was also attended by leaders of the Sukuma Union and the Lake Province Growers' Association, decided to send a delegation to complain directly to the Provincial Commissioner and to ask that tear gas never be used again in Tanganyika in situations where there was no real disturbance. The Provincial Commissioner replied that the gas had been used to disperse an illegal meeting because those in attendance had refused to disperse when requested to do so.

Meanwhile, Kandoro wrote to the Bukoban leaders advising them to "remain calm without provoking further disturbance" since the provincial headquarters of the Association had "taken steps." Nyerere, as territorial president of the Association, arrived from Dar es Salaam and he, Munanka, and Kandoro went to Bukoba to talk with the District Commissioner there about the tear gassing. They received the same answer. However, the Mwanzan leaders—who had been critical in the past of insufficient support from the Association in Dar es Salaam—were pleased that the matter received special attention from territorial headquarters and that Nyerere had "seen with his own eyes" the state of things in the Lake Province.[22]

At the end of 1953, Kandoro produced a report covering in outline the activities of the Lake Province branch of the Association over the previous year and a half. On the financial side, the Association had collected money through twelve local branches. With Bukoba's impressive

[21] Lake Province Annual Reports 1953 and 1954, Lake Province files.
[22] Kandoro, *Mwito wa Uhuru*, 29-31.

contribution of 6,200 shillings, total receipts came to over 9,300 shillings; expenditures were nearly 6,700 shillings. Although these sums were not all that had been hoped for, Kandoro congratulated branch leaders on their efforts and expressed his wish that Ali Migeyo's example in Bukoba would be emulated by others.[23]

No sooner had the new year begun than Kandoro and a special committee which had been appointed at the general meeting the previous November went off on a tour of the province. In twenty-five days they held public meetings in seventeen places in six districts, concluding at the end of January with another provincial meeting in Mwanza. The usual opposition to destocking, cattle tax, and cotton assessment was expressed, but the meeting became more heated with discussion of the December tear-gassing incident in Bukoba. Kandoro relates that at one point he said "to be governed by others . . . is shameful impotence." Emotions rose to such a pitch that Paul Bomani's father, Lazaro —who was then serving as the treasurer of the Lake Province Association—jumped up, tore his shirt, and exclaimed in the Sukuma language: "It is best that we control our own affairs with regard to land and livestock until we rule the country ourselves!"[24] Another Mwanzan leader tore off his tie and said he would not wear it again until independence had been achieved. The meeting decided to send a delegation to the Governor himself to dramatize the Association's opposition to destocking, cattle tax, and the cotton assessment. A telegram to this effect was dispatched to Dar es Salaam. Dar es Salaam replied that the Governor would be arriving in Mwanza on a scheduled tour February 12, and that the Association's representations could be submitted in writing to the Provincial Commissioner forthwith, together with a request for an audience with the Governor. Kandoro immediately sent copies of the telegram to all the Association's branches asking each to send its president and no less than six representatives to Mwanza by February 10 to prepare for the interview with the Governor.

The Governor arrived as scheduled, but on February 15 the Provincial Commissioner notified the Association that His Excellency had refused to grant an interview. Stunned, the Association sent representatives to the provincial office to make certain that this report was correct. It was. According to Kandoro's account, one officer of the Association suggested that the delegation follow the Governor to the house of the Provincial Commissioner where he was staying, but Lazaro Bomani said: "We are not fools! We do not follow a ruler to his house, but [see him] in his office only."[25]

[23] Ibid., 33.
[24] Ibid., 38.
[25] Ibid.

Munanka decided to contact the Association's headquarters in Dar es Salaam for advice. Headquarters replied that the Lake Province branch should take whatever "peaceful" steps it wished. The Lake Province Association then held a meeting and decided to cable directly to the Secretary of State for the Colonies in London, with copies to the Governor, the Provincial Commissioner, the Legislative Council members from the Lake Province, and the Association's headquarters in Dar es Salaam. The telegram, originally in Swahili, read:

> Citizens of Her Majesty the Queen cry out before you their distress at destocking of cattle, cattle tax, and cotton cess; also their distress at being tear-gassed during a meeting in the Lake Province, Tanganyika. Representatives refused interview with Governor when he visited Mwanza between 13th and 15th February. . . . We plead these difficulties be removed from our country quickly. We do not want trouble, but peace.

The telegram was signed "Executive Committee, Tanganyika African Association, Lake Province." Kandoro sent copies of the telegram to all the Association's members in the province with a letter sent out the same day. He asked all to remain calm, assured members that "we will get our rights and will pursue them by civilized means," and said "that members should await the reply to the telegram but be ready to come immediately to Mwanza when called." Kandoro ended his letter, "God is with us."[26]

The administration, meanwhile, made its position entirely clear. In a note to the Governor the District Commissioner of Mwanza portrayed the politicians as "discontented and self-seeking men who, by malicious propaganda [seek] to turn public opinion against [progressive] policies."[27] Seeking to shore up Native Authorities against the attacks of "irresponsible politicians," the Governor addressed the Mwanza Federation of Chiefs on February 17. He emphasized the authority and power of the chiefs and their role, together with the new councils, in implementing government policy. Speaking of the politicians, he said they were people

> who are trying to undermine the policy of the government and by trying to attract cheap-jack popularity they want to destroy the position of the chiefs and the native authorities. . . . They represent no-

[26] The telegram and the letter are reproduced in Kandoro, *Mwito wa Uhuru*, 39-40.

[27] "A Brief Note on Suggested Subject Matter for His Excellency the Governor's Address to the Chiefs of the Mwanza Federation," files of the Mwanza District Administration, now in National Archives, Dar es Salaam, Feb. 1954.

body except themselves. . . . I have read their papers about their complaints and they show that they are a lot of uneducated, ignorant people who either are unable to appreciate and comprehend what they are talking about, or they do not wish to hear the truth.

Indulging in a note of rural romanticism which would seem remarkable had it not been typical of colonial administrators at the time, the Governor commented that the politicians were "people who feel that they no longer want to have the traditional work of Africans living in the country, developing their land, and tending their cattle, but who come to the towns to live lives of parasites."[28]

In a memorandum to the Provincial Commissioner after his return to Dar es Salaam the Governor emphasized the importance of "the fullest co-ordination and understanding" between district administrators and the Native Authorities and the necessity that the latter *"through whom the work must necessarily be done—are themselves as efficient as we can make them, have our full support and are acceptable to the people."* Noting the Lake Province's wealth and "remarkable progress over the past few years," Governor Twining added that the Lake Province "is very much alive and it needs to be driven with a firm if light rein: but if we are not careful it may still get away from us, with unexpected and undesirable results."[29] As events were to prove, he was correct.

Conflict and Impasse

The Governor's refusal to see the deputation of the Tanganyika African Association in February 1954 marked a turning point in the political history of the Lake Province. After the expectations which followed upon the February telegram from Dar es Salaam advising the leaders of the Association to seek an interview with the Governor, the Governor's decision seemed an astonishing exercise of prerogative. Clearly, Twining and the new Provincial Commissioner, S. A. Walden, decided that strong measures against "irresponsible politicians" were necessary to the government's policies and programs in the Lake Province and, in particular, to the continued functioning of the Native Authorities on which the fulfillment of those policies and programs had been made to

[28] "Address by His Excellency the Governor to the Chiefs of the Mwanza District at a Baraza Held on Feb. 17, 1954," Mwanza District files.

[29] "Minute to all Members and the Provincial Commissioner Lake Province forwarded to the Provincial Commissioner by the Member for Local Government, March 1954," in S. A. Walden, papers, privately held, London. I am indebted to Mr. Walden for permission to see this document and others from the years of his tenure as Provincial Commissioner, Lake Province.

depend. Yet, it would be difficult to imagine any single act which would have more inflamed the "opposition" and consolidated discontent behind the various leaders the government was trying to discredit, been more conducive to continuing misunderstanding and the hardening of positions, and been more likely to produce the collision course in Lake Province affairs which was followed over the next five years. The government's commitment to what Glickman has called "Twining's Burkean notion of consultation with the African masses through their 'natural' representatives" was not to die an easy death.[30]

Ironically, as has often been the case with nationalist movements in Africa and elsewhere, the emergence of the Tanganyika African Association into a position of unquestioned political leadership followed hard upon, and was causally related to, Twining's refusal to treat with it. Echoing the Governor's own remarks before the Mwanza chiefs, Provincial Commissioner Walden wrote a lengthy letter to the Association on February 22 combining an explanation of the government's policies with severe and strongly worded criticism of the Association's ignorance, foolishness, and "lying propaganda."[31]

But the leaders of the Lake Province Association were in no mood to listen to such advice. Tear-gassed in Bukoba and snubbed by the Governor in Mwanza, they were certain now that their protests and representations were receiving no consideration whatsoever from the government. In early March Kandoro fashioned a series of impassioned and eloquent proclamations addressed to "Members of TAA and all Africans who have not yet become members of TAA." He trumpeted an appeal to all Africans to answer the call to freedom, to seek all the good things of life together through the Association. He cited the examples of Napoleon, Bismarck, Gandhi, Nkrumah, and Aggrey as men of all races who had raised up their own people; he lauded British traditions of democracy which fostered free speech and the existence of political organizations such as the Tanganyika African Association, assuring the members that an answer to the Association's February telegram would be forthcoming "according to the custom of the British Government." Failing an answer, the Association would be justified in sending another appeal, together with a delegation, to England. He assured the presidents of the Association's branches that the Association was a legal organization and that they should pay no heed to "childish and stupid threats." Confident that the Association's officers knew and

[30] Harvey Glickman, "Traditional Pluralism and Democratic Processes in Tanganyika," unpublished paper delivered at the Annual Meeting of the American Political Science Association, Chicago, Sept. 1964, 6.

[31] Walden to the president of the Tanganyika African Association, Feb. 22, 1954, reproduced in the original English in Kandoro, *Mwito wa Uhuru*, 46-50.

understood the value of their work, Kandoro urged them to collect funds and prepare delegations of ten members from each branch to attend an important general meeting of the Lake Province branch of the Association in April.[32]

Munanka, Kandoro, and other officials of the Association also wrote to Governor Twining renewing their case and objecting to their treatment by colonial officials who reprimanded them in harsh language and scorned them as "ignorant" and "useless." If we are such, the Association argued, then there was no need for the British government to bring its people here in the first place. The Association emphasized that it was not the aim of the organization to "fight" with the government, but to bring petitions before the government. Yet, when petitions were brought, the Association was "threatened and told if we don't watch our actions we will be in danger." Pointing out that tear gas was only used by armies fighting their enemies, the Association asked that "if we Africans were enemies we should be told so." The letter asked for the Governor's sympathy and the abolition of the detested regulations.[33] Munanka also corresponded with sympathetic members of the Fabian Colonial Bureau and the Labour party in England,[34] and questions on the administration's handling of political problems in the Lake Province were put to the Colonial Secretary in Parliament.

While the conflict between the Association and the administration was being acted out at higher levels, the Association continued its penetration of the rural areas. In March and April, Kandoro and Lameck Bogohe, formerly general secretary of the Sukuma Union but now assistant treasurer of the Association, toured Maswa, Nassa, Musoma, Geita, and Biharamulo. Their message dealt with destocking, cattle tax, cotton assessment; the representations made by the Association on behalf of the people; and the refusal of the government to receive representations and make the desired policy changes. Again, in May, Bogohe toured for more than a month holding public meetings in every district, checking the books, finances, and membership of every branch at the same time. Not content with the main routes, Bogohe at times took a bicycle into some of the remote areas.

The Association's political activities in rural areas seemed always to imply conflict with Native Authorities. Insecure in the face of new political ideas and organizations and challenged by politicians who, in criticizing the status quo, all but presented themselves as leadership

[32] Kandoro, *Mwito wa Uhuru*, 41-44.

[33] Ibid., 45-46.

[34] For example, Munanka to Nicholson, May 10, 1954, Fabian Colonial Bureau files, London. I am indebted to the Fabian Colonial Bureau for permission to consult relevant documentation in their files.

alternatives to those of the chiefly regimen, Native Authorities looked increasingly to the colonial administration for support. The unequivocal stands taken by the Governor and the Provincial Commissioner in February 1954 together with the Association's late 1953 and early 1954 push into the countryside spread and intensified the conflict between chiefs and politicians. Chiefs worked with unusual vigor in an attempt to stem the rising political tide. District Commissioners and district officers made more frequent appearances at local council meetings. The Provincial Commissioner distributed copies of the Governor's February speech to District Commissioners and all Native Authorities in all districts "so that the chiefs are left in no doubt of the attitude of Government both towards them and towards people whose sole desire it is to stir up disaffection."[35] The speech was read often at council meetings, where only the most intrepid individuals raised questions or objections.

In April 1954 the Legislative Council passed the Registration of Societies Ordinance to permit closer governmental regulation of political associations. The ordinance gave the government the power to define what was and what was not to be considered "lawful"; it was designed precisely for the suppression of political activities, such as those of the Tanganyika African Association in the Lake Province, which the government was not willing to tolerate. Speaking to the Legislative Council in May the Governor said:

> My attention has been drawn to attempts which have been made in some parts of the territory by self-seeking individuals, usually men of straw, who, having appointed themselves as political leaders, have tried to stir up the people against their Native Authorities, and in some cases the Central Government, by exploiting local grievances real or imaginary. They do not hesitate to collect money; indeed, large sums of money, from many ignorant or unsuspecting people which they have little qualms in using, or rather misusing, for their own benefit and aggrandizement. This cannot be allowed to continue and Government will not tolerate such activities which are contrary to the best interests of the people and are designed to damage, if not destroy, good government. Respect for authority, which is an inherent trait in the African character, must be preserved.[36]

Later in the month Nyerere, the president of the Association and a temporary member of the Legislative Council, spoke to the issues raised by the Governor's speech. Nyerere

[35] Provincial Commissioner to all District Commissioners, Apr. 22, 1954, files of the Geita district administration of the Government of Tanganyika (transferred from Geita to the National Archives, Dar es Salaam, in 1965).

[36] Tanganyika, *Proceedings of the Legislative Council*, May 12, 1954. The Ordinance was No. 11 of 1954, signed into law by the Governor on Apr. 24, 1954.

considered that all sensible Africans would support the Government in dealing with trouble makers; but he drew attention to the great difference between trouble-mongering and criticizing the Government justifiably. . . . He hoped that people were not going to take the Governor's warning as meaning that from that time onwards no criticism of either local or central government was going to be tolerated. If that happened a large number of people were going to be without their only means either of making useful suggestions to the authorities or of merely expressing their views.[37]

In accord with the Registration of Societies Ordinance, however, the administration notified Native Authorities in the Lake Province that registration requests were required before the end of June for all associations. At the same time, the Provincial Commissioner reproduced Swahili copies of the section of the Governor's speech quoted above, entitled the excerpt "Governor Warns Political Troublemakers," and forwarded copies to all District Commissioners and chiefs asking that the speech be given "the widest—and most telling—publicity."[38]

The Tanganyika African Association's third provincial meeting of the year convened in Mwanza in late June. Under increasing pressures from Native Authorities, from district and provincial officers, and now from the Governor himself in Dar es Salaam, the Association decried the harassment of its members and of its organization. Munanka noted that the president and secretary of the Association in Bukoba had been jailed "for standing up for our rights" and that leaders in Nassa, Malampaka, and Geita had also found themselves in difficulty with the government in previous weeks.[39] Reaffirming that the purpose of the Association was not to oppose the government but only to seek the correction of errors where they existed, Munanka—following Nyerere's lead in the Legislative Council—regretted the equation which the government and others were making between criticism and troublemaking. He struck out at non-Africans who, he said, lobbied for the suspension of a sort of political troublemaking which did not exist. Munanka said he would not like to see anyone abandon the political fight because of harassment.

Kandoro addressed himself to the usual issues regarding livestock and land, buttressing his arguments for man's freedom to use the land

[37] Summarized in United Nations Visiting Mission, 1954, 77. Nyerere's speech appears in full in *Proceedings of the Legislative Council,* May 25, 1954.

[38] Provincial Commissioner to all District Commissioners, June 2, 1954, files of the Maswa district administration of the Government of Tanganyika (transferred from Maswa to the National Archives, Dar es Salaam, in 1965).

[39] Munanka's speech quoted in Kandoro, *Mwito wa Uhuru,* 63-65. Ali Migeyo, the president of the Tanganyika African Association's branch in Bukoba, was imprisoned for one year for holding illegal meetings.

and to govern its animal and vegetable kingdoms with quotes from the
Bible and the Qur'an. Complaining that Africans were being held back
and discriminated against in relation to the other main races, he argued
that Africans suffered from separate and unequal schools, poorer hospital facilities, bad roads, low wages, no loan provisions, less justice in
the courts, and expulsion from their own lands. He maintained that the
government's proposed policy of parity in the Legislative Council and
nonracial graduated taxation must be accompanied by real equality for
Africans in all others areas. As Munanka summarized the Association's
view in a letter to the Fabian Colonial Bureau: "In a country like this
when absolutely nothing of importance is being done by the Government, it is . . . our loss to find that we are being taxed heavily without
getting increased facilities from the Government."[40] Kandoro deplored
the 1954 increase in cattle tax by 200 per cent (from half a shilling to
a shilling and a half per head) and queried once again the purpose of
the cotton assessment. Finally, citing the United Nations Declaration
on Human Rights, he spoke of freedom of speech and assembly and
of equal representation for all individuals in the government of the
country.[41]

While the Association in the Lake Province had on its own initiative
stepped up the pace of its activities in 1953 and early 1954, Nyerere
had been giving considerable thought to the necessity of transforming
the Association territorially into a potent nationalist organization which
would "fight relentlessly until Tanganyika is self-governing and independent."[42] With a Master of Arts degree from the University of Edinburgh, Nyerere had taken a teaching position at a Roman Catholic
school at Pugu, near Dar es Salaam, which he left when he was elected
territorial president of the Association in 1953. As president, he set out
to remodel the Association's constitution on more political lines. In 1954
he invited a group of the Association's members to Dodoma to discuss
his proposals, and in July a four-day conference of the Association convened in Dar es Salaam to act on the proposals. A new constitution was
adopted, and the Tanganyika African Association became the Tanganyika African National Union. Of the seventeen men who gathered for
this historic meeting, five, Kandoro and Bogohe among them, were from
the Association's Lake Province branch.

The agenda, as well as the attendance, reflected the importance of
the Lake Province branch of the Association, but it also revealed that

[40] Munanka to Nicholson, July 27, 1954, Fabian Colonial Bureau files,
London.

[41] Kandoro, *Mwito wa Uhuru*, 60-63; 66-70.

[42] Quoted from the Tanganyika African National Union constitution in Bennett, "Outline History of TANU," 3.

the branch's uncompromising militancy may have posed problems for the Association's territorial president as well as for the government.

The first item on the agenda was a discussion of the Lake Province branch's by-passing of territorial headquarters by sending telegrams and letters outside the territory without first notifying or clearing the letters with the Association in Dar es Salaam. According to Kandoro, Nyerere had sent a letter to Mwanza criticizing the Lake Province action as "very bad politics." When the question was discussed by the full meeting of the Association in July, it was decided that the Lake Province branch "had the right to act in this manner because the problems had not received attention from headquarters." On the other hand, however, the meeting decided to dismiss the general secretary of the territorial organization for having brought charges of peculation against Ali Migeyo, president of the Bukoba branch, without first consulting with territorial *or provincial* headquarters.

Apparently, the Lake Province representatives were strong enough in this last meeting of the Tanganyika African Association and first meeting of the new Tanganyika African National Union to assure that decisions and judgments relating to the Lake Province went in their favor. The meeting requested the leaders of the Lake Province organization "to continue with their good work as they had done in the past." In the future, however, all representations to the United Nations were to pass through Dar es Salaam. Respecting the Lake Province's favorite issues of destocking, cattle tax, cotton and coffee assessments, a committee headed by Nyerere was picked to make representations to the Ministry of Local Government.[43]

Meanwhile, events in the Lake Province moved rapidly toward the sort of political impasse between protest and authority which seemed, at least to the colonial administrators, to require the outright suppression of the protesters. The possibilities for compromise—or if compromise were too much to hope for, at least for dialogue—became the more remote to the extent that the political activists successfully penetrated the rural areas. Although the colonial regime might indefinitely have tolerated the vocalizing of dissident sentiment among a few politically oriented gadflies in the towns, it believed that it could not countenance what it perceived to be the undermining in the countryside of the very system of administration through which it exercised political control and implemented its development programs. As more local political activists—inspired by their leaders in Mwanza—made real the hitherto latent opposition to the administration's programs in the countryside, mutual suspicion and distrust increased and the relations

[43] Kandoro, *Mwito wa Uhuru,* 71-82.

between governmental authorities and politically active groups deteriorated further.

Open conflict broke out in Musoma when the District Commissioner attended a meeting of the Association, berated the leaders for "stupidity" and "lies," and unwittingly carried off a portion of the minutes on which he had jotted notes for some of his questions.[44] Attendance at the first all-Sukumaland Agricultural Show in Kwimba failed to reach expected levels because rumors spread that people who entered the fairgrounds would be conscripted for service in the military and sent to Kenya to fight the Mau Mau. However, the most intense conflict between the politicians and the Native Authorities occurred in Maswa where a new branch of the Tanganyika African Association made strong inroads into the territory of some of Sukumaland's strongest and longest reigning traditional chiefs.

The Association's branch at Malampaka, an entrepôt on the rail line to Tabora and Dar es Salaam, had opened in January after Kandoro's tour of the Maswa district. Under the leadership of Stanley Kaseko, a Sukuma trader who had for some years worked for the government as a medical assistant, the Association quickly encountered opposition from the District Commissioner and from the more powerful Native Authorities. In a meeting in March 1954, the Maswa Federation of Chiefs decided that persons known to be members of certain political organizations were "to be among the first called out for communal labor"; refusal to work would be followed by prosecution and imprisonment without option of a fine. The District Commissioner told the chiefs that the government in the past had shown great tolerance toward such unions as the Tanganyika African Association, but that "stronger action must now be taken against their attempts to spread civil disobedience and discontent among the Sukuma."[45]

Between April and September, Kaseko found himself continually at odds with the chiefs and with the administration over his requests for permission to hold public political meetings. First the District Commissioner refused permission to Kaseko because the latter "refused to cease spreading lies about destocking, soil erosion, and tribal labour."[46] Later, after Kaseko disclaimed any subversive intent, the District Commissioner agreed to the meetings, provided that the chiefs in whose

[44] Musoma Tanganyika African Association to Provincial Commissioner, July 23, 1954, and subsequent correspondence. Also a file note by the District Commissioner in question, Lake Province files.

[45] Minutes of a meeting of the Federation Council of Maswa district, Mar. 8, 1954, Maswa district files.

[46] District Commissioner to Kaseko, Apr. 24, 1954, Maswa district files. (Original in Swahili.)

chiefdoms the meetings were to be held would give their consent.[47] But then often—partly because of the District Commissioner's attitude and partly out of anxiety to sustain their own authority in their home areas—the chiefs themselves refused permission for Kaseko's meetings. One particularly celebrated instance resulted in the exchange of indignant and accusatory letters by Kaseko and Chief Ndaturu after the latter had countermanded the District Commissioner's provisional approval for a meeting in Ndaturu's home chiefdom.[48] Kaseko and Kandoro took the matter to the Provincial Commissioner, but to no avail. In September, when chiefs again refused to approve Kaseko's application for a set of public meetings after the District Commissioner had said that he had no objection, Kaseko held the meetings anyway. He was arrested; the evidence against him was collected and presented by the Maswa Federation of Chiefs; he was tried for holding illegal meetings and sentenced to jail for a year. Eight years later, after Tanganyika's independence, Kaseko was to become the Area Commissioner of Maswa District.

Having decided that the Lake Province was Tanganyika's "No. 1 security risk,"[49] the Governor, soon after Kaseko's imprisonment, instructed the authorities to move against the Tanganyika African National Union's entire Mwanza-based organization. Police confiscated all the books and records from the Union's office and from the homes of Munanka and Kandoro. On November 1, the Provincial Commissioner informed the two leaders that the Registrar of Societies had refused to register the Lake Province branch of the Union on the grounds that it "is being or is likely to be used for purposes prejudicial to or incompatible with the maintenance of peace, order, and good government."[50] The Mwanza District and Malampaka branches were also closed, and no other branches were permitted within Sukumaland. Kandoro was deported from Mwanza and prohibited from returning to the area. Though the administration subsequently permitted the registration of Union branches elsewhere in the Lake Province, the closing of the provincial headquarters and of the active branches within Sukumaland deprived the provincial Tanganyika African National Union of its vital organizational center for the next four years.

[47] District Commissioner to all chiefs, May 1, 1954, Maswa district files. (Original in Swahili.)

[48] Kaseko to Ndaturu, n.d. (Aug. 1954), Maswa district files. (Original in Swahili.) Kaseko had requested the meetings in a July 21 letter to the District Commissioner. Permission was given by the District Commissioner in a letter to Kaseko, July 27, Maswa district files.

[49] Twining to the Chief Secretary, Sept. 11, 1954, Walden papers, London.

[50] Registrar of Societies to the Lake Province, Oct. 27, 1954, Fabian Colonial Bureau files, London.

Retrospect

Two months before the ban, the United Nations Visiting Mission of 1954 had begun its tour of Tanganyika in the Lake Province where, by its own account, the Mission received "an intensive introduction to present-day African political thought and organization." Although at various points during its tour the Mission had found that the most active political force—the Tanganyika African National Union—was described as "the former African Association in a reorganized form,"[51] the Lake Province organization which the Mission encountered was not so much the Tanganyika African Association "reorganized" as the Association rebaptized. In the Lake Province the Union—in all but name—was a virtually undifferentiated continuation of the active, organized, intensely political Tanganyika African Association which had developed over the previous several years. Indeed, the Association in the Lake Province was at the height of its activity and influence when the Union was born. In July and August, existing branches of the Association had simply notified the government of the change of name and carried on with their activities as they had in the past. In late August, Kandoro was still using the Association's provincial stationery with "Association" crossed out and "National Union" added in ink. The Provincial Tanganyika African National Union's memorandum to the 1954 Visiting Mission was presented by the same people and elaborated many of the same arguments which previously had been presented by the Tanganyika African Association—opposition to alienation of land, particularly in the Meru case; opposition to destocking, cattle tax, and cotton assessment; protest against discrimination against Africans in education, health, hotels, loans, and employment; and a desire for better education, hospitals, and communications.

The Association in the Lake Province had pushed explicitly for "independence in the near future" in 1951 and, as early as 1948,[52] for greater African representation. Now in 1954 the Union's memorandum "pressed for a timetable of steps to be taken, in consultation with the people, towards the goal of self-government." Munanka and Kandoro headed a delegation of twenty Union leaders who presented the memorandum in person to the Visiting Mission. The delegation "pointed attention to the fact that the United Nations had already given Somaliland a target-date for independence." Insisting that Tanganyika was an African country and "not a country of all races, as people of other races

[51] United Nations Visiting Mission, 1954, 10, 74.
[52] See above, 647-48.

say," the Union's memorandum stated: "We are the owners of this country; there are more of us than of any other race . . . therefore it is just and proper that there should be African majorities in such councils as the Legislative Council, county councils, and town councils, and that the African representatives on these councils should be elected by the people." The Union objected to "loose references to Tanganyika as if it were a colonial possession of the United Kingdom," asked that the flag of the United Nations be flown with the British flag, and that a United Nations office be established in Tanganyika with a branch in each of the eight provinces. Unlike the previous petitions by the Association which had been presented in English, the Union's memorandum of 1954 was presented in Swahili—symbolic, perhaps, of a more conscious insistence on the separateness, distinctiveness, and rightness of being African.[53]

At the time of the proscription of the Union's Lake Province headquarters and its branches in Sukumaland, the Union claimed nearly ten thousand members in the province.[54] The actual figure may have been smaller; but, as the United Nations Visiting Mission pointed out, "the general following which the Union's leaders may command now or in the future is a matter of greater importance than its numerical strength." Certainly since thousands of people who never paid membership fees heard the Association's, and then the Union's, message in the Lake Province sympathetically, its total impact can hardly be assessed. It was the Mission's judgment that "if put to a test, its following would prove to be large, and its emergence as an important political force must therefore be recognized."[55]

The Lake Province leadership confidently held this view. On one occasion, after the Provincial Commissioner had fulminated against Munanka for opposing the British administration and "making-off" with people's money via the Association, Munanka is reported to have challenged the Provincial Commissioner to allow the people of the province to choose by which of the two of them they would prefer to be governed. Similarly, he proposed that the people of Tanganyika be allowed to choose between Governor Twining and Nyerere, the territorial president of the Association. Of course, the administration's decision to proscribe the Union in late 1954 was a testament to the Union's actual and potential strength. Further, though the administration rationalized the ban as a measure for safeguarding its planned programs of local government reform and natural resources' development, the wisdom of the ban was questionable even on the administration's own terms. Given

[53] United Nations Visiting Mission, 1954, 13.
[54] Lake Province Annual Report, 1954, Lake Province files.
[55] United Nations Visiting Mission, 1954, 13.

the Union's actual and potential strength, any policy of repression could not help but have a time limit—and a sequel.

Thus, in 1953–54 the Tanganyika African Association made itself *the* political force in the Lake Province and, in so doing, made the Lake Province the focal point in Tanganyika for the development of a radical new brand of organized political nationalism. The Tanganyika African National Union was born in Dar es Salaam in July; but, since the territorial Union's foremost leaders, Nyerere and Oscar Kambona, did not begin extensive political touring in Tanganyika until 1955, the nationalist movement in the Lake Province—notwithstanding its assumption of the Union's name in mid-1954—continued to develop independently. For a while political activity mushroomed in reaction to the government's increasingly repressive offensive; then it was cut short by the proscription of the Union's provincial headquarters and all of the Sukumaland branches in November 1954. By the end of the year the administration had disarmed the Lake Province activists of their platform, office, and organization. While Union branches were registered at Bukoba and Musoma, the reopening of the Union in Mwanza and Sukumaland had to wait until after widespread outbreaks of civil disobedience in Sukumaland, and the arrival of a new Governor in 1958.

As with nationalist movements elsewhere in colonial Africa, protest was the foundation stone of politics in the Lake Province of Tanganyika. Although a host of specific grievances provided the spur to action, effective action required unity and organizational strength. The task of a nationalist political organization—like that which "emerged" in the Lake Province in the years before it was officially to be known as part of the Tanganyika African National Union—was precisely to incorporate a variety of parochial and particular interests and desires into a focused drive toward national self-determination. With remarkable foresight, the precocious politicians of the Lake Province understood well before 1954 that the consolidation of a popular mass movement bent on self-government would provide their most important political weapon in any prolonged struggle with the colonial regime.

It is in this perspective that the activities of Lake Province organizers in the early 1950's must be viewed; it is this perspective which casts doubt on the too facile acceptance of the administration's characterization of the activists in the Lake Province as "wild," "misguided," and "irresponsible."[56] The Lake Province politicians were the first in Tanganyika both to define the principal issue as that of national self-determination versus colonial rule *and* to build tangible public support

[56] See Listowel, *Making of Tanganyika* 233, 236; also, for a similar problem of interpretation four years later, see Taylor, *Political Development of Tanganyika*, 176-77.

for their propositions by attempting to deal in the most concrete way possible with the complaints of people in a variety of localities. As forerunners of a revolution, they were the first to taste the fruits of the administration's displeasure. It should be recalled that Nyerere himself was vilified by the government as utterly irresponsible until the government did an about-face in 1958 after changing both its key personnel and its policies. But there was not this flexibility on the administration's side in the Lake Province in the early 1950's—political organizers either had to keep quiet and not organize or they were by definition "irresponsible rabble-rousers" who were to be dealt with accordingly.

Nor, it should be observed, is an appeal to law and order particularly compelling to those who oppose the very system which makes the laws and defines order. Especially is this true when, objectively considered, many of the specific grievances—as well as the more general desire for freedom—were valid and just. The people of the Lake Province wanted to farm their land, produce their coffee and cotton, and raise their cattle as they saw fit. They wanted to be freed from what they regarded as excessive burdens of taxation. They became impatient with Native Authorities and discontented with colonial administrators who—whether or not in their own "best interests"—interfered in too many aggravating and finally intolerable ways with their lives. Finally, reflecting the fact that the most exalted touchstones of twentieth-century political ideology—democracy, nationalism, and self-determination—had penetrated even to remote rural areas, they had begun to insist that an alien regime which by its very existence precluded personal and corporate self-determination for its subjects could not be tolerated indefinitely. In the Lake Province of Tanganyika—as elsewhere in Africa and the colonial world—all grievances merged ultimately into one, all the specific issues were less important than the call to freedom itself. It was this that the political organizers in the Lake Province before 1954 understood. It was this which provided the spark for their ideological and organizational anticipation of the Tanganyika African National Union.

THE *UNION DES POPULATIONS DU CAMEROUN* IN REBELLION: THE INTEGRATIVE BACKLASH OF INSURGENCY

WILLARD JOHNSON

It is commonplace to say that almost every one of the independent states of black Africa won its independence with a minimum of struggle. In Ghana, Nigeria, and the Ivory Coast—even in Guinée—the leadership did not have to organize and sustain a violent war effort in order to liberate their peoples. Theirs was primarily a job of organizing public opinion, of creating a broad and vociferous front of groups demanding accelerated progress toward goals already established or rather easily accepted by the colonial powers. As a result, independence came to most of the new states of black Africa before the will and mutual confidence of the leaders had been tested, and the weak, self-serving, and less efficient ones among them sifted out. Furthermore, organizing against colonial rule provided only superficial demonstrations to the people of the cost of dissidence and division. Nor did the imperatives of this struggle wed the military to the political leadership. There was no Thirty Years War or Hundred Years War, no Great Revolution or Long March in black Africa. The nation remains inchoate: that its will to exist is the product of independence is as true as the converse.

Cameroon's experience is an exception to this pattern. Though it achieved independence according to a schedule and form agreed upon by the colonial power, this did not happen before militant nationalists had clashed with that power in violent and protracted conflict. Will this difference in the experience of the nationalist movement make for any difference in the independent life of the country? Will national integration proceed at a faster pace than in countries having had no pre-independence experience with rebellion and intensive internecine strife?

How these questions are to be answered, or whether they can be

671

answered at all, depends upon the character of the strife ·and the context in which it occurs. It is not my purpose to fit the Cameroonian experience into a logically tight and widely agreed upon typology of internal warfare; it is important, however, to identify the degree to which this violence was controlled, and the nature and consistency of the objectives it served. Such an identification will permit us to assess the experience in terms of its net impact on national integration.

Development of the Rebellion

It is convenient to date the rebellion from April 22, 1955. On that day the leader of the *Union des Populations du Cameroun,* the most militantly nationalistic of the political parties in the Cameroon Trust Territory under French administration, and several other closely affiliated organizations,[1] issued a Joint Proclamation declaring the termination of the Trusteeship and calling for (a) general elections for a constituent assembly before the year's end, (b) the immediate installation of a United Nations Commission to supervise the establishment of national institutions, and (c) the immediate establishment of an African executive committee which would serve as a provisional government.[2]

This declaration came on the heels of a series of hurried but large public meetings throughout the major towns of Southern Cameroon, at which the leadership of the *Union* (Reuben Um Nyobé, Felix Roland Moumié, Ernest Ouandié, and Abel Kingué) had whipped up strong popular protest against the newly appointed Commissioner, Roland Pré, and repeated long-standing claims for full independence and for reunification of all the territory of the former German Kamerun. Demands for political independence had placed the militant leaders of the *Union* in direct conflict with the French administration from the time of the *Union*'s founding in 1948. Though they attempted to hide their real goals from the administration, their aspirations had always been for full independence, a goal which was incompatible with French intentions for the French Union, in which Cameroon was to be included on almost the same terms as France's colonies. As for reunification, it was considered a prerequisite to independence because the militant leaders thought that only by joining French interests and control with those of the British Trusteeship administration would it be possible to avert

---

[1] Namely the *Jeunesse Démocratique Camerounaise,* the *Union Démocratique des Femmes Camerounaises,* and the *Union des Syndicats Confédérés du Cameroun.*

[2] See Adalbert Owona, "Le Mouvement d'Inspiration Marxiste: UPC" (Yaoundé, 1962?, mimeo.); V. T. Le Vine, *The Cameroons: From Mandate to Independence* (Berkeley, 1964), 154.

the complete and lasting incorporation of Cameroon into the French colonial empire. Their opposition to Commissioner Pré's appointment stemmed from the fact that he came to his post charged with breaking up the *Union* and reversing popular attitudes toward its program.

After the Joint Proclamation, in early May of 1955, the public meetings of sympathizers grew larger and the demands of their spokesmen more violent. Speaking in tones of elated but premature confidence, *Union* President Moumié announced that he was no longer obliged to deal with the French Commissioner. He declared himself available for discussions with the French Ministry of Foreign Affairs. He also announced that like Mao Tse Tung and Ho Chi Minh, Reuben Um Nyobé had already taken to the "maquis."[3] Thereupon, together with affiliated youth, women's, and trade union groups, the *Union* stepped up its program of mass meetings and wildcat strikes throughout the southern towns. A general strike was scheduled for mid-May 1955, but failed for lack of sufficient time and organization. In May and June these groups launched a series of riots and mass demonstrations in the capital, the major port city of Douala, and a number of towns throughout regions of the country settled by the Bamiléké, Mungo, Douala, and Bassa peoples. One of the leaders shouted to an assembly of sympathizers: "You are authorized to stop all foreigners, commis saires of police, and gendarmes. Kill them! I am responsible."[4] And, armed with nail studded clubs, machetes, axes, and some firearms, rioters in Douala did burn down houses, attack Europeans and Africans on the streets, overturn cars and put a number of them to the torch, attack the radio stations, and block the major roads.[5] Similar occurrences wracked the other large cities. It took the government ten days to pacify these areas. By then, twenty-six persons had lost their lives, nearly two hundred were officially declared wounded, and thousands were homeless. Several weeks later the administration imposed a legal ban on the Union and its youth and women's organizations. The great popular uprising which the militant leadership had expected to follow upon the forceful suppression of the riots had failed to materialize. However, the leadership had acquired a vast following as a reward for bearing the brunt of the administration's opposition to nationalist aspirations.

Within a couple of months most of the top *Union* leaders had fled secretly into the sanctuary of Kumba, across the border, in the Southern British Cameroons. Soon thereafter the executive secretary, Reuben Um Nyobé, and his close associate and head of the youth wing, Theodore Mayi Matip, initiated a guerrilla-type campaign among their fellow

[3] Owona, "Mouvement," 10.
[4] Ibid.
[5] See Le Vine, *Cameroons*, 156.

Bassa[6] in the Nyong-et-Kélé division. Over the course of the next three years, until late 1958, bands of mainly Bassa *maquisards,* taking their orders from Um Nyobé, perpetrated acts of arson and murder, terrorism, and sabotage. They operated in a fairly delimited stretch of territory which the government called the *Zone de Pacification,* north from Douala through Ngambé to Yaoundé, and south to Eséka. Occasionally the Bamiléké and Mungo districts would fall victim to rebel incursions from across the border of the British Cameroons.

Among the most violent and widespread terrorist campaigns was that waged in late 1956 and early 1957 to discourage participation in the general elections for a new Legislative Assembly. The Assembly had been established under the provisions of the *loi cadre* passed in June 1956 by the French National Assembly. Militants among the *Union* leadership and their sympathizers, now under the direction of Moumié, rejected the reforms of the *loi cadre* as "bogus."[7] During the election campaign two candidates were assassinated. One report states that the *Union* made good on its threat to eliminate "les valets de colonialistes" in ninety cases.[8] In addition, the *Union* derailed trains, cut telegraph wires, burned houses, blocked or otherwise cut off roads, burned polling places, and intimidated prospective voters; but they failed to reduce the voting turnout markedly in any but the Wouri (Douala) and Sanaga Maritime (Bassa) divisions.[9]

Following the elections the region was relatively quiet for nearly

[6] The initial uprising was actually stirred up by the Bamiléké *Union* leader, Abel Kingué, working among Bassa-related groups in the Sanaga Maritime division.

[7] The issue of participation in the elections was argued among *Union* elements on two occasions, both with the same results. The first occasion was the Congress of the *Courant d'Union Nationale,* a recently formed grouping of nationalist elements under the leadership of Paul Sopp Priso, the former President of the Territorial Assembly. Moderates, although opposing the *loi cadre* and suspicious of French intentions, nevertheless anticipated real power and progress through the elections. *Union* militants sought to bring down the administration through violence and pressure from the outside. The *Union Nationale* failed to survive the split, and the *Union* continued the discussion immediately thereafter in a clandestine meeting of their own in Ebolowa, December 2–3, 1956. Moumié and the militant wing won the argument and the *Union* decided to boycott the elections. Um Nyobé is reported to have favored participation at that time because the *Union* was at the height of its popularity. He followed the force of numbers, however, and immediately set about organizing the rebellion. See Le Vine, *Cameroons,* 158, and J. Lamberton, "La Pacification de la Sanaga Maritime–Décembre 1957–Janvier 1959" (Centre des Hautes Études d'Afrique Moderne, Paris, *c.* 1961), Étude 3760, typescript.

[8] Lamberton, "La Pacification."

[9] See Le Vine, *Cameroons,* 161, and Appendix B; Marcel Nguini, "La Valeur Politique de la Tutelle Française" (Docteur ès lettres thesis, Aix-en-Provence, Faculté de Droit, 1956).

a year, until the final months of 1957. Thereafter for about a year, the Sanaga Maritime and Nyong-et-Kélé divisions were terrorized by *maquisards* and government armed forces alike. In mid-September 1958 a military patrol surprised and killed Um Nyobé and ended this phase of the rebellion.

Mayi Matip, who escaped detection despite the fact that he was with Um Nyobé at the time of his death, soon turned himself in to the authorities and launched an appeal to fellow rebels to do likewise. He, like others in the Bassa group, was weary of clandestine operations and questioned their efficacy. In the next three months, with Matip and other Bassa leaders aiding the government, a *ralliement* (return to legal life) campaign succeeded in enticing about 1,300 rebels out of the forest. The *ralliement* campaign organized by the government and army in March 1958 had already produced about 800 defectors.[10] Despite severe condemnation and threatened assault by the exiled leadership in Cairo (soon to locate in Accra and Conakry), Mayi Matip enjoyed continued and impressive success with the *ralliement,* although later he was to break with the government. By April 1959 the rallied contingent was strong enough to run six candidates successfully in by-elections throughout the troubled areas.

By this time, too, the first African government in Cameroon, which had been installed in May 1957 with André Marie Mbida as Prime Minister, had fallen into disarray. Its support had disintegrated because Mbida, by renouncing both early independence and reunification, had adopted an unpopular program and because of his imperious style of leadership. His successor, in 1958, was the half-Fulani northerner, Ahmadou Ahidjo, who pressed for the realization of the two principal planks of the original *Union* program, reunification and independence, and proceeded to negotiate an agreement with the French setting January 1, 1960 as the date of Cameroon's independence. With its principal hero, Um Nyobé, now dead, its program usurped, and its most devoted followers among the Bassa rallied, the leadership of the exiled *Union* became desperate. They shifted their focus to the United Nations General Assembly to whose Fourth Committee they had turned twice before, in 1952 and 1953 when Reuben Um Nyobé had appeared personally to argue his party's claims for reunification and independence, and again in 1955 when they had flooded United Nations organs with thousands of petitions protesting both the forceful measures the French used to terminate the strikes and riotous demonstrations of May, and the subsequent legal banning of the party and affiliated organizations. In the spring of 1959 so many issues concerning the Cameroon Trust Territories were before the United Nations that a special

[10] David Gardinier, *Cameroon: United Nations Challenge to French Policy* (London, 1963), 87, states that 2,500 had rallied by the end of 1958.

session of the Thirteenth General Assembly was convened with an agenda dealing exclusively with Cameroonian problems.

The *upécistes* (members of the *Union des Populations du Cameroun*) and their sympathizers, eighteen petitioners in all, demanded that the United Nations require that new elections be held in Cameroon prior to its approving the independence of Cameroon, which a Franco-Cameroonian agreement, ratified by both governments, had scheduled for the first day of the following year. The dissident forces also wanted guarantees of an honest and completely unconditional and general amnesty before such elections. Radical African states in the Assembly attempted to promote this cause, but met with considerable opposition from moderate, anti-colonialist delegations which thought it embarrassing and unwise to repudiate the report of a United Nations Visiting Mission which had recently visited the Territories and had failed to find any need in the French-controlled territory for new elections or any other special consultations prior to independence, or even prior to reunification. They also thought it unwise to oppose a resolution whose sponsors included respected and anti-colonialist India, and which would bring the fifth black African country, the third in this century, into the community of sovereign states. Rather than opposing the restriction, or complimenting a government so vehemently castigated by a militant nationalist party they supported, twenty-three delegations sympathetic to the *Union des Populations du Cameroun* abstained from voting on the resolution approving the Franco-Cameroonian arrangements for the country's accession to independence on January 1, 1960.[11] The militant rebel leaders had failed utterly to regain influence through external assistance. They had even failed in their demand that they be restored to legal status and protected by the General Assembly.

On the eve of independence the exiles turned once again to familiar tactics and initiated a new wave of terrorism and sabotage. This, the final stage of the rebellion, centered in the Bamiléké areas, or neighboring regions heavily settled by Bamiléké (such as Wouri, Mungo, Nkam, and Mbam). The attacks, although initially concerted, dwindled in number, degree of co-ordination, and brutality. In 1961 the incidence of attacks was quite high and was concentrated on the eve of and immediately following independence.

[11] Resolution 1349 (XIII). The vote was 56-0-23. Eight African-Asian states had given initial support to the *upécistes* in their effort to delay Cameroon's independence until new elections could be held in which they could demonstrate their popular support. But as India and other moderate states backed off, and as the Soviet bloc also cooled in their support of Moumié, these states attempted to persuade Moumié and Ahidjo to achieve a reconciliation on their own. Failing one, they simply abstained in the final voting.

The exiled leaders not only failed to remove, if not replace, the government of Ahmadou Ahidjo prior to independence, but the atmosphere of insecurity that they created only provided Ahidjo with an excuse to demand *full* governmental powers during a six-month period of transition to independence and a new constitution. Ahidjo then caught the exiled group by surprise on the eve of the April 1960 elections for the first National Assembly by suddenly rescinding the legal ban against the *Union* and affiliated organizations. Only the *ralliés*, already on the spot and well organized, could take advantage of it by running a slate of candidates. Rallied members or sympathizers of the *Union,* explicitly using that party's name, won nine seats in the one-hundred-seat assembly. In addition, five of the eighteen Bamiléké deputies, who had formed a separate organization shortly after the election, were former *maquisards* or party members.

From Accra and Conakry came charges of collusion with the government, puppet-like service to colonialism, and treason to the cause of true Cameroonian nationalism. The exiled leadership no doubt feared that the amnesty was not intended for them, and so they continued to provide encouragement and support to those terrorists who remained active in the country. In Accra they attempted to establish a revolutionary government of the Cameroon and to stir up a general revolt back home. In addition to more frequent assaults on the towns and the workers' camps in the Bamiléké, Mungo, and Douala areas, the rebels adopted a scorched earth policy, hacking down banana and coffee trees, and burning crops.

Atrocities at the hands of government troops and gendarmes seem to have stimulated some continued rebel activity, but the general revolt that the exiles in Accra had hoped for never materialized. In fact, the influx of diplomatic personnel and businessmen, the ceremonies connected with the transfer of power, and the subsequent dispatch of Cameroonian diplomats to the United Nations and to foreign capitals, made the charge that the Cameroon's independence was fictitious seem less and less justified despite the continued presence of French military troops and advisers in plain view throughout the troubled areas.

The Destructiveness of the Rebellion

The tangible costs of six years of intensive violence in the Cameroon were considerable. No official estimates of the loss of life or property have been issued. Minimal estimates can be made, however.

Victor Le Vine gives various figures for the number of persons killed by rebels or government forces or by accident; he suggests that the number might be anywhere from 6,000 to 15,000, and arbitrarily selects 10,0000 as a reasonable estimate.[12] Published estimates from people with access to government documents and/or personal experience in the area at the time suggest that the accurate number may fall closer to Le Vine's minimum.[13]

More precise figures concerning the destruction of public services and property due to the rebellion are available for the Bamiléké areas alone, as there the *Fond d'Aide et de la Coopération* took an inventory of the damage in order to determine the cost of a rebuilding program.[14] According to this report, seventy-four public schools (116 school buildings and an equal number of teacher's lodgings) were destroyed, as well as 3 hospitals, 46 dispensaries, about 40 bridges, and 12 agricultural stations. Over 750 kilometers of road were also destroyed or truncated and several hundred kilometers of telegraph line pulled down. Although the water systems were not systematically destroyed, most of them served as a source of pipes which the rebels used to manufacture guns. The estimate of monetary damage done to public services and to private institutions offering social services, such as missionary schools, churches, and health facilities, was put at 1.6 billion francs (CFA), or about $6.5 million.

Organization and Objectives of the Rebellion

For a rebellion effectively to challenge governmental authority, it must be controlled so as to serve particular objectives.[15] Violence may arise out of generalized, diffuse grievances over the general allocation of

[12] Victor Le Vine, "The Course of Political Violence" (mimeographed version presented to the Colloquium on French Speaking Africa, Washington, D.C., August, 1964). Portions of this paper also appear in W. H. Lewis (ed.), *French Speaking Africa: The Search for Identity* (New York, 1965). See also Le Vine, "Insurgency and Counter-Insurgency in the Cameroun, 1955–1962," unpublished paper for Special Operations Research Organization, American University, 1965.

[13] Owana, "Le Mouvement," states that between 1956 and 1959 the Sanaga Maritime maquis took 1,000 lives; on the other hand, George Horner, "Togo and Cameroon," *Current History*, XXXIV (February 1958), 84-90, suggests the figure 2,000 for the three-month period December 1956 to March 1957. The Bamiléké maquis in the three months immediately prior to and following independence caused the deaths of about 540 persons, including government military casualties. See *La Presse du Cameroun*, Jan. 1–Apr. 25, 1960. Violence perpetrated by rebels then tapered off, but casualties from government operations increased. Two thousand are unreliably reported killed in one operation at Lowe, Dec. 1961. See *Cameroon Times*, Dec. 22, 1961.

[14] See "Les Regroupements en Pays Bamilékés," *Fond d'Aide et de la Coopération*, Republic of France, Oct. 1962–Jan. 1963.

[15] See Nathan Leites and Charles Wold, Jr., "Rebellion and Authority: Myths and Realities Reconsidered" (Los Angeles: Rand Corp. paper, mimeo.); see also Lucian W. Pye, "The Roots of Insurgency and the Commencement of Rebellions," in Harry Eckstein (ed.), *Internal Warfare* (New York, 1964), 157-79.

values and the pattern of social and political stratification, out of quite specific grievances about a regime's performance, or out of a personal or group situation. Those supporting the rebellion may seek to alter the status or leadership of the whole territory or only a portion of it. Each kind of motive tends to affect the course of violence in a particular way, with a distinctive impact on the political life of the country.

The Cameroonian experience involved elements of each of the above-mentioned motives, and more. As a result, it was not possible to bring the rebellion under effective control. Although at first making it more difficult for the central government to stop the violence, ultimately this lack of control discredited the rebellion and strengthened the authorities. Thus, one may say that the most important failing of the rebellion was its inability to control its own course. During the entire rebellion, the *Union des Populations du Cameroun* was rent into at least two factions which operated with a minimum of co-ordination and co-operation. The theoretical split came primarily from a difference of opinion as to whether the rules and structures of the Administering Authority could ultimately accommodate nationalist objectives or whether this accommodation would require a violent showdown with the regime.[16] This was complicated and at times dominated by differences which sprang from specific social and ethnic characteristics peculiar to certain groups.

Let us turn now to some of these specific differences as they appear in the ethnic groups of the Bassa and the Bamiléké. Thus, we can see that from 1955 on those who argued within party ranks for increasing violence were almost all Bamiléké. One of the ironic facts about the *Union,* and an element that seriously affected its impact, was that despite its universal objectives—reunification, independence, and modernization—it was quite particularistic in its organizational base. Although its appeal reached far beyond, its structure and leadership came almost exclusively from the Bamiléké, Douala, and Bassa peoples, and these groups reflected very different outlooks and conditons. Whether the Bamiléké and Bassa wings of the party differed much in their policy preferences during the early phases of the rebellion is less certain than that the organization of the guerrilla activity in these areas was closely wedded to and shaped by their widely differing tribal cultures and structures.

The relevance of the traditional structures to the rebellion is best documented in the case of the Bassa maquis.[17] Despite the fact that Um

[16] Allegedly, Um Nyobé believed accommodation with the administration was possible. But the Bamiléké leadership rejected his position.

[17] See Lamberton, "La Pacification." The discussion of Bassa clans and secret societies is taken from this source. This view of the organization of Bassa society is confirmed in G. H. Schwab's monumental study of the Bassa, "Études sur les Coutumes Bassa," 1936 (typescript as yet unpublished).

Nyobé, the secretary of the *Union*, personally preferred participation in the 1956 elections,[18] he nevertheless set about organizing rebel bands and he effectively controlled guerrilla warfare and terrorist organizations among the Bassa of the Sanaga Maritime and Nyong-et-Kélé divisions. His success depended upon his ability to incorporate the maquis into the traditional structure of the Bassa peoples and to utilize traditional symbols of authority and influence. To quarter, feed, and train guerrilla bands, for example, it was crucial that he have control of land. All land suitable for these purposes was already owned, if not used, by corporate lineage groups. Obtaining access to these lands, and usufruct rights in them, required the co-operation of various lineage notables. Um Nyobé obtained access by relying on connections and influence among members of various Bassa secret societies. Although he was not himself a member of the most powerful of the societies, *Um Nkoda Nton* (*Jôn?*), Um Nyobé was able to buy membership in one of the societies next in importance. This particular society was no longer a secret one and held public meetings in which eloquence in public speaking, at which Um Noybé was a master, was of considerable importance. Its members, and especially notables in the clan groups, were influential figures in lower but more secret societies, which served to recruit personnel and supplies.

In addition, Um Nyobé acquired influence indirectly in the most important society, the *Um Nkoda Nton*, through the traditional status of his young associate, Theodore Mayi Matip. Notables from only a small number of clans of the so-called Grand Bassa belonged to this society, and among these the clan of Ndog-Njoué from Eséka-Boumyébel stood preeminent; at the head of this clan was the Matip family. The last of the authentic chiefs of this clan, Matip Ma Mbondol, had been succeeded by someone designated by the French and never properly invested in the post according to Bassa custom. Theodore Mayi Matip happened to have possession of family fetishes and other symbols of authority. He used these to good advantage in reasserting the traditional influence of his family in the Ndog-Njoué clan and claimed successorship to the titles of Mbondol; thereby, he marshaled the influence of Bassa tradition behind the *Comité Nationale d'Organisation* which Um Nyobé had established to direct the maquis.

The meshing of the *Comité* and the traditional Bassa institutions gave the maquis in the Bassa regions a coherence and effectiveness which was unmatched elsewhere in the country. Um Nyobé was not especially interested in stirring up general chaos, in contrast to the tactics of the exiled *Union* leadership in the Bamiléké areas. Even before

---

[18] Interview with participants in the 1956 meetings, confirmed by a former member of the *Union des Populations du Cameroun*, Yaoundé, Mar. 1963.

the maquis was organized, Um Nyobé had implored party branches to put good organization over polemics concerning "the great problems of the hour." "We know by experience that all political problems can be resolved with good organization," he wrote in a letter to the Eséka *Union* bureau, "whereas, all sorts of failures and even catastrophes are possible in a poorly organized movement."[19] The extent of his control over the maquis, its support among the populace, his personal displeasure with unnecessary bloodshed, and his understanding of who the enemy was, are all reflected in the fact that contact with the military was avoided and the general level of terrorism was relatively low. Sabotage of government facilities, intimidation of would-be voters, and attacks on Europeans were commonplace, however. "It is less a question of overthrowing legitimate authority than of leading it imperceptibly to disinterest itself in Bassa problems, which should be resolved among Bassa." Pursuing this logic, Um Nyobé instructed his forces, after January 1957, "to avoid all contact with the military and the guards in order to pursue the organizational effort without being disturbed."[20]

The external wing of the *Union* gave little effective help to the Bassa maquis. The various bands of *maquisards*, most of which seem to have contained fewer than fifty persons, often had only a dozen guns. Many of the *maquisard's* weapons were of their own fabrication, and many of their supplies were stolen from the military, or provided by well placed sympathizers in the service of the government. Very few of their supplies and, apparently, very little money came through the exiled contingent.[21] The autonomy of the Bassa element of the *Union* from the exiled group, and the effectiveness of its leaders' control over the rebels were most dramatically indicated by the quick success of the 1958–59 *ralliement* campaign and their victory at the polls during the elections of April 1960.

The Bassa leaders of the *Union* seem to have pursued different objectives than those sought by the exiled leadership. Reunification and, especially, independence were always the central goals for the former; they had previously refused to participate in the legal structure because they believed to do so would not endow Cameroonians with real power or permit them to gain independence. When the Mbida government was installed in May 1957, they had ample proof that their

[19] Quoted in Lamberton, "La Pacification," 5 (translation by the author).

[20] Ibid., 6.

[21] Zbigniew Brzezinski, in *Africa and the Communist World* (Stanford, 1963), 163 ff., suggests that Communist aid did not become substantial until Moumié moved to Conakry and established contact with the Chinese, probably in mid-1959. Gardinier, *Cameroon*, 93, indicates that it was in May 1959 that modern weapons and supplies began arriving for the Bamiléké rebels.

own objectives were not those animating the government. Yet there was always a certain measure of faith in the popularity of the *Union* and the possibility that the system would respect that popularity. With the coming of the Ahidjo government in February 1958, the coming into power in France of De Gaulle in June 1958, and a new status for Cameroon, Um Nyobé wearied of the maquis and questioned its efficacy. He is known to have approached colleagues and friends in Douala shortly before his death to consider terminating the rebellion; he was advised to continue the struggle. It is not impossible that the location of his headquarters was made known to the authorities by more extremist "friends" within the party, since he was discovered only a few days following his clandestine meeting in Douala.

The development and character of the rebellion in the areas settled by the Bamiléké was very different from that just discussed, with the exception of the fact that both rebellions were profoundly affected by the conditions and nature of the traditional society in which they occurred. Violence had beset the Bamiléké areas for a great many years; the political and social structures and the social and economic situations of these peoples were the contributing factors. Rather than constituting a single cohesive ethnic group with a sense of common identity, the Bamiléké, about 750,000 strong, are divided into over ninety chieftaincies and speak thirteen distinct languages.[22] Each chieftaincy is tightly organized into a powerful hierarchy headed by a chief who, although his power traditionally was buffered by a *kamveu* (council of notables), became rather autocratic due to French favor.[23] Thus, in every chieftaincy there has tended to be a number of notables with special grievances concerning the customary influence that had been usurped by the chief. More important is the fact that their practice of primogeniture, the rather limited territory that they occupy, and the high population growth among the Bamiléké have created very severe demographic pressures on the land. Violence arising from conflicting land claims is endemic to the society.[24] Another result of these conditions has been a massive emigration of Bamiléké away from their homeland into the towns and cities of Southern Cameroon; over 100,000 migrated there between 1930 and 1958.[25]

Among the most energetic and resourceful peoples of West Africa,

[22] Margaret Littlewood, "The Bamiléké of the French Cameroons" in Merran McCulloch, Margaret Littlewood, and I. Dugast (eds.), *Peoples of the Central Cameroons* (London, 1954), 87-131. Also see Claude Tardits, *Les Bamiléké de l'Ouest Cameroun* (Paris, 1960).

[23] Enoch Kwayeb, *Les Institutions de Droit Public du Pays Bamiléké* (Paris, 1960), 142-43.

[24] Tardits, *Bamiléké,* 17.

[25] Le Vine, *Cameroons,* 59.

the Bamiléké émigrés increasingly incurred the animosity of their hosts. They came to outnumber the Douala in the latter's home area and to constitute the largest single group in the capital. Moreover, they tended to dominate petty trade and to rise rapidly in the expanding middle-class occupations. Thus, not only was Bamiléké society in turmoil in its home areas, but migrant Bamiléké found themselves exposed to hostility in the towns. Often a sense of "being Bamiléké" emerged among these people only because of this experience of hostility, common to the émigrés from all the chieftaincies. A strong sense of ethnicity developed, especially among many of the young Bamiléké embedded in the organizational base of émigré chieftaincies in the towns. This preserved and strengthened the ties to the home area but did not prevent serious estrangement from the chiefs and other aspects of traditional society. It was relatively easy for the *Union* to exploit these sentiments and to utilize these émigré organizations. Even among the traditional rural elements, a ready-made reservoir of grievances existed into which the rebels could dip at will.

The grievances of a young deposed Bamiléké chief provided the exiled leadership of the party with its first opportunity to stir up widespread violence in the Bamiléké region. Kamdem-Ninyim Pierre, a militant young nationalist student in Paris and a member of the pro *Union* student group (*Union Nationale des Étudiants Kamerunaises*), inherited the throne of the chief of Baham in 1954. He then joined a study group and set about organizing *comités de base* for the party. His attitudes led the French to depose him a year or so later. The *Union* leadership encouraged him to organize a terrorist campaign against the new chief and his supporters. After the *Union* was banned, Kamdem-Ninyim and his colleagues established a front organization, the *Courant d'Action Nationale*. The leaders of this group (Tchoumba Isaac, Singap Martin, Peze Marcel) established the first Bamiléké maquis. Kamdem's activities were soon discovered; in November of 1956 he was imprisoned and the *Courant d'Action Nationale* suppressed. Singap and Tchoumba continued the rebellion in connection with the exiled leaders, however. Unlike the situation in the Bassa areas, there existed no pan-Bamiléké set of societies which could impose discipline. Within each chieftaincy, however, there did exist a number of associations and political strata from which the party could recruit members and acquire access to territory.

The Bassa terminated their guerrilla operations in late 1958 and early 1959, and Moumié settled in Conakry. These events were followed by sharply increased terrorist attacks in the areas settled by Bamiléké and among a number of holdovers from the earlier Sanaga Maritime operations. But here again, the *Union* was unable to achieve effective co-ordination. The *Armée de Libération Nationale du Kamerun,* under the leadership of Singap Martin, was established to direct the operations. Soon thereafter another maquis sprang up under Momo Paul, another of Kamdem's colleagues and one who remained loyal to him. It became official knowledge that Momo was not taking his orders from Moumié[26] though he continued to portray himself as the real head of the *Armée* instead of Martin. He was repudiated, along with Kamdem-Ninyim,[27] by the exiled leadership.

The various separate maquis outfits, organized into major districts and a number of rebel bands (typical names included Algeria, Morocco, Cuba, Accra), often felt the strain of conflicting ambitions. Many of them split up. Conflict among the local maquis leaders became so bitter that on several occasions some had to be pulled out of the field for a meeting with the exiled leadership at headquarters. One of these bitter conflicts occurred between Tankou Noé, head of the Douala District, and Tomo Henri, who had been sent out from Conakry to assist in the Douala campaign. The former accused the latter of having diverted arms being sent to Tankou Noé and of spreading false rumors that he was pocketing $40 a month for each rebel in his command. Tankou later claimed that he had never received any subvention from the exiled contingent. This dispute occasioned the establishment of a Bureau of Liaison at Kumba to facilitate communication with Accra and Conakry and to provide accessible help in Conakry on July 14, 1960 to clarify the jurisdiction and prerogatives of the *Armée* and Tankou Noé as one of the commanders.[28]

Many of the local districts were poorly co-ordinated, if at all. Tankou Noé never succeeded in establishing a general staff, for example, because the head of the Liaison Bureau never gave him the necessary confirmation for his nominations. Although the Yabassi district was supposed to be under his command, he never had any contact with the rebel groups in that area. The equipment he received from Conakry was hardly sufficient to support his operations: eight Czech pistols. The very few twelve-gauge shotguns in his group's possession were either stolen in Douala or procured from customs officials. Money was raised through periodic "dues" payments from well placed sympathizers, a number of highly placed government people among them.[29]

Contact between the exiled leadership and the several marauding

26 President Ahidjo announced this fact in a speech on Jan. 19, 1960. *New York Times* (Jan. 20, 1960).

27 Interviews with Abel Kingué and other exiled leaders, Accra, Dec. 1963.

28 Judgment No. 85, Tribunal Militaire Temporaire de Douala, Sept. 6–9, 1963.

29 Ibid.

bands of terrorists who remained active in the areas of the old Bassa maquis was especially infrequent. Control over these groups, commanding perhaps as many as five hundred persons, was nearly nonexistent, and so was their equipment.[30] However, control over, if not contact with, the groups operating in the Bamiléké areas was almost as rudimentary. The principal division was that between the exiled group and those loyal to Kamdem-Ninyim. He and the one-time member of the *Comité Directeur*, Tagne Mathieu, both "turned traitor" and not only rallied to but joined the Ahidjo government. Kamdem was made Minister of Health, but while occupying this post he continued to direct guerrilla forces in the Bamiléké districts. In this he seems to have been joined by other members of the *rallié* list who later would regroup with all the Bamiléké deputies into a *Front Populaire pour l'Unité et la Paix*. These leaders were accused by the exiled group of organizing their own maquis.[31]

It is clear from the turmoil and competition among Union sympathizers in the Bamiléké areas, and from the significantly greater number of casualties and amount of property damage there, that objectives were less specific and impersonal than in the earlier Bassa rebellion. Although the rebellion was used as a cover for the violent settlement of many personal disputes in both areas, this aspect seems to have been central in the Bamiléké case. Moreover, sporadic assassination, pillage, and murder continued into 1968, long after the *Union*, externally or internally, maintained any real organization; this suggests that the violence is now, and perhaps always was, largely anomic. The targets of the violence were only remotely related to the sources of strength of the central government; in fact, quite the reverse. The extensive destruction of public welfare services, and the limited number of Europeans attacked, suggests a campaign designed simply to intimidate local residents.

Impact of the Rebellion

With the sequential development and the organizational and motivational aspects of the rebellion in mind, we can return to our initial questions regarding the significance of this experience. Has the net effect of these years of turmoil and strife been to enhance or hinder Cameroon's potential to achieve a politically integrated society?

[30] Rev. Bijeck, a former prisoner of Bassa *maquisards*, in an interview with this author, June 1963, at Ebolowa, claimed that when he was able to flee from the *maquisards*, about 500 of them were in a camp near Ngambé in 1960. Official and other estimates suggest this number for all rebels, Bamiléké and otherwise,
[31] Interview with Kingué, Abel, and others, Accra, Dec. 1963.
at the end of 1960. This latter figure is probably too conservative.

I conceive of integration as a condition of interdependence among political actors in the society, ranging from those patterns of interaction requiring a high level of coercion to persist to those which arise perhaps gratuitously. I wish to emphasize two analytical dimensions to the patterns of interdependent interaction in my consideration of the integrative implications of the Cameroonian rebellion. These correspond to the qualitative and the quantitative aspects of those patterns and have to do either with the kinds and numbers of interactions that occur in the society (the connections that are formed between particular people acting in the society) or with the quality of those interactions and connections. One dimension can be labeled the "conjunctive" dimension and concerns the extent to which people are brought to participate in a common web of interaction, perhaps in collaborative undertakings or at least in those that have some effect on the rest of the society, even if it be a negative effect. The second dimension is the qualitative one, which can be labeled the "complementary-incompatibility" dimension. It concerns the nature of the consequences of interaction—whether they be positive or mutually supportive for the actors involved and thus complementary, or whether they be negative and result in injury to one or more actors or in conflict between them. Although certain kinds of conflict may carry integrative consequences, on balance, for the whole system or even for those parties involved directly in it, integration on a societal level usually demands the achievement of a minimum amount of compatible behavior among the most powerful groups in the society, those strong enough to affect the viability of the society as such. These various aspects of the two dimensions give us four basic modal categories of actions or factors which might affect the level of integration in a society: (1) conjunctive, (2) disjunctive, (3) complementary, and (4) incompatible.[32]

The Cameroonian insurgency resulted in certain integrative gains with respect to the first and last mentioned types of factors and realized some limited gains with respect to the third. Beyond the fact that the resettlement programs among the Bamiléké brought isolated villages and families into closer proximity, we have little evidence from which to judge the possible integrative factors of the second mentioned category. Of course, we must keep in mind the frightful cost of any such gains in terms of lives lost (perhaps 10,000) and property and capital

[32] For a further elaboration of these points, see my "National Integration in Africa: Some Analytical Dimensions," a paper presented to the Fifty-First Annual Meeting of the Association for the Study of Negro Life and History, Baltimore, Oct. 21–23, 1966. Papers on file at the Library, Morgan State College, Baltimore, Maryland; and *The Cameroon Federation: Political Integration in a Fragmentary Society* (Princeton, 1970).

destroyed (about $8 million). It is not my intention to imply that these represent *net* gains when measured against such costs; I know of no way such measurements can be made.

Incompatible Action: As of 1968, no significant political leadership in Cameroon has pursued a course of action incompatible with the objectives and program of the ruling circles of the only active party, the *Union Nationale Camerounaise.* Political conflict of a violent sort, or even assertive competition, has been at its lowest ebb since the late 1940's.[33] This is due in large part to a widespread weariness with factionalism, tribalism, and political dissidence which had, for over a decade, constantly drenched portions of the country in blood. This is not to say that all political tendencies have been harmonized and fused into an enthusiastic collaboration, merely that none of them seemed willing any longer to threaten a populace fatigued with violence with any really forceful pursuit of their own goals.

One of the *Union* directors, Ernest Ouandié, was thought (direct proof is lacking) as of 1968 to want to pursue the guerrilla campaign against the government of Ahidjo. The head of the rallied *Union,* Theodore Mayi Matip, and the Douala sympathizer, Bebey Eyidi, in 1967 still refused to embrace the party of Ahidjo, but their organizations stood literally for themselves alone. These leaders, together with André Marie Mbida, the former Prime Minister and head of the Democrats, and Charles Okala, the former Foreign Minister and head of the Socialists, in 1965 emerged from three years of detention on charges of subversive activities. By 1968 all save Eyidi, who died an independent, carried their organizations (only the former was substantial) into the ruling party. All the parties of West Cameroon, including a splinter of the Kamerun National Democratic party formed only a year before, had fused completely with the ruling *Union Nationale Camerounaise* in mid-1966.

The acquiescence in the consolidation of power in the hands of the formerly much maligned President Ahidjo was only the final outcome

[33] Certain elements of the Bamiléké leadership may have considered attempting a coup in November 1966 following the arrest of Victor Kanga, the only Bamiléké in a federal ministerial position, on charges of misusing state funds and fomenting subversion in response to his demotion from the post of Minister of Finance to that of Tourism, and his subsequent dismissal from that post. Kanga claimed that he was demoted for attempting to crack down on embezzlers, and that he had nothing to do with the pamphlets circulated by close associates claiming that he had been a victim of duty. In December he was sentenced, along with two former aides, to four years' imprisonment. If armed units placed around the radio station and other strategic points in Yaoundé indicate an attempted coup, it failed, and has not produced any significant stirring of the people, at least not enough to attract the attention of the external press.

of what had become an established tendency. Not only the rest of the southern population but the Bamiléké themselves have perceived opposition to the government as a threat of violence. This has been so since the formation of the block of eighteen Bamiléké deputies as the *Front Populaire pour l'Unité et la Paix*. Bamiléké leaders have actually come to the point of expressing shame that their region was unique in its propensity for violence, though such an admission was long and hard in coming.[34] Considerable resentment was generated just a few years ago when the Bamiléké were singled out as terrorists, and when the "troubles" associated with the *Union* seemed to come only from the Bamiléké and not the Bassa wing of the party. Appeals to end the rebellion switched from pre-1960 themes which stressed governmental reforms (such as the declaration of complete amnesty, the conduct of a round table to establish a provisional government, the removal of foreign troops, and the holding of elections open to all factions) to straightforward and unadorned demands for an end to violence. Efforts of Bamiléké sympathizers to achieve a round table conference of hostile Cameroon political factions changed to appeals for a round table among hostile Bamiléké factions.[35] The claims of the exiled *Union* increasingly fell victim to evidence, and the *Union*'s perfidy in supporting continued violence was increasingly exposed by purposeless brutality. The extent of the estrangement between the troublesome elements of the *Union* and the Bamiléké generally was reflected in the fact that no one protested President Ahidjo's announcement in mid-1963 that there would be no further liberalization of the terms of amnesty already offered to former rebels.

The government's response to the rebellion in the Bamiléké departments was not only to make heavy use of repressive measures, but also to initiate a large developmental and social reorganization program. Termed the "Regroupement en pays Bamiléké," this scheme had a predecessor on a smaller scale among the Bassa; it was, however, really more akin to the British relocation of the Kikuyu in Kenya during the Emergency of 1952–60. It sought to bring together the widely scattered Bamiléké homesteads into villages which could be policed and protected. These settlements could also more easily profit from medical and educational services than could the scattered communities. More

---

[34] Vice-President John N. Foncha, widely though incorrectly perceived as a Bamiléké, waged a "cold war against terrorism" in which he repeatedly reminded the Bamiléké that they "stood alone in perpetrating terrorism." Federal Republic of Cameroon Press Release 2512, July 1963. It should be mentioned that Foncha was fired upon during this tour.

[35] See *La Presse du Cameroun,* Jan. 18, 1963—appeal by a Bamiléké Deputy and the Minister of Husbandry.

important, in terms of reducing the level of conflict among the people, is the fact that the regroupments constituted an effort to establish administration and government on a new basis among the Bamiléké. As one young Bamiléké official put it: "the regroupments have also permitted a break with not only the traditional isolation [of Bamiléké families] but also with the encroaching hold of the chiefs."[36] The expectation was that these measures would reduce the conflict between traditional authorities and the younger elements.

Conjunctive Action: One of the recognized functions of internal conflict is to strengthen or create loyalties and identifications within if not between the conflicting groups.[37] The Cameroonian rebellion(s) resulted in some important gains of this sort. Although the conflict which gave rise to and resulted from the rebellion divided some groups, it united others and in the end enhanced the commitment among most groups involved to the larger political order that is the Cameroon federal state.

The consolidation of Bassa identification and solidarity was quite notable. The utilization of the moribund secret societies and the intense loyalty to Um Nyobé that developed gave an organizational coherence to Bassa public life that it had not known for a great many years. Although initially there was considerable resistance to the claims of the Union, and no small amount of vengeance concerning longstanding feuds which motivated some of the violence, the Bassa came to act essentially as a single organization. The Bassa rebel leaders (at least among the Protestants) were able to turn the rebellion on and then off again with remarkable effectiveness. Once rallied, these ex-"terrorists" were able to command the overwhelming support of the Bassa electorate. The pay-offs for relative loyalty have been meager for the Bassa, however. No massive development program has been launched, and no important Bassa leaders are members of the government.[38] Mayi Matip was once offered a cabinet post but turned it down. It is hard to imagine that the Bassa will long remain tranquil if their "good behavior" continues to go unrewarded.

There is nothing among the Bamiléké approaching even the rudimentary level of organizational solidarity and collaborative political action we have noted among the Bassa. No pan-Bamiléké organization

[36] Dina Lobe, "Mission dans la Region administrative de l'Ouest—14–21 Septembre, 1962" (Ministry of Planning, Yaoundé, 1962).

[37] See Georg Simmel (trans. K. H. Wolff and R. Bendix), *Conflict* (Glencoe, 1955), 13-15. See also the work of Lewis Coser, *The Functions of Social Conflict* (New York, 1956), based on Simmel.

[38] The director of the Sûreté is a Bassa but he has no personal political following among this group.

emerged to co-ordinate and control the ninety-odd chieftaincies. However, Bamiléké leaders have become more unified than they were during the seminal period of Cameroonian politics. In the late 1940's, the party did have some success in wedding itself to tradition-based structures which tended to span the breadth of the Bamiléké chiefdoms; one of the most important of the Bamiléké chiefs, Mathias Djoumessi, the first president of the party, created an organization called Kumze which he touted as "the traditional association" of the Bamiléké, but it had no historical justification. Though Djoumessi did succeed in implanting the organization into most of the chieftaincies, he used it more to aggrandize his own personal following than to increase that of the *Union*. As other Bamiléké chiefs became fearful of a certain anti-traditional, anti-chief orientation among the *upécistes*, Djoumessi found it more convenient to break with the party. The Kumze did not survive this split and the subsequent conflicts on which the rebellion fed, although Djoumessi continued to head a loose parliamentary group consisting mainly of Bamiléké deputies, the *Paysans Indépendents*. Following independence, Bamiléké representation in the central legislature was consolidated, however, in a way never before achieved among their elected leadership. This is a direct outcome of the rebellion in that the rallied Bamiléké *Union* Deputies and those who did not run on a party list, but who tended to share the *upécistes'* suspicions of the Mbida and Ahidjo regimes, all grouped into a single front in the legislature. This was the *Front Populaire pour l'Unité et la Paix*. As a Bamiléké deputy exclaimed, "They use the Bamiléké like a piece of wood; when they are cold they use us to warm up, but when they are warm they throw us out the window."

The really significant example of increasing conjunctiveness in Cameroonian political activity is, however, the growth of the *Union Camerounaise,* or the *Union Nationale Camerounaise* as it is now called after regrouping all other major parties. At the time when Ahmadou Ahidjo took over as Prime Minister in 1958, his party, the *Union Camerounaise,* could claim only thirty seats in an assembly of seventy members. The first accretion to his party's strength came when Charles Assale and his *Mouvement d'Action Nationale* joined the *Union Camerounaise,* first in coalition and later in fusion, in 1958 and 1960 respectively. Shortly after a government was formed for independent Cameroon in 1960, the Bamiléké deputies declared for the *Union Camerounaise,* bringing its parliamentary strength to about three-fourths of the one-hundred-man *Assemblée Nationale*. A skillfully played game of carrot and stick soon enticed or drove various members of the remaining parties into the ranks of the dominant party. Finally, in desperation, the "big four," Bebey Eyidi of the *Travaillists,* Mayi Matip of the

Union, Charles Okala of the Socialists, and Mbida of the Démocrats, published a joint manifesto accusing the President of pursuing a course that would lead to a fascist-type dictatorship, but in doing so they were careful to condemn and dissociate themselves from violence and terrorism. Their internment for three years followed the elections for the East Cameroon Assembly in June 1965 (the former Republic having become East Cameroon in the Federal Republic inaugurated October 1, 1961). The *Union Camerounaise* captured every seat unopposed; the Démocrats were convinced of the futility of running a list of candidates.

Complementary Action: Enthusiasm is not one of the hallmarks of the coalition of forces which now supports the Ahidjo regime. This coalition is rapidly growing in size and effectiveness, however. Without extensive attitudinal surveys or other measurement of the psychological orientation of important Cameroonian groups, it is hazardous to attempt to assess the degree to which their action and predispositions complement each other. There is some evidence which suggests that there is a growing body of shared values among formerly hostile political forces in the country.

One important value which constantly gained support was the value of the peaceful resolution of conflict. No public speech or publicly circulated pamphlet (and in fact no private conversations known to this writer) contained any calls to arms or appeals for a forceful pursuit of political objectives. This has been so since 1965. As has been pointed out, even the manifesto and open letter of the opposition United National Front, which resulted in the imprisonment of the principal opposition leaders, denounced the use of violence for political ends (especially by the government).

Another value which gained ground was the legitimacy of an independence which continued to involve large-scale aid from the former colonial power. Former *upécistes, maquisards* among them, came to accept the fact that the Cameroon was independent, at least as much as the other states of the former French Union. It must be mentioned that many remained dissatisfied with the extent of French influence in government circles, but most of these dissidents seemed to anticipate a gradual but steady loosening of these ties.[39] Indeed, Ahidjo became more forceful and autonomous over the years and incorporated a great many former opponents into the government. French troops were withdrawn, and there were fewer French advisers. The

[39] President Ahidjo himself claimed that French subsidies to the recurrent budget compromised the Cameroon's true independence, and he began to cut down the size of these subsidies from 1964 on, until they were eliminated in the budget of 1966–67. Significant French aid for development projects continued.

major source of criticism of French influence in Cameroonian affairs then emanated from the English-speaking community, whose attachment to institutions and symbols associated with their former Administering Authority has, as among the Francophones, deepened since reunification.

Ultimately the regime which the *Union*(s) sought to destroy was strengthened. The consolidation of national identity was advanced as a result of this most vivid demonstration of the costs of factionalism, tribalism, internal dissidence, and strife. The Ahidjo regime could claim with increasing effectiveness that it embodied the country's best hope for domestic justice, peace, and progress.

PART FIVE

THE ECONOMIC EXPRESSION

OF DISCONTENT

TRADE UNION, POLITICAL PRESSURE GROUP, OR MASS MOVEMENT?

THE INDUSTRIAL AND COMMERCIAL WORKERS' UNION OF AFRICA

SHERIDAN W. JOHNS, III

"We are aiming at the building up in Africa of a National Labour Organisation of the aboriginals, through which we shall break the wills of white autocracy. We must prevent the exploitation of our people on the mines and on the farms, and obtain increased wages for them. We shall not rest there. We will open the gates of the Houses of legislation, now under the control of the white oligarchy, and from this step we shall claim equality of purpose with the white workers of the world to overthrow the capitalist system of government and usher in a co-operative Commonwealth one, a system of Government which is not foreign to the aboriginal of Africa."[1]

With those words, widely reported in the South African press, and subsequently adopted as the objective of the Industrial and Commercial Workers' Union of Africa (ICU), Clements Kadalie, its national secretary, challenged white South Africa in the name of its nonwhite working force. At the time when Kadalie spoke (April 1925), the ICU was only six years old, and within three years it was to disintegrate into a handful of squabbling local factions. Yet, during its decade of prominence, the ICU came to dominate African politics in South Africa; during its brief, but often spectacular, existence, the ICU wrote an important chapter in the history of nonwhite protest in South Africa.

The author gratefully acknowledges the generous help of Professor Gwendolen Carter, Director of the Program of African Studies, Northwestern University, in making available to him the large collection of South African documents at the Program of African Studies. He is also indebted to Louise Antell Halper for valuable assistance and suggestions. All unpublished documents cited, unless otherwise noted, are located at the Program of African Studies, Northwestern University.

[1] *Cape Times*, Apr. 15, 1925; *The Workers' Herald*, May 15, 1925.

Violent organized resistance by the old African tribal order to the relentless advance of the whites had largely ceased by the end of the nineteenth century. Its futility was further demonstrated by the ease with which the Natal authorities were able to end the Bambatha rebellion of 1906 in Zululand.[2] Henceforth the struggle between black and white to determine the terms of racial co-existence was to be within the confines of a single, white-dominated political unit.

The forces of white might and technical organization wanted to limit closely the options of the nonwhites in the new system. In the vision of society held by Afrikaner nationalists, nonwhites were to be given subordinate positions in a patriarchal, rurally-based society with no possibility for advancement to, or full participation in, the institutions of the white society. Within the modernizing economic order dominated by the British, untrained nonwhites were both enticed and indirectly forced to take positions as unskilled or semi-skilled laborers under the command of imported English skilled workers or recent Afrikaner migrants to the cities, the latter being often as unprepared for labor in the mines and factories as the nonwhites themselves. A network of governmental regulations tied the nonwhites closely to these different hierarchical answers to South Africa's "racial problem."

Yet the imposition of white power over South Africa also brought new ideologies and institutions which offered the promise of a more egalitarian version of the new order to those nonwhites who would fully accept it. The diffusion of Christianity, mostly by English missionaries, brought a faith which preached the possibilities of joint participation in a common society; and, at the same time, the schools and churches of the missionaries began training a new group of nonwhites oriented, in one way or another, to this ideal. The gradual transplantation of English political institutions introduced another element conducive to hopes of eventual equality for all South Africans, regardless of color. Under the terms of the franchise granted to the inhabitants of the Cape Colony (and, in theory, of Natal) qualifications were merely stated in terms of property and education; a common standard of law was established for all "civilized" men. Although the terms of the Act of Union accepted the Afrikaner segregationist political practices in the Transvaal and the Orange Free State, they also entrenched nonwhite political rights elsewhere. Within this framework nonwhites, especially those trained by the missions, could participate in politics with whites and hope for the eventual expansion of opportunities to all nonwhites throughout South Africa.

The potentially color-blind dimensions of religion and politics

[2] See above, Shula Marks, "The Zulu Disturbances in Natal," 213-57.

were complemented by the growth of certain attitudes on the part of the key white participants in the modern, industrializing sector of the economy. On one side, capitalist entrepreneurs, concerned to maximize profits, admitted the possibility of a labor force in which skill and a willingness to accept lower wages, rather than skin color, would determine job placement. In practice, this meant a direct challenge to the legislatively buttressed color bar in the economy. On the other side, white labor, in its struggle to secure its position, introduced effective models of organization and socialist ideologies. Few among the white capitalists and white laborers actively pushed for full application of the implicitly egalitarian aspects of their economic assumptions—in both cases too many of the other premises of their South African existence would have been strongly undermined. Yet it was these implicitly color-blind features in the white-dominated economic order which gave a promise of greater and more equal participation to the other significant new social group—the growing number of nonwhite workers who had begun to cluster in South Africa's cities.

Reflecting the impact of white-imposed institutions and ideologies, and responding to the egalitarian potential of both, a new type of African organization had begun to appear in the Cape Colony in the latter part of the nineteenth century. Composed for the most part of Christian Africans who had received their training in the mission stations, the new organizations represented a small, but growing, group of African voters who organized for the furtherance of their interests, primarily through bloc voting and informal lobbying. In the wake of the Anglo-Boer War, congresses and voters' organizations of this type sprang up in all of the four colonies which were to make up the Union of South Africa in 1910. Although denied the vote everywhere but in the Cape Colony, these new groups through petitions and deputations actively campaigned for an extension of political and civil rights to nonwhites throughout South Africa. They were joined by organizations of Coloureds, the most prominent of which was the African Peoples' Organization.[3] The leadership and membership of these groups was dominated by a new nonwhite "middle-class" hopeful of full participa-

[3] At this time in South Africa the features of Indian politics were quite distinct from other nonwhite politics. Although Indians, led by Gandhi, had achieved world-wide notice through their passive resistance campaigns in the early years of the century, their campaigns were carefully conducted in terms of Indian-South African relations with the British Indian government, which was seen as the most important agency for intervention on behalf of South African Indians. Thus, unlike the Coloureds and the Africans, the Indians at this time redressed their grievances by actions directed at diplomatic intervention and not primarily through efforts to participate in the South African political system. See below, Leo Kuper, "Nonviolence Revisited," 788-804.

tion in South African society, yet willing, for the most part, to exhibit patience, respectability, and moderation to achieve its ends by strictly constitutional and peaceful means in line with its Christian and "British" faith.

The formation of new "integrationist" organizations was paralleled by the spread of a rival form of African organization born in frustration and resentment at the unfulfilled promise of equality within Christianity. Disillusioned African Christians, denied an equal voice in church government and policy-making, formed separatist churches which retained the basic creed and dogma of Christianity while asserting that Africans, not whites, should control African churches. Other Africans went further in their questioning of established white Christianity. Not only did they argue that Africans should control African churches, but they also asserted that African churches should adhere to syncretistic beliefs incorporating both traditional African and Christian practices. In separatist churches, these groups carried their message to the nonwhites. Separatists did not attempt to challenge white domination directly, yet within the fact of that domination they chiselled out areas in which Africans could exercise limited autonomy. In contrast to the "integrationist" congresses and voters' bodies, their appeal was directed less to the most educated and to those most likely to find acceptance from sympathetic white liberals.

With the establishment of the South African Native National Congress in 1912 (in the wake of the restricting terms of the Act of Union and in the face of the threat of the deprivations promised in the Natives Land Act of 1913), a partial fusion of the two approaches, integrationist and separatist, was realized. The leadership and the membership of the Congress were overwhelmingly drawn from the preexistent congresses and voters' bodies. The program of the Congress, in its aspirations to full civil and political rights and in its dedication to nonviolent and generally constitutional methods, also followed closely those of its predecessor congresses and voters' bodies. Yet the Congress appealed broadly to all Africans to join in a united front to achieve these goals—if necessary through African organization and pressure outside the accepted limits of the system in which the Congress demanded full participation for all South Africans. With this emphasis, the new Congress incorporated elements of the concerns of the separatists. From its foundation it seemed clear that the Congress represented a new type of challenge to the white domination of South Africa. Excluded from recognized participation in the political structure of the Union of South Africa, the Congress, nevertheless, asserted the right of Africans to participate in politics in accord with the Christian and democratic goals to which white South Africa professed allegiance.

In the initial decades of its existence, however, the Congress (from 1923, the African National Congress) remained largely the instrument of the "middle class" which made up its leadership and membership. It relied upon deputations, proclamations, and respectful pressure group tactics. Only during the passive resistance campaign against passes in early 1919 did the Congress apparently attempt to conduct mass agitation or to extend itself significantly among large numbers of Africans. Yet it continued to express, often in forceful language, the argument that Africans were entitled to proper attention from governmental authorities and to an extension of political rights, even if gradually. Although its middle-class leadership by training and temperament was apparently reluctant to embark upon an activist effort involving significant numbers of Africans who did not fully share its outlook, the Congress did provide a focal point for those who sought a political approach for solving African problems. In Coloured politics it was paralleled by the African People's Organization.

Yet the concerns and tactics of the Congress and the African People's Organization remained, for the most part, inadequate as vehicles for expression of the grievances which affected the new nonwhite "proletariat." In the more racially tolerant Cape Province a considerable number of Coloureds were advancing to skilled and semiskilled positions in the work force. Throughout South Africa, Coloureds and Africans made up the overwhelming majority of the unskilled laborers. Although many of the Africans were still migratory workers, an increasing number had begun to settle around the cities and towns. The demands of these men were primarily economic—for higher wages and better working conditions. Yet the restrictions of the pass laws and the contract labor system also agitated nonwhite workers. In the South African context, then, nonwhite economic demands inevitably became nonwhite political demands. Implicitly and explicitly, they challenged the basic hierarchical assumptions and the governmental regulations issuing from them upon which white domination rested. It was through the articulation and organization of these demands that the ICU, founded in 1919, exploded into a mass movement which threatened to reach even beyond the urban workers to the rural Africans with whom so many of the urban Africans were still closely linked.

As the first nationwide organization of the new "proletariat" of South Africa, the ICU faced a variety of organizational and tactical problems. Its potential membership was considerable,[4] yet most African workers were still only part-time residents in the towns or full-time agricultural laborers on white-owned farms. Properly trained leaders,

---

[4] In 1921 there were approximately 587,000 Africans and 250,000 Coloureds in urban areas. These figures are derived from data in D. Hobart Houghton, *The South African Economy* (Cape Town, 1964), 221.

familiar with the skills necessary for the operation of a rapidly expanding organization, were scarce. Existing African "middle-class" groups
with educational and organizational talent were uncertain of their
attitude toward a "working-class" body. In its membership and its pronouncements, the ICU for the most part proclaimed itself an organization for all nonwhite workers, yet in practice divergent interests of
various groups, particularly Coloureds and Africans, created friction
within the organization. In terms of its own operations the ICU never
resolved whether it was primarily a bona fide trade union or whether
it was a political pressure group. At times it also took on the character
of a mass movement of protest. Its efforts to further its programs vacillated between respectful representations to governmental authorities
and threats of mass strikes. It alternated between hopes of reform with
the aid of sympathetic whites in South Africa and reliance upon international pressures to bring about change within South Africa.
Throughout its existence the crucial question of its relationship to the
white workers of South Africa and their trade union and political
bodies agitated the leadership. The basic question of the place of the
ICU and its membership within white-dominated South Africa remained an unresolved issue, the terms of which shifted according to
alignments within the ICU and within white society. Inconsistencies,
internal strife, and both militancy and moderation marked the life of
the ICU; yet in these contradictions it is possible to ascertain the nature of the organization and its significance for the development of
new forms of political action among the nonwhites of South Africa.

The ICU was born in the maelstrom of unrest which seized South
Africa in the wake of World War I.[5] In the interests of the "war effort,"
capitalists and white labor leaders had papered over the deep differences which had divided them during the first decade of the twentieth
century. The white working force, dominated by immigrant skilled
workers of British origin but increasingly composed of Afrikaners at
the lower levels, was organizationally represented by growing trade
unions and the South African Labour party. With the end of the war
and the aggravation of economic difficulties, the mutual antagonisms
of white labor and capital could no longer be contained; strikes and
lockouts finally escalated into a general strike in 1922 on the Witwatersrand after the Chamber of Mines had threatened to lower wages
and to decrease the proportion of white workers employed. Ultimately,
the government of General Jan Christiaan Smuts declared martial law

[5] For an examination in detail of the origin of the ICU as a national organization see Sheridan W. Johns, III, "The Birth of Non-White Trade Unionism in
South Africa," Race, IX (1967), 173-92. The following account is a condensed
version of the analysis presented there.

and intervened to break the "Red Revolt" on the Witwatersrand. Defeated in their efforts to use direct action, the militant white workers then attempted to fashion a political alliance which would oust the Smuts government and replace it with a sympathetic administration. Throughout, the primary concern of the white workers was the protection of their privileged status atop the labor pyramid of South Africa. The assertive discontent of the white workers was paralleled by the continuing animosity of the rurally-based Afrikaner Nationalists to General Smuts and the imperial connection which he defended. Buoyed by post-war electoral gains, the Nationalists saw new possibilities. Postponing their commitment to an independent republic outside the British Empire in return for the temporary withdrawal of the "Socialist objective" of the Labour party, the Nationalists made an electoral pact with the Labour party which promised victory at the next election.

Like the white workers, Africans, too, had muted their demands during the war. In the years immediately before the outbreak of the war, African opinion had successively been disturbed by the establishment of the Union of South Africa (under terms which limited the possibility of nonwhite participation in government to the inhabitants of the Cape Province) and by the Natives Land Act of 1913 (by which African land ownership was restricted to thirteen per cent of the land of South Africa). Yet in an expression of spontaneous loyalty to the Crown, African leaders agreed not to press their grievances until the successful conclusion of the war.

During the war large numbers of Africans were sucked into the urban labor force as South African industry expanded rapidly and unexpectedly. At the bottom of the labor pyramid, Africans were poorly paid and restricted by a network of government regulations, including the Masters and Servants Act and various pass laws. At the end of the war this group, even more than their white co-workers, felt the impact of the post-war economic dislocations. Yet neither they, nor the "loyal" Africans as a group, received any immediate concessions from white-governed South Africa. Only a rash of demonstrations forced the white public to hear their grievances. In the Transvaal in 1918 African mineworkers boycotted shops, and there also were several limited strikes. Finally in February 1920, some 40,000 struck unsuccessfully against the mineowners. In Bloemfontein, Cape Town, and Port Elizabeth nonwhite workers also demonstrated and struck to support demands for higher wages. During early 1919 the South African Native National Congress conducted a campaign of passive resistance against passes in the Transvaal. Government and management yielded little to African demands, and organized white labor, for the most part, became increasingly hostile. Successive shootings of Africans (demonstrating urban workers in Port Elizabeth in 1920, defiant Israelite separatists at Bulhoek in 1921, and rebellious Bondelswarts tribesmen in Southwest Africa in 1922) reinforced African resentment—particularly against the Smuts government.

Against this backdrop the first African trade unions were organized in widely separated centers of South Africa. In Johannesburg in 1917 a small number of anti-war white Socialists had encouraged the organization of the Industrial Workers of Africa, but the union did not take root despite the apparently fertile soil turned up by the post-war demonstrations of African workers on the Witwatersrand. In Cape Town a sympathetic Labour party politician had spurred the organization of the Industrial and Commercial Union among the African and Coloured dockworkers in early 1919. Two months later, Selby Msimang, a clerk and court interpreter who had been closely associated with Dr. Pixley Seme in the establishment of the South African Native National Congress, led the African inhabitants of Bloemfontein in a series of demonstrations which brought police intervention and national attention. In Port Elizabeth nonwhite workers were also being encouraged to press wage demands by Sam Masabalala, a former teacher who was employed by a local pharmacist.

Clements Kadalie, the African leader of the trade union in Cape Town, was the only one of the new nonwhite trade unionists who was not South African.[6] Born in the mid-1890's to the Christianized son of a chief of the Tonga tribe of Nyasaland, Kadalie had been educated in Scottish mission stations, where, according to his account, he was among the brightest students. Upon completion of his schooling in 1912, Kadalie taught briefly in mission schools in Nyasaland. In 1915, however, he left Nyasaland "in quest of a higher civilized life." Making his way through Moçambique and Southern Rhodesia, Kadalie took a series of minor clerical jobs, finally arriving in Bulawayo in 1916. There Kadalie found work as a clerk in a private insurance firm run by a sympathetic white who placed great trust in him. In his spare time Kadalie organized social affairs for Africans in Bulawayo. When a substitute for his vacationing employer demanded that Kadalie perform domestic service in addition to his clerical duties, Kadalie decided to resign his post and migrate to South Africa, where many Africans from Nyasaland, including Kadalie's elder brother and a number of other relatives, had gone in search of work.

In early 1918 Kadalie arrived in Cape Town and shortly thereafter

[6] The following information about Kadalie's childhood and experiences prior to 1919 is taken from his unpublished autobiography. Clements Kadalie, "Memoirs" (unpublished typescript), 1-8.

found work as a messenger. For the next twenty months he held several jobs as messenger and clerk, occasionally encountering difficulties from fellow white employees who resented taking orders from him. His determination to protest an incident of discrimination brought him to the attention of A. F. Batty, a white Socialist member of the South African Labour party. Batty had been a witness to an incident in which Kadalie had been pushed off the sidewalk by a white policeman. He endorsed Kadalie's intention to complain about the matter to higher authorities. Shortly afterward, when Batty decided to run in a parliamentary by-election in a racially mixed district in Cape Town, he asked Kadalie to serve with his campaign team. Although Batty was defeated, he had found Kadalie's work useful. Perhaps with an eye to votes in future elections Batty asked Kadalie to continue organizing nonwhite workers. In January 1919, at a meeting of African and Coloured workers presided over by Batty, the Industrial and Commercial Union was founded. Kadalie was elected secretary of the new union; henceforth its affairs increasingly occupied his time. In October 1919, Kadalie led the union in an initially effective, but largely unsuccessful strike on the Cape Town docks. Through the strike Kadalie and nonwhite trade unionism gained prominence.

In July 1920, delegates from the various local trade unions (including Kadalie's union) met in Bloemfontein to co ordinate nonwhite trade union activity. Agreement was reached among the delegates to form the Industrial and Commercial Workers' Union of Africa. Resolutions were passed which asserted that the new nation-wide body would organize all types of nonwhite workers for the purposes of bettering their working conditions by peaceful negotiations with employers. In apparent deference to the South African Native National Congress, it was specifically stated that the Workers' Union would eschew political activity. It emphasized its legitimacy as a trade union, yet it also condemned the pass laws and the system of contract labor. Although governmental policies were thus challenged, the conference declared its main enemies to be protectionist white trade unions and white capitalists. When the conference turned to the election of officers, however, satisfactory agreement apparently proved impossible. Msimang was named president, but the conference passed over Kadalie for the post of general secretary. In resentment against the failure of the conference to name him to the post to which he believed he was entitled, Kadalie led the Cape Town delegates out of the conference, thus depriving the new organization of a branch in that important town. Nevertheless, the framework for a national nonwhite trade union organization had been established.

In the ensuing two and a half years the new Workers' Union was buffeted by a series of factional struggles and regional readjustments which altered the nature of the union. Kadalie continued to organize his union in Cape Town, primarily among African and Coloured dock-workers, yet he apparently initially remained aloof from the Workers' Union presided over by Msimang. In October 1920, the spotlight fell upon Port Elizabeth when twenty-four persons (including one white) were killed in disturbances following the arrest of Masabalala; Selby Msimang stepped in to represent the nonwhite workers and to prevent further disorder in the wake of the shootings. Through mid-1921 Msi-mang retained control of the national organizational structure of the Workers' Union, which continued to organize among Africans in the Orange Free State and the eastern Cape Province. On the first anni-versary of the shootings, Kadalie traveled to Port Elizabeth where he joined Masabalala in memorial demonstrations. Shortly thereafter a national conference of the Workers' Union was called at which a man from Cape Town was elected to the presidency while Kadalie and Masabalala were elected to the key posts of general secretary and or-ganizer-in-chief respectively. Msimang did not challenge the takeover and withdrew from the Workers' Union. His departure apparently sig-naled the end of activity in the Orange Free State.

In 1922 and 1923 the activity of the union was largely confined to the Cape Province, with increasing emphasis upon Cape Town. Masa-balala and Kadalie subsequently disagreed over administrative ques-tions and Kadalie successfully installed one of his Coloured supporters as the head of the Port Elizabeth branch of the Workers' Union.[7] By the end of 1924 Kadalie, an African immigrant from Nyasaland who spoke none of the African languages of South Africa, was clearly recog-nized as the dominant personality of the first national nonwhite trade union. It became known simply as the ICU, the initials of the original Cape Town trade union founded by Kadalie in 1919. The ascendancy of Kadalie, whose base of support was initially Cape Town, also meant a shift in the "racial" balance of union leadership and membership to-ward the Coloureds who had played an important role in Cape Town from the inception of nonwhite trade unionism there.

Under Kadalie's leadership the ICU did not depart from the broad outlines of the program which had been enunciated at the first confer-ence of the Workers' Union at Bloemfontein in July 1920. The ICU re-mained committed to the organization of all nonwhite workers and representation of their interests through constitutional means. Simul-taneously, the ICU attacked elements of governmental policy, in par-ticular the pass laws. Yet it repeatedly asserted that it was an apolitical

---

[7] Kadalie, "Memoirs," 23. The final break with Masabalala came in 1924. *The Workers' Herald,* May 15, 1924.

trade union whose "objectives are solely to propagate the industrial, economic, and social advancement of all the African workers through industrial organization on constitutional lines."[8] To this end it started irregular publication of a newspaper, *The Workers' Herald*, in May 1923.[9] Furthermore, it agreed to provide limited social and welfare benefits for its members.[10]

Developments in white South African society brought further elaboration of ICU attitudes and strategy. When the protectionist white trade unions of the Transvaal succeeded in getting the government to name Archie Crawford as the workers' representative to the newly established International Labor Organization in Geneva, Kadalie sparked the ICU to protest that it was more representative of the South African workers and henceforth that it should represent them in international councils.[11] Thus Kadalie early enunciated the desirability of links with overseas workers, a theme on which he was to become increasingly insistent in the mid-1920's. In 1923–24 he sought to realize his hopes by exchanges of correspondence with labor organizers in Australia and Great Britain.[12]

Relations with fellow white workers in South Africa, however, were less easily handled. The proximity of the militant, Socialist-oriented white trade unions which had challenged both the government and management repeatedly in their two decades of existence provided on the-spot evidence of the potentialities of trade union organization. With their calls for workers' solidarity and their various

[8] Industrial and Commercial Workers' Union of Africa, ICU, *Official Report of Proceedings—Third Annual Conference, Industrial and Commercial Workers' Union of Africa, ICU* (Cape Town, 1923), 3, 19. This policy was enunciated at the second annual conference of the ICU in Port Elizabeth, Oct. 1921, and reaffirmed at the third annual conference of the ICU in Cape Town, Jan. 1923.

[9] There is no complete file of *The Workers' Herald* available. The most extensive file is to be found on microfilm in the New York Public Library.

[10] The constitution of the ICU included the following:
   b) To provide legal assistance to the Organisation, and to its members in matters connected with their daily employment.
   c) To establish sick, unemployment, old age, and death benefits for its members.
   g) To establish Clubs, Debating Societies, etc., with the object of educating the workers, especially on Labour Questions.
   h) To publish pamphlets, newspapers, or any other literature that may be deemed necessary by the National Council or the Board of Arbitration, for the material and spiritual welfare of the members of the Organization.
Industrial and Commercial Workers' Union of Africa, ICU, *1925 Revised Constitution* (Johannesburg, 1925), 3.

[11] At an interview with the Minister of Mines and Industries in May 1922, Kadalie devoted particular attention to the matter of international representation for the ICU. *The Cape Times*, May 22, 1922.

[12] *The Workers' Herald*, July 21, 1923; Jan. 9, 1925.

formulas for reform and revolution, the white trade unionists offered attractive models to the nonwhite workers. Yet the bulk of the same white workers and their leaders also supported a privileged status for themselves, including a discriminatory wage structure and segregation. During the general strike on the Witwatersrand in 1922, the threat inherent in their position was made real when elements among the strikers attacked African workers whom they regarded as potential scabs.

In reacting to the contradictory features of the white labor movement, the ICU revealed ambiguous feelings of identification and rejection. In the repeated assertions that the ICU was strictly a legitimate trade union, it can be suggested that the ICU was attempting to emulate the established white trade unions. Support from individual white Socialists was accepted—perhaps most spectacularly when Tom Mann, the fiery British Communist trade union leader, was invited to open the ICU conference in January 1923, during a visit to Cape Town.[13] The ICU retained in its constitution a preamble based on Daniel De Leon's introduction to the constitution of the Industrial Workers of the World.[14] It spoke of itself as a part of the world-wide movement of the working class. Yet the ICU showed itself ready to break away from organized white labor in South Africa. During the heat of the Witwatersrand general strike, the ICU supported the efforts of the government to restore law and order and deplored the attacks of white workers upon Africans. When the white trade unions subsequently continued to demand replacement of nonwhite workers by whites and a "civilized" labor policy, the ICU reiterated its determination to organize "one Big Union movement" of Africans "with a view to protect our people."[15] Opposition to white trade unions, enunciated first in July 1920, was reaffirmed in the face of clear hostility from the white workers of the Transvaal.

[13] For an official statement on the ICU attitude toward Tom Mann's participation see Industrial and Commercial Workers' Union of Africa, ICU, *Official Report of the Proceedings*, 10. For further contemporary comment see *The Cape Times*, Jan. 10, 1923.

[14] The preamble was included in the original constitution of the ICU in 1919. Edward Roux suggests that the preamble was adapted by the ICU at the urging of Communists in Cape Town. Edward Roux, *Time Longer Than Rope* (2nd ed., Madison, 1964), 168. Yet at that time left-wing militant Socialists, who later became Communists, were antagonistic to the ICU run by Kadalie. See Johns, "The Birth of Non-White Trade Unionism in South Africa," 179. Thus it seems likely that the preamble came from another source, very probably from A. F. Batty, the Cape Town Socialist who had urged Kadalie to form a trade union.

[15] For an examination of the reaction of the ICU to protectionist white trade unionism in 1922–23 see Johns, "The Birth of Non-White Trade Unionism in South Africa," 187, 189.

In the political sphere the ICU displayed a cautious and partially contradictory policy. The organization continued to reject any explicit political role. Yet some of its leaders apparently identified with the South African Native National Congress, and the ICU was careful to assert that "it does not foster or encourage antagonism towards other established bodies, political or otherwise, of the African peoples."[16] In its attitude to white politics the ICU faced a dilemma. On one side the Smuts government had moved to protect Africans during the strike on the Witwatersrand. But it was also linked to the Chamber of Mines and the Port Elizabeth, Bulhoek, and Bondelswarts affairs. On the other side, the Nationalists represented the traditionally segregationist position of the Afrikaners, and their allies, the Labour party, generally endorsed the protectionism of the white workers of the Transvaal—although some of their Cape Town supporters remained protagonists of a nonracial platform for all workers. Even the tiny Communist party of South Africa was split, with only a minority group within the party anxious to encourage the ICU.[17] The ICU refrained initially from any identification with white political groupings. Yet as the prospect of the defeat of Smuts became greater, Kadalie began to lean toward support of the Nationalist-Labour pact.

Kadalie's inclination reflected the tactical difficulties of the newly formed ICU. After the first flush of strikes which preceded the organization of a national trade union, the ICU did not encourage any further strikes. The strike weapon was never rejected, but the ICU leadership, preoccupied with the problems of establishing a firm base from which to launch a successful national effort, placed its emphasis upon representations to governmental authorities. It demanded the enactment of legislation favorable to it and ICU representation upon labor bureaus for Africans.

When ministers of the government began to receive delegations from the union in 1922-23, it seemed that a policy of insistent, but respectful, moderation might gain a hearing for the ICU.[18] Such a position also suited the inclinations and experiences of the leaders of the ICU, many of whom had been educated by white missionaries and

[16] Industrial and Commercial Workers' Union of Africa, ICU, *Official Report of the Proceedings*, 19.

[17] A detailed discussion of the ambivalent position of the Communist Party of South Africa at this time may be found in Sheridan W. Johns, III, "Marxism-Leninism in a Multi-Racial Environment: The Origins and Early History of the Communist Party of South Africa, 1914–1932" (unpublished Ph.D. dissertation, Harvard University, 1965), 288-310.

[18] After the Minister of Mines and Industries first met an ICU deputation in May 1922 (see n. 11), ICU deputations were also received by the Minister of Education and the Minister of Railways and Harbours in Jan. 1923. Kadalie, "Memoirs," 27.

shared some of their assumptions about the possibilities for gradual expansion of African opportunities in South Africa.[19] It was also a tacit recognition of the superior power of white government against any direct nonwhite challenge to its authority; the Port Elizabeth, Bulhoek, and Bondelswarts events had underlined this point. At this stage the ICU expressed strong dissatisfaction with the existing position of the nonwhite workers in South Africa; in the preamble to its constitution it even proclaimed its ultimate commitment to a universal "Socialist objective." Yet the pattern of its actions delineated a strategy for reform which aimed to work within the white-dominated South African system. With the further consolidation of Kadalie's position within the union and the calling of a general election for June 1924, new opportunities arose for the testing of the ICU's assumptions.

Electioneering and Expansion

Although nonwhite participation in parliamentary elections was limited to the Cape Province, there were a number of constituencies in which the nonwhite vote was important.[20] As early as 1919, before the formation of the ICU, Kadalie had served on Batty's election committee during his unsuccessful campaign for Parliament in a district with a large registration of nonwhite voters.[21] After the formation of the ICU, the Cape Town section of the Labour party showed some interest in it.[22] More surprising was the fact that General James Barry Munnik Hertzog, the leader of the Nationalist party, made a contribution to the Bulhoek Memorial Fund of the ICU; at the same time he wrote a sympathetic letter to Kadalie on the need for mutual faith and understanding.[23] In early 1924 the Nationalists and the Labour party apparently

[19] Kadalie received his education in mission schools in Nyasaland. See above, 702. An examination of the biographies of ten other ICU leaders listed in a "Who's Who" of 1932, shows that all but one had attended mission schools; of the ten half had attended Lovedale Institute, the prominent secondary school in the Cape Colony. T. D. Mweli Skota (ed.), *The African Yearly Register* (Johannesburg, 1932).

[20] The racial composition of the Cape Province electorate in 1929 was the following: whites, 167, 184; Coloureds, 25,618; Africans, 15,780. Leonard Thompson, *Politics in the Republic of South Africa* (Boston, 1966), 65. African voters were concentrated in the Ciskei and Transkei; the Coloured voters were concentrated in and around Cape Town.

[21] Kadalie, "Memoirs," 10.

[22] Roux reports a meeting called by the Cape District Committee of the Labour party to encourage support from nonwhite workers. Roux, *Time Longer Than Rope*, 198-99.

[23] The text of the letter was first made public by political opponents of Hertzog in the South African Parliament. *House of Assembly Debates*, 1926, Col. 2064. It is reproduced in Roux, *Time Longer Than Rope*, 183-84.

renewed their expressions of sympathy and indicated that help would be forthcoming if Kadalie campaigned among non-whites on behalf of the anti-Smuts coalition.[24] Kadalie was willing to ignore the segregationist record of the Nationalists and the protectionist insistence of the Transvaal Labour party; instead he focused upon the association of the Smuts government with the Chamber of Mines and its shooting of Africans in Port Elizabeth, Bulhoek, and Southwest Africa. Kadalie traveled to Bloemfontein to the annual meeting of the African National Congress (the South African Native National Congress had changed its name in 1923). There he successfully obtained passage of a resolution asserting the desirability of a change in government; subsequently, he met General Hertzog who expressed appreciation for the resolution. Kadalie then obtained passage of a similar resolution at a meeting of the Cape Native Voters' Convention. In the Cape Town area he appeared at campaign rallies for Labour party and Nationalist candidates; Nationalist headquarters arranged for the printing and distribution of ICU literature in support of the Nationalist-Labour pact. Thus, with the success of the pact in the elections in June 1924, Kadalie had reason to hope for a sympathetic hearing from the new government.

Perhaps the best measure of the strength of the hopes of the ICU is the slowness with which it turned against the pact government—despite the latter's increasingly explicit segregationist program. Kadalie was initially heartened when Tielman Roos, the Nationalist Minister of Justice, in response to a challenge in Parliament, defended Kadalie's right to organize a legitimate trade union.[25] But the new Ministry of Labour was headed by Colonel F. H. P. Creswell, the leader of the parliamentary wing of the Labour party, who had been since the turn of the century one of the most outspoken proponents of a "civilized" labor policy. The pact government inherited the Industrial Conciliation Act passed by the Smuts government in 1924. This Act provided mechanisms for collective bargaining between employers and trade unions recognized under the Act; by its terms all "pass-bearing natives" (that is, almost all Africans outside the Cape Province) were explicitly excluded from the provisions of the Act. Nevertheless, the ICU persisted in the hope that it would eventually receive recognition under the Act.[26] The government moved to implement a "civilized" labor policy on other fronts. In government-owned enterprises, the railways in par-

[24] The following account of Kadalie's activities on behalf of the Nationalist-South African Labour party pact is taken from Kadalie, "Memoirs," 29-33. He also justified the stand of the ICU in support of the pact almost a year after the ICU broke with the pact. See The Workers' Herald, Sept. 14, 1926.

[25] Kadalie, "Memoirs," 34-35; The Workers' Herald, Sept. 14, 1926.

[26] A number of interviews were held with the Secretary of Labour in Pretoria to discuss the possibility of registration of the ICU as a recognized trade union under the Act. Kadalie, "Memoirs," 46.

ticular, nonwhite workers in semiskilled and some unskilled positions were replaced by whites. In early 1925 the pact government proposed new legislation—long desired by the white workers of the Witwatersrand—to give the color bar legal standing in the mining industry. According to the Mines and Works Act of 1911 Amendment Bill, all nonwhites were to be excluded by law from listed skilled and semi-skilled occupations. Invoking labor solidarity, the ICU urged the parliamentary delegation of the Labour party to vote against the law to "prove itself worthy as a party representing the labouring class of South Africa irrespective of colour."[27] When, as might easily have been predicted, the Labour party declared its full support for the proposed legislation, the ICU pinned its hopes on Hertzog:

> As for Colonel Cresswell, all we can say is that we have known him for years to be an industrial crank. Most of his theories and ambitions are as void as vacuum. . . . We have only one hope, and that is, that the Prime Minister who is a farsighted, just and influential personality will put his foot down and check the extremist wing of his colleagues. . . .[28]

Earlier that year the ICU had absolved Hertzog from responsibility for a proposal to extend the Transvaal pass laws to African women,[29] hitherto exempt, and then credited him with the postponement of the enforcement of the measure.[30] But he failed to fulfill the trust placed in him; the Nationalists, of course, gave full support to the color bar bill.

Nevertheless, the ICU persisted in its efforts to turn to its own interests the concern of the pact government for the protection of white labor. When, later in 1925, the pact government proposed a minimum wage bill, the provisions of which were to extend to certain categories of Africans, the ICU welcomed the move. It was clear, however, that the government's intention was to plug loopholes in the Industrial Conciliation Act which had permitted the large-scale employment of Africans at low wages in place of poor white workers, and the exclusion of agricultural and domestic labor categories from the minimum wage bill showed that the government had no desire to protect Africans in jobs regarded below the dignity of whites. The ICU protested at the lack of coverage for agricultural and domestic workers, but to no avail.[31] Later

[27] *The Workers' Herald*, Feb. 20, 1925.

[28] *The Workers' Herald*, July 20, 1925. Cresswell's name was misspelled.

[29] *The Workers' Herald*, Jan. 9, 1925.

[30] *The Workers' Herald*, Feb. 20, 1925.

[31] *The Workers' Herald*, May 15, 1925; "Resolution and Data Submitted by the Industrial and Commercial Workers' Union of Africa, I.C.U., to the Honourable Select Committee on the Minimum Wage Bill, House of Assembly, Cape Town, May, 1925" (mimeographed).

in the year the ICU seized the opportunity to make further representations to the government through the Economic and Wage Commission which the government had established to obtain evidence and recommendations for further action on behalf of labor.[32] The ICU was heard respectfully, but there were no signs of a shift in governmental policy in the wake of the ICU's appearance before the Commission.

Progressive disillusionment with the performance of the pact govment in its first year was offset by a new self-confidence inspired by strategic organizational advances. Almost immediately after the 1924 election, Kadalie had embarked upon a national tour.[33] Visiting first the established branches of Port Elizabeth, Kingwilliamstown, and East London, Kadalie then pushed on to Durban in Natal. Dismayed initially by what he regarded as Zulu passivity and obstructed by local white authorities, Kadalie was, nevertheless, able to establish a branch in Durban by September 1924. In November he came to Johannesburg, the home of the Chamber of Mines, regarded by Kadalie as the key symbol of capitalist oppression. In defiance of unfavorable publicity from the white press, Kadalie helped to swell the ranks of a branch which had been started by young enthusiasts before his arrival. From there he traveled to Bloemfontein where he sparked the establishment of an ICU branch in the location where Selby Msimang had led demonstrations five years earlier. After a quick trip to headquarters in Cape Town, Kadalie returned in early 1925 to Johannesburg to focus his organizational work in the center of South African economic life. By September 1925, the ICU claimed a membership of 30,400 with branches in all of the major South African cities.[34] Although the bulk of the membership remained concentrated in the Cape Province where Coloureds played an important role in the nonwhite work force, the ICU was poised to intensify its efforts throughout South Africa where Africans constituted the bulk of the "proletariat." The ICU could legitimately claim that it had begun to realize its aspiration to become a nation-wide nonwhite trade union organization.

Rapid organizational gains were magnified by a new interest in the ICU on the part of white South Africans. Kadalie's travels and speeches were reported widely in the white-owned press and his activities became the object of concern to opposition members in Parliament. The Chamber of Mines paid him the compliment of inviting him to their offices to request that he withdraw an attack upon them; Kadalie re-

[32] Kadalie, "Memoirs," 47-48.

[33] For Kadalie's account of the national tour from which the following is drawn see ibid., 33-43.

[34] Ernest Gitsham and James Trembath, A First Account of Labour Organisation in South Africa (Durban, 1926), 125.

fused.[35] In the eyes of Kadalie it was clear that the ICU was becoming a power with which white authorities would have to deal.

Kadalie's advances also brought attention from rival sources of potential white support. Liberals, Communists, and Socialists offered platforms and advice to the ICU. The combined impact of these conflicting pressures was sufficient to sustain Kadalie's hope that the ICU could work for nonwhite goals within and through a multi-racial society despite rising animosity from "established" white South Africa. At the same time, the strength of any one influence was insufficient to resolve the uncertainties of the attitudes of the ICU toward white society.

White liberals, both the "first generation" centered in church organizations and a new generation of professional men, were showing a new interest in direct approaches to African middle-class leaders. Through local Joint Councils, established in a number of South African cities after the visit of the Gold Coast educator, James Emman Kwegyir Aggrey in 1921, whites and Africans were brought into regular contact in biracial committees for consultation and discussion.[36] While in Durban, Kadalie was invited to speak before the local Joint Council; in his speech he attacked the restrictions placed upon him and reasserted the bona fide trade union status of the ICU.[37] It seems, however, that his experiences in Johannesburg made him skeptical of the potential of the Joint Councils. Africans in Johannesburg who were prominent in the local Joint Council were also closely associated with *Umteteli wa Bantu*, a newspaper established for Africans by interests close to the Chamber of Mines. These same Africans were among the leaders of the African National Congress who snubbed Kadalie.[38] It was probably these features of the Johannesburg situation which impelled Kadalie, who had been influenced by the rhetoric of white-led trade unionism in South Africa, to warn:

> . . . it is there [Johannesburg] where the English capitalists have succeeded to capture men of the African race—men with intellectual ability—to preach the gospel of cooperation between white exploiters and the exploited blacks—Let the African worker not be deceived, nothing tangible can come out from the "Joint Councils of Europeans and Natives." An exploited race has not to look to the exploiter for emancipation from the shackles of slavery. . . .[39]

[35] Kadalie, "Memoirs," 44.

[36] For a brief history of the Joint Councils, see Quintin Whyte, "Inter-Racial Cooperation," in Ellen Hellman (ed.), *Handbook on Race Relations in South Africa* (Cape Town, 1949), 653-54.

[37] *The Cape Times*, Sept. 4, 1924.

[38] See below, 715.

[39] *The Workers' Herald*, Jan. 9, 1925.

In 1925, then, Kadalie rejected the Joint Council approach.

His animosity was warmly endorsed by another Johannesburg group which regarded the growth of the ICU with enthusiasm. The general strike in 1922 on the Witwatersrand had spurred a realignment within the small Communist party of South Africa, the membership of which was concentrated in Johannesburg.[40] Sidney P. Bunting and a new group of Young Communists, supported by Communists from Cape Town, argued that white labor was no longer the primary progressive force in South Africa; in their estimation the more numerous, but hitherto unorganized, nonwhite workers represented the true "proletariat" and should be the first object of Communist activity. At the Third Congress of the Communist party in December 1924, their viewpoint was adopted by a narrow majority after a heated debate among the delegates. This significant shift in the policy of the Young Communist party took place shortly after Kadalie's arrival on the Witwatersrand. There he found that an ICU branch had been organized by young African enthusiasts, probably with the aid of the Communists.[41] When Kadalie approached white trade union leaders he found that many of them were unsympathetic.[42] In contrast Communists were among the few white trade union leaders who did encourage the ICU—even though most of them, including William H. Andrews, the most widely respected Communist labor organizer, had opposed the majority decision at the Third Congress of the Communist Party.[43] In the prestige of the Communist trade union leaders, the enthusiasm of the Young Communists, and the determination of Sidney P. Bunting, the ICU encountered a forceful new argument for the emphasis on the international Socialist plank of its own program.

Other more diffuse influences also pushed the ICU toward a continuation of its identification with the cause of labor throughout the world. A few non-Communist white trade union leaders, including Archie Crawford, who had represented the white workers abroad at the first meeting of the International Labor Organization, indicated that

[40] For a detailed account of developments leading to the shift of policy in the Communist party of South Africa see Johns, "Marxism-Leninism in a Multi-Racial Environment," 288-324.

[41] On June 20, 1924, the newspaper of the Communist party announced the "successful beginning" of an ICU office in Johannesburg. *The International,* June 20, 1924. It appears that young Communists in Johannesburg had helped to start the office. Edward Roux, *S. P. Bunting, A Political Biography* (Cape Town, 1944), 70.

[43] In his autobiography Kadalie gives particular credit to William H. Andrews for his help to the ICU. Ibid., 153.

[42] Kadalie, "Memoirs," 40-41.

they supported the organization of nonwhite workers.[44] Yet an encounter with an important member of the British Labour party provided the most dramatic example of the potential of white support. Kadalie's difficulties with the local white authorities in Durban brought him to the attention of Mrs. Mabel Palmer, a member of the local Joint Council. Through her Socialist connections she was subsequently to be important as a channel to trade union circles in Britain.[45] In 1924 she arranged for Kadalie to meet John H. Thomas, the Colonial Secretary in the British Labour government, who was then heading a visiting Empire Parliamentary delegation in South Africa. With public encouragement from Thomas, Kadalie was able to gain official permission to hold ICU meetings in Durban.[46] Thomas's intervention indicated the utility of drawing the attention of representatives of overseas white labor groups to the ICU. To further his cause Kadalie continued to correspond with a few British labor leaders with whom he had established contact.[47] In April 1925, the National Council of the ICU voted to send a representative to Britain to study the world labor movement.[48] Three months later Kadalie urged the British labor movement to take a stand on the color bar bill.[49]

Kadalie's links with African politics were also reshaped in 1924–25. He claims that he resisted attempts by West Indians resident in Cape Town (including James G. Gumbs, the president of the ICU from 1924 to 1929) to use the ICU for the ends of the Universal Negro Improvement Association headed by Marcus Garvey.[50] Yet Kadalie did not reject association with African politics in South Africa. In late 1923 he had received support from Thomas Mapikela, the respected Speaker of the African National Congress, who had helped to organize a series of meetings for Kadalie in Bloemfontein.[51] As the ICU grew it was treated with new respect by the leadership of the African National Congress, although not always with enthusiasm. In May 1924, at the time that Kadalie successfully persuaded the annual meeting of the Congress to

[44] Ibid., 40. Perhaps this fact and the interest of the Communists explain in part why its 1925 Revised Constitution contains an addition to the preamble which specifically states that the ICU does not foster or encourage antagonism toward established groups of "organized European Labour." Industrial and Commercial Workers' Union of Africa, I.C.U., *1925 Revised Constitution,* 2.

[45] See below, 721.

[46] For Kadalie's account of his meeting with Thomas and the results which followed see: Kadalie, "Memoirs," 35-37; *The Workers' Herald,* May 15, 1925.

[47] *The Workers' Herald,* Jan. 9, 1925.

[48] *The Workers' Herald,* June 15, 1925.

[49] *The Workers' Herald,* July 20, 1925.

[50] Kadalie, "Memoirs," 197.

[51] *The Workers' Herald,* Oct. 22, 1923.

pass his anti-Smuts resolution, he was designated Provisional Secretary of Labour and Railways in a "shadow" cabinet elected by the delegates.[52] When he arrived in Durban to organize the ICU he was helped considerably by James T. Gumede, the leader of the Natal branch of the Congress.[53] Yet in Johannesburg, some of the more important leaders of the Transvaal, including Sefako M. Makgatho, the past national president, were hostile to what they regarded as Kadalie's "unauthorized" invasion of the Transvaal. Despite their antagonism, Kadalie found support for his work among some officials of the Congress in the Transvaal.[54] In Cape Town he found an ally in James Thaele, although it would seem that because he believed in working with sympathetic whites he did not fully agree with Thaele's enthusiasm for Garveyism and the slogan, "Africa for the Africans."[55] By April 1925, relations between the Congress and the ICU were so close that the Reverend Zaccheus R. Mahabane, the president of the Congress, was designated to open the annual conference of the ICU.[56] In mid-May Kadalie was urging ICU members to join the Congress, "the only political body we recognize."[57] When the pact government later in the month announced its intention of extending pass laws to African women in the Transvaal, the ICU considered advocating a campaign of passive resistance and a general strike in conjunction with the Congress. The leadership of the Congress finally balked (although agreeing in principle) and the plan was dropped.[58] Nevertheless, in apparent violation of the ICU's proscription against political commitment, Kadalie was edging into more direct involvement in African politics.

[52] *The Friend,* May 31, 1924.

[53] Kadalie, "Memoirs," 34, 37; *The Workers' Herald,* Jan. 9, 1925.

[54] Kadalie, "Memoirs," 39.

[55] In April 1925, Thaele was listed as the subeditor of the ICU newspaper. *The Workers' Herald,* Apr. 2, 1925. Shortly thereafter, Thaele started publication in Cape Town of *The African World,* a short-lived newspaper in which Thaele preached Garveyism and "Africa for the Africans." Kadalie states specifically that he opposed the slogan. Kadalie, "Memoirs," 197. This may have led, in part, to the subsequent break between the two men.

[56] *The Workers' Herald,* Apr. 2, 1925. At the last minute, however, the Mayor of Johannesburg apparently agreed to open the conference. *The Workers' Herald,* May 15, 1925.

[57] Ibid.

[58] At the end of May *The African World* endorsed a joint campaign of passive resistance by the ICU and the Congress, including the threat of a strike at the end of six months, if the pass regulations for women in the Transvaal were implemented. *The African World,* May 30, 1925. At about the same time the white press reported that the ICU was to call a general strike on the question of the passes. *The Cape Times,* May 28, 1925. In his autobiography Kadalie asserts that the reluctance of the leadership of the Congress led the ICU to call off plans for a general strike. Kadalie, "Memoirs," 50.

In April 1925 the ICU was on the verge of becoming an organized movement of mass protest. For the first time a single organization claiming to speak for all nonwhite labor had branches in the major centers of South Africa. Trade union in form, the ICU made efforts to strengthen its trade union organization through the establishment of specific industrial and craft branches.[59] Yet in a situation where any question regarding nonwhite labor was inevitably a political one, the pronouncement and actions of the ICU and its leader took on an increasingly political color. Its faith in the pact government shaken but not destroyed, the ICU was turning to the exploration of the possibilities of links with a color-blind world labor movement at the same time that it paid new attention to African political activity in South Africa. Buoyed by apparent organizational success but frustrated in efforts to obtain results for its membership, the ICU was veering toward a more direct confrontation with the white power structure of South Africa. It was in this spirit that Kadalie issued the challenge to white South Africa cited at the opening of this essay.

The Search for a New Strategy

It was not long before General Hertzog laid down his own version of the proper solution to the "native question." In a well publicized speech on November 13, 1925, at Smithfield, a small farming center in the Orange Free State, the Prime Minister proposed a four-point program in which the segregationist intent of the government was made unmistakably explicit. In an elaboration of views which he had held for many years, General Hertzog proposed the following four-point program: 1) removal of Africans from the common electoral roll in the Cape Province; 2) final delimitation of the land to be made available to Africans under the Natives Land Act of 1913; 3) within these areas the establishment of partially-elected, partially-nominated local "Native Councils" with provision for a similarly chosen "Union Native Council"; and 4) representation of African interests in Parliament by seven white representatives elected by Africans enrolled upon a special, separate voters' roll. To complete his scheme of segregation, Hertzog proposed

[59] In the 1925 Revised Constitution it was asserted that the ICU "shall cater for the following sections under its aegis: Municipal Workers, Waterside Workers, Miner Workers, Building Workers, Agricultural Workers, Marine Workers, Transport Workers, Railway Workers, Factory Workers, Domestic Workers, Warehouse Workers." Industrial and Commercial Workers' Union of Africa, ICU, *1925 Revised Constitution*, 2. Although subsequent developments suggest that efforts to sectionalize ICU members into these categories were unsuccessful, it seems that an effort was made to do so in 1924–25. *New Africa*, May 25, 1929.

a special status for the Cape Coloureds, in terms of privileges fixing them between whites and Africans. Eventually, Hertzog dropped the plan for local "Native Councils" as well as the proposals regarding the Coloureds, but the remainder of his program was presented to Parliament by the pact government in what came to be known as Hertzog's native bills.

With these proposals the fragile faith of the ICU in the pact government was irrevocably shattered. Although the ICU welcomed any proposal to extend African land ownership, even on a limited basis, it indignantly regarded the Hertzog plan as a blatant attempt to force the Africans back into tribalism. In the pages of *The Workers' Herald*, Hertzog and the pact government came under steady attack in the strident language previously reserved for the Chamber of Mines and capitalists. The ICU talked of a "second Ireland" should the "Native Bills" be adopted.[60]

As a ground swell of African resentment swept the country, the ICU moved to translate this antagonism into strength for the ICU. Kadalie embarked upon another national tour; by August 1926 the ICU claimed to have raised its membership over twenty-five per cent to 39,400.[61] Kadalie explained the ICU expansion in terms of a single factor:

> The consolidation of our forces was inevitable, and at the opening of the current year, 1926, one witnessed a campaign to organize all African labour into ONE BIG UNION becoming a reality. What brought about this yearning among the proletariat? It was no other than the infamous Smithfield declarations in which it was said that the black men and women of this land should remain forever as "hewers of wood and drawers of water."[62]

Unequivocally angry at the pact government, the ICU recruited trade union members upon a primarily political platform of opposition to the Hertzog native bills.

Mere verbal opposition, even if backed by an expanding membership, was clearly insufficient to deflect government intentions. Several options, or combinations of options, seemed open. The ICU, which claimed to be a trade union, could have threatened strike action by its membership. Or, in keeping with its growing political orientation, the ICU could, either in alliance with the Congress, or in isolation, have

---

[60] *The Workers' Herald*, Feb. 20, 1926.

[61] Gitsham and Trembath, *A First Account of Labour*, 125. In March 1926, James G. Gumbs, the president of the ICU, had reported a membership of 45,000. *The Cape Times*, Mar. 12, 1926.

[62] *The Workers' Herald*, Sept. 14, 1926.

embarked upon a series of demonstrations to underline its demands. Yet because of its small size (as well as its "ideology"), the ICU still needed white allies in order to enhance its strength. With the pact government, which the ICU helped to elect, revealed as unqualifiedly segregationist, and the opposition South African party still regarded as the creature of the Chamber of Mines, the major political parties offered nothing for the ICU. Only the miniscule Communist party and scattered white liberals showed interest in the ICU within South Africa. Outside South Africa, however, were various organizations which presented untried, but potentially attractive, possibilities. During the course of 1926 the leadership of the ICU attempted to formulate a strategy from these various, and often conflicting, alternatives. Internal frictions, related to the rapid expansion of the ICU, and external threats, related to the mounting concern of the pact government, intruded to complicate the process and to provoke a spiral of tension within the organization. Before the end of 1926, controversy within the ICU exploded into a public confrontation at the uppermost levels of the organization. The outcome was a significant reorientation of the ICU.

In early 1926 the ICU placed its emphasis upon joint action with the Congress. At a meeting in January, the Congress had resoundingly protested against the native bills.[63] James Thaele was apparently appointed as a special organizer to co-ordinate a nation-wide agitation against the Hertzog proposals. The ICU was asked to join and, at a meeting on January 31 in Johannesburg, Kadalie launched the campaign.[64] Yet it appears that it quickly fizzled. Poorly organized nationally and accustomed to deputations and resolutions, the leadership of the Congress was unable to implement any sustained commitment to mass action. The limitations of joint African political pressure were again made evident. Kadalie and the ICU grew skeptical about the determination of the African National Congress.[65]

Behind the scenes in the ICU a "racial" crisis threatened to disrupt the organization. Coloureds were reported to represent over twenty per cent of the membership of the ICU, concentrated in Cape Town and the western Cape Province. Friction developed on the Cape Town docks when Coloured ICU members began to replace African ICU members in a Cape Province version of a "civilized" labor policy.[66] At the same time the Cape Town leaders of the ICU learned that Kadalie intended to propose the removal of the headquarters of the ICU to

63 *The Cape Times,* Jan. 5, 1926.
64 *The Workers' Herald,* Feb. 20, 1926; *The Friend,* Feb. 2, 1926.
65 *The Workers' Herald,* Feb. 20, 1926; March 27, 1926.
66 *The Cape Times,* March 12, 1926.

Johannesburg. To thwart the move the Cape Town members of the National Council, the majority of whom were Coloured, arranged to transfer the funds of the national ICU to the account of the Cape Town branch of the ICU. Through the financial secretary of the ICU, who was an African, Kadalie learned of the action. At a meeting of the full National Council in Johannesburg prior to the annual conference in April 1926, Kadalie confronted the Cape Town members with his knowledge of their intentions. African members from the eastern Cape Province and Natal immediately urged that the Cape Town members be arrested for theft. Confident of majority support, Kadalie maneuvered between the two factions. The Cape Town members were saved from possible legal action in return for their promise not to secede should the national conference endorse Kadalie's proposal for a transfer of the headquarters to Johannesburg.[67] Kadalie's move kept the union intact as a single national nonwhite organization; yet the basic causes of friction between the Coloureds and the Africans, and between Cape Town and the rest of the country, remained unresolved.

The shift of the headquarters to Johannesburg (approved overwhelmingly by the national conference) set the stage for an intensification of efforts on the part of white sympathizers to woo the ICU. Kadalie had wanted to move the headquarters to the Witwatersrand in order to be at the center of both capitalism and trade unionism in South Africa. In addition, he was impressed with the promises of help from a few white trade unionists (most of whom were Communists).[68] By moving its headquarters to Johannesburg the ICU placed itself in proximity to the headquarters of the Communist party, which was controlled by the party members who were most anxious to work closely with the ICU. The impact of these new associations became evident during the next few months. In a circular from headquarters, Kadalie urged all branches of the ICU to celebrate May Day as the workers' holiday, at which time resolutions were to be passed declaring solidarity with the workers of the world and with the Russian workers in particular.[69] Communists were welcomed to ICU meetings.[70]

Kadalie's new tack aroused the concern of white liberals associated with the Joint Council in Johannesburg. Mrs. Ethelreda Lewis, a novelist, boldly took the initiative in approaching Kadalie. Her straightforward technique was described by a friend:

> Mrs. Lewis had a happy idea. If the native Trade Unionists won't go to the white people, the whites must go to the Trade Unionists. She is

[67] The above account is derived from Kadalie, "Memoirs," 52-55.
[68] Ibid., 52.
[69] "Circular Letter No. 2-26" (mimeographed), Apr. 27, 1926.
[70] For a report of such a meeting see The Workers' Herald, Sept. 14, 1926.

getting together a small body of really expert and able men . . . and they are going down for a series of meetings with the ICU at Workers' Hall. She herself has got into close touch with Kadalie. . . .[71]

Through Mrs. Lewis, Kadalie and the ICU were put into direct contact with important white members of the Joint Council. Mrs. Lewis also made arrangements for a series of lectures by white speakers upon such subjects as "Social Advancement" and "Bantu History."[72] It appears that Mrs. Lewis and her supporters hoped to wean Kadalie away from association with the Communists at the same time that they hoped to temper his speeches. In their view the ICU should have placed full emphasis upon its legitimate trade union activity; political matters were to be the subject of discussions with sympathetic Europeans who would in turn present the African case in reasonable terms to the proper authorities.[73]

The courtship of the ICU by the Communists and the liberals took place against a backdrop of continuing harassment on the part of the government and white society. Hertzog reiterated his intention to present the native bills to Parliament. The white trade union organization of the Transvaal, the South African Trade Union Congress, meeting concurrently with the ICU national conference, refused to send a fraternal delegation upon the invitation of the ICU.[74] Faced with hostility and rebuffs within South Africa, Kadalie placed new hope in overseas support. At the annual conference of the ICU in April 1926, he obtained the passage of a resolution which directed the ICU to attempt to affiliate with the British Trades Union Congress:

That in view of the rapid development in the introduction of fundamental changes in the Native Policy under consideration, and in view of the seemingly compromising attitude of the European population as a whole, particularly in regards to the Prime Minister's Smithfield declaration, this Conference instructs the National Council of the ICU to enter negotiations for the affiliation of this Organization to the

[71] Letter from Winifred Holtby to Vera Brittain, June 6, 1926. Vera Brittain and Geoffrey Handley-Taylor (eds.), *Letters of Winifred Holtby and Vera Brittain (1920–1935)* (London, 1960), 136-37.

[72] Letter from Ethelreda Lewis to Winifred Holtby, July 27, 1926, Winifred Holtby Collection, Hull Public Library.

[73] An example of this line of thought may be found in letters written by Winifred Holtby while visiting South Africa, where she was in touch with white liberals. See Brittain and Handley-Taylor (eds.), *Letters of Winifred Holtby,* 105, 136-37.

[74] Clements Kadalie, *The Relation Between White and Black Workers in South Africa* (London, 1927), 6.

British Trades Union Congress, with the further object of bringing the case of the African workers before the League of Nations and public opinion throughout Europe.[75]

With this resolution Kadalie's long-time concern for international affiliations received new elaboration. It was clear that Kadalie saw international links as a device to overcome white hostility within South Africa. Through affiliation with the trade union movement in Britain, the ICU could attempt to bring the British trade unionists to persuade the white, English-speaking trade unionists of South Africa to modify their attitude toward the ICU. At the same time the ICU might have hoped to enlist the support of the powerful British Labour party to exert pressure on the South African government through Commonwealth channels. In addition, the ICU explicitly saw its move as a step toward the "internationalization" of the nonwhite problem of South Africa before European public opinion and the League of Nations.

The question of the "internationalism" of the ICU was rapidly joined to the unfolding struggle for influence between the local white liberals and the Communists. In the course of 1926 the white liberals were able to put Kadalie in touch with important British Socialists who gave him practical advice on how to implement the resolution passed by the national conference of the ICU in April 1926. Communists, on the other hand, offered Kadalie and the ICU prospects of participation in a rival international pressure group.

When Winifred Holtby, the English author, visited South Africa in early 1926, she was introduced to Kadalie by Mrs. Lewis; probably through Mrs. Mabel Palmer she also met A. W. George Champion, the ICU leader in Durban. Impressed with their cause, and concerned about their "Bolshevism," Miss Holtby agreed upon her return to Britain to contact the Independent Labour party and the editors of *The New Leader* with a view to encouraging their involvement in the problems of the ICU.[76] At about the same time, Mrs. Palmer visited England where she talked with several prominent socialists about the ICU.[77]

Through the initiative of the two women, Kadalie began to receive advice from important British Socialists. When the British Trades Union Congress failed to respond to the application of the ICU, Kadalie wrote to Miss Holtby soliciting her advice on whether the ICU

[75] "Circular Letter, October 21, 1926" (mimeographed).

[76] For Winifred Holtby's account of her visit to South Africa see Brittain and Handley-Taylor (eds.), *Letters of Winifred Holtby*, 87-139. Vera Brittain has also written about Miss Holtby's involvement with the ICU. Vera Brittain, *Testament of Friendship* (London, 1940), 199-239.

[77] Brittain, *Testament*, 239.

should turn to either the Labour party or the Independent Labour party for affiliation in accord with the April resolution of the ICU.[78] He noted that Mrs. Palmer had informed him that Sidney Webb had recommended that the ICU should apply for affiliation to the International Federation of Trade Unions (the non-Communist international trade union center in Amsterdam). Miss Holtby consulted with Arthur Creech Jones, then secretary of the Transport and General Workers' Union, who noted that neither the Labour party nor the Independent Labour party accepted overseas affiliates; he urged, instead, that the ICU seek links with international trade union centers, including the International Federation.[79] This advice was apparently communicated to Kadalie at about the same time that he received a polite refusal from the British Trades Union Congress in which it was also suggested that an application be made to the International Federation.[80] In accordance with the advice which he had received, Kadalie informed the membership of the ICU in a circular letter, in October 1926, that negotiations had been initiated with the International Federation.[81] During this period Kadalie and Creech Jones also entered into direct correspondence.[82]

The efforts of sympathetic English Socialists to steer the ICU toward an appropriate international labor body were paralleled by a Communist effort to secure the representation of the ICU at the Congress of Oppressed Nationalities, the first international "anti-imperialist" conference organized under the inspiration of the Communist International. It was to take place in Brussels in early 1927. In September 1926, Kadalie received an invitation to attend, along with an offer of funds from the Secretariat of the Congress.[83] Subsequently, the Communist newspaper urged that Communists in the ICU should push for the acceptance of the invitation to the Congress.[84] In the same issue the

[78] Letter from Clements Kadalie to Winifred Holtby, Sept. 10, 1926, Winifred Holtby Collection, Hull Public Library.

[79] Letter from Arthur Creech Jones to Winifred Holtby, Oct. 8, 1926, Winifred Holtby Collection, Hull Public Library.

[80] "Circular Letter, October 21, 1926" (mimeographed).

[81] Ibid.

[82] Apparently the first letters between the two men crossed one another. Letter from Arthur Creech Jones to Clements Kadalie, Sept. 23, 1926. Letter from Clements Kadalie to Arthur Creech Jones, Oct. 6, 1926, Winifred Holtby Collection, Hull Public Library.

[83] Kadalie announced that he had received an invitation to attend the Congress in September. *The South African Worker,* Sept. 3, 1926; *The Workers' Herald,* Sept. 14, 1926. It was later confirmed that he had also received a promise of funds from the organizers of the Secretariat of the Congress. *The Star,* Jan. 24, 1927.

[84] *The South African Worker,* Nov. 19, 1926.

ICU was warned to reconsider its intention to affiliate with the International Federation, which was labeled an agent of "labor reformism."[85]

The question of ICU representation overseas provoked disagreement between the Communist party and the ICU. Yet the root of their differences concerned the operation of the ICU within South Africa. In 1925–26 important white Communists had appeared regularly on ICU platforms and contributed articles to the ICU newspaper. Bunting had provided valuable legal advice when the government banned Kadalie from entering Natal and threatened to confine him to the Cape Province under existing pass regulations should he leave Johannesburg for Cape Town.[86] More importantly, the Communists had enthusiastically urged nonwhite workers to join the ICU.[87] Some of the few African Communists joined the ICU and other ICU members were recruited into the Communist party. In 1926 those associated with the Communist party led a campaign at the annual conference to strengthen the language of the resolutions of the conference.[88] Communists came to occupy a number of key positions in the ICU. Among them were James La Guma (general secretary), John Gomas (western Cape provincial secretary), Edward Khaile (financial secretary), Thomas Mbeki (Transvaal provincial secretary), and Ralph de Norman (secretary, Cape Town).[89] From positions close to and within the ICU, the Communists had an excellent opportunity to observe what they regarded as the crucial instrument for raising the political consciousness of the "proletariat" of South Africa. Yet what they saw also moved them to rising criticism of Kadalie and other leaders of the ICU.

From its first years of existence, the ICU had been plagued by mismanagement at the branch level and peculation by local officials.[90] As the union expanded, it needed officers to sustain the work of branches established in the wake of tours by Kadalie. Yet there were no Africans trained specifically for trade union work. According to Kadalie the following situation resulted:

[85] Ibid.

[86] Kadalie, "Memoirs," 153–54.

[87] *The South African Worker*, Aug. 13, 1926.

[88] For the roles of John Gomas, Thomas Mbeki, and Thomas Thibedi, see the proceedings of the conference as reported in *The Workers' Herald*, Apr. 28, 1926; May 15, 1926.

[89] The above list of Communist officers of the ICU is comprised of those who resigned from the ICU after Kadalie forced Communists either to resign membership in the party or their offices in the ICU. (See below, 725.)

[90] For discussion of the problem at the annual conference of the ICU in 1923, see Industrial and Commercial Workers' Union of Africa, ICU, *Official Report of the Proceedings*, 25. For difficulties encountered in the Orange Free State in 1925, see *The Workers' Herald*, Apr. 28, 1926.

> . . . young men, particularly teachers, flocked to the ICU, where they
> occupied remunerative positions in various branch offices at better
> wages than they received as teachers. In many cases . . . these young
> men were not all well-equipped or trained for elementary trade union
> work.[91]

It was this group which came under attack from La Guma, the Communist general secretary of the ICU, after an official ICU tour of thirteen branches in early 1926. In an internal memorandum to the ICU
he explicitly asserted that corruption was extensive throughout the
ICU, largely as a result of irregular and unconstitutional practices.[92]

La Guma did not confine his criticism merely to irregularities in
financial management and administration. He was also dissatisfied with
the widespread disregard of the ICU constitution by officials at all
levels of the organization, including "such highly placed officials as the
National Secretary [Kadalie]." He specifically attacked Kadalie's frequent bypassing of the National Council of the ICU and suggested that
"from appearances recently it seemed that a dictatorship is in embryo."
La Guma's criticism very possibly was directed at Kadalie's decision to
move the headquarters of the ICU to Johannesburg (La Guma was a
Coloured based in Cape Town), but it might also have reflected a concern held by other Communists that the leadership of the ICU was unresponsive to the demands of the rank and file for direct action.

La Guma's criticisms of the ICU were echoed in Durban by a non-
Communist critic of the administration of A. W. George Champion in
Natal. As the head of the Transvaal Mine Clerks' Association, Champion (an African) came to the attention of Kadalie in Johannesburg in
1925. Kadalie persuaded him to join the ICU and shortly thereafter
assigned him to revive the Durban branch of the ICU which had become shaky in the wake of disclosures of financial irregularities involving its first secretary, Alexander P. Maduna. Returning to his native
Natal, Champion embarked upon an organizational campaign among
the Zulu workers of Durban and vicinity. Through a network of auxiliary organizations largely under Champion's personal control, including
small businesses, a newspaper, and a social club, Champion was able
to provide a variety of services for ICU members. He also was able
to negotiate successfully with the Durban authorities to alleviate a
series of minor grievances of African workers. In this fashion the ICU
membership in Durban and southern Natal expanded rapidly. Toward

---

[91] Kadalie, "Memoirs," 199.

[92] The following discussion of La Guma's criticisms of the state of the ICU
is drawn from the report which he wrote after his tour. "General Secretary's Report of Inspection of Branches" (mimeographed), Mar. 6, 1926.

the end of 1926, however, one of the early members of the ICU in Durban, George Lenono, began to challenge Champion's methods publicly, particularly his integration of personal and ICU finances.[93]

During the latter months of 1926 the Communists also began openly to question developments within the ICU. From Natal a white Communist who had joined the ICU questioned the size of the ICU initiation fee and the preoccupation of the Natal leadership with expensive legal challenges in place of strikes.[94] When Kadalie was banned from Natal in mid-1926, the Communists apparently urged that he challenge the pass laws and Hertzog's native bills by calling a general strike of ICU members.[95] The Communists began to attack corruption and bureaucracy within the ICU.[96] They questioned both the methods of the ICU and its failure to use the strike weapon.

The arguments of the Communists were damaging to Kadalie, Champion, and the non-Communist leadership of the ICU. Although the motives of the Communists might have been considered by some to have been ulterior, it was clear that their criticisms spotlighted genuine grievances and organizational weaknesses. They provided a platform around which discontented elements within the ICU might have rallied to challenge the leadership, in particular Kadalie and Champion.

Aroused by Communist criticism and new efforts to push the ICU into naming La Guma as its representative to the Congress of Oppressed Nationalities, Kadalie resolved to act against the Communists within the ICU. At a meeting in Port Elizabeth in late 1926 (attended by thirteen of nineteen members of the National Council) Kadalie secured a narrow six to five majority for a motion which barred all officers of the ICU from holding membership in the Communist party. La Guma,

[93] For Champion's account of his efforts in Durban through 1927, see The Industrial and Commercial Workers' Union of Africa, ICU, *The Truth About the ICU* (Durban, 1927), 20-28. Kadalie gives his estimate in his autobiography See Kadalie, "Memoirs," 138-139. George Lenono's differences with Kadalie were aired in a pamphlet which he published in 1927. George Lenono, *The ICU Funds —Mr. Allison Champion, Provincial Secretary ICU (Natal) and the ICU Funds* (Durban, 1927). On the basis of this pamphlet, Champion sued Lenono for libel, but lost. The judgment of the court confirmed that Champion had mixed ICU funds with his own funds. *The Cape Times*, Dec. 2, 1927. Further details about the confused and complex state of the finances of Champion and the Natal and Durban branches of the ICU were given in the report of a private auditor subsequently engaged by Kadalie (see below). J. T. Windram and E. C. Hooper, "Investigation and Report: Natal Provincial and Durban Offices of the Industrial and Commercial Workers' Union (I.C.U.)" (typewritten). The above account is derived from these sources.

[94] *The South African Worker*, Aug. 6, 1926; Aug. 13, 1926.

[95] *The Cape Times*, Dec. 22, 1926; *The Workers' Herald*, Jan. 12, 1927.

[96] *The South African Worker*, Dec. 24, 1926, Jan. 7, 1927.

Gomas, Khaile, and Mbeki refused to resign from the party. They were immediately expelled from the National Council, but they and other rank-and-file Communists within the ICU attempted to outflank Kadalie and the National Council by summoning branch meetings to demand the reinstatement of the ousted officials and reconsideration of the decision of the National Council.[97]

In reaction to the threat to their positions, Kadalie and Champion were brought closer together. They resorted to a theme which deflected the strength and legitimacy of the Communist critique—they argued that *white* Communists were trying to dictate to Africans.[98] Supporters of Kadalie also apparently played upon anti-Coloured sentiment, attacking ICU members who were not "full-blooded natives," a category which included La Guma and Gomas, as well as de Norman, the secretary of the ICU in Cape Town.[99] The Communist party, with a membership of only one thousand, proved unable to rally the rank and file within the ICU machinery controlled by Kadalie and Champion. By the time of the annual conference in April 1927, held in Champion's stronghold of Durban, Kadalie was able to obtain confirmation of the decision of the National Council and to extend the ruling to bar all ICU members from simultaneously belonging to the Communist party.[100]

The sharp break with the Communist party had a twofold impact upon the ICU. On the international plane the ICU cut itself away from the Marxist-Leninist version of international Socialism offered by the Communists. When the International Federation accepted the affiliation of the ICU in early 1927, it seemed that the alternative option of

[97] For a detailed account of the confrontation between Kadalie and his allies and the Communist members of the National Council of the ICU, see Johns, "Marxism-Leninism in a Multi-Racial Environment," 359-63. A closely parallel account appears in Roux, *Time Longer Than Rope*, 163-67. Kadalie's immediate explanation appears in *The Cape Times*, Dec. 22, 1926. A lengthier statement, in the form of an ICU manifesto, appears in *The Workers' Herald*, Jan. 12, 1927. Another brief account, written much later, appears in Kadalie, "Memoirs," 71-72. The latter version reports that all the members of the National Council were in attendance. Newspaper reports at the time, however, indicated that only thirteen of the nineteen members were in attendance. See *The South African Worker*, Dec. 24, 1926. The first two sources cited here (Johns and Roux) rely greatly on this report. The above account is taken from these two sources and the ICU manifesto which appears in *The Workers' Herald*.

[98] Champion's public allegations were made before the break with the Communists at Port Elizabeth. *The South African Worker*, Aug. 20, 1926. Kadalie implied after the break that the Communists were dictating to the ICU as whites. *The Cape Times*, Dec. 22, 1926; *The South African Worker*, Dec. 31, 1926.

[99] *The South African Worker*, Jan. 14, 1927.

[100] *The Cape Times*, April 20, 1927; Roux, *Time Longer Than Rope*, 169.

links with overseas labor through anti-Communist British Socialists was proving a good approach.[101] Domestically, the break with the Communists moved the ICU closer to the "liberal" approach to non-racial politics. Support offered by Mrs. Lewis and her white associates was of a sort familiar to the ICU leaders, most of whom had been educated in mission schools run by white liberals. It was particularly welcome at a moment of crisis when the bulk of white South Africa remained hostile to the ICU.

In explaining the ouster of the Communists, Kadalie carefully emphasized that the move was made to preserve the ICU as a bona fide trade union operating within constitutional limits in the face of a Communist threat to convert the ICU into a revolutionary organization subject to the dictates of the Communist party. He further suggested that the use of strikes was outmoded.[102] Yet the ICU also sharply reiterated its opposition to the Hertzog program for Africans.[103] Kadalie seemed anxious to reassert that the ICU was a legitimate trade union—but a trade union also concerned with political measures affecting the interests of nonwhites.

Accordingly, the ICU quickly moved to strengthen the overseas ties which had been established. In December 1926, the National Council nominated Kadalie to represent the non-white workers of South Africa at the forthcoming conference of the International Labor Organization at Geneva.[104] The nomination was confirmed in a resolution of the annual conference of the ICU in April 1927, in Durban. Kadalie was instructed "to proceed to Geneva to submit the claims of the non-European workers who are the victims of merciless exploitation of both capitalism and the white labour policy of the Pact Government."[105] Sure that he would not get the official nomination of the South African government, which had alternated between representatives of the all-white South African Trades Union Congress in Johannesburg and the overwhelmingly white Cape Federation of Labour Unions in Cape Town, Kadalie urged Miss Holtby to arrange that the International Labor Organization accept his credentials as a representative of the African workers.[106]

---

[101] In mid-February it was announced that the ICU had been admitted to the International Federation, *The Cape Times*, Feb. 17, 1927.

[102] *The Cape Times*, Dec. 22, 1926.

[103] *The Workers' Herald*, Feb. 15, 1927.

[104] *The Cape Times*, Dec. 23, 1926.

[105] Roux, *Time Longer Than Rope*, 172.

[106] Letter from Clements Kadalie to Winifred Holtby, Jan. 27, 1927, Winifred Holtby Collection, Hull Public Library.

The ICU at the Peak of its Influence

The ICU seemed to be riding the crest of a new wave of popularity among Africans. The organizational deficiencies, financial irregularities, and unwillingness to strike pointed out by the Communists at best only tarnished the popular image of Kadalie and the ICU. As a counterweight, Kadalie could (and did) present himself as a successful defier of governmental authority. Although banned from Natal by the government in mid-1926, Kadalie (after consultation with legal advisers through Bunting) deliberately twice traveled to Pietermaritzburg and Durban. When arrested by the government Kadalie won his case on appeal.[107] The accompanying publicity, including a rising crescendo of attacks from whites, enhanced the status of the ICU. In Durban, Champion continued to seek action on local grievances, and, in particular, was able to persuade the municipality to end the obnoxious practice of dipping all new African arrivals into the city into disinfectant tanks. The Durban branch of the ICU became the largest section of the union, claiming a membership of 26,000 in April 1927.[108] In the rural Orange Free State the ICU also seems to have expanded rapidly during this period. When the annual conference met in Durban in April 1927, about 200 delegates were present; Kadalie stated that they represented a membership of 100,000. At the same time, however, he admitted that the internal structure of the ICU had been weakened by organizational, financial, and factional difficulties in 1926, some of which still remained.[109]

In the lively discussions of the ICU conference a new assertiveness was evident.[110] When the Mayor of Durban refused to open the conference because of the socialistic preamble in the ICU constitution, Kadalie and Champion refused to ask another white dignitary; they proudly asserted that the ICU was strong enough to conduct its affairs without the blessing of whites. More explicit racial overtones came to the fore when a narrow majority of the delegates voted to override

---

[107] For Kadalie's account of his trips to Natal in defiance of the ban and the subsequent legal battle (including the judgment given by the judge of the Natal Supreme Court), see Kadalie, "Memoirs," 62-66. A more contemporary account by Kadalie in exultant and triumphant language appears in The Workers' Herald, Sept. 14, 1926.

[108] The Workers' Herald, May 17, 1927.

[109] Ibid.

[110] The discussion of the annual conference which follows is based upon The Workers' Herald, May 17, 1927; The Weekend Advertiser, Apr. 16, 1927; Roux, Time Longer Than Rope, 167-72.

Kadalie and bar a friendly white supporter from the floor. Yet the delegates did not reject association with whites. They demanded, however, that they be recognized on their own terms. Instead of merely requesting the exchange of fraternal delegates with the white trade union organization, they endorsed a resolution that requested that the white trade unionists should join the ICU to form a single national trade union body. The constitution was revised to eliminate a clause which specifically barred Europeans from holding office in the ICU.[111]

Traditional trade union concerns received little attention. The delegates were completely preoccupied with the government's segregation bills, including new measures of control clearly aimed at the ICU. Perhaps in keeping with his heightened concern for constitutionality, Kadalie urged a day of prayer in protest against the native bills and the use of deputations and legal challenges of the pass laws before taking any further action. In response to opposition arguments from the floor in favor of direct action and strikes, Kadalie accepted endorsement of a day of formal protest to be followed by a passive resistance campaign against passes if an ICU deputation failed to receive satisfaction from the government. Kadalie's authority remained intact, but his emphasis upon accepted constitutional methods was tempered by threats of direct action. Poised at a new peak of membership and prestige, the ICU seemed less and less a trade union and more and more a national political pressure group. By comparison, the older African National Congress seemed a tiny federation of small local bodies.

At this juncture Kadalie embarked upon a five-month trip to Europe. It marked a crucial turning point in the history of the ICU. Kadalie's European experiences convinced him that the ICU had to be reorganized on the model of established European trade unions. But developments within the rapidly expanding ICU in South Africa were transforming its internal organization in a variety of ways uncongenial to the implementation of the reforms which Kadalie envisaged. In order to appreciate the spectacular fireworks within the ICU which erupted after Kadalie's return, it is necessary to understand the nature of Kadalie's trip to Europe and the state of the ICU during his absence.

Wherever Kadalie went in Europe new horizons and possibilities

[111] The old clause had read: "Europeans are eligible for membership, but under no circumstances shall such member hold office in this Organisation." Industrial and Commercial Workers' Union of Africa, ICU, *1925 Revised Constitution*, 4. In the revised constitution of 1927 there was no specific mention of "Europeans" either in the clause concerning officeholders or in the clause concerning membership. Industrial and Commercial Workers' Union of Africa, ICU, *Constitution and Rules* (Durban, 1927), 11-12, 27.

were opened to him.[112] For the first time in his life he was generally treated with respect and kindness by whites. At the meeting of the International Labor Organization in Geneva he was accepted as an observer and made many contacts with sympathetic delegates from throughout the world—despite the efforts of the official South African delegates to discredit him. In Paris at the annual congress of the International Federation of Trade Unions and at its headquarters in Amsterdam, Kadalie received encouragement and promises of further support. During trips to Holland, Germany, and Austria, Kadalie found European trade union leaders anxious to listen to his analysis of the South African situation and willing to send messages of support on behalf of the ICU.

The bulk of his time was spent in Britain where his links with Winifred Holtby and Creech Jones opened to him the doors of influential Socialists, national trade unions, and parliamentary groups. He gave speeches and wrote articles in a foredoomed effort to mobilize British opinion to prevent the passage of the native administration bill by the South African Parliament. In consultations with Socialist politicians and trade union leaders, Kadalie learned details about the operation of the established British trade unions at first-hand. From many sources he received advice and offers of help. His closest contacts were with Fenner (later Lord) Brockway, Creech Jones, and Winifred Holtby. Through Brockway and the Imperialism Committee of the Independent Labour party, Kadalie was scheduled for speaking tours throughout Britain and given office space and help. Creech Jones impressed upon Kadalie the necessity of reorganizing the ICU as a proper trade union, with particular emphasis upon the development of a sound organization and the limitation of its activities to the representation of workers' grievances. In this vein he drafted a new constitution for the ICU which Kadalie also discussed with Harold Grimshaw, director of the Colonial Division of the International Labor Organization. Throughout Miss Holtby helped with introductions and advice.

In late October 1927, Kadalie set sail for Cape Town. Although he had attempted to find a European adviser to accompany him, he had been unsuccessful. It had been agreed, however, that Brockway and Winifred Holtby were to select a suitable British trade unionist to send to South Africa temporarily as an adviser to the ICU. Kadalie carried with him promises of scholarships for ICU members at labor

---

[112] The following account of Kadalie's experiences in Europe is taken from Kadalie, "Memoirs," 74-116. Kadalie's narrative is clearly drawn, in part, from articles which appeared in *The Workers' Herald* on July 15, 1927 and Sept. 15, 1927.

colleges in England and Denmark, and in his luggage was the draft of a new constitution for the ICU written by Creech Jones. Many years later Kadalie described his feelings upon his departure from Britain:

> My mission to Europe had now ended. I must now return home to South Africa to work harder than ever before. To me it now appeared I was in the role of the biblical Moses, who had gone to Mount Sinai, returning with the new commandments to the children of Israel below. To Africa I must now return with new ideas to further the cause of the new trade unionism.[113]

Very quickly Kadalie was to realize that Aaron and his henchmen had been active in his absence.

To a regular reader of the South African press in 1927, it might well have seemed that branches of the ICU were being organized all over South Africa. Most striking was the continuing advance of the ICU into rural areas in the Orange Free State and Natal.[114] From small farming towns came reports of ICU meetings at which enthusiastic audiences often heard strident attacks upon the government. Farm laborers were being urged to join the union. In Natal the ICU particularly concerned itself with African squatters who were being ejected from European-owned land. Although there was no effort to organize a passive resistance campaign against the pass laws, it was reported (and denied by ICU headquarters) that the ICU was planning a general strike if its demands were not met within three months.[115] In both Johannesburg and Durban there were brief flash strikes by ICU members.[116]

To counter this threatening wave of African discontent, the government prepared new legislation. It easily secured passage of a native administration bill containing a clause clearly directed at the ICU:

> Any person who utters any words, or does any other act or thing whatever with intent to promote any feeling of hostility between Natives or Europeans, shall be guilty of an offence and liable on conviction to imprisonment for a period not exceeding one year, or to a fine of £ 100, or both.[117]

[113] Kadalie, "Memoirs," 115.

[114] For reports of meetings of the ICU in rural areas in the Orange Free State and Natal and the alarm which it caused among white farmers see: *The Cape Times,* May 12, 1927; June 14, 1927; July 19, 1927; Aug. 6, 1927; Aug. 8, 1927; Aug. 12, 1927; Aug. 18, 1927. For an African viewpoint of the atmosphere in which the ICU drive in the rural areas of Natal was conducted see: Gilbert Coka, "The Story of Gilbert Coka, of the Zulu Tribe of Natal, South Africa," in Margery Perham (ed.), *Ten Africans* (2nd ed., London, 1963), 293-97.

[115] *The Cape Times,* July 19, 1927; July 25, 1927.

[116] Roux, *Time Longer Than Rope,* 173.

[117] Ibid., 203.

After promulgation of the legislation, the Secretary for Native Affairs specifically directed the attention of the ICU to the terms of the "hostility clause."[118]

Signs of Crisis Amidst Hopes for Reform

Behind the scenes in the ICU, however, the structure of the union was not monolithic nor were the concerns of its leadership constantly focused upon plans for a direct confrontation with white authority. Champion, the acting national secretary in Kadalie's absence, complained about drunkenness and other improprieties by the staff at the headquarters in Johannesburg.[119] In the western Cape Province the leaders were fighting among themselves rather than strengthening and extending the organization.[120] In the eastern Cape Province the acting provincial secretary reported sadly that he found enthusiasm widespread but that competent secretaries could not be found to run new branches once they were established; he confessed that he had been unable to revive the important Port Elizabeth branch.[121] Complaints were made that Keable Mote, the provincial secretary of the Orange Free State whose speeches particularly disturbed white South Africa, was spending union funds illegally and that he refused to heed advice from the headquarters in Johannesburg.[122] In Natal a civil suit was instigated against Sam Dunn, Champion's temporary successor as provincial secretary, for his misappropriation of £415 of ICU funds for his own personal business affairs.[123] Shortly thereafter, Champion himself instituted a libel suit against George Lenono for attacks which the latter had made upon Champion's business practices—the court found that Champion had, indeed, used substantial ICU funds for his own private purposes.[124]

The ICU itself also toyed with business ventures. By 1925 *The Workers' Herald* had endorsed business activity by the ICU. In early 1927 the ICU branch at Alexandria in the eastern Cape Province bought a small farm upon which its members were to settle. In August 1927, the National Council authorized that union funds be used to purchase grain (presumably for resale to members). The ICU in the

[118] Kadalie, "Memoirs," 119.

[119] Minutes of the Meeting of the National Council, Industrial and Commercial Workers' Union of Africa, ICU, Nov. 18-25, 1927.

[120] Ibid.

[121] Letter from A. P. Maduna to A. W. G. Champion, Oct. 13, 1927.

[122] Minutes of the Meeting of the National Council, Industrial and Commercial Workers' Union of Africa, ICU, Nov. 18-25, 1927.

[123] *The Cape Times,* Nov. 11, 1927; June 5, 1928.

[124] See above, n. 93.

Orange Free State (without authorization of the National Council) used some of its funds to purchase rights to lots for its members in urban locations. The president of the ICU gave his endorsement to a co-operative scheme being launched in Natal.[125]

Instead of concentrating on narrow trade union concerns and careful organizational work, many leaders of the ICU were preoccupied with local squabbles and schemes for personal advancement. In Kadalie's absence the malpractices, organizational weaknesses, and fissiparous tendencies which had previously plagued the ICU gained new momentum—although their extent was not fully visible to the outside observer.

Amid widespread publicity from the white press, Kadalie returned to South Africa in November 1927. Admitting that in the past some might have justifiably thought that the ICU was anti-white, he affirmed his intention to end grounds for this suspicion. He announced his determination that the ICU should join the South African Trades Union Congress in a united front of labor. He warned the Labour party and the Trades Union Congress to recognize the ICU or to face ostracism from overseas labor organizations. Yet he also emphasized his intentions to make the ICU a well-organized legitimate trade union in which the ultimate goal of international Socialism would be ro tained. Specifically, he talked of a research depaitment, a publicity department, an expanded newspaper, and the need for a parliamentary obsei ver to be stationed in Cape Town.[126]

At a meeting of the National Council called immediately upon his return and at a subsequent specially convened national conference in December, Kadalie pushed the ICU to implement his proposals.[127] It was unanimously agreed by the National Council that formal application should be made to the all-white Trades Union Congress for the affiliation of the ICU on the basis of a membership of 100,000. Kadalie's request for a British trade union adviser was also approved. With

[125] The above discussion of ICU business efforts is derived from *The Workers' Herald*, July 20, 1925; Feb. 15, 1927; Minutes of the Meeting of the National Council, Industrial and Commercial Workers' Union of Africa, ICU, Nov. 18-25, 1927; Minutes of the Meeting of the National Council, Industrial and Commercial Workers' Union of Africa, ICU, Jan. 6, 1928.

[126] *The Star,* Nov. 16, 1927; *The Cape Times,* Nov. 17, 1927.

[127] The following analysis of developments within the ICU immediately after Kadalie's return is drawn from: Minutes of the Meeting of the National Council, Industrial and Commercial Workers' Union of Africa, ICU, Jan. 6, 1929; "Re-Organisation of the ICU" (mimeographed); "Proposals for Curtailing Expenditures at Head Office, Report to the National Secretary by the General Secretary" (typewritten). Champion's differences with Kadalie at the special national conference were subsequently explained in more detail. A. W. G. Champion, *Mehlomadala, My Experiences in the I.C.U.* (Durban, 1929), 22-23.

only minor changes the constitution which Kadalie brought from Britain was adopted by the National Council and then, largely as recommended by the National Council, it was adopted by the special national conference. Kadalie was elected without opposition to the key post of general secretary, the new name for the position which he had held since his takeover of the ICU in 1921.

Yet at both meetings, and at a January session of the National Council, there were signs of impending difficulties. From delegates from the four provinces Kadalie learned of various frictions and grievances. He was quickly apprised of the union's precarious financial position; although income had risen to £12,000 in 1927, over £11,500 had been spent, particularly large sums going for legal fees in Natal. The new pressure for satisfaction of the demands of the displaced squatters expressed itself most dramatically when a Zulu chief appeared at the national conference in December 1927 to plead that the ICU should act on behalf of his tribe in Natal. In response to the plea of the chief and others, the ICU agreed that it would embark upon a crash program to purchase land for the ejected Africans with whatever funds it could muster.

More ominous for Kadalie were the rumblings of discontent which were directed at him. At the meeting of the National Council which voted to seek affiliation with the Trades Union Congress and which endorsed the idea of a British trade union adviser, Kadalie found himself alone when he suggested that Europeans should be able to hold office in the ICU. At the national conference, Coloured delegates from Cape Town, supported by Africans, demanded to know whether Kadalie had returned a black man from England, or whether, like General Smuts, he had come back an Englishman. This group led an unsuccessful battle to insert a clause in the constitution barring Europeans from holding office in the ICU. Kadalie further antagonized the Cape Town representatives in an acrimonious debate over their charge that Afrikaans (the language of the Coloureds) had been unjustly neglected in the pages of *The Workers' Herald*. Keable Mote showed hostility to Kadalie (and to other members of the National Council as well). Kadalie and Champion disagreed over the means to raise funds for the land purchase project endorsed by the conference; Kadalie further implicitly criticized Champion and other leaders when he suggested that officials of the ICU were receiving excessive salaries. When Kadalie moved that the next national conference of the ICU should be held in January 1929, he was overwhelmingly outvoted; the delegates instead adhered to previous plans to meet again in April 1928. Kadalie's authority was challenged and, implicitly, key provisions of his plans for a reformed and revitalized ICU were questioned.

Meanwhile, the white trade unionists were debating their response to the application of the ICU. Although a number of trade union leaders in the Trades Union Congress were sympathetic to the ICU, they were also well aware of the strong segregationist views of the white rank and file, particularly among the growing Afrikaner component. They were also amazed at the ICU demand for affiliation on the basis of 100,000 members; if they accepted the ICU on its terms, it would have overwhelmingly outvoted the white trade unions, which only had a total of 30,000 members. At the time that the ICU made its application to the Trades Union Congress, the latter was involved in negotiations with the Cape Federation of Labour Unions upon the terms for a possible merger of the two groups. Thus, after discussion in the South African Trade Union Co-ordinating Committee, a group representing the leadership of both organizations, a reply was sent to the ICU in January 1928, rejecting affiliation upon the terms requested but offering, instead, that periodic consultations between the ICU and the white trade unions be undertaken. Indignantly, the ICU rejected the offer. It was convinced that the South African Trade Union Coordinating Committee had exposed its prejudice and racialism to the view of the international trade union movement; ultimately, the ICU believed that because it was based upon the proper principles of international workers' unity, it would triumph.[128]

At headquarters Kadalie worked to refashion the ICU into an instrument of trade unionism which could command respect from white unionists in South Africa and from supporters overseas.[129] In an attempt to regularize the chaotic financial practices of the ICU, he tried to establish a new system of weekly dues payments. In the fashion of British trade unions, he organized weekend schools at which he lectured the local officials upon proper trade union practices. He talked of making provincial secretaries into functional specialists on particular aspects of the economy. Over Champion's initial objections, he persuaded the Natal branch of the ICU to dispense with some of its in-

[128] For the text of the offer of the South African Trades Unions Co-ordinating Council and the ICU reply to it see: Industrial and Commercial Workers' Union of Africa, ICU, *I.C.U. Reply to Racial Declaration of South African Trades Union Congress* (Johannesburg, 1928). For the attitudes of the white trade union leaders, see: Minutes of the Special Meeting of the National Executive Council, South African Trades Union Congress, Dec. 8, 1927, Winifred Holtby Collection, Hull Public Library.

[129] Information for the following description of Kadalie's efforts at internal reform within the ICU is taken from: Minutes of the Meeting of the National Council, Industrial and Commercial Workers' Union of Africa, ICU, Jan. 6, 1928; "Report and Recommendations by General Secretary" (mimeographed); "Proposals for Curtailing Expenditures at Head Office, Report to the National Secretary by the General Secretary" (typewritten); Kadalie, "Memoirs," 123.

flated office staff. Upon his own initiative Kadalie engaged a firm of accountants to investigate the financial affairs of Champion and the Natal branch.

Kadalie was also anxious to revise the public platform of the ICU in line with his new image of proper trade unionism. In an "Economic and Political Program" released before the opening of the ICU's annual conference, it was announced that the ICU would seek a minimum monthly wage of £5 and a five-and-one-half day working week for all nonwhite workers, urban or rural, based upon a working day of eight hours only. "Friendly negotiations" would be sought with employers' groups, including farmers' associations, to be backed by national agitation. The Program also asserted that the ICU should become an active intermediary in reporting illegal practices to magistrates and the Native Affairs Department, particularly in the rural areas.

However, other provisions of the Program showed that, although Kadalie was anxious to strengthen trade union practices, he had no intention of abandoning political activity where he felt that it was relevant to the interests of nonwhite workers. In a demand which reflected the new concern of the ICU with rural grievances, the Program urged that Parliament be petitioned to increase the size of the native reserves and that agitation be undertaken against laws prohibiting African squatting. Passes were again made a central issue. The Program suggested that the government be petitioned to suspend the pass laws for a six-month trial period, and if no increase in lawlessness resulted, to repeal the pass laws in their entirety. If this petition failed, then the Program proposed the calling of a day of national protest at which passes were to be burned and all were to pledge that henceforth they would refuse to carry passes or recognize any pass laws. Proposals for economic demands and anti-pass action were accompanied by more specific suggestions for electoral activity; it was advocated that the ICU move to select candidates for seats in the Cape Provincial Council (technically open to nonwhite candidates). In an accompanying policy proposal, drafted for the forthcoming parliamentary election in 1929, Kadalie recommended that the ICU should replace its previous routine of backing a single party, or parties, with a policy of selective support of parliamentary candidates according to their positions upon key issues of interest to the ICU.[130]

Kadalie's proposals seem to have met with general approval from

130 For a summary of Kadalie's "Economic and Political Program" see *The Cape Times*, Mar. 22, 1928. His more specific program for parliamentary elections was contained in "Parliamentary General Elections, 1929—A Policy to be Submitted to Congress by the National Council" (mimeographed).

the delegates at the annual conference in April 1927. Fraternal greetings were sent to the South African Trades Union Congress, and it was reasserted that the Trades Union Congress would soon be compelled to admit the ICU. In political matters the ICU turned to the African National Congress which was simultaneously meeting in Bloemfontein. The National Council of the ICU and the National Executive of the African National Congress agreed to co-operate in working against the native bills and the pass laws; Kadalie's proposals with regard to the latter were apparently accepted as the basis for action.[131]

In keeping with the announcement of joint action with the African National Congress, Kadalie traveled to Pretoria where he made a sharp speech in favor of an end to passes and endorsed mass pass burning by Africans to bring about this goal. The speech was widely reported in the white press, and shortly thereafter, Kadalie was arrested and charged under the "hostility clause" of the Native Administration Act. In the subsequent trial Kadalie's contention that he was merely making a sharp criticism of governmental policy was upheld by the white judge. Again, Kadalie had successfully challenged the government—but this time any increment to his prestige was eclipsed by spreading turmoil within the ranks of the ICU.[132]

The Final Disintegration

The center of attention at the annual conference had not been Kadalie's new "Economic and Political Program," but the question of Champion's relationship to the ICU. Shortly before the meeting Champion had sent a thinly veiled warning to Kadalie:

> I have a feeling that you have a tendency of diminishing our solidarity. If you have such tendency I may just as well at this juncture warn you of the serious consequences. During your absence in Europe I did all in my power and thank God with success to keep that solidarity intact, and since you came back you seem to treat me with grave suspicion.[133]

At about this time Kadalie received a long report from the auditors in which it was made clear that Champion had hopelessly intertwined ICU monies with his own personal funds, and that some of the former

[131] The above account of the ICU annual conference is drawn from: *The Cape Times,* Apr. 9, 1928; Apr. 10, 1928; Apr. 11, 1928.

[132] For Kadalie's account of this brush with the law (including the statement of the judge who acquitted him) from which the above was taken see: Kadalie, "Memoirs," 143-50.

[133] A. W. G. Champion, "A Big Blunder" (mimeographed), 2.

had been used for private purposes.[134] At the annual conference Kadalie read the report of the auditors to the National Council. Immediately, some of the members, including some whom Champion had accused of improprieties during his stay in Johannesburg, demanded that Champion be arrested. According to Kadalie, he finally intervened to offer a compromise motion that Champion be suspended from office pending the results of an investigation by a special ICU commission. The motion was passed by the annual conference with only one negative vote.[135]

Champion returned to his home in Natal. The Zulu rank and file in Durban refused to accept the decision of the National Council. When Kadalie made an attempt to explain the position to them, he was denied a hearing at a tumultuous post-midnight meeting of the Durban membership. On May 17, the Durban branch of the ICU seceded from the national ICU. Supported by thirteen other branches of the ICU in Natal, the Durban branch (with the knowledge of, but not necessarily the encouragement of, Champion) formed the ICU yase Natal on May 31 upon a platform of provincial autonomy. In June Kadalie and Champion attempted to negotiate a *modus vivendi* based upon an end of Champion's suspension and a new federal structure within the ICU, but final terms could not be arranged. Champion then accepted the post of general secretary of the ICU yase Natal. Thus, the ICU lost its largest and potentially richest section.[136]

Champion's suspension, and the subsequent breakaway of the

134 Windram and Hooper, "Investigation and Report: Natal Provincial and Durban Offices of the Industrial and Commercial Workers' Union (I.C.U.)" (typewritten).

135 The contemporary accounts of the annual conference in the white press did not at the time carry news of Champion's suspension. The above account is taken from two sources which are in substantial agreement: Letter from Clements Kadalie to Norman Leys, Aug. 8, 1928; Kadalie, "Memoirs," 135-37. From these accounts it does not appear that there was a "disciplinary tribunal appointed by the Executive to carry out a wholesale 'cleansing' of the ICU." Roux, *Time Longer Than Rope,* 177. Instead the National Council and then the entire annual conference made the decision to suspend Champion.

136 It is impossible on the available evidence to determine who provoked the secession of the Durban branch. Champion's case rests on the argument that the rank and file in Durban made the initial move to secession which he accepted only after it was clear that they would not turn back. He then accepted the post of general secretary of the ICU yase Natal. Champion, "A Big Blunder," 1-2; Letter from A. W. G. Champion to Mrs. Mabel Palmer, May 23, 1928; *The Natal Advertiser,* June 20, 1928. Kadalie, on the other hand, claims that the National Council, at his urging, agreed to reinstate Champion upon the basis of a formula which would have allowed considerable financial autonomy. Yet the formula was rejected, and the ICU yase Natal formed. Kadalie argues that Champion instigated the secession. Letter from Clements Kadalie to Norman Leys, Aug. 8, 1928;

ICU yase Natal, were merely two incidents in a wave of troubles which threatened to engulf the ICU. In Natal indignant whites, aroused by a graveyard desecration falsely attributed to the ICU, sought out the ICU's branch headquarters, in some instances to destroy them. Africans were intimidated and in many cases were ejected from white-owned farms.[137] The rank and file, which had joined the ICU in the belief that the leadership would provide land for them, ceased to pay their dues and indignantly demanded their money back. At headquarters creditors appeared with regularity, and it was difficult to pay the salaries of many officials.[138] Friction grew among the ICU leaders. On June 26, eleven members of the National Council, including some who had been attacked for drunkenness or financial irregularities, challenged Kadalie's rule. In a "Clean Administration Manifesto," released to the white press, they condemned maladministration and demanded Kadalie's ouster.[139]

In a situation of spreading chaos, Kadalie still had one hope—the white trade union adviser who was being sent from Britain. After some difficulty, his supporters had finally found a willing candidate, William G. Ballinger, a young member of the Independent Labour party from Motherwell, Scotland. Creech Jones was disturbed about Ballinger's relatively limited experience in trade union work and by his lack of national recognition, yet he felt that his careful, cautious, and balanced approach would make him a "good type of man for this work."[140] With advice and a small sum in cash from British well-wishers, Ballinger set sail for South Africa. It was his belief that he was coming to the aid of a growing, solvent, but inexperienced, trade union harassed only by hostile and misunderstanding whites. Ballinger was appalled by what he found on his arrival. Nevertheless, with the support of Mrs. Lewis and a few white liberals in Johannesburg, he doggedly tried to right the tottering ICU. Kadalie, who was preoccupied with national policy matters and intra-union politics, allowed Ballinger great latitude, particularly in organizational matters.

Ballinger's strategy was two-pronged: on the one hand he wanted to obtain the support of sympathetic whites and the toleration of the government for a "respectable" and moderate trade union; on the

---

Kadalie, "Memoirs," 140-41. The terms of a tentative agreement between Champion and Kadalie were published in the white press. *The Natal Advertiser,* June 15, 1928.

[137] Roux, *Time Longer Than Rope,* 190.

[138] For a description of conditions both in the branches and in headquarters at this time, see Coka in Perham (ed.), *Ten Africans,* 306-10.

[139] *The Cape Times,* June 26, 1928.

[140] Letter from Arthur Creech Jones to Winifred Holtby, Mar. 28, 1928.

other hand, he wanted to reorganize the ICU internally in accord with his idea of a proper trade union structure.

In line with his first concern, he carefully presented himself and the ICU to the public as moderates who were concerned to right past excesses in the interests of African advancement.[141] He leaned particularly on the white liberals in the Joint Council who advised the ICU on proper approaches to the government about the pass laws.[142] Some of these white liberals even joined in a conference called by the ICU to discuss the organization of a campaign against passes.[143] Ballinger also established links with sympathetic white trade unionists. With William H. Andrews he discussed plans for white trade unionists to advise branches of the ICU.[144] About a month after Ballinger's arrival, it was announced that the ICU had reversed itself; it would enter into consultative meetings with the Trades Union Congress.[145]

In pursuit of his other goal, Ballinger drew from his experience in Scottish local government and adult education schools. He urged Kadalie to dismiss the provincial secretaries and reorganize the ICU on the basis of smaller districts. A new system of dues collection was advocated. Ballinger attempted to organize adult education classes for the members of the ICU. He also informed the incumbent provincial secretaries that their continuance in office was dependent upon their satisfactory specialization in the problems of a particular section of the economy. Shocked by the financial disorder which prevailed (to the extent that creditors even removed part of the office equipment at headquarters), Ballinger appointed a new financial secretary at headquarters and put him directly under his supervision. Ballinger also joined Kadalie in an unsuccessful approach to Champion for reunification.[146]

[141] For an example of his approach, see: *The Cape Times*, Oct. 3, 1928.

[142] Letter from William Ballinger to Winifred Holtby, Aug. 14, 1928.

[143] *The South African Worker*, Sept. 19, 1928.

[144] Letter from William Ballinger to Winifred Holtby, Aug. 14, 1928.

[145] *The Cape Times*, Aug. 23, 1928. The reversal, however, was not Ballinger's work alone. Shortly after the ICU had indignantly rejected the offer of the white trade unions to meet periodically for consultations, Creech Jones wrote to Kadalie urging that the ICU reconsider its position. In his reply Kadalie agreed that the ICU had made a "technical blunder" and a "political blunder." He stated that he would request a review of the question by the annual conference in Apr. 1928. Apparently, the matter was crowded out by other business, including the question of Champion's suspension. Letter from Creech Jones to Clements Kadalie, Feb. 27, 1928; Letter from Clements Kadalie to Creech Jones, Mar. 21, 1928, Winifred Holtby Collection, Hull Public Library.

[146] For more details on the reforms introduced by Ballinger, see: Letter from William Ballinger to Winifred Holtby, Aug. 14, 1928; "I.C.U. Adviser's Report, July 1928 to June 1929" (mimeographed); *The Workers' Herald*, Aug. 18, 1928. For reports of the attempts to negotiate with Champion, see *The Cape Times*, Nov. 20, 1928; Nov. 22, 1928.

In the midst of the bustle of encouraging activity which had been stimulated by Ballinger, the ICU achieved its first (and last) recognition from the government as the representative of African workers. In early October, ICU members at the Onderspoort Research Station in Pretoria went on strike. The Nationalist Minister of Agriculture refused to receive Kadalie with an ICU delegation and the workers were arrested, fined, and discharged. Meanwhile, the ICU was moving to organize African postal workers. Walter Madeley, the Labour Minister of Posts and Telegraphs, refused to receive an ICU delegation directly, but he agreed to meet with Kadalie and Ballinger through the recognized agency of the white Trades Union Congress. His willingness to challenge the remainder of the cabinet (Hertzog had forbidden all ministers to receive the ICU) was closely bound up with an internal struggle within the Labour party. Nevertheless, a meeting was arranged with William H. Andrews as intermediary. Its sequel brought spectacular publicity to the ICU and Madeley, but no gains for the African postal workers. When Hertzog learned that Madeley had received the ICU, he demanded his resignation, which Madeley refused to give. Hertzog then resigned and reconstituted a new government without Madeley. Kadalie could thus claim that the ICU had been responsible for the fall of a government.[147]

Yet in its own house, the ICU was still experiencing tensions, in part accentuated by Ballinger's moves within its weakened structure. In 1928 the ICU had reaffirmed its belief in its own self-generated non-white strength—particularly in its reaction to the rebuff from the white trade unionists. Anti-white feeling was latent in the ICU. Yet Ballinger, an alien white, wasted no time in attempting to reshape the nonwhite ICU into a model of the established proper trade union which he had known in Britain. He moved quickly against many long-time members of the ICU whose practices and attitudes he felt had contravened acceptable canons of trade unionism. His activist interventions carried him beyond the role of an adviser into that of an executive officer. Disgruntled officers began to attack him as a "dictator."[148] In October, the Cape Town branch, the center which had most actively opposed the idea of a white officer, seceded; its secession was accompanied by that of another branch in the Cape Province and a

---

[147] For accounts of this incident, which also provide further details about its significance in terms of the inner politics of the Labour party, see: Roux, *Time Longer Than Rope,* 181-83; R. K. Cope, *Comrade Bill* (Cape Town, 1943), 309-11.

[148] *The Cape Times,* Oct. 23, 1928. Kadalie also asserts that several members of the National Council called Ballinger a "dictator" upon his first appearance before the Council in July, 1928. Kadalie, "Memoirs," 153. There is confirmation of this suggestion in earlier articles by Kadalie. See: *New Africa,* May 25, 1929.

branch in the Transvaal.[149] In the Orange Free State Keable Mote was organizing a secession movement on the basis of provincial autonomy.[150] It is not clear whether the rash of secessions was a direct reaction to Ballinger's position or a delayed by-product of opposition to Kadalie, such as that expressed after the latter's return from Europe. Yet they did indicate that Ballinger's presence had not immediately succeeded in halting the disintegration of the ICU.

Kadalie had been personally offended immediately after Ballinger's arrival by the latter's refusal to share a train compartment with Kadalie on the trip from Cape Town to Johannesburg.[151] Yet once Ballinger arrived in Johannesburg and set to work Kadalie was full of praise for him.

> Mr. Ballinger is now two weeks with us and he has given us satisfaction already. You could not have made a better choice. In such a short space of time, he has won many friends for the ICU. You sent him at the right moment.[152]

In the pages of *The Workers' Herald* Ballinger's efforts were strongly endorsed.[153] By the last months of 1928, however, a coolness had developed between Kadalie and Ballinger. It seems that Kadalie's personal conduct was put under scrutiny by Ballinger and his supporters within the ICU. Ballinger learned that Kadalie's financial and family affairs were not fully in order; furthermore, Ballinger and the ICU staff with whom he worked were not satisfied by Kadalie's accounting for the substantial expenses incurred on his European tour of the previous year. With Ballinger's blessing, Kadalie apparently asked for and received leave from his job. At a meeting of the National Council on January 5, 1929, it was agreed that he would be granted a year's leave of absence, although he would still be available for propaganda work at the request of both headquarters and the branches.[154]

[149] *The South African Worker*, Oct. 24, 1928.

[150] Roux reports that Mote seceded early in 1928. Roux, *Time Longer Than Rope*, 178. Yet from discussion at a meeting of a subcommittee of the National Council in early 1929, it appears that Mote did not organize for secession until late 1928 and early 1929. Minutes of a Meeting of the Sub-Committee of the Industrial and Commercial Workers' Union of Africa, ICU, Feb. 28, 1929.

[151] *New Africa*, May 25, 1929; Kadalie, "Memoirs," 152.

[152] Letter from Clements Kadalie to Winifred Holtby, Aug. 1, 1928. Another letter in the same vein followed in mid-September. Letter from Clements Kadalie to Winifred Holtby, Sept. 12, 1928.

[153] *The Workers' Herald*, Aug. 18, 1928.

[154] The following account of Kadalie's departure from the ICU is taken from two sources: Minutes of a Meeting of the Sub-Committee of the National Council of the Industrial and Commercial Workers' Union of Africa, ICU, Feb. 28, 1929; Roux, *Time Longer Than Rope*, 184-87.

By this time Kadalie had apparently decided that he could no longer work with Ballinger. On January 25, Kadalie announced his resignation from the post of general secretary; he characterized his action ". . . as a protest against the Head Office Administration generally and against the assumption by Ballinger of the duties and power not only of the National Council but of the Annual Congress itself."[155] He moved to identify himself with the radical opposition to Ballinger's policies by reverting to criticisms of the Joint Council and asserting that, under its influence, Ballinger had diverted the ICU from militancy to a moderate policy acceptable to the Chamber of Mines.

In a *volte-face* on February 10, Kadalie renounced his resignation and announced his intention to resume the post of general secretary on February 13. Appealing for support from a broad spectrum of anti-Ballinger critics, Kadalie announced a new slate of officers including James La Guma (whom he had ousted for Communist activity in 1926), Alexander Maduna, H. D. Tyamzashe, Doyle Modiakhotla (who had signed the "Clean Administration Manifesto" against him in June 1928), and Keable Mote (who was threatening to secede from the ICU). When the pro-Ballinger officers in headquarters refused to heed his announcement, Kadalie then took over the post of provincial secretary in the Transvaal which was offered to him by a group of supporters on the Witwatersrand. Finally, called to order by an apparently *ad hoc* subcommittee of the National Council on February 28, 1929, Kadalie heard Ballinger assert that "there was no room in the ICU for Kadalie and himself." When it became clear that Ballinger's supporters controlled the machinery of the ICU at headquarters, Kadalie agreed to resign again from the post of general secretary. He could not immediately dislodge Ballinger and his supporters from their control of the top organs of the ICU, yet he had no intention of retiring from the ICU.

With the support of the secretaries of ICU branches on the Witwatersrand and with promises of support claimed from the Orange Free State and Natal, Kadalie issued a call on March 13 for a national conference to be held in Bloemfontein in April for the formation of the Independent Commercial and Industrial Workers' Union of Africa.[156] Standing on an anti-Ballinger platform studded with criticism of his subservience to the Joint Council and the Chamber of Mines, Kadalie also conspicuously promised that the new organization would be based upon provincial autonomy. A further section of the summons to Bloemfontein featured a scheme for the purchase of land for ICU members.

[155] Letter from Clements Kadalie to the Executives and Members of the ICU, Mar. 13, 1929 (mimeographed).
[156] Ibid.

Kadalie's program seemed carefully tailored to attract maximum support for a new national organization. Through criticisms of Ballinger, Kadalie sought to rally the many members who had been alienated by him. An appeal to the left and radicals was contained in his renunciation of the Joint Council and the attacks on the Chamber of Mines. Talk of a land purchase scheme reflected a sensitivity to the rural discontent which had manifested itself so strikingly since 1927. Promises of provincial autonomy were attractive to Mote, and might even have been devised to lure Champion with his substantial following in Durban. In the interests of reestablishing his position at the head of the ICU, Kadalie seemed willing to accept a decentralized coalition of all those who had broken from the ICU dominated by Ballinger.

For a brief period in 1929–30, Kadalie seemed on the verge of success. At the inaugural conference of the Independent ICU in April, Kadalie obtained the support of Maduna, Tyamzashe, Modiakhotla, and Mote. A newspaper, *New Africa*, was started with Tyamzashe as editor. Plans were announced for an African Native Land Settlement Corporation, Ltd., a shareholding company to purchase land for Africans.[157] In a play to obtain funds from overseas, Kadalie attempted to link up the Independent ICU with the League Against Imperialism, the Comintern-supported organization whose inaugural Congress of Oppressed Nationalities Kadalie had refused to attend. The wary South African Communists warned the League against traffic with Kadalie.[158] Nevertheless, in November, Kadalie joined with the Ballinger ICU to appear at a Communist-organized rally for African rights in Johannesburg.[159] In 1929, the Independent ICU succeeded in organizing, at least on paper, a network of branches throughout the Orange Free State, in parts of Natal and Transvaal, and in a few cities in the eastern Cape Province, including Port Elizabeth and East London. Alexander P. Maduna set up an office in Durban to challenge Champion on his home ground.[160] In November, however, Champion and Kadalie met and negotiated an agreement under which the ICU yase Natal was to affiliate with the Independent ICU with guarantees

[157] *New Africa*, May 25, 1929; July 29, 1929; Monica Hunter (Wilson), *Reaction to Conquest* (2nd ed., London, 1961), 568.

[158] Roux, *Time Longer Than Rope*, 187-88.

[159] "Joint Meeting—ICU of Africa, African Congress, Non-European Federation of Trade Unions, Communist Party, League of African Rights, Independent ICU" (typewritten). It is not clear why Ballinger consented to join with the Communists.

[160] For a list of the offices claimed by the Independent ICU in mid-1929, see: *New Africa*, July 29, 1929. An article by A. P. Maduna, hostile to Champion and the ICU yase Natal, appears in *New Africa*, June 29, 1929.

of full provincial autonomy. The Ballinger section was invited to join.[161] Yet the agreement was never implemented—and Ballinger, of course, remained aloof. The local branches of the Independent ICU, for the most part, did not take root. Kadalie's new trade union apparently could not gain sufficient momentum to establish itself on a firm national basis. With Maduna and Tyamzashe, Kadalie retired to the Independent ICU branch in East London.

The Aftermath

The failure of the Independent ICU to create a national organization was paralleled by the inability of the Ballinger-led ICU to resurrect the financially pressed national structure over which it claimed jurisdiction. The ICU remained a number of isolated units, to one degree or another carrying on in the name of the past reputation of the movement. Yet in the separate experiences of the local ICU units are further clues to the nature of the nonwhite protest which the ICU represented.

Ballinger's section in 1929–30 continued small-scale efforts to reestablish ICU branches. In mid-1930, Ballinger left the ICU to concentrate upon independent research and new welfare schemes for Africans. In the early 1930's the ICU headquarters in Johannesburg continued to maintain tenuous links with about fifteen branches, mostly in the Transvaal and the northern Orange Free State. Yet each branch ran itself as an autonomous body with small but stable memberships. By the mid-1930's the ICU office in Johannesburg was run by a small coterie of Africans loyal to Ballinger. Its focus was upon his efforts to start a co-operative among Africans in Johannesburg.[162]

From his new base in East London, Kadalie achieved brief national recognition once again in January 1930, when he led a strike of railway and harbor workers in the port of East London.[163] The strike spread among the African workers of East London and, for a limited period, over eighty per cent of the African workers stayed away from

[161] New Africa, Nov. 23, 1929.

[162] The above description of developments in the section of the ICU which remained loyal to Ballinger is taken from: "The Industrial and Commercial Workers' Union of Africa," Feb. 1933 (typewritten); Roux, Time Longer Than Rope, 188.

[163] For accounts of the strike and its aftermath, see: Roux, Time Longer Than Rope, 194-96, 247; Hunter, Reaction to Conquest, 568-70; The Cape Times, Jan. 13, 1930; Jan. 15, 1930; Jan. 16, 1930; Jan. 17, 1930; Jan 21, 1930; Jan. 24, 1930; Jan. 27, 1930; Jan. 28, 1930; Jan. 30, 1930; Kadalie, "Memoirs," 158-77. The following analysis is also derived from these sources.

their jobs. Kadalie, throughout the strike, exhorted the workers to solidarity, yet he equally strongly urged nonviolence. Only toward the end of the strike, when financially pressed Africans were beginning to drift back to work and the strike committee started to use pickets, did Kadalie suggest that authority should be defied if forces of the government attempted to break up the picket lines. Finally, Kadalie and eight other leaders were secretly arrested. From prison Kadalie urged the strikers to return to work, a call which many reportedly opposed. Nevertheless, the strike was broken. A number of strikers lost their jobs, although a few received small wage increases.

In the subsequent trial in Grahamstown, Kadalie was found guilty of incitement to public violence and was sentenced to a fine of £25 or three months' imprisonment with hard labor. He returned to East London to a tumultuous reception from four thousand supporters. Uneasy white employers urged further governmental action against Kadalie. The government reportedly moved to deport Kadalie to Nyasaland. It was rumored that in the face of these threats, Kadalie reached an understanding with the authorities[164]—later in 1930 he dramatically appeared in Bloemfontein to oppose a pass-burning campaign organized by the Communist party—and it has been argued that Kadalie lost both national and local support because of the unsuccessful strike.[165] Subsequently, the East London branch of the ICU was wracked by a series of factional quarrels between Kadalie and his lieutenants over personal and financial issues.[166] Nevertheless, Kadalie survived to maintain his leadership of a local organization which seems to have played an important role in East London as a welfare body and as a political party in elections for the local advisory board in Duncan Township.[167] Thus, within greatly reduced confines, Kadalie was able to establish a local ICU which retained the support of a significant number of Africans in one urban location.

In the Orange Free State, Mote labored to keep together several branches of the ICU in one organization. Negotiations were opened with the authorities in Bloemfontein for a wage raise for African workers.[168] When, later in 1930, it seemed that a Communist organizer was rallying support for a pass-burning demonstration on Dingaan's Day,

---

[164] Roux, *Time Longer Than Rope*, 196.

[165] Hunter, *Reaction to Conquest*, 570; Roux, *Time Longer Than Rope*, 196.

[166] In February 1933, Ballinger reported that the Independent ICU in East London had split between Kadalie and Maduna in a dispute over irregular financial practices. "The Industrial and Commercial Workers' Union of Africa," Feb. 1933 (typewritten).

[167] Kadalie, "Memoirs," 194-96.

[168] *The Cape Times*, Feb. 5, 1930.

December 16, Mote identified himself with this more specific political campaign.[169] Yet the pass-burning campaign failed, possibly in part because of Kadalie's intervention on the side of the government which, in any case, was determined to stamp out the campaign at all costs. Mote subsequently repudiated the Communists.[170] In April 1931, he convened a conference in Kroonstad of ICU branches in the Orange Free State and the western Transvaal. At the meeting fifty-seven delegates formed the Federated Free State ICU of Africa. Selby Msimang, attending as an invited delegate from the African National Congress, was elected to the presidency while Mote received the key post of general secretary.[171] The new organization was stillborn. Mote, at best, only retained the loyalty of a small group in Kroonstad.

In the western Cape Province it seems that the ICU disintegrated rapidly after the secession of the Cape Town branch in late 1928. In Cape Town a hard core of ICU members among the dockers, the first supporters of the ICU, clung to the Industrial and Commercial Workers' Federation.[172] It continued to represent their interests as a local trade union and also, upon one occasion, participated in a non-European conference where it urged mass demonstrations against governmental legislation.[173] It apparently made no effort to extend itself beyond Cape Town.

Only in Natal did the ICU yase Natal briefly threaten to establish itself firmly on a provincial basis.[174] Unrest resulting from the eviction of African squatters in Natal was aggravated in 1928 by demonstrations over new regulations governing the making of *utshwala* (African beer). When municipalities in Natal undertook to ban home brewing and to center all manufacture and sale of *utshwala* in municipally-owned canteens (the proceeds being channeled to funds for African urban locations), African women organized a boycott of the canteens which threatened their most important source of income. ICU members became involved. The disturbances came to a head in Durban in June 1929, when whites attempted to storm ICU's headquarters. Clashes between whites and Africans broke out throughout the city, resulting in the deaths of six Africans and two whites.

Peace was restored, yet unrest continued to simmer in Natal, often

[169] Roux, *Time Longer Than Rope*, 247.

[170] *Umteteli wa Bantu*, Oct. 3, 1931.

[171] *Umteteli wa Bantu*, Apr. 18, 1931.

[172] "The Industrial and Commercial Workers' Union of Africa," Feb. 1933 (typewritten).

[173] *The Cape Times*, Jan. 4, 1930.

[174] The following account of the ICU yase Natal is drawn from: Roux, *Time Longer Than Rope*, 189-94.

focused around ICU offices. It was alleged that Africans were failing to pay taxes. In November 1929, the national government, also fearful of a rash of Communist-sponsored demonstrations, decided upon a show of force and the enactment of new restrictive legislation. Armed police battalions, equipped with new tear gas bombs, paraded and conducted house-to-house searches, punctuated by judicious demonstrations of the effectiveness of tear gas. In Parliament the government obtained passage of the Riotous Assemblies Amendment Act, which among other things, empowered the Minister of Justice to order an individual to leave any part of the country if he considered that his presence there would cause "hostility" between the races. Undoubtedly in reaction to the threat to his activities, Champion held aloof from identification with Communist efforts to organize pass-burning. In June he issued an almost abject statement proclaiming his loyalty to the Nationalist government. His tactical shift was to no avail; in September 1930, he was banned from Natal Province. Only in 1933 was he allowed to return.

The show of force by the government and its deportation of Champion throttled the ICU yase Natal. Yet the organization was not disbanded and, upon Champion's return to Durban, he was able to breathe new life into it as a local body which attempted to gain limited advances for Africans within the existing system. The municipality of Durban tolerated the weekly meetings of the ICU yase Natal, and Champion built up a loyal following which subsequently helped him to become an important figure in African politics in Natal. With the advent of the Nationalist government in 1948 he continued to attempt to work within the system. He is presently the leader of the elected African representatives in the Combined Native Advisory Boards in Durban.[175]

Several times during the 1930's efforts were made by Kadalie and other ICU leaders to create a new national organization. Yet every attempt proved unsuccessful.[176] Meanwhile, many of the local branches

[175] Leo Kuper, An African Bourgeoisie (New Haven, 1965), 323-27. Further correspondence with Professor Kuper confirms that Champion still held this post in 1968.

[176] In June 1933, a Re-Union Conference met in Bloemfontein, apparently under Kadalie's inspiration. It formulated an agreement for reunification. "I.C.U. Re-Union Conference, Unanimous Agreement to Unification" (mimeographed). Yet no subsequent meeting seems to have been held in 1933. In 1936, at a meeting of Kadalie, Champion, Tyamzashe, Lujiza, and Mzazi (the latter two from the group previously oriented to Ballinger), a new call for reunification was issued. "Resolution of the United ICU" (mimeographed), Mar. 28, 1936. The resolution called for a conference of ICU delegates to be held in Bloemfontein in June after the meeting of the All-African Convention. There is no report that such a conference was ever held.

lost their members and went out of existence. Only in Durban and East London did the remnants of the ICU continue in effective operation. As in the initial period of nonwhite trade unionism, the only organizations which sustained themselves were those ICU groupings which satisfied limited local interests and restricted the scope of their operations. They were no threat to the status quo of white South Africa.

The ICU as a national nonwhite trade union organization was dead. In its place new locally based, non-white trade unions began to take root in the late 1930's. In sharp contrast to the practices of the ICU, they restricted themselves to specific industries and concentrated quite narrowly upon economic demands.[177] The days of a single "National Labour Organisation of the aboriginals" were no more.

The Significance of the ICU

Although the ICU left no national organizational legacy, its meteoric rise and fall marked the advent of a new type of nonwhite expression in South Africa. It reflected the reactions of newly created, nonwhite social groups to the terms of their rapid "integration" within a multi-racial society into which they had been thrust by the successful conquest of South Africa by overwhelming white power. At the same time it anticipated features of nonwhite political and economic action which did not become common until the decades following World War II.[178]

The post-World War I local trade unions which coalesced into the ICU were both an example of, and a reaction to, the protest of non-white workers against the conditions in which they found themselves. The ICU represented an attempt to adapt the egalitarian potential within the economic system to the needs of nonwhite workers. Seeing the possibility of advancement within the system on the basis of skill and performance rather than color, the nonwhites organized to further their consideration as workers like the whites. Borrowing the models of labor organization at hand, the ICU sought to fashion an instrument which would place nonwhites in the ranks of the working class.

[177] For an account of the growth of new nonwhite trade unions in the 1930's and 1940's, see: Roux, *Time Longer Than Rope*, 326-42.

[178] The following discussion relies heavily upon material drawn from Gwendolen Carter, Sheridan W. Johns, III, and Thomas Karis (eds.), *From Challenge to Protest: A Documentary Survey of African Politics in South Africa* (forthcoming), and Leo Kuper, "African Nationalism in South Africa, 1910–1964" (mimeographed). Reference was also made to Mary Benson, *African Patriots* (London, 1959); Jordan K. Ngubane, *An African Explains Apartheid* (New York, 1963); Roux, *Time Longer Than Rope*.

Although trade unionism had proved an effective vehicle for the advancement of the interests of white workers, its strict application to the problems of the nonwhites was thwarted by the intractable features of the South African racial situation. On the one hand, it met the determination of much of white South Africa to deny nonwhite workers the possibility of equality. On the other hand, the transitional state of nonwhite life helped to deny to trade unionism the chance to root itself firmly.

At the time of the establishment of the ICU, white trade unions were aggressively asserting their protectionist interests. The Chamber of Mines and other key white employers, including white farmers, displayed open hostility to the efforts of the ICU to organize. They maintained the system of contract labor which made it doubly difficult for sustained trade union work to be carried out among nonwhites. From the statute book the government could draw a wide variety of legal measures to hinder or threaten the activities of the ICU. In the few instances when the ICU attempted to call strikes, the police and military power of the government was applied to cripple and crush them. In addition, "scab" labor could easily be mustered. Even though the ICU at this stage carefully avoided any direct political activity, it was still seen as a threat, and treated as such, by crucial powers within white South Africa.

Although the nonwhite work force was numerous and growing, much of it was still migratory and remained oriented to the problems of the tribal areas. Grievances against the new urban system were deep (as testified by the largely spontaneous demonstrations immediately after World War I), yet it was difficult to organize nonwhite workers into a stable trade union dedicated to the painstaking and piecemeal struggle for improvements in working conditions. Furthermore, there were few nonwhite organizers who were willing and competent to maintain any elaborate organizational structure if, indeed, it could have been carefully established. This may help to explain why the ICU during its first years finally found some organizational stability among the Coloured workers of the western Cape Province. It was there that there was a substantial body of settled workers as well as a greater number of potentially competent officers to build a solid structure after the more flamboyant campaigns which initially launched the union in any particular area.

Yet the intention of Kadalie and the leadership of the ICU was that the organization would become "one Big Union" for all nonwhites throughout South Africa. Kadalie spurred the extension of the ICU into all four provinces. In pursuit of his goal Kadalie was drawn into explicitly political activity. The prospect of immediate benefits may have been the greatest spur to Kadalie's efforts on behalf of the Nationalist-Labour pact; at the same time, he was responding to the promise of a meaningful participation for all South Africans which was offered within the "liberal" tradition. Kadalie also saw himself as a leader of workers who was joining with other representatives of workers to oust a government regarded as favorable to the Chamber of Mines. When the actions of the pact government finally revealed that Kadalie's faith had been misplaced, he still did not reject the ideal; rather he continued his involvement through association with the African National Congress and the pressure group approach which it represented. When the Congress proved reluctant to embark upon political activity on the issues which agitated the ICU membership, the ICU leadership talked of independent efforts to conduct campaigns among Africans. Thus, in 1926–27 the ICU seemed to be evolving into an organization increasingly oriented to political action. Throughout its existence, the ICU had engaged in informal lobbying and petitioning to governmental authorities for redress of economic grievances; this practice was not abandoned, but its scope was extended and other forms of more explicit political pressure techniques were considered.

With the expansion of the ICU upon a platform which promised attention to the frustrations and demands of all African workers, including those in rural areas, the reputation of the ICU was enhanced in many areas even before it began specific organizational campaigns. During the flying visits of Kadalie and other ICU propagandists, great enthusiasms were aroused and large memberships enrolled, particularly in 1926–27. At this point it seemed that the ICU was on the verge of converting itself into the first nation-wide mass movement of Africans. A nonwhite group, appealing not only to Africans but also to Coloureds, was attempting to mobilize demonstrations and mass action in protest against and in challenge to the discriminatory bases of the South African system.

However, a combination of developments diverted and ultimately fragmented the ICU mode of organization—a mode which would have been, in any circumstance, extremely hazardous, if not inevitably doomed to destruction at the hands of white authority. Kadalie, in keeping with his faith in an ultimately nonracial society based upon justice for all workers, had always made reference to, and sought aid from, universalistic ideologies and sympathetic whites and their organizations. Rebuffed by the established white-dominated political system in South Africa, he had continued to search for, and accept support from, those few whites in South Africa who offered it to him.

Yet he also continued to believe that he and the leadership of the ICU, not sympathetic whites, should be the final arbiters of policy. When the alliance with the Communists challenged Kadalie's position within the ICU and seemed to expose the organization to more intensive attack from its white enemies, Kadalie broke with the Communists. The strength of his commitment to both the idea and the utility of links with white labor was such, however, that he took the proffered hand of white liberals in South Africa who facilitated his access to international labor circles. Through alliances with these groups, which he had always regarded as potential champions of his nonracial ideal, Kadalie anticipated that he could further his aims within South Africa. The white liberals did express their opposition to established South African practices, but most crucially they persuaded Kadalie that his wisest course was a reorientation of the ICU to the more limited trade union format—this time more strictly in accord with the model for established European trade unions.

With this new vision Kadalie returned to South Africa at the very time that the experiences and expectations of the burgeoning ICU membership were fixed primarily upon larger political grievances or concerns outside the realm of an occupationally divided urban trade union. Simultaneously, the leadership of the ICU was torn by internal disputes engendered to a large degree by maladministration and inadequate attention to the immense organizational problems resulting from the changing character of the demands and membership of the ICU. Further pressure was added through the measures of the government which clearly indicated that it would not hesitate to penalize the key leaders of the ICU should they move in the direction of an organized frontal assault upon the existing pattern of white society. In effect, the government expressed its determination to maintain the hierarchical order of society and to protect the recently entrenched position of white laborers and farmers.

Caught in a situation quite impossible to master, Kadalie could only frantically preside over the disintegration of the organization which he had labored so long to establish as a force for the betterment of the conditions of the nonwhite majority of South Africa. Talk of a bona fide trade union was inadequate—either to a membership which sought more than bread-and-butter trade unionism or to an aroused white society which viewed the ICU as a threat to its privileged position. The hastily constructed and shakily secured organizational structure of the ICU collapsed as its inexperienced and improperly trained leaders proved inadequate for their jobs. Demands for local autonomy, inimical to the continuation of the organization as it had been (and as Kadalie envisaged it), apparently could not be resisted. Even limited political campaigns could not be sustained. Disillusioned ICU members, although still unreconciled to the terms of their participation in the South African economy, deserted the organization. Isolated segments of the organization were able to capture the temporary loyalty of sections of the legion which had flocked to the ICU banners. But even these groupings—denied a national base, plagued with continuing factionalism, and, most crucially, harassed by anxious white authorities—were unable to maintain themselves except in a few instances where they carefully accepted the narrow limits within which they were allowed to operate as local welfare organizations and political pressure groups loyal to a single leader.

In the perspective of time the ICU can be seen as another dimension of the form of organization represented by the African National Congress. Its leadership shared a common background of training in mission schools. It accepted many of the crucial features of the new modernizing order, but it demanded that nonwhites be accommodated within it on an equal basis. Like the Congress it asserted its belief in the eventual full participation of all South Africans in a nonracial society. To achieve its ends, it asserted that the accepted practices of respectful lobbying must be accompanied by extra-parliamentary action and mass campaigns. To varying degrees, it looked to white or European models, yet, in the fashion of the separatist churches, it insisted that nonwhites be in control of the ICU. It urged a united front of all nonwhites (not at all times easily maintained) to put pressure upon white authority.

Yet the ICU made its distinctive contribution as a catalyst for the aspirations of the nonwhite "proletariat" which was being formed within the crucible of South African industrialization. In the decade before South Africa achieved economic "take-off," the ICU contradictorily and irregularly expressed the economic demands of the majority of the South African working force—often in an explicitly political context. Where the African National Congress (and the African Peoples' Organization) proved reluctant to take up the particular demands of the nonwhite workers, the ICU filled the gap—and for a brief period it eclipsed the more "moderate" groups as *the* nonwhite political organization. Yet as a political organization, it was weak, particularly under the pressures applied to it by the South African government. For the same reasons, it could never establish itself firmly as a mass movement.

Throughout its life the ICU was a changing, but permanently unstable, combination of trade union, political pressure group, and mass movement. In the contradictions between these forms of organization, the ICU expressed the demands of a shifting nonwhite population increasingly involved in the new urban economy. Its efforts at systematic trade union organization, sustained mass demonstrations, and a united front of all nonwhites set precedents which were to be taken up by other South African nonwhite opposition organizations in later decades. Its legacy, then, was not as a specific organization, but rather as an imperfect model of protest upon which succeeding generations could improve.

THE BUGANDAN TRADE BOYCOTT:

A STUDY IN TRIBAL, POLITICAL,

AND ECONOMIC NATIONALISM

DHARAM P. GHAI

Economic boycotts occupy an important and honored place in the long history of protest movements. They have an advantage over other forms of protest in that they can be conducted in a legal and nonviolent fashion, a fact which no doubt explains their continued popularity in the face of a high rate of failure. Seeking their objectives primarily through a disruption of certain vital services, economic boycotts are usually not allowed to proceed to a point where they can wreak devastation on an economy. At the same time, the inconvenience and hardship that they cause provide strong financial incentives for evasion, among both supporters and opponents. Once substantial evasion occurs, the collapse of the boycott becomes a matter of time. Another reason for the failure of boycotts is that their success can only be guaranteed by a sustained stand by the masses, and this is exceedingly difficult to achieve.

The Bugandan trade boycott of 1959 was an attempt to achieve certain political and economic goals through a boycott of alien traders. Its study provides an illuminating lesson on the strength and limitations of the boycott as a medium of protest.

Outline of the Boycott

On 1 March 1959 Augustine Kamya, the chairman of the newly formed Uganda National Movement, announced that his organization was planning a one-year boycott of non-African shops outside the main towns of Uganda.[1] With the conspicuous exception of a few outstanding persons, the Movement embraced most prominent Bugandan politicians.[2] By the time that the boycott was formally declared on 8 March, its scope had been broadened to include non-African shops throughout Uganda and the time limit had been extended indefinitely. In addition, it was to apply to certain services and products provided or manufactured by non-Africans, such as bus transport, and beer and spirits. The boycott achieved an immediate success in most parts of Buganda; its effects were also felt for some time in certain towns in the Eastern Province.

The organizers followed up their early success by arranging a meeting with two hundred African traders to approve a list of some thirty wholesalers to supply goods directly to them. However, the traders refused to accept the list presented to them because it had been drawn up without prior consultation. At a subsequent meeting on 18 March, however, agreement was reached between leaders of the movement and representatives of the African traders on a mutually agreed list of importers. Meanwhile, violence and intimidation were reported from various parts of Buganda and the Protectorate government moved to call a halt to the boycott.

A few days later, Kamya, the chairman of the Movement, was held for trial after pleading not guilty in a Kampala magistrate's court to charges "of threatening violence and watching and besetting an African trader to prevent him from selling beer."[3] However, as incidents involving assault, intimidation, and arson continued to multiply, the government of the Protectorate resolved to take sterner measures. On 11 April, in the Mengo and Masaka districts of Buganda, restrictions were placed on meetings of more than 250 people; this ban was later extended to the Busoga district and the Mbale township district in the Eastern Province. After being convicted of threatening vio-

---

[1] This story has been pieced together from the accounts of the boycott appearing in the national daily, the *Uganda Argus*, between March 1959 and April 1960. Unless otherwise stated, therefore, the *Uganda Argus* is the source of the factual material presented in this essay. I am grateful to Ali Mazrui, Robert Rotberg, Donald Rothchild, and Yash Ghai for helpful comments on an earlier draft of this paper.

[2] Among the early supporters were such prominent persons as I. K. Musazi, founder of the Uganda National Congress; Dr. E. Muwazi, secretary-general of the Uganda National Congress; D. Lubogo, president-general of the United Congress party; Godfrey Binaisa, secretary-general of the United Congress party; Eridadi M. K. Mulira, president of the Progressive party; Y. Sekabanja, president of the Uganda Nationalist Party Movement; A. D. Lubowa, member of the Lukiiko (Bugandan Parliament) and the editor of a Lugandan paper, *Uganda Eyogera*.

[3] *Uganda Argus*, 2 Apr. 1959.

lence, Kamya was sentenced to eighteen months' imprisonment. On 22 May, the Movement was declared an unlawful society and the whole of Buganda a disturbed area. Two days later leading members of the Movement were served with orders restricting them to their own *gombolola* (subcounty).

Soon after the proscription of the Movement, Mulira announced the formation of a new party—the Uganda Freedom Movement. This was little more than the old party under a new name. The sponsors of the "new" movement as well as the manifesto issued in its name made this evident. The next few months were to witness the bizarre spectacle of the repeated proscription and rebirth of the old Uganda National Movement under a variety of guises. Thus, the Uganda Freedom Movement gave way to the Uganda Freedom Convention, which was in turn converted into the Uganda Freedom Union and the Uganda League. The last were finally banned on 7 October.

By this time most of the original leaders of the Movement had been arrested, deported, or restricted. At the end of May, six prominent leaders of the Movement—Mulira, P. Muwanga, R. K. S. Muwagi, I. K. Musazi, H. Busungu, and Y. Sekabanja—had been detained by the police. At the subsequent inquiry on deportation at which the accused were defended by the eminent British lawyer Sir (now Lord) Hartley Shawcross, they were found guilty and deported to areas outside Buganda. Later in the year, in October 1959, Godfrey L. Binaisa, another leader, was arrested and also deported to an area outside Buganda.

Throughout this period of some eight months, the boycott remained largely effective. This was at least in part due to the continued campaign of intimidation, violence, and destruction of property waged by its supporters. The months of May, June, and July were particularly bad. Thousands of coffee trees were slashed, several houses were set on fire, and scores of cases of personal assault were reported. On 4 June a Roman Catholic school was set on fire because the scientific apparatus for the school had been purchased from a non-African shop. The same day the police opened fire on a mob in Katwe after a party of police, surrounded by several hundred Africans, had been stoned and shot upon. In the ensuing fight, nine policemen and seven demonstrators were seriously injured.

The Katwe incident, as it came to be known, became a major political issue and was at least in part responsible for the subsequent split in the Uganda National Congress—the faction led by A. Milton Obote supporting an inquiry into the incident and that led by Joseph W. Kiwanuka opposing. The sense of violence, fear, and insecurity increased in intensity with each day. Fear of the imminent collapse of law and order in Buganda, and renewed pressure from the Protectorate government, at last forced the Kabaka's government to come out openly and strongly against the intimidation and violence unleashed by the trade boycott. On 2 June, the Katikkiro (Prime Minister) of Buganda broadcast a statement calling for an end to violence and lawlessness and told people to buy their goods wherever and from whomever they wished. He said that his declaration had the authority of the Kabaka's government and of the Kabaka himself. This was followed by meetings addressed by the Katikkiro and his ministers urging the people to be peaceful.

These meetings apparently had little effect. The worst incident of the entire boycott occurred on 22 July when seven Africans were killed at Bulemezi, about twenty-five miles from Kampala, in a series of fights between supporters and opponents of the boycott, a division which coincided neatly with Gandan and non-Gandan. The next day the Kabaka (King) felt constrained to intervene personally and to condemn the violence at a special meeting of Buganda's Lukiiko (Parliament). The Lukiiko then passed a resolution urging chiefs and legislators to co-operate in bringing about an end to the continuing violence, and the Kabaka's government began to work actively with the central government in an effort to bring the Movement under control. It was this co-operation which was largely responsible for beating the "matoke ban" (an effort to disrupt trade in bananas) started by the organizers of the boycott.

Between late March and early September 1959 a total of 513 cases of intimidation and violence had been reported. However, the security situation began to improve about this time. In August seven Bugandan counties were released from the disturbed area order. By the end of November, the disturbed area declaration was lifted from the whole of Buganda except for Kyadondo and parts of Buddu Saza. Yet it was not until the middle of the next year that the intimidation and violence associated with the boycott were brought to an end. Meanwhile the pattern of threats and violence had undergone a slight change. In the first quarter of 1960, the supporters of the boycott shifted the focus of their campaign from their African opponents to the Asian traders. Asian-owned shops were burned and handmade bombs hurled into shops and public places. In February, an Asian trader was shot dead at Natwetwe, about seventy miles from Kampala. In the following month several attacks on Asian traders in the rural areas were reported, including another shooting incident. But by the end of May, the situation was becoming normal again, and the government of Uganda felt confident enough to lift almost all the restrictions imposed during the earlier phase of the boycott. By the end of July most of the persons imprisoned or deported in connection with the boycott had been allowed to return to their homes. The boycott may, therefore, be said to have come to a virtual end by the middle of 1960.

The broad outline of the history of the boycott has been sketched above; yet most of the fundamental questions remain unanswered. What was the boycott all about? Who were the men behind it? What were its consequences, both short-term and long-term? What in the final analysis were its achievements and failures?

The General Objectives

From its beginning, the Uganda National Movement pledged itself to pursue multiple and apparently contradictory objectives. Different leaders on different occasions stated that the aims of the Movement were to fight for the immediate independence of the country, to oppose any minority rights for the non-African communities resident in Uganda, to frustrate the working of the Wild Committee which had been established by the central government to consider the next steps in the constitutional evolution of Uganda toward independence,[4] to secure the economic independence of the country, and to safeguard the position of the hereditary rulers in the various kingdoms and districts of Uganda. In the months that followed, these aims crystallized into demands for immediate independence, Africanization of the economy, and the disbanding of the Wild Committee. Boycott was the instrument chosen to bring about the Africanization of the economy and the realization of the Movement's various political demands. But why should the Movement have clamored for the disbanding of the Wild Committee, which was set up to do precisely what its leaders were demanding, namely the speeding up of Uganda's progress toward independence? Similarly, it was surprising that the leaders of the Movement should have chosen to achieve their political objectives by a boycott of non-African shops rather than by the employment of more legitimate means. In order to understand the Movement's choice of strategy and objectives, it is necessary to look briefly into the history of Buganda's relationship with the central government of Uganda.[5]

[4] The Constitutional Committee (Wild Committee) was appointed by the Governor in 1958 to consider the situation arising from Buganda's boycott in 1958 of direct elections to the Legislative Council and to propose the next steps in Uganda's advance to self-government. It was also asked to advise on the question of the special representation of non-African minorities in Uganda. It was composed of thirteen members of the Legislative Council and two others, making ten Africans and five non-Africans in all.

[5] For a more detailed treatment of Buganda's relationship with the Protectorate government, see D. Anthony Low and R. Cranford Pratt, *Buganda and British*

The 1950's were a critical time for Buganda. Hitherto, in contrast to other kingdoms and districts, Buganda had enjoyed a special relationship with the Protectorate government. This relationship was symbolized by the 1900 Buganda Agreement.[6] Over the years, the Ganda had not only succeeded in retaining and consolidating traditional institutions such as the Kabaka and the Lukiiko, but had also enjoyed a wide measure of internal autonomy. This factor, coupled with the concentration of wealth and educated manpower in the kingdom and its geographical location, had made Buganda the dominant region in Uganda. It had also helped to create a strong sense of Gandan nationalism, which was nourished and sustained by ancient tribal institutions and rites. The *modus operandi* worked out between the Protectorate and the Kabaka's government was subject to serious strains from time to time; but it was reasonably successful in integrating Buganda into the rest of the country.

It was this delicate arrangement which seemed to be threatened by the spirit of nationalism which swept through the colonial world during the post-World War II period. The liberation of Asian countries from colonial rule had stimulated the growth of national movements in most African colonies. But the Gandan response to these ideas of nationalism and independence had characteristically been ambiguous. Many individual Ganda were caught up in this world-wide anticolonial movement and took the initiative in establishing radical, nationalist political parties such as the Uganda National Congress—Ganda such as Abu Mayanja, Joseph W. Kiwanuka, Musazi, and Mulira were prominent among early nationalists in Uganda. But the nationalist outlook represented by these individuals was in potential conflict with the interests of Buganda as viewed from Mengo, the seat of the Kabaka. The ambivalent attitude of the Kabaka's government toward nationalist movements was a manifestation of Buganda's parochialism—the fear of being submerged in a wider entity coupled with a refusal to forego Bugandan hegemony. No Gandan could entirely resist the pull of this mystique; the few who attempted to do so soon found themselves in the political wilderness. It has been aptly remarked that "in Uganda political parties of a populist, nationalist, anti-imperialist type, have constantly splintered to pieces on the rock of Buganda's

---

Over-Rule, 1900–1955 (London, 1960). The more recent developments are discussed in Donald Rothchild and Michael Rogin, "Uganda," in Gwendolen M. Carter (ed.), *National Unity and Regionalism in Eight African States* (Ithaca, 1966), 337-440; Audrey I. Richards, "Epilogue," in Lloyd A. Fallers (ed.), *The King's Men* (Oxford, 1964), 357-94.

[6] See Low and Pratt, *Buganda*, 84-159, for detailed discussion of this agreement.

separatism."[7] The result was that by the late 1950's there were several small parties in Buganda clustered around a few prominent Gandan politicians.

This conflict between orthodox nationalism and Bugandan traditionalism could only be resolved in an independent Uganda dominated by Buganda. However, as independence drew nearer, this outcome became more and more uncertain. Faced by this prospect, the Ganda acted in an uncertain and contradictory manner, clamoring for immediate independence and at the same time subverting every move which seemed to lead in the direction of independence for the larger Uganda. This was the explanation of Buganda's boycott of the 1958 elections. This is also the clue to the Movement's demand for independence and its simultaneous opposition to the Wild Committee.

The Uganda National Movement represented an attempt at this critical juncture to unify the Ganda in an effort to reassert their dominance in Uganda. From the outset, it was largely successful in bringing within its fold a wide range of the political parties and personalities of Buganda. It has already been mentioned that almost all prominent Ganda politicians, with the exception of leaders of the Democratic party and the Obote-Uganda National Congress wing, associated themselves with the Movement and the trade boycott. The original sponsors of the Movement included traditionalists such as Sekabanja, the president of the Uganda Nationalist Party Movement, a short-lived Buganda-based party; nationalists of varying convictions such as Musazi, the founder of the Uganda National Congress who, earlier in the year, was expelled from the party which he had founded; and younger moderate nationalists like Binaisa, secretary general of the United Congress party, which had left the National Congress Progressive party, "a party of the responsible and leading citizens."[8] In addition to these groups, the Movement drew support from groups of emerging African merchants.

The success of the organizers in welding these diverse elements into a united movement can only be explained by Gandan fears of being left out of the march toward independence. At the same time, as we shall explain, the boycott of non-African shops was potentially an immensely popular issue. The heterogeneous nature of the Movement's activists was also responsible for the apparently contradictory objectives of the Movement. The nationalists within the Movement were more preoccupied with quickening the pace of progress toward independence. Immediate independence was the theme of many speeches made by Binaisa, Musazi, and Mulira. On the other hand, the tradi-

[7] Richards in *The King's Men*, 378.

[8] David Apter, *The Political Kingdom in Uganda* (Princeton, 1961), 337.

tionalist element within the Movement was more anxious to reassert the dominance of Buganda and to preserve the position of the Kabaka's government. Its fears of the attempts then being made to prepare Uganda for self-government through direct elections to the Legislative Council led them to oppose the working of the Wild Committee, to advocate the abolition of the Legislative Council, and to seek safeguards for Buganda's traditional rulers.

Before we turn to a consideration of the demands made by the leaders of the Movement it is necessary to clarify the role played by the Kabaka's government in this episode. From the outset, the government of Buganda was placed in a quandary: It was in obvious sympathy with many of the demands made by the Movement, such as the preservation of the dignity and status of the hereditary rulers and opposition to the Wild Committee. On the other hand, as the governing body in Buganda, it could not condone the flouting of law and order by the activists. The exact role played by Mengo in the establishment and subsequent activities of the Movement is still a matter of conjecture. It has been alleged that the Kabaka's government gave strong covert support to the Movement in its earlier phase.[9] At any rate, the officials of the central government were convinced that the Kabaka's government had never been earnest in its condemnation and suppression of the activities of the Movement.[10] Whatever may have been its attitude at the start of the boycott, there is no doubt that the Mengo authorities were badly shaken by the rapidly spreading waves of violence and terrorism in the country, and before long threw the weight of their authority and resources behind the attempts to bring the boycott to a speedy end.

The Political Objectives of the Movement

How legitimate and relevant were the Movement's declared political objectives of independence and opposition to special rights for the non-African minorities? Long before the boycott, the government of

[9] Rothchild and Rogin, among others, have taken this line; they write, "What then were the roles of the Chiefs and of the Kabaka's Government? Although they had not organised the boycott, they gave it strong covert support"; in Carter, *National Unity*, 355.

[10] Richards in *The King's Men*, 371-72, states: "The Government believed that the Kabaka's Ministers were implicated, since the Katikkiro did not formally intervene to stop disorder till 10 April, when the boycott of Asian shops had become very effective, and since two Ministers, Mr. Sempa and Mr. Basudde, were financial contributors to a new vernacular paper *Munasi* ("The Citizen"), which supported the boycott."

the Protectorate was publicly committed to a policy of moving Uganda swiftly toward independence. Indeed, as we have seen, the Wild Committee was specifically charged with the responsibility of proposing the next steps in the constitutional evolution of Uganda into a self-governing state. The most important national parties such as the Uganda National Congress, the Democratic party, and the Uganda People's Union, had pledged support for the Wild Committee. All of these parties were also committed to securing rapid independence for Uganda. In the circumstances, it is difficult to see how the emergence of yet another party could have significantly contributed to this objective. Indeed, as we shall show later, the Movement may in the end have delayed the achievement of independence.

What of the other claim that the Movement was created to oppose the granting of minority rights to the non-African communities? It is indeed true that the Wild Committee was required by its terms of reference to consider the issue of special rights for non-African minorities. But it would be difficult to argue that there was a need to create a new organization and to impose an economic boycott in order to express opposition to the principle of special rights for minorities. Although it is true that certain influential elements in the non-African communities favored the establishment of some kind of special rights for minorities, the issue was hardly ever in doubt. All the national political parties were strongly opposed to the granting of any kind of minority rights, as indeed was the Uganda Action Group, a pressure group formed by a number of progressive and enlightened young Asians. Even the more conservative Central Council of Indian Associations, which may be considered more representative of Asian public opinion in Uganda, came out in favor of a common roll and against reserved seats for minorities. It is therefore difficult to believe that the Movement organized the trade boycott solely or even mainly to force the hand of the government in the interests of a democracy undiluted by minority rights or safeguards. On the contrary, the violence and intimidation unleashed by the trade boycott may have strengthened the position of the conservative elements among the non-African communities who were demanding special minority safeguards. It certainly gave them a reason for so doing.

What, then, were the real issues which united such a disparate group of individuals? And against what was the Movement protesting? It has already been suggested that the Movement came into being at a time when the special status enjoyed by Buganda was being threatened by the transformation of the Protectorate into an independent, unitary state, when the Ganda were divided into a number of small, ineffective parties formed around a few individuals, and when the Kabaka's government was engaged in a prolonged conflict with the central government over the nature of future constitutional developments. The Uganda National Movement was created to forge unity among the Ganda and to enable them to preserve their identity and protect their vital interests. Hence its opposition to the Wild Committee and to the Legislative Council, and its concern with the prestige and status of the traditional rulers.

The Economic Objectives

The strategy adopted by the Movement to further its aims was significant and imaginative. The boycott of non-African businesses, and particularly those of Asians, was expected to achieve several objectives. In the first place, because of the widespread dislike of Asian traders throughout Uganda, it was hoped that a trade boycott would command popular support. In this expectation the organizers were not disappointed. As has been suggested, the boycott was an immediate success throughout large parts of Buganda. But, contrary to the expectations of the organizers, it did not take root in areas outside Buganda, except to a limited extent in parts of the Eastern Province. Secondly, it was hoped that the boycott, by creating economic instability, would compel the government of the Protectorate to make concessions to the political demands of the Movement. Finally, and most importantly, the boycott was intended to be used to facilitate the entry of Africans into the world of commerce and industry, hitherto dominated by non-Africans, especially Asians. Thus the Movement must also be seen as an expression of Gandan economic nationalism, and the boycott as a weapon to end the dominance of foreigners in the economy of the country. In order to understand the full force of this argument, it is necessary to provide some background on the position of Asians in Uganda's society and economy.[11]

Although the boycott was directed against all non-African shops, and, as we shall see later, a few European firms like the Uganda Breweries and the Kampala and District Bus Services were hit hard, it was the Asian traders who were from the outset the primary target of the organizers. This was in part due to Asian dominance of wholesale and retail trade. But it was also a reflection of strong anti-Asian sentiments prevailing in the country.

Although individual traders from the Indian subcontinent had been trading in Uganda since the middle of the last century, Asian

[11] For a detailed discussion of the "Asian problem" in East Africa, see Dharam P. Ghai (ed.), *Portrait of a Minority: Asians in East Africa* (Nairobi, 1965), 91-111, 129-54.

settlement in any substantial numbers began only after the completion of the Kenya-Uganda Railway in 1905. By 1910, the number of Asian residents in Uganda had reached a figure of 2,000; this had risen to 13,026 by 1931, 36,300 by 1948, and 72,900 by 1959.[12] Soon after their arrival, the Asians established themselves firmly in the retail and wholesale trades. Asian traders became a familiar feature of the urban and rural landscape. With the growth of African-grown cash crops, which consisted principally of cotton until the 1930's, the Asian merchants combined their retail trade with produce marketing. In the 1920's and 1930's, they extended their interests to cotton ginning, so that by 1924 Asians came to own 100 ginneries out of a total of 164 and by 1930 they handled 68 per cent of the cotton crop.[13] With the development of marketing boards during World War II, and the growth of co-operatives in the 1950's and 1960's, the Asian role in the cotton and coffee industry was greatly diminished. But throughout much of the history of cotton and other cash crops, the Asian merchants played a key role in their collection, processing, distribution, and export. In combination with their dominance of retail trade in the townships and rural areas, this role brought them into intimate commercial contact with large sections of the African population.

Inevitably, this dominance led to a widespread feeling against the Asian mercantile community. There were complaints, often justified, of unscrupulous dealings, exploitation, short weights, and overcharging. Between the world wars, there were repeated clashes between African peasant growers and Asian ginners. This hostility was exacerbated by the failure of peasants to understand the complexities of the international markets for agricultural products. Often the blame for fluctuations in world prices of cotton and coffee was laid at the door of the Asian merchants. It was natural that Africans were hostile toward Asians, Uganda not being unique in this respect. Indeed the prevalence of a deep hatred against alien mercantile groups is a world-wide phenomenon, ranging from Jews in Europe to Chinese and Indian minorities in much of Southeast Asia.

It was therefore natural that, to a group of politicians casting about for a popular rallying cry, the boycott of Asian-owned shops should appear obvious. Not only was the boycott of Asian shops a popular cause, but it could also prove to be an immensely profitable one. And there is no denying the fact that among the supporters of the boycott there was a generous sprinkling of opportunists who saw in it a chance to make a quick fortune. Allied to this group was a much bigger group consisting of African petty traders struggling to establish a foothold

[13] L. W. Hollingsworth, *The Asians of East Africa* (London, 1960), 71.
[12] Statistical Abstract, Uganda Government, various years.

in the highly competitive world of commerce. For them the boycott could prove an easy and painless method of effecting African entry.

The post-war period had seen a rapid increase in the number of African petty traders. The sustained commodity boom of the 1940's and 1950's, increasing urbanization and the spread of education, and heightening ambitions had attracted large numbers of recruits to trade and commerce. In his study of the kingdom of Buganda, David Apter vividly describes the growth of an African trading class: "African trading outlets developed in Katwe, near Mengo, the seat of the Buganda government, and the palace, and Wandegeya, adjacent to Makerere College. Large numbers of petrol sellers, bakers, and small printers were packed in cheek by jowl with Asians in crowded slum conditions." Again he writes, "No longer were unsuccessful and partially successful traders a small group allied with the farmers. Their ranks were swelled. Each small trading stall and 'duka' now became a focal point of organization. Farmers who bought their grains and implements at these dukas or came to repair their bicycles remained to discuss matters of cotton and coffee prices. The result was that an increase in economic transactions also meant an increase in political organization."[14] The heightened sense of grievances and increased political consciousness on the part of African traders was undoubtedly an important element in the origin and subsequent sustenance of the boycott movement, though, as we shall have occasion to remark later, the very success of the boycott was to generate intra-African conflict.

One question remains: Why did the boycott fail to take root in areas outside Buganda? It has already been shown that, at the outset, the entire Movement became associated exclusively with the Ganda. We have seen that the leadership of the Movement came wholly from Buganda. In addition it was envisaged by its organizers as at least in part a vehicle for the furtherance of Buganda's special political interests, and the latter were to some extent at variance with the political objectives of the rest of the country. Thus the confusion of political with economic objectives, or at any rate the simultaneous pursuit of both by the Ganda, must be held primarily responsible for the surprising failure of the boycott movement to make much headway in areas outside Buganda. Also, it must not be forgotten that the African commercial class outside Buganda was relatively small and unsophisticated. The Africanization of the economy was to assume primacy in public policy soon after the attainment of independence. The trade boycott waged by the Ganda may be looked upon as a pioneering and, as it turned out, a premature effort in that exercise. But political leaders at the time were too preoccupied with constitutional and political

[14] Apter, *Political Kingdom*, 240.

bickering to devote much thought to problems of economic transformation. Thus it turned out that, despite its obvious potential as a rallying cry, the trade boycott remained to the end an essentially Bugandan affair.

Economic and Political Consequences of the Boycott

The boycott had considerable short-term economic repercussions, and it succeeded in a limited way in advancing the role of Africans in the economy of the country; but it failed to bring about any major transformation in the racial pattern of economic activity. It did provide African aspirants to commerce in Buganda with unique opportunities to establish or consolidate their businesses. Because of fear or intimidation there also was a considerable exodus of Asian traders from smaller townships to larger trading areas in and outside Buganda. African petty traders did indeed establish themselves in many parts of Buganda. But, typically, their economic mortality rate proved very high. And many of those who survived the birth pangs of their businesses went bankrupt once competition with Asian traders was revived. The reasons for the failure of a sustained upsurge in African commercial activity are not really different from the ones which have frustrated government-sponsored attempts to enlarge the African role in trade and commerce in the post independence period. These derived from lack of commercial acumen and know-how, and lack of capital. In addition, the very operation of the boycott made it difficult for African traders to obtain credit and supplies on easy terms. Nevertheless, the boycott did serve a useful educational function for large numbers of budding African entrepreneurs.

Actually, two trades saw a flowering of African entrepreneurship. The effective boycott of the Kampala and District Bus Services was a boon to African taxi and small passenger transport operators. The marked Africanization of the transport sector in Uganda originates from boycott days. Similarly, the boycott of European-type beer gave a stimulus to the production and consumption of local brews. It is quite likely that the tastes acquired for the stronger indigenous brew survived the demise of the boycott and may well have resulted in a permanent boost in the demand for the indigenous product. This, however, probably was a dubious blessing, as witness the determined efforts made by the government in recent years to prohibit or, at any rate, to bring under control the production and consumption of African-manufactured beer.

The minor advances recorded above were, however, greatly outweighed by the adverse economic effects of the boycott. Many of the established African traders who had built up close commercial ties with Asian businessmen suddenly found themselves cut off from their normal sources of both credit and merchandise. Those who dealt in the boycotted goods were hit particularly hard. The most obvious example is that of bar-owners, an occupation peculiarly suited to African enterprise. It was for this reason that almost from the outset there developed a bitter dispute between African bar owners and the organizers of the boycott. Although in the beginning many African bar operators were persuaded to close their bars, they soon had second thoughts, and many bars were reopened despite the threats of supporters of the boycott. Indeed, many of the violent incidents reported in connection with the boycott involved brawls and bottle-throwing in bars which continued to operate in defiance of the trade boycott.

The Africans who suffered most from the operation of the boycott were the individuals who lost their jobs. The acting Labor Commissioner estimated that by 14 July 1959, four months after the start of the boycott, the number of people rendered jobless by the boycott had risen to 10,000. Most affected were employees of breweries and soft drink bottlers, the transport industry, and, of course, the retail and wholesale traders. It is not surprising, therefore, that the unemployed became the most vociferous opponents of the boycott. On 12 April 1959, over 150 unemployed persons in the Kampala area signed a petition asking the Kabaka to intervene to stop the boycott. Later, during May, these unintended victims of the boycott organized a mass meeting in Naguru, near Kampala, where appeals were made for "determined and united efforts" to end the boycott.[15] It is thus ironic that the very people whom the boycott was intended to benefit turned into its most bitter opponents. As we shall see, this was an important factor in the ultimate failure of the boycott.

There were other ways in which Africans suffered from the boycott. There were scores of incidents of arson, destruction of livestock, uprooting of valuable coffee and banana trees, and loss of life. In a wider sense, everybody suffered as a consumer: first because of the restricted choice of goods and services, and second through the increase in price of the available commodities. Moreover, the country suffered a setback from the reduced revenue for both the Protectorate and the Kabaka's government brought about by the reduction in sales of beer and imported dutiable goods as well as through a general fall in people's incomes. It was revealed at the budget session of 1960 that the trade boycott had caused losses of about £750,000 in Protectorate revenues. The latter in turn reduced its grant to the Kabaka's government, and thus the consequences of the boycott were painfully brought

15 *Uganda Argus,* 18 May 1959.

home to the employees of the Kabaka's government—each had to accept a ten per cent cut in his salary. The fall in revenue of the central government also necessitated a reduction or a slowing down in the expansion of social and economic services.

The boycott and the accompanying violence, intimidation, and destruction of property also had a traumatic effect on the Asian community. Many feared that independence would bring worse developments. The resultant insecurity and widespread fear led to a flight of capital which assumed enormous proportions as independence drew nearer. Apart from this, many investment decisions were either shelved or postponed. In addition, a few firms were forced to close down: An important example was the closing down of the non-African-owned gramophone record and battery factory with a total investment amounting to about £200,000. The reason given was that the sales of records and batteries had been affected by the boycott.

Many Asian traders, especially those in rural trading centers, also suffered considerable hardship. In the course of the hearings preceding the deportation of the six Movement leaders in June, evidence of Asians being deprived of water and milk was produced; and we have already seen that during later stages of the boycott, attacks on Asian traders became frequent. One effect of the Movement was to drive Asian traders from smaller rural areas in Buganda to larger townships, particularly to Kampala and Jinja, and to areas outside Buganda, to the Eastern and Western Provinces. A spokesman of the Indian Merchants Chamber stated on 8 March 1960, almost exactly a year after the origin of the boycott, that nearly half of the Asian traders in the rural areas of Buganda had been forced to move elsewhere. At Kwampe, four miles from Kampala, out of thirty-one Asian traders, only two or three remained. In Mukono, there had been about twenty-six Asian traders, but all of them had vacated the area by the end of April.[16] Many who moved out of rural areas had to sell their property and stocks at very low prices; others suffered through reduction or cessation of business. On the whole, however, although there was financial hardship among Asian traders, few suffered genuine poverty. As in all encounters of this nature, the greater resourcefulness and mobility of Asians enabled them to emerge from the trial relatively unscathed.

Conclusion

What were the political achievements of the boycott? Uganda attained independence in August 1962; but it would be rash to credit the Move-

[16] *Kenya Weekly News,* 11 Mar. 1960.

ment with its achievement. By creating fear and insecurity among the immigrants, as well as by diverting attention from constitutional progress, the Movement may well have delayed the achievement of independence. It is possible that the strong opposition of the Movement had some effect on the recommendations of the Wild Committee. But, here again, we have seen that all the Africans serving on the Committee had expressed opposition to the principle of special safeguards for minorities. Indeed the representatives of the Asians—the most important minority—had themselves lost faith in the efficacy of such devices as protectors of minority interests. It is, therefore, equally plausible to argue that the activities of the Movement had little effect on the recommendations of the Wild Committee regarding minority safeguards.

The Movement was certainly successful in cementing Gandan unity, though even here it is necessary to point out that several prominent Gandan politicians to the end remained bitter opponents of the boycott. However, the newly found unity among warring factions and ideological opponents did not survive for long. The divisions among the Ganda reappeared and continued until they were momentarily resolved by the emergence of the Kabaka Yekka (Kabaka Alone) movement in 1961, which, though like the Uganda National Movement short-lived, proved far more successful in obtaining for the kingdom major political and economic concessions at the time of independence.

On the whole, the Movement failed in its economic objectives. Its professed political demands were realized in time, but it has been the burden of the author's argument that the Movement cannot claim much glory for their achievement. Was the Movement doomed to failure in its economic aspirations? Was its choice of strategy at fault? Boycotts are easy to start but difficult to sustain. For their prolonged effectiveness, they must either be backed by intense discipline and emotion, or be supported by a reign of terror. The Buganda trade boycott lacked the first and could never really achieve the second. The efforts to secure compliance through violence and intimidation soon provoked swift and stern response from the government, and, in time, lost it the support of those who might have been expected to sympathize with the Movement. Since Africans turned out to be the main victims of the boycott, the expected racial solidarity never materialized. To the end, the Uganda National Movement and the trade boycott remained very much a tribal affair. In its economic manifestation, the Movement is of interest primarily as an expression of long simmering resentment and frustration against an alien trading minority. In its political aspects, it was an attempt to create unity among disunited Ganda to safeguard the interests of the tribe at a time of momentous constitutional change.

NIGERIAN POLITICS AND THE

GENERAL STRIKE OF 1964

ROBERT MELSON

Not since 1945, when workers struck for forty-five days, had a general strike in Nigeria been as successful and as portentous as the General Strike of June 1964. Starting on the first day of June and continuing for two weeks, the strike brought the economic life of Nigeria to a halt. From 4,200,000 to 14,000,000 man-days were lost in this period.[1] To understand the significance of the strike, one must locate it in the sequence of political crises which beset Nigeria after independence.[2]

In retrospect it seems clear that the crises in the political sector stemmed from the coincidence of regional, ethnic, and economic cleavages. Thus the Northern region was populated largely by Hausa-speaking peoples, whose per capita income and level of educational

The author wishes to acknowledge the financial support received from the Carnegie Corporation, the Foreign Area Fellowship Program, and the National Science Foundation, which made possible a field trip to Nigeria in 1964–65. He would also like to thank the Department of Political Science and the African Studies Center at Michigan State University for their generous support. Above all the author wishes to thank Professors Richard L. Sklar and Howard Wolpe for invaluable criticism.

[1] This estimate assumes that the number of strikers equalled the number of wage earners. According to Ministry of Labour publications such as the *Annual Report of the Federal Ministry of Labour*, the number of wage earners in units hiring over 10 workers was 300,000 and the total number of wage earners was estimated to be 1,000,000. See the reports for 1961, 1962, and 1964.

[2] For details, see below, James O'Connell, "The Fragility of Stability: The Fall of the Nigerian Federal Government, 1966," and references there, 1012-34. See also William H. Friedland, "Paradoxes of African Trade Unionism: Organizational Chaos and Political Potential," *Africa Report*, X (June 1965), 6-10; Richard L. Sklar, "Contradictions in the Nigerian Political System," *Journal of Modern African Studies*, III (1965), 201-13.

attainment was significantly lower than that of Western region Yoruba peoples and Eastern region Ibo peoples. Moreover, in each region there existed minorities who felt that they were being discriminated against by the majority peoples, on economic and political grounds. Real and felt differences in culture, economic development, and political power led to interregional and inter-ethnic competition both in the economy and in the polity. Such competition came to be known as "tribalism" and it was felt that tribalism was disintegrating the political system. We shall contend in this paper that however bitter tribalism may have been at the time of the strike, tribalism did not cause the strike.

In trying to get at some of the causes of the strike, one must consider the relationship between the political elites and the strikers. Here, the differences were not tribal ones, but, broadly speaking, those of class and status. We shall try to show below how objective differences in income and life styles between workers and political elites were perceived by workers, and how this affected their willingness to strike.

Tribalism and conflict among party elites did not cause the strike. On the contrary, the relationship among these elements, if there were one, lay in the possible consequences that the strike may have had for the tribalism issue, and thus, indirectly, for the crises among the party elite. It was not in its causes but in its implicit consequences that the strike took on meaning and significance.

In the political climate of crisis and tribalism, the General Strike, paradoxically, seemed to be a hopeful event. Seeing in the strike the manifestation of class conflict crosscutting tribe and region, people who were worried about the effects of tribalism on Nigerian integration suggested that in the long run, albeit the very long run, class struggle might halt the process of balkanization and dissolution.

Implicit in such questions and suggestions were at least three assumptions. First, it was assumed that the workers went on strike because of their consciousness of class. Second, it was assumed that tribalism was incompatible with class consciousness, and that if workers struck against the party and governmental elites, they would cease to support such elites in the political sphere. Third, if workers withheld support from political elites, in the long run such elites would be compelled to make appeals on economic, not just regional and tribal grounds. Since we have no data with which to test this third assumption and since, in any case, it is dependent on the first two, we shall mainly concern ourselves in this paper with testing the first two assumptions—that the strike was a manifestation of class conflict and that workers who were class conscious rejected tribalism in politics.

There is historical evidence and survey data collected immediately after the strike which can help to clarify both assumptions. In examining the assumption of the workers' motives in going on strike, we will attempt to show that, from the beginning, labor leaders had formulated the strike in more than simply economic terms; moreover, the extent to which the rank and file saw the strike in class terms can be partially surmised from the survey data. As to the question of how workers viewed tribalism, and how this affected their support for the political elites, the timing of the strike provides a clue. The strike came only five months before the critical federal election of December, 1964. In preparation for this election, Marxists in the labor movement launched a labor party. It can be assumed that to the extent that workers were willing to support such a party, which was not based on tribal or regional sentiments, they were willing to translate their strike motives into political motives and opposition to the regional elites.

Before turning to a description of the strike and a discussion of the two assumptions, let us consider the principal actors in the drama —the workers, their organizations, and their employers.

In this paper the term "workers" signifies wage earners. As of 1963 about 800,000 to 1,000,000 Nigerians were wage earners; about 4,000,-000, or 10 per cent of the population, lived in towns having 20,000 or more inhabitants [3] Assuming that most wage earners lived in towns, about one quarter of the urban population consisted of wage earners. This is not counting their dependents.

Taking as urban areas only towns with a population of 20,000 or more, wage earners constituted about 30 per cent of the population of Lagos, 5 per cent of the urban population of the Northern region, and 20 per cent of the urban population of the Eastern region. [4] Thus, although the wage-earning population constituted at most 3 per cent of the Nigerian population, in urban centers such as Lagos, Port Har-

[3] The 800,000 to 1,000,000 figure is quoted by National Manpower Board, *Manpower Situation in Nigeria 1963* (Lagos, 1963). The 4,000,000 figure is used by the *Annual Abstract of Statistics 1963* (Lagos, 1963). The population figure assumes a rate of growth of 2 to 4 per cent from the 1953 census figures. In 1953, the population of Nigeria was, to the nearest ten million, 30,000,000 and the population in urban areas of 20,000 or more was, to the nearest million, 3,000,000.

[4] These figures are correct to the nearest 10 per cent. Starting with the 1963 census we have assumed a rate of growth of 2 to 4 per cent. The low figure for the Western region can be explained by two factors. First, Lagos draws many Yoruba wage earners. Second, the Yoruba Western region, unlike other regions of Nigeria, is largely populated by traditional towns whose growth preceded the modern wage-earning economy. The generalization that about one-fourth of urban centers consists of wage earners is therefore not true for the Western region without Lagos.

court, and Zaria, wage earners constituted a more sizable proportion.

Simple numbers tell us a great deal about the political significance of the workers. From the perspective of the political elites who needed numbers to win elections, it was clear that workers were an insignificant segment of the population. It comes as no surprise, therefore, that in the deliberations of the major regional parties in the full bloom of regionalism, workers and their leaders carried very little weight, when compared with peasants. To those politicians who had a long-range view of Nigerian developments, however, workers were somewhat more important.

To Marxist labor leaders especially, it was clear that, in time, the ratio between peasants and workers would shift in favor of workers. For the "Youths" (as Marxist labor leaders were called), Lagos with its urban workers was a future Nigeria writ small. If they could capture the wage-earning vote in Lagos, the "Youths" argued, economic interest and not the tribalism of the peasants would be "the coming thing." The strike of 1964 seemed to give the "Youths" an opportunity to prove their point.

However, the "Youths" were not the only labor leaders. In 1964, there were approximately 300,000 trade union members organized into about 300 active unions, which were in turn organized into four superordinate central labor body organizations. These were the United Labour Congress, the Nigerian Workers' Council, the Nigerian Trade Union Congress, and the Labour Unity Front. The leadership of the labor movement during and after the strike closely corresponded to that of the four central labor bodies.

Cutting across the four central labor bodies were two major factions. One was the "Youths"; the other, for want of a better term, we shall call the "Neutralists." The "Youths" were the Marxist, anti-federalist admirers of Ghana under Nkrumah, determined to launch a labor party.[5] The "Neutralists" were, on the whole, not explicitly Marxist. They had made their peace with the federalist system, and they tried strenuously to keep the labor movement out of politics. Although it is a gross oversimplification, in this paper we shall identify the Nigerian Trade Union Congress and the Labour Unity Front with the "Youths" and the United Labour Congress and the Nigerian Workers' Council with the "Neutralists."

The vulnerability of government, stemming from its heavy involvement in the economy, was not lost on the labor leaders. On the eve of the strike, the various governments—federal, regional, and local—em-

---

[5] For a more extensive discussion, see Robert Melson, "Marxists in the Nigerian Labour Movement" (unpublished Ph.D. dissertation, Massachusetts Institute of Technology, 1967).

ployed 54 per cent of all Nigerian wage earners. Any widespread unrest in the labor movement would necessarily involve some level of government. (Adding to the problem was the fact that European-owned private firms employed another 38 per cent of the wage-earning population.[6]) Workers asked: "It is the Nigerian government; why do the politicians not raise our wages?" It was bad enough that the government could not raise wages; at the same time, it was paying European-type salaries to higher civil servants. Furthermore, if the government could not support Nigerian workers in their demands for higher wages from European, mostly British, employers, then it laid itself open to accusations of corruption and "neo-colonialism." Such was the situation on the eve of the General Strike.

By 1964, four years after independence, Marxists and non-Marxists had reached a high level of consensus and unity of purpose. It is possible that nothing would have happened had the "Youths" and "Neutralists" refused to co-operate in fomenting the strike.

In what follows, we shall describe: (1) the changed political climate after independence which made possible joint action among the various labor factions; (2) the events of September 1963 and the formation of the Joint Action Committee and the Morgan Commission; (3) the Joint Action Committee memorandum to the Morgan Commission and the sequence of events leading up to the strike action itself; and (4) some observations on the strike. In a concluding section, we shall return to the motives which led workers to strike and shall consider the political consequences of the strike.

The peaceful struggle for independence had some unforeseen and unintended consequences for post-independence politics. The colonial system left behind, not only regionalism, the administrative and political structure highly resented by the unitary nationalists, but also a class of privileged civil servants and parliamentarians. Ironically, many of their privileges had been won by popular strikes in the 1940's and 1950's.[7] With the exit of the colonial power, the difference between the standard of living of this privileged class and that of the mass of Nigerian workers became a point of great resentment among the workers and their leaders.

During the 1950's most of the leaders of the "Neutralist" faction had co-operated with federal and regional governments and had sup-

[6] See Table 3.6 of the *Annual Abstract of Statistics 1964* (Lagos, 1965).

[7] For example, the "Emerson Must Go" strike of 1959, led by Michael Imoudu, forced the retirement of Sir Ralf Emerson as chairman of the Nigerian Railway Corporation and his replacement by a Nigerian, Dr. Michael Ikejianni. See *Report of the Elias Commission of Inquiry* (Lagos, 1960).

ported their affiliation to the International Confederation of Free Trade Unions. By the early 1960's, however, the neutralist United Labour Congress split into two factions, both still supporting the confederation, but one increasingly anti-regionalist. The issue uniting "Youth" and "Neutralist" and, indeed, the whole labor movement, was the gap in wages and life styles between the ordinary workers and the political class which profited from the regionalist system.

Therefore, it is not surprising that in 1962, barely seven months after independence, the United Labour Congress, the faction affiliated with the ICFTU and opposed to the "Youths," published a pamphlet indicating that, at least on domestic issues, its views were not far from those of the anti-ICFTU and anti-regime factions:

> Independence Day, October first 1960, freed us from colonial domination. It did not, unfortunately, free us automatically from colonial institutions. The edifice of privilege remains; only its proprietors are different. . . . This situation, in which a senior official may receive fifty times the salary of a junior official, or a daily labourer, is politically explosive and economically intolerable. . . . The United Labour Congress of Nigeria will fight against the continuation of this exploitation of class by class as fervently as it fought against imperialism. . . .[8]

When their grievances were articulated in terms of economic class rather than international politics, all factions could unite on a program.

As a result, in September 1963, the United Labour Congress, the "Youths" in the Nigerian Trade Union Congress and the Labour Unity Front, as well as others, came together to form the Joint Action Committee. This committee pressured the government to form the Morgan Commission, the terms of reference of which included the examination of wage structures in the governmental and private sectors of the economy.

The formation of the Joint Action Committee came after a year of attempts to persuade the federal and regional governments to negotiate a new wage agreement. By September 1963, the United Labour Congress decided "to prepare for industrial action":

> We know from experience that very often Nigerian employers including government, will always wait for workers' patience to be exhausted and attract industrial action before the workers are taken seriously about their demands. . . .[9]

On September 16, representatives of all labor factions met at the

---

[8] United Labour Congress Policy Statement, "A Programme for the Future" (Lagos, May 25, 1962).

[9] United Labour Congress memorandum, Sept. 6, 1963, signed by L. L. Borha. The memo was distributed to all central labor bodies, including the Labour Unity Front. It called for a meeting of "all unions to signify their support for a country-wide industrial action."

invitation of the United Labour Congress at its headquarters and agreed to form "a joint action committee in order to prosecute the wage issue."[10]

By that time, too, the United Labour Congress had made a distinction, crucial in this context, between the "government" and the "authority of the state":

> The Governments are unwilling to grapple courageously with the basic and fundamental question raised by the Congress' demands . . . it is necessary to re-emphasize that the Congress did not address its demands to the Governments necessarily as employers, but as the authority of the state which not only has direct responsibility to protect workers in all sectors [an allusion to the private sector] . . . but also the obligation to bring about a more rational economic structure the first steps towards which in our view is a complete overhaul of the existing colonial wage structure. . . .[11]

By making this distinction, the United Labour Congress came closer to the position of the Nigerian Trade Union Congress and the "Youths" in general. Labor was now ready to confront the government, not as an employer, but as "the authority of the state." Under such a slogan, both the "Youths" who wanted to destroy that authority and the less radical trade unionists could and did unite.

By September 19, 1963, the United Labour Congress, with the concurrence of the Joint Action Committee, called on the government to appoint:

> a high-powered commission for the carrying out of an upward revision of salaries and wages . . . the complete overhaul of the existing colonial wage structure . . . the introduction of a national minimum wage and the abolition of the zonal wage-rates and the daily rated labour systems.

The Joint Action Committee warned that if such a commission was not appointed by September 25, it would call on all its member unions to go out on strike "with effect from 00 hours 27 September 1963."[12] With

[10] Memorandum from H. P. Adebola, president of the United Labour Congress, to affiliated unions, Sept. 1963. Note that on Sept. 16 the term, "joint action committee" was still used informally, but by Sept. 17 a meeting was called under the direction of the "Joint Action Committee." From Sept. 21, the informal Alliance between the United Labour Congress and the other central labor bodies was called "JAC." JAC 1/63. Note that on the initial "memorandum committee" of the Joint Action Committee at least four of the ten members were Youths. The committee consisted of W. O. Goodluck (chairman), L. L. Borha (secretary), S. U. Bassey, G. Nzeribe, F. N. Kanu, A. Kalejaiye, Senator Chief Fagbenro-Beyioku, E. N. Okongwu, S. O. Oduleye, and Dr. M. E. Kolagbodi.

[11] L. L. Borha, "Government on Workers' Demand," Sept. 12, 1963.

[12] Resolutions passed by the Federal District Council of the United Labour Congress, Sept. 19, 1963.

excellent public relations, the Joint Action Committee rejected all the government's proposals and called for a strike for the week preceding the anniversary celebrations of Nigeria's Independence Day.

However, on September 26, 1963, without consulting the Joint Action Committee, the Ministry of Labour published the terms of reference of the committee which was to study the Joint Action Committee's demands. The next day, Borha received a letter from the Permanent Secretary which chastised him for not attending a meeting with the Minister of Labour. "The purpose of the meeting was to explain the terms approved by the government."[13]

In answer to this letter, Borha, writing in the name of the Joint Action Committee, had this to say: "You . . . released to the general public the terms of reference before they were brought to the notice of this committee. You will admit in all honesty that your action constitutes a serious breach of faith."[14] Contrary to the terms of reference suggested by the government, Borha, in the name of the Joint Action Committee, made the following demands:

> There should be appointed a high-powered Commission to be assigned the task of carrying out . . . (a) an investigation into the existing colonial wage structure, remuneration and other conditions of service . . . (b) an examination of the demands for (1) a general upward revision of salaries and wages of junior employees in both Government and *Private Establishments;* (2) the abolition of the daily wage system and the introduction of a national minimum wage. (c) On the basis of (a) and (b) above the Commission should make recommendations. . . .[15]

In his letter, Borha restated a principle which was to become the major theme of the General Strike of 1964:

> The Commission's work should result in the complete overhaul of the existing wage structure arbitrarily drawn up by colonialist exploiters of the past so that the politically dangerous and economically and so-

[13] ML.Co/128/Sec. 80: Federal Ministry of Labour. Signed A. I. Obiyan, Sept. 27, 1963. The terms of reference that the government proposed were as follows: (1) To examine the principles and system of wage fixing in all parts of Nigeria and to make recommendations with a view to removing any defects, including the differentials between federal and regional wage rates in the same area, and ensuring an effective basis consistent with national economic welfare; (2) To examine the principles underlying the employment of daily paid labor, and to consider whether any adjustment of present wage rates is justified and to make recommendations; (3) To examine the existing salaries and wages to indicate whether there were, in fact, inequities.

[14] JAC2/63. Letter to Hon. Minister of Labour. Signed L. L. Borha, Sept. 27, 1963.

[15] Ibid.

cially harmful effects inherent in the imbalance between the foreign-oriented upper stratum and the domestic-oriented lower stratum vis a vis the national economy may be permanently removed.[16]

Special attention should be given here to the explicit nature of the Joint Action Committee's demands for an upward revision of wages, including those of the private sector. This is quite an important point because, from the beginning, a major bone of contention between the Joint Action Committee and the government was the inclusion of the private sector in future negotiations. The Joint Action Committee claimed to represent all the unions, including those in the private sector. However, the government was legally not empowered to negotiate in the name of the private sector. The Joint Action Committee tried to solve this problem by the distinction which we have already noted between "government" on the one hand, and "the authority of the state" on the other. Thus, when Borha made demands on the government, he was making them on the "authority of the state." Too much should not be made of this point, but one should note that because the Joint Action Committee was trying to represent all the workers, it placed the government in the embarrassing position of insisting on the law and risking a major strike, or of not insisting on the law and having to risk its already weakened authority.

At first the government rejected the terms of reference suggested by the Joint Action Committee. For his own part, Borha regretted that the strike "will proceed to take effect in certain sectors and may spread unless our demands are met without further delay."[17] Some unions were alerted to go on strike by September 30, 1963. The government backed down. On October 3, 1963, Borha announced that the countrywide strike had been called off. Negotiations then took place between the Joint Action Committee and representatives of the Ministry of Labour, the Ministry of Establishments, and the Ministry of State, in the office of the Prime Minister. Finally it was announced that "The governments have agreed to set up a high powered commission for the purpose of revising wages and salaries on terms of reference to be agreed upon."[18]

[16] Ibid.

[17] Ibid.

[18] United Labour Congress files 1963. In the circular of Oct. 3, Borha commended the following unions for effective action during the September strike warning: Railway and Port Transport Staff Union (Alhaji Adebola's union in the United Labour Congress), Lagos Municipal Transport Workers' Union (bus drivers in the United Labour Congress), Aeronautical Workers' Union (United Labour Congress branch), but he also singled out Wahab Goodluck's Meteorological Workers' Union (Nigerian Trade Union Congress) and the John Holt's African Workers' Union (private sector, United Labour Congress). This showed that at the time Borha was willing to avoid ideological quarrels with the "Communist" Goodluck.

And on October 14, 1963, in consultation with the regional governments, the government did appoint a commission of inquiry chaired by Sir Adyinka Morgan, the Chief Justice of the Supreme Court of the Western region. The terms of reference of the Morgan Commission were as follows:

> (i) To investigate the existing wage structure, remuneration and conditions of service in wage-earning employment in the country and to make recommendations concerning a suitable new structure, as well as adequate machinery for a wages review on a continuing basis. (ii) To examine the need for (a) a general upward revision of salaries and wages of junior employees in both Government and private establishments; (b) the abolition of the daily-wage system; and (c) the introduction of a national minimum wage; and to make recommendations.[19]

The Commission held a private meeting in Lagos on October 23, and its first public meeting the next day.

For seven months the Morgan Commission listened to a variety of witnesses and deliberated. In a memorandum to the Commission, the Joint Action Committee stated its case. Above all, the memorandum argued, there existed an income gap between the very rich and the bulk of Nigerian workers. The memorandum strongly argued for "closing the gap." As an illustration of what is meant by "income gap," the Joint Action Committee report noted that:

> in the Federal Ministry of Works . . . six watchmen and gatekeeps earn between them £710 . . . by contrast the Minister of Works earns £2,700, the Director of Federal Public Works £3,180 and the Technical Engineering Office £3,640 . . . earnings of salaried persons range from more than £10,000 p.a. to less than £48 p.a. in Nigeria.[20]

Tracing the beginnings of the gap to the colonial period and to "prestige factors," the memorandum further pointed out that administrators had had to be induced to join the colonial service and to do service in Nigeria. Part of this inducement had been high salaries and allowances. Thus colonial administrators and other European civil servants had created a privileged caste in colonial Nigeria. It had been one of the goals of the independence movement to open this caste to Nigerian ambitions:

---

[19] *Report of the Commission on the Review of Wages, Salary and Conditions of Service of the Junior Employees of the Governments of the Federation and in Private Establishments,* Federal Ministry of Information (Lagos, 1964).

[20] The Joint Action Committee Memorandum to the Morgan Commission, United Labour Congress, 1963, 10.

When Nigerians became Ministers of State and Parliamentarians they argued that they should maintain a social status at least equal to that of the top colonial higher civil servants. Again when Nigerianization started, Nigerian officers insisted on not being paid any incomes lower than those of their expatriate equivalents.[21]

While ministers, parliamentarians, and senior civil servants had replaced the Europeans as a new privileged class, ordinary workers were still living on colonial wages. The problem was not only one of income but of style of life and relations between the two groups.

There was a pronounced master-servant relation expressed not only in a prestige income structure but in social snobbishness. All this has been carried into the new period. The task of the Commission . . . is to overhaul this structure.[22]

In order to close the gap, the Joint Action Committee recommended a minimum annual wage of £180 and an upper income scale varying between £500 and £960. This reorganization of the wage and salary structure was to be effected by cutting high salaries and by establishing the principle that "Nigerians can and should earn less than expatriates of equal skill and experience."[23]

Having heard evidence from the Joint Action Committee, the government, the Nigerian Employers' Consultative Association,[24] and various experts, the Morgan Commission presented its findings (with two minority reports) to the government on April 30. It was then up to the government to release the report and publish a White Paper, which would include the steps the government was prepared to take as a result of the report. On May 27, the report was released, but without a White

[21] Ibid.

[22] Ibid.

[23] Ibid.

[24] NECA was an employers' association formed in 1957 in Lagos: "The Association aims at providing a means for consultation and exchange of information on questions arising out of relations between Employers and their work people, and promoting co-operation . . . between Associations of Employers . . . and between individual Employers." *NECA News*, Jan. 1965. The significant point about NECA during the Okotie-Eboh negotiations held after the strike, was its lack of constitutional or any other powers either to enforce or even to represent the various employers in Nigeria. NECA sent representatives only at the insistence of the government after it had been warned that the Joint Action Committee would not come to a meeting unless employers in the private sector were also represented. Once NECA did attend the poststrike meetings, the Joint Action Committee argued that the wage raise accepted by the government was equally binding on all employers who were NECA members. Many employers refused to accept this interpretation, and in the private sector strikes went on for another two months.

Paper.[25] On Monday, June 1, the Joint Action Committee called the workers out on strike. The General Strike had begun.

Within a week, the government published its White Paper. The wage increases that it suggested were well below those demanded by the Joint Action Committee and recommended by the Morgan Commission. Consequently, the recommendations of the White Paper were rejected out of hand by the Joint Action Committee and the strikers. The strike lasted for another week, at which time it was agreed to hold tripartite negotiations among the Joint Action Committee, representatives of all the governments, and the Nigerian Employers' Consultative Association.

The results of the Okotie-Eboh negotiations (as they came to be known after the chairman, the late Chief Festus Okotie-Eboh, the then Minister of Finance) were favorable to the strikers. One can compare the Morgan Commission, the White Paper, and the Okotie-Eboh recommendations in Table 1.

My observations and those by Wolpe on the strike in Ibadan, Port Harcourt, and Lagos may be summarized under five headings.[26]

1.   Strike leaders were not selected by tribe.

Duplicating the pattern in Lagos, the various regional labor factions became united as a consequence of the strike. Neither the original division, nor the new found unity, however, had anything to do with tribalism. Unlike the political party leadership which was largely Yoruba in Ibadan and Ibo in Port Harcourt, the leadership of the Joint Action Committee at the regional level was truly Nigerian. But this was not a new phenomenon which stemmed from the strike, for the leadership of the labor movement was not selected on the basis of tribe. For example, the general secretary of the Western regional United Labour Congress and joint secretary of the Joint Action Committee in Ibaban was an Ibo, while the secretary of the Joint Action Committee in Port Harcourt was a Yoruba.[27]

[25] Jacob Obande, Minister of Establishments, was in charge of dealing with the Joint Action Committee. At this time, both the Minister of Labour and the Prime Minister were out of the country.

[26] See Howard Wolpe's excellent discussion of the strike in Port Harcourt in his "Port Harcourt: A Community of Strangers" (unpublished Ph.D. dissertation, Massachusetts Institute of Technology, 1967).

[27] Reporting on Port Harcourt, Wolpe was struck by the non-Ibo and minority group aspects of the Joint Action Committee leadership: "Six of its ten members, including the three most senior officials were non-Ibo. Its Chairman, E. I. Bille was from the Ijaw-speaking community of Old Bakana; its secretary, J. Alajo, was a Yoruba-speaking Lagosian; its vice president, Watson Gabriel, was an Ijaw-speaking Kalabari; and its treasurer, financial secretary, and auditor were, respectively, from Benin City, Calabar, and Western Nigeria." "Port Harcourt," 433.

TABLE 1 Government Minimum Monthly Wage Rates*

Final Agreed Zones	Previous Rates		Morgan Recommendation		White Paper		Final Agreement	
	Per Month	Index	Per Month	Index	Per Month	Index	Per Month	Index
1. I Lagos	7.11.8	100	12.0.0	158	9.2.0	120	10.0.0	132
2. II Ibadan, Benin, Burutu urban areas	7.11.8	100	10.0.0	132	7.16.0	103	8.2.6	109
3. II Western Nigeria and Mid-Western Nigeria excluding 2	7.11.3	100	8.0.0	105	7.16.0	103	8.2.6	109
4. II Port Harcourt urban area	6.10.0	100	12.0.0	185	7.16.0	120	8.2.6	127
5. II Enugu, Aba, Onitsha, and Umuahia urban areas	6.10.0	100	10.0.0	154	7.16.0	120	8.2.6	127
6. II Eastern Nigeria excluding 4 and 5	6.10.0	100	8.0.0	123	7.16.0	120	8.2.6	127
7. III Kaduna and Kano urban areas	5.10.6	100	10.0.0	181	6.12.2	120	6.18.8	125
8. IV Jos (including mines field) and Zaria urban areas	5.1.10	100	10.0.0	196	6.1.4	119	6.7.10	125
9. IV Soloto, Gusau, Bauchi, Gombe, and Lokoja urban areas. Katsina, Benue, and Kano Provinces (excluding urban areas above) Kabba Div.	5.1.10	100	6.10.0	128	6.1.4	119	6.7.10	125
10. V Zaria, Plateau, Sokoto, and Bauchi Provinces (excluding urban areas above) Gashaka/Mambilla N.A.	4.8.10	100	6.10.0	146	5.6.2	120	5.10.6	124
11. VI Northern Nigeria excluding 7, 8, 9, and 10	4.2.4	100	6.10.0	158	5.15.4	116	5.4.0	126
Effective date of increases	—		1-10-63		1-4-64		1-1-64	

* Adapted from table titled "Government Minimum Monthly Wage Rates," *Economic Trends*, Lagos Chamber of Commerce (August 1964), 9.

783

2.   The strike began in the public sector.

Both in Ibadan and Port Harcourt, the first organizations to be affected by the strike were the statutory corporations of the federal government, such as the Nigerian Railways, the Nigerian Ports Authority, and the Post Office. Port Harcourt's expatriate mercantile firms, such as the United Africa Company, were also affected on the first day. In Ibadan, such firms closed down by the second day. By the third day, the strike was almost universal; everything was shut down except some schools, hospitals, and petrol stations. By the end of the week, even the schools and hospitals (in Ibadan, at least) went on strike; only petrol stations and the African markets continued to do business.

3.   There was very little violence.

In Lagos, Ibadan, Port Harcourt, and even in the North, workers participated in mass rallies. There they were informed of the previous day's events, kept in touch with the strike in other parts of the country, and exhorted not to quit, to keep united, and to remain nonviolent. Except for the "Carter Bridge Incident" which occurred on the first day of the strike in Lagos, and in which workers trying to cross into Lagos were struck by police, no serious violence occurred in any other part of the country. Writing about Port Harcourt, Wolpe notes that "no loss of life resulted, destruction of property was virtually nil, and looting was non-existent."[28] He argues that newspaper reports suggesting widespread violence in Port Harcourt during the strike were incorrect—it is "one of the myths that has survived the General Strike."[29]

So little violence occurred because, at least in the beginning, there was hardly any opposition to the strike. Government and expatriate firms reacted very hesitantly. Furthermore, the high visibility of the army and police at all major intersections and gathering places, such as the racecourse in Ibadan, probably discouraged violence. The only act of near violence which the author witnessed was in a school compound in Ibadan during the negotiations between factions of the Western regional branch of the Nigerian Union of Teachers and representatives of its Lagos headquarters. Teachers milling outside the building where negotiations were taking place threatened to do violence to anyone not supporting the strike. Nevertheless, when the leaders of the Nigerian Union of Teachers emerged and called for a return to work, the crowd muttered, but dispersed.[30]

[28] Wolpe, "Port Harcourt," 441.
[29] Ibid., 443.
[30] Although the Nigerian Union of Teachers was represented in the Joint Action Committee by the members of the Labour Unity Front, of which the union was a member, in actuality the Nigerian Union of Teachers set its own strategy during the strike. In Port Harcourt, for example, the Council of Labour was sym-

4.   The magnitude and saliency of the strike affected the nature of the government's reaction.

From the perspective of the government, the very magnitude of a general strike was significant. Since there was no collective bargaining machinery to deal with a general strike which involved approximately 800,000 workers in the governmental and private sectors, the government was forced to negotiate at levels high enough to ensure authoritative decisions which would satisfy the strikers and stop the strike. Thus, the responsibility for dealing with the strike shifted dramatically from the offices of permanent secretaries to those of the Minister of Labour and the Minister of Establishments and, finally, to the office of the Prime Minister and then, to the Prime Minister himself.

In his response to the strike, the Prime Minister was not at his best. He miscalculated the seriousness of the event and the fortitude of the strikers. When he issued an ultimatum demanding that the workers return to work, no one budged; instead the Joint Action Committee itself began work on an ultimatum to the government.[31]

The events of the strike filled the radio and newspapers and thus raised the issues involved to national issues and focused national attention on the strike leaders—Borha, Goodluck, Imoudu, Adebola, Gogo Nzeribe, and others on the Joint Action Committee. It was lost on only a few that the Joint Action Committee was led by Southerners, most of whom supported the Action Group or the National Convention of Nigerian Citizens, and that it was in confrontation with a government which was dominated by the Northern Peoples' Congress.

5.   As the strike continued, it became political.

Although there was no violence, as the strike dragged into its second week labor's economic demands began to fuse with political denunciations of the regime and the governing elites. This became especially clear after the Prime Minister's ultimatum and the Nigerian Employers' Consultative Association's threats to fire or penalize workers who did

---

pathetic to the mayor's pleas that teachers should return to work, but the Council made it clear that it was the teachers who had decided to strike and only they could rescind the decision. Similarly, in Ibadan, the Joint Action Committee had no real control over the Nigerian Union of Teachers, although the more radical faction within the Ibadan branch of the union did stay in contact with the Joint Action Committee.

[31] On June 9, the late Prime Minister Sir Abubakar Tafawa Balewa warned the strikers: "In the present circumstances, my government will be failing in its duty to the nation if it does not take all necessary steps in its power to avoid a dislocation of the economic life of this country . . . The present position cannot be tolerated any longer." *Nigerian Daily Times*. In response, the Western regional branch of the Joint Action Committee called on the Prime Minister "to resign within 48 hours." *Nigerian Daily Times*, June 10, 1964.

not return to work. In Port Harcourt, Wolpe reports that "In the mass rallies, attacks upon corruption and the privileges enjoyed by the political establishment became more heated and references to the need for a labor party more frequent."[32]

Indeed, as the strike progressed into its second week, it began to attract not only the "Youths," but dissident elements from every section of the regionalist system; dissident members of the National Council of Nigerian Citizens, Action Group members, and members of the Zikist National Vanguard who opposed the Northern Peoples' Congress. Members of the National Council of Nigerian Citizens coalition began to converge on the headquarters of the Joint Action Committee in the regions. They brought with them not only advice and support, but the money and cars essential to the continuation of the strike.[33]

Finally, with respect to the private sector, the Joint Action Committee placed the government in the embarrassing position of having to choose between Nigerian workers and expatriate employers. The "Youths" had a field day pointing out how the government was "pocketed" by imperialists. For the duration of the strike, the government had to defend itself against accusations of "neo-colonialism."

In concluding, two questions in particular concern us: (1) Was the strike linked in any way to the crises besetting the political system of the day? (2) Was the strike a manifestation of class consciousness, and did workers reflect this attitude in the political sphere?

From workers' attitudes surveyed during and after the strike, it would seem that, in a general way, workers were opposed to the difference between their life style and that of the political elites ruling the nation. Thus, when asked about the causes of the strike, more than 90 per cent indicated low salaries and more than 70 per cent stressed the *difference* between the salaries of workers and the salaries of senior civil servants and politicians.[34]

Moreover, a majority of workers indicated that since independence, and especially after the strike—in spite of its success—their trust in politicians had diminished. Nevertheless, they would not explicitly link the strike with any one political crisis or series of crises then besetting the

[32] Wolpe, "Port Harcourt," 447.

[33] We infer such party activity from personal observation in Ibadan and Lagos. However, we cannot establish that the same pattern repeated itself in the East, the North, and the Mid-West regions.

[34] These results are based on a survey of trade unionists in July 1964, a month after the strike. The sample was a non-probabilistic quota sample of sixty-one trade unionists (with no significant differences between members of the United Labour Congress and the other central labor bodies).

Federation. Thus, only 3 per cent cited the census issue and no one mentioned the crisis in the Western region as causes of the strike.[35]

Conversely, workers did not derive from the strike a willingness to abandon regionally-based political parties for a party based on labor interest.[36] Although only 6 per cent of the sample indicated unequivocal support for the regionalist parties and 30 per cent indicated that "trade unionists should form a labour party," most chose to separate their labor and political interests. That is to say, workers most frequently chose the option: "Trade unionists, as trade unionists, should not mix in politics, although as private citizens, they may do so."[37]

These results lead us to believe that, while the strike may have exacerbated a division between the political elites and the workers, the latter were, nevertheless, not willing to abandon their political parties for a labor party. This can best be understood if we keep in mind that most workers were tied to the political parties through their tribal unions and regional loyalties. Workers may have been opposed to the politicians as corrupt individuals, but they were not opposed to the institutions and interests that the politicians represented. In his capacity as a member of this or that ethnic group or region, the same worker who denounced all politicians in one breath, supported *his* man in the next.

Returning to the hypothesis that class struggle as manifested in the strike was antagonistic to tribalism, it would seem from these findings that a direct conflict between ethnicity and class consciousness need not take place. By differentiating the institutions of ethnicity from those occupying positions in these institutions, egalitarian workers could support the first, while rejecting the second. We conclude, therefore, that the General Strike may have loosened workers' loyalties to politicians but not necessarily to the ethnic groups and institutions which these politicians represented; and that, in the long run, African states cannot rely on the processes of economic modernization and class struggle to solve problems of political modernization and national integration.

[35] These results are based on a quota sample of thirty-eight trade unionists interviewed in Oct. 1964. For the census issue, see below, O'Connell, "Fragility," 1019-20.

[36] These results are based on a quota sample of eighty-nine trade unionists interviewed in April 1965. Fifty-two were members of the radical wing and thirty-seven were members of the Neutralist wing of central labor bodies. It should be mentioned in passing that the question asked was meant to identify labor party supporters in general, not to gauge the potential support of a particular labor party, such as that of Mr. Imoudu, the Nigerian Labour party, or that of Dr. Tunji Otegbeye, the Socialist Workers' and Farmers' party of Nigeria.

[37] Ibid. For a fuller discussion of the survey see Robert Melson, "Marxists in the Nigerian Labour Movement."

NONVIOLENCE REVISITED

LEO KUPER

The Campaign for the Defiance of Unjust Laws

The South African Campaign for the Defiance of Unjust Laws of 1952 marked a critical point in interracial political relations. Unlike other movements for the liberation of oppressed peoples which brought independence to many countries after World War II, the Campaign for the Defiance of Unjust Laws brought even greater oppression in South Africa. It seemed to be an event in the unfolding of history as the story of reaction, not history as the story of freedom. It gave the governing Nationalist party the opportunity to test already assumed powers for excluding nonwhites from political participation, and it initiated a period of continuing contraction in the area of permitted action and of increasing efficiency in repression. The campaign's consequences imposed on many nonwhite leaders and on many observers the conclusion that, in South Africa, only violence could bring about political change.

Almost a generation has passed since the launching of the Defiance Campaign. There is now sufficient distance from the events to give a wider perspective and greater detachment. At the same time, the events can still be seen with clarity since they have not been overlaid with myth: perhaps it is too early for the elaboration of myth, or perhaps, given the new independent and militant African states, African politicians have been little inclined to recall a nonviolent campaign. It may therefore be a good time to revisit the Defiance Campaign, to seek anew to interpret its significance, and to inquire, at an abstract level, into the nature of the social conditions which either indicate or exclude the possibility of fundamental political change by nonviolent means.

The main protagonist in the Defiance Campaign was the African National Congress, which had been founded in 1912 in reaction to the constitution of the newly established Union of South Africa. The objectives of the Congress were to promote African unity and African political rights. At that time Africans were fragmented into diverse ethnic groups, largely following their traditional ways of life in different regions of the country. There was little urbanization and industrialization to provide conditions for interethnic contact and for mass mobilization. Almost inevitably, the Congress became a small, elite organization, its members being recruited mostly from the stratum of the Western-educated; political activity took the defensive form of petitions and deputations. There were periods of militant action in the decade after World War I, but by the depression of 1929–32, the Congress had greatly declined and was indeed almost extinct. However the passage of the Representation of Natives Act of 1936, which curtailed and segregated African political participation almost to the point of total exclusion, revived political activity and renewed the determination to achieve national freedom. This determination was further strengthened by the ideological conflict of World War II and more particularly by the Atlantic Charter, which the Congress applied to South African society in "The Atlantic Charter from the African's Point of View" and in a "Bill of Rights."[1]

In the vanguard of the new movement was the African National Congress Youth League, formed in 1943 under the authority of a resolution of the Congress. It drafted a "Programme of Action" for freedom from white domination and for direct representation on all governing bodies, to be secured by such means as boycotts, strikes, civil disobedience, and non-co-operation. This was adopted by the Congress in 1949 and initiated a period of militant action. Urbanization and industrialization were now much advanced, providing more favorable conditions for mass participation of Africans and for co-operation between Africans, Indians, and Coloureds. Working in the same direction were the apartheid policies of the Nationalist party which came to power in 1948 and threatened all nonwhite groups with systematic and total racial discrimination.

There followed a series of demonstrations, and in July 1951 the African and Indian Congresses and the Franchise Action Council, an organization of Coloureds, appointed a Joint Planning Council. Its mandate was to co-ordinate the efforts of the national organizations of the African, Indian and Coloured peoples in a mass campaign for the repeal of the pass laws, the Group Areas Act (for racial segregation), the Separate Representation of Voters Act (for further curtailment of the political rights of Coloureds), and the Bantu Authorities Act (for retribal-

[1] African National Congress, *Africans' Claims in South Africa* (Johannesburg, 1945).

ization of Africans), and for the withdrawal of the so-called rural rehabilitation scheme, including the policy of stock limitation. The plan submitted by this Council, as amended by the African National Congress, became the basis of the Defiance Campaign.[2]

The Joint Planning Council recommended that the government should be called upon to repeal the offending laws and policies. If this action failed, African and Indian Congresses should embark upon mass action for the redress of the just and legitimate grievances of the majority of the South African people. It described industrial action as the best and most important weapon in the struggle for the repeal of the unjust laws, but opposed its use in the initial phase in favor of civil disobedience. Three stages of disobedience were suggested: first, selected and trained persons would go into action in the big urban centers, then the number of volunteer corps and centers of operation should be increased, and finally there would be mass action on a country-wide scale in both urban and rural areas. Selection of the laws to be defied by each group was a problem since the unjust laws weighed with varying oppressiveness on the different groups. The obvious targets for urban Africans were the pass laws, for Indians the laws for compulsory segregation, and for all nonwhites the discrimination in public services and amenities; rural Africans could be asked to resist the policy of stock limitation which they so deeply resented. Though the immediate objectives were the repeal of these unjust laws and regulations, the final objective was freedom with full and equal rights.

In accordance with the recommendations of the Joint Planning Council, the President General and Secretary General of the African National Congress addressed a letter of demand to the government for the repeal of the unjust laws. In the same letter, they informed the government that the Congress had been established to attain freedom from all discriminatory laws for all the African people, and that the elimination of the exploitation of man by man, and the restitution of democracy, liberty, and harmony in South Africa were such vital and fundamental matters, that they were fully resolved to achieve them in their lifetime. Following the refusal of the government to comply with their demand, the African and Indian Congresses launched the Defiance Campaign on June 26, 1952.

The acts of defiance were directed against the pass laws and apartheid regulation of public amenities. The resisters courted arrest and submitted willingly to punishment. They sought to sustain trial and

---

[2] See Leo Kuper, *Passive Resistance in South Africa* (New Haven, 1957), 97-121. This gives a detailed account and documentation of the resistance movement, including copies of letters exchanged between Congress leaders and government officials.

punishment with good humor and to plan their defiance so as not to arouse undue bitterness among whites. These were clearly elements derived from the *satyagraha* of Mahatma Gandhi. Resistance took a somewhat ritual form with vicarious participation by the masses at public gatherings. Over 8,500 resisters defied the laws, and resistance was at its height in June when a number of violent disturbances, between police and Africans, blunted the spirit of defiance, and the campaign trailed off into suspension. The government banned and prosecuted leaders under the Suppression of Communism Act; it exercised its powers under the Riotous Assemblies Act; it persistently harassed the Congress organizations; and it introduced further repressive legislation—the Criminal Law Amendment Act with heavy penalties for civil disobedience, and the Public Safety Act for the declaration of states of emergency.

Political campaigns in the forms of demonstrations and boycotts, and spontaneous resistance and revolts, continued for a decade. The congresses sought to develop their capacity to mobilize the masses, and the government responded by liquidating their leaders and by attacking and finally suppressing their alliance. In the process, the government added to its wide range of oppressive laws. It declared a state of emergency; it proscribed political organizations; it exercised new arbitrary powers of imprisonment, thereby suspending the due process of law; and it subjected political opponents, without trial, to solitary confinement and other forms of torture. Paradoxically, in the short run at any rate, the struggle of the Congresses for freedom had plunged the nonwhites more deeply into impotent political subjugation and had raised the government in an exaltation of fascist domination.

Among Africans, three main political trends were to be observed in the decade which followed the Defiance Campaign. There was a strong movement toward interracial co-operation which reached its climax in 1955 in the Congress of the People and in the Freedom Charter adopted at that Congress. This declared that South Africa belonged to all who lived in it, black and white, thus implicitly denying the conception of Africa for the Africans, and it sought not the rule of the African majority but a democratic state based on the will of all the people.[3] The government responded by indicting most of the leaders for high treason in a mass trial which dragged a tortuous course for over four years, thereby further debilitating the Congress alliance.

The second trend was toward an exclusive African nationalism. This was expressed by a secession from the African National Congress

[3] See my discussion in "African Nationalism in South Africa—1910–1964" in Leonard M. Thompson and Monica Wilson (eds.), *History of South Africa* (forthcoming), II, and in *An African Bourgeoisie* (New Haven, 1965), ch. 23.

and the founding of the Pan-Africanist Congress in 1959. The idea of an exclusive African nationalism was always present in African political thought, but it had been subordinate to hopes for interracial co-operation. Exclusive nationalism now received reinforcement from the outside world through the rapid movement toward independence on the African continent and the growing strength of pan-Africanism as an international force. As a result, aspirations for African rule in South Africa became more realistic. Nationalism was also encouraged—positively by sentiments of Africanism, and negatively by racial antagonism directed against whites and Indians. The Pan-Africanist Congress rejected not only the multi-racial policies of the African National Congress but also its methods of struggle. And yet, in the only campaign launched by the Pan-Africanist Congress, it followed the almost traditional form of civil disobedience by defying the pass laws. This was all the more surprising given the recent history of civil disobedience and the fact that the Pan-Africanist Congress was in no way committed to nonviolence: if anything it believed in the necessity for violence as the instrument of change.

The third political trend among Africans was toward violence. It was organized as *Umkonto we Sizwe* (Spear of the Nation), an offshoot, in 1961, of the African National Congress engaged in sabotage, and as *Poqo,* an offshoot, in 1962, of the Pan-Africanist Congress consisting of anti-white terrorist groups. In its ideology, the movement toward violence stressed the conclusion that violence was already present in white domination, that only violence could effect democratic change, and that events had already established the futility of nonviolent struggle against a government and a white settler caste committed to the maintenance of white domination, impervious to moral persuasion, and ruthless in its own recourse to violence.

With the suppression of these organizations for violence, militant political activity by nonwhites inside South Africa virtually ceased. Outside South Africa the ideology of violence now determines the strategy of refugee African leaders seeking the liberation of their people in the context of a world divided by the conflicts between the great powers.

The Commitment to Nonviolence

The preceding narrative would perhaps generally be accepted as not too controversial an account of the campaign and its aftermath; but its interpretation is a different matter and certain to be controversial under conditions in which sharp ideological differences separate political parties of the same racial group as well as parties of different racial groups. There would, however, be wide agreement that in choosing civil disobedience the Campaign for the Defiance of Unjust Laws was largely influenced by considerations of political expediency, rather than by commitment in principle to nonviolence. Let us assume this for the present and apply the test of political expediency, though with a knowledge of the actual consequences denied to those who had planned the campaign.

What the Congresses in fact planned was not simply a civil disobedience campaign but a social, economic, and political revolution by graded steps. This was carefully communicated to the government— with meticulous concern that it should not be misled or taken unaware —by the initial demand for the repeal of certain unjust laws. The graded steps by no means implied a process of evolutionary change. On the contrary, the abolition of unjust laws was merely a sort of trailer for the main piece, a revolution to achieve racial equality; and this revolutionary goal was made quite explicit in the notices of intention communicated by the Congresses to the government. But even if the Congresses had announced only quite modest reforms, their goal would still have been a revolution for racial equality. In the post-war world, leaders of subordinate peoples had only a dichotomous choice of political objectives, freedom or bondage, and not a graded choice of degrees of bondage.

So too for the Nationalist party government the choice was dichotomous, white domination or black domination: modest reforms in the exercise of power were inevitably projected as a revolutionary reversal of power. It was in these terms that the Prime Minister, through his Private Secretary, immediately responded to the African National Congress: they were not making a genuine offer of co-operation, he wrote, but attempting to embark on the first steps toward, in the course of time, supplanting European rule.[4] The ends were thus interpreted as revolutionary; and so too were the means. To defy "unjust laws" was to deny the legitimacy of the whole structure of domination which rested on the sanctity of law enacted by due parliamentary process; and the pass laws were especially symbolic of, and fundamental to, domination by law. Moreover, at a time when the government's apartheid policy was pulling asunder the different ethnic and racial groups, their joining together in united political action was inevitably seen as subversion of authority.

When it had gained power in 1948, the Nationalist party had already instituted a counter-revolution against the possibility of revolution. It sought to legislate (and enforce by severe penalties) a reversal of those processes which were drawing the different sections together in a com-

[4] Letter, 29 Jan. 1952, in appendix to Kuper, *Passive Resistance.*

mon society, and to perpetuate white domination through control of social change—monopolizing for whites the parliamentary power to bring about change by legal means, and equating the promotion of political, industrial, social, or economic changes by illegal means with the heavily sanctioned statutory offense of communism. It was this counter-revolution which impressed nonwhite political leaders with a sense of the desperately urgent need for militant action.

In these circumstances, ruthless suppression of the Defiance Campaign by the government was surely to be expected. The African National Congress, in its letter to the Prime Minister, had declared that its decision was taken in full appreciation of the consequences which it entailed. The Prime Minister, in his reply, emphasized the punitive nature of these consequences, informing the Congress that should it adhere to its expressed intention of embarking on a campaign of defiance and disobedience, and in implementation thereof incite the Bantu population to defy law and order, the government would make full use of the machinery at its disposal to quell any disturbances, and would thereafter deal adequately with those responsible for initiating subversive activities of any nature whatsoever. There was also the voice of the Non-European Unity Movement, a rival political organization, which warned the Congress that the ruling classes would never modify any laws just because it had been brought to their notice that the nonwhites hated them. The Unity Movement argued that the rulers were fascists who knew that the nonwhites hated them and their laws: that there was only deception and self-deception in dealing with "Malanazis" as though they were "democrats" and "Christians" who would suffer pangs of conscience because certain nonwhite "leaders" were in jail; that the function of leaders was to lead; the jails were there to hinder and not to help the cause of freedom; and that it was the duty of everyone to keep out of jail as long as possible and especially of the leadership not to find freedom from responsibility in jail.[5] The government suppressed this campaign with great severity, introducing two further repressive laws to strengthen its already formidable armory of preventive and police sanctions.

Was the Defiance Campaign, then, an expedient method of struggle? Since the Congress had assumed that the African masses were not yet ready for revolutionary action, was it expedient to surrender the militant cadres to the prisons of the land? And in a society in which hundreds of thousands of Africans were annually sentenced for pass and similar statutory offenses, was there good reason to suppose that deliberate breach of the pass laws and voluntary and dignified sub-

[5] Kuper, *Passive Resistance,* 152-53.

mission to punishment would serve as a ritual sacrifice and act as a catalyst of revolution? And if the intention were to bring together urban and rural Africans, Indians, and Coloureds, in revolutionary struggle, was it really tactically expedient to choose civil disobedience as the method when the laws weighed with such varying effect on the different sections as to impose the need to select different targets of defiance?

There is no clear answer to these questions. The Coloureds remained largely peripheral to the Congress movement, but the Defiance Campaign brought Indians and Africans together in a close political association, which reached its climax in the Congress of the People. It would have been difficult to anticipate that the very closeness of this association would cause an anti-Indian political reaction among Africans and contribute to the founding of the Pan-Africanist Congress by secession from the African National Congress. But even if this possibility had been anticipated, the Defiance Campaign seems to have been a particularly appropriate political technique for promoting broader co-operation between Indians and Africans. Certainly nonviolence was indicated, given the objective of interracial co-operation: violence could only have taken the form of a racial war against whites and would have proved a hazardous basis even for the interracial co-operation of nonwhites.

Among Africans, the Defiance Campaign raised the general level of political activity and involvement, with consequences which are certainly not easily measured. The campaign must have contributed to the support later given to the demonstrations and boycotts organized by the Congresses, to the spontaneous movements of nonviolent protest, and to the peasant revolts in the Transkei and other reserves. But the response to the Defiance Campaign fell far short of the mass mobilization which might have provided the means of revolutionary change. The technique of civil disobedience seemed alien to the African masses and failed to fire them with revolutionary ardor. In contrast to the spontaneous movements of violence and the threatened proliferation of terrorist groups in 1962 and 1963, there were no spontaneous movements of civil disobedience. The result was an insufficient stimulus to launch the revolution, but a sufficient stimulus to strengthen the counter-revolution.

The selection of civil disobedience would seem then a somewhat doubtful expedient, measured by its consequences inside South Africa. But outside the country, it aroused international concern, and this may prove in the long run to have been a most significant contribution to political change. In South Africa itself, it almost certainly helped to bring about a profound deterioration in the political situation of nonwhites. Probably the Congresses overestimated the responsiveness of the African masses and underestimated the repressive force of the government. But the situation did appear to be revolutionary. Apartheid policy was clearly incompatible both with internal developments and with world ideologies of human rights, so that it was by no means politically unrealistic to believe that change was imminent.

Interpretation in terms of political expediency is thus quite plausible, save however in one crucial respect. It does not explain why civil disobedience, in the form pioneered by Gandhi, should have been chosen as the technique of nonviolent struggle instead of, for example, legal forms of noncooperation. There was little in the South African situation to indicate that it was an appropriate technique; in some ways, the indications were quite the reverse. And civil disobedience is a most unusual technique for launching a revolution. Moreover, calculations of expediency are not made in a vacuum, and they are not guided by pure rationality. They are shaped by historical experience and influenced by values.

In the present case, the historical experience was the civil disobedience campaign of 1906–8, under the leadership of Gandhi, against laws in the Transvaal which required Indians to carry registration certificates. Seemingly this method of struggle made a strong impression on Africans. In 1913 it was used by African women in Bloemfontein against the extension of pass laws to them by municipalities in the Orange Free State, and it spread to other towns, continuing for some years. It was used again by the Johannesburg branch of the African National Congress in 1919, by the Communist party in Durban in 1930, and its use was proposed in a number of campaigns which were never launched.[6] The Indian resistance campaign against the Asiatic Land Tenure and Indian Representation Act of 1946 must have helped further to establish civil disobedience in the African repertoire of militant resistance; the struggle in India itself had also demonstrated the power of nonviolence as a means to national liberation.

But values were also influential. The values were those of a commitment to nonviolence by many of the leaders. This can be documented from their speeches. It is also shown in the slowness of the movement toward violence, and in the selection by *Umkonto we Sizwe* of sabotage against property rather than violence against persons, so as to spare human life and not needlessly to embitter race relations. Nonviolence was certainly a positive value for these leaders. They were men of a broad humanity and a deep compassion. They had the

[6] In *Passive Resistance,* 9, I wrote, in error, that passive resistance ceased to be used as a method of struggle from the beginning of World War I, when Gandhi returned to India, until the end of World War II.

liberal faith in the fundamental goodness of man, and they sought a common society in which men of different races could live together in harmony and dignity. They were not driven by deep hatred of the white man and the desire to avenge themselves in blood. Murder would have been deeply repugnant to them. I think that there can be no doubt that among the considerations which led the Congresses to the Campaign for the Defiance of Unjust Laws, the commitment to nonviolence, as a matter of deep concern and principle, must have exercised a powerful influence.

Effectiveness of Nonviolence as a Technique

The question remains whether the course of events described above justifies the conclusion that change in the system of white domination in South Africa cannot be brought about by nonviolent means. This conclusion is usually linked with what is assumed to be the obvious corollary that change can only be brought about by violent means. But it by no means follows logically that because nonviolence is in-effective, violence must therefore be effective. Both may be ineffective as the means to immediate change, and this is the situation in South Africa, if the society is viewed as a relatively closed system. If, how-ever, the resources of the outside world are included in the analysis, then change in South Africa can easily be effected by violence, but at a heavy cost in lives and suffering—perhaps comparable to that in Viet-nam. But if the resources of the outside world for bringing about non-violent change are taken into account, then nonviolent techniques are also certain to be effective and at a much lower cost in human lives and suffering.

The conclusion that nonviolence cannot be effective rests on an analysis of South African society as a relatively closed system. The assumption as to the efficiency of violence draws in the resources of the outside world. There is thus a basic difference in the approach to violence and nonviolence which cannot be explained by the pure logic of analysis. Other motives, and especially punitive motives, are present and find expression in the conviction of the necessity for violence. Apartheid is so oppressive a system that men are driven to avenge its inhumanity. It is not difficult to understand that in their desire to pun-ish the white man they should be ready to destroy innocent whites with the guilty, as is inevitable in a racial war. But it is more difficult to understand the willingness, and the moral justification, for sacri-ficing vast numbers of those who are to be liberated from white dom-ination. In the resort to violence against well armed rulers, a much greater sacrifice is exacted from the dominated, as from the Arabs and

Berbers in Algeria and the Kikuyu in Kenya. What grounds are there for declaring that they prefer death to oppression, the finality of annihilation to the indeterminacy of existence?

If, to offer comparable situations, the comparison between the relative efficacy of violence and nonviolence is confined to South African society, then it is impossible to draw any valid conclusions from the experience in South Africa. The argument that experience has demonstrated the ineffectiveness of nonviolence is superficially persuasive. It rests on stronger grounds than a simple correlation between the resort to nonviolence and deterioration in the political situation of Africans, Coloureds, and Indians. A causal relationship can readily be demonstrated between a nonviolent campaign and repressive legislation or punitive action. But this is true also for the relationship between the brief excursions into sabotage and terrorism, and the government's counteraction by way of anti-sabotage laws, extensive reprisals, and brutal repression. Indeed, there was probably greater deterioration in the political situation of nonwhites following the resort to violence than after the nonviolent campaigns. The repression was more intense, and the solidarity of whites more assured. It cannot be said, therefore, that South African experience has established the ineffectiveness of nonviolence and the greater effectiveness of violence. The position is rather that both the nonviolent and the violent campaigns were backed by insufficient power to challenge the regime, and that they therefore provided the government with the opportunity to test and strengthen the structures of white domination.

There is a further difficulty in deriving the conclusion that South African experience has established the ineffectiveness of nonviolent techniques for changing the structure of domination. The conclusion, if it is to be meaningful, assumes that nonviolent techniques were used efficiently and vigorously. If this is not the case, then the failure may be in the manner of use rather than in the nature of nonviolence. Now it is precisely this assumption of vigorous campaigns which has been challenged by advocates of nonviolence. They argue that the organization and strategy of the African National Congress were weak;[7] they suggest that the leaders were insufficiently willing to sacrifice themselves in the nonviolent campaigns and that they acquiesced in the suppression of their activities;[8] and they comment that there was mili-

[7] See, for example, William Robert Miller, *Nonviolence: A Christian Interpretation* (London, 1964), 282-83. Miller writes that though it is to some extent true that the nonviolent movement was defeated by sheer force and violence, the African National Congress cannot be absolved from a share of blame for the defeat.

[8] Gene Sharp, "Can Non-Violence Work in South Africa?" *Peace News*, June 21, 28, and July 5, 1963.

tant, positive, nonviolent action, as distinct from mere passive nonviolence, for only a brief period. These seem valid comments but they may be controversial. Certainly campaigns of militant nonviolent direct action were of very short duration and received modest support. They are hardly an adequate basis for conclusions as to the efficacy of nonviolent techniques of struggle.

It is perhaps not too fruitful to speculate what the course of events might have been under different conditions of struggle. Rather, in the remainder of this paper, I shall ask what social conditions indicate the feasibility of fundamental political change by nonviolent means, and shall discuss three such conditions: the interdependence of the antagonists, the possibility of some point of reconciliation in the conflict of values and goals, and the mediating role of a third party.

The Feasibility of Nonviolence

Interdependence of the antagonists is a social condition which indicates the possibility of political change by nonviolent means. To the extent that the parties are interdependent, they may be expected to resist the disruption of the relationships on which they depend. This may take the form of the suppression of the disturbing elements by the dominant party, as in South Africa, or of the search for a new basis of relationship acceptable to both parties. Beyond this somewhat obvious proposition, the relationship between interdependence and nonviolent change seems quite obscure. I shall spell out the nature of the obscurity by raising a number of questions.

Interdependence is clearly not a determinant of political change by either violent or nonviolent means. All that can be said is that interdependence may be conducive to change by nonviolent means in certain circumstances. But what are these circumstances? Presumably they relate to the nature of the interdependence as this is expressed by its extent, its quality, the availability of other means for satisfying the needs met by the interdependent relationships, and the attitudes toward the continuance of these relationships. In extent, there may be relatively few interdependent relationships between the groups, and these may rest almost like an irrelevant superstructure on the main structures of the society, capable of being readily detached, as in some of the African colonies; or all aspects of life may be so deeply penetrated by innumerable ties of interdependence that their severance would utterly destroy the society. In quality, the nature of the interdependence may be like that between the rider and the horse, in which the dominant party largely determines and controls the performance of the subordinate; or initiative, skill, and deliberate co-operation may be required from both parties. There may be no possibility of meeting, from other sources, the needs satisfied by the interdependent relationships; or they may be met readily in other ways, as for example, by the importation of labor from neighboring African territories in the event of a strike by African miners in South Africa. In the attitudes of the groups toward the interdependent relationship and toward each other, there may be such revulsion that the dissolution of the society and holocausts of violence seem preferable to a continuation of the relationships; or there may be a readiness to reduce the interdependence and modify the style of life, as by a reduction in the standard of living; or the contribution of the interdependent relations may be so highly valued, that the dominant group is willing to seek new solutions or is prepared to exert maximum pressure to maintain the traditional relationships.

If South African society is analyzed in these terms, then it is clear that there is a high degree of interdependence. It is very marked in the economy. In 1964–65, there were over one and a half million non-whites employed in mining, manufacturing, construction, transportation, communication, and public authorities, and they constituted three-quarters of the employed population in these sectors.[9] Their purchasing power is a significant factor in the economy. The interdependence is marked also in the political system, where nonwhites co-operate in the "instruments of their own oppression" as policemen, informers, court interpreters, court messengers, jailers, and chiefs, and as members of a multitude of tribal authorities, advisory boards, and councils. It is present in the field of religion in many Christian denominations, and, though the interdependence may seem readily expendable from a secular point of view, it is no doubt deeply significant for those who kneel together, and even for many who kneel separately but in the same rituals.

The interdependence does not call for such a low order of performance from subordinates, such as from drawers of water or hewers of wood, that workers are quite interchangeable and may be almost totally regulated. The expanding sector of the economy is private manufacturing industry, which requires from many of its workers a measure of skill, commitment to a work ethic, and reliability and continuity in employment: there are now about half a million Africans employed in private manufacturing industry. The unskilled migratory workers may readily be replaced by workers from adjoining territories, but this is not true for the urbanized industrial core of nonwhite workers. And the country cannot replace the many nonwhites who contribute skilled services and who act as auxiliaries to the government in education, police work, and administration.

[9] Republic of South Africa, *Monthly Bulletin of Statistics* (Dec. 1966).

There can be no doubt that the withholding of nonwhite labor would entirely disrupt the country. Perhaps the withholding of co-operation in government and administration would be sufficient to make apartheid, in its present form, unworkable. Whether the dominant group would then be willing to renounce certain of its values so as to maintain racial domination, and whether it would be willing to revert for example to more primitive modes of subsistence with reduced standards of living, is difficult to say. But the latter seems highly doubtful. One of the major trends in South African society has been toward an increasingly positive affirmation of the values of a modern industrial society. The indications are that the interdependent relationships are so necessary to the dominant group for the realization of many of its most important values that a profound disturbance in these relationships may be expected to generate political change.

The second condition is that of the possibility of some reconciliation in values and goals. Presumably conflict and the desire for a violent confrontation result from incompatibility in the values sought by the contending groups. To the extent that it is possible to find some point of reconciliation by which the incompatibility is so reduced as to permit a measure of political change, nonviolent techniques become potentially effective.[10] This reconciliation may be achieved by a restructuring of the situation, or a redofinition of the values. Alternatively the values may permit a mutual accommodation, without redefinition, or a restructuring of the situation. This depends on the nature of the values. They may be based on assumptions of scarcity, resulting in theory in zero sum concepts of social relationships, and in practice in dialectical opposition; or they may be conceived as infinitely available. And again, the values may be dichotomous, or graded; in the former case, they are either achieved or not achieved, and in the latter case, they may be achieved in part or to some degree. Presumably the possibility of reconciliation is increased to the extent that values are perceived as infinitely or abundantly available: it would seem also that there is more scope for reconciliation of conflict where values are graded than where they are dichotomous.

It is very difficult to analyze the compatibility of the values of such large social entities as racial and ethnic groups in complex interaction. In the first place, the values of each group must be specified, and a hierarchy of these values established, since they are likely to have quite variable significance for the relationships between the groups. In the second place, there is certain to be considerable varia-

[10] I am drawing here on ideas developed by Johan Galtung, "Institutionalized Conflict Resolution," *Journal of Peace Research*, II (1965), 348-97, and on discussions and seminars at the International Peace Research Institute, Oslo, Norway.

tion in the values of strata within each group. There may be greater incompatibility in values between an elite stratum of a subordinate group and the mass of its members than between the elite and the mass of the dominant group. However, it will be assumed for the purpose of this discussion of nonviolence in South Africa that the major values are those relating to the political and economic systems, that these values are homogenous within each of the groups, and that they may be described in terms of the antithesis between white domination and racial equality in the political sphere, and between extreme discrimination and equality in the economic sphere.

The problem then is whether some point of reconciliation can be found in this conflict of values. The difficulties are slightly less insuperable in the economic system than in the political. There is a zero sum quality in the relationship to ownership of land, since to the extent that whites monopolize ownership nonwhites are excluded. The history of land policies in South Africa shows that there is little possibility of compromise here, though it is conceivable that with continuing urbanization of the white population, more land might become available for nonwhites. Ownership of mineral rights has the same characteristic of monopoly and exclusion, and this is true also for ownership of most of the means of production. But with an expanding industrial economy, there could be an opportunity for nonwhites to acquire ownership of new productive resources. Moreover, the relationship between the returns of industrial expansion for whites and for nonwhites is by no means dialectical. Increased profits, salaries, and wages for whites do not bring increased poverty for nonwhites. However extreme the discrimination, there are small increments for nonwhites in the industrial expansion of the country, and these increments could readily be made appreciable and stimulate further industrial expansion. But access to new resources and increases in wages do not touch the present extreme inequality in the distribution of land and other means of production. They offer some small space for maneuver and change, but not a basis for reconciliation of the conflict in values.

In the political system, there is even less room for reconciliation. In the first place, white domination imposes a dialectic of increasing concentration of power in the hands of whites and a correspondingly increasing subjugation for nonwhites. Where a resource is abundantly available, as for example salvation in some religions, there is no difficulty in distributing it to members of all groups, even under systems of racial domination. But power, in the form of domination, cannot be generated more abundantly so that there will be plenty available for distribution to all groups. In the second place, political relations are conceived by many whites as a dichotomy between white domination and black domination, thereby excluding the possibility of compromise by evolutionary processes of change. By contrast, in the movement toward independence in the British colonies, many of the conflicts could be readily resolved, since they related to such graded values as the tempo of change, or the proportion of nominated to elected members, or proportional representation for different racial groups. In the third place, the incompatibility in values is extreme—between equal rights and the denial of civil rights, and between conceptions of the racial or ethnic group as the politically relevant unit and conceptions of the inalienable rights of the individual. My comments here refer to dominant ideological tendencies and ignore some of the convergences in values held by members of different racial groups as, for example, in the commitment to democratic values among sections of the dominant group, and in the adoption of group definitions and concepts of separate development among sections of the subordinate groups.

In the form in which I have expressed the conflict in values concerning political relations, there is only one aspect which seems to offer some slight possibility of change by nonviolent means. This is in the government's declaration that Africans will be entitled to the exercise of full rights in their own areas. It is on this basis that the government claims moral justification for the general denial of political rights. The declaration is thus an important element in the ideology of apartheid. It may provide Africans with the means to acquire something more than the present fictitious rights in their own small overpopulated and impoverished reserves. This is no doubt of minor significance. But it may also provide the means to exercise some pressure for change in the general political situation of Africans in South Africa. The same possibility arises in the neighboring independent African states of Lesotho, Botswana, and Swaziland; they may be able to exert pressure for change in the status of the many Sotho, Tswana, and Swazi living in South Africa, and thus generally of all Africans in the Republic. These are very minor possibilities for nonviolent change in a situation in which there is an exceedingly sharp conflict of values, but they are not entirely without significance.

The third condition affecting the possibility of political change by nonviolent means is that in which an outside third party performs a mediating role. This seems to be one of the important conditions for the effective use of nonviolence in situations of sharp internal conflict between racial or ethnic groups. In the ultimate success of Gandhi's nonviolent campaigns in India, there was a significant contribution by pressure groups in England, detached from direct confrontation and involvement and able to serve in a role comparable to that of a mediating third party. In some of the British territories of Africa, the British colonial power, being somewhat removed from direct involvement in the conflicts between racial and ethnic groups prior to independence, was able to mediate with a measure of temporary or more lasting success. Where the third party identifies with one of the parties to the conflict, then the probability of violence may be increased, or change may be imposed by nonviolent means. Where the third party is able to relate to both parties to the conflict, then there is a greater probability of nonviolent change acceptable to both parties. The structure of the situation is altered. Instead of a polarization of the conflict between the two parties, narrowly restricting the range of their interaction and inclining them toward violence, the situation becomes more fluid with new possibilities of relationship and resolution of conflict.

Now there is a very considerable involvement of third parties in South African affairs. Some of this involvement encourages the resort to violence. In other cases, third parties seek to mediate in a great variety of fields. Each such involvement of a third party may be conceived, for analytical purposes, as creating a new system of social relationships. Thus the interest of international sports associations in ending racial discrimination in South African sports introduces a new structure consisting of separate white and nonwhite sports associations in South Africa, both belonging to the international sports associations. There are similar structures in religion. The involvement of the neighboring independent African states creates new possibilities of relationship. And above all, there is the involvement of the United Nations and of some of its agencies. In the cumulative effect of the mediating role of these third parties in a great variety of situations there is some potential for nonviolent change.

Clearly the search for a nonviolent solution in a situation characterized by extreme and enduring racial discrimination and by sharp conflict in values is not easy. But the search for a violent solution is not easy either, and the argument that only violence can bring about change is by no means conclusive. There are elements in the situation which offer some possibility of change by nonviolent means. The increasing interdependence of the races in South Africa provides a basis for internal pressures for change. New potentialities for bringing external influences to bear on the South African government flow from the changing structure of states, and consequently of international relations, in southern and central Africa. The role of third parties can be extended by drawing different sections of the South African population into structures which transcend national boundaries—thus affording opportunity for mediating roles—as in international agencies in trade, science, religion, sports, and so on. In the combination of these elements, and in the constructive use of their potentialities, it may be possible to bring about racial equality by nonviolent means.

PART SIX

THE LITERARY EXPRESSION
OF PROTEST

LITERARY PROTEST

IN FRENCH-SPEAKING AFRICA

GERALD MOORE

The first black writer to turn the weapon of literature against the French colonial system in Africa was the Caribbean Negro, René Maran. His novel, *Batouala*,[1] which won the Prix Goncourt in 1921, provoked an outcry in official circles and led to his removal from the French colonial service. Maran's path back to the Africa of his ancestors had been a complex one. Born in Martinique of Guyanese parents, he was brought up and educated almost entirely in France. Consequently, in many ways, he had a French outlook, and as a young man his attitude toward his own color was, if anything, apologetic. The full impact of French colonial methods, which were seen at their worst in Equatorial Africa, was needed to arouse in him a profound sense of his difference from the French people among whom he had hitherto lived. Following immediately upon centuries of slave raiding, these exploitative policies seemed likely to threaten the actual survival of certain tribal groups in the Lower Congo region. Though Maran had no personal sense of brotherhood with the poor, illiterate, and exhausted Africans of Ubangi-Chari among whom he worked, his novel displays an objectivity of which few, if any, white novelists were then capable. He refused to accept the rationalizations for brutality and neglect which were common currency among his fellow administrators. His knowledge of the people—based on travel, observation, and a grasp of their languages—enabled him to expose their bewildered fear and their contempt for their strange, dehumanized, and aloof French protectors.

Maran's novel was the first manifestation of the intellectual and literary concern of French-speaking Negroes in the New World for the conditions of Africans. In the Caribbean area their daily struggle with

[1] René Maran, *Batouala* (Paris, 1921).

the presence and values of the white world was far more direct and unrelenting than that of the average colonized African in his mercifully remote village or settlement. Consequently they came to feel that only the resurgence of the common African motherland from subjection would enable black men everywhere to hold their heads a little higher. It was the concern of men whose knowledge of Africa was patchy, romantically interpreted, and generalized, but it was nonetheless the expression of a genuine, powerful emotional and intellectual demand. This demand was further stimulated by the example of the American Negro writers of the Harlem Renaissance, notably Langston Hughes, Countee Cullen, and Claud McKay (the last of whom was actually a Jamaican), who were the first black poets anywhere in the world to stand up and proclaim their blackness, their difference, their exclusion, and their hope. They were not simply demanding acceptance into white society, but a recognition that America had been physically and culturally shaped by its black peoples as well its white.

During the 1920's and 1930's other voices from the French Caribbean were joined to Maran's in protest against the existing scheme: Gilbert de Chambertrand from Guadeloupe; Étienne Léro, Gilbert Gratiant, and Aimé Césaire from Martinique; Léon Damas from Guyana; Roussan Camille, Jacques Roumain, and Jean Brierre from Haiti —all swelled the chorus with their increasingly militant and revolutionary notes. By the mid-1930's their demand was unequivocally for the complete transformation—political, social, and economic—of Caribbean society. Surrealism and communism, twin weapons snatched from the hands of the West, were now to be used against it. While surrealism challenged the huge weight of European logic and scientific achievement which had been piled upon their heads for so long, communism would, they thought, realize the true equality of man as man. Surrealism was to re-establish the purity of emotion and the force of spiritual insight, communism to bring every race out of bondage and allow human dignity to flower.

While thought and action among Carribbean Negroes was undergoing this rapid evolution, the vanguard of French-educated African intellectuals was reaching the shores of Europe. With the foundation in 1934 of the review *L'Étudiant Noir* in Paris, the voice of Africa itself began to be heard in literary protest. Even at that early point it introduced a perceptibly new note. Whereas the Caribbean Negro was insisting upon the primacy of total revolution—the breaking and remaking of the existing world—the African early displayed a primary concern with culture. The Caribbean Negro was protesting against his total deprivation: his culture, name, place, and religion had all been stripped from him by slavery, yet the new scheme of values which was offered to him in their place relegated him to the lowest level in every sphere of action or expression. In the words of Damas:

> ils ont cambriolé l'espace qui était mien
> la coutume
> les jours
> la vie
> la chanson
> le rythme
> l'effort
> le sentier
> l'eau
> la case
> la terre enfumée grise
> la sagesse
> les mots
> les palabres
> les vieux. . . .
>
> [they have stolen the space that was mine
> custom, days, life,
> song, rhythm, effort,
> pathways, waters, words, palaver,
> ancestors. . . .][2]

In contrast, the African intellectual did not feel himself deprived in the same sense. He had grown up in the midst of his own living culture. But he saw that culture increasingly threatened by the joint assaults of missionary and educator, by military conscription and forced labor, by the deliberate spreading of Western material and technological values. He did not seek to change the whole order of things, only to rescue African civilization from the obloquy that had been heaped upon it and to celebrate its real values and its neglected achievements. In this work he was assisted by the discoveries of certain European ethnographers and sociologists who were beginning to restore the balance: men like Leo Frobenius, Maurice Delafosse, Michel Leiris, Marcel Griaule, and Georges Balandier. The impulse of the African intellectual was thus in many ways conservative rather than revolutionary: not conservative in the sense of seeking to restore the past, but in seeking to liberate its finest values and enable them to inform the new social order. The talk was not yet of total independence, but of a relationship with France which should be more just, more equal, and

[2] From "Limbé" in Léon Damas, *Pigments* (Paris, 1937), 42. Translation by Ulli Beier, *Black Orpheus*, II (1958), 24.

hence more fruitful. Africa, too, must be allowed to pour its riches into the common fund of human civilization. President Léopold S. Senghor expressed it as recently as 1959:

> Il n'est pas question de ressusciter le passé, de vivre dans le musée négro-africain; il est question d'animer ce monde, *hic et nunc*, par les valeurs de notre passé.

> (It is not a matter of reviving the past, of living in a kind of African museum; it is a matter of animating the world, here and now, with the values of our past.)[3]

These different tendencies within Caribbean and African protest should not be overstressed. Both sprang from common experiences of color discrimination expressed in social, residential, occupational, and economic terms. Both were reacting against colonial domination and a policy of "assimilation" which assumed that the black man was simply a *tabula rasa* on which the words of French metropolitan culture must be written to rescue him from barbarism. Both tendencies continually interacted, shared the same platforms (*L'Étudiant Noir,* the anthologies of Damas and Senghor devoted to colored poets of French expression, the debates in the French National Assembly and, from 1947 onward, the pages of *Présence Africaine*), operated in the same intellectual world, and marched together under the banner of *négritude.* But whereas the Caribbean Negro almost had to manufacture an alternative to the model offered him by assimilation, the African had one at hand in the vindication of his traditional civilization. Consequently, he was less likely to succumb to the temptation of exalting primitivism and assaulting the whole structure of Western rationalism with the volcanic ferocity of Aimé Césaire:

> Des mots?
> Ah oui, des mots!
> Raison, je te sacre vent du soir.
> Bouche de l'ordre ton nom?
> Il m'est corolle du fouet.
> Beauté je t'appelle pétition de la
> pierre.
> Mais ah! La rauque contrebande
> de mon rire
> Ah! mon trésor de salpêtre!
> Parce que nous vous haïssons vous et
> votre raison, nous vous réclamons de la

[3] L. S. Senghor, "Eléments constructifs d'une civilisation d'inspiration négro-africaine," *Présence Africaine,* XXIV/XXV (1959), 291. Translated by Gerald Moore.

démence précoce de la folie flambante
du cannibalisme tenace.

> (Words?
> Ah yes, words!
> Reason, I pronounce you wind of evening.
> Mouthpiece of order your name?
> To me it is a crown of whips.
> Beauty I call you a petition of stone.
> But ah! the raucous contraband
> of my laughter
> Ah, my treasury of gunpowder!
> Because we hate you, you and
> your reason, we reclaim from you
> our precocious madness our burning folly
> our triumphant cannibalism.)[4]

Allowing that this, like much of Césaire's *Cahiers*, is a rhetorical flourish full of humorous mockery, it nevertheless represents an exultant, full-blooded rejection of rational achievement seldom to be found in French African writing.

To trace the progress of literary protest in Africa itself, I propose to look at three works produced over a period of roughly twenty years. The first is Senghor's poem, *Prière aux Masques*,[5] published in 1945 but written several years earlier; the second is Sembene Ousmane's novel, *Le Docker Noir*,[6] published in 1956; and the third is a passage from Tchicaya U Tam'si's long poem, *Epitomé*,[7] which appeared in 1962. Senghor's poem, which I quote in its entirety, contains many of the major themes of his poetry as a whole and many of the elements embraced by his concept of *négritude*, a label which he gradually replaced by that of *africanité*. It may be significant that the first word originated with Césaire, while the second is Senghor's. The shift which is here evident, from the international fact of blackness to the continental fact of Africanness, was related to the approaching end of colonialism in tropical Africa and the consequent search for a basis on which the unity of free Africa might be constructed. Hence the increasing preoccupation with Africa itself, rather than with the Negro world in general. The renaissance of Africa would, in turn, vindicate the black man everywhere.

[4] Aimé Césaire, *Cahiers d'un retour au pays natal* (Paris, 1939), 47-48. Translation by Gerald Moore.

[5] L. S. Senghor, "Prière aux Masques," *Chants d'ombre* (Paris, 1945), 31-42. Translation by Gerald Moore.

[6] Sembene Ousmane, *Le Docker Noir* (Paris, 1956).

[7] Tchicaya U Tam'si, *Epitomé* (Tunis, 1962).

Prière aux Masques

Masques! O Masques!
Masque noir masque rouge, vous masques blanc-et-noir
Masque aux quatre points d'où souffle l'Esprit
Je vous salue dans le silence!
Et pas toi le dernier, Ancêtre à tête de lion
Vous gardez ce lieu forclos à toute rire de femme,
            à toute sourire qui se fane
Vous distillez cet air d'éternité ou je respire
      l'air de mes Pères.
Masques au visage sans masque, dépouillés
      de toute fossette comme de toute ride
Qui avez composé ce portrait, ce visage mien
      penché sur l'autel de papier blanc
À votre image, écoutez-moi!
Voie que meurt l'Afrique des empires—c'est
      l'agonie d'une princesse pitoyable
Et aussi l'Europe à laquelle nous sommes
            liés par le nombril
Fixez vos yeux immuables sur vos enfants
            que l'on commande
Qui donnent leur vie comme le pauvre son
            dernier vêtement.
Que nous répondions présent à la renaissance
            du Monde
Ainsi le levain qui est nécessaire à la farine blanche.
Car qui apprendrait le rythme au mond défunt
            des machines et des canons?
Qui pousserez le cri de joie pour réveiller morts
            et orphelins à l'aurore?
Dites, qui rendrait la mémoire de vie à
            l'homme aux espoirs éventrés.
Ils nous disent les hommes du coton du café de l'huile.
Ils nous disent les hommes de la mort.
Nous sommes les hommes de la danse, dont
         les pieds reprennent vigueur en
            frappant le sol dur.
(Masks! Oh Masks!
Black mask, red mask, you black-and-white masks,
Rectangular masks through whom the spirit breathes,
I greet you in silence!
And you too, my lionheaded ancestor.
You guard this place, that is closed to any feminine
            laughter, to any mortal smile.
You purify the air of eternity, here where I breathe
            the air of my fathers.

Masks of maskless faces, free from dimples and
          wrinkles,
You have composed this image, this my face that bends
          over the altar of white paper.
In the name of your image, listen to me!
See how the Africa of empires is dying—it is the
          agony of a pitiable princess—
And so is Europe to whom we are joined at the navel.
Fix your unmoving eyes upon your children who
          have been called
And who sacrifice their lives like the poor man
          his last garment.
So that we may cry "here" at the rebirth of the world
Like the leaven the white flour needs.
For who else would teach rhythm to a world that has
          died of machines and cannons
For who else should ejaculate the cry of joy to arouse
          the dead and fatherless in a new dawn?
Say, who else could return the memory of life to
          men with a torn hope?
They call us cotton-heads and coffee men and oily men,
They call us men of death.
But we are the men of the dance whose feet only gain
          power when they beat the hard soil.)[8]

The opening lines evoke the atmosphere of an ancestral shrine to which the poet-prodigal is returning. The colors of the masks remind us of the many moods and passions which have coursed through and been molded by them. The lion mask suggests a complex allusion, for apart from its usual heroic associations the lion is both the heraldic beast of Senegal and the name of Senghor's father, Diogoye. The secrecy and peace of the shrine breathe the air of eternity, even as the masks transcend mortality through the frozen gesture of art. For the mask dances not only through space but through time, carrying the breath of the spirit from generation to generation, transmitting those values with which the past seeks to inform the present and future. These lines show the impulse toward classical expression of the mortal and ephemeral which is common in Senghor's poetry. In the same way the beauty of the sleeping woman in his poem *Masque Nègre*[9] resides in her approximation to a mask of bronze and he implores her not to awaken and "move his flesh."

But Senghor has come to the shrine for a purpose. As a poet-magi-

[8] Senghor, *Chants d'ombre*, 31-32. Translated by Ulli Beier and Gerald Moore.
[9] Ibid., 23.

cian his art shares with that of the sculptor the ability to create fixed images which will nonetheless dance rhythmically through space and time. Composing his face to mirror the mask of his ancestor, he speaks to it from the agony of a war in which black soldiers are dying beside white in the name of a freedom that they have not tasted. (This poem clearly belongs to the war years when many volunteer and conscripted African soldiers perished.) The "Africa of empires" is almost certainly the Africa of the old indigenous empires, whose last representatives were still vividly remembered in Senghor's childhood. Al-hajj 'Umar and Samori were not long dead, and N'Dofene Dyouf, the last king of Serere, had visited the compound of Senghor's father with all his retinue. But Europe, cut off by its own domineering will from "the memory of life," is itself dying like the old Africa which Europe ravaged. As the old, divided world sinks into ruin under the blows of the conflict, Senghor declares that Africa must be present, with its own freedom and dignity, at the promised rebirth. In that world the old colonial insults (cotton, coffee, and oil refer both to favorite physical insults—that is, cotton-heads, oily men—and to the role of Africa as a perpetual supplier of cheap raw materials) will have no place. The last line of the poem, which beautifully captures the myth of Antaeus and harnesses it to the total meaning of rhythm and the dance in African culture, forms one of Senghor's most effective images, since it is through contact with the native earth and the rhythmic articulation of all the arts that this culture will be revivified.

It is Senghor's Catholic piety, which he shares with Alioune Diop, Bernard Dadié, and Birago Diop among the first generation of French-speaking African writers, that partly explains his feeling of being tied to Europe by the navel—a significantly filial image. The same piety profoundly modifies his acceptance of Marxism. It places him far from the pagan religions which are central to much of Africa's traditional culture, though he would doubtless argue that these can now somehow be embraced by a new enlarged Catholicism. Finally, surrealism, which directly challenges the whole basis of Western rationalism, can have little genuine appeal to a classically trained grammarian like Senghor, with his ingrained respect for formal sequences and connections. It is significant that his French influences are mainly from an earlier generation of poets, such as Claudel and Péguy.

Little wonder, then, that the political policies which after independence stemmed from these cultural attitudes proved to be largely conservative. Little wonder, either, that the next generation should demand stronger meat and should look to Marxism rather than UNESCO to achieve a new universality and a rationale for human progress. Beside the angry expostulations of the young Senegalese-Camerounian poet, David Diop, (1927–60)[10] we may set the novels of Sembene Ousmane as equally representative of this more radical phase. Born in 1923 in the Casamance, the more tropical southern corner of Senegal, Sembene had only a primary education before plunging into the harsh, bitter life of a black docker on the Marseilles waterfront. His personal history thus offers the strongest possible contrast to that of the university-educated, elitist first generation. Senghor, for example, was the first African anywhere to complete his *agrégé* at a French university. And Sembene Ousmane was certainly the first African docker to become a novelist.

The plot of his novel, *Le Dooker Noir*, concerns a young Senegalese who drifts to postwar Marseilles and joins the growing group of unskilled colored workers there. The city has been heavily damaged by the war, and housing and other social services are appalling. The work on the docks is hard, dangerous, and poorly paid, but out of a feeling that this is "a white man's affair" and that the unions are as hostile to them as the employers, most of the Africans seem to hold themselves apart from the consistent efforts of the trade unions to fight for better conditions. Sembene's hero, Diaw Falla, writes a novel about the slave trade in his evenings and, after many unsuccessful attempts to find a publisher, takes it to Paris and entrusts it to a young French novelist, Ginette Tontisane, with whom he has a casual affair. Relying on her assurances of finding him a publisher, he returns to Marseilles and to the docks. His militancy there causes him to be shunned by the employers and ignored by his fellow black workers. He becomes more and more withdrawn and embittered, dividing his time between interminable walks through the slums at night and fitful bursts of writing on a new novel. During one of his rare social visits, a little party in the crowded bedroom of a married friend, he hears that his novel has just been published and has won an important prize, but all in the name of the woman to whom he had entrusted it!

Rushing straight from the party, he takes a train to Paris, seeks out Ginette, and forces her to admit him to her apartment. Blind with rage, he accuses her and, when she attempts to buy him off with some of the cash prize, rapes her and knocks her down. In falling, she cracks her skull against a table and dies. Diaw flees to Marseilles and locks himself in his room. He refuses either to escape or to give himself up and drives away everyone, including his sweetheart, Catherine. After his arrest his uncle in Africa manages to pay for his defense, but the press and the prosecution make great play of the racial aspects of the case, especially the raping and hitting of the young woman. They pour scorn on the idea that Diaw could possibly have written the prize-

[10] David Diop, *Coups de Pilon* (Paris, 1956).

winning novel and, despite the efforts of the defense, he is convicted of premeditated murder and sentenced to life imprisonment at hard labor. The last pages of the book consist of a grim, lonely, and courageous letter to his uncle in Senegal, giving the state of his mind and feelings as he counts the slow steps to oblivion and death. We learn that his mother has died of grief at the news of his conviction and his sweetheart has become a whore to support the twin boys born soon after his arrest. He ends with the cry: "J'ai vu plus que mon âge et n'ai vécu qu'un printemps." (I have seen beyond my age and have lived only a springtime.)

In its anatomy of homicidal despair, this plot appears to owe something to Dostoievsky. But it suffers from improbabilities resulting from its author's determination to make his indictment of French society as bleak as possible. Diaw Falla makes no attempt to produce the manuscript of his second novel as evidence of his literary skill, nor to call friends who have read and seen him at work on the first. Furthermore, there is no reason why the very idea of an African writing a novel should be so incredible in post-war Paris, where African writings had been known since the 1930's. Similarly, the difficulties of finding a publisher should not have been quite so formidable as they appear here if the book really was of prize-winning quality. Finally, the raping of Ginette, though explained by the author as intended to humiliate her, seems needlessly inflammatory as a plot device.

On the whole, however, these are minor blemishes in a novel which is original and effectively written. Sembene writes of a group of people he knows intimately, a group which is forced to evaluate for itself the place of the black man in a white man's world. For Africa has been able only to color exotically the streets and markets of certain quarters of Marseilles: it cannot alter the terms of life there and has to either accommodate itself to them or perish. The force of this experience is behind the words of Diaw's friend when he sees the reaction of the popular press to the crime:

> Vois-tu, maman, commença l'homme, s'asseyant sur la chaise, c'est pas l'enfant qui est coupable, ce sont plutôt ceux qui contribuent à répandre le sadisme pour degrader la vigueur morale d'une génération qu'ils veulent asservir, ceux qui sèment le racisme en bouillon de culture pour assurer leur régime de profit, fondé sur la misère et ses conséquences les plus extrême. Ils restent impunis, ceux-là!

> (See here, mother, the man began, seating himself, it's not the young one who's guilty, but rather those who help to spread sadism, so as to weaken the moral vigor of a generation they seek to enslave. It's those who throw racism into the boiling pot of culture so as to guarantee

their own profits, founded on misery and its vilest consequences. But that lot will never be punished!)[11]

In the same scene another character rejects the whole concept of his French nationality—the keystone of assimilation as a policy—and exclaims: Même s'ils devaient m'enlèver chaque matin un morceau de ma chair, je maintiendrai que je ne suis pas Français. (Even if they cut off a piece of my flesh every morning, I shall still insist that I am no Frenchman.)[12]

It is clear that, in Sembene's view, any cord connecting France and Africa is to be severed rather than strengthened and that it is probably attached to the wrists rather than the navel. Since Sembene is a Marxist convert from Islam, he can hardly be expected to radiate gratitude to France for bringing the Christian Gospel to Africa. The missionary influence must be as unwelcome as French capitalist activities, French military use of colonial troops, and French cultivation of an indigenous elite to perpetuate the stratified and partially segregated society built under colonialism. The whole concept of the French Union can be nothing to him but a monstrous fraud, aimed at creating a string of client states whose independence, if it ever comes, will in no way disturb the status quo.

In comparing this attitude to Senghor's, we are looking at a difference of experience just as much as one of generation. The first group of African students in Paris did, it is true, know loneliness, misunderstanding, and occasional insult, but they did not know poverty, squalor, insecurity, and unequal, savage competition as they were known by the unskilled African or Arab laborers in the ports and industrial cities of France. The action in Sembene's novel implies that the cultural struggle cannot be primary since it can only be resolved in the context of a more just and more equal social order. Primacy must go to the political and economic transformation of African society, and to the reshaping of Africa's relations with Europe. Nor does anything in the book suggest that Marxism needs some special adaptation to the peculiar characteristics of African social tradition or to the demands of religious faith. Indeed, Sembene appears critical of the aloofness of Diaw's fellow workers from trade union efforts to better general working conditions. Insofar as these efforts are a part of the class struggle within French society, the novel seems to imply that African workers have enlisted in that struggle by joining the metropolitan work force and that they must face the consequences of their decision.

None of Sembene's reflections on the black proletariat in Mar-

[11] Sembene Ousmane, *Le Docker Noir*, 34. Translated by Gerald Moore.
[12] Ibid., 35.

seilles can be literally transposed from France to the situation in Africa itself. But the reader must ask himself whether the social worker-employer relations on the dockside in Abidjan or Dakar have been significantly altered by African tradition, even if we concede that the dialectical class wars of Marxism formed no part of that tradition in the rural or pastoral life of past centuries. In a later novel, *Les Bouts de Bois de Dieux* (1960), Sembene specifically transposes the struggle of unionism to Africa by telling the story of the Dakar-Niger railway strike of 1947. In this novel, the nature of his activity gradually forces a railwayman to modify his relations with his clan and cultural tradition so that he may through disciplined and united action gain a measure of control over working conditions. This change springs solely from his position within a modern industry and not from any extraneous demand. Thus the trend toward a definition of an African socialism stemming from Senghor's insistence on the central importance of culture and of certain unique features of Africa's traditional civilization, appears to be challenged by Sembene Ousmane's thinking. Similarly, although Diaw defends the dignity and coherence of Africa's existing customs against European misunderstanding, he does not suggest that they possess some enduring validity unrelated to the existing social and political order.

The year when *Le Docker Noir* appeared—1956—marked something of an explosion in the realistic African novel in French. The first two novels by Ferdinand Oyono and Mongo Beti's *Le Pauvre Christ de Bomba* all belong to that year. Both writers are Camerounians and both have set their novel a few years back in time, so that they belong to the era of "high colonialism." What all three novels have in common is a central hero who becomes utterly disillusioned by his exploration of the colonial world. Oyono's hero in *Une Vie de Boy* is a young "houseboy" whose enthusiasm for his employers, the French commandant and his pretty, loose, young wife, gradually gives way to sorrowful contempt when he observes the real quality of their lives at close quarters. Finally the white world he has so admired destroys him when he is mortally beaten in prison after being sent there on a false charge by the commandant: Both the commandant and his wife come to hate and fear him because of his knowledge of their weakness.

Meka, the old negro of Oyono's second novel, *Le Vieux Nègre et la Médaille,* has been a devoted ally of the French imperial authorities all his life. He has given his land to the Catholic mission and both his sons to the French army. The award of a medal by the colonial authorities promises to be the climax to his faithful services. This event, however, leads to his humiliation before all his friends and relatives since the discrimination made between him and the other re-

cipients, who are all white, is too blatant to be overlooked. Furthermore, he is arrested later the same night for blundering into the European area and suffers still further humiliation at the police station, in
the course of which he loses both his medal and the self-respect it was
supposed to represent.

In *Le Pauvre Christ de Bomba,* it is a European hero who suffers
disillusionment. The Reverend Father Drumont, who is the "poor
Christ" of the title, finally abandons his mission and quits Africa forever when he is forced to recognize by the events of the novel that for
twenty years he has been the unwitting ally of colonialism. However
he may have viewed his own role, French administrators saw it as one
of "softening up" the Africans, rendering them docile and uncritical,
and hence assisting the general work of "civilization." Although Drumont's pride and irascibility still blind him to many truths even at the
end of the book, he is too high-principled and sincere to remain in
Africa once he is convinced that his work is open to this kind of exploitation. Colonial Cameroun, Beti seems to imply, is not a place in
which an honest man can work.

The thinking of Sembene Ousmane, Oyono, and Beti, that of realistic novelists rather than discursive writers, lies relatively close to the
surface of their work and is not difficult to decipher. Sembene Ousmane, in particular, is by intention a popular writer of books for men
like him in education and background, as well as for those sophisticates he despises as too "bourgeois" and Westernized in their social
manner and outlook. It is quite different with Tchicaya U Tam'si, the
poet of the Middle Congo, who has developed a profoundly esoteric
style much influenced by surrealism and by the magical conjurations
of Rimbaud and Aimé Césaire. Tchicaya's poetry is difficult in the
same way and for the same reasons as theirs. He is deeply convinced
of the power of words to change the world by imposing new patterns
upon experience. But words can do this only if they are organized
with the greatest subtlety, complexity, and skill. Obscurity arises from
the effort to define meanings which are genuinely difficult and half-
hidden even from the poet himself. It is not perverse and not altogether avoidable; it is permissible because a tradition of esoteric
poetry which needs some interpretation is ancient everywhere, not
least in Africa where the poetry of diviners and certain religious cults
has long been of this character.

Tchicaya U Tam'si was born in 1931 near Pointe Noire and received his early education in the Middle Congo; at fifteen he accompanied his father, who had been elected to the French National Assembly, to Paris. He attended a French lycée and has lived mainly in
France ever since. Yet his poetry is not filled with that sense of phys-

ical and emotional distance from Africa that we find in Senghor or in
David Diop. His fourth book of poèms, *Epitomé*, published in 1962,
is filled with the immediacy of the Congo tragedy then unfolding itself on the other side of the river from his home. Although he spent
three months in the Congo at the height of the crisis, the poet writes in
Paris, where he experiences the full incomprehension and apparently
racialist garbling of these events by the Western press. His own relative distance and safety from the struggle do not give him a unique
sense of guilt. Rather, he divides his guilt with all those, black and
white, whose responsibility may range from bloody involvement to
sheer indifference. He is by turns bitter, compassionate, humorous,
and despairing. And his poetry works entirely through imagery, offering little in the way of narrative or progressive argument.

Under the impact of events in the Congo in the summer and au-
tumn of 1960, however, Tchicaya's language takes on a new edge of
specific anguish:

> Or face à Kinshasa
> Sainte-Anne à son heure critique
> Hausse l'échine
> Et n'a plus la chair fine du messie
> Ni le sang clair du messie . . .
>
> Sainte-Anne ton sang ton chair
> à quels saints les vouer
> Et si ce désir devient le brandon du peuple
>
> A Kinshasa . . . de Kamina
> Trois escouades d'une forêt celeste en parachute
> sans fleurs au canon de leurs ramures
> ayant aux bottes la même boue qui absorba
> face à Kin ton triste sang menstruel
> Anne conçois-tu leur diarrhée
> s'ils font des ombres partout
> tous feux éteints?
>
> Es-tu femme toi qui as si mauvaise conscience
> de ton sexe
> que tu le veux de pierre
> aux coeurs les plus fervents?
> On ne vivra plus ni de chair ni de sang
> Je dine d'un plat de viande de soir
> pourquoi n'est-ce pas la chair de mes frères
> en holocauste?
>
> (Now opposite Kinshasa
> Saint Anne at her critical hour

arches her spine
and no longer has the delicate flesh of the Messiah
nor the clear blood of the Messiah . . .

Saint Anne your blood your flesh
to what saints should we dedicate them
If this desire became the firebrand of the people

At Kinshasa . . . from Kamina
Three gangs from the heavenly forest of parachutes
without flowers upon the barrels of their branches
with the same mud on their boots that absorbed
opposite Kin your sad menstrual blood
Anne think of their sickness
if they make of the shadows everywhere
nothing but stifled fires?
Are you a woman you with such a guilty conscience
about your sex
that you wish it made of stone
to even the most fervent hearts?
We shall live no more on flesh or blood
I am eating a dish of meat this evening
why not the flesh of my brothers
burnt in the holocaust?)[13]

Here the figure of Saint Anne seems to represent the spirit of the Congo in the agonies of birth. But her travail is not a clean one, fouled as it is by violence, cunning, and greed on the part of all those who seek to manipulate the new Congo for their own purposes. The waiting people become almost like the lovers of the woman on whom their hopes depend, but their desire may become the firebrand which will burn them all. Saint Anne lies now at Kin (Kinshasa) but her agony embraces the whole Congo basin. It was at Kinshasa (Léopoldville) that she shed her "sad menstrual blood," and it is there that the Belgian paratroopers come raining from the sky—a sky that should bring blessings rather than destruction and death. The poet's compassion extends even to them, however. How chronic will be their sickness when they learn to fear the hatred crouching in every shadow! In the last lines a profound physical disgust rises in the poet's gorge. Flesh and blood have been so violated, so contaminated, that even the dish of meat before him becomes a reminder and a reproach.

Thus events that at the time produced so much bad popular doggerel and song all over Africa also moved one of her finest living poets to protest with the whole reach of his being. Unlike both Senghor and Sembene, Tchicaya is not concerned with defining Africa in relation

[13] Tchicaya U Tam'si, *Epitomé*, 40-41. Translated by Gerald Moore.

to "The Other"—be it France, be it the Western world in general. Nor, since he is still concerned with the exploration of his own consciousness, does he feel obliged to take up any constant ideological position. His poetry speaks to the world from the center of contemporary African experience, and his satire is just as likely to pour over his "obedient black brothers" as over any other actor upon the scene. In this respect it is typical of an attitude now found among many of the younger African writers: "protest" no longer necessarily implies protest against Europe or colonialism. The new rulers are often satirized as fiercely as the old and in more specific terms. Thus, the gentle Camara Laye points out in his latest novel, *Dramouss* (1966), that some of the leaders who extol Africa's traditions of neighborly solidarity, humanism, and brotherly love are capable of sponsoring violence against their political opponents in open defiance of those traditions. Several writers clearly feel that the luxury of blaming all Africa's ills upon some single external cause is something one can no longer afford. But while Africa remains the cockpit of so many contending forces, and while events as emotive as guerrilla warfare against white settlers or foreign mercenaries are likely to recur, the writer must be ready to chronicle such things as Africa sees them. When the passions of the day have subsided and contemporary half-truths are forgotten, his witness will remain, and it is through him that most of his countrymen will experience their history.

POLITICAL PROTEST IN

THE AFRICAN NOVEL IN ENGLISH

JOHN POVEY

African literature in English is still extremely new, dating as it does from the late 1950's. It is still difficult, therefore, to point out its dominant themes or to discuss it in terms of a real *tradition* of protest. Nor do we yet know enough about the links which may exist between the new literature and the traditional oral African literature to be knowledgeable about the elements of protest which may have been contained in the latter.

On the other hand, one must be on guard against the deceptive expectation of similarity which may arise from the fact that the works here to be discussed were all written in English. Such expectation has undoubtedly caused a distorted emphasis. Critics approaching these works after training in English literary disciplinary methods have overstressed those attributes of contemporary African writing which derive most clearly from English traditions. This explains the excessive time that has been spent in discussing the degree to which African writers can be fitted into the general context of twentieth-century British writing—in insisting upon the obvious stylistic influences of, say, Gerard Manley Hopkins or T. S. Eliot upon the Nigerian, J. Pepper Clark. This insistence conceals our general ignorance of the equally significant African influences upon his work. In spite of these problems of criticism, however, there is justification for declaring that African literature in English is a separate and new area which may be considered in relation to contemporary Africa, and without reference to vernacular writing.

By virtue of its practically worldwide extension, English has become an international vehicle for protest. Whatever the goal of protest, English provides the essential tool with which to escape from the limitations imposed by a single tribal vernacular in a linguistically fragmented society. English can reach outward. Black South Africans write in English only partly because the Bantu language presses are government controlled. They write in English because the protest appeal they intend to make must be directed not to the tribe but to the outside world. The Sotho or the Shangaans do not have to be told of their oppressions; it is the outside world that must learn. For African authors, English thus becomes the international language, and the message of these writers often seems to be protest.

Even if in African literature there is no "tradition," in the narrow sense, either of protest or of any other continuing theme, it is nevertheless possible to demonstrate, within the decade and a half of that literature's existence, the concern of African writers for their multifarious societies. There are no ivory towers in Africa; merely to record contemporary circumstances is to make a critical statement about the social justice of a society. The writers' reactions will vary in response to the varieties of their political experiences and to the multiple administrative systems of their countries. Yet in the final analysis, there is a kind of generalization that seems infinitely hopeful. All African writers, whatever their national allegiance, seem to be asserting their inalienable rights: to a government that should be just, honest, and humane, and that should permit its people to exist with dignity and security. This is the basic cry, whether in the bitter complaints against racial oppression in Alex La Guma's South African novels or in the sarcastic repudiation of the self-seeking and vulgar Nigerian politicians found in the novels of Cyprian Ekwensi. This striking fundamental unity indicates the premise of moral justice from which all protest literature must derive. For the true protest is not merely an ephemeral rejection of a certain government, or protest would have terminated with independence; it aims rather at the continuing injustices derived from the nature of man when he uses government to dictate to his fellows.

It is worthwhile to point out that the deepest protests in Africa are not found among those writing in English but among those writing in French. Thus the concept of *négritude*, which penetrates so much more deeply than political assertion and comprehends the entire African being. When Léopold Senghor, the arch-apostle of the creed, repudiates the "hygienic loves" of Manhattan for the "sword blade breasts" of Harlem, his condemnation has a totality which goes beyond a concept of political change:

New York! I say to you: New York let black
blood flow into your blood

That it may rub the rust from your steel
joints, like an oil of life,
That it may give your bridges the bend of
buttocks[1]

Senghor's emotion rests in the affirmation of Negro values, in the necessity of blackness in a Western-dominated world that he considers sterile and overintellectualized. This reassertion of humanity is the Negro role: "For who else would teach rhythm to the world that has died of machines and cannons?" This emotional revolt may call for political activism because a belief in blackness requires an attendant rejection of colonialism if it is to be successful. By its nature colonialism assumes a hierarchy of cultural values and the inferiority of the "primitive" non-Western culture of colored peoples. Such belief often remains when an African government takes over from a colonial power.

In contrast to the sweeping indictments of the *négritude* writers, the concern of writers in the ex-British areas have invariably been more immediately pragmatic and functional. Such differences may be rooted in the political histories of the two colonial areas. The French administered their colonies by direct rule based upon the concept of France Outre-Mer, that is, that the French colonial territories were parts of France which simply had the misfortune of being distant from the motherland. With the administration centered in Paris, the policies of metropolitan France intruded directly into its colonies. French colonial policy also had the declared aim of assimilation—the ultimate ideal for the African colonial was to become a Frenchman, black it is true, but when educated and exposed to the language and metaphysics of French intellectualism, a civilized man. There seems no equivalent for English-speaking educated Africans of the Senegalese intellectual's discovery that he had become French. This is what has to be repudiated—and this is the essence of *négritude*—yet it ironically uses the very spirit of French intellectualism to make its denunciation. It is not accidental that like many French movements, *négritude* derives from Montmartre café discussions, that its opening blasts come from an impassioned pamphlet called *Défense Légitime*.[2]

The British never made assimilation a declared colonial aim. They always paid lip service to the ideal of ultimate self-government no matter how conveniently distant that day might have to be. Africans in the ex-British colonies may reject the cultural imperialism of Britain

[1] Léopold Senghor, "New York," in Gerald Moore (ed.), *Modern Poetry from Africa* (London, 1963), 53. See also above, Gerald Moore, "Literary Protest in French-Speaking Africa," 807-22.

[2] Published by students from the French Antilles. (Paris, June 1932).

but they have not been totally drained of their own cultural nation-hood. The intellectual impetus that led to *négritude*, on the other hand, came from the recognition that except for the imported spirit there was nothing. This is the source of its violence.

The difference in cultural allegiance arising from the two colonial administrations decisively influences the nature of protest writing. Yet it is only a part of the difference between the areas dominated by the two major European languages. It is a coincidence, but a highly re-vealing one, that the first major work of Nigerian literature in English was not the ringing manifesto of a *Défense Légitime*, but a weird and grisly folk tale by the unfairly abused Amos Tutuola, *The Palm-Wine Drinkard*.[3] Though the main direction of development was to lead away from Tutuola's eccentric, illiterate but imaginative prose, nevertheless he demonstrated that the cultural freedom permitted by the British ad-ministration was only equalled by the freedom implicit in the English tongue. The British attempt no deliberate control over the develop-ment of their language, they have no equivalent of the French Acad-emy with its serious (if ultimately powerless) committees to decide that *le parking* and *le week-end* are not French and are to be prohibited. The flexibility of English, with its prodigious power of vocabulary as-similation, has been demonstrated across the centuries. This flexibility has resulted in what may prove to be a regrettable variety of Eng-lishes, a point which is especially true in the second-language situation, where a mother-tongue vernacular presses its syntax and tonal pat-terns upon the structure and pronunciation of the more recently acquired English. Yet that very flexibility has undoubtedly permitted a more ready assertion of literary nationalism through the develop-ment of characteristic and individual, localized English.

As a result of these divisive features, English-language writing tends to be more national than racial in its concerns. However, when contrasting the French and English attitudes from which protest de-rives, it should in fairness be mentioned that French writing in Africa began in the 1930's, in other words in a period that marked the cul-mination of colonial aggrandizement in Africa, with Mussolini's attack on Ethiopia proving the last European land grab. Thus, in the 1930's there was an enemy to oppose. Colonialism was rampant and power-ful. The conflict was direct, both socially and historically. But the first major work in English from Africa appeared only in 1958, when Chi-nua Achebe published *Things Fall Apart*.[4] By then certain post-war political truths had become apparent which directed the literature of

[3] Amos Tutuola, *The Palm-Wine Drinkard* (London, 1952).
[4] Chinua Achebe, *Things Fall Apart* (London, 1958).

protest into channels very different from the ones the French writers had pioneered in the 1930's. In the late 1950's, although independence for African countries might have been delayed by the power of the settlers or the significance of a country's primary production to the European power, its inevitability was clear. In West Africa, where African literature in English began, the situation was not bedeviled by white settlers and the capitalist economics of mining. There was no evidence that activism would have greatly accelerated the inevitable and willing departure of the colonial governments.

Thus, the timing of the beginning of African writing in English (in the context of twentieth-century political history) must account for the specific nature of the protest writing which does exist. If the literature of, say, Ghana or Nigeria had developed twenty years earlier, it might well have taken on different overtones of protest, perhaps especially that angry rejection of alien government that now marks South African literature. Given the chronological sequence of political events and literary beginnings, colonialism could not be a topic of major concern for the new writers in English since they themselves postdated independence. Although some novels do recreate the colonial past, they do so without marked recrimination and their real concerns are with the problems that beset the newly independent states—with their tribal incohesion and their as yet fragile economies.

Four Reactions of Protest

Within the historical framework it is possible to see four reactions that might generally be termed protest. Their pattern follows—in a general way—the sequence of African rejection of colonialism and establishment of viable and legitimate regimes. Yet because the historical events and the literatures did not develop at the same pace in individual African countries, the range of reactions becomes evident only in the context of the entire continent and not within the tradition of a single country's writing. In other words, the four stages of protest in African literature in English are discernible if one takes evidence from all the regions.

The pattern might begin with protest at the loss of innocence—at the supplanting of a dignified traditional life by questionable Western values. In a sense this has to be a historical position since the loss can only be perceived in retrospect, through historical perspective, and indignation is diluted by time. But the sense of loss may also be seen as establishing a tone that would have preoccupied the local novelists had they been writing at that time. Achebe's two powerful novels—

two of the few that have attempted historical reconstruction—are examples of such themes. By its very title, *Things Fall Apart,* especially in the context of Yeats's poem, "The Second Coming," from which its title is derived, is a declaration of deprivation because "the center cannot hold" in an environment which brings Christian missionaries to destroy the established order of things.

The second stage is direct political protest, not as a loss perceived by looking backward, but as a response to the day-to-day oppression of events under a colonial regime which is both alien and inherently exploitative. This protest is implicitly revolutionary since it demands change within the unjust system of the regime. As stated above, this is not a theme of the West African novel because the writing postdates anti-colonial agitation. Britain withdrew from Ghana and Nigeria with a fair degree of decency in method and timing. An antagonistic mood hardly had time to develop in West Africa. It did to some extent in East Africa. Although the first East African novel is comparatively recent (James Ngugi, *Weep Not, Child*), it does, as one might anticipate, reflect resistance and colonial rejection.[5] However, even though the author is old enough to remember the events of Mau Mau which he records, the book was written after Kenyan independence, and this dilutes the immediacy of the anger that would undoubtably have suffused such a novel had the society still been under colonial control.

As for the south, though South Africa is not precisely a colonial regime, it is obvious that a situation in which an oppressed majority is ruled by a European minority presents many elements comparable to an imperial occupation. And it is from South Africa that that direct cry of protest comes which exhibits the outraged rejection of oppression which might well have been the theme of literature in other countries had their independence been delayed. It is in South Africa that we find the revolutionary rhetoric, the bitter angry despair of the disenfranchised, the condemnation of a regime made with such passion that many of the writers are in political exile. The tone of this writing ranges widely, from the visceral anger of Alex La Guma to the rapier irony of Nadine Gordimer and the Christian reconciliation of Alan Paton. Preoccupation with racial antagonism, provoking writers to record the bitter and insoluble nature of their situation, is an inescapable and even monotonous theme in any serious writing from South Africa.

The third form of protest is turned inward—not against neocolonialism or the exploitation of the national economies by large-scale foreign capital investment. The anger turns to the exposure of the

---

[5] James Ngugi, *Weep Not, Child* (London, 1964).

shattered illusions; to the failure of the new regimes which had been thought to represent the utopian hopes of the young nations. Here the governments were local and African, usually elected by at least some fair approximation of democratic voting; and yet they seemed to owe no allegiance to the people who had allocated power to them. Many Africans came to feel that there had only been a transposition of elites. The unattractive struggle among African ministers for "European" housing and for the prestige of imported limousines seemed to offer no discernible advantages to the populations of the newly independent African states. They had been encouraged to see their liberation as a step on the road to some glorious opportunity for wealth and ease for all, but instead their new rulers behaved like the old colonial ones, or worse. Anger, ridicule, and exposé became the devices used by Ekwensi, Achebe, and others to display the miserable incompetence and greed of the new politicians, who are pictured as rapacious, cruel, and self-seeking. It seems likely that the arbitrary power of the governments involved, plus a certain desperately retained loyalty to local rulers during the initial stages of national development, until very recently prevented this tone from being given completely free rein.

The fourth stage of this historical outline may seem too constructive to be called protest; yet protest is not only negative. By its nature, protest presupposes some positive social or moral concept, for the criticism comes when the regime fails to match a political standard that is considered to be of higher moral integrity. At present this form of protest is only the most incipient of ideals, and is often expressed in that kind of platitudinizing prose that makes it clear that it cannot yet be taken very seriously. Nevertheless, to see the circle of protest—exploitation, rejection, reform, and reaffirmation—in its entirety, one must note that there have been a few occasions when, for example, the pan-African ideal has been held up as an honest solution to the appalling divisions that weaken Africa in the international arena. Ekwensi talks of the great ideal of African union in *Beautiful Feathers*.[6] This reunion would, it is thought, solve the problem of African diversity—if it could be established as ideally envisaged. A similar utopian South African theme stresses racial brotherhood, viewing disintegrative color antagonism as the West Africans see narrow nationalism—as the ultimate source of immoral incohesion.

The lament at deprivation, the pain of colonial rule, and the injustices of incompetent local administration—these are the protests which have so far been found in African English-language writing. The implicit moral assertion of good government and a new spirit of

[6] Cyprian Ekwensi, *Beautiful Feathers* (London, 1963).

union is the force that drives their protests toward a solution which would bring to Africa a just resolution of five centuries of abuse.

The Novelists

It is Onuora Nzekwu who best expresses what might be called the issue of colonial cultural deprivation. Works by Chinua Achebe (*Things Fall Apart* and *Arrow of God*)[7] on a similar theme are more subtle in their presentation and allow a wider grey zone between the two antagonistic systems: the traditional belief of the Igbo-speaking tribes and the destructive foreign ideas introduced by soldiers and missionaries. Achebe does not assume that right and wrong are easily attributed. Because he is a more subtle writer than Nzekwu, the polemic element of protest is less evident in his work. Thus, in *Arrow of God*, the battle of systems is seen as a personal conflict between the old chief priest, Ezeulu, and the British administrator, Winterbottom. Both are noble men and, in the process of asserting their admirable integrity, both are inevitably destroyed. The victors are the quisling adjusters, the African hangers-on of the administration, the corrupt messengers, and the cruel police who make no pretence at morality. This interpretation of events that does not attribute a simple villainy to their side is profoundly honest and is the stuff of tragedy. But the attitude implicit in the tragic view of life is not the material of direct protest, for it contemplates an existence that is, in the final interpretation, unchangeable.

Such works as *King Lear* and *Oedipus Rex* may be considered as a total complaint to the gods about the human condition that has been allocated to us, but that is a metaphysical approach far removed from political protest. Nevertheless, for all his general tragic profundity, Achebe's protest is inherent in his clear accusation of causality. Achebe insists on an initial blame:

> The white man is very clever. He came quietly and peaceably with his religion. We were amused at his foolishness and allowed him to stay. Now he has won our brothers, and our clan can no longer act like one. He has put a knife on the things that held us together and we have fallen apart.[8]

This theme is equally apparent in *Arrow of God* which contains the following significant analogy: When Suffering knocks at your door and you say that there is no seat left for him, he tells you not to

[7] Chinua Achebe, *Arrow of God* (London, 1964).
[8] Achebe, *Things Fall Apart*, 160.

worry because he has brought his own stool. The white man is like that.[9] Nevertheless, there is a sense in which Achebe's two historical novels may be considered laments rather than protests.

This quality is shared by Okot p'Bitek's long poetic lament, *Song of Lawino*,[10] which records the sadness of a wife who cannot change to satisfy the new cultural patterns. "I cannot dance the rumba." Her complaints, however, are really directed personally as much as culturally toward a husband who demands from her the most meretricious adaptation to modernization in the form of wigs, lipstick, and the rumba. In Lawino's innocent wifely despair there is evidence of the loss of the harmonious tradition to which she was born. Her protest challenges the contemporary priorities even though her song is directed not at impositions by the colonial power, but at the acculturating change actively sought by the Africans themselves. Lawino's society too has "fallen apart."

As for Nzekwu's earlier two novels, published in the early 1960's, *Blade Among the Boys*, and *Wand of Noble Wood*,[11] they make a more specific challenge. In spite of their excessive anthropological and autobiographical detail, they demonstrate the reaction of the intelligent young African to the attempted destruction of his heritage and the despising of his culture. The themes of the novels overlap without apology, and their protest is directed at the missionaries, who were in the vanguard of social change. It was the new religion that undermined the continuity of tribal tradition, a point Achebe also makes in his two historical novels. At first the alternative belief propounded by the missionaries appealed only to outcasts of society, such as women rejected for bearing twins. Later the missionary appeal became wide enough to reach even the holders of titles. At the end of *Arrow of God*, with an irony which within the context of the novel grows into sardonic force, Achebe announces the death of the old belief. Christian Harvest Festivals are to replace the pagan yam festival. "Thereafter any yam . . . in the man's fields was harvested in the name of the son."[12] The forces of social dissolution have been willingly embraced.

The issue of belief is complex and there is often a sense that with some modernization a kind of genuine compromise would have been possible. But for the missionaries there could be no middle ground; anything outside their theology was deemed to be heathen and repre-

---

[9] Achebe, *Arrow of God*, 104.

[10] Okot p'Bitek, *Song of Lawino* (Nairobi, 1966).

[11] Onuora Nzekwu, *Blade Among the Boys* (London, 1962) and *Wand of Noble Wood* (London, 1961).

[12] Achebe, *Arrow of God*, 287.

hensible. When a young hero is, for example, caught playing in the village orchestra at a non-Christian funeral he is caned on the bottom by the priest for "participating in things idolatrous."[13] The refusal of the missionaries to accept any element of African belief as legitimate may be a matter for abstract argument.

Yet in practice the root of African complaint was not in theological debate but in the whip hand that the missionaries had through their control of English language education:

> The white man's medicine was quick in working. Mr. Brown's school produced quick results. A few months in it were enough to make one a messenger or even a court clerk.[14]

But such educational advantages had a price tag: to pray or to remain illiterate was the simple alternative. Nzekwu describes the scene with the scathing exactness of personal memory. The children arrive hopefully at a new Roman Catholic school for the first day's teaching. They are ordered to go to opposite ends of the football field according to their parents' beliefs—the sheep and goats of the Roman Catholic and the heathen. The priest then turns to the unbaptized, sinful group and announces: "You non-Catholics, you'll go and try other schools in town. . . . If you are keen on coming to this school, then become a Catholic and come back for admission next year."[15] Amidst the laments and promises of the unsanctified, the holy are ordered to bring their baptismal certificates as the one essential document for academic registration. The young hero is properly outraged by such patent maneuverings but his old uncle has a cynicism that comes from years of experience with the white man's actions in Africa. His knowledge of history is shrewd. He sees an elementary continuity in the bribery; only the gifts have become more sophisticated—and more vital. He talks to the young man about the early days of the missionaries:

> We found them and their sermons unattractive and boring; but still we went and listened to them because, at the end of each religious service or lecture, they distributed dresses, bottles of kerosene, heads of tobacco.[16]

Now in exchange for dreary rote learning and unjust punishments you gain the infinite largesse of the School Certificate. The cynical uncle indicates that for these Africans the only self-defense is a kind of stoic

[13] Nzekwu, *Blade Among the Boys,* 85.
[14] Achebe, *Things Fall Apart,* 162.
[15] Nzekwu, *Blade Among the Boys,* 85.
[16] Ibid., 86.

passive resistance—there is as yet no alternative: "You must continue to go to school. Suffer in silence and, when you finally leave school, choose and live by your own standards . . . when they punish you at school always remember that there is no glory without thorns."[17] There is irony, probably accidental, in the uncle's choice of the Christian metaphor, but his attitude is very clear. There could be no open protest for the African could not exist without the missionary's education. One day the joyous opportunity would come when the whole matter could be repudiated. This protest is now found in the novels of those educated in the missionary schools.

The reason for the lack of protest writing outside South Africa has been explained above. Yet there is an underlying sense of protest in the first novel from Kenya, by Ngugi. As the history of the white settlers of Kenya would lead us to expect, there are two sources of protest—racism and land policy and, inevitably, in settler-influenced communities the two go together.

Although the narrator of the book is too young to have participated in the Mau Mau rebellion, as was Ngugi himself, there is evidence of the attitudes which must have sustained those rebels' anger. On every side there are comments which demonstrate the deprivation and loss that Africans had suffered after the intervention of the settlers. "You could tell the land of Black People because it was red, rough and sickly, while the land of the white settlers was green and not lacerated into small strips."[18] The lines which express this sense of theft make a very simplistic catechism:

> Do you think it's true what father says, that all the land belongs to black people?
>
> Yes. Black people have their land in the country of black people. White men have their land in their own country. It is simple. I think it was God's plan.
>
> Are there black people in England?
>
> No. England is for white people only.
>
> And they all left their country to come and rob us acres of what we have?
>
> Yes. They are robbers.[19]

But if the tone is at this point naïve, there is a more virulent conversation later in the book in which the attendant anger of protest is clear: "Don't you believe in anything? No. Nothing. Except revenge."[20]

[17] Ibid., 87.
[18] Ngugi, Weep Not, Child, 8.
[19] Ibid., 48-49.
[20] Ibid., 115.

The political assumptions of this first novel are simplistic, yet the characters are not entirely divided into heroes and villains by color alone. The corrupting force of disappointment in a white farmer's action is made credible. The decision of the hero's brother to join the Mau Mau movement is not discussed solely as a heroic decision for liberation. In him, too, a decay of character is seen in the violence, even savagery, of the life that has to be led in the bush by guerrillas existing off the land. This is a measure of the responsible attitude of the writer who is a novelist and not merely a propagandist.

This balanced attitude is also found in *No Easy Task,* the first novel written by a Malawian, Aubrey Kachingwe.[21] This book actually concerns the period of the gaining of independence from the British yet, even here, critical attention is focused upon African-interaction—foreshadowing themes similar to those employed by Achebe and Ekwensi. There is the cocktail party type of settler who mouths such views as: "We brought here everything—wealth, health, and the little civilization that there is. But what do the few ambitious boys want? To spoil everything and return back to the darkness."[22] But other Englishmen seem quite benevolent, particularly Peter Brown, the newspaper editor, who has accepted financial losses to keep an honest African paper in circulation. Even though events culminate in a state of emergency and then independence, Kachingwe also shows the disaffection and corruption within the first-generation elite as they seek to secure their own slippery positions in the midst of rapidly changing local events. There is an idealized portrait of the national leader in the description of the hero's father, but the portrait of the shrewd politician Dan Dube is more realistic. He has gained wealth and power, allegedly from illegal earnings at "Sleepy Aunt's" dubious hostelry. Many fear and despise him: " 'Do you admire Dan Dube?' 'I think he is clever. Don't you admire his brains?' 'Me!' He said it as if I had asked him to love a snake. 'He is a politician and politicians are a tribe of their own.' "[23] Dube is craftily trying to make sure of his own continuing advantage whichever way the national struggle should turn out. Like a political chameleon he responds to events without principle. " 'Dan Dube is our man.' 'He certainly behaved differently today,' I said. 'He can't afford to do otherwise.' "[24] But later an editorial announces that Dube has become "the devil's own brother."[25]

---

21 Aubrey Kachingwe, *No Easy Task* (London, 1966). Earlier novels had been written in the vernacular.
22 Ibid., 98.
23 Ibid., 88.
24 Ibid., 135.
25 Ibid., 147.

The problem that drives the nation (as well as Kachingwe's plot) is the desire for independence. But even while this is being fought for, the novelist has already begun to indicate the factional rivalries and the corruption of the coming national regime. Presumably a further book will make the link with the internal political challenge discussed in the first novel of another writer from Malawi, David Rubadiri, *No Bride Price*.[26]

But this type of protest is rare in East Africa, for literature in English there is in its infancy. Things are different to the south. Protest preoccupies every major writer as it preoccupies many other men of good will in that unhappy country. The racial classification of the author makes little difference to the actual sense of protest. What differs is only the stance, the degree of specific resentment and rejection. In this a distinction can be made between white and black novelists in terms of the direction in which their protest moves. Although both groups of writers begin with the same premises of liberal justice, the white writer, even if as politically indignant as Harry Bloom, can write with a shade more detachment. Irony is a possible mode. After all, there cannot be quite the same physical conviction when you do not need to carry a pass or search for the "non-European" entrance to a post office or a railway station. Whites make intellectual commitments that are, in the ultimate analysis, withdrawable. Africans are permanently committed by color. For African writers protest is more openly political and more specific in its demand for immediate change. They describe the violence of arrogant policemen, the savage conditions of labor on mines and farms, and the daily humiliations in the Johannesburg streets. In their protest we see from the receiving end what happens when the dispassionate racial logic of governmental policy becomes translated into daily living in a world of *slegs vir Blankes* (For Whites Only).

In contrast to the understandable immediate social protest of Africans, written protest as illustrated by whites is directed more deeply at the human fiber of events. For them what needs protesting is not the occasional violence nor even the physical restraints that they rarely have to share, but the continuing and eternal emotional deprivation which precludes the possibility of real humanity in the need for love. We see this emphasis on "love" in such titles as *Cry, the Beloved Country*,[27] *Occasion for Loving*,[28] and *Evidence of Love*.[29] In the last Dan Jacobson answers the implicit question of what is evidence of love. In

[26] David Rubadiri, *No Bride Price* (Nairobi, 1967).
[27] Alan Paton, *Cry, the Beloved Country* (London, 1948).
[28] Nadine Gordimer, *Occasion for Loving* (London, 1956).
[29] Dan Jacobson, *Evidence of Love* (London, 1959).

the South African environment he believes it to be the willingness to be jailed.

The assertion can be applied as widely in the South African context as Jacobson certainly intends it to be. In the events of his novel it is doubly ironic that it is marital love that brings a man to a jail where he demonstrates the nature of love. He is willing to sacrifice himself to display how the South African regime deliberately undermines the most immediate and tender of relationships. Kenneth, the young hero of the book, is very light-skinned but legally "coloured." He is intelligent enough to know what he has been denied, for his father is the supreme example of the "adjuster" who apes with agonizing urgency the bourgeois standards of the whites. He is humble in the face of white patronage—"sah punctuated Cornelius's speech like a tick." In London the son marries a white South African girl. They could stay on and live happily there but they decide to return to South Africa and face their situation even though this act can only be a temporary gesture without utility in any practical sense, for the results are a foregone conclusion. On arrival, Kenneth and his wife move into a hotel and, knowing that they have violated the racial laws which do not permit the cohabitation of colored and whites—married or not—they wait fully dressed for the inevitable arrest. When the police come, the hotel manager spews out a stream of abuse, spits on Kenneth, and curses him. Yet in a way the reader remains immune. We know such fanatics are the aberrations of any society; they are the monsters from whom ordinary men are divided.

This is where protest becomes supreme art: we learn of South African racial feeling, not from the committed racist whom we despise, but from the reactions of well-meaning liberals such as we imagine ourselves to be. There is the court case for offenses against the morality laws (these neat reversals between the titles of acts and their intent are straight from Orwell). Kenneth is sentenced to six months' imprisonment at hard labor and twelve strokes of the cane. The mind must boggle at this penalty in all of its horrible dimensions. But the shock is not so powerful as the emotional protest that comes after the remark of the defending counsel—a man of genuine sympathy, or how else could he take such an unpopular case? He remarks offhandedly: "That'll be four months, if they behave themselves." . . . "It could have been worse, [the judge] is a good stick at heart."[30] It is in such cheerful gossip that the true enormity of the South African situation is best exposed. It is important to stress that this is art, for propaganda, however justifiable, lacks this emotional quality. Art is more vital for propaganda

---

[30] Ibid., 182.

than the pamphleteers will recognize. We reject the perorations of the political theorists, but we cannot reject the statement of a generous man who finds that the sentence for a married couple spending a night in a Cape Town hotel of six months in jail and a whipping "could have been worse."

Dan Jacobson's technique of allowing the speakers to condemn themselves and to expose their society in innocent talk is even more subtly handled by Nadine Gordimer, who is a finer writer. She has an exact ear for dialogue and does not moralize and expound editorially upon the situation. She lets her characters speak in their natural way and in doing so she draws up the most profound condemnation that has yet been made of the South African situation. Some have criticized Nadine Gordimer because of her lack of ostentatious political commitment. This is to argue from ignorance of the role of a writer in a society which demands protest. Miss Gordimer's protest is the more total because it is not shallow. She exposes the hearts of her characters and lays bare the total disintegration of spirit that racialism creates. It is the spirit that she feels must be protected.

We may expect the openly vicious:

> "Yoo can't bring kaffirs in my bullding," she screamed. "Sitting there like this is a bloody backyard location, I mean to say, the other tenants is got a right to 'ev yoo thrown out. Kaffir women coming here, behaving like scum, living with decent people. Wha'd'yoo think, sitting here with kaffirs? . . . This is my flat, d'you hear, you've no right to walk in here." . . . "look in your lease and you'll see. . . . Read it and see. No natives unless they're in the capacity of servants."[31]

There are other characters in the same tone who become burlesque because of an arrogance that in another context could be comic. These are not shabby apartment managers but the confident wealthy of South African society. "Here! Come on, get my boots off! . . . These lazy bastards! How long d'you think this wood will last, eh? That's no good all that small stuff. . . . Makulu, Makulu eh! Plenty big logs."[32] This fatuous abuse later provokes the comment: "John really is unbelievably patient with them. I felt like giving that one careless little bastard a kick in the pants this morning—if he'd been my own boy."[33]

What Nadine Gordimer does so well is to let her characters betray themselves. What makes ordinary conversation sting is our acceptance of some external standard that exposes the ugliness of these

[31] Nadine Gordimer, *A World of Strangers* (London, 1958), 205-6.
[32] Ibid., 224.
[33] Ibid., 230.

people. Her protest is in a sense tangential. She does not say that her characters are villains; they are the ordinary people—businessmen and good fathers and husbands too. Miss Gordimer's protest is more passionate. This is, she says, what our society does to ordinary people; it makes them monsters to the outside world. Her caricatures range widely to encompass many narrow-souled people exhibiting their racial arrogance:

> "You know, I can't imagine it—I mean, a black man next to me at table, talking to me like anyone else. The idea of touching their hands. . . ." Her hand came out in the imaginary experiment and hesitated, waved back.[34]

Every bit as bad is the racial distortion of false praise. The fundamental truth which may be lost in *négritude* is that white and black are equal and that to be patronizing is to insist upon inferiority no less strongly than to be abusive.

> "The Africans were an absolutely marvelous audience. Quite the best audience we've ever had. D'you know that they actually picked up points that white audiences missed?" This was the standard comment of white companies when interviewed by the Press after a performance before a black audience, even if they had presented Anouilh to a hall full of black school children.[35]

There is anger here but it is all the more pointed and effective for two reasons. It is superbly controlled so that it does not spill over into an authorial denunciation. And it does not make its points by means of improbable puppets of unredeemed evil and unimaginable good, such as crudely represent the issues in a social realist drama. These are living people and there can even be compassion mixed with condemnation.

> "They're a strange people really. There's very little dignity left in them; they're passionate Nationalists of course, in the narrowest, most superannuated sense; they hate the English, they hate the blacks. . . . They hate and fear everything and everyone except themselves—what a miserable way to exist."[36]

This last comment is not political protest; it is an appalling record of the life these people lead in their racial prejudice and, as such, it is the artist's protest against humanity.

[34] Ibid., 251.
[35] Ibid., 203.
[36] Ibid., 184.

The other side of South African protest comes from the "non-whites," of whom the coloured novelist Alex La Guma must be considered the best to date. His novel, A *Walk in the Night,* illustrates a specific dimension of protest writing.[37] He implies that irony is a luxury reserved for the whites. His novels burn and surge with the hate that daily frustration has engendered. This mood and tone are only too understandable, but the author's inevitable antagonism produces only caricatures of people—sterile white monsters, the usual and inevitable policemen. In these circumstances there is only color and color hate. The hero is fired from his job for being impertinent but the terms of the abuse are color. "Called me a cheeky black bastard. Me, I'm not black. Anyway I said he was a no-good pore-white and he calls the manager."[38] Inevitably sex also spills across the color line. There is fierceness in the repartee when the hero refuses to share the enthusiasm of his friend for the shapely white girl walking by. " 'I don't give a damn for a bastard white arse,' [said] Michael. . . . 'That's politics,' Greene said. 'Cut out politics.' "[39] There is a violent kind of comedy here but the underlying truth is that in District Six—that area of Cape Town set aside for coloured inhabitants—everything is politics. Its daily life is a demand for protest against individual social injustice, but this can only be done through literature—through the novels of these writers—for other forms of protest are impossible. Protest becomes an impotent internal anger, never openly expressed, for the power of the authorities is too strong. The staggering discrepancy between the verbalized admission and the inner anger in the following dialogue places this bitter protest in focus. Michael, the hero of the novel, is stopped by the police on the way home. He avoids their eyes for

> It was only the very brave, or the very stupid, who dared look straight into the law's eyes, to challenge them or question their authority. . . .
>
> Yes, (you mucking boer)
>
> Yes, what? . . .
>
> Yes, baas. (you mucking bastard boer) . . . Deep down inside him the feeling of rage, frustration and violence swelled like a boil knotted with pain.[40]

This anger rings truer than the vicious scenes of corrupt police who shoot in cold blood and punch the faces of the same people who bribe them. These things do happen but the true horror rests not in the oc-

[37] Alex La Guma, A *Walk in the Night* (Evanston, 1962).
[38] Ibid., 4.
[39] Ibid., 17
[40] Ibid., 11-12.

casional sadist but in the honest man calmly going about his normal day's duty—even though that duty denies the remotest element of humanity. Here again the significant moral basis of protest is clear. Protest against the monsters who arise in any society, in the final analysis, adds up to a statement about the psychotic. Protest against a society that destroys the integrity of its ordinarily decent if apathetic citizens is another issue, and it is this more fearsome, comprehensive, and dismaying accusation that the South African novelist makes.

Criticism of the New Political Situation

With independence came the development of literature in English which often recorded contemporary events in the recently established states. Since the novels' plots were often close to autobiography, they demonstrated the attitudes of intellectuals to a particular nation's independence. Even unintentionally they were very close to the pulse of social events. In an interesting radio interview in 1964 Dennis Duerden of the Transcription Center in London questioned Cyprian Ekwensi as follows:

> Duerden: Do you see your novels as some kind of social commentary, I mean, saying something about the state of present-day Nigeria or present-day Lagos?
>
> Ekwensi: Yes, but my novels are social commentaries incidentally. I don't set out to make my novels social commentaries. If any social commentary emerges then this is something which the reader is left to get out himself. I am primarily a story teller.[41]

Ekwensi may have been a little disingenuous here in keeping with his declared aim of being a popular narrator who deplores preaching in novels. Yet what he says is true enough. Social condemnation is not usually the central element in his novels but is deduced by the reader from his portraits of politicians and the political and economic exploitation which he records.

In recent West African writing, for example, the single theme of political protest centers not so much on the direction of national policy—that receives only passing attention—as on the individuals who run the country. To this extent West African writing is diametrically opposed to the protest of South African writers. In fact, West Africans appear to have little generalized objection to the system, in spite of

[41] Africa Abroad No. 106, Recorded at the Transcription Center, London (Nov. 2, 1964).

its occasional aberrations. They say, rather, that it is man who abuses a potentially adequate system of organization. Achebe, always a superb handler of the ironic tone, clearly expresses this recognition. The following example is fascinating in that the irony cuts in at least three different directions. Sam, a successful, prosperous, and not excessively corrupt politician remarks:

> "I used to have a Nigerian as my assistant but he was an idiot. His head was swollen like a soldier ant because he went to Ibadan University. Now I have a white man who went to Oxford and he says 'sir' to me. Our people have a long way to go."[42]

Presumably his people have to learn their proper humility in the face of successful politicians like Sam!

Although the condemnation of West African writers falls upon the figures who pretend to rule them, there is also at the heart of their work a rejection of virtually all political activity. Nzekwu has one of his characters remark: "I don't play politics. It is a dirty game. I shall not be your tool in the mean job of dragging the names of people, societies and properly constituted authority in the mud."[43] It is a pessimistic view of politics and one might comment, in passing, on the odd logic, since presumably the authorities were politicians too. However, the view is repeated when a lovelorn man bewails his inadequacy in comparison with the smooth techniques of his city rival, and he is encouraged by the remark: Isn't he the little troublesome politician? He hasn't got a chance with any literate girl in town . . . No decent girl . . . would marry him."[44] Though demonstrably one-sided, this must be a very widespread view because it is repeatedly found in West African novels, an attitude going beyond the condemnation of a corrupt politician to a blanket rejection of political activity itself. Remarks of this tenor occur again and again in Ekwensi's *Jagua Nana*:

> "Politics not for you, Freddie. You got education. You got culture. You're a gentleman an' proud. Politics be game for dog."[45]

> "Since he don' wan' to fight, I must fight him firs'. Das politics. Spare no foe!"[46]

> She was thinking . . . how ordinary people she knew became transformed by this strange devil they called politics.[47]

[42] Achebe, *No Longer at Ease* (London, 1963), 69.
[43] Nzekwu, *Wand of Noble Wood*, 27.
[44] Ibid., 117.
[45] Cyprian Ekwensi, *Jagua Nana* (London, 1961), 103.
[46] Ibid., 106.
[47] Ibid., 116.

Although the attack is launched against the corruption of politicians, the general basis for criticism is a sense of disappointment and of frustrated expectation. The feeling of being let down by events is brilliantly and wittily exposed in Wole Soyinka's intensely complex, symbolic play, *A Dance of the Forest*,[48] which was written for Nigeria's independence ceremonies. Never one for sycophantic presentations, Soyinka wrote a drama which is partly a parody—a satire on false expectations. The people ask their ancestors to return from the dead to help them celebrate the glorious occasion. They assume that the dead will represent the great African glories of the empire of Songhai. Instead, they appear in the historical flashbacks as corrupt, vicious, greedy, and lecherous, and, since each character played a duplicate part in sequences dealing with the present, the message was clear. The present is the same as the past. Human beings play out the same follies and the same sins throughout the centuries.

The relevance of this statement to the theme of protest is seen when one considers how this obvious comment must have shocked the dignitaries and the people gathered for the first production. The degree of disappointed anticipation was a measure of the hypocrisy and unjustified optimism with which independence was being greeted. Clearly, for all African states, independence was a supreme moment; yet as a stage in nation building it was the beginning, not the climax, of social change. Misunderstanding of this fact created the sense of letdown. The shiny mirage of wealth and progress that was implicitly promised, proved on inspection to be a society where only a few could gain the fruits of independence, at least immediately.

As Achebe sharply wrote of it in retrospect:

A man who has just come in from the rain and dried his body and put on dry clothes is more reluctant to go out again than another who has been indoors all the time. The trouble with our new nation . . . was that none of us had been indoors long enough to be able to say, "To hell with it " We had all been in the rain together until yesterday. Then a handful of us—the smart and the lucky and hardly ever the best —had scrambled for the one shelter our former rulers left, and had taken it over and barricaded themselves in. And from within they sought to persuade the rest through numerous loudspeakers, that the first phase of the struggle had been won and that the next phase—the extension of our house—was even more important and called for new and original tactics; it required that all argument should cease and the whole people speak with one voice and that any more dissent and argument outside the door of the shelter would subvert and bring down the whole house.[49]

[48] Wole Soyinka, *A Dance of the Forest* (London, 1963).
[49] Chinua Achebe, *A Man of the People* (London, 1966), 34.

For those who had not had the good fortune to establish them-selves under the cover of an elite governmental position, independ-ence brought a less than happy existence. There were the slums of too rapid urbanization, and disillusionment with the false metropolitan glamor that had brought young people into the shanty towns of Lagos. As the people contemplated the difference between their hopes and their actual situations, they looked to their government and saw the rich, idle, and corrupt politicians shamelessly preying on the populace and allowing the whole administrative structure to descend to the cor-ruption which had battened upon the possibilities of honorable change in Nigeria.

Cyprian Ekwensi speaks for these people. His situations are melo-dramatic, his characters are sometimes puppets, his plots are often only a plethora of uncontrolled events, but his books are the best mirror of modern Lagos. The shabby slums with their stinking water and slime, the battle for survival against rich Syrian landlords, the frenetic energy of dancing the High Life in a hundred dismal bars, all these show the dissatisfaction that explodes the dream-form of national freedom. His first novel, *People of the City*,[50] is not a very coherent book but its title may be taken literally. These are the people of the new city and their way of life is the frenzied way in which they must live. The protest here is largely unfocused; it makes only occasional passing complaints about grasping landlords, and these are Syrian, not African. Mainly the book is concerned with a sense of wretchedness that is hardly amenable to control. It is indicative that, in the rather simplistic ending of the novel, Amuso Sango, the hero, and his new wife seek to leave the coun-try in order to find a happier world abroad (ironically enough in Ghana). This relieves Ekwensi of the need to postulate alternative so-cial improvements within Lagos itself.

It is not until his second novel, *Jagua Nana*, that Ekwensi takes the investigation a step beyond the description of social malaise and toward a specifically political protest. This element in Ekwensi's work has largely been overlooked, partly because a general scorn of his se-riousness as a writer has prevented his books from receiving their due consideration, and partly because the character of Jagua Nana her-self has caught the attention of readers so exclusively that they are not sufficiently aware of the attendant dramatic figure of Uncle Taiwo, the politician. For all her energy, Jagua Nana is a stereotype. The meaning of the name Nana, implying the borrowed tradition of the prostitute on the make, is not greatly changed by being transplanted to Lagos. The implication of Jagua, the second part of her name, is a fascinating social comment for it derives not from the sleek jungle cat

[50] Cyprian Ekwensi, *People of the City* (London, 1954).

but from the prestige in Lagos of owning the British sports car. Jagua reflects the tinsel glitter which the city exemplifies—the glamorized way in which the lure of the lights and cars of Lagos draws the village girl to the excitement of the town. But Ekwensi's criticism is directed not at her folly, not even at the city and its need for administrative reform, but at the politicians.

Uncle Taiwo symbolizes all of them. Uncle Taiwo is a magnificent creation. Hugely profligate and grossly demanding in all his appetites, he dominates the book like an evil version of Falstaff, confident, vulgar, corrupt, vicious, and unashamed. He has adopted the political maneuvering of the West and, with the addition of African violence, raised it to a corrupt art. He is almost a total villain. His opinion of African society is brilliantly established in a few lines during a scene in a night club to which he has taken Jagua. Instead of the typical secondhand jazz, the management has brought in a folk dance troupe which performs impressively. Taiwo's reaction is a cameo of his character.

> On Uncle Taiwo's face she saw a look of boredom. "Is all nonsense! We don' come here to see dat. We come to hear High Life and jazz, das all.". . .
>
> A man began arguing with him telling him that jazz had its origins in that kind of fetish dancing, that this was a throw-back to the birthdays of jazz. Uncle Taiwo yawned, "Music! Give us real music!" "You jus' heard real music," Jagua told him. "Jus' like in me own country. We get nearly de same kin' of dance."
>
> "Is bushman dancing!" said Uncle Taiwo. He roared with laughter.[51]

This significant repudiation of any remnant of African tradition is symptomatic of the new politicians, ignorance fostering contempt. Taiwo's method of political activity is striking and utterly cynical:

> When Uncle Taiwo had acknowledged the cheers, he mounted the rostrum. Then he opened his black bag and coming down moved among the people, scattering handfuls of ten shilling notes, like rice grains on a bride. The election ground had become a rugger ground with the printed notes as the ball. . . . Loyally Jagua followed him, and as they moved on the wild ones closed in behind them, scrabbling and fighting.[52]

Later Jagua asks him where the money came from and he says: "Is party money. I give dem de money like dat, so them kin taste what we

[51] Ekwensi, *Jagua Nana*, 132.
[52] Ibid., 196.

goin' to do for them if they vote us into power." "The campaign continued."[53] This scornful statement is sufficient indictment.

The death of Uncle Taiwo after losing an election—after so much strong-arm violence and corruption and murder—is most powerful, more so than the end of Achebe's last book, *Man of the People*. There the much praised irony verges on the cheaper effect of sarcasm. But in Taiwo's death scene, Ekwensi's lines have a controlled power.

> Lagos was in a state of chaos that day. It seemed as if the ghost of that corpse had gone abroad among them. The body was lying there twisted and swollen; one knee was drawn up against the chest, the arms were clutching at the breast, rigid like a statue. . . . In Africa you see these things. . . .[54]

The political issue is broached more directly in Ekwensi's third novel, *Beautiful Feathers*. Again critics have ignored his sharp political observations because they reject the fundamental sentimentality of the novel's plot which has diluted its valid elements. Here there is no huge monster of the ilk of Taiwo. There are small ratty men like the hero's brother-in-law, Jacob, who is more a sniveling hyena than a ferocious lion. Brother Jacob could change two votes into a thousand—"for a consideration"—and for him the peaceful demonstrations for African unity conceived by Wilson, the idealistic hero, are only occasions for looting and rape. When Wilson's new pan-Africanist party begins to carve out a place for itself, and a cautious millionaire offers some financing with a view to being able to exert pressure should Wilson by chance become influential in the government, Wilson is morally scathing in rejecting the funds and the attendant control. The answer of the unfazed millionaire is crushing in its simplicity: "And I thought you were serious." To be serious is to be corrupt, for how else is power achieved? More comic, though no less politically trenchant, is the portrait of the minister called, in a title worthy of Evelyn Waugh, the Minister of Consolation. His toadies and sycophants haunt his office, seeking the consolation of the handout. He is vain and disagreeable, patronizes his white secretary while he practices his photogenic grin before the mirror. The situation is comic; the implications are ugly. Surrounded by supplicants, he hands out some money, accepts some appeals, and preens himself in the attendant gratitude.

> "Thank you, sir. Next election you will go in—by the power of our vote."
> "By the power of God," corrected another man, breaking into the room,

53 Ibid., 196.
54 Ibid., 214.

and now there were twenty of them waving envelopes addressed to the Minister. "It is God who is above everything."

"Just so. Next time you go in by the power of God—and our vote."[55]

Here is democracy at work—in the scathing interpretation of Cyprian Ekwensi.

In almost all African novels, the theme of bribery and corruption is omnipresent. It is seen in Thomas Aluko's *Kinsman and Foreman*,[56] in which the family which had struggled to educate its son anticipates its reward; the corruption and bribery conventionally attendant on his newly earned position are to be kept within the family group. Also relevant is Obi, the young hero of Achebe's second novel, *No Longer at Ease,* which is concerned with contemporary Lagos. Obi's initial shock comes when he returns to Nigeria and a customs officer offers to allow him duty-free concessions for cash. But this distaste is lost when he later takes advantage of the chances for gain which are attached to his position as secretary to the scholarship board: "Had not a Minister of State said, albeit in an unguarded, alcoholic moment, that the trouble was not in receiving bribes, but in failing to do the thing for which the bribe was given?"[57] Obi treads a slippery road to disaster as bribe leads to bribe and his conscience, grown more flexible, becomes acquiescent. The final irony of the judge's humiliating remark becomes clear: "I cannot comprehend how a young man of your education. . . ." And this is reminiscent of Onuora Nzekwu's young hero, Patrick, in *Blade Among the Boys,* whose first application for scholarship ends up in the wastepaper basket for lack of a "dash." His aggrieved recognition that nothing is achieved without bribery assures his seeking his share when he finally buys himself a position as a railway clerk. A farmer requests the most ordinary service of goods delivery to the town, and, wordlessly, Patrick's hand is held out, the palm significantly up. Again and again this theme is a motivating factor—the pernicious and continuous undermining of the efficiency of government through bribes. The only honest man in *No Longer at Ease* is Mr. Green, the expatriate, and he despises all Africans.

Contemporary fiction does not contain a single optimistic interpretation of recent West African history. There always is the cry against the elite, now African, but as hungry for power and as contemptuous of "locals" as ever the colonial administrators had been. The painfully admitted irony is in the recognition that the new elite is more self-seeking than the old who, at least, had a pompously su-

---

[55] Ekwensi, *Beautiful Feathers,* 76.
[56] Thomas M. Aluko, *Kinsman and Foreman* (London, 1966).
[57] Achebe, *No Longer at Ease,* 88.

perior sense of the white man's duty with which to sustain their integrity.

The climax of this rejection of political maneuvering comes in the latest novels of Ekwensi and Achebe. Each contains vicious indictments. Ekwensi generalizes, finding wider complaint:

> The generation of today; a generation that was in a hurry to live, to make progress, to accumulate wealth, to bed girls, to eat, drink, be promoted to fill fat-salaried posts, to be in power only to line one's pockets. A generation of greed, never satisfied, never leisurely.[58]

Achebe is more scornful in the sarcastic denunciation that concludes his novel, talking of "the fat-dripping, gummy, eat-and-let-eat regime."

> A regime which inspired the common saying that a man could only be sure of what he had put away safely in his gut or, in language ever more suited to the times: "you chop, me self I chop, palaver finish"; a regime in which you saw a fellow cursed in the morning for stealing a blind man's stick and later in the evening saw him again mounting the altar of a new shrine in the presence of all the people to whisper into the ear of the chief celebrant.[59]

Ekwensi, in *Iska*, particularly concerns himself with the Igbo-Hausa rivalry that was soon to break into massacres and civil war. There are numerous moments of moralizing of the variety: "People are only human. There is no tribe which is all bad. . . . In the same way there is no tribe which is all good."[60] Such platitudes do not alter the direction of blame: Hausa and Igbo "both had lived peacefully together for a hundred years. Then came politics—the vulture's foot that spoils the stew."[61] But now along with the common accusation there is a new note of violence which in Achebe's novel culminates in the military coup, a literary device which coincidentally paralleled the actual one. Ekwensi sees other evidence of the violence of the situation. The dialogue with a drug-smoking youth exposes the savagery latent in the political and social frustration so regularly recorded:

> "Why do you wreck people's cars?"
> "Is the instruction."
> "Why?"
> "People have done nothing for us, that's why. We have independence. They just leave us to suffer and they get all the big money and everything."[62]

[58] Cyprian Ekwensi, *Iska* (London, 1966), 73.
[59] Achebe, *Man of the People*, 141.
[60] Ekwensi, *Iska*, 39.
[61] Ibid., 14.
[62] Ibid., 108.

The violence that concluded the two last novels of Nigeria's and Africa's best known novelists was only a premonition of the explosion that was going to shatter their society. The diagnosis of corruption and violence was sharp enough, although they could not have anticipated the direction that it was going to take in their country.

From Central Africa, Rubadiri's recent first novel is no more optimistic. Unlike Achebe's prescient recognition, Rubadiri's terminal coup is as yet fictional, but the sustaining tone of the book links it identifiably with the theme of *A Man of the People* and *Iska*. Rubadiri's country came to the threshold of independence later and so more resentment remains against the residue of the colonial regime. Promotion often remains blocked by expatriates:

> "It looks like the break I've been waiting for. But what a hell of a time to wait for it. . . . Independence so far away behind. . . . [and your promotion?]
>
> Not a hope. Two more whites arrived today. Contracts for four years."[63]

Yet independence has brought changes. Those who were identified too closely with the colonial regime have been ostracized. The subcontractor to whom "easy money had given the colonial mentality that believed that the whiteman was there forever. . . . " was now being called The Stooge, "a kind of pox to the people." His power ended ironically when, with intentional moderation, he sought compromise by joining "a party started by a dyed-in-the-wool white liberal."[64]

But Lombe, the hero, is not above temptation; rather, he lacks opportunity. Being given a ride in a chauffeur-driven Mercedes, "Lombe suddenly wished he was a Minister. No wonder these people did everything they could to get votes from the people."[65]

Rubadiri's conclusion invites mere moralizing, which compares ill with Achebe's authoritative irony, but it makes the same point.

> "Poor Africa," said Lombe, "Isn't it tragically funny that after all those glorious days of fighting for freedom, now that we have it we behave like a couple of dogs—fighting when there is enough food and to spare for everyone."[66]

The radio announcement of the coup mouths the inevitable truisms which are no less true for having become clichés in the African context.

[63] Rubadiri, *No Bride Price*, 16.
[64] Ibid., 97.
[65] Ibid., 28.
[66] Ibid., 153.

Not only has there been corruption, murder, and injustice but their policies and love of power have forced them to use all means to destroy the people . . . the ambitions of a handful of people to whom the only achievement was power and the retention of power.[67]

Against this recognition and our experience of contemporary events, the cheerful optimism of Sammy, Rubadiri's successful young nationalist, seems suspiciously thin.

Present Striving

We cannot yet be certain what the tone of the next novels to come from these areas will be. However, the strict honesty of the artist has refused to be impressed by the pretences of his society, and it is likely that other regimes will receive the same scathing condemnation should they lack the integrity which is so desperately desired.

The issue that establishes the direction of the protest writing is the utopia toward which the African writer aspires. Failure to achieve this ideal provokes that social criticism which is the basis of protest. From the discussion thus far the issues are clear enough: the continuing colonial racial oppression and the greedy inadequacy of present administrations. The sought-for alternative is a series of nations so free from external intervention and so responsible in their internal organization that they would be able to plan for a pan-African union worthy of the potential of that continent. The trouble is that this prospect is so remote, given present conditions in contemporary Africa, that the writers lack the conviction from which comes the authority to create plausible dialogue and character. The classic example of this inadequacy is a novel from Sierra Leone by William Conton simply called *The African*.

It begins with a rather warm and detailed biographical account, and allows the hero to reach an improbable pinnacle of political success which he then throws away in a quixotic impulse for revenge. In England he meets a girl from Pretoria.

"That makes us both Africans. Small world isn't it?" She smiled a little sadly. "There's more difference than that of pigment between a West African and a South African I'm afraid."

"Not fundamentally, you know," I insisted staunchly.[68]

The girl is deliberately murdered by a racist character horrified by even potential miscegenation. Our hero obtains a visa to South Africa.

[67] Ibid., 156
[68] William Conton, *The African* (London, 1960), 63.

In a scene redolent with sentimentality and devoid of the reality from which credibility derives, he meets the assassin, who happens to be dead drunk in the gutter. The hero takes no revenge. "It was pity I found in my heart for him not hate. I stooped quickly, lifted him gently, and bore him through the easing rain to the safety of his home."[69] Racial conflict will not be eliminated by such Dickensian gestures and this is why few South African writers have paid even lip service to the early prospect of racial unity. But there are exceptions.

The most obvious advocate of the necessity for human reconciliation between the races is found in the famous novel by Alan Paton, *Cry, the Beloved Country*. He is right, of course, in calling for a willingness in men to honor each other, and yet in the Christian humility of his African protagonist there is an almost unbelievable quantity of spiritual forgiveness in the face of the consistent enmity of oppressors. Paton must be correct at the deepest moral level, but such is the ferocity of the South African struggle that one almost questions the relevance of so much generosity in a land where there is so little of it left on either side.

With some qualifications, this mood can be detected in the first major work of Peter Abrahams, *Mine Boy*. Both these books were published relatively early in the 1950's. Perhaps now there would inevitably be less generosity of spirit and more open protest. Yet *Mine Boy*, which concerns the urban assimilation of a kind of noble savage—an innocent African who comes to Johannesburg seeking work in the mines—may betray elements unintended by the writer. The affirmation of the noble equality of men is found in the lines quoted at the opening of the book. Ironically they are by Rudyard Kipling, the poet of British imperialism.

> But there is neither East nor West,
> Border, nor breed nor birth,
> When two strong men come face to face,
> Though they come from the ends of the earth![70]

In this case the ends of the earth are the ultimate oppositions of black and white in South African society. Paddy, the white miner, and Xuma, the mine boy, try their best to establish a relationship based on mutual manly respect. To some small extent they succeed even though a strike brings police intervention and jail. This is the hopeful element in the novel. Yet there is a kind of sad irony in a discussion which runs:

[69] Ibid., 213.
[70] "The Ballad of East and West," as quoted in Peter Abrahams, *Mine Boy* (London, 1954).

"[Chris] wants to be your friend. . . ."

"He is white," Xuma said.

The smile faded from her face and there was sadness in her eyes. . . . "And so you cannot be friends," she said.[71]

It is indicative of our own sentiments that the most powerful character is not the moral Xuma nor the honorable Paddy nor the loving and uncomplaining girl friend Maisie. It is the educated Zulu girl whose learning has only extended her recognition of all that she is denied. Her words echo as a bitter protest long after the hopeful ending and Paddy's self-denial seem merely gestures. She exemplifies the corrosion of the color bar. "Inside me there is something wrong. And it is because I want the things of the white people. . . . Inside I am not black and I do not want to be a black person."[72] Here one suspects is a more authentic cry of deprivation. Men can only manage so much altruism. Few have attempted generosity in novels which are rather concerned with angry protesting cries of revenge for daily humiliation. The issue of color prejudice against which so many African writers have protested is so deep-seated that they make little attempt to suggest remedies. Lewis Nkosi's drama, *The Rhythm of Violence*,[73] for all its romantic self-sacrifice, shows only the perniciously damaging effect of racial prejudice throughout society.

A complaint of the West African writer is that the selfishness of the despised national politicians has prevented the union of the fragmented nations of independent Africa. As Conton writes of his admittedly fictional land: "Some of our leaders are ruining our country even now. Look at the way they want to split my country up."[74] Again it is the dishonesty and hypocrisy of the politicians which are challenged. One is made to admit sardonically in *Iska*, "My business is to capitalize—on anything, any situation. That's politics. . . . I don't tell my voters that. I talk to them about unity, solidarity, brotherhood of man, things like that. They like it."[75]

One can only have a most pessimistic view of the prospects for pan-Africanism in the immediate future. The writers recognize this too, so in a sense only lip service is paid to this prospect. It is not that narrow nationalism should not be protested, but that the chance of change is so utopian that it is not easy to present it as a functioning, motivating force. Perhaps this is why, in Ekwensi's *Beautiful Feathers*,

[71] Ibid., 96.
[72] Ibid., 89.
[73] Lewis Nkosi, *The Rhythm of Violence* (London, 1964).
[74] Conton, *The African*, 129.
[75] Ekwensi, *Iska*, 182.

Wilson has such an element of ineffectiveness in him for all the false confidence of the artificial ending, which contradicts so much that the novel has cleverly established. A speech such as Wilson makes on behalf of his political party, the Nigerian Movement for African and Malagasy Solidarity, has that hollow political ring of the impractical even without the sad extra irony of our present insight. "Colonialism is gone but separatist influences are at work. Let Nigeria set an example by smashing them before all Africa. We are already united internally. . . ."[76] In this novel the desire for African union is expressed by a rather muddled symbolic hunt. The lack of decisive clarity, and the choice of the hunt image, makes its own comment upon the distant, elusive nature of the quarry—pan-African union. Wilson is sent by the rather idealized prime minister of his country to a conference on unity in a nearby French-speaking African country. The delegates are treated to a hunt, and the symbolism appears. All of the delegates shoot, and someone manages to shoot a strange beast apparently unknown in Africa.

> It was a very rare specimen and no one could name it, but everyone believed it was highly prized. Some of the hunters wanted the horns, some wanted the whole beast preserved in a museum and immediately an argument arose and voices became loud. . . . Confusion spread. Wilson saw the white man carrying off the beast and running down the slope. He aimed at the retreating white man, but a shot struck him in the ribs and he fell.[77]

It is all rather obscure, but the intention is clear enough; and if we do not readily grasp the point the president of the country visits Wilson in the hospital to tell us all. "You know . . . it is like the struggle for African Unity. While Africa burns, interested parties carry away the loot. We must be on our guard."[78]

Protest in African writing concerns the present. There is little time to offer recriminations about the past, to speculate about the might-have-beens. "Now" is the concern of writers. Their nows are different, and it is this that marks the differences within their literary protests. For South Africa the present is an oppression which must be challenged by every line, by every device of literary condemnation. In West Africa in many ways the situation is not much less gloomy. Their protests are differently directed, but equally scathing. Both protests are based on moral principles—upon the necessity of brotherhood in

[76] Ekwensi, *Beautiful Feathers*, 48.
[77] Ibid., 135.
[78] Ibid., 136.

South Africa and upon political integrity in West Africa. When these deeply sought ideals are directly incorporated into novels they appear hollow. Politically such changes are too remote for even the most optimistic to expect them to come soon or to come without attendant social upheaval. For this reason contemporary African writers have avoided speculating about that future utopia which is too distant and visionary to allow a realistic expression. Their reality is their existing society, which demands impassioned criticism and protest. Nevertheless, it is important to insist that the degree of anger and the quality of the criticism which mark the protest theme in the new African literature in English are measures of belief in the principles which are so outrageously being violated in these countries. Criticism is sterile without an attendant moral certainty. Implicit in so much African writing is an assertion of the kind of life which would offer the individual the dignity and honor sought passionately by all Africans even though they are still confronted with such disconcerting hurdles of greed and violence.

AN EARLY ANGOLAN PROTEST:

THE RADICAL JOURNALISM OF

JOSÉ DE FONTES PEREIRA (1823-1891)

DOUGLAS L. WHEELER

Protest against Portuguese activities has been a hardy perennial in Angola. Until the nineteenth century much of it was initiated by tribal Africans—black men with no European education. Increased Europeanization and education, however, led to a more varied and complex pattern. Thus, since about 1850, both Europeans and *assimilados*[1] have also taken part in expressing dissatisfaction.

The traditional form of protest against Portuguese rule was one of armed rebellion. In this way a kind of "micro-nationalism" had been expressed in the ancient Kongo kingdom in northern Angola, where Portuguese activities had often produced a negative and violent reaction. On occasion, however, the Kongo reaction was limited to written protests. Thus, starting in the sixteenth century, several kings of Kongo wrote letters of royal protest against the Portuguese slavers of São Tomé and Principe to the King of Portugal and to the Pope. In a sense, they were a "national" expression of protest. More modern instances may also be found in the actions of several Kongo princes, *assimilados*, and members of the Agua Rosada dynasty. Thus, Prince Nicolas[2]

---

[1] The Portuguese word *assimilado* (literally "an assimilated one") originally meant simply a native who had assimilated some Portuguese culture. This term came into use in the nineteenth century. In the 1920's and 1930's, however, the term was given a legal meaning in Portuguese law: a statute of 1929 divided the colonial population into "natives" and "non-natives." Among "non-natives" were Europeans and *assimilados*, both of whom enjoyed rights of Portuguese citizenship. To become an *assimilado* after this law, then, one had to pass certain qualifying tests. For an explanation of one aspect of this practice, see James Duffy, *Portuguese Africa* (Cambridge, 1959), 293-97. For a discussion of the position of the *assimilado* in Angolan history, see the forthcoming book by Douglas L. Wheeler and René Pélissier, *Angola* (London, 1970).

[2] For a discussion of Prince Nicolas of Agua Rosada e Sardonia, see Douglas L. Wheeler, "Nineteenth Century African Protest in Angola: Prince Nicolas of Kongo (1830?–1860)," *African Historical Studies*, I (1969), 40-59.

(1830?–60), a son of the King of Kongo, wrote letters to the King of Portugal and the Emperor of Brazil and to a Lisbon newspaper in 1859, protesting Portuguese activities in the Kongo and asserting his own candidacy for the throne of Kongo. His protests broke the traditional pattern since they were in the form of written, legal, European-inspired arguments, and not in the form of violence.

With the exception of Nicolas's celebrated dissents, however, the leading mode of nonviolent protest in Angola was journalism. Such writing took place mainly in Luanda, the capital, from 1870 to 1922, a period in which rigorous and systematic censorship of the Portuguese press in Angola had not been instituted. Indeed, before 1922 the numerous if ephemeral journals of the "free press" era (1866–1922) in Angola[3] suffered only occasionally from the censor's pencil. There are several reasons to help explain the relative freedom of this era: liberalism in Portuguese domestic politics, an "open" atmosphere in the colonial territory's press, and the fact that literacy in Portuguese was limited to all but a handful of Europeans and assimilados. However, this relative freedom was conditioned by the mood of the day and by the character of the Governor General in charge.

In its early stages, modern African nationalism in Angola derived some of its inspiration and development from the feverish press activity of this period. Writers and editors of all races participated. Many of the protesters were inspired and aided by Europeans. But most of them were largely self-educated; they had not visited Europe, but had been employed at one time or another in the Portuguese colonial and civil service. They informed themselves of public affairs in Africa and Europe through contemporary literature from Brazil, the United States, and Western Europe. In general, their interests and concerns seemed to coincide with those of the political dissenters, mainly republicans, in Portugal and Brazil. The educated sons of Angola learned from the increasingly effective attacks of Portuguese republicans on the dying Bragança monarchy in Portugal. In dealing with issues in Angola some assimilados used many of the same arguments, polemical methods, and styles. In a sense, therefore, early Angolan nationalism included a great deal of republican, or anti-monarchical, content and style.

Prominent among early Angolan assimilado journalists was the mestiço (mulatto) lawyer, José de Fontes Pereira (1823–91).[4] A writer as well as a civil servant in Luanda, Fontes Pereira achieved the comfortless reputation of enfant terrible of the volatile Luandan press. He

[3] Júlio de Castro Lopo, Jornalismo de Angola. Subsídios Para A Sua História (Luanda, 1964), 19. All translations from the Portuguese are by the author.

[4] Mestiço, in Portuguese ("a mixed one"), means a person of mixed blood, the offspring of a Portuguese and an African, or a Portuguese and a mestiço.

was at once sensational, "fighting reporter," political polemicist, social critic, African champion, and reformist. It is difficult to place this remarkable spirit in any definite category for he was a man of many interests and his protests were sometimes contradictory. Nevertheless, his place as a protester is assured by his radicalism, his identification with Angola and Angolans as opposed to Portugal and Portuguese, and by the reaction he elicited from the conservative Portuguese interests of his day. Fontes Pereira influenced only a small circle of educated Angolan *mestiços* and Africans, and a few liberal Europeans, mainly in the coastal region around Luanda. A brief examination of his life and an analysis of the significant articles he wrote in the Portuguese press in Angola can serve to indicate his historical significance.

Born in or near Luanda in May 1823, José de Fontes Pereira was the offspring, probably, of a Portuguese father, one João de Fontes,[5] and an African mother. Young José was raised in Luanda, attended a local primary school, and faithfully attended the Luanda Cathedral, Our Lady of Remedies. As a man he lived in a time of economic and social upheaval in Angola. By the time he was forty-three, he had witnessed the beginning of the revolution in Angolan life brought about by abolition of the Atlantic slave trade (1842–45), which had been Angola's major source of revenue; the institution of Portuguese reforms to replace the slave trade with legitimate sources of revenue from new taxation of Africans and customs duties (1850–60); the attempt to abolish the ancient institution of slavery in Angola (1858); the opening of Angolan ports to foreign commerce with the resulting appearance of foreign representatives (1844); steam navigation on the Cuanza River; and the establishment of the first regular private weekly newspaper in Luanda (1866).

José de Fontes Pereira did not begin his career in Angola as a journalist. By reading history and law he obtained a *carta*, a license to practice law, probably in the 1850's, and entered the government service as a clerk or scribe in Luanda.[6] He married Izabel Josephina de Fontes Pereira, about whose ethnic background we know nothing, and had several children. His associates were mainly people of color. A religious man and a devout Roman Catholic linked by training and

---

[5] Castro Lopo, *Jornalismo*, 76. A photograph of Fontes Pereira in this book shows him to be a mulatto, fairly light in skin, but with some Negroid facial features.

[6] *O Desastre* (Luanda weekly), 30 May 1891; *A Verdade* (Luanda), 3 Feb. 1888.

friendship to the Luanda clergy, he defended the Church and later criticized anti-clerical activities in his articles.[7]

Much of Fontes Pereira's personal life remains a mystery, but the year 1875 stands out as a tragic landmark. At that time his sixteen-year-old son, Manuel, was for no apparent reason murdered by an African servant or slave who had been brought up in their Luanda household. The father's bereavement was deepened by the death of his young daughter, Maria, which followed the shock of hearing the news of her brother's murder.[8] The third unfortunate event of the year was Fontes Pereira's dismissal from his government post and the loss of his lawyer's license.[9] The Governor General of Angola, the tough and uncompromising José Baptista de Andrade, dismissed him summarily as punishment for his violent attacks on the government in the republican weekly, O Cruzeiro do Sul ("The Southern Cross").[10] Two years later Fontes Pereira had, however, regained his position with the civil service and his lawyer's license.[11] But history foreshadowed further conflict with the Portuguese authorities and settlers—his position as a lawyer and his career as a journalist were both to get him into further trouble.

Meanwhile the fledgling Luandan press, which had begun to appear on a regular weekly basis only in the late 1860's, had already attracted the talented mestiço because it was a forum for the expression of grievance and protest.[12] Fontes Pereira began to write occasional letters to the press, probably in the late 1860's. His name first appeared in the Angolan press, however, on September 1, 1870, when

[7] O Ultramar (Luanda), 1 Aug., 1 Sept. 1882; O Cruzeiro do Sul (Luanda), 31 July 1875. Unless otherwise indicated all these Angolan newspapers were consulted in the collection held in the Library of the Câmara Municipal, Luanda, Angola.

[8] O Cruzeiro do Sul, 27 Aug. 1875, 27 Sept. 1875.

[9] Ibid., 30 Dec. 1875.

[10] Ibid., 26 Feb. 1876.

[11] Ibid., 8 Nov. 1877.

[12] Until the 1880's European journalists had dominated the press, because the few papers were European-run and financed, with only a few Angolan mestiços writing occasional articles. After 1881, however, an African press developed, the earliest probably being O Echo D'Angola, which appeared in November 1881 in Luanda. (See Castro Lopo, Jornalismo, 75). Though it rarely used the local African vernacular, Kimbundu, but tended to publish in Portuguese, this pioneer African press did publish some articles in Kimbundu and did use a few African titles. Although a recent article published in Angola suggests that the pioneer African press did publish entire papers in the Kimbundu language (Carlos Alberto Lopes Cardoso, "Dois Jornais Quimbundos De Luanda No Último Quartel Do Século XIX," Boletim Cultural Da Câmara Municipal De Luanda, XVI [July-Sept. 1967], 26-29), I examined these newspapers in the collection used by Cardoso, and found that Portuguese was used more than Kimbundu in these numbers.

he signed a letter-petition to the government praising an interim Governor General, J. J. de Graca, for work in Luanda and earlier in Moçâmedes, and requesting that Portugal appoint Graca as permanent Governor General "for the prosperity and well-being of Angola."[13] His first protest writing dates from 1871 or 1872. In an article appearing in 1873 he noted that he had, one or two years earlier, in the European-run journal *O Mercantil,* attacked the scandal of the export of African forced labor to the island of São Tomé.[14]

Fontes Pereira's most active period of journalism was in the twenty years from 1870 to 1890. He wrote not only for the Luandan press but also for several republican papers in Lisbon and Oporto. Until 1873 and the appearance of the pro-Republican weekly paper, *O Cruzeiro do Sul,* he had, however, no vehicle for radical, extreme criticism in Luanda. The first regular private weekly, a government gazette begun in 1845, was from 1866 called *A Civilização d'Africa Portugueza* and was financed and edited by Europeans. Reflecting a moderate, European-settler point of view, the editors favored more Portuguese aid for Angola—more autonomy and reforms—but *A Civilização* was pro-monarchist. *O Cruzeiro do Sul* was a radical departure from the earlier journals, for, though it was owned by Europeans, it espoused republicanism and took a muckraking approach to most issues. This sheet manufactured controversy. Inspired by rising Republican agitation against the Portuguese monarchy at home, this radical weekly began its tortured existence in 1873. In number twelve,[15] Fontes Pereira began his active crusade against the inefficiency, injustice, and corruption of Portuguese rule in Angola. His program of attack and assertion suggests a rather deep liberal conscience combined with skepticism, tempered by loyalty to Portuguese culture and liberalism in the tradition of King Pedro IV and his liberal constitution.[16]

What was the course of Fontes Pereira's extracurricular career of journalism, and how did this affect his life and times? First, it is important to understand the nature of his criticism and the development of his radicalism vis-à-vis Portuguese colonial rule.

The subject matter of his journalism may be divided into the following topics: social-humanitarian criticism, political reformism, and the assertion of African rights. In the area of social-humanitarian criticism,

[13] *O Mercantil* (Luanda), 1 Sept. 1870.
[14] *O Cruzeiro do Sul,* 1 Sept. 1873.
[15] Ibid., 1 Sept. 1873.
[16] Ibid., 9 Apr. 1874; *O Ultramar,* 5 Oct. 1882; for material on Pedro IV, see Harold Livermore, *A New History of Portugal* (Cambridge, 1966), 268-79.

he consistently attacked the widespread practices of forced labor and slavery in Angola, and of labor export to São Tomé; the low status of Angolans as opposed to metropolitan Portuguese; the lack of educational facilities for both Europeans and Africans; economic inequalities; the wretched conditions in local prisons, and the treatment of prisoners. Throughout his writings he stressed the need for an adequate educational system: he claimed that there was not "one regular primary school" up to good European standards in Angola.[17] In attacking what he once referred to as "recruitment by the whip,"[18] he touched on a major problem in Angolan history which has angered (sometimes for different reasons) generations of Portuguese and Angolan nationalists alike. Fontes Pereira's approach was at once challenging and penetrating. His writings connected forced labor and slavery to the syndrome which characterized what he considered the poor quality of Portuguese colonization. He suggested that the system of lingering illegitimate enterprise, though abolished or reformed on paper, actually ruined free enterprise and undermined trade between Luanda and the hinterland. The stagnation of agriculture in Angola, he believed, was also a result of this syndrome. To Fontes Pereira, the much discussed shortage of labor in Angola was due in part to the growing export of African workers to São Tomé's coffee and cocoa plantations. This was, in his words, "completely opposed to the interests and the economy of Angola."[19]

To this radical writer lack of education was only partly the result of Portuguese poverty and weakness. He argued that it was also a matter of "false civilization," a term and critical approach later developed further by African and *mestiço* dissenters.[20] His interpretation of why there was little educational activity in Angola was startling and subversive. As he wrote in an article in 1886, the Portuguese had not developed education because "they understand that the son of Angola who learns brutal [Portuguese] customs will be able to proclaim the independence of his country."[21]

Fontes Pereira's attacks on prison conditions in Luanda were a less controversial yet equally iconoclastic act. His writing on the dun-

[17] *O Futuro D'Angola*, 11 Mar. 1882.

[18] Ibid.; *O Cruzeiro do Sul*, 22 Sept. 1873.

[19] *O Futuro D'Angola*, 10 Nov. 1886.

[20] In a remarkable tract published by a number of African and *mestiço* writers of Angola as a protest against increasing Portuguese pressures against their advancement. Anonymous, *Voz D'Angola Clamando No Deserto* (Lisbon, 1901). For a discussion of its contents, see Douglas L. Wheeler, "Origins of African Nationalism in Angola: Assimilado Protest Writings, 1859–1929," in Ronald H. Chilcote (ed.), *Brazil and Portuguese Africa* (Berkeley, 1970), forthcoming.

[21] *O Cruzeiro do Sul*, 11 Sept. 1875.

geon prisons of Fort São Miguel was among his most effective muck-raking. In a series entitled "The Cemetery of Live People," he painted a chilling picture of living death below ground for over fifty civil and political prisoners. "Although it may seem fiction," he wrote, "what I am about to describe is, unfortunately, pure reality."[22] In a similar article later, he blasted the wretched conditions found in the nearby civil jail of Luanda, where some seventy-three persons were rotting away.[23]

When Fontes Pereira turned to ideas of political reform, he attacked a field rich in potential criticism. In a way open to few European critics of his day, he gave a new perspective through his revelations of the corruption, inefficiency, and chicanery in the system. In so doing, he was influenced by his reading of liberal tracts in French, Brazilian, and Portuguese newspapers and by observing the deeds of European explorers and missionaries in Africa. In an editorial of 1882, for example, he praised the explorer Henry Morton Stanley and the French missionaries in the Congo who "are going to do what the Portuguese have not wanted or known how to do."[24] In the same mood he criticized the current Governor General of Angola, the Banco Nacional Ultramarino in Luanda ("that rat-hole"),[25] as well as the failure of the Portuguese to expand along the coast north of Luanda or even to hold the line in Dembos territory, only a few miles north of Luanda, where an African rebellion in 1872–73 had again smashed Portuguese sovereignty. He favored Portuguese expansion into the interior of Angola for trade purposes, since he felt that such expansion would aid the Angolan economy.[26] Fontes Pereira went further, however, and praised the occupation campaigns of a fellow *assimilado,* the *mestiço* officer Colonel Geraldo A. Victor, who was the hero of military campaigns against Africans in Portuguese Guinea and Dembos.[27] Fontes Pereira asserted that Victor had not received adequate reward for his expansion efforts.[28]

[22] Ibid.

[23] Ibid., 7 June 1876.

[24] *O Futuro D'Angola*, 25 Mar. 1882.

[25] Ibid., 15 Apr. 1882.

[26] Ibid., 8 May 1886; see Alfredo de Sarmento, *Os Sertões D'Africa* (Lisbon, 1880), 156-57. For a discussion of Portuguese expansion in nineteenth-century Angola, see Douglas L. Wheeler, "Portuguese Expansion in Angola since 1836: A Re-examination," in *Local Series* pamphlet No. 20 of the Central Africa Historical Association (Salisbury, Rhodesia, 1967), 1-16.

[27] *O Ultramar,* 1 Aug. 1882.

[28] Colonel Geraldo António Victor was one of the few Angolan *assimilados* to achieve a high military rank. He was a folk hero among Angolans of all races; immortalized in African songs in Angola after his death, he was known to the

While he favored Portuguese expansion, he attacked the Portuguese tradition of charging heavy customs duties and imposing trade restrictions at Angolan ports. These restrictions he attacked in the spirit of the Brazilian independence of 1822, an event which undoubtedly inspired his generation in Angola, and his words resembled those of an American patriot: "Either liberty of commerce or nothing."[29]

To this "fighting reporter" of Luanda, the existing Portuguese political system in Angola was both useless and inhumane. He protested the corrupt method of electing deputies to the Portuguese Parliament. Africans in Angola had, he wrote, enjoyed more freedom when he was a youth in the 1830's than later, when the so-called liberal monarchy became more despotic. On the Portuguese national holiday of December 1, commemorating freedom from Spanish "captivity" in 1640, he wondered why Angolans should celebrate the day when in fact they had "lost their freedom 100 years ago," when their land and freedom were taken away and their fellows were "sold like meat."[30]

The language of his articles in the Portuguese colonial press was usually strong and violent. The tone was inflammatory. But the violence of language and verbal controversy did not exist in a vacuum. Violence emerged periodically throughout the period of Fontes Pereira's career. The very year this radical writer began his sustained protest in *O Cruzeiro do Sul,* the Luandan community was shaken by African rebellions in the north and by violence in the streets of the capital. The Governor General himself, José Maria da Ponte e Horta (in office 1870–73), was attacked and beaten on the streets of the city by "unknown persons," very probably Africans. In retaliation, several Africans were arrested and later deported to the southern coast of Angola.[31] The language used in the press merely reflected the charged atmosphere of daily life.

The verbal barbs of Fontes Pereira, therefore, were not unusual in this atmosphere of conflict, suspicion, and hatred. Nevertheless, they were often interpreted by his contemporaries as being libelous. Fontes Pereira's own lack of formal education perhaps compounded his sensitivity. He was snubbed by the better educated, especially those from metropolitan Portugal. There is more than a hint of frustration mixed with self-assertion in his statement: "It is not necessary to attend naval

---

Swiss-American missionary, Heli Chatelain, who mentioned him in his *Folk-tales of Angola* (Boston, 1894), Introduction. Chatelain claims that Victor was the offspring of an Italian father, one of a number of exiled Italian convicts sent to Angola after 1815, and an African mother in Angola. See E. E. Sarot, "The Contribution of the Italians to the Knowledge of Angola," *Zaire,* IX (1955), 825-48.

[29] *O Futuro D'Angola,* 25 Mar. 1882.

[30] *O Arauto Africano* (Luanda), 6 Jan. 1890.

[31] *O Cruzeiro do Sul,* 14 July 1873.

schools, nor be a student of Coimbra, or a pseudo-Frenchman to discover. . . ."[32]

For his strong stand on issues and his frequent attacks on personalities, Fontes Pereira suffered censorship, threats of jail, court proceedings, and social ostracism. He lost his job on at least two occasions—in 1875 and again in 1890—and his life was at times threatened. It is not surprising, then, that he sometimes assumed a *nom de plume*. In one series of articles, "Notes for the History of Angola," in 1873, he wrote under the names of "O Anciao Indigena" ("The Old Native"), "Um Veterano miliciano" ("A Veteran Militiaman"), and "F.J.F. Farto da Costa" (or "F.J.F. Fed Up with Costa"—a Portuguese he apparently disagreed with on some issue).[33]

His radicalism and his temper naturally lent an uncertainty to his position with Luandan papers and editors. The fragility and volatility of the pioneer press were increased by the poverty of newspaper backers and by the apathy and negligence of a tiny subscribing public. Many colonial papers in Luanda lasted only a few issues; many could not manage to get their subscribers to pay for their papers on a regular basis. Fontes Pereira's fragmented journalistic career reflects this instability, for from 1871 or 1872 he wrote for at least eight weekly papers. His journalism was not restricted to Angola, however, as he submitted articles to at least four metropolitan journals in Lisbon and Oporto.[34] His first writing for the "African press" appeared in *O Futuro d'Angola* in 1882; his last articles were apparently published in *O Arauto Africano* in 1890.

Fontes Pereira's radicalism may be explained in part by his association with a small circle of educated *mestiços* and Africans, as well as with moderate and liberal Europeans who desired change in Angola. A number of his friends favored a republican solution to Portugal's political problems. Fontes Pereira knew the Brazilian physician, scholar, linguist, and teacher, and sometime consul for Brazil, Dr. Saturnino de Sousa e Oliveira, who taught Fontes Pereira's son in a primary school in Luanda in the 1860's. While he was acting consul for Brazil,[35] Sousa e Oliveira had been implicated in the Prince Nicolas affair of 1859–60. Sousa e Oliveira was in sympathy with liberal, republican ideas and

---

[32] *O Futuro D'Angola*, 11 Mar. 1882.

[33] *O Cruzeiro do Sul*, 26 Nov., 1 Dec., 8 Dec. 1873; 2 Oct. 1875.

[34] Metropolitan journals he wrote for included *O Século* (Lisbon), *Voz do Minho* (Oporto), and *Campeão das Províncias* (Lisbon). See *O Futuro D'Angola*, obituary, 16 May 1891.

[35] See Wheeler, "Prince Nicolas of Kongo," *African Historical Studies*, 50-54, for material on Sousa e Oliveira in Angola. Since much of the correspondence of this Brazilian has not been located or studied, it is difficult to ascertain all of his activities in Angola.

encouraged ideas of political autonomy among educated Angolans. A number of other Brazilians, including several liberals who got into trouble with the Portuguese authorities because of their opinions;[36] a small circle of educated Angolans, including the eminent writer and philologist, J. D. Cordeiro da Matta (1857–94); and Portuguese figures like Alfredo Mantua, Alfredo Trony, and Urbano Monteiro de Castro who were involved in politics and in supporting the colonial press were all also among Fontes Pereira's associates. Even though many in this small circle of educated individuals were not radical revolutionaries, they did favor and work for changes in the status quo in Angola. In this way, they encouraged some of Fontes Pereira's thoughts. Angolans interested in reform found the colonial press one of the few outlets of expression, as there was no regular representative or elective government with meaningful power. The Governor General was often virtually omnipotent, and the few elected deputies to the Libson Parliament from Angola were invariably recent arrivals from Portugal.

African rights frequently concerned Fontes Pereira. Protest against European abuses, ironically, was partly supported by the tradition of European opposition to metropolitan Portuguese rule in Angola. In one of several articles based on original historical research, Fontes Pereira recounted tales of Angolan citizens of all colors rising against hated Lisbon-appointed officials. In incidents in 1667, 1836, 1839, 1851, 1865, and in the 1870's, officials ranging from lowly *chefes do posto* to Governors General had unceremoniously been expelled by irate Angolans.[37] The obvious lesson of the series of articles was that, given the opportunity and the grievance, Africans would do the same in the 1880's.

And African grievances were many. Fontes Pereira deplored the lack of job opportunities in the 1880's and contrasted this situation with more flexible arrangements in pre-1860 Angola. By producing statistics on African employment in skilled jobs in 1824 and 1832, he showed how recent administrations practiced more discrimination than had previous ones. In one case, the government had failed to promote an African with twenty-two years of service in one department.[38] To Fontes Pereira, "the enemies of progress" opposed African advancement. He alleged that only a few Europeans, the "foreign missionaries," favored progress, and in an article of 1882 he praised their activities in southern Angola.

[36] The Brazilian editor of *O Commercio de Loanda*, Francisco P. Dutra, was arrested by the Governor General and sent to Lisbon for his "abuse of freedom of the press" in 1867. See *O Commercio de Loanda*, 27 Nov., 4 Dec. 1867 (Luanda).

[37] *A Verdade* (Luanda), 14 Apr. 1888, from collection held in library of Arquivo Histórico de Angola (Luanda).

[38] *O Futuro D'Angola*, 13 May 1882.

It appeared to the Luandan writer that Africans would become a major factor in the territory in coming decades. He observed the efforts of foreign missions to "civilize" (a word he was very fond of) the African peoples of the interior. Such "civilized" Africans would then "occupy" the Angolan coast "in less than 10 years." At that time, he believed, "the sons of Angola can receive the education and social and political position denied them by their government."[39]

How would change come to Angola? Would the Portuguese government alter its policies? Earlier in Fontes Pereira's journalism, his protests had envisioned a possible Portuguese initiative for change. The change would come from Portugal, he hoped, and the Portuguese would reform their policies and improve conditions in Angola. He attacked Portuguese indifference and asserted that "there is not one man of courage in Portugal who understands the sad situation to which this province [Angola] has been reduced, a province which is also Portuguese and deserving of a better fate!"[40] In assailing what he termed an "empire of immorality,"[41] he hoped to move the authorities to change. As a good nineteenth-century liberal he defended the major political institutions of change: the free press and the vote. Later he despaired of reform coming from the Portuguese hierarchy and withdrew whatever remaining trust he had in the system. He became convinced that significant change would not come from the Portuguese government without extraordinary new methods of pressure and new proposals which would lay a foundation for Angolan self-assertion.

As little change occurred, as he found that his ideas were not adopted, and as his own advancement was not forthcoming, Fontes Pereira became discouraged with the Portuguese. His articles then began to reflect a more strident, embittered tone. In one written attack in 1882 he combined Portuguese cynicism and sarcasm with an Angolan perspective:

> How has Angola benefited under Portuguese rule? The darkest slavery, scorn, and the most complete ignorance! And even the Government has done its utmost to humiliate and vilify the sons of this land who do possess necessary qualifications for advancement. . . . What a civilizer, and how Portuguese![42]

His growing opposition to conditions in Angola was illustrated by his attack on the social and political discrimination practiced against African Angolans:

[39] Ibid.
[40] *O Cruzeiro do Sul,* 27 Sept. 1875.
[41] Ibid., 20 Oct. 1875.
[42] *O Futuro D'Angola,* 8 Apr. 1882.

Generally considered as being outside the accepted social circle [of Metropolitan Portuguese], the sons of the colonies are allowed a significant role only when the Portuguese need them to elect to Parliament that gang of rogues which the Government chooses to give it a vote of confidence; that mess of pastry-cooks which robs the official ministers of the action of justice. The sons of the colonies, moreover, possess no nationality because the government of the metropole and their delegates are those most interested in condemning them [the Africans] as foreigners, depriving them of the exercise of the first public offices now filled by certain rats they send us from Portugal . . . they do not use their intelligence in the civilization of a people for whom they have no respect, and this is proved by the saying that

com preto e mulato
nada de contrato ! ! !
[With mulattoes and blacks
no need for contracts]

those sons of the country who are at the mercy of miserable crumbs from the budget table, so that it is necessary to dismiss them. . . .[43]

In an article written seven years later, Fontes Pereira continued to expound his thesis that education was a requisite for progress in Angola for both colonizer and colonized alike· "It is very clear that we can expect nothing good from Portugal, since, even there [in Europe], education of the people does not exist."[44] The Portuguese, therefore, could not be expected to act as the necessary instrument of change in Angola when their own credentials for being "civilized" were highly suspect!

In several articles during his journalistic career, Fontes Pereira advocated that Angola should become an independent territory. This theme became more common in his writing after 1880. Other writers in the early colonial press had discussed independence for Angola, but Fontes Pereira was probably the first "son of Angola" to propose that Angolans should *organize* in a modern way to assert their rights. His suggestion in 1882 that the "sons of the country" should "league together" to discuss what he termed "Angolan nationality" was published in a Luandan weekly.[45] His employment in an article of the term "Angolan nationality" was probably the earliest instance of an Angolan thinking of one, unified territory of Angola. In 1889 Fontes Pereira's suggestions were followed with a similar idea expressed by his colleague, Carlos da Silva, a *mestiço* editor and writer.[46] There is no evi-

[43] Ibid., 29 Apr. 1882.
[44] *O Arauto Africano*, 26 May 1889.
[45] *O Futuro D'Angola*, 13 May 1882.
[46] *O Arauto Africano*, 17 Mar. 1889. Editorial by Silva.

dence, however, that Fontes Pereira or Silva actually formed such an association or league in Angola.

Rebellion now began to occupy a major place in the lexicon of Fontes Pereira's protests. To his mind, reform seemed less and less likely under the existing regime: by 1890 he had become perhaps the most radical of his contemporaries in journalism. Portuguese officials were shocked to read his suggestion that Portugal's record as a colonizer during 400 years of activity overseas was bad; they were appalled by his thought that perhaps Angolans should reject Portuguese rule. From their point of view his most treasonous writings dealt with the idea of exchanging Portugal for another colonial power in Angola. These ideas coincided with a serious conflict between Britain and Portugal over certain areas of tropical Africa. Officials in Angola and Moçambique feared that educated Africans and *mestiços* would betray them at a time when the greatest unity was required in the effort to uphold and defend Portuguese territorial claims in Nyasaland and Rhodesia against the British.[47]

In January 1890, just as Great Britain handed Portugal a formal "ultimatum" over Portuguese activity in Nyasaland, Fontes Pereira discussed the crisis in certain articles for the journal *O Arauto Africano*, an Angolan enterprise. These articles provoked a powerful reaction among Portuguese officials and settlers in Angola which virtually ended Fontes Pereira's journalistic and civil service careers and probably led indirectly to his physical decline and death not long afterward. In what was, in effect, his parting shot in the Luandan press, the radical *mestiço* journalist, learning of an uncomfirmed report (later discovered to have been false), wrote that an English fleet had blockaded Lisbon: although it never occurred, the threat of an English blockade was implicit in the English ultimatum to Portugal.[48] One of the articles in this controversial series was entitled "The Colonial Party" and referred to the colonial regeneration sparked by an active group of Portuguese explorers, soldiers, and officials who, in Portugal, were considered to be liberals. In the colonial press in Angola, however, their reputation was something other than liberal. Fontes Pereira's protest in *O Arauto Africano* deserves extensive quotation:

> . . . one does not wonder that foreigners, understanding all this [Portuguese weaknesses] would try to take over Portuguese lands which are still preserved in a state of nature, and that they would

[47] For a full discussion of the 1889–90 Anglo-Portuguese conflict and crisis in Africa, emphasizing Moçambique, see Eric Axelson, *Portugal and the Scramble for Africa 1875–1891* (Johannesburg, 1967), 117-258.

[48] *O Arauto Africano*, articles of 6 Jan., 20 Jan., and 29 Jan. 1890.

take advantage of them as potential wealth in order to exploit them and to civilize the natives, making them useful citizens for them and for the rest of humanity. For our part, we would advise these foreigners not to waste time discussing in Europe matters which would benefit them in Africa; it is necessary for them only to address themselves to Africa's inhabitants, the natural lords that they are of their lands, and make with them all the necessary treaties of commerce and reciprocal protection. If they do this, they will be received with open arms for it has been proved that we have nothing to expect from Portugal except the swindles and shackles of slavery, the only means she has in order better to brutalize and subjugate the natives! And with this conclusion, we declare that we trust neither in the good faith nor in the sincerity of the Portuguese Colonial Party, whose members are only crocodiles crying in order to lure their victims. We know them only too well. Out with them! [49]

Great was the fury of the Portuguese officials and settlers who read this article. Guilherme Capelo, Governor General of Angola at the time and the object of a number of Fontes Pereira's earlier editorial attacks, wrote a confidential letter to the Minister of the Colonies in Lisbon,[50] in which he recounted how a group of some ninety angry Portuguese had marched on the offices of the African newspaper demanding a retraction and apology from Fontes Pereira and insisting that the editor of the paper, Carlos da Silva, change the name of the paper to a title less offensive than *Arauto* ("Cry").[51] The Governor General roundly denounced this *mestiço* "republican" as "a traitor with the title of lawyer," who wrote in what he called "bad Portuguese." Furthermore, the Governor General deplored the action of the British consul in Luanda in this heated incident. (The British consul had apparently read Fontes Pereira's article and sent translations of it to his superiors in London.) Capelo surmised that the English interpretation of the affair would be that the Angolan journalist was "an illustrious man and a faithful interpreter of the feelings of the natives." The Governor General then went on to describe Fontes Pereira as "that degenerate son of Angola" who had stirred up a hornet's nest with his writing. Legal

[49] Ibid., 20 Jan. 1890.

[50] File A-16-6 (Angola): Capelo to Lisbon, 30 Jan. 1890, Arquivo Histórico de Angola (Luanda).

[51] Editor Carlos da Silva did change the name of the paper to O *Polícia Africano* in the very next number, 4 Feb. 1890. The number of 27 Jan. 1890 was the last of O *Arauto Africano*. O *Polícia Africano* was a more moderate title as it meant something like "The African Civilization" or "The African Sentinel." The second volume of the *New Michaelis Illustrated Dictionary* (Wiesbaden, 1961), 979, cites three meanings for *Polícia* in current usage, in order of occurrence, "police, civilization and polity." A further definition of *policiado* reveals the meaning of "policed, civilized, moderate."

proceedings would be taken against him by the government, and his lawyer's license would be revoked. To the highest ranking Portuguese official representing Lisbon in Angola, then, this incident seemed just one more example of the unfortunate effects of the current "law of un-limited freedom of the press" in overseas Portugal. "Orderly rule," he wrote, was impossible under such circumstances.[52] The Governor General concluded his interesting letter to Lisbon by stating that patriotism in Angolan society was in general strong enough to overcome the temporary but pernicious influence of the likes of Fontes Pereira!

This important series of articles in January 1890 was probably the last published work of the radical protester. Within sixteen months, on May 2, 1891, he was dead, a victim of pneumonia.[53]

José de Fontes Pereira was buried in the main Portuguese cemetery of Luanda. The funeral was attended by a substantial group of citizens —of all colors—including many of his most persistent journalist enemies in the press. The obituary articles were generally laudatory.[54] He was, in the words of a present-day Angolan intellectual, Mário António, "the most combatted and most combative of African journalists."[55] A writer in a weekly Fontes Pereira had once worked for, O Futuro d'Angola, made this tribute: "He left among the sons of this land a vacuum which will not be filled very soon." Bordered in black, this article and others recorded the passing of an important Angolan intellectual and pioneer protester. Another contemporary mestiço journalist, Mamede de Sant'-Anna e Palma, writing in O Desastre, mourned the death of Fontes Pereira by writing of "the dean of Angolan journalists, the most strenuous champion of this province, which was his beloved place of birth!"[56] Sant'Anna e Palma praised him for his work in the administration, as "escrivão da administracão do concelho de Luanda," as a lawyer, and as a member of the local army militia, where he was reputed to have aided Luandan youth in escaping from the widespread "vice of gambling."

What was the historical significance of this Angolan protester? What

---

[52] The problem of the freedom of the colonial press was a continual controversy in late nineteenth-century Angola. The rising republican agitation and pressure in Portugal (which had its repercussions in Angola, of course) prompted the government to pass the stronger censorship law of March 29, 1890. This increased official censorship in Europe as well as in the colonies. José Tengarrinha, História Da Imprensa Periódica Portuguesa (Lisbon, 1965), 225-30.

[53] Castro Lopo, Jornalismo, 76.

[54] Obituaries include those found in O Mercantil, 7 May 1891; O Futuro D'Angola, 16 May 1891; and in O Desastre, supplement to No. 16, 30 May 1891. There may be others in Portuguese newspapers.

[55] Mário António F. de Oliveira, A Sociedade Angolana Do Fim Do Século XIX E Um Seu Escritor. Ensaio (Luanda, 1961), 15-18, 56, 69.

[56] Sant'Anna e Palma errs in citing Fontes Pereira's birthdate as the year 1826. Cf. Castro Lopo's excerpt from the obituary in Jornalismo, 79.

was his legacy to future generations? What impact did his writings have in his own time?

It is difficult to give a clear and complete answer to these challenging questions. What little we know of Fontes Pereira derives from a fragmentary collection of Portuguese colonial newspapers and from a few letters from the government archives. Yet to be examined are private collections of letters and more metropolitan newspapers and journals. And for his career in the civil service and law, the judicial records of the Municipality of Luanda and the Governor General have yet to be studied. Archives in Brazil might well reveal new material. Nevertheless, given the basic sources it is possible to outline some of the major ways in which he was significant.

An understanding of Fontes Pereira's role as an *assimilado,* as an Angolan who was culturally Portuguese, is crucial to an insight into his protest. Although he was sympathetic to the plight of the mass of Africans, he usually accepted them as a part of Angola only to the extent that they were "civilized." Fontes Pereira's standards of "civilization" were remarkably similar to those of the Portuguese in control of the territory. Despite his bitter attacks on Portuguese failings in the education of both Europeans and Africans, his values were essentially Portuguese.

Fontes Pereira was not alone in his protest in the last quarter of the nineteenth century in Luanda. Among Angolans who possessed some European education, there were several dissenting writers. This *mestiço* radical, however, was unique in the extreme nature of his protest and in his solution to the problem of Angolan autonomy and *assimilado* and African rights. His vicious attacks and his subversive proposals were unusual, but not unique, since other angry writers in the colonial press of Luanda had suggested Angolan independence and more rights for Angolans. Where Fontes Pereira's protests differed was on the key question of ultimate loyalty to Portugal. At the end of his career he apparently made the decision to explore a different path to Angolan rights by seeking aid from another colonial power, perhaps Britain, and by instituting a republic instead of remaining with a decaying European monarchy.

Unlike his younger but more famous colleague, the *mestiço* intellectual J. D. Cordeiro da Matta, Fontes Pereira was not an accomplished literary figure. Cordeiro da Matta was not a radical protester but a political moderate who, during his short lifetime, concentrated on literary creation. However, Fontes Pereira was known to be more learned than most of the Angolan journalists of his day.[57] Although he

---

[57] Castro Lopo, *Jornalismo,* 75-79; see Mário António, *A Sociedade Angolana* for a study of J. D. Cordeiro da Matta.

does not seem to have written poetry or novels or compiled grammars and dictionaries like his younger friend Cordeiro da Matta, he had a definite interest in writing history, and he produced several valuable articles based on unpublished documents as well as official gazettes. He thought of Angola as one territory with a common history rather than as a number of regions with different backgrounds.[58]

Fontes Pereira was a radical and particularly striking voice in the chorus of discontent and unrest which welled up in post-1860 Angola. The Angolans were discovering themselves through the new influences coming from Europe and Brazil in the form of republican ideas, liberalism, economic reform, and new social and political institutions. Not the least of the new institutions was the new colonial press. Controversial writing was the order of the day for all writers who sought both excitement and instruction in a stagnant atmosphere. Often the protest was more destructive than constructive. Few writers offered more than utopian plans and facile visions for reform. Even Fontes Pereira himself rarely wrote of viable alternatives for the harassed Portuguese officials who were strapped by bankruptcy, corruption, and a deadly climate.

Fontes Pereira's articles did not go unread, but their effect upon the decision-makers was often counter-productive. Often the very radicalism and tone of his writing would alienate Portuguese officials and settlers alike. Although his attacks could sometimes be dismissed as the emotional outpourings of a republican *assimilado,* the effect on authorities was to convince them that education for Africans and *mestiços,* unless carefully controlled, was dangerous and subversive to Portuguese sovereignty. There was a definite feeling among some Portuguese officials that the educational system of Angola, weak as it was, nevertheless produced a group of educated Angolans who were misfits in colonial society. One effect of the protest writings in the press was to cause some re-thinking of the Portuguese commitment to education in Angola. The statement of a Governor General in a letter of 1885 to the Lisbon government suggested that thus far Angolan education had produced only "useless visionaries, detestable clerks."[59] This assertion referred, at least indirectly, to the case of Fontes Pereira, and perhaps to the earlier case of Prince Nicolas of Kongo as well as to other "rebels."

Angolan writers, invariably employed in the colonial civil service like Fontes Pereira, were influenced by his writings. Some were bold enough to protest and to assert Angolan rights despite the probability that they would be attacked and even punished by the government for

[58] See series of articles (Oct.–Dec. 1875) in *O Cruzeiro do Sul.*

[59] Gov. Gen. to Lisbon, 14 Oct. 1885, Angola, Pasta 4, *Arquivo Histórico Ultramarino,* Lisbon.

their actions. Even though there was no strict censorship law or regular censorship of the press before 1922, governors not infrequently prosecuted Angolans—of all races—for their "abuse of the liberty of the press." For example, an associate of Fontes Pereira, the Angolan editor-journalist Arcénio Pompílio Pompeu de Carpo, a one-time councilman in the Luandan municipal government, was in March 1890 brought to trial for his writings. Like Fontes Pereira, he too lost his job.[60]

Any fair analysis of the life and writings of Fontes Pereira must balance his championship of Angolan rights with the atmosphere of invective in the press and with his obvious interest as an *assimilado* office seeker under increasing pressure from metropolitan European competitors. The educated African and *mestiço* groups in the Portuguese service were placed in an increasingly vulnerable position after the regeneration of Portuguese effort and interest in Africa in the 1870's and 1880's and by the increased Portuguese immigration which followed.[61] Furthermore, the Angolan involved in European society deeply resented being discriminated against in social life. Hence, Fontes Pereira's attack on the nonacceptance of Angolans by metropolitan Portuguese in an article of 1882.[62] On the other hand, the educated *assimilado* felt socially superior to the "bush African," the tribal Angolan, and in this feeling Fontes Pereira was no exception. At least culturally, he was a Portuguese. In his own household in Luanda he had experienced the conflict between the privileged master and the less privileged servant and slave. Fontes Pereira's own social and political ambitions and his interest in the advancement of his own caste and class must be balanced with his humanitarian and social liberalism.

The *assimilado* community, like the others in Angola, was divided in opinion on major questions. Fontes Pereira's opinions were not completely supported by his colleagues in his own time. His last editor, Carlos da Silva, disavowed connection with and responsibility for Fontes Pereira's opinion on the Anglo-Portuguese crisis and the resulting controversy in Luanda in early 1890.[63] Nor were other African writers unanimous in supporting the controversial lawyer's writings. In 1889 several of his criticisms of the Portuguese regime had been attacked in the press both by Europeans and by a few *mestiços*.[64]

[60] *Boletim Official* (Luanda), 1 Mar. 1890.
[61] Compare figures of population in G. A. Pery, *Geographia e Estatística Geral de Portugal E Colónias* (Lisbon, 1875), 356-57; and in *Annuário Estatístico da Província de Angola*, II (Lisbon, 1900), IX-X.
[62] *O Futuro D'Angola*, 27 Apr. 1882.
[63] *O Polícia Africano*, 4 Feb. 1890. Silva wrote that on the question of ultimate loyalty he was in disagreement with Fontes Pereira, and that he had changed the name of his newspaper "to prove that we were not party to such ideas."
[64] See articles in the journal *Muen'Exi* (Luanda), 2 June, 23 June 1889.

Opinion in the educated community was fragmented and divided —pro-monarchist versus pro-republican, conservative versus liberal. In Luanda there was no unified front of *assimilado* opinion. The Conservative *mestiços* attacked liberal ones; friends of the Bragança monarchy in Portugal attacked the republicans who wanted to create a new, more liberal republic in Portugal and in Angola. The Angolan Republican party was encouraged and excited by the news that Brazil had declared itself a republic in 1889. But the more conservative Luandans stuck to their guns and maligned the critics. Cornélio Castro Francina, a *mestiço* writer for a paper with a Kimbundu title, *Muen'Exi* (roughly "Lord of the Land"), criticized Carlos da Silva's paper and defended the Portuguese government in Lisbon and the Câmara Municipal in Luanda against what he considered irresponsible and undeserved attacks.[65] Included in his counterattack was a typically Portuguese value judgment that Silva's paper had "used bad Portuguese," an accusation also leveled against Fontes Pereira by the Governor General in the 1890 incident.

From the storm raised in the Luandan press in reaction to Fontes Pereira's sensational and essentially treasonous articles of January 1890 it would appear that he was in a minority among his *assimilado* colleagues on the issue of ultimate loyalty to Portugal. Not only did the Portuguese settlers attack him for this heresy, but some African officials in the Portuguese service lashed out at him with arguments which have since become common fodder for the Portuguese case. One António De Paula Brito, an African official in the Post Office in Luanda, attacked Fontes Pereira by asserting that only in the Portuguese areas of Africa would "a black be able to raise himself to such a position" as both he and his enemy enjoyed in the Luandan civil service.[66] Thus an *assimilado* staunchly defended Portugal against the strictures of another *assimilado* who was a radical and a republican.

Did the memory of Fontes Pereira's protest reach to later generations? A significant number of Angolan *assimilados* during the generation and a half following his death did think of his example and did show some familiarity with his writing. There is a reference to him in an article contained in the bitter but inspired collection entitled *Voz D'Angola Clamando No Deserto. Offerecida Aos Amigos Da Verdade Pelos Naturaes* (Lisbon, 1901). This tract, edited by several *mestiço* and African journalists in Luanda, was published a decade after Fontes Pereira's death. Following the tradition of his dissent, one article declared that the late champion of Angolan rights would have been

[65] *Muen'Exi*, 2 June 1889.

[66] *O Mercantil* (Luanda), 30 Jan. 1890. The article entitled "Partido Colonial" was a rebuttal by A. De Paula Brito of Fontes Pereira's recent articles.

gravely disturbed by recent Portuguese injustices and poor race rela-tions.[67] His name appeared again in the title of a *mestiço* social club, *Centro de José de Fontes Pereira,* founded in his honor in the 1920's by an offspring or relative in Luanda.[68]

This brief survey of the life and writings of an *assimilado* protester in Angola suggests a number of interesting factors. It can illustrate the complexity of political opposition to Portuguese rule in Angola. Oppo-sition as it appeared in 1890 in Angola was by no means unified. Its message was often conditioned by the protester's position vis-à-vis the dominant European hierarchy of officialdom or by its position on key political issues of the day. Would the social critic José de Fontes Pe-reira have sweetened the gall of his attack if the Portuguese had ac-cepted him socially and had advanced his career in their service? Or was he accepted—at least provisionally—and found that his victory was empty of satisfaction? Were the Angolan moderates, who could tone down their editorials and the names of their newspapers to please the Portuguese community, completely satisfied with their roles? In any event, the mainstream of Angolan society was so dependent upon Por-tuguese patronage that for the most part it did not follow the narrow path of Fontes Pereira in opposition to Portuguese rule.

The early protest tradition led by Fontes Pereira and his colleagues in Luanda was also dependent upon an atmosphere of relative flexibil-ity and pseudo-liberalism. Without a "free" approach to press censor-ship, the journalism of Fontes Pereira would never have been seen in print or on the streets. Although some governors did censor issues and papers at times, this censorship was like the ephemeral newspapers they undermined, short-lived and often casual. Liberalism was on trial but not yet convicted.

Perhaps the most remarkable factor of all is the style of Fontes Pereira's protest. This early protest exhibited intense feelings and a fund of talent. His compositions were marked by a determination and singleness of mind which must have unnerved his enemies and inspired his friends. This Luandan was doubtless the outstanding Angolan journalist of his generation. His message was important. The very fact that he had emerged and had risen in society and that he had educated himself in a culturally deprived atmosphere and then had rebelled against Portuguese rule made his case both controversial and poignant.

His bold suggestions that Angola should perhaps exchange Portu-gal for another colonial power guaranteed his place in the future as an extraordinary—if unorthodox—dissenter. His conscience transcended

[67] *Voz D'Angola,* 77.
[68] Oscar Ribas, *Izomba. Associativismo E Recreio* (Luanda, 1965), 38-39.

874 THE LITERARY EXPRESSION OF PROTEST

ordinary concerns and sought to understand great questions fundamental to the future of Angola. His profoundest dream was to see lasting peace and prosperity in Angola. He wished, through the medium of his writing, to change society for the better. If he were not alone in his dreams for an autonomous and "civilized" Angola, he was unique in his radical tone, in the solution he put forward in his controversial 1890 editorials, and in his breadth of treatment.

Fontes Pereira linked his protests with European ideologies being discussed currently in Portugal as well as in Angola. These were vehicles which he hoped would bring reform to Angola. His adherence as an Angolan *assimilado* to the foreign ideology of republicanism, more for pragmatic than for intellectual reasons, suggests modern parallels with the adoption by African nationalists of socialist doctrines. To this Angolan champion, republicanism meant freedom and social acceptance for the *assimilado*. To him the end of the Portuguese monarchy, seemingly so close during the 1890–91 crisis, would mean almost inevitable improvement for Angola and Angolans. The Republic of Portugal was established nineteen years after his passing. If he had lived to experience its operation, he would probably have been disillusioned and his republican faith might well have been destroyed. For the republic did not realize the essence of the dreams of this remarkable journalist.[69]

His protest, however, remains on record. It may or may not be claimed and immortalized—with all its ambiguities and excesses—by a newer and better prepared generation of Angolans. Nevertheless, in this early voice crying in the wilderness one can hear the stirrings of modern Angolan nationalism.

Fontes Pereira's particular contribution to the tradition of black protest in Angola was his strong language, his criticism of what he interpreted as Portuguese exploitation of Angola and the weaknesses of Portugal as a colonial power. Some of his criticisms have been echoed in the writings of modern Angolan nationalists. Thus, in a 1967 book by a black Angolan nationalist, Dr. Américo Boavida, recent Portuguese reforms after the 1961 insurgency in northern Angola are attacked as "a desperate attempt to save the Portuguese presence in Angola, by means of new forms of pillage and parasitism."[70] In many ways, the verbal battle over Angolan nationalism—now accompanied by gunfire—was begun by Fontes Pereira and is carried on by men who employ a remarkably similar vocabulary of protest.

[69] A competent study of the Portuguese republic is Jesus Pabón (trans. Manuel Emídio and Ricardo Tavares), *A Revolucao Portuguesa* (Lisbon, 1961); for Angola under the republic (1910–1926) see Wheeler and Pélissier, *Angola*, ch. III.

[70] Américo Boavida, *Angola:cinco séculos de exploração portuguêsa* (Five Centuries of Portuguese Exploitation) (Rio de Janeiro, 1967), 85.

PART SEVEN

REVOLUTIONS, COUPS, AND READJUSTMENTS IN THE POST-INDEPENDENCE ERA

THE COUP IN RWANDA

RENÉ LEMARCHAND

What became known as the "coup de Gitarama" took place on January 28, 1961, in the central Rwandan town of Gitarama. It is from this day, rather than from their formal accession to independence on July 1, 1962, that most Nyarwanda date their "real independence." Although the event attracted very little attention in the outside world, anyone in Gitarama on that day in January 1961 would have sensed its special quality. From the early hours of the morning, dozens of trucks from all parts of the country converged on the town. Their passengers were almost all the recently elected communal councillors and burgo-masters—some three thousand of them—coming together, it was said, to discuss matters concerning "the maintenance of peace and order" during the first (and last) general elections to be held before independence. But many of those present suspected, with reason, that a more momentous decision was in the offing and it was with a sense of keen expectancy that the dense crowd in the market place watched a group of Rwandan officials flanked by a handful of Europeans, for the most part local administrators, making their way toward an improvised platform. The first speaker, Jean-Baptiste Rwasibo, Minister of Interior in Rwanda's provisional government, "set the tone" of the meeting; after a long diatribe against Rwanda's monarchical regime, he held up the vision of a brave new world in which democracy and equality would reign supreme; Rwasibo asked: "What will be the solution given to the problem of the monarchy? When shall we abandon the realm of the 'provisional'? It is incumbent upon you, burgomasters and councillors,

I wish to record my indebtedness to Miss Rachel Yeld and Mrs. Alison Des Forges for their valuable comments on an earlier version of this chapter. Neither is responsible, however, for the opinions expressed in it.

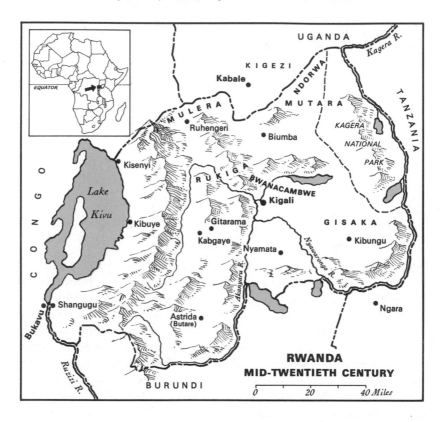

RWANDA
MID-TWENTIETH CENTURY

representatives of the Rwandan people, to answer these questions." It was the stocky, bespectacled Joseph Gitera, President of Rwanda's provisional council, who gave the definitive answer to the first question. Speaking in Kinyarwanda, Gitera calmly announced the abolition of the monarchy and all its symbols, including the royal drum, and went on to proclaim the birth of "the democratic and sovereign Republic of Rwanda." His words were greeted by thunderous applause from the crowd, punctuated by repeated cries of "Vive la République!" Next came the turn of Grégoire Kayibanda, the provisional Prime Minister; when he translated the news into French, new waves of enthusiasm moved over the audience. Then, sitting as a constituent assembly, the 3,126 councillors and burgomasters present proceeded to elect a President of the Republic and to co-opt among themselves the members of the Legislative Assembly. Finally, in line with Belgian constitutional practice, the newly elected President of the Republic, Dominique Mbonyumutwa, called upon Kayibanda to act as a *formateur* of the future government; by 7 P.M. a cabinet of ten members had been set up, headed by Prime Minister Kayibanda. A new phase had begun in the history of Rwanda.[1]

Today in Rwanda January 28 has the same symbolic significance as July 14 has in France. Every year on this occasion official speeches commemorate the coup of Gitarama in typical July 14 oratory—as "the dawn of a new era," as the day on which "the Rwandese chose, with enthusiasm and determination, to become a free and democratic society."[2] But just as the fall of the Bastille can only reveal a small fraction of the events surrounding the French Revolution, the coup of Gitarama was only the surface symptom of a much deeper transformation.

Actually, the events of Gitarama carried to its penultimate stage the social and political revolution which had begun in late 1959, and which involved nothing less than a conscious effort on the part of the Hutu elites to cast off the age-old domination of the Tutsi oligarchy. This kind of racial upheaval is not unknown in Africa. The Zanzibari revolution of January 1964 offers many striking parallels with developments in Rwanda, not the least significant being the overthrow of a racially distinct minority by a group of leaders who claimed to represent the hitherto forgotten and oppressed majority.[3] Whether carried out by the military or civilians, whether motivated by military or ethnic self-interest, or a combination of both, coups have occurred not only in Rwanda and Zanzibar but also in Dahomey, Togo, the Congo (Kinshasa), Nigeria, Ghana, and the Sudan, to cite but a few examples.

But if the phenomena of revolution and coups have become common occurrences in Africa, the case of Rwanda does present some interesting peculiarities. Unlike other African coups, the coup of Gitarama occurred a year and a half *before* Rwanda's accession to independence, when the country was still a trust territory of the United Nations and Belgium was the administering authority. Because of this peculiar timing, and, more specifically, because a coup more usually occurs not in a colonial situation but against incumbents who have already gained full control of the machinery of the state, some observers may well challenge the use of this term to describe the

---

[1] The foregoing account is based on information contained in the interim report of the U.N. Commission for Ruanda-Urundi of Mar. 8, 1961 (*Question of the Future of Ruanda-Urundi, U.N. General Assembly*, A/4706, 27 ff.), and on personal interviews.

[2] *Rwanda Carrefour d'Afrique*, Feb. 1965, 2; Feb. 1966, 4.

[3] See René Lemarchand, "Revolutionary Phenomena in Stratified Societies: Rwanda and Zanzibar," *Civilisations*, XVII (1968), 1-34. See also below, Michael Lofchie, "The Zanzibari Revolution: African Protest in a Racially Plural Society," 924-67.

seizure of power which took place at Gitarama.[4] They might also object that this seizure of power was not only remarkably peaceful but, from all appearances, far more limited in its implications than might be gathered from the more conventional use of the term "coup." The Belgian authorities were still formally in charge of administering the territory, even though a transfer of power had already occurred at the local level. Unlike the more orthodox pattern of African coups, Gitarama was only one stage in the long and complicated sequence of events that led to the consummation of independence under Hutu hegemony—that stage when the overload of revolutionary current passes from one circuit to another, but with the safety switches still firmly in Belgian hands. The point to be stressed here is that the timing of these events in itself constituted a strong presumption of connivance on the part of the administering authorities. As we shall see, the Rwandan revolution was not the massive and spontaneous uprising that some might imagine; it began as a jacquerie, transformed itself into a localized rebellion, and wound up as a social and political revolution directed against the monarchy. All along the Belgian administration played a decisive role, gradually destroying or neutralizing all sources of resistance to the revolutionary movement and at the same time creating new institutions through which further transformations could be generated. In brief, whether examined in terms of its timing, of its participants, or of the multiple forms of social protest which it called forth, the Rwandan revolution may well be regarded as a unique phenomenon.

Background to Gitarama

Like all revolutions, the Hutu revolution had its origins in the inequities of the social and political order that it sought to destroy. The basic conflict over values involved democracy, justice, and equality on the one hand, and a feudal system based on an all-pervading "premise of inequality on the other."[5] It was, in a sense, a Jacobin revolution, aiming at a fundamental and irreversible shift of relationships between rulers and ruled. Yet in another sense the Hutu revolution was also a war of independence, fought against an alien minority for the sole purpose of retrieving from the past a way of life which the

[4] See Victor T. Le Vine, "The Course of Political Violence," in William H. Lewis (ed.), *French-Speaking Africa: The Search for Identity* (New York, 1965), 61.

[5] The expression is borrowed from J. J. Maquet, *The Premise of Inequality in Ruanda* (London, 1961), 160-72.

Tutsi conquest had almost obliterated. To understand how these two different sets of motivations—one aiming at renovation, the other at restoration—culminated in the fall of the Rwandan monarchy, something must be said of Rwanda's precolonial and colonial history.

For the sake of analysis it may be convenient to consider the history of Rwanda in four distinctive phases: (1) *Until 1889: The pre-colonial period*, characterized by the emergence of a small nuclear kingdom in central Rwanda, under the leadership of a ruling Tutsi clan, followed by the gradual absorption of the neighboring Hutu populations into an expanding territorial unit; (2) *From 1899 to 1945: The early colonial period*, during which the logic of indirect rule led to a further centralization of authority in the hands of the Tutsi chiefs and the king, and to the consolidation of Tutsi hegemony in the north; (3) *From 1945 to 1959: The post-war colonial period*, during which a belated attempt was made to mitigate the effects of indirect rule through constitutional reforms aimed at setting up representative organs at the central and local levels; (4) *From 1959 to 1962: The terminal phase of colonial rule*, ushered in by the so-called "revolution of November 1959" and characterized by an abrupt transfer of power to the newly emerging Hutu elites and the substitution of a republican form of government in place of monarchical rule.

Although we are primarily concerned in this discussion with the forms of protest that were brought to light during the fourth phase of Rwanda's evolution, these cannot properly be understood independently of earlier forms of agitation and of the patterns of interaction that have taken place over the years not only between Hutu and Tutsi but also between each of these two groups and the European colonizer.

The Pre-colonial Period

If the social and political objectives of the Jacobin revolution can be easily inferred from the social and structural rigidities inherent in the feudal system, the "conservative" revolution is intimately related to Rwanda's historical tendency to expand territorially and, in the process, to absorb and amalgamate new societies. Although both features were in some ways reinforced during the early phase of the colonial period, the basic trends were set long before the Europeans came into the country.

Of all the conquest states that have emerged in the lacustrine region of Africa, the kingdom of Rwanda was among the most centralized and rigidly stratified. In Rwanda's caste-like society, social rank was determined by membership in one of three distinctive racial groups—Tutsi, Hutu, and Twa. Although constituting a small percentage of the total population, the Tutsi, a group of nomadic pastoralists reputed to have come originally from Ethiopia, were unquestionably a dominant minority, politically, socially, and economically. Partly through sheer political astuteness and superior military strength, and partly because of the influence of the institution of kingship among segmentary societies, they managed to impose some of their own institutions, customs, and prejudices upon the indigenous Hutu tribes. In so doing they gained a monopoly not only of power but of wealth and social prestige. The Hutu agriculturalists, representing approximately 83 per cent of the population, share the physical characteristics of other Bantu people; they were accurately described by the Duke of Mecklenburg as "a medium-size type of people, whose ungainly figures betoken hard toil, and who patiently bow themselves in abject bondage to the later arrived, yet ruling race, the Tutsi."[6] The last group, the pygmoid Twa, stood at the bottom of the social pyramid. Representing less than one per cent of the population, they held an essentially marginal position in the traditional society; they were hunters and potters, and sometimes offered their services at the court where they served as cooks, buffoons, torturers, and executioners. Rwandan society was thus based on a hierarchy of interior-superior relationships in which the ranking of various *standen,* or status groups, tended to coincide with ethnic differences.

The central figure in the political system was represented by the *mwami* (a hereditary and divine king), who stood at the apex of a complex hierarchy of army chiefs, land chiefs, and cattle chiefs. Subordinate to this echelon was a vast number of subchiefs from whom tribute was exacted for the higher chiefs and the king. How much power the chiefs and subchiefs could claim for themselves was entirely dependent upon the king's grace.

Although the analogy with medieval Europe should not be pressed too far, in traditional Rwanda, as in medieval society, relationships among individuals were essentially based on ties of personal dependence. At the core of this relationship lay the institution of *buhake* (vassalage or clientship), an institution through which "an individual Hutu or Tutsi who had inferior social prestige, and who was less well provided with cattle, offered his services to and asked protection from a person whose status was higher and his wealth greater."[7] More than a purely economic transaction, the *buhake* involved reciprocal ties of

[6] Adolphus Frederick, Duke of Mecklenburg, *In the Heart of Africa* (London, 1910), 47.

[7] Maquet, *Inequality,* 129.

personal loyalty between patron and client: Just as in feudal Europe "the count was the 'man' of the king, and the serf the 'man' of his manorial lord," in Rwanda the chief was the king's "man" in the same fashion that the chief's client was the chief's "man."[8]

The economic base of this relationship helps to explain why the Hutu were generally at the bottom of the social pyramid and almost never at the top. Because the Tutsi minority was the sole possessor of cattle, and, because cattle therefore came to be regarded as the only significant symbol of wealth and prestige, the Tutsi as a group were bound to hold a dominant position in the power structure. Political power was inseparable from economic wealth, and economic wealth was inseparable from the ownership of cattle.

But a monopoly of wealth alone would not have sufficed to maintain the Tutsi elite in power. One does not need to subscribe to Helen Codere's intriguing thesis—that the struggle for power going on within the ranks of the Tutsi oligarchy served as a deterrent against Hutu-led revolts and thus "seems completely functional in maintaining Tutsi dominance and the old order"[9]—to recognize the inadequacy of a strictly Marxist interpretation of Rwandan society. As much as through the dispensation of wealth and the use of naked force, the Tutsi were able to maintain themselves in power because their traditional value system legitimized the premise of inequality on which their social and political institutions were built. Deeply rooted in Rwanda's "mythical charter" was the belief that the Tutsi were in fact a master race. Superlatively endowed by the *Imana* (Creator) with military skill, courage, and *ubwenge* (intelligence), they were "born" to rule over the Hutu, just as the *mwami* was "born" to rule over the country as a whole. To rebel against the established social order would have been no less sacreligious than to rebel against the *mwami* himself.

In recent times cultural attitudes toward "the premise of inequality" have tended to vary not only according to the subculture of each caste but particularly in relation to the intensity and duration of its exposure to the dominant ideology—acceptance or rejection of Tutsi values on the part of the Hutu peasantry depended on both the density of Tutsi in relation to Hutu in any given area, and on the duration of contact between the two. The little that we know about early Rwandan history suggests a three-phase process of territorial expansion: At first small bands of Tutsi pastoralists infiltrated among the local Hutu clans or lineage groups, using their cattle as a lever of economic power to gain ascendancy over the host population; then came

[8] See Marc Bloch, *Feudal Society* (London, 1962), I, 145.
[9] Helen Codere, "Power in Rwanda," *Anthropologica*, IV, 2 (1962), 45-87.

the amalgamation of a few autonomous chieftaincies into a small nuclear kingdom in the Bwanacyambwe region of central Rwanda; a final stage saw the incorporation of the outlying areas into a single territorial unit.[10]

It was in the northern region (Rukiga), where the density of Hutu elements is the highest, that the extension of the Tutsi imperium met with the greatest resistance. Thus the effective annexation of the small Hutu kingdoms of the northern and northeastern marches was not completed until the late 1920's and would probably have taken even longer had it not been for the timely assistance proffered at first by the Germans and later by the Belgians.[11] Indeed, despite close ethnic affinities with the Hutu of central Rwanda, the northern tribes (sometimes referred to collectively as the Kiga) have never been fully assimilated into the national culture of Rwanda; to this day they remain conspicuously aloof and culturally self-conscious, some of them insisting that their homeland is not really Rwanda but Rukiga. "The proud boast of the Kiga," wrote P. T. W. Baxter, "is that they never were, as a people, subjugated by either Tutsi or Hima."[12]

Although Baxter is here referring primarily to the Kiga of Kigezi (Uganda), this attitude is, nevertheless, surprising when one considers how strikingly similar their own indigenous institutions were to those of their Tutsi neighbors. Not only did the Kiga of Rwanda have their own ruling clans and *bahinza* or *bami* (kings) endowed with divine powers, but their own form of clientship. Clientship among the Kiga was a kind of land-lease contract between the original owners of the land, who were also the ruling families, the so-called *bakonde*, and the lineages or families who opened it for cultivation, the so-called *bagererwa*. Relationships between *bakonde* and *bagererwa* were in many respects similar to those existing between *shebuja* (patrons) and *bagaragu* (clients) in central Rwanda but with a major difference—it did not imply the subordination of one caste to another but only of one or several families to another. With the extension of Tutsi hegemony to the north this situation underwent a radical transformation: the lands of the ruling Hutu lineages were in most cases expropriated and turned over to Tutsi immigrants who then used their newly acquired property, and the backing of the European administration, to play the role of the old *bakonde* families. More than anything else, it

[10] See Jan Vansina, *L'Evolution du Royaume du Rwanda des Origines à 1900* (Brussels, 1962), 74-79.

[11] See William Roger Louis, *Ruanda-Urundi: 1884–1919* (Oxford, 1963), 156 ff.

[12] P. T. W. Baxter, "The Kiga," in Audrey Richards (ed.), *East African Chiefs* (New York, 1959), 281.

was their resentment of this status reversal attendant upon the extension of Tutsi hegemony to the north which caused the descendants of certain *bakonde* families (some of whom hold prominent positions in Rwanda's republican government) to join the revolutionary crusade against the *ancien régime*, and this in spite of the fact that they shared none of the leveling aspirations of the Westernized Hutu elite of central Rwanda.

Equally important from the standpoint of subsequent developments was the tradition of messianic activity which followed in the wake of the Tutsi conquest. This tradition is associated with the Nyabingi movement, a spirit-possession cult which came to express, in some respects, a struggle of the northern Hutu against Tutsi domination.[13] Although its origins can be traced back to the eighteenth century, its rapid development among the Kiga was directly related to the expansionist drive of Mwami Rwabugili in the late nineteenth century; in time the Nyabingi added to its purely magico-religious trappings the qualities of a subversive sect directed against all established authority, and in particular against Tutsi authority.

No doubt the continuing appeal of the sect was attributable in a large measure to the frustrations and economic hardships produced by the imposition of Tutsi rule; it also derived considerable impetus from the incidence of dynastic rivalries which developed within the Tutsi camp during the last decade of the nineteenth century. The facts, briefly stated, are as follows: After the famous and bloody palace revolution that took place in Rucuncu in 1896 a bitter struggle for power ensued between the representatives of the royal clans, the Bega and the Banyiginya; after the death of Mwami Rutalindwa at Rucuncu, members of the defeated Banyiginya clan sought asylum in the north, where they tried to enlist the support of the Kiga in their fight against the new *mwami*, Musinga, whom they regarded as a usurper. One of the most famous rebel chiefs thrown up by the coup of Rucuncu was a certain Ndungutsi, who came to be regarded by the local Hutu peasantry as their savior. Though himself of Tutsi origins his name became, and remains to this day, a symbol of anti-Tutsi sentiment. Typically, Ndungutsi saw himself as the protector of the oppressed peasantry, as a "social bandit" who posed as "the people's champion against the gentry and the foreigners."[14] At the same time, much of his success as a leader stemmed from his skillful exploitation of the opportunities offered by the Nyabingi—from his own efforts to

[13] See above, Elizabeth Hopkins, "The Nyabingi Cult of Southwestern Uganda," 258-336.

[14] See E. J. Hobsbawm, *Primitive Rebels* (New York, 1959), 32.

identify his immediate political objectives with those of the sect in the hope that it might be converted into an instrument to excite the latent animosities of the northern peasantry against the Tutsi.[15]

Thus, behind northern opposition to Tutsi rule lies a complex mixture of economic, political, and religious motives, stemming in part from the conditions in existence in the north prior to the Tutsi penetration, and in part from the growth of internal rivalries within the ruling oligarchy. But no matter how diverse the motives, the results were everywhere the same. A kind of latent agrarianism, directed against the Tutsi chiefs and actuated by a sense of class solidarity reminiscent of populism, spread throughout Kigaland. Though lacking an explicit ideology or program, this early form of unrest had a dual impact on subsequent protest movements: For one thing it evidently predisposed the northern Hutu populations to challenge the legitimacy of Tutsi overrule and thus enabled the northern Hutu politicians to mobilize support more quickly and effectively than anywhere else in the country; secondly, it served as a "carrier movement" through which the traditional Hutu elites of the north were able to reassert, albeit under the guise of a modern egalitarian ideology, their customary claims to authority. Hence, it is no accident that the northern Hutu leaders should have been drawn from traditional leadership groups, that is, from the descendants of the old *bakonde* families; nor is it very surprising that the northern revolt, far from being a social revolution, should have been primarily a rebellion against Tutsi imperialism and only secondarily against Western imperialism.

The Early Colonial Period

Inasmuch as the northern awakening can be traced to the conditions of stress engendered by an indigenous form of imperialism, these conditions bear a direct relationship to the territorial expansion of Tutsi hegemony brought into effect by European colonialism. The commitment of the German colonizer to the principle of indirect rule had meant not only a strengthening of the *mwami's* authority in central Rwanda but a conscious effort to ease and accelerate Tutsi penetration in the north, more often than not through punitive expeditions directed

[15] Much of the revolutionary potential harnessed against the monarchy in 1959 and 1960 stemmed from the heritage of resistance to alien rule which the Nyabingi left in its wake and which continued to make itself felt long after the banishment of its leaders and prohibition of its practices by European colonizers. Not that the Nyabingi as such was openly receptive to republican ideals. Its whole eschatology was clearly monarchical in inspiration. Yet there can be little doubt that the fiercely anti-Tutsi character of its orientation did provide an important link in the transition from monarchical to republican rule.

against the "rebel" tribes. The same implications can be read into the Belgian version of indirect rule as "it drew its inspiration from the line of conduct followed earlier by the German authorities."[16]

The forceful imposition of Tutsi rule in those areas that were still relatively "independent" at the time of the European conquest naturally sharpened the animus of the northern tribes against their masters; but more than this fact alone it was the extreme harshness of the methods used to achieve this rule which predisposed these tribes to rebel against the Tutsi invader. In this connection one only needs to recall the punitive expedition launched by Gudovius, the German Resident, in 1912, against Ndungutsi, which resulted in the wanton destruction of villages and crops and the loss of probably hundreds of human lives. Described as "the worst example of German brutality,"[17] the expedition against Ndungutsi was by no means the only one. Although the Belgians eventually succeeded in pacifying the region more or less permanently, the memory of previous repressions was bound to leave its mark on the attitudes of the local inhabitants.

In their effort to promote the "Tutsification" of the north the German and Belgian administrations not only encouraged Tutsi immigration but gave the imported Tutsi chiefs an even greater latitude in the exercise of their prerogatives than was ordinarily the case in other areas. Simultaneously, every effort was made to get rid of the last remaining Hutu kings, and by the late 1920's the entire region had become part of the *mwami's* domain. Difficult though it may be to generalize about the attitude of Tutsi authorities in the conquered provinces of the north, there is an obvious causal relationship between the arbitrariness of their rule and the feelings of intense hatred occasioned by some. The northern region soon became the Achilles' heel of the Belgian administration; indeed, W. R. Louis's statement that "the German authorities never found an entirely adequate solution for the stormy and rebellious northern part of Rwanda" would seem to apply equally well to the Belgian authorities.

For the sake of indirect rule, then, the whole northern region was in fact placed under direct rule and Tutsi supremacy; elsewhere, however, indirect rule had quite different implications as it presupposed "the unqualified recognition of the sultans [*mwami*] from us, [the German Residency], whether through taxes or other means, in a way that will seem to them as little a burden as possible."[18] As elsewhere in Africa, the intention of indirect rule was to use the traditional political institu-

---

[16] *Rapport sur l'administration belge au Ruanda-Urundi* (Brussels, 1921), 8.
[17] Louis, *Ruanda-Urundi,* 204.
[18] Ibid., 119–20.

tions as instruments of local government; but in Rwanda the preservation of these institutions had as its corollary the perpetuation of Tutsi supremacy in every walk of life. It meant, in Richard Kandt's words, "upholding the supremacy of the Tutsi and the corresponding extreme dependence of the great masses of the population."[19] The success of indirect rule, in other words, was conditioned by the strict maintenance of the caste system and the careful avoidance of all measures likely to upset the traditional social order.

The inception of the Belgian mandate, after World War I, saw the introduction of a series of administrative reforms intended to temper, systematize, and formalize the system of indirect rule inaugurated by the Germans. Early in 1917 the Belgian Resident decided to deny the *mwami* the powers of life and death heretofore exercized over his subjects, and in July 1917 the Belgian administration proceeded to further limit the Crown's authority through what amounted to a re-enactment of the Edict of Constantine: Discrimination against Catholic converts was declared illegal, especially in matters concerning appointments to office. Royal powers were curtailed even more drastically in 1923, when the dismissals of chiefs from office required the preliminary approval of the Resident. Finally in 1926 the Belgian Resident decided simply to eliminate the previous hierarchy of cattle chiefs, land chiefs, and army chiefs and substitute for it the rule of a single chief appointed by and responsible to the European administration.

Without in any way minimizing the importance of what was later referred to by Louis De Lacger as "a decisive and resolute entry into the sphere of constitutional reforms,"[20] these reforms had little effect on the existing social structure of Rwandan society. Not only was no effort made to promote racial integration but the social and economic gap between Hutu and Tutsi widened substantially as a result of specific policies and practices. Not until 1933 was a conscious effort made by the Residency to alter the structure of customary dues and taxation; meanwhile, however, the system was rendered even more burdensome by the laissez-faire attitude displayed by the administration toward the chiefs. As early as 1916 Mgr. Léon Classe reported that the *butaka* (land tax), which traditionally involved one day's labor out of five on the chief's property, was raised to two and in some places to three days' labor out of six.[21] Moreover, new *corvées* were introduced

19 Richard Kandt, *Caput Nili* (Berlin, 1905), 483.
20 Louis De Lacger, *Ruanda* (Kabgaye, 1959), 466.
21 Léon Classe, "L'Organisation Politique du Ruanda au début de l'Occupation belge" (unpublished document, Kabgaye, 1916), 5.

which had not before existed, such as the construction of houses in durable material for the chiefs and the *mwami*. Then the regular taxes were often supplemented through the most arbitrary methods: "Where there is a predominance of 'small' Tutsi," wrote Mgr. Classe in 1916, "the chief or his wife consider themselves entitled to take anything they please [from the Hutu taxpayer]—bananas, yams, etc., and the Hutu must comply lest he be expelled from his field."[22]

Evidence that such abuses continued long after these lines were written can be inferred from the decision of the administration, in 1933, to substitute a fixed monetary tax for the system of dues in kind paid to the *mwami* and the chiefs. From then on the tribute owed to the *mwami (ikoro)*, the chiefs, and the subchiefs *(ibihunikwa)* amounted to a total of 3 francs per taxpayer. Yet the system of *corvée* labor remained unchanged. In fact the expression *prestations coutumières* came to serve as a magic label under which a multitude of additional *corvées*, including compulsory cultivation of food crops, was thrust upon the peasantry under the pretext that custom somehow conferred automatic legitimacy upon all forms of work. This, along with the introduction of a head tax levied by the chiefs on behalf of the European administration, sharply increased the demands made upon the masses. The result was that the lot of the Hutu masses was unquestionably worse under Belgian rule than at any other time in the past. Few Belgian administrators would have conceded this fact without emphasizing the advantages derived from the imposition of the *pax Belgica*—the construction of roads, hospitals and dispensaries, the improvements in the quality and quantity of crops, and the margin of economic security which this provided for the peasant masses. But if these were indeed appreciable gains, their cost in terms of human labor and taxation was extremely heavy. Coming on top of customary tithes, tributes, and *corvées*, the "civilizing" aspects of the Belgian presence made the rule of the chiefs a singularly uncivilized one.

But if the requirements of administrative efficiency and economic viability undeniably added to the deprivations suffered by the peasantry, the same factors were equally instrumental in altering the position of the chiefs in society. The point here is that the legitimacy of chiefly rule, as distinct from monarchical rule, was threatened not only by the additional constraints which it involved for the Hutu masses but also by the structural innovations introduced into the political system. The abolition of the army chiefs and the cattle chiefs in the 1920's, and their replacement by a single officeholder within each chiefdom, destroyed the system of checks and balances which

[22] Ibid.

until then had provided certain structural safeguards against abuses of power. Furthermore, because they were expected to discharge a host of functions for which there was no counterpart in traditional Rwandan society, and for which they remained ultimately accountable to the administration, the Rwandan chiefs were to all intents and purposes cast in the role of functionnaires. Before long they had to choose between two equally unpalatable alternatives—either they would redefine their role and position so as to meet the requirements of bureaucratic rule, or they would simply ignore the new imperatives and face the consequences. At first many chiefs preferred to be dismissed from office rather than to adapt themselves to the new system. In time, however, a new generation of chiefs emerged to replace the old ones. They tended to act as the obedient servants of the authorities of the mandatory power and no longer exclusively as the "king's men." The resulting situation was one in which administrative efficiency was not only synonymous with the application of uniform bureaucratic standards but very often with sheer brutality and arbitrariness.

Although the chiefs and the subchiefs continued to represent a distinctive elite group within the dominant Tutsi stratum, both in terms of their specialized training and the positions they held in society, the social distance separating this political elite from other members of the aristocracy was not nearly as wide as that which separated them both from Hutu "commoners." Being generally exempt from corvée labor and other customary dues, the Tutsi as a group were able to assume the status of a "leisure class" to an unprecedented extent; and because they remained (at least until the early 1950's) the sole beneficiaries of Western educational opportunities, they were able to "objectify" their elite status through a markedly Western style of life, including Western patterns of household behavior and more than occasional traces of "conspicuous consumption." More important still, their supremacist claims were openly recognized by the Catholic church and the administration and acted upon accordingly. They became more and more visibly differentiated from the "lower orders," culturally, socially and economically, so that whatever grievances were eventually directed against the chiefs inevitably tended to reverberate upon the entire Tutsi stratum.

In short, the early period of colonial rule created a revolutionary potential on which subsequent generations of Hutu leaders could capitalize in order to attain their own political ends. A situation of dysfunction, to use Chalmers Johnson's expression,[23] was bound to develop betwen a political system based upon an extreme form of

[23] Chalmers Johnson, *Revolution and the Social System* (Stanford, 1964), 5.

bureaucratic-oligarchical rule and a social system that could not forever be kept insulated from, or made invulnerable to, Western influences. Yet for many years after the intrusion of colonial rule, Rwanda remained an island society, immune from the unsettling influences of industrialization and large-scale commercialization, and hence largely devoid of modern forms of political self-expression. Not until after World War II did Rwanda begin to show signs of an incipient social and political transformation.

The Post-war Colonial Period

Of all the post-war changes that have contributed to the growth of a revolutionary consciousness, at least three deserve mention: to begin with, trusteeship status involved a fundamental change in the ultimate political objectives of the administering authority, that is, to a commitment "to promote the political, economic and social and educational advancement of the inhabitants of the trust territory, and their progressive development toward self-government and independence."[24] This led in the early 1950's to the introduction of social and constitutional reforms aiming at the abolition of the feudal regime and the implantation of governmental structures more representative of the "lower orders." Secondly, this overall reappraisal of policy objectives was paralleled by similar changes in the attitude of the Roman Catholic church: Whereas until World War II the educational policy of the Church had remained closely attuned to the social requirements of indirect rule, by the early 1950's the European clergy of Rwanda was almost unanimously committed to the policy of gradual democratization advocated by Belgium. In practice this meant the opening of facilities for secondary and higher education to the Hutu and a concurrent attempt at widening the bases of recruitment of native priests irrespective of their ethnic affiliations. Finally, and as a consequence of the foregoing, the post-war years saw the emergence of a new educated Hutu elite, profoundly dedicated to democratic ideas and increasingly anxious to make good its claims to equal rights and opportunities for all regardless of caste differences. It is important to stress the interconnection between these various changes in the social and political setting: The revolutionary dispositions of the new Hutu elites cannot be disassociated from the part played by the Roman Catholic church in bringing the Hutu into contact with a new set of values and metaphysical beliefs any more than the decision of the Church to reverse its traditional stand on the question of Hutu-Tutsi

24 U.N. Charter, Art. 76.

relations can be divorced from changes in the official thinking of the administering authorities.

Until the post-war period the policy of the Roman Catholic church was based on the assumption that Tutsi supremacy should be maintained in every walk of life, as prescribed by the "natural laws" of Rwandan society. "The greatest disservice which the government could render to itself and to the country as a whole," wrote Mgr. Classe, Rwanda's first Apostolic Vicar, "would be to suppress the Tutsi caste. A revolution [sic] of this kind will surely lead the country straight to anarchy and to a fiercely [haineusement] anti-European Communism. . . . As a general rule we will never find better and more intelligent chiefs, more amenable to progress, and more acceptable to the people, than among the Tutsi."[25]

By the mid-1950's, however, the Roman Catholic church seemed to take precisely the opposite view and tended to associate the danger of a "fiercely anti-European Communism" with the continued withholding of social and political rights from the Hutu masses. In part this attitude seemed to reflect certain changes in the social background of the European clergy. Among the Belgian missionaries who came to Rwanda after World War II there were many of relatively humble social origins, which, together with their Walloon background and and previous experience of social conditions in the French-speaking provinces of Belgium, led them to sympathize with the plight of the Hutu peasantry. It is equally pertinent to note in this connection that it was in 1955 that Mgr. Jean Perraudin, a Swiss citizen, arrived in Kabgaye to assume the functions of Apostolic Vicar for Rwanda. If Perraudin's nationality helps to explain his strong personal commitment to democratic reforms, his position in the Catholic hierarchy suggests that he enjoyed considerable influence to help in bringing them into effect. Significantly, to this day the personality of Mgr. Perraudin evokes diametrically opposed, although equally emotional, reactions from Hutu and Tutsi. The former view him as nothing short of a savior, and the latter see him as a hateful sycophant guilty of spreading racial hatred and violence among the people of Rwanda.

Because the Church dominated the schools, this reversal of attitude led in 1955–56 to the extension of new educational opportunities to the members of the Hutu caste. Simultaneously, positive efforts were made by the European clergy of Rwanda to influence the policy of the Belgian government and to inform Belgian public opinion of the social and political problems of Rwanda. Thus the Church made itself felt at two levels: Psychologically, it served as the main vehicle through

[25] Lacger, Ruanda-Urundi, 524.

which new ideas and values—which sometimes held revolutionary implications—were introduced among the Hutu; organizationally, it served as the main intermediary through which this nascent, educated Hutu elite came into contact with the outside world.

Through its links with Church-affiliated metropolitan organizations the European clergy made it possible for some leading Hutu politicians, like Grégoire Kayibanda (later President of the Republic) and Aloys Munyangaju (a former deputy who became Vice-President of the Constitutional Court), to establish connections with Belgian politicians and interest groups and to seek and receive the moral and material support they so badly needed to sustain them in their fight for equality. One might mention in this connection the substantial, although undetermined, financial support which these leaders received from the pro-Catholic Belgian trade union organization, the *Confédération des Syndicats Chrétiens*, and from the *Boerenbound*, the all-powerful, Flemish-led agricultural union affiliated with the *Confédération*. In retrospect, it seems doubtful that the Hutu leadership would have become so actively engaged in revolutionary activities unless they had reason to expect continued support from the Church, and unless they felt that this support could elicit a favorable response to their cause from the metropolitan authorities as well as from certain segments of Belgian public opinion.

Despite the coming to power in 1954 of an "anti-clerical" government, made up of a coalition of Liberals and Socialists, in general the official thinking of the metropolitan authorities after World War II was highly favorable to the policy of democratization advocated by the Church. Belgium's adherence to the political aims of the trusteeship signaled a radical departure from her previous policies. By 1948 Belgian officials freely admitted that "Belgian policy ought to bring to an end the feudal system." Even though the administering authorities in Rwanda approached the whole question of self-government with characteristic prudence, repeatedly emphasizing the danger of premature reforms, democracy and self-government were now being envisaged as legitimate alternatives to the *status quo*. This drastic revision of the traditional goals of Belgian policy led to the gradual introduction of constitutional reforms, beginning in 1952 with the establishment of representative organs at each level of the administrative hierarchy. But it was not until 1956 that a form of indirect male suffrage was introduced. Instead of giving the chiefs a free hand in the appointment of the electoral colleges, as had been the case under the decree of July 14, 1952, they were to be indirectly elected by the entire adult male population.

Although the reform did lead to a substantial increase of Hutu representation in the lower councils (chiefdom and subchiefdom councils), the membership of the higher councils continued to reflect an overwhelming majority of Tutsi, which testified to the continued subservience of the Hutu peasantry and to the social norms operative in Rwandan society. Very much the same kind of conservative attitude was brought to light by the reform of the *buhake* (cattle contract) in 1954, which, in theory, provided that the obligations attendant upon the clientage system could be waived unilaterally or by mutual consent. In some parts of Rwanda the reform was received with great enthusiasm, but there were a number of cases where the clients would, after dividing up their cattle between themselves and their patron, remorsefully offer one of their remaining cows to their former patron as a sign of continued allegiance.

In short, however instrumental they may have been in bringing about a limited change in the power relationships between Hutu and Tutsi, the social and constitutional reforms of the 1950's failed to achieve the basic transformations which the Hutu leaders had hoped for. As they became conscious of the enormous lag between the very slow pace of social change in Rwanda and the increasing pressures brought to bear upon Belgium to give the country its independence (pressures which originated from international public opinion as well as from the more educated Tutsi elites), their disappointment suddenly gave way to an intense fear that self-government might be thrust upon Rwanda before the Hutu had a chance to reap the benefits of democracy, that is, the benefits of majority rule. In this case self-government could only mean the perpetuation of Tutsi hegemony. Thus a major inducement to revolutionary activity came from a growing conviction on the part of the Hutu leadership that only through the use of violence would they be able to awaken the political consciousness of the masses in time to build a power base of their own in the countryside.

But this did not make the revolution inevitable. Thus far we have deliberately emphasized those factors and circumstances which favored the rise of a revolutionary consciousness: (1) the emergence of a new "alienated" class of Hutu intellectuals who could no longer fit themselves into the context of traditional Rwandan society; (2) the spread of a leveling, egalitarian ideology, based on new metaphysical beliefs; (3) the determination of these new elites to achieve by revolutionary means what could not be attained through constitutional reforms; (4) the presence in the north of a class of *bakonde* (traditional land-owning families) who, for cultural and historical reasons, were already predisposed to rebel against Tutsi overrule. A fifth element, to be discussed more fully in the next section, was the persistent refusal of the incumbent Tutsi elites to yield to the demands voiced by the Hutu intelligentsia. Without in any way minimizing the importance of these factors, it is well also to bear in mind some of the forces working in the opposite direction: (1) a general lack of popular support for the democratic ideas advocated by the Hutu leadership and a corresponding absence of revolutionary zeal among the rural communities; (2) the enormous obstacles raised by the absence of proper communications and a physical environment which is so mountainous and isolated as to make any large-scale political mobilization extremely difficult to achieve; (3) the fact that the Belgian presence could presumably be relied upon to prevent, or at least minimize, the incidence of violence. This, however, is precisely where the paradox lies: Instead of denying the Hutu the facilities which they needed to carry on a successful revolution, the administering authorities were, through a series of unanticipated events, led to throw their weight on the side of the insurgents, thereby decisively altering the balance of power between Hutu and Tutsi. But this is not to say that the Belgian authorities intended the revolution. The improvised character of the Belgian responses to the Hutu revolution can best be understood by looking at the chain of circumstances that led to the outbreak of the revolution.

The Road to Violence: 1957–59

The years immediately preceding the outbreak of rural rioting, in November 1959, saw a worsening of Hutu-Tutsi relations. As previously noted, a major element in the "social tinder" characteristic of this pre-revolutionary period was the social disaffection of an increasing number of Hutu intellectuals whose sense of identity had undergone a profound erosion with their exposure to Christianity; another was the intransigence of the ruling elites and their consequent failure to make expected changes. Commenting on "the great changes" which took place in Rwanda during the five years preceding the revolt of 1959, an Anglican bishop who had spent many years in Rwanda wrote that during this period "the traditional feudal system of master and servant had been broken by giving every servant his share of cattle as his personal property and by abolishing the duties usually attached to the possession of cows. . . . Government obligatory labor—a long-standing grievance—had been ended. . . . Local councils have been given powers previously exercised by the chiefs and the administration. . . . There were elections in 1956, to the Mwami's council which has considerable powers."[26]

[26] Bishop Brazier, "Ruanda's Fiery Trial," *Ruanda Notes,* 147 (Mar.–May, 1960), 12.

The truth is, however, that these changes were more apparent than real and in no way altered the position of supremacy traditionally held by the Tutsi oligarchy. Thus the abolition of the *buhake* was quickly circumvented by the perpetuation of clientage ties through land tenure —in particular through the famous *ibikingi* system which allowed the original owners of cattle to retain control over pasture lands; certain forms of *akazi* (compulsory labor) continued until at least 1959; the local councils remained purely advisory and thus made it possible for the chiefs to ignore the desires of their constituents; as for the Mwami's Council, not only were its powers also advisory, but its membership remained almost exclusively made up of Tutsi elements, with a clear majority of chiefs. What needs to be stressed here is *not* that "objective" social conditions were substantially different from what they were, say, in 1949, but, rather, that a whole series of expected changes failed to materialize so that conditions that were still perceived as tolerable in 1949 were no longer so by 1957.

The Hutu Manifesto

The turning point came in March 1957, shortly before the arrival of the United Nations Trusteeship Visiting Mission, with the publication of the Manifesto of the Bahutu.[27] In it, for the first time in the history of Rwanda, a group of Hutu intellectuals, all nine of them former seminarians, systematically challenged every conceivable feature of the feudal system. The heart of the matter, they said, lay in "the political monopoly of one race, the Tutsi race, which, given the present structural framework, becomes a social and economic monopoly." After citing specific examples of political, social, economic, and cultural injustices, they concluded: "From all this to a state of 'cold' civil war and xenophobia, there is only one step. From all this to the popularity of communist ideas there is only one step." To remedy the situation they proposed a series of measures designed to achieve "the integral and collective promotion of the Hutu," that is, the abandonment of caste prejudice, the recognition of individual landed property, the creation of a Rural Credit Bank *(Fonds de Crédit Rural)* to promote rural initiatives, the codification of customs, the promotion of Hutu elements to public office, and the extension of educational opportunities at all levels to Hutu children. Never before had such a devastating critique of the *ancien régime* been publicly set forth by its opponents.

The authors of the manifesto had few organizational ties to hold them together. They formed a loose network of young people who

[27] See *Rwanda Politique: 1958–1960* (Brussels, 1961), 20-29.

knew one another, had attended the same seminary (at Kabgaye) and who, in some cases, belonged to the same chiefdom or subchiefdom council. Of the various personalities, the one who possessed the greatest ambition and the surest touch for politics was Kayibanda.

Born in 1924 in the vicinity of Kabgaye, some say of a Mushi father from the Congo and a Hutu mother, Kayibanda attended the *petit séminaire* of Nyakibanda and subsequently found employment as a primary school teacher at the Institut Classe, near Kigali, where he stayed until 1952. While serving at the institute he showed sufficient initiative to become secretary of the literary committee in charge of awarding prizes for the best literary essays written by Rwandan students; to this function he added that of secretary of the *Amitiés Belgo-Congolaises,* a cultural association founded in Kigali by a Belgian settler named J. F. C. Goossens. In 1952 Kayibanda was allowed to attend the *grand séminaire* at Kabgaye. In 1956 he was editor in chief of a local newspaper, *Kinyamateka,* personal secretary to Mgr. Perraudin, the Apostolic Vicar of Rwanda, and a member of the chiefdom council of Marangara. These three roles he apparently exploited with consummate skill: the first to propagandize his ideas, the second to enlist the support of the Church, and the third to recruit potential adherents to his cause. Thus, when in June 1957 Kayibanda launched the *Mouvement Social Muhutu* an all-Hutu party whose program was indistinguishable from that set forth in the Manifesto—he had already established valuable contacts and gained considerable respect from the local peasantry as well as from the literate Hutu elites.

Yet the *Mouvement* remained a rather weak and ineffectual organization which failed to generate anything like grass roots support in areas other than Gitarama and Kabgaye. The main asset of the Hutu leadership lay in the almost unconditional support which it received from the Roman Catholic church—indeed from Mgr. Perraudin himself whose sympathies for the *menu peuple* soon became an open secret. This support enabled them, among other things, to gain control over the vernacular press and to use the daily newspaper *Temps Nouveaux d'Afrique,* then published by the White Fathers of Bujumbura, as a vehicle for the diffusion of their ideas among Europeans and literate Africans of both Rwanda and Burundi. Many of these leaders first caught the attention of the public by their pamphleteering journalism, and it was principally through their journalistic activities that they first sought to enlist support for their crusade against the feudal system.

From the very beginning the Hutu leadership was faced with several major obstacles. One of the most serious stemmed from the absence of cohesion among the various personalities who claimed to represent the Hutu masses. This is why a man like Joseph Gitera—one of Rwanda's most erratic personalities—found it expedient in November 1957 to bolt the *Mouvement* in order to found his own association, the *Association pour la Promotion Sociale de la Masse* (in short, Aprosoma). Gitera's attempt to pre-empt the themes, if not the tactics, of the *Mouvement* encountered partial success in and around Astrida (now Butare), but on the whole Aprosoma achieved no significant results, save perhaps that of weakening the still very fragile supports of its parent organization.

Another liability confronting the Hutu leadership was that they had relatively little contact with the rural communities of the hills. Not only did they lack the necessary means of communication but there was little they could do to break the rigorous surveillance of the chiefs and subchiefs. True, in some areas they took advantage of the so-called *réunions de colline*—the judicial and administrative meetings held on the hills at the request of the local ruling families—to propagate their ideas; but this practice was restricted to northern and northwestern regions. Elsewhere only in the vicinity of the main mission stations and commercial centers were the Hutu leaders able to establish effective contacts with the peasantry. Thus until 1959 the Hutu movement had relatively few adherents, although certainly a great many potential sympathizers, outside the Ruhengeri-Gitarama axis.

A third handicap was created by the apparent indifference of the administering authorities to the demands of the Hutu. Although the manifesto had urged the Belgian administration to take "more positive and unambiguous measures to achieve the political and economic emancipation of the Hutu," at first nothing of substance was accomplished to mitigate racial tension. Not until December 1958 did Vice-Governor Jean-Paul Harroy concede that "the Hutu-Tutsi question poses an undeniable problem," but even so one may wonder if the proposed solution—the abolition of the official usage of the terms Hutu and Tutsi—did more than provide a convenient way of dodging the issue. Indeed, as one reflects upon the attitude of the Belgian authorities during these years, one cannot fail to be struck by their seeming passivity in the face of the impending crisis. Although many Belgian officials probably sensed the gravity of the situation, the impression that one gains is that they simply did not know how to handle it. Whatever the cause may be, the silence of Belgian officialdom added significantly to the climate of tension and uncertainty which characterized this transitional period. In addition to arousing the anxiety of the Hutu leadership, the attitude of Belgian authorities was readily interpreted by some Tutsi as tacit approval of their claims to supremacy.

The Monarchist Reaction

In time, however, tensions were bound to develop between the indigenous Tutsi elite and the European administration. At the root of the conflict lay two radically divergent estimates of the Hutu-Tutsi problem and thus two basically incompatible approaches to its solution. By 1958 the consensus among Belgian administrators and members of the European clergy was that a profound social transformation was taking place, one that should be activated and controlled through appropriate institutional reforms. Implicit in this view was the assumption that the Belgian presence should be maintained in Rwanda for as long as the exigencies of the situation required. In the minds of the Tutsi elite, on the other hand, a social transformation on the scale envisaged in the Manifesto was inconceivable. By and large they felt that the demands voiced by the Hutu leadership were only representative of the views of a tiny minority of hotheads, and that most of the trouble came from the errors made by the administration in the application, or misapplication of indirect rule; such being the case, only through "full independence" could a lasting remedy be found to the social ills generated by the Belgian presence. The strategy laid out by the Tutsi oligarchy, in brief, was to seek the eviction of the Trust authorities at the earliest possible date so as to reassert their control over the destinies of the country. Once this was done, the future of the monarchy seemed assured.

But in spite of their quasi-unanimous agreement on the desirability of independence within the shortest possible time, the tactics employed by the monarchists underwent some significant changes of emphasis between 1957 and 1959. From an almost exclusive preoccupation with the reassertion of traditional values and institutions, the Tutsi elite in early 1959 veered to a position of increasing hostility toward the administration, and eventually to active involvement in party politics.

These tactical shifts must be viewed against the background of two major events: One was the appointment of a parliamentary commission *(groupe de travail)* by the Belgian government, in April 1959, to investigate the conditions under which a transfer of authority could safely be accomplished; the other was the sudden death of Mwami Mutara Rudahigwa in July of the same year. Given the terms of reference of the commission, one can easily see why its arrival in Rwanda should have caused such deep anxieties among the ruling elite; the introduction of democratic processes implied the organization of popular elections and the substitution of majority rule, ascertained through the ballot box, for the rule of the minority. In the climate of racial tension which had prevailed since the publication of the Manifesto, this initiative was bound to increase further the suspicions of the Tutsi group.

What brought these suspicions to the point of near-explosion was the news of the death of Mwami Mutara, on July 25, in circumstances that were never completely elucidated. The official explanation of the Belgian authorities—that Mutara had died of a heart attack—did not sound very convincing to the Tutsi, and to this day the opinion of most Tutsi is that their *mwami* was assassinated by the Belgians—"like Rwagasore of Burundi, and Lumumba," as one of them said to this writer. That Mutara's death should have occurred shortly after he had an exchange of views with Belgian officials in Bujumbura, and only two days before he was scheduled to issue what everyone expected to be an important policy statement, seemed to them to confirm this opinion. Predictably, the immediate reaction of the ruling caste took the form of a violent denunciation of the alleged duplicity of the Belgian authorities.

But Mutara's death did not signify the death of the monarchy. It was during the burial of Mutara, in the vicinity of the royal capital of Nyanza, on Mwima hill, that the name of his successor was first revealed to the public. What came to be known as the Mwima coup marked the beginning of a new phase in Rwandan politics, characterized by a sudden upsurge of organized political activity and a further deterioration of the relations between the Crown and the administration.

Limitations of space preclude a detailed analysis of the tortuous sequence of events triggered by Mutara's death; suffice it to note here that the nomination of Mutara's successor, his half brother Jean-Baptiste Ndahindurwa, came as a complete surprise to the administration, and under circumstances which gave the Vice-Governor no choice but to accept the decision as a *fait accompli*. Although the Residency had been vaguely told of the possibility of "unforeseen developments" during the *mwami's* funeral, it had no inkling of the nature of these developments. In strict conformity with tradition the choice of Mutara's successor had been kept secret until the very last moment. In these conditions special security measures seemed not only unnecessary but inappropriate for the occasion. As it turned out the main security forces present at the *mwami's* funeral were scores of armed Tutsi and Twa elements who had come from various surrounding localities to pay their last respects to their deceased sovereign. Confronted with this improvised militia the Resident opted for the safest course. As he himself later told this writer, "we [Belgians] had no way of telling what might have happened had we tried to interfere with the succession. The atmosphere at Mwima was extremely tense. The wrong move could well have triggered a reaction of violence of some sort or another." Not only did this cause the administration to suffer a considerable loss of face, but it also conveyed the distinct impression that real power now lay in the hands of the monarchists.

The next point to be stressed is that the new *mwami* could not possibly hope to play the unifying role that circumstances and natural ability had conveyed upon his predecessor; at the time a twenty-one-year-old youth, and intellectually not a very gifted one, Ndahindurwa—better known under the dynastic name Kigeli—lacked the experience and prestige of his brother; he lacked Mutara's adeptness at reconciling divergent viewpoints and tendencies, at giving a measure of harmony and unity to his following. Thus as the need for unity became all the more pressing, an alternative source of cohesion had to be found. This is what led to the creation of the *Union Nationale Rwandaise* (Unar) on August 15, 1959. Though ostensibly dedicated to "the union of all Rwandese for the purpose of achieving true progress in all spheres," and under the nominal presidency of a Hutu—François Rukeba—the Unar was clearly intended to serve as the instrument of Tutsi supremacy.

From the very outset the doctrine, tactics, and leadership of the Unar seemed to reflect the circumstances that led to its foundation. Party doctrine was consciously fashioned to extol the values of kingship, as if to reassure the masses that the passing of Mutara had in no way compromised the strength and continuity of monarchic institutions. This theme found expression in a multitude of manifestos, tracts, and newspapers, in which the notion of kingship was consciously related to the unity of all Rwandese—Hutu, Tutsi, and Twa—with the suggestion that all three castes had always lived in total harmony with each other, and that therefore the existence of racial tensions could only be attributed to the evil hand of the administration.

Though incarnating the continuity of monarchic institutions, Kigeli was only a figurehead. The most dynamic if not the most influential personality in the Unar leadership was its President, François Rukeba, the man who had dramatically revealed himself at Mwima as a potential leader by boldly stepping forth in front of the assembled crowd to proclaim the name of Mutara's heir. Besides having shown on this occasion considerable courage and initiative, as a Hutu Rukeba was an ideal choice to lend credibility to the ideological claims of the party. Rukeba, however, was justly said to represent the "emotional and prophetic element in the party, whereas some of the important chiefs of Rwanda constituted its braintrust."[28] These were Michel Kayihura, Pierre Mungalurire, and Chrysostome Rwangombwa. All three were men of considerable standing, whose official status as chiefs was further enhanced by their membership in the Mwami's Council (*Conseil Supérieur du Pays*). That these men did in fact constitute the core of the Unar leadership was made abundantly clear by subsequent events; as we shall see, it was in response to the administrative sanctions taken against them that, in November 1959, a group of young members of the Unar decided to resort to "direct action."

The Jacquerie of November 1959

The political spark that set off the jacquerie of November 1959 originated from the decision of the Belgian authorities to take disciplinary measures against Chiefs Kayihura, Mungalurire, and Rwangombwa, on the grounds that their participation in a meeting of the Unar at Kigali, on September 13, 1959, was in flagrant violation of the instructions issued by the Residency. At first they were told they would be dismissed from office; but after a review of the sentence by the Resident they learned that they would be simply transferred to other chiefdoms. As much as the substance of the decision itself, the timing and the procedure employed by the administration were critical elements in the chain of events that led to the riots.

It should be noted, first, that the decision of the administration was not made final until October 12, exactly a month after the Kigali meeting. In the meantime some important developments had taken place. The Kigali meeting had been the occasion for a brilliant display of nationalist oratory on the part of Rukeba and the three chiefs. Before a crowd estimated at two thousand, Rukeba had read out the party's program and ended with a long panegyric on the Rwandan monarchy, punctuated with scathing attacks against Belgian colonialism: "The whole of Africa," said Rukeba, "is struggling against colonialism, the same colonialism which has exploited our country and destroyed our ancestral customs in order to impose alien ones upon us. . . . He who does not belong to this party will be regarded as the people's enemy, the Mwami's enemy, Rwanda's enemy!"[29]

So successful was the meeting that it encouraged similar organizational moves on the part of both Hutu and Tutsi. Thus on September 14 a new party sprang up, the *Rassemblement Démocratique Rwandais* (in short, Rader). Led by Chief Prosper Bwanakweli, the Rader came

[28] *U.N. Visiting Mission to Trust Territories in East Africa: Report on Ruanda-Urundi*, T/1551 (New York, 1960), 22.

[29] Cited in "Memoire sur la révolution Ruandaise," anon., mimeo. (Kigali, 1960).

to represent the views of moderate Tutsi elements and for this reason never succeeded in attracting more than a marginal following. Then on October 19, 1959, Kayibanda converted his original *Mouvement* into a more militant and tightly-knit organization, the *Parti du Mouvement de l'Emancipation Hutu*, better known as Parmehutu. Unlike the Rader, the Parmehutu emerged as a fairly strong organization, fully committed to populist ideals, and with considerable support among the Hutu masses of Gitarama; yet like the Rader, the Parmehutu was regarded by the more conservative Tutsi politicians as a creature of the colonial establishment. What gave this accusation a peculiarly convincing ring is that the birth of the Parmehutu had been predicted in a Unar circular of September 16, in which Rukeba warned "the people, friends and children of Rwanda [that] in a few days a new party will be born, supported by the government and the priests: This movement will be said to have come from Christ to preach charity . . . Rwandese, children of Rwanda, subjects of Kigeli, rise up! Let us unite our strength! Do not let the blood of Rwanda be spilled in vain. There are no Twa, Hutu or Tutsi: we are all brothers; we are all descendants of Kinyaranda!"[30] If the tone of the circular is any index, the foundation of the Parmehutu, or better, the circumstances of its foundation, only served to bring racial tension to a new high.

As for the procedure employed by the administering authorities, the point which needs to be emphasized is that there were no legal grounds on which charges could be brought against the three chiefs at the time that the Kigali meeting was held. Indeed, what made the decision of the administration so patently unfair is that the instructions of the Residency concerning the extent to which indigenous authorities could participate in political activities had not been issued until well after the Unar meeting (although statutory regulations concerning the right to organize and participate in political associations had been in existence long before the Unar meeting, these did not specifically debar indigenous authorities from participating in such associations; all that was needed was a preliminary authorization from the adminis-tration—the so-called *agréation préalable*—which the Unar had in fact received); what made it especially harsh on the chiefs is that all three held important chiefdoms and enjoyed considerable prestige among their own people, including the local Hutu inhabitants. In the words of a United Nations report, "the affair of the three chiefs was a decisive turning point, indicating a break between the administration and the Unar. It led to the voluntary exile of the three chiefs and made it extremely difficult for talks to be resumed."[31]

[30] Ibid.
[31] U.N., *Report on Ruanda-Urundi*, 27.

In this highly volatile atmosphere the slightest provocation could set off an explosion. Thus, when on November 1 the news came that a band of young Unar militants had attacked a Hutu subchief in the vicinity of Gitarama, the incident became the signal for a violent reaction by the Hutu population. From Gitarama, violence and arson spread like wildfire through the whole of Rwanda, and in the weeks that followed literally thousands of Tutsi huts were pillaged and set aflame. To quote from the report of the United Nations Visiting Mission, "the incendiaries set off in bands of ten. Armed with matches and paraffin, which the indigenous inhabitants use in large quantities for their lamps, they pillaged the Tutsi houses they passed on their way and set fire to them. On their way they would enlist other incendiaries to follow the procession, while the first recruits, too exhausted to continue, would give up and return home. Thus day after day fires spread from hill to hill."[32]

Despite the striking uniformity of methods used by the insurgents, the revolt was more in the nature of a spontaneous uprising than the result of careful premeditation. "They burned and pillaged because they had been told to do so, and because the operation did not seem to involve great risks and enabled them to seize loot in the victims' huts."[33] Nonetheless, the potential for violence varied in character and intensity depending on the regions, carrying the revolutionary crusade in strange and sometimes conflicting directions. At least two separate strands can be identified: one, reflecting the situation of latent unrest created in the north by the carry-over of messianic influences, has tended to impart to the northern rebellion some of the qualities of a millenarian movement—"the hope of a complete and radical change," along with a "fundamental vagueness about the actual way in which the new society will be brought about."[34] If the first of these characteristics goes far in explaining the success of the northern uprisings in achieving a swift and massive mobilization of local energies against Tutsi rule, and indeed in virtually annihilating its local agents, the second accounts for the inability of the movement to restructure the political environment it had destroyed. The millenarian thrust behind the northern uprisings was thus extremely short-lived and almost wholly negative in its effects. Its energies were at once absorbed into a very different type of movement—localized, anarchistically oriented,[35] and exhibiting a relatively high quotient of pre-Tutsi tradi-

[32] Ibid., 78.
[33] Ibid.
[34] Hobsbawm, *Primitive Rebels,* 57.
[35] The expression is here used to denote a movement toward a *status quo ante,* though not necessarily leading to the actualization of the pre-existent situation. See Johnson, *Revolution,* 42.

tionalism. The rapid disintegration of the Tutsi-implanted superstructure in the north cleared the way for the partial resurgence of pre-Tutsi institutions and the re-establishment of the old *bagererwa-bakonde* type of clientelism.

The second strand, confined to the central and southern regions, revealed the restorative-egalitarian element common to all jacquerie situations. Unlike the former, which initially sprang from a collective quest for the millennium and rapidly transformed itself into a nostalgic search for a pre-Tutsi identity, its aim was to appeal to the legitimacy of the existing monarchical order against the illegitimacy of chiefly exactions –in short "to purge the regime of its violators, and, so to speak, to set it back on the tracks."[36] As we shall see, the weaving of these threads into a more or less unified movement was a long and arduous endeavor, involving, among other things, a redefinition of the ethnic context of clientage networks and their adaptation to common revolutionary goals.

Meanwhile, and in contrast with the rather amorphous, unstructured quality of the Hutu uprising, the following Tutsi repression was not only better organized but more specifically related to political aims. The main target of the repression was the Hutu leadership, widely regarded by the incumbents as the principal agent of subversion Thus before the administering authorities had a chance to intervene, a veritable manhunt got underway, organized from the *mwami*'s palace in Nyanza, under the guidance of a handful of chiefs. Beginning on November 6, a number of Twa- or Tutsi-led commandos were sent out from Nyanza with specific instructions to kill or capture certain Hutu leaders. The first victim was a certain Secyugu; the next day, on November 7, several other influential Hutu were killed in the Nyanza and Gitarama districts. While some were killed on the spot, others were taken to the *mwami*'s palace and judged before an improvised military tribunal, composed of Unar leaders, before being handed over to the Twa executioners. Although the Residency had taken urgent steps to reinforce the security forces available on the spot, it was not until November 14, approximately two weeks after the Gitarama incident, that temporary calm was restored to the country by the deployment of Belgian paratroopers and Congolese troops.

If the exact number of casualties is impossible to determine, the contention of a Belgian authority, J. R. Hubert, that "this was not a *bloody* revolution"[37] flies in the face of the evidence; further, Hubert's statement that "in the course of events the number of people killed by

[36] Ibid., 32.

[37] J. R. Hubert, *La Toussaint Rwandaise et sa Repression* (Brussels, 1965), 40. (My italics.)

the Tutsi amounted to thirty-seven and those killed by the Hutu to thirteen" is difficult to reconcile with the estimates of the United Nations Visiting Mission, according to which "approximately 200 persons were killed." The same mission goes on to note that "the actual figure is surely much higher, for the people, when they can, prefer to carry off their dead and bury them silently. An official communique issued on November 23 stated that at that date the number of persons wounded in the disturbances who were hospitalized or given first aid had reached 317, but probably many wounded had left without seeking attention."[38] To this must also be added thousands of huts destroyed and an undetermined number of plantations plundered, livestock killed, and belongings pillaged.

The Revolution from Below

Because of the rather indiscriminate use of the term "revolution" to describe the jacquerie of November 1959, there has been a tendency among certain scholars and commentators to read into these events a far greater political significance than they actually deserve. As noted earlier, this so-called "revolution" was little more than a peasant revolt, ignited by the force of example. Like the Luddite riots of nineteenth-century England, it was primarily focused against property rather than against persons or institutions, and where violence did carry some political implications, as in the Gitarama and Ruhengeri districts, it was aimed against individual chiefs, not against the monarchy. The actual revolution, which brought about a fundamental change of social, economic, and political relationships, occurred after the uprisings; but even then this transformation did not proceed everywhere at the same speed. Indeed, whether the Hutu revolution can be said to have run its full course remains an open question even to this day.

In a sense the forces which propelled dissent from one phase to the next—from the stage of anomic violence to that of organized political action—were self-generating. The mere experience of violence was enough to set the stage for further violence, as well as for the emergence of a new set of psychological orientations on the part of both Hutu and Tutsi. But it is well to remember that these forces did not operate in a vacuum, and that until the very end of its mandate the administration acted as the prime regulator, indeed as the accelerator, of the revolutionary forces unleashed by the revolt of November 1959.

The attitude of the Belgian authorities in the days which followed

[38] U.N., *Report on Ruanda-Urundi*, 31.

the disturbances emerges with striking clarity from the terms of a semiofficial memorandum submitted to the United Nations in late 1960, entitled "L'Attitude de l'Administration Belge à l'égard de l'Unar" [*Union Nationale Rwandaise*]. Commenting on the "social and political upheaval of November 1959," the administration admitted that "it found itself faced with a redoubtable alternative: To either crush the authentic democratic drive animating the masses of Rwanda, in collaboration with the indigenous authorities . . . or else to canalize this claimant movement while publicly recognizing its existence." The first alternative was automatically ruled out, as it was "in contradiction with the program of emancipation adopted by Belgium"; therefore the only conceivable course was "to inaugurate a *protectionisme éducateur*, by no means intended to eliminate once and for all the representatives of the old order but to permit the popular forces to organize themselves, free of the old feudal constraints." In practice this *protectionisme éducateur* meant the progressive elimination of the Tutsi elite from the political scene through a series of measures intended, on the one hand, to weaken or suppress the influence and capacity for violence of the Unar, and on the other hand, to facilitate the entry of Hutu elements into the political arena.[39]

Among the several measures that contributed to neutralizing the influence of the ruling casto, one of the most effective was the rustication of the three leading Unar personalities, Chiefs Mungalurire, Kayihura, and Rwangombwa—in part because it led to their exile and thus opened the way for potential rifts between the local Unar branches and its leadership in exile. Even more decisive was the role played by the administration in preventing the Unar from making full use of its repressive apparatus. Without the intervention of the administering authorities, the Tutsi repression might well have succeeded in decapitating the Hutu movement; as it happened, however, the repression proved sufficiently ruthless to intensify the hatred of the peasantry and their leaders against the ruling oligarchy, and yet not nearly as effective as it needed to be to yield the intended results. A third majority liability came from the eviction of a substantial number of Tutsi chiefs from the northern districts, where the hostility of the local population against the feudal regime had reached its highest level of intensity. In the period immediately following the disturbances, no less than twenty-one Tutsi chiefs and 332 subchiefs were either killed by the security forces, arrested, or forced to resign in the face of local Hutu opposition; of these well over 50 per cent held office in the northern districts. Even though in some cases the administration had

[39] See "L'Attitude de l'Administration Belge à l'égard de l'Unar," official document, mimeo. (Usumbura, 1960).

no choice but to bow to the popular verdict, it is equally true that Belgian officials sometimes encouraged the local population to get rid of their chiefs. The least that can be said is that no effort was made to restore the authority of the chiefs despite the fact that the arbitration of the administering authorities still carried a decisive weight.

At the same time a number of positive steps were being taken to achieve an effective transfer of authority to the hands of the Hutu peasantry. One of these consisted in the installation of "interim authorities," all of Hutu origin, to fill the vacancies left by the desertion of Tutsi chiefs and subchiefs. Another was the organization of communal elections in June and July 1960. Still another contributory factor, perhaps the really decisive one, lay in the very active role played by the administration in accelerating the process of institutional transfer to the central organs of government.

The Installation of Interim Authorities

The appointment of some two hundred Hutu chiefs and subchiefs to occupy the posts which the Tutsi authorities had left vacant inaugurated a period of profound instability, marked by considerable administrative inefficiency, mutual provocations, and recurrent violence. Countless examples of administrative incapacity were reported by various *administrateurs de territoire* in early 1960, all of them involving interim authorities. Of the Hutu chief of Rukiga, for instance, Ducène said in May 1960 that he was "absolutely incapable," and of the Hutu chief of Ndorwa that he was, likewise, "incapable," and that the situation there was rapidly getting out of hand. "They have created a Committee of Public Safety," Ducène added, "with Ministers, etc." In the Budaha, Buhoyi-Lac, and Cyesha regions the interim authorities were either unable or did not even try to prevent acts of incendiarism. Thus, in the Budaha alone, more than five hundred Tutsi huts were set on fire between May 16-18, 1960. In an attempt to absolve the arsonists, it was said that "the actions of the incendiaries were primarily directed against violent Tutsi elements who were already implicated in different affairs," but one is impelled to wonder whether certain instances of Tutsi violence were not the outcome of previous Hutu provocations.[40]

To understand why the authorities allowed this situation to de-

[40] The information contained in this paragraph and the next is drawn from the *procès-verbaux* of the *réunions de cadres* held under the auspices of the Special Resident, Colonel Bem Logiest, in late 1959 and early 1960. I am grateful to the *préfet* of Ruhengeri, M. André Mpakanyie, for making these documents available to me.

velop, it is necessary to recall that in their minds the exigencies of the situation made it imperative to hasten the politicization of the Hutu masses, no matter how high the cost. The official viewpoint of the local authorities is perhaps best illustrated by the declaration made by the Special Resident, Colonel Bem Logiest, in the course of a *réunion de cadres* in January 1960: "What is our goal? It is to accelerate the politicization of Rwanda. In Urundi politics are avoided; one would like to have elections before political parties are brought into being. This may be all right for Urundi, but here the situation is different. Not only do we want elections but we want everybody to be aware of this. People must go to the polls in full freedom and in full political awareness. *The result is that we must undertake an action in favor of the Hutu who live in a state of ignorance and under oppressive influences. By virtue of the situation we are led to take sides. We cannot stay neutral and sit.*"[41] Far from being neutral or passive the Belgian administration became the prime legitimizer of Hutu rule.

The main significance of these "interim appointments" is that they afforded the Hutu leadership a unique opportunity to expand their activities to areas where popular support for their cause had yet to be awakened. In many places these authorities became the self-appointed leaders of local Parmehutu branches; elsewhere they preferred to wait and see which of the major Hutu parties would come out on top. But as a rule they seldom missed an opportunity to demonstrate their anti-Tutsi feelings. Since they did not conceive of their role as involving any particular obligations save that of promoting the interests of their caste, they naturally tended to act more like political agitators than civil servants, and in so doing they hoped to establish political credentials that would enable them to hold their positions on a more permanent basis.

One of the most notable consequences of these appointments was to accelerate the flight of Tutsi refugees from their native regions to safer areas. Thus from about 7,000 at the end of November 1959, the total number of refugees rose to 22,000 by April 1960. Of these about 7,000 were installed at the Nyamata camp for refugees, while the remaining 15,000, distributed through the districts of Bymba, Kisenyi, and Astrida, sought refuge in mission stations and government buildings, or simply wandered over the countryside in a vain quest for shelter, food, and security. The mere presence on the hills of thousands of Tutsi refugees, most of them lacking the bare necessities of life, was bound to exacerbate intercaste animosities; in fact, the Unar consciously exploited the refugee problem to mobilize support for its

[41] "Réunion des Administrateurs de Territoires, January 11, 1960" (Kigali, mimeo.), 2. (My italics.)

cause by continually stressing the element of human tragedy apparent in the situation. On the other hand, the massive exodus of Tutsi families from various parts of Rwanda caused a rapid shrinkage in the territorial spread of the Unar, thereby making the prospects of a Unar victory at the polls even more remote. And since many of these refugees failed to meet the residence requirements stipulated in the electoral law, the Hutu leaders had every reason to anticipate a massive victory over their opponents.

The Communal Elections

In line with the official declaration made by the Belgian government on November 10, 1959, the administration began in early 1960 to lay the groundwork for the communal elections scheduled for June and July of the same year. The commune, headed by a burgomaster assisted by a popularly elected communal council, was to take the place of the subchiefdom as the basic political unit; the existing chiefdoms would be converted into purely administrative entities; at the central level legislative powers would be vested in an indirectly elected Legislative Council that would exercise its functions jointly with the *mwami*. It was understood that the administration would nonetheless retain a veto power over the decisions made at each of these levels.

Contrary to what the United Nations Visiting Mission had hoped, the approach of the electoral campaign saw no let-up in the racial tension. If anything, the constitutional reforms envisaged by the government, together with the attitude of the local administration, helped reinforce the Unar's conviction that Belgian officialdom was doing its best to crush the Tutsi and promote the Hutu. Although there is little basis for the view that *all* official actions were systematically aimed at destroying Tutsi hegemony, the mere fact that they came to be regarded by the Tutsi as prejudicial to their interests was enough to bring racial antagonisms to a new pitch of tension.

What further intensified the exasperation of the Unar leaders were the strenuous efforts of the administration to advertise the merits of democracy in such a way as to cast discredit upon the Tutsi caste. Thus the Residency used the full weight of available communication media to urge the people "to vote in full freedom," "to denounce the saboteurs of democracy," and "to demand that government circulars be read out to them, for this is their right." One such circular cautioned the electorate against "the propaganda, deceit and flattery of some individuals who have everything to lose from the democratization of the country's institutions, of those who enjoyed absolute powers, of the feudal elements who once possessed all of the land and who abused their *bagaragu* and *bagererwa*, of the bad chiefs and subchiefs who saw in their mandate an opportunity to exploit the people."[42] The circular continued: "These are the men who demand immediate independence, knowing full well that after the withdrawal of Belgian authority they would all the more easily go back to their obscure feudal practices, to their devious intrigues, to corruption and complicity." Even under the best of circumstances the Unar leaders could never hope to match the weight and pervasiveness of the official propaganda machine; moreover, after the Resident decided on July 6 to ban all political meetings under the pretext that "certain leaders had abused their freedom of speech by advocating a boycott of the elections," official propaganda became the only legitimate propaganda.

Under these conditions, a landslide victory for the Parmehutu was a foregone conclusion. With 2,390 seats out of a total of 3,125, the party clearly held a dominant position in the communal councils. Its nearest opponent, the Aprosoma, only claimed 233 seats. With a mere 56 seats the Unar had no choice but to concede defeat.

These figures, however, cannot be taken as an accurate index of the electoral strength of the contestants partly because they do not take into account the heavy percentage of Unar abstentions.[43] About 21.8 per cent of the registered electorate abstained from voting, but the actual percentage must be much higher since a good many voters failed to register. In specific areas—in the whole eastern sector, corresponding roughly to the Gisaka region, and in the vicinity of Nyanza —less than 50 per cent of the electorate went to the polls. In the region of Nyanza, for example, the administration-sponsored newspaper *Imvaho* reported that "the saboteurs of democracy" managed to keep electoral participation down to 30 or 40 per cent, "or even less in certain other localities." Then there were numerous instances of electoral irregularities. The fact that the polling officers were in many places chosen by interim authorities, that is by Hutu politicians who belonged for the most part to the Parmehutu, was bound to favor the Hutu.

The above analysis is not meant to minimize the part played by the electoral struggle in advancing the revolution to a stage where pressure from below prepares the ground for legalization from above. The only point here is that revolutionary fervor was still unevenly felt throughout the country. Rwanda was still, formally speaking, a monarchy. And in many places the organizational apparatus of the

---

[42] "Circulaire No. 7 à la population d'Astrida," mimeo.

[43] For an excellent discussion of the communal elections of 1960, see Marcel d'Hertefelt, "Les élections communales et le consensus politique au Ruanda," *Zaire*, XIV (1960), 403-38.

revolution remained embryonic if not altogether nonexistent. The real significance of the elections is that they made it technically possible for the newly elected burgomasters to achieve virtually unlimited control over local affairs. Thus they were able to make full use of their prerogatives to accelerate the tempo of revolutionary change.

The Burgomasters in Action

The immediate result of the communal elections was to bring about a radical shift in the distribution of power at the local level: Of the 229 communes set up under the Interim Decree of December 1959, 210 were headed by Hutu burgomasters, of whom 160 were members of the Parmehutu. Although the *chefferie* was still recognized as a formal administrative unit, the position of the chief was, legally speaking, reduced to that of a figurehead.

But this transformation of the old feudal power structure, no matter how far-reaching, did not everywhere imply a corresponding shift of loyalties. In certain areas serious conflicts developed between the newly elected authorities and those Hutu elements who, for some reason or another, felt that it was in their interest to support the old ruling caste; these were generally the chief's personal clients and landed tenants, the latter sometimes referred to by the Belgian authorities as *bagererwa politiques*. Another source of conflict stemmed from the existence of socio-economic disparities between the burgomasters and their constituents: In this connection it is interesting to note that the overwhelming majority of the burgomasters possessed at least a primary education or some technical skills which separated them sharply from the ordinary peasant. Except for the northern region, where achieved status often corresponded with traditional claims to authority, status differences between the incumbents and their constituents were, and still are, a major source of tension at the local level.

In the face of this opposition, some burgomasters did not hesitate to resort to violence and intimidation to assert their authority. In some places they instigated local disorders in order to provoke the exodus of Tutsi families, and once this was accomplished they proceeded to sell the refugees' land and property to their supporters. Elsewhere individual Tutsi were arrested on the flimsiest grounds, tried before an improvised tribunal, and thrown into jail. Meanwhile the raids organized by isolated bands of Tutsi refugees became a pretext for arbitrary Hutu retaliation against the local Tutsi population. Although some administrators deplored "the objectionable decisions of the burgomasters" and freely admitted that they had a "tendency to go too far," very few were actually prepared to do more than reprimand.

Certainly, the expectation of continued support from the administration was a major asset in the hands of the burgomasters, and it
constituted a tacit encouragement to violence. But there are other factors to consider. One is that the burgomasters' powers were as yet undefined in legal terms. Not until two months after they were in office was
a decree passed which set statutory limitations on the exercise of communal authority. Until then, as one *administrateur de territoire* put
it, "neither the burgomasters nor the councillors knew the exact limitations of their powers." Another positive element was the massive
replacement of Tutsi auxiliaries such as clerks, accountants, and *moniteurs agricoles* by Hutu elements chosen on the basis of recommendations made by the burgomasters. (Each had been given permission to
hire three policemen, three *moniteurs agricoles,* and one secretary.) Simultaneously, specific instructions were issued by the acting Resident to
insure the incorporation of Hutu elements into the higher echelons of
the administrative hierarchy. Eventually a whole new group of political
aspirants gained entry into the administrative superstructure, thereby
providing the burgomasters with a new base on which to rest their
authority. Finally, in an effort further to solidify their bases of power,
some burgomasters organized something resembling a personal militia,
often recruited from among their own "clientele" or, in the north, from
among the members of their own clan.

The procedure used by the burgomasters to eliminate residual
opposition to their rule is nowhere better illustrated than in Pierre
Gravel's account of the situation he witnessed in Remera, in the
eastern part of Rwanda. There the burgomaster at first carefully
avoided involvement in local disputes, "but after gathering together a
small band of opportunists . . . he tried out his authority—first by
prohibiting hunting and then by forbidding people to leave their homes
after 6:00 P.M. He and his gang patrolled the hill at night to see to it
that his orders were obeyed. He bragged that he was out to get the
Tutsi who had jobs with the administration, that he would see that
they lost them. . . . The administration, through fear of subversive
political meetings, allowed the burgomasters to forbid hill and lineage
meetings. This served further as a pretext for arrests. He arrested more
and more Tutsi. It seemed that three Tutsi drinking together was
a meeting. He pressured the Hutu into buying party membership cards
by telling them they could profit by signing and suffer by not. . . .
Eventually he began to trample on people's customary rights, and
yet they would not file complaints against him because, they explained,
the administration would support him in any case. It was better to
say nothing than to be harassed further. To obtain the burgomaster's
favor, people brought him gifts of beer. He started to put pressure

on the cow-keepers to bring him gifts of milk. . . . He was well on his way to claiming the prerogatives of the old regime's chieftain."[44]

Of special relevance in this connection was the part which the recasting of patron-client relationships played in activating the revolutionary process. The re-establishment of clientage ties within the framework of the Hutu caste was both the cause and the symptom of the political transformations which followed in the wake of the November uprisings. A major stimulus to the prosecution of the northern crusade against Tutsi hegemony came from the convergence of interests between *bakonde* and *bagererwa* in reasserting their traditional patron-client roles vis-à-vis each other. The rapidly created—or recreated— solidarities between the *bakonde* and their landed clients were soon converted into the leader-follower nexus which, precisely because its origins were so deeply rooted in the culture and history of the northern region, played a major role in the mobilization of the northern peasantry against Tutsi rule. At the same time, the social dislocations engendered by the flight of Tutsi authorities made it all the more imperative for the peasantry to look for alternative sources of protection, a need felt with ever-increasing intensity as the threats to their security became more frequent.

Thus even where no such prior form of organization existed among the Hutu, as in the central and southern regions, a somewhat similar type of client-patron relationship developed between the burgomasters and their local supporters. The former's control of the communal institutions enabled them to tap new sources of patronage, whether in the form of jobs or administrative favors of one kind or another, and in this fashion to build up a body of trusted lieutenants whose role was, and still is in some ways, strongly reminiscent of the chiefs' traditional clients.

Yet, instrumental as this type of relationship may have been in creating new solidarities to replace the old, the evidence shows that the adaptation of clientage ties for revolutionary purposes did not everywhere proceed at the same speed, nor without causing some major conflicts of interests and questioning of loyalties among the peasant masses. In the north the political clientele of the evicted chief was understandably reluctant to surrender their privileges to the *bakonde's* traditional clients, and, with the reassertion of the *bakonde's* claims over the land, a major conflict of interest developed between "political" and "traditional" clients. Elsewhere a similarly tense situation attended the displacement of interim authorities by elected burgo-

[44] Pierre B. Gravel, "The Play for Power: Description of a Community in Eastern Rwanda" (unpublished Ph.D. dissertation, University of Michigan, 1962), 263-64.

masters as the change of officeholder also implied a transfer of "benefices" from one set of clients to another. Then in specific areas (and in the eastern region in particular) the influence of pre-existing habits acted as a major disincentive to the transfer of personal allegiances. Even as late as 1960 pockets of residual allegiance to the Tutsi oligarchy could still be encountered throughout the country. Social or ethnic integration through political clientelism thus proceeded very slowly, and, even where the peasantry was no longer the captive of traditional constraints, the result has often been to facilitate the emergence of new forms of primordial loyalties, centered upon kinship ties, local or regional affiliations, and competing clientele networks.

A major consequence of the coup of Gitarama has been to create the conditions for the extension of clientage ties from the top to the base of the political structure, thus making possible the establishment of control mechanisms with which further to accelerate the shift of popular loyalties to local Hutu patrons. This, however, was by no means the sole motive actuating the revolutionary elites. A growing fear of disaffection, rumors of impending aggression by Tutsi exiles, and a vague suspicion that the Belgian government might withdraw its authority before the consummation of the revolution were key elements in the background of the coup of January 1961.

The Coup from Above

Having captured control over the local institutions, the next logical step, in the minds of the Parmehutu leaders, was to attempt to extend their hold to the central organs of government. In presenting their case for holding legislative elections as soon as possible after the communal elections, they argued that since the Parmehutu had so clearly revealed itself as the "party of the masses," and in fact held a dominant position in almost every communal council, there was no reason to defer legislative elections until early 1961, as recommended by the United Nations Visiting Mission after its passage through Rwanda in March 1960. To allow for a "cooling-off" period that would pave the way for national reconciliation was, in their view, utopian. Any attempt on the part of the metropolitan authorities to delay the installation of an autonomous government through popular elections would necessarily be interpreted as a sign of bad faith by the masses and thus would provoke new outbursts of violence.

Yet, a more candid look at Rwanda's political scene in the months following the communal elections tells a somewhat different story. Not the strength but rather the very weakness of their bases of support is what caused the Parmehutu leaders to press their claims for an accelerated transfer of power. As they saw their position being gradually undermined by internal dissension and incipient popular resentment against the communal authorities, the temptation to consolidate their electoral gains "from above" became increasingly difficult to resist.

Between August and November 1960 a radical shift in the balance of forces within the country occurred. In November 1960 the leaders of the Aprosoma, Rader, and Unar agreed to form a *front commun* in opposition to the Parmehutu; the spokesmen of the *front commun* unanimously denounced the "dictatorial regime" of the Parmehutu, which they went on to describe as "racist, racial and antidemocratic . . . deliberately attempting to crush all other parties through corruption and intimidation." "This kind of feudalism," they concluded, "is worse than the old one."[45] Meanwhile in a number of localities the communal authorities were faced with recurrent acts of terrorism instigated by groups of Tutsi refugees from Uganda and the Congo—the so-called *inyenzi*, or cockroaches. Usually aimed at Hutu officials, these border raids led to a cruel repression of the local Tutsi population by the Hutu officials. Tutsi-instigated terrorism at first resulted in a strengthening of caste solidarity among the Hutu, but in time the sheer arbitrariness of retaliatory measures caused considerable disaffection among the Hutu peasantry.

Nor was the international scene all that encouraging to the Hutu leaders. The presence at the United Nations of an extremely able and articulate group of Unar petitioners, led by Michel Kayihura, coupled with the inherently anticolonialist nature of their case, assured them a favorable hearing in the General Assembly. But perhaps the main source of anxiety was the apparent unwillingness of the Belgian government to recognize the Hutu case. The initial reluctance of Brussels to yield to local pressures for a rapid transfer of sovereignty to the Hutu is to be explained in part by reference to the personal preferences and inclinations of the then Minister of African Affairs, Auguste de Schrijver, leader of the *Parti Social Chrétien*. Whether because of his own aristocratic background or because of his conservative leanings, Schrijver had always felt a deep sympathy for the Tutsi culture; in fact, having once privately admitted to this writer his admiration for Tutsi artistic traditions, he went on to express strong misgivings as to whether such a magnificent cultural heritage could be allowed to be swept away in the name of a democracy whose merits, in any case, remained dubious. But the attitude of the metropolitan authorities

[45] *Rwanda Politique,* 347.

was also conditioned by the nature of their international obligations under the United Nations Charter. The Belgian government could ill afford to antagonize international public opinion further so soon after the secession of the Katanga and at a time when it was drawing considerable and well-deserved criticism from the United Nations.

Given these circumstances one can appreciate the sense of frustration and bitterness felt by the Hutu leadership when they learned that the General Assembly, in its resolution of December 20, 1960, had recommended postponing legislative elections to a date to be decided at the resumption of its fifteenth session, in the summer of 1961. General Assembly resolution 1579, passed on December 20, 1960, urged the administering authorities "to implement immediately measures of full and unconditional amnesty, to enable political workers and leaders who are still in exile or imprisoned in the territory to resume normal democratic political activity before the elections."[46] In addition, it was suggested that "a conference fully representative of political parties, attended by U.N. observers, be held in early 1961, before the elections, in order to compose the differences between parties and to bring about national harmony." While noting that this unexpected turn of events placed the Belgian government "in the very serious dilemma of having to choose between immediately satisfying the urgent request of the people under its trusteeship or taking into consideration the new General Assembly recommendation,"[47] Brussels grudgingly agreed to comply with the terms of the resolution. In Rwanda, however, the Parmehutu reacted to the news by a violent denunciation of the United Nations, saying, in effect, that the postponement of the elections was nothing less than a deliberate attempt to delay the setting up of democratic institutions. What the party leadership failed to mention, however, was that the "cooling-off" period envisaged by the United Nations would, in all probability, be used by their opponents to increase their following, and that the measures of amnesty, if implemented, would surely turn to the advantage of the more conservative wing of the Tutsi population.

By then, however, the role of the United Nations in Katanga had put diplomatic relations between Brussels and New York under considerable strain, with the result that the Belgian government was not prepared to adopt a somewhat more flexible stance toward either the Hutu leadership or the administering authorities in Rwanda. However, the determining element was the appointment, in September 1960, of Count Harold d'Aspremont Lynden to the post of Minister of African Affairs. A staunch supporter of Belgian policies in Katanga,

[46] *Question of the Future of Ruanda-Urundi*, 6.
[47] Ibid., Addendum I, Annex XV.

d'Aspremont had little sympathy for United Nations objectives in Africa. If only as a reaction against United Nations policies, he naturally felt inclined to give his support to the Hutu against the Tutsi. This, in practice, meant that the local administration would be given virtually a free hand in preparing the accession of Rwanda to independence under Hutu rule.

Prior to the appointment of d'Aspremont to the Ministry of African Affairs, the Special Resident, Colonel Logiest, had gone to great lengths to persuade the Belgian government to satisfy Hutu demands for internal autonomy, but with little success. As early as August 29, 1960, the Resident General, Jean-Paul Harroy, had sent a cable to the Minister of African Affairs in which he called attention to the gravity of the situation and intimated that the installation of a provisional government was the only way to restore stability and check Communist penetration into the country. At about the same time Colonel Logiest went to Brussels to present the Hutu case to the Belgian government. Upon his return from Brussels, in the course of an impromptu meeting of *administrateurs de territoire*, Logiest gave the following account of the political situation: "The Hutu," said Logiest, "have asked us that a Government or a Parliament be set up, or in any case, the organs which would permit them to achieve internal autonomy. The Resident General, Mr. Harroy, and myself had agreed to this request. This was the purpose of my trip to Belgium, which, on the whole, yielded no positive results. You must remember that our delegate to the U.N., in order to sweeten the pill *[afin d'atteneur la chose]*, had said that the communal elections would carry no political consequences and had no other purpose than to set up the communal infrastructure. . . . The objective of our government, drawing a lesson from the Congo, is to have before independence a U.N. representative in Rwanda. . . . It favors the presence of a Permanent U.N. Commission and a few 'blue helmets'. . . . It is purely and simply *la politique du parapluie*. . . . All that we can expect is a Visiting Mission from the U.N. and nothing else. The action of the U.N., though ill-intentioned, cannot harm us. Furthermore, we are going to set up a kind of government which will gain practical experience *[qui s'aguerrira]* and will take up positions."[48] Clearly, as anxious as they were to seize the initiative, the local Belgian authorities could not disregard entirely the views of their government; consequently the policy of the administration remained to a considerable degree subject to the limitations imposed from Brussels, and, to a lesser extent, from New York. After the appointment of d'Aspremont as Minister of

[48] *Réunion des Administrateurs de Territoire, Procès-Verbaux* (Sept. 2, 1960), 10.

African Affairs, however, a close working relationship developed between Brussels and Kigali, the result of which was to substitute what one might call a *politique d'entente* for the *politique du parapluie*.

Yet, until the very last minute, the Belgian government carefully avoided showing its hand. It obligingly paid lip service to the decisions of the General Assembly and stated in early January that it hoped to set up an autonomous government *after* the general elections, around June 1961. Meanwhile, from January 7 to 12, 1961, forty delegates, representing each of the main parties of Rwanda, held "round-table" discussions in Ostend with representatives of the Ministry of African Affairs on the political future of the territory. Ironically, it was at the Ostend Round Table, held at the request of the United Nations, that final arrangements were made to circumvent the obstacles raised by the General Assembly's resolution of December 20, 1960. Although the evidence is admittedly lacking, there seems little question that the metropolitan government did co-operate on a fairly close basis with the Residency in planning the coup of January 28, 1961; if nothing else, the Special Resident must have received unofficial assurance from the Ministry of African Affairs that Brussels would not interfere with the course of action upon which the Hutu leaders were about to embark, no matter how serious the legal implications.

It is clear that the authors of the coup know beforehand that they would enjoy complete immunity from the Residency. As the United Nations Commission for Ruanda-Urundi subsequently observed: "The Commission cannot escape the impression that the local administration, finding itself no doubt too much bound by promises to its favored political parties, and considering that its prestige was at stake, was reluctant to comply with the decision [initially] taken by the Belgian government to cooperate in giving effect to the recent U.N. resolutions on Ruanda-Urundi. . . . It is hard to believe that the coup d'etat of Gitarama could have taken place without the knowledge of the Belgian authorities in the Territory, and indeed without certain European members of the administration taking part in it. Without help from the administration, the actual organization of a meeting of some 3,000 burgomasters and communal councillors, convened by the Minister of Interior, as early as January 25, is barely conceivable."[49]

If so, one cannot fail to detect an element of deliberate distortion in the explanations offered by the Resident General to the United Nations Commission: "The Resident," states the report of this Commission, "considered that the action had resulted in part from the feeling of the political leaders that they had been betrayed by the Administering Authority, from the conviction that the U.N. was hostile to them

[49] *Question of the Future of Ruanda-Urundi*, 46, 48.

and from a fear that the disorders in the neighbouring Republic of the Congo might extend to Rwanda. The Resident General said he had to choose, on the one hand, between the use of force to suppress the new regime—a course that was inconceivable and, moreover, impossible in view of the very small armed forces which the metropolitan country had placed at his disposal—and, on the other hand, the possibility of advising the Belgian government to negotiate with the new authorities. Though characterizing the action of Rwanda's burgomasters and municipal councillors as illegal, he noted that such action was in accordance with the Interim Decree of December 25, 1959, which, at the time, had provided for indirect legislative elections."[50] Certainly, the motives invoked by the Resident General cannot be overlooked; the only point he did not mention, however, was that the Hutu leaders may not have resorted to such drastic action unless they had excellent reason to believe that the administration was on their side. This alone was enough to spell the difference between a successful and an abortive coup.

For some, the coup of Gitarama marked the beginning of an entirely new phase in the history of Rwanda, in effect symbolizing the birth of a new social and political order during which the forces of democracy finally emerged triumphant from their fight against feudalism. Taking a more realistic view of the situation, the United Nations Commission for Ruanda-Urundi stated in March 1961: "A racial dictatorship of one party has been set up in Rwanda, and the developments of the last eighteen months have consisted in the transition from one type of oppressive regime to another. Extremism is rewarded and there is a danger that the [Tutsi] minority may find itself defenseless in the face of abuses. . . . Taken as a whole the political situation in Rwanda is distinctly disquieting."[51] Whether Rwanda's republican regime can be said to be as oppressive for the Tutsi as the feudal system was for the Hutu is debatable; what is beyond question is that the Rwandan revolution was essentially negative in character, its main objective being the destruction of the caste system and the caste privileges associated with it, and only secondarily the erection of a democratic polity. One might press the point even further and argue that the type of social system and political organization associated with the Tutsi oligarchy would probably have remained untouched if the racial issue had not intruded itself so forcefully. At worst, the real target of the Rwandan revolution was Tutsi feudalism rather than feudalism per se; at best, its key objective was democracy for the Hutu rather than democracy per se.

50 Ibid., 29, 30.
51 Ibid., 51.

TABLE 1   Typology of Protest Movements in Rwanda, 1898-1961*

Chronology	Type of Protest	Orientation	Target	Localization	Origins
Before 1900	Messianism-cum-Social Banditry	Xenophobic	Tutsi Chiefs	Northern Region (Rukiga)	Northern Kiga
1900-1920	Same	Same	Tutsi Chiefs and Europeans	Same	Northern Kiga
1957-1958	Social Reform Movement	Egalitarian-Democratic	Tutsi Elites (modern and traditional)	Central Region (Gitarama)	Hutu Intelligentsia
1959	Jacquerie	Anomic	Tutsi-Undifferentiated	Countrywide	Hutu Peasantry
1960	Political Revolution	1) Xenophobic-Conservative	Tutsi Chiefs	Northern Region (Rukiga)	1) Northern *Bakonde* Families (Kiga)
		2) Xenophobic-Jacobin	Tutsi-Undifferentiated	Central Region	2) Communal Authorities (Hutu)
1961	Coup	Republican	Tutsi Monarchy	Gitarama	Parmehutu Leadership and Belgian Administration

* The above typology offers a rough synthesis of the principal spacial and temporal variations that have conditioned the growth and development of protest movements in Rwanda since the beginning of the century. Historically, these types of manifestation form a closely woven texture whose separate strands are sometimes difficult to unravel. Nonetheless, in this table two major types of protest are discernible which, although originating in different regions and at different times, have converged in the same direction: One, xenophobic-conservative in orientation, came into being at the turn of the century in the northern region, and expressed itself through a combination of messianism and social banditry. Its main objective was the eviction of Tutsi chiefs from areas recently brought under their domination, and their replacement by Hutu chiefs. Another, egalitarian-democratic in character, described here as a social reform movement, is that which developed in 1957–58 in central Rwanda, and which first manifested itself through the so-called Manifesto of the Bahutu. Though aiming at the abolition of caste privileges, this social reform movement was by no means xenophobic. By 1960, however, these two separate forms of protest had coalesced into a more or less unified revolutionary movement which now shared the characteristics of both. It is this combination of conservative (i.e., elitist) and Jacobin (i.e., egalitarian) orientations, each arising from a different set of historical circumstances, each identified with a distinctive type of leadership and limited to a special region, which makes the Hutu revolution something of a unique phenomenon in the history of African protest movements.

What makes the aims and general orientation of the Rwandan revolution so difficult to define with any degree of precision is that the intensity of revolutionary fervor, as well as the sources from which it drew its inspiration, varied enormously from one region to the next. As already noted, it was in the district of Gitarama, near the Kabgaye mission station, that revolutionary sentiment reached its peak; elsewhere the attitude of the Hutu peasantry was, at least until 1959, overwhelmingly conservative. As one reflects on the revolutionary dispositions of the peasant masses of Rwanda on the eve of the revolution, one is reminded of Marx's description of the French peasantry in mid-nineteenth century as forming "a vast mass, the members of which lived in similar conditions but without entering in manifold relations with one another," living "in stupefied bondage to the old order," and wishing "themselves and their small holdings saved and favored by the ghost of the monarchy."[52] Of course this is not to imply that the Hutu peasantry had always placidly accepted Tutsi domination. As shown in the typology in Table 1, Rwanda had been the scene of anti-Tutsi revolts long before the intrusion of European influences; but these were circumscribed to specific areas and were generally lacking in political content. One can assume that even as late as 1960 the vast majority of the Hutu peasants remained loyal to the symbols of the monarchy, if not to their chiefs.

Finally there is another peculiar trait of the Rwandan revolution—it received its initial impetus from a variety of motivations, ranging from pure xenophobia to a vague sense of anomie associated with a general state of social and political disorientation; from economic grievances rooted in the traditional land-tenure system to what can be described as a "transfer of allegiance" on the part of the educated Hutu elite, and the development by them of a democratic mythology. This fundamental ambiguity of motives is nowhere better illustrated than in the resurgence in the north of the *ubukonde* (leased-land contract) system, so obviously reminiscent of the old feudal order but nonetheless tolerated by the Rwandan government as a necessary evil. One might also recall in this connection a story which this writer heard from an informant whose good faith cannot be questioned. Kayibanda, in his effort to earn the support of the peasant masses, went about the countryside around Kabgaye presenting the revolution as nothing more than an attempt to provide the Hutu with an opportunity to elect their own *mwami*. That a similar technique was used to mobilize the populations of the north, centered upon the traditional land rights of the old *bakonde* families, is not implausible.

[52] Karl Marx, *The Eighteenth Brumaire of Louis Bonaparte* (New York, 1963), 109.

In a recent article on "the etiology of internal wars," Harry Eckstein observed that "if there is an art of revolution, it involves, largely at least, not making or subduing it, but capitalizing on the unallocated political resources it provides."[53] The Rwandan revolution offers the example par excellence of a situation in which a variety of more or less latent motivations were consciously activated and forced into revolutionary channels. However, a good deal of the credit for this must go to the European administration, for no matter how sensitive the Rwandan elites may be on this matter, one can hardly exaggerate the part played by Belgian officials in accelerating and extending the revolutionary process, in structuring its development along coherent political lines, and in facilitating the seizure of power from above. The point here is not that Hutu revolutionary sentiment was an artificial creation of the Europeans but rather that the European presence served as a guarantee of success for the revolutionary elite.

Hence the supreme paradox of the Rwandan revolution: Aimed at an indigenous form of imperialism, it drew its sustenance and inspiration from one of the imperial powers which had in the past been the strongest supporter of the *ancien régime*.

[53] Harry Eckstein, "On the Etiology of Internal War," *History and Theory*, IV (1965), 139.

THE ZANZIBARI REVOLUTION:

AFRICAN PROTEST IN

A RACIALLY PLURAL SOCIETY

MICHAEL F. LOFCHIE

Between 2:00 and 3:00 A.M. on Sunday morning, January 12, 1964, a small, secretly organized army of about 250 men attacked the Zanzibari government's major police armory at Ziwani, one mile south of Zanzibar Town. This was the decisive moment in the overthrow of an oligarchic Arab dynasty which had governed Zanzibar for nearly a century and a half. It enabled the revolutionaries to capture the government's principal supply of arms and ammunition, and, thereby, to cripple seriously any further resistance. John Okello, the obscure figure in Zanzibari politics who had organized and then led the revolutionary group, has described the capture of the Ziwani armory at length:

> A few minutes before 3:00 A.M. we cut through the barbed wire fence at Ziwani and entered the police compound. At this moment, all but 30 or 40 men became frightened and ran back through the fence; the enormity of our predicament and its dangers was suddenly obvious to them: we, armed with pangas, spears and a few motor car springs, were going to face the risk of close combat with men armed with automatic rifles, pistols and tear gas. It is no surprise that many men balked; those who stayed can only be praised as natural-born soldiers. . . . We got down in the grass and began to crawl towards the building, surrounding it and breaking open the doors. As we stood up, one sentry shot three of my men, killing two outright. Albert, a Kenyan, wounded a second sentry with a bow and arrow. I jumped the sentry with the rifle, pushing him, and got hold of the gun; we fought, and I managed to hit him on the cheek with the gun butt wounding him badly. I killed him with the bayonet. The front doors had been opened, but by this time the Government police, who had been upstairs sleeping, began to rush towards the stairs. Some forty of them were under

attack by my men, who used mainly bows and arrows and stones to hold the men upstairs while we broke into the armory. The rifle which I had taken from the sentry had three shots in it—this was the first "modern" weapon in our Revolution, but it was the most important one for it gave us an advantage for a few minutes.[1]

The revolutionaries' seizure of power had been remarkably easy and swift. Zanzibar possessed no army and the small police force was obviously unprepared for a surprise assault. Although it required several days to suppress sporadic resistance in the rural areas, the revolutionary army was, in fact, in effective control of the entire country by early Sunday afternoon.[2]

Myths of the Revolution

The speed and decisiveness of Okello's coup, together with the fact that Okello himself was virtually unknown before the revolution, have led to numerous rumors and myths about the nature of the revolutionary army. Inasmuch as many of these myths involve a conspiratorial theory of the Zanzibari revolution, it may be useful to deal with those which have become most widespread. One widely publicized report stated that Cuban millitiamen had been present among the revolutionaries, presumably in a planning and leadership capacity. There is no evidence available to substantiate this report. The Cuban rumor probably originated as a result of the conspicuous visibility, during the first few days after the coup, of a small number of Zanzibaris who wore Cuban-style dress and who, in general, affected a Cuban appearance. One of Zanzibar's principal parties, the Zanzibar Nationalist party, had maintained an office in Havana for several years, largely for international propaganda purposes. In June 1963, the Nationalist party split. Most of the members of the Havana contingent resigned to join a radical splinter movement called Umma ("The People") and returned to Zanzibar to participate in Umma's organizational activity. Since members of this group commonly wore a Castro-like beard and uniform, since many were of Arab or mixed-Arab

[1] John Okello, Revolution in Zanzibar (Nairobi, 1967), 31-32.

[2] As an independent country until its merger with Tanganyika in late April 1964, Zanzibar had comprised two large islands and a number of adjacent smaller ones with a total population of about 300,000. Zanzibar Island, roughly 640 square miles in area, contained approximately 55 per cent of the population (165,000) and was the center of government and commerce. Zanzibar Town, the capital, is located at about midpoint on the western coast of this island. Pemba Island, about 25 miles to the northeast, is roughly 380 square miles in area and has a population of about 135,000.

descent and therefore of markedly lighter skin color than most Africans, and since some even used the Cuban victory cry *venceremos* ("we shall conquer") as a political slogan, their presence on the streets of Zanzibar after the fall of the old regime gave rise to the belief that Cubans had had an active part in executing the coup. In the frantic moments of post-revolutionary upheaval, on-the-spot observers probably forgot or did not know that this indigenous band of Castroites moved quite openly in the capital for several months before the coup.

The most widely circulated report concerning the Zanzibari revolution was, however, that the conquering army had been recruited, equipped, and trained on the mainland, with the secret co-operation of one of the mainland governments. This report was based on the fact that by daybreak on Sunday morning, the revolutionary army consisted of several hundred well-armed soldiers. Because it would have been impossible to conceal, supply, and train such a large group on Zanzibar, and because the nearby African countries were known to be generally unsympathetic to the former regime, the notion of mainland involvement became a feasible explanation for the number of revolutionaries and their modern armament. The report of mainland African participation in the revolutionary army has, however, been denied by Okello.[3] In his book, he explains that the modern arms acquired by the revolutionaries had been taken from the Government of Zanzibar's armories and distributed by the first group of revolutionaries to well-known sympathizers of the Afro-Shirazi party—the major African political party in Zanzibar. This explanation accords with the observation, made by several reporters on the scene, that very few of the Africans with modern weapons were skilled in their use. This factor is inconsistent with the idea of previous training.

The most effective refutation of the theory of mainland African governmental participation in the Zanzibari revolution has been offered by the experienced British correspondent, Keith Kyle, who conducted an extensive series of interviews in Zanzibar and in Dar es Salaam shortly after the fall of the Sultan's government. Kyle asserts that mainland African political leaders were planning an entirely separate revolutionary coup, completely unrelated to Okello's. In an article entitled "Gideon's Voices" he states that:

> There were two revolutionary plots in Zanzibar, not one. . . . The first plot was planned by the Afro-Shirazi Party almost certainly with knowledge and approval of some leading politicians on the mainland. It relied to some extent on outside help. . . . The second plot was Okello's. This did not have outside help, was completely unknown in

[3] See *Revolution in Zanzibar*, ch. 8.

advance to the mainland (and to most of the island) politicians, and was timed for the night of January 11–12 in order to anticipate the date of the first plot by one week.[4]

The significance of Kyle's "two plot" theory is that it allows for the decision by a few mainland political leaders to overthrow the former Zanzibari regime and also provides a thoroughly plausible explanation for the political autonomy of Okello's army.

A third widespread myth about the Zanzibari revolution is that it was accomplished by fierce fighting between Okello's army and the government police. In the annals of the revolution, the Malindi police station, which sits astride the major intersection leading to the Stone-town section of the capital (the center of government and commerce and the location of the Sultan's palace), was the scene of a furious battle which raged throughout Sunday morning. "The battle of Malindi" has been seized upon by spokesmen representing various attitudes toward the revolution.

Okello himself, writing from political exile approximately two years after the event, was captivated by the image of a battle at Malindi. He describes the fighting as follows:

> We surrounded the station and used Bren and Sten guns, and other automatic weapons, to spray bullets liberally in all directions. The scene was terrible and a large number of people were killed; fire spread and there was extensive damage. When there was no longer any sound from inside I entered the building and found no life. As in the prison [captured previously] the defenders had withdrawn from the rear just as we were about to overwhelm them. Blood was splattered on the walls and lying in pools on the floors. There would have been no point in going for the Sultan when we had not yet captured Malindi but he was now the only possible focus of resistance left in the town.[5]

Spokesmen for the old regime have used "the battle of Malindi" in a desperate attempt to salvage a semblance of respectability for the government's forces. Here, they claim, an embattled but determined group of reserve police constables, courageously loyal and fighting against overwhelming odds, managed to put up a last-ditch resistance long enough to allow the Sultan and his family to escape. This battle has thus taken on a kind of epic quality as a legendary moment even in opposing accounts of the revolution.

Conspiracy theorists of the Zanzibari revolution have also seized on

[4] *The Spectator*, Feb. 6, 1964.
[5] *Revolution in Zanzibar*, 146.

"the battle of Malindi" as evidence to support their case. No ragtag and bobtail army such as Okello's, so the argument runs, would ever have been capable of the organizational precision, extraordinary discipline, and tactical skill necessary to win a sustained fight against a well-entrenched emplacement. These qualities could only have been acquired through extensive training by military advisers with long experience in such combat. In this theory, "the battle of Malindi" demonstrates that foreign military personnel must have had a hand in the overthrow of Zanzibar's old regime.

No such battle ever occurred. Several journalists who visited Zanzibar during the week following the revolution found the Malindi police station almost completely undamaged. Kyle, among others, reported that not only were there practically no shell holes in the walls of the building, but not a single window had been broken. The Malindi station was observed by this author four years after the revolution; it evinced no signs of reconstruction or repair, appearing just as it had during the pre-revolutionary period. Moreover, the Malindi police station could not possibly have constituted a defense for the Sultan's palace for there is a second route into the Stonetown area. This second route, which by-passes the former High Court and the entrance to the Zanzibar Hotel, would have enabled the revolutionaries, had they so chosen, completely to avoid the Malindi intersection. The basic reason for Okello's delay in entering Stonetown was not a delaying action at Malindi by government police but fear of a counterattack by armed government loyalists from the rural areas. Though such an attack never materialized, the possibility that it might delayed Okello's occupation of the capital by several hours.

It is, of course, intrinsic to the nature of most conspiracy theories that they can never be finally and conclusively disproved. Since they rarely contradict the known facts of any given situation, factual evidence can rarely be cited to prove conspiracy theories wrong. In addition, conspiracy theories thrive on a sort of paradoxical anti-logic: the very absence of evidence to support the conspiracy notion becomes positive evidence in its favor. For the lack of visible proof merely indicates that the conspiratorial plot, by its nature sinister and hidden, was successful in preserving the secrecy of its existence. For example, in the case of a man killed in what is apparently an accident, this anti-logic would make it impossible to show that the "accident" was not deliberately and ingeniously contrived by business and professional rivals. A similar anti-logic helps to perpetuate conspiracy theories of the Zanzibari revolution implicating such diverse countries as Cuba, the Soviet Union, China, and Tanzania despite the lack of positive evidence.

Much of Okello's narrative as related in *Revolution in Zanzibar* is clearly a sort of *post hoc* romanticization (for example, his account of "the battle of Malindi"), and much is also reflective of the mystical thinking of a messianic political figure. For these reasons, Okello's story will probably fail to dispel the lingering uncertainties about conspiracy. Nevertheless, if taken together with the reports of journalists, diplomatic observers, and other foreign by-standers, Okello's book makes an impressive case that Okello was the central figure in the revolution itself and the prime architect of the seizure of power from the former government. It seems reasonable to assume that at least the skeletal outlines of Okello's version of the coup constitute a fairly accurate account.

Okello's Role

The only remarkable feature of Okello's story is its utter simplicity. He had come to Zanzibar in 1959, at the age of 21, where he worked as a painter, stonecutter, and occasional laborer. As a mainland African (Okello was born in the Lango district of northern Uganda), he was attracted to the Afro-Shirazi party and became a minor branch official in the small village of Vitongoji in east-central Pemba. Okello's conviction that only by direct revolutionary action could the Afro-Shirazi party come to power seems to have developed as early as mid-1961. He moved from Pemba Island to Zanzibar Island in early 1963 but, because of the general election scheduled for July, he did not begin to plot revolution actively until late summer. The Afro-Shirazi's defeat in that election dispelled any lingering doubts about the necessity for revolution.

Among Okello's earliest supporters were members of his former union, the Zanzibar and Pemba Paint Workers' Union, and a small number of militant members of the Afro-Shirazi Youth League, but the most critical recruiting was done among former policemen. Just before independence, the government had initiated a police reorganization program and had discharged a substantial number of African policemen whose loyalty it suspected. These men constituted a perfect revolutionary element. They not only harbored a bitter sense of personal grievance against the government but were familiar with the organization of the Zanzibari police and experienced in the use of arms. Their importance to Okello is best indicated by the fact that a number of them were among the attackers at the Ziwani armory.

Okello kept his revolutionary plans a secret from the top leader-

ship of the Afro-Shirazi party. As a branch leader he had been personally exposed to the organizational weakness of the party and, like many
other minor party officials, had probably blamed a succession of
electoral defeats on the ineptitude of its highest leaders. There was no
doubt that bickering and rivalry in the Afro-Shirazi executive committee had been a major factor in preventing the party from developing a
viable and effective nation-wide organization. Feelings of resentment
at the apparent incompetence of Afro-Shirazi leadership became even
more acute after July 1963 when the party failed to gain a parliamentary majority in the last general election held before independence.
Okello may well have felt that to place the revolution in the hands of
the Afro-Shirazi leadership would be to invite disaster.

But to maintain the secrecy of his plans was very difficult. On
an island as small and as densely populated as Zanzibar, there was
simply no isolated area where it might be possible to conceal a
revolutionary element, even one as small as two or three hundred
men. Okello's solution to this problem was to recruit only among
the most militant opponents of the government, to keep any sort of
formal training at an absolute minimum, and to meet only in villages
known to be overwhelmingly loyal to the Afro-Shirazi party. Several
factors facilitated the success of this strategy of secrecy. In the rural
areas of a society as small as Zanzibar, people become very well
known to one another. This meant that screening out potential police
informants was not nearly so difficult as it had been for revolutionary
African movements in other, larger countries. In addition, the government was concentrating its intelligence efforts on the known political
opposition, the Afro-Shirazi party, Umma, the African trade unions,
and the Afro-Shirazi Youth League. There is quite reliable evidence
that the government had discovered the existence of the revolutionary
plot between Afro-Shirazi and mainland African political leaders. If
so, this probably would have led government security personnel to
believe that they would be able to anticipate an attempted coup. In
any case, the sheer implausibility of a revolutionary army being
organized independently of the existing partisan opposition furnished
a splendid decoy for Okello's activities and may well have been the major factor enabling him to achieve the element of secrecy and surprise.

The timing of the revolution was also a matter of some difficulty.
Clearly, no revolution was possible before independence. The continuing British presence, however small, was an almost certain guarantee of failure. On the other hand, it would also be hazardous to wait
very long after independence. This would give the government an
opportunity to consolidate its control over the society and to proceed

with such security measures as police reorganization and the arming of loyalists in the rural areas. The date chosen was only slightly more than four weeks after official independence. On the evening of Saturday, January 11, a special Ramadan festival was being held in Zanzibar Town. Using the festival as a cover, the revolutionaries entered Zanzibar Town individually and assembled at a pre-arranged point in the African quarter just prior to the assault on the Ziwani armory.

After the Ziwani armory had been seized, Okello distributed the captured supply of arms to members of his army and to a sizable number of militant sympathizers in the African community. The revolutionaries then laid siege to the government's only remaining potential center of resistance, a police station in the northern corner of Zanzibar Town at a location known as Mtoni. Although it was unnecessary to capture this station since the revolutionary army, substantially enlarged by this time in both numbers and weapons, was clearly the dominant military and political force in the country and had placed the government completely on the defensive, Okello's forces, officered by former policemen, maintained the siege to prevent any counterattack by government forces. In the meantime, a unit of Okello's army had occupied the government's radio station, which was completely undefended, and by midmorning on Sunday Okello had begun a series of broadcasts appealing for the voluntary surrender of government officials and warning against popular resistance.

Early Sunday afternoon, a majority of the government ministers surrendered collectively as an official gesture of capitulation. In order to minimize loss of life, several of the ministers made a radio broadcast calling for the surrender of any government forces which were still offering resistance and asking the people of Zanzibar to accept the revolution.

Even if Okello's revolutionary strategy had been part of a broader conspiracy, this would not be adequate to explain why the revolution achieved such astonishingly rapid success or why the previous government could be toppled and a new one installed within a matter of hours. The answer to these far more basic questions lies in the nature of Zanzibari politics. Zanzibari society in early 1964 had become highly vulnerable to revolutionary activity. The success of Okello's revolution was the culmination of years of intense and often violent partisan conflict. The end product of pre-revolutionary conflict in Zanzibar was a governmental and social structure characterized by so many symptoms of weakness and instability that practically any well planned coup, even one far less cleverly executed than Okello's, would probably have had a reasonably good chance of success.

The Character of the Community

The basic source of political conflict in pre-revolutionary Zanzibar was racial pluralism, and, in particular, the fact that there was a pronounced tendency for racial divisions to coincide with socio-economic and political inequalities. Since the early nineteenth century, Zanzibari society had been dominated politically and economically by non-African immigrant minorities. An Arab community of just under 50,000 persons, or about 16 per cent of the total population, not only owned the vast bulk of Zanzibar's arable land but was the society's dominant political stratum. A small Arab elite, composed largely of the wealthiest land owners, high-ranking civil servants, and influential members of the Sultan's family, controlled the legislative and administrative organs of government and the police. Furthermore, an Asian minority of Indo-Pakistani descent, numbering just under 20,000 or about 6 per cent of the population, formed an exclusive economic elite which controlled most of the country's commerce and trade. The African community, which numbered over three-fourths of the total population, was the vast underprivileged mass of Zanzibari society.

This socio-economic and political structure determined the basic pattern of Zanzibari politics during the pre-revolutionary period: a struggle by Africans to gain a position of social equality with other communities, and a countervailing attempt by the Arab political elite to resist any serious diminution of its elite status. The Zanzibari revolution brought Arab supremacy to an abrupt end and began the erosion of the Asian community's economic predominance.

Arab political domination of Zanzibar dated from about 1830 when the Sultanate of Oman, a small state on the southeastern corner of the Arabian peninsula, transferred its capital to the island principally in order to have a better vantage point from which to control Indian Ocean commerce and the slave trade. This launched a heavy Arab immigration into Zanzibar which continued throughout the nineteenth century. Though Arabs had been in contact with eastern Africa since pre-Islamic times, and Arab traders had established numerous settlements along the coast, the Omani penetration of Zanzibar represented a more oppressive form of colonization. The Arab immigrants formed a closed colonial community which included aristocratic and military strata as well as a merchant class. Since it was their intention to settle permanently, they created a separate cultural and social life into which Africans were introduced only as servants and laborers. Moreover, in order to insure the security of their colony, the Arab settlers established an extensive administrative system to exercise political control over the indigenous African population of the interior areas of the island.

One particularly repressive feature of Arab settlement on Zanzibar Island was the forcible acquisition of arable land. In order to provide a means of livelihood for successive waves of colonists, the Arab regime began to take possession of large areas of fertile territory outside Zanzibar Town. Because of the peculiar geographical configuration of the island, land alienation led to a pattern of conspicuous residential segregation between Arabs and Africans. Zanzibar Island is bisected by a ridge running somewhat irregularly north and south. The land to the west of this ridge is extremely fertile and suitable for intensive cultivation. To the east of the ridge, the land is rocky and sparse, the soil of poor quality, and an agricultural economy not easily sustainable. The Arab colonists settled entirely in the fertile western sector where they gradually came to enjoy exclusive occupancy, and where they established a richly productive plantation agriculture devoted largely to export crops such as cloves and coconuts. The African population became progressively confined to the eastern area, residing primarily in coastal villages where it was possible to supplement a meager subsistence agriculture by fishing. The visible inferiority of the African community's agricultural land quickly became a deeply resented symbol of its enforced subordination to an Arab colonial class.

The establishment of a British Protectorate over Zanzibar in 1890 did little to alter the social relationship between Arab and African. Having signed a Protectorate Agreement with the Sultan and having recognized him as the legitimate head of an Arab state, British authorities in Zanzibar interpreted the protectorate relationship as involving a special obligation to protect the interests of the Arab community. Until shortly before independence, they pursued this policy. The Arab Association was given disproportionate representation in the Legislative Council and on other government bodies, Arabs were given preferential treatment in civil service recruitment, and, through informal contacts, Arab leaders had a major voice in Protectorate affairs. Even the gradual introduction of a representative electoral system was not viewed as affecting the Arab community's dominant role in Zanzibari politics. In general, British officials tended to perceive representative government in somewhat narrow terms, primarily as an arrangement which would transform the Sultanate into a constitutional monarchy with elective Arab leadership, not as an institutional change which would lead to the creation of an African state. Moreover, the authorities of the Protectorate tended to see the creation of representative government in Zanzibar as an extremely long-range affair in which Arabs would play an important tutelary role.

On the economic level, the position of the Asian minority as the paramount element dates from the earliest years of Arab rule. At that time, the Sultan's government encouraged Asian immigration as a means of creating a commercial and clerical class. Asians were, by ancient tradition, the bankers, financiers, and managers of the Indian Ocean trade, and their entrepreneurial skills were an invaluable economic asset to the emergent Arab state. Before the revolution, Asians owned virtually all of Zanzibar's largest business firms, they controlled the country's import, export, and tourist trades, and they operated the vast majority of its urban retail shops. A few Asian businessmen also possessed extensive agricultural holdings, and some of Zanzibar's largest plantations were in Asian, not Arab, hands. Asian predominance in the upper economic strata of the society also had important political consequences, as it was a major factor in preventing the emergence of an African elite until quite recently. It was thus an object of intense political resentment among Africans. The Asian community also formed the majority of Zanzibar's middle class, and it virtually monopolized the intermediate grades of the Protectorate's civil service and the clerical and managerial sectors of business and trade. Though only a small fraction of the entire population, Asians clearly controlled the vast bulk of the nation's wealth.

Despite its economic status, the Asian community was not able to exercise effective political influence on a long-range basis. First of all, the essentially middle-class positions of most Asians fostered a sense of political insecurity: as a community of shopkeepers and civil servants, Asians were dependent upon the good will of other racial groups and, since friendly personal relations were often necessary to maintain their economic status, they were reluctant to become involved in political disputes. In addition, the Asian community were divided into a host of highly particularistic communal and caste subgroups, to which most Asians felt a far stronger personal loyalty than to the community as a whole. This fragmentation of loyalties made it practically impossible for the Asian community to function as a unified political group, even when important economic interests were involved. Perhaps the most important cause of the Asian community's political noninvolvement, however, was a strong tendency to remain culturally oriented toward the Indian subcontinent. Even families which had resided in the Protectorate for several generations often retained strong social and family ties to India and Pakistan. The cultural separation of the Asian minority was reflected in a number of ways, such as in a preference for segregated living quarters and a low rate of intermarriage with other racial communities. Its most concrete manifestation was a widespread unwillingness among Asians to become active in Zanzibar's political conflicts.

The elite status of the Arab and Asian minorities had a strong self-perpetuating quality. Both communities, for example, enjoyed a significant educational advantage over Africans, since the educational system of the Protectorate tended to favor the well-to-do at the expense of the poverty-ridden and the urban dweller at the expense of the rural farmer. Moreover, both communities had become culturally acclimated to upper-class status, an attitude which was in striking contrast to the sense of abject powerlessness felt by most rural African villagers. Outright discrimination was also highly important in preserving the basically racial configuration of socio-economic and political stratification. Few Asian business firms would employ Africans except in the most menial tasks, and Arab and Asian officials in charge of recruitment for the civil service consistently gave preferential treatment to members of their own community. This combination of factors—educational imbalance, cultural apathy, and racial discrimination—effectively prevented all but a tiny handful of Africans from gaining access to the upper stratum of Zanzibari society during the pre-revolutionary period.

The African Majority

The African majority furnished Zanzibar with its agricultural laborers, manual workers, fishermen, and semi-skilled craftsmen. In general, Africans provided the lowest-paid workers in government and commerce, the smallest number of students in the upper grades of the secondary schools, and the fewest land holders in the Protectorate's agricultural system. African relations with other communities were usually conducted in the idiom of superior-inferior. Africans were the servants in Asian and Arab homes, the squatter-laborers on Arab-owned farms and the menial workers in Asian-owned stores. The African community was also the least represented element in the Protectorate's political system. No Africans were nominated to the Zanzibar Legislative Council until after World War II, and, for years afterward, African representation was far smaller, in absolute numerical terms, than that of either the Arab or Asian communities. The result of this general pattern of subordination was a deep sense of socio-economic frustration and political resentment.

At the same time, politically significant ethnic and socio-economic cleavages did exist within the African community. The basic division was between those Africans who considered themselves the indigenous inhabitants of the islands and an immigrant African community of more recent, mainland, origin. The former, who constitute just under four-fifths of the total African population of about 240,000, have preferred to describe their community as "Shirazi" rather than "African," in order to differentiate it from the mainland group in terms of descent and length of residence. The concept of a Shirazi, or mixed Afro-Persian, ancestry had originally been used only by those indigenous Africans who claimed a particularly high Persian admixture.[6] During the twentieth century, the term has been adopted by virtually all indigenous Africans as a communal category of self-description. Nevertheless, the original distinction continues to exist. The Shirazi community is composed of three quasi-tribal subgroups—the Pemba, the Tumbatu, and the Hadimu. The Pemba reside on Pemba Island (from which they have taken their name) and on the smaller adjacent islands; the Tumbatu live on Tumbatu Island, just off the northwestern coast of Zanzibar Island, and have spread to southern Pemba and the northern peninsula of Zanzibar; the Hadimu reside primarily in the rural areas of central and southern Zanzibar but a large number have taken up urban residence in Zanzibar Town. Although each of these groups regards itself as Shirazi, each also possesses a strong sense of separate tribal and regional identity.

The presence of a substantial mainland African community of about 50,000 persons is largely attributable to the enormous demand for labor in the clove industry. When, during the second half of the nineteenth century, the Sultan's government encouraged the extensive cultivation of cloves as an export crop, many slaves were imported to work as agricultural laborers on the plantations. After the abolition of slavery at the end of the century, most of the freed Africans remained in Zanzibar Town and took up employment, either as manual laborers in Zanzibar Town or as paid workers on the agricultural estates. A heavy African immigration to Zanzibar has continued to modern times, with large numbers of mainland Africans coming to Zanzibar to seek employment in the clove plantations. Since Zanzibar generally enjoyed a somewhat higher standard of living than the nearby mainland countries, many of the migratory workers took up permanent residence in the Protectorate. The mainland African population of Zanzibar is thus composed of members of a wide range of tribes from virtually all the countries of Eastern Africa—Malawi, Tanganyika, and even the Congo being heavily represented. Among the most numerous tribal groups are Nyamwezi and Yao, but there are also significant numbers of Makonde, Sukuma, and Kikuyu. Regardless of their widely diverse origins, the mainland Africans of Zanzibar have developed a strong sense of common identity, especially in political matters.

A strong sense of separate ethnic identity has been perpetuated

[6] For a recent assessment of the character and timing of early contact with the off-shore islands of East Africa, see Neville Chittick, "The 'Shirazi' Colonization of East Africa," *The Journal of African History*, VI (1965), 275-94.

by socio-economic and residential differentiation between the two groups. The mainland African population has been heavily urbanized and a majority resides in Zanzibar Town. Typically, mainland Africans have worked in the lowest-paid occupations, either as domestic servants or as daily paid laborers in government and commerce. Those who resided in the rural areas were usually squatter-farmers on the large Arab estates, where they performed certain obligatory services in return for a small plot of land. The Shirazis, on the other hand, are an almost entirely rural agricultural community, working on land which they themselves own either communally or individually. Many Shirazis are also part-time fishermen and thus able to supplement their farming income. Although the actual cash income of most Shirazis is frequently not as large as that of the mainland group, their standard of living is almost invariably better since they are able to combine subsistence and cash pursuits in a way which the more urbanized mainland Africans cannot.

The clear tendency of socio-economic cleavages to parallel communal divisions has intensified the tensions and antagonisms normally present in a racially plural society. Members of different ethnic communities have been estranged not only by alien cultural practices and traditions but by opposed economic and class interests. The degree of alienation has been so great that it has tended to affect all areas of life; even such activities as recreation and sports have normally been organized along racially divided lines.

The one potential bond of unity among the different racial groups has been religion. More than 95 per cent of all Zanzibaris are Muslim. Adherence to Islam is virtually unanimous among Arabs and Shirazis, including all but a handful of mainland Africans, and nearly three-fourths of the Asian community. During the decade of agitational politics before the revolution when the Arab community was seeking to preserve its dominant status by attracting the voluntary support of Africans and Asians, it consistently employed Islam as a symbol of Zanzibar's multiracial unity.

Pre-revolutionary Politics

The most provocative question about the Zanzibari revolution is why fundamental changes in the pattern of political and economic stratification have had to come about through violent and convulsive means. Many observers, both within Zanzibar and abroad, had predicted that the establishment of a majoritarian form of government would bring the African community to power through orderly electoral processes. There was ample occasion for this to occur. Between 1957 and 1963

Zanzibar had four national elections based on a non-racial franchise and broad popular participation. However, an Arab-led party was able to attract sufficient African support to win the last two of these elections. Thus, the most conspicuous feature of Zanzibari politics when independence was achieved in December 1963 was that a status reversal between Arabs and Africans had failed to occur and that Arab political leaders, exercising power through an elected parliamentary majority, were in decisive control of the political life of the country. This was, in a sense, *the* basic cause of the Zanzibari revolution. Africans overthrew Arab rule by forceful, violent means because they had been unsuccessful in doing so in a constitutional manner.

Maintenance of Arab Supremacy: 1954–57

The Arab community's success in maintaining its supremacy despite the establishment of representative government was in large measure the result of its ability to seize and maintain the political initiative by organizing a nationalist movement which capitalized on ethnic divisions within the African community. Zanzibari nationalism was, at its inception and for a considerable period thereafter, the creation of the Arab minority.[7] Thus, in early 1954, the Arab Association rejected British government proposals for communal representation and demanded an immediate common roll election as a means of hastening Zanzibar's progress toward independence. In order to dramatize the urgency of this demand, the Association boycotted the Legislative Council and, between June 1954 and early 1956, mounted a militant press campaign in favor of immediate constitutional reform. The paradoxical feature of Arab nationalism was that Arabs apparently had the most to lose if constitutional liberalization should occur. Liberal changes could only mean a diminution of the Arab Association's large nominated representation in the Legislative Council and other government boards. Moreover, Arab leaders were fully aware of the danger that, if a common roll election were held, their candidates could easily be swamped by the overwhelming African majority in the Protectorate.

The basic predicament confronting the Arab Association was that by 1954 Great Britain had already made it clear elsewhere in Africa that it was committed to the eventual introduction of parliamentary government in all those colonies which did not have large resident white populations. Although Britain was willing to delay the implementation of this policy in Zanzibar and to qualify it temporarily by such measures as communal representation, these could at best be

[7] A book-length treatment of Zanzibari nationalism appears in Michael F. Lofchie, *Zanzibar: Background to Revolution* (Princeton, 1965).

short-range safeguards of Arab political dominance. The more far-sighted leaders of the Arab Association could not have avoided the conclusion that if their community's elite status were to be permanently preserved, this would have to be done within a context of parliamentary democracy. As a matter of sheer political strategy, the Arab leadership knew that it would eventually need to depend upon substantial electoral support from Africans and Asians. This conclusion would suggest that Arab nationalism in Zanzibar was, at least in part, an attempt to gain the confidence of the African and Asian communities. Timing was a critical factor if this strategy were to be successful; it was necessary to wrest control of the country from Britain before African nationalism from the mainland could spread to Zanzibar and arouse the African population in opposition to Arab as well as British rule.

Arab nationalism was also a product of complex patriotic and religious considerations. Before the establishment of the British Protectorate, Zanzibar had been a full-fledged Arab state with its own civil service, military cadre, judiciary, and system of African administration. Moreover, under the Sultan, Zanzibar had exercised extensive territorial claims over the mainland of eastern Africa. Therefore Arabs had always felt an especially heavy sense of loss because of the British intrusion, and many believed that in Zanzibar British colonialism had subordinated an independent Arab, not African, country. Islamic religious beliefs further stimulated Arab resentment of the British presence. In particular, Islam postulates an inevitable and obligatory conflict between Muslims and nonbelievers. The concept of *jihad*, or holy war, enjoins all Muslims to wage an eternal struggle in behalf of their faith. In this perspective, anticolonialism took on something of the quality of a crusade and became a species of holy war against *alien* religious infidels.

The Arab Association's demand for a common roll election was finally accepted by the British authorities toward the end of 1955 and an election for a limited number of seats in mid-1957 was announced. This confronted the Association with an awkward dilemma. It was imperative to organize a national campaign for multi-racial support, but, if the Association itself founded a political party, Arab leaders would be suspected of trying to dominate it. This would cause the Arab community to lose whatever popular acceptance had been gained by its nationalistic boycott of the Legislative Council. In early 1956, therefore, several members of the executive committee of the Arab Association began to join a small peasant protest movement called the National Party of the Sultan's Subjects, which had been organized in response to certain local grievances. The Sultan's Subjects fitted the Association's need for a political party which could be presented as having purely African origins. But once Arabs became members, they easily dominated the organization and soon became its most influential political leaders. Although an African was retained as party president, relations within the party were characterized by the dominance of Arab intellectuals over relatively uneducated and politically unsophisticated African villagers. Within a short span, the Arabs had changed the name of the movement to the Zanzibar Nationalist party, had proceeded to create a nationwide organization, and had begun to campaign for African support throughout the Protectorate.

The Nationalist party enjoyed several important advantages in its efforts to recruit African members. As the first nationalistic party in the Protectorate, it was able to pre-empt the symbols of nationalism and to identify itself exclusively with the demand for "freedom, now." The Nationalist party was also able to draw on Islamic religious precepts as a vehicle for recruiting African supporters. Two Qur'anic precepts were of particular significance. The social teachings of the Qur'an are quite explicit in endorsing the necessity of cordial and co-operative relations between members of different racial groups. One passage, for example, reads: "Men, we have created you from a male and a female and divided you into nations and tribes so that you might get to know one another."[8] The party's leaders argued that their effort to draw on a racially diverse body of supporters was an obligatory fulfillment of this scriptural commandment and asserted that it compelled African and Asians of the Muslim faith to support them as well. The political doctrine of Islam was also employed in this way. The Qur'an does not possess an explicit theory of the state but one passage reads: "Obey God and His Apostle and those who have authority over you."[9] Since the Sultan and the Arab community constituted Zanzibar's closest approximation to an established ruling class, this passage could be made to appear as if it created an obligation to support Arab leadership.

The Nationalist party's most important advantage was the quality of its top leadership. As a party of the rural gentry and the urban well-to-do, it was able to draw upon a large number of persons with considerable experience in government and administration, including a substantial group of retired civil servants. Not only were leaders of this caliber able to provide it with a strong financial base but, being economically independent, they were able to devote a considerable portion of their time to its activities. As a result the central and rural leadership of the Nationalist party represented an enormous reservoir

[8] Qur'an, 49, 13.
[9] Ibid., 4, 62.

of organizational skill and financial backing, resources which were never equalled by any rival African party in the Protectorate. Rural Arab landowners were especially valuable in the party's drive to recruit African members. As the employers of large numbers of African laborers, they could apply enormous economic pressure on prospective recruits.

Attempts to Create an African Party: 1957

No serious effort to form an African political movement was made until almost a year after the Nationalist party had begun its election campaign. In February, 1957, only six months before the scheduled election, leaders of the mainland African and Shirazi communities met to try to form a united party in response to the threat of Arab domination posed by the Nationalists. However, their efforts had little success. On Zanzibar Island, it was agreed that the African and Shirazi Associations would co-operate for electoral purposes and form a loose Afro-Shirazi Union; there was, however, to be no merger and each association was to retain a separate organizational identity. Even this modest degree of agreement did not extend to Pemba where the African and Shirazi Associations decided to contest the election as rival organizations.

The inability of mainlanders and Shirazis to form a single, unified, political party revealed the depth of cultural and ethnic separatism between the two communities. That the social and occupational differences between immigrant and indigenous Africans had fostered a strong sense of separate identity has already been mentioned. More important was the fact that the two groups tended to have widely differing attitudes toward Zanzibar's Arab minority, the mainland Africans being by far the more bitter against it. The mainland Africans were deeply conscious that their very presence in Zanzibar had originated in the Arab slave trade or in the need for migrant labor on the Arab clove plantations. Many of the older mainlanders had personal recollections of slavery: their stories of harsh treatment at Arab hands fostered a deep sense of antagonism toward Arabs throughout the entire community. Many generations removed from their countries and communities of origin, the mainlanders were unable to return home or, because of their status as a subordinated immigrant minority, were unable to identify completely with Zanzibar. They frequently held the Arabs to blame for their general condition of statelessness and estrangement. Moreover, as a servant class of domestic workers and agricultural laborers, the mainland Africans were often in direct personal contact with Arab superiors. This heightened their sense of subordination and deprivation. For all these reasons, the mainlanders could see little reason for entering politics except to defeat the Arab oligarchy and to establish an African-ruled state.

Within the Shirazi community, only the Hadimu tended to share the mainland Africans' profound antipathy toward the Arab minority. As the resident African community of Zanzibar Island, the Hadimu had borne the full brunt of the Arab immigration of the nineteenth century. Most Hadimu felt that the agricultural areas occupied by Arabs had once been theirs; the contrast between highly productive Arab plantations and their own section of the island had for many years generated bitter resentment. In addition, the Hadimu had been subjected to stringent administrative control by the Arab state and had experienced a rapid breakdown of their own tribal institutions. In addition, large numbers of Hadimu resided on a temporary basis in the African quarter of Zanzibar Town, where they were exposed to the mainlanders' political sentiments; those who returned to the rural areas often acted as carriers of militantly anti-Arab attitudes.

On the other hand, the Pemba Shirazis, and, to a certain extent, the Tumbatu as well, looked back on a history of warm and friendly relations with the Arab settler community. This was largely the result of Pemba's unusual pattern of historic and social contact between indigenous Africans and immigrant Arabs: the Arab penetration of Pemba had been much more gradual than that of Zanzibar and had in fact been undertaken at the explicit invitation of the Pemba Shirazi community.[10] The consent of the local population made it comparatively unnecessary for the Sultanate to impose a repressive system of social control. For this reason, the rather autocratic character of Arab colonial rule was not nearly as visible in Pemba as it was on Zanzibar, the Arab presence did not precipitate a breakdown of traditional political institutions, and the Pemba Shirazis never developed a strong sense that the Sultan's regime represented a sudden and forcible subordination to alien domination. As a result, Pemba and Tumbatu Shirazis were profoundly reluctant to enter a political movement whose basic premise was the overthrow of the Arab oligarchy.

The land question had also been much less tense in Pemba than in Zanzibar. Fertile soils are almost ubiquitous throughout Pemba Island and there is no conspicuous geographical demarcation of areas of good and poor quality soil. Therefore, although a substantial amount of

[10] Before the establishment of the Omani Sultanate on Zanzibar Island in 1828, Pemba had been harshly ruled by Arabs from Mombasa. Around 1821, the Pemba Shirazis sent a small delegation of local leaders to the Sultan's government and requested it to occupy their island as a means of ending Mombasan rule. For a full history see John Gray, *History of Zanzibar From the Middle Ages to 1856* (London, 1962).

Arab land alienation did occur, Arab settlers became widely scattered over the island and there was no massive dispossession of the Pemba Shirazis from their indigenous areas of habitation. Whereas Zanzibar Island had been characterized by conspicuous residential segregation, in Pemba Arabs and Shirazis became neighbors living side by side on soil of roughly equal quality; close personal relations were common. Indeed, because Pemba Shirazis remained in possession of large areas or arable land, the establishment of a clove industry enabled them to prosper along with the Arab immigrants, a phenomenon which fostered a sense that Shirazis and Arabs had mutual economic interests. Many of the more well-to-do Shirazi families were also large employers of seasonal mainland African labor and this fact, together with their voluntary acceptance of Arab settlement, led to a strong sense that the mainlanders, not the Arabs, were the alien presence in Zanzibar. Indeed, most Pemba Shirazis felt that they had little in common with mainland Africans, historically or politically.

The First Election: 1957

The first election campaign, which occurred between February and June 1957, brought to the surface of Zanzibari political life racial and ethnic attitudes which had hitherto been latent. The Afro-Shirazi Union, which was effectively organized only on Zanzibar Island, presented itself as the party of the impoverished African masses and campaigned on a militantly anti-Arab basis. Its leaders asserted that Zanzibari Africans suffered from two colonialisms, British and Arab, and argued that if Africans were ever to advance socially and economically, Arab as well as British rule had to be overthrown. One conspicuous theme in the Afro-Shirazi campaign was the need for gradual constitutional progress. Many Africans in Zanzibar viewed Britain sympathetically as the power which ended slavery in East Africa, and they felt that the British presence prevented the Arab regime from engaging in autocratic and harsh practices toward the African community. Afro-Shirazi leaders feared that if British rule were removed before Africans had had an opportunity to catch up with other racial communities in educational and other attainments, the Arabs would be able to consolidate their privileged position permanently.

The Nationalist party, which had a nationwide organization and was able to nominate candidates in five of the six constituencies, presented itself as a militantly nationalistic, multi-racial party. Its leaders urged Zanzibaris of all races to unite in order to end British colonial rule and demanded immediate and rapid progress toward independence. The Nationalist leaders were bitterly critical of the racialism of the Afro-Shirazi Union which, they argued, was in violation of the Islamic creed. In the Nationalists' view, racial divisions were a colonial contrivance—a result of British tactics of "divide and rule"—and the party admonished members of all racial communities to identify themselves only as Zanzibaris. Nationalist party spokesmen were also highly critical of the rather conservative, "gradualist" constitutional position taken by the Afro-Shirazis and argued that such a position amounted to an admission of racial inferiority. The Nationalist party campaign was not without racial overtones of its own however. The party's press, in particular, attacked mainland Africans as an alien and divisive element in Zanzibar and sought to appeal to Shirazis on the grounds that indigenous Africans should be given preference for urban employment.

Meanwhile, Shirazi Association candidates in Pemba advocated a multiracial doctrine somewhat similar to that of the Nationalist party. The major difference was that they sought to present the Shirazi Association as a moderate third force in Zanzibar politics, one which would avoid the racial emphasis of the Afro-Shirazi Union and the predominant Arab influence of the Nationalist party. Its principal appeal was to Shirazi voters who were a majority in Zanzibar and—the argument ran—should unite in opposition to both Arabs and mainland Africans.

At the polls, the Nationalist party was completely defeated; although it had campaigned as a multi-racial movement it gained less than one-fourth of the popular vote and did not win a single seat. The Afro-Shirazi Union won all three seats which it had contested on Zanzibar Island, where it gained a decisive majority of the vote. The differing fortunes of these two parties were widely interpreted, at the time, as evidence that the African community had achieved a constitutional revolution and ended Arab hegemony through sheer electoral strength. This was not the case, and it is quite erroneous to view this election as a portentous display of African electoral strength. The Afro-Shirazi Union's victories gave it only half of the elective positions in the Zanzibar Legislative Council and, on a Protectorate-wide basis, it was far from achieving a majority of the popular vote. In Pemba, anti-Arab views were known to be rather unpopular. An African Association candidate whose racial views corresponded closely to those of the Afro-Shirazi Union was defeated by an overwhelming plurality. The fact is that the election results as a whole did not reveal widespread support for anti-Arab sentiments. They may simply have indicated a strong tendency among Zanzibaris to remain politically loyal to their separate ethnic communities.

Actually, communalism did emerge as the decisive factor in all three constituencies not contested by Afro-Shirazi candidates. The two victorious candidates in Pemba had been officially endorsed by the Pemba Shirazi Association and the winning candidate in Zanzibar Town had been chosen to represent the Muslim Association, a communal interest group of Asians of the Muslim faith. Communal loyalties, rather than anti-Arab sentiment, may also have been the most important source of the Afro-Shirazi Union's victories: despite the party's avowedly anti-Arab campaign, it had been able to present itself as the legitimate heir of the African and Shirazi associations and had clearly profited greatly from an ability to draw on long-standing loyalties to those two bodies.

Of course, communal separatism had become an entrenched feature of Zanzibari life long before the era of competitive partisan politics. It was best exemplified by the widespread popular acceptance of the British practice of racial representation in the Legislative Council, and by the presence of innumerable communal and ethnic associations. The distinction between anti-Arab sentiment and communal separatism as a basis for electoral victory was of decisive importance to the subsequent history of the Nationalist party. It meant, in practical terms, that anti-Arab sentiments were neither sufficiently intense nor sufficiently widespread among Zanzibari Africans to constitute a decisive obstacle to the electoral prospects of an Arab-led political party. This message was not lost on the Arab leaders of the Nationalist party, and in later elections the party sought merely to discredit the established traditions of communal voting in favor of the Nationalist party's concept of multi-racial affiliation. This strategy proved fruitful and in Zanzibar's last three national elections the Nationalist party was able to recover completely from its defeat in 1957 and eventually attracted sufficient African and Asian support to win parliamentary majorities in co-operation with a small Shirazi-led party.

Post-election Maneuvers: Mergers and Splits

Several months after the election, the Shirazi and African Associations of Pemba reached an agreement: the two elected Shirazi leaders from Pemba joined the Afro-Shirazi Union, which was renamed the Afro-Shirazi party, and sat in the Legislative Council as its members, though they insisted on the Shirazi Association's right to continue to maintain separate organizational facilities. This demand graphically symbolized the deep disagreement between Pemba Shirazis and other Africans over the issue of race relations with the Arab minority. Throughout its subsequent history, the Afro-Shirazi party remained an ethnically divided party and, in organizational terms, never became more than a loose electoral coalition between Shirazis and mainland Africans. Organizational weakness together with a chronic inability to conceal the political tensions between Shirazis and mainlanders consistently made it extremely difficult for it either to establish itself effectively on a nationwide basis or to conduct well planned election campaigns.

The period following the 1957 election was marked by a severe intensification of racial and communal tensions throughout the Protectorate. Competitive partisan politics were a new phenomenon in Zanzibar, and the political culture of the society lacked an established set of norms and principles which defined the boundaries of party conflict and set politics clearly apart from other modes of social behavior. As a result, the communal and racial antagonisms which had been aroused by the election campaign infused all areas of life. Members of opposed political parties boycotted one another's shops, organized rival bus companies, and in the rural areas went so far as to refuse to share the same wells. The Afro-Shirazi party constructed an entirely separate market place in the African quarter of Zanzibar Town and the party's Youth League began to establish a nationwide chain of African co-operatives so that Africans would not have to patronize stores owned by Arabs or Asians. The African co-operative movement was so successful that, within a year, it had forced hundreds of Arab shopkeepers out of business. In their turn, Arab landowners sympathetic to the Nationalist party evicted large numbers of mainland African squatter-farmers from their plantations and refused to employ African agricultural laborers who would not consent to join their party. The religious life of the country was also deeply affected. Weddings, funerals, and worship itself were subjected to a nearly universal pattern of partisan segregation in which members of one party refused to attend ceremonies initiated by or identified with the opposite party. By the end of 1958, race relations had deteriorated to a point where sporadic outbreaks of violence had become common and the British authorities feared that rioting on a national scale would imminently engulf the entire society in open racial welfare.

At this point, an attempt to avert a racial clash and to unify Zanzibar's political parties was made during the fall of 1958, by the Pan-African Freedom Movement of East, Central and Southern Africa, an international organization of African nationalists. After hearing representations from both parties, Pan-African Freedom Movement officials concluded that the Afro-Shirazi party was allowing its racial animosity toward the Arab community to stand in the way of Zanzibar's struggle for independence. They were particularly critical of the constitutional conservatism of the Afro-Shirazis and recommended that the African party change its position and form a common front with the Nationalist party to work for immediate progress toward independence.

The Freedom Movement recommendation was a major political victory for the Nationalists, for it placed the Afro-Shirazi party in an awkward and embarrassing position. If the Afro-Shirazi leaders agreed, they faced the humiliating task of publicly revising their constitutional policy to accord with that of a rival party which their party had far surpassed at the polls.[11] If they refused, they would not only be cutting themselves off from the mainstream of East African nationalism but would lend credibility to the Nationalist party's claim to be the only genuine nationalist movement in the Protectorate. After a bitter internal struggle, the Afro-Shirazis chose the former course and, in late 1958, joined with the Nationalist party to form a national "Freedom Committee." For nearly fifteen months, Afro-Shirazi leaders toured the country, frequently appearing on the same platform with Nationalist party leaders, and urged their followers to forget old racial differences for the sake of national independence. Throughout this period, the Afro-Shirazi party presented the spectacle of a party which was repudiating the very grievances on which it had recently based its sole claim to support—the socio-economic and political subordination of the African majority. It found itself compelled to concede publicly the superior merit of the multi-racial and constitutional policies of its chief rival. As a result, the Nationalist party was able to increase its stature immeasurably among members of all racial communities.

An internal dispute among the Afro-Shirazis over the Freedom Committee eventually led to a major split in the party in the late fall of 1959. Opposition to the Freedom Committee had originated primarily in the party's Youth League and among a small minority of its executive committee. Some of the dissidents refused to accept the notion of a united front with the Nationalists, and formed a splinter group which sought to persuade the Afro-Shirazi leadership to withdraw from the Freedom Committee and to resume its former policy position. Although the split within the party had initially crossed Shirazi-mainland African lines, it gradually took on the complexion of a disagreement between two ethnic groups. It is a common experience of many ethnically plural party organizations for issue conflicts, regardless of their substance, to follow previously existing lines of cleavage. In the Afro-Shirazi party, the tension between mainland African and Shirazi leaders was so great that these groups were almost invariably opposed to one another over matters of strategy and tactics that had little to do

[11] In the election of 1957, the Afro-Shirazi Union gained 12,800 votes to 6,200 for the Zanzibar Nationalist party on Zanzibar Island. On Pemba Island, where the Afro-Shirazi Union as such did not stand, the Nationalist party gained 4,700 votes. Two Shirazi Association candidates, who subsequently joined the Afro-Shirazi Union, received 9,200 votes there.

with ethnic considerations. Ultimately, it became clear that support for the Freedom Committee was concentrated primarily among the mainlanders and opposition, among the Shirazis.

Thus, toward the end of 1959, Ameri Tajo, a Hadimu Shirazi member of the Afro-Shirazi executive committee and one of the party's elected members in the Legislative Council, was accused of publicly opposing the Freedom Committee and was, under humiliating circumstances, expelled from the party. His expulsion was deeply resented by the two elected Shirazis from Pemba, Mohammed Shamte, a retired school teacher, and Ali Sharif, a well-to-do landowner. Since joining the Afro-Shirazi party in late 1957, both men had been uncomfortable in their close relationship with mainland Africans and took this opportunity to resign in order to show sympathy with Tajo. The three Shirazis formed a new political party, the Zanzibar and Pemba People's party. Although the People's party declared itself officially multiracial and open to members of all racial communities, it appealed primarily to Shirazis. From its very beginning the People's party could depend upon the complete support of the Pemba Shirazi Association, which had continued to maintain its separate organization, and in which both Sharif and Shamte were highly influential figures. The relationship between the Pemba Shirazi Association and the People's party was so close that the two became organizationally virtually indistinguishable. This meant that, although a fledgling party, the People's party possessed a highly viable organization of local branches and regional committees throughout Pemba Island.

The split over the Freedom Committee was paradoxical in several respects. Although mainland African leaders had harbored by far the deepest sense of grievance against the Arab minority, they were the most conspicuous element in favor of multi-party co-operation. The Shirazis, who were personally well disposed toward the idea of a multiracial nationalist movement, had opposed the Freedom Committee largely because they felt that the Afro-Shirazi party's participation in the Committee resulted from autocratic mainland African domination of the party. In addition, popular opposition to the Freedom Committee among Afro-Shirazi supporters had become so great that the party had been compelled to curtail its participation drastically several months before the split. Ironically, the Freedom Committee would probably, in any case, have ceased to function by the end of 1959. Zanzibar's second national election had been scheduled for mid-1960 and both the Afro-Shirazis and the Nationalists were anxious to conduct independent campaigns.

The split in the Afro-Shirazi party meant that it would face the impending election in an extremely poor condition, bereft of both leadership and organization in Pemba and with significantly reduced popular support in Zanzibar. In addition, large numbers of party supporters had become demoralized and disillusioned by the Afro-Shirazi leaders' abrupt shifts in policy and by their open conflicts.

Two Elections in 1961

The second election campaign did not differ strikingly from the first. The Nationalist party once again laid heavy emphasis on its multiracial character and on the religious sanctification of its principles. By presenting itself as the preferred party of the Sultan's family, the Nationalist party was able to tap widespread popular loyalty to the Sultan and to identify itself unequivocally with the Islamic precept of deference to established authority. The party's appeal to Arabs and Asians was particularly effective. In constituencies inhabited predominantly by these communities, the Nationalist party asserted that it would conduct governmental programs in a nondiscriminatory fashion, a pledge which was calculated to relieve minority fears of social and economic policies that might give special preference to members of the African majority. Among Shirazi voters, Nationalist spokesmen played on the tension between Shirazis and mainlanders, arguing that the mainland African community was a disruptive element which had upset the historically cordial relationship between Zanzibar's indigenous population and the Arab settlers.

The Afro-Shirazi campaign was based on the need to create a sense of common interest and identity between Shirazis and mainland Africans. The party stressed the generally low socio-economic status of all Africans in the Protectorate and argued that Arab colonialism had subordinated indigenous as well as immigrant Africans. Afro-Shirazi leaders also sought to establish the common character shared by Zanzibari African and continental African nationalism. Thus, party branches prominently displayed a variety of symbols which linked the Afro-Shirazi party with nationalist movements in Tanganyika and Kenya. Pictures of Julius Nyerere and Jomo Kenyatta were placed beside those of Abeid Karume, the Afro-Shirazi President. The party's flag and anthem were similar to those of Tanganyika. Moreover, well-known nationalist leaders from Tanganyika were invited to Zanzibar to address Afro-Shirazi meetings. Although the Afro-Shirazi party also to a certain extent sought to present itself as a multi-racial party loyal to the Sultan, its gestures in this direction were perfunctory. Most Afro-Shirazi leaders spoke of the need for Zanzibar to become a constitutional monarchy, but a few party spokesmen openly treated the Sultan as the arch symbol of Arab domination and, as a result, they were generally viewed as being hostile to the Sultanate.

The third party, the People's party, had considerable difficulty in distinguishing its campaign from those of its two larger rivals. The official party policies—multi-racialism, rapid constitutional progress, and loyalty to the Sultanate—were closer to the program of the Nationalists than of the Afro-Shirazis but the party also stressed its status as the sole organization representing the indigenous African majority. In reality, the People's party made its basic appeal to Shirazi voters, and most of its supporters were attracted more by its close identification with the Pemba Shirazi Association than by its official campaign principles.

Although the election was eventually postponed from mid-1960 to January 1961 because of administrative difficulties in organizing the polling, the delay did little to help the Afro-Shirazi party recover from the disastrous after-effects of the Freedom Committee period. Of the 22 places in the Legislative Council (13 from Zanzibar, 9 from Pemba) the Afro-Shirazis won only 10. Their greatest weakness was in Pemba where they won only 2 seats and gained less than one-fourth of the popular vote. The most significant and portentous feature of the election was the extent to which the Nationalist party had been able to improve its popular standing. It won 9 seats (5 in Zanzibar, 4 in Pemba), only one less than the Afro-Shirazis. Although the Nationalists did extremely poorly in the mainland African and Hadimu Shirazi areas, their support among Arabs, Asians, and Tumbatu Shirazis enabled them to do nearly as well as the Afro-Shirazi party even on Zanzibar Island. The People's party won only three seats, all on Pemba, but prevented either of the major parties from gaining a parliamentary majority, thereby creating a constitutional deadlock. Both the Afro-Shirazi party and the Nationalist party initiated negotiations with leaders of the People's party to form a coalition government but the People's party itself split, one member joining the Afro-Shirazis and two, the Nationalists. This meant that there was no clear parliamentary majority and another election had to be scheduled for June, only six months later.

The only major difference in the conduct of the June 1961 election campaign was that for this election the Nationalist party and the People's party formed an electoral coalition. In part, the coalition simply reflected the Pemba Shirazi leaders' profound personal mistrust of mainland African leaders. More important, the formation of a Nationalist-People's party coalition symbolized the fact that Pemba Shirazis had never sympathized with the anti-Arab sentiments of the Afro-Shirazis and had always preferred a multi-racial doctrine far closer to that of the Nationalists. By forming an alliance, the Nationalists and People's party were able to avoid opposing each other in any constituency and could support a common candidate against the Afro-Shirazi party. The coalition also enabled the two parties to pool their popular support since party loyalties in Zanzibar had become sufficiently strong to ensure that supporters of either party would generally vote for a coalition candidate regardless of which party he officially represented. The regional distribution of popular support for the various parties remained almost exactly the same in June as it had been in January and this, together with the effectiveness of the coalition's electoral strategy, made it impossible for the Afro-Shirazi party to improve upon its parliamentary strength. Afro-Shirazi candidates gained only 10 seats out of 23.[12] Coalition candidates won the remaining 13 seats (10 Nationalists; 3 People's party) and were able to form a government. The President of the People's party, Mohammed Shamte, became Prime Minister, but a majority of the most important cabinet posts, including the Ministries of Education and Agriculture, were assumed by Arab leaders of the Nationalist party. With only minor changes in personnel, the Nationalist-People's party coalition government remained in power in Zanzibar until the revolution.

However, the intensity of racial and partisan animosities had by this time become so great that the June election touched off several days of widespread rioting on Zanzibar Island, with two patterns of violence distinguishable. On election day, June 1, the disturbances consisted primarily of street-fighting in Zanzibar Town between Afro-Shirazi and Nationalist supporters. Being confined to certain sections of the urban area, this outbreak was fairly easily controlled by British troops flown in from the mainland to assist the Zanzibar police. On June 2, however, the violence spread to the rural areas and increased radically in intensity. Enormously exaggerated reports of the election day urban fighting and news of the coalition's victory had spread to villages where Afro-Shirazi sentiment was strong. For nearly five days, a large number of spontaneously organized bands of Africans roamed the plantation areas of the island where Arabs resided and engaged in wholesale destruction of life and property. Many clove plantations were completely devastated; the exact number of Arabs killed has not been firmly established. The government's official estimate placed the number killed at sixty-eight, of whom sixty-four were Arabs, but reliable unofficial estimates indicate that the death toll was probably twice this figure, nearly all Arab. The pattern of rural violence which followed the June election—the murder of Arab families who were exposed and essentially defenseless because of their isolated residence in remote areas—closely resembled the pattern after the January 1964 revolution. The latter was, however, somewhat more effectively organized and was unrestrained by the presence of British soldiers. It was, therefore, of a far greater intensity.

[12] The Protectorate authorities had added an additional constituency to prevent the possibility of still another constitutional deadlock.

The Atmosphere and Results of the Fourth Election: 1963

The basic cause of the June 1961 riots lay in the extent to which several years of intensely competitive partisan politics had aroused and inflamed racial hatreds. The two major political parties had since early 1957 been engaged in ardent efforts to recruit supporters; during this period, party and racial conflict had become practically synonymous. The tendency for opposed parties to become identified in purely racial terms was so prevalent that throughout the Protectorate the Swahili terms for Arab and African were used by nearly everyone as shorthand euphemisms for the Nationalist party and Afro-Shirazi party respectively. The campaigning which preceded the June 1961 election had begun as early as late 1959 and had increased steadily in intensity. In the effort to maintain the enthusiasm of their supporters, the parties had resorted to appeals of a more and more virulent sort. By mid-1961, Zanzibari society was being saturated almost daily with partisan propaganda whose essential ingredients were hysterical accusation and gross racial stereotypes.

Speakers representing the coalition parties sought to stigmatize the Afro-Shirazi party as a pernicious agent of mainland African infiltration in Zanzibar. They argued that an Afro-Shirazi victory would mean domination of the country by Tanganyika, the suppression of the Muslim faith, and violent persecution of all minority groups. Some coalition leaders went so far as to assert that the Afro-Shirazi party was secretly a Christian movement and that its branches were used to hold covert church meetings at which forcible conversion of Muslims was preached. On the other hand, a large proportion of Afro-Shirazi electioneering had been devoted to accusations that the Nationalist party was the political front of Zanzibar's entrenched Arab oligarchy. Afro-Shirazi speakers interpreted this to mean that a Nationalist victory would bring about the return of slavery, with all its attendant cruelties. One of the most frequently discussed subjects in Afro-Shirazi leaders' speeches was the brutal physical treatment of Africans under slavery. Stories of such treatment were widely circulated among Afro-Shirazi supporters on a person-to-person basis. This form of communication lent them a quality of such historical authenticity that numerous party members began to claim that they would even prefer death to life under an Arab government. The cumulative impact of this sort of campaigning was to create a pervasive atmosphere of hysteria, terror, and racial hatred.

This atmosphere of racial antagonism continued to pervade Zanzibari society until the revolution. Although the British authorities declared a state of emergency after the June riots and placed stringent limitations on party activities and political meetings, the Protectorate remained in a state of extreme political tension. A fourth general election was scheduled for July 1963, six months before independence, so that the parties would have one final opportunity to contest for political power. The outcome of this election, however, was never in serious doubt. The Nationalist-People's party coalition had hardened into a virtual merger of the two parties, and there were few changes in the regional distribution of popular support. The coalition parties gained 18 of the 31 constituencies into which the country had been divided, thereby retaining control of the government. The coalition maintained its unchallenged predominance in Pemba where it won 12 of the 14 seats. The Afro-Shirazi party, which gained the remaining 13 seats, was unable to make significant inroads among the ethnic and communal groups which supported the Nationalists and the People's party. Its popularity among mainland Africans and Hadimu Shirazis was unrivaled but, with the exception of its two victories in Pemba, it did consistently badly not only among Arabs and Asians, but among Pemba and Tumbatu Shirazis as well.

The most ominous feature of the 1963 election was that the Afro-Shirazis had in reality gained more than 54 per cent of the popular vote and had outpolled their rivals by over 13,000 votes. In the mythology of the revolution, the Afro-Shirazis party's popular majority led to the charge that the British government intentionally gerrymandered the constituencies in order to insure an Arab victory. Commemorating the first anniversary of the revolution, the Tanganyikan newspaper, *The Nationalist*, for example, commented that "these elections had been deliberately rigged by the British colonial regime to prevent any chance of the national liberation movement, led by the Afro-Shirazi Party, winning a majority of seats."[13] Both myth and accusation are untrue.

Close inspection of the constituency boundaries and popular figures reveals not only a remarkable uniformity in population but an absence of the distorted and tortuous boundaries symptomatic of gerrymandered areas.[14] The peculiarity of the election results stemmed from the fact that the Afro-Shirazis' popular support was densely con-

[13] *The Nationalist*, Jan. 12, 1965.
[14] Constituency maps and census figures may be found in Sir Robert Arundell, *Report of the Delimitation Commissioner, Zanzibar, 1962* (Zanzibar, 1962). Two constituencies in Zanzibar Town won by the Zanzibar Nationalist party did have a somewhat smaller number of eligible voters than all the others. This was due to the presence of a great many Asian residents who did not possess Zanzibari nationality. Even if these two constituencies had been consolidated, the result of the election would not have been appreciably affected.

centrated in a few areas—the African quarter of Zanzibar Town and the central and southern rural areas of Zanzibar Island. The party won seats in these areas by overwhelming majorities, often capturing more than 80 per cent of the popular vote and, thereby, accumulating its massive electoral total. In the rest of the Protectorate, however, Afro-Shirazi support was scattered and sparse, and the coalition was able to win a number of close contests, especially in Pemba. However, the Afro-Shirazis' ability to win a popular majority while losing the election increased the sense of political frustration among Africans and added to the general political instability of the country.

Working Up to Revolution

The Zanzibari revolution was not altogether unexpected, for the strength and militancy of anti-government sentiment and the government's inability to respond effectively to the challenge it posed, were the most conspicuous features of Zanzibari politics during the months before independence. The most active and militant of anti-government groups was a new political party, called Umma ("The People"), which had splintered off from the Nationalists just before the July election. Umma had been organized by Abdul Rahman Muhammad (Babu), the general secretary of the Nationalist party, after a long and bitter disagreement with his party's executive committee. The Nationalist party had, for some time, been split by a deep-seated ideological cleavage between radical and conservative elements. The radicals, led by Babu, had consistently sought to persuade the party to move away from its religiously based, multi-racial theory of national community which, in their view, had profoundly conservative political and social implications. They felt that Nationalist party leaders should face up to the fundamental racial inequalities in Zanzibari society, adopt a more socialistic position, and offer concrete proposals for thorough-going social reform. Babu was also opposed to the party's long-standing practice of nominating candidates on a racial basis: in constituencies where the majority of Nationalist supporters were Arab or Asian, the party had nearly always nominated Arab or Asian candidates. He felt that it should demonstrate its commitment to fostering closer relations between the races by appointing Shirazi candidates in these areas.

Babu had proposed these changes at a pre-election meeting of Nationalist leaders held in May 1963, but the bulk of the party's executive committee had felt that it was politically inexpedient to introduce novel and unfamiliar politics in the midst of a critical election campaign. The rejection of the radicals' suggestions led to Babu's resignation and the formation of Umma. Umma was unable to attract popular support in the brief time remaining before the election and therefore did not even nominate candidates of its own. Its significance was in its ability, after the election, to act as a revolutionary rallying point for a wide range of anti-Nationalist party sentiment.[15]

Umma's initial support came from disaffected radical elements within the Nationalist party organization. Several Shirazi members of the party's executive committee, virtually the entire youth movement, and a large number of trade union leaders who had been affiliated with the party structure, shifted to Umma and, almost immediately, began to participate in its bitter attacks on the coalition government. During the months following the election, Umma was also successful in attracting radical segments of the Afro-Shirazi party. Several members of the Afro-Shirazi executive, a large number of the party's most influential journalists, and a large proportion of its affiliated trade union leadership became actively involved with Umma. Under Babu's leadership, Umma was able to achieve a high degree of organizational unity and ideological discipline among these inchoate elements. By sponsoring a network of affiliated groups of its own such as a new trade union movement and a national journalists' organization, Umma created the appearance that it was the spearhead of a broad popular front with widespread organizational and popular support. Umma and its affiliates launched a massive propaganda campaign condemning the Nationalist party as the political tool of the feudal, landowning class. The basic thrust of their argument was that the coalition represented a narrow bourgeois stratum, that its multiracial sentiments were a deceptive façade designed to conceal social inequalities, and that revolutionary action was the sole method which could achieve social progress. In its ability to harass the government, to dramatize the opposition cause, and to maintain a sense of political enthusiasm among the African population, Umma was incomparably more effective than the Afro-Shirazi party which had been so demoralized by electoral defeat that many of its top leaders were apathetic.

Umma, however, was unable to gain the full confidence of the vast majority of Afro-Shirazi leaders and supporters. Most Afro-Shirazi members were deeply distrustful of a new party composed predominantly of persons who had, until recently, been high-ranking leaders of their chief rival. Moreover, despite the two parties' common opposition to the coalition government, there were marked ideological differences between them. Umma articulated its sentiments in the stylized jargon of doctrinaire Marxist ideology; its leaders preferred to depict

[15] Much of the following material in this essay has been based upon a series of interviews conducted with Zanzibaris in Dar es Salaam during the summer of 1965.

the problems of Zanzibari society in class, rather than racial, terms and proposed violent change as the only solution to such divisions. The Afro-Shirazi party had never identified itself with a fixed ideological posture. As a protest movement of the African population, its political position had usually consisted of a straightforward enumeration of the socio-economic hardships suffered by Africans. Though radical in outlook, Afro-Shirazi leaders approached social reform as a matter of working for governmental acceptance of specific measures to alleviate the deprivations suffered by the African community. Perhaps most important, there were significant ethnic differences between Umma and the Afro-Shirazis. Most Umma leaders were not African, and, although several Shirazis had resigned from the Nationalist party to join it, Umma's ethnic composition clearly reflected its origin as a splinter group from an Arab-dominated organization. Many Afro-Shirazi leaders feared that if Umma were to obtain political power, Africans would continue to experience difficulty in gaining access to top governmental positions.

The Afro-Shirazi party had emerged from the July election more demoralized and disunited than ever and was almost wholly unable to act as an effective opposition. In addition to long-standing ethnic tensions, the party was wracked by mutual recriminations over responsibility for the electoral defeat and by deep divisions over policy toward the coalition government. At least three separate bodies of opinion could be discerned. One group of Afro-Shirazi parliamentary leaders felt that the party should function as a loyal and responsible opposition and should avoid giving the government any justification for imposing repressive controls over its political activity. They felt that a period of respite would give the party an opportunity to reorganize and would enable the nearby mainland African countries to exercise diplomatic pressure in its favor. A second group of leaders felt that the party should engage in intensive efforts to persuade the government to form a national three-party coalition and that it should employ the party's vast popular support as a political weapon by organizing legal forms of political protest such as street demonstrations, strikes, and boycotts. This group broke openly with the party's top leadership and, calling itself the "Progressives," formed an autonomous opposition within the party structure. A third group favored close co-operation with Umma and believed that the Afro-Shirazis' only hope of eventual success lay in outright revolutionary activity. These disagreements virtually paralyzed the party and, until the revolution, most of the party's attention was devoted to efforts to resolve internal difficulties. Since no common policy could be agreed upon, the party became, by default, a mild parliamentary opposition.

In response to the revolutionary threat represented by Umma, the Nationalist-People's party coalition undertook a series of measures designed to stabilize its political position and to insure a maximum degree of social control. It imposed severe limitations on the activities of all opposition leaders, drastically curtailing their right to travel outside Zanzibar, began to recruit politically loyal Arabs into strategically important positions in the bureaucracy, and began a major reorganization of the Zanzibar police. Among the government's most authoritarian acts was the passage of legislation enabling it to exercise complete regulatory authority over any opposition group. The Registration of Societies Ordinance, passed just before independence, authorized the Minister of Internal Affairs, at his own discretion, to ban any organization he considered inimical to "peace, order and good government." This law was so broadly and vaguely worded that it could easily have been applied to a peaceful opposition such as the Afro-Shirazi party had become, as well as to a subversive organization such as Umma. Its effect was probably to weaken, rather than strengthen, the government's stability since it undermined the position of those Afro-Shirazi leaders who were urging restraint and lent credence to the arguments of the revolutionary elements.

The government also sought to reorganize the Zanzibar police but this action, as well, led to a situation of short-term weakness. The rank and file of the Zanzibar police was filled largely by mainland Africans who had been recruited by British authorities in Kenya, Tanganyika, and Nyasaland. Nationalist party leaders feared that these police were so sympathetic to the Afro-Shirazi party that they could not be relied upon if a political crisis were to occur. The Ministry of Internal Affairs initiated a program of repatriating the mainland police to their countries of origin and began to replace them with Arabs, Asians, or carefully screened Shirazis known to be loyal to the government. The flaw in this policy was that the mainland African police represented the most skilled and experienced element in the police force while the new recruits could, at best, be hastily and inadequately trained. Moreover, the repatriation program led to widespread demoralization of the police, since many African policemen who remained were led to feel insecure about their positions. The hasty induction of inexperienced recruits and the sense of political resentment generated by the repatriation program severely reduced both the will and the ability of the Zanzibar police to maintain social control. As has already been shown, the single most important factor in the success of the revolutionary army was the ineffectuality and swift collapse of police resistance.

It may well be argued that, in the few months before the revolution, the Zanzibari government was pursuing a suicidal policy. On the one hand it unequivocally refused to form a national coalition which would include Afro-Shirazi leaders and, possibly, reduce the political tension in the country. Instead the governing coalition was implementing repressive measures which made violent protest the only course of action open to opposition groups. At the same time, however, its policy toward the police critically reduced the will and the ability of its security forces to cope with the dangerously unstable political situation that its restrictive legislation had created.

Independence and Revolution: 1963–64

When independence occurred, in early December 1963, the government of Zanzibar exhibited a number of symptoms of extreme weakness and fragility. A major source of the weakness of the regime was the contemporary Arab elite's lack of autonomous mechanisms of political control. When Arabs had first established their political supremacy in Zanzibar, it was on the basis of absolute military and technological supremacy over the African population and upon an ability to suppress any resistance by coercive means. During the seven decades of British protection—when Great Britain could be depended upon to furnish ultimate military sanctions for Arab rule—the character of the Arab oligarchy had, however, undergone a profound transformation: The militarily powerful, baronial aristocracy lost its dominance to an urbanized intellectual elite composed primarily of civil servants, journalists, and parliamentary politicians. Whereas Arab dominance in the past had rested upon decisively superior armed force, it now depended upon the organizational and tactical skills of Nationalist party leadership and upon the voluntary acquiescence of a large proportion of the African population.

However, the split in the Nationalist party described earlier had gravely weakened the principal basis of Arab political dominance; the defecting group included the party's most skilled strategists and tacticians. Babu himself had universally been recognized as the organizational genius of Zanzibari politics; he was often called the chief architect of the Nationalists' electoral victories. Several other defectors had also been key figures in the smooth functioning of the Nationalists' party apparatus. Moreover, the collective resignation of the radical group left the party largely in the hands of a conservative "old guard" element which was far less adept at the intricate maneuverings of competitive agitational politics. This group was composed largely of rural Arab landowners and leaders of the Arab community in Pemba. Its members were insular in their outlook, most being fully convinced that simple repressive measures, unalloyed by any concessions to the African community, would enable the Nationalist party to remain in power. The old guard's control over the party during the six months before the revolution was so great that even Ali Muhsin, the Nationalists' most respected and hitherto most influential leader, was unable to persuade the party's executive committee of the strategic need for a more progressive attitude. The high degree of rigidity in the government's pre-independence position, its inability to develop a flexible policy which might accommodate some African demands until power could be consolidated, and the coalition parties' failure to engage in effective counter-revolutionary propaganda or organizational activities could all, in large measure, be attributed to the dramatic change in the quality and outlook of Nationalist party leadership after the formation of Umma.

The defection of the Nationalists' radical element also did considerable damage to the party's credibility among its African supporters. Many Shirazis had been willing to affiliate with the party on the grounds that it contained an influential group of leaders committed to fundamental social change in the country. Once the radical group had resigned and unchallenged power within the party had been assumed by conservative Arab leaders, many Shirazi members began to entertain serious doubts about the reality of their party's declared commitment to radical social reform.

On their part, Nationalist party leaders reinforced the mounting suspicion by an open willingness to act in the narrow interests of the Arab oligarchy during the final months of the coalition regime. This was particularly evident in the government's agricultural and land policy. As an independence gift, Great Britain had offered Zanzibar a large sum of money with which to modernize the agricultural economy. The Minister of Agriculture, an Arab, then proposed to establish a land bank which would offer loans to farmers who agreed to diversify their crops in accordance with government recommendations. The politically relevant feature of the land bank proposal was that the amount of the loan for which any farmer would be eligible was to be proportional to the size of his farm, since land was to be offered as collateral for borrowed funds. This meant that large Arab landowners would receive the overwhelming share of the British gift while African farmers, whose farms were mostly of peasant size or communally owned, would receive very little assistance. When the Nationalist-People's party government introduced legislation to establish the land bank in the late fall of 1963, Afro-Shirazi leaders pointed out the racially discriminatory features of the proposal. They argued that fundamental land reform should take precedence over crop diversification and that the money should be used first to bring about a more equalitarian distribution of agricultural land in the country. The government's spokesmen responded that the Afro-Shirazi party's objections were racially motivated and thus inimical to the political stability of the society. There was also a veiled threat that the Afro-Shirazis' opposition to the land bank would be considered sufficient reason for suppression of the party under the Registration of Societies Ordinance. By forcing the land bank program through the Assembly without considering the merits of the Afro-Shirazi spokesmen's position, the coalition ministers not only dispelled any lingering illusion about the possibility that they might undertake social reform voluntarily, but demonstrated the utter futility of parliamentary opposition.

Economic depression also impaired the viability of the Nationalist-People's party regime. Since the early 1950's, Zanzibar's economy had been in a state of chronic stagnation due to falling world clove prices. India and Indonesia, the principal markets for cloves, were experiencing critical foreign exchange difficulties and had sharply reduced clove imports in order to conserve their supplies of hard currency. This situation, together with stiffened competition from new clove producers, caused a precipitous drop in the price of cloves. Since the Zanzibari government's revenue was drawn largely from an export duty on cloves, this condition had resulted in chronic budget deficits.

In order to place the administration on a sound financial basis the coalition parties began to cut down on government services; they closed schools, discharged teachers, reduced hospital facilities, and cut back welfare programs. Although these measures were necessitated by declining government revenue and would have had to be introduced eventually in order to avoid complete bankruptcy, they came at a time when African fears of governmental policy had already been aroused. Against the background of successive election campaigns in which the Afro-Shirazi party had predicted that an Arab government would place the African population in a condition of permanent misery and inferiority, the retrenchment of social services added enormously to the atmosphere of desperation within the African community.

The government's greatest physical weakness was the indefensible location of its capital. Zanzibar Town is situated on a small triangular peninsula on the western coast of Zanzibar Island. The central locus of all governmental activity was at the outer extremity of this peninsula in an area called Stonetown. All the major office buildings, the ministerial residences, and the Sultan's palace were located in the Stonetown area. A sprawling African slum called Ngambo stretched across the peninsula between Stonetown and the main portion of Zanzibar island. Both Ngambo and the adjacent rural areas of the island contained overwhelming majorities of Afro-Shirazi supporters. Thus, the government was physically isolated from its nearest substantial body of popular support, a community of Tumbatu Shirazis resident on the remote northern peninsula of Zanzibar Island. With the Nationalist party's trade union movement thrown into disruption by the resignation of its leadership to support Umma, and without a defense agreement with Great Britain or any of the mainland countries, the coalition parties could rally no one to their cause once an outbreak of violence had begun.

The Nationalist party had sought to compensate for this weakness by distributing arms to Arab plantation owners and shopkeepers in the rural areas of the island nearest the town. These people, however, were isolated from one another, were completely enclosed within areas of massive Afro-Shirazi support, and were not given even rudimentary training in how to respond to an emergency situation. As a result, the rural Arabs were not only unable to group together for a defense of the Sultan's regime, but were completely unable even to defend themselves when the revolutionary army struck. Indeed, precisely because rural Arabs were known to possess arms and, therefore, represented a potential counter-revolutionary threat, they became the principal target of Okello's forces during the week after the seizure of power and, as a group, suffered the heaviest death toll of any segment of the population.

The distribution of the government's principal defenses displayed an additional aspect of geopolitical weakness. The two major police stations and the Zanzibari radio station were located in the African area of Zanzibar Town. Once the Ziwani armory had been captured and the police station at Mtoni placed under siege, the Stonetown area was defenseless. Since the radio transmitter was also in revolutionary hands, government officials were unable to communicate with their supporters either on Zanzibar Island or in Pemba.

Very little is known with certainty of what went on within the government of Zanzibar on the morning of the revolution. Apparently, the government ministers spent the early hours of Sunday morning in vain efforts to mount a counter-revolutionary strategy. It has been reported, though not confirmed, that there were appeals to the British and American governments for military assistance. If so, these were obviously declined, most probably for reasons embedded in the complexities of international politics. It has also been reported that considerable thought was given to fleeing to Pemba where the majority of the population was felt to be loyal to the Sultan and the Nationalist party regime, where local police detachments were still intact, and from where it might be possible to launch a counter-revolutionary assault. The principal reason generally offered for the rejection of this idea was the fear that nearby mainland African governments would come to the immediate and forceful assistance of an embattled revolutionary regime on Zanzibar Island. In fact, officials of the old regime probably believed that mainland African countries were already deeply involved in the revolution. Their knowledge of an Afro-Shirazi plot in collusion with mainland African political forces has been fairly well confirmed, and they might simply have felt that they had been misinformed as to its exact date. It was virtually impossible for Nationalist party leaders to have known that Okello's plot was a separate one, organized independently of the Afro-Shirazi party and, at least initially, unsupported by mainland countries.

It was of decisive importance to the events following the revolution that Okello's army was not tied to either of the opposition parties. This meant that the immediate seizure of power did not result in a clear and unambiguous transfer of authority to either the Afro-Shirazi party or Umma. Initially at least, political power was held exclusively by Okello. His decision to establish a Revolutionary Council composed of leaders of both the former opposition parties accounts for the fact that Umma, though a new party and one conspicuously lacking in popular support, formed an important part of the post-revolutionary government.

Okello's decision to include Umma leaders in the Revolutionary Council has been the subject of considerable speculation. Inasmuch as Okello himself has not explained his decision in *Revolution in Zanzibar*, the reasons can only be surmised. The basic factor was probably the same as had prompted his determination to keep the revolutionary army a secret from the Afro-Shirazi party: a strong sense of disillusionment with the Afro-Shirazi leadership. There is little doubt that Okello had for some time thought of the Afro-Shirazi leaders as inept and ineffectual. In the weeks before the coup, the party had become more paralyzed than ever by petty internal bickering. In contrast, Umma presented a picture of organizational discipline and ideological unity. Inclusion of Umma in the Council may thus have been seen as a kind of guarantee that the social objectives of the revolution would not be corrupted or compromised by organizational vacillation.

However, in fact, the differences between Umma and the Afro-Shirazi party were so great that Umma has been able to play a major, if not decisive, role in determining the policies of the Revolutionary Council. Thus, in the Council's deliberations, Umma leaders who possessed a clear-cut ideology and a strong collective viewpoint have had an important advantage over the more disunited and desultory Afro-Shirazi leadership. Umma leaders have also had the advantage that the radical social progress which they advocate seems far more adapted to rapid social reconstruction than the more moderate outlook of the Afro-Shirazi group. Moreover, the very success of the revolution was, in a sense, a final blow to the dwindling status of political moderation and constituted a powerful validation of the revolutionary viewpoint which Umma had consistently espoused.

The radicalism of the post-revolutionary government has manifested itself in a variety of ways—in the nationalization of land and many of the country's largest business firms, in the extent of administrative control imposed over the entire economic life of the society, in the closeness of foreign policy ties with Eastern bloc countries and Communist China, and in the attempt to infuse the population with militantly Marxist political attitudes. These policies are, in part, the product of Umma's influence in the Revolutionary Council, but they are also a result of the immoderate and unrestrained character of political conflict during the previous decade. Ten years of intensely competitive partisan politics, interrupted at several points by widespread racial violence, had created a legacy of extreme bitterness and animosity. Leaders of all political parties were determined to pursue victory to its ultimate conclusion. Had the Nationalist-People's party coalition remained in power, there is little doubt that it would have created an authoritarian police state, with social and economic policies favoring the Arab elite. When Umma and Afro-Shirazi leaders gained power, they were determined to change the character of the society in the shortest possible time. Revolutionary ideas originating in Cuba and China were less a determinant than a rationale for this policy.

Since 1964, popular support for the revolution and for the radical policies of the Revolutionary Council has been extremely irregular, both in the regions and among the various racial communities in the society. The new regime's greatest acceptance comes, not unexpectedly, from those groups which had always supported the Afro-Shirazi party—mainland Africans and the vast majority of Hadimu Shirazis. Although the new government's economic programs have failed to stem Zanzibar's economic recession, the Council has, by redistributing land and elite positions among the different races, been able to bring about substantial social restratification. Mainlanders and Hadimu Shirazis have been the primary beneficiaries of these measures and many have experienced a markedly improved standard of living due to the Council's policy of awarding confiscated Arab plantations to African settler-farmers and to its deliberate recruitment of Africans into the highest positions in the civil service. As a result of the dramatic status reversal between these two African communities and the former Arab and Asian elites, there is almost unanimous support for the new government in the African quarter of Zanzibar Town and in the nearby rural areas.

But the Revolutionary Council's popular base is far less secure among Tumbatu and Pemba Shirazis, especially among those who were strong supporters of the Nationalist or People's parties. The present political attitude of these communities is one of latent discontent. Although they were not involved in the actual fighting during the revolution, and although, as agricultural and fishing communities, their day-to-day lives have not been seriously affected by the political changes which have occurred, Pemba and Tumbatu Shirazis have indicated an undercurrent of deep resentment at the violent destruction of the old regime. This resentment has expressed itself primarily in the form of tacit noncooperation or subdued hostility. Open resistance has been extremely rare but, in Pemba, there have been sporadic acts of limited disobedience. Villagers in areas where the Nationalist party was strong have, on occasion, refused to participate in self-help schemes sponsored by the government. In these areas, the Revolutionary Council has been compelled to resort to coercive techniques to achieve popular compliance.

The Asian and Arab communities have suffered the heaviest losses from the revolution and, as a result, their support for the new regime is the most limited of all the society's racial groups. The Asian community's loss has been primarily economic. (Although a substantial number of Asians were beaten or molested during the revolution, the number killed was small and the vast majority of Asians were physically undisturbed.) The community's economic misfortune has assumed several forms. The immediate destruction or theft of Asian property was considerable as many Asian shops, stores, and homes were looted before the government could restore order. After the revolution, several hundred Asian civil servants were discharged as part of the Revolutionary Council's policy of Africanizing the bureaucracy and most of these have found no other work. The government's decision to establish quasi-monopolistic state enterprises in basic sectors of the economy such as import and export and the distribution and marketing of staple goods, together with the outright nationalization of the largest retail and industrial firms, has also deprived Asians of their most remunerative sources of income and radically reduced the wealth of the community.

Despite these losses, Asians have, to a certain extent, been able to cushion the shock of the revolution. Those who have retained their governmental positions or businesses operate an *ad hoc* welfare system to care for impoverished communal brethren. The extended family structure of the Asian community has also functioned as a sort of wel-

fare agency and has absorbed countless numbers of jobless and unemployed. Many Asians have been able to emigrate from Zanzibar, to
join family businesses or to re-establish professional careers in mainland East Africa, in Britain, or in India and Pakistan. Thus, although
most Asian families have suffered severe economic adversity, few have
been reduced to absolute penury, and the community as a whole has
been able to withstand its losses without widespread destitution or
despair.

The Asian community in Zanzibar today occupies a peculiar and
complex position in the political system. Asian refugees report that
below-the-surface hostility to the revolution is considerable but partly
because of the community's residence in the center of Zanzibar Town,
where the revolutionary regime is able to exercise its most effective
forms of social control, and partly because of the Asian community's
tradition of political noninvolvement, this resentment remains unex-
pressed and unrevealed. Most Asians adopt a watch-and-wait attitude,
hoping that international pressure may compel the Revolutionary
Council to mitigate the extreme severity of its economic and racial
policies.

For the Arab community, the revolution has been a physical catastrophe. The exact number of Arabs who were killed is unknown, but
conservative estimates indicate that the figure is probably well over
5,000. Immediately after the revolution, the Revolutionary Council instituted a forcible repatriation program and shipped many hundreds
of Arab families by dhow to port cities on the Arabian peninsula.
Large numbers of Arabs also fled from Zanzibar on their own, either
to the East African mainland or to the Middle East where, as political
refugees, they constitute a stateless population. The total number of
Arabs who have been killed or expelled, or have fled the country is
thus well over 10,000 –more than one-fifth of the Arab population.
Moreover, this figure includes virtually the entire Arab political, economic, and intellectual elite. The fact is that the Arab community as
such has virtually ceased to exist in Zanzibar. Those who remain have,
for the most part, been completely stripped of their homes, farms, and
sources of employment. They exist as a pariah group, on the sufferance
of racial communities who hate them, and live on prostitution, beg-
gary, and charity. Leaderless and without organization or other means
of political expression, they are atomized and apathetic. Though seething with resentment at the new era, they are powerless to affect their
political condition.

The most debated issue concerning the Zanzibari revolution is
whether it was essentially an expression of racial or class protest. In
a society whose various racial communities are socio-economically dif-

ferentiated, this question cannot be answered with precision. The most fundamental political characteristic of such a society is that racial and class antagonisms often become synonymous and indistinguishable since the various racial groups are also opposed as rival economic strata. This was the case in pre-revolutionary Zanzibar. Each racial and ethnic community had economic interests which differed appreciably from those of the others. Economic and ethnic differences were thus mutually reenforcing dimensions of political conflict.

On the purely subjective level, however, most Zanzibaris perceived the pattern of political conflict primarily in communal rather than in economic terms. For Africans and Arabs alike, the emotive stimulus of solidarity and the symbolic ingredient of self-identification were to the ethnic community rather tnan to the economic class. This was apparent not only in the competitive partisan propaganda but in the private attitudes of party leaders and followers. Most Arabs were not members of the established political elite but the Arab community was virtually unanimous in its support for the Nationalist party because of its identification as an "Arab" organization. In the case of the African community, economic subordination generated a sense of collective grievance against Arabs, but, once established, that grievance came to be defined almost entirely in racial terms. "The Arabs have oppressed us Africans," or a close variation on this theme was a far more common African description of the political and economic structure of Zanzibari society than one phrased in class categories. Thus, to the extent that the basic character of a political conflict can be defined in terms of the subjective perceptions of its participants, the Zanzibari revolution was primarily a racial phenomenon.

Merger with Tanganyika

In late April 1964, Zanzibar merged with Tanganyika and became, in formal constitutional terms, an integral part of the United Republic of Tanzania. The reasons for the merger were highly complex. As a tiny isolated country, Zanzibar would have experienced considerable difficulty in maintaining its economic and political viability. By merging with a large and highly sympathetic neighbor, Zanzibar would help insure the security of the revolution and would benefit from Tanganyika's greater economic resources. Moreover, the Afro-Shirazi party had always had close ties with the Tanganyika African National Union and many Afro-Shirazi officials undoubtedly saw in this relationship an opportunity to use the Tanganyika Union's influence to strengthen their own position in the Revolutionary Council. The most frequently stated reason for the merger was the presumed desire on the part of Tanganyika's leaders to exercise a moderating and restraining influence within Zanzibar. Ironically, the merger has had exactly the opposite effect. A large number of moderate Afro-Shirazi leaders, several of whom had begun to reestablish their influence in the months following the revolution, left Zanzibar to take up positions in the United Republic capital at Dar es Salaam. Their departure left the Revolutionary Council more firmly than ever in control of its radical wing.

Although the constitution of the United Republic calls for a substantial degree of political integration of the two countries, Zanzibar continues to practice considerable independence in both domestic and foreign affairs. Its budgetary arrangements are entirely separate from those of Tanganyika and its economic policies are decided upon with a minimum of consultation with the United Republic government. Zanzibar maintains separate ministerial and bureaucratic structures for a whole range of government services—health, education, agriculture, and commerce and trade. Perhaps most important, Zanzibar possesses an entirely separate system of defense. Its army, formally organized with the help of Chinese advisers after the revolution, is completely independent of United Republic control and even exercises autonomy with respect to such matters as equipment, foreign advisors, and political education

The prospects for a closer integration of Zanzibar and Tanganyika appear slim. Tanganyika's political leaders are heavily preoccupied with their own country's problems of development and modernization and are, for this reason, content to allow the present *modus vivendi* to continue. Moreover the leadership of Zanzibar's Revolutionary Council is determined to complete its political revolution unfettered by outside restraints.

THE CONGO IN REVOLT
1960–1964

– – – Province boundaries 1960

······· Boundaries established
after 1960

KUMU Ethnic groups
prominent in rebellion

Approximate maximum extent
of rebel advance

0   300 Kilometers

0   300 Miles

REBELLION AND THE CONGO

M. CRAWFORD YOUNG

Insurrection engulfed the Congo (Kinshasa)[1] in 1964. The tides of rebellion swept away central authority in five provinces out of twenty-one, and in portions of eight more. At high-water mark in August 1964, the complete collapse of the Kinshasa regime appeared a real possibility. Rebel success created the image of unified purpose and revolutionary promise. Only in its subsequent phases of decay and disintegration did the basic characteristics of rebellion become fully evident: a dramatic lack of cohesion, a disparity in purpose and perception, and a remarkable range of phenomena incorporated into the syndrome of insurrection.

The object of this essay is to examine the rebellion from 1964 to 1967 for those dimensions which place it in comparative perspective. In doing so, one immediately encounters the fundamental fact that the Congolese rebellion was not a single movement, but a series of parallel, partly overlapping dramas, which do not have one history, but several.[2]

[1] In 1966 and 1967, the place names of a number of Congolese cities were altered. In this essay, we have exclusively used the current names. The changes are as follows: Kinshasa (ex-Léopoldville); Kisangani (ex-Stanleyville); Lubumbashi (ex-Elisabethville); Bandundu (ex-Banningville); Mbandaka (ex-Coquilhatville); Isiro (ex-Paulis); Kalemie (ex-Albertville); and Lukasi (ex-Jadotville).

Another alteration since the rebellion has been the consolidation to eight of the twenty-one provinces existing in 1964–65; in this essay, we retain the twenty-one as labels of convenience. In addition to the sources cited this study is based upon interviews in Jan. 1965 in Kisangani and Kinshasa and June 1967 in Kalemie, Mbuji-Mayi, and Kinshasa.

[2] This is reflected in the fact that the most valuable sources to date all treat either one geographic zone, or several in sequence. The most ambitious study is Benoit Verhaegen, *Rébellions au Congo*, I (Brussels, 1966); a second volume is forthcoming. Other valuable accounts include J. Beys, P. N. Gendebien, and

Therefore, as a preamble, a highly compressed synopsis of the rise and fall of the rebellion will be offered to enable the reader to "place" the analysis which follows. Subsequently, we will consider the accumulation of an insurrectional potential, the stratification of values and participation, patterns and limits of diffusion, exercise of powers in zones under rebel control, and the process of disintegration.

Rebellion: A Brief Summary

In the Congo, barely perceptible symptoms of rebellion first appeared in mid-1963, at the crest of a wave of relative euphoria: the country had been reunited; it seemed to have survived the disastrous events of 1960. Economic upsurge seemed to be accompanying a slow but steady improvement in Congolese administration. Not the least of the paradoxes to follow was the fact that the first violence appeared in Kwilu, the province which had been widely advertised as a "pilot province" and a local incarnation of the recovery process.[3] Actually, in spite of the smiling surface of events, two important developments were already at work which were to help to precipitate insurrection. One was the declining ability of the Adoula government to absorb or provide outlets for opposition. Thus, though paralyzed by the utter fragmentation of political groupings, Parliament had provided a forum for the expression of opposition and a reasonable guarantee against arrest through parliamentary immunity. The decision, in September 1963, to adjourn Parliament indefinitely was therefore an important encouragement to rupture. The second development was the prospec-

---

Benoit Verhaegen, *Congo 1963* (Brussels, 1964); J. Gérard Libois and Jean van Lierde, *Congo 1964* (Brussels, 1965); *Congo 1965* (Brussels, 1966); *Congo 1966* (Brussels, 1967); Renée Fox, Willy de Craemer, and Jean-Marie Ribeaucourt, "La deuxième Indépendance—Étude d'un cas: La rébellion au Kwilu," *Études Congolaises*, VIII (Jan.-Feb. 1965), 1-35; Crawford Young, "The Congo Rebellion," *Africa Report*, X (Apr. 1965), 6-11; Charles W. Anderson, Fred R. von der Mehden, and Crawford Young, *Issues of Political Development* (Englewood Cliffs, N.J., 1967), 120-39; Thomas Turner, "Ethnicity and the Congo Rebellions" (unpublished seminar paper, University of Wisconsin, 1968). Journalistic accounts include Paul Masson, *La Bataille pour Bukavu* (Brussels, 1965); Jean Kestergat, *Congo Congo* (Paris, 1965); Georges de Bosschere, *Rescapés de Watsa* (Brussels, 1966); David Reed, *111 Days in Stanleyville* (New York, 1965).

[3] For example, "Nearly all the new provinces now have functioning institutions. Some, like Kwilu . . . operate with impressive effectiveness," in Crawford Young, "The Congo's Six Provinces Become Twenty-One," *Africa Report*, VIII (Oct. 1963), 13. See also J. C. Williame, "Les Provinces du Congo: I Kwilu-Luluabourg-Nord Katanga-Ubangi," *Cahiers Economiques et Sociaux* (May 1964), 17-50.

tive withdrawal of United Nations forces by June 1964, a factor to which we shall return later.

The second half of 1963 saw two groups taking a dissident position. The first was the result of the efforts of Pierre Mulele, who had in July 1963 returned to the Congo after more than two years abroad, spent in part in China and Eastern Europe. Immediately upon his return he had gone to his home province of Kwilu and there begun the organization of a rural maquis. And at the beginning of October, a number of political figures who had been associated with the Lumumbist alliance in 1960, and the Kisangani Gizenga government in 1960–61, crossed the river to Brazzaville, where a *Conseil National de Libération* was proclaimed. The Mulele maquis and the *Conseil* were entirely separate efforts, although some *Conseil* elements subsequently claimed a link with Mulele.

The first violent incidents occurred in January 1964, with Mulelist insurgents attacking government outposts, mission stations, and, in some cases, palm oil mills and other company installations. By the end of January, large parts of Idiofa and Gungu territories were under siege. On 5 February, the chief of staff of the *Armée Nationale Congolaise*, Colonel Eugene Eleya, was ambushed and killed by a poisoned arrow. Army reinforcements were rushed to Kwilu; they succeeded in reopening the roads, and holding the towns of Gungu and Idiofa. By April 1964, the army had clearly gained the upper hand. But despite the complete lack of modern arms for Mulelist insurgents, and lack of access to external supplies, many months passed before the army was able to isolate the partisan bands and administrative reoccupation could occur.

As for the *Conseil*, it had initially concentrated its hopes on a coup in the capital and on external diplomatic and material support. Solicitations were made to radical African governments and to the Soviet Union and China; some modest financial support was forthcoming with a more abundant supply of advice. A coup in November 1963 narrowly failed; for a short time Sûreté head Victor Nendaka and army commander General Joseph Mobutu were captured. By the end of 1963, a series of camps had been established in Congo (Brazzaville), where ideological instruction and rudimentary military training were given primarily to residents from Kinshasa, Kwilu, and the Lac Léopold II area.[4] A campaign of urban terrorism in Kinshasa was initiated in

[4] For a fascinating account of the nature of the instruction at the camps, see the document *Les Cahiers de Gamboma* (Brussels, 1965). These are based upon the notebooks of a participant and clearly demonstrate the influence of a Marxist-Leninist-Maoist analysis of Congolese society and the requirements for revolutionary change.

1964 and reached a peak in May. The attacks consisted mainly of plastic bombings of public places carried out by commandos based in Brazzaville. But the bombings were insufficient in scale or duration to have a major impact. The last armed incursion from the Brazzaville base occurred in July 1964, when a small group from one of the Gamboma complex of insurgent camps seized the small towns of Bolobo, Kwamouth, and Mushie. The invasion lasted only six days; this band had disappeared by the time military reinforcements arrived.

Meanwhile, insurrection was making spectacular progress in the eastern Congo. Gaston Soumialot, in 1960 Lumumba's lieutenant for the Maniema area, in February 1964 arrived in Bujumbura to establish a *Conseil* office. He had traveled widely in the area between Kalemie (North Katanga) and Kisangani, had served as a provincial minister in the Kivu-Maniema government of Adrien Omari in 1961, and had spun a network of political relationships throughout this zone. His initial breakthrough came in linking to the broader cause of rebellion a local chieftaincy dispute among the Fulero, a small but strategically situated ethnic group living in the Ruzizi plain, along the Burundi frontier, and in the surrounding mountains. The first armed clashes in the eastern Congo occurred in April 1964. However, the crucial event was the seizure on 17 May of the town of Uvira. This opened the way to the Burundi border, and became a point of diffusion for insurgent initiatives. Fizi, at the heart of Bembe country, was captured ten days later, the Bembe rallying as an ethnic community to the rebellion. At the same time, two army battalions were routed by rural insurgents equipped with only a handful of firearms.

North Katanga was the next focus for dissidence. The backdrop for insurrection in Kalemie, then the North Katangan provincial capital, was a factional dispute within the provincial government between Jason Sendwe and Prosper Mwanga Ilunga. Both had been Balubakat (the dominant political party in the North) leaders in 1960, and were identified with the Luba resistance to the Tshombe regime in Katanga from 1960 to 1962. However, in late 1962 a split had developed which, by 1966, dominated all North Katangan political life. Sendwe had the support of the central government, but by May 1964 he led a virtually paralyzed provincial administration. In an atmosphere of total demoralization, an uprising led by Balubakat "youth" occurred on 27 May, fomented by a small group of young Luban leaders who had established liaison with Soumialot in Bujumbura. The national army units initially remained inactive, expecting the "youth" to be joined by a rebel force from the exterior. However, two days later, when the promised rebel army failed to appear and instigators of the uprising were unable to direct it, the army suddenly turned on the insurgents.

A restored Sendwe government undertook a pitiless repression in the three weeks that followed. On 18 June, a small rebel column under the command of General Nicolas Olenga arrived from Fizi. The national army units simply evaporated: the bulk of the government troops had commandeered a train the evening before, and ordered three European railwaymen to conduct them to safety.

At this time, the remainder of North Katanga proved a veritable suction pump, the vacuum created by the disappearance of government authority providing unanticipated opportunities for expansion. Baudouinville was captured by forty-five men on 19 July. (The rail line, after the flight of the army, was used by withdrawing Europeans and, finally, by members of the Congolese civil administration who feared assassination by insurgents.) Small insurgent bands followed up this initiative, establishing a superficial and ephemeral suzerainty over most of North Katanga during July. In this zone, the population remained passive and indifferent and the rebel bands were mostly drawn from outside North Katanga.[5]

Soumialot arrived in Kalemie on 28 June and briefly established an insurgent government claiming authority for the eastern Congo. However, by early July the center of gravity was shifting to the Lumumbist heartland in Maniema. The insurgent army, the *Armée Populaire de Libération*, which had first taken shape in the Uvira area in late May, coalesced in early July as a military force, faithfully replicating the structure and nomenclature of the national army. The popular army advanced along the old Zanzibari trade route from Fizi via Kabambare to Kasongo, which fell 15 July. Kindu was taken on 24 July, and the Lumumbist capital of Kisangani came under rebel control on 5 August. Thereafter, rebel columns fanned out in all directions, gorged with the armaments abandoned by the fleeing national army, vehicles confiscated from traders and companies, and money seized in the banks. During the six weeks which followed, all of Uele and Kibali-Ituri were overrun. One column following the north bank of the Congo River penetrated as far as Lisala, then the capital of the Middle Congo province, and another reached Boende, in Cuvette Centrale. Most of Sankuru was briefly overrun in September, and one group penetrated as far as Sentery in Lomami.

A major turning point occurred between 15 and 20 August, when General Olenga and a motorized column of six thousand men assaulted Bukavu. Government forces, reinforced by hastily remobilized Katangan gendarmes, held their ground, and the popular army suffered its first

[5] For a sensitive eyewitness account of the rebellion in North Katanga, see E. Lejeune, "Une page de l'histoire de la Révolution congolaise," *Remarques Africaines*, 245, 247, 249 (June, Aug., Sept. 1965).

serious reverse. The balance of force was tipped by the decision, made under duress at the last moment, of Mwami Alexandre Kabare, paramount chief of one section of Shi, to back the central government. Because of repeated conflicts with Kinshasa-supported provincial authorities, Kabare had contacts on the rebel side, and Olenga had had reason to hope for his support.[6] The Kabare chieftaincy lay athwart the approaches to Bukavu, and the Mwami's warriors decimated the insurgent invaders. An important central government redoubt along the eastern frontier, including portions of Central Kivu and North Kivu provinces, thus remained.

The zenith of rebel self-confidence was marked by the proclamation of 5 September of a revolutionary government in Kisangani under the leadership of Christophe Gbenye.[7] (Two short-lived rebel "governments" had preceded the arrival of Gbenye in Kisangani.) At the moment of its establishment, the revolutionary government derived continuous succor from its very success and the sense of triumphant momentum. But when the swollen rebel armies encountered a level of resistance with which they could not cope and began to fall back, the aura of invincibility soon vanished. Troubles crowded in upon the Kisangani leadership, and the gossamer fabric of unity was rent. Bitter conflict soon emerged between Gbenye, Soumialot, and Olenga.

By early September, the balance of force had clearly altered. The Tshombe government[8] had reinforced the demoralized national army with a few hundred white mercenaries, and most of the former Katangan gendarmerie had been integrated into the national army. Meanwhile, by late August, the rebel leaders had recognized that European residents in the towns under their control might be a shield against aerial bombardment. Subsequently, the concept of the "white umbrella" was enlarged to include using the nationals of countries aiding the central government, that is, Belgium and the United States, as negotiating counters to halt the columns closing in on Kisangani. The hostage policy led to the Belgian-American parachute operation at Kisangani and Isiro. "Dragon Rouge" began at dawn on 24 November in Kisangani, and on the same day the first national army-mercenary column

[6] Paul Masson gives an extremely thorough account in *La Bataille pour Bukavu.*

[7] Gbenye had been a major *Mouvement National Congolais*/Lumumba leader in Kisangani, and Lumumba entrusted to him the key post of Minister of the Interior. He played a crucial role in the 1960–61 Gizenga regime in Kisangani, then served for six months as Minister of the Interior under Adoula before rejoining the opposition.

[8] On 5 July 1964, President Kasavubu had invited Moise Tshombe to form a government to replace the cabinet of Cyrille Adoula, who had served as Prime Minister from 1961 to 1964.

reached Kisangani. Some two thousand hostages, mainly Belgian and American, were evacuated. Five days later the Belgian paratroopers were withdrawn from the Congo. However, Kindu had already been retaken on 6 November.

The loss of the capital of Lumumbism, the proclaimed seat of the revolutionary government, was a mortal blow to the rebellion in the eastern Congo. The three most important leaders asserting a pan-rebel authority—Gbenye, Soumialot, and Olenga—made their way into exile. The enormous indignation in many African states at the Belgian American intervention with "Dragon Rouge" was translated into a major flow of military supplies via the Sudan, Uganda, and Tanzania. But the loss of central direction, which had emerged in the period between July and November 1964, shriveled the rebellion into localized pockets. The perspectives of the insurgents had profoundly altered, prospects of success were nil, and demoralization was widespread. Nevertheless, in the zone around Kisangani, in Buta-Aketi, Bafwasende, Opala, and several other areas, rebel groups rendered key roads insecure for many months.[9] The most substantial zone of continued dissidence was the Fulero-Bembe pocket, located in inaccessible mountain terrain. This group (although marked by internal tensions between Fulero and Bembe) received more regular moral sustenance from external insurgent leadership cliques, and had access to arms supplies across Lake Tanganyika.

The bitter factionalism which characterized rebel exile politics, combined with military defeat on the terrain, led to a progressive loss of external credibility for the rebellion, and thereby to diminishing support. The final blow was the removal of the Tshombe stigma by Kinshasa. At the Organization of African Unity (OAU) summit conference in Accra in October 1965, President Kasavubu, fresh from his abrupt removal of Tshombe as Prime Minister, was welcomed back into grace. On 25 November, Kasavubu and Tshombe were both overthrown by General Mobutu, whose political style placed the Congo even closer to the mainstream of African diplomacy.[10] The consequence of this takeover was to compound the isolation, frustration, and internal tensions of diverse rebel exile groups.

---

[9] See, for example, the revealing map indicating zones of insecurity in December 1965, in "Rébellion: situation militaire," Études Congolaises, IX (Jan.-Feb. 1966), 51.

[10] Although Mobutu was initially suspect to many because of his close early American connections, he consciously embraced the language of African nationalism, continued to give facilities to Angolan insurgents, brought some radical young intellectuals into his entourage, and, over a period of time, established his regime as one with which both radical and moderate states could work.

Antecedents: Relative Deprivation

The history of the 1964 revolt is thus described in brief. More important than the chronological skeleton is the comparative significance of this drama, seen against the historical regularities in African protest movements and the contemporary patterns of post-independence politics. The first set of questions which arises relates to the emergence of an insurrectionary potential. One of the most striking aspects of the rebellion was the incredible speed of its transmission in responsive areas. Herbert Weiss ably summarized the situation:

> The speed with which the rural population rallied to the rebellion in virtually every region touched by it is probably the most important common denominator of all the local uprisings. It is inconceivable that such massive and rapid support was the result of laborious organization by a trained revolutionary elite. . . . Thus, the only alternative explanation is that a great degree of protest potential already existed and that the rebellion, insofar as it was organized at all, presented a framework within which this protest could express itself.[11]

One useful conceptual prism for examining the emergence of an insurrectionary potential is the sociological workhorse of relative deprivation.[12] The sense of grievance must have a reference point. Similarly consciousness of deprivation has meaning only in terms of some vision or recollection of non-deprivation. In the Congo, we may suggest that a sense of deprivation was not only widespread, but measured along three dimensions: in temporal space, in vertical social space between strata, and in horizontal communal space between ethnic groupings.

The time dimension had two aspects: the immediate recollection of a more ordered and materially prosperous life situation, and a

[11] Herbert Weiss, in *Congo 1964* (Princeton, 1965), xi-xii. Weiss is preparing a major study of the Kwilu phase of the rebellion, supported by a particularly rich documentation on the internal operation of the Mulelist movement.

[12] David Aberle formulates this sociological concept in a particularly useful form, defining it as "a deprivation that stems from change, actual or anticipated. It is where conditions decline by comparison with the present, and where shifts in the relative conditions of two groups occur, that the deprivation experience becomes significant for efforts at remedial action. . . ." "A Note on Relative Deprivation Theory as Applied to Millenarian and Other Cult Movements," in Sylvia L. Thrupp (ed.), *Millennial Dreams in Action* (The Hague, 1962), 209-10.

utopian vision of future well-being briefly generated by the explosion of terminal colonial nationalism. A paradoxical nostalgia for certain aspects of the colonial order was encountered with surprising frequency in the Congo in 1961–64. This was not, of course, a yearning for the myriad vexations of the authoritarian Belgian colonial system—for a restoration of European authority—but simply a faintly gilded memory of an epoch when jobs were more plentiful for the unskilled, when rural marketing mechanisms worked reliably, when roads were kept in good repair, and when local dispensaries had possessed both personnel and medical supplies. Compounding the disappointments of the present was the seismic effect of the electoral promises of 1960. Consider, for example, the following campaign poster widely distributed by the party dominant in Kwilu, the *Parti Solidaire Africain:*

1. Complete elimination of unemployment and work for all.
2. Expansion of school facilities, especially in rural areas. Elimination of all school fees for primary and secondary schools.
3. Salary raises for everybody.
4. Improvement of housing of rural areas.
5. Free medical care for all non-wage earners.[13]

Fatuous as these pledges were, they were outstripped in apocalyptic content by the rhetoric employed at local election meetings. Mechanization of peasant agriculture, price rises for peasant crops, a style of life modeled on that of the Belgian rulers—all of these aims were said to be within reach in the *anno mirabilis* of 1960.

In the best of circumstances, a sense of disappointment would have been inevitable. Independence brought the worst of circumstances to most rural and many urban areas. Except for the poles of relative prosperity in the Kinshasa-Lower Congo and Southern Katanga areas, commercial networks shriveled and the embryonic welfare apparatus of the terminal colonial state atrophied. Diminished well-being opened an enormous chasm between promise and performance, past and present.

The social stratification dimension of relative deprivation refers to the rapid development after independence of a vast differential in access to material rewards between those able to move into the formerly Belgian-occupied roles and those who lacked opportunities for status mobility. Stratification of African society prior to 1960 was primarily on a prestige and educational/occupational basis and was not marked

---

[13] Herbert Weiss and Benoit Verhaegen, *Parti Solidaire Africain* (Brussels, 1963), 9.

by large disparities in wealth or power.[14] The highest prestige occupations, in both the public and private sectors, were clerical positions. The very lexicon of stratification is revealing. Prior to independence the Congolese elite was generally referred to as *évolués*, a term descriptive of their educational rather than their economic status. After independence the elites decolonized the vocabulary but preserved the same basis of distinction by relabeling themselves "intellectuals."[15]

Until the eve of independence, a dual reward system had been in effect in the civil service which maintained the remuneration of Congolese petty functionaries at a very modest level, not far removed from the wage levels of the urban worker.[16] The flight of Belgian functionaries and army officers in 1960 suddenly opened up ten thousand top positions, which were swiftly filled by clerks and noncommissioned officers. In addition, several thousand highly paid "political" positions were created in 1960 at the central and provincial levels. Certain categories of persons, such as the military and police forces and teachers, were in good positions to enforce claims for sharp increases in pay. Finally, the achievement of independence opened up entirely new opportunities to the Congolese commercial sector, through special assistance available from the state. For example, in Kinshasa since independence, the thriving Congolese commercial entrepreneurial group accumulated much of its initial capital either through direct political activity or through favored access to import licenses and foreign exchange quotas—highly profitable commodities during periods of currency instability.[17]

Table I offers a general picture of the pattern of salary increases from the time of independence to the period of the rebellions. During this time, the exchange value of the Congo franc fell to one-seventh of its

[14] A full discussion of concepts of social stratification and "class" as applied to the African environment would be beyond the scope of this essay. Treatments of this subject which I have found particularly stimulating include the various essays collected in Reinhard Bendix and Seymour M. Lipset, *Class, Status and Power* (2nd ed.; New York, 1966); "Les Classes sociales dans le monde d'aujourd'hui," *Cahiers Internationaux de Sociologie*, XXXVIII, XXXIX (1965); Melvin M. Tumin, *Social Class and Social Change in Puerto Rico* (Princeton, 1961); and Richard L. Sklar, "Political Science and National Integration," *Journal of Modern African Studies*, V (May 1967), 1-11.

[15] *La Gazette* (Kisangani), December 15-16, 1964, contains an illuminating article entitled "Lorsque les intellectuels Stanlcyvillois prennent conscience d'eux-mêmes." This was a response to the treatment accorded "intellectuels" by the rebel government.

[16] For more detail, see Crawford Young, *Politics in the Congo* (Princeton, 1965), 95-100, 195-216.

[17] Prominent examples are Gaston Diomi, Joseph Ngalula, and Albert Kalonji, all former provincial presidents, and now (1968) businessmen in Kinshasa.

pre-independence level. In evaluating the relative position of different groups, one must recall that top functionaries had enjoyed a swift vertical ascent up the scale, from a clerical position in 1959, drawing perhaps 40,000 Congo francs ($900) annual salary, to a rank earning perhaps five times that figure in 1960.[18] The extent to which the politician-functionary strata monopolized the resources of the state is indicated by the fact that in 1965 payment of political personnel consumed 10 per cent of the operating budget, and an additional 20 per

TABLE I   Rise in Salaries by Social Categories, 1960–65 (Indices as of 31 December 1965 have as their base 30 June 1960 = 100.)

Category	Nominal	Real
Civil servants		
Auxiliaries (messengers, etc.)	498	102
Clerks	678-1073	139-219
Bureau chiefs	241	49
Permanent secretaries	153	31
Military		
Privates	414	85
Sergeants	571	117
Teachers		
Teachers	333	68
Primary teachers without degree	566	116
Private sector		
Legal minimum (bachelor)	306	63
Legal minimum (married, 3 children)	255	52

Source: Forthcoming study on economic change in the Congo 1960–65 by the *Institut des Recherches Economiques et Sociales,* Université Lovanium, quoted in Jean Louis Lacroix, *Industrialisation au Congo* (The Hague, 1967), 203.

cent of the operating budget went for provincial political sectors or for "irregular expenditures"—political payments occurring outside the regular budgetary channels. Another 29 billion of the 55 billion franc total went to cover central administration, education, and subsidies to provinces. Most of these disbursements were for salary payments.[19]

The rapid polarization of the socio-economic strata was rendered

[18] See Young, *Politics in the Congo,* 402-14.

[19] Jean Louis Lacroix, *Industrialisation au Congo* (The Hague, 1967), 204-5; "Situation économique et financière du Congo en 1965 et en 1966," *Etudes Congolaises,* X (May–June 1967), 2.

dramatic in its impact by the frequently conspicuous display of new wealth. The opulent life style of the colonial establishment served as a reference point for the administrative bourgeoisie. The very spatial structure of colonial towns tended to enhance the visibility of stratification. The well manicured European quarters had been carefully demarcated from the African quarters by green belts, golf courses, zoos, or other appropriate buffer areas. Politicians and civil servants in large numbers inherited the housing that was attached to ranking position in the state hierarchy and then became removed from the humbler strata by the devices which had once served to preserve the segregated character of colonial society.

A rough estimate of those benefiting materially from independence might total 150,000. Awareness of the new gap between the political-administrative class and laborers, unemployed, and peasantry was general by 1962. The vexations of the deprived were multiple. For urban workers who had jobs, wages did not keep pace with inflation. But mere employment was a blessing, as unemployment rates in the towns shot up. From the depression until 1956, involuntary urban unemployment had been a marginal phenomenon only; the 1957 recession in the Congo produced cyclical unemployment, then assumed to be temporary; the 1960 crisis converted this pressure into massive structural unemployment. Pressure on employment opportunities was exacerbated first by a vast flight to the cities after independence, when administrative controls on this kind of influx were removed, and second by a reduction in the number of jobs available. The population of Kinshasa had at least doubled since independence, some estimates placed it as high as 1,500,000, and most towns had experienced similar growth. The magnitude of the drop in the number of employment outlets is suggested by figures for Kinshasa, although the capital, along with the cities of the Copperbelt, was a center of relative prosperity. On 31 December 1959, 87,000 were employed; on 15 December 1961, only 58,000 jobs existed. Unemployment rose in that period from an estimated 29 per cent to 58 per cent of the wage earning population.[20] Paradoxically, the unemployment rate was also affected by a trend toward the mechanization of industry; government-imposed minimum wage rates had risen to a point where industrial enterprises could no longer afford to employ a superabundance of unskilled hands.[21]

One apparent outlet for the unemployed was the administration itself. There was an enormous inflation of the lower ranks of government public works and other departments employing the unskilled,

[20] Paul Raymaekers, *L'Organisation du zones de Squatting* (Paris, 1964), 35-47.
[21] Lacroix, *Industrialisation*, 33-90.

particularly in the provinces. However, these were legally on "contract" rather than enjoying civil service status. The number of *sous-contrats* was estimated as high as 300,000; the elasticity of the lower reaches of the administration is suggested by the sixty-three chauffeurs who had been hired in the North Katangan territory of Kongolo to drive the one inoperative administrative vehicle attached to the territory.[22] But such employment was often sheer illusion. Pay arrearages became a general pattern in the provinces, especially in the lower ranks of the administration. By the time of the rebellion, arrearages of up to two years were common. The *sous-contrats* were a large and inflammable group in provincial capitals, particularly receptive to the argument that the political-administrative elite consumed all public resources and thus deprived them even of the modest wage which was their nominal right.

The tensions generated by new stratification patterns were most acute for the young men who were recruited into the rebel armed forces. Students of social stratification elsewhere have observed that a crucial factor reconciling lower strata with their status is a belief in the possibilities of mobility, either inter-generational, or, for the young, within their own careers.[23] The post-war period produced a generation of young men who developed new aspirations through the availability of primary education and the opportunity for migration to the towns. This group was particularly vulnerable to the pressure of diminished employment opportunities beginning in 1957, and was threatened with forcible return to the villages by the colonial administration. The promise of nationalism reopened vistas of mobility for these young men, and they responded with militant enthusiasm. Most parties developed large and volatile youth wings in 1960 which provided paramilitary muscle for the election campaign. Correspondingly intense was the bitterness when, after independence, the youth found that the unlimited horizons of the campaign for independence had suddenly contracted. Boundless hope was replaced by unrelieved despair. It was in this setting that judgment was passed against the members of the new elite who had found fulfillment in independence. It is within this context that the social logic of the extraordinary violence unleashed by the rebellions against "intellectuals" becomes clear,[24] as does the appeal of a call for a "second independence."

[22] Interviews with district officials, Kalemie, June 1967.

[23] Tumin, *Social Class*, lays great stress on this factor. He found that a surprising degree of legitimacy was given to extant social class arrangements in Puerto Rico. See also Lipset in Bendix and Lipset, *Class, Status and Power*, 170.

[24] For an illuminating picture of the frame of mind of Kinshasan youth, see Raymaeker, *Squatting*. His inquiry was in large part conducted after independence.

For many in the older generation, "independence" had never had the credibility which it had enjoyed with the youth. Alan Merriam, describing the pre-independence year in a Songye village where he was resident, suggests a pattern that was widespread: "Independence was conceived as something with which the young men were concerned, and the older people were not vitally interested. When they spoke of it, it was with a certain diffidence and even boredom; the problem was simply not theirs to solve and they preferred to give their attention to other matters."[25] For the generation over thirty, one may suggest that the idea of the limited good had taken full hold. For those who endure it, rural poverty begets highly limited expectations. The resource "pie" is constant and small; rural life is a zero-sum economic game.[26] The actual shrinkage of rural resources after independence was perhaps an unanticipated disappointment, but the sense of relative deprivation which it generated was attenuated by the far more modest expectations of change.

A little explored facet of stratification is that involving sex differences in mobility opportunities. Its potential significance is suggested by the important role that townswomen played in northeastern Congo. *Femmes nationalistes* formations appeared in a number of places, and in Bunia played a central role in driving the national army out in August 1960. In Isiro, Kisangani, and Kindu, women were in evidence, both in the violence and in claiming some share in power. For example, in Kindu Olenga promised the *femmes nationalistes* a place in the governing council for Maniema shortly after the rebel triumph; women apparently participated, particularly when judgments were being rendered against adversaries of the rebel regime.[27] Young women who had fled the village enjoyed meager prospects. The highly functional colonial educational system had placed little stress on educating girls, who were unlikely to enter the economy as units of production. Thus, only a handful of townswomen possessed the educational credentials which governed access to most high-status roles, or, for that matter, spoke French, the language of the modern sector. A study in Luluabourg shortly before independence showed that 25.6 per cent of the males over five spoke French, as compared to 1.08 per cent of the females.[28] The only occupational outlets in the town were petty trade

[25] Alan Merriam, *Congo: Background to Conflict* (Evanston, 1961), 177.

[26] This idea is given interesting treatment in James Scott, *Political Ideology in Malaysia: Reality and the Beliefs on an Elite* (New Haven, 1968). See also George M. Foster, "Peasant Society and the Image of the Limited Good," *American Anthropologist*, LXVII (Apr. 1965), 293-315.

[27] "The Rebellion in Maniema," typescript, draft of Verhaegen, *Rébellions au Congo*, II.

[28] André Lux, "Luluabourg, Migrations, Accroissement et Urbanisation de sa population congolaise," *Zaire*, XIII (1958), 77.

and prostitution or concubinage. Although it would be misleading to speak of "women" as a categoric group which nurtured collective resentments, the social situation of townswomen did generate a striking degree of female militant action.

The third axis of relativity in the perception of deprivation runs horizontally across the Congolese polity and is cut into ethnic and regional segments. The dynamics of rebellion and, most central of all, the causes of its failure can be understood only when this dimension is appreciated together with the other two. The gradual expansion of social and political consciousness in the cities in the post-war years was marked by the crystallization of ethnic as well as Congolese/African self-awareness.[29] The politicization of the rural areas, which diffused from urban-political nodular points, followed the same pattern. Thus, the cognitive map through which groups evaluated the distribution of social and material rewards gave a prominent place to the ethnic landscape. The new political class, compelled by the electoral time-table to develop a rural clientele at breakneck speed, necessarily relied on the ethnic linkages. The political lexicon which developed was heavily laden with ethnic terminology because the infinite complexity and incomprehensible fluidity of both provincial and national politics could be diminished by the application of ethnic labels to contending groups. The inaccuracy inherent in this process could in turn be reduced by the self-fulfilling prophecy: once labels became current, groups often tended increasingly to resemble their sterotypes. Kwilu is the clearest example. Two important groups, the Pende and the Bunda, came to see provincial and national politics as offering privileged access to other groups in the area bearing the generic label of "Mbala."[30] The dominant party in the region had been openly split, since 1960, between a faction led by Cleophas Kamitatu, a Ngongo but labeled Mbala, and Antoine Gizenga, a Pende. Mulele, the apostle of insurrection, was a Mbunda. Despite the fact that the Kwilu provincial government was headed by Norbert Leta, a Pende, at the moment of rebellion, it was a Mbala regime in the eyes of most Pende and Mbunda. And this perception in turn meant that the Kwilu insurrection was a "Pende-Mbunda" movement in the eyes of other Kwilu groups, so that despite the fact that rural Mbala shared the same social and material grievances in the name of which Mulele raised his banner, their perception of the movement precluded their rallying to it.

[29] For a detailed presentation of the thesis that ethnicity in African politics is a correlate of modernization and social mobilization, see Anderson, von der Mehden, and Young, Issues, 15-83. See also Clifford Geertz, "The Integrative Revolution: Primordial Sentiments and Civil Politics in the New States," in Geertz (ed.), Old Societies and New States (New York, 1963), 105-57.

[30] Including, in addition to the Mbala, the Ngongo and some others.

The horizontal segmentation process in the eastern Congo was necessarily far more complex, as the rebellion affected a far greater area. It is nonetheless true that close investigation reveals the importance of the ethnic thread in the texture of revolt. Throughout the eastern Congo, a central place in the rebel elite which became a factor of polarization was held by Tetela-Kusu. In the Uvira-Fizi area, the massive participation of the Bembe generated a hostile response on the part of the Rega in the Mwenga area. Shi in the Bukavu area, who had grown restive under alleged "Kusu" domination during the Kashamura-Omari regimes in 1961, and had in turn purged the Kusu from the Kivu administration when Kinshasan control was reasserted, were, a priori, reserved about a new movement in which Kusu leaders were prominent.

In a broader sense, there were marked disparities in well-being between the two zones of prosperity—Kinshasa/Lower Congo and the Katangan Copperbelt—and the "interior." In geopolitical terms, the poles of prosperity happened to coincide with the two most strategic areas. To the extent that rebellion was also a movement of the "interior" against the "capital," and had some continuities with the 1960–62 uprising of the impoverished north versus the opulent south (Katanga), the people at the prosperity poles saw themselves as threatened and were therefore immune to rebel solicitations.

The tridimensional nature of relative deprivation helps to make clear the pattern of response to the appeal to arms. Insurrectional potential accumulated in most parts of the country during the vicissitudes of the early post-independence years. Response, however, was sharply different from one zone to the next. The fragmented perception of grievance suggests at least a part of the explanation. Deprivation was relative in geographic as well as social space and time.

Antecedents: Power Deflation

To the catalog of grievance must be added the diminishing capabilities of the political system. Chalmers Johnson has offered a useful set of categories for analyzing these aspects of the antecedents to rebellion. Revolution, Johnson suggests, occurs when social systems have become "disequilibrated." As a part of this process, governments experience a "power deflation," sharply reducing their ability to cope with an armed challenge to their exercise of power. The final catalyst to insurrection is an "accelerator," which Johnson describes as "The event which triggers revolution in a society that is disequilibrated and that has a discredited base of authority." "Accelerators are," he continues occurrences that make revolution possible by exposing the inability of the elite to maintain its monopoly of force. They are not sets of conditions but single events—events that rupture a system's pseudo-integration based on deterrence. Accelerators always affect an elite's monopoly of armed force, and they lead either mobilized or potential revolutionaries to believe that they have a chance of success in resorting to violence against a hated system.[31]

We have already considered the "disequilibration" of the post-independence social system in the Congo. A profound power deflation occurred in the immediate aftermath of independence with the mutiny of the army and the flight of the European cadres who had operated the authoritarian structures of the colonial system. However, the presence of United Nations forces as a surrogate for the normal governmental monopoly of coercion in a polity, added to the sheer speed of the transformations effected by independence, delayed the period when power deflation became an invitation to insurrection. Further, rebellion could only develop when the full social consequences of 1960, in terms of "disequilibration," could work themselves out. In a compelling metaphor, Parsons has suggested that the coercive sanctions available to governments are analogous to the gold basis of a monetary system. Power, like money, is dependent on confidence, which "implies vul nerability to certain types of disturbances analogous to inflation and deflation in the economic case. A highly developed power system cannot meet all of its presumptively legitimate obligations at once."[32]

The nature of the coercive instruments available to the government after independence led to the capricious, unpredictable, and irregular application of force. This replaced the more regularized colonial practice. Colonial order, of course, reposed upon overwhelming force. This force was frequently used at the local level to quell minor disturbances and the occasional substantial revolts which marked the Belgian period. As an instrument of colonial control, coercion was predictable in its operation. The July 1960 mutiny, and the improvised Africanization which followed, meant that a new random factor of arbitrarily imposed violence appeared. Perpetuation of the colonial practice of distributing troops to every district and territory meant that the army was omnipresent. Brutality was not new to the national army, but the frequent lack of relationship between application of coercion and the requirements for public order was an innovation. The capricious use of force by local commanders, or administrators, or even troops on their

[31] Chalmers Johnson, *Revolutionary Change* (Boston, 1966), 98-99 and *passim*.

[32] Talcott Parsons, "The Place of Force in Social Process," in Harry Eckstein (ed.), *Internal War* (New York, 1964), 69.

own, diminished the effectiveness of coercion as an instrument of government control.[33] Force was arbitrary, unpredictable, and inexplicable. The ability of the army to secure rural co-operation was thereby gravely compromised.

Power deflation also occurred because of the transmission of instability down the various echelons of the administration. The crisis was initially centered at the national level, but the provinces were soon affected. Provincial conflicts were multiplied by the splintering of the six original provinces into twenty-one in 1962. Many experienced paralyzing disputes; divisions within groups surfaced which had never previously even been visible (Tetela of the savannah versus Tetela of the forest in Sankuru and Bena Tshibanda versus Bena Mutu wa Mukuna among the Luba of South Kasai). Provincial conflict in turn resulted in frequent purges of district commissioners and territorial administrators; at the lowest level, rivalries over chieftaincies were abetted by the new opportunities for claimants to enlist the support of provincial political factions. Changes of provincial regime then often meant changes in chiefly personnel.

To instability must be added the contraction of the capabilities of the field administration. Administrative vehicles broke down, and repair was often impossible in areas distant from Kinshasa or Lubumbashi. Administrators were consequently confined to their headquarters and lacked the material means to maintain the array of services and controls previously exercised. In 1962 in Gungu territory, later a focal point of the Kwilu rebellion, the local administrative offices had virtually exhausted their supply of paper.[34] There were substantial variations in degree from one region to another; however, as a rule of thumb, the greater the distance from Kinshasa or Lubumbashi, the more substantial was the deflation of administrative power.

The accelerator was an interlocking set of circumstances which offered vivid evidence of the weakness of the government's deterent force. The first aspect was the spectacular success of Mulelist bands in Kwilu in suddenly sweeping administrators, missionaries, and plantation operators out of Gungu and Idiofa territories in January 1964. The partisan bands possessed only spears, machetes, and bows and arrows, yet they overwhelmed the police and army detachments in the area. Although the Kwilu rebellion had been contained by April 1964, its capacity to generate massive participation, and to pit spear against firearms, had a major demonstration effect.

More decisive was the rout of the national army in the eastern

[33] See the excellent article by Benoit Verhaegen, "L'Armée Nationale Congolaise," *Etudes Congolaises,* X (July–Aug. 1967), 1-31.

[34] Interviews with Gungu administrative personnel, Apr. 1962.

Congo. The defeat in May of two government battalions in the Ruzizi plain by predominantly Fulero warriors began the process, and events in North Katanga and Maniema in June and July completed it. The national army, terrorized and demoralized, simply evaporated. The fleeing troops explained their headlong retreat with horrifying tales of the prowess of the rebel bands, thus cumulating the terror. A Congolese account of an engagement along the Kabambare-Kasongo road in July is a prototype of national-popular army combat:

> . . . The horde continued to advance, inexorably, like the tentacle of an octopus sliding toward a man to seize and strangle him. The soldiers fired, without interruption. Defying the bullets, the "mulele" came toward them, chanting at the top of their lungs: Mulele-Mai [water]! Mulele-Mai! Mulele. . . . Our gendarmes began to doubt the effectiveness of their weapons. The distance diminished: 200 meters . . . 150 . . . and fear built up in our ranks. . . .
>
> At their waist hung all sorts of leaves: banana or palm fronds. These leaves concealed their shorts. Branches placed here and there in their belt gave them an even more savage and ferocious appearance. Their chests were covered with animal skins. . . . As they marched, their headdress, made of feathers and skins, shook like the mane of a lion. At their neck and waist, oscillating at the cadence of their step, were diverse amulettes and packets of "dawa"[35]. . . . The horde approached like a sinister monster. They were now only 100 meters—very close. A shiver of fear ran through the ranks of the soldiers. Then suddenly, the firing stopped, with only the chants of the rebels breaking the silence. A moment of hesitation—and the same idea came like a flash to the mind of all our gendarmes: "They are invulnerable . . . invulnerable . . . Run for your lives!" The order was not given, but it was executed. . . . The simba[36] found it beneath their dignity to pursue.[37]

In appearance, despite the magnitude of power deflation, the disproportion between government force and the insurgent arsenal was still overwhelming. A crucial aspect of the accelerator was a supernatural multiplier which at this juncture utterly transformed the balance of force. A faith in magic as a power resource is rooted in traditional cosmology and appears to be a universal attribute of human communities before a scientific viewpoint becomes dominant (and for that matter frequently co-exists with theories of material rational

[35] *Dawa* is a Swahili word meaning medicine or potion, but in the eastern Congo the term referred to supernatural curative and protective powers.

[36] Swahili for "lion," and the name given to popular army troops in the eastern Congo beginning in June 1964.

[37] Verhaegen, "The Rebellion in Maniema."

causation).[38] The folklore of African resistance is filled with remarkably parallel responses to the uniform problem: how can men with spears, bows, and arrows overcome the force of enemies with firearms? No material counterforce was available; help could only come from the pantheon of supernatural forces. A superior force within the hierarchy of causation could transform the lethal agent of the rifleman, his bullet, and render it as harmless as a raindrop. The keys to the kingdom of magic were held by those with the specialized knowledge of and access to occult forces; the continuous intercession and collaboration of wizards was indispensable to insurgent power.[39] The utility of magical armament was enormously enhanced by the fact that it was equally plausible to government troops, who shared the same belief system as the insurgents.

The decisiveness of magic as the pivotal component of force during the zenith of the eastern rebellion is underlined by the fact that the only real military defeats suffered at this stage were at the hands of hostile rural bands who could more readily counter this force on its

[38] See the penetrating discussion of this question by Robin Horton, "African Traditional Thought and Western Science," *Africa*, XXXVII (1967), 50-71, 155-87.

[39] Renée Fox has an important contribution on this subject forthcoming, delivered as a lecture on "Patterns of Thought and Belief in the Congo Today," Madison, Wisconsin, 22 March 1968. The list of rebellions in which this belief is present is too long to cite here. For Maji-Maji, which presents many striking parallels with the Congo rebellion, see A. R. W. Crosse-Upcott, "The Origins of the Majimaji Revolt," *Man*, LX (May 1960), 71-73; R. M. Bell, "The Maji-Maji Rebellion in the Liwali District," *Tanganyika Notes and Records*, 28 (1950), 38-57; John Iliffe, "The Effects of the Maji Maji Rebellion of 1905–1906 on German Occupation Policy in East Africa," 557-76, and Robert I. Rotberg, "Resistance and Rebellion in British Nyasaland and German East Africa, 1888–1915: A Tentative Comparison," in Prosser Gifford and Wm. Roger Louis (eds.), *Britain and Germany in Africa* (New Haven, 1967), 667-90. For Haji Muhammad Abullah Hassan (the "Mad Mullah"), see Saadia Touval, *Somali Nationalism* (Cambridge, Mass., 1963), and Douglas Jardine, *The Mad Mullah of Somaliland* (London, 1923). Tawia Adamfio, former Secretary General of the Convention People's party in Ghana, attested to a similar belief in his first treason trial, Accra Radio, Oct. 13, 1965. Reuben Um Nyobé, *Union des Populations du Cameroun* guerrilla leader, cultivated the mystique of his own invulnerability to bullets; when he was shot, the rebellion melted away in his (Bassa) district. Willard Johnson, "The Union des Populations du Cameroun in Rebellion: The Integrative Backlash of Insurgency," above, 671-92. The 1947 Madagascar insurrection had a similar pattern. O. Mannoni, *Prospero and Caliban* (London, 1956), 59-61. On the role of magic in Congolese societies, the pioneering and still classical study is E. E. Evans-Pritchard, *Witchcraft, Oracles and Magic among the Azande* (Oxford, 1932). The analysis of Luba cosmology by the Rev. Placide Tempels, *Bantu Philosophy* (Paris, 1959), is also useful in understanding this aspect of rebellion. See also W. P. P. Burton, *Luba Religion and Magic in Custom and Belief* (Tervuren, 1961); J. van Wing, *Etudes Bakongo* (2nd ed.; Louvain, 1959), 345-443.

own terms. The defeat of Olenga's August assault on Bukavu was determined to a large extent by the decimation of his forces at the approaches to the city by Mwami Kabare's Bashi warriors. Particularly enlightening is the account given to a popular army council meeting in July 1964 of the stinging defeat suffered by a predominantly Bembe insurgent group attacking Rega irregulars who were defending their home territory of Mwenga; participants in the council were four rebel officers, two "advisers," and two *docteurs-feticheurs*. An officer who had taken part in the Mwenga battle reported that "the war which we carry on with soldiers and that with populations are two different wars . . . when we fight with the inhabitants who utilize Urega fetishes." On the third assault wave against the Rega forces, the insurgents found themselves "fighting against devils, not men." The combat was marked by extraordinary phenomena; the Rega possessed a gigantic dog, which required sixty-one bullets to bring down. When an assistant fetish doctor broke ranks and fled, scattering the *dawa* upon the ground behind him, the young *simba* took fright and fled in turn. Rebel troops, when they discovered that the Rega possessed unknown fetishes and knew the secret of their own, would only resume combat when a fetish of higher quality was brought into play. The popular army war council unanimously decided that a colonel would be dispatched immediately to Kalemie to secure this assistance.[40]

There were other new capabilities offered by the utilization of magic. In Kwilu, the mystique of Mulele's leadership rested in part upon his extraordinary powers. He was said to be invulnerable to bullets and to demonstrate his force by firing blank cartridges at himself. He could move long distances through government lines, by rendering himself invisible, or by transporting himself as a bird, or by using a tiny airplane no bigger than the palm of a hand.[41] Not only could the force of a government bullet be reduced but arrows could be transformed into cartridges in flight.

The potency of magic as force rested upon the universality of its plausibility. For those on both sides, at least partly enmeshed in the traditional belief system, social reinforcement operated through the sharing of these convictions with all the others in the group, and the inadequacy of alternative sources of explication. E. E. Evans-Pritchard gives a lucid summary in his Zande study:

> In this web of belief every strand depends upon every other strand, and a Zande cannot get out of its meshes because it is the only

[40] Verhaegen, "The Rebellion in Maniema."

[41] Fox, de Craemer, and Ribeaucourt, "La deuxième Indépendance," 20-21; James Bertsche, "The Congo Rebellion," *Practical Anthropology*, XII (Sept.–Oct. 1965), 218.

world he knows. The web is not an external structure in which he is enclosed. It is the texture of his thought and he cannot think that his thought is wrong.[42]

The system provided explanations for its own failures. In the popular army in the east, its use was systematized, sanctioned by a range of taboos, many of which had clear social control functions (such as the prohibition against sexual intercourse during a campaign), and administered by a cadre of fetish doctors attached to every unit. An elaborate ritual was developed, including "baptism" of new recruits— a laying on of hands to transmit invulnerabilty from the supernatural domain to the *simba* through the agency of the specialist in wizardry. Thereafter, certain proscriptions such as the prohibition against turning one's head in combat, provided explanation for a reasonable number of failures. Beyond a certain threshold, however, as the Mwenga example suggests, a conviction of collective failure of magic could develop. However, questioning did not extend to the larger issue of the efficacy of magic in general, but rather to the shortcomings of the particular fetishes in hand.[43] The national army itself, when the rebellion was in decline, became increasingly effective against residual pockets in part because *simba dawa* (although not magic in general) lost its credibility.

Value-Orientations: From Marx to Mama Marie Onema

Thus by 1964 an insurrectionary potential had been realized. The precarious legitimacy of the post-independence regime had been gravely impaired, and the credibility of its coercive power severely devalued. For those persuaded that the construction of a new Congo required the destruction of the existing regime, possible success nurtured hopes which expanded in tandem with the shrinkage of government capability. For rebel leaders, the revolutionary hour was at hand; in July 1964, the road from Kasongo to Kinshasa was paved with dazzling prospects of imminent triumph. We must now shift our focus from cause to process and suggest the essential dynamics of the rebellion in order to seek insight into its decomposition and collapse.

A first part of the answer to the failure of the rebellion lies in the extraordinary internal diversity of insurgent forces. This can be seen

[42] Evans-Pritchard, *Witchcraft*, 194.

[43] One could argue by analogy with Max Gluckman's thesis of the integrative role of conflict over a given chief in the name of chieftaincy that even failures become reinforcing, as they require explanation in terms of the institution itself. See *Order and Rebellion in Tribal Africa* (London, 1963), 84-136.

through the ideological and value spectrum and through the stratification of participation in rebellion. As a syncretic mélange of ideas and symbols drawn from many sources, the ideology of rebellion displays evident continuities with the multitude of separatist churches, messianic sects, witch-finding movements, and other religious expressions of the tensions of social change during the colonial period.

At the summit, there was an infusion of Marxist-Leninist, and to some extent Maoist, patterns and categories of analysis. To those prepared to accept the premises and the selective use of evidence, this provided an apparently coherent explanation of why the first achievement of independence had gone awry. Reduced to its simplest terms, this analysis argued that the Kinshasa regime incarnated the national bourgeoisie, definitively corrupted by its alliance with imperialist forces. Capitalist imperialism in the Congo was represented by Belgians and Americans; increasingly, the Kinshasa regime was dependent upon the support of its external protectors. The *compradore bourgeoisie* (those who have linked their class status to imperialism in Maoist parlance) joined hands with Belgian and American capitalist/imperialist forces in the systematic exploitation of the impoverished masses and the national resources.

The infusion of Marxist-Leninist-Maoist thought into the ideological panoply of the rebellion came primarily through the agency of a small number of leaders who, between 1960 and 1964, had the opportunity for travel and study in China, the U.S.S.R., and Eastern Europe, and thus gained exposure to revolutionary currents of political thought. As ideology hunters, these young men were favorably predisposed to a system of analysis offering a radical critique of the existing regime which also provided an identification of the enemy that corresponded with their own perceptions. Another source of ideological exposure were the Communist embassies situated in Brazzaville and Bujumbura, the two key sanctuaries for rebel leaders. The Chinese were particularly evangelical in their efforts to improve the ideological sophistication of the rebel elites. Also, in the guerrilla training camps of Congo/Brazzaville, ideological instruction was part of the program, with some participation by Chinese instructors.

Pierre Mulele was probably the most ideological of the rebel luminaries. Mulele had enjoyed only modest visibility in 1960; in the national elections, he had, with only 5,520 votes (compared to 60,511 for Kamitatu and 52,445 for Gizenga), stood ninth among *Parti Solidaire Africain* candidates in the number of preferential votes received. He was Minister of Education in Lumumba's government and then fled to Kisangani with the Gizenga group. However, by December 1960 he was disillusioned with Gizenga and left for Cairo with the designation of ambassador. On 21 March 1961, he wrote to Nkrumah to ask support from Ghana, because he "considered himself the sole person to assume leadership in trying to halt the sad course of events which followed the illegal dismissal of Lumumba." According to Nkrumah, Mulele kept in close touch with the Chinese embassy in Cairo and in 1962 traveled via Prague and Moscow to Peking, where he underwent a training course in guerrilla warfare.[44] Upon his return to Kwilu in mid-1963, Mulele soon assumed the dimensions of a regional prophet. Curiously, he never put his political philosophy in writing, nor did he publish a manifesto or program. As reconstructed from numerous accounts of those who lived in the forest camps which he and his lieutenants organized, Mulelist ideology had three main themes. There were two main classes in society, capitalists and impoverished masses. In the Congo, the capitalist class was divided into foreigners and those associated with the Kinshasa government—the "reactionaries." Two sorts of struggle existed: reformist, to be avoided as only alleviating and not rectifying the sufferings of the mass; and revolutionary, whereby the masses assumed control over their own destiny. Thirdly, in tactical terms, the revolutionary struggle had to be conducted by partisans whose relationship to the villages had to be "as fish in water"; village support and integration of partisans into the village milieu were the indispensable prerequisites to success.[45] Mulelist partisans had as their tactical primer a document entitled "Ordre de mission des partisans." This partisan bible was largely inspired by the classic writings of Mao on guerrilla warfare; Benoit Verhaegen demonstrates the point-by-point literal correspondence between Mulele's text and Mao's military thoughts.[46]

The Marxist-Leninist contribution to the rhetoric of insurrection in the eastern Congo was much more fragmentary. The fabric of rebellion was far more complex in design, and no charismatic leader enjoyed the ascendancy which Mulele had in Kwilu. The only close equivalent to the partisan training camps deep in the forested valleys of Kwilu were centers of political instruction organized by Antoine Marandura, son of the sometime Mwami Musa Marandura, in the mountainous part of Fulero country. A few second-rank leaders, such as Laurent Kabila in North Katanga, or Tony Nyati in Kisangani, had studied in Eastern Europe, and had formulated their thoughts with some concern for ideological sophistication. Also, in the predominantly Bembe redoubt in the Uvira-Fizi area there were a large group of Cuban ideologists and military technicians during much of 1965, when

[44] Kwame Nkrumah, *Challenge of the Congo* (New York, 1967), 153-54.
[45] Verhaegen, *Rébellions au Congo*, 129-30.
[46] Ibid., 122-23, 153-56.

the rebellion was in decline; included in this latter group, the evidence suggests, was the late Ernesto "Che" Guevara.

The next layer of political thought was the radical but vague nationalism epitomized by Lumumbism in 1960.[47] Areas in which widespread response to the call of rebellion occurred were all dominated by parties displaying an aggressive response to terminal colonial rule. Militant nationalism at this stage, however, was largely measured in terms of style and tone. The only really defined goal was unitary government and immediate and total independence, and degrees of militance were measured by the level of commitment to these simple aims, whose consequences and further implications went largely unexplored.[48] Most of the leadership in the eastern Congo spoke primarily in the Lumumbist idiom. The destruction of the Kinshasa regime, a vigorous reassertion of Congolese control over its own destiny, and a vague socialist commitment were recurrent themes. But at bottom it appeared far more a frame of mind and a style of expression, than an interrelated set of ideas.[49]

Finally, there was incorporated into the value spectrum a range of ill-defined norms and orientations which rendered the movement intelligible to the audience of rural and urban youth to which it appealed. Characteristic was, in Kwilu, the curious extension of Maoist logic, to extol the pristine virtues of the rural village; the working class, as a revolutionary force, disappeared altogether. Vehicles of acculturation such as the Christian missions, European artifacts, and the use of French were rejected. Indeed, the Mulelists also proscribed the "state Kikongo," a simplified, detonalized version of Kikongo used by the administration and in primary schools in the Kwilu-Kwango area, in favor of Lingala (an equally deformed, river-trading lingua franca which had been standardized and simplified by the colonial administration). The new society, Renée Fox and others suggest, "is conceived as a gigantic village, composed of smaller villages where people will recover their own authentic identity, the satisfaction of all their material needs, justice, creative activity, and joy in working the soil in common."[50] The importance of traditional cosmologies has been described

[47] Note the extraordinarily vague character of Lumumba's political thought in the collection of his speeches in Jean van Lierde (ed.), *La pensée politique de Patrice Lumumba* (Brussels, 1963); the emotional radicalism is obvious, but the economic and social content remained undefined.

[48] See the set of criteria elaborated by Herbert Weiss to suggest a typology of 1960 parties, in *Political Protest in the Congo* (Princeton, 1967), 64-73.

[49] Perhaps the flavor of 1964 Lumumbism is most readily available in the newspaper published in Kisangani, *Le Martyr*, Aug.–Nov. 1964.

[50] Fox, de Craemer, and Ribeaucourt, "La deuxième Indépendance," 19. See also Bertsche, "The Congo Rebellion," 216. Fox *et al.* note the coincidence between these themes and a Catholic movement, "Savoir-Vivre."

previously. Of particular interest is the effort to systematize and employ in a uniform manner a composite of beliefs and practices borrowed from a variety of groups. The North Katanga rebellion of 1960–62 and the Luba refugee camp in Lubumbashi in 1961–62 saw frequent exploitation of magic as a control mechanism; Balubakat *jeunesse* played some part in south Maniema before and during the rebellion, and one of the two most renowned fetish doctors was a Luba. The *simba* initiation rites were similar in a number of respects to Kumu ceremonies, and this may have been a source of the technology of magic.[51] But traditional cosmologies were specific to given cultural areas in their detail, even if broadly similar in outline. Thus, the effort to standardize magic in the popular army was, in its context, a radical innovation.[52]

Skill Groups and Diversity in Participation

Functional and social stratification in participation also played an important part in the rebellion. The rebellion was a multi-dimensional drama enacted in many different ways at different levels of society. Each category of participant differed in perspective, political resources, and action capabilities. The simultaneous pursuit of varying aims by interlocking and overlapping circles of participants lies at the very heart of the process of violence.

At the top was the rebel elite, composed predominantly of political leaders spawned in the tumults of 1959–60. They had in common a thorough hostility to the political formula which had emerged in 1961 in Kinshasa national politics, even though some, such as Gbenye, had held ministerial posts. Most had been associated with the Gizenga regime in Kisangani in 1960–61, although not with Gizenga's subsequent adventure at the end of 1961.[53] Most had committed themselves to national politics since 1961. This group launched the *Conseil National de Libération* in October 1963 in Brazzaville. From the outset, it was rent by debilitating factionalism. The significance of simple personal incompatibilities is impossible to overestimate; the messiah complex was common to the 1960 political generation. Mulele mistrusted Gizenga; Egide Bocheley-Davidson detested Gbenye, who was in turn sharply critical of Gizenga's leadership in Kisangani in 1960–61. Anicet Kashamura, who never rallied to the rebellion despite

[51] Verhaegen, "The Rebellion in Maniema."

[52] I am indebted to Thomas Turner and Jan Vansina for this observation.

[53] See *Congo 1961; Congo 1962*, for the most thorough account of the Gizenga dissidence in Kisangani and Maniema, 1961–62.

his apparent ideological sympathy for its cause, published highly un-flattering views of Gbenye and Thomas Kanza, among others.[54] Soumialot split with Gbenye and Olenga; Olenga in turn had a violent altercation with Gbenye in Khartoum in mid-1965 and promised a Uganda Commission of Inquiry that he would reveal the "whole truth" about other rebel leaders before he was forcefully rusticated by Ugandan police in 1966. Neither a sense of shared political goals nor a common ideology was sufficient to generate sustained collaboration among the elite.

The rebel elite had differing audiences. Kanza, designated "Foreign Minister" of the revolutionary government in Kisangani in September 1964, had a slender domestic base among university students and intellectuals, and a much more important constituency in the African diplomatic sphere, where, during his period of service, he was a persua-sive advocate. However, his commitment to rebellion only came after he had agreed to enter the Tshombe government as Foreign Minister, and the appointment had been vetoed by President Kasavubu, with whom the Kanza family had a personal vendetta.[55] Mulele refused to take any part in exile politics in Brazzaville, and operated from his Kwilu redoubt. Bocheley-Davidson remained in Brazzaville, and op-erated from the *Conseil* secretariat which was situated there; the *Parti Solidaire Africain* Gizenga group for the most part did likewise.

The rebel elite did have in common their aspiration to operate at a national level. They were thus, of necessity, coalition builders, seeking to aggregate regional pockets of discontent. As regional auxiliaries, the elite worked with a set of leaders whose aspirations and operations were more local. Most belonged to the 1960 political class, and many had served as provincial ministers or even national deputies, but had failed to achieve prominence. At the time that insurrection broke out, many found advantage in an alliance which offered to reverse existing provincial power arrangements. Virtually all had been associated with the "Lumumbist bloc" of parties in 1960, and so found congenial the symbols and rhetoric of rebellion. What is striking about this group, however, is the extent to which the structure of provincial conflict as it stood in 1964 tended to shape their options. In North Katanga, Ildephonse Massengo and Roger Kabulo established their links with rebel leaders at a moment when the province was literally paralyzed by the bitter Sendwe/Mwamba-Ilunga struggle. In Sankuru, Louis Lumumba, brother of the late Prime Minister, served as a re-luctant and ambiguous ally of the rebels during their five-day occupa-tion of Lodja in August. The provincial government established for

[54] Anicet Kashamura, *De Lumumba aux Colonels* (Paris, 1966).
[55] Moise Tshombe, *Quinze mois du gouvernement au Congo* (Paris, 1966), 20.

Maniema after the rebel conquest of Kindu was, according to Verhaegen, "by its composition neither a People's Government, nor a
revolutionary one. It could perfectly well have been elected by the
provincial assembly of the preceding regime. Its principal characteristic
was to be drawn from the 'counter elite'—that is, that fraction of the
politico-administrative elite which, while possessing the same characteristics as the group in power, had previously been thrown into
opposition."[56] In Kisangani, François Sabiti played a similar role; his
father and grandfather had served as chiefs of the *arabisé* quarter of
the African town.

From July 1964 on, a distinctive military elite emerged in the
eastern Congo, as the popular army became a substantial organization
replicating the national army in structure and nomenclature. The
popular army took shape in the Fizi area in the first part of June when
three columns were formed under the command of Jean-Bosco Ka-
lisibe, Victor Tshombaz, and Olenga, all three Tetela-Kusu. Soumialot, also identified as a Kusu (although his father was a Songye),
initially invested the officers with their functions, but by late July
Olenga had become the dominant and autonomous force within the
insurgent constellation, deriving his authority from his relative control
of a potent political resource, the popular army. There was a marked
predominance in the insurgent officer corps of Tetela-Kusu. A number
had once served in the national army, but had been purged, as members of Lumumba's ethnic group, for suspected disloyalty to the
Kinshasa regime. The homogeneity of the rebel officer corps no doubt
contributed to the cohesiveness of the popular army, and to its effectiveness as a pressure group. At the same time, as the possible instrument
of Tetela-Kusu ethnic hegemony, this homogeneity ultimately rendered
the army suspect in areas outside the Maniema core.

The popular army rank and file were of a very different origin.
Initially, the troops were heavily drawn from certain groups, above
all the Bembe of Fizi. Fulero and Rwanda Tutsi refugees were also
numerous at first. As the insurgent columns marched through Maniema,
many others were enrolled, with Ngubangu of Kabambare and Zimba
of Kasongo particularly numerous. Subsequently, as the rebel force
snowballed in size, its composition became rather more diffuse, but
at bottom it was a Maniema army. Once outside the areas in which the
predominant groups had local attachments, it became an alien force,
with its separation from the civilian population reinforced by its own
taboos. It was a crusade of rural youth, mainly in the twelve to twenty
age group.

56 Verhaegen, "The Rebellion in Maniema."

The organization of Mulelist partisan bands was sharply different. These were structured into small teams, each team led by "political commissioners" and based in a village, or a forest camp. Not every villager was integrated into the teams, but every village in the core areas of the Mulelist movement had a team. There was no effort to constitute larger units, and no distinctively military elite emerged; the partisans remained more firmly linked with the political apparatus.

The urban-based "youth" groups were both an asset and a liability to rebel elites. The Kisangani situation was the prototype. The *Mouvement National Congolais*/Lumumba "youth" had been given major responsibilities in party organization in 1960; flying squads of young men had seen to the establishment of the party in the Orientale-Maniema hinterland of the Lumumbist capital by achieving the co-operation of chiefs and local leaders where possible, and by intimidation where necessary. By 1964, Kisangani was full of very angry young men, cheated in their own eyes of the birthright of independence; their leaders had been in and out of prison as successive weak administrations in Kisangani tried to maintain a tenuous social peace. For a time after independence, the *Mouvement National Congolais*/Lumumba "youth" had been led by Bernard Salumu, "boss" of Kisangani city in the Gizenga period.[57] He had been succeeded by Victor Benanga[58] and Alphonse Kingis;[59] the latter was also a Kitawalan pastor, leading a religious community on the left bank of the Congo River at Kisangani. Benanga and Kingis were ruthless, violent, and sanguinary, and their "youth" gangs were responsible for much of the indiscriminate slaughter of "intellectuals" which occurred during the rebel administration. They belonged to a *tsotsi* subculture,[60] and were never brought under the control of the rebel leadership. The first "revolutionary provincial government" constituted at Kisangani at the time it was first captured by rebel forces was led by Kingis and Benanga; Olenga, upon his return from the unsuccessful assault on Bukavu, sacked the "youth" leaders, declaring: "Well-founded complaints had been registered denouncing actions in violation of the most elementary notions of the rights of man, such as arbitrary arrests, kill-

[57] For a portrait of Salumu, see Young, *Politics in the Congo*, 427-30. Salumu rallied to Kinshasa and was killed in an automobile accident in 1966.

[58] Benanga, at last report, in 1967 still led one of the last rebel bands at large deep in the forest north of Kisangani.

[59] Kingis was assassinated, apparently by his own followers, at the time of the reconquest of Kisangani in Nov. 1964.

[60] *Tsotsi* is a slang term of the South African slums, referring to the disoriented, bitter young men bred in the slum yards whose frustration and despair is reflected in juvenile delinquency and violence.

ings; in a word barbarity and vandalism have made their appearance."[61]
(Olenga at the same time personally executed the army commander he
had left in charge, Col. Kifakio, in front of the leading hotel.)

Competing rural elites were an important part of the mosaic of
rebellion at local levels. The Belgian version of local administration,
although officially based upon respect for traditional criteria in the
selection of the chiefs who were the capillaries of rural governance,
placed a higher value on efficiency and productivity. Consequently,
there was a substantial reservoir of potential claimants to official
investiture when competitive provincial politics injected new opportunities for ousting incumbents. Rival claimants to chieftaincies frequently had a significant clientele and were, in the context of electoral
politics, attractive allies for town-based politicians. The sharp conflicts
which arose at the provincial political level after independence further
complicated many local situations, as ephemeral regimes used chieftaincies as a reward for their followers and removed those conspicuously identified with rival factions. The rebellion provided an
opportunity for those deprived of office to reverse their status.

In Opala territory, southwest of Kisangani, a local chief who had
been ousted by Belgian officials the year before independence had,
initially in 1960, become a rural organizer for the *Mouvement National
Congolais*/Lumumba "youth." When the Lumumbist regime in Kisangani was displaced in 1961, he found himself again excluded from office.
When the Opala region was overrun by insurgent forces, he had a
new opportunity to recover power. Indeed, at this stage he enlarged
his ambitions by proclaiming himself paramount chief of the entire
Mbole ethnic group, which was dominant in Opala territory. To assure
the permanence of his new title, he assassinated eight of the nine incumbent local chiefs in the area. The acephalous Mbole tradition lent
no sanction to his claim, but the invocation of fidelity to Lumumbism
provided a partial surrogate.

Another specimen of the interaction between local leadership conflicts and the rebellion lies in the chieftaincy struggle among the
Fulero. The Fulero had a relatively centralized traditional political
structure, which initially had a royal caste of alien origin, in common
with many kingdoms in the interlacustrine area. However, the Belgians
had deposed this group, when it proved insufficiently pliable. At the
end of the colonial rule, Henri Simba, the invested *mwami* of the
Fulero chieftaincy, claimed his office on the basis of customary sanction, but the traditional rules had undergone a major mutation. Simba
chose to oppose the militant nationalist parties, *Centre de Regroupe-*

[61] *Le Martyr*, 1-2 Sept. 1964.

ment Africain and *Mouvement National Congolais*/Lumumba "youth," which sought to organize the Uvira area in 1960. The foremost Fulero spokesman of the politically militant was Musa Marandura, who was elected provincial councillor from the area. Under the Kashamura-Omari regime in Bukavu in early 1961, Simba fled to exile in Burundi, and Marandura was declared "President" of the chieftaincy; he immediately proceeded to purge most of the subordinate chiefs and replace them with the politically faithful. Simba, however, had his revenge when Jean Miruho came to power in mid-1961; he was reinstalled as *mwami* and chased the Marandura men. By late 1963, Marandura, aided by his son Antoine, began organizing the residual political "youth" branches of 1960 vintage, and isolated attacks upon subordinate Simba chiefs began at the end of the year. Soumialot already had close contacts with Marandura. When he arrived in February 1964 to organize an insurrection in the east from Bujumbura, he had little difficulty in hitching the local purposes of the Marandura faction to the broader aims of the *Conseil National de Libération*.[62]

The importance of magic in the rebellion made those specializing in its invocation and control a skill group of some importance, especially in the eastern Congo.[63] Wizards from certain cultural groups had particular reputations extending far beyond their own ethnic areas; fetish-manipulators did not need to come from the group whose needs they were serving. (Kusu-Tetela have a particular notoriety in this regard.) The high priestess of the eastern rebellion, Mama Marie Onema, had a reputation throughout the Maniema-Kisangani area even before the rebellion offered her new opportunities. She was a wizened, one-breasted woman of very short stature whose startling appearance enhanced her effectiveness. She was resident at Kindu at the moment of the rebellion, and General Olenga, after the capture of Kindu, sought her out immediately to enlist her services. She held court in Kisangani during the period of the revolutionary government. After the fall of the rebel capital, she was captured by forces of the central government. Sûreté chief Victor Nendaka induced her to change her allegiance, and in early 1965 the former rebel zones were saturated with government posters announcing Mama Onema's switch. The specialists in magic operated within the popular army; every unit was

---

[62] Verhaegen, *Rébellions au Congo*, 268-70.

[63] A similar process has been noted in the Maji Maji rebellion. Those controlling occult forces achieved new prominence in a context which made their function critically important. An interesting discussion of this point is found in Terence O. Ranger, "African Reaction and Resistance to the Imposition of Colonial Rule," in Lewis H. Gann and Peter Duignan (eds.), *Colonialism in Africa* (Cambridge, 1969).

anxious to have a technician of occult forces in order to be able to offer continuous protection from the dangers of combat.[64]

The multiplicity of values and elites helps to clarify the complex molecular structure of the rebellion. At any given time and place, the valence of the component value and elite elements could vary within a considerable range. No single group or belief system could dominate the rebellion across the whole area in which the insurrection occurred. Further elucidation of this point requires some consideration of symbols of rebellion, orbits of influence of particular groups and individuals, and arenas of conflict.

Symbols and Diffusion of Rebellion

In general, one may suggest that, particularly for rural populations, modern politics required translation into locally meaningful symbols if the populace at large were to be able to relate thereto.[65] In the Congo, the three most important types of symbols were heroes, ethnic labels, and political parties. The diffusion of the rebellion, and the attraction of the local population to it, depended upon local populations finding within the symbolic language which announced the insurrection a basis of identity with the rebellion. Conversely, symbols can be negative; where the labels by which the option of rebellion was presented evoked hostility, resistance occurred.

The memory of Lumumba, the martyr, and the luminous living legend of Mulele were the two most conspicuous hero symbols for

[64] Rebel documents provide abundant evidence. The following order from Soumialot is reproduced as a specimen:

> OS/MJC
> République Révolutionnaire du Congo
> Cabinet du Président de l'Est
> Défense Nationale
>
> ORDRE DE MISSION
>
> Je Soussigne Gaston Soumialot, Président du Conseil National de Libération —Section Est du Congo, charge Monsieur Kakoni Mahunon, Docteur dans l'Armée Révolutionnaire Populaire de Libération à l'Est du Congo la mission d'aller accompaner et traiter les militaires dans les opérations pour le MANIEMA, LOMAMI, SANKURU et STANLEYVILLE.
>
> Donné à Albertville, le 11 juillet 1964
> Le Président de l'Est
> G. SOUMIALOT
> Charge de la Défense Nationale

Reproduced ibid., 480.

[65] For a stimulating survey of this subject, see Murray Edelman, *Symbolic Uses of Politics* (Champaign, Ill., 1964).

rebellion, although they operated in a somewhat different fashion. In 1960, Lumumba had, in most parts of northeastern Congo, become the human incarnation of the inchoate hopes and aspirations of the first independence. His name had infused with a palpable, human symbolism both the dominant party (the *Mouvement National Congolais*/Lumumba "youth") and the visceral nationalism which swept the area (Lumumbism). Lumumba, Lumumbism, and Lumumbists were omnipresent in the catechism of the eastern rebellion. The new party cards issued in 1964 contained a red spot, symbolic of the blood of the patron saint. The centrality of Lumumbism helps to clarify the boundaries of rebellion. In North Katanga, rural populations which rose against the Tshombe regime in Lubumbashi in 1960–62 were quiescent in 1964, even when rebel warriors arrived, because neither Lumumbism, nor any of the other symbols of rebellion, had a binding appeal. But when the rebel columns reached the fringes of the Ubangi district, sharp resistance was encountered as they left the radius of Lumumbist appeal. The possibility of a rebel push toward central Kasai was abandoned because of the necessity to pass through territory of the Luba of Kasai; here the Lumumba symbol evoked not just indifference, but violent antipathy.[66] The Lumumba symbol was peculiar to the eastern rebellion; it was not utilized in Kwilu.

Mulele was a new entry in the symbolic lexicon. His role in 1960 was too slight to achieve wide public visibility; his personality was invested with legendary attributes only when the Mulelist maquis exploded into view at the beginning of 1964. For Kwilu, he was a charismatic guerrilla leader, with prophetic, superhuman qualities. In the eastern Congo, Mulele was less a person than an omnipotent force. Rebel forces marching into battle chanted "Mulele mai! Mulele mai!" (Mulele water); the chant reinforced the potency of the ritual immunizations provided for the troops by the unit *docteur-feticheur*, with the terrible powers of the man-spirit, Mulele. Gbenye, when he reached the eastern Congo in late August, ordered the popular army to chant "Lumumba mai!" rather than invoke Mulele. However, this order was not fully executed, presumably because of the specific symbolic properties which the name of Mulele had come to incorporate, even though as a real person he was wholly unknown in the eastern Congo.

Political party labels also offered a mechanism for relating peasant populations to the rebellion, as well as determining the boundaries of the rebellion's appeal. Party as a symbol was not much used in

[66] In 1967, when President Mobutu addressed a public meeting in Mbuji-Mayi, the Kasai Luba capital, references to the Lumumbist heritage, which the present regime seems to embrace, still engendered a sullen silence.

Kwilu, where the zone of the Mulele maquis was roughly co-terminous with the Gizenga wing of the *Parti Solidaire Africain.* Mulele, because of the far more thorough infusion of a whole new symbolic system in his forest training camps, did not need the 1960 symbols. But in the east, party labels served to objectify both friend and foe. *Mouvement National Congolais*/Lumumba was the principal party symbol of the rebels, possession of a paid-up party card was indispensable to personal security, and prior association with the party was a requisite criterion for appointment to political office in Kindu, Kisangani, Isiro, and Bunia, where "provincial" administrations were established. Other parties of the 1960 Lumumbist coalition, *Centre de Regroupement Africain* (Kivu), Balubakat and Cartel (North Katanga), served as accessory symbols. The enemy bore the *Parti National de Progrès* (PNP) label after the 1960 administration-supported moderate movement which had, by the time of the May 1960 elections, been literally liquidated in the Lumumbist zones. (Those labeled for execution were "PNP," which was virtually a residual category for functionaries, politicians, and chiefs identified with the Kinshasa regime, or for those who failed to establish their *Mouvement National Congolais*/Lumumba *bona fides.*) Radeco, the short-lived national coalition which former Prime Minister Adoula sought to erect, was also a designation of the "social enemy" and identified as a functional equivalent of the "PNP."

Ethnic labels as symbols of conflict were also crucial to the pattern of diffusion. The importance of ethnicity in the cognitive process converted the abstract idea of insurrection into the specific message "group X is in revolt." Reaction to the opportunity of rebellion then depended, in part, on whether or not group Y saw itself threatened by group X. In Kwilu, the perception of Mulelism as a Mbunda-Pende movement rendered it self-containing, although fragments of some other neighboring groups took part in the early stages, when, among other things, they had to consider the greater risks of not joining a movement which might prove victorious. In North Katanga, rebel columns were largely composed of Bembe, with an infusion of Rwandan refugees and Fulero. Although some Luba leaders, such as Ildephonse Massengo and Laurent Kabila, played a part, the government briefly constituted in Kalemie was not rooted in North Katangan ethnic realities. In Kalemie itself, the dominant townsmen, the Tumbwe, played almost no part in the bitter factionalism of provincial politics, nor were they represented in the rebellion. Both the Luba-dominated factions of Sendwe and Mwamba-Ilunga, and the insurgent government, were equally alien.

In Kivu and Maniema, Fulero, Bembe, Ngubangu, Zimba, and Kusu-Tetela participated heavily. Rega found themselves cast in the role of enemies, of Bembe in Mwenga, Zimba in Kasongo, and Kusu in Kindu, and were thrown into opposition. For Kivu, Olenga's invading column was a Maniema force, and both major Shi factions, Kabare and Ngweshe, resisted. In North Kivu, provincial politics was dominated by a conflict between Rwandan immigrants and Nande, embittered by a dispute over the territories of Goma and Rutshuru. The sympathies of Rwandans for the rebellion rendered it a threat to the Nande.[67] In northern Maniema, the Kumu initially rallied to the rebellion. Kumuhood was bound up with the syncretic movement of Kitawala, which had been absorbed into the segmentary structure of Kumu society.[68] Kitawala had been the object of repressive measures by the colonial administration and the post-independence government. Rebellion initially offered the possibility of support to Kitawala, and therefore Kumu identification with the movement was strong. However, Kitawala came into sharp conflict with rebel leaders and the popular army and Kumu support for the insurgents melted; the national army had little difficulty reoccupying the Kumu area.

The Tetela-Kusu label played a pivotal role in the dialectic of rebellion in the east. From the earliest days of the colonial period, a Tetela-Kusu myth had developed. Tippu Tip claimed to have received the keys of the Maniema kingdom from Kasongo Rushie, whom he described in his memoirs as the "Sultan of Utetera."[69] Subsequently, Tippu Tip's legendary lieutenant, Ngongo Lutete, led marauding bands of Tetela-Kusu on raiding expeditions throughout the Maniema-Sanguru-Lomami areas. A large percentage of the *wangwana* (free men) who settled around the Swahili outposts of Kasongo, Nyangwe, Kibombo, and Kisangani, and were labeled by the Belgians as *arabisés*, were of Tetela-Kusu origin.[70] Ngongo Lutete allied himself with Congo Independent State forces in 1892, and many of his men joined the *Force Publique*. Two major mutinies, in 1895 at Luluabourg and in 1897 in the Ituri forest, were described as "Tetela revolts."[71] The group was divided by colonial administrative boundaries, with those in

[67] J. C. Willame, "Nord-Kivu," in "Les Provinces du Congo," *Collections d'Etudes Politiques*, Oct. 1964, 27-66.

[68] Daniel Biebuyck, "La Société Kumu face à Kitawala," *Zaire*, XI (1957), 7-40.

[69] *Maisha ya Hamed bin Muhammed el Mujebi yaani Tippu Tip*, trans. by Wilfred Whiteley, supplement to the *East African Swahili Committee Journals*, 28/2 (July 1958) and 29/1 (Jan. 1959) §99.

[70] See Crawford Young, "Islam in the Congo," in James Kritzeck and William Lewis (eds.), *Islam in Africa* (New York, 1969).

[71] See the interesting effort by a Soviet historian at identifying these mutinies as proto-nationalist episodes in A. Zousmanovitch, "L'insurrection des Batetelas au Congo Belge au XIX Siècle," *Présence Africaine*, 51 (1964), 159-69.

Maniema labeled "Kusu" and those in Sankuru (Kasai) as "Tetela." A congress called in March 1960 asserted the cultural unity of the group, designated it "Ankutshu-Anamongo," and pledged its support to the party of its favorite son, Lumumba.[72] The ethnic solidarity of the Tetela-Kusu, and its affinities with the eastern portion of the much vaster Mongo culture cluster, was one pillar of the electoral success of the *Mouvement National Congolais*/Lumumba "youth" in 1960.

In 1960, a tract appeared which played a major part in establishing the political legend of the Tetela-Kusu. Entitled "Parchemin que tout Ankutshu doit avoir et connaitre par coeur," the document is a statement of extravagant ethnic chauvinism.[73] Its origin is obscure, but the improbable extremism it expressed led most observers to believe it to be a forgery. In 1964, the "Parchemin" reappeared throughout rebel areas in the eastern Congo. Its concordance with the fears and suspicions evoked by the striking pre-eminence of Tetela-Kusu in rebel leadership ranks, and above all in the popular army officer corps, gave it a subjective authenticity. Whatever its origins, it came to be widely believed in intellectual circles.

The tendency to identify the rebel elite with Tetela-Kusu became more pronounced with the establishment of a revolutionary government in Kisangani. Gbenye, president of the revolutionary government, was a Bua, but the other two designated ministers actually in Kisangani, Soumialot and François Sabiti, were both identified as Kusu. In Kindu, the designated provincial regime had eight of twelve Tetela-Kusu ministers who dominated the government. Gbenye was led to communicate an order to the commander of the "3rd Groupement" of the popular army at Kisangani warning, "There could be no question of being Mutetela to be promoted, and we must not limit the success of our citizens because of their ethnic origins."[74] Particularly in the northeast, mutterings about the "foreign" character of the revolutionary regime were frequent.

Curiously, the Tetela-Kusu saliency in the eastern rebellion did not achieve massive support for the rebellion in Sankuru. Provincial politics in Sankuru had catalyzed a division between Tetela "Eswa" and Tetela "Ekonda" which had not previously been perceptible to students of the area. The "Eswa" group, roughly speaking, lived in the savannah lands, and had experienced some acculturative contact with the Arab-Swahili trading states of the nineteenth century. The "Ekonda" were

[72] The resolutions of this Congress are reproduced in Jules Gérard-Libois and Benoit Verhaegen, *Congo 1960* (Brussels, 1961), III, 7-18.

[73] The text of the tract is reprinted in Paul Ribeaud, *Adieu Congo* (Paris, 1961), 22-25.

[74] *Congo 1964*, 312.

forest dwellers who occupied a more inaccessible area where opportunities for economic and social change had been less. By 1963, bitterness between the two reached the point where a large part of the principal town of Lodja was burned. The legacy of this dispute appears to have precluded a unified response to the rebellion, despite the identification with all of its symbols. Rebel operations in Sankuru were ephemeral and superficial.

Structure and Leadership: Political Resources and Radius of Influence

There were a number of instances where ethnic communities did not respond as a single group to the rebellion. In these instances, a dialectic of local factionalism frequently operated. The choice of a given leader or faction tended to be determined by the choice made by the alignment of the local faction with whom conflict was most salient; it was in terms of this symbiosis of hostility or alliance that the rebellion would be perceived. (A similar pattern has been widely remarked upon in choosing between co-operation and resistance in the initial phase of colonial penetration, and in the diffusion patterns of rebellious movements such as Maji Maji.[75]) By adding this factor, one may complete the analysis of diffusion in Kwilu. The Mbunda and Pende wholly identified with the symbols of the rebellion, and rallied en masse. The Mbala and Ngongo were so threatened that they opposed as communities. In other small groups in the area, neither attracted by nor totally repulsed by the ethnic identifications of Mulelism, the local dialectic prevailed—examples of this reaction were found at least in some degree among the Ding, Lori, Nkutshu, Shilele, Suku, Wongo, and Yanzi.[76]

At the leadership level, the rebellion was far too diverse for any single man to assert personal ascendancy; the most prominent individuals, such as Gbenye, Soumialot, Olenga, Bocheley-Davidson, Mulele, and Gizenga, each had orbits of influence determined by their range of activities. Gbenye had two key assets: regional support from the Bua area, in the Aketi-Buta zone of Uele, and an intimate familiarity with the complex social relationships in Kisangani deriving from pre-independence prominence in the city. Soumialot had a radius of activity with Kindu as its hub, and Maniema, South Kivu, and part of North Katanga enclosed within its circumference. However, he had

---

[75] Leonard Thompson has found a similar pattern in his study of southern African resistance movements. Oral communication.

[76] Fox et al., "La deuxième Indépendance," 24.

never lived in Kisangani so that when the Lumumbist capital became the central place of the eastern rebellion, Soumialot was partly eclipsed by Gbenye. François Sabiti could be effective within the Kisangani urban area, but nowhere else. Bocheley-Davidson held as his precarious political resource the Brazzaville exile machinery, but could not have challenged Gbenye, Soumialot, or Olenga on the ground in the eastern Congo.

The rebellion produced a growing number of structures which served as resources in the matrix of interpersonal rivalry. The Mulelist maquis possessed its own infrastructure, not linked to any other. The *Conseil National de Libération* in Brazzaville was split into Gbenye and Bocheley-Davidson factions within a month after its foundation. When Soumialot established operations in Bujumbura, he set up a "CNL-East." After the establishment of the revolutionary government in September 1964, Gbenye and Soumialot quickly came into conflict over their respective prerogatives. Gbenye argued that the revolutionary government had superseded the *Conseil*, while Soumialot maintained that his responsibilities as head of "CNL-East" gave him separate sanction for his exercise of authority.[77] At the same time, at the OAU summit conference in Addis Ababa which took place simultaneously with the proclamation of the revolutionary government in Kisangani, Bocheley-Davidson reaffirmed that the *Conseil National de Libération*/Brazzaville was the sole representative of the Congolese revolution and that Gbenye had been expelled from his office in the Conseil. The *Mouvement National Congolais*/Lumumba "youth" re-emerged as yet another structure, with two committees, led by Victor Benanga and Gustave Ifefeko, respectively, appearing in Kisangani the day after the *simba* conquest. In Kindu, a Conseil des Sages was constituted as a quasi-provincial assembly, as well as a new provincial government. *Mouvement National Congolais*/Lumumba "youth," and the *femmes nationalistes* were other structures offering organizational resources to local leaders. Finally, the popular army under Olenga was to all intents and purposes an autonomous body.

The organizational picture became even more complex in the declining phase of the rebellion, when much of the activity was carried on in the vacuum of exile. Brazzaville, Accra, Conakry, Algiers, Cairo, Khartoum, Kampala, Dar es Salaam, and Bujumbura provided the changing loci for shifting alignments of rebel personalities and their

---

[77] On the very day of the proclamation of the revolutionary government, Gbenye wrote Soumialot a curt official letter informing him that, "from the moment that the Revolutionary Government was officially invested, the activities of CNL-East which you direct are terminated." Soumialot never accepted this interpretation.

diminishing clientele. In April 1965, Soumialot established in Cairo a *Conseil Suprême de la Révolution* which included Gabriel Yumbu and some other members of the Bocheley-Davidson wing of the *Conseil National de Libération*, but excluded Gbenye and Olenga. Bocheley-Davidson himself at this juncture had a temporary reconciliation with Gbenye. Col. Vital Pakassa, a former national army officer who had been a close associate of Gizenga, rallied to the Gbenye camp and was assassinated in Cairo by Soumialot's men. Gizenga, driven by a curious obsession as the self-anointed successor of Lumumba, in 1965–66 became an important part of the mosaic. After his release from prison by Tshombe in July 1964, he declined to join the *Conseil National de Libération*; instead, he sought to organize his own United Lumumbist party, repeating an unsuccessful initiative of 1961. In September 1966 in Cairo, he formed a *Front Congolais de la Révolution*, which won over some of the exile clientele. The remaining pockets of internal rebel resistance had their choice of soliciting external support from the Gbenye, Soumialot, or Gizenga factions.[78]

The arena of conflict determined what political resources could be brought to bear. In 1964, when the decisive action occurred on the sundry battlegrounds of insurrection within the Congo, leaders able to provide direction and relative control within this framework were predominant. The metamorphosis into the murky world of exile politics compelled rebel elites to base their actions upon other foundations. Access to moral backing and financial support from states committed to at least covert support of Congolese revolutionaries was one key. In this type of world, Olenga was simply unable to compete. On the other hand, Gizenga by 1965–66 could appear as the most plausible revolutionary alternative to external supporters. His absence of grass roots revolutionary capability was less important than it had been at the peak of rebellion.

Rebellion in Power

The dilemmas of the deprived in the Congo were illuminated by the record of the rebellion in power. A paradoxical aspect of the rebellion was that its greatest success was its greatest disaster. The capture of Kisangani led to the erection of the form and structure of a regular government, but the rebel regime in its three months of power demonstrated that, although it might make things worse, it had neither the ideas nor the capacity to make them better. The surfacing of latent

[78] For details on the labyrinthine history of exile cliques, see C.R.I.S.P., *Travaux Africains*, 61(1968); *Congo 1965*, 170-200; *Congo 1966*, 421-30.

personal tensions, the multiplicity of organizational structures, the unleashing of the most violent and dangerous rebel support groups, and the vaguely politicized urban youth, all combined to lead to an inevitable and disastrous result.

The Kisangani problem was foreshadowed by the train of events in Kalemie, the first significant town under prolonged rebel administration. At the beginning of the two months of insurgent rule in late June, Soumialot imposed a tenuous order upon the town, and popular army units kept themselves and the terrorist groups under some control. Soumialot, who had never lived in Kalemie, tried to maintain his version of personal rule; his days were passed in continuous audience, listening to the complaints and pleas of the unemployed, functionaries, schoolmasters, pastors, thieves, and company representatives. But personal rule and improvisation were inadequate to sustain the city. After a little more than a month, Soumialot left in despair, and the town sank into total chaos. It was described by one witness: "There is no longer any authority whatsoever in Kalemie; the so-called rebels have barely heard of Soumialot, who has in any case left for Kindu. Everyone has equipped himself with a scrap of paper, bearing the title he has given himself. Colonel, Chief of Special Branch, Police Commissioner, etc. It is the most total anarchy, which encourages theft and pillage, the ultimate aim of these disoriented young men, transformed for the instant into insurgents."[79]

In Kisangani, the insurgent regime was initially sustained by the euphoria of success, the new hopes for a genuine second independence which had been generated, and the confiscation of the liquid capital available in bank vaults, company cash boxes, and shop inventories. The first rebel authority was a triumvirate of "youth," which proved to be literally a *tsotsi* regime; "youth" power was turned to the task of unrestrained vengeance against all who were labeled as "PNP." The installation of the revolutionary government under Gbenye saw an effort by an older generation of politicians to assume charge and to reassert social control over the forces unleashed by the rebellion. What is striking about the Gbenye period is the effort to restore precisely the patterns of administration which had prevailed before. Aside from new personnel and an alteration in rhetorical style, the rebel regime came empty-handed to its rendezvous with the millennial dreams of its following. The only innovation was the further diminution of administrative capabilities, produced by the purge of "PNP" elements from the public service and the assassination of others, the rupture of supply routes, and the confusion resulting from multiple claimants to

[79] Quoted in Verhaegen, *Rébellions au Congo*, 465.

the various segments of authority. The seriousness of the deterioration of the situation was concealed by the depletion of stocks of all sorts —monies, vehicles, fuel, and other goods. In Kisangani and Isiro, "People's Co-operatives" were opened and confiscated goods were sold at 1960 prices. The supplies, obviously, did not last long, and there was no possibility of replenishment. The devastating impact of these destructive policies was not fully felt until after the rebel authority had evaporated from the towns of the northeast. Even the modest pre-rebellion level of economic activity in this vast area has been impossible to restore, and in 1968 the prospects were dreary.

Concluding Remarks

Strategists of rebellion for the Congo would appear to be faced with an insoluble dilemma. At the present stage in the evolution of society and polity, there would appear to be no navigable channel between the Scylla of ethnic encapsulation and the Charybdis of incapacity to govern urban areas. The Mulelist strategy, despite its far greater sophistication in formulating ideology and exploiting the technology of guerrilla warfare developed in China, Vietnam, Algeria, and Cuba, was in the last analysis a failure when judged against its presumed goal of overturning the Kinshasa regime. Mulelism defined its own orbit of action. Once the movement had set its limits, the government could at its leisure wear it down by slowly breaking the crucial links between partisan teams and village support bases. The village populations could not indefinitely withstand the tremendous hardships caused by their forcible relocation in the forest with the partisans; little by little they succumbed to the blandishments of the government to leave the encumbering presence of the guerrilla units. The process took a heavy human toll, as both the government and partisans directed their reprisals at the most vulnerable group, the villagers.[80] In the eastern Congo, the whole flimsy superstructure centered on Kisangani was extremely vulnerable to counterattack by even a modest military force. An illusion of omnipotence tottered upon incorporeal pillars of magic. The sorcerer's apprentices of terror and demoralization swept away the national army units and the legal administration in front of the advancing *simba*. But the process was halted where the attainment of the perimeter of insurgent appeal was combined with the injection of a small but decisive counterforce of mercenaries who were impervious to the primary weapon of the insurgent army. The effective force of white mercenaries which went into action at the beginning of September

[80] On the pacification campaign in Kwilu, see *Congo 1965*, 89-134.

was four hundred; in addition, the capabilities of the national army were enhanced by a modest number of Belgian military advisers, and a handful of aircraft secured through the good offices of the United States. The added force input was infinitesimal when contrasted to the 500,000 French troops in Algeria, or a similar number of American in Vietnam. Presumably the warnings of Debray to Latin American revolutionaries concerning the illusions of liberated zones, and the dangers of false analogies with the Chinese situation, are germane.[81]

The conclusion to be drawn from the Congo rebellion would seem to be an empirical invalidation of Chou En-lai's classic observation that "Africa is ripe for revolution." More germane is Zolberg's penetrating observation:

> . . . it is unlikely that movements such as these will be able to translate their revolutionary aspirations into the institutionalization of a new regime and of new social structures. African society does not have a center; its syncretic character insures that it cannot be turned upside down, or that if an attempt is made to do so, some groups will shift their relative positions but the society as a whole will remain very much as it was before.[82]

The very lack of integration of a polity as vast and diverse as the Congo means that all roads to rebellion lead to the same impasse. Neither China nor Cuba—nor Zanzibar—can serve as a political model for the Congo. The millennial dreams of the deprived have given way to renewed despair, as the devastation and destruction remaining from the aborted rebellion are visible to all in the affected zones. A post-rebellion song from the Pende areas of Kwilu which gave strong support to Mulele suggests that those who paid the enormous price of embarking upon unsuccessful revolt will be reluctant soon to repeat the experience:

> Quand je vous vois, la honte me prend
> Oh vraiment, quand je vous vois
> la honte m'etreint;
> Car nous avons été
> Trois années entières dans le bois
> Parce que Mulele avait donné
> de mauvaises directives.
> Pour avoir donné de mauvaises directives

[81] Regis Debray, *Revolution in the Revolution?* (New York, 1967), 59-68. I am indebted to Thomas Turner for this observation.

[82] Aristide Zolberg, "The Structure of Political Conflict in the New States of Tropical Africa," *American Political Science Review*, LXII (1968), 85.

Gatshinga fit périr une multitude d'hommes
et à sa suite
Funji avait aussi montré
une mauvaise voie
Qui fait périr une multitude d'hommes.[83]

The very disparities which created the insurrectionary potential in the first place are redoubled; nothing could be more vivid than the contrast between the relative opulence of the Lower Congo, and the hopelessness of Kisangani. No doubt the illusion of the apocalypse will be reborn, and new prophets will bear the message. Only the most consummate leadership can forestall yet another rendezvous with rebellion.

[83] C. Gudijiga, "Poèmes pende," *Voix Muntu,* 2 (1967), 20-32. Gatshinga and Funji were leaders of the 1931 Pende rebellion.

THE FRAGILITY OF STABILITY:

THE FALL OF THE NIGERIAN

FEDERAL GOVERNMENT, 1966

JAMES O'CONNELL

In retrospect it is possible to explain why the Nigerian federal government that emerged out of the independence settlement of 1960 proved fragile.[1] Stability is closely linked with political integration. But such integration cannot be easily achieved in multi-ethnic (multi-national is a better term) states where the different groups have no long history of association with one another.[2] Economic development and the expectations it arouses also condition integration and stability. And not least is the caliber of the political leadership that sets out to create integration and foster economic growth. By analyzing these factors it is possible to outline a simple, theoretical framework[3] that helps to explain why Nigeria—as well as other African countries—has proved politically unstable.

A number of conditions need to be taken into account. For one thing, the presence of a referee falsifies the power struggle before independence. Not only do the officials of colonial power represent an interest group in the pre-independence settlement but, no matter how

---

[1] See the optimistic remarks on Nigeria's political leaders in Margery Perham, *The Colonial Reckoning* (London, 1961), 77-78. A conviction that the existing governments were strongly in control and hardly likely to be removed by what opposition existed runs through the generally shrewd commentary of John P. Mackintosh in his *Nigerian Government and Politics* (London, 1966). The final stages of preparing the book were overtaken by the January coup. The hasty revisions leave a number of glaring anomalies behind.

[2] On Nigeria as one state and many nations, see O'Connell, "Senghor, Nkrumah and Azikiwe: Unity and Diversity in West African States," *Nigerian Journal of Economics and Social Studies,* V (1963), 77-93.

[3] This framework is outlined at greater length in James O'Connell, "The Inevitability of Instability," *Journal of Modern African Studies,* V (1968), 181-91.

fairly they act, their presence has the effect of creating artificial conditions for the struggle for power: they determine the rules of the game and they back them with their power. Often the nationalist leaders add to the artificiality of an independence settlement by being more bent on hastening independence than on definitively settling the location of power. This restricted political process may produce a constitutional framework that fails to reflect the relative strength of the various groups within a state. It also tends to keep politicians from gaining the experience which could teach them that power must normally be limited in its use to prevent politics from destroying those who take part in it. This experience is all the more important for men accustomed only to the autocracy of a colonial government which combined the exercise of executive, legislative, and judicial powers.

Furthermore, the failure of economic growth to meet expectations creates frustrations that explode more easily against the government than against other institutions. Moreover, growth leads to a scramble for its benefits and seldom fails to increase tensions among ethnic and other groups. Nigeria offers illustrations of this revolt against authority in the context of the bitterness that arose with the competitive modernization of the elite groups of the most socially and politically advanced of her peoples.

Finally, in a developing country political skills are no more abundant than any other skills. Political leaders with traditional backgrounds do not easily acquire attitudes that enable them to correlate financial expenditure and economic development, to understand the potentialities and exigencies of machine technology, and to cope with the highly structured and relatively impersonal bureaucratic procedures that are required for decision-making in societies that are striving to modernize rapidly.

Any one of these three broad factors is capable of threatening the stability of political authority in a developing country. But the social conditions indicated by these variables can also occur simultaneously. When that happens, the factors threatening stability exercise a reinforcing effect on one another and make instability an ever more likely outcome. This is precisely what happened in Nigeria.

The Erosion of a Constitutional Settlement and Constitutionalism

For practical purposes the Nigerian anticolonial front, which was on occasion able to stir up the socially mobilized classes against the colonial administration, broke down in 1950–51 when the revision of the Richards constitutional arrangements offered the prospect of effective power to political leaders.[4] Political parties quickly came into being. Their founders sought support mainly from among their own ethnic groups. The local communities within each ethnic group grasped the advantage of organizing along ethnic lines to promote their own welfare and interests and to protect their own social identity against the encroachment of other groups. Three main parties—the Action Group, the National Council of Nigeria and the Cameroons, and the Northern People's Congress—emerged. Each came to control the government of the region where the ethnic group that was its main support was in a majority.[5]

For some ten years, as their representatives modified the country's constitutional structure in the direction of increased regional autonomy and as they worked out issues such as the timing of independence and the status of Lagos as the federal capital, the activities of the parties fostered considerable bitterness among the different peoples who supported them and among the leaders who were competing for power. The parties sought to consolidate their base areas of support, to win over minority groups, and to eliminate opposition. Yet by and large they exercised considerable restraint on issues which might easily have provoked violence among their followers. If they strayed sometimes from the spirit of the law by using unfair methods—such as the selective distribution of social services—to attract support or to intimidate opposition, mostly they stayed within the letter of the law. Behind this observance of the law lay a realization that the British authorities could in an emergency deploy enough force to overcome the violent opposition of any section of the country. There also was among the political elite a genuine regard for the law. But the weakness of the observance of law was exposed as it gradually became clear that at least some of the leaders were only waiting for the British to leave to settle accounts among themselves.

The restraint imposed in part by the implicit threat of colonial force, and in part by the presence of large numbers of colonial officials in key administrative posts, was complicated by the role that the British played in constitutional evolution. The central political issue during

[4] Governor Richards's proposals were put forward in *Proposals for the Revision of the Constitution of Nigeria*, 6599 (1945). They were the first constitutional move to independence. For a discussion of the proposals and political reaction to them, see James S. Coleman, *Nigeria: Background to Nationalism* (Berkeley, 1958), 271-95; Kalu Ezera, *Constitutional Developments in Nigeria* (London, 1960), 64-81.

[5] The National Council of Nigeria and the Cameroons, however, retained and sought Yoruba, Edo, and other non-Ibo support. But the Action Group and the Northern People's Congress in their beginnings leaned heavily on Yoruba and Hausa support respectively.

the 1950's quickly became that of the relative size and constitutional powers of the regions that made up the federation.[6] In 1947 the British had retained the existing administrative arrangements when they divided the country into Northern, Eastern, and Western regions. This division was to govern the country's entire subsequent development up to independence. The regions were already in existence in 1951 when the first broad-based voting took place. They polarized the voting. And so they determined the patterns of the alliances of the local communities.

There is some evidence to show that the colonial officials, when making preparations for the Richards constitution of 1947, set out deliberately to maintain the existing administrative boundaries in order to protect the Northern emirates and to enable them to collaborate with one another and with other Northern groups against the more educationally developed Southern peoples.[7] They argued—and not without reason—that in building up legislative institutions it was necessary to link together the two existing levels—the Native Authority councils and the Legislative Council in Lagos—and that to do this the nascent regional councils of chiefs and residents should be used as a consultative mechanism. But it is also true that the officials simply did not think beyond the already existing administrative structures. Administrative inertia and the understaffing of the war period hardly contributed to the devising of difficult, innovative reforms. And the British officials in the South, and particularly in the Yoruba-dominated West, felt much less affinity with and sympathy for the forest peoples among whom they worked than did their Northern-based counterparts for the Hausa-Fulani aristocracy. They were consequently a less forceful lobby at Whitehall and elsewhere for Southern claims.

The Southern politicians were initially more concerned with consolidating their base areas than with criticizing the boundaries of those

[6] On main issues in Nigerian politics between 1951 and 1960, see O'Connell, "Political Integration: the Nigerian Case," in Arthur Hazlewood (ed.), *African Integration and Disintegration* (London, 1967), 151-57.

[7] A former Governor of Nigeria, Sir Bernard Bourdillon, contended that the Richards constitution, far from representing separatist tendencies, ". . . represents not the division of one unit into three, but the beginning of the fusion of innumerable small units into three and from these three into one . . . The [regional] Houses of Assembly will encourage not only a very useful interchange of ideas, but the beginning of that widening of the social, economic and political horizon which is essential if the unity of Nigeria is ever to have any real meaning to its inhabitants." "Nigeria's New Constitution," *United Empire*, XXXVII (1946), 78. Mackintosh quotes from letters, which he says he found in an open file in a Northern department, passages which reveal how strongly the Northern colonial officials were determined to defend Northern traditions and interests as they saw them. Mackintosh, *Government*, 32-33. See also Ezera, *Constitutional*, 64-66.

areas. The revision of the Macpherson constitution in 1954 that turned Nigeria into a properly federal structure was meant by the politicians to protect their bases of support and their possibilities of patronage.[8] The Southern leaders realized much too late that the patterns of regionalization were permitting the Northerners to make their position impregnable. All of the earlier reflexes of the Northerners had been defensive because the Southerners were so far ahead of them in educational attainment.[9] Only much later, on the eve of independence, were they to come to understand that they could make use of their political power in the federation to develop their own communities and areas positively. In the earlier defensive constitutional bargaining the Northern politicians made extensive use of the skills and influence of their British officials. Not the least asset that the latter possessed was that they had an experience and detachment that enabled them to look beyond the immediate political battles. They were valuable allies at a critical juncture when the Northern leaders, for all their political acumen, were short of the skills needed to translate it into constitutional propositions and language. The Southern politicians neither sought nor received equivalent help from their officials.

[8] It was the constitution drawn up under Sir John Macpherson which provided for the setting up of elected legislatures in each region and the formation of regional governments. Macpherson replaced Richards in 1948 when the British government realized that a more liberal approach to political development was necessary. On the Macpherson constitutional provisions, see *Report of the Drafting Committee on the Constitution* (Lagos, 1950), *Review of Constitutional Proposals by Colonial Secretary* (Lagos, 1950), Sess. Paper No. 20; *Nigeria (Constitution) Order in Council*, 1951, S. I. 1172 of 1951.

[9] The contrast between Northern and Southern rates of socio-economic development can be best brought out by contrasting the levels of schooling reached by the different parts of the country and by the employment of skilled manpower. The statistics given are all from 1963, which is the last year in which they are available for all regions.

Enrollment in Primary Schools		Enrollment in Secondary Schools	
North	410,706	North	9,881
East	1,278,706	East	39,938
West	1,099,418	West	30,630
Lagos	107,552	Lagos	11,372

Skilled Manpower (excluding teaching and research)

Senior Category		Intermediate Category	
North	2,220	North	11,549
East	2,640	East	6,341
West	3,132	West	8,713
Lagos	5,738	Lagos	17,560

Source: Federal Office of Statistics, *Economic Indicators* (Lagos, 1966).

In the constitutional discussions that took place after 1954 the British government opposed the changing of the existing regional arrangements—whether by redrawing boundaries or by creating new regions or states. In the 1958 resumed constitutional conference the Secretary of State for the Colonies made clear to the Nigerian participants that if they were to insist on changes in the existing regional boundaries, independence would have to be delayed.[10] Earlier in 1957 the British government had reluctantly agreed to set up a commission to look into the claims of minorities, but it gave the commission terms of reference that were weighted against the creation of new regions.[11] Divided against and unwilling to trust one another, afraid of being outflanked by radicals who might claim that they had held up independence treacherously, and in any case anxious to take over power without colonial supervision, the Southern leaders accepted the British conditions for the timing of independence. These conditions left the Northern region with a population larger than the other two regions together and therefore with greater political influence in a country where representation was tied to population. The Northern leaders had made this settlement their own condition for staying in the Nigerian federation at a time when they had not yet clearly grasped how much the North stood to gain from the unity of the country.[12] In

---

[10] At the 1957 constitutional conference the position of the British government was that the creation of even a single new state "would create an administrative problem of the first order, the creation of more than one such state in any region could not at present be contemplated." *Report by the Nigerian Constitutional Conference, Held in London in May and June, 1957* (London, 1957), par. 24. At an earlier stage the Colonial Secretary, Alan Lennox-Boyd, had opposed states on the grounds of "fragmentation," see *West Africa* (May 28, 1955). The same Colonial Secretary insisted at the resumed conference in 1958 that were new states created independence might have to be held up, *Report by the Resumed Nigeria Constitutional Conference* (London, 1958). There were a variety of reasons for the British stand: the British considered that the Northern leaders (who were the ones that might most be weakened by a new state) were more sympathetic to continuing good relations with the British than were the Southern leaders; they were afraid of a fragmentation that might take the form of a proliferation of states or even the disintegration of the country; they were afraid that the Northern leaders might try to secede if they were threatened with the breakup of their territory; and they reckoned that the administrative and financial costs of new regions would be prohibitive.

[11] GB, Colonial Office, *Nigeria: Commission Appointed to Enquire into the Fears of Minorities and the Means of Allaying Them, Report*, MND 505 (1958).

[12] It took several years of the experience of ruling to convince the Northern leaders that proper access to the coast was vital to the economy. Ironically, the blockade imposed on the North by Colonel Odumegwu Ojukwu after September 1966 again brought home the same point to Hausa leaders who had been more than toying with the idea of confederation.

the minds of the Southern leaders there was the hope that once the British withdrew, they would use their control over the more developed parts of the economy and their lead in manpower skills to wrest power from the North. But whatever the longer term intentions and hopes of the Southerners, the first effect of a settlement that owed much to the administrative shape of colonial occupation and the exercise of colonial influence was a situation that is an anathema to federal theorists: a federation in which one unit predominates even when the others combine.

Independence was achieved without any serious squall. The first turning point in post-independence politics came with the Northern regional election in May 1961.[13] A combination of an appeal to Hausa-Fulani and Kanuri tradition, conciliation of the Middle Belt and non-Muslim peoples, and judicious resort to a mixture of force and intimidation, enabled the Northern People's Congress to win 160 of 170 seats. The scale of the victory made it clear that in any future general election the Congress would be able to win an absolute majority of the seats in the federal House of Representatives. Southerners saw the signs but they still thought that the greater freedom of a federal election—and the conduct of the 1959 federal election seemed to offer some support for this view—would allow the Southern-based parties and the Northern Elements' Progressive Union, the Hausa-Fulani opposition party, to win more seats than in a regional election.

The second critical turning point came in 1962 when the Prime Minister used a bout of fisticuffs in the Western House of Assembly as a pretext to summon parliament and put through legislation to declare a state of emergency, suspend the government of the Western region, and impose a federal administrator on the region. The federal government acted within the letter of the law: parliament could decide when a state of emergency existed in a region. But the government had departed from the spirit of the law and broken the rules of the game by using its majority in the federal parliament to crush a disliked opposition. No objective circumstances existed that would have justified the declaration of a state of emergency. Later the federal government aided dissident Action Groupers and the National Council of Nigerian Citizens opposition party to form the regional government.[14] But the

13 On this election, see O'Connell, "The Northern Regional Elections, 1961: An Analysis," *Nigerian Journal*, IV (1962), 181-87.

14 See Richard S. Sklar, "Nigerian Politics: the Ordeal of Chief Awolowo, 1960–65," in Gwendolyn M. Carter (ed.), *Politics in Africa* (New York, 1966), 119-66, for a most readable general account of the crisis and its immediate sequel. An account that is closer to the events and that is full of vivid detail is John P. Mackintosh, "Politics in Nigeria: the Action Group Crisis of 1962," *Political Studies*, XI (1963). These two groups later combined to form the Nigerian National Demo-

Action Group continued to command the support of the majority of the people of the region.

Once the rules of the game—those willed restraints on competitiveness that prevent politicians from destroying one another—are broken, there is implicit in the actions of those concerned an appeal to the manipulation of law and control of situations through superior force. Those who possessed power legally in Nigeria were to push to the utmost limits the advantages conveyed by this possession and were to ignore considerations that could not claim the protection or the support of the letter of the law. The logic of such actions leads toward the breakdown of the sense of justly ordered relations between individuals and groups, the rejection of and contempt for legality, and provocation of retaliation outside the law. The emergency in the Western region was the major step in the breakdown of constitutionalism—that mixture of just or acceptable law and the rules of the game without which the ultimate appeal is to force.

Once voting is linked to population, the census takes on political importance. Abundant evidence existed to show that the 1952 census (on which the distribution of seats for the 1959 election had been based) had undercounted the Southern areas. Hence, many Southerners hoped that the 1962 census might show changed population proportions between the regions. Before the census was held, vigorous propaganda to encourage registration was carried on in all parts of the country. Before long, however, suspicions were aroused that the count had not been fair and that many results had been inflated. The upshot was that the results were never released. Nearly all of the non-Northern members of the federal House of Representatives walked out in protest when Waziri Ibrahim, the Minister of Economic Planning who was in charge of the census, defended what the protesters considered an inflated figure for the North. In a move to reach a compromise, Sir Abubakar Tafawa Balewa declared that the government would sponsor another census. This time the results pleased the non-Northerners even less. Though the Northern proportion of the population fell by a small fraction, the proportions between the regions stayed much as they had been in 1952. The Eastern, mostly Council, members contested the figures in the federal cabinet. But the Prime

---

cratic party. As later resistance suggests, it picked up little support. Pamela Day, in a survey of student opinion at the University of Ife, found that only one student in eighty-three sympathized with the Nigerian National Democratic party, "An Opinion Survey of the Students in the University of Ife: 1962-63," *Nigerian Journal,* VIII (1965), 333-46. In this context it might be noted that the National Council of Nigeria and the Cameroons had changed its name after Cameroonian independence to the National Council of Nigerian Citizens but retained its initials.

Minister accepted them on behalf of the government.[15] The Eastern government tried to contest them in the Supreme Court but lost.[16]

Many individuals and groups in the South felt that they had been cheated both by the executive and the judiciary. Southerners in the federal and regional civil services were openly contemptuous of the population statistics that they were expected to use for various purposes. Educated opinion in the North remained exceedingly defensive over the results. Economic planners (including visiting experts from the World Bank) made no secret of the fact that the census was useless for planning purposes and that they were using private assumptions to calculate population size and growth. The central conclusion that politically minded Southerners drew was that there would be no change in the balance of power through population counting. This conclusion helped to deepen their resentment against Northern domination and their growing conviction that it was becoming increasingly difficult to secure a change of government through constitutional action.

The 1964 federal election was to test the Southern politicians' hypothesis that enough seats could be detached from the Northern

[15] The figures in the suppressed census (1962–63) were: North, 22.5 mil., East, 12.3 mil., West, 10.5 mil., and Lagos, 0.8 mil. There was probably some inflating of figures in the North but it was hardly considerable. There was considerable inflating carried out in the East and the West. There was evidence to show that the 1952 census in the North had been relatively accurate—it correlated well with tax figures and other statistics. But evidence existed, especially from school registration, that the 1952 census had undercounted the Southern peoples. For example, on the basis of the 1952 census it was estimated that 170,000 children of the six- to seven-year age group would register in the Western region during 1954 to enter school in 1955. It may be argued that some of these children did not belong to the age-group that was supposed to register. But it is also true that school registration and attendance were far from complete in many Western areas. There is a good discussion of the politics of the Nigerian censuses by Mackintosh, *Nigerian Government*, 547-56. He also gives some unpublished figures.

Population of Nigeria by Region

Region	Population, Present Boundaries			
	1931 Census	1952–3 Census	1963 Census	Per sq. mile
	(000)	(000)	(000)	
Northern	11,434	16,840	29,809	106
Western	2,743	4,595	10,266	337
Mid-Western	986	1,492	2,536	170
Eastern	4,266	7,218	12,395	420
Lagos (Township)	126	272	665	24,639
TOTAL	19,555	30,417	55,671	156

[16] The Eastern solicitor general had been instructed by his government to claim that the census was invalid because there had been irregularities in various procedures but the federal Supreme Court rejected the case after a short hearing.

People's Congress in the North to put it in a minority vis-à-vis the two main Southern parties and their allies. The Action Group and the Council had teamed up with the opposition parties in the North to form the United Progressive Grand Alliance. The Northern People's Congress had joined with the Western region governmental party, the Nigerian National Democratic party, which was made up of the former Council opposition members in the West and the Action Groupers who broke with Chief Obafemi Awolowo, the Action Group leader, at the time of the emergency to form the Nigerian National Alliance. United Progressive Grand Alliance tempers flared quickly when a mixture of the hopelessness of the struggle and administrative and other intimidation permitted the Northern People's Congress to return sixty-eight members unopposed in the North, where 167 seats had been at stake. These unopposed returns and the other difficulties that they ran into in campaigning finally convinced the leaders of the Grand Alliance that they were almost certain to lose the federal election. Eastern leaders were also upset by anti-Ibo declarations in the North and by the flood of refugees who had become nervous over a possible outbreak of communal fighting and who poured back into the East from the North.

In their last minute panic, the leaders of the Grand Alliance made the strategic mistake of boycotting the election. This gave the Nigerian National Democratic party more than half the seats in the West—they won by means of small polls and falsified returns—and an opportunity to conceal the strength of Yoruba opposition to the regional government. After the election the National Alliance claimed to have detached the West from the Southern camp and to be a genuinely national alliance that held a comfortable majority in the federal parliament. Though there was a constitutional skirmish between the President and the Prime Minister about inviting the latter to form a government (the President expressed doubts about the legality of the election), there was little that could be done constitutionally except to recognize the constituency results that had been declared.[17] To crown the fiasco, the Council's former federal ministers, anxious to retain personal prestige and patronage, persuaded their party that it

[17] There is an excellent account of the 1964 federal election and the constitutional quarrel between the President and Prime Minister that followed it by Mackintosh, *Nigerian Government and Politics*, 563-609. Yet the final reflection by such an acute commentator was extremely unperceptive: "Having stared the consequences of open conflict in the face, and knowing the legal and physical forces available to the government, southern politicians show all signs of being resigned to the situation and of being prepared to do the very considerable amount of good for themselves, their parties and their constituencies which the easy and moderate leadership of Sir Abubakar Tafawa Balewa permits," 609.

should join the government, and, at Sir Abubakar's invitation, went back into the cabinet. In a "broad-based" government that had a cabinet of twenty-six, and some eighty ministers in all, the Council played a role subordinate to that of the Democratic party, which had then become the prime ally of the Northern People's Congress.

On the level of elections there was one final opportunity left to show that the large National Alliance majority in the federal parliament did not reflect the real political divisions in the country and that the distribution of governmental power needed to be renegotiated. The opportunity lay in the regional election that was to be held in the West before the end of 1965. The outcome of this election, however, made clear that the Democratic party government was willing to use all of the opportunities that the possession of power made available to save itself from losing the election. It simply administered the election in such fashion as to make an overwhelming victory inevitable. Electoral officers hid to avoid receiving opposition nomination forms; ballot papers were distributed to government supporters; local government policemen and thugs were used to drive opposition supporters from the polls; counting of votes was falsified; and when everything else failed (it came to that in the majority of the constituencies), the government-controlled news media announced to a compliant electoral commission that the candidates of the Democratic party had won by handsome majorities.[18]

The only legal recourse left was to the courts. But, first, people had lost confidence and doubted that the courts would provide justice for the opponents of the government. Second, there were so many cases to be fought, the task of assembling evidence in the face of intimidation was so overwhelming, and legal procedures were likely to be so slow and expensive that the courts, even were they to be fair, offered little effective hope of redress.

The government dominated by the Democratic party had made a calculated gamble. They were prepared for some reaction to the falsified election. But they believed that their control over the administrative apparatus and the security forces would cow the Yoruba people, who were thought to respect the possession of power more

[18] There is as yet—though one is promised—no study of this election. Provided one allows for its bias, a great number of facts can be found in the issues of this period of the Action Group newspaper, the *Tribune*, published at Ibadan. The writer taught at the same period in the University of Ibadan and can bear out the descriptions in the text from personal observation and from interviewing. No final result of the election was ever published by official sources. Results were even being changed up to a late date after the election according to whether a candidate had opted for the government party or not! Further details are given below of the disturbances that followed the election.

than anything else. Protests in the form of disorders broke out, however, almost immediately. Instead of yielding to repression they grew worse and spread to most parts of the region. The federal government supplied police and soldiers to quell the disturbances. Balewa, who had initiated the emergency legislation for the West in 1962, now declared that he had no constitutional power to intervene against his ally, Chief S. L. Akintola, the Western premier. The revolt in the West was still on when the army coup of 15 January 1966 brought down both governments.

In short, the arbitrary use of power discredited its constitutional distribution between the regions and the peoples. The arbitrary use itself had been made possible by the artificial division of power in the independence constitutional arrangements which, by largely ignoring the minority peoples in each region, left the main control of power in the hands of the Northern political leaders. The federal system had been intended to safeguard the diversity of the country's peoples. But, in practice, it offered guarantees only to the majority groups. And even then it proved no defense against a central decision to break an opposition that controlled a regional government. Once the regional powers had been mobilized to create regional bloc voting, the size of its population gave the North a built-in parliamentary majority. But representation based on population was itself discredited by two abortive censuses. Elections are the main alternative to the forcible seizure or retention of power, but the Nigerian elections were discredited by malpractices. The courts offer another alternative to forcible efforts to secure redress, but in Nigeria the courts had become discredited, being considered either biased or ineffective. If the executive, legislature, and judiciary were discredited in these ways, power was soon likely to lie with those who could mobilize the men and the skills to hold it, or to take possession of it by force. In practice in the Western region effective power lay with the security forces on which the regional government was dependent for its survival. When a substantial minority of the army revolted in January 1966, constitutional order at the center failed to hold. Though the originators of the revolt did not succeed in taking over control of the government, the remnants of the army supreme command itself were obliged to fill the power vacuum.

The Tensions of Economic Growth

The 1950's were a period of economic buoyancy in Nigeria. The Korean War and other factors had kept the prices of the country's principal export commodities high. External reserves rose in the early part of that period. There was large-scale internal public spending which went mainly into economic infrastructure and education. Though the 1955–60 educational expansion in the Southern regions absorbed some forty per cent of the regional recurrent expenditures, these regions still had enough money available to keep the other parts of their economies moving and to absorb those job seekers who were emerging from the existing schools to enter the labor market. With rapid Nigerianization taking place in the public services, the future looked bright for prospective candidates not only with regard to entry into the services but also as to prospective promotions. Those years were the last years of the colonial era and they were also the first years of Nigerian internal self-government. They were prosperous years. Later they were obviously the years that Nigerians—consciously or unconsciously—were going to contrast with the first years of independence.

In a developing country whose peoples are as heterogeneous as those of Nigeria, two problems in particular arise in the course of economic growth. The first problem is the slow rate of economic growth in relation to the general level of expectations. The second is the sharing of the benefits of growth among the various socially mobilized groups. The late 1940's and the early 1950's had already seen the second problem posed acutely. After effective Nigerianization of the public services had begun, ethnically aligned competitiveness broke out among the educated members of the main Southern groups, particularly the Ibo and the Yoruba. The latter had been educated first and had for long almost monopolized the higher posts to which Nigerians had access in Lagos and the other coastal towns. Educated Ibo began arriving on the scene in the 1940's and were soon in a position to challenge the Yoruba quasi-monopoly, though hardly the Yoruba dominance. Bitterness grew apace in a modernizing situation in which interethnic competition for posts extended down to the meanest clerkship. What intensified the conflict was the realization in the early 1950's that those Nigerians who managed to get into the public service were getting in on the ground floor at a most crucial time. The social and economic struggle was inevitably part of, and exacerbated by, the political tussle for power that was taking place during the same period.

As the public services were regionalized and continued to expand, and as nearly all of the firstcomers moved up in the ranks, there seemed to be reasonable prospects for everybody. The extreme bitterness of the first struggle subsided. But if the later 1950's were in many ways notable for their absence of tribal conflict, changes were occurring that contained the seeds of later trouble. Universal primary education schemes were filling schools with millions of hopeful pupils. The secondary schools were also multiplying. But the top ranks of the senior civil service were nearly filled, and in a service that was no longer expanding rapidly there came to be less room in the lower and intermediate ranks than there had been. At the same time commodity prices were falling. With the arrival of independence, foreign capital grew cautious and there was less foreign private investment than had been hoped for by economic planners. The export of oil had not yet begun to make an impact on the economy. The cities were being crowded and their social facilities strained by ill-educated young job seekers who remained unemployed indefinitely or for long periods and who depressed the standard of living of the working brothers and cousins with whom they lived.

Discontent built up gradually and came to a head in several sectors of the economy at much the same time. In each instance social discontent was complicated by political sentiments, mainly but not exclusively Southern resentment and fear of Northern control. Three episodes merit special comment: the general strike that took place among the town workers; the revolt of the peasant farmers of the Western region; and the unsavory dispute over the vice-chancellorship of the University of Lagos that definitively split the Southern intelligentsia.

The Town Workers

By 1963–64 the workers in the towns had begun to feel the pinch of prices that had risen steadily from the time of the Mbanefo awards in 1959.[19] They began to press governmental and private employers for salary increases. Some ill-tempered strikes took place, notably a strike of dock-workers in Lagos during 1963 which the police repressed with some brutality. These strikes broke out in scattered industries and places and by and large met with little success. But a sense of working-class solidarity was gradually developing. In places like Lagos it was nourished in no small way by the opulent life of the top members of the political class. Workers began to think that they were being denied the gains of independence. Significantly the union leaders chose the celebration of Nigeria's declaration of republican status on 1 October 1963 as the moment to call a general strike. The timing was chosen on purpose to embarrass the government internationally. But it also

[19] *Report of the Commission Appointed by the Governments of the Federation, the Northern Region, the Eastern Region, and the Southern Cameroons for the Review of Salaries and Wages* (L. N. Mbanefo, Chairman), Lagos, 1959. The Western regional government had set up its own commission.

showed that by this time the working-class people possessed little senti-ment for the frills of nationalism. The government gave ground and the strike was called off on the condition that a commission would be set up to look into wages and salaries. Some nine months later, after the commission had reported and the government had in part rejected its recommendations, a general strike broke out.

Three factors, at least, lay behind the strike: (1) The workers wanted to improve their standard of living by obtaining salary in-creases. (2) The Southern workers—and it was in the South that the strike was successful—were increasingly bitter about Northern control of the federal government. Many speeches during the strike were di-rected against the North. And antagonism toward the Northern leaders was deepened by the repressive tactics used against the strikers in the North. (3) The workers generally resented the arrogance, the conspic-uous consumption, and the corruption of the politicians. They also re-sented the difference in the standard of living between themselves and the senior civil servants.

It took time for the government to realize that the strike was a serious matter. Several ministers whose departments were intimately concerned with labor affairs were either out of the country or absent from the capital. The White Paper issued by the government to give its views on the commission's recommendations was slow in prepara-tion, lacked political finesse, and provided the strike leaders with both the time and provocation they needed to mobilize support. A threaten-ing broadcast by the Prime Minister and excessive use of force by the police against the union leaders solidified the labor ranks. A great part of the modern sector of the economy, particularly transport and com-munications, was brought to a halt. The government was shaken by the strength that the unions were able to muster against it. After a strike of twelve days it agreed to raise its offer to the workers.[20] But inflation-ary trends in the economy were boosted by the settlement that was reached, and the workers lost within a few months a good part of the gains that they had made. No salary increases were given to the senior civil servants. The group that lost out most in the settlement was the nonunionized workers who were employed by small private enterprises and whose wages were not raised—private industry and commerce were technically outside the agreement but tacitly the larger employers had in the past tended to follow government policy. The strike did, how-ever, give workers generally a sense of their strength. And it suggested the strength of populist reaction against privilege and its alienation from the possessors of political power.

[20] See above, Robert Melson, "Nigerian Politics and the General Strike of 1964," 771-87, for a fuller account and documentation.

The Peasants

Rural dwellers are usually slower than town dwellers to perceive a sense of relative deprivation. They are also less subject to the tensions of social change because traditional authority patterns tend to hold rural communities together internally. But in the Nigerian countryside frustrations were beginning to become evident. In the Eastern region in 1957, for example, when the government reintroduced school fees for primary education, widespread anti-taxation riots broke out.

The Tiv, who lived in the Middle Belt (the southern and largely non-Muslim part of the Northern region) rose in revolt twice—in 1960 and again in 1964—in protest against an imposed, inefficient, and corrupt local government authority that did not offer them value in return for the taxes they were obliged to pay.[21] In the Ishan communities of the Mid-West, politically inspired rioting broke out in 1962 against the Western regional government for the part the latter had played in supporting injustice in the customary courts and in the unfair distribution of tax levies within the communities. In the North a minor Mahdist uprising took place and a detachment of police was wiped out. But the most serious uprising of all took place among the relatively well-to-do and largely cocoa-growing farmers of the Western region.

The immediate cause of the Western revolt—as we have already seen—was the falsification of the results of the 1965 regional election, coming as it did on the heels of the disputed federal election of the previous September. The Yoruba communities generally rejected the leadership of Akintola, the Premier, and gave their allegiance to Awolowo, the imprisoned Action Group leader, who became increasingly a symbol of Yoruba political identity. But the roots of the dissension went much deeper than matters of personal allegiance. The peasants looked back nostalgically to the period of Action Group government as an era of prosperity and associated the successor government with lower cocoa prices and falling standards of living. Were it not for this contrast, Akintola might at least not have provoked violent resistance; he had, in fact, won over a large section of the more well-to-do members of the Yoruba communities (though by and large he had not won over the teachers, small traders, clerks, professionals, and academics). Not only did the farmers consider that they were less well-off than before in terms of actual income, but they felt themselves increasingly burdened by edu-

---

[21] On the Tiv riots in 1960 and 1964, see Martin J. Dent, "A Minor Party—' The United Middle Belt Congress," in Mackintosh, *Nigerian Government*, 493-507; *A White Paper on the Government's Policy for the Rehabilitation of the Tiv Native Authority* (Kaduna, 1965).

cational expenses for their children. They were also concerned with the apparent waste of money in sending children to secondary modern schools which proved little better than primary schools as a preparation for employment.[22] There is some evidence, too, that the expansion of primary schooling had helped to make labor scarce and expensive on the farms. An effect of the scarcity of labor was a fall in food production that began to make itself felt in 1964 and 1965 and that led to considerably higher food prices during the "hungry season" before the harvest.

Running through all these issues was a sense of neglect. Government information services were not geared to the farmers, and they were poorly informed of the improvements being made in the rest of the country. They had only rudimentary medical facilities. In many areas they did not have proper water supplies, good roads, or electric light. Rumors of corruption in the marketing boards convinced them that their hard-earned money was being made off with by "chop-chop" politicians.[23] When their votes failed to oust Akintola, they seemed locked in hopelessness and despair. If they rose in revolt, it was in one last attempt to better their lot. Their revolt was given an edge by the petty bourgeois elements of the Democratic party that had ranged themselves around Akintola—little men on the make who violated justice within small communities, defied redress, and upset the sense of hierarchical order dear to Yoruba hearts. When the farmers rose in revolt, they hounded party representatives from their farms, their villages, and their towns; they burned crops, houses, cars, and persons; they were themselves killed in considerable numbers as they resisted the police and the army; they built road blocks, destroyed local government buildings, and cut themselves off from other communities; they halted travelers and held them for ransom. Hired thugs, some from outside the region, were paid by the leader of the Grand Alliance to help stimulate and keep alive the disorders.[24] Though aggravated by the

[22] The secondary modern schools offered three years of schooling after primary school but, unlike attendance at primary schools, attendance at secondary modern schools had to be paid for. In practice they did not impart the commercial or other skills that they had been intended to impart. For most pupils they simply prolonged the period of schooling at considerable cost to their families. Yet there were 110,000 pupils in those schools in 1962. The numbers subsequently began to fall off steeply.

[23] There were good grounds for their beliefs. See the *Report of the Commission of Inquiry into Certain Statutory Corporations in Western Nigeria* (Chairman: Mr. Justice Coker), (Lagos, 1962); Charles V. Brown, *Government and Banking in Western Nigeria* (Ibadan, 1964).

[24] The descriptions in the text have been put together from personal experience and from interviewing. How far feeling had gone may be gauged from the calm manner in which a man described to an academic colleague of the writer's

thugs, the disorders would nevertheless have continued without them.

The federal government gave its support to the regional government. No serious steps were taken by the Prime Minister to conciliate the alienated groups and communities. There were frequent meetings between Akintola and Sir Ahmadu Bello, the Northern Premier, who was also the leader of the Congress, the political party to which the Prime Minister belonged. Ahmadu Bello openly proclaimed his support for Akintola and the Western government. An entire region was alienated. Increasingly, the regional government depended on the security forces, and its writ did not run where they were not operating. But if the security forces enabled the government to stay in power, they could not enable it to govern. It also became more and more clear that the Southern members of the police force were disaffected and that the employment of Northern police drafted into the West was more provocative of bitterness than effective in curbing disturbances. By and large, an atmosphere of violence was building up in the country. And in that atmosphere it was easier for a group of impatient and frustrated men to move from constitutional action to the use of force to determine the possession of power.

The Intelligentsia

Discontent among the educated elite groups sprang in no small way from the political and social situation that has been described. But they had their own reasons for being discontented. Those who entered the public service in 1965 had little hope of climbing the promotion ladder as rapidly as those who had entered earlier. Yet the climate of rapid promotions persisted. Moreover, a scramble for the remaining top posts revived an atmosphere of competitive bitterness resembling the period after 1948 when the public service opened up to Nigerians. Inevitably the bitterness was greatest among the two main competing groups, the Ibo and the Yoruba.[25]

This hostility came to a head not within the public service but in a dispute over the vice-chancellorship of the University of Lagos. By devious but legal methods a Yoruba-dominated university council replaced an Ibo, Dr. Eni Njoku, with a Yoruba, Saburi O. Biobaku, who had already agreed to become the first vice-chancellor of the University of Zambia. More than most other posts the few vice-chancellorships available in the Nigerian university system underlined how limited the prospects were in the public service system generally and heightened

---

the practical problems involved in endeavoring to get a match to the clothes of a person who had already been drenched in petrol.

[25] On this general issue, see O'Connell, "The Political Class and Economic Growth," *Nigerian Journal*, VIII (1966), 129-40.

the importance of immediate advancement. When Njoku was ousted, the university staff split along Ibo-Yoruba lines. Into that combat went all of the pent-up feelings of men who were insecure in a situation of ethnically competitive social change. A press war was sparked such as had not been witnessed since the early days of the breakup of the nationalist front.[26] Both sides in the dispute found themselves appealing to a Northern Prime Minister for support and arbitration; neither side was particularly happy at having to do so. But Balewa's failure to intervene effectively revealed his incapacity to understand the issues that were at stake and his general lack of resolution in arriving at decisions.

After long months of controversy during which the university was closed, it opened under a Yoruba vice-chancellor and with its reputation badly tarnished. The Nigerian intelligentsia by and large divided into Yoruba and non-Yoruba factions in the dispute. At the other federal university, the University of Ibadan, social relations and academic co-operation among Nigerian members of staff (who were in the main Ibo and Yoruba) never recovered from the controversy. Morever, it left bitter and deep scars within the federal civil service. Few case studies so clearly illustrate the aggressive ethnicity and political ineptitude endemic to the last year of the first Nigerian republic.

The Southern scramble for appointments and promotions was complicated by the arrival on the scene of educated Northerners. The staff of the federal public service was less than five per cent Northern in origin. But the small number of Northerners who were in the public service held posts disproportionately important to their numbers. Moreover, many Northerners were being advanced faster than their Southern counterparts. From the viewpoint of federal logic and social equity it made a lot of sense to increase the proportion of Northerners in the service and to offer them definite prospect of advancement. But other civil servants whose personal prospects were threatened by the policy were little consoled by its national justification. Specific examples of Northern advancement in the latter part of 1965 evoked bitter feelings in Lagos. There was something close to mutiny in the federal ministries when in November fifteen Northerners were transferred, with promotion, from the North to the center—and it was known that more were to arrive in the new year. In the customs service a strike broke out when preference over others was given to five Northerners, and the strike was settled only by the promotion of five Southerners. By and large a dis-

[26] There was a spate of publications from both sides in the dispute. Typical were titles like the following: *The Crisis over the Appointment of Vice-Chancellor of University of Lagos by the Senior Members of the Staff* (Lagos, 19 Mar. 1965); *Appointment of a Vice-Chancellor*, University of Lagos Official Publication (Lagos, 16 June 1965).

tinct malaise swept through the Southern-dominated federal service and damaged morale.

The young army officers were in no way insulated from the reactions of the educated intelligentsia in the civil service and elsewhere. In 1962 almost three-quarters of the army officer corps was Ibo.[27] By 1965 the corps had been considerably enlarged—army recruitment generally had been agreed to on a fifty-fifty basis between the North and the South. The Ibo officers still formed nearly half the officer corps, but they had the impression that Northerners were being recruited and promoted in such fashion as to damage their prospects of advancement. When the army revolt came, some of its psychological origins among the Ibo officers who formed the core of the rebel group lay in this discontent over promotions in an army that was intended to stay small. Yet the revolt would not have been possible for this kind of reason only. It must be placed in the context of the erosion of constitutionalism and the lack of esteem for the political class.

The Vicissitudes of Tradition

The final element in the Nigerian political breakdown lay in the difficulty which the political leaders experienced in adjusting traditional attitudes to the exigencies of the contemporary situation. Not only were traditional attitudes inadequate, but they degenerated in contact with situations for which they were not originally devised.

In a state composed of many nations the political class must lead the way in forging links between the communities and in founding or deepening a sense of nationalism on the level of the state. But those who led Nigeria had made their way up in politics by appealing to communal traditions. They themselves remained communal in outlook, and few of them came to think effectively in terms of the state which they represented and whose affairs they directed. In a sense, the Nigerian ethnic communities went on living with one another within one state in the kind of international relationship that they had lived traditionally with "stranger" communities. But in living within the one state they no longer possessed the safeguards of a genuine international situation; there were constant possibilities for uneasiness and tension between the communities. In a tribalistic situation—one in which bitter competition for posts and promotions occurred between the different elite groups of the most rapidly modernizing peoples—interethnic relations worsened considerably. Once such acrimonious relations existed and once constitutional safeguards appeared insufficient to the politically active members of ethnic groups, the conflicts within the state

[27] On the ethnic composition of the officer corps of the army in 1962, see William Gutteridge, *Armed Forces in New States* (London, 1962), 36-37.

quickly turned into a challenge to leaders who came from communities other than those of the challengers. The January cabal was based on an almost completely Southern plot. But it was a logical outcome of the distrust and resentment that had grown up in Southern communities against the Northern leaders who controlled authority in the state but who had been no better than any other leaders in acquiring a sense of Nigerian political identity.[28]

The politicians also failed to come to terms with the administrative and technological requirements of government in a large modernizing country. They were more interested in political infighting than in governing. They failed to grasp the tight connection between financial accounting, allocation of resources, and the growth of the economy. They delayed indefinitely, for example, decisions such as the one on the timing and location of a steel mill. They went ahead with educational schemes against the concerted advice of officials who said that their budgets would not stand the expense.[29] Yet for all their arbitrary use of power, these leaders were psychologically insecure in their possession of it, and they were both unwilling and afraid to display the tolerance which is essential to the pluralism of a multi-ethnic country. In short, most of them had neither the temperament, experience, nor education that would have enabled them to cope with tasks that would have tried the world's finest leadership.

As the 1960's went on, political leaders alienated the socially mobilized sectors of Nigerian society more and more. The latter had learned from Western nationalism to idealize to a considerable extent the traditions of their country. They also possessed a pride in pan-African possibilities. But they could have little pride or confidence in

[28] There is a sophisticated and able article by a Southern academic, Billy J. Dudley, that criticizes the pattern of Northern control, "Federalism and the Balance of Political Power in Nigeria," *Journal of Commonwealth Political Studies,* IV (1966), 16-29.

[29] The writer bases his knowledge of the advice of the officials on interviews with civil servants in both the Eastern and Western regions. A speech by Dr. Nnamdi Azikiwe in the regional Legislature in late 1957 on reintroducing school fees acknowledges what his civil servants had earlier told him but which had not been believed. An extract from the speech is found in L. Gray Cowan, James O'Connell, and D. G. Scanlon, *Education and Nation-Building in Africa* (New York, 1965), 157-58. The following figures give the percentage of educational spending as a percentage of governmental recurrent expenditure during the years 1955–62.

	1955	1956	1957	1958	1959	1960	1961	1962
North	20.1	25.4	24.0	24.5	24.4	23.0	22.4	23.3
East	37.6	42.5	59.0	43.4	45.2	44.9	41.5	38.2
West	40.7	36.5	42.8	41.3	40.8	43.9	44.6	47.3
Federation	16.4	18.7	22.0	21.2	21.4	22.6	21.3	..

men who were openly corrupt, who had used their positions to grow rich, and who had turned their riches into forms of conspicuous consumption that grated upon the poverty of the masses. In other words, the intelligentsia came to despise the leaders as arbitrary, ignorant, and corrupt. They not only possessed no confidence in the rule of the political leaders within the country but they were embarrassed that these men should project its image without. As this contempt was constantly voiced in the news media and in private conversations, the politicians had no illusions about the low esteem in which they were held. They finally cherished little respect for themselves and lost confidence in their own legitimacy. It is not surprising that at a moment when the majority of the army was still loyal, the morale of the members of the cabinet remaining in Lagos—who had failed to agree on naming an acting Prime Minister—broke down and thus permitted the army commander, Major General J. T. U. Aguiyi-Ironsi, to take over. The political leaders had already lost the will to rule.

Conclusion

Though this paper emphasizes one set of factors at a time—constitutional imbalance and the decay of constitutionalism, the frustrations of insecure or disappointed economic expectations, and the poor caliber of political leadership—it is impossible to separate the various factors from one another. They were interconnected and mutually reinforcing factors of instability. The decay of constitutionalism not only added to the social dissatisfaction that was already present from economic competition for scarce posts and benefits, but diverted political attention and energy from the tasks of economic growth. Reactions to a pace of economic growth that did not match the production of skills, particularly in Southern Nigeria, exacerbated dissatisfaction with the distribution of power and the manner of its exercise. And no leadership emerged that had an upright and competent image, transcended communalism, and avoided the worst pitfalls of the abuse of power.

This Nigerian case study emphasizes—as do similar studies of other developing countries—the superficial roots of the legitimacy of a modern-type authority in postcolonial, multi-national, and economically developing states.[30] Legitimacy requires a subtle combination of con-

[30] See, for example, Crawford Young, *Politics in the Congo* (Princeton, 1965); Dennis Austin, *Politics in Ghana 1946–1960* (London, 1964); Lucian W. Pye, *Politics, Personality, and Nation-Building* (New Haven, 1962); Clifford Geertz, "Primordial Sentiments and Civil Politics in the New States," in Geertz (ed.), *Old Societies and New States* (New York, 1963), 105-57; Hugh Tinker, *Ballot Box and Bayonet* (London, 1964).

sent and conciliation between rulers and ruled that results in the acceptance by the ruled that the proper persons are ruling and that they are ruling properly. Without this legitimacy government is—to say the least—not likely to prove stable. With the firm backing of the security forces a government may survive a temporary lapse in acceptance. But more than that is most improbable.

At this stage of the evolution of political events in Nigeria it would be easy to write with excessive hindsight about earlier events. The fall of the governments that the federation had at independence, which has been analyzed in this paper, led to a military regime that later fell as the army split. The result of this split was a challenge not only to the stability of political authority but to the unity of the political community. Factors came into play that had roots deep in the situation that led to the demise of the independence regime. They took on, however, a different pattern under the military regime, and they are not our concern here.

There are few grounds for optimism in the analysis of the Nigerian situation contained in this paper. Inevitably the question arises: Will Nigeria face a Latin American situation in which army coup succeeds army coup whenever social tensions cross a certain threshold? It is true that where the army has once intervened it will be tempted to do so again. Yet there is a case for stressing the positive elements that are to be found in the situation of instability that this paper analyzes. There is in Nigeria a genuine sense of constitutionalism that is based on a regard for law and order among peoples who are extraordinarily sensitive to the ill effects of disorder. The foresight and ambition of peoples who put a high premium on rapid economic achievement suggest that they also have a capacity to grasp with time that there are built-in limitations to the pace of growth and the spread of benefits in an economy that is developing rapidly by comparative standards. The military officers themselves are not allied to religious or economic reaction in an old-fashioned Latin American style but are what Hugh Seton-Watson has called "the intelligentsia-in-uniform."[31] And not the least effect of the growth of education in Nigeria should be the greater future availability of political skills.

[31] Hugh Seton-Watson, *Neither War Nor Peace* (London, 1960), 175-76.

THE COUPS IN UPPER VOLTA, DAHOMEY, AND THE CENTRAL AFRICAN REPUBLIC

VICTOR T. LE VINE

By March 1969 twelve of Africa's forty-two independent states were ruled by military governments that had come to power by unconstitutional means. The twelve regimes were, however, only the most recent and visible aspects of a mounting wave of domestic military intervention. Three of these regimes and the coups that brought them to power are the focus of this study. They are of interest not only because they took place within the short span of thirteen days (December 22, 1965–January 3, 1966), but because each case sheds some light on both the nature of recent African military intervention and the character of political instability on the continent. Since this study deals with three separate sets of events, the chapter will, in the interests of expository clarity, be organized into five sections: first, a summary of the salient facts in each case; second, a discussion of the broader, African context of the three coups; third, an examination of several of the relevant variables in each of the political systems; fourth, a discussion of the after-effects of the coups; and fifth, a summary and conclusions.

The Three Coups

Dahomey

In October 1963, the then Colonel Christophe Soglo had taken power from Hubert Maga, Dahomey's first President. Soglo ruled a provisional regime until January 1964, when he retired from politics and turned the government over to the country's leading—but feuding—politicians,

Sourou-Migan Apithy and Justin Ahomadegbé. Ahomadegbé had been freed from prison, where he had been committed by the Maga government for allegedly plotting a coup, and Apithy, nominally Vice-President of Dahomey, had returned from Paris, where he served as the Dahomean ambassador.

On November 29, 1965, in view of the fact that conflict between President Apithy and Prime Minister Ahomadegbé had blocked the operations of government, General Soglo forced the resignations of both men and extracted a promise of negotiations for a new civilian governing coalition including ex-President Maga. The President of the National Assembly, Tahirou Congacou, under the terms of the constitution became the provisional chief of government. On December 1 Congacou announced that he had formed a government, and on December 7 he and his cabinet were confirmed by the National Assembly. (Two years later, virtually to the day, Soglo himself was forced out by a junta of junior officers, without having reached his goals. The new rulers, perhaps taking a page out of Soglo's January 1964 book, restored civilian rule.)

On December 21, the National Assembly, summoned to Cotonou, dispersed without meeting. Open partisan violence had begun to flare up in various parts of the country, and, in Cotonou, massed demonstrators demanded the dissolution of the Assembly and the intervention of the military. The next day, General Soglo, by then chief of staff of the Dahomean Army, took power again. To justify his reintervention, he invoked "the spectacle of conflict between the political leaders," affirmed that he "would not be a dictator," and set himself a year to bring things back to normal by writing a new constitution and creating a unified, single party.

On December 24 a decree created a *Comité de Rénovation Nationale* of twenty-five members, including a new government composed of both technicians and military men. On January 3, 1966, the Soglo government broke diplomatic relations with mainland China.

Central African Republic

During the night of December 31, 1965–January 1, 1966, a group of officers headed by Colonel Jean Bedel Bokassa, chief of staff of the Central African Republic Army, wrested power from President David Dacko. Earlier, Commandant Henri Izamo, chief of the Republic's gendarmerie, had invited Colonel Bokassa and some of his officers to usher in the new year with him at his home, there allegedly hoping to arrest the lot and stage his own coup. Bokassa, apparently suspicious, instead invited Izamo to his office, and there arrested him. Shortly thereafter, Bokassa called out his troops and, after a brief exchange of fire with some gendarmerie units, gained full control of the situation. On January 1 President Dacko submitted his resignation to Colonel Bokassa and, together with most of his ministers, was placed under house arrest. Colonel Bokassa then dissolved the National Assembly and the Economic and Social Council, and proclaimed himself head of a government composed of three former ministers of the Dacko cabinet, plus six new ministers, of whom three were military officers. Colonel Bokassa also announced that his mission was exclusively to restore order and to prepare the country for free general elections, but he did not set a date for the latter event.

There had been very little resistance to the coup (save from the gendarmerie) and no counter-demonstrations. During the night of December 31, Colonel Bokassa's troops had placed roadblocks within Bangui and on routes into the capital; several people, including a Frenchman who had sought to pass them without showing proper identification, were shot. Also killed was Clement Hassan, secretary-general of the government. On January 6, the new regime broke diplomatic relations with mainland China, preparatory work was begun on a new constitution, and the detained ministers were freed. On February 1 ex-President Dacko was transferred from the military camp where he had been held to a villa next door to that of Colonel Bokassa (the two men are cousins). Dacko declared that Bokassa had saved his life, and Bokassa, in return, praised the former President. The chief of security, Jean-Prosper Mounounbai, was arrested, and Jean-Christophe Nzallat, the ex-chief of the political section of the presidency, was tried and convicted for complicity in a plot to train—with Chinese help—a "people's liberation force" and overthrow the Dacko regime. Mounounbai was shot and Nzallat imprisoned.

Upper Volta

President Maurice Yaméogo returned to Ouagadougou on December 6, 1965, following a Brazilian honeymoon with his second wife, whom he had married in October despite criticism by the local Roman Catholic clergy. On December 30 the Upper Voltan National Assembly passed Yaméogo's "austerity budget" that included, among other things, a 10 per cent to 20 per cent reduction in salaries of government employees and cuts in the *allocations familiales*. However, the budget included no reductions in the president's salary or perquisites. On January 1, 1966, a general strike of civil servants was decided upon and, in Ouagadougou, demonstrations were organized by students and trade unionists. Various delegations attempted to see Yaméogo, but were not received. Sometimes they were even brutally evicted from the grounds of the presidential palace. President Yaméogo declared the strike set for January 2 to be illegal, and broadcast a communique in which he claimed to have proof that a "communist-inspired movement," headed by a labor leader trying to hand the country over to Red China and Ghana, was seeking to create disorder in the capital. The demonstrations became more agitated during January 2, and both demonstrators and trade unionists began to demand that the army should take power.

On January 3 Lieutenant Colonel Sangoulé Lamizana, representing the army, did take power. Colonel Lamizana immediately issued orders that all agitation cease, singling out the trade unionists for particular warning. All remained peaceful. Ex-President Yaméogo himself issued a plea for the restoration of order, declaring that he was pleased with Colonel Lamizana's accession to power. Colonel Lamizana installed a "consultative committee" composed of civilians and military men to run the government and declared that even though the military wanted to "return to our barracks" as soon as possible, it would not do so until it could be sure that it would not have to come out again within a short time. The new regime immediately reduced both salaries and perquisites of government officials (20 per cent to 50 per cent cuts in salary, elimination of free automobiles, housing, utilities, and so forth) and placed a moratorium on all party activity.

On January 5 Colonel Lamizana suspended the constitution and dissolved the Upper Voltan National Assembly.

The Coups in Context

Between September 14, 1960 and March 1, 1969, no less than twenty-six unconstitutional changes of government took place in independent Africa.[1] (See Table 1 for the full list.) Eight of the twenty-six changes occurred during the six-month span from November 11, 1965 to April 14, 1966, sometimes referred to as "the winter of discontent." The twenty-six coups, putsches, mutinies, and revolts were notable because

---

[1] *The New York Times,* Jan. 3, 1963, 3; "Crisis in Upper Volta," *West Africa* 2536 (Jan. 8, 1966). By "unconstitutional changes" are meant changes for which no provision was made in the constitutions of the countries concerned. Even though many of these changes were almost immediately or subsequently legalized by the formal resignation of the head of the government or chief of state, the circumstances surrounding these resignations still permit the term "unconstitutional" to be used. "Independent Africa," as used hereinafter, refers to African states excepting the Republic of South Africa. Rhodesia, still formally in revolt against Great Britain as of this writing, is also excluded.

they succeeded; they were not, however, isolated instances of political disturbance in an otherwise calm continent. Since November 1958, when General Muhammed Abboud overthrew the government of the Sudan, major political disturbances have affected all but four or five of Africa's independent states. These disturbances have included not only the changes in government noted above, but such events as the secession of Eastern Nigeria (May 29, 1967); revolts (Algeria, 1963; Burundi, 1965; Congo/Kinshasa, 1960–65; Ethiopia, 1960; Mali, 1963–64; Sudan, 1963–present; Uganda, 1963); mutinies (Kenya, Uganda, Tanzania, 1964; Nigeria, 1966; Somalia, 1961); various abortive coups, plots, and putsches (Chad, Congo/Brazzaville, Congo/Kinshasa, Gabon, Ivory Coast, Guinée, Liberia, Mali, Nigeria, Senegal, Sudan, Togo, Tunisia); assorted alleged coups and plots; several successful and unsuccessful assassination attempts; and various instances of communal violence, riots, and border fighting (the last involving, notably, Algeria, Morocco, Tunisia, Uganda, Kenya, Somalia, and Ethiopia). Obviously, the three coups discussed here were not singular events. Given the increasing political instability throughout Africa, they were neither unusual nor exceptional.[2]

If the three coups were neither exceptional nor unusual, were they part of some broader pattern of increasing political instability on the continent? Given the frequency of military coups during the "winter of discontent," were the three coups connected in some way? There are no clear-cut, satisfying answers to either question. However, a careful reading of the available evidence does suggest some tentative answers:

1. What discernible patterns do emerge are rather limited, but, in any case, they do not suggest that any individual instance of instability

[2] Using the concept of "political violence," this writer, surveying 40 African polities between 1946 and 1964, found between 300 and 400 instances falling under this rubric. Victor T. Le Vine, "The Course of Political Violence in Africa," in William H. Lewis (ed.), *French-Speaking Africa* (New York, 1965), 58-79. Other general treatments of political instability in Africa include: Ronald Matthews, *African Powder Keg* (London, 1966); I. William Zartman, "The Limits on Violence and Intervention," in his *International Relations in the New Africa* (Englewood Cliffs, N. J., 1966), 87-104; Victor D. Du Bois, "African Ferment 1966," *American Universities Field Staff Reports*, IX (West Africa Series, 1966); "Après les militaires," *Afrique*, 54 (1966) 9-15; Ronald Matthews, "Forecast for Africa: More Plots, More Coups," *The New York Times Magazine* (Apr. 10, 1966), 10; Edmund Schwarzenbach, "Military Coups in Africa," *Swiss Review of World Affairs*, XV (Feb. 1966), 6-8; W. Arthur Lewis, "Africa's Officers Take Command," *The Reporter* (Mar. 24, 1966), 33-36; Aristide Zolberg, "The Structure of Political Conflict in the New States of Tropical Africa," *American Political Science Review*, LXII (1968), 70; Dennis Austin, "The Problem of Africa's Spate of Coups," *Times of Zambia* (Aug. 1, 1966).

TABLE 1 Unconstitutional Governmental Changes in Africa, 1960-1968

Date	Country	Summary of Changes
1. 9/14/60	Dem. Rep. of Congo	General Joseph Mobutu temporarily "neutralizes" politicians, takes power.
2. 1/13/63	Togo	Mutinous army elements topple government, kill President Sylvanus Olympio, recall Nicolas Grunitsky and Antoine Méatchi to head new regime.
3. 8/15/63	Rep. of Congo	Civilian-military coup forces President Foulbert Youlou to resign; new government headed by Alphonse Massemba-Débat.
4. 10/28/63	Dahomey	Col. Christophe Soglo deposes President Hubert Maga in military coup, returns government to civilians Sourou-Migan Apithy and Justin Ahomadegbé.
5. 1/12/64	Zanzibar	Bloody revolt overthrows regime of Sultan Abdulla bin Khalifa; Abeid Karume becomes president.
6. 10/30/64	Sudan	Civilian countercoup overthrows government of President Muhammed Abboud.
7. 5/19/65	Algeria	Col. Houari Boumedienne ousts President Ahmed Ben Bella in coup.
8. 7/7/65	Burundi	Prince Charles Ndizeye (later Mwami Ntare V) takes power from his ailing father, Mwami Mwambutsa.

❧   ❧   ❧

"Winter of Discontent"

Date	Country	Summary of Changes
9. 11/25/65	Dem. Rep. of Congo	Gen. Mobutu takes power from President Joseph Kasavubu.
10. 11/29/65	Dahomey	General Soglo removes President Apithy, Vice rule.
11. 12/22/65	Dahomey	General Soglo removes civilian government, takes President Ahomadegbé, seeks new civilian coalition power.
12. 1/1/66	Central African Republic	Col. Jean-Baptiste Bokassa overthrows government of President David Dacko in military coup.
13. 1/3/66	Upper Volta	Col. Sangoulé Lamizana overthrows government of President Maurice Yaméogo in military coup.
14. 1/15/66	Nigeria	Military junta headed by General J.T.U. Aguiyi-Ironsi overthrows federal government headed by President Nnamdi Azikiwe and Prime Minister Abubakar Tafawa Balewa.
15. 2/24/66	Ghana	Military coup overthrows government of President Kwame Nkrumah; General J. A. Ankrah heads junta.

Table 1   (*continued*)

Date	Country	Summary of Changes
16. 4/15/66	Uganda	Prime Minister A. Milton Obote ousts President Edward Mutesa, takes all executive power.

☼   ☼   ☼

Date	Country	Summary of Changes
17. 7/29/66	Nigeria	Army mutiny overthrows junta of General Ironsi; Lt. Col. Yakubu Gowon heads new Government.
18. 11/28/66	Burundi	Capt. Michael Micombero deposes Mwami Ntare V in military coup.
19. 1/13/67	Togo	Lt. Col. Etienne G. Eyadema seizes power from President Nicholas Grunitsky in military coup.
20. 3/21/67	Sierra Leone	Brig. David Lanzana seizes power from newly-invested Prime Minister Siaka Stevens in military coup.
21. 3/22/67	Sierra Leone	Military triumvirate arrests Lanzana, takes power; Lt. Col. Juxon-Smith becomes head of military government.
22. 5/27/67	Nigeria	Eastern Nigeria, headed by Col. Odumegwu Ojukwu, secedes from federation, declares itself Republic of Biafra.
23. 12/17/67	Dahomey	Junta headed by Maj. Maurice Kouandété seizes power from Col. Soglo, six months later turns government over to civilians, headed by Pres. Emile Zinsou.
24. 4/17–18/68	Sierra Leone	Military and police units, headed by two warrant officers, seize power, oust Brig. Juxon-Smith, within eight days restore civilian government, headed by P. M. Siaka Stevens.
25. 8/68	Congo/Brazza	Military group headed by Capt. Marien Ngouabi removes government of Pres. Massemba-Débat.
26. 11/19/68	Mali	Military Junta headed by Lt. Moussa Traoré overthrows government of Pres. Modibo Keita.

was necessarily related to any other. Although it is true that the major military figures in the three coups knew one another, having served under the same French flag and having been officers in the army of the Community, there is nothing to indicate that they plotted with one another or that the coup led by one influenced the coup led by another. Further, although it is tempting to argue that the example of one successful coup may have stimulated military men elsewhere to try the same thing, there is no evidence available as yet to show that during 1965–66 some sort of "demonstration effect" operated to motivate military men to topple one regime after another. This does not, of course, leave out the possibility that that may have been the case in one instance or another; as of December 1967, however, only one major military figure involved in a recent coup—Colonel A. A. Afrifa of Ghana—had published his memoirs, and there is nothing in his book to suggest that events elsewhere impelled him to join in plotting the downfall of the Nkrumah regime.[3] What the evidence *does* suggest is that the *causes* of most of Africa's political post-independence instability were and are largely *internal* to the countries concerned.

A corollary proposition may also be advanced at this point: in no case has it been proven that "foreign intervention" contributed directly to the fall of any African government; it is possible that indirect foreign pressures may have been exerted in one or two cases, but if so, such pressure did not determine the actual events themselves. It *is* true that "foreign intervention" was a factor in several *attempts* to bring down independent African regimes; one such attempt was certainly the so-called "Stanleyville revolt" in 1963–64 in Congo/Kinshasa, which would hardly have begun or been sustained without considerable help from "friendly" African states and "socialist" governments outside the continent.[4] The fact remains, however, that some of the better known cases of "foreign intervention" in Africa were supported by African states against each other; as examples one need only cite the several "national liberation movements" trained and supported by Ghana against the African governments of Niger, Cameroon, Senegal, the Ivory Coast, and Togo.[5]

2. Whether the three coups of this study were part of some general pattern of political instability depends, of course, on the extent to which one is willing to generalize about the events themselves. This much, at least, can be said: First, instances of major political instability and/or violence increased notably *after* independence was attained by most states. Coups, it is obvious, could not take place until Africans themselves held the reins of power. Other forms of political instability also became more frequent, if for no other reason than that most new Africans could not—or had no desire to—achieve at once the level

---

[3] A. A. Afrifa, *The Ghana Coup, 24 February 1966* (London, 1966).

[4] See above, M. Crawford Young, "Rebellion and the Congo," 969-1011.

[5] See, for example, *Nkrumah's Subversion in Africa* (Accra, 1966). Among those harbored, supported, and often trained in Ghana for subversion against Ghana's Organization of African Unity neighbors were members and leaders of such groups as Cameroon's *Union des Populations du Cameroun*, Niger's Sawaba party, and Senegal's *Parti Africain d'Indépendance*. The would-be assassin and his accomplices involved in an attempt to kill Niger's President Hamani Diori in April 1965 were in fact Sawaba members trained in sabotage in Ghana and infiltrated into Niger from Ghana. See also below, 1179.

of authoritarian control possible to colonial governments. Second, a common aspect of the major changes in regime in 1965–66 is that they all occurred in situations of extreme economic or political uncertainty and stress. The three coups of this study are certainly representative examples of this proposition. Whether the situation of political or economic stress in fact contributed to a particular regime's instability is something to be determined in each case. However, at least in the case of the military coups, there is evidence that military men felt—rightly or wrongly—that things had become so bad that they had to intervene to "save" their countries. Even a cursory reading of the post-coup statements of Afrifa, Kotoka, Ironsi, Bokassa, Lamizana, Soglo, and others suggests that this was the case. Third, the involvement of the African military *on its own initiative* is becoming more frequent, particulary in situations of political instability. Eighteen of the twenty-five unconstitutional governmental changes listed in Table 1 were led by military men; the last ten (July 1966 to November 1968) were wholly military initiated. Other reasons aside, it appears in most cases that when either or both the economic and political systems seemed on the verge of breakdown, the military men saw themselves as the only remaining organized force capable of taking charge and avoiding national catastrophe. And again, it should be stressed that what counted in each situation was the perceptions of the military men, not whether their vision was or was not true. In most cases, it must be added, the military men were not far off in their assessment. Whether their interventions were justified on that basis is, of course, another matter. Fourth, thus far, three military coups (Dahomey, October 1963; Dahomey, December 1967; and Sierra Leone, April 1968) and one civilian coup (Sudan, October 1964) have led to the restoration of civilian rule. Given the widely differing circumstances surrounding these events, it is impossible to tell if they represent a trend. They do testify, if they show anything, to the fact that military men are not always comfortable with the reins of power, and can be persuaded to turn them over to civilians with seemingly "right"—that is, uncorrupted— values. That disagreement over these values can result, however, was apparent during May 1968, when the Dahomean Army invalidated the results of a widely boycotted presidential election.

This, then, is the political context within which the three coups took place. The context has been sketched with only the broadest strokes, but it is enough to suggest that the events of December 1965 to January 1966 in the Republic, Dahomey, and Upper Volta were not unique, or isolated, and that they were a reflection of a more widespread continental political malaise.

Upper Volta

As long as ten months before the collapse of the Yaméogo regime it had become apparent to many members of the Upper Voltan political elite—both in and out of the government—that the country's political and economic prospects were far from encouraging. Five years of independence had not brought Upper Volta relief from its pressing economic and social problems, nor—it seemed to many—had an increasingly authoritarian regime, which lined its pockets while it issued ringing calls for public sacrifices and renewed dedication, done much to change the situation.[6] The judgments of the government's critics were certainly harsh, but any objective assessment of the situation in 1965 could not but confirm a considerable basis for pessimism, disillusionment, and frustration. It was the release of these tensions that finally brought down the Upper Voltan house of cards.

Except for the period from 1919 to 1932, Upper Volta did not exist as a territorial entity until 1947, when nationalist pressures from the traditional rulers of the Mossi people—a people numbering about 1.7 million, or about half of the country's population—persuaded the French to sever the area's administrative and political ties with the neighboring territories of French West Africa.[7] Mossi nationalism, which aimed at the reunification of the various tribes and clans that comprised the once great Mossi empire, was preempted by politicians —some of them Mossi—who saw the future of the territory as a multi-ethnic, modern political community in which they, rather than the traditional forces, would hold power. During the early post-war period a number of political parties, including several openly sponsored by the Mossi chiefs, competed for the allegiance of the growing electorate which had been created in the wake of France's post-war colonial reforms. Eventually, the *Union Démocratique Voltaique*, a branch of the regional *Rassemblement Démocratique Africaine*, came to dominate the political scene. The *Union* was led by Ouézzin Coulibaly, a close friend and old political ally of the Ivory Coast's Félix Houphouët-Boigny. Coulibaly, heading an alliance made up of non-Mossi and some Mossi, won the March 1957 elections to the Territorial Assembly, one result of which was to dash the Mossi chiefs' hopes of retaining special powers within the new government. Coulibaly died suddenly in 1958, just before the referendum on the new constitution,

[6] These observations emerged from a series of interviews with political leaders conducted by the author in Ouagadougou during Mar. 1965.

[7] The rise and decline of the Mossi as a political force is traced by Elliott P. Skinner, *The Mossi of Upper Volta* (Stanford, 1964), 179-203.

and the Assembly, meeting in extraordinary session later in October, elected Maurice Yaméogo[8] Prime Minister. The extraordinary session was unusual for another reason; its initial meeting was conducted under siege by the Mossi king (the Mogho Naba) and three hundred of his warriors. The Mossi chiefs hoped to force the creation of a government which Mossi traditional interests might dominate, but the demonstration was swiftly dispersed by French troops and the Mogho Naba and his followers were forced into humiliating submission. Not long afterwards the Yaméogo government stripped the Mogho Naba of all but his ceremonial powers.

The virtual elimination of traditional ethnicity as a salient factor in Upper Voltan politics had the two-fold effect of reducing the key political actors to those operating in the modern sectors of the polity and of bringing into sharp focus those issues of greatest importance to the country, that is, issues having to do with the bread and butter of Upper Volta's political and economic survival.

The creation of the first Yaméogo government in 1958 signaled not only the decline of traditional politics on the national level, but the beginning of a process whereby the active Upper Voltan political parties were gradually reduced in number so that by independence, in 1960, the *Union* remained the only effective, legally sanctioned party. Early in 1958 three main political groups were active on the national Upper Voltan scene: first the *Union/Rassemblement*, headed by Coulibaly and Joseph Ouedraogo,[9] the local branch of the *Rassemblement;* second, a group led by Joseph Conombo[10] that had splintered from the *Union* over the issue of affiliation with the *Rassemblement;* and third, a coalition of small political groups called the *Mouvement*

---

[8] Maurice Yaméogo. Born 1921 in Koudougou of Mossi peasant stock; attended the Catholic mission secondary school at Pabré; became a clerk in the government health services; served in the Territorial Assembly 1947–52; re-elected 1952, 1957; member of the *Grand Conseil* of the AOF; Vice-President of the local *Confédération Africaine des Travailleurs Chrétiens;* Minister of Agriculture, 1957; Minister of Interior, 1958; Prime Minister, 1958–59; President of the Republic, 1959.

[9] Joseph Ouedraogo. Former mayor of Ouagadougou (up to 1959); former member of Upper Volta Assembly, 1947–60; President of Territorial Assembly, 1952–53; Minister of Finance, 1957–58; Minister of Interior, 1958-59; former *Union* General Secretary; Vice-President of the *Confédération Africaine des Travailleurs Chrétiens* trade union; chairman of Trade Union Joint Action Committee, 1965–66.

[10] Joseph Conombo. Medical Doctor; member of Upper Volta Assembly, 1952–65; former member of French Government (Secretary of State of Interior, later Secretary of State for Economic Affairs, 1954–55); Mayor of Ouagadougou since 1961; first Vice-President of Upper Volta National Assembly; Organizational Secretary of *Union.*

du Regroupement Voltaique, operating as the local wing of the regional "federalist" *Parti du Regroupement Africain,* and led by Nazi Boni.[11] By mid-1958, the *Union/Rassemblement* had regained the support of five "opposition" (Conombo group) deputies led by Maurice Yaméogo, a move that gave the government a majority in the Assembly and undisputed possession of political power. Conombo "rallied" soon thereafter, but two months before independence Joseph Ouedraogo was jailed for his pro-federalist views and was not released until 1961. The *Mouvement du Regroupement Voltaique* transformed itself in September 1959 into the *Parti National Voltaique,* which was banned by the government two months later. Nazi Boni then created the *Parti Republicain de la Liberté,* but it too was promptly dissolved in January 1960 and its leader forced into exile. Also during 1960 a small, ultra-nationalist opposition party, the *Movement National de Libération,* led by Joseph Ki-Zerbo,[12] made a brief appearance.

The process whereby Upper Volta was transformed into a single-party regime is not uncommon in Africa; some of the consequences of that process, also seen elsewhere, soon became evident as well. Immediately after independence the *Union Démocratique Voltaique* had included most of the politically relevant leaders of the country; within a short time, however, the unity forged en route to independence began to break down, and opposition to the regime began to take shape both inside and outside the government and the party. By 1965 three distinct groupings of forces had emerged, each representing a polarized focus of political activity and/or involvement:

1. The "ins"—the "members of the establishment"—including the president, his closest political advisers, those occupying the highest positions of government, plus the leaders of the *Union Démocratique Voltaique* (including most government leaders) at both national and local levels.

2. The "outs," including a large number of excluded, disaffected politicians (most had fallen from favor in the wake of over ten government reshuffles between 1959 and 1965),[13] the principal trade unions, the leaders of the proscribed or *sub rosa* parties (some, like Nazi Boni, in exile), and many "intellectuals" (including most teachers, students

---

[11] Nazi Boni. Deputy to French National Assembly, 1951–56; member of Upper Volta Assembly, 1947–60; leader of MPA, MRV/PRA, PFA; emigrated to Mali July 1960, following proscription of his *Parti Republicain de la Liberté* (Jan. 7, 1960); died in an automobile accident, 1969.

[12] Joseph Ki-Zerbo. Upper Volta's leading intellectual; Professeur Agrégé of History, teacher at Lycée Ouézzin Coulibaly (Inspecteur d'Academie of Upper Volta); writer, poet, leader, and founder of *Mouvement National de la Libération.*

[13] The last reshuffle took place in Dec. 1965.

in the local secondary schools, students pursuing studies abroad, plus various independent professionals). Opposition to the regime had, by 1965, gravitated toward the trade unions and student organizations, inasmuch as these groups had become the only remaining organized centers of relatively free political expression. The excluded politicians, the leaders of proscribed parties, and the "intellectuals" constituted reservoirs of support for anti-government activity and organization, both overt and clandestine. Probably the two most important figures in this constellation of groups and individuals were Ouedraogo, to whom the trade unions looked for leadership, and Ki-Zerbo, who set the tone for the "intellectuals."

3. The sporadic and/or marginally involved, including the army, which remained ostensibly loyal to the regime until called to power, the Ouagadougou-Bobo Dioulasso business community (a loose, functional coalition of local and French interests), and the Roman Catholic hierarchy, headed by Paul Cardinal Zoungrana. The business community, mainly represented by the Upper Volta Chamber of Commerce, tended to keep out of active politics, though it was willing, for the sake of its collective health, to make the necessary obeisances to the regime. The Catholic hierarchy, restrained from overt political participation by its own rules, nevertheless lent strong, though muffled support to the opposition once the excesses of the Yaméogo regime became public knowledge. The local hierarchy was reportedly quite outraged by the manner in which President Yaméogo, a nominal Catholic, callously shed his first wife in mid-1965, sent her back to her village, then ostentatiously married a twenty-two-year-old former "Miss Ivory Coast," and hastened off to a honeymoon in Brazil. Cardinal Zoungrana was away at the Vatican Council at the time, a fact that lent support to the suggestion that the President was trying to "put one over" on the local clergy.

Had the Yaméogo regime merely become authoritarian and corrupt during the six years of its existence, it might not have fallen as readily as it did. What weakened it beyond recall, what almost forced a mutually irreconcilable polarization of political forces, was a combination of the regime's centralization of power, its political blundering during 1965, and the stark fact of an economy becoming less, rather than more, viable.

The economic facts of 1965 could only add fuel to the fires of discontent. Upper Volta has few natural resources save cattle, has never had a positive balance of trade (the $28 million deficit in 1964 represented an amount totaling over *half* of the total value of the country's trade), and is completely dependent upon its coastal neighbors for access to the sea. This dependence persuaded Yaméogo to enter into a brief flirtation with the Mali Federation (1959–60), but the country's ties with the Ivory Coast (Abidjan is the principal port for Upper Volta) and Houphouët's hostility to Mali forced Yaméogo to reconsider.[14] In 1961, in the face of an economic disagreement with the Houphouët government, Yaméogo tied his country to Ghana in an effort to overcome its fiscal difficulties.[15] That marriage, never wholly consummated by either side, was abandoned early in 1965 when the *Conseil de l'Entente* (the economic union of the Ivory Coast, Dahomey, Niger, Upper Volta, and Togo, formed in 1959) was revived and relations between Houphouët and Yaméogo improved.

Yaméogo's preoccupation with relations with his southern neighbors had yet another basis in the fact that an average of perhaps 325,000 persons per annum leave the Upper Volta for months, and sometimes years, to seek work in the coastal countries, particularly in the Ivory Coast and Ghana. In 1961 when a sample survey census was taken, migrants, the majority male, represented some 7 per cent of the total Upper Voltan population.[16] Estimates in 1965 suggested that the total migrant population had risen to about 400,000 in 1967.[17] Among other aspects of the country's unhappy economic picture was the necessity for continued—and to many, galling—financial dependence on French subsidies of various kinds. In 1965, for example, *visible* French aid amounted to about $5 million, or approximately 15 per cent of the total budget; the value of *all* French aid, including the cost of French technical aid personnel, invisible subsidies, and so forth prob-

[14] That story is discussed in William Foltz, *From French West Africa to the Mali Federation* (New Haven, 1965), 108-10.

[15] Immanuel Wallerstein, "Background to Paga," *West Africa*, 2304 (July 29, 1961), 819; 2305 (Aug. 5, 1961), 861.

[16] There are no accurate figures for either the volume or rate of flow of these migrations. Official figures are mere guesses, the closest being those mentioned, drawn from La République de Haute-Volta, Service de Statistique, *La Situation Démographique en Haute Volta* (1962). Official French figures, given in 1960, are even higher: an estimated 460,000 migrants (including 100,000 absent 3 to 6 months, 260,000 absent from 1 to 5 years, and 100,000 gone for good, many with their families). (Documentation Française, *Notes et Études Documentaires*, 2 [19 August 1960], "La République de Haute-Volta," 49). The 1962 Census report (above) listed the causes of migration as "the presence of high population densities in those regions where the soil is not particularly fertile and often shows signs of exhaustion, characteristically poor remuneration for traditional economic activities, and the country's lack of employment opportunities for its surplus rural labor. This excess manpower thus contributes, in a large measure, to the prosperity of Upper Volta's neighbors. She herself receives but a very small part of the surplus value thus created, since the remittances sent home by the emigrants are always very modest." (7)

[17] Unpublished figures provided the author by the Upper Voltan Ministry of National Economy.

ably approximated $10 million a year.[18] It is hardly necessary to embellish the picture. The economy, if not on the verge of bankruptcy, certainly appeared—at least to the government's critics—to be lurching in that direction. Further, it made little difference to the government's critics that small but encouraging gains had in fact been registered in some sectors of the economy, or that the Yaméogo regime could not, in all justice, be blamed for the fact that circumstances and nationalist fervor had brought into existence a state with only marginal prospects for economic improvement. By mid-1965, there was no question but that "a head of political discontent was already building up" against Yaméogo and his regime,[19] but it had not become sufficiently strong or widespread to deny Yaméogo massive popular support and reelection in the presidential balloting of October 3.

Yaméogo's first mistake of 1965, according to a post-coup story in the government-owned paper *Carrefour Africain,* was that he put up a list of "yes men" as candidates for the legislative elections on November 7. In this way, he dashed hopes that he might be making a fresh start.

> The list offended not only those who had hoped to be on it, but were not, but also those who had been in the previous Assembly and were now excluded. The paper recounts an eve of poll meeting in the party HG in Ouagadougou, which was so ill-attended that party stalwarts had to rustle up street traders to make a presentable audience for the President. And in the voting there was a visible boycott, especially in Ouagadougou.[20]

The municipal elections of December 5 confirmed the boycott trend, although the official figures, as in the Assembly elections, showed spectacular numbers of voters. Here offense had also been given by the imposition of *Union* candidates without prior consultation with local interests. About half of the capital's voters stayed away from the polls. It is almost certain that in both elections party officials were instructed to be sure that the official slates received overwhelming support. In the meantime, the affair of the President's divorce and remarriage had become common knowledge, a fact that probably contributed to the December ballot boycott in Ouagadougou, where the

---

[18] The estimate of visible aid is a composite figure drawn from data given in "L'Afrique d'expression française de Madagascar, 6e édition," *Europe-France-Outremer,* 435, Special Issue (Apr. 1965), 133-38; *Memento de l'économie africaine au sud du Sahara, 1965* (Paris, 1965), 215-26. The estimate for *all* French aid was suggested by a French technical counsellor in a conversation with the author in 1965.

[19] "The Colonel in Ouagadougou," *West Africa,* 2540 (Feb. 5, 1966), 139.
[20] Ibid.

seat of the Ouagadougou archdiocese is located and where a substantial percentage of the city's 105,000 people are Roman Catholic. (The Upper Voltan Roman Catholic population is officially estimated at 220,000.)

> Add to this the extravagance of the presidential ways [*Le Carrefour* cites a new Mercedes 600; others have mentioned the large country villa at Yaméogo's home town of Koudougo], despite the economic plight of the country [also very much in evidence was the splendidly furbished presidential palace, an ultra-modern luxury hotel in Ouagadougou, and government salaries and benefits exceeding 60 per cent of the annual budget], and the ascendancy of government by caprice (there were frequent government reshuffles. . .). Note also the charge of nepotism, and the return to the Ministry of the Interior of Denis Yaméogo, the President's cousin, whose strong-arm methods with the unions did much to provoke the general strike.[21]

Yaméogo's final political blunder of 1965 was the so-called "austerity" budget passed by the National Assembly on December 30. Given the situation, the budget was incredibly impolitic since it managed to offend almost all persons directly affected by it: civil servants were to be subject to a decrease in salary and perquisites of between 10 and 20 per cent, family allowances were to be made uniform for all wage earners (constituting, in effect, a reduction for most), and reciprocal preferential tariffs on locally produced goods were to be abolished (a move which angered most small businessmen in the country). The new budget proved to be the final straw. On January 1, 1966, the trade unions, coalesced in an interunion Joint Action Committee under the chairmanship of Ouedraogo, decided on a general strike to be launched the next day. Yaméogo's next moves all but decided his fate: in a nation-wide broadcast on January 1 the President accused Ouedraogo of trying to hand over Upper Volta to Ghana and mainland China; a few hours later he announced a country-wide state of emergency and curfew and declared the proposed strike illegal. "Subversion," claimed the President in his first broadcast, "inspired by Communists, has entered the country with its leader Joseph Ouedraogo, who is in hiding."[22] Evoking the Communist bogey

---

[21] Ibid. Walter Skurnik noted that Denis Yaméogo's "chief qualifications for that sensitive job [Interior Minister], aside from family ties, appear to have been an inadequate education and a penchant for pugilism. Rumor has it that his boxing talent was used freely as a means of persuading union leaders of the nobility of government policy." ("Political Instability and Military Intervention in Dahomey and Upper Volta," unpublished paper, 1966.)

[22] *The New York Times*, Jan. 3, 1966, 3.

gained the President neither sympathy nor support. In fact, his statements so enraged the trade unionists that they redoubled their efforts to topple him.

One last note must be added to this discussion of the events and causes of the coup. It is important to recall that the army did not actively enter the picture until the evening of January 2, *after* the leaders of the strike and demonstrations had visited Lamizana and his officers and implored them to intervene. Whether the military had in fact already decided to move against the regime is difficult to know, but at least two pieces of evidence bear on the question. One is a report that even though regular troops were on guard at the presidential palace at the height of the demonstrations, it was the forces under the control of the Ministry of the Interior who were most active in trying to quell the disturbances.[23] The other is that in March 1965 two senior army officers with whom the author spoke expressed serious misgivings about the longevity of the regime. It was, they intimated, thoroughly corrupt, unresponsive to the army's needs, and rather cavalier in its attitude to the several thousand Upper Voltan veterans (of service in the French Army) who depended on the French and Upper Voltan governments for financial assistance. However the question of the army's intentions is answered, this much is clear, that Lamizana and his officers showed little reluctance to assume power, and that they did virtually nothing to prevent the strike and demonstrations that led to the call for a military take-over.

Dahomey

The situation preceding the third (and last) coup by General Christophe Soglo was not unlike that in Upper Volta. The country's economy could, at best, be described as stagnant, at worst, as undergoing catastrophic deterioration. The government and the trade unions regarded each other with ill-concealed hostility. Opposition groups, in the persons of excluded politicians, disgruntled and frustrated students and intellectuals, as well as angry trade unionists, were actively engaged in undermining the government. Rather than mobilizing enthusiastic support for the regime, the single-party system succeeded only in evoking *pro forma* acquiescence or alienating those leaders most necessary to its survival. Two elements of the Dahomean situation, however, were quite dissimilar and made Dahomey even more explosive

---

[23] Denis Yaméogo, as Minister of the Interior, controlled the *Garde Republicaine* and the *Compagnie Republicaine de Sécurité*. Laminzana, responsible to the Minister of Defense, had charge of *both* the army and gendarmerie. The report was in a letter to the author from a responsible eyewitness, who declined to be identified.

than Upper Volta. There was, first of all, ethnic hostility of long standing between Dahomey's main tribal groups: this hostility, only lightly
covered by the tissue of statehood, periodically erupted into violence
and was openly cultivated by the country's warring political factions.
Second, there was a continual power struggle among Dahomey's leaders, a struggle unresolved during the short period of the country's
independence. The first three elements would have sufficed to rend
the Dahomean polity, but the five combined brought the country to
the point where its military men felt that only their intervention could
prevent complete collapse.

By every indicator of economic activity, Dahomey was something
of a pessimist's paradise. The country had not had a positive balance
of trade since 1950, and, after independence (1960), the negative
balance between imports and exports increased from 26 per cent
(1960) to 40 per cent (1965).[24] Shortly after the formation of the new
Soglo regime in 1965, Finance Minister Nicephore Soglo revealed that
Dahomey was the only state in former French Africa whose exports
had declined since independence—the decline was estimated at between 10 per cent and 50 per cent in terms of the cash crops that provide most of the country's revenue.[25] Unemployment was endemic and
growing at an alarming rate, in part because of the repatriation between 1958 and 1965 of several thousand Dahomean *fonctionnaires*
who had been ousted from positions elsewhere in French-speaking
Africa.[26] (The French government usually provided a major share of
the annual budgetary funds—in addition to subsidizing the country's
feeble output on the world market. The major Dahomean export, at
least until 1963, was intellectuals, who sought and found jobs as administrators and teachers elsewhere in French-speaking Africa when
they could not be absorbed at home.) The government was unable to
collect all of its taxes or attract development capital. Most damaging,
it devoted extraordinary percentages of the national budget to pay
its civil servants, the national civil service swelling from 12,000 in
1960 to over 18,000 in 1965.[27] In 1964, for example, salaries and perquisites for government employees consumed 64.3 per cent of the
national budget.[28]

[24] *Memento de l'économie africaine au sud du Sahara, 1965* (Paris, 1966),
185.

[25] Skurnik, "Political Instability," 2.

[26] Virginia Thompson, "Dahomey," in Gwendolen Carter (ed.), *Five African
States* (Ithaca, New York, 1963), 196. Professor Carter describes the expulsion of
Dahomeans from Abidjan in her *Independence for Africa* (New York, 1960),
106-17.

[27] Skurnik, "Political Instability," 2.

[28] *Memento*, 181.

The net result of these various drains on the treasury was an accumulated budgetary deficit greater than the annual budget in 1965; the total economic picture could, in fact, support the suggestion that in 1965 Dahomey was disintegrating. Not even the construction of a deep-water port at Cotonou or the infusion of massive French aid helped the situation. For one thing, the Germans undertook the building of a deep-water port in Lomé, the capital of Togo, barely eighty miles along the coast, and whatever benefits Dahomey could have derived from its own port were diluted even before the Cotonou harbor was completed. Though the comparison was certainly unintended, some Dahomeans considered it something of a portent that an American motion picture company chose Cotonou as the site for filming scenes from a novel set in Haiti.[29]

Seen against this grim economic backdrop, the long conflict between the trade unions and the government takes on added focus. Well organized and well led, the trade unions, though representing only a small minority of the country's work force (no more than 3 per cent of salaried workers), were nevertheless a formidable political force.[30] They included nearly all the members of the oversize civil service plus most of the craftsmen and industrial workers employed in Cotonou's factories and the country's four palm oil mills.[31] Two federations contained most of the trade unions: The *Union Nationale des Syndicats des Travailleurs du Dahomey* (the local branch of the trans-territorial *Union Générale des Travailleurs d'Afrique Noire*) and the *filiale* of the *Confédération Africaine des Travailleurs Chrétiens*. Of the two, the first was by far the more powerful, particularly since it enjoyed the close support of Justin Ahomadegbé's *Union Démocratique Dahoméene*, the territorial branch of the *Rassemblement Démocratique Africaine*. In fact, several of the *Union's* senior officers were also prominent members of the *Mouvement Démocratique Dahoméen*.

Though labor unrest was nothing new in Dahomey, it was not until after the territorial elections of March 1957 that open hostilities between the government and the trade unions became a regular feature of Dahomean political life. The March 1957 elections had been won by a coalition of Sourou-Migan Apithy's *Parti Républicain du Dahomey*, based in the south, and Hubert Maga's *Mouvement Démocratique Dahoméen*, with northern support. The coalition went on to form the first Dahomean government, with Apithy as Premier. In

[29] Graham Greene, *The Comedians* (New York, 1966).
[30] Mrs. Thompson's discussion of the political role of the trade unions is the basis of much that follows. "Dahomey," 213-34, *passim*. See also Ioan Davies, *African Trade Unions* (Harmondsworth, 1966), 104-7.
[31] Thompson, "Dahomey," 106.

October 1957, the *Union Démocratique Dahoméene*, with *Union Générale des Travailleurs d'Afrique Noir* support, launched a campaign of strikes and boycotts against the *Société des Huileries Modernes du Dahomey*, the territory's principal employer, ostensibly in protest against its policy of reducing the numbers of workers at its Avrankon mill. On February 4, 1958, the Avrankon mill closed abruptly and Apithy resigned, but not before riots and other violence had claimed several lives and scores of wounded, and troops had been called in to stem the disorders. Governor Casimir Biros managed a temporary settlement between the government and the unions, and Apithy formed a new government with the promise of various reforms in wage and work conditions. New grievances, nevertheless, kept relations between the new Apithy government and the trade unions strained throughout 1958: the delayed release of trade unionists involved in the January violence; hesitant—and tardy—attempts to implement the government's earlier promises; opposition to the September 1958 referendum (to decide participation in President De Gaulle's new French Community); the local formation of the *Union Nationale des Syndicats des Travailleurs du Dahomey* (seen by the *Confédération Africaine des Travailleurs Chrétiens* as an attempt to aggrandize *Union Générale des Travailleurs d'Afrique Noir* strength); and opposition to projected Dahomean membership in the Mali Federation. Several local strikes broke out in July, and in December the *Union Nationale des Syndicats des Travailleurs du Dahomey* called a general strike to protest Dahomean membership in the Community, approved by the vote in September, and the country's pending entrance into the Mali Federation. Not even Apithy's declaration against entrance into the Federation, his resignation in January 1959, a temporary coalition between the *Union Démocratique Dahoméene* and the *Parti Républicain du Dahomey* and the *Mouvement Démocratique Dahoméen*—which brought Hubert Maga to power—could temper the conflict.

By September 1959 the unions were again up in arms, and in October 1959 they were joined by the *Union Démocratique Dahoméene* (now disenchanted with the coalition) in a general strike that tied up Cotonou and Porto Novo until Maga called in troops, armed police, and archers from the north to quell the disturbances. In the December elections Maga's new party, the *Parti Démocratique de l'Unité*, captured 69 per cent of the votes and all the seats in the new Assembly. Thus strengthened, Maga moved first to break Ahomadegbé and the *Union Démocratique Dahoméene* and then to tame the trade unions. In April Maga dissolved the *Union Démocratique Dahoméene* and in May Ahomadegbé and eleven of his closest associates were arrested and charged with allegedly planning to murder Maga and his ministers. Ahomadegbé's trial did not take place until December 5; he was convicted and sentenced to five years in prison, and his co-defendants received terms of imprisonment ranging from one to ten years.[32] (Ahomadegbé—after serving eighteen months of his sentence—was released because of changes in the country's political climate.) Five days after the *Union Démocratique Dahoméene* had been dissolved, Maga also dissolved the *Union Nationale des Syndicats des Travailleurs du Dahomey,* creating in its place a trade union federation more amenable to government control, the *Union Générale des Travailleurs du Dahomey.*

The new federation into which the unions had been forcibly drafted maintained a relative calm which, however, only masked the continuing discontent of its component organizations. That discontent emerged into the open when, in October 1963, the unions issued a successful call for a general strike and asked the army to take over the government.[33] Maga fell, but neither during General Christophe Soglo's short interregnum (October 1963 to January 1964), nor during the succeeding Apithy-Ahomadegbé regime did it prove possible to bring the trade unions to heel. Not even the inclusion of Théophile Paoletti, former secretary general of the *Union Générale des Travailleurs du Dahomey,* in Ahomadegbé's cabinet as Minister of Labor, nor various concessions to the workers, could heal the breach (Paoletti, in fact, was considered something of a traitor to labor's cause when he agreed to enter the government.) By May 1965, the trade unions once again saw themselves completely at odds with the government, and it was no surprise when trade union leaders again took the lead in organizing the downfall of the Ahomadegbé-Apithy regime at the end of 1965.

The question may legitimately be asked if any Dahomean regime between 1957 and 1965 could have enjoyed trade union support. (As a matter of fact all did, but for very short periods of time.) Given the country's basic economic difficulties, attempts by the government to impose austerity measures (more often than not including reductions of civil servants' salaries and perquisites) were bound to run head-on into the union's desire to improve conditions for their own members. The conclusion is difficult to avoid that the conflict between governmental and trade union economic priorities could not have been resolved save in the context of a general improvement of economic conditions. Certainly, as a relatively fat and privileged minority in the society, salaried workers were the obvious targets of government attempts to curtail seeming affluence. But adding fuel to the fire were

[32] Ibid., 232.

[33] The first Dahomean coup (Oct. 1963) is discussed in "What Happened to Dahomey," *West Africa,* 2422 (Nov. 2, 1963), 1239.

the not infrequent misallocations by the government of scarce resources to sumptuous displays and prestige projects: the glittering presidential palace in Cotonou, the vacant secretariat building for the defunct *Union Africaine et Malagache,* and an enormous (and as yet unfinished) independence monument were just a few examples of what the unions perceived as wasting resources that could have been used to better the workers' lot. But, as successive Dahomean governments discovered—each to its own chagrin—the trade unions not only resisted attempts to curtail their power, but actively helped to bring down offending regimes.

The trade unions' continual warfare with the government was only one—albeit a major one—of the several internal conflicts that have long afflicted Dahomean politics. Equally corrosive to the system was the long-standing, three-cornered feud between Apithy, Ahomadegbé, and Maga, the three political leaders who, with their allies and organizational adjuncts, almost completely dominated Dahomean politics after World War II.

The rivalry between the three men was based upon a complex of personal and historical circumstances, the most important of which was that each built his political base upon effective representation of regional ethnic interests. The three major ethnic groups in the country are the Fon in the south, center, and west (Ahomadegbé's constituency), the Yoruba and related groups in the southeast (Apithy's fief), and the Bariba, Fulani, and other related northern groups (organized by Maga). The three major groups have a long history of mutual distrust and antagonism, and, as regional politics became national, as regional political groups moved into the territorial arena, and as economic and social interest aggregates such as trade unions and student groups began to seek political outlets and affiliations, it was almost inevitable that the three should come into conflict in the modern Dahomean political arena.

Apithy built his political base in Porto Novo, among the Yoruba and related people in the south and southeast. He was the oldest of the trio and one of the founding fathers of the Dahomey nationalist movement.[34] A devout Roman Catholic, Apithy initially found it relatively easy to collaborate with other southern Roman Catholic politicians, such as Paul Hazoumé, Emile Zinsou, and Louis I. Pinto, in various political cliques and groups. (As a matter of fact, during the

[34] Sourou-Migan Apithy. Accountant; b. Apr. 8, 1912, at Porto Novo; Deputy for Dahomey, French National Assembly, 1946–58; Deputy in Dahomean Constituent Assembly, President of Dahomean Executive Council, 1958–59; Foreign Minister, then Minister of Finance in Government of Hubert Maga; Vice-President, Ambassador to Paris, 1959–63; President of Dahomey, 1964–65.

first post-war decade in Dahomey, it was difficult to find a local politician who was *not* a Roman Catholic.) By 1951, Apithy and his collaborators were confronted by the emergence of a strong northern political force organized by Maga, centered in Parakou and grouping Bariba, Fulani, Dioula, and other northern Dahomean interests under the banner of the *Groupement Ethnique du Nord*.[35] The first electoral test of strength between the two in 1951 found northern and southern constituencies each following its leader in almost equal numbers. Virtually the whole south voted for Apithy (about 53,000 votes), and all the north for Maga (some 49,000 votes).[36]

So long as Apithy and Maga could effectively divide the territory's political forces between them, some sort of equilibrium was possible. By 1956, the long dormant Dahomean branch of the *Rassemblement Démocratique Africaine* had been revived by Ahomadegbé as the political spokesman of Cotonou's radical trade unions, and Apithy's southern coalition had begun to disintegrate. Ahomadegbé, a former dentist and a descendant of the Abomeyan royal family,[37] rallied not only the trade unions and some of Apithy's allies, but also most of the powerful Fon-Abomeyan ethnic constituency. In time, both Ahomadegbé and Apithy came to head their own political parties, and they found themselves split, in various and shifting ways, on matters of ideology, on the great issues of Community versus Federalism, and on local programs and policies. Whatever the heuristic substance of their disagreement, their conflict, at root, cut across regional-ethnic, and, often, class lines.

Only for two relatively short periods of time, during the second Apithy government (April 1958 to January 1959) and the early months of the Maga government (after April 1959), were Maga, Apithy, and Ahomadegbé together as a group within the government. They were "together," it must be added, in only the most nominal sense of the word. Their conflict, as a matter of fact, took on new dimensions after the April 1959 elections.

Already in trouble at the beginning of 1959, Apithy so gerrymandered the electoral districts that the results of the April 2 elections

[35] Hubert Maga. Schoolmaster; b. Aug. 1910, at Parakou; Deputy for Dahomey in French National Assembly, 1951–58; Secretary of State for Labor in French government of Félix Gaillard, Nov. 1957–Apr. 1958; Premier, then President of Dahomey, 1959–63; in detention, Oct. 1963–Nov. 1965; voluntary exile, Dec. 1965.

[36] Thompson, "Dahomey," 176.

[37] Justin Ahomadegbé. Dentist; b. 1917 at Abomey; Mayor of Abomey, 1956; President of National Assembly, 1959–60; Senator of French Community, 1959; in jail for alleged plot against government of Hubert Maga, 1961–62; Prime Minister and Vice-President of Dahomey, 1964–65.

favored him and his party. Ahomadegbé's party received 44 per cent of the votes (162,132) but only 11 of the 60 seats in the new Assembly; Apithy's *Parti Républicain du Dahomey* polled 144,038 votes and took 37 seats, and Maga's *Parti Démocratique de l'Unité* received 62,132 votes and 22 seats.[38] When the results became known, rioting broke out in which over one hundred persons were injured. Apithy compromised with Ahomadegbé, but the upshot of their negotiations was to bring in Maga as a compromise Prime Minister—an outcome neither Apithy nor Ahomadegbé wanted, but which neither could really avoid. Rather than being named Vice-Premier in Maga's new cabinet, Apithy found himself only a minister of state without portfolio—a serious affront. The Maga-Ahomadegbé alliance lasted only until the labor unrest of October 1960, which led to Maga's arrest and imprisonment in May 1961. By mid-1960, Maga and Apithy had once again been reconciled, and in the wake of the December 1960 elections, Apithy was named Vice-Premier. At the beginning of 1961, the old antagonisms between the two men threatened to erupt again, but to avoid another open break Apithy consented to go to Paris as Dahomey's ambassador.

With Apithy in Paris and Ahomadegbé under arrest, Maga tried to put the politics of the country on a more solid footing. A single party, a consolidated trade union organization, and a unified youth movement were to be his instruments to achieve national unity. Maga had nearly three years in which to pull the pieces of his country's splintered politics together; in October 1963, Colonel Soglo and his colleagues decided that Maga had failed and that his regime needed replacement. In January 1964, Soglo withdrew from politics and Apithy (back from Paris) and Ahomadegbé formed a new government as President and Vice-President, respectively.

Between January 1964 and December 1965 the new regime tried, albeit unsuccessfully, to deal with the country's increasingly serious economic and financial problems. By the end of 1965, the President and Vice President, again at political swords' points, were actively engaged in undercutting each other in the councils of government. Mitinkpon Nignon, writing in *Afrique Nouvelle,* pungently summarized the rise and fall of the Apithy-Ahomadegbé biumvirate:

> Finally the two rivals found themselves alone, united by circumstances and by the desire of the people of the south to have a stable regime, capable of governing. A party was created (the PDD) which boasted reconciliation and union. But, the new union proved too fragile to contain the two fighting crocodiles without breaking. The struggle continued until Apithy reigned without governing, and Ahomadegbé governed without reigning. . . . Everyone knows what followed.[39]

[38] Thompson, "Dahomey," 221.
[39] Jan. 29, 1966, 6. (Author's translation.)

What followed led directly to military intervention. At the beginning of November 1965, unable to agree on the appointment of a judge to head the Supreme Court, the two men precipitated a constitutional deadlock. On November 24, 1965, Ahomadegbé moved against Apithy through the *Parti Démocratique Dahoméen,* which formally dismissed the President from its ranks and called upon him to give up his powers. Ahomadegbé succeeded Apithy as President, but his tenure was cut short when General Soglo, who had become chief of staff, and the army took over on November 29, forcing both men to resign. Soglo made one last attempt to get Apithy, Ahomadegbé, and Maga (released from detention for the occasion) to compromise their differences. To no one's surprise, they could not—or would not—agree, and their partisans immediately took to the streets. On December 22 Soglo decided that he—and the country—had had enough and launched his third, and last, coup.

Dahomey has had the dubious distinction of experiencing three coups led by the same military man. Soglo demonstrated a restraint rare in such cases. In 1964 he had given up power voluntarily and in November 1965 he once again sought to turn over the government to the three men responsible for its collapse. Moreover, the three coups were accomplished without firing a shot or staging mass purges. Once again the effort to have a democratic government failed, and General Soglo himself took over the government in December 1966.

Central African Republic[40]

The military coup which—during the night of December 31, 1965–January 1, 1966—brought about the collapse of the government of David Dacko, had its antecedents in circumstances that, in retrospect, look distressingly like those that preceded the coups in Dahomey and Upper Volta. There certainly was considerable erosion of public confidence in the regime, a consequence of the gradual disintegration of the single party that had virtually ruled the country since 1960; there was dissent and often open conflict among the country's ruling elite; and finally, as the ominous backdrop to political troubles, there was the country's general economic stagnation, the effects of which further undermined confidence in the regime so that the government's attempts to apply economic palliatives were unpopular and unsuccessful. Again, as in Dahomey and Upper Volta, it was not any single circumstance or set of circumstances that persuaded Bokassa to act; more probably, it was the cumulative effect of the Republic's general political and

[40] Portions of this discussion are rephrased and recast from a previous article. Victor T. Le Vine, "The Central African Republic: Insular Problems of an Inland State," *Africa Report,* X (Nov. 1965), 17-23.

economic malaise, plus several specific events that precipitated his intervention. Unlike Upper Volta and Dahomey, there was not in the Republic a large, discontented, and politically volatile trade union movement; trade unionism in the Republic was never more than minimal, and even then it was subordinated to the single party. There was not, as in the other two cases, a core of alienated and hostile political leaders waiting impatiently in the wings for the government to fumble its lines; discontented members of the political elite there were, but—with the possible exception of the leader of a defunct opposition group, Dr. Abel Goumba and his few followers—they were all *within* the establishment. But, as a Republic leader wrote to the author, "Our troubles were enough—you don't have to suffer *all* the punishment of Hell to be damned."[41]

Perhaps the most important element contributing to the air of political uncertainty characteristic of the several years preceding the coup was the unfilled void left by the death of Barthélemy Boganda,[42] simultaneously the first chief of government, the founder of the *Mouvement d'Évolution Sociale de l'Afrique Noire* (by constitutional amendment in 1963 the sole legal authority and only party in the Republic), and the architect of his country's independence. Boganda was killed in an airplane crash on March 3, 1959, during a tour of the country. He was, by all reports, a man of considerable charismatic attributes. He possessed highly developed political and organizational skills and, by a combination of ruthlessness and finesse, had succeeded in welding the *Mouvement* into a political machine of overwhelming strength and organizational depth. Boganda had founded his party in April 1950 in an attempt to provide an "Ouabanguian" alternative to the local branch of the *Rassemblement Démocratique Africaine* and the administration-dominated branch of the Gaullist *Rassemblement du Peuple Français*. The *Mouvement d'Évolution Sociale de l'Afrique Noire* had grown in strength during the elections of 1951 and, following the elections of 1952 (in which the *Mouvement d'Évolution Sociale de l'Afrique Noire* won seventeen of the twenty-six second college-African-seats), had come almost completely to dominate politics in the territory.

During his lifetime Boganda assumed almost legendary proportions. He was the territory's first ordained priest, but left the priesthood to marry his French secretary and enter politics. The priestly aura of his earlier days never quite left him, and to it he added quasi-

---

[41] Confidential letter to the author dated Aug. 8, 1965.

[42] Barthelemy Boganda. b. Apr. 4, 1910, d. Mar. 3, 1959; Catholic Priest, 1938–1946; Deputy for Ubangui-Shari in French National Assembly, 1946–59; Mayor of Bangui, 1955; President of Grand Conseil of AEF, 1957–58; President of Executive Council of the Republic, 1958.

mystical pretensions: he was not beyond pretending to perform a miracle when an eclipse of the sun occurred, nor did he try to dissuade people from believing that he was immortal. (Only a few months before his death, a large crowd gathered on the banks of the Ubangui River near the capital, fully expecting to witness Boganda cross the river by walking upon the waters.) His political methods were at times undeniably crude but they were effective: he made extensive use of strong-arm squads to enforce the writ of the *Mouvement d'Évolution Sociale de l'Afrique Noire* and not a few political opponents felt the physical consequences of his displeasure. Because Boganda was, in every sense of the term, the embodiment of Central African nationalism, his death introduced the classic situation that often follows the disappearance of a charismatic leader—uncertainty, policy gaps, and a struggle for the mantle of legitimacy now vacated but too large for those contending for it.

The party floundered after Boganda's death; it did, however, manage to pull itself together sufficiently to win the 1959 elections over weak opposition. David Dacko, Boganda's nephew, was elected head of government in May.[43] In June 1960, however, *Mouvement d'Evolution Sociale de l'Afrique Noire* split. One splinter, led by Dr. Abel Goumba, Boganda's finance minister, and Minister of State in Dacko's cabinet, formed the *Mouvement d'Evolution Démocratique de l'Afrique Centrale*, and the others, led by Dacko, appropriated the *Mouvement d'Evolution Sociale de l'Afrique Noire* machinery. Both factions tried to legitimize their positions by appeals to Boganda's memory. Eventually the Dacko faction won, suppressed the *Mouvement d'Evolution Démocratique de l'Afrique Centrale* (December 26, 1960), imprisoned Goumba and several of his followers, and installed itself in power. The remaining small political parties were formally dissolved in 1962. By the beginning of 1963, all visible political opposition had been crushed, had disappeared, or had been integrated into the *Mouvement d'Evolution Sociale de l'Afrique Noire*. In 1963, the Republic's constitution was amended to make the *Mouvement d'Évolution Sociale de l'Afrique Noire* the sole legal party in the country *(parti unique)*, and legislation was passed which imposed severe penalties on anyone seeking to organize another "party, movement, group, or organization of a political nature." As for Goumba, he was released shortly after his arrest in 1960, but was rearrested for six months in 1962, and then

[43] David Dacko. Schoolmaster; b. Mar. 24, 1930, at Bouchia-M'baiki; Deputy to Territorial Council, Mar. 1957; Minister of Agriculture, May 1957–Aug. 1959; Minister of Administrative Affairs, Aug.–Dec. 1958; re-elected to Republic Assembly, Dec. 1958; Minister of Interior, Dec. 1958–Mar. 1959; President of Republic, May 1959–Dec. 1965; overthrown by coup, Dec. 31, 1965.

sent to France on an extended scholarship, ostensibly to "complete his medical training."[44]

Dacko, a relatively young man of thirty when he became President, and a former schoolmaster, tried to govern pragmatically and to move the party leadership from autocratic to collegial decision-making. He appeared to some to see himself as *primus inter pares* in the councils of state and of the party and permitted, even encouraged, his ministerial colleagues to share political power in the widest sense. A post-coup commentary saw Dacko's style in a totally different light:

> David Dacko's power had already begun to dissipate a good many months [prior to the coup]. [This occurred], moreover, to some extent through the fault of the young president, who, in order to dominate them better, had surrounded himself with colorless collaborators. [He] oversaw the least actions of his ministers, who became, in effect, mere agents without power of decision.[45]

Whatever the truth about Dacko's style of governing, its consequences were still the same: general disaffection within the regime, coupled with a gradual erosion of the militant solidarity of the *Mouvement d'Evolution Sociale de l'Afrique Noire* machine. Individual ministers and deputies began to carve out political fiefs of their own, and as a result, the *Mouvement d'Évolution Sociale de l'Afrique Noire* began to disintegrate into rival factions. In this situation, the venal often found welcome opportunities. For example, "At the base, its [the party's] representatives made their own deals, selling the party insignia for as much as 8,000 francs CFA [approximately $33.00]."[46] Not surprisingly, during 1964 and 1965, the party's membership became increasingly resistant to calls to action by the party's leadership. One example of the *Mouvement d'Évolution Sociale de l'Afrique Noire's* declining vitality was the feeble response to the *Kwa Ti Kadro*, a voluntary "human investment" program by which people were expected to donate free time for civic improvement projects. When some 2,000 Bangui citizens turned up for the May 1, 1965, *Kwa Ti Kadro* session to join with President Dacko and high government dignitaries to clear brush and grass from a tract destined for a national park, official enthusiasm ran high.[47] Popular enthusiasm, however, did not match official enthusiasm; subsequent turnouts in Bangui were feeble, a pattern duplicated throughout the

[44] The quote is from one of the author's confidential informants, a cabinet minister, interviewed in May 1965, in Bangui.

[45] "La République Centrafricaine," *Jeune Afrique*, 309 (Dec. 11, 1966), special section, ix. (Author's translation.)

[46] Ibid.

[47] *Terre Africaine* (Bangui), May 14, 1965.

country. In some villages, in fact, *Kwa Ti Kadro* appeared to have evoked memories of the days of French forced labor, and local party militants aroused considerable antagonism with some of the heavy-handed methods that they used to persuade people to volunteer for the program.

Another example of the difficulties in communication between national planners and the citizenry was seen in the response to a so-called National Loan, the objective of which was to raise $2,000,000 for local improvement projects. As of June 1965, perhaps one-fifth had been subscribed, and a good deal of that by a forced levy of 10 per cent on civil servants' salaries. Party leaders in many areas used pressure to meet local goals, which had often been set unrealistically high in relation to the ability of the inhabitants to meet them. The author was repeatedly told in May 1965 that resistance to the loan was growing, and that increasingly forceful methods were being used to stimulate participation.

Also symptomatic of the political and economic uncertainty that pervaded the Republic in the months before the coup was an alarming increase in instances of bribery, embezzlement, and misappropriation of public funds by government personnel at all levels. Diamond concessions, for example, a source of considerable profit, were sold "under the table" for 2 to 3 million CFA (approximately $8,000 to $12,000); some 25 million francs CFA (approximately $104,000) was apparently illegally offered for a permit to open a "private diamond-buying office." Between 1963 and 1965 twenty prefects and subprefects were imprisoned for embezzlement.[48]

> [This state of affairs] reached such proportions that inspectors [of finance] refused to drop prosecutions unless they received a *trou* [gift] of at least 250,000 CFA [approximately $1,000]. It was all common knowledge: a child was heard to declare that "he didn't want to become a prefect, so that he wouldn't have to go to prison."[49]

Nevertheless, by mid-June 1965—according to unofficial reports current in Bangui—several hundred officials had been brought to prosecution, fined, or sent to jail. Among these were a postmaster and the directors of the Offices of Currency Exchange, of Tourism, and of the National Development Bank. Exhortation by President Dacko and a Cabinet decision to apply "draconian" and "exemplary" punishments did not improve the situation perceptibly.

Yet another source of tension in local politics was the insistent

[48] "La République Centrafricaine," ix.
[49] Ibid.

pressure of the "Young Turks" within the administration and the army for more radical governmental policies on a wide range of domestic and foreign policy matters.[50] The "Young Turks" comprised a small group of well educated, highly placed young men nominally integrated within the party's youth wing, the *Jeunesse Nationale Centrafricaine*, but openly restive and critical of what they termed the conservative and bourgeois policies of the *vieux turbans* (that is, the older nationalists of Boganda inspiration and vintage). The "Young Turks" acclaimed the recognition of Communist China by the Republic in 1964, followed the revolutionary turn of events in Congo/Brazzaville with intense interest, and made little effort to conceal their anti-European, that is, anti-French and anti-American, views. If the revelations of the Bokassa regime are to be believed, a number of them were involved in a plot to overthrow the Dacko regime and in the formation of a so-called revolutionary "Army of National Liberation" with the assistance and logistical support of the Communist Chinese embassy in Bangui. Among the most active of the "Young Turks" was Jean-Christophe Nzallat, the chief of President Dacko's *Cabinet Politique*. Nzallat was one of the first people arrested and tried by the Bokassa regime in the wake of the coup.

By mid-1965 the Republic, in addition to its political troubles, had worked itself to an economic cul-de-sac from which escape was extremely doubtful. It simultaneously confronted (a) a decline in agricultural production, including a drop in its prime export crop, cotton; (b) a diamond boom of uncertain future, which drew thousands from farming to the mines in the hope of quick profit, but which the government had been unable either to control effectively or capitalize upon for revenues; (c) budgetary instability derived from increased costs of services, widespread corruption, excessive salaries to civil servants, poor tax yields, a decline in the international development capital market, and increased resistance to temporary measures designed to raise money quickly (including the National Loan); and (d) a capital drain involving resident foreign companies, many of which were quietly withdrawing in the face of increased taxes, declining profits, and what they saw as a progressive deterioration of the economy as a whole.[51]

[50] Le Vine, "The Central African Republic," 19.

[51] The data on which this discussion is based derive from the following sources: Miscellaneous mimeographed handouts from the Republic Ministry of National Economy (1965); "Basic Data on the Economy of the Central African Republic," *Overseas Business Reports* (U.S. Department of Commerce), Dec. 1963; *Memento de l'économie africaine au sud du Sahara, 1965;* "L'Afrique d'expression française et Madagascar," 133-38.

Of the above aspects of the Republic's economic troubles, the diamond boom probably had the most damaging impact upon the economy. Diamonds were first discovered in the Bria region of Oubangui Province, but it was not until 1936 that production was put on a commercial basis. Between 1936 and 1960, about 2,000,000 carats were mined, of which perhaps half were of gem quality; in 1952 alone, 147,000 carats were mined. Since 1961, production increased steadily and stood, in 1965, at about 500,000 carats a year. By 1968, it was estimated, production would reach about one million carats per year. In 1965 diamonds became the Republic's most valuable export ($20,-000,000), accounting for about 75 per cent of the total value of exports.

The diamond boom, which brought in considerable new revenue for both the government and those involved in mining, paradoxically tended to *depress*, rather than stimulate the economy, mainly because it pulled thousands of individuals from traditional and commercial agriculture. Perhaps 80,000 to 100,000 individuals were involved in diamond mining, a sizable percentage of them mining illegally and smuggling stones out at a rate of about $10 million a year. Most of the mining, it must be added, was done by individuals using simple hand tools, a circumstance that tended both to stimulate recruitment to the mines and to encourage illegal mining. The Republic sought—unsuccessfully—to stem the tide of smuggling by imposing strict controls and by opening a government mining office.

Not only were the diamond-bearing beds of uneven quality, but it was not certain how much longer the country could continue to depend on the boom, which, as was noted, provided 75 per cent of the total value of the Republic's exports. Moreover, and much more dangerous for the economy, farmers lured to the diamond mines tended to take their fields and plantations out of production, creating not only a decline in exports but a potentially dangerous situation both for them and the government should the diamonds give out. It was not hard to imagine the crisis that might face the country should thousands of individuals be thrown upon their own resources or those of the state at a time when cash-crop agriculture was likely to be in a disastrous condition and much of the farm land returned to bush.

The problem of the diamond industry, coupled with the other economic difficulties in which the Republic found itself in 1965, persuaded the government to seek new ways of raising the needed revenues. The National Loan was one device, and higher taxes and levies on domestic producers and foreign firms was another. Although returns from these new imposts rose at the beginning of 1965, their net effect was, on the one hand, to accelerate the flight of capital, and, on the other, to convince many farmers and planters that they were better off taking their fields out of production, going back to subsistence agriculture, or trying their luck in the diamond fields. Moreover, an additional irritant was represented by the ubiquitous party militants and tax collectors who showed up at cotton purchasing centers to exact "voluntary" contributions for the National Loan, the *Mouvement d'Evolution Sociale de l'Afrique Noire,* and, often, for themselves. A farmer's reaction at Berberati, after he had been paid for his crop and then been forced to give most of his money back to various party and government officials, typified much of the popular reaction to the economic problems of the government: "Je m'en fou du gouvernement; mieux pas venir [ici] que revenir chez moi sans sou. La femme va croire que je l'ai bouffe."[52] ["To hell with the government; it's better that I shouldn't come here than go back home without a cent. My wife will think I've used the money for drink."]

Although it is true that in 1965 the Republic continued to receive foreign aid from France in the form of technical assistance, grants, and subsidies for its cotton crop (as well as aid from other Western countries), had negotiated a $4 million credit with mainland China (of which only half had become available in 1965), and had been promised an eventual extension of the Trans-Cameroon Railway to Bangui, the economic situation gave little grounds for optimism. More important, the situation contributed to the prevailing political uneasiness, serving to undermine public confidence in the regime still further.

All in all, by the end of 1965 the cumulative effect of the country's political and economic troubles appeared to have been great enough to persuade at least two groups—the Izamo faction in the military, and the "Young Turks"—to seek to replace the regime by force. It is worth repeating that it was not, apparently, any *one* thing that triggered Bokassa's intervention during the night of December 31–January 1, but an accumulation of circumstances, plus the imminence of the projected Izamo coup. Whether Bokassa himself had been planning his own intervention is not known, but it is a possibility that cannot, in light of what actually happened, be ruled out.

After-effects of the Coups

Military coups in Latin America have tended to be exercises in political musical chairs; the ruling personnel changes, but, since the new rulers are almost invariably drawn from the same social strata from which their predecessors came, the system as a whole experiences little change

[52] Remark overheard by the author at Berberati in May 1965.

save, perhaps, for a short-lived increase in the volume of governmental exhortation and propaganda.[53] The long-standing, almost traditional, class relationships between the landed aristocracy, the middle class, the church, and the military that characterize much of Latin American politics, and which give Latin American coups such low systemic impact, are totally lacking in Africa. This point is worth making for three reasons: (1) to suggest that analogies between Latin American and African military coups—often made—are generally false, (2) to reinforce the point that African coups, including the three here discussed, have virtually no basis in social class divisions, and (3) to suggest that African coups have tended to be unique since they, in fact, effect sharp, almost revolutionary changes in the political systems within which they take place. Three of these changes come at once to mind.

First, and most obvious, the three coups changed the constitutional basis of each state. In each country, the new military rulers undertook to write new constitutions designed, hopefully, at least to overcome the structural weaknesses of the older ones. The three earlier constitutions were modeled to a very large extent on the French Constitution of 1958, which—consonant with the personal style of General de Gaulle—gave very extensive powers to the presidency. And it was presidential excess that was cited to justify the Soglo coup of 1963 and was said to be one of the causes of the Upper Voltan coup. The process of elaborating post coup constitutions was well underway by the beginning of 1969. One apparent trend seemed to be toward a curtailment of executive powers, a shift undoubtedly representing a reaction to alleged presidential excesses of the past. The new Ghanaian constitution, for example, creates a dual executive dividing powers between a President and a Prime Minister, but reserves such powers of judicial supervision to the judiciary so as to make the Supreme Court virtually the final arbiter within the political system.[54] In any case, the sense of these attempts at constitution-making was that the coups ushered in new political eras, second republics, as it were, that would operate under a better set of rules than their predecessors. Constitutional revision, it must be added, has become a matter of highest priority for the military rulers of Nigeria, Sierra Leone, Togo, Burundi, and Congo/Brazzaville, and for much the same reasons.

Second, the three coups either dissolved or suspended such structural features of the three countries' political systems as legislatures and political parties. In the Republic, the *Mouvement d'Evolution*

[53] Merle Kling, "Towards a Theory of Power and Political Instability in Latin America," *Western Political Quarterly,* IX (1956), 21-35.

[54] Emily Card, "Ghana Prepares for Civilian Rule," *Africa Report,* XIII (Apr. 1968), 9.

Sociale de l'Afrique Noire apparatus was reduced to skeletal proportions following a purge of its leadership; it was not abolished outright, although President Bokassa was said to have considered doing so. In 1967 Bokassa assumed the presidency of the *Mouvement d'Evolution Sociale de l'Afrique Noire*, but by then the party had ceased to have any significant influence on the government. In Upper Volta, President Lamizana at first banned political activity, then relented, and finally, after political agitation threatened to get out of hand, banned all political activity in September 1966. Affected was not only Yaméogo's *Union*, but also the *Mouvement de Libération Nationale* of Ki-Zerbo, the old *Parti du Regroupement Africain* of exiled leader Boni, and the *Groupement d'Action Populaire*, of Muslim initiative.[55] In Dahomey, Soglo simply dissolved all political parties, though he did not—or could not—affect the status of Dahomey's troublesome trade unions. Legislatures in all three countries were *mis en congé*, a phrase that conveys the meaning of suspension without dissolution, and dissolution without abolition. In effect, legislatures and legislators were simply put into constitutional limbo pending the formulation of new constitutional principles and the holding of new elections, without specific dates given for either event. It is clear from the published statements of the three military regimes that they intended to revive the legislatures at some later date, but not before the *hommes valables* (to which Lamizana repeatedly alluded) could be found to man them.

The third effect is a consequence of the second: a drastic change—perhaps sometimes only transitory, as political fortunes shift—in both the predicates and the bases of leadership recruitment. It is significant to note that in all three countries the coups were directed against the ruling politicians, because they were seen by the military as unable to rule effectively and as being thoroughly corrupt. The new military governments, therefore—and not unexpectedly—were manned by combinations of military men and technically competent civilians, most of whom occupied their positions on the basis of particular expertise, experience, or skills. Among this latter group were to be found a large number of "younger" men, that is, men who had risen to positions of leadership shortly before or, more likely, after independence. Their distinguishing characteristic is that, by and large, they were not identified with the agitational political style of the "old"—that is, pre-independence vintage—leaders. Those who had such an identification, such as Dr. Emile Zinsou, Dahomey's Foreign Minister, had nevertheless usually managed to retain at least the appearance of honesty and probity at the time when their contemporaries seemed to be becoming

[55] "Haute Volta, quatre partis dans la course," *Jeune Afrique*, 309 (Dec. 11, 1966), 19.

increasingly venal and corrupt.[56] The suspension of parties and legislatures, considered in conjunction with the stated motives of the new military rulers (that is, to save the system from its civilian rulers), had the effect, therefore, of discrediting a whole generation of leaders and of removing most of them, at least in the first two years after the coups, from the pool of potential recruits to high governmental positions. At least initially the new military rulers of the three countries turned to the technocrats to assist them in the tasks of reconstruction.[57]

Summary and Conclusions

The three coups considered in this essay are not, admittedly, a sufficient sample from which to draw wider generalizations about either the causes or the effects of recent political upheavals in Africa. Nevertheless, examination of the coups reveals antecedent conditions, certain key group involvements, and contextual circumstances that have a considerable degree of similarity to events elsewhere on the continent. Some of these conditions, involvements, and circumstances were mentioned earlier in this study. It is worth recapitulating them and adding whatever dimensions and further illustrations our examination of the three coups has provided.

Antecedent conditions

Casual connections between political upheavals and political, economic, and social conditions must be sought within the particular systems involved. General economic and political deterioration appeared to provide at least a pretext for military intervention. In all three instances there is strong evidence to suggest that both the

[56] Dr. Emile Derlin Zinsou (b. 1918) is the only one of the old-timers who survived the 1965 coup in a position of authority. The government reshuffle of Dec. 1966 did not eliminate all of the top personnel in the Apithy-Ahomadegbé regime; Arsene Kinde, former Minister of Justice, became Director General of the National Oilworks Company; Marcel Dadjo, Minister of Posts, Transport, and Communication, retained his position, and Nicephore Soglo, a high functionary in the Finance Ministry, became Minister of Finance and Economic Affairs on Dec. 30, 1966, but resigned the next day, following the appointment of Bertin Borna—a minister in Maga's government—as Finance Minister. Zinsou was serving as President of Dahomey in late 1969, when his government was overthrown by Colonel Maurice Kouandété.

[57] The author has elsewhere discussed the rise of the technocrats in French-speaking Africa. Victor T. Le Vine, *Political Leadership in Africa: Post-Independence Generational Conflict in Upper Volta, Senegal, Niger, Dahomey, and the Central African Republic* (Stanford, 1967); "Political Elite Recruitment and Political Structure in French-speaking Africa," *Cahiers d'Études Africaines*, VIII (1968), 369-89.

national economy and political system were either on the point of collapse or in serious difficulty. Examination of the conditions preceding the upheavals in Congo/Brazzaville (1963), Algeria (1965), Ghana (1966), and Togo (1967) suggest a similar dual disintegration. A period of political instability (in some instances, violence) without corresponding economic deterioration preceded, and provided a pretext for, unconstitutional action in the Biafran secession (Nigeria, 1967), in Burundi (1966), Nigeria (1966), Congo/Kinshasa (1965), the Sudan (1964), Zanzibar (1964), and Congo/Kinshasa (1960).[58]

Group participation

Trade unions were instrumental in the downfall of the Maga government (1963) and the Apithy-Ahomadegbé regime (1965) in Dahomey, as they were in the removal of the Yaméogo regime in Upper Volta. Similar trade union involvement, in varying degrees, occurred in the political upheavals in Congo/Brazzaville (1963), the Sudan (1964), Togo (1967), and the first Nigerian coup of General Ironsi (1966). It appears that wherever trade unions have had some degree of autonomous strength within a political system, they have been crucially involved in changes of government. Similarly involved, though on a less well organized scale, have been youth, student, and "intellectual" groups. Their participation appears to have been important to the coups in Upper Volta and Dahomey; they lent support, in somewhat less organized fashion, to the Republic coup. Elsewhere, notably in Togo (1967), Congo/Brazzaville (1963), and the Sudan (1964), they provided demonstrations, agitators, and conspirators for the groups that seized power. In almost every instance, moreover, they demonstrated support (*post hoc*, to be sure) for the revolutionary, reformist, or broadly reconstructionist goals enunciated by the successor regimes.

Context

Whether it comes as an identity crisis,[59] as the widening of the systemic expectation-performance gap,[60] or as a sort of "morning after" effect,[61]

58 See above, Michael F. Lofchie, "The Zanzibari Revolution: African Protest in a Racially Plural Society," 924-68; Young, "Rebellion and the Congo," 969-1011; James O'Connell, "The Fragility of Stability: The Fall of the Nigerian Federal Government, 1966," 1012-34.

59 Lucian Pye, *Politics, Personality, and Nation-Building* (New Haven, 1963), 187-88.

60 Raymond Tanter and Manus Midlarsky, "A Theory of Revolution," *The Journal of Conflict Resolution*, XI (1967), 264-80.

61 Brian Crozier, *The Morning After, a Study of Independence* (London, 1963), *passim*.

some sort of political trouble appears to be the unhappy lot of most new countries within three to five years of their independence.[62] Only those few fortunate new African states that have somehow managed to maintain relatively popular regimes and a reasonable, visible improvement in the social and economic lot of their citizens have thus far escaped serious internal political crisis.[63] It is in these countries that political succession can be achieved without rending the fabric of the polity; indeed, successful post-1960 regime change has been accomplished only in the Gambia. (Sierra Leone might have been the second instance were it not for ex-Prime Minister Albert Margai and his military collaborators.) In any case, the three coups here discussed fall well within a period of increasing political instability in Africa. The list in Table 1 is only a partial compendium of post-1960 political instability; all save four or five of Africa's thirty-seven independent states had, by mid-1967, experienced some variety of serious internal political disturbance. The coups in Upper Volta, Dahomey, and the Central African Republic did not appear to have been externally generated, nor was there any evidence that Soglo, Lamizana, or Bokassa took any particular inspiration from each other's activities. It is reasonable to suppose that with each successful military coup the likelihood of more such coups increased. The examples of success might well prove persuasive for military men seeking to change their regimes. This may have been the case, but, thus far, there is no evidence to support such a hypothesis, nor to support the corollary supposition that some sort of "demonstration effect" persuaded politicians out of power that their national military could accomplish for them what they had been unable to accomplish themselves.

[62] For a general discussion of the problem of political succession in the contemporary world, see Dankwart A. Rustow, "Succession in the Twentieth Century," *Journal of International Affairs*, XVIII (1964), 104-13.

[63] Trying to predict which African states will manage to survive the first crucial post-independence years without major political troubles is a task best left to professional odds-makers. By the end of 1967 a few African states had, however, managed to retain both stability and considerable promise for the future: Niger (ind. 1960) had successfully resisted the inept attempts of the Sawaba party to kill President Hamani Diori and seize control; the Cameroon Federal Republic (ind. 1960) had weathered and overcome a long-standing revolt begun by the *Union des Populations du Cameroun* in 1955; Zambia (ind. 1964), Kenya (1963), and Tanzania (1963) appear to be on stable courses despite the Jan. 1964 army mutinies in the latter two countries. The Malagasy Republic should be included in the list, since it was fortunate in having had its nationalist revolt much earlier, in 1947, and has experienced relative stability since.

PRIVILEGE AND PROTEST AS INTEGRATIVE FACTORS: THE CASE OF BUGANDA'S STATUS IN UGANDA

ALI A. MAZRUI

The first half of 1966 saw a decisive confrontation in Uganda. In February Daudi Ocheng, a member of the Kabaka Yekka political party, made a speech in Parliament virtually accusing the Prime Minister, the Minister of Defense, and the Deputy Army Commander of complicity in corrupt practices involving the transfer of gold from the Congo (Kinshasa), then in the throes of a rebellion, to Uganda. The accusation against these leaders led to a motion for the setting up of a commission of enquiry. This motion was openly debated in Parliament, but it was even more dramatic that, when the vote was taken, both the government side and the opposition voted overwhelmingly in favor of establishing a commission to investigate the allegations against the Prime Minister and his two prominent colleagues.

The political career of A. Milton Obote appeared to undergo a serious decline; the ruling party, the Uganda People's Congress, was apparently on the verge of changing its leadership. A motion by a member of the opposition could have become the means for the ruling party to (1) clear its name of the insinuations made by the opposition which would discredit the opposition, or to (2) change its own leadership and replace Obote with someone else.

At the time Prime Minister Obote was himself on tour in another part of the country. He took a few days to collect himself and then left for the capital, Kampala. Soon after his arrival Obote reasserted control and suspended the constitution. Five of his cabinet ministerial colleagues—those suspected of being the initiators of the move within

This essay could not have been written without the help and stimulation of several colleagues of Makerere University College. But responsibility for the views expressed herein is, of course, exclusively mine.

the ruling party to replace the leadership—were, unexpectedly, arrested while at a cabinet meeting. Prime Minister Obote also relieved the President, Sir Edward Mutesa (also then the Kabaka of Buganda), of his office as President because Sir Edward was suspected of being in league with those who wanted to replace the leadership of the Uganda People's Congress and thus change the Prime Minister of the country. Later accusations compromised Sir Edward even more seriously when it appeared that he had explored the possibility of getting external help from Britain to overthrow the Prime Minister by force if necessary.

After the arrests and the suspension of the constitution, Obote declared himself Executive President of the country and, in addition, proceeded to appoint the commission of enquiry into his own behavior which Parliament had already approved of in his absence. The commission itself was indisputably an independent commission consisting of British judges brought from outside Uganda. Its full report has never been made public but enough was revealed to exonerate Obote and his colleagues of some of the most serious charges brought against them.

Meanwhile, events had been gathering momentum in other spheres of national life since Obote's return and his suspension of the constitution. The arguments between him and Sir Edward Mutesa led finally to a confrontation between the central government under Obote and the government of the region of Buganda under Sir Edward when the region gave the central government notice to quit Kampala, the capital, which had once formed a part of the Kingdom of Buganda. The central government treated this ultimatum as an act of rebellion.

From then on events gathered momentum, culminating in the Battle of the Palace on May 24, 1966, when the national army, on Obote's orders, attacked the Kabaka's residence, and, after a sustained exchange with its defenders, captured it. The Kabaka himself escaped and found his way to Britain, where he was to remain in exile. But Buganda as an autonomous entity seemed at last to have come to an end. In fact, when the new constitution was promulgated a year later, Buganda was split into four districts and denied the distinctive personality that it had legally enjoyed for so long.

The distinctive personality and privileged position of Buganda had been one of the more dramatic consequences of the British colonial policy of indirect rule. While permitting significant changes in the nature of local institutions, that policy had encouraged the survival of an effective traditional kingship in Buganda. A degree of autonomy was granted to Buganda which in time both preserved Buganda's militant loyalty to itself and secured the region's favored position in the Protectorate of Uganda as a whole. The Ganda themselves added to this pre-eminence by a marked response to modernity in selected areas of life. Their acceptance of Western education, their sophisticated links with Christian missions, and the commercialization of some of their agricultural activities, all helped to give the Ganda a lead in national affairs as compared with other groups. Thus, the pre-eminence which size and history had already conferred upon them was given additional stimulus by the Ganda themselves through their modernizing tendencies. And modernity was in turn made to serve the cause of tribal identity. To use David Apter's words, the ethos of the Ganda was "sufficiently adaptable to allow innovation to be traditionalized and thereby sanctified."[1]

It has often been suggested that, by helping to maintain Buganda's privileged identity, British colonial policy made the task of national integration more difficult. Kenneth Ingham represented a whole school of thought when, in his comment on the arrangements of the Uganda Agreement of 1900 for the administration of Buganda, he argued that "the weakness of the Agreement from a long-term point of view lay in the very completeness of the arrangements made for Buganda as a separate unit while at the same time making it a province of the Uganda Protectorate."[2] Many years later this agreement was revised and replaced by the Buganda Agreement of 1955. Commenting on the latter, R. C. Pratt admitted that it contained a formula which satisfied Buganda's separatist loyalties without driving it into full isolation from the rest of Uganda, but he expressed some reservations about the possibility of achieving a united Uganda in the future. He contended that the ability of the Ganda to win their Kabaka's return from exile in 1955 might heighten their separatist sentiments no matter what the formal constitutional arrangements were.[3] Apter, particularly in his concluding chapter, also refers to Buganda's resistance to participation in the central government.[4]

Finally, even the Uganda Relationships Commission, which in 1961 studied the future form of government best suited to Uganda and the question of the relationships between the central government

---

[1] David E. Apter, *The Political Kingdom in Uganda* (Princeton, 1961), 27. This point is discussed in similar terms by G. S. Engholm and Ali A. Mazrui, "Violent Constitutionalism in Uganda," *Government and Opposition*, II (1967), 585-99. For the period 1959 to 1960 in Buganda see Dharam P. Ghai, "The Bugandan Trade Boycott: A Study in Tribal, Political, and Economic Nationalism," above, 755-70.

[2] Kenneth Ingham, *The Making of Modern Uganda* (London, 1958), 92.

[3] D. Anthony Low and R. Cranford Pratt, *Buganda and British Overrule, 1900–1955* (London, 1960), 348-49.

[4] Apter, *The Political Kingdom*, 435-79.

and the other authorities in Uganda, pointed to the Buganda problem, and to the British policy responsible for it, as the main stumbling blocks to the creation of a united, democratic, political system in Uganda.[5] Clearly, then, the contention that British colonial policy, by helping to maintain a privileged identity for Buganda, made the task of national integration more difficult, has behind it a formidable array of authorities.

We maintain, however, that although such a thesis has been widely accepted, the evidence for it must, for the time being at least, be regarded as inconclusive. In fact, there is evidence to support a contrary thesis, and it is to this contrary thesis that we address ourselves here. We hope to demonstrate that the existence of a large, militant, and prestigious region within Uganda was by no means always a negative factor in terms of national integration. We feel that a situation of power imbalances between regions, while generating a good deal of hostility and rivalry, can also be a positive factor in the integrative process. We argue, therefore, that the very privileged position which Buganda enjoyed for so long, when coupled with the very protests which this position evoked from other parts of the population, constituted an important element on the positive side of Uganda's national growth.

In the pages which follow, we shall discuss the role of this special kind of inequality in the integrative process, as well as the impact of Buganda on the cultural homogenization of Uganda; the relationship between ethnic rivalries and political alignments in nation building; and the degree to which Buganda's dominant position facilitated pluralistic competitive politics and helped to encourage certain habits of conflict resolution in the political style of the country as a whole.

There are occasions when the cause of unification is well served by a situation in which one member of the group enjoys a decisively leading role. This applies as much to international forms of integration as it does to certain domestic processes of a similar kind. Altiero Spinelli, the Italian leader in the European integration movement, once argued, for example, that all true confederations which have meant something in history were viable only because they contained one member "more equal than the others."[6] This argument was concerned with European matters, as he was suggesting that American hegemony in the Western alliance provided an·important foundation for the viability of the alliance. For only so long as Europe accepted that

[5] Uganda Government, *Report of the Uganda Relationships Commission 1961* (Entebbe, 1961), 42.

[6] Altiero Spinelli, "Atlantic Pact or European Unity," *Foreign Affairs*, XL (1962), 543.

hegemony and America continued to be concerned about the security of Europe, could the Western alliance exhibit enough cohesiveness to be internationally meaningful.

Buganda's position in Uganda was not, however, really analogous to that of a dominant partner in an alliance. On the contrary, there often were isolationist tendencies in Buganda's political style which appeared to loosen bonds rather than to tighten alliances. Yet in a sense this was a case of one dominant region being forced to share life within a single national entity; and at times, as the partner of an imperial presence, that region did attempt to exercise hegemony over the rest of the country. In other words, there is a sense in which Buganda did attempt to be, and perhaps partially succeeded in becoming, the Prussia of modern Uganda. Prussia in the nineteenth century under Chancellor Otto von Bismarck took the lead in uniting the German states. Bismarck, a member of the Prussian rural nobility, virtually created the Second German Reich, and made it an extension of Prussian power.[7]

Like Buganda in Uganda, Prussia had its critics among the German states. Prussia's leadership was often challenged or resented. But, unlike Buganda, Prussia had the military power to assert supremacy over the other German regions. For Prussia it was not simply a case of persuading the rest of the confederation that this particular region was pre-eminently qualified to lead. In the words of the nineteenth-century German historian Heinrich von Treitschke:

> Often as we have tried by theory to convince the small States that Prussia alone can be the leader in Germany, we had to produce the final proof upon the battlefields of Bohemia and the [river] Main [in 1866].[8]

As long as imperial order prevailed in Uganda, Buganda was supreme on the metaphorical battlefield of politics within the imperial system. *Pax Britannica* itself was, after all, a form of protection which prevented the resort to arms in Uganda of the kind which in the nineteenth century had decided which subregion would emerge supreme in Germany. For, as long as colonial rule prevailed, Buganda's skill in political battle within the colonial political system continually ensured its privileged position in relation to the other national regions.

With independence, however, it became increasingly clear that the support of the security forces was an important factor in internal

[7] A useful introduction to the modern phase of German history is Koppel S. Pinson, *Modern Germany* (New York, 1954).

[8] See Heinrich von Treitschke (trans. Blanche Dugdale and Torben de Bille), *Politics* (New York, 1963), 38.

domestic hegemony, and the balance of power was significantly tilted. In the course of 1965 and 1966 in Uganda leading politicians of different parties attempted to recruit the guaranteed support of the security forces in the country. And the Kabaka of Buganda, who was also President of the country, did—as he himself subsequently admitted —consider the question whether a British military presence in Uganda might not restore the system which in the colonial period had enabled Buganda to assert a neo-Prussian hegemony in the country as a whole.[9] But no external military support was forthcoming.

The military forces in Uganda were overwhelmingly composed of northerners, the Ganda having been at one time too proud to seek a career in the army. The result was the military defeat of the Kabaka in May 1966 and the eclipse of Buganda, at least for a while. Buganda had not succeeded in continuing to play Prussia after independence.

But now, to turn to the integrative process: Buganda's brief enjoyment of a neo-Prussian dominance during the colonial period had already exerted an influence on this process. Privilege and prestige compel both emulation and resentment. But the effects of emulation and resentment on the process of national cohesion are not identical. Both emulation and shared resentment are elements of homogenization—as the model to be emulated from its pedestal commands a growing likeness to itself from those who are below. But resentment, when it is shared, is a process of horizontal homogenization. Those who indulge in the same resentment find a bond in that factor. And so non-Ganda, by emulating the Ganda, established a growing likeness among themselves and the model on its pedestal; at the same time, those non-Ganda who sense a common antagonism against the Ganda are united among *themselves* by that shared attitude.

It should be pointed out that vertical homogenization, when it encompasses several communities at the base which are seeking to emulate the same pinnacle, results in horizontal homogenization as well. If A, B, and C at the base of the social structure are all emulating the ways of D at the pinnacle, success would imply that A, B, and C become similar to each other at the same time that individually they become similar to D. Three small tribes in Uganda all imitating certain aspects of Gandan culture may in the process themselves acquire similar characteristics.

---

[9] See E. W. Oryema, Inspector General of Police, televised admonition to politicians, "Don't Tamper with Security Forces," reported in *Uganda Argus,* Mar. 3, 1966. See also Sir Edward Mutesa's *Desecration of My Kingdom* (London, 1967), 179, on his painful awareness of the changed balance of forces in the country after independence. Refer to *Uganda Argus* of Mar. 4, 5, 1966, pages 1 and 2 respectively, for the request for external troops by Sir Edward.

The phenomenon of one community or one region acquiring so much influence and prestige that the rest of the nation turns to follow its direction is by no means unique in the growth of nations. In fact, it is the rule rather than the exception. England, in relation to Great Britain, is an example of one region or subgroup acquiring so much power, influence, and prestige that in cultural evolution much of the rest of the country takes its cue from England. The Scots and the Welsh, and, indeed, the Irish continue to retain personalities of their own; the Welsh have even retained a live language. Nevertheless, the Anglicization of Scotland, Wales, and Ireland has made a number of gains throughout the ages. England is, of course, a bigger segment of the United Kingdom than Buganda is of Uganda. But the analogy between England and Buganda does not necessarily depend on comparable size or ratio of importance. What needs to be grasped is that Buganda was for a while attempting to play England to Uganda's Great Britain—just as the term "England" has often been used to refer to the United Kingdom as a whole, so had Bugandan interests sometimes been equated with the interests and views of Uganda as a whole.[10]

Finally, it should be noted that all these matters are connected with the process of forming a consensus in a growing nation. And here it is worth distinguishing between *primary consensus*, implying long-term agreement on the fundamentals of the society, and *secondary consensus*, implying *ad hoc* agreement on individual policies or individual leaders of political parties at a given moment in time. In 1964 and 1965 President Johnson succeeded in creating a wide consensus in the United States both for his foreign policy and for the new domestic policies of greater welfare and wider opportunities. But by 1968 this consensus had virtually evaporated. Yet the American people rejected Johnson's policies without rejecting his legal right to be President. There was, in other words, a primary consensus for the legitimacy of Johnson's being President.

The quality of nationhood implies a capacity for a high degree of

[10] Nationalism in Scotland and Wales has been increasing in the last few years. (See, for example, a special feature article on the subject in *The Sunday Times* [London], Apr. 21, 1968.) A less clear but no less suggestive example of the supremacy of one subculture in a nation as a whole is the supremacy of English in the United States. We have referred to Bismarck and the growth of Prussia. It was in fact Bismarck who said that one of the most important accidents in world politics was the simple fact that Americans spoke English. Today only a minority of Americans can, in fact, trace their origins to England. But the supremacy of the English language and the "Anglo-Saxon" subculture is attributable to the prestige and influence which the original English-speaking component of American society continued to enjoy even in the face of a sizable invasion of people speaking other tongues.

primary consensus. And this capacity might, in fact, only mean that a people have at least managed to accumulate a large number of continuing common prejudices. Some prejudices are simply a part of secondary consensus if they are likely to disappear rather quickly with the changing mood of public opinion. But other prejudices which might have started as secondary prejudices can, if they survive long enough, assume the quality of being primary. Common enemies of a particular people can, for example, be either transient or long-term and traditional. A shared prejudice against a certain people can itself become a part of the long-term process of prejudice-consolidation which is much a part of nation-building.

It is our contention that anti-Gandan prejudice may for a while have contributed to the diffuse growth of shared aversions elsewhere in the country. To that extent protest and resentment of the privileged community acquired an additional significance for national integration.

But before we look more closely at the alignment of forces which resulted from protest and resentment, we need to examine the cultural context by outlining Buganda's impact on the process of cultural homogenization in the country as a whole. Of course this process is still in its initial stages, but there is little doubt that the prestige which Gandan political culture had accumulated during the colonial period had by 1966 begun to command the emulation of a number of other regions.

First there was the process of institutional reproduction: Some of Buganda's institutions found replicas elsewhere. Several examples might be cited, but the spread of the institution of "traditional" *ruler* was perhaps the most conspicuous example of Buganda's cultural impact on the surrounding areas. Although Bunyoro had always been credited with a long line of rulers who at one time had even been more powerful than those of Buganda, and in Toro and Ankole the rulers consolidated their powers over their respective areas more as a result of British than of Bugandan intervention, it remains true that during the period of British colonial rule the prosperity, prestige, and splendor of Buganda's Kabaka served both as a focus of resentment and a model for imitation. The ambition to be as "Buganda-like" as possible was particularly strong in the kingdom of Toro where, before independence, the district went so far as to demand a constitution similar to that of Buganda.[11]

Elsewhere the tendency to imitate the Bugandan institution of the Kabaka resulted in the creation of ceremonial figures. Busoga, which had no tradition of a hereditary, paramount ruler, created the ceremonial post of "Kyabazinga" in 1940 and, on the eve of independence,

[11] Uganda Government, *Report of the Relationships Commission,* 50.

found itself demanding that the post be made hereditary.[12] Other districts created posts for ceremonial figures; but unlike the situation in Busoga these figures were elected. In Lango it was the post of the "Won Nyaci"; in Acholi the post of the "Laloyo Maber"; in Kigezi the post of the "Rutakirwa"; Bugisu had its "Omuinga"; Bukedi its "Senkulu"; Sebei its "Kingoo"; and Madi its "Lopirigo." Only the districts of Teso, West Nile, Madi, and Karamoja managed to resist the temptation of creating these ceremonial posts. Behind these moves lay the desire to achieve parity of esteem with Buganda;[13] the practical impact on the country, however, was to spread the cult of "traditional" rulers, and hence to universalize the esteem for such rulers all over the country. In this regard it may be revealing that even a party such as the Uganda People's Congress, led by a man like Obote, who comes from an area without a paramount hereditary ruler, found it had to pledge itself in its manifesto "to uphold the dignity and prestige of the hereditary rulers and the other heads of African Governments."[14] The Democratic party included a similar pledge in its manifesto.[15]

Another instance of Buganda's cultural impact on other areas was the spread of its local governmental system to all the districts of Uganda. Rural Buganda before and after the introduction of British rule had been divided into administrative and council units, descending in size from the county or *saza*, headed by a *saza* chief and a council, through the subcounty, or *gombolola*, headed by a *gombolola* chief and a council, and the parish or *miruka* headed by a *miruka* chief and a council, down to the village or *mutongole* (or *nyampara*) headed by a *mutongole* chief and council. These units and chiefly hierarchies had also existed in the three kingdom areas of Bunyoro, Toro, and Ankole and, to some degree in Busoga, but not in the other areas. During the British era this system of local government spread over the whole country. In many parts of the country the British employed Gandan agents when setting up the first administrations; they naturally made use of the local governmental system with which they were familiar, namely the Bugandan system. The system remained even after these agents had been replaced by Africans from the areas con-

---

12 Ibid., 54.

13 In 1959 the first constitutional committee detected this feeling in Madi and Acholi, where a demand was made for the creation of a Northern Province assembly, "the object being to deal with Buganda on an equal basis." The assembly was to be the equivalent of the Buganda Lukiiko or legislature. Uganda Government, *Report of the Constitutional Committee* (Entebbe, 1959), 42.

14 Uganda People's Congress, *Policy Statement* (Kampala, 1960), 3.

15 The Democratic Party, *Forward to Freedom, Being the Manifesto of the Democratic Party* (Kampala, 1960), 16.

cerned. Therefore, structurally[16] Uganda had benefited from a uniform system of local government.

In some areas the adoption of these Gandan political structures has been accompanied by the adoption, also, of the communication medium in which the governing is done, namely the Luganda language. In nearly the whole of the Eastern region, particularly in Busoga, Bukedi, and Bugisu (and even in Teso among older chiefs) the day-to-day language of government until perhaps recently has been Luganda. Outside local government administration, the Luganda language is widely spoken in the Eastern and Western regions and to some extent even in the Northern region, where many former migrant laborers who had learned the language during their sojourn in Buganda now live.

The other Bantu regions were to some extent "hypnotized" by some of the ways of the Ganda. The Gandan costumes of the *busuti* for the women and the *kanzu* for the men are far more widely used in the Bantu regions than in the Nilotic north. The Gandan staple of *matoke* (mashed boiled plantain) is, on another front, busy conquering other Bantu cultural areas at the expense of staples like millet, which the people of these areas traditionally consumed. Perhaps the most impressive evidence of Buganda's "hypnotic" impact on Bantu culture is the occasional practice among low-level, working class Western region people (notably Rwandans) of trying to pass themselves off as Ganda rather than as members of their own tribe.

The problem of integration in Uganda was for many years not so much a problem of integrating the various districts of Uganda—Bantu and Nilote—as it was one of integrating these districts and the central political unit of the country, namely Buganda.[17]

Before independence these other parts of the country, their Bantu or Nilotic labels notwithstanding, feared Bugandan domination; Buganda, for its part, feared being dominated by a coalition from the Eastern, Northern, and Western Provinces (now Regions).[18] Even on the eve of independence, the Relationships Commission found these areas virtually unanimous in their acceptance of a united Uganda, in contrast to the ambivalence of Buganda between secession and a federal union. Another indicator of this contrast lay in the distribution of support for the political parties. Both the Uganda People's Congress and the Democratic party were, in policy and intention, trans-tribal

[16] I.e., as opposed to the *powers* the structures carried—which would tend to differ before 1966 between Buganda and other areas.

[17] See n. 1 above.

[18] Uganda Government, *Report of the Constitutional Committee*, 42-43. See also Apter, *The Political Kingdom*, 19.

parties. They achieved a substantial measure of success in being accepted as trans-tribal almost everywhere but in Buganda. The composition of the leadership of these two parties reflected a Bantu-Nilote mixture. Obote, a Nilote, found wide acceptance of his leadership both in his Nilotic north and in the Bantu areas; and so did many of his colleagues, both Bantu and Nilote. They were not, however, accepted in Buganda. The Democratic party had a Ganda for its leader. He too was accepted quite widely in the areas outside Buganda but not in Buganda. In short, if political parties integrate people, the Uganda People's Congress and the Democratic party managed to integrate the Nilotic and Bantu peoples of the areas outside Buganda but, except maybe for the short-lived alliance between the Uganda People's Congress and Kabaka Yekka,[19] they failed to integrate these areas and Buganda. Why was there this co-operation between the Bantu and Nilotic peoples in areas outside Buganda? Why did the Bantu-speaking people not unite with their fellow Bantu, the Ganda, rather than with the Nilotes? Here again Buganda's privileged status and the protest of others against it were perhaps central. To a large extent it can be argued that political co-operation between disparate groups outside Buganda was itself a kind of protest against Buganda's position of aloofness from both its Nilotic and Bantu neighbors. To that extent Buganda may have unwittingly contributed to national integration by preventing or delaying the development of a more primary political cleavage—the Bantu-Nilote cleavage. This ethnic boundary was potentially more deeply divisive than anything the country had so far seen.

There was a time when Uganda as a whole seemed willing to accept Buganda's leadership. People alert enough to join the early political parties of the 1950's, for example, easily accepted Gandan party leaders. However, by 1958 all this had changed. In that year a party was established with the aim of uniting the country's anti-Buganda forces. This party was called the Uganda People's Union. In contrast to earlier parties, the new party's leadership contained no prominent Ganda. Its leadership included people from both the other Bantu areas and from Nilotic areas—from Bunyoro, Acholi, Busoga, Toro, and Bugisu. Apter suggests that one important impetus for the creation of this party was the more or less open assumption of political superiority by the Ganda. This was brought home sharply when a one-time Omuwanika (Minister of Finance) of Buganda indicated that the

---

[19] Kabaka Yekka or "Kabaka Alone" was the party which was set up in Buganda to protect the autonomy of the region and the status of the Kabaka. The party ceased to exist after the events of May 1966, and some of the members either withdrew from politics or joined the ruling party.

Kabaka should be the king of Uganda; non-Ganda took sharp exception.[20] The party later amalgamated with a splinter group of an older party, the Uganda National Congress, to form the Uganda People's Congress under the leadership of Obote. Unlike Buganda, much of the rest of the country—both Bantu and Nilote—accepted the new Congress. Unwittingly, therefore, Buganda, by its protests against the curtailment of its own privileges, provoked people in the rest of Uganda to co-operate in their fight for a common political program. A shared suspicion of the Ganda as an ethnic group thus first helped to give birth to the Uganda People's Union and then to make the Uganda People's Congress a success in some Bantu areas.

Within Buganda itself suspicion of the Bugandan ruling class— which was largely Protestant in composition—gave birth and sustenance to the Democratic party. According to the 1900 Agreement a tradition was established that the Kabaka and his first and third Ministers should be Protestant, while the second Minister should be Roman Catholic. Of the twenty counties, ten were to be administered by Protestant chiefs, eight by Catholics, and two by Muslims. This Protestant preponderance in the ruling class was reinforced by the common practice of appointing civil servants in the three ministries of the same denomination as the Minister concerned.[21] The 1955 version of the 1900 Agreement did little to alter the balance of the two Christian denominations in the ruling class. The result was that the Catholics came to regard themselves as an underprivileged majority. It was probably such a consideration that gave a measure of strength to the Democratic party, which to some extent continues (in 1968) to be commonly associated with the Catholics despite attempts by the party to neutralize its denominational origins. At the time of the 1961 elections in which the Kabaka's government declared that all of those who registered and voted were disloyal, 4 to 5 per cent of the potential Bugandan electorate defied the order. Of those registered, 76 per cent voted, and 67 per cent voted for the Democratic party.[22] The boycott thus made it possible for the Democratic party to win twenty out of the twenty-one Bugandan seats. The determination of the party in Buganda was taken as a clear case of the Roman Catholics standing against the Protestant establishment and its desire to secede. Buganda had staged

---

[20] Apter, *The Political Kingdom*, 346-47.

[21] F. B. Welbourn, *Religion and Politics in Uganda* (Nairobi, 1965), 7.

[22] R. C. Peagram, *A Report on the General Election to the Legislative Council of the Uganda Protectorate held in March, 1961* (Entebbe), 3; *Uganda Argus*, Mar. 27, 1961, 3, for detailed election results in all areas for the 1961 General Elections. If the results for the three seats in metropolitan Kampala are excluded, the percentage of those who registered that voted for the Democratic party in rural Buganda is higher than the 67 per cent quoted here.

a "secession" the previous year, but the British colonial authorities had supremely ignored this ceremonial secession and life went on as usual. But the issue of Buganda's separatism remained in the background in the 1961 election.

The party's success in Buganda enabled it to maintain a link between Buganda and the rest of Uganda just at a time when the Kabaka's establishment was most indisposed to have anything to do with the rest of the country. Both the Democratic party and the Uganda People's Congress, being national parties, have played important roles in bringing together the different peoples of Uganda. To the extent that the former's success arose out of internal suspicion of the ruling class within Buganda, it can rightly be said that internal protest against the privileges of the Bugandan ruling class promoted the Democratic party's integrative role in the country. In other words, both the intra-Buganda protest (as exemplified by the Democratic party) and the extra-Buganda protest (as illustrated by the Uganda People's Union and the then Uganda People's Congress) helped the two national parties in the struggle to create some degree of co-operation and unity among the different peoples of Uganda.

The above conclusions bring us to the relevance of ethnic pluralism to a liberal style of politics. Precisely by strengthening the autonomy of Buganda and contributing to the self-consciousness of other regions, British policy had helped to prepare the way for *competitive* politics in the country. Here again "a latent violence and a vigorous constitutionalism" found a meeting point.[23] In much of Africa ethnic pluralism tends to be among the most politically sensitive of all social issues. The risk of violence between tribes is at the center of Africa's twin crises of legitimacy and integration. Britain's indirect rule, where it was successful, tended to sharpen ethnic loyalties. To that extent it probably increased the risk of violence between tribes. But at the same time that policy created the framework for genuinely competitive politics and for a spirit of energetic dissent in at least the first few years of independence. Nigeria has provided perhaps the most dramatic example of these two related consequences of indirect rule. The country started off with an almost furious liberal ethos in its national politics, with the wrangles of strong rival political parties, the excitement of dissent, and strongly competitive political journalism. Perhaps even in its present tragedy much of Nigeria is more of an open society than almost any other in West Afri But the tragedy is the other consequence of indirect rule. By institutionalizing ethnic pluralism in Nigeria, the British created the potential for a meaningful competitive democracy in the years ahead and also the framework for latent violence. Institu-

[23] See Engholm and Mazrui, "Violent Constitutionalism in Uganda" where this idea is discussed more fully.

tionalized ethnic pluralism in a polity like Nigeria or Uganda was functionally, to some extent, in the same tradition as the old doctrine of "separation of powers." By creating a number of subcenters of power within the polity, institutionalized ethnic pluralism tended to avert the danger of absolute government. Within each region of Nigeria, and perhaps preeminently in the north, there was an intolerance of dissent; this intolerance characterized internal Bugandan politics as well. However, the strength of the regions was a form of devolution which has continued to make centralized authoritarianism in both Nigeria and Uganda less likely than it has been elsewhere in Africa.

In at least one respect Uganda until 1966 was even more of a liberal polity than the old Nigeria. This point can best be understood if we first remind ourselves that while the most successful application of indirect rule in Nigeria was in the isolationist north, the most successful application of the policy in Uganda was in the centrally situated and dynamic Buganda. The Northern Region of Nigeria was permitted to remain more traditionalist, more autonomous, and more authoritarian internally than Buganda ever was. Buganda's position at the center of the country and of the national administrative machinery forced upon the region a degree of openness and national accountability never demanded of the northern emirates of Nigeria. Even so, Buganda as a subpolity remained, it must be admitted, relatively illiberal. But its centrality saved Buganda from being a closed society, and Buganda's energetic defensiveness prevented the country in turn from being too easily subjected to unitary control.

What all this meant for a time was that relations between groups in Uganda, and between Uganda and the central government, were highly politicized. And extended experience of political activity does itself have relevance for integration. It is not always remembered that no national integration is possible without internal conflict. Although conflict has a propensity to force a dissolution, the *resolution* of conflict is an essential mechanism of integration. The whole experience of jointly looking for a way out of a crisis, of seeing each other's mutual hostility subside to a level of mutual tolerance, of being intensely conscious of each other's positions and yet sensing the need to bridge the gulf—these are experiences which, over a period of time, should help competitive groups in a nation move forward into a relationship of primary consensus, even if secondary dissensus continues to divide them. Like the Conservative and Labour parties in Britain, rival groups in a country may hate each other over certain policy issues (secondary dissensus), and yet the long experience of peaceful political rivalry and the sharing of a particular mode of political activity can still result in cumulative primary consensus about the system itself.

Therefore, the fact that Buganda's privileged position helped to politicize the political system in Uganda to a degree rarely matched elsewhere in Africa was yet another contribution which the ethnic imbalance in Uganda happened to make to the integrative process in the country. But the case for this particular aspect is not as yet fully proven. By politicizing the system Buganda's strong stand might indeed have contributed to the experience of conflict resolution. But there are occasions where rivalries are too acute to be solved politically. The resort to arms takes place when politics as a mode of conflict resolution fails. It might well be true that in 1966 Buganda strained the system too far. There was a resort to arms—and the style of open politics in Uganda was seriously interrupted.

Perhaps it is here that the weakness of the previous balance of forces within Uganda is to be found. While the system allowed for vigorous political dissent, it also held the seeds of serious political disorder. In Africa, conditions can still require a strong government even at the expense of certain liberal ideals. It is often assumed that stability and national integration are similar national aims. But national policies sometimes have to choose between them. Political integration is often destabilizing because new stresses are created by the very process. Conversely, integration presupposes the accumulated experience of certain forms of internal conflict and their resolution. A government in an African country, therefore, might have to choose between the ideal of enforced stability, even at the expense of slowing down integration, and the ideal of competitive politics, however integrative it might be.

In short, a case can be made for the proposition that African governments should put stability before rapid integration, and internal peace before liberal dissent. For those who hold this position, it was right to have ended Buganda's special position in 1966 even if this was at the expense of the liberal polity and of the accumulation of experience in certain forms of conflict-resolution.[24]

[24] The question might still be asked whether the experience of the past was too deep to have been permanently ended by the events of 1966. Will Uganda's competitive pluralism reassert itself as a style of political activity in the days ahead? There are signs of lingering openness of dissent. The country still has an opposition party, the Democratic party, which is probably stronger in the country than its handful of members in Parliament would indicate. In April 1968 President Obote resumed a series of "Meet the People" rallies which he addressed in different parts of the country. Alexander Latim, the leader of the opposing party, promised counterrallies with or without government permission. See *The People*, Kampala, Apr. 27, 1968. The debate on the new Uganda Constitution the previous year had been one of the frankest and most open constitutional wrangles in Africa since independence. The Kampala-based magazine *Transition* continued to publish opposing views on how Uganda was ruled well into 1968. Meanwhile, the decline

In 1966 Buganda was humbled. Was this a gain for national integration? It may well be, but our concern in this paper has not been to demonstrate the consequences of May 1966 when Buganda's pre-eminence was brought to an end. Rather it has been with the consequences of that pre-eminence for as long as it lasted. We have sought to demonstrate that the previous relations between groups in Uganda were not devoid of national functionality. On the contrary, as we have tried to show, a situation in which one particular group was "more equal than the others" might itself have constituted one route toward national integration. Both *privilege* and *protest against privilege* have in moments of history interacted to create greater interpenetration between groups. Nor indeed has it been merely protest *against* privilege which has had such potential. A continuing posture of protest in *defense* of privilege—the kind which Buganda for so long adopted—might have contributed to the politicization of Uganda and to greater interpenetration between groups.

A curious factor to be borne in mind is that Buganda contributed to national integration in spite of itself. There was a recurrent isolationist tendency in Buganda's behavior as well as a style of political condescension toward other groups. The region even staged a formal secession in 1960 and declared itself independent. If Buganda had had its conscious will, there would be no Uganda today as presently defined. Nor must it be forgotten that units of the size of Buganda, by their insistence on maintaining their specialness and particularism in a situation where competitive liberal democracy was supposed to prevail, could often be distinctly disruptive. Buganda's privileged position was sometimes a strain on national cohesiveness, rather than an aid to it.

But after these important allowances are made it might still be found that the region's neo-Prussian preeminence over a number of decades was more functional than is sometimes assumed. On balance, Buganda might have contributed more than a variant rendering of its own name to the identity of the Uganda nation.

---

of Buganda seemed to raise the possibility of a realignment of ethnic forces in Uganda, though this was not as yet fully clear. The intra-Northern clash between the Acholi and the Lango, though having long-standing roots, reasserted itself openly during the first few months of 1968. See *Uganda Argus,* Kampala, Mar. 27 and Apr. 4, 1968. See also Colin Leys, *Politicians and Politics: An Essay on Politics in Acholi, Uganda 1962–65* (Nairobi, 1967). For further discussion of some of the historical and theoretical problems of integration raised here see A. G. G. Gingyera-Pinycwa, "Uganda Outlaws the Royalists," *East Africa Journal,* IV (Nov. 1967), 9-14; Ali A. Mazrui, "Pluralism and National Integration," Proceedings of the Colloquium on Pluralism, University of California, Los Angeles, 1966; Mazrui, "Thoughts on Assassination in Africa," *Political Science Quarterly,* LXXXIII (1968), 40-58.

KUMANYANA AND RWENZURURU: TWO RESPONSES TO ETHNIC INEQUALITY

MARTIN R. DOORNBOS

Introduction

This essay is concerned with the contrasting development of political protest in Ankole and Toro, two neighboring societies in western Uganda. A comparison may be useful because, in their origins, the two cases are quite similar but, in their conduct of protest, they are markedly different. Further, as Ankole and Toro are subsystems within the more extensive political entity of Uganda, an analysis of their internal conflicts may throw light on some special problems of national integration.

Ankole and Toro are situated in the western lacustrine area, which also includes Buganda, Bunyoro, Rwanda, and Burundi. Until recently, Ankole and Toro were kingdoms with a quasi-federal relationship to the national center of Uganda. With the adoption of a republican constitution for Uganda in 1967, however, monarchy was abolished, and Ankole and Toro became districts similar to the other administrative districts of Uganda. Both societies comprise different ethnic groups, and in each of them social status and privilege were for a long time distributed unevenly among the various ethnic groups: In Ankole[1] there were the dominant cattle-keeping Hima and the subordinate Iru

The author is grateful to the East African Institute of Social Research for the support which made this essay possible and to Michael Faltas, René Lemarchand, and Michael Lofchie for their helpful comments.

[1] On Ankole, see John Roscoe, *The Banyankole* (Cambridge, 1923); K. Oberg, "The Kingdom of Ankole in Uganda," in Meyer Fortes and E. E. Evans-Pritchard (eds.), *African Political Systems* (London, 1940), 121-62; A. G. Katate and L. Kamugungunu, *Abagabe d'Ankole, Ekitabo I and II* (Kampala, 1955); D. J. Stenning, "The Nyankole," in Audrey I. Richards (ed.), *East African Chiefs* (London, 1959), 146-73; H. F. Morris, *A History of Ankole* (Nairobi, 1962).

cultivators, and in Toro there were the politically dominant Toro and the subordinate Konjo and Amba. Although it has been widely assumed that these relationships are of long standing, the historical evidence now suggests that, as far as the Amba and the Konjo were concerned, they were not subordinated before the early part of this century, after Britain had begun to rule.[2] However, in recent years, the premises of hierarchy and subordination embedded in the political structures of Ankole and Toro have been seriously challenged. Just as inequality had in both cases been defined mainly in ethnic terms, so protest was expressed along correspondingly salient, ethnic lines. In Ankole, a reaction among the Iru against Hima overrule culminated in a movement which has become most widely known as *Kumanyana* (from an Ankole expression meaning "To get to know one another"). In Toro, the Konjo and Amba mobilized fierce resistance against Toro domination in the *Rwenzururu* movement, which derived its name from the Lukonjo term for the "Mountains of the Moon," the Ruwenzori range on the Uganda-Congo border, which forms the habitat of most Konjo and which separates the Amba from the Toro.

In a variety of ways the two movements had common origins. To start at the most general level, in both cases protest developed as a concomitant of some basic structural transformations characteristic of the process of modernization.[3] In this sense, they can be related to the imbalances arising out of the shift from ascriptive patterns of role allocation to more functionally specific types of recruitment. More particularly, protest in Ankole and Toro was an attempt to redress ethnic inequalities in the two societies: inequalities in the distribution of power; in access to the political center for the allocation of benefits; in wealth and welfare; and in dignity and social status. Hence, in both cases, protest was concerned with redefining the political framework and changing the distribution of power, with enlarging social and

---

[2] On Toro, see Julien Gorju, *Entre le Victoria l'Albert et l'Edouard, Ethnographie de la Partie Anglaise du Vicariat de l'Uganda* (Rennes, 1920); Audrey I. Richards, "The Toro," in Richards (ed.), *East African Chiefs*, 127-45; Brian K. Taylor, *The Western Lacustrine Bantu* (London, 1962). Much relevant background information on Toro is also available in the literature on Bunyoro, e.g., John Beattie, *Understanding an African Kingdom: Bunyoro* (New York, 1965); A. R. Dunbar, *A History of Bunyoro-Kitara* (Nairobi, 1965).

[3] Cf. S. N. Eisenstadt, *Modernization: Protest and Change* (Princeton, 1966), 32-34. In regard to the divergent development of the two cases, cf. William Kornhauser, "Rebellion and Political Development," in Harry Eckstein (ed.), *Internal War, Problems and Approaches* (New York, 1964), 153; Harry Eckstein, "On the Etiology of Internal Wars," *History and Theory*, IV (1965), 133-63; Henry A. Landsberger, "The Role of Peasant Movements and Revolts in Development: An Analytical Framework," *Bulletin of the International Institute for Labour Studies*, IV (1968), 8-85.

economic opportunities, and with a search for new dignity and social identity. In the actual course of affairs, however, these objectives were to a large extent fused.

During the first half of this century, social and political inequality in Ankole and Toro were not only comparable in a general sense, but there were even some significant specific similarities in their manifestation. Politically, for instance, the most visible sign of ethnic inequality was in the fact that members of the ethnically distinct elites of Ankole and Toro had for a long period held all the key governmental posts and the senior chieftainships. At another level, the elites in both areas frequently used the same derogatory terms to refer to the subordinate ethnic groups. On the whole both elites also treated Iru, Konjo, and Amba as "unclean"; they did not, for instance, permit them to eat in their houses, at most giving them some food outside. In both societies there was a taboo on intermarriage, which became even stronger as ethnic conflict increased. Such similarities could be anticipated since the two adjacent societies shared a number of cultural traits and traditions. In addition, underlying similarities were reinforced by the application of what was by and large the same pattern of colonial rule: administratively the Ankole and Toro kingdoms both formed part of the Western Province of Uganda.[4]

The formulation of protest against inequality also was spurred by comparable factors in Ankole and Toro. Thus, the economic and social transitions which took place during this century were basic to the emergence of protest in both kingdoms. In recent decades, following the introduction and cultivation of cash crops such as coffee and cotton, incomes rose more generally than heretofore. Progressive increases in school enrollment diffused skills and modern orientations and widened the social basis for recruitment of qualified personnel in various sectors of the societies. In turn, new employment opportunities created an increasing number of positions outside the chiefly hierarchy. As a result, the Iru in Ankole and the Konjo and the Amba in Toro gradually began to share in social advantages previously concentrated in the dominant groups. Rising material welfare, increased access to education, and an infusion of more egalitarian values thus militated increasingly against continued acceptance of social and political inequality. Although the actual incidence of discriminatory practices did decline in recent times, especially in Ankole, this did not necessarily mean a decline in indignation over remaining, as well as remembered, inequalities. To the contrary, development in the economic and social

---

[4] Not least significant was the support the British initially gave the ruling classes. In both kingdoms this had the effect of solidifying the ethnic hierarchies and perpetuating them until about the middle of this century.

fields stimulated a heightened self-awareness and a desire for general, and especially political, equality among the emergent groups. The Kumanyana and Rwenzururu movements were expressions of these sentiments and, from the outset, their protest accordingly had strong emancipatory characteristics.

The emergence of both movements was also stimulated by the process of constitutional development initiated during the final phase of colonial rule in Uganda. During this period an increasing range of powers and functions was delegated to the governments of kingdoms and districts and, step by step, these bodies were also made responsive to the popular will. Moreover, the relationships between constituent units were revised.[5] One effect of these measures was to enhance the district-centered basis of politics in Uganda, already strong as a result of over half a century of largely separate development. However, they also created new political arenas in which long-standing grievances between conflicting groups could be transposed into modern political terms and issues. Above all, however, they fostered definite interest in the future distribution of power among hitherto excluded groups and thus provided new foci for political alignments and conflicts: in other words, subgroups in the several kingdoms and districts of Uganda became aware of the relative gains and losses in political influence which wider local jurisdiction, increasing representation, and a redefinition of realtionships might entail for them. Clearly, minority concerns emerged as a natural corollary of the advance to independent statehood. The Kumanyana and Rwenzururu movements were as much products of this development as of the social and economic transitions which were taking place in Ankole and Toro.

Major distinctions between the two situations lay, however, in the nature of contact between the ethnic groups in Ankole and Toro, and in differences in the relative size of the various components of the two societies. In Ankole, Hima and Iru by and large shared the same territory and lived in close physical proximity to one another. In Toro, on the other hand, the subordinate Konjo and Amba occupied distinct and separate areas, large parts of which were characterized by a con-

---

[5] The major documents of this process include: *African Local Government Ordinance* (1949); *District Administration (District Councils) Ordinance* (1955); *Local Administration Ordinance* (1962); *Administration (Western Kingdoms and Busoga) Act* (1963); the renegotiated *Agreements* with the kingdoms of Buganda, Ankole, Toro and Bunyoro (appended as *Schedules* to the *Independence Constitution* of Uganda); *Report of an Inquiry into African Local Government in the Protectorate of Uganda* [Wallis Report] (1953); *Report of the Constitutional Committee* [Wild Report] (1959); *Report of the Uganda Relationships Commission* [Munster Report] (1961); *Report of the Uganda Independence Conference* (1962).

siderable degree of isolation. Moreover, in Ankole the dominant Hima elite formed only a small minority of the population (about 5 per cent), whereas the Iru constituted the vast majority of a population of roughly 700,000. In Toro, however, the dominant Toro comprised more than half of the population, which totalled about 350,000, whereas the Konjo and Amba together numbered only about 40 per cent.

As we shall see, various important factors of history and culture must be added to the distinctions made here. Nonetheless, it is the contention of the author that the divergent development of the two protest movements evolved largely from the different social contexts within which inequality was expressed in Ankole and Toro. Although the two movements both strove for political emancipation, they came to define their targets in entirely different, if not contrary, terms. While the Kumanyana movement pressed consistently for the inclusion of the Iru into the Ankole political elite—to them the most strategic and most obvious way of attaining equality in that kingdom—the Rwenzururu movement pursued the same general objective by seeking the exclusion of the Amba and Konjo from the Toro political framework. Indeed, from the outset the establishment of a separate district for Konjo and Amba was the principal goal of the Rwenzururu movement. The most militant section of the Rwenzururu movement actually created its own autonomous, and still (1969) surviving, state.

As for the development of political protest in Ankole and Toro, it differed in three more significant respects. First, whereas the Kumanyana movement sought its objectives by continuous and steady pressure for integration, the Rwenzururu movement made a sudden and revolutionary bid for power. Second, the Rwenzururu movement broke out as a mass movement, whereas the involvement in Kumanyana remained by and large restricted to the level of notables. Third, the Rwenzururu movement continued to be more exclusively preoccupied with political concerns; Kumanyana was stimulated to promote Iru emancipation along a much wider range of fronts.

The Iru movement, on the one hand, and the Konjo and Amba movement, on the other hand, took very different forms: the Iru demanded inclusion into Ankole's political elite, the Konjo and the Amba insisted on separation from Toro. The reasons for such a difference may be found in a number of social factors: a contrasting structure of ethnic cleavages; the different proportions of the dominant and subordinate strata, and the varying degree of cultural affinity of the conflicting groups in Ankole and Toro. Thus, for example, Ankole's ethnic structure directed Iru aspirations toward some form of participation within the established framework because the Iru and the Hima constituted two horizontal social layers, spread out through most of the kingdom. Hence there was no territory but Ankole—and none but the whole of Ankole—which the Iru could consider their own. As a result, they had virtually no alternative but to seek equality within Ankole. The fact that the Iru formed the vast majority of the population also fostered a certain confidence among them that political emancipation could be achieved in the process of a general constitutional transition. Moreover, notwithstanding the differences in their customs, there were important cultural links between the Iru and Hima: they shared the same language and many traditions and had for many years been living with each other in a symbiotic relationship. Together, these factors strengthened an Iru allegiance to Ankole as a political unit, though this allegiance did not necessarily reflect an affection for the regime, nor for the political community. Using anthropological speculation, Iru radicals have looked upon the Hima as "Hamitic" invaders who should go back whence they came and on themselves as the "pure Banyan-kore," a distinction which in its extreme implication emphasizes exclusive Iru claims on Ankole. The general effect of these conditions has been to stimulate demands by the Iru for their due influence within Ankole.

In contrast to the Ankole situation, the relationship of the Konjo and the Amba to the Toro has been marked by a vertical-territorial cleavage in addition to the horizontal-hierarchical one. As the Konjo and Amba lived in physical separation from the Toro, it is easy to see that they would consider the best way to overcome Toro domination to be political autonomy in their own areas. (The inaccessibility of Ruwenzori strengthened this outlook to the extent that the Konjo in the mountains eventually seceded from Uganda.) The desire to separate was strengthened by Konjo's and Amba's minority position in Toro. Since they constituted no more than 40 per cent of the total population of Toro, the Konjo and the Amba thought it extremely unlikely that they would ever be granted full equality with the Toro within the existing structure. Finally, there were few cultural and historical links between them and the Toro which could minimize their desire to be divorced from Toro. Not only were their languages and customs markedly different, but the Konjo and the Amba retained a vivid memory of an independence which had been destroyed by their inclusion within Toro. Indeed, it was largely due to this heritage that the outburst of conflict in Toro was accompanied by a pervasive cultural renaissance. Nothing of this magnitude happened in Ankole; the few Iru leaders who took an interest in folk tales and history in the 1950's mainly recorded traditions which were not essentially different from those handed down by the Hima. But the special conditions of the Konjo and the Amba prompted them to claim separation from Toro as a means of achieving equal rights with the Toro. Hence, Kumanyana was an assertion of equality, Rwenzururu an assertion of independence.

There were also other aspects of the composition and position of the subject populations which enhanced the potential for revolutionary tendencies in Toro, in contrast to the more gradual trend in Ankole. These conditions did not by themselves cause the differences in phasing, but they restrained or accelerated the two movements when they were being influenced by other, more immediate factors. Thus, in Ankole, the adoption of a slow but sustained pressure for integration was induced by an important religious division among the Iru as well as by their close proximity to the Hima. This division—a cleavage between Protestant and Roman Catholic Iru—had weakened their numbers as well as their power and had introduced an element of competition among them which tended to prolong the influence of the traditional Hima elite. Moreover, possibilities for the development of radical programs among any one of the Iru groups were diminished by the fact that the two religious groups lived side by side, though in varying proportions, over most of Ankole. This destroyed their homogeneity and reduced the ease with which the two sections could be mobilized. Of even greater importance was the fact that the Hima and the Iru lived together in the areas where grievances were most articulate and where protest eventually originated. The physical proximity of the Hima as well as their political and economic influence imposed a considerable constraint on Iru activities. The vulnerability of those Iru who challenged the regime thus induced cautious and secret stratagems which were not to be given up until the Iru had achieved a substantial amount of influence in the government of Ankole.

In contrast to Ankole, the potential for open protest was much greater among the Konjo and the Amba. Although political agitation preceding the Rwenzururu movement usually occurred separately in each tribe, the initial articulation of radical attitudes was not checked by divisions within either of them. Also, the marked physical distance of the Konjo and the Amba from the Toro increased the possibilities for the organization of open opposition and stimulated the development of distorted stereotypes on each side. Besides, the Konjo and the Amba could generally expect fewer administrative posts and other benefits from the Toro government than could the Iru in Ankole. The discontent arising from this discrimination could more easily lead to an outburst of hostility. But the most important factor leading to the formulation of a revolutionary stand by the Rwenzururu movement lay in the nature of the redoubtable Ruwenzori mountains.

Three other factors were of more direct influence in causing Iru protest to take the form of continuous pressure for participation while Konjo and Amba protest became an abrupt attempt to throw off Toro overrule. One significant difference was that the ruling class in Ankole was generally more accommodating to pressure for integration than was the Toro political elite. This was in large measure due to the numerical weakness of the Hima, as well as to the fact, as has been mentioned, that they were gradually losing their educational and economic advantages over the Iru. The Toro ruling class, on the contrary, retained a much wider and stronger social basis. Thus, while the Hima elite was compelled to give consideration to Iru discontent, the Toro elite could more easily resist—and indeed ignore—Konjo and Amba claims for equal privileges. Iru demands for governmental positions and other benefits thus had been accommodated in a piecemeal fashion since the late 1940's, whereas the Konjo and Amba lacked any prospect of this happening until the early 1960's. Although the accommodations made in Ankole did not prevent Kumanyana's emergence, they did cause that movement to be less revolutionary than it might have been in the absence of any concessions, and, for that matter, to be less revolutionary than Rwenzururu.

Iru protest also remained more limited in scope than Konjo and Amba dissent because of the more gradual constitutional development in Ankole, as compared with that in Toro. The application of new constitutional instruments in Ankole had progressively widened Iru political representation in the 1950's, whereas in Toro this process had virtually stagnated during the same period. In part because of its relative weakness, the Hima elite in Ankole was unable to resist the introduction of the 1955 District Administration Ordinance, which was the most critical constitutional innovation of the period, whereas the Toro elite persisted in its opposition until the possibility of its application was superseded by the Toro Agreement of 1961. Hence, during the years when the Iru were beginning to participate in the affairs of government of Ankole, the Konjo and the Amba remained virtually without any sense of involvement in the political system in Toro. As a result, the legitimacy of the regime was far more radically challenged by Rwenzururu than by Kumanyana. Indeed, the confrontation in Toro was not only more open, but also much more severe than in Ankole. Moreover, due to the deadlock which resulted from the Rwenzururu demand for a separate district, the issue in Toro remained more narrowly focused on the definition and structure of the political framework, and problems of social and economic accommodation were largely left in abeyance until a political solution could be found. In Ankole, on the other hand, the relatively high level of political adjustment of the ethnic groups, although piecemeal, gave rise to the development of relatively diffuse objectives on the part of the Kumanyana movement. Indeed, throughout most of its existence, the Kumanyana movement was almost as actively concerned with problems of social and economic inequality as it was with political issues.

The final and perhaps most decisive factor underlying the divergent development of the two protest movements stemmed from some central axioms for nation-building. In Africa, as elsewhere, it has often been thought that two basic requirements for the growth of a stable polity are the promotion of equitable popular participation in public affairs and the maintenance of territorial unity. For these reasons, efforts have commonly been made to foster the representation of subgroups in political institutions, but at the same time to resist the creation of new political divisions. Over and above the immediate impulses and more general preconditions in each of the two cases, it is adherence to these postulates which motivated Kumanyana to press for integration and Rwenzururu to resort to rebellion. The principle of increasing participation held out promises to the Kumanyana movement which were attainable within the Ankole framework, whereas the insistence on maintaining existing district boundaries was a severe obstacle to the fulfillment of Rwenzururu aspirations. Iru emancipation, it can be argued, has been promoted by the force of these principles, and Konjo and Amba advancement victimized.

Protest in Ankole: The Assertion of Equality

In 1949, a small incident touched off protest in Ankole. An Iru had, under British sponsorship, been appointed Enganzi, or chief minister. Four Hima students at Mbarara High School, believed to have been instigated by influential elders, wrote a letter to the Omugabe, the ruler of Ankole, protesting against this encroachment upon positions to which, as Hima, they considered themselves entitled. Even though its various provisions had long since been disregarded, they based their position on the Ankole Agreement of 1901, which had given the principal chiefs the right to nominate their own successors. The letter was intercepted and circulated by the Iru. Its effect was to crystallize latent antagonisms into concrete alignments, both among the Iru and the Hima. It was at that moment that the Iru protest movement which was eventually to be known as Kumanyana emerged.

The situation following the 1949 incident differed from earlier protests because the expression of Iru discontent was far more explicit in 1949 than it had been in the past and because the sense of grievance and indignation was shared by more Iru than ever before. This is of course not to say that there had been no antecedents in the Iru movement. In fact, the earliest organized expression of Iru aspirations goes back to the Church Missionary Society Association Club of the 1930's. Under this name, selected to minimize vulnerability, a handful of educated Iru had met to discuss matters of common concern. One of the most important matters so discussed was to remain a continuing, indeed major, theme of protest: that appointment to public service should be on merit. Although the Club's direct influence was minimal, it was nevertheless significant as an early discussion ground for an incipient Iru elite and because it stimulated reflection on discrepancies in Ankole's political structure. One should also mention the fact that in 1940 the Iru students at Mbarara High School had organized themselves into an association named *Obutsya Ni Birwa* (after a Kinyankore proverb meaning "The daughter will equal her mother"). They had done so in answer to an organization founded by the Hima students, called *Kamwe Kamwe* ("One by One," an abbreviation of a proverb meaning "One by one together make a bundle"). After this, regular meetings among small numbers of Iru leaders, of Iru "old boys" of Mbarara High School, as well as of student organizations at the school itself, had continued discussions of the position of Iru in Ankole society.

By 1949, however, circumstances were quite different. In that year, a new African Local Government Ordinance had been issued which was designed to expand local administrative functions and to induce greater local involvement in local affairs. Although it remained basically an advisory body, the Ankole Eishengyero (the legislative assembly of the kingdom) was enlarged to include more official and unofficial members, and expectations were fostered that the Iru would be allowed steadily widening participation in local government. That the Iru believed that the Protectorate had come to support their political advancement was clear from their pleas during the next years addressed to the District Commissioner, the Governor, and British Members of Parliament and designed to promote their participation in the local government. They also had reason to believe, however, that the Hima ruling class did not favor such changes. And indeed the Hima continued their substantial influence on the recruitment of personnel for local government.

Against this background, education became increasingly important. Since early in the century the Mbarara High School had been the main training ground of Ankole's elite; by the 1940's the high school had become more and more mixed in make-up. As its graduates normally took the positions of leadership, the question whether educational qualifications would be allowed to supersede ethnic criteria as the principal consideration for admission into government service became very critical. The dilemma was especially acute because the administrative positions constituting the Ankole establishment were limited in number and not likely to be expanded to a significant extent.[6] If Iru were really to have equal opportunities, a major change would have had to take place. And this was not likely. Increasingly the Iru became convinced that the Hima were determined to change the direction of Iru advancement. Suspicion grew.

Thus, in the climate of expectations which had come to exist in Ankole in 1949, a minor incident such as the students' letter had consequences which would have been inconceivable in an earlier period: protest and the start of Iru organization. Significantly, the chain reaction that this event produced was closely linked with past events. Thus, when protest was articulated, it was often in terms of a reinterpretation of the historical relationship between the Iru and the Hima in the light of what the Iru increasingly saw as unjust Hima domination. Indeed, discontent about a wide variety of matters became more consciously linked than before and social grievances, whether based in reality or history, fact or fiction, were more fully explained in terms of Hima supremacy. There appeared to be one important qualification, however, and that was that the base line of Iru grievances generally tended to be drawn at the time of the establishment of British rule in Ankole. This was so because, although Ankole had for centuries been a hierarchical society, the foundations of the political framework as it operated in the 1940's and 1950's had to a significant extent been laid by the British on their assumption of overrule in 1901.

One effect of British rule appears to have been the increased exposure of ethnic cleavage between Hima and Iru, partly because colonial rule tended to make redundant the few mitigating structures that had existed. In the pre-colonial past, though the cattle-keeping Hima had for long exercised authority and enjoyed privileges not accorded to the Iru,[7] some of their institutions had reduced the visibility of the ethnic distinction. Most of the clans, for instance, had both Iru and Hima sections and used to be major units of identification as well as serving important protective functions. In addition, a substratum called Mbari, consisting mainly of privileged Iru who were accorded high status as a reward for distinguished services or ability and whose descendants could eventually be assimilated as Hima, formed a thin social layer between the Hima and Iru. However, the security pro-

---

[6] There were ten county chieftainships, about an equal number of senior posts at Kamukuzi, the local government headquarters, and lastly between forty and fifty subcounty chiefs.

[7] Oberg, "The Kingdom of Ankole," 126-32.

vided by British rule in large measure removed Hima needs for clan support in political affairs. At the same time this security weakened the Hima elite's feeling that they were obliged to allow minimal opportunities for social mobility to the Iru. Whereas previously the security of office of the traditional elite had been partly dependent on their readiness to accommodate Iru demands for benefits and status, after the British had assumed control and incorporated the chiefs into their administrative structure, the tenure of chiefly positions rested on British sanction rather than on responsiveness to grass roots demands. Despite an early struggle for influence among leading clans at the turn of the century, the fact that chiefly positions were safeguarded by a colonial framework soon began to foster a certain congruence of interests among the Hima incumbents which came increasingly to supersede previous rivalries among them.

Initially, British authority also reaffirmed and entrenched the ethnic hierarchy in a more direct way. On the establishment of colonial rule, the Hima ruling class was granted a number of privileges, the most important of which were formally laid down in the Ankole Agreement of 1901. Chieftainships were the most important of these benefits. Since they were for a long time, with the tacit concurrence of Protectorate officials, largely filled by co-optation, Hima remained quite firmly established in these ranks and, indeed, as late as 1966 held five out of the ten county chieftainships. Also, in the colonial period the British allowed the Hima chiefs to participate in the collection of tax and the employment of labor; this not only enhanced their political authority, but also significantly promoted their economic welfare. Tax and labor excises from the Iru were often quite considerable and were in no small part used for personal enrichment. The distribution of mailo land—a term adopted from Buganda, where "mailo" had developed as the local expression for the square "miles" also allocated there—similarly tended to accentuate the social and economic gap between the chiefly Hima and the Iru. Contrary to the terms of the Ankole Agreement, which read that the mailo estates should be created from "waste lands," the Hima allottees were allowed to carve them out in the most densely populated, central parts of the kingdom. This enabled them to levy rent as well as to demand food and services from the Iru peasants living on their mailos. And since a substantial part of the mailo land was irrevocably issued as freehold grants, the system of landlord-tenant relationships which developed on estates of this type has continued to exist, with relatively minor modifications, and in 1967 still affected over 20,000 Iru in Ankole.[8]

[8] *Ankole Agreement* (1901), par. 7; *Report of the Commission of Inquiry into Mailo Land* (Mbarara, 1965).

During the following decades, each and every advantage given to the Hima when British authority began became an object of Iru discontent. The disproportionate allocation of chiefly positions became a focus of Iru grievances as soon as qualified Iru were available to occupy such ranks. Indeed, the creation as well as the activities of the Kumanyana movement in the 1950's was to a large extent stimulated precisely by discrimination in this sphere. In addition, the tax and labor contributions which were demanded from Iru were often felt to be excessively burdensome, and frequent transgressions of authority by Hima chiefs in these matters increased the feelings of discrimination among the Iru.[9] A sense of injustice was also prompted by the fact that the non-chiefly, pastoral Hima, who were generally wealthier than the Iru, were usually not only excluded from labor duties but were able to avoid taxation over a long period. As late as 1967, these facts were mentioned by Iru as grievances against Hima chiefs. The distribution of mailo land holdings also became an irritant to the Iru because of the preference given to Hima, as well as for other reasons. For a long time Iru tenants on the mailo estates lacked any security of tenure and were not infrequently evicted at the whim of their landlords. In addition, property rights on their crops and belongings were often found difficult to uphold, and severe restrictions were frequently imposed on the improvement of their houses and gardens by their landlords. The arrangement was even more anomalous because Iru who did not live on mailo land were free to develop their plots without excessive interference.

Generally, during the first half of this century, Hima domination was maintained by a surprisingly small chiefly class and met with a great deal of submissiveness from the Iru. This was largely because the Iru had little conception of a different order and because opportunities to express discontent were very limited. It is often argued in Ankole that the Hima made conscious efforts to minimize the pace of social development of the Iru to maintain their political supremacy. Examples cited include discouragement of Iru from seeking an advanced education and discrimination in the allocation of school bursaries. And a number of myths have developed about the behavior of Hima chiefs. There is now a widely circulated assertion, for instance, that they first burnt the cotton seed before distributing it among the Iru peasants.

---

[9] It should be noted that during the first three decades of this century the chiefs who were found guilty of such breaches of jurisdiction were not only Hima, but included a substantial number of Ganda. However, far from unifying the indigenous population in opposition, as happened in neighboring Kigezi, it seems that the Iru of Ankole have regarded the role of the Gandan chiefs as being basically supportive of the Hima superstructure.

Although this remains unproven, it is no exaggeration that the Hima chiefs, who traditionally had not been involved in agriculture and had little more than disdain for their subjects, have taken only a limited interest in the agrarian development of the kingdom. As a result, Ankole remained for a long period a relatively backward corner of the country. Perhaps also in consequence of this situation, it took at least half a century of slow social and economic change before Iru protest against traditional Hima overrule began to gain momentum.

When protest finally emerged, it originated mainly among Protestant Iru, Kumanyana therefore being principally a Protestant movement. Basically, the Protestant Iru were more alert to the differences which separated them from the Hima elite than were the Roman Catholics. Paradoxically, this seems to have resulted largely from the social advantages which the Protestant Iru had over the Roman Catholics, as well as from their closer contacts with the Hima.[10]

Educational differences were also important. Whereas Roman Catholic missions combined broadly based, low-level education with specialized, mainly seminary-type, training for a selected few, the Protestants had from an earlier date offered wider opportunities for intermediate and extended instruction. In the tradition of schools for chiefs' sons, the Protestant curriculum was more closely geared to the requirements of the administration. In part as a result of these differences, the Roman Catholic population of Ankole has produced relatively few—though some outstanding—social leaders, in contrast to a fairly substantial leadership stratum among the Protestants. Initially, the Protestant facilities for education benefited the Hima most, adding

---

[10] The result of missionary activity to 1968 has been that, with no more than five exceptions, all converted Hima are Protestants, belonging to the (Anglican) Church of Uganda. However, the majority of Hima (who, it will be recalled, now total approximately 5 per cent of Ankole's population of 700,000) have not become Christians. On the other hand, most Iru have become Christians, and slightly more are Roman Catholic than Protestant. These facts are explained by the way in which Christianity made its entry into Ankole society. Protestant missionaries had the advantage of arriving first, and, moreover, they enjoyed the support of the authorities. Initially, they concentrated their efforts on the Hima ruling stratum at the center, whereas the Roman Catholics started among the Iru in more distant locations. As a result, the Protestants gained a virtual monopoly of Hima converts. Besides, following the pattern of establishment of mission stations by the two denominations, Protestants have become relatively predominant in the central counties of Shema, Igara, Kashari, and Rwampara, whereas Roman Catholics tend to be concentrated in the northern peripheral areas of Bunyaruguru, Buhweju, and Ibanda as well as, though to a lesser extent, in Isingiro to the south. It is important to note that the two ethnic strata of Hima and Iru both happened to be more fully represented in the central parts of the kingdom, while in the outlying counties to the north there were either few or no Hima.

a strong buttress to the perpetuation of their chiefly class.[11] From the 1930's on, however, there has been progressively increasing school attendance by Protestant Iru, which has resulted in the growth of an especially vocal element.

An equally crucial factor in the growth of different orientations and levels of achievement among Protestant and Roman Catholic Iru lay in the Protestant complexion of Ankole's ruling group after 1900. Not only did this group, with the tacit consent of the British District Commissioners, generally support the interests of the Native Anglican church and its schools; it also gave relatively better chances of employment to the Protestant Iru than to the Roman Catholics, as Protestant Iru were appointed in greater numbers than Roman Catholics as lower ranking chiefs, clerks, and askari. A few were even able to rise to important positions before the 1940's. On the whole, therefore, the opportunities open to Protestant Iru, though far more limited than those of the Hima, were invariably better than those of the Roman Catholics. As a result of these conditions, the Roman Catholic Iru remained engaged longer in self-sufficient traditional cultivation while Protestant Iru began to respond to visions of individual and collective improvement.

The factors which differentiated the Protestant Iru from the Roman Catholics were most pronounced in the centrally located counties of Ankole, where a majority of the Protestants lived. Physical proximity to the center enabled them to keep more easily in touch with developments in public affairs and facilitated the marketing of the cash crops that they had begun to cultivate. Indeed, the introduction of coffee in the 1930's stimulated a rise of incomes, especially in the counties of Shema and Igara, as well as in parts of Rwampara. In turn, this rise provided a financial basis for increasing school attendance which helped to develop new skills and orientations. Shema and Igara especially have competed, for many years, in claiming the largest numbers of graduates at various levels. Eventually, a majority of the leaders of the Kumanyana movement who entered the scene in the 1940's and thereafter were also from Shema and Igara; most of them in fact attended the same primary school—that of the Native Anglican church at Kabwohe in Shema.

Thus, it was the Protestant Iru, and not the Roman Catholics, who stood up against Hima domination, precisely because their relatively greater opportunities, their economic welfare, and their educational

[11] During the first few years of Mbarara High School, opened in 1911, over 75 per cent of the student body were Hima, 8 per cent Ganda, and the remainder were Mbari and Iru. (From an analysis of the Register of Mbarara High School by Richard Kaijuka and the author.) Many of these early students were appointed to high positions, and several of them are still influential in Ankole affairs.

attainments gave them stronger incentives and better means to strive for further social advancement. Moreover, their closer contacts with the Hima made them more sensitive to the advantages given to their Hima schoolmates, fellow church members, and government colleagues than were the Roman Catholics, who had least in common with the Hima. In addition, since the majority of Protestant Iru were concentrated in the central areas, they experienced more directly some of the negative aspects of Hima supremacy, such as the relationships between mailo landlords and tenants. As greater numbers of them reached higher levels of economic and educational achievement, such instances of Hima privilege became increasingly exasperating. For these reasons, it became more and more evident that the fringe benefits granted to Protestant Iru had laid only a fragile bridge, not a firm basis for concurrence between the two Protestant groups. Although the Protestant Iru had become the most favored of the underprivileged stratum in Ankole, their pressure for greater participation ultimately led to an attack on the principle of Hima rule.

Notwithstanding the depth of animosity which increasingly came to characterize Iru-Hima relationships, ethnic conflict in Ankole did not lead to open confrontation. Indeed, in striking contrast to the developments in nearby Rwanda, or to the violent clashes resulting from ethnic antagonism elsewhere in Africa, the tension between Iru and Hima has throughout remained singularly devoid of spectacular events.[12] This absence of landmarks was not unrelated to the basically accommodationist quality of protest in Ankole. In fact, there appears to have been a fairly general conviction that incidents were to be avoided because they would serve no purpose. This point is perhaps borne out most clearly by the role which the Kumanyana movement chose to play.

Generally, the Kumanyana movement opted for indirect strategies rather than for any open onslaughts on what it considered to be the wrongs of Ankole society. Throughout the 1950's when Kumanyana was actively engaged in the assertion of Iru interests, it certainly sought to remain as inconspicuous as possible. Its members did not stage demonstrations or become engaged in fights; nor were reputations established or enhanced by prison terms. Perhaps most significant, the

---

[12] Some distinctions between Rwanda and Ankole in regard to the potential for revolutionary tendencies are made in the author's paper, "Protest Movements in Western Uganda: Some Parallels and Contrasts," *Proceedings of the University of East Africa Social Science Conference* (Nairobi, 1966), 3-5. For an interesting comparison of ethnic relationships in traditional Rwanda and Ankole, see Jacques Maquet, "Institutionalisation féodale des relations de dépendance dans quatre cultures interlacustres," *Colloque du Groupe de Recherche en Anthropologie et Sociologie Politique* (Paris, 1968), 10-13.

Kumanyana movement never initiated a large-scale mobilization of the peasant masses. Through preliminary meetings, the movement tried to influence votes in the Eishengyero, the Ankole Public Service Commission, or other official bodies; it definitely did not put itself up as a bargaining group. On occasion, it would call upon its members to submit protests and petitions to Ugandan and British authorities if the situation demanded; again, however, these people were expected to do so as individuals and not in the name of the Iru or of the Kumanyana movement. One reason for this circuitous approach was, no doubt, that Kumanyana was for a long time of necessity an underground movement. Challenging Hima supremacy amounted to questioning the traditionally sanctioned ethnic hierarchy and could easily have invoked retaliation. In this regard, it was of no small significance that many who were in Kumanyana's vanguard occupied, and depended economically on, government positions. This made them particularly vulnerable to official sanctions and caused them to refrain from bringing their actions into the open.

Other factors, however, tended to lead in the same direction. One of them lay in the paradoxical fact that, notwithstanding the pervasive nature of Hima domination in the Ankole political and social framework, there was no legal or other concrete basis of recognition for this hegemony. Despite the long prevalence of ethnic co-optation in the Ankole government service, the formal structure of government designed by the British was theoretically neutral, and recruitment supposedly took place on consideration of merit alone; even the signatories to the Ankole Agreement of 1901 had been recognized in their individual capacity rather than as Hima. Thus, the Kumanyana movement, whose very existence was rooted in the problem of Hima domination, might well have found itself at a loss if it had been required to point to any explicit code or procedure as evidence of a willfully maintained Hima supremacy. Given this lack of "proof," discontent could not easily be directed in any concrete direction; it could also not be displayed as openly as it might have been with a more clear-cut cause. (Hence, too, the rather disproportionate importance attached to a minor but at least tangible piece of evidence, such as the 1949 letter.) In addition, however, no Iru movement could afford openly to propagate the doctrine of Iru ascendancy if it did not want to lay itself open to accusations of ethnic partiality similar to that of which it was accusing the Hima. If they did not want to weaken their argument, the Iru could, at least publicly, only justifiably stress broad egalitarian principles and the need for merit and qualifications as criteria of recruitment. Underground, far more particularistic, and at times petty, interests were nonetheless expressed.

Kumanyana's organization was in keeping with its strategies. Basically, it was a loose assemblage of Iru leaders, without formally designated officeholders or any other explicit framework. There was clear consensus, however, as to which individuals exercised overall leadership in the movement. Kumanyana's underground quality was perhaps best revealed by the fact that for a long time contact was maintained by secret gatherings, usually irregularly called by person-to-person communication to confront immediate issues. In a very real sense, Kumanyana *was* these meetings, and vice versa. Indeed, the term "Kumanyana" itself has connotations of fellowship, to "get to know one another." Never were more than about seventy people present at any of the meetings, but large sections of the Iru population were nonetheless effectively kept in touch with what evolved. The most important convocations were usually held in or near Mbarara. The participants in these meetings served as links with various areas of Ankole and subgroups of Iru as they communicated the results of the discussions to the meetings which were subsequently held in the counties. To reach the grass roots, at the latter meetings individuals were often assigned to contact Iru in various corners of the counties. This was frequently done after Protestant church services, which was one reason why a strong parallel emerged between Kumanyana's network and that of the Native Anglican church. Once relationships had been established with parish congregations, such groups were asked to send delegates to future meetings at the next higher level.

Kumanyana's leadership consisted mostly of relatively modern and educated Iru. In addition, its leaders were men who had already achieved a certain prominence. Most of the key figures held positions of some significance in Ankole, and these were generally the highest that had been attained by Iru. Conversely, virtually all Iru who now hold high-ranking offices were at one time engaged in the Kumanyana movement. The central personality in the movement was Kesi Nganwa, supervisor of the Native Anglican schools in Ankole. Nganwa was sometimes called Ruterengwa ("Nothing compares with him in nature"), a name which was objected to by royalist circles because it implied superiority over the king. Another prominent figure was C. B. Katiti, one of the first members of the Uganda Legislative Council and later a Uganda cabinet minister. Katiti was one of the people who established a relationship between party politics and the movement. Many of the leading participants were teachers, the one profession in which Iru had been able to fill the great majority of positions. In addition, there were clerks, traders, medical assistants, farmers, some chiefs who disregarded the ban on political activities, and several Protestant clergymen. The latter had a particularly strong incentive to become involved since the hierarchy of the Anglican church in Ankole, like that of the government, was dominated by Hima. With dramatic sermons and references to Christian doctrine, they contributed greatly to the spiritual basis of the movement. Although Kumanyana was basically a Protestant group, a few Roman Catholics remained regular members over the years. Most participants, at any rate those in the central and county level gatherings, were notables in their areas and had considerable influence over local opinion. A number sat in the Eishengyero and were thus in a position directly to represent Iru interests as formulated at the Kumanyana meetings, as well as to influence fellow councillors. After 1955, when Iru influence in the Ankole government was substantially increased, Kumanyana's political role became largely that of a shadow parliament, in which alternative policies were sounded out before they were officially launched and from which an important source of support emanated for the Iru leadership, whose position in the government remained precarious.

Not the least compelling of the movement's objectives was to instill a greater sense of self-confidence among Iru generally. One of the most important driving forces of the Kumanyana movement was undoubtedly the resentment, especially among educated Iru, of continuing attitudes of superiority and arrogance of the Hima. This prompted the movement's assertion of equality of status and dignity in many areas of life, and greatly strengthened the impetus of the movement's activities in the political and economic spheres. It certainly appears to have been realized that the strength of the movement would rest not only on its ability to give expression to Iru grievances, but also on its capacity to awaken the Iru to the possibility of change.

A perception of the relationship between social welfare and political influence was strongly evidenced in Kumanyana's preoccupation with the educational progress of the Iru. Because it was realized that the future position of the Iru depended largely on the attainments of the student generation, Kumanyana exerted much pressure on the allocation of bursaries and itself maintained a relief fund which was largely used to pay the school fees of needy children. It also encouraged parents to build schools in remote areas which did not have educational facilities. Similarly, its supporters campaigned for the erection of more hygienic and permanent houses, for the adoption of more productive methods of cultivation, and generally tried to awaken the people to the idea of higher standards of living. Kumanyana was of no less importance in articulating the grievances of mailo tenants and it played an active part in stimulating, without official sanction, resettlement from the densely populated counties of Shema and Igara to Kashari. It also was a strong promoter of the establishment and growth of many co-operative societies. Lastly, it was in several counties instrumental in the creation of local welfare societies which addressed themselves to the needs of the Iru. Basic to all this activity was an urge to demonstrate that the Iru were capable of attaining increasing economic and social prosperity. As they had for ages been subordinate and regarded as inferior, there was a compulsion to assert their equality with the Hima and to imprint this same notion upon much larger numbers of Iru. Kumanyana was at once exponent, symbol, and radiator of these sentiments.

Notwithstanding its wide range of involvements, the most critical goals of Kumanyana remained in the realm of political participation. The movement was particularly concerned with trying to increase and strengthen Iru representation in the Ankole Eishengyero and in the corridors of the Ankole government. In a closely related way, the movement also sought to influence the appointment as well as the transfer of chiefs and other public servants. After the initial stimulus of 1949 and subsequent skirmishes in 1952–53, peak times in its fluctuating role as a political pressure group were reached whenever major choices were imminent—such as in 1955, at the nomination of a second Iru Enganzi, and again around 1958 when a growing entente between Protestant Hima and Roman Catholic Iru created an entirely new political situation. The 1955 crisis was decisive for much more than the selection of an Enganzi alone. The Hima group, including the Omugabe, were determined to have a Hima county chief who had a rather unfavorable reputation among Iru. Under the then existing constitutional procedure, laid down in the 1949 African Local Government Ordinance, the Enganzi would be appointed in agreement between the Omugabe, the incumbent Enganzi, and the District Commissioner. Kumanyana mobilized fierce opposition to the proposed nomination, and a deadlock ensued which was solved only by altering the constitutional framework of the Ankole administration. Protectorate officials speeded up the process by which Ankole, as the first district, could come under the regulations of the District Administration (District Councils) Ordinance which was being prepared in 1955. This ordinance considerably broadened the area of jurisdiction of the local government; expanded the Eishengyero by enlarging the number of directly elected members; and provided for an Enganzi elected by the Eishengyero. As a result, the Iru henceforth obtained a substantially increased influence in the Eishengyero, and Kesi Nganwa, the man who had emerged as the leader of Kumanyana, was elected Enganzi.

Once this was achieved, however, Kumanyana's political role began to change markedly. One result was an increase, rather than a decrease, in the number of its meetings and the size of its following. Another was that, during the following years, the focus for the movement's political action became increasingly narrowed to securing positions for its more active supporters who, as it was locally expressed, "had killed the animal and wanted to eat it." Their desire to be rewarded with sinecures was, however, thwarted by two conditions. One of these was that the tenure of most posts held by Hima was protected by civil service regulations; the other was that Roman Catholic Iru expressed an increasing interest in having a share in the benefits. Roman Catholic Iru had begun to constitute a third political force in Ankole and by the mid-1950's they had been attracted to Catholic Action and other lay organizations. Through the working of electoral mechanisms, they obtained a substantial representation in the Eishengyero. In 1955, they considered it in their best interests to support the Protestant Iru in the Nganwa election, thus bringing about a complete Iru alignment against the Hima. They became disenchanted, however, when they felt that the Protestant Iru were gaining most of the advantages for the achievement to which they had given their support. Protestants, on the other hand, considered that they had borne the brunt of the struggle for Iru advancement, that they had more qualified people available to take positions, and that there was thus a stronger justification for distributing chieftainships and other posts among themselves than among the Roman Catholics. As a result, the initial alignment between Protestant and Roman Catholic Iru was followed by a widening estrangement between the two groups. Kumanyana, which had originated as an expression of protest against conditions affecting all Iru, played an increasingly partisan role in matters of appointment, and, since the spoils were limited by the protection of tenure, its pressure to gain appointments for its own group became more intense. Whereas in a different context the Kumanyana movement might have unified all Iru, it now grew into one of the factions dividing them.

Political developments in the late 1950's and early 1960's reaffirmed the tripartite nature of Ankole politics and further restricted the scope of the Kumanyana movement. A convergence of interests gradually led to a coalition between the Protestant Hima and the Roman Catholic Iru. This was first manifested in 1958 in the Eishengyero, during the nomination of representatives to the Uganda Legislative Council; its organizational basis became the Ankole branch of the Democratic party. As for the Protestant Iru, they were subsequently attracted into the Uganda People's Congress, which then used Kumanyana's organizational network. In keeping with other parts of Uganda, the religious cleavage assumed major dimensions in the immediate pre-independence period and forced the two Iru groups to compete for Hima support in the 1962 Ugandan elections. As a result, Hima received only half of the six elective Ankole seats in the National

Assembly (Uganda People's Congress: 1; Democratic party: 2); in addition they had substantial influence on each party's executive. Clearly, this enabled them to gain a much stronger position than their numerical strength among the population of Ankole would have made probable under conditions of proportional representation. Nevertheless, the vast majority of Hima had remained loyal to the alignment between Hima and Roman Catholic Iru and voted for the Democratic party. Kumanyana was temporarily eclipsed in this process; later it underwent a minor revival as one of the factions in the Uganda People's Congress in Ankole. Although this revival was not solely concerned with Hima-Iru differences, these questions did form an important part of its *raison d'être*.

Despite the changing political situation, the following years brought frustration to many Iru, who had expected to enjoy more visible and complete fruits from their victory. Instead they saw continued over-representation of the Hima in high political, administrative, and clerical positions; the Hima continued to form a wealthy class based on cattle ownership; differences continued between Iru and Hima on matters concerning land tenure, cattle ranches, and other questions. Though losing much of its sharpness, social distance also remained, in some peripheral areas, such as Buhweju and Nyabushozi, even taking the old patriarchical form. However, in spite of the lingering grievances cited above, the Hima could no longer seriously be regarded as a political force of much consequence. To this result the Kumanyana movement had made an important contribution. As fewer and fewer issues were left which corresponded with the ethnic devision, there was no practical or "sociological" reason for an ethnic movement to persist.

Therefore, when the new Uganda Constitution of 1967 abolished the kingship and made it possible for that faction of the Uganda People's Congress which claimed direct descent from the Kumanyana movement to take office, this was hardly as momentous and revolutionary an event as it was made out to be. But in more ways than one it did mark the end of an era by underlining how the earlier process of change had gradually moved ethnic issues into the background. Today, in Ankole, modernization has made economic class differences the major focus of political discontent. Ethnic inequality seems to have become outmoded as a vehicle for protest.

Protest in Toro: The Assertion of Independence

Among the secessions that followed independence in Africa, the Rwenzururu movement is perhaps one of the most extreme as well as one of the least noticed: One of the most extreme because the Govern-

ment of the Rwenzururu Kingdom, as the secessionist offshoot of the
wider Rwenzururu movement is called, represents a virtually complete
rupture from the state of Uganda and has been able to maintain its
own, however crudely organized, government from the time of its
establishment in 1962 until the present (1969); one of the least noticed,
mainly because, in its splendid isolation, it has not posed an immediate
security problem to the government of Uganda and has therefore remained relatively ignored.

The Rwenzururu movement also represents a tragic example of
an unresolved local dispute which has become so bitter that it is very
difficult to imagine any genuine reconciliation. Originally an attempt by
the Konjo and Amba tribesmen on the Congo border to shake off Toro
political domination, the movement sought to redress the minority status which had been imposed on them around the turn of the century
when the British re-established and enlarged the Toro kingdom. (Unequal social development has since then considerably widened the social
distance between the Toro and the Konjo and Amba.) In a variety
of respects, the Konjo and the Amba were neglected over a long period,
and it was not until the 1950's that significant economic development
began to take place in their areas. The ensuing changes, combined with
expectations created by constitutional transitions, stimulated discontent
among the Konjo and Amba over their inferior position in Toro society, and eventually led to a desire for independence.

For a better perspective on the development of the movement, it
will be useful to look first at the wider Toro context from which it
emerged. For, while the Rwenzururu movement was certainly the most
dramatic, it was by no means the only reaction to regional disparities
in Toro. To put it very briefly, when the British re-established Toro
around 1900, they added to it certain peripheral areas in an effort to
bolster Toro against Bunyoro, which had resisted the imposition of British rule and which had earlier ruled over Toro. Apart from Busongora
and Bwamba counties, the habitat of most Konjo and Amba, these included Kyaka county to the east, Kibale to the south, the non-Konjo
parts of Busongora, and smaller entities elsewhere. However, the people
of the central and original part of Toro, in Mwenge county, continued to
think of themselves as the only real Toro and therefore to look down
on the peoples in the other areas. At the same time, educational and
economic opportunities were centered in the areas around Fort Portal,
which was the district headquarters. The most conspicuous regional
differences lay, however, in the composition of the kingdom's government, since most senior officials, including the chiefs posted in other
counties, were recruited from Mwenge and Burahya and thus from the
core area of Toro.

Toro's regional distribution of social advantages was thus not unlike that in Ankole, where the central areas had also provided the
nucleus from which the system was expanded. But whereas in Ankole
the juxtaposition of ethnicity and religion fostered the growth of a
major political cleavage at the center, this did not happen in Toro.
The relationships between the three status categories among the Toro
—the ruling Bito clan, presumed to be of Nilotic origin; the cattle-
keeping Huma, who correspond to Ankole's Hima; and the Iru—have
been less hierarchical than in Ankole. Historically, Iru status in Toro
appears to have lacked the stigma of inferiority attached to it in Ankole, largely because the Bito sought to counteract Huma influence
by promoting the Iru.[13] In this century, there has also been more social
integration between these strata than in Ankole, as a number of Huma
have taken up agriculture, and intermarriage among Bito, Huma, and
Iru has been on the increase. Consequently, although some prestige is
still attached to Bito and Huma descent, the influence of ethnic distinctions has been much less pervasive than in Ankole. One result of
this lack of distinction has been that, although a disproportionate
number of the chiefs from Mwenge and Burahya have been of Bito
and Huma ancestry, rivalry for rewards at the center was not seen
as ethnic conflict. Instead, during the first half of this century, it was
mainly perceived as competition between clans, some of which were
closer to the Omukama, the ruler of Toro, and others which were less
"known" to him. Similarly, although chiefly prerogatives introduced
by the British had induced a differentiation of social and economic welfare comparable to that in Ankole, these differences in Toro were
not commonly associated with ethnic status distinctions. In the outlying
counties populated by Toro, the ethnic descent of the metropolitan
chiefs remained a matter of considerable indifference; it was their
area of origin which became the crucial focus of attention. In turn,
the attitudes toward other people incorporated in Toro, such as the
Konjo and the Amba, enhanced the status of the lower stratum among
the Toro themselves. Whereas in Ankole the Iru were looked down
upon as inferiors, their counterparts in Toro (who are, incidentally,
only infrequently referred to as "Iru") were regarded, and regarded
themselves, as far superior to the Konjo and the Amba.

Religious divisions in Toro also had different consequences and
did not accentuate and multiply social cleavages as much as in Ankole.
Although the majority of the Toro ruling elite has also been Protestant,
a number of Bito and Huma have become Roman Catholics, and some

---

[13] The author is indebted to Professor M. L. Perlman for drawing his attention to this point.

of them have held high offices. Moreover, Roman Catholics and Protestants have been more evenly distributed in the various parts of Toro than in Ankole, and in fact Roman Catholics, who form a greater majority in Toro than in Ankole, are concentrated in large numbers around Fort Portal. Roman Catholic educational institutions, such as St. Leo's College near Fort Portal, have for some time promoted the social advancement of Roman Catholics in Toro, and cursory evidence suggests that Toro Roman Catholics have generally had a larger share in economic prosperity and perhaps a somewhat larger number of sinecures than their coreligionists in Ankole. Party politics based on religion in the early 1960's did, nevertheless, cause increased friction between Protestants and Roman Catholics in Toro. It reached a climax when the Protestant government dismissed some Roman Catholic chiefs. The protests that this action provoked in some cases ran parallel with regional disaffection, but among the Toro they were not clustered together with ethnic grievances as had been the case in Ankole. On the whole, therefore, regional disparities produce the most pronounced distinctions in Toro.

In the 1950's and early 1960's, discontent over regional discrepancies began to be voiced in several areas, its special focus being the distribution of chieftainships and other government posts. In some areas, such as Kyaka and Kibale, thought was even given to association with Bunyoro or Ankole if no amelioration were forthcoming. This tendency to evaluate political representation in terms of the number of chiefs appointed from an area was made even stronger by the particular way constitutional developments occurred in Toro during these years. Persistent demands by the government of Toro, led by the Omukama, for federal powers similar to those possessed by Buganda kept the 1955 District Administration (District Councils) Ordinance from being applied to Toro: this ordinance would have given a greater sense of popular political involvement. Instead Toro until 1961 remained under the 1949 Local Government Ordinance which vested authority more exclusively in the chiefly hierarchy. Meanwhile, however, the political climate in Uganda in the years before independence was leading to a general expectation of increased political participation and greater political equality. One of its effect in Toro was to stimulate demands that the chiefly hierarchy itself become more representative of the various regions.

The first protests were from east, south, and southwest Toro. For a number of reasons they were much milder than the somewhat later protest of the Konjo and the Amba were to be. For one thing, the customs, language, and traditions of the people of Kyaka, Kibale, and Busongora were much closer to the central Toro than were those of either the Konjo or the Amba. Although they were not considered proper Toro by the inhabitants of the central areas, neither were they ostentatiously treated as inferiors, as were the Konjo and the Amba, and the name of "Batoro" has never been seriously questioned in respect to them. In addition, in contrast to the relative isolation in which most Konjo and Amba lived, their areas were linked to the center of Toro by several main communication lines, a fact which had promoted more extensive contacts and a greater overlap of interests. However, probably the most important reason why protest in east and south Toro remained relatively mild lay in the abrupt appearance of the Rwenzururu movement in 1961–62. In reaction, the Toro government accelerated efforts to accommodate grievances in other areas so as to enlarge its basis of support against the movement. The relative affinity between the center and the south and east of Toro facilitated such an alignment, although regional demands did not altogether disappear in those areas either. Thus, when, in an attempt to quiet the disaffection, Konjo and Amba were installed as chiefs in Busongora and Bwamba, the interest of other groups in similar appointments increased.

The immediate background for the movement may be described as follows. The decade preceding the outbreak of the Rwenzururu movement had brought revolutionary economic developments in Busongora and Bwamba, making them the two richest counties of Toro as well as the areas with the greatest tax yield. Large numbers of Konjo had come down the slopes of the Ruwenzori to cultivate cotton in the plains of Busongora, while they also grew coffee on the mountain spurs. In addition, the economic significance of Busongora was enhanced by a flourishing fish industry, salt mining at Katwe, and copper mining at Kilembe, all of which increasingly offered employment opportunities to Konjo. The Amba, for their part, took up the cultivation of coffee, though in their area an increasing number of plots were bought by Toro who subsequently employed Amba as laborers. The important point here is that the Konjo and the Amba were thus provided with greatly increased cash incomes and brought into more frequent contact with the Toro. Moreover, the concrete results of their industriousness gave them a crucial sense of achievement, and provided at least economic proof of their equality with the Toro, who had never considered them capable of any productive pursuits. With progress, however, came increasing sensitivity to discrimination in the allocation of benefits. Although in the 1950's government services had expanded in their areas, the fact remained that the Konjo and the Amba had never provided a county chief and only very few subcounty chiefs. As late as 1962, only six out of thirty-eight subcounty chiefs in all Toro were Konjo or Amba.[14] There were also far fewer teachers, medical staff, and other government personnel among them than among the Toro, and it was even alleged that there were no Konjo or Amba clerks in the central office.[15] Besides, there was evidence that until immediately before the emergence of the Rwenzururu movement, both peoples had been discriminated against in the allocation of scholarships, bursaries, and government development loans.[16]

Such discrepancies strengthened the opinion of the Konjo and the Amba that the Toro were not prepared to deal with them on a basis of equality. At the same time, political developments in Toro, as well as elsewhere in Uganda, alerted them to the possibility of seeking a political solution to their predicament. Prior to independence, the Toro government advanced quite exaggerated demands as to the future status of the kingdom within Uganda. Not only did it want a federal relationship with the center and the recognition of Toro "as a nation first" before its constitutional position could be considered,[17] it also started a campaign for the recovery of a large part of Kivu Province in the Congo, which had been "lost" as a result of the Anglo-Belgian boundary settlement of 1910. Most of the people in the area concerned were Konjo and Amba, a few of whom had at some time in the past been in a very loose tribute-paying relationship to Toro; but most of them had never in any real sense been part of the kingdom. Thus, although the claims of the Toro government for enhanced prestige and increased autonomy directly involved the Amba and the Konjo, they had no voice in the formulation of these demands. The demands did, however, create an impression among them that bids for alterations in constitutional status would provide an appropriate avenue for the redress of their political grievances.

Another important factor was that during the term of office of the Democratic party as the government of Uganda (1960 to 1962), the Sebei in eastern Uganda were granted separate district status. The Sebei had for a long time been in a rather similar position with regard to the Gisu in the Bugisu district as were the Konjo and the Amba to the Toro. Numerically, the Sebei had been a minority in the Bugisu district, living in more or less isolation in the higher regions of Mount Elgon and being regarded as socially inferior by the dominant Gisu. The Konjo and the Amba hence regarded the Sebei solution as a pre-

---

[14] Uganda Government, *Report of the Commission of Inquiry into the Recent Disturbances among the Baamba and Bakonjo People of Toro* (Entebbe, 1962), 8. This document is hereafter cited as the *Ssembeguya Report,* after the Chairman of the Commission, Dr. F. C. Ssembeguya.

[15] *Ssembeguya Report,* 8.

[16] Ibid., 7, 9.

[17] *Uganda Argus,* 19 July 1961.

cedent which should also be adopted in their own case. Moreover, after a visit to the Konjo and Amba areas, Benedicto Kiwanuka, the leader of the Democratic party, left the impression, rightly or wrongly, that a Democratic party government would further their demands for a separate district in exchange for support at the polls in 1962. Although the Democratic party did obtain support in this way, the Uganda People's Congress was victorious in the country as a whole, and, in addition, the new constitution made it infinitely more difficult to change the existing boundaries of districts and kingdoms. These facts were to be an obstacle to the achievement of Konjo and Amba aspirations. It is conceivable that if the Amba and the Konjo had begun to press half a year earlier for a separate district, they would have had a fair chance of achieving it under a Democratic party government.

For a long time, however, the Konjo and the Amba had lacked effective means to express themselves. Only in 1961, when the first direct elections to the Toro Rukurato (Council) were held, did it become possible for them to voice their discontent. Significantly, the Rukurato was not only a convenient body for the airing of grievances, but it was also a meeting ground of the greatest significance for the two tribes and the place where the alliance between the Konjo and the Amba was forged. Their joint membership in this body made them see clearly the common interest they had against the Toro, and in a very real sense the Rwenzururu dispute was sparked in the Rukurato. In 1961–62, both groups realized that they could put up a meaningful case for a separate district if they did it together. Moreover, the Amba, who were far outnumbered by the Konjo, had only one choice, to follow the Konjo, their area being separated from Toro proper by the Ruwenzori range, which was populated by the Konjo, and accessible only by an easily blocked escarpment road.

Dissent in the new Rukurato, in which there were twenty-one Konjo and Amba members out of a total fifty-eight seats, precipitated the crisis. Lack of familiarity with parliamentary procedures among the Toro, as well as the Konjo and the Amba, encouraged conflict. Amba and Konjo had not been included in a constitutional committee appointed from among members of the Rukurato to negotiate a final agreement on Toro's constitutional relationships with the central government; only after complaints had been made, were two representatives from among them admitted to the discussions. At that time, the Amba and the Konjo demanded that the new constitution should explicitly recognize the Amba, Konjo, and Toro as the three tribes of Toro. When this demand was refused, the Amba and Konjo walked out of the proceedings and henceforth took no further part in the negotiations. Isaya Mukirane, the principal Konjo leader, subsequently submitted the aspirations of the Konjo and the Amba to the Governor of Uganda, at the same time asking for a separate district.[18] At the next meeting of the Rukurato, in March 1962, all the Konjo and Amba members walked out, and immediately thereafter Mukirane and the Amba leaders Kawamara and Mupalaya were arrested on charges of having insulted the Omukama. While they were imprisoned, it was decided to hold by-elections for a number of Konjo and Amba seats which had been declared vacant. This decision caused a tense situation, as large sections of the populations considered the announced elections invalid. Violence broke out in the Karambi subcounty of Busongora in August 1962. Shortly before nomination day, a new Toro chief was molested on a tax-collecting tour which the local Konjo regarded as a provocation. This sparked a series of similar incidents throughout the Ruwenzori mountains which, as it turned out, were only the prelude to far more violent conflict during the next few years.

Until the end of 1964, engagements primarily took place between Rwenzururu forces and the Toro. The Konjo and the Amba made numerous attacks on the Toro in retaliation for rustications and other punitive measures enforced by the Toro government and the Ugandan army and police troops which were sent to the area. Rwenzururu forces burnt houses and chased Toro out of Bwamba and some other areas which were predominantly populated by Konjo. Toro chiefs were the foremost targets but many other Toro who took a stand against the movement were also assaulted. Most of the violence occurred during night raids. Night after night, selected homesteads were attacked, but not many Toro were killed. Largely because of their unpredictability, these raids stirred a sense of insecurity among large numbers of Toro. Rwenzururu forces would stage a minor incident at one end of the Ruwenzori range to attract Ugandan security forces away from areas where they would subsequently launch a larger attack. Such actions showed a marked capacity for strategic co-ordination and for fast communication over long distances.

Violence in the first year or two did not originate exclusively from among the Amba and the Konjo. For many incidents the Toro bore primary responsibility. But in June 1964, the initiative clearly shifted to the Toro. Apparently instigated by Toro government officials, the Toro made a ten-day onslaught, primarily on the Konjo, which was unprecedented in its brutality and indiscriminate killing. Brought from Mwenge and other Toro counties to the plains and lower slopes of the Ruwenzori, hundreds of spearmen together with local Toro killed numerous Konjo men, women, and children. Official figures give a few hundred casualties, but there is a widespread conviction that the actual

[18] *Ssembeguya Report,* 3.

number was many times more. Police and army arrived too late to intervene effectively, and even then they were often powerless or unwilling to stop the Toro. This civil war caused a wholesale flight of Konjo into the mountains; only recently have they gradually begun to return. Social life was completely disrupted and even now a legacy of hatred persists which almost defies any return to normal relations.

Although not endorsing the demand for a separate Rwenzururu district, the report of the Ssembeguya Commission, which was convened to inquire into the disturbances among the Amba and Konjo, placed the responsibility for the emergence of the Rwenzururu movement firmly on the Toro government. In its opinion, the government had handled the complaints of the Konjo and the Amba without tact.[19] Despite the seriousness of the grievances and the extremely sensitive feelings among wide sections of its population, the Toro government in the Commission's judgment had made no constructive attempts to conciliate the dispute. Instead, even after the conflict had come out into the open, it still met moderate Konjo and Amba leaders who sought to arrive at a settlement "with intimidation and high-handedness," while the request for a separate district itself "was dealt with in a most obtuse and insensitive manner."[20]

Acting upon the recommendations of the report, which was published on October 10, 1962, one day after independence, the government of Uganda also rejected the demand of the Konjo and Amba for a separate district.[21] The most compelling reason for this decision was the desire, in the interest of national unity, to avert fragmentation of the country's political structure. Moreover, it was considered that the proposed district would prove uneconomical and, given the prevailing shortage of staff, would also prove difficult to administer, especially since large areas of Bwamba and Busongora (particularly in the higher mountain regions) were undeveloped and inaccessible. Though unmentioned, an additional factor of significance appears to have been the concern of the central government, which was controlled by the Uganda People's Congress, not to jeopardize its chances of strengthening its political support among the Toro.

It is open to question, however, whether the economic and staffing arguments were as compelling as they were purported to be. In comparison to the Sebei, for instance, whose control of a district had enabled them to obtain a modern hospital, more schools, and an improved road system, the Konjo and the Amba were not only several times more numerous but also economically far more advanced. In-

[19] Ibid., 14.
[20] Ibid., 12.
[21] Uganda Government, *Sessional Paper No. 1 of 1963*, 1.

deed, some of the country's major sources of revenue, e.g., copper, lay in their areas. In addition, their total population, which in 1959 amounted to nearly 137,000 (Konjo 103,868; Amba 32,866),[22] exceeded that of other districts such as Bunyoro (126,875) and Madi (50,627), and by Ugandan standards included a relatively high proportion of tax-payers (26,435). Although staffing would have presented certain problems, it was no easier in Sebei, Madi, or in Karamoja, the most undeveloped area of the country. The situation which evolved, at any rate, prevented the continued employment of Toro staff in Konjo and Amba areas. Increased conflict forced the central government in early 1963 to take over the administration of the services in Busongora and Bwamba for which the Toro government had been responsible, and, since then, these functions have been entrusted to an administrator appointed by the central government and aided by Konjo and Amba appointees.

Whereas the underdeveloped state of sections of the Konjo and the Amba areas was advanced as an argument against a separate district, this condition might perhaps have been used more convincingly to argue in favor of it. Quite apart from the question of whether or not the nature of social relationships in Toro would have allowed fruitful co-operation within the existing framework, the special problems of terrain and communication, as well as the economic potential of the Ruwenzori region, might have been considered a strong argument for the creation of a special district as the most effective form for its development. Lastly, though the decision to reject the claim for a separate district may have forestalled similar demands in other parts of the country, the effect of the policy in respect to the Amba and the Konjo has not been to strengthen national unity. The Amba and the Konjo who had pleaded, solely on account of their adverse relationships with the Toro, for the establishment of a Rwenzururu district as an integral part of independent Uganda, became increasingly disaffected from the national framework after the announcement of the government's position. Not only had the government not concurred in their wishes for autonomy, but, in addition, it did not act upon some of the major recommendations of the Ssembeguya Commission. Thus, the Commission had urged the calling of new elections throughout Toro to reestablish the representativeness of the Rukurato, the levying of a special tax on all the people in Toro to compensate for damage caused during the initial disturbances, and the encouragement of the Toro government to make a formal public pronouncement, in the nature of an addendum to the Toro Agreement, that the three main tribes of Toro were the Amba, the Konjo, and the Toro.[23] On the

[22] *Uganda African General Census* (1959).
[23] *Ssembeguya Report*, 14-15, 17, 18.

contrary, the Ugandan government, although not absolving the Toro government from all blame, took the position that it was "unable to accept the view of the Commission of Inquiry that the present Toro government is largely responsible for the recent disturbances."[24] The Commission's call for a "change of heart," which was not followed up by any dramatic gesture by the national political leaders, remained an exceedingly feeble basis for reconciliation. In consequence, the basis of Konjo and Amba protest, which had been essentially emancipatory, shifted to one of frustration. The escalation of regional demands into secessionist aspirations soon followed.

One of the common features of African protest movements is a tendency toward fragmentation and disunity when strong resistance is encountered. Internal divisions quite often assume the form of bitter disagreement over strategy and tactics. This pattern was also manifested in the Rwenzururu movement. The shattering of expectations which followed the government's refusal to consider Rwenzururu's claims not only spurred the movement, it also stimulated divergent tendencies within it. Indeed, the government's position later provoked an anti-climactic disintegration of the Rwenzururu movement, the basic reason for which was that, in the new and increasingly complex situation which came to prevail, there was great difficulty in developing any single Rwenzururu strategy which could hold out hopes for eventual success. Amba and Konjo had joined hands in the movement for a separate district as a means of gaining independence from and equality with the Toro. To both of them this target had not only seemed a straightforward and desirable solution, but it had also appeared that its early fulfillment was within reach. The depth and the genuineness of the grievances had, moreover, caused virtually all sections of the Konjo and of the Amba to support Rwenzururu's goals.

Once the central government took a firm stand against the movement's aims, however, the critical question became one of strategy. As the government's denial had not been accompanied by clearly constructive alternative measures to accommodate Konjo and Amba discontent, a subsiding of the movement was hardly to be expected. Yet, as all constitutional channels and targets for the promotion of the Rwenzururu cause had been exhausted, none of its leaders was able to offer prospects which could continue to attract the support of all shades of Konjo and Amba opinion. Various elements adopted contrasting and indeed conflicting policies, of which the only common basis remained opposition to the Toro. Over the years, these different positions multiplied following severe clashes with the Toro, the standard of living deteriorated for a very considerable part of the population, and

[24] *Sessional Paper*, 1.

the central government increased its involvement in the Konjo and Amba areas. In the complex array of attitudes which resulted, two were of major import: the thrust toward the creation of a secessionist state— the Rwenzururu kingdom—and the persistent pressure for some alternative arrangement for remaining within Uganda but outside Toro. Both of these tendencies, it should be noted, were commonly referred to as "Rwenzururu." The Rwenzururu kingdom was no doubt the more spectacular of the two, but not necessarily the more important.

Major determinants of the growing divergence within the movement were geographic and social. The independent Rwenzururu state found its support among the Konjo of the higher Ruwenzori regions, whereas the continued claims for autonomy within Uganda emanated mostly from the Amba as well as from the Konjo on the lower mountain spurs. As noted above, the terrain in the higher Ruwenzori was a crucial factor in the establishment and survival of a secessionist government. The fact that there were no roads, only an intricate maze of steep footpaths connecting homesteads over a large area, had for a long time prevented government administrators from permanently establishing their influence. It still constitutes a major impediment to any government or military action intended to bring an end to the resistance movement. In addition, the fact that the area bordered on the Congo increased the possibility—which has actually been exploited—of hiding from the Ugandan security forces. (It did not, however, lead to an enduring *rapprochement* between the Konjo of Uganda and those living in the Congo.) In contrast, the few roads leading into the Ruwenzori foothills and into Bwamba have made the Konjo and the Amba living there more exposed to government sanctions and hence less free to support a move for outright secession. Besides, the same environmental factors had also resulted in the higher regions being educationally and economically relatively less developed, and thus in a sense less vulnerable, than Bwamba and the lower Ruwenzori areas. All these conditions seem to have stimulated the willingness of highland Konjo to take greater risks and to be more militant, whereas the realities of the situation in Bwamba and the foothills, where people had jobs and possessions to lose, induced them to adopt a more flexible approach. Moreover, it was also due to the comparative inaccessibility of the mountain regions that a more pronounced spirit of independence had lingered on there over the years and was more easily reasserted.

The splits between the Konjo and the Amba which emerged in the movement appear to have corresponded roughly with the situation before 1961–62, when the common front between the two tribes was formed. They were reflective of wider differences between the two peoples who, though occupying adjacent areas, had by and large led separate existences. Historically, the neutrality which characterized their relationship seems to have been based on countervailing deterrents: the Amba did not encroach upon the mountain for fear of being stoned by the Konjo, and the Konjo did not intrude into the plains of Bwamba in consideration of the superior arrows of the Amba. Although both are basically noncentralized societies, the Amba and the Konjo have different traditions and customs, social contact has been limited, and intermarriage has remained rare. There are also considerable differences in their languages which force them at times to use Rutoro—the language whose imposition upon them had been one of the sources of their discontent—in their communications within the Rwenzururu movement. (Apart from the difficulty of understanding each other in Rukonjo, Kwamba, or any of the other Amba languages, an additional reason appears to have been that no agreement could be reached as to which should be the official Rwenzururu language.) In the decade before the formation of the Rwenzururu movement there was a certain degree of reciprocal influence between Amba agitation and that of the Konjo, though basically it took the form of separate organizational activity in each of the two tribes. During that period, most of the ferment originated not on the Ruwenzori, but in Bwamba county, with Harugali, a subcounty on the mountainside predominantly populated by Konjo, serving as a contact point with the Amba. Eventually, it was their leadership which spread the movement further up the mountain. At the same time, that is, in the 1950's, a succession of new Amba organizations also developed.[25] One of the most important was the outspoken Musana ("Sun") Society, founded by Erisa Nyamuseesa, an Amba clergyman. In 1957, the Musana Society split into two equally militant groups, the Baamba Students' Progressive Association led by H. M. Kibulya, and the more mature Balyebulya Society (meaning "one day they [the Toro] will be caught unaware"). The importance of these organizations lay in their articulation and stimulation of a consciousness of social inequality and the reflections which they induced about the future role of the Amba in Toro society.[26] An indication of

[25] The earliest organized expression of discontent occurred in the 1940's among the Amba when Mikairi Nturanke, a clerk and later a clergyman, led the influential Baamba Native Association.

[26] Although the nature of the concerns of these groups caused them, at that time, to avoid official (i.e., Batoro) scrutiny, it is surprising that an anthropologist who spent considerable time during the early 1950's in Bwamba did not notice anything of this activity. Edward H. Winter writes in *Bwamba, A Structural-Functional Analysis of a Patrilineal Society* (Cambridge, 1956): "Of enormous importance, since it affects almost all contemporary questions, is the fact that the Amba, far from resenting the attitudes which the Toro hold toward them, admit that they are inferior people. Their greatest desire at the present time is to

Nturanke's, and especially Nyamuseesa's, influence can be seen in the fact that the leaders who had the task of formulating Rwenzururu's goals had almost all earlier been under their influence. These included not only Yeremiya Kawamara and Petero Mupalya, the principal Amba spokesmen, who have led in pressing for the separate district solution rather than for the secession alternative, but also Mukirane, the Konjo leader, who, when the other two were restricted, adopted the more extreme line of establishing an independent state in the Ruwenzoris.

Among the Konjo, a man of early influence, though not of undisputed popularity, had been S. R. Bukombi, a former chief of Harugali. In the early 1950's he took it upon himself to record the history of the Konjo, and in 1954 he was one of the main initiators of the Bakonjo Life History Research Society. This society was an example of the transformation of a cultural organization into an influential political action group which was frequent in the pre-independence periods of African countries. Very soon after the Society's establishment Mukirane, who was then a primary school teacher, and had been assisting Bukombi in the organization of the Society, took over its leadership.[27] Immediately after assuming the presidency of the Bakonjo Society, Mukirane began to alter its organization and goals. He established a network of branches, staged numerous meetings, and enlarged the membership from among younger people, by and large ignoring the elders. The historical pretensions and research interests of the Society served as an excellent cloak for political activity. Mukirane even obtained official introductions from the District Commissioner, Toro, to organize his research. The major pre-occupation of the association was, inevitably, with past and present relationships between the Konjo and the Toro. Traditions of lost independence and memories of insults inflicted upon the Konjo were revived to form an illuminating background to current grievances about discriminatory treatment. Just

---

emulate the Toro and to become as fully Toro-ised as possible. One very important implication of this is that the Amba are by no means restive under the rule of the Toro but are more than willing to submit to their authority." (p. 7) One is inclined to see in this observation food for the argument that the structural-functional approach in the social sciences induces the analyst to perceive the society he studies as a harmonious equilibrium.

[27] Axel Sommerfelt, "First Impressions from Bukonjo," paper read at the 1958 Conference of the East African Institute of Social Research, available at the Makerere Institute of Social Research Library. For some time Mukirane also served as a research assistant to Tom Stacey, a British journalist interested in the history of the Konjo. Their close relationship prompted the Ugandan government, at the end of 1962, to invite Stacey to try to persuade the separatist leader to change his course of action. An account of Stacey's abortive mission can be found in his *Summons to Ruwenzori* (London, 1965).

as in the case of the Amba, a central concern was the future status of the Konjo within the political framework of Toro. As early as 1955 and 1956, the Bakonjo Life History Research Society presented to the Toro government the demands which were to become an increasingly important focus of their disaffection: direct representation in the Rukurato, and recognition of the Toro, the Konjo, and the Amba as the three tribes of Toro.[28]

Until 1961, the Amba and Konjo organizations operated independently of one another and their grievances were by and large ignored by the Toro government and unnoticed elsewhere in the country. Sensitivities steadily increased in both groups during this period until, shortly before independence, their collaboration in the Rukurato and the prospects of constitutional rearrangements induced them to align themselves within the Rwenzururu movement against the Toro. But however dramatic the appearance of their unity, they had entered the movement from different perspectives. Ironically enough, after a brief honeymoon, the Amba and Konjo leaders of the Rwenzururu movement found themselves in conflict over such elementary matters as which grievances they should submit in a joint memorandum to the Prime Minister of Uganda.[29] Both sections, nonetheless, continued to pose as the representatives of all Konjo and Amba, in the process denouncing each other's legitimacy and tactics. It does not necessarily follow, however, that all Konjo could be identified fully and solely with the secessionist policy, or the Amba population as a whole with the goal of a separate district. Certainly, lowland Konjo in the populous Busongora area in time clearly disassociated themselves from the Rwenzururu kingdom, and viewpoints in Bwamba have for long been markedly ambiguous and susceptible to change. But, by and large, the Amba leaders remained faithful to the original policy of pressing for a separate district, at least in public, whereas the Konjo faction led by Mukirane supported all-out independence, first in a republican arrangement, and finally as a kingdom with Mukirane himself as Omukama.

Both courses were perhaps no more than acts of desperation; in the final analysis, both seemed to have had equally little to offer. They shared one important characteristic, however, and that was their singularly prolific propaganda. Whereas in the 1950's it had been necessary to move cautiously so as to avoid being branded as subversive, once

[28] Correspondence from the Bakonjo Life History Research Office, Kasulenge, Ruwenzori, Uganda, to the Katikiro (chief minister) of Toro, Dec. 1955 to Feb. 1956 (author's files).

[29] Correspondence between Rwenzururu leaders, 28 July and 14 Aug. 1962 (author's files).

their complaints had become an open political issue, the main weapon available to the Rwenzururu leaders was an informed public and international opinion. In addition, popular feelings in the Konjo and Amba areas had been aroused to such an extent that the very existence of either wing of the movement depended on its providing an outlet for and, later, a means of sustaining those emotions. Consequently, both groups were prolific sources of innumerable memoranda, letters, and pamphlets—an assertion of bureaucratic proficiency, if nothing else. The Amba group directed this material mainly to Ugandan cabinet ministers, government officials, and embassies, the Mukirane group to a standard mailing list of heads of foreign governments, the Secretaries-General of the United Nations and the Organization for African Unity, and, invariably, the British Colonial Secretary. Indeed, so compelling was the need to communicate that one of the first actions of the secessionist Rwenzururu government was to establish a training school for typists.[30] Meanwhile, grievances against the Toro, the elections, and the constitutional developments leading up to the crisis; the encounters with Ugandan security forces; and the heroic deeds of the leaders were recounted all through the Ruwenzori in numerous songs and recitations, especially among the Konjo. Also songs were composed on such subjects as the scenery of Rwenzururu country and the virtues of its citizenry, thus adding to the cultural renaissance which had been evoked by the conflict.

Over the years the symbolic expression of independence took on ever more exalted forms in Rwenzururu kingdom. Ministries and chieftainships were created and adorned with neotraditional titles, a god of Rwenzururu, to whom great protective powers were attributed, made his entry, and Mukirane became surrounded with various emblems of royalty. The monarchy even became hereditary after Mukirane, the victim of dysentery, died at the end of August 1966. His fourteen-year-old son Wesley Charles, a primary school pupil, was crowned as Rwenzururu's new Omukama Kibanzangha, while a regency of three senior ministers took over responsibility for the affairs of government. Monarchical symbolism in order to assert independence from and parity with Toro kingdom had become very pervasive. But expressive of revealing after-thoughts were some Rwenzururu songs which ended with the phrase "What will happen to us?"

Rwenzururu was a mass movement involving men, women, and children in what was generally considered a "just" war. Until 1963–64, its stand against Toro domination attracted widespread response and

[30] From "A Full Report on what Omukama Isaya Mukirane has done since Rwenzururu came to Power," Office of the Omulembera (chief minister), Buhikira Central Office, Rwenzururu Kingdom Government, 25 Oct. 1966.

support throughout the Ruwenzori region. Its leaders were comparatively young and educated. A good number of them, at any rate among the Konjo, belonged to clans of such relatively high status as the Baswaga, Bahira, and Basukale. A majority were Protestants, suggesting again a greater Protestant propensity for militancy even in areas far removed from the origin of the idea of the "Protestant ethic." In other words, the leadership came from the elite which had been the most modern element in the population and which could therefore pose, and command support, as the group which should tackle essentially contemporary issues. After 1967, however, as the conflict dragged on without solution and at great cost to the population, a profound sense of weariness enveloped more and more people and a growing cynicism confronted both those who propagated a separate district solution as well as those who persisted in secession; most of the rank and file, even many of those who had actively supported the movement, longed to see the end of conflict and to return to their normal daily pursuits. Although only a few Konjo and Amba were prepared to accept renewed integration with Toro, there has in recent years been a growing disbelief in the ability of the leaders to extort a settlement. Until 1967, this dilemma was perpetuated by a weird immobility of the position of each of the parties in the dispute, leaving creeping disaffection virtually the only element of change.

The Ugandan government, for its part, has not yielded in its opposition to a separate district, but otherwise its policy has remained exceedingly vague. It established county councils in the Amba and Konjo areas to foster a sense of involvement among them in the running of their own affairs. This involvement was not forthcoming, however, because their authority, the source of their revenue, and their relationship to the Toro and central government's administration were not clearly spelled out. Consequently, these bodies remained by and large devoid of meaningful functions. The resulting indifference was matched by the suspicion with which government officials were met in their attempts to restore Amba and Konjo participation within the Toro political framework. A great many Amba and Konjo were ready to collaborate with agencies of the central government as an interim measure or even as a permanent solution. Government representatives, however, saw their involvement as a transitory stage toward the reincorporation of Rwenzururu within Toro. This divergence of attitudes and objectives prevented a full *rapprochement* between the central government and the Amba and the Konjo, so that for a long period the government's policy resulted mainly in a continuing impasse.

The government of the Toro kingdom added to the deadlock by insisting on at least *de jure* recognition of its authority over the Amba and Konjo areas. Basically, it expected the Ugandan government to restore order in the areas and then to return them to the Toro administration. On various occasions, it showed its impatience with the apparent slowness with which the Ugandan government approached the Rwenzururu problem. Despite the fact that the administration had been placed in the hands of agents of the central government, the Toro government maintained its own chiefs, stripped of all functions, in the two major centers of the areas.[31] They constituted a heavy drain of financial resources and served as a constant reminder of Toro claims to rule the Konjo and the Amba.

Rwenzururu had reached a point of no return. Concessions less than the granting of a separate district could not divert it from its course, and to capitulate short of this goal would have constituted gross political and moral defeat for the secessionists. Its leadership, moreover, developed obvious interests in self-created ministerial positions and chiefly sinecures, and their maintenance became even more crucial in the face of the alternative prospect of severe punishment. The basis of the kingdom's authority, however, shifted progressively from popular acceptance to coercion and exploitation. Opportunities to raid the Toro became limited by a buffer of Ugandan security forces along the mountainside, so that after 1964 Rwenzururu gangs increasingly directed their attacks against the Konjo and the Amba living down the mountain and in the plains. The motives of these raids, in which people have been assailed, houses burned, and crops, money, and livestock confiscated, have been to ensure loyalty to the Rwenzururu regime, to inflict punishment for co-operation with central government officials, and especially to levy tribute for the maintenance of the kingdom. The population in the foothills therefore found itself between two governments, both of which demanded taxes and compliance. The Rwenzururu kingdom increasingly came to be regarded as the greater threat of the two, and the Amba—as well as a growing number of Konjo —have become disaffected from it. In 1968 there were indications that the Rwenzururu regime, leaning·upon minority support, was actually crumbling into a loose alliance of powerful chiefs exercising control over their immediate surroundings and themselves wielding considerable influence over and against the central Rwenzururu government. The gradual fragmentation of the movement did not necessarily mean that its demise was near, however, as it was able to survive the death of

[31] This arrangement was not dissimilar to that made by the Rwenzururu government, which also appointed nominal chiefs for some of the counties of Toro outside its immediate control. With this measure, it apparently sought to affirm its claim that Rwenzururians were the original inhabitants of Toro who were pushed on to the mountainside as a result of Toro invasions from Bunyoro. The Rwenzururu position is that the Toro must vacate the area for Rwenzururians.

its founder and leader[32] and its armed strength combines to give additional life to its physical control of the inhabitants of Ruwenzori. Although there were sporadic outbreaks of Konjo resistance against the secessionist state, the Konjo who live on the mountain spurs were generally not well enough organized to bring an end by themselves to their subjection to Rwenzururu power. In some areas they organized vigils and, at times, they succeeded in reconquering mountain spurs from the Rwenzururu forces. Large numbers of them, however, continued to be exposed to Rwenzururu threats, in the face of which they were usually powerless. Their precarious position has remained basically unchanged for years, as it was rooted in the wider deadlock over the Rwenzururu dispute.

At least till 1967, the leaders of the Amba and Konjo who were prepared to co-operate with the central government found themselves in an unenviably restricted position. If anything, failure to achieve their original promises, and their resultant insecurity, tended to make them more dogmatic. A separate district, or some alternative form of independence from the Toro, has remained a stringent standard against which new proposals have been judged. Deviations from it, for example, calling for reconciliation with the Toro or too loud displays of agreement with central governmental policies, have been penalized by immediate ostracism. This happened in 1963 with the kidnapping of E. Bwambale, the Konjo Member of Parliament, and again in 1965 and 1966. At the same time, renewed demands for separation from Toro could hardly elicit a favorable response from the Ugandan government. In the absence of more constructive gestures from the central government, the predicament of the more conciliatory Rwenzururu leaders has thus remained their inability to provide a clear sense of direction. Their situation is perhaps best illustrated by the fact that quite a few have been punished by both the Ugandan and the Rwenzururu kingdom governments. Indeed, in various instances the same individuals have been in turn restricted by the Ugandan government because they were suspected of furthering the secessionist cause, and by the Rwenzururu government because they were considered dissident elements who had betrayed Rwenzururu solidarity, as defined by the secessionist kingdom. Within the extremely narrow range left between these two poles, virtually the only suggestions which these leaders could make were for the transformation of the county councils in Konjo

[32] The possibility of the collapse of the movement was anticipated after Mukirane's death. The conclusion of the Rwenzururu government report on his accomplishments said: ". . . Let us go forward, let us not deceive ourselves that since Mukirane has died, . . . also the Rwenzururu movement is dead. Not at all, the Rwenzururu movement lives and will always be kept alive, even by our sons and daughters."

and Amba areas into more executive and autonomous bodies and their amalgamation, if only for certain purposes, into a larger joint assembly. Proposals to this effect, which were made with the hope of ultimately achieving a separate district in all but name, came especially from the Konjo leadership in the Busongora lowlands—but without any result. Some support of this line was also forthcoming from Bwamba, but conditions there left possibly even less room for new departures. In recent years, the decisive factor in Bwamba has been the simultaneous operation of two competing structures. Behind the façade of co-operation with central government agents, Rwenzururu forces have exercised enormous power over the local population, in no small measure based on terror. This has increasingly reduced the possibility of the emergence of a different point of view.

All these positions remained basically unchanged until the fall of 1967. Unfortunately, during the first five years after Uganda's independence none of the attempts made to solve the deadlock had a genuine chance of succeeding. Primary responsibility for breaking out of the impasse rested with the Ugandan government. While it did not retreat from its decision to resist the Konjo and Amba claims, neither did it initiate any serious actions to end the movement. This was not least because of the considerable expense involved in a major military operation in the Ruwenzoris, and also because Uganda was confronted with more immediate problems of security in Buganda. There also seemed to be a feeling in high places that an effort to end the secession movement might result in a consolidation of support for Rwenzururu. The Ugandan government appeared to entertain hopes that the Rwenzururu movement would die a natural death. Its passivity, however, sustained the immobility which surrounded the dispute and tended to infuse the movement with additional life.

Important modifications in the situation seemed to occur with the introduction of the new republican constitution for Uganda in September 1967. Most significant in Rwenzururu terms were the abolition of kingship in Toro and a considerable increase of central control over district administrations—among other things, in matters of appointment. Moreover, these measures were followed by changes in the key officeholders in the new Toro district, a process which was clearly guided by a decision to distribute the major posts among the three tribes. The newly appointed secretary-general was a Toro, his deputy an Amba, the chairman of the new District Council a Konjo, and his deputy a Toro. In addition, it was planned to withdraw both the redundant Toro chiefs and the central government agents who had substituted for them from the Amba and Konjo areas, and to replace them with a single hierarchy of officials. Thus, a variety of new elements began to exercise a certain effect on the situation, although exactly how important they will be is as yet (in 1969) hard to establish. Nonetheless, a few facts stand out. The abolition of the Toro kingship was a cause of considerable rejoicing throughout the Ruwenzori; Amba and lowland Konjo have welcomed the moves toward a more unitary form of government in Uganda as they decreased the significance of local government and hence the importance of Toro control. Reception of the new appointments was perhaps more mixed, since at least one important case concerned a man who had for some time been ousted by Uganda-oriented Amba because of his conciliatory views. The Konjo and the Amba were also disappointed because the constitution did not remove the obstacles to the creation of new districts in Toro. Their frustration was all the more bitter because the constitution did create four new districts to replace the kingdom of Buganda.

The new constitution prompted a considerable amount of soul-searching among the Amba and the Konjo. No doubt one major consideration was that whatever the precise structural changes and possible improvements, co-existence, and indeed collaboration, with the Toro would continue to be necessary. For many Amba and Konjo this was a sour prospect. Besides, giving their support to the new governmental structure would also imply abandoning any further aspirations for a Rwenzururu district and disbanding whatever popular forces remained available to press for this goal. On the other hand, any reconsideration of attitudes was bound to be influenced by the pervasive weariness resulting from years of misery and insecurity; by the expectation that the Ugandan government would not, in future, give in to demands for a separate district; and by a realization that the changes offered were, under the circumstances, probably as good as any for which the Amba and Konjo could hope. The attitudes of the Amba and the Konjo have thus been pulled in different directions as a result of the Ugandan government's decision, and it is perhaps not surprising that acceptance of the constitutional changes of 1967 has been regarded by some as a defeat, and by others as a victory for the movement and its Rwenzururu goals.

The fluctuations in attitude occurred primarily among the Konjo in the Busongora lowlands and the Amba. Indications are that large numbers of these people have now become prepared to accept the new governmental arrangements as a fresh basis for co-operation. Their leadership has already shown its willingness to participate in the new framework and to renounce the movement altogether an instrument to achieve further goals. In Bwamba and the Busongora plains, therefore, the movement is basically dead, even if social relationships with Toro continue to be marked by considerable distance. This trend signifies an important step toward the achievement of ethnic reconciliation in Toro district and, by implication, it should enhance central Ugandan authority. The Rwenzururu kingdom's government has, meanwhile, remained adamant in the face of the new constitutional structure and, eschewing any contact with Ugandan authorities, persists in its secession. Their continuing secession has no long-term basis of viability, however, and eventually the mountain Konjo organized in the Rwenzururu kingdom will have to return to the larger unit. Renewed efforts currently undertaken by Ugandan education officers and other officials to reopen schools and provide badly needed services are already inducing a change of attitudes among the rank and file Bakonjo on the mountains. The Rwenzururu secession, whose record from 1962 till 1969 has made it the most enduring separatist movement in all of Africa, is therefore bound to reach the end of its days in the foreseeable future.

Conclusion

In the foregoing, the focus has been mainly on specific local conditions of protest in two subunits in a wider political framework. What is the significance of such conflict when seen in the context of national unification? The polity under consideration is basically pluralistic and pragmatic. The problem is not merely a derivative one; there is not necessarily a one-to-one relationship between integration at the local level and the national level. For instance, to say that a secession of local origin, such as that of the Rwenzururu movement, subtracts from national unity in Uganda may be correct in a sense, but perhaps only superficially so. If we were able to delve more deeply into the policy determinants surrounding the issue, it is conceivable that we would conclude that the Rwenzururu secession is the price which the Ugandan government pays for political unity elsewhere in the country, and that it has hence contributed to national unification. The fact is that the processes of integration within subunits do not occur in isolation from those operating at the next higher, or national, level. Rather conflict and integration at these two levels affect one another in a complex fashion—at times being mutually supportive, at times working in contrary directions.[33]

Two possible ways of approaching this relationship, starting from opposite ends, seem to suggest themselves. One is to ask what is the effect of the national context on the conduct of protest and the outcome of conflict within subunits. The second is to try to assess the effect of conflict within subunits on unity at the national level. The first of these questions is, in a sense, inordinately speculative because what it asks is

[33] Cf. Amitai Etzioni, *Political Unification: A Comparative Study of Leaders and Forces* (New York, 1965), 83.

essentially what difference would it have made had Ankole and Toro not been parts of a more comprehensive political system. Yet we can hardly avoid putting the question this way if we hope to obtain even a brief glimpse of the special conditions of protest and conflict that derive from the subunit level in which they occur. Moreover, by beginning with this dimension, we can at least start to formulate questions about the implications of subunit conflict for national unity.

Our data suggest that the existence of a wider national context affects subunit conflict in various ways. Certain aspects seem to diminish and others to perpetuate the propensity for protest and, hence, the potential for conflict within subsystems. The national context appears to mitigate the sharpness of protest if and insofar as it opens alternative outlets for individual and collective aspirations. It also does so to the extent that the center can effectively act as an arbiter in local disputes. On the other hand, a wider national framework may perpetuate the grounds for protest by sustaining specific local social discrepancies as they become, as it were, "protected" by general rulings applicable to the country as a whole. Evidently, both these tendencies can, and often do, occur simultaneously. The cases of Ankole and Toro seem to provide examples of both effects.

The "mitigating outlet" characteristic of a wider framework is perhaps clearest with regard to the transfer of personnel which it allows. Over and above the more overt ideological aims of protest, such as equal recognition or participation in decision-making, protest may often be considered as competition for elite positions between the incumbents and the leadership of newly emergent groups. In situations of subsystem conflict, the very existence of a national center is bound to draw many of the educationally most qualified members of both contending parties into central government positions and thus away from the local competition for posts and sinecures. This tends to let off some of the steam of local protest, and the resulting decreased demands may make conflict less intense and abrupt. In the two cases of ethnic protest which we have looked at, this spillover effect is clearest in Ankole, where a good many years of educational opportunities for Iru as well as Hima had fostered the growth of modern, qualified cadres in both groups. Increasing numbers of highly educated Hima and Iru have found employment in Kampala, Entebbe, and elsewhere in Uganda. Had these people been confined to competing for the already limited number of elite positions within Ankole, they would probably have aggravated local tension considerably. In Toro, on the other hand, this outlet was provided to a much smaller degree, primarily because educational advancement among the Konjo and the Amba had not progressed sufficiently to make their recruitment into the middle and higher ranks of the Ugandan government service a factor of much

significance. It was not until 1968, for instance, that the first Amba
to receive a university degree graduated from Makerere University
College. As a result, an Amba and Konjo leadership aspiring to greater
individual advancement was on the whole induced to seek this goal
in Toro itself rather than within the larger Uganda. But this goal was
blocked by the Toro who held the leading positions. Even if part of
the educated Toro, similar to the modern Ankole elite, had benefited
from employment opportunities elsewhere in Uganda, they felt sufficiently strong in Toro to disregard and resist Amba and Konjo aspirations for occupational mobility.

The absorptive capacity of the center may also be looked at in a
somewhat different light. If the center tends to draw away some of the
best qualified elements of conflicting groups, it may in an important
sense deprive these groups of their most effective potential leadership.
Such policies could lame the movement concerned, especially in cases
where an elite is relatively small. In certain cases, the overall result
may then still be the same: a diminution of tension because of the lack
of an organizing cadre. But other examples are conceivable, particularly
where conflict is generated by grass roots resentment that is so strong
that the presence or absence of an educated elite makes little difference
to the articulation of protest, and where the drawing off of a potentially
more manipulative leadership may only result in more anomic and
irreconcilable expressions of discontent. This tendency seems to have
also manifested itself in the Rwenzururu movement.[34]

A wider national framework may also mitigate conflict at the local
level by enabling the center to play the role of arbiter. This role is
possible as long as the issue does not shift from the subunit level to
the national level, thus threatening the center's viability. It is not
merely that a central government is often an outsider at the subunit
level; normally, the center also exhibits a vital interest in the prevalence
of tranquility throughout its territory. Perhaps most decisive, however,
is the fact that, in contrast to international conciliatory bodies, a
national center is generally better equipped to seek and enforce com-

[34] There is of course yet another way in which the center can divert pressure from subunit conflict, but this implies major changes in the system as a
whole. The kinds of ethnic dissension with which this paper has been concerned
can be typically found in what David Apter has called "reconciliation systems."
The solutions sought for them have mainly been incremental and do not alter, but
rather sustain, the basic format of the structure. Ethnic conflict, either at the
subunit or at the national level, can be countered, however, if a government
chooses to shift from a pluralistic bargaining type of polity to one that presupposes far greater unity of values, Apter's "mobilization systems" for instance. In
their ideal form, the popular identifications with the national community which
these systems mobilize would render regional ethnic differences more or less
meaningless. See David E. Apter, *The Politics of Modernization* (Chicago,
1967), 36.

promises at the subunit level. With varying degrees of clarity, this assumption is borne out by the cases of Ankole and Toro. In Ankole, the timing of the Protectorate's decision in 1955 to alter the constitutional basis of the district as a means of easing the dilemma surrounding the nomination of the Enganzi is a case in point. With respect to the Rwenzururu conflict, the center may not have fully exploited its opportunities for arbitration; nonetheless, the Ugandan government's involvement in the administration of the Amba and Konjo areas in Toro since 1963 falls largely within this category.

However, the center's ability to act as arbitrator is closely linked to, and circumscribed by, the fact that it is also the body which defines the rules of the game: it determines what rights can be maintained and what actions are permissible. But in doing so it also sets the terms for conflict in a wider sense because it simultaneously to a large extent predetermines what issues will be contended next, legally or illegally. Seen in this light, the rules are more than just "legal" prescriptions; they also fix the boundaries for actions to change or uphold the status quo. The major turning points in the development of protest in both Ankole and Toro, for instance, were brought about by central government rulings which defined, redefined, or reaffirmed the issues and, by implication, the targets. In other words, the center establishes the objects of competition by the opposing groups in a subsystem. This exemplifies the perhaps somewhat contradictory fact that it was not against the Ugandan government but primarily against the Toro and the Toro government that Konjo and Amba antagonism was directed; nonetheless, it was the Ugandan government which finally ruled against a separate Rwenzururu district.

The center's function of laying down rules is restricted but also strengthened by the general applicability which they must have. According to this principle, the center is in a position to induce basic adjustments in certain instances of subsystem inequality but is prevented from doing so in others. The refusal to create a separate district for the Konjo and the Amba, for instance, followed largely from this requirement of the general applicability of rules—granting Rwenzururu demands was not considered compatible with policies designed for the system as a whole. One may argue that, if Toro had been a national system, its center, theoretically speaking, would have been less limited in its jurisdiction by a regard for the wider validity of lawmaking. On the other hand, political democratization in Ankole was fostered and implemented, in keeping with trends in the country at large. In this regard, Ankole is a clear illustration of the positive role of a national context in the relatively smooth solution of inequality in subunits. It contrasts markedly with Rwanda where the attainment of political equality was accompanied by violent upheaval. But Ankole also offers some contrary evidence, without which protest could not have persisted. Although the political supremacy of the Hima might have been eroded by the more general constitutional transitions, their economic advantages and their predominance in positions of public service did not disappear, or at least not so quickly. These aspects of Hima status have been supported by statutes applied throughout Uganda. Civil service regulations ensure the tenure of Hima chiefs until they reach the age of retirement; legislation regarding land tenure upholds the property rights of mailo landowners; and a progressive tax system which would level the wealth and incomes of various economic categories only exists in embryonic form, is probably still superfluous for many parts of the country, and hence perpetuates marked economic differences. Basically, pronounced social and economic inequality in subsystems of a wider political entity may endure because the larger system cannot adopt special measures to solve local discrepancies. To exercise the flexibility necessary for such adjustments would be contrary to the development of uniform policies for national political unification. Paradoxically, subsystem nonintegration may thus be congruent with system integration.

If we now reverse the perspective and look at the effect of disaffection and conflict within subunits on national unification, it is clear that the problems here are quite different from those involved in the integration, on a national or even an international plane, of subunits exhibiting basic internal consensus on policy alternatives.[35] Where such consensus is lacking, it is obviously not very meaningful to discuss the integration of the subunits into a wider framework while disregard-

[35] Ernst Haas argued that European integration is being facilitated by the existence of considerable agreement on objectives among the elites of various social and economic groups within each of the participating states as well as among the elites at the interstate level. Moreover, roughly identical social and economic structures would allow a linking up of these national systems at various levels. The elite consensus, manifesting itself in "the end of ideology," is made possible by virtue of the fact that in each of the European states the major political questions, that is, those involving social and economic questions, have by and large been solved. See Ernst B. Haas, "The Uniting of Europe and the Uniting of Latin America," *Journal of Common Market Studies,* V (1967), 320.
When contrasting the integration process in Europe to that of a single African state, it should, of course, be kept in mind that there is a fundamentally different starting point. In African countries, integration begins at the center, sometimes perhaps merely with a center, whereas in Europe the center is the end product of integration. Such distinctions, however, should not deter us from looking for generally relevant conditions facilitating or hampering integration. If the conditions sustaining European integration are applied to individual African states, the latter's chances of political development of any significance would be very dim indeed. To search for alternative ways of achieving integration is thus a *sine qua non* for policy-makers in Africa.

ing the political divisions within them. One cannot talk of the integration of Toro, as such, into Uganda if an important section of Toro secedes from Uganda. Problems of integration may be most critical not at the national level, but at a level one step removed from the center. We must adjust our focus. However, it may be erroneous to leave the matter with the assumption that nonintegration at the subunit level implies nonintegration at the national level. For it is conceivable that in some situations conflict within the subsystem may induce a strengthening, rather than a weakening, of national allegiances among one or even both parties engaged in dispute. Moreover, it is possible that an absence of local integration is compatible with integration of elite interests at the national level.

As regards the first of these possibilities, at this stage our data on Ankole and Toro allow little more than an indication of areas for further exploration. In Ankole, the preoccupation of Iru and Hima with the local political framework would seem to have shifted the focus away from the national system; yet, in a different fashion, both groups manifested increasing dependence upon the national center for support in, as well as an alternative to, the local dispute. In Toro, the Rwenzururu kingdom evidently provides an example of the negative consequences of subunit conflict in terms of national allegiances. Nonetheless, large numbers of Konjo and Amba, not belonging to the Rwenzururu state, have increasingly identified with Uganda and are now probably the most nationally minded group in the district. In their case, positive attitudes toward the center have followed from conflict within the subunit. The extent to which the Toro "belong" to the national system is more difficult to assess; although it is plausible that the conflict has in some ways strengthened a sense of Toro identity, the Toro have also, though not quite so voluntarily, become more dependent on the center as a result of the Rwenzururu issue. Thus again we see that an opportunity for the center to intervene may create a greater national involvement. At an earlier stage, marked by the resistance to the application of the 1955 District Ordinance to Toro as well as by such acts as calling for the recognition of Toro as a nation, sentiments were fostered in Toro which were detrimental to national integration in Uganda. These moves were not only a way of demanding a higher price for Toro's integration into Uganda but, in addition, had the effect of perpetuating the political supremacy of the Toro elite within Toro.

With this last point we have arrived at what has perhaps been the most crucial connection between conflict, integration, and protest in Uganda during the years before and immediately after independence. Until quite recently at least, Uganda was noteworthy for the district-centered basis of its politics. To a very significant extent the districts and kingdoms were the centers of political influence, and the national center basically reflected this pluralism. National leadership was largely composed of elites with a strong district basis and, to fit the multi-centered power structure, took the form of a coalition. The fact that the subunits were in various respects the most meaningful sources and places of action meant that basic political alignments and counter-alignments occurred to a large extent at the level of internal district and kingdom politics. Although sharp political cleavages thus existed within a majority of the subunits, the national coalition tended to reflect the groups in power in most of the districts and kingdoms. National integration as it existed in Uganda, therefore, was largely based on the consensus of these power elites. But in a number of sub-units, and certainly in the two with which we have been concerned, the position of the political elites did not remain unchallenged. Pressure and protest from groups claiming a larger share of influence and benefits were not uncommon in a number of local areas. Although challenges were made, they did not affect the system as a whole be-cause by and large they remained as localized as were its component parts. Perhaps the major reason why this system has been able to continue to function is to be found in its pluralist characteristics. In a sense, the national system could bear the occurrence of protest and conflict within subunits, even of the extreme variety of Rwenzururu, because its very pluralism prevented a spill-over effect in adjacent areas. Protest could put one of a series of watertight compartments out of order, but it could not make the ship sink. From the national center, which derived its strength from the district elites, these elites could expect a certain willingness to back them up if trouble arose. The perpetuation of this system, however, implied the continuation of a relatively weak center which, in the long run, might prove too fragile for its tasks. Since 1967 there have been cautious moves to alter the format of the system. Steps are being taken toward the creation of a stronger center, toward a unification that reaches downward to en-compass more levels, and toward the growth of a fuller sense of Ugandan identity. One of the most difficult transitions involved is the reversal of relationships of influence between the center and the dis-trict elites. In turn, this implies the need for a modification of the local political leadership. Significantly, these moves have not been prompted by the subunit conflicts found in many parts of Uganda, but rather by developments in Buganda, the one area which was in a position to pose a direct threat to the center. Of at least equal significance is the remark-ably smooth, hence also unspectacular, manner in which this transforma-tion has thus far been carried out.

PART EIGHT

SOVEREIGNTY AND DIPLOMACY

IN POST-INDEPENDENCE AFRICA

SOCIALISM AS A MODE OF INTERNATIONAL PROTEST: THE CASE OF TANZANIA

ALI A. MAZRUI

In January 1967 in Arusha, the National Executive Committee of the Tanganyika African National Union discussed measures of economic policy which were to have far-reaching consequences for Tanzania. These discussions culminated in the Arusha Declaration, which set forth the party's newly invigorated policies on socialism and self-reliance. Accompanying the Declaration were socialistic measures which included the nationalization of banks, breweries, flour mills, and import and export enterprises, as well as stiffer policies imposing austerity as a life-style for party leaders and as a directive for official behavior at large.[1]

It is all too easy to see the Declaration exclusively as a program for domestic action. This paper argues that such an interpretation is inadequate. It is true that the new ethic propounded and implemented after the Declaration significantly affected internal events in Tanzania and the style of Tanzanian politics as a whole. But I hope to demonstrate that the Arusha Declaration was not just a statement of domestic policy but also a pronouncement of foreign policy. The Declaration, its background, and its aftermath constituted one of the meeting points between ideology, domestic policies, and international relations.

[1] The authoritative version of the Declaration is: *The Arusha Declaration and TANU'S Policy on Socialism and Self-Reliance* (Dar es Salaam, 1967). For the beginning of TANU see above, Andrew Maguire, "The Emergence of the Tanganyika African National Union in the Lake Province," 639-70. See also Ahmed Mohiddin, "Ujamaa na Kujitegemea," *Mawazo*, I (1967), 24-88. For some initial attempts at analyzing the implications of the Declaration see articles in *East Africa Journal*, Mar., Apr., May, and June issues, 1967. See also A. A. Mazrui, "Political Superannuation and the Trans-Class Man," *International Journal of Comparative Sociology*, IX (1968), 81-96.

I will start by examining socialism itself as pre-eminently an ideology of protest. I will then go on to the background of Tanzania's frustrations with donor countries in connection with conditions for aid, and to the place of Rhodesia's Unilateral Declaration of Independence in the upsurge of a new militancy in Tanzania. Finally, I will discuss the Arusha Declaration itself as a response to these events and as a fusion of President Julius Nyerere's own socialism, Lenin's theory of imperialism, and simple, hard-headed pragmatism.

To the extent that the Arusha Declaration was a reaffirmation, at a more militant level, of Tanzania's socialistic ideals, it fell within an ideological tradition which has for a long time been associated with protest. Leftist tendencies in politics have more often than not displayed a leaning toward opposition to the establishment. It is almost a part of the definition of leftist socialism that the establishment of any regime should be suspect. Marxism itself defines its utopia in terms of the complete withering away of the established state. During the stage of the proletarian dictatorship the state would indeed remain necessary, as it has done in those countries which have already established socialist regimes. But, fundamentally, even in a proletarian country the state remains an instrument of class oppression. It is inherent in socialism therefore, to wage a constant struggle toward the final elimination of the state.

Within Africa the attraction of modern socialistic ideas has also been partly traceable to psychological leanings toward protest. To understand the nature of this attraction we should perhaps look more closely at some of the postulates of African nationalism at large. In the ultimate analysis, nationalism has been a movement whose main inspiration has been a desire for *equality*, rather than freedom. This is not to underestimate the logical complications in any attempt to disentangle the concept of equality from the concept of liberty—complications that may be suggested by recalling that the first Declaration of Independence from British colonial rule opened with the premise that "All men are created equal." And yet one can attempt to disentangle the two concepts at least to the extent of suggesting that whereas the Americans proclaimed "equality" in pursuit of independence, the African nationalists have now sought independence in the pursuit of equality. Indeed, the development of African nationalism is a progressive metamorphosis in the general attitude as to what would be acceptable as an adequate expression of racial equality.[2]

But the equality which has inspired African nationalism has been an equality primarily between *races*, while the equality which inspired

[2] This point is discussed more fully in A. A. Mazrui, "On the Concept of 'We are all Africans,'" *American Political Science Review*, LVII (1963), 83-97.

European socialism was, in the first instance, equality between *classes*. And yet the egalitarian element in socialism, however different in emphasis, was sufficient to make this ideology attractive to African nationalists. To protest against racial inequality might indeed have been different from protesting against disparities between classes, but a fusion occurred when both aspects became a joint protest against inequality at large.

Another factor which made socialism attractive to African nationalists before independence was not something in socialism itself, but something attributed to *capitalism*. Hobson's and Lenin's theses on the nature of imperialism might have oversimplified the phenomenon. It was not only capitalists who wanted to build empires; individual empire builders were a mixed bag, ranging from well meaning missionaries to calculating businessmen. All the same, historically the growth of capitalism, and its need for markets and raw materials, did have some connection with imperial expansion. Out of this link between capitalism and imperialism emerged the links between European socialists and Afro-Asian nationalists. And these ties in turn later led, in some cases, to a marriage of the ideologies of nationalism and socialism in the new states. The reasoning behind the transition from stage to stage was perhaps of the following order:

> Socialism is against the capitalist;
> Nationalism is against the imperialist;
> But the capitalist and the imperialist are either the same man or two men in alliance;
> Therefore nationalism and socialism in Africa can either be the same ideology or two ideologies in alliance.[3]

Sometimes the case was aggravated by the bogey of communism, which imperial powers used to make legitimate their suppression of African nationalistic agitators. This bogey now persists in Rhodesia and in South Africa—the latter using the umbrella of the Suppression of Communism Act to deal severely with any major manifestations of anti-apartheid protest.

In the face of this bogey of communism, nationalists gradually developed the kind of defiance which made them accept the charge of being at least "Marxist-oriented." Their conversion to Marxism or neo-Marxism was sometimes out of sheer reaction to the anti-Marxist policies of the colonial regimes. (The British Parliament at home might indeed have included a number of distinguished Marxists, but in the colonial countries the local administrators were quick to resort to cor-

[3] See Ali A. Mazrui, *Towards a Pax Africana* (London, 1967), 98-99.

rective or preventive measures against "agitators" as soon as there were any suggestions of leftist influences operating among "innocent natives.")

In short, socialism, even when uncomplicated by colonial situations, has remained basically a protest-oriented ideology. But in Africa this tendency toward protest has been sharpened by the presumed connection between capitalism in metropolitan countries and imperial expansion abroad; by the alliance which sometimes has grown up between socialists in metropolitan countries and nationalists in Afro-Asian colonies; by the basic egalitarian orientation shared by socialism as an opposition to class distinctions and African nationalism as a protest against racial inequality; and, finally, by the monotonous bogey of communism which colonial governments in Africa and racialistic regimes generally have used to justify their suppression of nationalist activities.

The attraction of socialistic ideas for Tanzania had its roots in the factors mentioned above. But when Nyerere first propounded the doctrine of "African Socialism" as a factor of political life in Tanzania in 1962, the emphasis was more on the "African" than on the "socialistic" component of the doctrine. There was a constant search for ways of providing a native base for some of the socialistic principles which were gaining increased respectability. Nyerere argued that *Ujamaa*, a Swahili word denoting the fellowship of kinship ties and tribal solidarity, provided in its essence a collective basis for socialism. Traditional African life, he argued, had been predicated on the principle of reciprocal relationships and on the ethos of sharing. There was a loyalty to the larger society, and the subordination of individual prejudices to collective well-being. Hospitality was a persistent obligation to one's fellow beings, and care of the aged and the sick was taken for granted. The acquisitive instinct was tamed, and parasitism, or the tendency to live on others, was severely frowned upon.

On the basis of this idealized interpretation of life in traditional African societies, Nyerere asserted "We, in Africa, have no more need of being 'converted' to socialism than we have of being 'taught' democracy. Both are rooted in our past—in the traditional society which produced us."[4]

At this stage *Ujamaa* was more an expression of cultural nationalism than an assertion of militant socialism. For some time the image of Nyerere in the capitals of the Western world was that of a "moderate" with a strong leaning toward the West. He talked about socialism, but he behaved like a liberal in a recognizable Western sense. He believed in a one-party state but at first spoke almost apologetically—

[4] Nyerere, *Ujamaa: The Basis of African Socialism* (Dar es Salaam, 1962).

pointing out that he could not help it if his own ruling party were overwhelmingly supported by the people. Nyerere reiterated the values of individual freedom and of the open society, and simply argued that these were not incompatible with the situation of one-party dominance in a particular country.[5]

But *Ujamaa* gradually changed from being in essence an exercise in cultural nationalism to becoming a program of radical social transformation culminating in the Arusha Declaration. Of course, even if *Ujamaa* were basically a romanticization of traditional Africa, it did maintain the theme of keeping the best of what was valuable from the African heritage and translating this theme into policy decisions in contemporary Tanzania. But although these ideas had been formulated on the eve of independence and immediately after, there at first seemed to be little inclination toward any vigorous implementation of planned change. In fact Colin Leys, then teaching at Kivukoni College in Dar es Salaam, had occasion to lament that Tanganyika was suffering from four social ills—"poverty, ignorance, disease and empiricism."[6]

But then radicalizing tendencies began to affect the political ethos of Tanzania. One major contributory factor was Tanganyika's union with Zanzibar. The revolution in Zanzibar had been a Marxist revolution with a greater commitment to social transformation than Dar es Salaam envisaged for the mainland. The actual revolution which overthrew the Sultan's regime took place in January 1964; the union with Zanzibar was accomplished in April of that year.[7] By the time the union was brought into being, Zanzibar had already established significant diplomatic contacts with the East Germans and the mainland Chinese—thus indicating the radical orientation of Zanzibar. Some of these contacts were later to cause difficulties for and embarrassment to the Dar es Salaam government.

Nyerere was understandably reluctant to let the union collapse as a result of divergent tendencies between the inhabitants of the mainland and the islanders. In a bid to ensure that the Zanzibaris remained relatively contented, a significant degree of autonomy and latitude was allowed to accrue to them. Representation of Zanzibar in the Parliament in Dar es Salaam was vastly disproportionate—forty-four members represented 300,000 islanders as against 145 members for the 10,000,000

[5] For the evolution of Nyerere's views on the one-party system consult, *inter alia,* Julius Nyerere, "One Party Government," *Transition,* 1 (Dec. 1961), 9-11; *Democracy and the Party System* (Dar es Salaam, 1962); *Report of the Presidential Commission on the Establishment of a Democratic One-Party Democracy* (Dar es Salaam, 1965).

[6] See Colin Leys, "The Need for an Ideology," *Kivukoni Journal* (1961), 4.

[7] See above, Michael F. Lofchie, "The Zanzibari Revolution: African Protest in a Racially Plural Society," 924-68.

people of mainland Tanzania. According to the constitution, Abeid Karume, a Zanzibari and the First Vice-President of the Republic, was entitled to act as President whenever Nyerere was out of the country. There have also been up to seven other Zanzibaris who have been members of the union government; four of them were at one time cabinet ministers and three parliamentary secretaries.

We might therefore say that the union with Zanzibar introduced a significant radical pressure group into the politics of Dar es Salaam, strengthening these radical elements among those Tanganyikans who had been in any case so oriented. Some of these radicals later, however, came to be discredited or were even detained. Preeminent among the Zanzibaris was A. Kassim Hanga, who had become Vice-President of Zanzibar after the revolution in January 1964 and had then become Minister of State for Union Affairs in Dar es Salaam. Hanga, a Marxist, was associated both with Oscar Kambona, after the latter had quarreled with Nyerere, and with the small group of leftist Tanzanians who in 1967 had allegedly tried to subvert the armed forces in a bid to push Tanzania even further to the left. But the fact that a number of these Tanzanians fell from favor, because they were both a threat and Marxist, was not by itself an indication that they had not been an important influence on Tanzania's evolution toward a more radical ethos. On the contrary, the importance which these dissidents assumed in the second half of 1967, as Nyerere argued with Kambona, then in self-imposed exile in England, and with local critics, was itself a measure of their significance as an interest group within the ruling party prior to the actual break with the leadership.

It might even be said that although the Arusha Declaration constituted the triumph of *radicalism,* it was soon followed by the eclipse of *radicals* within Tanzania. In other words, the Declaration constituted a high watermark for socialistic measures adopted by the government as a basis for internal transformation, but the leading figures of the leftist movement in Tanzania were soon to decline in importance. Abdul Rahman Mohammed (Babu), the leading Zanzibari Marxist, moved from the important Ministry of Commerce after the banks and industries were nationalized in 1967 to a more modest portfolio; Kambona, who had at one time been politically the second strongest man in Tanganyika, soon departed in somewhat suspicious circumstances to go to Europe and from there conducted an altercation with Nyerere on the direction of change in the country; A few younger Marxists were accused of attempting to subvert the armed forces in pursuit of revolutionary change and were placed in detention; and Hanga followed them into detention after his return from a trip during which he apparently attempted to persuade President Sékou Touré of Guinée to exercise his influence in assuring the security of some of the leftist dissidents of Tanzania. President Nyerere referred to Hanga's and Kambona's contacts with Touré in a speech which he gave in Zanzibar on January 12, 1968—the fourth anniversary of the island's revolution. Nyerere indicated that his former colleagues had had their own new "plans for a revolution in Tanzania" which had now been frustrated. These events made the Arusha Declaration and its aftermath both the climax of radical policies and the beginning of a decline of Tanzania's traditional leftists.[8]

But as Tanzania was moving from *Ujamaa* as a mild form of cultural nationalism to *Ujamaa* as a radicalized program of action leading to the Arusha Declaration, there were forces which were also helping to give her ideology a significant international dimension. Of course cultural nationalism itself presupposes the challenges of other nations and must therefore be presumed to include a comparative international perspective. One romanticizes one's own traditions as opposed to the traditions of other societies. But the radicalization of Tanzania was partly inspired by more direct international complications. These concerned the place of aid in relations between recipient and donor countries and touched upon the kinds of tensions which sometimes arise between the political sensibilities of a recipient country and the political demands of the donors.

In order to understand the relevance of Rhodesia's Unilateral Declaration of Independence of November 1965 to the socialist formulations which issued forth from Arusha in January and February 1967, it is important to understand not simply the question of relationships between big powers and small countries but also the moral tone of Nyerere's whole approach to both domestic and international politics. In the words of Leys, ". . . We have to understand Nyerere's style— the relentless magnification of the moral aspects of each and every policy decision—in terms of his need to sustain the *moral* basis of his own leadership, vis-à-vis both the cadres and the public at large; *it is his stock-in-trade*, as it was also Gladstone's."[9]

Leys here seems to imply that "moral magnification" was an emphasis in a mode of rationalization rather than a determinant of policy. But in fact moral considerations as an influence on Nyerere's political choices have been a reality in themselves. In other words, this is not simply a question of Nyerere using moral arguments to rationalize policies chosen for other reasons; it is a case of Nyerere making those choices partly on moral grounds. It might even be argued that Nyerere

[8] *East African Standard,* Jan. 13, 1968.
[9] See Colin Leys, "Inter alia—or Tanzaphilia and All That," *Transition,* 34 (Jan. 1968), 51-53.

has all too often permitted too large an intrusion of the ethical into the political sphere.

On 15 December 1965 Tanzania broke off diplomatic relations with Britain over the issue of Rhodesia. The foreign ministers of the Organization of African Unity at Addis Ababa had earlier demanded that Britain should take effective action against the illegal Rhodesian regime or face a collective severance of diplomatic relations by all independent African states. By 15 December, the date when the ultimatum was to expire, it was clear that a large number of African countries would not in fact carry out this resolution. But Tanzania took the lead in ensuring that it, and as many as its example could persuade, fulfilled the Organization's resolution. Nyerere further committed himself by publishing an article in *The Observer* explaining why the severance of relations was necessary if Britain failed to act. Tanzania and Nkrumah's Ghana were the only two Commonwealth countries that fulfilled the Organization's resolution; and Tanzania was the first to take the plunge.

Reports indicate that the break with Britain was a commitment undertaken on President Nyerere's own initiative, and that his cabinet was not consulted. And there even is evidence to suggest that not all of his ministers would have supported such a move had they been consulted. Some critics in East Africa saw the act as an *expensive* moral gesture, other critics abroad saw it as an *empty* moral gesture. In the words of *The Times*, "Breaking relations with Britain was hardly a requirement of non-alignment. It was a burnt offering to the purity—or rigidity—of Dr. Nyerere's principles on the Rhodesian issue."[10]

The cost of these principles concerning Rhodesia was the loss of an interest free loan of £7.5 million which had been agreed upon (but not in writing) between Britain and Tanzania. This amount was frozen when Tanzania broke off diplomatic relations. The high cost of this moral gesture might well have been the most important link between the Rhodesian issue and the Arusha Declaration which followed some thirteen months later. For a number of years Nyerere had been feeling the "painful" constraints of economic dependence both on domestic planning and on foreign policy. The disenchantment with foreign aid as a method of achieving domestic purposes came quite early.

When Tanganyika launched a three-year development plan soon after the attainment of independence, it was in optimistic expectation of significant external underpinning. The country's gross national product

---

[10] See *The Times*, June 6, 1966. See also William Tordoff, *Government and Politics in Tanzania* (Nairobi, 1967), 176-77.

in 1961 was £168,000,000 and its per capita income £18. A persistent alternation between floods and drought, combined with the more common phenomenon of declining terms of trade, helped to make the economic future of the new state look ominous indeed. The value of exports fell in 1961 by 11 per cent while staple food prices fell by 16 per cent.[11]

Nyerere, then Prime Minister, went overseas shortly thereafter to try to obtain as much external aid as possible. Even then he was complaining that external donors were less interested in stable countries like Tanganyika than they should perhaps have been. Soon after, Tanganyika started up the long road toward a position of self-sufficiency. At first this was limited to self-help schemes that were launched as a part of the attempt to meet the targets of the first three-year plan. When regional commissioners took office on March 1, 1962, they had been charged by the then Prime Minister, Rashidi Kawawa, with their "first job" of "interpreting the Three Year Development Plan in practical terms right down to the village level which has not so far been done." The original plan had included the small amount of £70,000 to provide for self-help schemes under the Community Development Programme, but partly because resources were revealed to be more limited than had been hoped, internal self-help activities assumed extra importance in the Plan. By February 1963 Paul Bomani, the Minister of Finance, told the Economic Commission for Africa that self-help schemes had saved Tanganyika £500,000.[12]

This early experience of inadequate aid and the need to resort to self-help schemes was the beginning of Nyerere's quest for relative self-sufficiency. He was beginning to feel that there was a fundamental indignity in being indigent. In September 1963 he said that although Tanganyikans had won the right to international equality when the country became independent, a man who was ignorant, who could not produce enough food for himself, or who suffered from disfiguring diseases could not really stand on terms of equality with all others.[13]

Foreign policy preferences as well as domestic plans were sometimes frustrated by an inadequate external response. For instance, domestic and international considerations became intertwined on the

[11] Speech by Minister of Finance to the National Assembly, June 5, 1962. Consult Joseph S. Nye, Jr., "Tanganyika's Self-Help," *Transition,* 11 (Nov. 1963), 35. See also Nye, *Pan Africanism and East African Integration* (Cambridge, Mass., 1966), 167-69. Henry Bienen, *Tanzania: Party Transformation and Economic Development* (Princeton, 1967), 264-73.

[12] See *Tanganyika Standard,* Feb. 3, 1962, and Mar. 5, 1963. See also Nye, "Tanganyika's Self-Help," 35-39.

[13] See "The Stress Is Now on Dignity," *Sunday News* (Dar es Salaam), Sept. 8, 1963.

issue of diplomatic representation from the two Germanys in Tanzania. Soon after the revolution in Zanzibar, East Germany had established itself on the island. However, when the union with Tanganyika was formed, external affairs as well as external trade and borrowing were constitutionally entrusted to the Parliament and Executive of the United Republic. Therefore, if there were to be East German representation in the new United Republic of Tanzania, the East German Ambassador had to be accredited to the union government in Dar es Salaam and not to the island's regime. However, at that time, Dar es Salaam had a fully accredited West German Embassy; and the Federal Republic's "Hallstein Doctrine" implied that the new United Tanzania could not combine West German representation with a fully accredited East German Embassy transferred from Zanzibar to Dar es Salaam. The Tanzanian union government, as a concession to the Federal Republic's "Hallstein Doctrine," denied East Germany full diplomatic representation and granted it status only as a consulate-general. But the West Germans were still not satisfied with this concession. As an expression of their reservations they stopped all military aid to Tanzania. Nyerere reacted by saying that if the West Germans were going to withdraw military aid, they might as well withdraw all forms of aid.[14]

The problem of the two Germanys and the problem of Rhodesia's declaration of independence in fact occurred in the same year, 1965. Because of the issue of representation Tanzania sustained the loss of West German aid at a time when much of the Five-Year Development Plan depended on it, and, on the Rhodesian issue Tanzania sacrificed £7.5 million aid when she broke off diplomatic relations with Britain. The two events strongly reinforced a feeling that Nyerere had been developing ever since he returned relatively empty-handed from his travels for aid in 1961. In 1964 Nyerere had, in a speech at Tukuyu, asserted that Tanganyikans were enjoying only one fourth self-government. "Complete independence means being in a state of self-supportment."

This quest for "self-supportment" was the starting point of the doctrine of *self-reliance* which was enunciated by the Arusha Declaration in 1967. With the Arusha Declaration Tanzania said to itself that its previous development plans had assumed too readily the presence of outside capital in Tanzania. The Declaration asserted that two contradictions were involved in this assumption. One contradiction lay in the simple fact that capital was precisely what a poor country did not

---

[14] See *The Nationalist* (Dar es Salaam), Aug. 20, 1964; *The Standard* (Dar es Salaam), June 10, 1966.

have access to. "We are trying to overcome our economic weakness by using the weapons of the economically strong—weapons which in fact we do not possess." The second contradiction which the Arusha Declaration pointed out was an alleged confusion of means and ends. The Declaration argued that the availability of money was the fruit of development for a poor country rather than the means toward it.

> We will continue to use money; and each year we will use more money for the various development projects than we used the previous year because that will be one of the signs of our development. What we are saying, however, is that from now on we shall know what is the foundation and what is the fruit of development. Between MONEY and PEOPLE it is obvious that the people and their HARD WORK are the foundation of development, and money is one of the fruits of that hard work.[15]

Signs of this disenchantment with the policy of relying too heavily on foreign aid are scattered throughout the pages of the Arusha Declaration. The implications of Tanzania's severance of relations with Britain over the Rhodesian Declaration of Independence were particularly galling. The £7.5 million lost as a result of the break with Britain was certainly a major blow; but at least as insulting were the forms of foreign aid which British indulgence allowed to continue in Tanzania. An impressive proportion of the technical assistance received by Tanzania, ranging from teachers in the villages to economic advisers to the government, continued to be from Britain. In other words, the implication was that Tanzania could afford the moral gesture of breaking diplomatic relations with Britain only because it was thought that Britain would not be intolerant enough to do to Tanzania what General de Gaulle did to Guinée when the latter voted for independence in 1958. Furthermore, Guinée had, after all, been prepared to exchange aid for independence whereas Tanzania's moral gesture in support of a somewhat unrealistic resolution by the Organization of African Unity was therefore more daring.[16]

For a leader with the proud sensibilities of Nyerere, the continued

---

[15] The Arusha Declaration, 5, 16-17.

[16] Nyerere virtually admitted this lack of realism of the Organization of African Unity ultimatum in the article he wrote for The Observer on the eve of the ultimatum's deadline. The resolution had demanded that Britain should, by 15 December 1965, have taken action which had resulted, or was about to result in the overthrow of the regime in Rhodesia. But by the time Nyerere wrote his article for The Observer all that he was demanding was, in fact, a new toughness in Britain's policy toward the problem. See The Observer, 12 Dec. 1965.

reliance on British tolerance was embarrassing and demeaning. When Tanzania first broke off diplomatic relations with Britain it was in the company of eight other countries. By the spring of 1968 most of these eight countries had reestablished or were about to reestablish links with Britain, but Tanzania seemed determined to be the last to resume relations. And yet of the nine countries that broke off diplomatic relations, Tanzania had been the greatest beneficiary of British aid. Again, the break must have resulted from Nyerere's conception of what Tanzania ought to do to become self-reliant. As we indicated, he had, after all, himself equated indigence with indignity in situations of dependent relationships.[17]

These factors, joined with the problem of the two Germanys and with the earlier inadequate external response to Tanzania's requests for aid, helped to make the aftermath of Rhodesia's Declaration of Independence an extra catalyst in the process of Tanzania's militant reappraisal of itself.

A subsidiary factor was the thriving business of transporting oil to Zambia, which rapidly assumed significant proportions in the wake of Rhodesia's Declaration. In absolute terms, the commerce of transporting oil to Zambia from Tanzania was perhaps negligible; but in the context of Tanzania's commercial underdevelopment and relative paucity of enterprises of this kind, the transportation and marketing of oil provided a dramatic new economic boost. A number of political leaders in Tanzania soon established a stake in this new enterprise; there was good money to be made with proper organization and handling. There is reason to believe that the dramatic introduction of this new commercial enterprise, and the greed which characterized the response of some important Tanzanians, were additional considerations prompting Nyerere's reexamination of the whole problem of conflict of interest as a factor in the conditions for holding public office. The resolutions of the Arusha Declaration relating to leadership demanded that those who held governmental or party jobs, and even those who were simply Members of Parliament, were to relinquish commercial sources of income, second salaries, directorships of business firms, and houses that they let for profit. Nyerere had, in fact, for some time been feeling his way toward this kind of leadership ethic. The National Service, which was announced in October 1966 and which was designed to involve university graduates and the graduates of comparable institutions in the activities of nation-building, was partly inspired by a desire to mitigate the dangers of self-aggrandizement

---

[17] The other countries which broke off diplomatic relations with Britain on the issue of Rhodesia were Ghana, Mali, Guinée, the United Arab Republic, Algeria, Mauritania, Congo (Brazzaville), and the Sudan.

which higher education might promote in those who were privileged to receive it.[18]

What was significant about the transportation of petroleum products to Zambia was that it highlighted the compelling temptation of any new possibilities for profit-making. The petroleum trade to Zambia was, in other words, something of a last straw; it re-emphasized the temptations which the possibility of rapid money-making could present to officeholders. Here again a factor connected with the aftermath of Rhodesia's Declaration reinforced the mounting case for the kind of militant reappraisal set out in the Arusha Declaration.

Conclusion

I have attempted to demonstrate not only that socialism as a radical approach to social change is itself a form of protest, but also that in the particular case of Tanzania the need for socialist measures was emphasized by domestic underdevelopment and the politics of international contact.

The Arusha Declaration shows the influence of Leninist notions of exploitation and imperial dependence. The concept of "neo-colonialism" is, after all, itself derived from the kind of economic interpretations of imperialism which we associate with Hobson and Lenin. Lenin had described imperialism as the highest stage of capitalism, and Nkrumah entitled one of his books *Neo-Colonialism, the Last Stage of Imperialism*.[19]

Nyerere, in line with many other nationalist leaders in Africa, has often made two assumptions which are or can be mutually contradictory. One assumption is that real political independence is impossible without economic independence. The other assumption underlies the demand that aid to small countries should come with no strings attached. If it is possible for a small country to obtain aid with no political strings attached, then it is possible to receive aid and still remain politically independent. Yet, because the country needs aid it cannot claim full economic independence. It follows, therefore, that it is possible to be genuinely independent politically while remaining economically dependent.

This conclusion reinforces African assumptions about neo-colonial-

[18] See Lionel Cliffe, "Education in Socialist Tanzania," *Mawazo*, I (1967), 73-80; Julius K. Nyerere, *Education for Self-Reliance* (Dar es Salaam, 1967). Refer also to A. A. Mazrui, "Political Superannuation and the Trans-Class Man," 81-96, and A. A. Mazrui, "Political Hygiene and Cultural Transition in Africa," *Journal of Asian and African Studies,* forthcoming.

[19] See Mazrui, "Nkrumah: the Leninist Czar," *Transition*, 26 (1966), 9-17.

ism. Many nationalists have believed that any aid—be it from the East or from the West—is at least *by intention* neo-colonialist. How is it then that Africans can accept aid without being overcome by neo-colonialism? For an answer we have to refer to what one might call the Doctrine of Balanced Benefaction—the idea that the great defense against neo-colonialism is to diversify one's benefactors. In this case both the East and the West are deemed to be neo-colonialist in intention—but one could prevent them from being neo-colonialist in actual practice by balancing the aid of one side with aid from the other.

Tanzania has taken a decisive lead in trying to live up to the Doctrine of Balanced Benefaction. Over the years the country's benefactors have included the United States, the Soviet Union, the Communist Chinese, the West Germans, Israelis, Egyptians, and others. Even on specific projects Tanzania has sometimes, either by accident or design, ended up dividing one project between two ideological camps. The preliminary survey for the Tanzania-Zambia railway was to be paid for by the West (Britain and Canada), while the actual railway was scheduled to be financed by mainland China.[20]

But in the Arusha Declaration the Doctrine of Balanced Benefaction is less conspicuous than the Doctrine of Self-Reliance. There is in the Arusha Declaration more of a conviction that aid, even when balanced in its sources, tends to favor the dissolution of national autonomy. In the words of the Declaration "Independence means self-reliance. Independence cannot be real if a Nation depends upon gifts and loans from another for its development. Even if there was a Nation or Nations prepared to give us all the money we need for our development, it would be improper for us to accept such assistance without asking ourselves how this would affect our independence and our very survival as a nation."[21]

In response to this assumption, Tanzania embarked, as I have noted, on a new and militant program of public ownership, collective economic exertions, and national austerity. It entered a new stage of socialistic organization. What ought to be remembered is that this was partly due to a domestic revolt against Tanzania's own indigence and complacency, and partly to an international protest against the constraints of economic relationships with others.

[20] See *East African Standard*, Mar. 27, 1968. The preliminary Anglo-Canadian *feasibility* survey is not to be confused with the subsequent *operational* survey by the Chinese in readiness for construction. The former survey produced the Maxwell Stamp Report which found the project viable. But the West was still not keen on participating in the actual construction.

[21] *Arusha Declaration*, 9.

THE ORGANIZATION OF AFRICAN UNITY

AS AN INSTRUMENT AND FORUM

OF PROTEST

YASHPAL TANDON

On January 13, 1963, Togo's President Sylvanus Olympio was assassinated. President Kwame Nkrumah of Ghana was alleged to have been implicated in the assassination. Coming as it did at a crucial moment in Africa's history, the incident had considerable political impact. Thus, at the meeting of the African heads of state held in Addis Ababa in May 1963 to launch the Organization of African Unity (OAU), Nkrumah was relatively isolated. Since he was the champion of the radical African states that had formed the Casablanca group during the Congo crisis, his relative isolation weakened the impact of the radical group at the crucial drafting stage of the OAU Charter. In addition, the host country of the Casablanca Conference, Morocco, was not even present at Addis Ababa because Mauritania, a country that Morocco then considered had no right to an independent existence, was in attendance. The impact of the Casablanca group was therefore doubly weakened at this significant moment.

The Casablanca group had propagated revolutionary norms for African international relations, one of them being that the real enemies of independent Africa were the foreign colonial powers who continued to control Africa by virtue of their economic power, which they manipulated through "client" governments in "nominally independent" African states. After the death of its first nationalist leader, Patrice Lumumba, Congo (Léopoldville)[1] was held to be a paradigm of such a state.[2] But the new Africa was not going to let itself be a victim of

[1] On 30 June 1966 the name Léopoldville was changed to Kinshasa. In this article we deal with events in the Congo before this date. It is proper therefore to retain the old name Congo (Léopoldville).

[2] Congo's central place in African international politics was underlined by Guinée's delegate to the United Nations: "We are convinced that if the policy of territorial division were to succeed in the Congo the entire world would undoubt-

neo-colonialism. And the only way to achieve and ensure freedom was through concerted effort. In such a context, one could describe the concern of a genuinely independent state with the affairs of another controlled by neo-colonialism as a legitimate act of "intervention." In other words, according to the rhetoric of the radical states, intervention designed to deliver a state from the neo-colonial control of other states was not illegal.[3]

But this radical doctrine of African international relations was not accepted at Addis Ababa. The only concession to radicalism in the OAU Charter was the clause that would have had the Organization eradicate "all forms of colonialism" from Africa. Relations between independent African states were to be governed by the same classical rules of international behavior that governed relations in other parts of the world. Thus, the first three out of the seven principles of the Organization of African Unity Charter referred to sovereign equality, noninterference in internal affairs of other states, and mutual respect for sovereignty and territorial integrity. The Charter was largely a triumph of conservatism.[4]

In a sense, the OAU itself was more important than its Charter, for only it could deal with concrete issues. By providing rules for dealing with interventions the Charter created the possibility of real tests of the relevance of the Organization. A study of how the OAU functioned as an instrument of protest against the outside world and as a forum in which members protested against each other is the purpose of this paper. We shall take four concrete situations—two in relation to the external world, and two dealing with inter-African practices —as test cases.

The OAU as an Instrument of Protest Against External Interference

Two critical instances of OAU involvement with powers outside Africa were the Congo crisis of 1964–65 and the Rhodesian crisis of 1965–67.

---

edly be a spectator to the destruction and breaking up of Africa to the satisfaction of the colonial powers. . . . As far as we are concerned, Guinea could well be the Congo, and the Congo, Africa." Quoted in L. W. Martin, *Neutralism and Nonalignment* (New York, 1962), 51.

[3] For a description of the revolutionary body of thought in African diplomacy, see Robert C. Good, "Changing Patterns of African International Relations," *The American Political Science Review*, LVIII (1964), 632-34. For a text of the Charter of Casablanca, see Colin Legum, *Pan-Africanism* (New York, 1962), 187-92.

[4] See T. O. Elias, "The Charter of the Organization of African Unity," *The American Journal of International Law*, LIX (1965), 243-67.

The Congo was a case of protest against what many African states regarded as unwarranted and unsolicited interference by external powers in the affairs of an African country, an interference which had implications for the peace and stability of the whole continent. Rhodesia was a case of protest against what virtually all African states regarded as a betrayal of British responsibility toward the African majority in Rhodesia. The issue of foreign power intervention in Africa was common in both cases. But whereas in the Congo the central problem facing the OAU was how to *prevent* foreign intervention, in Rhodesia it was how to *encourage* foreign intervention. How and with what success did the OAU Africanize the Congo crisis and internationalize the Rhodesian crisis?

Foreign Interventions in the Congo, 1964 to 1965

The Congo continued as a testing ground for African international relations by providing the OAU with its first major conflict with foreign powers. The first Congo crisis, from July 1960 to May 1963, had virtually split Africa into two camps.[5] The Congo reconciliation of 1963 prepared the stage for a reconciliation on the continental scale in Addis Ababa in May of that year; but it did not last long. By March 1964, the Lumumbist members of the Congolese Parliament had deserted and had formed a government-in-opposition, the National Liberation Council. By June, the National Liberation Council had "liberated" wide areas of Kwilu, North Katanga, and Maniema, and the Upper Congo, and had established their headquarters in Stanleyville, symbolically important since it was there that Lumumba's immediate successor, Antoine Gizenga, had formed the first radical secessionist regime in 1962.[6]

The precarious central government led by Cyrille Adoulla was then dissolved by President Kasavubu, who called Moise Tshombe to power from exile in Spain. Only Tshombe had the resources—the connections with mercenary organizations, with arms-supplying Western governments, and with international financial concerns interested in the economy of the Congo—and the tenacity to raise a strong enough military force to fight against the insurgents.

Immediately upon assuming power on June 26, 1964, Tshombe sent for the 2,000 Katangese gendarmes who had been waiting in Angola. He recruited white mercenary soldiers from South Africa, Rhodesia, and Europe; appointed Michel Struelens, a Belgian, as his

[5] For an account of the first Congo crisis, see Catherine Hoskyns, *The Congo Since Independence* (London, 1965).

[6] See above, M. Crawford Young "Rebellion and the Congo," 969-1011.

personal adviser on foreign affairs; and made a successful deal with the United States for military assistance. On 19 August, the Pentagon confirmed that it had sent 30 aircraft and a "small number" of B-26K bombers, piloted by Americans and Cubans and guarded and maintained by 50 United States paratroopers and 56 Air Force maintenance men, to the Congo.[7]

In the normal course of international relations, Tshombe's request for foreign military assistance would not have been regarded as the OAU's concern. Its Charter, as indicated earlier, had recognized rights normally claimed by sovereign states including, presumably, the right to seek foreign assistance. And yet, a month after the first major supply of American arms to the Congo, the OAU called its Council of Ministers into extraordinary session to discuss the Congo situation.

If the OAU could describe the Congo situation as one of civil war, it could then make a good case for seeking to prevent foreign intervention. There was a good precedent in the United Nations efforts from 1960 to 1963 to restrict unilateral foreign intervention in the Congo. Not surprisingly, therefore, Tshombe argued that the National Liberation Council was a group of "rebels" which it was the government's duty to suppress, with foreign assistance if necessary. The Tshombe thesis was not, however, acceptable to a number of the OAU states. While none actually recognized the government of the National Liberation Council, they refused to accept the Congo government's description of it as "rebellious." In the words of Milton Obote, Uganda's Prime Minister:

> Now regarding Gbenye . . . we in Uganda cannot call this man a rebel. How do we prove that he is a rebel? We know that he has political differences with the Government in Leopoldville and our concern is to try to bring this man and the others round the table to talk together. . . .[8]

And at the OAU meeting itself, Kenya's Foreign Minister, Joseph Murumbi, had appealed to the "warring factions" in the Congo to negotiate a peaceful settlement.[9] Murumbi had, thus, in one phrase, raised the status of the activities of the National Liberation Council to acts of "war" and had reduced the status of the central government to that of a "faction."

Two further factors helped to obtain a consensus in the OAU

[7] Keesing's Contemporary Archives (1963–64), 20424.
[8] *Uganda Parliamentary Debates,* XXXIX, Third Session, 2nd meeting (15 Feb. 1965), 671.
[9] Keesing's Archives (1963–64), 20425.

seeking to raise the moral and political status of the National Liberation Council to that of the government and to prevent foreign intervention in the Congo. The first was the personality of Tshombe. Arguments advanced by states critical of Tshombe's regime, to the effect that Tshombe had come to power "undemocratically," were in the main rationalizations to deny his authority as chief executive of a sovereign state to seek foreign assistance. After all, Tshombe's was not the only government in Africa whose legitimacy or authority was questionable. The aversion to Tshombe was personal and ideological rather than legalistic. The crude simplicity of the Moroccan delegate's argument against Tshombe's seating at the July 1964 meeting of the OAU was broadly representative:

> "How can you imagine that as a representative of our national conscience I can be seated at a conference table or at a banquet at the same time as a representative of this state of rebellion and secession?"[10]

In other words, the Moroccan delegate found the memory of the man who had led the secession in Katanga stronger than the respect that was now due him as the Prime Minister of the Congo. Katanga had become for many a symbol of the covert reimposition of colonial or quasi-colonial authority in a newly independent African country, and Tshombe was identified as the African prophet of neo-colonialism.[11] That Tshombe was now not a secessionist, but the head of a central government, probably only made matters worse, since the whole of the Congo was now in danger of being subverted by neo-colonial forces. Whether justified or not, this line of thinking obviously had a significant impact on the deliberations of the Council of Ministers in Addis Ababa.

The second factor that helped to build up the image of the National Liberation Council and lower that of the central government was Tshombe's use of white mercenaries; this seemed to negate the whole ethos of African renaissance. After all, the African liberation movement was as much a protest against white domination in Africa as it was a protest against colonialism. The fact that a large number of the mercenaries employed by Tshombe came from South Africa was

[10] Quoted in Immanuel Wallerstein, *Africa: The Politics of Unity* (New York, 1967), 84.

[11] On 5 Oct. 1964, Tshombe left Léopoldville to attend the Non-Aligned Conference in Cairo, but his plane was not allowed to land at the Cairo airport. The organizers of the conference, President Nasser of the United Arab Republic, President Tito of Yugoslavia, and Mrs. Bandaranaike of Ceylon, explained this action as a "sincere desire to avoid unnecessary difficulties liable to impede the normal work of the Conference." See *The Times* (London), 6 Oct. 1964.

a source of great humiliation: African states were frustrated by not being able to help Africans in white-controlled South Africa, but South Africans could come into an independent black-controlled African state and indulge in acts of massacre. Very few states considered the sovereign right of the government of the Congo to employ mercenaries ethically superior to their own collective right to protect Africans from indignities imposed by white soldiers. Many states accordingly felt themselves morally justified in rendering assistance to the *simba* (popular army troops) in their fight against the mercenaries.

Therefore, at the Council of Ministers meeting in Addis Ababa, in September 1964, Tshombe fought a losing battle. A large number of normally moderate states joined the ranks of the radical states in identifying the internal situation in the Congo as of legitimate concern to the OAU. In order to have a wide consensus, however, direct condemnation of Tshombe was avoided.[12] (The final resolution of September 10 was passed by a vote of twenty-seven in favor, with seven abstentions.) In fact, Tshombe's right to seek foreign assistance was not directly challenged, the Council of Ministers deciding instead to call upon foreign powers to cease interference in the Congo, a general request that in fact was aimed at the United States. The Council also called upon Tshombe to expel all mercenaries from the Congo.[13]

But if the Congolese government were to be deprived of support from both mercenaries and the American government, was not the OAU really asking the Congolese government to underwrite its own demise at the hands of the National Liberation forces? Clearly, the government of the Congo was unlikely to accept this decision unless the OAU could also ensure that the National Liberation Council, too, ceased receiving assistance from outside sources. As a price for expelling the mercenaries, Tshombe furthermore demanded that his government's attempt to restore order be assisted by troops from African states. The idea of an OAU peace-keeping force, however, was stillborn. The Council of Ministers decided instead that a ten-nation commission of the OAU would be set up to attempt to mediate between the Congolese government and the National Liberation Council.

The ten-nation Conciliation Commission, consisting of the Cameroon, Ethiopia, Ghana, Guinea, Kenya, Nigeria, Somalia, Tunisia, the United Arab Republic, and Upper Volta, and headed by President Jomo Kenyatta of Kenya, failed completely in its mediation between the Congolese government and the National Liberation Council. But we are for the present concerned only with how it handled the question of foreign interference in the Congolese civil war.

[12] OAU Resolution of 10 Sept. 1964, ECM/Res.5(III).
[13] Ibid., par. 1.

One of the first acts of the Conciliation Commission was to send a delegation headed by Joseph Murumbi, Kenya's Foreign Minister, to the United States to persuade the United States government to stop supplying military assistance to the Congo. The Congolese government not unexpectedly protested that such a mission was a manifest interference in the sovereign affairs of the Congo. From a purely practical point of view it was clearly inconceivable that the delegation could succeed in breaking the Léopoldville-Washington axis unless arrangements were made at the same time to stop aid allegedly reaching the National Liberation Council from Communist sources, and unless alternative means were found to help the central Congolese government to restore its authority. On 23 September, the United States government advised the Conciliation Commission it could not meet the Murumbi mission without the participation of the Congolese government. Tshombe, of course, was not inclined to take part in the discussion. When the Murumbi mission arrived in Washington, it was accordingly not even received by President Johnson—an incident interpreted by the mission as a serious affront to the OAU. As an act of courtesy, however, Dean Rusk, the Secretary of State, saw the mission on 30 September, and issued a communiqué of dubious worth promising United States support in bringing about Congolese national reconciliation.[14] The question of military assistance to the Congo was not discussed, the United States holding that a similar mission should have been sent to Peking to stop Communist assistance to the National Liberation Council.

What may we say, at this point, about the OAU as an instrument of protest against foreign interference in the Congo? This particular experience may be reduced to the proposition that a good political case, supported by a considerable majority of the OAU members, had been carried through to a very poor diplomatic payoff.

As it happened, the rhetoric of protest was in this case mainly that of what Immanuel Wallerstein has called the radical "core" of the African unity movement.[15] The "periphery" of the movement, which believed in preserving the traditional norms of international behavior, curiously enough acquiesced in the demands of the radical "core." Thus, the alleged agents of external assistance to the National Liberation Council—African states like Algeria and the United Arab Republic and non-African states like China—were not condemned. Therefore, it was not surprising that the Conciliation Commission should have sent a mission only to the United States. Obviously, the personality of Tshombe and his use of mercenaries had agitated almost everyone,

[14] See *East African Standard* (Nairobi), 2 Oct. 1964.
[15] See Wallerstein, *The Politics of Unity*, 21.

and thus made it possible for the leaders of the radical states to gain support of the more conservative states. Considerations of emotion based upon an understandable aversion to white mercenaries inflicting indignities on black *simba,* and on equally understandable fears that continued American support for the government of the Congo might plant American power, exercised through an African agent, in a large and rich territory in the heart of Africa, superseded considerations regarding the "sovereign" rights of the Congo state.[16]

But while the rhetoric of protest was politically understandable, it contained its own seed of diplomatic failure. Clearly, protest by itself was not likely to prevent Tshombe from using mercenaries and American power. But the OAU had no means of pressuring Tshombe, who was peculiarly immune to mild threats of diplomatic isolation. Furthermore, the OAU had lost whatever moral authority it had over the Congolese government by taking a too openly anti-Tshombe position. The idea of an OAU peace-keeping force, which might conceivably have persuaded Tshombe to expel his mercenaries, was killed at birth by a situational dilemma that required the OAU force, had it been created, to be deployed against the very forces toward which the radical African states were sympathetic. The Organization clearly was not going to be used to impose on the Congo the authority of a man widely identified as an agent of a foreign power. There was a certain circularity about it all. The less the OAU was willing to help Tshombe because he was dependent on foreign powers, the more he was driven into the hands of foreigners.

The failure of the OAU in September 1964 to stop the Congolese government from using mercenaries and American power produced, barely two months later, the most explosive situation yet to involve the OAU. This was the Stanleyville incident. In the middle of November, in an attempt to stem the tide of war which was going against them, the National Liberation "government" in Stanleyville captured an estimated 1,400 white residents of the area and held them as hostages. The intent clearly was to put pressure on the United States to persuade Tshombe to cease hostilities. On 24 November, in the midst of attempts by the OAU to get the hostages released, 600 Belgian paratroopers—transported in American aircraft from British-held Ascension Island—made a dramatic landing at Stanleyville airport. On seeing the paratroopers the National Liberation Council soldiers opened fire on the hostages, killing about thirty. The rest were rescued. Afterward there was a massive onslaught on National Liberation Council forces, which led to the death of thousands of

[16] See above, Young, "Rebellion and the Congo," 974-75.

Africans. Was the landing justified? Why could the OAU not do anything about the situation?

Even if the paratroop landing were justified, and a great majority of African states thought that it was not, the cry of protest that followed in Africa had little to do with the legal rights and wrongs of the situation. The Stanleyville operation was a kind of revelation, a demonstration of the dire vulnerability of Africa to the power of the former colonial powers and their ally, the United States. If the colonial powers decided at any time to intervene militarily in an African state to secure their interests, there was very little Africans could do to prevent the enforcement of their will. An unidentified African diplomat, presumably French-speaking, told *Le Monde:*

> We discovered fairly soon that independence had little meaning and that economically things were worse than under the colonial regime. Yet we had hoped that independence, UN membership, a flag, a Government, a President of the Republic, Ministers and a small national army would all give us human dignity we had not known for centuries. But at Stanleyville this dignity was made mockery of. We were shown that we were not really masters in our own house.[17]

Certainly, the Western powers had international law on their side and could legally justify their intervention on the grounds that they had the authority of the Tshombe government. But this act only confirmed African fears that, because of the economic and political power which the West possessed, it could bring regimes to power in Africa which would sanction every act of Western intervention. And there could always be a legal pretext, like the right under traditional law to intervene to protect the lives and property of Western nationals in Africa.

Nkrumah accordingly described the operation as "a flagrant act of aggression."[18] President Julius Nyerere considered it "reminiscent of Pearl Harbor"[19] in that the West had committed aggression right under the noses of the Africans just as the Japanese had done against the Americans in 1941. Haile Selassie of Ethiopia, more mindful of tradition, saw it as a "veritable manifestation of neo-colonialism on the African scene."[20]

But why could the OAU not have prevented the operation by securing the release of the hostages? One Western rationale for dealing with the matter directly was that the OAU had made no progress

[17] Quoted in Keesing's Archives (1965–66), 20563.
[18] Ibid.
[19] Ibid.
[20] Ibid.

in freeing the hostages.[21] As a matter of fact, President Kenyatta, chairman of the Congo Conciliation Commission, had begun to use his influence with the National Liberation Council "government" of Stanleyville immediately on learning of the existence of the hostages. Having secured from Stanleyville an agreement that the hostages would not be harmed, he arranged a meeting between Thomas Kanza, the Foreign Minister of the Stanleyville regime, and William Attwood, the American ambassador to Kenya. The purpose of the meeting was to negotiate a settlement between the United States and Belgium which demanded an unconditional release of the hostages, and Stanleyville's demand for a political *quid pro quo* in exchange for freeing the hostages.

Was such a negotiated settlement possible? Was it really true, as the United States claimed, that it had no power over Tshombe and therefore could not really "buy" the release of the hostages? Could the Stanleyville regime be relied upon to free its prisoners after it had secured political concessions from the United States? An answer to these questions will never be known. Kanza arrived in Nairobi on 22 November for the talks—two days earlier a battalion of Belgian parachute troops had been flown to Ascension Island. On 21 November, Tshombe had announced that his government had authorized the Belgian government to "send an adequate rescue force to accomplish the humanitarian purpose of evacuating civilians held as hostages by the rebels and authorize the American government to furnish the necessary transport."[22] Thus, even before the talks had begun in Nairobi, Belgium and the United States had secured both the capacity to intervene and the authorization. On 23 November, a day after the talks had begun, a Belgian paratroop battalion was flown to the Kamina base in the Congo.

According to Attwood, he had no authority to negotiate anything other than the unconditional release of the hostages. If these were his instructions, then obviously Kanza could not have hoped to get political concessions in return for the release of the hostages. From the point of view of the OAU, the significant thing was that the paratroop operation should have begun while negotiations were still ostensibly in progress. Attwood obviously knew that the operation was planned for the early morning of 24 November, since before the news of the paratroop landing had even reached Nairobi he had declared that Kanza's proposals were "totally unacceptable."[23] The American-Belgian action took Kenyatta by surprise. What he did not know, or refused to

21 William Attwood, *The Reds and the Blacks* (New York, 1967), 206-16.
22 Keesing's Archives (1965–66), 20561.
23 Attwood, *The Reds and the Blacks,* 215.

believe, was that the West had already ruled out a negotiated settlement in favor of military action.[24] The OAU therefore not surprisingly felt humiliated at having its efforts toward a negotiated settlement prematurely frustrated by Western military action.

The United States, however, denied that it was a military solution. On the very day of the landing, the State Department declared that the paratroop action was "a humanitarian and not a military one."[25] In this statement there is obviously a confusion, probably deliberate, between the purpose of the mission and the means used. The purpose might have been humanitarian, but the means used were undeniably military. One might even question whether the purpose of the mission was purely humanitarian. In the light of the aftermath of the Stanleyville operation, it would appear not. The blow that the Stanleyville "government" suffered in November 1964 was one from which it could never recover. It lost hundreds of its men as well as its headquarters in Stanleyville. Before it could revive, Tshombe, with the help of mercenaries, carried the operation through to a vigorous conclusion and, by March 1965, the National Liberation forces were badly routed in the northern Congo.

The OAU did not, as one might have expected, meet in a hurriedly called emergency meeting to protest this action of the Western powers. Such a protest would have been of no consequence to the West. What was needed was the condemnation of the West in a world body, not in the OAU. There was a widespread demonstration of support in countries of Asia and the Communist world (American embassy windows were broken in places as distant as Jakarta and Moscow); and the best forum for merging their sympathies into a collective global protest was obviously the United Nations.

But what the African states gained in globalizing the protest, they lost by being forced to tone down the language of protest, for at the Security Council, the Western nations stood in defense of their action and were ready with their veto (any one of the three—the United States, Britain, or France—could have used it) to resist any strong condemnation of their action. Thus, while the OAU could conceivably have condemned the Belgian-American action as an act of "aggression," such a resolution was impossible in the Security Council. Thus the Council resolution of 30 December 1964, passed five weeks after the operation, made no reference to Stanleyville and simply called on foreign states to refrain from interfering in the Congo.[26]

The Western defense of its action was even supported by African

[24] Ibid., 216-20.
[25] Keesing's Archives (1965–66), 20562.
[26] Security Council Resolution 199 (1964). UN Document S/6129.

states. To the utter consternation of the radical African states, Jaja Wachuku of Nigeria dismissed the African complaint in the Security Council as inadmissible on the grounds that the Western action had a proper legal basis because it had been authorized by the sovereign government of the Congo. Instead, he condemned the African states which continued to interfere in the affairs of the Congo.[27] Clearly, there were states in Africa which, whatever the basis of their moral indignation, were still prepared to uphold the principles of international law. African protest against the Stanleyville operation thus lacked the force of unanimity. Nevertheless the loudest voices in the OAU were the ones that were indignantly critical of the Stanleyville operation. States like Ethiopia and Kenya, usually not identified as radical states and considered as marginally conservative in the language of African diplomatic parlance, were particularly shocked at the American lack of faith in the OAU. Ghana, Guinée, Algeria, and the United Arab Republic were probably expected to be a priori anti-American, but the reactions of Kenya, Ethiopia, and several French-speaking African states were not a priori anti-American.

Kenya's pride was particularly wounded because Kenyatta's attempt to mediate between the rival parties in the Congo had been thwarted by the Stanleyville operation. Thus, Murumbi protested to the Security Council: "The American-Belgian intervention, with British collaboration . . . was an insult to my President, an attempt to humiliate the OAU, and to disregard African interests. At best, it was a very poor and impatient exhibition of diplomatic negotiation."[28]

For the OAU the Stanleyville operation dramatically confirmed the weakness of the Organization as an effective forum of protest against external intervention: The OAU had dismally failed to prevent United States intervention.

The Rhodesian Problem, 1965 to 1967

On 11 November 1965, in defiance of the British government, the white minority in the self-governing British colony of Rhodesia declared independence. From the very outset, African states took the position that since Britain was still constitutionally answerable for Rhodesia, it was

[27] Security Council, *Official Records*, 19th Year, 1176th mtg. (15 Dec. 1964), 2-14. Jaja Wachuku, of Nigeria, said: "I will ask this Council to throw out the first charge—it is of no consequence whatsoever—and to concentrate its attention on the second, which presents a substantial case, because we know as a matter of fact—I know, as the Foreign Minister of Nigeria—that there is intervention."

[28] Security Council, *Official Records* (15 Dec. 1964), 13.

up to Britain to end the white rebellion and to restore the due process of law that should in time transfer power to the black majority in the country.

The position made sense in legal terms. Britain had itself declared that, although Rhodesia had enjoyed internal self-government since 1923, the final act of granting Rhodesia independence was Britain's. London was therefore committed to deal with this act of rebellion. If the African states had taken it upon themselves to roll back the rebellion by military action, such a step could conceivably have been technically interpreted as an act of war against Britain itself. However, it can be assumed that, had Britain been prepared to use force against Rhodesia, it would have been possible to work out a joint Anglo-African military operation. (The African contribution would really have been only an ancillary one, but it would have served the purpose of legitimatizing the joint Anglo-African Commission.) Clearly the more relevant consideration was a practical one: could an effective, *African* force have been raised?

In absolute numbers, the total strength of the African armies was greater than that of the army of Rhodesia.[29] But there were political as well as logistical obstacles to the effective raising of an OAU force against Rhodesia. Many of the African armies were already tied down, either in quelling domestic disorder or rebellion, as in the Southern Sudan, or in keeping guard over unhappy frontiers, as in the case of Ethiopia's and Kenya's borders with Somalia. Countries like Ghana, Guinée, and Algeria had pledged their forces for use by the OAU, but immense logistical problems would have proved an effective barrier to their deployment against Rhodesia. Malawi's President Kamuzu Banda's description of the Ghanaian "paper air force" was probably too harsh a judgment, but the Ghanaian air force was certainly no match for the Rhodesian air force.[30] There was always the danger, furthermore, of involving South Africa in the defense of Rhodesia, a move which would not only have escalated the conflict but would have placed it beyond African power altogether.

In fact, the OAU Defense Committee—consisting of Kenya, Tanzania, Nigeria, the United Arab Republic, and Zambia—met in Dar es Salaam between 19 and 23 November 1965, but, not surprisingly, nothing was heard of its deliberations. One possible alternative to undertaking a conventional war was for the OAU to have organized a resistance movement. But the Rhodesian African population did not appear to be ready to undertake guerrilla operations, even with Algerian assistance.

[29] See David Wood, *The Armed Forces of African States* (London, 1966).
[30] Keesing's Archives (1965–66), 21088.

The only recourse open to the OAU, therefore, was to put pressure on Britain to end Ian Smith's rebellion, by force if necessary, and to join with Britain in imposing sanctions against Rhodesia. Once this decision was taken, however, the OAU ceased to be the most appropriate organ to exert pressure on Britain. The fact of the matter was that over half the members of the OAU, particularly the French-speaking ones, had virtually no means of exerting pressure on Britain. It would matter very little to Britain, for instance, if the Ivory Coast or Gabon were to break diplomatic relations with London. The one act of diplomatic blackmail attempted by the OAU in its first two years—namely the Council of Ministers' recommendation made at the extraordinary session in Addis Ababa on 5 December 1965, that member states sever diplomatic relations with Britain unless the Rhodesian rebellion was crushed by 15 December—was a dismal failure. Only nine states carried out the recommendation—Algeria, Congo (Brazzaville), Ghana, Guinée, Mali, Mauritania, Sudan, Tanzania, and the United Arab Republic.[31] A tenth, Somalia, had already, in March 1963, severed its diplomatic relations with Britain on another issue.

At the sixth regular session of the OAU Council of Ministers in February 1966, members were divided on the question of what attitude they should take toward Britain. The Council's resolution did not refer to the question of relations with Britain, but created a five-member "Committee of Solidarity for Zambia" to "seek appropriate measures of technical and economic assistance by Member States to Zambia."[32] It also recommended that interested governments not recognize any of the Rhodesian nationalist parties and "give aid only to such groups of Zimbabwe fighters who are actively engaged within Rhodesia in the fight to liberate their country from the colonialist and racist yoke." Subsequent meetings of the OAU reiterated African opposition to the continuation of the white regime in Rhodesia, condemned British inaction, and urged it to take all measures, including the use of force, to end Smith's rebellion. But besides this minimum exertion of pressure on Britain, there was very little that the OAU could do in practice.

Organizationally speaking, the initiative had passed from the OAU to the Commonwealth and the United Nations. Among the African states themselves, the Commonwealth members were probably the only ones with some potential influence over Britain. Furthermore, a gesture of support from India or Pakistan or Canada in Commonwealth

---

31 See R. Cranford Pratt, "African Reactions to the Rhodesian Crisis," *International Journal*, XXI (1966), 186-98; for the effect of this action on Tanzania see above, Ali A. Mazrui, "Socialism as a Mode of International Protest: The Case of Tanzania," 1146.

32 OAU Resolution of 4 Mar. 1966, CM/Res.75(VI).

meetings, or an expression of encouragement from the Soviet Union in meetings of the Security Council, would probably have had a greater impact on Britain than a vote by the Ivory Coast or Gabon in the meetings of the OAU.

Even though it did not accept their demands Britain had persisted in continued relations with the African Commonwealth states. During the last few days of the negotiations between Prime Minister Harold Wilson and Ian Smith which had preceded Rhodesia's bid for independence, Britain had held continuous consultations, especially with Ghana, Kenya, Nigeria, Tanzania, Uganda, and Zambia. Most of these states had emphasized that Britain should not rule out the use of force to prevent Rhodesia's Declaration of Independence. Zambia had gone so far as to threaten to leave the Commonwealth and to withdraw its sterling balance from London should Britain, by failing to take a tough line against Smith, permit independence to be realized. Nigeria, however, had cautiously approved of a negotiated settlement. Yet Britain had ruled out the use of force from the very outset, a decision which placed on Britain a considerable measure of blame for Rhodesia's act of defiance.[33] There are times when a state may be physically unable to implement a threat to use force but should make it nonetheless, for the purposes of diplomatic effect. Wilson had, however, in his conversation with Smith before the Unilateral Declaration of Independence, repudiated the threat to use force directly. Was this a deliberate act of encouragement to Smith?

Considering the financial and diplomatic loss that Britain subsequently suffered in trying to impose economic sanctions against Rhodesia, it would seem unlikely that Britain deliberately, as against unwittingly, encouraged Smith's rebellion.[34] What is perhaps more significant is that some of the African states had begun to question Britain's credibility. Referring back to Britain's repudiation of the use of force, Simon Kapwepwe, then the Zambian Foreign Minister, said to the United Nations General Assembly on 22 October 1966: "One still

[33] Along with several observers, Wilson probably exaggerated the potency of British economic and monetary sanctions against Rhodesia as a means of breaking Smith's will. See Jane Symonds, "The Rhodesian Crisis," *The World Today*, XXI (1965), 453-59.

[34] The cost to Britain of sanctions against Rhodesia is, of course, very difficult to compute. Estimates of £90 to £120 million a year have been made, but these are justifiably criticized by *The Economist* (10 Dec. 1966), 1106, as misleading. Some of the exports withheld from Rhodesia found markets elsewhere and might well have seeped back into Rhodesia through third parties. Nonetheless, sanctions involved definite economic risks for Britain.

wonders whether this was a tactical error of Wilson's or a plot. Time will give us the true verdict."[35]

By January 1966, however, when the Commonwealth ministers met in Lagos—for the first time outside of the United Kingdom—even the Nigerian government was convinced that force against Smith could not be ruled out. The final communiqué of the conference stated that force "could not be precluded if this proved necessary to restore law and order." In return for this statement, Wilson was able to buy time in which to try out the economic sanctions that Britain had imposed on Rhodesia. The conference did, however, set up a sanctions committee under Canadian chairmanship to study the effect of the sanctions and to review the situation periodically. By the time that the Commonwealth Conference again met in London in September, it was apparent that economic sanctions had not succeeded. Thus Wilson's hope that the sanctions might prove sufficiently painful for Rhodesia to force Smith to negotiate a settlement of the dispute was not carried out. Once again he was able to buy time from the Commonwealth. The final communiqué restated Britain's "Six Principles" which formed the basis of its policy in Rhodesia, and which gave Britain until December 1966 to reach some solution.[36] If by that time the rebellion was not ended, Britain was to sponsor a resolution in the Security Council for "effective and selective mandatory economic sanctions" against Rhodesia.[37]

Actually, the African members of the Commonwealth were opposed to a negotiated settlement between Wilson and Smith. They feared that Wilson might legalize Smith's regime on the basis of some vague promises of future constitutional reforms, which Smith might later simply refuse to carry out. The Wilson-Smith talks aboard H.M.S. *Tiger*, 1 to 3 December 1966, nearly vindicated African fears. The main thrust of the "Working Document" that was made public at

[35] General Assembly, *Official Records*, Meeting of 22 Oct. 1966.
[36] The "Six Principles" are:

1. Unimpeded progress toward majority rule already enshrined in the 1961 Constitution;

2. guarantee against retrogressive amendment of the Constitution;

3. immediate improvement in the political status of the African population;

4. progress toward ending racial discrimination;

5. assurance by the British Government that any basis proposed for independence was acceptable to the people of Rhodesia as a whole;

6. assurance by the British Government that, regardless of race, there is no oppression of the majority by the minority or of the minority by the majority.

[37] See *The Economist* (17 Sept. 1966), 1099-1100.

the end of the discussions was to provide Smith a chance to return to legal status. As Wilson explained it in a television broadcast on 6 December, "Mr. Smith could have signed aboard H.M.S. *Tiger,* and he could have left Gibraltar as Prime Minister–designate of Rhodesia . . . Within four months . . . Rhodesia would have been independent."[38] In effect, in an unprecedented imperial act, Britain had promised to give Rhodesia independence even before majority rule had been achieved. In return, Britain would restore its rule under a Governor-General for the four months preceding the granting of independence. According to Leo Baron, the "Working Document" was "a constitutional formula which must rank as one of the major betrayals of history, and one infinitely more cynical than the 1961 Constitution which it purported to improve."[39]

The Rhodesians, however, considered their prospects better as they were and on 6 December rejected the "Working Document" on the grounds that the proposed four months of interim government by Britain would be a "Trojan Horse for the introduction of armed forces by which Britain would endeavor to control the Rhodesian Armed Forces."[40] Britain was thus compelled to withdraw its proposals to Rhodesia, and to prepare to implement that part of the Commonwealth communiqué which required it to propose selective mandatory sanctions to the United Nations Security Council.

What is significant in assessing the impact of African states on the handling of the Rhodesian question through the Commonwealth is that, although they were in large measure successful in maintaining constant pressure on Britain and in turning the Commonwealth into an instrument of such pressure, Britain very nearly succeeded in resisting all such pressures. In the final analysis, it decided to accept the recommendations of the Commonwealth only because the two prongs of its policy toward Rhodesia—economic sanctions and a negotiated settlement—had both manifestly failed.

If this, then, was the impact of African states on the handling of the Rhodesian question by the Commonwealth, how should we assess their impact on the United Nations handling of the situation? Condemnatory resolutions either against the illegal regime of Smith, or against Britain's refusal to resort to force were easy to obtain as long as the United Nations organs concerned were the "Committee of Twenty-four" (that is, the Committee on the Situation with Regard to the Implementation of the Granting of Independence to Colonial

[38] Wilson's television broadcast of 6 Dec. 1966 as reported in *The Times* (7 Dec. 1966).

[39] "Rhodesia: Taking Stock," *The World Today,* XXIII (1967), 372.

[40] Keesing's Archives (1965–66), 21759.

Countries and Peoples), the Trusteeship Committee, or the General Assembly. But under the United Nations Charter, no decision on mandatory sanctions can be taken except by the Security Council. And there Britain had a veto.

Britain did not have to use its veto to prevent action in the Council, since the African states were unable to secure a sufficient number of Council votes. A case in point was that of the two Greek ships, *Joanna V* and *Manuela*, which was discussed in the Council in April 1966. The two ships had attempted to carry oil to Rhodesia and Britain had sought Security Council authorization to use force, if necessary, to stop the two ships from arriving at the port of Beira in Moçambique. The African states attempted on this occasion to make the authorization to use force more generally applicable. In other words, the African states wanted the use of force against the *Manuela* and the *Joanna V* to be extended to deal generally with Smith's regime. But they could not secure the necessary votes in the Council to force this issue, and a British-sponsored resolution authorizing the use of force for strictly limited objectives was passed by the Council.[41] Again, in December 1966, following the collapse of the *Tiger* talks, African states attempted to include oil as one of the twelve key items proposed by Britain in imposing mandatory selective economic sanctions against Rhodesia. In the Council resolution of 16 December 1966, the African states were able to include a request to all states to prevent their ships from supplying oil products to Rhodesia, but only after Britain had accepted the proposal.[42] But their attempt to include an invitation to Britain to prevent, "by all means," the transport of oil to Rhodesia failed to secure the necessary votes. Thus, although for the first time the Security Council undertook to impose mandatory sanctions against Rhodesia, the African states had no cause to be pleased with the resolution.

What may we then say of the African states' handling of the Rhodesian question? The most that can be said is that their undiluted opposition to Smith's regime put marginal pressure on states like South Africa and Portugal, and possibly on Australia, not to recognize the Rhodesian Declaration of Independence; even so, this decision was more likely a result of United Kingdom diplomatic activity than of African opposition. On the other hand, the African states could not really have prevented a negotiated settlement between Wilson and Smith had the two men been able to carry their electorates along with them. The African impact on the United Nations was similarly very modest: the issue of mandatory sanctions was raised much later than

[41] Security Council Resolution #221 of 9 Apr. 1966. See *U.N. Monthly Chronicle*, III (May 1966), 11.
[42] *U.N. Monthly Chronicle*, IV (Jan. 1967), 21.

the Africans had wanted, and the final result was a greatly watered-down version of their demands.

What were the factors limiting the impact of African diplomacy? The influence of the OAU on Britain was necessarily minimal, and the Organization found it necessary to transfer the burden of responsibility to the Commonwealth members of the OAU. But even the collective diplomacy of African Commonwealth states had an only marginal influence on British policies. It is conceivable that if all the African Commonwealth states, including Nigeria and Malawi, had acted in concert in severing diplomatic relations with Britain or in threatening to disrupt the Commonwealth by leaving it, they might have made of themselves a much more powerful pressure group. It is unlikely, however, that they would have necessarily been able to push Britain into resorting to force against Rhodesia. They might only have hastened the decision on mandatory sanctions by the United Nations. In any event, such concerted action was politically impossible.

None of the states could contemplate so drastic an action as leaving the Commonwealth, even though Zambia and Ghana had occasionally threatened to do so. The disruption of the pattern of economic relations that such a withdrawal would have entailed was obviously a serious deterrent factor, although had there been a sufficient will to face up to the costs of leaving the Commonwealth, as indeed Rhodesia itself did, it would not have been impossible to have done so.

Furthermore, there was also the consideration that, if drastic action were contemplated against Britain, there was a very real possibility that Britain might have been driven to legitimize the Smith regime with bigger concessions than those offered on the H.M.S. *Tiger*. Wilson seemed, in the short run, to be solely concerned with restoring the constitutional regime in Rhodesia, and, to achieve this result, he could easily have qualified or deferred his pledges to the "Six Principles" to make them seem consistent with the restoration of a constitutional government in Rhodesia. The *Tiger* talks had already demonstrated Wilson's flexibility in this matter. Once Rhodesia's 1961 Constitution was restored, there was nothing more than the dubious British will to prevent a future prime minister from declaring yet another independence.

But African resources with which to make an impact on international diplomacy were as limited as their resources to influence Britain directly. The United States had virtually committed itself to the British position and had therefore placed itself beyond independent African influence. France consistently maintained that Rhodesia was essentially a British problem and almost always abstained from voting in the United Nations debates. If there was any scope for diplomatic or material support, the Communist states were propably the only substantial sources of supply. It was the threat of a "red army in blue berets," a phrase used by Wilson when referring to the danger (from the Western point of view) that the United Nations might create a peace-keeping force manned by Soviet soldiers, that constituted for Britain and the United States the most disturbing aspect of the whole situation.[43] But the question was not even raised in the United Nations, for, although the veto in the Security Council could have been circumvented by resorting to the General Assembly, the proposal would almost certainly have been blocked by a combined vote of European, American, and Latin American, and, indeed, several African and Asian states. In any case, there was no real possibility of introducing a United Nations peace-keeping force which would have fulfilled the demands of the African states.

On the other hand, there was no inducement for, and numerous risks involved in, any direct intervention, solicited or otherwise, by the Communist states in Rhodesia. Thus, when Britain refused to accede to Zambia's request to place British troops on the Rhodesian side of the Kariba dam—a proposal which was calculated to involve British troops in a possible conflict with Rhodesian troops—Zambia turned for assistance to Moscow and Washington. Envoys sent to the two capitals on 4 December ostensibly to "sound out" the idea of a United Nations contingent returned empty-handed except for platitudinous pledges of sympathy and support. In terms of international power politics, the African states had nothing substantial to offer to induce unilateral Communist intervention in Rhodesia, or did not want to offer what they had. A base for Soviet missiles in Zambia might, for instance, have been a powerful inducement, but the price was too high for Zambia.

Some Conclusions

For the OAU, the Congo and Rhodesian problems had some features in common. Both demonstrated the power of the white nations over events in Africa. There were racial overtones in both situations, the Stanleyville operation having been mounted to rescue white hostages even at the cost of hundreds of black lives.[44] A Rhodesian military operation was ruled out by Britain for reasons that appeared to many African and several nonwhite non-African states to be connected with an unwillingness to risk white Rhodesian lives for the sake of the black

[43] House of Commons, *Parliamentary Debates*, 672 (12 Nov. 1965), 637.

[44] For a discussion of the implications of the crisis for the United States, see Kenneth W. Grundy, "The Stanleyville Rescue: American Policy in the Congo," *Yale Review*, LVII (1967), 242-55.

majority. "It has become clear to us," the Zambian Foreign Minister had protested in the General Assembly on 22 October 1966, "that the motivations of the British Government were racialist."[45]

In both situations, again, African states, with few exceptions, felt collectively humiliated by their inability to control the development of events in their continent. The powerlessness was a product of the lack of the arms, men, and economic infrastructure necessary to impose one nation's will upon another. But it was also a product of a lack of solidarity among the member states of the OAU. The interrelationship between a lack of effective power and the absence of solidarity is central to any analysis of the OAU.

The OAU as a Forum of Protest

Any international organization which deals with the political re-lations of its members must inevitably become a forum of complaints by one against another. Since its creation, the OAU has heard several cases of mutual recrimination by its members. The list, in fact, is a long one. It includes persisting conflicts, like Somalia's border disputes with Ethiopia and Kenya, and transient conflicts, like Guinée's protest in February 1966 against Ghana's detention of its Foreign Minister and other diplomats who were then proceeding to the OAU meeting in Addis Ababa.

Only two instances are selected for closer examination; they raise issues similar to the ones that were dealt with above. The first once again involves the Congo situation in 1964–65, but this time in terms of the Congo's protests against African intervention in its affairs. The second concerns protests in 1965 by Ghana's French-speaking neigh-bors—principally, the Ivory Coast, Dahomey, Niger, and Upper Volta —against what they alleged were Nkrumah's attempts to subvert their regimes.

African States' Intervention in the Congo, 1964–65

Traditionally in international law, the advantage in a situation of civil strife lies with the incumbent government.[46] Legal restraints against foreign assistance to the rebellious opposition are greater than against assistance to the incumbents. Assistance to rebels is not completely excluded, but, to justify it legally, certain conditions have to be satisfied,

---

[45] General Assembly, *Official Records*, Meeting of 22 Oct. 1966.

[46] See James N. Rosenau, "Internal War as an International Event," in James N. Rosenau (ed.), *International Aspects of Civil Strife* (New York, 1964), 45-92. See also above, Young, "Rebellion and the Congo," 1007-10.

among them the requirement that the rebels be accorded some kind of a recognized status: that of "insurgents" if they have a well organized resistance and control of some part of the territory, or that of "belligerents" if the situation is recognized as a case of civil war.[47]

As we indicated earlier, the OAU Charter had approved the regulation of inter-African relations according to traditional international law. Article II, paragraph 2, of the Charter forbade members to interfere in each other's affairs. Under traditional international law, the Charter presumably permitted states in Africa to render assistance to an incumbent regime and obliged them to refrain from assisting rebellious elements in a member country unless the rebels were accorded a proper legal status for receiving assistance. At no time were the rebels in the Congo given such a proper legal status by the OAU or by its members. There were times when the National Liberation "government" was treated as a "party" to the "civil war" in the Congo and when its representatives were heard at the OAU meetings. But its status was never really made clear in any formal declaration.

Paradoxically, however, more African states rendered assistance to the National Liberation forces than to the central government. The only time a member assisted the central government was after the departure of the United Nations forces in June 1964, when, at the request of the government of the Congo, Nigeria sent four hundred policemen to help keep internal order until the end of the year. But these men were not deployed against National Liberation troops, and allegations to this effect by the National Liberation Council were vigorously denied by Nigeria. The Congolese government's further requests that the OAU send an all-African peace-keeping force were, however, not acceded to by the Organization.

Assistance to the National Liberation Council, on the other hand, was not only given but in some cases openly admitted, especially after the Stanleyville operation of November 1964. Thus Egypt made no secret of a camp at Heliopolis near Cairo which provided three-week training courses for recruits of the National Liberation Council. Algeria publicly declared on 8 March 1965 that it was sending arms to the National Liberation Council.[48] Arms were also known to have come from Ghana and Uganda. And the Sudan, following the overthrow of the military government in November 1964, became an important supply route for the National Liberation forces and a significant headquarters (in Khartoum) for the leaders of the National Liberation Council. Congo (Brazzaville) and Burundi allegedly also provided

[47] See Hersh Lauterpacht, *Recognition in International Law* (Cambridge, 1947), 270.

[48] Keesing's Archives (1965–66), 20803.

bases of operation for the National Liberation forces, although these allegations were denied.

There is a danger in exaggerating the amount of aid given to the National Liberation Council by, or through, the neighboring countries. The total material assistance never, in fact, reached the level and quality of United States assistance to the Congolese government (at least 30 aircraft, pilots, maintenance men, and paratroopers). In any case, the question at issue is not the quantity of aid, but its propriety in the light of the provisions of the Charter of the OAU.

There were two areas of ambiguity which cried out for clarification by the OAU: First, were the National Liberation forces in the Congo in fact receiving assistance from other African states, as was alleged, and, if so, from which countries? It is true that Algeria and Ghana openly admitted their activities, but there were others, like Uganda and Congo (Brazzaville), which vigorously denied having intervened in Congolese affairs. This ambiguity naturally caused strained relations between the Congo and its neighbors. An impartial inquiry by the OAU could at least have alleviated the tension that arose out of mutual allegations which had no basis in fact.

The second area of ambiguity with which the OAU might have concerned itself was the status of the civil strife in the Congo, and the rights and obligations of third-party member states therein. In other words, the situation demanded some kind of regulative action by the Organization. It could have taken the form of an open declaration that the situation was a civil war in which the National Liberation forces enjoyed insurgent or belligerent rights. Such a statement would have legitimized the otherwise irregular aid given to the National Liberation forces. Alternatively, the OAU could have declared the situation one in which the incumbent government was pursuing its legitimate function of putting down an act of rebellion within its borders. The Organization could, in the latter case, have then gone on to set up the necessary machinery to isolate the Congo strife from all outside intervention. Indeed, theoretically it could have gone further and assisted the Congolese government with an all-African police force to quell internal rebellion in the Congo.

In another time and in another country, it is conceivable that the OAU might have taken one of the above courses of action. But the Congo posed a difficult problem. The OAU could not openly describe the situation as one of civil war in which the rebels enjoyed the same rights as the incumbents vis-à-vis third states. Such a step might not only have exacerbated the conflict, but it would also have set an unfortunate precedent with regard to the status of rebel groups in other countries. The Congo, after all, was not the only country in Africa that had an organized opposition. In a sense, it was a lesser evil for all concerned to leave it to individual states to determine the nature of the situation in the Congo. Furthermore, it was thought sufficient to describe the situation as a threat to peace in Africa: immediate steps could thus be taken to alleviate the conflict and to obviate interminable debates about the legal status of the National Liberation Council.

But while the OAU was reluctant to give any kind of formal recognition to the National Liberation government, it was still less prepared to do the opposite, namely, to recognize that the Congolese government could exercise its sovereign rights to deal with the "rebels" as it pleased, and that, therefore, all other African states should refrain from interfering in the affairs of the Congo. Earlier, reasons were advanced for the noncommittal attitude of the OAU toward the Congolese government. For the OAU the Congo situation was really in a twilight zone: it was neither a formally determined civil war—in which both parties enjoyed equal rights—nor a situation in which the OAU could accept the full implications of the rights of the Congolese government as the executive arm of a sovereign state.

The obvious way for an international organization to deal with such twilight situations is for it to offer to mediate between the contending parties within the national state, while making it clear that this does not in any way constitute formal recognition of the "rebel" party. The OAU, in fact, took just this step by setting up the *ad hoc* Conciliation Commission headed by President Kenyatta. But what is less easy to handle in a twilight situation is the problem of interference in the situation by foreign states. Tshombe quite naturally insisted that the OAU should respect his rights as the chief executive of a sovereign member of the Organization, and, accordingly, that it should take immediate steps to stop foreign assistance to the "rebels."

The OAU's response was irresolute. The Conciliation Commission decided on 20 September 1964, ten days after it was created, that it would visit Congo (Léopoldville), Congo (Brazzaville), and Burundi in order to inquire into the Congo's allegations of interference from neighboring states. No action was immediately taken, however, the Conciliation Commission preferring to give priority to its mediatory rather that to its investigatory functions. By the middle of November, the Commission's mediatory activities were overtaken by the Stanleyville crisis, which virtually paralyzed the Commission. It was not until 30 January 1965 that the Commission finally set up a subcommittee to go to Léopoldville to prepare the ground[49] for the investigation by the Commission.

[49] The subcommittee was still not asked to institute actual investigation into the situation, only "to prepare the ground" for future investigation.

What was interesting about this subcommittee was its composition and the timing of its creation. It consisted of representatives of Nigeria, Ghana, and Guinée. The propriety of including the latter two states, both known to be among the most critical of Tshombe, must be seriously questioned. If impartial investigation at the very least requires the confidence of the host state in which investigation is to be conducted, then Ghana and Guinée were undoubtedly not the best choices.

But the timing of the creation of the subcommittee was equally unpropitious. Although it was set up more than two months after the Stanleyville crisis, emotions in most African states were still extremely hostile to Tshombe. More significantly, the Stanleyville crisis provoked still more interference by foreign states in support of the National Liberation Council. What was particularly daunting to the conduct of an impartial investigation by the OAU was that President Kenyatta, the chairman of the Conciliation Commission, himself met with the leader of the National Liberation Council, Christopher Gbenye, in January 1965 and, in conjuction with Uganda and Tanzania, pledged support to him.[50] The whole rationale behind investigating Tshombe's protests against interference by African states was thus shaken.

In any event, on 7 February 1965 three representatives of Nigeria —as members of the subcommittee—arrived in Léopoldville. Finding no one from Ghana or Guinée there, they returned home on 11 February; they went back on 21 February after Guinée decided to send its representatives. Ghana still did not comply. But by this time it was almost too late to do anything since the OAU itself was scheduled to meet on 26 February in Nairobi. The question of investigation lay in abeyance until the OAU finished its business on 9 March. By that time, however, troops of the Congolese government had inflicted severe losses on the National Liberation forces which were now fast retreating toward whatever refuge was provided by the neighboring states. Not surprisingly, Tshombe was no longer interested in what the OAU did about investigating his allegations or about the whole question of foreign state interference in the Congo.

What may we say, then, of the OAU as a forum of protest for the Congo against African interventions in its affairs? Clearly, the OAU did not provide an adequate forum as far as the Congo was concerned. The OAU resolution of 10 September 1964 calling upon foreign states to stop intervening in the Congo said nothing specifically about intra-African interventions.[51] If the organization was not sure about the truth of Congolese allegations, it could at least have provided an adequate machine with which to conduct investigations. But the investigations

[50] See *East African Standard* (Nairobi), 15 Jan. 1965.
[51] OAU Resolution of 10 Sept. 1964, ECM/Res.5(III).

were not seriously undertaken. Foreign state interference in the Congo not only continued after the matter was brought to the OAU; it increased after the Stanleyville crisis.

When interference by African states in the Congo's civil strife did stop in March and April 1965, this came about less as a result of action by the OAU than as an outcome of two other factors. The first was the gradual elimination of the National Liberation forces by Tshombe's government and mercenary forces. The second pertained mostly to the domestic politics of the aid-supplying countries. The Sudan, to give one example, discovered that some of the aid that the National Liberation forces had acquired was filtering into the Southern Sudan and into the hands of the secessionist forces that the Sudan itself was fighting.[52]

If the Congo situation of 1964–65 is of any importance for an understanding of the character of the OAU, the lesson is that the Organization really was a weak forum of protest for states which were compelled to rest their case on legalistic norms. This is not to say that these norms are not important. It is to argue that, although the OAU Charter is an embodiment of the principles of the traditional norms of international relations, certain kinds of situations could create pressures within the OAU that could lead to the substitution of the revolutionary code of inter-African relations for more traditional norms. The Congo provided such a situation.

Protest by French-speaking States Against Ghana, 1965

The country in Africa that suffered most foreign interference in its affairs was the Congo. The one country in Africa that was most often alleged to have interfered in the affairs of other African states was the Ghana of Kwame Nkrumah.

On 12 February 1965, the French-speaking African states formed the *Organisation Commune Africaine et Malgache* out of a rump left by its predecessor, the *Union Africaine et Malgache*. On the same day, the new organization issued a communiqué which strongly condemned "the action of certain states, notably Ghana, which offer a welcome to agents of subversion and organize training camps on their territory."[53] Three months later at the Abidjan meeting of the *Organisation Commune Africaine et Malgache*, nine of its member states announced that they would not attend the forthcoming meeting of the OAU, scheduled for Accra in September (later delayed to October), on the grounds that Ghana was sheltering subversive elements against

---

[52] Personal information from embassy of the Sudan.
[53] OCAM communiqué of 12 Feb. 1965. See *West Africa* (20 Feb. 1965), 203.

four of them—Upper Volta, Niger, the Ivory Coast, and Dahomey.[54] The other five—Chad, Gabon, Malagasy, Togo, and the Cameroon—presumably joined in sympathy. The incident that had provoked this boycott was an abortive attempt on the life of President Hamani Diori of Niger. The assassin was captured; he allegedly confessed that he was a member of the Sawaba party (which was banned in Niger but which had its headquarters in Accra), and that he had been trained for subversive action in Ghana.[55]

The charge against Ghana was obviously a serious one. The OAU Charter had specifically mentioned assassination and subversion as acts in which African states were not to indulge.[56] But the threat by the *Organisation Commune Africaine et Malgache* states not to attend the OAU meeting was equally serious, since it could prove centrifugal, particularly when the Ivory Coast, Niger, and Upper Volta began sending emissaries to Guinée, Mali, Nigeria, Liberia, Sierra Leone, and other countries to persuade them to boycott the OAU meeting at Accra as well. How did the OAU deal with this double threat—the threat of Ghana's alleged activities, and the threat of a boycott?

At the initiative of Nigeria an extraordinary meeting of the OAU Council of Ministers was called in Lagos from 10 to 13 June 1965. Niger, the Ivory Coast, and Upper Volta presented dossiers on subversive actions allegedly perpetrated by Ghana. Ghana denied the charges and claimed that its training camps were for African nationalists who were fighting in South West Africa and other nonindependent states.

The Council decided that, under the circumstances, the most appropriate step was to examine the charges against Ghana and to persuade Nkrumah to give assurances against intervening in the affairs of his neighbors. Accordingly, it set up a subcommittee consisting of Ethiopia, the Gambia, Mali, Nigeria, and Tunisia to implement the Council's decision. The five-nation subcommittee engaged in negotiations with Ghana and, by 13 June, elicited from President Nkrumah assurance to the effect that (a) he would expel all refugees residing in Ghana who were considered undesirable by any member state, and (b) that he would forbid the formation of any political group in Ghana whose aims were opposed to any member state.[57]

The report of the subcommittee was received with relief by the Council of Ministers. It decided that with Nkrumah's assurances the

[54] *West Africa* (15 June 1965), 619.

[55] *West Africa* (24 Apr. 1965), 455. See above, 1042.

[56] Article III, paragraph 5 of the Charter makes an "unreserved condemnation, in all its forms, of political assassination as well as of subversive activities on the part of neighbouring states or any other states."

[57] *East African Standard*, 14 June 1965.

OAU would now be able to meet in Accra as scheduled. Murumbi and OAU Secretary General Diallo Telli were appointed to ensure that Ghana kept its pledges. The two visited Ghana in August. On 24 August, Diallo Telli declared in Addis Ababa that Ghana had taken great pains to fulfill its promises.[58] Nonetheless to obtain further assurances from the French-speaking states that they would attend the OAU meeting in Accra, Nkrumah met with President Félix Houphuët-Boigny of the Ivory Coast, President Maurice Yaméogo of Upper Volta, and President Hamani Diori of Niger in Bamako on 4 September. The assurances were obtained. But when the OAU session began in Accra on 22 October, eight *Organisation Commune Africaine et Malgache* member states decided to remain absent—Chad, Dahomey, Gabon, the Ivory Coast, Malagasy, Niger, Togo, and Upper Volta.

What had gone wrong? Nkrumah seemed to have made unprecedented concessions in order to placate his neighboring heads of state. Personally, he had decidedly taken a backward step in renouncing all protection to political refugees from states that he had consistently regarded as less than fully independent. He had also gone on to take the initiative in meeting the presidents of some of these states. And yet they refused to come to Accra for the OAU meeting. They said that the "conditions demanded of Ghana had not been fulfilled to their satisfaction."[59]

Were the *Organisation Commune Africaine et Malgache* states simply planning to prevent the OAU from meeting in Accra lest it should acquire the status of OAU's "regional headquarters" in West Africa? It is true that Nkrumah had hoped that Accra would become some kind of a center to the OAU, and it was known that he was lavishly using the scarce resources of his treasury to build the sumptuous Africa Hall. But to frustrate such ambitions as Nkrumah had for Accra would seem to have been too petty a reason for the boycott by the French-speaking states.

The clue to their attitude is most likely to be found in the way in which the OAU handled their protest against Nkrumah's alleged subversive activities. Perhaps the Lagos meeting of the OAU Ministerial Council was less of a triumph for the *Organisation Commune Africaine et Malgache* states than it was at the time believed. The Council at Lagos acted strictly pragmatically. In May 1965 the threat posed by the *Organisation Commune Africaine et Malgache* to the organizational interests seemed greater than the threat to the security of these states inherent in the alleged activities of Ghana. The Lagos meeting did indeed extract concessions from Ghana in order to placate the *Organisa-*

58 *West Africa* (4 Sept. 1965), 991.
59 *West Africa* (23 Oct. 1965), 1178.

tion Commune Africaine et Malgache states, but one suspects that this was done more in order to salvage the unity of the OAU than to guarantee the security of *Organisation Commune Africaine et Malgache* states.

The concessions that were extracted from Nkrumah were really short-term only. There was no guarantee that once the OAU had concluded its meeting in Accra Nkrumah would not resume the practice of providing a base for opposition elements from the neighboring states. Also the machinery that the OAU created in Lagos, the five-nation subcommittee, was set up for the short-term purpose of getting assurances from Nkrumah rather than as a permanent supervisory body over Nkrumah's future activities. The five-nation subcommittee did not even seriously investigate the charges against Ghana which were contained in the dossiers provided by the Ivory Coast, Niger, and Upper Volta. The *Organisation Commune Africaine et Malgache* states also failed to obtain a specific condemnation of Nkrumah by the OAU.

Indeed, the convergence of the interests of Ghana and of the OAU Council meeting in Lagos was the crucial factor. Ghana did not want to jeopardize the OAU meeting in Accra. And the Lagos meeting hoped that it could trade Nkrumah's concessions for assurances by the *Organisation Commune Africaine et Malgache* states that they would attend the Accra conference. Both Ghana and the OAU were prepared to take the retrogressive step of denying the generally recognized right of sovereign states to grant asylum to political refugees in order temporarily to placate the French-speaking states.

When the entirely short-term basis of the formula became apparent to the *Organisation Commune Africaine et Malgache* states, they realized that the concessions made by Ghana were politically insignificant. By this time, however, it was too late for them to protest that the Lagos Conference had not extracted a long-term commitment from Nkrumah to refrain from subversive activities against them. Yet the OAU could now meet in Accra as scheduled. If the *Organisation Commune Africaine et Malgache* states decided not to attend the meeting, the onus of the decision was on them. Neither the OAU nor Ghana could, after Lagos, be accused of having ignored the protests of the *Organisation Commune Africaine et Malgache* states. Thus, between May, when the threat by the *Organisation Commune Africaine et Malgache* states was first made, and October, when the OAU finally met at Accra, the question of salvaging the OAU conference continued to claim priority. But whereas, before, the burden of weakening the OAU would have fallen on Ghana, now it was the original complainants, the *Organisation Commune Africaine et Malgache* states, who were to blame for the dissension.

If our analysis is correct, or substantially correct, it highlights the OAU's extreme pragmatism. The OAU serves as an efficient forum of protest if, as our analysis of the Congo situation suggests, the protest is justified not only on the basis of the traditional norms of international conduct, but also on the basis of something that might almost be called a "higher form of ethical conduct" that governs relations between African states. The use of mercenaries, for instance, would spoil the case for the party that uses them. The Ghana-*Organisation Commune Africaine et Malgache* conflict demonstrates, on the other hand, that the OAU serves as an efficient forum of protest not only if the protest is justified in terms of certain rules of conduct, traditional or revolutionary, but also if it falls short of jeopardizing the organizational interests or survival of the OAU.

Thus we can note the three variables that determine the political behavior of the OAU with regard to inter-African conflict: the traditional norms of inter-African intercourse recognized in the OAU Charter; a higher form of ethical conduct, unspecified and volatile in character but nonetheless politically significant in concrete situations; and the organizational survival of the OAU. This does not by any means exhaust the list of variables that affect the functioning of the OAU as a forum of diplomatic protest.

Conclusions

The first obvious observation is that the emotional context of protests against non-African interventions in African affairs is much more contentious than that of protests among African states. War or threat of war, political control of one people over another, and race are the three elements of human relations that trigger powerful and varying human emotions. A combination of all three in the Western interventions in the Congo in 1964–65 and the Rhodesian crisis since 1965 in both cases created explosive situations.

On the other hand, relations among African states are characterized by a relative absence of these three elements. They do indeed exist in situations like the Southern Sudanese secession and could create an explosive situation. But the rhetoric of African protests makes a distinction between, say, the control of one African people over another African people and the control of white over black or of a non-African power over an African state.

The second observation relates to the kind of resources the OAU would have needed in handling both protests. Both the Congo and Rhodesian crises illustrated the impotence of a strategy of protest in dealing with powerful foreign countries or racialist regimes. These adversaries do not belong to the same framework of ethical relationship to which the African states belong. Neither one, that is, would be responsive to an appeal for respect for the dignity of Africans.

The resources needed by the OAU in handling inter-African protests are of a different order of importance. The power of the barrel of a gun to impose the OAU's decisions on a member state has so far not become a relevant consideration in dealing with inter-African protests. Much more significant are arguments based on an appeal to the organizational interests of the OAU and to traditional norms of international relations, especially the more revolutionary norms that take the dignity of the African peoples as their starting premise.

The OAU's capabilities as an instrument and as a forum of protest are therefore varied. The Organization is a very weak instrument of protest against the outside world since it lacks the resources that are needed to impose its will upon the international community. It is more potent as a forum of protest within Africa itself provided, however, that the protest contains the ingredients necessary to evoke the response that the protesting party would want to elicit from the OAU. Such a response is based as much on the susceptibilities of individual states to invocations of ethical norms applicable only within the African context as on the objective merits of the case presented.

POSTLUDE:

TOWARD A THEORY OF PROTEST

We might divide major acts or movements of protest during the last hundred years of Africa's history into four broad categories: protests of conservation, protests of restoration, protests of transformation, and protests of corrective censure.

By protests of conservation we mean those acts or movements which are aroused by a sense of impending peril to a system of values dear to the participants. The reaction is a defensive action to conserve that system of values. Protests of restoration are, on the other hand, nostalgic—seeking to restore a past which has already been disrupted or destroyed.

Protests of transformation are a manifestation of a profound disaffection with an existing system of values, or system of rewards and penalties. The great impetus behind protests of transformation is a commitment to radical change. If protests of conservation and restoration are oriented toward the past and its preservation or revival, protests of transformation are oriented toward the future and its reformulation.

The fourth category is that of protests of corrective censure. In this case what is at stake is not a whole system of values, or of rewards and penalties, but an *ad hoc* demand for a particular modification in the system. Of course there is almost invariably an element of "censure" and "correction" implied in the other categories of protest as well. Those who are for conserving a pre-existent code of social arrangements are censuring those who are jeopardizing its continuation and seeking to censure or correct their ominous behavior. Those who are committed to restoring the past are censuring or seeking to correct a "mistaken" departure from it. And those who aspire to the transformation of social arrangements are seeking to correct those who are obstinately and rigidly upholding the *status quo*. But in these other broad categories of conservation, restoration, and change, the censure is not the primary motive of the protest nor is what is being corrected a mere detail. Whole systems are at stake, and the protests are directed toward determining the fortunes of those systems. But in the case of protests of corrective censure a system is not immediately at stake. A government may have incurred the anger of a particular group because of a new tax on cigarettes. Indeed the issue may even concern international affairs rather than domestic arrangements. It could be a problem of recognizing a new regime in a country which has just had a military coup, or a question of evaluating the behavior of a senator or other public figure. The censure sometimes is almost an end in itself, though it does take place within a system of values. Those who are protesting may be implying that a certain departure from those values has been committed and ought to be corrected. But they would not be worried about the survival of the system as a whole. They simply wish to make a point about an individual transgression.

Africa affords particularly rich material for assessing different functions of protest in diverse social situations and diverse moments of social development. It is a truism to observe that the last hundred years of Africa's history have telescoped many ages of social change. When we are discussing social systems and sub-systems in this period the range is from the life-style of the Karamojong and the Masai in East Africa to the life-style of the top French-speaking African elite in Dakar, or the African technocrats in the United Nations Economic Commission for Africa.

Protest can itself be an index of change from tradition to modernity. Tradition implies acceptance of what is sanctified by time. Traditional societies, almost by definition, are pre-eminently concerned with problems of social and moral conservation. Many of the more important forms of protest in traditional society are either protests of corrective censure or protests of conservation. In Africa the commitment to the past, personified in some societies by a profound loyalty to ancestors, resulted very often in the minimization of reform. Of course, all societies undergo important change, but the difference between change and reform is sometimes a difference between the unconscious and the conscious. Social change may take place even if those involved in it do not want it or are not even aware of what they are undergoing. But social reform is a commitment to conscious change in a specified direction.

The move from tradition to modernity is, in a fundamental sense, a move from resignation to reform. Resignation in this case is meant not necessarily in a fatalistic sense, but simply in the sense of a profound acceptance of the past as the ultimate legitimation of the present. When the spirit of social resignation succumbs to a spirit of social reform, the modernization process is underway. Protest is a necessary mechanism for this transition from a world of acceptance and conservation to a world of reform and development.

Protest acquires this significance because of its role as a mechanism for testing the elasticity of a social system. Conflict between individuals or between groups is an inevitable aspect of human society. But when a conflict of interest is still at the level of exchanging protests, a dialogue is still taking place. To protest is, after all, not only to express a point of view but also to assume some residue of a shared ethical language between those who are protesting and those to whom the protest is addressed. But when conflict escalates into combat, and all that is exchanged is violence, protest as a medium of discourse is suspended. And the survival of the whole system of conflict-resolution may be at stake.

It was Edmund Burke who once said that a constitution or government without the means of change was without the means of conservation. Burke was asserting that a certain elasticity in a system of government is necessary if it is to survive at all. The system of government must be capable of accommodating some degree of change, even if it remains economical in its permissiveness. A total inflexibility would risk a total revolution.

Along the coast of Kenya there is a parable about a baobab tree and a palm tree illustrating different responses to a night of violent winds. The coconut tree seemed the more frail of the two, thin and tall and seemingly vulnerable. The baobab tree was firm and thick and deeply grounded. The winds roared that night with the fury of godly indignation. The palm tree swayed, in apparent surrender to every push of the ferocious clouds of dust. It swayed to the right and to the left, forward and backward, in elegant servility to the storm.

But the baobab tree stood its ground. In a posture of massive defiance it confronted the winds of heaven. It met those winds, straight on, in rigid resistance to these violent dictates of the elements. The winds pushed and shoved, but the baobab tree stood its ground. The roar of the storm continued—and two tropical trees offered alternative responses to the challenge which was posed.

That night of divine fury came to an end. All was quiet as the sun rose, but much was revealed in ruins. The winds had taken their toll. As the shadows retreated and revealed the fortunes of the two trees, they uncovered the coconut tree tired and bereft of some of its leaves and all of its fruit, but still standing erect. But the baobab tree had fallen in defiant majesty. It had been uprooted altogether, and lay there a massive monument to the futility of total resistance to the elements.

The palm tree, from our point of view, stands for flexibility where the forces of the universe are too strong to resist. The baobab tree stands for proud rigidity—and both pride and rigidity are a prelude to a fall.

If we relate all of this experience back to social systems, we may say that traditional belief systems did allow room for changes when these had become too strong to resist. But on the whole the phenomenon of protest in traditional African societies took the form of either protests of conservation or protests of corrective censure. Protests of conservation were on the whole a manifestation of disturbed faith. They sought to protest what was being endangered by a spirit of innovation. But protests of censure sought to correct an *ad hoc* tendency toward transgression.

In the relationship between tradition and political change Michael Oakeshott presents a penetrating conservative point of view. In a famous sentence he has asserted: "In politics, then, every enterprise is a consequential enterprise, the pursuit, not of a dream, or of a general principle, but of an intimation." Oakeshott cites one important movement of protest in British history, the suffragette movement and its quest for the rights of women. He argues that the arrangements which constitute a society capable of political activity, whether they are customs, institutions, laws, or diplomatic decisions, are to *some* extent internally coherent, but they always include certain elements of incoherence. The pattern may be somewhat out of shape, but the very nature of the pattern "intimates" what kind of change would help to add greater coherence to that pattern. Where this intimation really comes from the very structure of the social arrangements already achieved, that intimation amounts to a sympathy for that particular change. "Political activity is the exploration of that sympathy; and consequently, relevant political reasoning will be the convincing exposure of a sympathy, present but not yet followed up, and the convincing demonstration that now is the appropriate moment for recognising it."[1]

This is where Oakeshott introduces the question of the legal status of women in English society. That status had for a long time been "in comparative confusion, because the rights and duties which composed it intimated rights and duties which were nevertheless not recognised." Oakeshott regarded it as irrelevant to have based the case for the technical enfranchisement of women on arguments about natural right, or justice between the sexes, or some general concept of feminine personality.

> . . . on the view of things I am suggesting, the only cogent reason to be advanced for the technical 'enfranchisement' of women was that in

[1] Michael Oakeshott, *Rationalism in Politics and Other Essays* (London, 1962), 124.

all or most other important respects they had already been enfranchised. Arguments drawn from abstract natural right, from 'justice', or from some general concept of feminine personality, must be regarded as either irrelevant, or as unfortunately disguised forms of the one valid argument; namely, that there was an incoherence in the arrangements of the society which pressed convincingly for remedy. In politics, then, every enterprise is a consequential enterprise, the pursuit, not of a dream, or of a general principle, but of an intimation.[2]

From the point of view of our own analysis, we may regard protest as one of the most important forms which this intimation takes. In a transitional society, protest or corrective censure is sometimes in reality the protest of reform which alleges a transgression from ancestral values when in fact the "transgressor" might be the more orthodox of the two sides in a dispute. But whenever that sort of change takes place it might be said, in Oakeshott's terms, that the social arrangements are ready to follow an intimation that a certain incoherence which had arisen as a result of change in other parts of those arrangements was now to be *corrected.*

But Oakeshott's theory as a description of what really happens is truer in traditional societies than in most modern societies. The ideal type of an Oakeshottian pursuit of a subtle intimation is probably to be found more in a society of silent social change than in a society of conscious social reform. If modernization is in part a movement from silent change to conscious reform, the concept of social incoherence becomes more difficult to pin down as the range of possible changes in society is *recognized* as broad, and the society in any case becomes more complex structurally.

On Africa's first contact with alien cultures it was inevitable that some of the first forms of protest should in fact have been protests of conservation. As we have indicated, protests of conservation are a sign of disturbed faith in the security of one's system of values and an attempt to protect those values and recover that pre-existent sense of security. The so-called movements of primary resistance were often protests of conservation. Later in the colonial period the religious movements in Africa often seemed to be animated by nostalgia for the past, real or imaginary. These latter were often protests of restoration.

If a militant impulse to conserve is often an indicator of disturbed faith, a militant impulse to restore or to transform is often an indicator of awakened consciousness. But what we find here is that the whole problem of trying to ascertain what is social or political consciousness in the study of African movements of protest touches a similar problem in the study of Marxism. In the latter, it touches, first, on whether an

[2] Ibid.

underprivileged class is conscious of itself as a class. It touches, secondly, on whether the underprivileged class is conscious of what it has to protest against, and, thirdly, on whether that class is conscious of how it can transform the situation to its own advantage. The first is simple self-awareness as a group; the second is the collective grievance; and the third is the popular revolutionary aspiration.

The same three levels of awareness are discernible in the development of African political consciousness and protest movements in the past hundred years.

Let us take an example almost at random. On 25 February 1947, the *Daily Express* of Nigeria reported that a West Indian working for the Colonial Office Welfare Department was refused accommodation by the white-owned Bristol Hotel in Lagos on the grounds that he was colored. It was not long before the editor of *Pan-Africa,* a nationalist journal published in London at the time, took up this incident and started to speculate on its broader significance for nationalism in Africa. Why had the African employees of the hotel failed to register their protest at this exclusion of a colored patron? The editor of *Pan-Africa* was convinced that in this, as in many other instances of apparent apathy or conformity by the masses of Africans, what was lacking was the ability to realize "the implications of such incidents." He therefore warned his fellow African intellectuals: "If we cannot arouse their consciousness we shall have lost a great battle."[3]

If the so-called primary resistance was an indication of disturbed faith, the so-called secondary resistance has often been an indication of awakened consciousness. But the relationship between consciousness and grievance is not always a matter of spontaneous perception, but must include an element of manipulated consciousness. We might indeed here distinguish African political consciousness from African national consciousness, and African national consciousness from African nationalism. African political consciousness in its modern phase was born out of a consciousness of the kind of common grievance illustrated by the incident at the Bristol Hotel. The incident symbolized a whole universe of inequality and humiliation. African *political* consciousness started with a consciousness of precisely such shared grievances.

The political consciousness became African *national* consciousness when the grievances were identified as "common" not only in the form they took ("We are *all* denied admission to the Bristol Hotel") but also

[3] J. R. Makonnen, "The Greek Word for Colour Bar," *Pan-Africa* (June 1947). This incident and its implications are discussed in similar terms in Ali A. Mazrui, "The English Language and Political Consciousness in British Colonial Africa," *Journal of Modern African Studies,* IV (1966), 295-311.

in the reasons behind them ("We are all denied admission to the Bristol Hotel because we are all black").

This kind of black national consciousness became a goal-oriented African nationalism when alternatives to the *status quo* began to be conceived and to be regarded as feasible. This was a move from protest of corrective censure against the color bar to protest of transformation in favor of changing the whole system. The stages of the process began with a consciousness of political status as a relevant factor toward explaining some of the grievances. ("We are all denied admission to the Bristol Hotel not merely because we are all black but also because we do not possess direct political power to force the Bristol to accept black patrons.") An alternative to the *status quo* became a matter of calculated possible modifications of the political status of the Africans. It began with an awareness of piecemeal alternatives to individual grievances. It then passed from this stage to a militant transformative one. ("The Bristol Hotel's insult against us stems from our whole dependent status. It is that status which must be changed completely.") By this time the politics of grievances had been transformed into a more positive force. Politics were now concerned with definable national aspirations.

If we are to identify the three most persistent psychological sources of protest, we would probably find that they are *anger*, *fear*, and *frustrated ambition*. Anger and fear on the part of individuals are emotional *responses*, while ambition is an emotional *drive*. Anger and fear are internal individual responses to external stimuli. One is angry at something or afraid of something usually as a result of an external provocation. Ambition, on the other hand, is often an instinctual quest for self-improvement, an internal impulse seeking external fulfillment. What a person is ambitious about, or what constitutes self-improvement, may be culture-bound or sociologically determined. But the actual desire for self-improvement—regardless of the form which that improvement is to take—is often a deeper human longing. It is an inner impulse in the nature of man rather than a trait acquired from the particular society in which an individual may live.

The self-improvement which is sought need not, of course, necessarily be material well-being. The quest may be for improved status, greater prestige, or what John Milton called "that last infirmity of noble mind," fame and immortality.

Protest arises where ambitions are frustrated or denied what are regarded as legitimate areas of fulfillment. Despres has argued that, with respect to many protest movements, the political character of the movement derives not so much from the nature of protest as it does from the structure of the society within which protest exists. He has gone on to assert that in a plural society the political character of protest is assured. His major example is Guyana. Any sense of deprivation experienced by the African group in relation to the Indian group, or vice versa, results not only in a posture of protest but in a form of protest which is fundamentally *political.*

> More precisely, any change capable of altering the structure of intersectional relations will have consequences for the political order of the society. Conversely, any change in the political order of the society will inevitably alter the structure of the intersectional relations. In short, the process of change in the plural society tends to be a political process at all levels of the social order.[4]

By way of illustration, the author cites the example of the construction of a new health center by the Guyanese government. The questions which arise in such a situation have important implications for intersectional relations. Will the facility be located in a predominantly African village or will it be constructed nearby in an Indian village? Who will be placed in charge of the facility, an African or an Indian? Similarly, where will the new school be located?

> Ultimately, these decisions affect the competitive advantage which individual Africans and Indians believe they have with respect to intersectional relations. . . . In view of these considerations, it would appear that practically all forms of protest will have political consequences in societies of plural type.[5]

In reality Despres mistakes the characteristics of *competitive* pluralism for attributes of pluralism at large. Where different cultural groups in a society feel they are in competition with each other, it is indeed likely that almost all significant forms of protest in that society will affect intersectional relations. Such a situation is one where the advantages enjoyed by one section are resented by another. Competitive pluralism implies that the outlets for the ambitions of the different groups are the same and must be shared.

But different cultural groups living in the same society need not aspire to the same things. Plural societies which have occupational specialization by racial or cultural groups, for example, need not be acutely competitive between those groups. Societies with a caste system, where legitimate ambitions for one caste are differentiated from the legitimate ambitions of another caste, need not have acute inter-caste rivalry. In such cases, pluralism consists of groups which are not mutually competitive. Protest therefore need not automatically be politicized. Caste

---

[4] Leo A. Despres, *Protest and Change in Plural Societies* (Montreal, 1969), 17.
[5] Ibid., 16-17.

societies are based primarily on *complementary* plurality rather than *competitive* plurality. When a particular caste is forced to protest in defense of its rights, it is likely to be defending rights exclusive to itself. Those exclusive rights may have been momentarily slighted or violated. Sometimes the demands may be from religious groups within a particular society, claiming not what the followers of another religion might have and which they lack, but claiming what is essential for the observance of their own religion or for the dignity of their religious institutions. The rights of each *millet* in the Ottoman Empire, for example, were unisectional rights, and the defense did not necessarily entail intersectional scramble for the same prize. Protest in defense of exclusively religious rights of a *millet* was not therefore automatically politicized in the sense postulated by Despres. Ambition is not always competitive. A poet's ambition to write an epic need not be at the expense of another poet. A woman's ambition to make her husband happy need not entail rivalry with another.

Here another observation needs to be emphasized. Protest arising out of *frustrated ambition* is always self-regarding. It tends to be protest in defense of the rights or interests of the protester. But protest arising out of the impulse of anger can be other-regarding. There is such a thing as altruistic anger, usually arising out of a sense of offended idealism. A European protester may be indignant at what is being done in Vietnam, or an American protester at what happened in Biafra. Their anger can be entirely other-regarding and altruistic in motivation.

As for protests arising out of fear, these could be either self-regarding or other-regarding. The protester may be fearful of what would happen to himself or fearful of what might happen to another. The motivation may be self-interest or anxious idealism. Protests of conservation tend very often to include a high component of fear. This is because the instinct to conserve carries with it latent anxieties and jealous protectiveness.

Protests of restoration and protests of transformation are often characterized by an ambitious drive. In the case of restoration, the ambition derives sustenance from deep nostalgia and the aspiration to bring back what has passed away. Protests of transformation are a commitment to innovative goals. There may be a component of anger at the inadequacies of the current state of affairs, but there is always in addition a conviction that new directions are feasible. The ambition takes the form of aspiring to have those directions followed in earnest.

Anger is a persistent source of corrective censure. But elements of fear and even of ambition may sometimes also be present in this kind of protest.

The three impulses of ambition, fear, and anger are all relevant to the process of national integration in the new Africa. And protest itself becomes also important in the wider process of modernization.

In *Representative Government*, John Stuart Mill defined a nationality in the following terms:

> A portion of mankind may be said to constitute a Nationality if they are united among themselves by common sympathies which do not exist between them and any others—which make them co-operate with each other more willingly than with other people, desire to be under the same government, and desire that it should be government by themselves or a portion of themselves exclusively. This feeling of nationality may have been generated by various causes. . . . But the strongest of all is identity of political antecedents; the possession of a national history and consequent community of recollections; collective pride and humiliation, pleasure and regret, connected with the same incidents in the past.[6]

Mill is here emphasizing the importance for nationhood of the kind of shared experiences which lead to shared prejudices and shared emotional dispositions. When a group of people begin to feel proud about the same things or humiliated by the same things, or pleased or saddened collectively by the same incidents, that group of people is acquiring the capacity for collective selfhood. The process of nation-building at the psychological level therefore entails the cumulative acquisition of common emotional dispositions and common potential responses to the same stimuli. To be capable of being angry about the same incident is to share an area of fellow-feeling.

Social engineering in the new African states has sometimes taken the form of purposeful collectivization of anger in a bid to make the populace share a moment of indignant empathy. The collectivization of anger sometimes results in the nationalization of protest. A capacity for what Mill calls "collective pride and humiliation" is a particularly important feature of a sense of shared nationhood. It is precisely because of this that anger as an emotion is so central to the growth of nationhood. After all, offended pride gives rise to anger. And collective humiliation, a deeper stage of offended pride, in turn generates anger, either overtly or in a silent, subdued form. Shared moments of collective anger by a group, by being connected with the cumulative acquisition of a capacity for collective pride and collective humiliation, become part of the process of national integration.

National integration is itself part of modernization in Africa, and the role of protest in the integrative process has relevance for moderni-

[6] *Representative Government* (London, 1861), Ch. XVI.

zation as a whole. But protest has other functions apart from that of national integration. It gives a social system the cumulative experience of tension management, and therefore permits it to increase its absorptive capacity for change. By testing the elasticity of a social or political system, protest may sometimes result in the disruption of that system. But that is one of the risks of growth and development. Social systems, like social beings, often have to experience the anguish of maturation. Moments of disruption followed by moments of readjustment may be inseparable from the process of growth.

We have indicated earlier that the move from a society of silent change to a society of conscious reform is one major indicator of modernization, and that protest constitutes an important aspect of it. But according to Eisenstadt the very definition of a modern society hinges on a capacity to absorb change. The changes which come with technology and improved modes of productivity, with better communications and new horizons of exploration, and with the conquest of disease and the increase of populations all generate important social consequences.[7] The modernity of a society is to be judged primarily in regard to that society's capability to absorb those changes effectively. And the demand for changes which need to be made in the social arrangements is often articulated through protest as a medium for reform. The institutionalization of protest, in ways which make conflict-management feasible and efficient, is one of the central features of political development and social integration.

If the two tropical trees are to remain valid analogies for social analysis, we might say that the move from tradition to modernity is the move from the mysterious rigidity of the baobab tree to the realistic flexibility of the coconut tree. The elements of the universe in their modern guise often attack all societies together. Some of the most modern are in a state of disruption. But that may well be because they are not modernized enough to absorb the changes, or have not as yet been given a chance to demonstrate their full absorptive capacity.

There are times when only protest can convincingly test the elasticity of a social system. The essays in this book were not primarily designed to demonstrate this proposition. But they were designed to illustrate protest as a social fact of wide implications. The theoretical inferences which constitute this conclusion are an attempt to assess the range of those implications. Yet, in the final analsysis, the primary source of thought and illumination on protest as a social fact in Africa across several generations must lie for the time being in the case-studies en-

---

[7] See, for example, S. N. Eisenstadt, *Modernization: Protest and Change* (Englewood Cliffs, 1966).

compassed in this book. Only against the background of the empirical data used here, and of the analysis of these specific cases, can protest as an area of social experience be expected to reveal itself in more concrete forms.

Ali A. Mazrui

BIBLIOGRAPHY

This is a select bibliography of articles and books which is designed to supplement the individual essays and sections of this volume and to provide a general list of the available literature on resistance movements, rebellions, and so forth in Africa. The editors make no claims for the completeness of the bibliography, but they do hope that it is at least suggestive, and that it encompasses a reasonably wide range of subject matter. Some items, although relevant to more than one category, are listed only once.

1. RESISTANCE TO CONQUEST

Alldridge, T. J., *The Sherbro and Its Hinterland* (London, 1901).

Archinard, Louis, *Le Soudan français en 1889–90* (Paris, 1891).

————, "Rapport sur la campagne de 1890–91," *Journal officiel de la République française* (10 and 28 October 1891), 4863-5214.

Arnette, Maurice, *Un voisin gênant: Samory* (Lille, 1898).

Baratier, A. E. A., *A travers l'Afrique* (Paris, 1910).

————, *Epopées africaines* (Paris, 1912).

Baratieri, Oreste, *Memorie d'Africa (1892–1896)* (Torino, 1898).

Battaglia, Roberto, *La prima guerra d'Africa* (Torino, 1958).

Bellavita, Emilio, *Adua, I Precedenti, La Battaglia—Le Conseguenze* (Genova, 1931).

Berete, Framoi, "Kankan," *Cahiers Charles de Foucauld*, IV (1956), 17-25.

Berkeley, George F. H., *The Campaign of Adowa and the Rise of Menelik* (London, 1902).

Bernus, Edmond, "Kong et sa région," *Etudes Eburnéennes*, VIII (1960), 239-324.

Besson, Maurice, "Borgnis Desbordes et Archinard," *Bulletin du Comité de l'Afrique Française*, XLIII (1953), 313-18.

Binger, Louis Gustave, *Du Niger au Golfe de Guinée par le pays de Kong et le Mossi* (Paris, 1892), 2v.

————, *Carnets de route* (Paris, 1938).

Boisboissel, Yves de, *Le capitaine Georges Mangin* (Paris, 1954).

Bonnier, Gaetan, *L'occupation de Tombouctou* (Paris, 1926).

————, "Au Soudan de jadis," *Revue internationale d'histoire militaire*, IV (1956), 87-112.

Borgnis-Desbordes, Gustave, "Au vieux Soudan," *Renseignements coloniaux*, XX (1910), 81-94, 145-50, 159-68.

————, "Un cinquantenaire," *Revue militaire de l'Afrique Occidentale Française*, XIV (1933), 33-41.

————, "Le cinquantenaire de Bamako," *Institut colonial du Havre*, XXXIX (1933), 3-5.

Bourelly, G., *La battaglia di Abba Garima* (Rome, 1896).

Ciasca, R., *Storia coloniale dell' Italia contemporanea* (Milan, 1940).

Colin, G., "La France dans le Soudan occidental," *Revue française de l'étranger et des colonies*, I (1895), 297-304.

Collieaux, Alfred, "Contribution à l'étude de l'histoire de l'ancien royaume du Kénédougou," *Bulletin du comité d'études historiques et scientifiques de l'Afrique Occidentale Française*, VII (1924), 128-81.

————, "Détails rétrospectifs sur l'histoire des dernières opérations contre Samory," *Bulletin du comité d'études historiques et scientifiques de l'Afrique Occidentale Française*, XXI (1938), 290-303.

Conti Rossini, Carlo, *Italia ed Etiopia dal trattato d'Uccialli alla battaglia di Adua* (Rome, 1935).

Crispi, Francesco, *La prima guerra d'Africa. Documenti e memorie dell' Archivio Crispi* (Milan, 1914).

Delafosse, Maurice, *Les frontières de la Côte d'Ivoire, de la Côte d'Or et du Soudan* (Paris, 1908).

————, *Haut-Sénégal-Niger* (Paris, 1912), 3v.

————, "Afrique occidentale," in Gabriel Hanotaux (ed.), *Histoire des Colonies françaises* (Paris, 1931), 1-356.

Demanche, G., "Le Soudan français et la campagne contre Samori," *Revue française de l'étranger et des colonies*, VIII (1893), 289-95.

Duboc, Albert Alfred, *L'épopée coloniale en Afrique Occidentale Française* (Paris, 1938).

————, *Samory le sanglant* (Paris, 1947).

Dubois, Félix, *La vie au continent noir* (Paris, 1893).

Ellenberger, D. F., and C. J. Macgregor, *History of the Basuto, Ancient and Modern* (London, 1912).

Ellenberger, Victor, *A Century of Mission Work in Basutoland* (Morija, 1933).

Faidherbe, Louis Léon C., *Le Sénégal* (Paris, 1889).

Farler, J. P., "England and Germany in East Africa," *The Fortnightly Review*, LI (1889), 157-65.

Fofana, Kalil, "L'Almamy Samori," *Recherches africaines*, V (1963), 3-28.

Frey, Henri, *Campagne dans le Haut Sénégal et le Haut Niger, 1885–86* (Paris, 1888).

Gallieni, Charles, *Voyage au Soudan Français* (Paris, 1885).

———, *Deux campagnes au Soudan Français* (Paris, 1891).

Gatelet, A. L. C., *Histoire de la conquête du Soudan français* (Paris, 1901).

Germond, R. C., *Chronicles of Basutoland* (Morija, 1967).

Giglio, Carlo, *L'Italia in Africa: Etiopia/Mar Rosso* (Rome, 1958), 3v.

———, "Article 17 of the Treaty of Uccialli," *Journal of African History*, VI (1965), 221-31.

Guèbrè-Sellassié, *Chronique du règne de Ménélik II, roi des rois d'Ethiopie* (Paris, 1930-32), 2v.

Guillaumet, E., *Project de mission chez Samory* (Paris, 1895).

Hebert, R. P., "Une page d'histoire voltaïque: Amoro, chef des Tièfo," *Bulletin de l'Institut Français d'Afrique Noire*, XX (1958), 377-405.

———, "Samory en Haute Volta," *Études voltaïques*, II (1961), 5-55.

Holas, B., "Un document authentique sur Samori," *Notes Africaines—Institut Français d'Afrique Noire*, LXXIV (1957), 52-55.

Humbert, G., *Le général Borgnis-Desbordes et le colonel Humbert* (Paris, 1896).

———, "Le Soudan français en 1897," *Nouvelle Revue*, I (1897), 18-37.

Humblot, P., "Kankan, métropole de la Haute Guinée," *Bulletin du Comité de l'Afrique Française*, XXXI (1921), 129-40, 153-61.

Ingold, (Général), *Samory, sanglant et magnifique* (Paris, 1961).

Jones, G. I., "Chiefly Succession in Basutoland," in Jack Goody (ed.), *Succession to High Office* (Cambridge, 1966), 57-81.

Jonquière, C. de la, *Les Italiens en Erithrée. Quinze ans de politique coloniale* (Paris, 1897).

Labouret, Henri, "Les bandes de Samory dans la Haute Côte d'Ivoire, la Côte de l'Or et le pays Lobi," *Renseignements Coloniaux*, XXXIII (1925), 341-55.

Lagden, Godfrey, *The Basutos* (London, 1909).

Legassick, Martin, "Firearms, Horses and Samorian Army Organization," *Journal of African History*, VII (1966), 95-116.

Mangin, C., *Lettres du Soudan* (Paris, 1930).

———, "Lettres de jeunesse," *Revue des Deux Mondes* (Jan. 1930), 102-25.

Mantegazza, Vico, *La Guerra in Africa* (Firenze, 1896).

Massaia, G., *I miei trentacinque anni di missione nell'alta Etiopia* (Rome, 1885–95).

Melli, T. B., *La colonia Eritrea dalle sue origini* (Parma, 1899).

Meniaud, Jacques, "Le général Borgnis-Desbordes," in *Les grands soldats coloniaux* (Paris, 1931), 247-58.

———, *Les pionniers du Soudan* (Paris, 1931).

———, *Sikasso* (Paris, 1935).

Mévil, André, *Samory* (Paris, 1899).

Monnier, L. P., *France Noire (Côte d'Ivoire et Soudan)* (Paris, 1894).

Monteil, Charles, *Une page d'histoire militaire coloniale, la colonne de Kong* (Paris, 1902).

Monteil, P. L., *Souvenirs vécus, quelques feuillets de l'histoire coloniale* (Paris, 1924).

Mordacq, J. J. H., *Le spahis soudanais* (Paris, 1912).

Müller, Fritz F., *Deutschland-Zanzibar-Ostafrika: Geschichte einer deutschen Kolonialeroberung, 1884–1890* (Berlin, 1959).

Pankhurst, Richard, "The Battle," and "How the News Was Received in England," *Ethiopia Observer*, I (1957), 349-57, 357-63.

———, "Fire-Arms in Ethiopian History (1800–1935)," *Ethiopia Observer*, VI (1962), 135-80.

Péroz, Etienne, *L'Empire de l'Almamy Emir Samory* (Besançon, 1888).

———, *Au Soudan français* (Paris, 1889).

———, *La tactique au Soudan* (Paris, 1890).

———, *Au Niger* (Paris, 1895).

———, *Par vocation* (Paris, 1905).

———, "Les ancêtres de Samori," *Cahiers d'Etudes Africaines*, IV (1963), 125-56.

Person, Yves, "La jeunesse de Samori," *Revue française d'histoire d'Outre Mer*, II (1962), 152-80.

———, "L'aventure de Porèkèrè et le drame de Waima," *Cahiers d'Etudes Africaines*, V (1965), 248-316.

———, "Correspondances de la résidence du Kissi relatives à l'affaire de Waima," ibid., V (1965), 472-89.

———, "Samori et la Sierra Leone," ibid., VII (1967), 5-26.

———, "L'empire de Samori, selon Péroz," *Notes africaines*, CXIII (1967), 31.

Pollera, Alberto, *La battaglia di Adua del 1° marzo 1896; narrata nei luoghi ove fu combattuta* (Florence, 1928).

Ranger, Terence O., "Connexions between 'Primary Resistance' Movements and Modern Mass Nationalism in East and Central Africa, I," *Journal of African History*, IX (1968), 437-53.

Redmayne, Alison, "Mkwawa and the Hehe Wars," *Journal of African History*, IX (1968), 409-36.

Rossetti, C., *Storia diplomatica della Etiopia durante il regno di Menelik II* (Turin, 1910).

Rubenson, Sven, "Some Aspects of the Survival of Ethiopian Independence in the Period of the Scramble for Africa," *University College Review* (Spring 1961), 8-24.

——, "The Protectorate Paragraph of the Wichale Treaty," *Journal of African History*, V (1964), 243-83.

——, *Wichale XVII: The Attempt to Establish a Protectorate over Ethiopia* (Addis Ababa, 1964).

——, "Professor Giglio, Antonelli and Article XVII of the Treaty of Wichale," *Journal of African History*, VII (1966), 445-57.

——, "The Adwa Peace Treaty of 1884," *Journal of Ethiopian Studies*, V (1967), 225-36.

Sabelli, Luca dei, *Storia d'Abissinia* (Rome, 1938), 4v.

Sevin-Desplages, L., "Le Soudan Français et sa colonisation," *Revue de Géographie*, XIV (1891), 216-23.

Shepperson, George, "The Military History of British Central Africa," *The Rhodes-Livingstone Journal*, XXVI (1959), 23-33.

Suret-Canale, J., "L'Almamy Samory Touré," *Recherches Africaines*, I (1959), 18-22.

Tordoff, William, *Ashanti under the Prempehs* (London, 1965).

Tylden, George, *The Rise of the Basuto* (Cape Town, 1950).

Valbert, G., "Un épisode inédit des campagnes du Soudan," *Revue des Deux Mondes*, CXXVI (1894), 697-708.

Wheeler, Douglas L., "Nineteenth-Century African Protest in Angola: Prince Nicolas of Kongo," *African Historical Studies*, I (1968), 40-58.

Woon, Harry V., *Twenty-Five Years' Soldiering in South Africa* (London, 1909).

Work, Ernest, *Ethiopia, a Pawn in European Diplomacy* (New Concord, Ohio, 1935).

Wylde, Augustus B., *Modern Abyssinia* (London, 1901).

Zaghi, Carlo (ed.), *Crispi e Menelich: nel diario inedito del conte Augusto Salimbeni* (Turin, 1956).

II. REBELLIONS AGAINST ALIEN RULE

Barnett, Donald, *Mau Mau From Within* (London, 1966).

Bessel, M. J., "Nyabingi," *Uganda Journal*, VI (1938), 73-86.

Collins, Robert O., *The Southern Sudan 1883–1898* (New Haven, 1962).

Crowder, Michael, *West Africa under Colonial Rule* (London, 1968).

Denzer, LaRay, "A Diary of Bai Bureh's War," *Sierra Leone Studies*, 23 (1968), 39-65; 24 (1969).

Gray, Richard, *A History of the Southern Sudan 1839–1889* (Oxford, 1961).

Gwassa, G. C. K., and John Iliffe (eds.), *Records of the Maji Maji Rising*, I (Nairobi, 1968).

Hasan, Said Muhammad, *Al Mahdiya fi al-Islam* (Cairo, 1953).

Hess, Robert, "The 'Mad Mullah' and Northern Somalia," *Journal of African History*, V (1964), 415-34.

Hill, Richard, *Egypt in the Sudan 1820–1821* (Oxford, 1959).

Holt, Peter M., *The Mahdist State in the Sudan, 1881–1898* (Oxford, 1958).

Iliffe, John, "The Organization of the Maji Maji Rebellion," *Journal of African History*, VIII (1967), 495-512.

Marks, Shula, "Harriette Colenso and the Zulus, 1874–1913," *Journal of African History*, IV (1963), 403-12.

———, "Christian African Participation in the 1906 Zulu Rebellion," *Bulletin of the Society for African Church History*, XI (1965), 55-72.

———, "Natal, the Nguni and Their Historians: A Review Article," *Journal of African History*, IX (1968), 529-40.

Mwase, George S. (Robert I. Rotberg, ed.), *Strike a Blow and Die: A Narrative of Race Relations in Colonial Africa* (Cambridge, 1967).

Onwuteaka, V. C., "The Aba Riot of 1929 and Its Relation to the System of 'Indirect Rule'," *Nigerian Journal of Economics and Social Studies*, VII (1966), 273-82.

Ranger, Terence, "The 'Ethiopian' Episode in Barotseland, 1900–1905," *The Rhodes-Livingstone Journal*, XXXVII (1965), 26-41.

Rotberg, Robert I., *The Rise of Nationalism in Central Africa: The Making of Malawi and Zambia 1873–1964* (Cambridge, 1965).

———, "Resistance and Rebellion in British Nyasaland and German East Africa, 1888–1915: A Tentative Comparison," in Prosser Gifford and Wm. Roger Louis (eds.), *Britain and Germany in Africa* (New Haven, 1967), 667-90.

Shepperson, George, "Pan-Africanism and 'Pan-Africanism': Some Historical Notes," *Phylon*, XXIII (1962), 346-58.

———, "External Factors in the Development of African Nationalism, with Particular Reference to British Central Africa," *Historians in Tropical Africa* (Salisbury, 1962), 317-32.

———, "Abolitionism and African Political Thought," *Transition*, 12 (1964), 22-26.

———, and Thomas Price, *Independent African. John Chilembwe and the Origins, Setting and Significance of the Nyasaland Native Rising of 1915* (Edinburgh, 1958).

Shibeika, Mekki, *Al-Sudan fi Qarn 1819–1919* (Cairo, 1947).

Shoucair, N. (Na'um Shuqayr), *Ta'rikh al-Sudan al-qadim wa al-hadith wa jughrafiyatuhu* (Cairo, n.d. [1903]), partially translated into German by E. L. Dietrich in *Der Islam*, XIV (1925), 199-288.

Stuart, James, *A History of the Zulu Rebellion, 1906, and of Dinuzulu's Arrest, Trial and Expatriation* (London, 1913).

Trimingham, John Spencer, *Islam in the Sudan* (Oxford, 1949).

Wingate, F. R., *Mahdiism and the Egyptian Sudan* (London, 1899).

III. THE RELIGIOUS EXPRESSION OF DISCONTENT

Abun-Nasr, J. M., *The Tijaniyya, a Sufi Order in the Modern World* (London, 1965).

Amara, I. B., "Possession: Its Nature and Some Modes," *Sierra Leone Bulletin of Religion*, VI (1964), 1-12.

Amos-Djoro, Ernest, "Les églises harristes et le nationalisme ivorien," *Le Mois en Afrique*, V (May 1966), 26-47.

Andersson, Efraim, *Messianic Popular Movements in the Lower Congo* (Uppsala, 1958).

Aquina, Mary, "The People of the Spirit: An Independent Church in Rhodesia [The Apostles]," *Africa*, XXXVII (1967), 203-19.

Baeta, C. G., *Prophetism in Ghana: A Study of Some "Spiritual" Churches* (London, 1962).

Balandier, Georges, "Contribution à une sociologie de la dépendance," *Cahiers Internationaux de Sociologie*, XII (1952), 47-69.

————, "Messianismes et nationalismes en Afrique Noire," ibid., XIV (1953), 41-65.

————, *Sociologie actuelle de l'Afrique noire. Dynamique des changements sociaux en Afrique centrale.* (Paris, 1955, revised edition, 1963).

Banton, Michael, "African Prophets," *Race*, V (1963), 42-55.

Barrett, David D., *Schism and Renewal in Africa: An Analysis of Six Thousand Contemporary Religious Movements* (Nairobi, 1968).

Bastide, Roger, "Messianisme et développement économique et social," *Cahiers Internationaux de Sociologie*, XXXI (1961), 3-14.

Bazola, E., *La conversion au Kimbangisme et ses motifs* (Léopoldville, 1964).

Beattie, J. H. M., "Initiation into the Chwezi Spirit Possession Cult in Bunyoro," *African Studies*, XVI (1957), 150-61.

Bernard, G., and P. Caprasse (trans. F. Monnier), "Religious Movements in the Congo: A Research Hypothesis," *Cahiers Economiques et Sociaux*, III (1965), 49-60.

Bertsche, James E., "Kimbanguism: A Challenge to Missionary Statesmen," *Practical Anthropology*, XIII (1966), 13-33.

Brown, Kenneth I., "Worshipping with the African Church of the Lord (Aladura)," *Practical Anthropology*, XIII (1966), 59-84.

Buerkle, Horst, "The Message of the 'False Prophets' of the Independent Churches of Africa," *Makerere Journal*, XI (1965), 51-55.

Cardaire, M., *L'Islam et le terroir africain* (Bamako, 1954).

Chome, Jules, *La passion de Simon Kimbangu 1921–1951* (Brussels, 1959).

Dallimore, H., "The Aladura Movement in Ekiti," *Western Equatorial Africa Church Magazine*, XXXVI (1931), 93-97.

Debertry, Léon, *Kitawala* (Elisabethville, 1953).

De Queiroz, Maria I. Pereira, "Maurice Leenhardt et les 'églises ethiopiennes'," *Le Monde Non-Chrétien*, LXXIV (1965), 84-101.

Fehderau, Harold W., "Kimbanguism: Prophetic Christianity in Congo," *Practical Anthropology*, IX (1962), 157-78.

Fernandez, James W., "The Lumpa Uprising: Why?" *Africa Report*, IX (1964), 30-32.

———, "The Idea and Symbol of the Saviour in a Gabon Syncretistic Cult: Basic Factors in the Mythology of Messianism," *International Review of Missions*, LIII (1964), 281-89.

———, "Politics and Prophecy: African Religious Movements," *Practical Anthropology*, XII (1965), 71-75.

———, "Symbolic Consensus in a Fang Reformative Cult," *American Anthropologist*, LXVII (1965), 902-29.

———, "Unbelievably Subtle Words: Representation and Integration in the Sermons of an African Reformative Cult," *History of Religions*, VI (1966), 43-69.

Foran, W. Robert, *A Cuckoo in Kenya* (London, 1936).

Froelich, J. C., *Les musulmans d'Afrique noire* (Paris, 1962).

Goldsmith, F. H. (J. M. Silvester, ed.), *John Ainsworth, Pioneer Kenya Administrator 1864–1946* (London, 1959).

Gorju, Julien, *Entre le Victoria l'Albert et l'Edouard* (Rennes, 1920).

Gouilly, Alphonse, *L'Islam dans l'Afrique Occidentale Française* (Paris, 1952).

Haliburton, G. M., "The Anglican Church in Ghana and the Harris Movement in 1914," *Bulletin of the Society of African Church History*, I (1964), 101-6.

Haywood, Victor E. W. (ed.), *African Independent Church Movements* (Edinburgh, 1963).

Heward, Christine, "The Rise of Alice Lenshina," *New Society*, IV (13 Aug. 1964), 6-8.

Holas, Bohumil, *Le séparatisme religieux en Afrique noire (L'exemple de la Côte d'Ivoire)* (Paris, 1965).

Kaufman, Robert, *Millénarisme et acculturation* (Brussels, 1964).

Köbben, A. J. F., "Prophetic Movements as an Expression of Social Protest," *International Archives of Ethnography*, XLIX (1960), 117-64.

Lanternari, Vittorio, *Religions of the Oppressed: A Study of Modern Messianic Cults* (New York, 1963).

———, "Syncrétismes, messianismes, neo-traditionalismes. Postface à une étude des mouvements religieux de l'Afrique noire. II. La situation post-coloniale," *Archives de Sociologie des Religions*, XXI (1966), 101-10.

Lehmann, Dorothea, "Alice Lenshina Mulenga and the Lumpa Church," in John V. Taylor and Dorothea Lehmann, *Christians of the Copperbelt* (London, 1961), 248-68.

LeVine, Robert A., "Omoriori: Smeller of Witches," *Natural History*, LXVII (1958), 142-47.

———, "Gusii Sex Offenses: A Study in Social Control," *American Anthropologist*, LXI (1959), 965-90.

———, "The Internationalization of Political Values in Stateless Societies," *Human Organization*, XIX (1960), 51-58.

———, "Witchcraft and Sorcery in a Gusii Community," in John Middleton and Edward H. Winter (eds.), *Witchcraft and Sorcery in East Africa* (London, 1963), 221-55.

———, "Socialization, Social Structure, and Intersocietal Images," in Herbert Klein (ed.), *International Behavior: A Social Psychological Analysis* (New York, 1965), 45-69.

———, and Barbara LeVine, "Nyansongo: A Gusii Community in Kenya," in Beatrice B. Whiting (ed.), *Six Cultures* (New York, 1963), 19-202.

Macpherson, Fergus, "Notes on the Beginning of the Movement," in "The Alice Movement in Northern Rhodesia," International Missionary Council Occasional Papers, I (London, 1958), 2-5, mimeo.

Mair, Lucy P., "Witchcraft as a Problem in the Study of Religion," *Cahiers d'Etudes Africaines*, IV (1964), 337-48.

Margarido, Alfredo, "L'église Toko et le mouvement de libération de l'Angola," *Le Mois en Afrique*, V (May 1966), 26-47.

Messenger, John C., "Reinterpretation of Christian and Indigenous Belief in a Nigerian Native Church," *American Anthropologist*, LXII (1960), 268-78.

Nottingham, John, and Carl C. Rosberg, *The Myth of Mau Mau: Nationalism in Kenya* (New York, 1966).

"Nyangweso," "The Cult of Mumbo in Central and South Kavirondo," *The Journal of the East Africa and Uganda Natural History Society*, 38-39 (1930), 13-17.

O'Connell, James, "Government and Politics in the Yoruba African Churches: The Claims of Tradition and Modernity," *Odu*, II (1965), 92-108.

Ogot, Bethwell A., "British Administration in the Central Nyanza District, 1900–1960," *Journal of African History*, IV (1963), 249-73.

Parrinder, E. G., *Religion in an African City* (London, 1953).

Pauw, B. A., *Religion in a Tswana Chiefdom* (London, 1960).

Pauwels, Marcel, "Le culte de Nyabingi (Ruanda)," *Anthropos*, XLVI (1951), 337-57.

Perrot, Claude-Hélène, "Un culte messianique chez les Sotho au milieu du 19e siècle, *Archives de Sociologie des Religions*, XVIII (1964), 147-52.

Philipps, J. E. T., "The Nabingi: An Anti-European Secret Society in Africa, in British Ruanda, Ndorwa and the Congo," *Congo*, IX (1928), 310-21.

Ringwald, Walter, "Westafrikanische Propheten," *Evangelische Missionszeitschrift*, I (1940), 118-22; 145-55.

Roberts, Andrew, "The Lumpa Tragedy," *Peace News* (4 September 1964).

Rondot, Pierre, "Le Mahdisme," *Le Mois en Afrique*, V (May 1966), 48-60.

Rotberg, Robert I., "The Lenshina Movement of Northern Rhodesia," *The Rhodes-Livingstone Journal*, XXIX (1961), 63-78.

Sangree, Walter, *Age, Prayer and Politics in Tiriki, Kenya* (London, 1966).

Sastre, Robert, "Christianisme et cultures africaines," *Tam-Tam*, VI (1957), 12-23.

Schlosser, Katesa, *Propheten in Afrika* (Braunschweig, 1949).

Shepperson, George, "Ethiopianism and African Nationalism," *Phylon*, XIV (1953), 9-18.

————, "The Politics of African Church Separatist Movements in British Central Africa, 1892–1916," *Africa*, XXIV (1954), 233-46.

————, "Negro American Influences on the Emergence of African Nationalism," *Journal of African History*, I (1960), 299-312.

————, "Nyasaland and the Millennium," in Sylvia L. Thrupp (ed.), *Millennial Dreams in Action* (The Hague, 1962), 144-59.

————, "Church and Sect in Central Africa," *The Rhodes-Livingstone Journal*, XXXIII (1963), 82-94.

Smith, Marion W., "Towards a Classification of Cult Movements," *Man*, LIX (1960), 63-76.

Stone, W. Vernon, "The 'Alice Movement' in 1958," in "The Alice Movement in Northern Rhodesia," International Missionary Council Occasional Papers, I (1958), 5-10, mimeo.

Sundkler, Bengt Gustaf M., *Bantu Prophets in South Africa* (London, 1948, revised and enlarged 1961).

Tangri, Roger K. "Early Asian Protest in the East Africa Protectorate, 1900–1918," *Africa Quarterly*, VII (Apr.–June 1967).

Thrupp, Sylvia L. (ed.), *Millennial Dreams in Action* (The Hague, 1962).

Thwaite, Daniel, *The Seething African Pot: A Study of Black Nationalism, 1882–1935* (London, 1936).

Turner, Harold W., "Searching and Syncretism: A West African Documentation," *International Review of Missions*, XLIX (1960), 189-94.

————, "Prophets and Politics: A Nigerian Test-Case," *Bulletin of the Society of African Church History*, II (1965), 97-118.

————, *History of an African Independent Church* (Oxford, 1967), 2v.

Vidal, Claudine, "Passé et présent des innovations religieuses au Congo-Léopoldville," *Le Mois en Afrique* (May 1966), 61-79.

Webster, James Bertin, *The African Churches Among the Yoruba 1888–1922* (Oxford, 1964).

Welbourn, F. B., *East African Rebels: A Study of Some Independent Churches* (London, 1961).

———, and Bethwell A. Ogot, *A Place to Feel at Home* (London, 1966).

Whisson, Michael, "The Will of God and the Wiles of Men," in Proceedings of the Conference of the East African Institute of Social Research (1962), 1-34, mimeo.

IV. THE EMERGENCE OF PRESSURE GROUPS AND POLITICAL PARTIES

Ansprenger, Franz, *Politik in Schwarzen Afrika* (Cologne, 1961).

Austen, Ralph A., "Notes on the Pre-History of TANU," *Makerere Journal,* IX (1964), 1-6.

Bates, Margaret, "Tanganyika: The Development of a Trust Territory," *International Organization,* IX (1955), 32-51.

———, "Tanganyika," in Gwendolen Carter (ed.), *African One-Party States* (Ithaca, 1962), 295-476.

Beck, Ann, "Some Observations on Jomo Kenyatta in Britain, 1929–1930," *Cahiers d'Etudes Africaines,* VI (1966), 308-29.

Bennett, George, "An Outline History of TANU," *Makerere Journal,* VII (1963), 1-18.

Benson, Mary, *African Patriots* (London, 1963).

Chidzero, Bernard T. G., *Tanganyika and International Trusteeship* (London, 1961).

Chilcote, Ronald H., "Les mouvements de libération au Mozambique," *Le Mois en Afrique* (July 1966), 30-42.

Coleman, James S., "Nationalism in Tropical Africa," *American Political Science Review,* XLVIII (1954), 404-26.

———, *Nigeria: Background to Nationalism* (Berkeley, 1958).

Dudbridge, B. J., and J. E. S. Griffiths, "The Development of Local Government in Sukumaland," *Journal of African Administration,* III (1951), 141-46.

Feit, Edward, *African Opposition in South Africa: The Failure of Passive Resistance* (Stanford, 1967).

Gardinier, David, *Cameroun, United Nations Challenge to French Policy* (London, 1963).

Hailey, William Malcolm, Baron. *Native Administration in the British African Territories* (London, 1950–53), 5v.

Hooker, James R., "Welfare Associations and Other Instruments of Accommodation in the Rhodesias Between the World Wars," *Comparative Studies in Society and History,* IX (1966), 51-63.

Jeffries, Charles, *Transfer of Power. Problems of the Passage to Self-Government* (London, 1960).

Johnson, G. Wesley, "The Ascendancy of Blaise Daigne and the Beginning of African Politics in Senegal," *Africa,* XXXVI (1966), 235-53.

Kandoro, S. A., *Mwito wa Uhuru* [The Call to Freedom] (Dar es Salaam, 1961).

Kilson, Martin L., *Political Change in a West African State* (Cambridge, Mass., 1966).

Kimble, David, *A Political History of Ghana* (Oxford, 1963).

Lang, Gottfried O., and Martha B., "Problems of Social and Economic Change in Sukumaland, Tanganyika," *Anthropological Quarterly,* XXXV (1962), 86-101.

Langley, J. Ayodele, "The Gambia Section of the National Congress of British West Africa," *Africa,* XXXIX (1969), 382-92.

Le Vine, Victor T., *The Cameroons: From Mandate to Independence* (Los Angeles, 1964).

————, "The Course of Political Violence in Africa," in W. H. Lewis (ed.), *French Speaking Africa: The Search for Identity* (New York, 1965), 58-79.

Liebenow, J. Gus, "Responses to Planned Political Change in a Tanganyika Tribal Group," *American Political Science Review,* L (1956), 442-61.

————, "The Sukuma," in Audrey I. Richards (ed.), *East African Chiefs* (London, 1959), 229-59.

Listowel, Judith, *The Making of Tanganyika* (New York, 1965).

Lonsdale, John M., "Some Origins of Nationalism in East Africa," *Journal of African History,* IX (1968), 119-46.

————, "The Emergence of African Nations; A Historiographical Analysis," *African Affairs,* LXVII (1968), 11-28.

Mackintosh, John P., *Nigerian Government and Politics: Prelude to Revolution* (Evanston, 1966).

Nye, Joseph S., Jr., "TANU and UPC: The Impact of Independence on Two African Nationalist Parties," in Jeffrey Butler and Alphonso Castagno (eds.), *Boston University Papers on Africa* (New York, 1967), 224-50.

Odinga, Oginga, *Not Yet Uhuru* (London, 1967).

Ranger, Terence, "African Attempts to Control Education in East and Central Africa, 1900–1939," *Past and Present,* XXXII (1965), 57-85.

Shaw, J. V., "The Development of African Local Government in Sukumaland," *Journal of African Administration,* VI (1954), 171-78.

Sklar, Richard L., *Nigerian Political Parties* (Princeton, 1963).

Taylor, J. Clagett, *The Political Development of Tanganyika* (Stanford, 1963).

Twining, Edward Lord, "The Last Nine Years in Tanganyika," *African Affairs,* LVIII (1959), 15-24.

Um Nyobé, R., "Caméroun, naissance du mouvement national," *Cahiers Internationaux,* VI (1954), 78-82; VII (1955), 81-88.

Wishlade, R. L., "Chiefship and Politics in the Mlanje District of Southern Nyasaland," *Africa,* XXXI (1961), 36-45.

Wright, Ian Michael, "The Meru Land Case," *Tanzania Notes and Records,* 66 (1966), 136-46.

V. THE ECONOMIC EXPRESSION OF DISCONTENT

Ballard, John A., "Les incidents de 1923 à Porto Novo: la politique à l'époque coloniale," *Études Dahoméennes,* IV (1965), 83-87.

Brittain, Vera, *Testament of Friendship* (London, 1940).

————, and Geoffrey Handley-Taylor (eds.), *Letters of Winifred Holtby and Vera Brittain (1920–1935)* (London, 1960).

Champion, A. W. G., *Mehlomadala, My Experiences in the I.C.U.* (Durban, 1929).

Forman, Lionel, *Chapters in the History of the March to Freedom* (Cape Town, 1959).

Friedland, William H., "Paradoxes of African Trade Unionism: Organizational Chaos and Political Potential," *Africa Report,* X (1965), 6-13.

Gitsham, Ernest, and James Trembath, *A First Account of Labour Organisation in South Africa* (Durban, 1926).

Hopkins, Anthony G., "The Lagos Strike of 1897," *Past and Present,* XXXV (1966), 133-55.

Houghton, D. Hobart, *The South African Economy* (Cape Town, 1964).

Johns, Sheridan W. III, "The Birth of Non-White Trade Unionism in South Africa," *Race,* IX (1967), 173-92.

Kuper, Leo, *Passive Resistance in South Africa* (New Haven, 1957).

————, *An African Bourgeoisie* (New Haven, 1965).

Nelson, Anton, *The Freemen of Meru* (Nairobi, 1967).

Perham, Margery (ed.), *Ten Africans* (London, 1938; 2nd ed. 1963).

Roux, Edward, *S. P. Bunting, A Political Biography* (Cape Town, 1944).

————, *Time Longer Than Rope: A History of the Black Man's Struggle for Freedom in South Africa* (London, 1948; 2nd ed., Madison, 1964).

Scott, Roger, *The Development of Trade Unions in Uganda* (Nairobi, 1966).

Trachtman, Lester N., "The Labor Movement in Ghana: A Study in Political Unionism," *Economic Development and Cultural Change,* X (1962), 183-200.

Warren, W. M., "Urban Real Wages and the Nigerian Trade Union Movement, 1939–1960," *Economic Development and Cultural Change,* XV (1966), 21-36.

VI. REVOLUTIONS, COUPS, AND READJUSTMENTS IN THE POST-INDEPENDENCE ERA

Albert, Ethel, "Socio-Political Organisation and Receptivity to Change: Some Differences Between Ruanda and Urundi," *Southwestern Journal of Anthropology,* XVI (1960), 46-74.

Anber, Paul, "Modernization and Political Disintegration: Nigeria and the Ibos," *Journal of Modern African Studies*, V (1967), 163-79.

Anderson, Charles, Fred von der Mehden, and Crawford Young, *Issues of Political Development* (Englewood Cliffs, N.J., 1967).

Attwood, William, *The Reds and the Blacks* (New York, 1967).

Ballard, John A., "Four Equatorial States," in Gwendolen Carter (ed.), *National Unity and Regionalism in Eight African States* (Ithaca, 1966), 231-336.

Baron, Leo, "Rhodesia; Taking Stock," *The World Today*, XXIII (1967), 369-74.

Bosschere, Georges de, *Rescapés de Watsa* (Brussels, 1966).

Centre de Recherche et d'Information Socio-Politique, *Rwanda Politique: 1958–1960* (Brussels, 1961).

Cliffe, Lionel, "Socialist Education in Tanzania," *Mawazo*, I (1967), 73-80.

Codere, Helen, "Power in Rwanda," *Anthropologica*, IV (1962), 45-85.

Crawford, Robert W., "Sudan: The Revolution of October 1964," *Mawazo*, I (1967), 47-60.

De Lacger, Louis, *Ruanda* (Kabgaye, 1959).

Dowdy, Homer E., *Out of the Jaws of the Lion* (New York, 1965).

Dudley, B. J., "Federalism and the Balance of Political Power in Nigeria," *Journal of Commonwealth Political Studies*, IV (1966), 16-29.

Elias, T. O., "The Charter of Organization of African Unity," *The American Journal of International Law*, LIX (1965), 243-67.

Engholm, G. F., and Ali A. Mazrui, "Violent Constitutionalism in Uganda," *Government and Opposition*, II (1967), 585-99.

Fox, Renée C., *et al.*, "The Second Independence: A Case Study of the Kwilu Rebellion," *Comparative Studies in Society and History*, VII (1965), 78-109.

Good, Robert C., "Changing Patterns in African International Relations," *American Political Science Review*, LVII (1964), 632-41.

Grundy, Kenneth W., "The Stanleyville Rescue: American Policy in the Congo," *Yale Review*, LVI (1967), 242-55.

Guilhelm, Marcel, and Jean Hebert, *Précis d'histoire de la Haute Volta* (Paris, 1961).

Gupta, A., "The Rhodesian Crisis and the Organization of African Unity," *International Studies* (July 1967), 55-64.

Hancock, I. R. "The Uganda Crisis, 1966," *Australian Outlook* (Dec. 1966), 263-77.

Hazoumé, Paul, *Doguicimi* (Paris, 1938).

d'Hertefelt, Marcel, "Les élections communales et le consensus politique au Rwanda," *Zaire*, XIV (1960), 403-38.

———, "Myth and Political Acculturation in Rwanda," in Allie Dubb (ed.), *Myth in Modern Africa* (Lusaka, 1960), 114-35, mimeo.

———— and Andre Coupez, *La royauté sacrée de l'ancien Rwanda* (Brussels, 1964).

Hoskyns, Catherine, *The Congo Since Independence* (London, 1965).

Hubert, Jean R., *La Toussaint Rwandaise* (Brussels, 1965).

Kestergat, Jean, *Congo Congo* (Paris, 1965).

Kiba, Simon, "La Haute Volta après quelques mois de liberté," *Afrique Nouvelle*, 994 (Aug. 31, 1966), 16; 995 (Sept. 14, 1966), 16.

Lebeuf, Jean-Paul, *Bangui* (Paris, 1954).

Lemarchand, René, "L'influence des systèmes traditionnels sur l'évolution politique du Rwanda et du Burundi," *Revue de l'Institut de Sociologie*, II (1962), 333-57.

————, "Power and Stratification in Rwanda: A Reconsideration," *Cahiers d'Etudes Africaines*, VI (1966), 592-610.

————, "Political Instability in Africa: The Case of Rwanda and Burundi," *Civilisations*, XVI (1966), 307-37.

————, "Social Change and Political Modernisation in Burundi," *Journal of Modern African Studies*, IV (1966), 401-33.

————, "Revolutionary Phenomena in Stratified Societies: Rwanda and Zanzibar," *Civilisations*, XVIII (1968), 1-34.

————, "La Relation de Clientèle comme Moyen de Contestation: La Cas du Rwanda," *Civilisations*, XIX (1969), 1-27.

————, *Rwanda-Burundi: A Tale of Two Kingdoms* (London, 1970).

Le Vine, Victor T., "The Central African Republic: Insular Problems of an Island State," *Africa Report*, X (1965), 17-23.

————, "The Trauma of Independence in French-Speaking Africa, *Journal of Developing Areas*, II (1968), 211-24.

Lofchie, Michael, "Party Conflict in Zanzibar," *Journal of Modern African Studies*, I (1963), 185-207.

————, *Zanzibar: Background to Revolution* (Princeton, 1965).

————, "Was Okello's Revolution a Conspiracy?" *Transition*, 33 (1967), 36-42.

Maquet, Jacques J., "Ruanda-Urundi: The Introduction of an Electoral System for Councils in a Caste Society," in Raymond Apthorpe (ed.), *From Tribal Rule to Modern Government* (Lusaka, 1960), 57-68, mimeo.

————, "La participation de la classe paysanne au mouvement d'indépendance du Rwanda," *Cahiers d'Etudes Africaines*, IV (1964), 552-68.

————, and Marcel d'Hertefelt, *Elections en société féodale* (Brussels, 1959).

Masson, Paul, *La Bataille pour Bukavu* (Brussels, 1966).

Mathews, Ronald, *African Powder Keg* (London, 1966).

Mazrui, Ali A., "The United Nations and Some African Political Attitudes," *International Organization*, XVIII (1964), 499-520.

————, *Towards a Pax Africana* (Chicago, 1967).

————, *The Anglo-African Commonwealth: Political Friction and Cultural Fusion* (Oxford, 1967).

————, *On Heroes and Uhuru-Worship: Essays on Independent Africa* (London, 1968).

————, *Violence and Thought: Essays on Social Tension in Africa* (London, 1969).

Mazrui, Ali A., and Donald Rothchild, "The Soldier and the State in East Africa: Some Theoretical Conclusions on the Army Mutinies of 1964," *The Western Political Quarterly*, XX (1967), 82-96.

Miller, Linda B., *World Order and Local Disorder: The United Nations and Internal Conflicts* (Princeton, 1967).

Mohan, Jitendra, "Ghana, The Congo, and The United Nations," *Journal of Modern African Studies*, VII (1969), 369-406.

Morgenthau, Ruth S., *Political Parties in French-Speaking West Africa* (London, 1964).

Mutesa, Frederick, Kabaka of Buganda, *Desecration of My Kingdom* (London, 1967).

O'Connell, James, "The Political Class and Economic Growth," *Nigerian Journal of Economics and Social Studies*, VIII (1966), 129-40.

————, "The Inevitability of Instability," *Journal of Modern African Studies*, V (1967), 181-91.

Pratt, R. Cranford, "African Reactions to the Rhodesian Crisis," *International Journal*, XXI (1966), 186-98.

Sklar, Richard L., "The Contributions of Tribalism to Nationalism in Western Nigeria," *Journal of Human Relations*, VIII (1960), 407-18.

————, "Contradictions in the Nigerian Political System," *Journal of Modern African Studies*, III (1965), 201-213.

————, "The Ordeal of Chief Awolowo: Nigeria's Political System in Transition," in Gwendolen M. Carter and Alan F. Westin (eds.), *Politics in Africa* (New York, 1966), 119-65.

————, "Nigerian Politics in Perspective," *Government and Opposition*, II (1967), 524-39.

Skurnik, W. A. E., "Dahomey: The End of a Military Regime," *Africa Today*, XV (1968), 21-22.

Symonds, Jane, "The Rhodesian Crisis," *The World Today*, XXI (1965), 453-59.

Tardits, Claude, *Porto Novo* (Paris, 1958).

————, "Parenté et classe sociale à Porto Novo, Dahomey," in Peter C. Lloyd (ed.), *The New Elites of Tropical Africa* (London, 1966), 184-98.

Thompson, Virginia A., "Dahomey," in Gwendolen Carter (ed.), *Five African States* (Ithaca, 1963), 161-262.

Tixier, G., "Les coups d'état militaires en Afrique de l'Ouest," *Revue de Droit Public et de la Science Politique*, LXXII (1966), 1116-1132.

Tshombe, Moise, *Quinze mois du gouvernment du Congo* (Paris, 1966).

Verhaegen, Benoit, *Rebellions au Congo*, I (Brussels, 1966).

Wallerstein, Immanuel, "The Early Years of the OAU: The Search for Organizational Pre-Eminence," *International Organization*, XX (1966), 774-87.

————, *Africa: The Politics of Unity* (New York, 1967).

Weiss, Herbert, *Political Protest in the Congo: The Parti Solidaire Africain During the Independence Struggle* (Princeton, 1967).

Welch, Claude E., "Soldier and State in Africa," *Journal of Modern African Studies*, V (1967), 305-22.

Wild, Patricia Berkoo, "The Organization of African Unity and the Algerian-Moroccan Border Conflict: A Study of New Machinery for Peace-Keeping and for the Peaceful Settlement of Disputes among African States," *International Organization*, XX (1966), 18-36.

Young, M. Crawford, *Politics in the Congo* (Princeton, 1965).

PROTEST AND POWER

IN BLACK AFRICA

THE AUTHORS

ROBERT I. ROTBERG is associate professor of history and political science, The Massachusetts Institute of Technology, and a research fellow of the Center for International Affairs, Harvard University. A graduate of Oberlin College, Princeton University, and the University of Oxford, he previously taught at Harvard University. He is the author of: *The Rise of Nationalism in Central Africa: The Making of Malawi and Zambia, 1873–1964* (Cambridge, Mass., 1965), *A Political History of Tropical Africa* (New York, 1965), *Christian Missionaries and the Creation of Northern Rhodesia, 1882–1924* (Princeton, 1965), and *Joseph Thomson and the Exploration of Africa* (London, 1970). He edited and introduced George S. Mwase, *Strike a Blow and Die: A Narrative of Race Relations in Colonial Africa* (Cambridge, Mass., 1967). He is the editor of *The Journal of Interdisciplinary History*.

ALI A. MAZRUI, a Kenyan, is professor of political science, Makerere University College. He received his D. Phil. from the University of Oxford and previously studied at the University of Manchester and Columbia University. He is the author of: *The Anglo-African Commonwealth: Political Friction and Cultural Fusion* (Oxford, 1967), *Towards a Pax Africana* (Chicago, 1967), *On Heroes and Uhuru-Worship* (London, 1968), *Violence and Thought* (London, 1969), and numerous articles. He edits *Mawazo*.

PIERRE H. ALEXANDRE was born in Algiers. He was an administrator in the French Colonial Service in West Africa from 1943 to 1955; the Secretary General of the Centre de Hautes Études Administratives sur l'Afrique et l'Asie Modernes, University of Paris, from 1955 to 1958; and later professor of Bantu Languages, École des Langues Orientales, and lecturer in sociolinguistics, École Pratique des Hautes Etudes. He is the former editor of *L'Afrique et l'Asie* and presently edits *Cahiers d'Etudes Africaines* and *Chronologie Politique Africaine* and is the coeditor of *L'Année africaine*.

He has written: *Manuel élementaire de langue bulu* (Paris, 1956), *Le groupe dit Pahouin* (Paris, 1958), *Systeme verbal et predicatif bulu* (Paris, 1966), *Langues et langage en Afrique noire* (Paris, 1967), and various articles.

ANTHONY ATMORE, a lecturer in the history of Africa at the School of Oriental and African Studies, University of London, previously served as an education officer in Nyasaland. He is joint author with Roland Oliver of *Africa Since 1800* (Cambridge, 1967).

LEON CARL BROWN, associate professor of Near Eastern studies at Princeton University, has spent several years in the Middle East and North Africa, first with the United States Foreign Service and recently in independent research under the auspices of the Ford Foundation and the Institute of Current World Affairs. He is coauthor with Charles A. Micaud and Clement H. Moore of *Tunisia: The Politics of Modernization* (New York, 1964), editor of *State and Society in Independent North Africa* (Washington, 1966), and author/translator of *The Surest Path* (translation with commentary of Khayr al Din al-Tunisi's *Aqwam al masalik li ma'rifat ahwal al mamalik*) (Cambridge, Mass., 1967).

MICHAEL CROWDER is research professor and director of the Institute of African Studies, University of Ife. He was formerly director of the Institute of African Studies, Fourah Bay College, University of Sierra Leone, and has held positions at the Universities of Ibadan, Columbia, and California (Berkeley). He is the author of: *A Short History of Nigeria* (New York, 1962), *Senegal: A Study in French Assimilation Policy* (London, 1962), and *West Africa Under Colonial Rule* (London, 1968). He has also been editor of *Nigeria Magazine* and *Sierra Leone Studies* and Executive Secretary of the International Congress of Africanists. He is an Officer of the National Order of Senegal.

LaRAY E. DENZER is currently engaged in research for a thesis entitled "Political Developments in Northern Sierra Leone: 1878–1907," which will be submitted for a Ph.D. degree at the University of Ghana. Since 1965 she has been employed as research assistant to the Director of the Institute of African Studies at Fourah Bay College, University of Sierra Leone.

MARTIN R. DOORNBOS is senior lecturer in political science at the Institute of Social Studies, The Hague. After graduating from Amsterdam University in 1960, he worked as a free-lance correspondent on African affairs. Awarded a Harkness Fellowship in 1962, he did graduate work in political science at the University of California, Berkeley, until 1965. From 1965 to 1967 he was a research fellow of the East African Institute of Social Research and part-time lecturer in the Department of Political Science at Makerere University College.

JAMES W. FERNANDEZ is professor of anthropology, Dartmouth College. He is the author of numerous articles on syncretist sects in Africa, and has done extensive research in Gabon.

DHARAM P. GHAI was born in Kenya and educated at the University of Oxford and Yale University. He taught at Makerere University College and now is deputy director of the Institute for Development Studies, Social Science Division, University College, Nairobi. He has edited *Taxation for Development: A Case Study of Uganda* (Nairobi, 1966) and is the author of *Portrait of a Minority: Asians in East Africa* (Nairobi, 1965).

ELIZABETH HOPKINS, associate professor of anthropology at Smith College, was a research associate of the East African Institute of Social Research from 1961–63 and did field work in Ankole and Kigezi. She is the author of several articles on East Africa.

ROBERT D. JACKSON received a Bachelor's degree from the University of California at Berkeley in 1965. He taught secondary school in Eastern Nigeria for two years and has also taught in the public schools of New York City. He is currently doing work toward a Ph.D. in history at Harvard University.

SHERIDAN W. JOHNS, III, a lecturer in political science at the University of Zambia, has also taught at Brandeis and Northwestern Universities. In 1962–63 he studied politics in South Africa under the auspices of the Ford Foundation Foreign Area Fellowship Program.

WILLARD R. JOHNSON is associate professor of political science at The Massachusetts Institute of Technology. He received his Ph.D. in government from Harvard University in 1965 and has done extensive research in West Africa. He is the author of *The Cameroon Federation: Political Integration in a Fragmentary Society* (Princeton, 1970).

MARTIN L. KILSON, professor of government and research associate of the Center for International Affairs, Harvard University, was a fellow in the Ford Foundation Foreign Area Training Program for Research in West Africa and visiting professor at the University of Ghana. His publications include *Political Awakening in Africa* (as coeditor with Rupert Emerson) (Englewood Cliffs, N.J., 1965), *Political Change in a West African State* (Cambridge, Mass., 1966), and *Apropos of Africa: Sentiments of American Negro Leaders on Africa from the 1800's to the 1950's* (as coeditor with Adelaide Hill) (London, 1969).

LEO KUPER is professor of sociology at the University of California, Los Angeles. He formerly taught at the University of Natal. His publications include: *Durban: A Study in Racial Ecology* (with Hilstan Watts and Ronald Davies) (London, 1958), *Passive Resistance in South Africa* (London,

1956), *An African Bourgeoisie* (New Haven, 1965), *Living in Towns* (with other contributors) (London, 1953), and *African Law: Adaptation and Development* (co-edited with Hilda Kuper) (Berkeley, 1965).

RENÉ LEMARCHAND, born in France, is associate professor of political science at the University of Florida. At one time he was a teaching assistant in the Faculty of Law at Lovanium and was subsequently a member of the research staff of the Institut de Sociologie Solvay in Brussels. He is the author of *Political Awakening in the Congo: The Politics of Fragmentation* (Berkeley, 1964), and numerous articles.

VICTOR T. LE VINE is associate professor of political science and chairman of the African Studies Committee at Washington University, St. Louis. He conducted extensive field research in West Africa, primarily in the French-speaking states, in 1959, 1960–61, and 1965. In 1969 he became visiting professor and head of the Department of Political Science, University of Ghana. He is the author of *The Cameroons from Mandate to Independence* (Berkeley, 1964), *Political Leadership in Africa* (Stanford, 1967), and numerous articles.

MICHAEL F. LOFCHIE is associate professor of political science and assistant director of the African Studies Center, University of California, Los Angeles. He has written *Zanzibar: Background to Revolution* (Princeton, 1965) and articles on other aspects of African politics. He has visited Africa several times, principally as a Foreign Area Training Fellow in 1962–63 and as a Fulbright-Hays Faculty Research Fellow in 1966–67.

JOHN M. LONSDALE, currently research fellow of Trinity College, University of Cambridge, received his Ph.D. from that institution in 1964. He was lecturer in history at the University College, Dar es Salaam, from 1964 to 1966. He is the author of *A Political History of Western Kenya, 1838-1958* (Oxford, 1970).

G. ANDREW MAGUIRE received his Ph.D. in government from Harvard University in 1966. He did research in England and East Africa on a Foreign Area Training Fellowship. He was an Advisor on Political and Security Affairs with the United States Mission to the United Nations from 1966 to 1969. He is now Director, Office of Jamaica Planning and Development, Queens, and author of *Towards Uhuru in Tanzania: The Politics of Participation* (Cambridge, 1969).

SHULA MARKS received her Ph.D. from the University of London and is lecturer in history with special reference to South Africa at both the School of Oriental and African Studies and the Institute of Commonwealth Studies, University of London. She is the author of *Reluctant Rebellion: An Assessment of the 1906-8 Disturbances in Natal* (New York, 1970).

ROBERT MELSON was born in Warsaw, Poland in 1937. He came to the United States in 1947 and became a citizen in 1952. From 1964 to 1965 he did field work in Nigeria where he was a research fellow of the Institute of African Studies at the University of Ife. His work was supported by grants from the Carnegie Corporation, the Foreign Area Fellowship Program, and the National Science Foundation. In 1967, he completed a doctoral thesis at The Massachusetts Institute of Technology. Since 1966, he has been assistant professor of political science and a member of the African Studies Center at Michigan State University.

ROBERT CAMERON MITCHELL is assistant professor of sociology at Swarthmore College and has made a detailed study of Aladura churches in Western Nigeria. With Harold W. Turner he has compiled *African Religious Movements: A Comprehensive Bibliography* (Evanston, 1966).

GERALD MOORE was educated at the University of Cambridge, where he read English. From 1953 to 1966 he worked at universities overseas, first in Nigeria and later in Hong Kong and Uganda. He is now teaching in the School of African and Asian Studies at Sussex University. His publications include *The Chosen Tongue* (London, 1969); *Seven African Writers* (Oxford, 1962); (ed.), *Modern Poetry from Africa* (Harmondsworth, 1963); and (ed.), *African Literature and the Universities* (Ibadan, 1965).

JAMES O'CONNELL, a Roman Catholic priest, received his M.A. at the National University of Ireland and his Ph.D. from the University of Louvain. He taught for nine years in the Department of Political Science of the University of Ibadan and is now chairman of the Department of Government at Ahmadu Bello University, Zaria. He is a contributing author and coeditor of *Education and Nation-Building in Africa* (New York, 1965).

YVES PERSON was born in France. From 1948 to 1963 he was an administrator in Francophone Africa, and from 1963 to 1967 he was with the Centre National de la Recherche Scientifique. He is now chairman of the Department of History, Université de Dakar. His doctoral thesis was on Samori.

JOHN POVEY, after many years in South Africa, came to the United States where he obtained his Ph.D. degree at Michigan State University. He is associate professor of English at the University of California at Los Angeles. He is the editor of *African Arts*.

ANDREW ROBERTS, who was born in Newcastle-on-Tyne, England, received his B.A. from the University of Cambridge in 1960, and his Ph.D. from the University of Wisconsin in 1966. He was a Leverhulme Overseas Research Scholar, Makerere University College, 1960–61, junior research fellow, University of Sussex, 1965–66, and research fellow in oral history, University

College, Dar es Salaam, Tanzania, 1966-68. He is presently research fellow in history, University of Zambia. He edited *Tanzania Before 1900* (Nairobi, 1968).

SVEN A. RUBENSON was born in Sweden and educated at the University of Lund where he received the degrees of C. Phil. in 1946 and L. Phil. in 1954. He went to Ethiopia in 1947 as an educational missionary of the Swedish Evangelical Mission and has spent the years since that time in teaching and school administration there. He has been head of the Department of History of the Haile Sellassie I University and has been dean of the Faculty of Arts. His publications include: *Wichale XVII: The Attempt to Establish a Protectorate over Ethiopia* (Addis Ababa, 1964); *King of Kings: Tewodros of Ethiopia* (Addis Ababa, 1966); and "The Lion of the Tribe of Judah, Christian Symbol and/or Imperial Title," *Journal of Ethiopian Studies*, III (1965), 75-85.

YASHPAL TANDON, who was born in Uganda, received his Bachelor's and Ph.D. degrees from the London School of Economics. In 1966–67 he was senior research fellow in international organization at Columbia University. He is currently senior lecturer in political science at Makerere University College and director of the Makerere Institute in Diplomacy and has written numerous articles in the fields of international affairs and international organization.

DOUGLAS L. WHEELER is a graduate of Dartmouth College and Boston University. Since 1965 he has taught African and Iberian history at the University of New Hampshire. He traveled and did extensive research in Angola and Moçambique during 1966–67 and taught in the History Department at University College, Salisbury, Rhodesia in 1967. He spent the year 1961–62 as a Fulbright scholar at the University of Lisbon, Portugal, doing research on colonial history.

AUDREY WIPPER is an assistant professor of sociology at the University of Waterloo, Ontario. She is completing a study of millenarian and prophetic movements in Kenya.

M. CRAWFORD YOUNG teaches political science at the University of Wisconsin, where he has been a member of the faculty since 1963. He is the author of *Politics in the Congo* (Princeton, 1965), and, in collaboration with Charles Anderson and Fred von der Mehden, *Issues of Political Development* (Englewood Cliffs, 1968), as well as a number of articles concerned with Congolese, Ugandan, and African politics. He served as chairman of the African Studies Program at the University of Wisconsin from 1964 to 1968, and, beginning in 1968, as associate dean of the Graduate School. In 1969 he became chairman of its Department of Political Science. During 1965–66, he was visiting lecturer in African Studies at Makerere University College.

INDEX

In this index modern geographical renderings are used for purposes of identification even where they might be anachronistic.